LEVITICUS
23–27

VOLUME 3B

THE ANCHOR BIBLE is a fresh approach to the world's greatest classic. Its object is to make the Bible accessible to the modern reader; its method is to arrive at the meaning of biblical literature through exact translation and extended exposition, and to reconstruct the ancient setting of the biblical story, as well as the circumstances of its transcription and the characteristics of its transcribers.

THE ANCHOR BIBLE is a project of international and interfaith scope: Protestant, Catholic, and Jewish scholars from many countries contribute individual volumes. The project is not sponsored by any ecclesiastical organization and is not intended to reflect any particular theological doctrine. Prepared under our joint supervision, THE ANCHOR BIBLE is an effort to make available all the significant historical and linguistic knowledge which bears on the interpretation of the biblical record.

THE ANCHOR BIBLE is aimed at the general reader with no special formal training in biblical studies; yet it is written with the most exacting standards of scholarship, reflecting the highest technical accomplishment.

This project marks the beginning of a new era of cooperation among scholars in biblical research, thus forming a common body of knowledge to be shared by all.

William Foxwell Albright
David Noel Freedman
GENERAL EDITORS

THE ANCHOR BIBLE

LEVITICUS 23–27

◆

A New Translation
with Introduction and Commentary

JACOB MILGROM

THE ANCHOR BIBLE
Doubleday
New York   London   Toronto   Sydney   Auckland

THE ANCHOR BIBLE
PUBLISHED BY DOUBLEDAY
a division of Random House, Inc.
1540 Broadway, New York, New York 10036

THE ANCHOR BIBLE, DOUBLEDAY, and the portrayal
of an anchor with the letters A and B are trademarks
of Doubleday, a division of Random House, Inc.

LIBRARY OF CONGRESS CATALOGING-IN-PUBLICATION DATA
Bible. O.T. Leviticus XXIII–XXVII. English. Milgrom. 2000.
Leviticus 23–27: a new translation with introduction and commentary /
by Jacob Milgrom.—1st ed.
    p.   cm.   (The Anchor Bible; v. 3B)
Includes bibliographical references and index.
1. Bible. O.T. Leviticus XXIII–XXVII—Commentaries.
I. Title: Leviticus twenty-three through twenty-seven.
II. Milgrom, Jacob, 1923– III. Title. IV. Bible.
English. Anchor Bible. 1964; v. 3B.
BS192.2A1   1964.G3 vol. 3B
[BS1253]   220.7′7 s—dc21
[222′.13077]   99-086528

ISBN 0-385-50035-1
Copyright © 2001 by Doubleday, a Division of Random House, Inc.

for my children and grandchildren
Shira, David, Talia, Noam, Yarm, Liore
Jeremy, Kinneret, Maor, Maayan
Etan, Deborah, Jonathan, Sarah, Hannah
Asher, Alice, Eliana, Chyelle

O House of Jacob, come,
let us walk by the light of YHWH
Isaiah 2:5

CONTENTS

◆

BIBLIOGRAPHY
(Cumulative Bibliography of Volumes 3A and 3B)

INDEXES
(Cumulative Indexes of Volumes 3, 3A, and 3B)

PREFACE

◆

A word of explanation regarding the Introduction. From the start, I decided not to repeat anything I had written in the Commentary. The Introduction is thus not a compendium, but a supplement. Frequent references to the Commentary are made throughout. Such is the case with H's distinct terminology (I B); style (I D); law and narrative (I G); polemic against P, JE, and D (I I); holiness (II G); ethics (II H); jubilee (II K); and reflections on the biblical *gēr* (II N). Hence, just as necessity dictated that the Commentary be *written* before the Introduction, so also the Commentary should be *read* before the Introduction.

Frequent reference is also made to three seminal books on H, which appeared during the past five years: Knohl (1995), Joosten (1996), and Schwartz (1999 Hebrew). Moreover, wherever chapters 17–27 (H) allude to or assume chapters 1–16 (P), I refer the reader to the discussion in my earlier work, *Leviticus 1–16* (AB3). The Introduction also omits the state of research, since it is thoroughly covered by Hartley (1992: 251–60) and Joosten (1996: 5–16).

The other commentators and studies I have consulted—Reventlow (1961), Kilian (1963), Feucht (1964), Elliger (1966), Cholowinski (1970), Zimmerli (1980), Hurvitz (1982), Levine (1989), Paran (1989), and Sun (1990)—have contributed to this Commentary and are gratefully acknowledged. As in volume 1, the insights of the medieval Jewish commentators and their rabbinic predecessors illuminate these pages. Once again, I have benefited from the perceptive questions and comments of my graduate students in both Berkeley and Jerusalem. They are noted by first initial and surname. Several of them have also contributed excursuses: The Missing Family Members in the List of Sexual Prohibitions (Dr. S. Rattray); Parallelism and Inversion in 21:1b–15 (C. E. Hayes); Hittite and Israelite Festive Calendars (Dr. S. Stewart); and Ancient Seed Mensuration (J. Sheldon).

The Introduction is in two parts. The first is called Structure, justifying reference to chapters 17–27 as H, a discrete priestly source, which differs from chapters 1–16 (P) in form (I A), terminology (I B), style (I D), and precision (I C). H exhibits inner growth (I F), supplements and revises P (I H), polemicizes against P (I I), and extends into Exodus and Numbers (I E). Hence the book of Leviticus remains a distinctive organic creation (I L), composed, with the exception of several verses, in preexilic times (I K). The second part, Theology, deals with topics found in H, such as revelation (II A), rationales (II B), ancestor worship (II C), idolatry (II D), covenant (II F), holiness (II G), ethics (II H), land (II I), Sabbath (II J), jubilee (II K), crime (II O), and YHWH (II Q).

My deepest appreciation is extended to the librarians of the Hebrew Union

College, Jerusalem, for their cooperative and efficient bibliographical help. I cannot close without expressing my thanks to my indefatigable and faithful editor, David Noel Freedman. My indebtednerss is implicit on every page by its improved style and clarity and is explicit on occasion by his perceptive comments.

The introduction is preceded by my translation of the entire book of Leviticus, thereby obviating the need to flip to volume 1 each time my rendering is sought. The volume concludes with appendices A–F, giving my comments to some of the scholarly reactions to volume 1.

tam weníšlam
April 23, 1999
This is the day YHWY made;
let us rejoice and exult in it.
Ps 118:24

ABBREVIATIONS

◆

'Ab.	'Abot
AB	Anchor Bible
ABD	Anchor Bible Dictionary
'Abod. Zar.	'Abodah Zarah
'Abot R. Nat.	'Abot Rabbi Nathan
ADD	C. H. W. Johns, Assyrian Deeds and Documents, 3 vols. (Cambridge, 1898)
AfO	Archiv für Orientforschung
AH³	Biblia hebraica stuttgartensia (3d edition)
AHw	W. von Soden, Akkadisches Handwörterbuch (Wiesbaden, 1965–81)
AJSR	Association of Jewish Studies Review
Akk.	Akkadian
AnBib	Analecta Biblica
ANET³	J. B. Pritchard, ed., Ancient Near Eastern Texts Relating to the Old Testament (Princeton, 1969)
AOAT	Alter Orient und Altes Testament (1069–)
AoF	Altorientalische Forschugen
'Arak.	'Arakin
Aristotle	
Polit.	Aristotle, Politius
ARM	Archives royales de Mari
ARN¹	Abot Rabbi Nahman, ms.1
ArOr	Archiv Orientalni
Aram.	Aramaic
ASOR Symposia	America Schools of Oriental Research Symposia
ASTI	Annual of the Swedish Theological Institute
b.	Babylonian Talmud
B. Bat.	Baba Batra
B. Meṣ.	Baba Meṣiʿa
B. Qam.	Baba Qamma
B. Soṭ.	Talmud Babli, Soṭah
BA	Biblical Archaeologist
BAM	F. Köcher, Die babylonisch-assyriache Medizin in Texen und Untersuchungen (Berlin, 1963–)
BAR	Biblical Archaeologist Reader
Baby.	Babylonian

bar.	baraita
BASOR	*Bulletin of the American Schools of Oriental Research*
BBR	H. Zimmern, *Beiträge zur Kenntnis der babylonischen Religion* (Leipzig, 1901)
B.C.E.	Before the Common Era; corresponds to B.C.
BDB	F. Brown, S. R. Driver, and C. A. Briggs, *Hebrew and English Lexicon of the Old Testament* (Oxford, orig. 1907; I cite the 1953 ed.)
Bek.	*Bekorot*
Ber.	*Berakot*
Beṣ.	*Beṣah*
BH	biblical Hebrew
BHS	*Biblia Hebraica Stuttgartensia*
BH³	Biblia hebraica stuttgartensia (3rd edition)
BI	*Biblical Interpretation*
Bib	*Biblica*
Bik.	*Bikkurim*
BIN	*Babylonian Inscriptions in the Collection of J. B. Nies*
BiOr	*Bibliotheca Orientalis*
BJRL	*Bulletin of the John Rylands University Library of Manchester*
BKAT	Biblische Kommentar: Altes Testament
BM	*Beth Mikra*
BN	*Biblische Notizen*
Bo	unpublished Boğazköy Tablets
BO	*Bibliotheca Orientalis*
BR	*Bible Review*
BWL	*Babylonian Wisdom Literature*
BZ	*Biblische Zeitschrift*
CAD	*The Assyrian Dictionary of the Oriental Institute of the University of Chicago*
CBC	Cambridge Bible Commentary
CBQ	*Catholic Biblical Quarterly*
CD	Damascus Document
C.E.	Common Era
CH	Code of Hammurabi
CJ	*Conservative Judaism*
Cowley	A. Cowley, ed., *Aramaic Papyri of the Fifth Century B. C.* (1923)
CT	*Cuneiform Texts from Babylonian Tablets*
CTA	A. Herdner, ed., *Corpus des tablettes en cunéiformes alphabétiques découvertes à Ras Shamra-Ugarid de 1929 à 1939* (Paris, 1963)
CTH	designation of compositions after Laroche 1971
D	Deuteronomist

DBAT	*Dielheimer Blätter zum Alten Testament*
DBSup	*Dictionnaire de la Bible, Supplément*
Dem.	*Demai*
Deut. Rab	*(Midrash) Deuteronomy Rabbah*
Deut. Re'eh	*Deuteronomy Rabbah,* parashat *re'eh*
DISO	C.-F. Jean and J. Hoftijzer, *Dictionnaire des inscriptions sémitiques de l'ouest* (Leiden, 1965)
DJD V	J. Allegro, ed. *Discoveries in the Judean Desert,* V (Oxford, 1968)
DJD	J. T. Milik et al., eds., *Discoveries in the Judaean Desert* (Oxford, 1955–62)
DNWSI	*Dictionary of Northwest Semitic Inscriptions*
E	Elohist Source
EBWL	*Encyclopedia of the Biblical World, Leviticus* (Jerusalem: Revivim) (Hebrew)
'Ed.	*'Eduyyot*
EI	*Eretz-Israel*
EJ	*Encyclopaedia Judaica*
EM	*Encyclopaedia Miqra'it*
EQ	*Evangelical Quarterly*
ERE	J. Hastings, ed., *Encyclopedia of Religion and Ethics*
'Erub.	*'Erubin*
ET	*The Expository Times*
Eth.	Ethiopic
fem.	Feminine
FF	*Forschungen und Fortschrifte*
frag.	fragment
GAG	W. von Soden, *Grundriss der akkadischen Grammatik samt Erganzungsheft,* AnOr 33/47 (Rome, 1969)
Giṭ.	*Giṭṭin*
GKC	W. Gesenius, ed. E. Kautsch, trans. A. Cowley, *Gesenius' Hebrew Grammar* (Oxford, 1983)
H	Holiness Code
Ḥal.	*Ḥallah*
Ḥag.	*Ḥagiga*
HALAT	*Hebräisches und Aramäische Lexikon zum Alten Testament*
HAL³	W. Baumgentmer et al, eds., *Hebräisches und aramäisches Lexicon zum Alten Testament,* 3 ed.
HAR	*Hebrew Annual Review*
HAT	Handbuch zum Alten Testament
Heb.	Hebrew
Heliod.	Heliodorus, *Aethiopica*
Herod.	Herodotus
Hitt.	Hittite

HL	Hittite Laws
Hor.	*Horayot*
HSS	Harvard Semitic Studies
HTR	*Harvard Theological Review*
HUCA	*Hebrew Union College Annual*
Ḥul.	*Ḥullin*
IBHS	B. Watke and M. O'Connor, *An Introduction to Biblical Hebrew Syntax* (Winona Lake, Ind: 1990)
ICC	International Critical Commentary
IDB	G. A. Buttrick, ed., *Interpreter's Dictionary of the Bible*, 4 vols. (Nashville, 1962)
IDB S	*Interpreters Dictionary of the Bible, Supplement*
inf. const.	infinitive construct
IEJ	*Israel Exploration Journal*
J	Yahwist Source
JAAR	*Journal of the American Academy of Religion*
JAOS	*Journal of the American Oriental Society*
JBL	*Journal of Biblical Literature*
JCS	*Journal of Cuneiform Studies*
JE	Jewish Encyclopedia
JEN	*Joint Expedition with the Iraq Museum at Nuzi*
JJS	*Journal of Jewish Studies*
JLAS	*Jewish Law Association Studies*
JNES	*Journal of Near Eastern Studies*
JNSL	*Journal of Northwest Semitic Languages*
JNWSL	*Journal of Northwest Semitic Languages*
Jos.	Josephus (Loeb Classical Library editions)
Ant.	*Antiquities of the Jews*
Con. Ap.	*Contra Apion*
Wars	*The Jewish Wars*
Life	*Life*
JPS	Jewish Publication Society
JQR	*Jewish Quarterly Review*
JSOT	*Journal for the Study of the Old Testament*
JSS	*Journal of Semitic Studies*
JTS	*Journal of Theological Studies*
Jub.	*Jubilees*
IDBSup	Interpreters Dictionary of the Bible Supplement
K./Q.	Ketib/Qri'
KAI	H. Donner and W. Röllig, *Kanaanäische und aramäische Inschriften* (Wiesbaden, 1968–71)
KAR	*Keilschrifttexte aus Assur religiösen Inhalts*
KAT	*Kommentar zum Alten Testament*
KB	L. Koehler and W. Baumgartner, *Lexicon in Veteris Testamenti libros* (Leiden, 1958)

KB³	Köhler Baumgartner, third edition
KBo	*Keilschrifttexte aus Boghazkoy*
Kel.	*Kelim*
Ker.	*Keritot*
Ket.	*Ketubot*
Kil.	*Kil'ayim*
KJV	*King James Version*
Koh. Rab	*Kohelet Rabbeh*
KTU	*Die keilalphabetischen Texte aus Ugarit*
KUB	*Keilschrifturkunden aus Boghazkoy*
LB	Late Bronze
LBH	late biblical Hebrew
LE	Laws of Eshnunna
lit.	literally
LKA	E. Ebeling, *Literarische Keilschrifttexte aus Assur* (Berlin, 1953)
ll.	Lines
LXX	Septuagint
m.	Mishna
MA	Middle Assyrian
Maʿaś.	*Maʿaśerot*
Mak.	*Makkot*
MAL	Middle Assyrian Laws
MAL A	Middle Assyrian Laws, Tablet A
MAOG	Mitteilungen der Altorientalischen Gesellschaft
MDP	Mémoires de la Délégation en Perse
Meg.	*Megilla*/construct *Megillat* (e.g., *Megillat Taʿanit*)
Meʿil.	*Meʿila*
Mek̲.	*Mek̲ilta*
Mekh.	*Mekhilta*
Men.	*Menaḥot*
Menaḥ.	*Menaḥot*
Meṣ.	*Meṣoraʿ*
Mid.	*Middot*
Midr. Exod. Rab.	*Midrash Exodus Rabbah*
Midr. Gen. Rab.	*Mirdash Genesis Rabbah*
Midr. Lev. Rab.	*Midrash Leviticus Rabbah*
Midr. Num. Rab.	*Midrash Numbers Rabbah*
MMT	*Maʿśê Miqṣat Hattôrâ*, Qumran Cave 4, 394–99
MMT B	*Miqṣat maʿśê Tôrâ*, B
Moʿed Qaṭ.	*Moʿed Qaṭan*
MSL	*Materialen zum sumerischen Lexikon*, (Rome, 1937–)
MS(S)	manuscript(s)
MT	Masoretic Text
MTZ	*Münchener theologische Zeitschrift*

NAB	*New American Bible*
Naz.	*Nazir*
Nbn	J. N. Strabsmeier, *Inschriften von Nabonidus, König von Babylon von der Thrintafeln des Britischen Museums* (Leipzig, 1989)
NEB	*New English Bible*
Ned.	*Nedarim*
Nid.	*Niddah*
NJPS	*New Jewish Publication Society Bible*
NRSV	*New Revised Standard Version*
Num. R.	*Numbers Rabbah*
OB	Old Babylonian
OB Gilg.	Old Babylonian text of Gilgamesh
OLA	Orientalia Louveniensia Analecta
Or	*Orientalia* (Rome)
ʿ*Or*	ʿ*Orlah*
OTL	Old Testament Library
OTS	*Oudtestamentische Studiën*
P	Priestly Source
PAAJR	*Proceedings of the American Academy of Jewish Research*
par(s).	paragraph(s)
Paus.	Pausanias
PEQ	*Palestine Exploration Quarterly*
Pesah.	*Pesaḥim*
Pesh.	*Peshitta*
Pesiq. R.	*Pesiqta Rabbati*
Pesiq. Rab Kah.	*Pesiqta de Rab Kahana*
Philo	Philo
Plant.	*De plantatione*
Virt.	*De virtutibus*
Vit. Mos.	*De vitae Mose*
Pirqe R. Kah.	*Pirqe Rab Kahana*
pl.	plural
PRU	C. F.-A. Schaeffer and J. Nougayrol, eds., *Le Palais royal d'Ugarit* (Paris, 1955–65)
Q	Qumran
Qidd	*Quiddishun*
QL	Qumran Literature
1QM	Qumran, *War Scroll*, Cave 1
Qoh.	*Qohelet (Eccl, Ecclesiastes)*
1QS	*Serek hayyaḥad* (Rule Of The Community, *Manual Of Discipline*) Cave 1
1QSa	Qumran, *Rule of the Congregation*, Cave 1
4Q	Qumran, Cave 4
4QDᵇ	Qumran fragment Dᵇ, Cave 4

4QD^e	Qumran fragment D^e, Cave 4
4QD^6	Qumran fragment D^6, Cave 4
4QLev^e	Qumran, Leviticus, fragment e
11QPaleoLev	Qumran, Paleo Leviticus, Cave 11
11QT	Qumran, Temple Scroll, Cave 11
11QT^a	Qumran, Temple Scroll fragment a, Cave 11
R.	Rabbi
RA	*Revue d'assyriologie et d'archéologie orientale*
RB	*Revue biblique*
rev.	reverse
Revq	*Revue de Qumran*
RHA	*Revue hittite et asianique*
RHR	*Revue d'histoire des religions*
RIDA	*Revue internationale des droits de l'antiquité*
RIH	J. de Rouge, *Inscriptions hiéroglyphiques en Égypte*, 3 Vols. Études égyptoloiques 9–11 (Paris, 1877–78)
RLA	E. Ebeling and B. Meissner, eds., *Reallexikon der Assyriologie* (Berlin, 1928)
RLAR	*Realexicon der aegyptischen Religionsgeschichte*
Roš Haš.	Roš Haššana
RS	Ras Shamra, field numbers of tablets
RŠbY	*Rabbi Simeon bar Yoḥai*
RSO	*Rivista degli studi Orientali*
RSV	*Revised Standard Version*
Ruth Rab.	*Ruth Rabbah*
Šab.	*Šabbat*
Šabb.	*Šabbat*
Sam.	Samaritan Pentateuch
Sam. Tg.	*Samaritan Targum*
Sanh.	*Sanhedrin*
SANT	Studien zum Alten und Neuen Testament
SBL	Society of Biblical Literature
SBLSP	*Society of Biblical Literature Seminar Papers*
SbTU	H. Hunger, ed., *Spätbabylonische Texte aus Uruk* (Berlin: Mann, 1976–)
Šebi.	*Shebi 'it*
SDB	*Supplément, Dictionnaire de la Bible*
Šebu.	*Šebu 'ot*
Seder Elijah Rab.	*Seder Elijah Rabbah*
Šek.	*Šekalim*
sing.	singular
SJOT	*Sandinavian Journal of the Old Testament*
Skt.	Sanskrit
Sop.	*Soperim*
Soṭ.	*Soṭah*

StBoT	*Studien zu den Bogazkoy-Texten*
Sukk.	*Sukkot*
Sum.	Sumerian
SVT	*Supplements to Vetus Testamentum*
Syr.	Syriac
t.	Tosefta
T. Levi	*Testament of Levi*
TA	*Tel Aviv*
Ta'an.	*Ta'anit*
Targ. Jon.	*Targum Jonathan*
Tam.	*Tamid*
Tanḥ	*Tanḥuma*
TCL	*Textes cunéiformes du Louvre*
TCS	Texts from Cuneiform Sources
TDOT	G. J. Botterweck and H. Ringgren, eds., *Theological Dictionary of the Old Testament*
Tem.	*Temura*
Ter.	*Terumot*
tg(s).	targum(s)
Tg. Neof.	*Targum Neofiti*
Tg. Onq.	*Targum Onqelos*
Tg. Ps-J.	*Targum Pseudo-Jonathan*
Tg. Yer.	*Targum Yerušalmi*
Th WAT	G. J. Botterweck and H. Ringgren, eds., *Theologisches Wörterbuch zum Alten Testament*
THAT	E. Fenni and C. Westermann, eds., *Theologisches Handwörterbuch zum alten Testament*, 2 vols. (München, 1971–76)
ThR	*Theologische Rudschau*
Tiq. Soph.	Tiqqun Sopherin
Tg. Onq.	*Targum Onqeles*
Tg. Sam.	*Targum Samuel*
Tos.	*Tosafot*
TS	M. M. Kasher, ed., *Torah Shelemah* (Jerusalem, 1927–)
UF	*Ugaritische Forschungen*
Ug.	Ugaritic
UT	C. H. Gordon, *Ugaritic Textbook* (Rome, 1965)
V	Vetus Latina
VAB	*Vorasiartische Bibliotek* (Lipzig, 1907–16)
VBW	B. Mazar, ed., *Views of the Biblical World* (Jerusalem, 1958–61)
Vg	Vulgate
VT	*Vetus Testamentum*
VTE	D. J. Wiseman, ed., *Vassal-Treaties of Esarhaddon* (London, 1958)

WHJP	*World History of The Jewish People*
WMANT	Wissenschaftliche Monographien zum Alten und Neuen Testaments
WO	*Die Welt des Orients*
Y.	Talmud Yerušalmi = Jerusalem Talmud
Yal.	*Yalquṭ*
YBC	tablets in the Babylonian Collection, Yale University Library
y.	*yerushalmi*
y. Pe'a	(Talmud) *yerushalmi, Pe'â*
Yeb.	*Yebamit*
Yelammedenu	Midrash Tanḥuma Yelammedenu
ZA	*Zeitschrift für Assyriologie*
ZABR	*Zeitschrift für Altorientalische und Biblische Rechtsgeshichte*
ZAH	*Zeitschrift für Althebräistic*
ZAW	*Zeitschrift für die alttestamentliche Wissenschaft*
ZDMG	*Zeitschrift der deuschen morgenländischen Gesellschaft*
Zeb.	*Zebaḥim*
Zebaḥ.	*Zebaḥim*
Zuṭ	*Zûṭâ*

Translation of
The Book of
Leviticus

◆

THE BOOK OF LEVITICUS
IN OUTLINE

◆

I. The Sacrificial System
Chapters 1–7
1. The Burnt Offering (1:1–17)
2. The Cereal Offering (2:1–16)
3. The Well-Being Offering (3:1–17)
4. The Purification Offering (4:1–35)
5. The Graduated Purification Offering (5:1–13)
6. The Reparation Offering (5:14–26)
7. Sacrifices: The Administrative Order (6:1–7:38)
II. The Inauguration of the Cult
Chapters 8–10
8. The Consecration of the Priests (8:1–36)
9. The Inaugural Service (9:1–24)
10. The Tragic Aftermath of the Inaugural Service (10:1–20)
III. The Impurity System
Chapters 11–16
11. Diet Laws (11:1–47)
12. Childbirth (12:1–8)
13. Scale Disease (13:1–59)
14. Purification after Scale Disease (14:1–57)
15. Genital Discharges (15:1–33)
16. The Day of Purgation (*Yôm Kippûr*) (16:1–34)
IV. The Holiness Source
Chapters 17–27
17. The Slaughter and Consumption of Meat (17:1–16)
18. Illicit Sexual Practices (18:1–30)
19. Ritual and Moral Holiness (19:1–37)
20. Penalties for Molek Worship, Necromancy, and Sexual Offenses
(20:1–27)
21. Instructions for the Priests (21:1–24)
22. Instructions for the Priests (Continued) and Lay Persons (22:1–33)
23. The Holiday Calendar (23:1–44)
24. Tabernacle Oil and Bread; The Case of Blasphemy (24:1–23)
25. Jubilee, the Priestly Solution for Economic Injustice (25:1–55)
26. Blessings, Curses, and the Recall of the Covenant (26:1–46)
27. Consecrations and Their Redemption (27:1–34)

PART I. THE SACRIFICIAL SYSTEM (CHAPTERS 1–7)

1. *The Burnt Offering (1:1–17)*

Introduction

¹YHWH summoned Moses and spoke to him from the Tent of Meeting, and said: ²Speak to the Israelites, and say to them: When any person among you presents an offering of livestock to YHWH, he shall choose his offering from the herd or from the flock.

The Burnt Offering: From the Herd

³If his offering is a burnt offering from the herd, he shall offer a male without blemish. He shall bring it to the entrance of the Tent of Meeting, for acceptance on his behalf before YHWH. ⁴He shall lean his hand on the head of the burnt offering, that it may be acceptable on his behalf, to expiate for him. ⁵The bull shall be slaughtered before YHWH, and Aaron's sons, the priests, shall present the blood and dash the blood against all sides of the altar that is at the entrance to the Tent of Meeting. ⁶The burnt offering shall be flayed and quartered. ⁷The sons of Aaron the priest shall stoke the fire on the altar and lay out wood upon the fire. ⁸Then Aaron's sons, the priests, shall lay out the quarters, with the head and suet, on the wood that is on the fire upon the altar. ⁹Its entrails and shins shall be washed with water, and the priest shall turn all of it into smoke on the altar as a burnt offering, a food gift of pleasing aroma to YHWH.

From the Flock

¹⁰If his offering for a burnt offering is from the flock, of sheep or of goats, he shall offer a male without blemish. ¹¹It shall be slaughtered on the north side of the altar before YHWH, and Aaron's sons, the priests, shall dash its blood against all sides of the altar. ¹²When it has been quartered, the priest shall lay out the quarters, with the head and suet, on the wood that is on the fire upon the altar. ¹³The entrails and the shins shall be washed with water, and the priest shall present all of it and turn it into smoke on the altar. It is a burnt offering, a food gift of pleasing aroma to YHWH.

From Birds

¹⁴If his offering to YHWH is a burnt offering of birds, he shall present a turtledove or a young pigeon as his offering. ¹⁵The priest shall present it to the altar, pinch off its head and turn it into smoke on the altar; and the blood shall be drained out against the side of the altar. ¹⁶He shall remove its crissum by its feathers, and cast it into the place of the ashes, at the east side of the altar. ¹⁷The

priest shall tear it open by its wings, without severing [them], and turn it into smoke on the altar, upon the wood that is on the fire. It is a burnt offering, a food gift of pleasing aroma to YHWH.

2. The Cereal Offering (2:1–16)

Raw Flour

[1]When a person presents an offering of cereal to YHWH, his offering shall be of semolina; he shall pour oil upon it, lay frankincense on it, [2]and present it to Aaron's sons, the priests. [The priest] shall scoop out therefrom a handful of its semolina and oil, as well as all of its frankincense; and this token portion the priest shall turn into smoke on the altar, as a food gift of pleasing aroma to YHWH. [3]And the remainder of the cereal offering shall be for Aaron and his sons, a most sacred portion from YHWH's food gifts.

Cooked: Baked, Toasted, Fried

[4]When you present an offering of cereal baked in an oven, [it shall be of] semolina: unleavened cakes mixed with oil, or unleavened wafers smeared with oil.

[5]If your offering is a cereal offering [toasted] on a griddle, it shall be a semolina mixed with oil, unleavened. [6]Crumble it into bits and pour oil upon it; it is a cereal offering.

[7]If your offering is a cereal offering [fried] in a pan, it shall be made of semolina in oil.

[8]If you bring to YHWH a cereal offering prepared in any of these ways, it shall be presented to the priest, who shall deliver it to the altar. [9]The priest shall set aside the token portion from the cereal offering and turn it into smoke on the altar as a food gift of pleasing aroma to YHWH. [10]And the remainder of the cereal offering shall be for Aaron and his sons, a most sacred portion from YHWH's food gifts.

Injunctions Concerning Leaven, Honey, and Salt

[11]No cereal offering that you offer to YHWH shall be made leavened, for you must not turn into smoke any leaven or any honey as a food gift to YHWH. [12]You may offer them to YHWH as a first-processed offering; but they shall not be offered up on the altar as a pleasing aroma. [13]You shall season all your cereal offerings with salt; you shall not omit from your cereal offering the salt of your covenant with your God: on all your offerings you must offer salt.

Natural Grain

[14]If you bring a cereal offering of first-ripe fruits to YHWH, you shall bring milky grain parched with fire, groats of the fresh ear, as a cereal offering of

your first-ripe fruits. [15]You shall add oil to it and lay frankincense on it: it is a cereal offering. [16]And the priest shall turn into smoke its token portion: some of its groats and oil, with all of its frankincense, as a food gift to YHWH.

3. The Well-Being Offering (3:1–17)

[1]If his offering is a sacrifice of well-being—

From the Herd

If he offers from the herd, whether male or female, he shall present it without blemish before YHWH [2]and lean his hand upon the head of his offering. It shall be slaughtered at the entrance of the Tent of Meeting, and Aaron's sons, the priests, shall dash the blood against all sides of the altar. [3]He shall then present from the sacrifice of well-being a food gift to YHWH: the suet that covers the entrails and all the suet that is around the entrails; [4]the two kidneys and the suet that is around them, that is on the sinews; and the caudate lobe on the liver, which he shall remove with the kidneys. [5]Aaron's sons shall turn it (this food gift) into smoke on the altar, with the burnt offering that is upon the wood that is on the fire, as a food gift of pleasing aroma to YHWH.

From the Flock

[6]And if his offering for a sacrifice of well-being to YHWH is from the flock, whether male or female, he shall offer it without blemish. [7]If he offers a sheep as his offering, he shall present it before YHWH [8]and lean his hand upon the head of his offering. It shall be slaughtered before the Tent of Meeting, and Aaron's sons shall dash its blood against all sides of the altar. [9]He shall then present, as a food gift to YHWH from the sacrifice of well-being, its suet: the broad tail completely removed close to the sacrum; the suet that covers the entrails and all the suet that is around the entrails; [10]the two kidneys and the suet that is around them on the sinews; and the caudate lobe on the liver, which he shall remove with the kidneys. [11]The priest shall turn it into smoke on the altar as food, a food gift to YHWH.

[12]And if his offering is a goat, he shall present it before YHWH [13]and lean his hand upon its head. It shall be slaughtered before the Tent of Meeting, and Aaron's sons shall dash its blood against all sides of the altar. [14]He shall then present as his offering from it, as a food gift to YHWH, the suet that covers the entrails and all the suet that is around the entrails; [15]the two kidneys and the suet that is around them on the sinew; and the caudate lobe on the liver, which he shall remove with the kidneys. [16]The priest shall turn these into smoke on the altar as food, a food gift of pleasing aroma.

The Law of Suet and Blood

All suet is YHWH's. ¹⁷It is a law for all time throughout your generations, in all your settlements: you must not eat any suet or any blood.*

4. The Purification Offering (4:1–35)

Introduction

¹YHWH spoke to Moses, saying: ²Speak to the Israelites thus:

When a person inadvertently does wrong in regard to any of YHWH's prohibitive commandments by violating any one of them—

Of the High Priest

³If it is the anointed priest who so does wrong to the detriment of the people, he shall offer for the wrong he has done a bull of the herd without blemish as a purification offering to YHWH. ⁴He shall bring the bull to the entrance of the Tent of Meeting before YHWH, lean his hand upon the head of the bull, and slaughter the bull before YHWH. ⁵The anointed priest shall take some of the bull's blood and bring it into the Tent of Meeting. ⁶The priest shall dip his finger in the blood, and sprinkle some of the blood seven times before YHWH against the veil of the shrine. ⁷The priest shall put some of the blood on the horns of the altar of perfumed incense, which is in the Tent of Meeting, before YHWH; and all the rest of the bull's blood he shall pour out at the base of the altar of burnt offering, which is at the entrance of the Tent of Meeting. ⁸He shall set aside all of the suet from the bull of the purification offering: the suet that covers the entrails and all of the suet that is around the entrails; ⁹the two kidneys and the suet that is around them, that is on the sinews; and the caudate lobe on the liver, which he shall remove with the kidneys—¹⁰just as it is set aside from the ox of the well-being offering. The priest shall turn them into smoke on the altar of burnt offering. ¹¹But the hide of the bull, and all its flesh, together with its head and shins, its entrails and dung—¹²all the rest of the bull—shall be taken away to a pure place outside the camp, to the ash dump, and burned with wood; it shall be burned on the ash dump.

Of the Community

¹³If it is the whole community of Israel that has erred inadvertently and the matter escapes the notice of the congregation, so that they violate one of YHWH's prohibitive commandments, and they feel guilt ¹⁴when the wrong that they committed in regard to it becomes known, the congregation shall offer a bull of the herd as a purification offering and bring it before the Tent of Meeting. ¹⁵The elders of the community shall lean their hands upon the head of the bull be-

---

*Italic block type here through page 1922 (Chaps. 3–16) stands for H.

fore YHWH, and the bull shall be slaughtered before YHWH. [16]The anointed priest shall bring some of the bull's blood into the Tent of Meeting, [17]and the priest shall dip his finger in the blood and sprinkle some of it seven times before YHWH, against the veil. [18]Some of the blood he shall put on the horns of the altar that is before YHWH in the Tent of Meeting, and all the rest of the blood he shall pour out at the base of the altar of burnt offering, which is at the entrance of the Tent of Meeting. [19]He shall set aside all of its suet from it and turn it into smoke on the altar. [20]He shall treat the bull as he treated the [first] bull of the purification offering; he shall treat it the same way. Thus the priest shall effect purgation for them that they may be forgiven. [21]The bull shall be taken away outside the camp, and it shall be burned as the first bull was burned; it is the purification offering of the congregation.

Of the Chieftain

[22]When the chieftain does wrong by violating any of YHWH's prohibitive commandments inadvertently, and he feels guilt [23]or he is informed of the wrong he committed, he shall bring as his offering a male goat without blemish. [24]He shall lean his hand upon the goat's head, and it shall be slaughtered at the spot where the burnt offering is slaughtered, before YHWH: it is a purification offering. [25]The priest shall take some of the blood of the purification offering with his finger and put it on the horns of the altar of burnt offering; and (the rest of) its blood he shall pour out at the base of the altar of burnt offering. [26]All of its suet he shall turn into smoke on the altar, like the suet of the well-being offering. Thus shall the priest effect purgation on his behalf for his wrong, that he may be forgiven.

Of the Commoner

[27]If any person from among the populace does wrong inadvertently by violating any of YHWH's prohibitive commandments and he feels guilt [28]or he is informed of the wrong he committed, he shall bring as his offering a female goat without blemish for the wrong he committed. [29]He shall lean his hand upon the head of the purification offering, and the purification offering shall be slaughtered at the spot (of the slaughter) of the burnt offering. [30]The priest shall take some of its blood with his finger and put it on the horns of the altar of burnt offering; and all the rest of its blood he shall pour out at the base of the altar. [31]All of its suet he shall remove, just as the suet was removed from the well-being offering; and the priest shall turn (it) into smoke on the altar as a pleasing aroma to YHWH. Thus the priest shall effect purgation on his behalf, that he may be forgiven.

[32]If the offering he brings is a sheep, he shall bring a female without blemish. [33]He shall lean his hand upon the head of the purification offering, and it shall be slaughtered for purification purposes at the spot where the burnt offering is slaughtered. [34]The priest shall take some of the blood of the purification offering with his finger and put it on the horns of the altar of burnt offering, and all the rest of its blood he shall pour out at the base of the altar. [35]And all of its suet he shall remove, just as the suet of the sheep of the well-being offering is

removed; and the priest shall turn it (lit., them) into smoke on the altar, with the food gifts of YHWH. Thus the priest shall effect purgation on his behalf for the wrong he committed, that he may be forgiven.

5. *The Graduated Purification Offering (5:1–13)*

The Four Cases

[1]If a person does wrong:

When he has heard a public imprecation (against withholding testimony)—and although he was a witness, either having seen or known (the facts)—yet does not testify, then he must bear his punishment;

[2]Or when a person touches any impure thing—be it the carcass of an impure wild quadruped or the carcass of an impure domesticated quadruped or the carcass of an impure swarming creature—and, though he has become impure, the fact escapes him but (thereafter) he feels guilt;

[3]Or when he touches human impurity—any such impurity whereby one becomes impure—and, though he has known it, the fact escapes him but (thereafter) he feels guilt;

[4]Or when a person blurts out an oath to bad or good purpose—whatever anyone may utter in an oath—and, though he has known it, the fact escapes him but (thereafter) he feels guilt in any of these matters—

Resolution: Confession and Sacrifice

[5]When he feels guilt in any of these matters, he shall confess that wherein he did wrong. [6]And he shall bring as his reparation to YHWH, for the wrong that he committed, a female from the flock, sheep or goat, as a purification offering; and the priest shall effect purgation on his behalf for his wrong.

[7]But if his means do not suffice for a sheep, he shall bring to YHWH as his reparation for what he has done wrong, two turtledoves or two pigeons, one for a purification offering and the other for a burnt offering. [8]He shall bring them to the priest, who shall offer first the one for the purification offering, pinching the head at its nape without severing it. [9]He shall sprinkle some of the blood of the purification offering on the side of the altar, and what remains of the blood shall be drained at the base of the altar; it is a purification offering. [10]And the second he shall sacrifice as a burnt offering, according to regulation. Thus the priest shall effect purgation on his behalf for the wrong that he committed so that he may be forgiven.

[11]And if his means do not suffice for two turtledoves or two pigeons, he shall bring as his offering for what he had done wrong one-tenth of an ephah of semolina for a purification offering; he shall not put oil upon it or place frankincense on it, for it is a purification offering. [12]He shall bring it to the priest, and the priest shall scoop out a handful as a token portion of it and turn it into smoke on the altar, with YHWH's food gifts; it is a purification offering. [13]Thus the priest shall effect purgation on his behalf for the wrong he committed in

any of these matters so that he may be forgiven. It shall belong to the priest, like the cereal offering.

The Reparation Offering (5:14–26)

For Sacrilege Against Sancta

5:14YHWH spoke to Moses, saying: 15When a person commits a sacrilege by being inadvertently remiss with any of YHWH's sancta, he shall bring as his penalty to YHWH a ram without blemish from the flock, convertible into payment in silver by sanctuary weight, as a reparation offering, 16and he shall make restitution for that item of the sancta wherein he was remiss and shall add one-fifth to it. When he gives it to the priest, the priest shall effect expiation on his behalf with the ram of the reparation offering so that he may be forgiven.

For Suspected Sacrilege Against Sancta

17If, however, a person errs by violating any of YHWH's prohibitive commandments without knowing it and he feels guilt, he shall bear his responsibility 18by bringing to the priest an unblemished ram from the flock, or its assessment, as a reparation offering. The priest shall effect expiation on his behalf for the error he committed without knowing it so that he may be forgiven. 19It is a reparation offering; he has incurred liability to YHWH.

For Sacrilege Against Oaths

20YHWH spoke to Moses, saying: 21When a person sins by committing a sacrilege against YHWH in that he has dissembled to his fellow in the matter of a deposit or investment or robbery; or having withheld from his fellow 22or having found a lost object he has dissembled about it; and he swears falsely about any one of the things that a person may do and sin thereby—23when one has thus sinned, and feeling guilt, he shall return that which he robbed or that which he withheld, or the deposit that was entrusted to him, or the lost object he found, 24or anything else about which he swore falsely; he shall restore it in its entirety and add one-fifth to it. He shall pay it to its owner as soon as he feels guilt. 25Then he shall bring to the priest, as his reparation to YHWH, an unblemished ram from the flock, or its assessment, as a reparation offering. 26The priest shall effect expiation on his behalf before YHWH so that he may be forgiven for whatever he has done to feel guilty thereby.

6. Sacrifices: The Administrative Order (6:1–23)

Introduction

1YHWH spoke to Moses, saying: 2Command Aaron and his sons thus:

The Burnt Offering

This is the ritual for the burnt offering—that is, the burnt offering that stays on the altar hearth all night until morning, while the altar fire is kept burning on it. ³The priest, having put on linen raiment, with linen breeches next to his body, shall remove the ashes to which the fire has reduced the burnt offering on the altar and put them beside the altar. ⁴He shall then remove his vestments and put on other vestments, and take the ashes outside the camp to a pure place. ⁵The fire on the altar shall be kept burning on it [the hearth]; it shall not go out. Every morning the priest shall feed wood to it, lay out the burnt offering upon it, and on top turn into smoke the fat parts of the well-being offerings. ⁶A perpetual fire shall be kept burning on the altar; it shall not go out.

The Cereal Offering

⁷This is the ritual for the cereal offering. Aaron's sons shall present it before YHWH, in front of the altar. ⁸A handful of the semolina and oil of the cereal offering shall be set aside from it, with all of the frankincense that is on the cereal offering, and this token of it shall be turned into smoke on the altar as a pleasing aroma to YHWH. ⁹The remainder Aaron and his sons shall eat; it shall be eaten unleavened in a holy place; they shall eat it in the court of the Tent of Meeting. ¹⁰It shall not be baked with leaven; I have assigned it as their portion from my food gifts; it is most sacred like the purification offering and the reparation offering. ¹¹Any male of Aaron's descendants may eat of it, as a due for all time throughout your generations from YHWH's food gifts. Whatever touches them shall become holy.

The High Priest's Daily Cereal Offering

¹²YHWH spoke to Moses, saying: ¹³This is the offering that Aaron and his sons shall present to YHWH from the time of his anointment: one-tenth of an ephah of semolina as a regular cereal offering, half of it in the morning and half of it in the evening. ¹⁴It shall be prepared with oil on a griddle. You shall bring it well soaked, and present it as tūpînê, a cereal offering of crumbled bits, of pleasing aroma to YHWH. ¹⁵And so shall the priest, anointed from among his sons to succeed him, sacrifice it; it is YHWH's due for all time; it shall entirely go up in smoke. ¹⁶So every cereal offering of a priest shall be a total offering; it shall not be eaten.

The Purification Offering

¹⁷YHWH spoke to Moses, saying: ¹⁸Speak to Aaron and his sons thus: this is the ritual for the purification offering. The purification offering shall be slaughtered before YHWH, at the spot where the burnt offering is slaughtered; it is most sacred. ¹⁹The priest who offers it as a purification offering shall enjoy it; it shall be eaten in a holy place, in the court of the Tent of Meeting. [20]Whatever touches its flesh shall become holy; and if any of its blood is spattered upon a garment, the bespattered part shall be laundered in a holy place. [21]An earthen vessel in which it is boiled shall be broken; if it has been boiled in a copper vessel, that shall be scoured and flushed with water. [22]Any male among the priests may eat of it: it is most sacred. [23]No purification offering, however, may be eaten from which any blood is brought into the Tent of Meeting to effect purgation in the shrine; it shall be consumed in fire.

7. Sacrifices: The Administrative Order (Continued) (7:1–38)

The Reparation Offering

[1]This is the ritual for the reparation offering: it is most sacred. [2]The reparation offering shall be slaughtered at the spot where the burnt offering is slaughtered, and he [the priest] shall dash its blood against all sides of the altar. [3]All of its suet shall be presented: the broad tail, the suet that covers the entrails; [4]the two kidneys and the suet that is around them on the sinews; and the caudate lobe on the liver, which shall be removed with the kidneys. [5]The priest shall turn them into smoke on the altar as a food gift to YHWH; it is a reparation offering. [6]Any male among the priests may eat of it; it shall be eaten in a holy place, it is most sacred.

The Priestly Prebends from the Most Holy Offerings

[7]The reparation offering is like the purification offering. There is a single rule for both: it shall belong to the priest who performs expiation therewith. [8]The priest who sacrifices a person's burnt offering shall keep the hide of the burnt offering that he sacrificed. [9]Any cereal offering that is baked in an oven, and any that is prepared in a pan or on a griddle shall belong to the priest who offers it. [10]Any cereal offering, whether mixed with oil or dry, shall belong to all the sons of Aaron alike.

The Well-Being Offering

[11]This is the ritual for the sacrifice of well-being that one may offer to YHWH. [12]If he offers it for thanksgiving, he shall offer together with the sacrifice of thanksgiving unleavened cakes mixed with oil, unleavened wafers smeared with oil, and well-soaked cakes of semolina mixed with oil. [13]This offering, with cakes of leavened bread added, he shall offer together with his thanksgiving sacrifice of well-being. [14]Out of this he shall present one of each [kind of] offering as a contribution to YHWH; it shall belong to the priest who dashes the blood of the well-being offering. [15]And the flesh of his thanksgiving sacrifice of well-being shall be eaten on the day that it is offered; none of it shall be put aside until morning.

¹⁶If the sacrifice he offers is a votive or freewill offering, it shall be eaten on the day he offers his sacrifice, and what is left of it shall be eaten on the morrow. ¹⁷What is then left of the sacrificial flesh shall be consumed in fire on the third day. ¹⁸If any of the flesh of his sacrifice of well-being is eaten on the third day, it shall not be acceptable; it shall not be accredited to him who offered it. It is desecrated meat, and the person who eats of it shall bear his punishment.

¹⁹Flesh that touches anything impure shall not be eaten; it shall be consumed in fire. As for other flesh, anyone who is pure may eat such flesh. ²⁰But the person who, while impure, eats flesh from YHWH's sacrifice of well-being, that person shall be cut off from his kin. ²¹When a person touches anything impure, be it human impurity or an impure quadruped or any impure detestable creature, and eats flesh from YHWH's sacrifice of well-being, that person shall be cut off from his kin.

No Suet or Blood May Be Eaten

²²And YHWH spoke to Moses, saying: ²³Speak to the Israelites thus: you shall not eat the suet of any ox, sheep, or goat. ²⁴The suet of an animal that died or was mauled by beasts may be put to any use, but you must not eat it. ²⁵If anyone eats the suet of an animal from which a food gift is presented to YHWH, that person shall be cut off from his kin. ²⁶And you must not ingest any blood, whether of bird or animal, in any of your settlements. ²⁷Any person who ingests any blood shall be cut off from his kin.

The Priestly Prebends from the Well-Being Offering

²⁸And YHWH spoke to Moses, saying: ²⁹Speak to the Israelites thus: the one who presents his sacrifice of well-being to YHWH shall bring his offering to YHWH from his sacrifice of well-being. ³⁰His own hands shall bring YHWH's food gifts: he shall bring the suet together with the breast, the breast to be elevated as an elevation offering before YHWH. ³¹The priest shall turn the suet into smoke at the altar, but the breast shall belong to Aaron and his sons. ³²And the right thigh from your sacrifices of well-being you shall give to the priest as a gift; ³³the one among Aaron's sons who offers the blood of the well-being offering and the suet shall receive the right thigh as his prebend. ³⁴For I have taken the breast of the elevation offering and the thigh of the contribution from the Israelites, from their sacrifices of well-being, and have assigned them to Aaron the priest and to his sons as a due from the Israelites for all time. ³⁵This shall be the perquisite of Aaron and the perquisite of his sons from YHWH's food gifts once they have been inducted to serve YHWH as priests, ³⁶which YHWH commanded to be assigned to them, once they had been anointed, as a due from the Israelites for all time throughout their generations.

Summary

³⁷This is the ritual for the burnt offering, the cereal offering, the purification offering, the reparation offering, the ordination offering, and the sacrifice of well-being, ³⁸which YHWH commanded Moses on Mount Sinai, when he commanded the Israelites to present their offerings to YHWH, in the Wilderness of Sinai.

PART II. THE INAUGURATION OF THE CULT (CHAPTERS 8–10)

8. The Consecration of the Priests (8:1–36)

¹YHWH spoke to Moses, saying: ²Take Aaron and his sons with him, the vestments, the anointing oil, the bull of purification offering, the two rams, and the basket of unleavened bread, ³and assemble the whole community at the entrance to the Tent of Meeting. ⁴Moses did as YHWH commanded him. And when the community was assembled at the entrance of the Tent of Meeting, ⁵Moses said to the community, "This is what YHWH has commanded to be done."

⁶Moses brought Aaron and his sons forward and had them washed with water. ⁷He put the tunic on him, girded him with the sash, clothed him with the robe, put the ephod on him, and girded him with the decorated band, which he tied to him. ⁸He put the breastpiece on him, and put into the breastpiece the Urim and Thummim. ⁹And he set the turban on his head; and on the turban, in front, he put the gold plate, the holy diadem—as YHWH had commanded Moses.

¹⁰Moses took the anointing oil and anointed the tabernacle and all that was in it, thus consecrating them. ¹¹He sprinkled some of it on the altar seven times, and he anointed the altar, all of its utensils, and the laver with its stand, to consecrate them. ¹²He poured some of the anointing oil upon Aaron's head, thereby anointing him to consecrate him. ¹³Then Moses brought Aaron's sons forward, clothed them in tunics, girded them with sashes, and tied caps on them—as YHWH had commanded Moses.

¹⁴He had the bull of purification offering brought forward. Aaron and his sons leaned their hands on the bull of purification offering, ¹⁵and it was slaughtered. Moses took the blood and with his finger put [some] on the horns around the altar, decontaminating the altar; then he poured out the blood at the base of the altar. Thus he consecrated it to effect atonement upon it. ¹⁶All of the suet that was about the entrails, and the caudate lobe of the liver, and the two kidneys and their suet, were then taken up and Moses turned [them] into smoke upon the altar; ¹⁷but the [rest of the] bull—its hide, its flesh, and its dung—was put to fire outside the camp—as YHWH had commanded Moses.

¹⁸Then the ram of burnt offering was brought forward. Aaron and his sons leaned their hands upon the ram's head, ¹⁹and it was slaughtered. Moses dashed

the blood against all sides of the altar. [20]The ram was cut up into its quarters, and Moses turned the head, the quarters, and the suet into smoke. [21]The entrails and shins were washed in water, and Moses turned all of the ram into smoke on the altar. This was a burnt offering for a pleasing aroma, a food gift to YHWH—as YHWH had commanded Moses.

[22]Then the second ram, the ram of ordination, was brought forward. Aaron and his sons leaned their hands upon the ram's head, [23]and it was slaughtered. Moses took some of its blood and put [it] on the lobe of Aaron's right ear, and on the thumb of his right hand, and on the big toe of his right foot. [24]Then the sons of Aaron were brought forward, and Moses put some of the blood on the lobes of their right ears, and on the thumbs of their right hands, and on the big toes of their right feet; and Moses dashed the [rest of the] blood against all sides of the altar. [25]He took the suet—the broad tail, all of the suet about the entrails, the caudate lobe of the liver, and the two kidneys and their suet—and the right thigh. [26]From the basket of unleavened bread that was before YHWH, he took one cake of unleavened bread, one cake of oil bread, and one wafer, and placed [them] on the suet pieces and on the right thigh. [27]He placed all of these on the palms of Aaron and on the palms of his sons, and presented them as an elevation offering before YHWH. [28]Then Moses took them from their palms and turned [them] into smoke on the altar with the burnt offering. This was an ordination offering for a pleasing aroma, a food gift to YHWH. [29]Moses took the breast and presented it as an elevation offering before YHWH; it was Moses' portion of the ram of ordination—as YHWH had commanded Moses.

[30]Then Moses took some of the anointing oil and some of the blood that was on the altar and sprinkled [it] upon Aaron's vestments, upon his sons, and upon his sons' vestments with him. Thus he consecrated Aaron's vestments, his sons, and his sons' vestments with him.

[31]And Moses said to Aaron and his sons: Boil the flesh at the entrance of the Tent of Meeting and eat it there with the bread that is in the basket of ordination—as I commanded: "Aaron and his sons shall eat it." [32]The remainder of the flesh and the bread you shall destroy by fire. [33]You shall not go outside the entrance of the Tent of Meeting for seven days, until the day that your period of ordination is completed; for your ordination will require seven days. [34]Everything done today, YHWH has commanded to be done, to make atonement for you. *[35]You shall stay at the entrance of the Tent of Meeting day and night for seven days, observing YHWH's prohibitions, so that you do not die—for so I have been commanded.*

[36]And Aaron and his sons did all of the things that YHWH had commanded through Moses.

9. *The Inaugural Service (9:1–24)*

The Sacrificial Procedure

[1]On the eighth day, Moses summoned Aaron and his sons and the elders of Israel. [2]He said to Aaron, "Take a calf of the herd for a purification offering and

a ram for a burnt offering, both without blemish, and bring [them] before YHWH. ³And speak to the Israelites, saying, 'Take a he-goat for a purification offering; a calf and a lamb, both yearlings without blemish, for a burnt offering; ⁴and an ox and a ram for a well-being offering to sacrifice before YHWH; and a cereal offering mixed with oil. For today YHWH will appear to you.'"

⁵They brought what Moses had commanded to the front of the Tent of Meeting, and the whole community came forward and stood before YHWH. ⁶Moses said, "This is what YHWH commanded that you do, that the Glory of YHWH may appear to you." ⁷Then Moses said to Aaron, "Come forward to the altar and sacrifice your purification offering and your burnt offering and make atonement for yourself and for the people; and sacrifice the people's offering and make atonement for them—as YHWH has commanded."

⁸Aaron came forward to the altar and slaughtered his calf of purification offering. ⁹Aaron's sons presented the blood to him; he dipped his finger in the blood and put [it] on the horns of the altar; and he poured out [the rest of] the blood at the base of the altar. ¹⁰The suet, the kidneys, and the caudate lobe of the liver from the purification offering he turned into smoke on the altar—as YHWH had commanded Moses; ¹¹and the flesh and the skin were consumed in fire outside the camp. ¹²Then he slaughtered the burnt offering. Aaron's sons passed the blood to him, and he dashed it against all sides of the altar. ¹³They passed the burnt offering to him in sections, and the head, and he turned [them] into smoke on the altar. ¹⁴He washed the entrails and the legs, and turned [them] into smoke on the altar with the burnt offering.

¹⁵Then he brought forward the people's offering. He took the he-goat for the people's purification offering, and slaughtered it, and performed the purification rite with it, as with the previous [purification offering]. ¹⁶He brought forward the burnt offering and sacrificed it in the prescribed manner. ¹⁷He then brought forward the cereal offering and, taking a handful of it, he turned [it] into smoke on the altar— *in addition to the burnt offering of the morning.* ¹⁸He slaughtered the ox and the ram, the people's sacrifice of well-being. Aaron's sons passed the blood to him—which he dashed against all sides of the altar— ¹⁹and the suet pieces of the ox and the ram: the broad tail, the covering [suet], the kidneys, and the caudate lobes. ²⁰They laid these suet pieces upon the breasts; and he turned the suet pieces into smoke upon the altar. ²¹Aaron presented the breasts and the right thigh as an elevation offering before YHWH—as Moses had commanded.

Blessing and Theophany

²²Then Aaron lifted his hands toward the people and blessed them; and he came down after sacrificing the purification offering, the burnt offering, and the well-being offering. ²³Moses and Aaron then entered the Tent of Meeting. When they came out, they blessed the people; and the Glory of YHWH appeared to all of the people. ²⁴Fire came forth from before YHWH and consumed the burnt offering and the suet pieces on the altar. And the people saw, and shouted for joy, and fell on their faces.

10. *The Tragic Aftermath of the Inaugural Service (10:1–20)*

Nadab and Abihu

¹Now Aaron's sons, Nadab and Abihu, each took his pan, put coals in it, and laid incense on it; and they offered before YHWH unauthorized coals, which he had not commanded them. ²And fire came forth from YHWH and consumed them; thus they died before YHWH. ³Then Moses said to Aaron, "This is what YHWH meant when he said: 'Through those near to me I shall sanctify myself, and before all of the people I shall glorify myself.' " And Aaron was silent.

⁴Moses called Mishael and Elzaphan, sons of Uzziel the uncle of Aaron, and said to them, "Come forward and carry your kinsmen away from the front of the sacred precinct [to a place] outside the camp." ⁵They came forward and carried them out of the camp by their tunics, as Moses had ordered. ⁶And Moses said to Aaron and to his sons, Eleazar and Ithamar, "Do not dishevel your hair and do not rend your clothes, lest you die and anger strike the whole community. But your kinsmen, all the house of Israel, shall bewail the burning that YHWH has wrought. ⁷You must not go outside the entrance of the Tent of Meeting, lest you die, for YHWH's anointing oil is upon you." And they did as Moses had ordered.

The Conduct and Function of the Priests

⁸And YHWH spoke to Aaron, saying: ⁹Drink no wine or ale, you or your sons after you, when you enter the Tent of Meeting, that you may not die; it is a law for all time throughout your generations. *¹⁰You must distinguish between the sacred and the common, and between the impure and the pure. ¹¹And you must teach the Israelites all of the laws that YHWH has imparted to them through Moses.*

On Eating the Priestly Portions

¹²Moses spoke to Aaron and to his remaining sons, Eleazar and Ithamar: "Take the cereal offering that remains from YHWH's food gifts and eat it unleavened beside the altar, for it is most holy. ¹³You shall eat it in the sacred precinct, inasmuch as it is your due and your sons' due from YHWH's food gifts; for so I have been commanded. ¹⁴But the breast of the elevation offering and the thigh of contribution you, and your sons and daughters after you, may eat in any pure place, for they have been assigned as a due to you and your children from the Israelites' sacrifices of well-being. ¹⁵Together with the food gifts of suet, they must present the thigh of contribution and the breast of the elevation offering, which shall be elevated as an elevation offering before YHWH, and which shall be a due to you and to your children after you for all time—as YHWH has commanded."

¹⁶Then Moses insistently inquired about the goat of the purification offering, and it had already been burned! He was angry with Eleazar and Ithamar, Aaron's remaining sons, and said, ¹⁷"Why did you not eat the purification offering in the sacred precinct? For it is most holy, and he has assigned it to you to remove the iniquity of the community to effect purgation on their behalf before YHWH.

¹⁸Because its blood was not brought into the interior of the sacred precinct, you certainly ought to have eaten it in the sacred precinct, as I commanded." ¹⁹And Aaron spoke to Moses, "See, this day they brought their purification offering and burnt offering before YHWH, and such things have befallen me! Had I eaten the purification offering today, would YHWH have approved?" ²⁰And when Moses heard this, he approved.

PART III. THE IMPURITY SYSTEM (CHAPTERS 11–16)

11. *Diet Laws (11:1–47)*

Introduction

¹YHWH spoke to Moses and Aaron, saying to them: ²Speak to the Israelites thus:

Quadrupeds

These are the creatures that you may eat from among all of the quadrupeds on the land: ³any quadruped that has hoofs, with clefts through the hoofs, and that chews the cud—such you may eat. ⁴The following, however, of those that chew the cud or have hoofs, you shall not eat: the camel—although it chews the cud, it has no hoofs: it is impure for you; ⁵the rock badger—although it chews the cud, it has no hoofs: it is impure for you; ⁶the hare—although it chews the cud, it has no hoofs: it is impure for you; ⁷and the pig—although it has hoofs, with the hoofs cleft through, it does not chew the cud: it is impure for you. ⁸You shall not eat of their flesh or touch their carcasses; they are impure for you.

Fish

⁹These you may eat of all that live in water: anything in water, whether in the seas or in the streams, that has fins or scales—these you may eat. ¹⁰But anything in the seas or in the streams that has no fins and scales, among all of the swarming creatures of the water and among all of the [other] living creatures that are in the water—they are an abomination for you ¹¹and an abomination for you they shall remain: you shall not eat of their flesh and you shall abominate their carcasses. ¹²Everything in water that has no fins and scales shall be an abomination for you.

Birds

¹³The following you shall abominate among the birds; they shall not be eaten, they are an abomination: the eagle, the black vulture, the bearded vulture, ¹⁴the kite, and falcons of every variety; ¹⁵all varieties of raven; ¹⁶the eagle owl, the

short-eared owl, and the long-eared owl; hawks of every variety; [17]the tawny owl, the fisher owl, the screech owl, [18]the white owl, and the scops owl; the osprey, [19]the stork, and herons of every variety; the hoopoe, and the bat.

Flying Insects

[20]All winged swarming creatures, that walk on all fours, shall be an abomination for you. [21]But these you may eat among all the winged swarming creatures that walk on all fours: all that have, above their feet, jointed legs to leap with on the ground. [22]Of these you may eat the following: locusts of every variety; all varieties of bald locust; crickets of every variety; and all varieties of grasshopper. [23]But all other winged swarming creatures that have four legs shall be an abomination for you.

Purification Procedures

[24]And you shall make yourselves impure with the following—whoever touches their carcasses shall be impure until evening, [25]and whoever carries any part of their carcasses shall wash his clothes and be impure until evening—[26]every quadruped that has hoofs but without clefts through the hoofs, or does not chew the cud. They are impure for you; whoever touches them shall be impure. [27]Also all animals that walk on flat paws, among those that walk on all fours, are impure for you; whoever touches their carcasses shall be impure until evening. [28]And anyone who carries their carcasses shall wash his clothes and remain impure until evening. They are impure for you.

[29]The following shall be impure for you from among the creatures that swarm on the earth: the rat, the mouse, and large lizards of every variety; [30]the gecko, the spotted lizard, the lizard, the skink, and the chameleon. [31]Those are for you the impure among all the swarming creatures; whoever touches them when they are dead shall be impure until evening. [32]And anything on which one of them falls when they are dead shall be impure: be it any article of wood, or fabric, or skin, or sackcloth—any such article that can be put to use shall be immersed in water, and it shall remain impure until evening; then it shall be pure. [33]And if any of those falls into any earthen vessel, everything inside it shall be impure and [the vessel] itself you shall break. [34]Any food that might be eaten shall become impure when it comes into contact with water; and any liquid that might be drunk shall become impure if it was inside any vessel. [35]Everything else on which the carcass of any of them falls shall be impure. An oven or a stove shall be smashed; they are impure, and impure they shall remain for you. [36]A spring or cistern in which water is collected shall remain pure, however, but whoever touches such a carcass [in it] shall be impure. [37]If such a carcass falls upon seed grain that is to be sown, it remains pure; [38]but if water is put on the seed and such a carcass falls upon it, it shall be impure for you.

[39]If a quadruped that you may eat has died, anyone who touches it shall be

impure until evening; [40]and anyone who eats of its carcass shall launder his clothes and remain impure until evening; and anyone who carries its carcass shall launder his clothes and remain impure until evening.

Land Swarmers

[41]All creatures that swarm upon the earth are an abomination; they shall not be eaten. [42]You shall not eat anything that crawls on its belly, or anything that walks on all fours, or anything that has many legs, comprising all creatures that swarm on the earth, for they are an abomination. [43]*You shall not defile your throats with any creature that swarms. You shall not make yourselves impure therewith and thus become impure,* [44]*for I YHWH am your God. You shall sanctify yourselves and be holy, for I am holy. You shall not contaminate your throats with any swarming creature that moves upon the earth.* [45]*For I YHWH am he who brought you up from the land of Egypt to be your God; you shall be holy, for I am holy.*

Summary

[46]These are the instructions concerning quadrupeds, birds, all living creatures that move in the water, and all creatures that swarm on the earth, [47]for discriminating between the impure and the pure, between creatures that may be eaten and creatures that may not be eaten.

12. *Childbirth (12:1–8)*

[1]YHWH spoke to Moses, saying: [2]Speak to the Israelites thus: When a woman at childbirth bears a male, she shall be impure for seven days; she shall be impure as during the period of her menstrual infirmity. — [3]On the eighth day the foreskin of his member shall be circumcised. — [4]She shall remain in [a state of] blood purity for thirty-three days; she shall not touch any consecrated thing, nor enter the sacred precinct until the period of her purification is complete. [5]If she bears a female, she shall be impure for two weeks, as at her menstruation, and she shall remain in [a state of] blood purity for sixty-six days.

[6]On the completion of her period of purification, for either son or daughter, she shall bring a yearling lamb for a burnt offering, and a pigeon or turtledove for a purification offering to the priest, at the entrance of the Tent of Meeting. [7]He shall offer it before YHWH and effect expiation on her behalf, and then she shall be pure from her source of blood. This is the ritual for the woman who bears a child, male or female. [8]*If, however, her means do not suffice for a sheep, she shall take two turtledoves or two pigeons, one for a burnt offering and the other for a purification offering. The priest shall effect expiation on her behalf, and she shall be pure.*

13. *Scale Disease (13:1–59)*

Introduction

[1]YHWH spoke to Moses and Aaron, saying:

Shiny Marks

[2]When a person has on the skin of his body a discoloration, a scab, or a shiny mark, and it develops into a scaly affection on the skin of his body, it shall be reported to Aaron the priest or to one of his sons, the priests. [3]The priest shall examine the affection on the skin of his body: if hair in the affection has turned white and the affection appears to be deeper than the skin of his body, it is scale disease; when the priest sees it, he shall pronounce him impure. [4]But if it is a white shiny mark on the skin of his body that does not appear deeper than the skin and its hair has not turned white, the priest shall quarantine [the person with] the affection for seven days. [5]On the seventh day, the priest shall examine him, and if the affection has retained its color and the affection has not spread on the skin, the priest shall quarantine him for another seven days. [6]On the seventh day, the priest shall examine him again: if the affection has faded and has not spread on the skin, the priest shall pronounce him pure. It is a scab; he shall wash his clothes, and he shall be pure. [7]But if the scab should spread on the skin after he has presented himself to the priest and been pronounced pure, he shall present himself again to the priest. [8]And if the priest sees that the scab has spread on the skin, the priest shall pronounce him impure; it is scale disease.

Discolorations

[9]When a person has a scaly affection, it shall be reported to the priest. [10]If the priest, on examining [him], finds on the skin a white discoloration and it has turned some hair white, with a patch of raw flesh in the discoloration, [11]it is chronic scale disease on the skin of his body, and the priest shall pronounce him impure; he shall not quarantine him, for he is impure. [12]But if the scales break out over the skin so that they cover all of the skin of the affected person from head to foot, wherever the priest can see—[13]if the priest sees that the scales have covered the whole body—he shall pronounce the affected person pure; because he has turned all white, he is pure. [14]But as soon as raw flesh appears in it, he shall be impure; [15]when the priest sees the raw flesh, he shall pronounce him impure. The raw flesh is impure; it is scale disease. [16]If the raw flesh again turns white, however, he shall come to the priest, [17]and the priest shall examine him: if the affection has turned white, the priest shall pronounce the affected person pure; he is pure.

Boils

[18]When a boil appears on the skin of one's body and it heals, [19]and a white discoloration or a reddish-white shiny mark develops where the boil was, he shall

present himself to the priest. [20]The priest shall examine [it]; if it appears lower than his skin and the hair in it has turned white, the priest shall pronounce him impure; it is scale disease that has broken out in the [site of the] boil. [21]But if the priest on examining it finds that there is no white hair in it, and it is not lower than his skin, and it is faded, the priest shall quarantine him for seven days. [22]If it has spread on the skin, the priest shall pronounce him impure; it is an affection. [23]But if the shiny mark remains stationary, not having spread, it is the scar of the boil; the priest shall pronounce him pure.

Burns

[24]When the skin of one's body sustains a burn by fire, and the patch of the burn becomes a reddish-white or white shiny mark, [25]the priest shall examine it. If some hairs in the shiny mark have turned white and it appears deeper than the skin, it is scale disease that has broken out in the burn. The priest shall pronounce him impure; it is scale disease. [26]But if the priest on examining it finds that there is no white hair in the shiny mark, and it is not lower than the skin, and it is faded, the priest shall quarantine him for seven days. [27]On the seventh day, the priest shall examine him: if it has spread on the skin, the priest shall pronounce him impure; it is scale disease. [28]But if the shiny mark has remained stationary, not having spread on the skin, and it is faded, it is the discoloration from the burn. The priest shall pronounce him pure, for it is the scar of the burn.

Scalls

[29]If a man or a woman has an affection on the head or in the beard, [30]the priest shall examine the affection. If it appears deeper than the skin and the hair in it is yellow and sparse, the priest shall pronounce him impure; it is a scall, scale disease of the head or jaw. [31]But when the priest examines the scall affection and finds that it does not appear to go deeper than the skin, yet there is no black hair in it, the priest shall quarantine [the person with] the scall affection for seven days. [32]On the seventh day, the priest shall examine the affection. If the scall has not spread, and there is no yellow hair in it, and the scall does not appear deeper than the skin, [33]the person [with the scall] shall shave himself, without shaving the scall; the priest shall quarantine him for another seven days. [34]On the seventh day, the priest shall examine the scall. If the scall has not spread on the skin, and does not appear deeper than the skin, the priest shall pronounce him pure; he shall wash his clothes, and he shall be pure. [35]If, however, the scall should spread on the skin after he has been pronounced pure, [36]the priest shall examine him. If the scall has spread on the skin, the priest need not look for yellow hair; he is impure. [37]But if [subsequently] the scall has retained its color, and black hair has grown in it, the scall has healed; he is pure. The priest shall pronounce him pure.

Tetters

[38]When a man or woman has numerous shiny marks on the skin of the body and they are white, [39]the priest shall examine [them]. If the shiny marks on the skin of the body are dull white, it is a tetter that has broken out on the skin; he is pure.

Baldness

[40]When a man's hair falls out from his head, he is bald [on the crown] but pure. [41]If the hair falls out from the front of his head, he is bald on the forehead but pure. [42]But if a reddish-white affection appears on the bald crown or forehead, it is scale disease that is breaking out on his bald crown or forehead. [43]The priest shall examine him: if the discolored affection on his bald crown or forehead is reddish white, like scale disease of fleshy skin in appearance, [44]the man has scale disease; he is impure. The priest shall not fail to pronounce him impure; he has an affected head.

The Comportment of a Certified Carrier

[45]As for the person stricken with scale disease, his clothes shall be rent, his hair shall be disheveled, he shall cover his mustache, and he shall call out, "Impure! Impure!" [46]He shall be impure as long as the affection is on him. He is impure: he shall dwell apart; his dwelling shall be outside the camp.

Fabrics

[47]When mold disease occurs in a fabric, either a wool or a linen fabric, [48]or in the warp or woof of the linen or the wool, or in a skin or in anything made of skin: [49]if the affection in the fabric or the skin, in the warp or the woof, or in any article of skin, is bright green or bright red, it is mold disease. It shall be shown to the priest. [50]The priest shall examine the affection and shall quarantine the [article with the] affection for seven days. [51]On the seventh day, he shall examine the affection: if the affection has spread in the fabric, or in the warp, or in the woof, or in the skin, for whatever function the skin serves, the affection is malignant mold disease; it is impure. [52]The fabric, or the warp, or the woof, whether in wool or linen, or any article of skin that contains the affection, shall be burned, for it is a malignant mold; it shall be destroyed by fire. [53]But if the priest sees that the affection in the fabric, or in the warp, or in the woof, or in any article of skin, has not spread, [54]the priest shall order the affected material to be washed, and he shall quarantine it for another seven days. [55]And if, after the affected material has been washed, the priest sees that the affection has not changed its color and that it has not spread, it is impure. You shall destroy it by fire; it is a fret, whether on its inner side or on its outer side. [56]But if the priest examines [it] and finds the affection faded after it has been washed, he shall cut it out from the

fabric, or from the skin, or from the warp, or from the woof; [57]and if it reappears in the fabric, or in the warp, or in the woof, or in any article of skin, it is breaking out afresh; you shall destroy the affected material by fire. [58]If, however, the affection disappears from the fabric, or warp, or woof, or any article of skin that has been washed, it shall be washed once more, and it shall be pure. [59]This is the procedure for mold disease of fabric, woolen or linen, or of warp, or of woof, or of any article of skin, for pronouncing it pure or impure.

14. *Purification after Scale Disease (14:1–57)*

Rite of Passage

[1]YHWH spoke to Moses, saying: [2]This shall be the ritual for a scale-diseased person at the time of his purification. When it is reported to the priest, [3]the priest shall go outside the camp. If the priest sees that the scale-diseased person has been healed of scale disease, [4]the priest shall order two wild pure birds, cedar wood, crimson yarn, and hyssop to be brought for the one to be purified. [5]The priest shall order one bird slaughtered into an earthen vessel over spring water; [6]and he shall take the live bird, along with the cedar wood, the crimson yarn, and the hyssop, and dip them together with the live bird in the blood of the bird that was slaughtered over the spring water. [7]He shall then sprinkle [the blood] seven times on the one to be purified of the scale disease. When he has thus purified him, he shall release the live bird over the open country. [8]The one to be purified shall launder his clothes, shave off all of his hair, and bathe in water; then he shall be pure. After that he may enter the camp, but must remain outside his tent for seven days. [9]On the seventh day, he shall shave off all of his hair—of his head, chin, and eyebrows—indeed, he shall shave off all of his hair. He shall launder his clothes and bathe in water; then he shall be pure.

Purification Sacrifices

[10]On the eighth day, he shall take two male lambs without blemish, one yearling ewe without blemish, three-tenths [of an ephah] of semolina mixed with oil for a cereal offering, and one log of oil. [11]The priest who performs the purification shall place the one to be purified, together with these [offerings], before YHWH at the entrance to the Tent of Meeting. [12]The priest shall take one of the male lambs and present it as a reparation offering, together with the log of oil, and offer it as an elevation offering before YHWH. [13]The lamb shall be slaughtered at the spot in the sacred precinct where the purification offering and the burnt offering are slaughtered. For the reparation offering is like the purification offering; it [goes] to the priest; it is most holy. [14]The priest shall take some of the blood of the reparation offering, and the priest shall put [it] on the lobe of the right ear of the one who is being purified, and on the thumb of his right hand, and on the big toe of his right foot. [15]The priest shall then take some of the log of oil and pour [it] into the palm of his own left hand. [16]And the priest

shall dip his right finger in the oil that is on his left palm and sprinkle some of the oil with his finger seven times before YHWH. [17]And some of the oil left on his palm the priest shall put on the lobe of the right ear of the one being purified, on the thumb of his right hand, and on the big toe of his right foot—on top of the blood of the reparation offering. [18]The remainder of the oil on the priest's palm shall be put on the head of the one being purified. Thus the priest shall make expiation for him before YHWH. [19]The priest shall then offer the purification offering and effect purgation for the one being purified for his impurity. After this, the burnt offering shall be slaughtered, [20]and the priest shall offer up the burnt offering and the cereal offering on the altar. And the priest shall make expiation for him. Then he shall be pure.

Purification Sacrifices for the Poor

[21]If, however, he is poor and his means are insufficient, he shall take a reparation offering of one male lamb for an elevation offering to make expiation for him, one-tenth [of an ephah] of semolina mixed with oil for a cereal offering, a log of oil; [22]and two turtledoves or two pigeons, whichever are within his means, the one to be the purification offering and the other the burnt offering. [23]On the eighth day of his purification, he shall bring them to the priest at the entrance of the Tent of Meeting, before YHWH. [24]The priest shall take the lamb of reparation offering and the log of oil, and elevate them as an elevation offering before YHWH. [25]When the lamb of reparation offering has been slaughtered, the priest shall take some of the blood of the reparation offering and put it on the right ear of the one being purified, on the thumb of his right hand, and on the big toe of his right foot. [26]The priest shall then pour some of the oil on the palm of his own left hand, [27]and with the finger of his right hand the priest shall sprinkle some of the oil that is on the palm of his left hand seven times before YHWH. [28]The priest shall put some of the oil on his palm on the lobe of the right ear of the one being purified, on the thumb of his right hand, and on the big toe of his right foot, on top of the blood spots of the reparation offering; [29]and the remainder of the oil on the priest's palm shall be put on the head of the one being purified, to make expiation for him before YHWH. [30]He shall then offer one of the turtledoves or pigeons that are within his means—[31]whichever he can afford—the one as a purification offering and the other as a burnt offering together with the cereal offering. Thus shall the priest make expiation before YHWH for the one being purified. [32]This is the ritual for the one who has scale disease [and] whose means are insufficient at [the time of] his purification.

Fungous Houses: Diagnosis and Purification

[33]YHWH spoke to Moses and Aaron, saying: [34]When you enter the land of Canaan, which I give you as a possession, and I inflict a fungous infection upon a house in the land you possess, [35]the owner of the house shall come and tell the priest, saying, "It appears to me that there is something like an infection in

my house." ³⁶*The priest shall order the house cleared before the priest enters to examine the infection, so that nothing in the house may become impure; after that the priest shall enter to examine the house. ³⁷If, when he examines the infection, the infection in the walls of the house is found to consist of bright green or bright red eruptions, which appear deeper than the wall, ³⁸the priest shall come out of the house to the entrance of the house, and quarantine the house for seven days. ³⁹On the seventh day, the priest shall return. If he sees that the infection has spread on the walls of the house, ⁴⁰the priest shall order the stones with the infection in them to be pulled out and cast outside the city into an impure place. ⁴¹The house shall be scraped inside all around, and the mortar that is scraped off shall be dumped outside the city in an impure place. ⁴²They shall take other stones and replace those stones [with them], and take other coating and plaster the house.*

⁴³*If the infection breaks out again in the house, after the stones have been pulled out and after the house has been scraped and replastered, ⁴⁴the priest shall come and examine: if the infection has spread in the house, it is a malignant fungus in the house: it [the house] is impure. ⁴⁵The house shall be demolished—its stones and timber and all of the mortar of the house—and taken to an impure place outside the city.*

⁴⁶*Whoever enters the house during the whole time it is quarantined shall be impure until evening. ⁴⁷Whoever lies down in the house must launder his clothes, and whoever eats in the house must launder his clothes.*

⁴⁸*If, however, the priest comes and sees that the infection has not spread in the house after the house was replastered, the priest shall pronounce the house pure, for the infection has healed. ⁴⁹To decontaminate the house, he shall take two birds, cedar wood, crimson thread, and hyssop. ⁵⁰One bird shall be slaughtered over spring water in an earthen vessel. ⁵¹He shall take the cedar wood, the hyssop, the crimson yarn, and the live bird, and dip them in the blood of the slaughtered bird and the spring water, and sprinkle on the house seven times. ⁵²Having decontaminated the house with the blood of the bird, the spring water, the live bird, the cedar wood, the hyssop, and the crimson thread, ⁵³he shall release the live bird over the open country outside the city. Thus he shall perform purgation upon the house, and it shall be pure.*

Summary of Chapters 13–14

⁵⁴This is the procedure for all [fleshy] scale diseases, for scalls, ⁵⁵for mold in fabrics and houses, ⁵⁶for discolorations, for scabs, or for shiny marks—⁵⁷to determine when they are impure and when they are pure. This is the procedure for scale disease.

15. *Genital Discharges (15:1–33)*

Introduction

¹YHWH spoke to Moses and Aaron, saying: ²Speak to the Israelites and say to them:

Abnormal Male Discharges

When any man has a discharge, his discharge being from his member, he is impure. ³This shall be his impurity in his discharge—whether his member runs with his discharge or his member is blocked by his discharge, this is his impurity. ⁴Any bedding on which the man with a discharge lies shall be impure; and every object on which he sits shall be impure. ⁵Anyone who touches his bedding shall launder his clothes, bathe in water, and remain impure until evening. ⁶Whoever sits on an object on which the man with a discharge has sat shall launder his clothes, bathe in water, and remain impure until evening. ⁷Whoever touches the body of the man with a discharge shall launder his clothes, bathe in water, and remain impure until evening. ⁸If the man with a discharge spits on one who is pure, the latter shall launder his clothes, bathe in water, and remain impure until evening. ⁹Any means for riding that the man with a discharge has mounted shall be impure. ¹⁰Whoever touches anything that was under him shall be impure until evening; and whoever carries such things shall launder his clothes, bathe in water, and remain impure until evening. ¹¹Anyone whom a man with a discharge touches without having rinsed his hands in water shall launder his clothes, bathe in water, and remain impure until evening. ¹²An earthen vessel that a man with a discharge touches shall be broken; and any wooden implement shall be rinsed with water.

¹³When a man with a discharge is healed of his discharge, he shall count off seven days for his purification, launder his clothes, and bathe his body in spring water; then he shall be pure. ¹⁴On the eighth day, he shall obtain two turtledoves or two pigeons and come before YHWH at the entrance of the Tent of Meeting and give them to the priest. ¹⁵The priest shall offer them up, the one as a purification offering and the other as a burnt offering. Thus the priest shall effect purgation on his behalf, for his discharge, before YHWH.

Normal Male Discharges

¹⁶When a man has an emission of semen, he shall bathe his whole body in water and remain impure until evening. ¹⁷All fabric or leather on which semen falls shall be laundered in water and remain impure until evening.

Marital Intercourse

¹⁸[This applies to] a woman, with whom a man has sexual relations; they shall bathe in water and remain impure until evening.

Normal Female Discharges

¹⁹When a woman has a discharge, her discharge being blood from her body, she remains in her menstrual impurity seven days; whoever touches her shall be impure until evening. ²⁰Anything she lies on during her menstrual impurity

shall be impure; and anything she sits on shall be impure. [21]Anyone who touches her bedding shall launder his clothes, bathe in water, and remain impure until evening; [22]and anyone who touches any object on which she has sat shall launder his clothes, bathe in water, and remain impure until evening. [23]If it [the object] is on the bedding or on the seat on which she is sitting when he touches it [the object], he shall be impure until evening. [24]And if a man proceeds to lie with her, her menstrual impurity is transmitted to him, and he shall be impure seven days; any bedding on which he lies shall become impure.

Abnormal Female Discharges

[25]When a woman has a discharge of blood for many days, not at the time of her menstrual impurity, or when she has a discharge beyond the time of her menstrual impurity, as long as her impure discharge lasts, she shall be impure, just as during her menstrual period. [26]Any bedding on which she lies while her discharge lasts shall be for her like bedding during her menstrual impurity; and any object on which she sits shall be impure, as during her menstrual impurity: [27]whoever touches them shall be impure; he shall launder his clothes, bathe in water, and remain impure until the evening.

[28]When she is healed of her discharge, she shall count off seven days, and after that she shall be pure. [29]On the eighth day, she shall obtain two turtledoves or two pigeons, and bring them to the priest at the entrance of the Tent of Meeting. [30]The priest shall offer up the one as a purification offering and the other as a burnt offering; and the priest shall effect purgation on her behalf, for her impure discharge, before YHWH.

Consequences for the Sanctuary and for Israel

[31]*You shall set apart the Israelites from their impurity, lest they die through their impurity by polluting my Tabernacle which is among them.*

Summary

[32]This is the procedure for the one who has a discharge: for the one who has an emission of semen and becomes impure thereby, [33]and for the one who is in her menstrual infirmity, and for anyone, male or female, who has a discharge, and for a man who lies with an impure woman.

16. *The Day of Purgation* (Yôm Kippûr) *(16:1–34)*

Introduction

[1]YHWH spoke to Moses after the death of the two sons of Aaron who died when they encroached upon the presence of YHWH.

Precautions and Provisions

²YHWH spoke to Moses: Tell your brother Aaron that he is not to come whenever he chooses into the adytum, inside the veil, in front of the *kappōret* that is upon the Ark, lest he die; for *by means of the cloud I shall appear on the* kappōret. ³This is how Aaron shall enter the adytum: with a bull of the herd as a purification offering and a ram for a burnt offering; ⁴he shall put on a sacral linen tunic, linen breeches shall be on his body, and he shall gird himself with a linen sash, and he shall don a linen turban. These are the sacral vestments he shall put on after bathing his body in water. ⁵And from the Israelite community he shall take two he-goats for a purification offering and a ram for a burnt offering.

The Purgation Ritual

⁶Aaron shall bring forward his own bull of purification offering to effect purgation for himself and for his household; ⁷and he shall take the two he-goats and set them before YHWH at the entrance of the Tent of Meeting. ⁸Aaron shall place lots upon the two goats, one marked "for YHWH" and the other "for Azazel." ⁹Aaron shall bring forward the goat designated by lot "for YHWH" to sacrifice it as a purification offering; ¹⁰while the goat designated by lot "for Azazel" shall be stationed alive before YHWH to perform expiation upon it by sending it off into the wilderness to Azazel.

¹¹When Aaron shall bring forward his bull of purification offering to effect purgation for himself and his household, he shall slaughter his bull of purification offering. ¹²He shall take a panful of fiery coals from atop the altar before YHWH, and two handfuls of finely ground perfumed incense, and bring [these] inside the veil. ¹³He shall put the incense on the fire before YHWH so that the cloud from the incense covers the *kappōret* that is over [the Ark of] the Pact, lest he die. ¹⁴He shall take some of the blood of the bull and sprinkle it with his finger on the *kappōret* on its east side; and in front of the *kappōret* he shall sprinkle some of the blood with his finger seven times.

¹⁵He shall then slaughter the people's goat of purification offering, bring its blood inside the veil, and manipulate its blood as he did with the blood of the bull; he shall sprinkle it upon the *kappōret* and before the *kappōret*. ¹⁶Thus he shall purge the adytum of the pollution and transgressions of the Israelites, including all of their sins; and he shall do likewise for the Tent of Meeting, which abides with them in the midst of their pollution. ¹⁷No one shall be in the Tent of Meeting when he goes in to effect purgation in the adytum until he comes out. Thus he shall effect purgation for himself and his household and for the entire congregation of Israel. ¹⁸He shall then come out to the altar that is before YHWH and effect purgation upon it. He shall take some of the blood of the bull and of the goat and put it upon the horns around the altar; ¹⁹and he shall sprinkle some of the blood upon it with his finger seven times. Thus he shall purify it of the pollution of the Israelites and consecrate it.

The Scapegoat Ritual

[20]When he has finished purging the adytum, the Tent of Meeting, and the altar, he shall bring forward the live goat. [21]Aaron shall lean both of his hands upon the head of the live goat and confess over it all of the iniquities and transgressions of the Israelites, including all of their sins, and put them on the head of the goat; and it shall be sent off to the wilderness by a man in waiting. [22]Thus the goat shall carry upon it all of their iniquities to an inaccessible region.

The Altar Sacrifices

When the goat is set free in the wilderness, [23]Aaron shall go into the Tent of Meeting, take off the linen vestments that he put on when he entered the adytum, and leave them there. [24]He shall bathe his body in water in a holy place and put on his vestments; then he shall go out and sacrifice his burnt offering and the burnt offering of the people, effecting atonement for himself and for the people. [25]The suet of the purification offering he shall turn into smoke on the altar.

The Purification of the High Priest's Assistants

[26]He who sets free the goat for Azazel shall launder his clothes and bathe his body in water; after that he may reenter the camp. [27]The purification-offering bull and the purification-offering goat whose blood was brought in to effect purgation in the adytum shall be taken outside the camp, and their hides, their flesh, and their dung shall be burned in fire. [28]He who burned them shall launder his clothes and bathe his body in water, and after that he may reenter the camp.

The Date: An Appendix

[29]*And this shall be for you a law for all time: In the seventh month, on the tenth day of the month, you shall practice self-denial; and you shall do no manner of work, neither the native-born nor the alien who resides among you.* [30]*For on this day shall purgation be effected on your behalf to purify you of all your sins; you shall become pure before YHWH.* [31]*It shall be a sabbath of complete rest for you, and you shall practice self-denial; it is a law for all time.* [32]*The priest who has been anointed and ordained to serve as priest in place of his father shall effect purgation. He shall put on the linen vestments, the sacral vestments.* [33]*He shall purge the holiest part of the sanctuary, and he shall purge the Tent of Meeting and the altar; he shall effect purgation for the priests and for all the people of the congregation.* [34]*This shall be for you a law for all time: to effect purgation on behalf of the Israelites for all their sins once a year.*

Summary

And he [Aaron] did as YHWH had commanded Moses.

PART IV. THE HOLINESS SOURCE (CHAPTERS 17–27)

17. *The Slaughter and Consumption of Meat (17:1–16)*

Introduction

[1]YHWH spoke to Moses, saying: [2]Speak to Aaron and to his sons and to all the Israelites and say to them: This is what YHWH has commanded:

No Nonsacrificial Slaughter

[3]If anyone of the house of Israel slaughters an ox or a sheep or a goat in the camp, or does so outside the camp, [4]and has not brought it to the entrance of the Tent of Meeting to present (it as) an offering to YHWH, before YHWH's Tabernacle, bloodguilt shall be imputed to that person: he has shed blood; that person shall be cut off from among his kinspeople. [5](This is) in order that the Israelites may bring their sacrifices which they have been sacrificing in the open field—that they may bring them to YHWH, at the entrance of the Tent of Meeting, to the priest, and offer them as sacrifices of well-being to YHWH; [6]that the priest may dash the blood against the altar of YHWH at the entrance of the Tent of Meeting, and turn the suet into smoke as a pleasing aroma to YHWH; [7]and that they may offer their sacrifices no longer to the goat-demons after whom they stray. They shall have this (statute) as an eternal law, throughout their generations.

No Sacrifices to Other (Infernal) Gods

[8]And say to them further: If anyone of the house of Israel or of the aliens who may reside among them offers up a burnt offering or a (well-being) offering, [9]and does not bring it to the entrance of the Tent of Meeting to offer it to YHWH, that person shall be cut off from his kinspeople.

[10]And if anyone of the house of Israel or of the aliens who reside among them ingests any blood, I will set my face against the person who ingests blood, and I will cut him off from among his kinspeople. [11]For the life of the flesh is in the blood, and I have assigned it to you on the altar to ransom your lives; for it is the blood that ransoms by means of life. [12]Therefore I say to the Israelites: No person among you shall ingest blood, nor shall the alien who resides among you ingest blood.

[13]And if any Israelite or any alien who resides among them hunts down a beast or bird that may be eaten, he shall pour out its blood and cover it with earth. [14]For the life of all flesh—its blood is with its life. Therefore I said to the Israelites: You shall not ingest the blood of any flesh, for the life of all flesh is its blood; anyone who ingests it shall be cut off.

Eating of a Carcass Requires Purification

[15]And any person, whether citizen or alien, who eats what has died or has been torn by beasts shall launder his clothes, bathe in water, and remain impure until the evening; then he shall be pure. [16]But if he does not launder (his clothes) and bathe his body, he shall bear his punishment.

18. *Illicit Sexual Practices (18:1–30)*

Opening Exhortation

[1]YHWH spoke to Moses, saying: [2]Speak to the Israelites and say to them: I am YHWH your God. [3]As is done in the land of Egypt where you dwelt, you shall not do, and as they do in the land of Canaan to which I am bringing you, you shall not do; you shall not follow their statutes. [4]My rules alone shall you observe and my statutes alone shall you heed, following them: I YHWH your God (have spoken). [5]You shall heed my statutes and my rules, which if one does them, he shall live by them: I YHWH (have spoken).

The Prohibitions

[6]No one shall approach anyone of his own flesh to uncover nakedness: I YHWH (have spoken). [7]The nakedness of your father, that is, the nakedness of your mother, you shall not uncover; she is your mother—you shall not uncover her nakedness. [8]The nakedness of your father's wife you shall not uncover; it is the nakedness of your father. [9]The nakedness of your sister, the daughter of your father or the daughter of your mother—whether of the household clan or of an outside clan—do not uncover her nakedness. [10]The nakedness of your son's daughter or of your daughter's daughter—do not uncover their nakedness; for their nakedness is your own nakedness. [11]The nakedness of your father's wife's daughter who is of your father's clan—she is your sister; do not uncover her nakedness. [12]The nakedness of your father's sister you shall not uncover; she is of your father's flesh. [13]The nakedness of your mother's sister you shall not uncover; for she is your mother's flesh. [14]The nakedness of your father's brother you shall not uncover, (that is,) you shall not approach his wife; she is your aunt. [15]The nakedness of your daughter-in-law you shall not uncover: she is your son's wife; do not uncover her nakedness. [16]The nakedness of your brother's wife you shall not uncover; it is your brother's nakedness.

[17]The nakedness of a woman and her daughter you shall not uncover; neither shall you marry her son's daughter or her daughter's daughter to uncover her nakedness: they are kindred; it is depravity. [18]And you shall not marry a woman producing rivalry to her sister, uncovering her nakedness during her (sister's) lifetime. [19]You shall not approach a woman during her menstrual impurity to uncover her nakedness. [20]You shall not have sexual relations with your neighbor's wife and defile yourself through her. [21]You shall not dedicate any of

your offspring to be sacrificed to Molek, and thereby not desecrate the name of your god: I YHWH (have spoken). 22You shall not lie with a male as one lies with a woman: it is an abomination. 23You shall not have sexual relations with any animal to defile yourself thereby; nor shall any woman give herself to an animal to mate with it; it is a perversion.

Closing Exhortation

24Do not defile yourselves in any of these (practices), for by all these (practices) the nations I am casting out before you defiled themselves. 25Thus the land became defiled; and I called it to account for its iniquity, and the land vomited out its inhabitants. 26You, however, must keep my statutes and my rules and commit none of these abominations, neither the citizen nor the alien who resides among you; 27for all these abominations the people in the land who (were) before you did, and the land became defiled. 28So let not the land vomit you out for defiling it, as it is vomiting out the nation that was before you. 29For all who commit any of these abominations—such persons shall be cut off from their kin. 30So you will heed my prohibitions not to commit any of these statutory abominations that were done before you, and not defile yourself by them: I (who speak) am YHWH your God.

19. Ritual and Moral Holiness (19:1–37)

Opening: Call to Holiness

1YHWH spoke to Moses, saying: 2Speak to the entire Israelite community and say to them: You shall be holy, for I, YHWH your God, am holy.

Religious Duties

3You shall each revere his mother and his father, and keep my sabbaths: I YHWH your God (have spoken).
    4Do not turn to idols, and molten gods do not make for yourselves: I YHWH your God (have spoken).
    5When you sacrifice a well-being offering to YHWH, sacrifice it so it may be accepted on your behalf. 6It shall be eaten on the day you sacrifice (it), or on the next day; but what is left by the third day must be consumed in fire. 7But if it is eaten at all on the third day, it is rotten meat; it will not be acceptable. 8Anyone who eats of it shall bear his punishment, because he has desecrated what is sacred to YHWH; that person shall be cut off from his kin.
    9When you reap the harvest of your land, you shall not destroy the edge of your field in reaping, and the gleanings of your harvest you shall not gather. 10Your vineyard you shall not pick bare, and the fallen fruit of your vineyard you shall not gather. For the poor and the alien shall you leave them: I YHWH your God (have spoken).

Ethical Duties

[11]You shall not steal; you shall not dissemble, and you shall not lie to one another. [12]And you shall not swear falsely by my name, lest you desecrate the name of your God: I YHWH (have spoken).

[13]You shall not exploit your fellow, and you shall not commit robbery. The wages of your hireling shall not remain with you until morning. [14]You shall not insult the deaf, and before the blind you shall not place a stumbling block, but you shall fear your God: I YHWH (have spoken).

[15]You shall not do injustice in judgment. You shall not be partial to the poor or favor the rich; in righteousness shall you judge your fellow. [16]You shall not go about as a slanderer among your kin; you shall not stand aloof beside the blood of your fellow: I YHWH (have spoken).

[17]You shall not hate your brother (Israelite) in your heart. Reprove your fellow openly so that you will not bear punishment because of him. [18]Rather, you shall not take revenge or nurse a grudge against members of your people. You shall love your fellow as yourself: I YHWH (have spoken).

Miscellaneous Duties

[19]You shall heed my statutes.

You shall not let your cattle mate with a different kind; you shall not sow your field with two kinds of seed; and clothing made of two kinds of yarn you shall not put on yourself.

[20]*If a man has sexual intercourse with a woman who is a slave betrothed to another man, but has not been ransomed or given her freedom, there shall be an inquest; they shall not be put to death because she has not been freed.* [21]*But he shall bring to the entrance of the Tent of Meeting, as his penalty to YHWH, a ram of reparation offering.* [22]*And the priest shall make expiation for him before YHWH with the ram of reparation offering for his wrong that he committed, so that he may be forgiven of his wrong that he committed.**

[23]When you enter the land and plant any kind of fruit tree, you shall treat its foreskin with its fruit as foreskin. Three years it shall be forbidden to you; it shall not be eaten. [24]In the fourth year, all of its fruit shall be sacred, an offering of rejoicing to YHWH. [25]In the fifth year, you may use its fruit that its yield may be increased for you: I YHWH your God (have spoken).

[26]You shall not eat over the blood. You shall not practice augury or divination. [27]You shall not round off the side-growth on your head, and you shall not destroy the edge of your beard. [28]Gashes in your flesh you shall not make for the dead, and tattoos you shall not put on yourselves: I YHWH (have spoken).

[29]You shall not degrade your daughter by making her a prostitute so that the land may not be prostituted and the land be filled with lewdness.

---

*Vv. 20–22 are an insertion from the P source.

Closing

³⁰You shall keep my sabbaths and my sanctuary you shall revere: I YHWH (have spoken).

³¹Do not turn to ghosts and do not search for wizard-spirits to become impure by them: I YHWH your God (have spoken).

³²In the presence of the elderly you shall rise, and thereby you will show respect to the aged; you shall fear your God: I YHWH (have spoken).

Appendix

³³When an alien resides with you in your land, you shall not oppress him. ³⁴The alien residing with you shall be to you as a citizen among you. You shall love him as yourself, for you were aliens in the land of Egypt: I YHWH your God (have spoken).

³⁵You shall not do injustice in judgment, (namely,) in measures of weight or capacity. ³⁶You shall have an honest scale, honest weights, an honest ephah, and an honest hin.

Closing Exhortation

I YHWH am your God who freed you from the land of Egypt. ³⁷You shall heed all my statutes and all my rules, and you shall do them: I YHWH (have spoken).

20. *Penalties for Molek Worship, Necromancy, and Sexual Offenses (20:1–27)*

¹And YHWH spoke to Moses: ²Say further to the Israelites:

Penalties for Molek Worship

Any man from among the Israelites, or among the aliens residing in Israel, who dedicates any of his offspring to Molek, must be put to death; the people of the land shall pelt him with stones. ³And I myself will set my face against that man and cut him off from among his people, because he dedicated his offspring, thus defiling my sanctuary and desecrating my holy name. ⁴And if the people of the land indeed shut their eyes to that man when he gives of his offspring to Molek by not putting him to death, ⁵I myself will set my face against that man and his family, and I will cut off from among their kin both him and all who whore after him in whoring after Molek.

Penalty for Necromancy

⁶And if any person turns to ghosts and wizard-spirits to whore after them, I will set my face against that person and I will cut him off from among his kin.

Opening Exhortation

[7]You shall sanctify yourselves and be holy, for I YHWH am your God. [8]You shall heed my statutes and do them: (Thereby) I YHWH make you holy.

Penalties for Sexual Violations

[9]If any man dishonors his father or his mother, he must be put to death; he has dishonored his father or his mother—his bloodguilt is upon him.
  [10]If a man commits adultery with a married woman—committing adultery with his (Israelite) neighbor's wife—the adulterer and the adulteress must be put to death. [11]If a man lies with his father's wife, it is the nakedness of his father that he has uncovered; the two of them must be put to death—their bloodguilt is upon them. [12]If a man lies with his daughter-in-law, the two of them must be put to death; they have committed a perversion—their bloodguilt is upon them. [13]If a man lies with a male as one lies with a woman, the two of them have done an abhorrent thing; they must be put to death—their bloodguilt is upon them. [14]If a man marries a woman and her mother, it is a depravity; by fire they shall burn him and them, that there be no depravity among you. [15]If a man has sexual relations with a beast, he must be put to death, and you shall kill the beast. [16]If a woman approaches any beast to mate with it, you shall kill the woman and the beast; they must be put to death—their bloodguilt is upon them.
  [17]If a man marries his sister, the daughter of either his father or his mother, so that he sees her nakedness and she sees his nakedness, it is a disgrace; they shall be cut off in the sight of their people. He has uncovered the nakedness of his sister; he shall bear his iniquity. [18]If a man lies with a woman in her infirmity and uncovers her nakedness, he has laid bare her source and she has exposed the source of her blood; the two of them shall be cut off from among their kin. [19]You shall not uncover the nakedness of your mother's sister or your father's sister, for that is laying bare his own flesh; they shall bear their punishment. [20]If a man lies with his uncle's wife, it is his uncle's nakedness that he has uncovered. They shall bear their sin: they shall die childless. [21]If a man marries the wife of his brother, it is repulsive. It is the nakedness of his brother that he has uncovered; they shall remain childless.

Closing Exhortation

[22]You shall heed all my statutes and all my regulations and do them, so that the land to which I bring you to settle in will not vomit you out. [23]You shall not follow the statutes of the nations that I am driving out before you. It is because they did all these things that I loathed them [24]and said to you: You shall possess their land, and I myself will give it to you to possess, a land flowing with milk and honey. I YHWH am your God who has set you apart from other peoples. [25]So you shall distinguish between the pure and the impure quadrupeds

and between the impure and the pure birds. You shall not defile your throats with a quadruped or bird or anything with which the ground teems, which I have set apart for you to treat as impure. ²⁶You shall be holy to me, for I YHWH am holy; therefore I have set you apart from other peoples to be mine.

Appendix: Penalty for Mediums

²⁷A man or a woman who is a medium for a ghost or wizard-spirit shall be put to death; they shall be pelted with stones—their bloodguilt is upon them.

21. *Instructions for the Priests (21:1–24)*

¹YHWH said to Moses: Say to the priests, the sons of Aaron, and say to them:

Mourning

None shall defile himself (mourning) for any dead person among his kin, ²except for his closest relatives: his mother, his father, his son, his daughter, and his brother; ³also for his marriageable sister, closest to him, who has no husband, for her he may defile himself. ⁴But he shall not defile himself among his kinspeople, thereby desecrating himself.

⁵They shall not make any bald patches on their heads, or shave off the edge of their beards, or make gashes in their flesh. ⁶They shall be holy to their God and not desecrate the name of their God; for they offer the gifts of YHWH, the food of their God, and so must be holy.

Marriage

⁷They shall not marry a promiscuous woman or one who was raped, nor shall they marry a woman divorced from her husband. For each (priest) is holy to his God, ⁸and you must treat him as holy, since he offers the food of your God; he shall be holy to you, for I YHWH who sanctifies you am holy.

Addendum on a Priest's Daughter

⁹When the daughter of a priest desecrates herself by harlotry, it is her father whom she desecrates; she shall be burned by fire.

The High Priest

¹⁰The priest who is preeminent among his fellows, on whose head the anointing oil has been poured and who has been ordained to wear the (priestly) vestments, shall not dishevel his hair or rend his vestments. ¹¹He shall not go in

where there is a dead body; even for his father or mother he shall not defile himself. [12]He shall not leave the sacred area so that he not desecrate the sacred area of his God, for the distinction of the anointing oil of his God is upon him. I (who speak) am YHWH.

[13]He is to marry a young virgin. [14]A widow, a divorcee, a raped woman, or a harlot: these he shall not marry. Only a young virgin of his kin may he take to wife [15]that he not desecrate his offspring among his kin, for I am YHWH who sanctifies him.

Blemished Priests

[16]YHWH spoke to Moses: [17]Speak to Aaron and say: A man of your offspring in any generation who has a blemish shall not be qualified to offer the food of his God. [18]No one at all who has a blemish shall be qualified: a man who is blind, lame, disfigured, or deformed; [19]a man who has a broken leg or broken arm, [20]or who is a hunchback, or a dwarf, or has a discoloration of the eye, a scar, a lichen, or a crushed testicle. [21]Every man among the offspring of Aaron the priest who has a blemish shall not be qualified to offer YHWH's gifts; having a blemish, he shall not be qualified to offer the food of his God. [22]He may eat the food of his God, of the most holy and of the holy. [23]But he shall not enter before the veil or officiate at the altar, for he has a blemish. And he may not desecrate my sanctums. (Thereby) I am YHWH who sanctifies them.

Subscript

[24]Thus Moses spoke to Aaron and his sons and to all the Israelites.

22. *Instructions for the Priests and Lay Persons (22:1–33)*

[1]YHWH spoke to Moses, saying: [2]Instruct Aaron and his sons to be scrupulous concerning the sacred donations that the Israelites consecrate to me so they do not desecrate my holy name, I am YHWH. [3]Say (further) to them: Throughout your generations, if any man of your offspring, while he is impure, encroaches upon the sacred donations that the Israelites may consecrate to YHWH, that person shall be cut off from my presence: I YHWH (have spoken).

Concerning Sacred Food

[4]Any man of Aaron's offspring who has scale disease or a chronic discharge [or is contaminated by a corpse], may not eat of the sacred donations until he is pure. [One who touches anything contaminated by a corpse, or] If a man has an emission of semen, [5]or if a man touches any swarming thing by which he is

made impure or any human being by whom he is made impure whatever (be) his impurity, [6]the person who touches any of these shall be impure until evening, and he shall not eat of the sacred donations unless he has washed his body in water [7]and the sun has set. Then, he shall be pure; and afterward he may eat of the sacred donations, for they are his food. [8]He shall not eat of any animal that died or was torn by beasts to become impure by it. I YHWH (have spoken). [9]They shall heed my prohibition lest they bear sin by it and die thereby when they desecrate it; I am YHWH who sanctifies them.

[10]No lay person shall eat sacred food; neither may a priest's resident hireling eat sacred food. [11]But if a priest purchases a person with money, he may eat of it; and those born into his household may eat of his food. [12]If a priest's daughter marries a layman, she may not eat of the sacred gifts; [13]but if a priest's daughter is widowed or divorced and without children, and returns to her father's house as in her youth, she may eat of her father's food. But no lay person may eat of it.

[14]If any (lay) person inadvertently eats of a sacred donation, he shall add one-fifth of its value to it and pay to the priests the (combined) sacred donation. [15]They (the priests) shall not desecrate the sacred donations of the Israelites that they set aside for YHWH [16]by causing them (the Israelites) to bear the penalty of reparation when they (the Israelites) eat their (own) sacred donations; for it is I YHWH who sanctifies them (the priests).

Concerning Blemished Sacrificial Animals

[17]YHWH spoke to Moses, saying: [18]Speak to Aaron, to his sons, and to all the Israelites, and say to them:

Whenever any person from the house of Israel or from the aliens in Israel presents an offering for any of his vows or any of his freewill gifts, which may be presented to YHWH as a burnt offering, [19]to be acceptable on your behalf (it must be) a male without blemish, from cattle, sheep, or goats. [20]You shall not present any that has a blemish, because it will not be acceptable on your behalf.

[21]And whenever any person presents, from the herd or the flock, a well-being offering to YHWH for an expressed vow or as a freewill offering, (it must be) perfect in order to be acceptable; it shall not have any blemish. [22]Anything blind, (has a) broken (limb), is maimed, (has) a seeping sore, a scar, or a lichen—such you shall not present to YHWH; you shall not put any of them on the altar as a food gift to YHWH. [23]You may, however, sacrifice as a freewill offering a herd or flock animal with an extended or contracted (limb), but it will not be accepted for a votive offering. [24]You shall not offer to YHWH (an animal) with bruised, crushed, torn, or cut-off (testicles). You shall not do (this) in your land. [25]And from the hand of a foreigner, you shall not offer the food of your God from any of these. Because of deformities and blemishes in them, they will not be accepted on your behalf.

Additional Criteria for Sacrificial Animals

²⁶YHWH spoke to Moses, saying: ²⁷Whenever an ox or a sheep or a goat is born, it shall remain seven days with its mother, and from the eighth day on it will be acceptable as a food-gift offering to YHWH. ²⁸However, no animal from the herd or from the flock shall be slaughtered on the same day as its young.

²⁹When you sacrifice a thanksgiving offering to YHWH, sacrifice [it] so that it will be acceptable on your behalf. ³⁰It shall be eaten on the same day; you shall not leave any of it until morning. I YHWH (have spoken).

Exhortation

³¹You shall heed my commandments and do them. I YHWH (have spoken). ³²You shall not desecrate my holy name that I may be sanctified in the midst of the Israelites. I am YHWH who sanctifies you, ³³your deliverer from the land of Egypt to be your God; I am YHWH.

23. *The Holiday Calendar (23:1–44)**

¹YHWH spoke to Moses, saying: ²Speak to the Israelites and say to them: **(As for) the fixed times of YHWH, which you shall proclaim as sacred occasions, these are my fixed times.**

The Sabbath

³Six days' work may be done, but the seventh day is a sabbath of complete rest, a sacred occasion. You shall do no work; it is a sabbath of YHWH throughout your settlements.

The Festivals

⁴These are the fixed times of YHWH, the sacred occasions, which you shall proclaim at their fixed times:

The Paschal Offering and the Unleavened Bread

⁵In the first month, on the fourteenth (day) of the month, at twilight, a paschal offering to YHWH, ⁶and on the fifteenth day of that month the Pilgrimage-Festival of Unleavened Bread to YHWH. Seven days you are to eat unleavened bread. ⁷The first day shall be for you a sacred occasion: You shall do no la-

---

*In chap. 23, italic block type (as in v. 1) stands for H, boldface block type (as in v. 2b) for H$_R$, standard type (as in v. 10b) for Pre-H$_1$, and boldface standard type (as in v. 11b) for Pre-H$_2$. For details see the commentary on chap. 23, COMMENT A.

borious work. *8Seven days you shall offer food gifts to YHWH. The seventh day is a sacred occasion: You shall do no laborious work.*

The First Barley Offering

9YHWH spoke to Moses, saying: 10Speak to the Israelites and say to them:

When you enter the land I am giving to you and you reap its harvest, you shall bring the first sheaf of your harvest to the priest. 11He shall elevate the sheaf before YHWH. For acceptance on your behalf **from the day after the sabbath-week** the priest shall elevate it. 12On the day that you elevate the sheaf, you shall sacrifice an unblemished male lamb in its first year as a burnt offering to YHWH. 13Its accompanying cereal offering shall be two-tenths of an ephah of semolina mixed with oil, a food gift of pleasing aroma to YHWH; and its accompanying libation shall be one-fourth of a hin of wine. 14Do not partake (from the new crop) of any bread or parched or fresh grain until the very day you have brought your God's offering—*a law for all time, throughout your generations, in all your settlements.*

The First Wheat Offering

15And **from the day after the sabbath-week,** from the day on which you bring the elevation offering of the sheaf, you shall count for yourselves **seven sabbath-weeks. They must be complete:** 16**You shall count until the day after the seventh sabbath-week** fifty days. Then you shall present a new cereal offering to YHWH. 17You shall bring from your settlements as an elevation offering of two bread (loaves), comprising two-tenths (of an ephah) of semolina and baked after leavening, as firstfruits for YHWH. *18With the bread you shall offer seven unblemished yearling lambs, one bull of the herd, and two rams; (they) shall be a burnt offering to YHWH, and with their cereal offerings and libations, a food gift of pleasant aroma to YHWH. 19You shall sacrifice one he-goat as a purification offering* and two yearling lambs as a sacrifice of well-being. 20And the priest shall elevate them *with the bread of firstfruits* as an elevation offering to YHWH *with the two lambs;* they shall be holy to YHWH for the priest. *21On that very day, you shall proclaim: It shall be for you a sacred occasion; you must do no laborious work—a law for all time, in all your settlements, throughout your generations. 22And when you reap the harvest of your land, you shall not complete (it) to the edge of your field, or gather the gleanings of your harvest; you shall leave them for the poor and for the alien; I am YHWH your God.*

The Festival of Alarm Blasts

23YHWH spoke to Moses, saying: 24Speak to the Israelites thus: In the seventh month, on the first day of the month, you shall observe a rest, a sacred occasion, commemorated with short blasts. 25You shall do no laborious work; and you shall present a food gift to YHWH.

The Day of Purgation

26YHWH spoke to Moses, saying: 27However, the tenth day of this seventh month is the Day of Purgation. It shall be a sacred occasion for you; you shall afflict yourselves, and you shall offer a food gift to YHWH; 28you shall do no work on that very day. For it is a purgation day, to effect purgation on your behalf before YHWH your God. 29Indeed, any person who does not afflict himself on that very day will be cut off from his kin; 30and any person who does any work on that very day I will cause that person to perish among his people. 31You shall do no work; it is a law for all time, throughout your generations, in all your settlements. 32It shall be a sabbath of complete rest for you, and you shall afflict yourselves; on the ninth day of the month at evening, from evening to evening, you shall observe your sabbath.

The Festival of Booths

33YHWH spoke to Moses, saying: 34Say to the Israelites thus: On the fifteenth day of this seventh month [there shall be] the pilgrimage-festival of Booths, [lasting] seven days to YHWH. 35The first day shall be a sacred occasion; you shall do no laborious work. 36Seven days you shall present food gifts to YHWH. On the eighth day, you shall observe a sacred occasion and present a food gift to YHWH. It is a solemn assembly; you shall do no laborious work.

Summary

37These are the fixed times of YHWH, which you shall proclaim as sacred occasions, to present food gifts to YHWH—burnt offerings, cereal offerings, sacrifices, and libations, the daily protocol on each day—38apart from the sabbath offerings of YHWH, and apart from your gifts, and apart from your votive offerings, and apart from your freewill offerings that you give to YHWH.

Addendum on the Festival of Booths

39However, on the fifteenth day of the seventh month, when you have ingathered the yield of the land, you shall celebrate the pilgrimage-festival of YHWH seven days: on the first day, rest and on the eighth day, rest. 40On the first day you shall take for yourselves the boughs of majestic trees: fronds of palms, branches of leafy trees, and willows of the brook, and you shall rejoice before YHWH your God seven days. *41You shall celebrate it as a Pilgrimage-Festival to YHWH for seven days in the year as a law for all time, throughout your generations. You shall celebrate it in the seventh month.* **42In booths you shall live seven days; all citizens in Israel shall live in booths, 43in order that your generations may know that I made the Israelites live in booths when I brought them out of the land of Egypt; I am YHWH your God.**

44Thus Moses declared the fixed times of YHWH to the Israelites.

24. Tabernacle Oil and Bread; the Case of Blasphemy (24:1–23)

Oil for the Tabernacle Lamps

¹YHWH spoke to Moses, saying: ²Command the Israelites to bring you clear oil of beaten olives for lighting, for kindling a flame regularly. ³Aaron shall set it up in the Tent of Meeting outside the veil of the Pact [to burn] from evening to morning before YHWH regularly; it is a law for all times, throughout your generations. ⁴On the pure (golden) lampstand shall be set up the lamps before YHWH [to burn] regularly.

Bread for the Tabernacle Table

⁵You shall take semolina and bake it (into) twelve loaves; two-tenths of an ephah shall be in each loaf. ⁶You shall place them (in) two piles, six to a pile, on the table of pure (gold) before YHWH. ⁷With each pile you shall place pure frankincense, which shall be a token offering for the bread, a food gift for YHWH. ⁸Every sabbath day it shall be set up before YHWH regularly, (a commitment) of the Israelites as a covenant for all time. ⁹It shall belong to Aaron and his descendants; and they shall eat it in a holy place; it is a most sacred portion for him from the food gifts of YHWH, a due for all time.

The Case of the Blasphemer

¹⁰There came out among the Israelites a man whose mother was Israelite and whose father was Egyptian. And a fight broke out in the camp between the son of an Israelite woman and a certain Israelite. ¹¹The son of the Israelite woman pronounced the Name, cursing it, and he was brought to Moses—now his mother's name was Shelomith, daughter of Dibri, of the tribe of Dan—¹²and he was put in custody, (until) the decision of YHWH should be made clear to them. ¹³And YHWH spoke to Moses, saying: ¹⁴Take the blasphemer outside the camp; and have all who were within hearing lean their hands on his head; then have the whole community stone him. ¹⁵And to the Israelites speak thus: Anyone who curses his God shall bear his punishment; ¹⁶but if he (also) pronounces the name of YHWH he must be put to death. The whole community shall stone him; alien as well as citizen, if he has (thus) pronounced the Name, he must be put to death.

The Talion Laws

¹⁷If anyone kills any human being, he must be put to death. ¹⁸But anyone who kills an animal shall make restitution for it, life for life. ¹⁹If anyone maims another, as he has done so shall it be done to him: ²⁰fracture for fracture, eye for eye, tooth for tooth. The injury he has inflicted on the person shall be inflicted

on him. [21]One who kills an animal shall make restitution for it; but one who kills a human being shall be put to death. [22]You shall have one law for the alien and citizen alike: for I YHWH your God (have spoken).

The Compliance Report

[23]Moses spoke (thus) to the Israelites. And they took the blasphemer outside the camp and pelted him with stones. The Israelites did as YHWH had commanded Moses.

25. Jubilee, the Priestly Solution for Economic Injustice (25:1–55)

Introduction

[1]YHWH spoke to Moses at Mount Sinai: [2]Speak to the Israelites and say to them:

The Sabbatical Year

When you enter the land that I give you, the land shall observe a sabbath to YHWH. [3]Six years you may sow your field, and six years you may prune your vineyard and gather in its produce. [4]But in the seventh year there shall be a sabbath of complete rest for the land, a sabbath to YHWH; you may neither sow your field nor prune your vineyard. [5]The aftergrowth of your harvest you shall not reap, nor the grapes of your untrimmed vines shall you pick; it shall be (a year of) complete rest for the land. [6]But the sabbath (-yield) of the land will be for you to eat: for you, for your male and female slaves, your resident hirelings, who live under your authority, [7]your livestock and the wild animals in your land—all of its yield will be (available for you) to eat.

The Jubilee Year

[8]You shall count for yourself seven weeks of years—seven times seven years—so that the period of seven weeks of years gives you (a total of) forty-nine years. [9]Then you shall sound the horn loud; in the seventh month, on the tenth day of the month—the Day of Purgation—you shall have the horn sounded throughout your land, [10]and you shall sanctify the fiftieth year, proclaiming release throughout the land for all its inhabitants. It shall be a jubilee for you, when each of you shall return to his holding and each of you shall return to his kin group. [11]That fiftieth year shall be a jubilee for you; you shall not sow, nor shall you reap its aftergrowth or pick its untrimmed vines. [12]Since it is a jubilee, sacred it shall be to you; you may only eat its produce (direct) from the field. [13]In this year of jubilee, each of you shall return to his holding.

[14]When you sell property to your fellow, or buy (any) from your fellow, you shall not cheat one another. [15]On the basis of the number of years since the jubilee shall you buy from your fellow; on the basis of the number of (remaining) crop years shall he sell to you; [16]the more such years, the more its purchase price; the fewer such years, the less its purchase price; for it is the number of crops that he is selling you. [17]Do not cheat one another, but fear your God; for I YHWH am your God.

[18]You shall perform my laws, and my rules you shall heed and you shall perform them, that you may dwell on the land in security. [19]The land shall yield its fruit and you shall eat your fill, and you shall dwell upon it in security. [20]And should you say, "What are we to eat in the seventh year, if we may not sow or gather in our crops?" [21]I will ordain my blessing for you in the sixth year, so that it will yield a crop (sufficient) for three years. [22]When you sow (in) the eighth year, you will (continue to) eat from the old crop; until the ninth year, until its crop comes in, you shall eat the old.

Redemption of Property: The Basic Principle

[23]Furthermore, the land must not be sold beyond reclaim, for the land is mine; you are but resident aliens under my authority. [24]Therefore, throughout the land you hold, you must provide redemption for the land.

The Three Stages of Destitution

Stage One: Sold Land and Houses and Their Redemption

[25]When your brother (Israelite) becomes impoverished and has to sell part of his holding, his closest redeemer shall come and redeem the sold property of his brother. [26]If a man has no redeemer but prospers and acquires enough for his redemption, [27]he shall compute the years since its sale, refund the difference to the man to whom he sold it, and return to his holding. [28]If he does not acquire sufficient means to recover it, his sold property shall remain with its buyer until the jubilee year; it shall be released in the jubilee, and he shall return to his holding.

[29]If a man sells a dwelling house (in) a walled city, it may be redeemed until the end of a year of its sale; its redemption period shall be a year. [30]If it is not redeemed before the completion of one full year, the house in the walled city shall belong to its purchaser beyond reclaim throughout the ages; it shall not be released in the jubilee. [31]However, houses in hamlets that have no encircling walls shall be classed as open country; they may be redeemed, and in the jubilee they shall be released. [32]As for the Levitic cities—the houses in the cities they hold—the Levites shall forever have the right of redemption. [33]Whoever of the Levites redeems (should know that) the house sold (in) the city of his possession shall be released in the jubilee; for the houses in the cities of the Levites are their holding among the Israelites. [34]But the field of

the livestock enclosures (about) their cities may not be sold, for that is their holding forever.

Stage Two: Lost Land

³⁵If your brother, being (further) impoverished, falls under your authority, and you (would) hold him (as though he were) a resident alien, let him subsist under your authority. ³⁶Do not exact from him advance or accrued interest. Fear your God, and let your brother subsist under your authority. ³⁷Do not lend him money at advance interest, or lend him food at accrued interest. ³⁸I, YHWH, am your God, who freed you from the land of Egypt, to give you the land of Canaan, to be your God.

Stage Three: "Slavery"

³⁹If your brother, being (further) impoverished under your authority, is sold to you, do not make him work as a slave. ⁴⁰He shall remain under you as a resident hireling; he shall work under you until the jubilee year. ⁴¹Then he and his children with him shall be released from your authority; he shall return to his kin group and return to his ancestral holding.—⁴²For they are my slaves, whom I freed from the land of Egypt; they shall not be sold as slaves are sold.—⁴³You shall not rule over him with harshness; you shall fear your God.

⁴⁴Male and female slaves as you may have—(it is) from the nations around about you, from them that you may buy male and female slaves. ⁴⁵Also from among the children of residents (aliens) who live under your sway, from them you may buy (slaves), or from their kin groups that are under your sway, whom they begot in your land. These shall become your property; ⁴⁶you may keep them as a possession for your children after you, for them to inherit as property for all time. These you may treat as slaves, but as for your Israelite brothers, no one shall rule over the other with harshness.

⁴⁷If a resident alien under you has prospered, and your brother, being (further) impoverished, comes under his authority and is sold to the resident alien under you, or to a branch of the alien's kin group, ⁴⁸after he is sold he shall have the right of redemption. One of his brothers shall redeem him, ⁴⁹or his uncle or his uncle's son shall redeem him, or anyone of his kin group who is of his own flesh shall redeem him; or if he prospers, he may redeem himself. ⁵⁰He shall compute with his buyer the total from the year he was sold to him until the jubilee year: the price of his sale shall be applied to the number of years, as the term of a hired laborer he shall be under the other's authority. ⁵¹If many years remain, he shall pay back (for) his redemption in proportion to his purchase price; ⁵²and if few years remain until the jubilee year, he shall so compute; according to the years involved, he shall pay back (for) his redemption. ⁵³As a worker hired by the year shall he be under his (the alien's) authority, who (however) shall not rule over him with harshness in your sight. ⁵⁴If he has not been redeemed in any of these ways, he and his children with him shall go free in the jubilee year. ⁵⁵For it is to me the Israelites are slaves.

They are my slaves whom I freed from the land of Egypt. I am YHWH your God.

26. Blessings, Curses, and the Recall of the Covenant (26:1–46)

The Essence of God's Commandments

¹You shall not make idols for yourselves, and a carved image or pillar you shall not set up for yourselves, and a figured pavement you shall not place in your land to worship upon it, for I YHWH am your God. ²You shall keep my sabbaths and venerate my sanctuary: I YHWH (have spoken).*

The Blessings

³If you follow my laws and keep my commandments and observe them, ⁴I will grant you rains in their season, so that the earth will yield its produce, and the trees of the field will yield their fruit. ⁵Your threshing shall overtake the vintage, and the vintage will overtake the sowing; you shall eat your fill of food and dwell securely in your land.

⁶I will grant peace in the land, so that you shall lie down, and no one shall make you afraid; I will eliminate vicious beasts from the land, and no sword shall traverse your land. ⁷You shall give chase to your enemies, and they shall fall before you by the sword. ⁸Five of you shall give chase to a hundred, and a hundred of you shall give chase to ten thousand; your enemies shall fall before you by the sword.

⁹I will look with favor upon you, and make you fruitful and multiply you; and I will uphold my covenant with you. ¹⁰You shall eat old grain long stored, and you shall have to clear out the old to make room for the new. ¹¹I will establish my presence in your midst, and I will not expel you. ¹²I will walk about in your midst: I will (continue to) be your God, and you shall be my people. ¹³I YHWH am your God who freed you from the land of Egypt from being their slaves; I broke the bars of your yoke and made you walk erect.

The Curses

¹⁴But if you do not obey me and do not observe all these commandments, ¹⁵if you despise my laws and loathe my rules, so that you do not observe all my commandments, thereby breaking my covenant, ¹⁶I in turn will do this to you: I will bring panic upon you—consumption and fever wearing out the eyes and

---

*Boldface block type (vv. 1–2, 33b–35, and 43–45) stands for H_R. For details see Chap. 26 NOTES.

drying out the throat; you shall sow your seed to no purpose, for your enemies shall eat it. [17]I will set my face against you: you shall be routed by your enemies, and your foes shall dominate you. You shall flee though nobody pursues you.

[18]And if, for all of that, you do not obey me, I will go on to discipline you sevenfold for your sins, [19]and I will break your proud strength. I will make your skies like iron and your earth like copper, [20]so that your strength shall be spent to no purpose. Your land shall not yield its produce, nor shall the trees of your land yield their fruit.

[21]And if you continue in opposition to me and refuse to obey me, I will go on smiting you sevenfold in measure for your sins. [22]I will let loose wild beasts against you, and they shall bereave you of your children and wipe out your cattle. They shall make you few (in number), and your roads shall be deserted.

[23]And if, in spite of these (things), you are not disciplined for me, and you continue in opposition to me, [24]I too will continue in opposition to you: Yes, I myself will smite you sevenfold for your sins. [25]I will bring a sword against you, executing vengeance for the covenant; and if you withdraw into your cities, I will send pestilence among you, and you shall be delivered into enemy hands. [26]When I break your staff of bread, ten women shall bake your bread in a single oven; they shall dole out your bread by weight, and though you eat, you shall not be satisfied.

[27]But if, despite this, you disobey me and continue in opposition to me, [28]I will continue in wrathful opposition to you; Yes, I myself will discipline you sevenfold for your sins. [29]You shall eat the flesh of your sons, and the flesh of your daughters you shall eat. [30]I will destroy your cult places and cut down your incense stands, and I will heap your carcasses upon your lifeless fetishes.

I will expel you. [31]I will lay your cities in ruin and make your sanctuaries desolate, and I will not smell your pleasant odors. [32]I myself will make your land desolate, so that your enemies who settle in it shall be appalled by it. [33]You, however, I will scatter among the nations, and I will unsheath the sword after you.

When your land will be a desolation and your cities a ruin, [34]then the land shall be paid its sabbath years throughout the time that it is desolate. When you are in the land of your enemies, then the land shall rest and pay off its sabbath years. [35]Throughout the time it is desolate, it shall have the rest it did not have on your sabbaths when you were living on it.

[36]As for those of you who survive, I will bring faintness in their hearts in the land of their enemies. The sound of a driven leaf will put them to flight. They shall flee as though from the sword, and they shall fall though nobody is pursuing. [37]They shall stumble over one another, as if (to escape) a sword, though pursuing is nobody. You shall not be able to stand (your ground) before your enemies. [38]You shall be lost among the nations, and the land of your enemies shall devour you. [39]And those of you who survive shall rot because of their iniquities in the land of your enemies; also they shall rot because of the iniquities of their ancestors (adhering) to them.

Remorse and the Recall of the Covenant

⁴⁰But if they confess their iniquity and the iniquity of their ancestors, in that they committed sacrilege against me and, moreover, that they continued in opposition to me—⁴¹so that I, in turn, had to continue in opposition to them and disperse them in the land of their enemies—if, then, their uncircumcised heart is humbled and they accept their punishment in full, ⁴²then I will remember my covenant with Jacob; also my covenant with Isaac and also my covenant with Abraham I will remember, namely, I will remember the land. **⁴³For the land shall be deserted by them that it may be paid its sabbath years by being desolate without them, as they accept their punishment in full for the very reason that my rules they spurned and my laws they loathed. ⁴⁴Yet, for all that, while they are in the land of their enemies I have not spurned them or loathed them so as to destroy them, annulling my covenant with them: for I YHWH am their God.** ⁴⁵But I will remember in their favor the covenant with the ancients whom I freed from the land of Egypt in the sight of the nations to be their God: I YHWH (have spoken).

Summation

⁴⁶These are the laws, rules, and the rituals that YHWH established between himself and the Israelites at Mount Sinai through Moses.

27. *Consecrations and Their Redemption (27:1–34)*

Vows of Persons and Animals

¹YHWH spoke to Moses, saying: ²Speak to the Israelites and say to them: When a person makes an extraordinary vow to YHWH concerning the (fixed) valuation of a human being, ³these shall be the valuations: If it is a male from twenty to sixty years of age, the valuation is fifty shekels of silver by the sanctuary weight. ⁴If it is a female, the valuation is thirty shekels. ⁵If the age is from five years to twenty years, the valuation is twenty shekels for a male and ten shekels for a female. ⁶If the age is from one month to five years, the valuation for a male is five shekels of silver, and the valuation for a female is three shekels of silver. ⁷If the age is from sixty years and over, the valuation is fifteen shekels in the case of a male and ten shekels for a female. ⁸But if he is too poor (to pay) a valuation, he shall be presented before the priest, and the priest shall assess him; the priest shall assess him according to what the vower can afford.

⁹If [the vow concerns] any quadruped that may be brought as an offering to YHWH, any such that may be dedicated to YHWH shall be holy. ¹⁰One may not exchange it or substitute it—a healthy with an emaciated one or emaciated with a healthy one; if one does substitute one animal for another, it (the vowed one) and its substitute shall be holy. ¹¹If [the vow concerns] any impure quadruped that may not be brought as an offering to YHWH, the quadruped

shall be presented before the priest, [12]and the priest shall assess it. Whether high or low, whatever is the valuation of the priest, so it shall stand; [13]and if he wishes to redeem it, he must add one-fifth to its valuation.

Consecrations of Houses and Fields

[14]If a man consecrates his house to YHWH, the priest shall assess it. Whether high or low, as the priest assesses it, so it shall stand; [15]and if he who consecrated his house wishes to redeem it, he must add one-fifth to the sum at which it was assessed, and it shall be his.

[16]If a man consecrates to YHWH any part of his tenured field, its valuation shall be according to its seed requirement: fifty shekels of silver to a homer of barley seed. [17]If he consecrates his field as of the jubilee year, its valuation stands. [18]But if he consecrates his field after the jubilee, the priest shall compute the price according to the years that are left until the jubilee year, and its valuation shall be so reduced; [19]and if he who consecrated the field wishes to redeem it, he must add one-fifth to the sum at which it was assessed, and it shall pass to him. [20]But if he does not redeem the field but has sold the field to another, it shall no longer be redeemable; [21]when the field is released in the jubilee, it shall be holy to YHWH, as a proscribed field; it belongs to the priest.

[22]If he consecrates to YHWH a field that he purchased, which is not of his tenured field, [23]the priest shall compute for him the proportionate valuation up to the jubilee year, and he shall pay the valuation as of that day, a sacred donation to YHWH. [24]In the jubilee year the field shall revert to him from whom it was bought, to whom the tenured land belongs. [25]All valuations shall be by sanctuary weight, the shekel being twenty gerahs.

Firstlings

[26]However, a firstling of quadrupeds—designated as a firstling to YHWH—cannot be consecrated by anyone; whether bovine or ovine, it is YHWH's. [27]But if it is of impure quadrupeds, it may be ransomed at its valuation, with one-fifth added; if it is not redeemed, it may be sold at its valuation.

Proscriptions

[28]However, anything a man proscribes to YHWH of what he owns, be it persons, quadrupeds, or his tenured land, may not be sold or redeemed; every proscribed thing is totally consecrated to YHWH. [29]No human being who has been proscribed can be ransomed: he must be put to death.

Tithes

[30]All tithes from the land, whether seed from the ground or fruit from the tree, are YHWH's; they are holy to YHWH. [31]If a man wishes to redeem any of his

tithes, he must add one-fifth to them. ³²All tithes of the herd or flock—of all that passes under the shepherd's staff, every tenth one—shall be holy to YHWH. ³³He must not seek out the healthy as against the emaciated and substitute (the latter) for it (the former). If he does provide a substitute for it, then it and its substitute shall be holy: they cannot be redeemed.

Summary

³⁴These are the commandments that YHWH commanded Moses for the Israelites on Mount Sinai.

TRANSLATION, NOTES, AND COMMENTS

◆

PART IV.
THE HOLINESS SOURCE
(CHAPTERS 17–27 CONTINUED)

◆

23. THE HOLIDAY CALENDAR*

TRANSLATION

¹YHWH spoke to Moses, saying: ²Speak to the Israelites and say to them: **(As for) the fixed times of YHWH, which you shall proclaim as sacred occasions, these are my fixed times.**

The Sabbath

³Six days' work may be done, but the seventh day is a sabbath of complete rest, a sacred occasion. You shall do no work; it is a sabbath of YHWH throughout your settlements.

The Festivals

⁴These are the fixed times of YHWH, the sacred occasions, which you shall proclaim at their fixed times:

The Paschal Offering and the Unleavened Bread

⁵In the first month, on the fourteenth (day) of the month, at twilight, a paschal offering to YHWH, ⁶and on the fifteenth day of that month the Pilgrimage-Festival of Unleavened Bread to YHWH. Seven days you are to eat unleavened bread. ⁷The first day shall be for you a sacred occasion: You shall do no laborious work. ⁸Seven days you shall offer food gifts to YHWH. The seventh day is a sacred occasion: You shall do no laborious work.

---

*In chap. 23, block italic type (as in v. 1) stands for H, boldface block type (as in v. 2b) for H$_R$, standard type (as in v. 10b) for Pre-H$_1$, and boldface standard type (as in v. 11b) for Pre-H$_2$. For details see the commentary on chap. 23, COMMENT A.

The First Barley Offering

⁹YHWH spoke to Moses, saying: ¹⁰Speak to the Israelites and say to them:
When you enter the land I am giving to you and you reap its harvest, you shall bring the first sheaf of your harvest to the priest. ¹¹He shall elevate the sheaf before YHWH. For acceptance on your behalf **from the day after the sabbath-week** the priest shall elevate it. ¹²On the day that you elevate the sheaf, you shall sacrifice an unblemished male lamb in its first year as a burnt offering to YHWH. ¹³Its accompanying cereal offering shall be two-tenths of an ephah of semolina mixed with oil, a food gift of pleasing aroma to YHWH; and its accompanying libation shall be one-fourth of a hin of wine. ¹⁴Do not partake (from the new crop) of any bread or parched or fresh grain until the very day you have brought your God's offering—a law for all time, throughout your generations, in all your settlements.

The First Wheat Offering

¹⁵And **from the day after the sabbath-week,** from the day on which you bring the elevation offering of the sheaf, you shall count for yourselves **seven sabbath-weeks. They must be complete: ¹⁶You shall count until the day after the seventh sabbath-week** fifty days. Then you shall present a new cereal offering to YHWH. ¹⁷You shall bring from your settlements as an elevation offering of two bread (loaves), comprising two-tenths (of an ephah) of semolina and baked after leavening, as firstfruits for YHWH. *¹⁸With the bread you shall offer seven unblemished yearling lambs, one bull of the herd, and two rams; (they) shall be a burnt offering to YHWH, and with their cereal offerings and libations, a food gift of pleasant aroma to YHWH. ¹⁹You shall sacrifice one he-goat as a purification offering* and two yearling lambs as a sacrifice of well-being. ²⁰And the priest shall elevate them with the bread of firstfruits as an elevation offering to YHWH with the two lambs; they shall be holy to YHWH for the priest. *²¹On that very day, you shall proclaim: It shall be for you a sacred occasion; you must do no laborious work—a law for all time, in all your settlements, throughout your generations. ²²And when you reap the harvest of your land, you shall not complete (it) to the edge of your field, or gather the gleanings of your harvest; you shall leave them for the poor and for the alien; I am YHWH your God.*

The Festival of Alarm Blasts

²³YHWH spoke to Moses, saying: ²⁴Speak to the Israelites thus: In the seventh month, on the first day of the month, you shall observe a rest, a sacred occasion, commemorated with short blasts. ²⁵You shall do no laborious work; and you shall present a food gift to YHWH.

The Day of Purgation

²⁶YHWH spoke to Moses, saying: ²⁷However, the tenth day of this seventh month is the Day of Purgation. It shall be a sacred occasion for you; you shall afflict yourselves, and you shall offer a food gift to YHWH; ²⁸you shall do no work on that very day. For it is a purgation day, to effect purgation on your behalf before YHWH your God. ²⁹Indeed, any person who does not afflict himself on that very day will be cut off from his kin; ³⁰and any person who does any work on that very day I will cause that person to perish among his people. ³¹You shall do no work; it is a law for all time, throughout your generations, in all your settlements. ³²It shall be a sabbath of complete rest for you, and you shall afflict yourselves; on the ninth day of the month at evening, from evening to evening, you shall observe your sabbath.

The Festival of Booths

³³YHWH spoke to Moses, saying: ³⁴Say to the Israelites thus: On the fifteenth day of this seventh month [there shall be] the pilgrimage-festival of Booths, [lasting] seven days to YHWH. ³⁵The first day shall be a sacred occasion; you shall do no laborious work. ³⁶Seven days you shall present food gifts to YHWH. On the eighth day, you shall observe a sacred occasion and present a food gift to YHWH. It is a solemn assembly; you shall do no laborious work.

Summary

³⁷These are the fixed times of YHWH, which you shall proclaim as sacred occasions, to present food gifts to YHWH—burnt offerings, cereal offerings, sacrifices, and libations, the daily protocol on each day—³⁸apart from the sabbath offerings of YHWH, and apart from your gifts, and apart from your votive offerings, and apart from your freewill offerings that you give to YHWH.

Addendum on the Festival of Booths

³⁹However, on the fifteenth day of the seventh month, when you have ingathered the yield of the land, you shall celebrate the pilgrimage-festival of YHWH seven days: on the first day, rest and on the eighth day, rest. ⁴⁰On the first day you shall take for yourselves the boughs of majestic trees: fronds of palms, branches of leafy trees, and willows of the brook, and you shall rejoice before YHWH your God seven days. ⁴¹You shall celebrate it as a Pilgrimage-Festival to YHWH for seven days in the year as a law for all time, throughout your generations. You shall celebrate it in the seventh month. **⁴²In booths you shall live seven days; all citizens in Israel shall live in booths, ⁴³in order that your generations may know that I made the Israelites live in booths when I brought them out of the land of Egypt; I am YHWH your God.**

⁴⁴Thus Moses declared the fixed times of YHWH to the Israelites.

Comments

The composition of chap. 23, COMMENT A; the sabbath-week, COMMENT B; the Festival of Booths in Neh 8, COMMENT C; the paschal sacrifice in Exod 23, 34,

COMMENT D; the firstfruits festivals of Qumran, COMMENT E; and the Israelite and Hittite festival calendars, COMMENT F.

NOTES

Each holiday begins with an introduction: Sabbath (vv. 1–3), Paschal Offering and Unleavened Bread (vv. 4–8), Firstfruits of Grain (vv. 9–22), Alarm Blasts (vv. 23–25), Day of Purgation (vv. 26–32), and Booths (vv. 33–43). These introductions betray the viewpoint of their author that Paschal Offering and Unleavened Bread, on the one hand, and Barley and Wheat, on the other, had each become fused into a single holiday (see NOTE on v. 6, and INTRODUCTION to vv. 15–22). A bipartite division can also be recognized by the subscript *ănî YHWH 'ĕlōhêkem*, which marks off the spring festivals (vv. 5–22) and the autumn festivals (vv. 23–43; Wenham 1979). The source division of this chapter is indicated by the translation and is discussed in the INTRODUCTION to vv. 15–22 and COMMENT A; the comparison with other calendars is reserved for COMMENTS E and F.

The contents of chap. 23 can be outlined as follows:

Introductory formula to the calendar (vv. 1–2)
I. The Sabbath (v. 3)

THE FESTIVALS

II. The Paschal Offering and the Unleavened Bread (vv. 4–8)
   A. Introductory formula (original) to the calendar (v. 4)
   B. The date of the Paschal Offering (v. 5)
   C. The Pilgrimage-Festival of Unleavened Bread (vv. 6–8)
III. The Firstfruits of Barley and Wheat (vv. 9–22)
   A. Introductory formula (vv. 9–10aα)
   B. The First Barley Offering (vv. 10aβ–14)
      1. Elevation offering of an *ʿōmer* on a Sunday (vv. 10aβ–11)
      2. Additional public sacrifices (vv. 12–13)
      3. Prohibition against eating of the new grain before the offering (v. 14)
   C. The First Wheat Offering (vv. 15–21)
      1. Two loaves offered fifty days after the barley offering (vv. 15–17)
      2. Additional public sacrifices (vv. 18–20)
      3. Laborious work prohibited (vv. 20–21)
   D. The poor benefit from the grain harvests (v. 22)
IV. The Festival of Warning Blasts (vv. 23–25)
   A. Introductory formula (vv. 23–24a)
   B. The date (v. 24b)
   C. Laborious work prohibited (v. 25)
V. The Day of Purgation (vv. 26–32)
   A. The introductory formula (v. 26)
   B. The date and individual self-denial (v. 27)

    C. All work prohibited (v. 28)
    D. Punishments for disobedience (vv. 29–30)
    E. Reprise (vv. 31–32)
  VI. The Feast of Booths (vv. 33–43)
    A. Introductory formula (vv. 33–34a)
    B. The date and laborious work prohibited (vv. 34b–36)
    C. Subscript to the original calendar (vv. 37–38)
    D. Appendix to the Festival of Booths (vv. 39–43)
        1. Reprise of date (v. 39)
        2. The four species (vv. 40–41)
        3. Dwelling in booths (v. 42)
        4. Rationale (v. 43)
  VII. Compliance report (v. 44)

This chapter is addressed to the Israelites. The priests are not included, as they were in the previous pericope (22:17–33), even though they are indispensably and inextricably involved in the cultic offerings (e.g., v. 11). Nonetheless, the priests' role is deliberately muffled. Center stage is occupied by the people. The manifold obligations falling on the individual Israelite in the observance of the festivals are prescribed: complete sabbath rest (v. 3), *pesaḥ* offering and unleavened bread (vv. 5–8), an *ʿōmer* of new barley before it may be eaten (vv. 10–11, 14), two loaves of new wheat (v. 17), a reminder to leave grain for the needy (v. 22), sounding alarm blasts (v. 24), fasting and complete rest (vv. 27–28), altar processions and home booths (vv. 40–42).

Yet these details should not mask an equally significant imperative of this chapter: Israel is responsible for maintaining the *public* cult. Note the repeated command addressed to Israel: *Wĕhiqrabtem ʾiššeh laYHWH* 'you shall offer food gifts to YHWH' (vv. 8, 25, 27, 36 [bis]). Where actual sacrifices are prescribed, address to Israel, in the second-person plural, is again employed (vv. 12, 18–19), in striking contrast to the third-person address referring to the priest (vv. 11, 20). To be sure, H, no differently from P, presumes that the sacrificial service is conducted exclusively by priests. However, maintenance of the public cult and, presumably, supervision over the priestly order ultimately are the people's responsibility.

Ibn Ezra observes that this chapter logically follows the previous one by keeping to the same theme of sacrifices: whereas chap. 22 concludes with Israel's lesser sacred offerings (the thanksgiving offering), chap. 23 deals with the most sacred offerings (the burnt offerings) prescribed for the festivals. This association is erroneous and, at best, forced. Burnt offerings are, in fact, a major theme in chap. 22 (cf. vv. 17–20), but are not expressly mentioned for most of the festivals in chap. 23. There is logical progression in chaps. 21–23: chap. 23 supplements the sacred persons (priests) and sacred offerings (sacrifices) with sacred time (festivals).

Leach's (1976: 77–93) division of ritual into rites of separation, liminality, and incorporation (based on van Gennup 1960; cf. vol. 1.566–69), is utilized by

Wright (1992: 247–48) to suggest that holy days may be similarly described; they serve temporally as rituals to "give meaning, direction and order to an otherwise undifferentiated and homorphous temporal continuum." Their restrictions may indeed be characterized as liminal rites of passage; they lack, however, rites of separation and incorporation, typical of postbiblical Judaism where the sabbath and festivals are sanctified (at onset) and desanctified (at close) by light and wine. Perhaps the blowing of the shofar from the Temple and the beginning and end of a holy day served the same function. To be sure, the use of the shofar for this purpose is attested for the Herodian Temple. Indeed, a fallen cornerstone that once stood atop its southwestern wall reads: *LBYT HTQY'H LH*[. . . 'To the Trumpeting Place to . . . '] (cf. *m. Suk.* 5:5; Jos. *Wars* 4.582). Nonetheless, since the festivals were "proclaimed" (see NOTE on v. 2), the proclamation was most likely performed by use of the shofar (Num 10:10; see NOTE on 25:9), initially at the major sanctuaries and, ultimately, at the central sanctuary, the Jerusalem Temple.

Vv. 1–2. Introductory Formula

The subject matter of the sabbath (v. 3) is bracketed by vv. 2aβ,b, 4 to form an introverted structure (M. Hildenbrand; J. Thompson):

A   *mô'ădê* YHWH *'ăšer-tiqrĕ'û 'ōtām*
   B   *miqrā'ê qōdeš*
     C   *'ēlleh hēm mô'ăday*
       D   *šēšet yāmîm*
         E   *ta'ăśeh mĕlā'kâ*
           X   *ûbayyôm haššĕbî'î šabbat šabbātôn miqrā'-qōdeš*
         E'   *kol-mĕlā'kâ lō' ta'ăśû*
       D'   *šabbāt hi' laYHWH bĕkōl môšbōtêkem*
     C'   *'ēlleh mô'ădê* YHWH
   B'   *miqrā'ê qōdeš*
A'   *'ăšer-tiqrĕ'û 'ōtām bĕmô'ădām*

A   (As for) the fixed times of YHWH, which you shall proclaim
   B   as sacred occasions,
     C   these are my fixed times (v. 2aβ,b)
       D   Six days'
         E   work may be done,
           X   but the seventh day is a sabbath of complete rest, a sacred occasion.
         E'   You shall do no work,
       D'   it is a sabbath of YHWH throughout your settlements (v. 3)
     C'   These are the fixed times of YHWH,
   B'   the sacred occasions,
A'   which you shall proclaim at their fixed times: (v. 4)

By dint of the threefold repetition of *miqrā' qōdeš* (BXB), this structure declares that the sabbath is a "sacred occasion," which is *šabbāt*, a day of rest for YHWH (D'), and a *šabbat šabbātôn* 'a complete day of rest' for Israel (X). It is also a *mô'ēd* 'a fixed time' (ACA'), namely, "each seventh day" (X). Thus X, the center pivot, emphasizes three aspects of the sabbath, which are echoed and reinforced by the surrounding structure: the sabbath is a sacred occasion of complete rest occurring every seventh day, as patterned by YHWH.

Admittedly, the innermost enclosure DEE'D' is anything but a flawless chiasm. The author, however, had no choice; he was citing Exod 35:2 (H): *šēšet yāmîm tē'āśeh mēlā'kâ ûbayyôm haššēbî'î yihyeh lākem qōdeš šabbat šabbātôn laYHWH kol-ha'ōśeh bô mēlā'kâ yûmāt* (see also Exod 31:15). The minor differences are easily explainable. Our hypothetical author had to adopt the terminology of Lev 23; hence, *yihyeh lākem qōdeš* becomes *miqra' qodeš*. He wishes to stress that although "the sabbath is to YHWH" (D'), the *šabbat šabbātôn*, the complete sabbath rest (Exod 35:2aγ), is incumbent on Israel (X).

There are two major differences between the two passages: the death penalty (Exod 35:2b; cf. 31:15b) is dropped, and the phrase *bĕkōl môšĕbōtêkem* 'throughout your settlements' is borrowed from the following verse (Exod 35:3; it does not appear in Exod 31:12–17). Both changes, I submit, betray the author's time and place—in the Babylonian Exile. To be sure, the latter phrase also occurs elsewhere in the chapter (vv. 14, 21, 31), and for this reason, the author felt constrained to use it in order to equate the sabbath with the other festivals. Similarly, as the following exegesis will substantiate, he desired to declare the sabbath a *mô'ēd*, which it is not, and a *miqrā' qōdeš*, which it is not (see below). However, he was not able to copy the requirement of sacrifices, *'iššê YHWH*, found in the other festivals (23:8, 12–13, 18–20, 25, 27, 36) because there were no sacrifices in the exile! By the same token, he had to drop the death penalty (Exod 35:2b; cf. 31:15b) because Israel was powerless to impose it while under foreign domination (the *hop'al yûmat* means "death by human agency"; cf. Milgrom 1970: 5–8; and the fact that the sabbath pericopes of Exod 31 and 35 [also H] carry the death penalty imply that they stem from an earlier preexilic H stratum). Thus despite the author's consummate artistry (typical of H) to link his interpolation (vv. 2aβ–3) with the superscription to the holiday calendar (v. 4), the seams still show (see further below). The artistry of v. 3 is further evidenced by viewing it as three intertwined *sorites* (D. Stewart):

D *šēšet yāmîm*

   E *tē'āśeh mēlā'kâ*

D' *ûbayyôm haššēbî'î*

      F *šabbat šabbātôn miqrā' qōdeš*

     E' *kol-mēlā'kâ lō' ta'śû*

       F' *šabbāt hî' laYHWH*

         G *bĕkōl môšbōtêkem*

Two *sorites* (DD' and EE') exhibit anadiplosis (*yôm* and *mělā'kâ*), and the third (FF') states that the sabbath is to be observed by Israel because it is YHWH's. This passage climaxes with the information that no work may be done (EE') on the seventh day (DD'), the sabbath (FF'), in Israel's settlements (G). Thus the build-up is six workdays, the seventh a sacred occasion, when no work may be done, wherever Israel resides.

2. *Speak to the Israelites.* H's address returns to the people after the digression to the priests (chaps. 21–22).

(*As for) the fixed times. mô'ādê YHWH.* The possibility exists that the previous word *'ālehem* originally read *'ēlleh hēm* (*'lhm* < *'lh hm*), as at the end of this verse, or that an original *'ēlleh* before *mô'ādê* fell out (Paran 1989: 225), in either case causing the error by haplography and thereby creating a chiastically structured v. 2 (abb'a'). Otherwise, we are left with a hanging open clause. However, by looking at the introverted structure of vv. 1–4, it will become clear that *'ēlleh* was deliberately omitted in order that AA' (*mô'ādê YHWH, běmô'ădām*) would be approximately equivalent. Paran's analogy with 14:54–57 does not hold. In the latter case, the repetition of *zō't hāttôrâ* / *tôrat* is for the purpose of creating an inclusio; in our case, however, v. 4aα is a new heading. Thus this structure is clearly the work of H_R, who skillfully attached vv. 2aβ–3 to vv. 2aα, 4.

Levinson (1997: 20) regards v. 1 as the heading of the original calendar and v. 4 as a resumptive repetition in order to form the introverted structure of vv. 1–4. This reconstruction is deceptively simple, but on examination proves erroneous. V. 2 by itself is both awkward stylistically and incorrect grammatically. As noted above, to make sense of this verse, one has to posit the omission by haplography of *'ēlleh hēm* after *'ālehem*. And even were these words restored, they would create a redundancy with *'ēlleh hēm* in v. 2b. Levinson glosses over these difficulties by rendering *'ăšer-tiqrě'û 'ōtām miqrā'ê qōdeš* 'which you shall proclaim *to them, are* sacred occasions' (my emphasis). This involves two incorrect renderings: *'ōtām* 'to them' and the main clause changed into a nominal sentence by adding "are." Nowhere does *'et* or *'ēt* mean "to," and a nominal sentence would have required the addition of *hēm* after *qōdeš*. Besides, *miqrā'* is always the direct object of *qārā'* (cognate accusative) and never the predicate in a nominal sentence.

As recognized by many critics (e.g., Dillmann and Ryssel 1897; Baentsch 1903; Noth 1977; Elliger 1966; Kochman 1987; Knohl 1995), vv. 2aβ–3, the passage on the sabbath, is an interpolation. The reasons are as follows:

1. The concluding summary (vv. 37–38) explicitly excludes the sabbath from the enumerated holidays (cf. Ramban).

2. The sabbath is neither a *mô'ēd* nor a *miqrā' qōdeš* (see below). Indeed, even the rabbis are puzzled: *mah 'inyan šabbāt lě'inyan hammô'ădôt* 'What has the sabbath to do with the festivals?' (*Sipra* Emor, par. 9:7; cf. Ramban, Abravanel). As indicated below, the sabbath is scrupulously distinguished from the *mô'ēd* in all the biblical sources, and since it is independent of the lunar month, falling on every seventh day, it is not a *miqrā'*, a proclamation day; its arrival need not be announced (see further below).

3. Abravanel remarks pointedly: " 'These are my fixed times' (v. 2b) . . . is an obvious repetition, also the entire section is in the third person [but see Knohl's qualification 1987: 73, n. 12; 1995: 15, n. 14], and only this phrase is presented in his Person, May He Be Blessed, as if he were speaking for himself." The use of the first person for the Deity is one of H's telltale signs (see Introduction I A).

Hoffmann (1953) tries to counter these arguments by pointing to Exod 35:1–3, which begins *'ēlleh haddĕbārîm 'ăšer-ṣiwwâ YHWH la 'ăśōt 'ōtām*, literally "these are the things that YHWH commanded to do them." This heading cannot re-fer to the sabbath, the subject that immediately follows (vv. 2–3) because on the sabbath one does not "do" anything. Rather, it applies to the following subject, the construction of the Tabernacle (vv. 4ff.). Similarly, contends Hoffmann, the heading *mô'ădê YHWH, mô'ădāy* (v. 2) refers not to the sabbath (v. 3), but to the following subject (vv. 4ff.). Unfortunately, Hoffmann's argument boomerangs. He is absolutely correct regarding Exod 35:1 as the true heading for the long story of the construction of the sanctuary (Exod 35:4–39:43) which, however, leads to the reverse conclusion: Exod 35:2–3 is also an H interpolation con-cerning the sabbath (as is Exod 31:12–17), emphasizing that even the sacred task of erecting the sanctuary may not take priority over the command to cease work on the sabbath.

Hartley (1992) argues that the addition of the sabbath is not an intrusion, since (1) it occurs in older festival calendars (Exod 23:12–17; 34:18–24); (2) the sabbath plays a role in determining the Festival of Weeks; and (3) certain festi-val days are observed like the sabbath. I shall respond:

1. The sabbath in Exod 23:12 is connected with the sabbatical year (v. 11), not with the festival calendar, and is separated from the calendar by an ex-hortation against idolatry (v. 13). It is also an intrusion in Exod 34:18–24 (v. 21), but there it serves an auxiliary function: to prohibit work on the sabbath during the agricultural season.
2. In chap. 23, the sabbath day means "sabbath-week" (see INTRODUCTION to vv. 15–22).
3. Not true: festivals are either a *šabbātôn* (vv. 24, 39) or a *šabbat šabbātôn* (v. 32), which bear a differing meaning (see NOTES).

the fixed times of YHWH. mô'ădê YHWH. The fixed times *for* YHWH—that is, to worship him—or *by* YHWH—that is, set by YHWH (Gen 1:14; Hartley 1992).

The noun *mô'ēd* stems from the root *y'd* 'designate' either a place (e.g., *'ōhel mô'ēd* 'the Tent of Meeting', Exod 27:21; *lĕmô'ēd dawid* 'to the meeting [place] of David', [1 Sam 20:35 ‖ *hammāqôm* 'the place', v. 19]) or a time (sing., 23:4; Gen 17:21; 21:2; Num 9:2, 3, 7, 13; 28:2; pl., Gen 1:14; Lev 23:2 [twice], 4, 37, 44; Num 10:10; 15:3; 29:39; cf. Exod 23:15; 34:18; see Rashbam, Wessely 1846). Thus it can mean "a fixed time." Pharaoh is challenged to set the time (Exod 8:5). Using the verb *qārā'* 'proclaim' (see below), the country of Judah cries out *qārā' 'ālay mô'ēd* 'He (YHWH) has proclaimed a set time against me' (Lam

1:15). In regard to the calendar, *mô'ēd* refers to a fixed annual observance, *běmô'ădām* 'each at its fixed time' (Lev 23:4).

As noted above, the sabbath is not a *mô'ēd*; neither is the new moon, as indicated by references throughout the span of the biblical period (e.g., Num 10:10; Isa 1:13–14; Hos 2:13; Ezek 44:24; 46:1, 6, 9, 11; Lam 2:6; Neh 10:34; 1 Chr 23:1; 2 Chr 8:13; 31). Both the sabbath and the new moon (and the daily offering) are included in the calendar of public sacrifices, Num 28–29 (28:3–15), but these are erroneously termed *mô'ădîm* in the heading and subscript (28:2; 29:39). That these verses betray the hand of H, note the first-person *qorbānî lahmî lě'iššay rēah nîhōhî* (Knohl 1987: 88; 1995: 30). Just as H uses the superscript to incorporate the sabbath into the list of *mô'ădîm* in Num 28, so it uses the same device in Lev 23. Indeed, it inserts the word *mô'ēd* twice (v. 2aβ,b) in order to make it crystal clear that the sabbath is included.

Why, then, has H found it so urgent to go against accepted usage and label the sabbath a *mô'ēd*? The only logical answer, I submit, is that the H redactor lived among the exiles in Babylonia, where the Temple and the sacrificially bound *mô'ădîm* of Lev 23:4–38 and Num 28–29 were inoperative. He therefore composed the passage Lev 23:2aβ–3 and the framework Num 28:2aβ,b; 29:39 to indicate that the sabbath is one of the *mô'ădê YHWH* 'the fixed times of YHWH' and should be scrupulously observed (v. 3). This deduction comports well with the emphasis given to the sabbath by the exilic prophets (cf. Isa 56:1–8; 58:13–14; Ezek 20:12–13, 20–21). Thus one need not go so far as to posit "a slackening in Sabbath observance" (Weinfeld 1993: 199) to account for the prophetic accentuation of the sabbath. For the prophets, as well as for the exilic H tradent, the sabbath was the only continual cultic act by which to express loyalty to God and his commandments. Supporting my thesis is the absence of any reference to the sabbath sacrifice (Num 28:7–10) in v. 3 (as noted by Abravanel), in contrast to the sacrificial references in all the other holiday prescriptions of Lev 23 (vv. 8, 12–13, 18–19, 25, 27, 36, 37). This striking omission is not due to error (Elliger 1966), but to the constraints of reality—Israel is in exile. For the significance of this finding in determining the composition of Leviticus, see Introduction I F, and the NOTES on vv. 39–44, especially v. 43.

H's editorial work proved decisive for Qumran. Unquestioningly, Qumran labels the sabbath a *mô'ēd* (WLMW'D HŠBT, 4Q512; Baillet 1982: 264) and, therefore, against rabbinic halakha, permits the blowing of trumpets, prescribed for the *mô'ădîm* (Num 10:10), also on the sabbath (4Q493Mᶜ; Baumgarten 1987a). Moreover, having the sabbath at the beginning of the festival calendar fits well into Qumran's system of numbering the sabbaths, starting in the first week of the first month—that is, ahead of *pesah* and the Festival of Unleavened Bread (vv. 5–8), falling on the fourteenth and fifteenth to the twentieth days, respectively.

you shall proclaim. tiqrě'û. The verb *qārā'* in this context has been variously rendered: (1) "set a time" (Rashbam); compare *qārā' 'ālay mô'ēd* 'set a time against me' (Lam 1:15); (2) "invite" (Ramban), as in *qěrū(y)ê hā'ēdâ*, literally "invited ones of the congregation" (Num 1:16; cf. 1 Sam 9:13); (3) "single out"

(Wessely 1846), as in *qārā' YHWH běšēm běṣal'ēl* 'YHWH has singled out by name, Bezalel' (Exod 35:30); (4) "call together, convene" (Ramban; Shadal; Dillmann and Ryssel 1897; Bertholet 1901; Elliger 1966), as in *lěmiqrā' hā'ēdâ* 'to summon the community' (Num 10:2); and (5) "proclaim" (*Tg. Onk.*; *Sipra* Emor, par. 9:2), as in *kî-qārā' šěmiṭṭâ laYHWH* 'the remission proclaimed is of YHWH' (Deut 15:2).

These claims will be analyzed briefly:

1. The sabbath occurs automatically, independently of any calendar; it need not be "set."
2. The same objection applies to "invite."
3. The meaning "single out" is possible, but it runs into difficulty if the object is the cognate accusative *miqrā'* (see below).
4. The same objection applies to "call together." Moreover, considering the sabbath restrictions, where and for what purpose would a convocation be convened? To be sure, on this day of rest, it would be possible to travel short distances—for example, to consult the prophet (2 Kgs 4:23)—but convening an entire community on the sabbath is unattested in Scripture.
5. The meaning "proclaim" fits the context best, particularly in view of its object *miqrā'*, as in *qěrō' miqrā'* 'proclaiming of solemnities' (Isa 1:13 NJPS). When *qārā'* appears with the root *qdš*, the meaning "proclaim" is particularly in evidence: *qadděšû 'aṣārâ labba'al wayyiqrā'û* ' "sanctify a solemn assembly to Baal" and it was proclaimed' (2 Kgs 10:20); *qadděšû-ṣôm qir'û 'aṣārâ* 'sanctify a fast, proclaim a solemn assembly' (Joel 1:14). Perhaps it is no mere coincidence that the Hittite king was expected, through an "overseer" to officially "proclaim" the onset of a festival (Haas 1970: 43–50).

The rabbis understood this verb as a license to set the beginning of each lunar month so that in a famous case in which the court erred and, as a result, Yom Kippur was set a day too early, this verse was mobilized to uphold the court's decision: God's appointed times are only those that the rabbinic court proclaims (*m. Roš Haš.* 2:8–9). This rabbinic license was forcefully opposed by the Qumran sectaries, who declared *L'LQDM 'TYHM WL'LHT'ḤR MKWL MW'DYHM* '(One must) neither advance their (the festivals') times nor be delayed in all their festivals' (1QS 1:14–15 [Schwartz 1992: 234–35]).

sacred occasions. miqrā'ê qōdeš. This priestly idiom is found eleven times in this chapter (vv. 2, 3, 4, 7, 8, 21, 24, 27, 35, 36, 37) and eight times elsewhere (Exod 12:16 [twice]; Num 28:18, 25, 26; 29:1, 7, 12). Since *miqrā'* is the cognate accusative of *qārā'*, the idiom should literally be rendered "sacred proclamations." But these proclamations were for the purpose of announcing the arrival of a festival day, so it is only natural that the term *miqrā'* became associated with the designated day itself; hence the rendering "occasion." This rendering is plausible in view of *qr'* II 'happen, befall' (e.g., Exod 1:10; Isa 51:19), in which case its nominal form *miqrā'* would mean "happening, occasion" (*Tg. Onq.*, *m'ar'ê qadîš*; cf. Dillmann and Ryssel 1897; Eerdmans 1912: 110–12; Kutsch 1953). This surely is its meaning in *ḥōdeš wĕšabbāt qĕrō' miqrā'* 'new moon and sabbath, proclaiming (sacred) occasions' (Isa 1:13), where *miqrā'* clearly connotes a period of time. I submit, however, that wherever *miqrā'* is found, *qārā'* 'proclaim' is implied, that is, the occasion is announced.

Seven days are designated as "sacred occasions" during the liturgical year: the first and seventh of Unleavened Bread (vv. 7–8), Weeks (v. 21), the first day of the seventh month (v. 24), the Day of Purgation (v. 27), and the first and eighth of Booths (vv. 35, 36). Sabbath as an eighth sacred occasion disrupts the sabbatical pattern—another reason for regarding it as an interpolation (J. Thompson). Since this phrase is common to all seven days, Gerstenberger (1996: 341) proposes that the sabbath here does not refer to the weekly cycle of sabbaths (despite v. 3a!), but to the seven sacred occasions in the calendar, which, he claims, fall mainly on the sabbath. His proposal, however, must presuppose that the lunar month always consisted of 28 days (actually, it is slightly more than 29.5 days) and the first day of the year was a sabbath (in defiance of Gen 2:1–3)! Interestingly, P records only six sacred occasions (this term is missing in Num 29:35), an indication that the sabbatical pattern is not as significant for P.

This term is not used for the new moon (Num 28:11–15), since work is not prohibited and, hence, that day is not sacred. This term is also missing in P's sabbath (Num 28:9–10) because, as mentioned above, it is not a *miqrā'*—it need not be proclaimed. This last stratum of H, however, speaks from the perspective of exile. Being subject to the Babylonian calendar, whose days are organized by the month, not the week, the exiles may have found it easy to overlook the advent of the sabbath; it had to be proclaimed. And the custom continued even after the return from exile. Josephus (*Wars* 4.582) records that the trumpet would be sounded from the Temple at the beginning and end of the sabbath, a claim that was verified by the discovery of an inscribed stone, which had fallen off the uppermost southwestern corner of the Herodian wall surrounding the Temple Mount, reading LBYT HTQY'H LHK[RYIZ] 'To the (trumpet) blowing room for announ[cing]', indicating the exact spot where the priest would proclaim the beginning and end of the sabbath (Israeli 1974: 165). In modern Israel, the shofar is sounded throughout the land before sunset on Friday.

Although the new moon, as mentioned, is not a *miqrā' qōdeš*, it certainly was a *miqrā'*. Its exact date had to be proclaimed. Indeed, the rabbis cite the superscript to Lev 23 to prove that the date of the new moon (and the intercalated month) was determined by the authorized rabbinic court. This is vividly illustrated by the reported clash between Rabban Gamaliel, the head of the court, and R. Joshua, who differed with him on the day he set the new moon:

Rabban Gamaliel sent to him (saying), "I charge you that you shall come to me with your staff and your money on Yom Kippur as it falls according to your reckoning." R. Akiba went to R. Joshua and found him sore perplexed. He said to him, "I can teach you (from Scripture) that whatever Rabban Gamaliel has done is done (aright), for it is written, *These are the fixed times of the Lord, the sacred occasions, which you shall proclaim* (Lev 23:4). Whether in their proper time or not in their proper time, I know no other 'fixed times' save these (which the court enjoins)." . . . He (R. Joshua) took his staff and his money in his hand and went to Jabneh to Rabban Gamaliel on the day which fell according to his reckoning on Yom Kippur. Rabban Gamaliel stood up and kissed him on his head and said to him, "Come in peace, my master and my disciple!—'my master' in wisdom and 'my disciple' in that you have accepted my words!" (*m. Roš. Haš* 2:9)

Another rabbinic statement expresses the rabbinic prerogative even more boldly: "In the past (before the divine revelation at Sinai), 'These are my fixed times' (Lev 23:2b). Henceforth 'which you shall proclaim' (vv. 2aβ,4b). If you have proclaimed them, they are my fixed times; if not, they are not my fixed times" (*y. Roš Haš.* 1:3). Indeed, because the lunar month is approximately 29.5 days long, it is for the recognized authorities to decide whether a month contains 29 or 30 days. Thus the entire calendar, even the setting of Yom Kippur, the holiest day of the year, must be the result of human, not divine, decision.

V. 3. The Sabbath

Six days'. šēšet yāmîm. This is an accusative of time, specifying the duration of an activity (GKC §118i).

may be done. tēʿāśeh. This is passive also in Exod 31:15; 35:2 (H). The LXX *poiēseis* 'you will do' reads *taʿăśeh* (active), as in the Decalogue (Exod 20:10; Deut 5:14; also Exod 23:12)—a reading that must be rejected, since the passive is clearly a usage of H.

but the seventh day. ûbayyôm. The *waw* is adversative.

a sabbath of complete rest. šabbat šabbātôn. The basic meaning of the verb *šābat* is "cease" (Gen 8:22; Exod 34:21; Josh 5:12; Isa 14:4; 24:8; 33:8; Jer 31:36; Job 32:1; Lam 5:15), the natural extension of which is "rest" (Gen 2:2; Exod 31:17; cf. Exod 20:11). In Scripture, the sabbath is most often described as observed in its breach (Jer 17:19–27; Ezek 22:8, 26; Isa 56:2; 58:13; Neh 10:32; 13:15–22).

The *ôn>ān* ending transforms *šabbātôn* from a noun to an adjective, as in *roʾš* 'head' > *riʾšôn* 'first' (Levine 1989). The construct chain *šabbat šabbātôn* is a superlative, literally "the most restful rest" (cf. *qōdeš qŏdāšîm*, lit. "the holiest holiness" or "most holy"). Falling under the category of *šabbat šabbātôn* are the sabbath (Exod 31:15; 35:2; cf. Exod 16:23), Yom Kippur (Lev 16:31; 23:32), and the sabbatical year (25:4). Accordingly, a total cessation of labor is enjoined for the sabbath and Yom Kippur (see below) and a total cessation of labor *on the land* for the sabbatical year. That is, on the sabbath and Yom Kippur, Israelites (and persons and animals under their control) must rest, whereas during the sabbatical year not persons but the land must rest. A *šabbātôn* is prescribed for the first, fifteenth, and twenty-second days of the seventh month (vv. 24, 39), but as indicated by the work prohibition for these days, only a partial rest is enjoined.

The sabbath is the only holiday commanded in the Decalogue (Exod 20:8–11) and the only command grounded in creation (v. 11). It is mentioned by all sources and genres: prophecy (Isa 56:2–6; Jer 17:21–27), history (2 Kgs 11:5–9), poetry (Ps 92:1; Lam 2:6), narrative (2 Kgs 4:23; Neh 13:15–22), and law (Exod 23:12; Neh 10:32–34).

In Akkadian, *šapattu* is a day defined as *ûm nuḫ libbi* 'a day of the resting of the heart', in which ceremonies were performed to soothe the gods. The *šapattu* falls on the fifteenth day of the month (i.e., the full moon). Hebrew *šabbāt*, however, is not and never was the full moon. The expression *ḥōdeš wĕšabbāt* (Isa 1:13) is not a reference to "new moon and full moon" (Lewy 1942–43; Tur-Sinai 1944; Fishbane 1985: 149–51); it is simply a progression from the less frequent holiday to the more frequent holiday, as in the sequence *ḥaggāh ḥodšāh wĕšabbātāh* 'her pilgrimage-festivals, new moons, and sabbaths' (Hos 2:13; cf. Tigay 1976: 512; see NOTE on "the day after the sabbath," v. 11). The *šapattu* and *šabbāt* may have the same ancient source, but would have radically diverged in both meaning and time of occurrence. Some have tried to relate *šabbāt* to the market days of other cultures, which likewise recur every set number of days and are not tied to the moon or the seasons. However, the sabbath is quite unlike a market day, since trade was actually forbidden. In sum, no other known culture has anything quite like the sabbath.

a sacred occasion. miqrā' qōdeš. Normally, this phrase would be followed by *yihyeh lākem* 'it shall be for you' (cf. vv. 21, 24 [split], 27, 36). Its inclusion, however, would contradict the following attribution "it is a sabbath of YHWH." That is, it is not for you to proclaim the day (cf. Exod 16:25; 31:15; 35:2; M. Hildenbrand).

You shall do no work. kol-mĕlākâ lō' taʿăśû. Examples of work from the Torah are gathering of food (Exod 16:29–30), plowing and reaping (Exod 34:21), kindling fire (Exod 35:3), and gathering wood (Num 15:32–36). Some would derive the prohibition against cooking on the sabbath and the command to prepare the sabbath meals in advance from the manna pericope "Bake what you would bake and boil what you would boil; and all that remains put aside to be kept until morning" (Exod 16:23b). However, the *ʿōdēp* 'the remainder' may refer to the uncooked manna, which on the sabbath was to be eaten raw (cf. Ramban). And the verb *wĕhēkînû* (v. 5) most likely means "when they measure" and not "when they prepare," in view of the remainder of the verse, "it shall prove double the amount they gather each day" (Rashi, Ehrlich 1908). The manna pericope also provides the source for the law that on the sabbath one may not leave one's premises or community (Exod 16:29; cf. *Mek. Bešallaḥ* 5). However, it is possible to argue that the purpose of this prohibition is to prevent the Israelites from doubting YHWH's word that on the sabbath no manna would fall (Weinfeld 1968: 109–10, 127–30). Other kinds of work prohibited on the sabbath mentioned elsewhere in Scripture include engaging in trade (Amos 8:5) and carrying burdens (Jer 17:21–27; cf. Neh 13:15–22). Since the work prohibition on the sabbath is missing in P's festival calendar (Num 28:9–10), in contrast to the other festivals (Num 28:18, 25, 26; 29:1, 7, 12, 35), Knohl (1995: 18–19) argues that according to P work was not forbidden on the sabbath.

In Deuteronomy, the prohibition against work is found in connection with the seventh day of the Festival of Unleavened Bread, where it is formulated *lō' ta'ǎśeh mělā'kâ* (Deut 16:8bβ). It gives the impression of a simplified conflation of the priestly *kol-mělā'kâ* for the sabbath and Yom Kippur (vv. 3, 30) and *měle'ket 'ǎbōdâ* for the seventh day of the Festival of Unleavened Bread and the other festival days (vv. 8, 21, 25, 35; see NOTE on "The seventh day is a sacred occasion," v. 8). Alternatively—and more likely—D was totally unaware of the priestly nuances of prohibited labor and simply wrote down what it knew, namely the prohibition against occupational work, which it termed *mělā'kâ* instead of the more precise priestly term *měle'ket 'ǎbōdâ*.

As to why D mentioned the work prohibition for the seventh day of the Festival of Unleavened Bread and not for the other days in the festival calendar of Deut 16, it must be borne in mind that the latter days must be spent at the centralized sanctuary, far from the Israelites' fields and other occupations (cf. Tigay 1996: 156), and only the seventh day of the Festival of Unleavened Bread is to be observed at an assembly (*'ǎṣeret*; see NOTE on v. 36) in their hometowns.

Qumran (CD 11:17–18) and, before it, *Jubilees* (50:10–11) apply the work prohibition to the Temple: all sacrifices are forbidden on the sabbath, except the prescribed sabbath and daily offerings. Wacholder (1983: 49–50) wrongly claims that Yadin (1983) held that the sect forbade the daily offering (Tamid) on the sabbath (cf. Baumgarten 1985: 398, n. 23). To be sure, the sect made certain that none of the festivals could ever fall on the sabbath (Jaubert 1953; Beckwith 1981). Yadin (1983: 1.117–18) maintains that the sect excluded the sabbath from its reckoning of the seven-day holidays, as reported by Al-Qirqisani concerning the practice of the Zadokites. It is more likely, however, that instead of adding an additional day, the seven-day festival was left intact, and on the sabbath (the fourth day of the Festivals of Unleavened Bread and Booths), no prescribed holiday sacrifices were offered (Wacholder 1983: 50). Baumgarten (1985: 398, n. 26) suggests that *šěmînî 'ǎṣeret*, the eighth day following the seven-day Festival of Booths, would have been regarded as the missing day, but admits that no such extra day is provided for the Festival of Unleavened Bread. Besides, the sacrifices prescribed for *šěmînî 'ǎṣeret* do not fit the sacrificial scheme for the Festival of Booths.

The people, however, did allow themselves short journeys (2 Kgs 4:23), and the changing of the guards at the palace and of the priestly courses at the Temple took place on the sabbath (2 Kgs 11:5–8; 2 Chr 23:4–8). In the Temple, the Bread of Presence was replaced every sabbath (Lev 24:8), the king would officiate on the sabbath (2 Kgs 16:18), and, in Ezekiel's visionary Temple, the king (*nāśî'*) would offer the sabbath (and new moon) sacrifices via a special entrance (Ezek 46:1–8). The sabbath was not just a day of abstentions; it was characterized by pleasure and joy (Isa 58:13).

Above all, the sabbath stood out from all other holidays by its egalitarian character. All laborers, regardless of status, even animals, rested on this day. It occasions no surprise to learn that in the Babylonian Exile it was the sabbath that attracted non-Israelites to cast their lot with the returning exiles (Isa

56:2–6) and that by the end of the second Temple period many Hellenistic communities had adopted the sabbath as a day of rest. As claimed by Josephus (*Con. Ap.* 2.282): "there is not one city, Greek or barbarian, nor a single nation to which our custom of abstaining from work on the seventh day has not spread."

it is a sabbath of YHWH. šabbāt hî'(Q) *laYHWH.* Is the *lamed* to be rendered "of" or "to"? Favoring the latter is the expression *ḥag laYHWH* 'a pilgrimage-festival to YHWH' (e.g., vv. 6, 41; cf. Exod 13:6; 32:5; Deut 16:10; see NOTE on vv. 5–6). However, the sabbath in priestly sources is part of God's creation and the day on which he rested (Gen 2:2–3; cf. Exod 20:11; 31:17). Therefore, the sabbath, by right of ownership, is "of YHWH," the Lord's. The notion generated by the creation account that the sabbath is YHWH's day of rest is expressed in Moses' rebuke of the Israelites who sought to gather manna on the sabbath: *šabbāt hayyôm laYHWH lō' timṣâ'ūhû bāśśādeh* 'today is a sabbath of YHWH; you will not find it in the field' (Exod 16:25). This highly anthropomorphic expression is clear: God is resting on this day; the sabbath is his day off (on the basis of the sabbath of creation when *wayyinnāpaš*, lit. "he caught his breath," Exod 31:17 [H]; D. N. Freedman, personal communication). Thus the rendering "of YHWH" is fully substantiated (see also the expression *šabbĕtōt YHWH* 'YHWH's sabbaths', v. 38; cf. 19:3, 30; 26:2; Exod 31:13).

Yet the distinction between the sabbath and the festivals provides full confirmation of the rendering "of YHWH." As pointed out above (see NOTE on "sacred occasions," v. 2), the festivals are fixed according to the lunar calendar. Hence it is not God but Israel that determines their dates (*tiqrĕ'û* '*you* shall proclaim'). The sabbath, however, is independent of the calendar; its occurrence has been predetermined by God.

This distinction is clarified further by focusing on the unusual term describing the first sabbath, *wayyĕqaddēš 'ōtô* 'and he (God) sanctified it' (Gen 2:3; cf. Exod 20:11b). In contrast to the Babylonian myth that the gods built Marduk a temple after he had created the world when he vanquished Tiamat and the other gods of chaos, the God of Israel builds for himself (other gods being nonexistent) a temple, not in space but in time—the sabbath (Heschel 1951; Weinfeld 1981). Never in Scripture do we find that God sanctifies space. Although the world is his creation, he does not hallow it. Even his land on which he settles Israel is never specifically called holy (see NOTE on "for the land is mine," 25:23). The sacred space occupied by the sanctuary and its priesthood is not sanctified by God, but by Moses (8:10–11, 12, 30). (There is one statement attributing the act of sanctification to God, Exod 29:44 [H]. But this is H's metaphoric, figurative notion of holiness. Indeed, even when H speaks of God continuously sanctifying Israel and the priesthood [20:8; 21:8, 15, 23; 22:9, 16, 32], the sanctification is actually done by the human recipients, through their obedience to God's commandments.) Thus the act of sanctifying time by the God of time makes it his exclusive possession. It is "of YHWH."

This point, I submit, is reinforced by the use of the possessive dative *laYHWH* 'to YHWH' exclusively with the sabbath (Exod 16:23, 25; 31:15; 35:2; Lev 23:3).

To be sure, the sabbatical year is also described as *laYHWH* (25:2, 4), probably on the analogy of the weekly sabbath, but its meaning there is probably "to YHWH"—that is, dedicated to YHWH (see NOTE on 25:2). Indeed, the sabbatical year, but not the weekly sabbath, can be expressed with a second-person-plural suffix *šabbĕtōtêkem* 'your sabbaticals' (26:35), because the onset and close of the sabbatical year is by the lunar calendar, which is determined not by God, but by Israel.

The term *môʿădîm* 'fixed times' can also be "of YHWH." However, in such cases it is expressed as a subjective genitive *môʿădê YHWH* (23:2, 4, 37, 44), never with the dative *lamed*, *laYHWH*. In fact, just as can the sabbatical, it can take a second-person-plural suffix, *bĕmôʿădêkem* 'in *your* fixed times' (Num 10:10; 15:3; 29:39), an indisputably logical choice, since the festivals, no differently from the sabbatical, are fixed by the lunar calendar, the determination of which is entirely in Israel's hands. (For the same reason, third-person suffixes can be attached to *môʿēd*, 23:4; Num 9:2, 3, 7, 13; 28:2.)

Nonetheless, the possibility may be reckoned with that on the analogy of *ḥag laYHWH*, Israel is instructed to observe a "sabbath *to* YHWH" by abstaining from work and having the priests perform the prescribed sacrificial service in the Temple (Num 28:9–10). It is not clear whether devotion to God in other ways was expected, but the offhand remark that people would consult the prophet on the sabbath (2 Kgs 4:23) may indicate that the leisure time afforded by the sabbath enabled the people (or some of them) to seek spiritual and religious instruction—the beginning of Torah study in Israel.

The structure of this sabbath injunction clearly formed the basis of H's prescription for the sabbatical year (parallels in boldface).

ûbayyôm **haššĕbîʿî** *šabat šabbātôn* . . . *kol-mĕlāʾkâ* **loʾ** . . . *šabbāt hi(w)ʾ* **laYHWH**
ûbaššānâ **haššĕbîʿīt** *šabbat šabbātôn yihyeh lāʾāreṣ šabbāt* **laYHWH** *śādĕkā* **lōʾ** . . .

but the seventh day is a sabbath of complete rest . . . no work; **it is a sabbath of YHWH** (v. 3aβ,b)
but in the seventh year the land shall have **a sabbath of complete rest, a sabbath to YHWH; no** field . . . (25:4)

The differences (the nonparalleled words) are slight; nevertheless, they are significant:

1. The sabbatical year is not YHWH's, but the land's (cf. *šabbat hāʾāreṣ*, lit. "the land's sabbath," 25:6).
2. The total rest (*šabbat šabbātôn*) falls on the land, not on the Israelites. Hence the latter may work at all other occupations but farming.
3. Whereas the sabbath existed from the world's creation, the sabbatical year is instituted not by God, but by Israel—to be implemented in the future (*yihyeh*). Hence the land's sabbath is not "of YHWH," but "to YHWH."

throughout your settlements. bĕkōl mô̂šĕbōtêkem. The rabbis register the following controversy: "Everywhere 'your settlements' is written, the passage refers (to your settling) in the land (not outside of it)—the statement of R. Ishmael. R. Akiba said to him: Since Scripture says, 'It is a sabbath of the Lord throughout your settlements' (Lev 23:3), I infer that it is both in the land and outside the land" (*Sipre* Šelaḥ 107).

The term *mô̂šābōt* is found sixteen times: Exod 12:20; 35:3; Lev 3:17; 7:26; 23:3, 14, 17, 21, 31; Num 15:2; 35:29; Ezek 6:6, 14; 1 Chr 4:33; 6:39; 7:28. These instances prove that R. Ishmael was right. But if, as I believe, H's passages on the sabbath (23:3; Exod 35:3) were composed in the exile, R. Akiba—who cites this sabbath passage—was also right. It should not go unnoticed that all the cited, pentateuchal passages are attributable to H (Knohl 1995: 104, 106; vol. 1.63). This term is indicative of the provincial provenance of H, which focuses on settlements and not on cities. That these, too, are discrete forms of housing is shown by Num 31:10 and Ezek 6:6, which speak of cities within settlements (Joosten 1996: 161, n. 88).

THE FESTIVALS

There are five festival calendars in the Pentateuch: Exod 23:14–17; 34:18–26; Deut 16:1–17; Lev 23; Num 28–29. Only the last two, the priestly calendars, can be considered complete. It shall be shown that Lev 23 (H) is based on Num 28–29 (P). For a convenient table conflating all the festival calendars, see Jensen (1992: 227–31).

The festival calendar (vv. 4–38) contains seven days of rest: the first and seventh days of the Festival of Unleavened Bread (vv. 7–8), the First Wheat offering (v. 21), the Festival of Alarm Blasts (v. 24), the Day of Purgation (v. 28), the first day of the Festival of Booths (v. 35), and the day following Booths (v. 36; Wenham 1979: 301)—additional evidence that the prescription for the sabbath (v. 3) is an interpolation. Possibly, the calendar also consisted of seven festivals: *pesaḥ, maṣṣôt, 'ōmer, minḥâ ḥădāšâ, zikrôn tĕrû'â, yôm hakkippûrîm, sukkôt.* Although *pesaḥ* and *maṣṣôt* are joined (vv. 5–6), originally they were discrete (see NOTE on a paschal offering to YHWH," v. 5), and the eighth day attached to *sukkôt* is not even described as a separate festival.

This calendar effectively divides into two parts: the festivals of the first month (and their fifty-day extension, vv. 5–22) and the festivals of the seventh month (vv. 23–36), flanked by an introduction (vv. 1–2aα,4) and a summary (vv. 37–38). These two halves are marked by the same closing formula "I am YHWH your God" (vv. 22bβ, 43b). Each half is further characterized by the phrase *laḥōdeš hazzeh / hazzeh laḥōdeš* (vv. 6, 27, 34), referring to the first and seventh month, respectively.

The Mesopotamian calendar, reflected in the priestly calendar, was lunar. The preference of the lunar over the solar year may go back to Sumerian mythology, which considered the moon the father of, and hence superior to, the sun. The eleven-day disparity between the solar and lunar years was overcome by intercalating an entire lunar month approximately every three years: "Thus, the

Mesopotamian year was, in effect, a solar year squeezed into a lunar 'strait-jacket' " (M. Cohen 1993: 4).

The year was divided into two periods. The first six months of summer (*ummātu*), or hot season (*umšum*), began with the vernal equinox. The second six months of winter (ENTEN), or cold season (*kuṣṣum*), began with the autumnal equinox. Ancient Israel was aware of this cycle by referring to the equinoxes as *tĕqûpat haššānâ* (Exod 34:22) and *tĕšûbat haššānâ* (2 Sam 11:1): "the turn of the year." The priestly calendar clearly reflects this bipartate division of the year by its concentration of festivals in the first and seventh months that largely parallel one another. For example, both these two months contain a seven-day festival beginning on the fifteenth day of the month to which an additional day is attached: the *pesaḥ* before the seven-day Festival of Unleavened Bread (Lev 23:5–8) and the eighth day after the seven-day Festival of Booths (v. 36). This symmetry is accentuated in the Septuagint of Ezek 45:20: "You shall do the same (as the first day of the first month) in the seventh month."

The term *mô'ēd* means "fixed time (or meeting or place)" and implies, perhaps, the time fixed by man (e.g., 1 Sam 9:24; 13:8, 11; 2 Kgs 4:16, 17) in contrast to the sabbath, the time fixed by God (see NOTE on v. 2).

The Mesopotamian calendar, probably introduced by Samsuiluna (ca. 1750 B.C.E.), was adopted by all of Mesopotamia by the end of the millennium and subsequently by the entire Asiatic Near East, including Israel. For details, see Rochberg-Halton (1992) and M. Cohen (1993: 239–305).

4. This verse with vv. 1–2aα, I hold, was the original heading of H's original, preexilic calendar (see COMMENT A). Telltale evidence is provided by the lack of the incipit "YHWH spoke to Moses, saying" for the Paschal Offering and the Festival of Unleavened Bread (cf. vv. 1, 9, 23, 26, 33; Scott 1993: 107).

at their fixed times. bĕmô'ădām, literally "in their fixed time." The plural rendering for the noun *mô'ēd* can be justified by comparing a similar usage of this term in another H passage: *'et-qorbānî laḥmî lĕ'iššay rēaḥ nîḥōḥî tišmĕrû lĕhaqrîb lî bĕmô'ădô*, literally "(Be punctilious in presenting to me) my offering, my food, as my gifts, my pleasing aroma, at its fixed time" (Num 28:2), which, however, clearly has a plural connotation: "my offerings, my food-gifts, my pleasing aromas, at *their* fixed time" (GKC § 145m), as expressly stated in the calendar subscript *bĕmô'ădêkem* 'in their fixed times' (Num 29:39).

The dates of the *mô'ădîm* that follow are according to the lunar month: *'āśâ yārēaḥ lammô'ădîm* 'He made the moon to (mark) the fixed times' (Ps 104:19; cf. Gen 1:14); "The moon, too, that marks the changing times, governing the seasons, their lasting sign, by which we know the feast days and fixed dates" (Sir 43:6–7a).

Vv. 5–8. The Paschal Offering and the Unleavened Bread

The details of the former are given in Exod 12:1–20, and the latter in Num 28:17–25, both of which are presumed here.

5. *In the first month. baḥōdeš hāri'šôn*. Also called *lĕmô'ēd ḥōdeš he'ābîb* 'at the fixed time of the month of the ripening grain' (Exod 23:15; 34:18; cf. Deut

16:1) or "the month when the grain is easily hulled" (Saadiah; *m. Kil.* 5:7; Gins-berg 1979–80: 151). This longer expression was also shortened to give the month its earlier name, which is mentioned in several places in the early narrative (Exod 13:4; 23:15; 34:18 [bis]; cf. Deut 16:1 [bis]). The first grain to reach the stage of ripening or hulling is barley (Exod 9:31; see NOTES on Lev 2:14). The im-precise dating in the Exodus and Deuteronomy calendars (see also Josh 5:10; 2 Kgs 23:21–22) is probably earlier than the fixed date given in the priestly texts (Lev 23; Num 28). The use of numbers for the months may represent a delib-erate attempt to avoid the polytheistic practice of using the names of gods (de Vaux 1961: 185).

A numbered-month calendar is employed throughout the priestly calendars (23:5, 24, 27, 39, 41; Num 28:16; 29:1, 7, 12) as well as elsewhere in the priestly texts (Gen 7:11; 8:4, 5, 13, 14; Exod 12:2; 16:1; 19:1; 40:2, 17; Num 1:1, 18; 9:1, 11; 10:11; 20:1; 33:3, 38). Levine (1989a: 267) argues that its use in Jere-miah, in 2 Kgs 25:1, 25, and in contemporary epigraphy shows that it came into existence close to the exilic period. De Vaux (1961: 191–92) contends that since the numbered-month calendar system assumes a spring New Year, its adoption is due to the influence of the Babylonian calendar, which also begins in the spring. This must have occurred, according to de Vaux, after the death of Josiah when Judah became a vassal state of Babylon. Elliger (1966: 312) holds that the calendar with a spring New Year first arrived under Assyrian influence in the seventh century B.C.E. Nonetheless, he argues that the numbered-month system was taken over from the Babylonians, but only in the exile. Ginsberg (1982: 67, 122–27) suggests the earlier date of the reign of Manasseh, who, as a submissive vassal of Assyria, also may have used the Babylonian calendar.

Possibly, the changeover would have occurred as early as the eighth century under Ahaz to curry favor with his Assyrian overlord (2 Kgs 16:7, 10). This would account for the few P references to the numbered-month system in the story of the Flood (Gen 7:11; 8:4, 5, 13, 14) and in P's cultic calendar (Num 28:16; 29:1, 7, 12), both of which may stem from the precentralized (pre-Hezekian) Jerusalem Temple. All the other numbered months in the Torah derive from H, and the possibility must be considered that the citations attributed to P may actually be the product of H's editing. In any event, it is clear that the spring calendar using a numbered-month system was in place by the seventh century and, possibly, as early as the eighth century.

Tadmor (1962: 264–67) maintains that the northern and southern kingdoms differed in their respective calendars in regard to the beginning of the year: the north in the fall and the south in the spring. Especially telling is his demon-stration that a number of synchronizations between the two, beginning in the eighth century—particularly between the reigns of Zechariah, the son of Jere-boam II, and Uzziah—can be reconciled only by positing a difference of six months in their calendrical reckoning (Tadmor 1962: 267). Indeed, it seems likely, with Tadmor, that this difference between the two calendrical systems was in evidence from the beginning of the history of the divided kingdom. In any case, it can be stated affirmatively that with the loss of the northern kingdom at the end of the eighth century, the spring calendar of Judah prevailed, and that is what is reflected in our priestly texts.

on the fourteenth (day) of the month. The LXX, Sam., and fifteen MSS add *yôm* 'day', as in Num 28:16. The biblical day, as the Egyptian day (Parker 1950: 9–23), began at dawn (Gen 1:5; 19:33–34; Lev 7:15; 22:30; Num 9:11; 33:3; Josh 5:10; Judg 19:4–9; 1 Sam 19:11; 28:18–19). The creation story requires justification, since most exegetes posit that Gen 1 proves the reverse, namely, that the day begins with evening (most recently, Levenson 1988: 123). Not so. God creates only during daylight; hence the first thing he creates is light. Each day ends with the refrain "And there was evening and there was morning, day——." This can only mean that the day was completed at the end of the *following* night. When morning arrived, God began his creative labors; it was a new day (see Ibn Ezra and Rashbam on Gen 1:5; Hartom and Loewenstamm 1958). That the term *'ereb* 'evening' refers to the evening that follows God's creative acts is proved by the refrain of the first day (Gen 1:5). Obviously, there was no evening preceding the creation of light.

Even stronger evidence that the day begins with daylight is the priestly text dealing with the manna. The key verses are "Tomorrow is a day of rest, a holy sabbath of YHWH. . . . So they put it (the manna) aside until the morning. . . ." Then Moses said, "Eat it today, for today is a sabbath of YHWH" (Exod 16:23–25). The plain meaning of these verses (despite the vigorous objections of Ibn Ezra, at v. 25) is that the day begins with daylight.

An ostensible objection is offered by one of the prescriptions for the Festival of Unleavened Bread: in the first month, from the fourteenth day of the month **at evening,** you shall eat unleavened bread until the twenty-first day of the month **at evening** [my emphasis]" (Exod 12:18). However, the fact that this festival begins and ends in the evening actually proves the reverse. If the day began in the evening, there would be no need to state, not once but twice, that the termini are the evenings. Rather, this statement is necessary because normally the day begins with morning. The reason that this festival begins (and, hence, ends) with the evening is that unleavened bread is an indispensable ingredient in the paschal sacrifice, which is offered in the evening and eaten during the night before the onset of the Festival of Unleavened Bread (Exod 12:8). Therefore, the seven-day span of this festival begins and ends in the evening. The exceptional timing of this festival is also responsible for the deuteronomic injunction *šēšet yāmîm tō'kal maṣṣôt* 'You shall eat unleavened bread for six days' (Deut 16:8a). That is, having eaten unleavened bread with the *pesaḥ* sacrifice the evening before, at the beginning of the first day of the festival, only six days remain for its completion (Ginsberg 1982: 57; Levine 1989a: 266). This change of date is even more manifest in Deuteronomy by its seemingly superfluous addition of *bayyôm hārī'šôn* 'on the first day' to *'ăšer tizbaḥ bā'ereb* 'which you sacrifice in the evening' (Deut 16:4). Its purpose is to emphasize that exceptionally for this festival the day begins the evening before. Similarly, the special stress on *hayyôm* 'this day' (Exod 12:14, 17) can be attributed to an attempt to fuse the *pesaḥ* (on the fourteenth) and the *maṣṣôt* (beginning on the fifteenth) into a single *ḥag* (Knohl 1987: 78;

1995: 20). The exceptional circumstances of the Day of Purgation also necessitate that it be an evening-to-evening observance (see NOTE on v. 32).

That the *pesaḥ* eaten at night and the *maṣṣôt* festival starting in the morning fall not on the same day but on consecutive days of the calendar is proved by Num 33:3: "on the fifteenth day of the first month, **on the morrow of the *pesaḥ* offering,** the Israelites started out boldly in **plain view** of all the Egyptians [my emphasis]." That is, on the day following the paschal offering (sacrificed and eaten on the fourteenth), Israel left Egypt in daylight, which marked the fifteenth day. Finally, the prophecy *haššîr yihyeh lākem kělêl hitqaddeš-ḥāg* 'Singing shall be yours as on a night when a festival is hallowed' (Isa 30:29a) probably refers solely to the evening of the paschal sacrifice, according to the commentators, ancient (*b. Pesaḥ* 85b; *y. Pesaḥ* 9:3) and modern (e.g., Kissane 1960; Watts 1985).

McKay (1972) offers this objection: if the month begins the day after the new moon is sighted, then the following night is part of the first day. His deduction is absolutely correct. This is precisely how the Egyptians, operating on a solar calendar, calculated their months. One must not confuse the preexilic calendrical system of the Bible with the near-total lunar calendar in evidence during the Second Temple period, when the first sighting of the new moon determined the beginning of the month.

When did this transition occur? The alternation day–night or night–day is not a reliable criterion, since both are attested throughout Scripture (for the former, see Gen 1:14; Exod 13:21–22; 1 Kgs 8:59; Ps 74:16; for the latter, Deut 28:66; 1 Kgs 8:29; Isa 27:3; Ps 55:18 [but cf. v. 11]) in both early and late texts (contra de Vaux 1961: 181). Ostensibly, the sabbath begins the preceding evening, according to Neh 13:19 (de Vaux 1961: 181–82; Stroes 1966: 460–65). However, as Tigay (1978a) has demonstrated, its expression *'aḥar haššabbāt* does not mean "Saturday evening" but "Sunday"; that is, the gates of Jerusalem, closed for the sabbath, were not opened until Sunday—in fact, until "the heat of the day" (Neh 7:3). Thus the sabbath may not have ended until Sunday morning, and it cannot be used as evidence that the changeover to the evening took place in the Babylonian Exile (Zeitlin 1945–46). Est 4:16; Dan 8:14, and Jdt 11:17 possibly indicate a shift to the evening, but the composition of these books cannot be dated earlier than the fourth century B.C.E. In any event, the sacrificial service at the Temple never changed; until the destruction of the Temple in C.E. 70, the day began in the morning (*m. Yoma* 3:1; *b. Ḥul.* 83a).

Elliger (1966) and Gerstenberger (1966) note the lack of historical grounding for the *pesaḥ* and *maṣṣôt* festivals (vv. 5–8) in contrast with the *sukkôt* festival (v. 43). The latter, however, stems from Hr, whereas the former as well as the basic calendar of chap. 23 stem from H, which presumes the historical basis detailed in Exod 12:1–20. Note that the prescription for the *sukkôt* festival within the H calendar (vv. 33–36) is also without historical reference. In this case, however there was none (see COMMENT A).

at twilight. ben hā'arbāyim. This phrase is added to its P *Vorlage* (Num 28:16; see below, and COMMENT A). It literally means "between the two evenings." The Tgs. render *bên / bênê šimšayā'*, literally "between the two suns" (Rabbinic Hebrew *bên haššěmāšôt*), which Jastrow (1943: 1602) interprets as "between the two services, between the rulership of the day and that of the night." The rabbis define it: "From the time that the sun sets (and) as long as the face of the east is red" (*b. Šabb.* 34b)—in other words, the twilight.

Ibn Ezra reaches the same conclusion on the basis of examining other attestations of this expression:

> Note the verse "When Aaron lights the lamps *bên hā'arbayim*" (Exod 30:8); there is no doubt that he lights the lamps when the sun is setting . . . and a moment within the *bên 'arbayîm* is called *'ereb*, for (regarding the quail miracle) it is written (both) "you shall eat meat *bên ha'arbayîm*" (Exod 16:12) and "when the Lord gives you meat to eat *bā'ereb*" (v. 8). And in kindling the lights it is written "Aaron and his sons shall set them up (to burn) from evening to morning" (Exod 27:21). And it is written "burnt offerings for the Lord for the morning and evening" (Ezra 3:3), and it is written "you shall offer the second lamb *bên hā'arbayîm*" (Exod 29:39). And behold for the *pesaḥ* we find "there alone shall you slaughter the *pesaḥ*, in the evening, at sundown, the time of day you departed from Egypt" (Deut 16:6). . . . Thus we have two sunsets, the first is the setting of the sun when it goes under the earth and the second is the disappearance of its light which is seen in the clouds. Between the two is about one-third of an hour. Then the man who had a nocturnal emission may enter the camp (Deut 23:12) and Aaron may kindle the lamps (Exod 27:21).

As pointed out by Ginsberg (1982: 57), D postpones the slaughter of the *pesaḥ* from the afternoon (at home) to *bā'ereb kĕbô' haššemeš* 'in the evening at sundown' (Deut 16:6), which leaves Levine (1989a: 267) perplexed: "It is not entirely clear why the Holiness Code reverts to this older [i.e., afternoon] pattern." His enigma is resolved once it is realized that H is consistent with the older (P) pattern (Exod 12:6); H, like P, presupposes multiple sanctuaries (see chap. 17, COMMENT D). Thus in the smaller, regional sanctuaries it is possible to contain all the *pesaḥ* sacrifices within the compass of twilight. D, however, which reflects the practice of the single, authorized sanctuary, probably the Jerusalem Temple, is intentionally vague in describing the time for the sacrifice as "in the evening at sundown." It provides ample room for legitimately offering the sacrifice *toward* sundown, precisely as practiced in the Second Temple.

The reason for specifying the twilight is not clear. I would suggest that it ensured that the *pesaḥ* would be eaten during the night. Since *pesaḥ* means "protection," it is critical that it should be eaten—that is, provide protection, as does the blood on the entrance of the houses—while the Destroyer is abroad carrying out his deadly work.

In later sources, we find that this expression is interpreted as the last third of the day (*Jub* 49:10, 19), after 3:00 P.M. (*m. Pesaḥ.* 5:1), or after high noon (Philo, *Laws* 2.145; R. Natan in *Mek.* Bo 5). The extension of "twilight" is perfectly understandable. After the centralization of worship under King Josiah, with all of

Israel commanded to offer the *pesaḥ* at the Temple (Deut 16:2, 5–6; 2 Kgs 23:21), the official time of twilight had to be extended to accommodate the throngs of pilgrims. It could only be extended earlier, since there were no sacrifices after dark. For the same reason, the evening Tamid, which also had to be sacrificed at twilight (Exod 29:39), was offered early in the afternoon before the paschal offering (*m. Pesaḥ.* 5:1; Jos. *Wars* 6.423; cf. Jos. *Ant.* 14.65): "In the Gospel of John, the Jewish leaders urge Pilate to make sure that the crucified prisoners are dead because the time for offering the paschal sacrifices is fast approaching, i.e., afternoon, because the time is about 3:00 P.M. and the sacrifices are about to begin very soon, i.e., long before evening. It is another indication that the writer of the Fourth Gospel was better informed about local Jerusalem customs and especially Temple practices than the other evangelists" (D. N. Freedman, personal communication).

Because the language of this verse is taken verbatim from Num 28:16 (P), the possibility must be considered that originally the *pesaḥ* was sacrificed at a local altar or at home (see NOTE on "a paschal offering"), as acknowledged by D: "you are not permitted to slaughter [*lizbōaḥ*; cf. Deut 12:15, 21] the *pesaḥ* in any of your settlements" (Deut 16:5). The prescription for the second *pesaḥ* (Num 9:9–14), however, implies a single sanctuary (see following NOTE).

a paschal offering. *pesaḥ*, meaning *nĕkîsat pishâ* 'the *pesaḥ* sacrifice' (*Tg. Neof.*) or *zĕman nîksat pishā'* 'the time of the *pesaḥ* sacrifice' (*Tg. Ps.-J.*); compare *zebaḥ pesaḥ* (Exod 12:27). The predicate *pesaḥ hû' laYHWH* (Exod 12:11, 27) or *ta'ăśû pesaḥ wĕ'āśā' laYHWH* (Num 9:10, 14) is missing (Boleh). However, this is the construction found in Num 28:16 and, hence, is evidence that the latter served as the model.

The root *psḥ* is shared by two homonyms: "limp, be lame" (2 Sam 4:4; 1 Kgs 18:26) and "protect" (Isa 31:5). Otto (1988: 31–35) holds that both meanings derive from the notion "strike, push back," which, however, cannot be substantiated. The common but erroneous rendering "Passover" was first introduced by the LXX on Exod 12:23 *pareleúsetai* 'he will pass by'; however, it renders *ûpāsaḥtî 'ălêkem* (Exod 12:13) *kaí skepásō humàs* 'and I shall protect you' and *pāsaḥ* (Exod 12:27) *esképasen* 'protected'. The rabbis, however, comment on Exod 12:13 and 23: "The word *pĕsîḥâ* means nothing but protection, as it is said 'Like the birds that fly, even so will YHWH of Hosts shield Jerusalem *gānôn wĕhiṣṣîl pāsôaḥ wĕhimlîṭ* 'shielding and saving, protecting and rescuing' (Isa 31:5)" (*Mek. Bo'*, par. 7 [Horowitz: 24, 39]). Only R. Josiah follows the tradition of the secondary LXX rendering: "Do not read *ûpāsaḥtî* 'I will protect' but *ûpāsa 'tî* 'I will step over'. The Holy One Blessed Be He skipped over the houses of his children in Egypt" (*Mek. Bo'*, par. 7 [Horovitz: 25]), but even R. Josiah has to admit that the true meaning of *pāsaḥ* in this context is "protect." To be sure, in Exod 12:13, 23, it makes no sense that YHWH skips over Israel's homes, thereby leaving them vulnerable to the *mašḥît* 'the Destroyer'. Rather, YHWH protects them against "the Destroyer" (reading *lammašḥît* for *lĕmašḥît* 'to destroy', v. 13).

Adopting the meaning "pass over" for *pāsaḥ*, Jub 49:2–4 records that God did not go forth at night, but commanded "all the forces of Mastema" to slay the

Egyptian firstborn and "pass over" the homes of the Israelites (cf. Loewenstamm 1992: 212). Nonetheless, *Jub* 49:15 also seems to adopt the notion of "protect," since it claims that the paschal blood on the house will protect its inhabitants from plagues for an entire year.

The apotropaic power of blood was widely attested in the ancient Semitic world, as evidenced by its survival in modern Arab tribes (details in Gray 1925: 360–63; Loewenstamm 1965: 84–94). It was pointed out that blood placed on the extremities of a person, such as the priestly consecrant and the healed *měṣōrāʿ*, also has an apotropaic purpose (vol. 1.528–29, 853). Perhaps, the crimson cord placed by Rahab outside her window (Josh 2:18, 21) also served symbolically as apotropaic blood against the "destroyer" Israel.

The prohibition against breaking a bone of the Paschal Offering (Exod 12:46; Num 9:12) also may serve an apotropaic function—so that Israel's bones will not be broken (*Jub* 49:13): "The same Scripture (Exod 12:46) is quoted by the Gospel of John in connection with the death of Jesus. John points out that the soldiers came and broke the legs of the other crucified prisoners in order to hasten their death, but didn't do so with Jesus because he was already dead when they came; cf. John 19:31–37, esp. v. 36" (D. N. Freedman, personal communication). Some peoples, such as American Indians and Siberian Inuit, engage in a similar practice in relation to hunted animals in the belief that they will come to life again, but the attempt to apply this theory to the pesaḥ (Stendebach 1973) falters on the obvious question: Why shouldn't a similar prohibition be employed with all the blood sacrifices and not just the *pesaḥ* (S. Rattray).

The time of the paschal sacrifice is not a *miqrāʾ qōdeš* 'sacred occasion' (but it is a *môʿēd* 'fixed time'), since work is not forbidden (see NOTE on v. 7). Dillmann and Ryssel (1897) add another reason: the observance is at home, not at a sanctuary. However, this reason is invalid: sabbath, as noted above, is a *miqrāʾ qōdeš* and is also observed at home and is totally severed from the sanctuary.

The brevity of this statement on the Paschal Offering is explicable, as noted above, on the assumption that its author copied P's similar statement in Num 28:16. There, however, it made sense, because it is ensconced in an exposition of the sacrificial calendar. Lev 23, however, is directed to the people, and one would expect an exposition of the laws concerning the consumption of the sacrifice. Thus there can be no question that the author of this verse presumed that the regulations of Exod 12:1–13, 21–27 were known (see Introduction I F).

Gerstenberger (1996: 343) is puzzled that the composer(s) of this calendar is silent concerning the three required festival pilgrimages (Exod 23:17; 34:23). However, the term *pesaḥ la YHWH* presupposes a sanctuary sacrifice in all other priestly texts (Exod 12:27, 48; Num 9:10, 14; 28:16; except Exod 12:11, which implies an improvised, temporary altar). For the Festival of First Wheat, a pilgrimage is indeed not mandated by H (see NOTE on "all your settlements," v. 21). The Festival of Booths (vv. 33–36) is ostensibly silent, but it is dependent on Num 29:12, where it is called *ḥag laYHWH* 'a pilgrimage festival'.

The *pesaḥ* and *maṣṣôt* festivals are discrete in all the early sources (Exod 12:1–13, 14–20, 21–28, 40–51; 13:3–10; Lev 23:5, 6–8; Num 28:16, 17–23).

They are fused together first in Deuteronomy (Deut 16:1–7) and in postexilic sources (Ezek 45:21; Ezra 6:20–22; 2 Chr 30:2, 5, 13, 15; 35:17).

The evidence for the discreteness of the two festivals is indisputable. The eating of *maṣṣôt*, according to the priestly texts, is not bound up with sacrifice and therefore does not mandate the state of purity regularly required for visits to the sanctuary. The Israelite and resident alien (Exod 12:48; Num 9:14) need but cleanse their homes of all leaven and eat *maṣṣôt* instead of bread during the seven-day period (e.g., Exod 12:15–20). Even impure persons, such as the corpse-contaminated (Num 9:6), could observe this practice in their homes. But they could not make the pilgrimage to the sanctuary in order to sacrifice the Paschal Offering. Those whose impurity had invalidated them from offering the *pesaḥ* are still enjoined to remove the leaven from their homes and eat *maṣṣôt* for seven days at the same time as their fellow Israelites, whereas their Paschal Offering is postponed for one month (Num 9:10–11). This inference is corroborated by the halakha of the rabbis that this second date for the *pesaḥ* is observed for one day (*t. Pesaḥ.* 3:7) and that leaven may be eaten (*m. Pesaḥ.* 9:3).

The severing of the *pesaḥ* from the *maṣṣôt* festival for impure persons points to the probability that the two festivals originally were discrete and were combined only in a later age. The two, however, could always have been conjoined. The seven-day NIN.DINGIR installation of the high priestess at Emar, for example, is preceded by a discrete one-day shaving rite, and Emar's seven-day *zukru* festival, which strikingly begins on the fifteenth day of the first month, is preceded by preparatory rites on the fourteenth day of the month (Fleming 1995: 144). And the priestly calendar itself enjoins the observance of a discrete eighth day of assembly immediately following the seven-day *sukkôt* festival (23:36; Num 29:12, 36).

The consensus holds that both the *pesaḥ* and the *maṣṣôt* originated as first-fruit festivals, the former observed by shepherds and the latter, by farmers, to ensure the fertility of their respective flocks and crops. Thus the Israelite transhumant pastoralists combined their observance of the *pesaḥ* (cf. Exod 5:1; 10:9) and the *maṣṣôt* festival after they had abandoned their wilderness wandering and had settled permanently in Canaan. Indeed, the fact that the two festivals originally were separate enabled the rabbis to enjoin the celebration of the seven-day *maṣṣôt* festival (subsequently termed Passover), even after the cessation of sacrifices with the destruction of the Temple.

The home observance—the blood of the lamb or kid on the lintel and door-posts (Exod 12:7, 22)—was, according to the rabbis, observed only once during the exodus (*m. Pesaḥ.* 9:5; *Mek. Boʾ* 3–5). However, as will be shown (see NOTE on "the Pilgrimage-Festival of Unleavened Bread," v. 6), this rite prevailed in Israelite homes in Canaan. But surely the home ritual would have come to an end with the enforcement of the deuteronomic injunction to observe the Paschal Offering at the single central sanctuary (Deut 16:2). Whereas, subsequently, sacrifices were slaughtered by Temple personnel (e.g., 2 Chr 29:24), the paschal sacrifices continued to be slaughtered by its offerers "raised for that particular day to the dignity of the priesthood" (Philo, *Laws* 2.145; cf. *Moses* 2.224) and eaten collectively (Exod 12:3–4, 21; cf. *m. Pesaḥ.* 8:7; *t. Pesaḥ.* 4:3; Jos. *Wars* 6.423), but it differed from the original practice in two respects: the animal could also be a bovine, and it was not roasted but cooked (Deut 16:2, 7). In other words, it was converted to a sacrifice of well-being, resembling more the thanksgiving offering than the Paschal Offering (Lev 22:29–30; Philo, *Laws* 2.146). However, whereas the thanksgiving offering could be eaten until the following morning, it became customary, and eventually the law, to eat the *pesaḥ* before midnight (*m. Pesaḥ.* 10:9; *m. Zebaḥ.* 5:8; "the first third of the night," *Jub.* 49:12; cf. Albeck 1930: 3). It is interesting that the Chronicler's account of the Josianic *pesaḥ* (2 Chr 35) harmonizes the discrepancies between the laws pertaining to the earlier, home observance and the texts ordaining or describing the later, Temple-centered *pesaḥ* by prescribing that both a bovine and an ovine should be sacrificed (vv. 7–9). The latter is termed the *pesaḥ*, roasted (*wayyĕbaššĕlû happesaḥ bā'ēš*, v. 13, a verbal harmonization of *ṣĕlî-'ēš* [Exod 12:8] and *ûbiššaltā* [Deut 16:7]), and the former is termed *qŏdāšîm*, also roasted (*biššĕlû*, v. 13; cf. Deut 16:7), a secondary sacrifice, which the rabbis called *ḥăgîgâ* (*m. Pesaḥ.* 6:3; *b. Pesaḥ.* 69b).

Once the *pesaḥ* obtained sacrificial status, however, ritually impure persons were ineligible to partake of it. Hence the priestly establishment (late H; Knohl 1995: 21–22) ordained the institution of the second passover one month later (Num 9:1–14; cf. 2 Chr 30:2–3). Corpse-contamination is singled out (and travel) as the cause for the month's postponement (Num 9:10) only because it was the original case (v. 6), but clearly all impurity bearers are intended (note *wĕhā'îš 'ăšer-hû ṭāhôr* 'But if a person who is pure', v. 13). Is the person who legitimately — that is, for either of these two stated reasons — cannot participate in the *pesaḥ* sacrifice required to observe the second *pesaḥ*, and failing that be subject to *kārēt* — the fate of those who inexcusably absent themselves from the first *pesaḥ* (v. 13)? The answer depends on the interpretation of the clause *wĕ'āśâ pesaḥ laYHWH* (v. 10bγ): Is it the end of the protasis and, hence, voluntary (Ramban; Noth 1977; *NJPS*) or the beginning of the apodosis and, hence, mandatory (Rashi, Shadal, *NRSV*)? The former seems correct. The text states that a sin is incurred only for deliberately not observing the *pesaḥ* at its appointed time, not, however, if there are extenuating circumstances. Nothing is stated regarding the Festival of Unleavened Bread: all must eat *maṣṣôt* and abstain from leaven during the prescribed time, even those who are impure or live too far from the sanctuary.

to YHWH. *la YHWH.* In contrast to v. 3, where the same expression must be rendered *of YHWH* 'for YHWH' (see its NOTE), here the preposition *la* denotes not possession, but direction: Israel is commanded to take itself *to* YHWH, namely, to his sanctuary. The same expression and connotation occurs twice again: *ḥag hammaṣṣôt la YHWH* 'a Festival of Unleavened Bread to YHWH' (v. 6aβ) and *ḥag haṣṣukkôt . . . la YHWH* 'a Festival of Booths . . . to YHWH' (v. 34bβ). It is no accident that these two cases are the only ones in H labeled a *ḥag*. This term signifies that the festival must be celebrated at a regional sanctuary. Since the *ḥag* was celebrated by the family, it entailed a pilgrimage. (For

H's exemption of *ḥag* for the Festival of First Wheat, see NOTE on "in all your settlements," v. 21.) Thus in H's festival calendar, there were only two occasions that required a journey to a (regional) sanctuary: 14–15/1 (Nisan) and 15–21/7 (Tishri). In the former case, the required *pesaḥ* offering was followed by a sacrifice on the *ḥag*. The nature of the sacrifices offered by each family on the *ḥag* is not mentioned. Those sacrifices alluded to in vv. 8, 36 (*wĕhigrabtem 'iššeh laY-HWH*) refer to the sanctuary's obligation (Num 28:19; 29:8–34). That a sacrifice from each family was required is implied by Exod 23:17; Deut 16:16. The rabbis refer to this family sacrifice on the pilgrimage festivals as *ḥaggîgâ*.

6. *and on the fifteenth day*. Beginning at daybreak (see NOTE on "on the fourteenth [day] of the month," v. 5). Knohl (1995: 20) ascribes vv. 5–6 to P because H elsewhere (Exod 12:18) expressly speaks of fusion. But Knohl (1995: 21) himself acknowledges that Exod 12:18–20 belong to a later stratum of H. Thus vv. 5–6 may stem from an earlier H (which I call H) before fusion took place. Subsequent Exod 12:18–20 would therefore reflect an H tradent living after the deuteronomic reform that began the first day of the *maṣṣôt* festival on the previous evening, thereby combining it with the consumption of the *pesaḥ* (see NOTE on "on the fourteenth [day] of the month," v. 5). Equally likely, the H tradent lived in the Babylonian Exile (H_R). The exiles offered no *pesaḥ* sacrifice. The only rite that could be observed was the command to eat unleavened bread together with bitter herbs (*maṣṣôt 'al-mĕrōrîm*, Exod 12:8), a reminder of the *pesaḥ* that Hr wanted to retain and that would account for the fusion of the *pesaḥ* and *maṣṣôt* festivals in Exod 12:18. The effect of the fusion is to condense eight days into seven (T. King). The fourteenth and fifteenth days of the month, so prominent in the priestly calendars (23:5, 6, 34; Num 28:16, 17; 29:12), also play an important role in the cultic calendars of Hattia (e.g., the AN.TAH.ŠUM festival; Güterbock 1960; Gurney 1977: 32–33) and Ugarit (e.g., *KTU* 1.112; cf. Weinfeld 1983a: 118–19).

the Pilgrimage-Festival. ḥag. The verb *ḥāgag* means "turn, twist, dance out of happiness" (1 Sam 30:16; Ps 42:5), and its nominal form in Arabic (*ḥaǧǧ*) means "pilgrimage, procession, festal gathering" (cf. Kedar-Kopfstein 1980: 201–3). The oldest cultic calendars of Israel prescribed three mandatory sanctuary appearances each year for all adult males, of which the Festival of Unleavened Bread was one (Exod 23:17; 34:23; cf. Deut 16:16).

The first time *ḥag* appears in Scripture is in Moses' demand of Pharaoh: "We will all go, young and old. We will go with our sons and daughters, our flocks and herds; for we must observe YHWH's *ḥag*" (Exod 10:9). Thus the *ḥag* is a family affair (see Deut 16:11, 14). But Pharaoh replies "No! You menfolk go and worship YHWH, since that is what you want" (Exod 10:11)—keeping with the requirement of Exod 23:17; 34:23! As pointed out by Scott (1993: 29–32), not all attestations of *ḥag* imply a pilgrimage (e.g., Exod 32:5; Judg 21:19). The chances are that the older, precentralization calendar (Exod 23:17; cf. 34:23) prescribed an appearance at a local sanctuary, which could hardly be called a pilgrimage (contra Haran 1978: 289–90). Thus Kedar-Kopfstein's (1980) rendering "community festival" is more precise. Nonetheless, all other calendars mandating centralization of worship, either regionally (P or H) or nationally (D), would have pilgrimages in mind.

Unleavened Bread. maṣṣôt. The etymology is obscure. It can hardly be from Hebrew *mṣṣ* 'suck' (BDB) or *mṣh* 'press out, sip up', but Greek *màza* 'barley bread' does suggest that it may be a loanword from Asia Minor, perhaps from Hurrian (details in Kellermann 1984: 1075). In fact, Anan ben David (eighth century C.E.), regarded by the Karaite sect as its founder, declared that the unleavened bread for this festival must be made of barley. However, it cannot be of the new crop, which may be eaten only after the subsequent *ʿōmer* offering (see NOTE on v. 10). If, then, barley of the previous crop must be used, why not wheat? Also, if the *maṣṣôt* festival was in reality a festival of firstfruits, why was the new barley celebrated for seven days but the new wheat, for only one day (vv. 15, 21; Dillmann and Ryssel 1897)?

Goldstein and Cooper (1990: 20–21; Cooper and Goldstein 1992: 27–28) suggest that "the basic meaning of the term *maṣṣôt* is 'strife,' from the root *n-ṣ-h* (cf. Isa 58:4, **rîb ûmaṣṣâ*)—specifically the strife between God and Death." Because Deuteronomy refers to the unleavened bread as *leḥem ʿōnî* 'the bread of distress', they conjecture that "the process of redemption entails a symbolic period of mourning without sacrifice, marked by the consumption of mourner's food (*leḥem ʿōnî*, Deut 16:3) . . . culminating with a *ḥag* that signifies the release from mourning (Exod 13:6)." In the more recent work, Cooper and Goldstein (1992: 29–34) speculate that *maṣṣôt* formed a quintessential part of the cultic meal with the ancestral spirits (*ʾĕlōhîm*), citing Gen 18–19, Judg 6:11–24; 13:2–24, and 1 Sam 28. Others surmise that the purpose of the *maššôt* was to make the new crop available for food; therefore, nothing of the old crop could be associated with it (e.g., Ringgren 1966: 187; Porter 1976).

These theories cannot be the origin of the festival. As observed by Margalit (1993), leaven was prohibited during the seven-day *maššôt* festival, but not in the making of the unleavened bread prescribed for the consumption of the *pesaḥ* (Exod 12:8). This latter *maṣṣâ* may have been prepared with oil, wine, and fruit juice (as enriched matzoh wafers today). Surely, as Margalit (1993: 329) asks: "Would Lot have entertained his guests with a feast (*mišteh*) containing flat unleavened bread?" Besides, I might add, if the *pesaḥ* was subsequently converted into a thanksgiving offering (2 Chr 35; see NOTE on "a paschal offering," v. 5), the bread accompaniment eaten by the worshiper would have to have been leavened (7:13). Also, the text states explicitly, "On the first day you shall remove leaven from your houses" (Exod 12:15). Since the day begins in the morning, the paschal meal, eaten during the previous night, may legitimately have contained leaven (see the rabbinic controversy on this verse in *Mek.* Bo', par. 8). In any case, Moses issued the command to prepare the *pesaḥ* and its *maṣṣôt* adjunct on the first of the month (Exod 12:2). Therefore, neither the rationale of Exod 12:39 nor that of Deut 16:3 can be original; they reflect a subsequent historization of this rite.

the Pilgrimage-Festival of Unleavened Bread to YHWH. ḥag hammaṣṣôt laYHWH. On what day(s) was the pilgrimage (*ḥag*)? The biblical sources provide three different answers: (1) *the first day* (Exod 12:14, 17 [H?]; Lev 23:6 [H]; Num 28:17 [P]; Deut 16:16 [D; by inference from vv. 2, 7–8]); (2) *the seventh day* (Exod 13:6 [JE]); and (3) *all seven days* (Ezek 45:21; Ezra 6:22; 2 Chr 8:12–13; 30:13, 21; 35:17).

Clearly, Exod 13:6, the epic source (JE), is the oldest. And since the two non-committal verses (Exod 23:15; 34:18 [before it was edited by D; cf. v. 25b; see COMMENT C]) are also from the same source, it is reasonable to conclude that they, too, posit that *ḥag hammaṣṣôt*, the pilgrimage prescribed for the seven-day festival, falls on the seventh day. The significance of this fact should not be overlooked. There can be only one reason why the pilgrimage takes place on the seventh day: the *pesaḥ* is observed at home, in keeping with the regulations of Exod 12:1–13, 22–27a, 28—all probably P (cf. Bar-On 1995)—which reflects the evidence of local altars and regional sanctuaries. The *pesaḥ* would be offered at a local altar or, more likely, at an improvised one (see chap. 17, COMMENT A), in any case, near enough to bring the paschal blood back home to smear it on the entrance. The shift to the first day already may have begun with P (Num 28:17), which posits a regional sanctuary (including the pre-Hezekian Temple) at which the *pesaḥ* may have been sacrificed and consumed (see below). The shift from the seventh to the first day was finalized by H (probably exilic Hr), which completely fused *pesaḥ* and *maṣṣôt* by declaring that the *maṣṣôt* festival should begin on the evening of the fourteenth day (overlapping the *pesaḥ* offering) and ending on the evening of the twenty-first (Exod 12:18). But there can be no doubt that the centralization of worship made a pilgrimage to the Temple for the *pesaḥ* mandatory and necessitated the shift of the *ḥag* to the first day.

Finally, it is hardly a coincidence that the extension of the one-day *ḥag* to embrace all seven days is documented in late biblical sources beginning with Ezekiel. For it is in the Babylonian Exile, when the pilgrimage (and to a destroyed Temple) could no longer be practiced, that the term *ḥag* changes its meaning, from "pilgrimage-festival" to "festival." Henceforth, *ḥag hammaṣṣôt* refers to all seven days during which the eating of leaven is proscribed. The Festival of Unleavened Bread in the spring now corresponds in length to the Festival of Booths in the autumn (v. 34).

It should not be considered "peculiar" that a historic rationale is lacking for this festival in contrast to v. 43, where a rationale is provided for the Pilgrimage-Festival of Booths (Gerstenberger 1996: 349). As indicated in the case of the *pesaḥ* (see NOTE on "a paschal offering," v. 5), the account of the redemption from Egypt and its association with the *maṣṣôt* festival is detailed in Exod 12–13 (see esp. 13:3, 7–8), which H *takes for granted.*

The rabbis derive from the verse "you shall remove [*tašbîtû*] leaven from your houses" (Exod 12:15) that the leaven must be destroyed (*Mek. Boʾ*, par. 8). However, evidence that this cannot be the intent of this injunction can be adduced from a letter to the Jewish garrison of Elephantine Egypt, referring to a rescript of Darius II (419 B.C.E.): [WKL ḤMYR ZY ʾYTY BBTYKM H]NʿLW BTWNYKM WḤTMW BYN YWMYʾ [ʾLH] 'And bring into your chambers [any

leaven which you have in your houses] and seal (them) up during [these] days'
(Cowley 21:8). This Aramaic papyrus also states (if the reconstruction is correct): *PSH' 'B]DW* 'ob]serve [the *pesaḥ*]' (l. 4), which may imply that this diaspora community offered animal sacrifices at its sanctuary, despite the objections of the Jerusalem priesthood (cf. Porten 1968: 128–33, 279–82, 311–14).

7. *The first day shall be for you a sacred occasion. bayyôm hāri'šôn miqra'-
qōdeš.* The first day, as stated explicitly by the P *Vorlage* (Num 28:17), is the
ḥag. This is plausible for D (Deut 16:2–16) on the grounds of its insistence on
centralization for the paschal sacrifice, but if P and H reflect a precentralization
stratum, as I have proposed, what is their motive for transferring the *ḥag* from
the seventh day to the first? My thesis does not conflict with this datum: P and
H do not demand a single sanctuary, but do endorse a central (i.e., regional)
sanctuary (see chap. 17, COMMENT D; vol. 1.29–35). Thus to avoid making the
journey twice, on the eve of the fourteenth day for the *pesaḥ* and on the seventh day for *ḥag hammaṣṣôt,* P (followed by H) also sets (rather, originates) the
ḥag on the first day. P, therefore, may be the first (before H and D) to record
the alteration of the home rite of the *pesaḥ* into a sacrificial rite at the sanctuary. Indeed, D itself admits that before centralization, the *pesaḥ* was offered at
local sanctuaries (Deut 16:5), precisely as presupposed by P. What, then, of the
home rite (Exod 12:1–13), which is also attributed to P? The answer is that P,
unlike D, did not make the Paschal Offering at the sanctuary mandatory. Thus
a household residing in the sanctuary town or nearby could observe the paschal
rite at home and the following morning observe the *ḥag* at the sanctuary.

shall be for you. yihyeh lākem. This is added to the citation from Num 18:18.
laborious work. měle'ket 'ăbōdâ. Both *mělā'kâ* and *'ăbōdâ* mean "work," but they
are not synonyms. Whereas the latter refers to physical labor, the former refers
to work that requires special skill. Thus *mělā'kâ* describes God's work in creation (Gen 2:2–3; Ps 73:28), the building of the Tabernacle and Temple (Exod
36:4, 8; 1 Kgs 7:14), and their cultic tasks (1 Chr 6:34; 9:19, 33; 25:1;
2 Chr 29:34). The Tabernacle construction texts are replete with the use of
mělā'kâ and *'ăbōdâ.* The latter, denoting physical labor, must be rendered "construction" or "building"; the former embraces those tasks that entail special skill
(details in Milgrom 1970: 76–87).

The construction *měle'ket 'ăbōdâ* is found eleven times in connection with
work forbidden on the festivals (Lev 23:7, 8, 21, 35, 36; Num 28:18, 25, 26; 29:1,
12, 35). The pericopes on the sabbath and the Day of Purgation, however, use
the phrase *kol-mělā'kâ* (Lev 23:3, 28; Num 29:7; cf. Exod 31:14–15). The same
distinction exists in regard to the word *šabbāt*: the sabbath and the Day of Purgation alone are described by *šabbat šabbātôn* (vv. 3, 32; Exod 16:23; 31:15;
35:2), whereas for festivals, only the term *šabbātôn* occurs (vv. 24, 39 [twice];
see NOTE on v. 24). Just as *šabbat šabbātôn* means "absolute rest," so *kol-mělā'kâ*
must be severer and more encompassing than *měle'ket 'ăbōdâ.* Therefore, *kol-
mělā'kâ,* the analogue of *šabbat šabbātôn* 'absolute rest', connotes that every conceivable kind of exertion, skilled or unskilled, heavy or light, is proscribed. The
festivals, though, are bound by the term *měle'ket 'ăbōdâ,* where *mělā'kâ* refers

to any enterprise and *ʿăbōdâ* is the physical labor attached to it, literally "an activity requiring labor" or "laborious work." Implied is that light work is not forbidden (Ramban). Is there any way of determining what this may be?

A clue is provided in one priestly text. The terminal days of the Festival of Unleavened Bread are characterized by an alternative description of *mĕle'ket ʿăbōdâ*: "no activity [*kol-mĕlā'kâ*] should be carried out on them; only what every person is to eat, that alone may be prepared for you" (Exod 12:16). This would imply that *mĕle'ket ʿăbōdâ* is equivalent to *kol-mĕlā'kâ* with the sole exception of food preparation! The medieval exegetes regard food preparation as an instance of a general principle (*binyan 'āb*; cf. Milgrom 1989a: 175) —for example, *mĕle'ket hănā'â* 'pleasure activity' versus necessity (Ramban); *mĕlā'kâ šellō' mištammeret laʿăbôdat qinyān* 'an activity that does not lead to acquisition' (R. Hananel, cited by Ramban on v. 7; cf. Ibn Ezra and Rashbam on Exod 12:16 and Deut 16:6). However, the unique phraseology of Exod 12:16 produces more problems than it can solve. Is, perhaps, the Festival of Unleavened Bread severer than other festivals in forbidding all activity except food preparation because food prepared before the holiday is liable to be contaminated by leaven? Or does Exod 12:16 (tentatively attributed to H; see Introduction I E), stemming from a source other than Lev 23:7 or Num 28:18, 25 (P), imply that H is severer than P regarding work during this festival? Unfortunately, the textual evidence is insufficient to draw any further conclusions.

For details concerning the etymology and historic development of the term *mĕlā'kâ*, see Milgrom and Wright (1984).

Why is work forbidden on the festivals? A rationale is provided for this prohibition on the sabbath: it is YHWH's day (v. 3b; Exod 20:10), on which he rested (Gen 2:3; Exod 20:11; 31:17), mandating that Israel, his covenant people, must also rest (Exod 20:10; 31:16). But this rationale does not hold for festivals; YHWH did not rest on these days. Hence work is prohibited because, as explained by the previous phrase, the festival is a *miqrā' qōdeš* (vv. 7, 8, 21, 24b–25a, 27–28a, 35, 36; Num 28:18, 25, 26; 29:1, 7, 12). Such days are holy. *Holiness mandates cessation from labor.*

Chap. 23 can be seen as an extension of chaps. 21–22. From sacred space (the sanctuary), one engages sacred time (the festivals). But whereas desecrated space is expressed by *mûm* 'blemish', desecrated time is expressed by *mĕleket ʿăbōdâ* 'laborious work'. Olyan (1996b) has cogently argued that the altar must be built with natural, unfinished stone (Exod 20:25; Deut 27:6) because any alteration of it desecrates it (*ḥll*, Exod 20:25). It must be built with stones that are *šelēmôt* 'whole / complete' (Deut 27:6; Josh 8:31; cf. 1 Kgs 6:7), a nonpriestly term that is the precise equivalent of priestly *tāmîm* 'whole / complete' (Lev 22:19). The analogy between sacred space and sacred time therefore holds. Just as the altar must be whole, so must sacred time. As human activity with stone desecrates the altar, so does human activity in time: work. Both space and time in their holy dimension must remain in their natural state; they may not be blemished or desecrated by human labor.

To be sure, blemished time is an abstraction. It is not visible, as are blemished space and the changed appearance of a blemished priest, sacrificial animal, or altar. But blemish is a broader concept than that expressed by *mûm*. All desecration is a "blemish," which would therefore embrace the two verbs for desecration: *māʿal* (P) and *ḥillēl* (H). Desecrated time is blemished time, and it would fall into the same category as the desecrated or blemished name of God in a false oath (see NOTES on 5:20–26; 19:12, and vol. 1.365–67). Both are invisible, but the desecration or blemish is real, and if committed deliberately, brazenly, it is punishable by *kārēt*. An analogous desecration is Molek worship or consulting the dead (20:2–6); although leaving no visible trace, each is a capital offense against the Deity and thus punished by *kārēt*.

8. *you shall offer food gifts to YHWH*. *wĕhiqrabtem ʾiššeh laYHWH*. The phrase *ʾiššeh laYHWH* occurs seven times in the original calendar (vv. 8, 13, 18, 25, 27, 36 [twice]). It represents a condensation of Num 28:19–23, indicating that Lev 23 (H) is referring to its source, Num 28–29 (P).

Heretofore, nearly every commentator has held, under the assumption that P is later than H, that the calendar of Num 28–29 (P) is later than that of Lev 23 (H). If that were the case, we would be at a loss to explain this expression, which recurs throughout the chapter (vv. 25, 27, 36 [bis], 37). What, indeed, could be its referent? Moreover, since H does take the pains to specify the sacrifices attached to the grain offerings (vv. 12–13, 18–19), we would have to conclude that the category, species, and number of sacrifices for the remaining festivals (Unleavened Bread, Alarm Blasts, Purgation, and Booths) would be left to the discretion of the sanctuary! The absurdity of this deduction suffices, in itself, to demonstrate that Num 28–29 (P) must be earlier than and the basis of Lev 23 (H) as well as a probable indication that H, in general, is the heir and redactor of P. The question arises: If P is earlier than H why is it found in the later book of Numbers? Ramban (on 23:2) suggests that since the festivals' public sacrifices were not instituted until Israel settled in the land, their instruction was given to the generation commanded to conquer the land (Num 33:51) and divide it among the tribes (Num 26:53).

The Numbers passage corresponding to v. 8 reads *wĕhiqrabtem ʾiššeh ʿōlâ laY-HWH . . . ûminḥātām . . . ûśĕʿîr ḥaṭṭāʾt . . . milbad ʿōlat habbōqer* (Num 28:19–23), implying, on the one hand, that the purification offering (*ḥaṭṭāʾt*) is not an *ʾiššeh*, a conclusion that is confirmed by v. 37, which omits the *ḥaṭṭāʾt* under the rubric *ʾiššeh* (see the even more explicit differentiation provided by Num 15:25). Is, then, 23:8 implying that only sacrifices qualifying as *ʾiššeh* are offered, but not the *ḥaṭṭāʾt*? This can hardly be correct, since H explicitly adds the *ḥaṭṭāʾt* to its roster of holiday sacrifices (v. 19a). Thus it must be concluded that H's use of *ʾiššeh* is its "compare," *referring to the MT* of Num 28–29. On the other hand, one might argue that the priest's privilege to offer *ʾiššê YHWH* (21:6, 21) surely includes the *ḥaṭṭāʾt*! Does this not mean that H regards the *ḥaṭṭāʾt* as an *ʾiššeh*? Not at all. As pointed out in the NOTE on 21:6, the very reason that 21:6 and 21 add the otherwise redundant apposite phrase *leḥem ʾĕlōhêhem / ʾĕlōhāyw* 'the food of their / his God' is in order to include the *ḥaṭṭāʾt*, which is not an *ʾiššeh* (see NOTE on 1:9). The term *ʾiššeh* here is probably being used imprecisely. H ignores the exclusion of the *ḥaṭṭāʾt* for the sake of a one-word "compare" covering all the sacrifices. Lev 23:7–8 is condensed from Num 28:18–25, as follows (square brackets indicate H's additions; parentheses, its deletions):

¹⁸*bayyôm hāri'šôn miqrā'-qōdeš* [*yihyeh lākem*] *kol-mĕle'ket 'ăbōdâ lō' ta'ăśû* ¹⁹*wĕhiqrabtem 'iššeh* (*'ōlâ*) *laYHWH . . .* ²⁴*šib'at yāmîm . . .* ²⁵(*û*)*bayyôm haššĕbî'î miqrā'-qōdeš yihyeh lākem kol-mĕle'ket 'ăbōdâ lō' ta'ăśû.*

The seventh day is a sacred occasion. Why? This is not true for the other seven-day holiday, the Festival of Booths (the eighth day, which is a sacred occasion, is a different festival, see vv. 34b, 36b). I submit that the sacredness of the seventh day is a remembrance and commemoration of an earlier period when the *ḥag*, the pilgrimage required during the Festival of Unleavened Bread (Exod 23:15; Deut 16:16), took place on the seventh day (Exod 13:6), which D also commemorates by referring to the seventh day as an *'ăṣeret* (Deut 16:8). Thus both D and P/H agree that the seventh day is a sacred (*qōdeš*) / special (*'ăṣeret*; see NOTE on v. 36) occasion on which limited work (*mĕle'ket 'ăbōdâ*) / no work (*mĕlā'kâ*; Deut 16:8) should be done.

As will be pointed out (see NOTE on "seven sabbath-weeks," v. 15), the fifty-day period following the Passover is fraught with peril to the ripening grain lest it be devastated by the dreaded sirocco / *ḥamsîn* (= *ḥămiššîm* 'fifty') winds. Equally significant, this period marks the onset of the dry season. The condensation of the dew each night is generally adequate to bring the crops to fruition. However, any diminution will also abort the ripening. Thus an *'ăṣeret* 'assembly' (D's term) on the seventh day would be convened in each city and town to supplicate God for a "safe passage" on behalf of the crops. Indeed, it is probably no accident that the *'ăṣeret* of the first month matches the *'ăṣeret* of the seventh month (see NOTE on v. 36) at the onset of the rainy season, to pray for adequate rain during the coming months when the seed is planted and nurtured. The memory of these two assemblies must have been so powerful that they echo in the synagogue liturgy to this day: the prayer for dew on the first day of the *maṣṣôt* festival, and the prayer for rain on the day following the Festival of Booths. I presume that originally the prayer for dew was the order of service on the seventh day of *maṣṣôt*, but when it lost its ritual character to the first day, it also surrendered its prayer for dew.

What of the intervening days? D explicitly states that on the second day, following the *ḥag*, the pilgrims return home (Deut 16:7; see below). Indeed, the fact that D goes out of its way to state that on the seventh day no work should be done means that it concurs with P and H that the work prohibition applies solely to the festival's termini, the first and seventh days. Reality could not be otherwise; the harvest has begun, and the farmer cannot be spared from the field. Contrast the Festival of Booths: although it limits the abstinence from work to only the first day (v. 35), it ordains all seven days as a *ḥag* before YHWH (vv. 39–41; Deut 16:15); the crop is in, and agricultural worries are at a minimum (for details, see NOTE on "seven days to YHWH," v. 34).

The more explicit account of the post-*ḥag* days of the *maṣṣôt* festival in D merits consideration: "in the morning (of the second day) you may go back to your

tents [*lĕ'ōhǎlêkā*]. For six days you shall (continue to) eat unleavened bread, and
on the seventh day (there shall be) a solemn assembly [*'ăṣeret*] for YHWH your
God; you shall do no work" (Deut 16:7b–8). The term *'ōhel* in D is used only in
regard to the wilderness sojourn (Deut 1:27; 5:30; 11:6), in poetry (33:8), and in
referring to the Tent of Meeting (31:15). It is never found in the law code. For
one's residence, D uses *bayit* 'house' (6:7, 11; 8:12; 11:19; 20:5, 6, 7, 8; 22:8, 21
[twice], 24:2, 5, 10; 26:13; 28:30), *'îr* 'city' (13:13, 14, 16, 17; 19:1, 2, 5, 7, 9, 12;
21:2, 3 [twice], 4, 6, 19, 20, 21; 22:15, 17, 24; 25:8), or *šĕ'ārêkā* 'your gates' (5:14;
6:9; 11:20; 12:15, 17, 18, 21; 14:21, 27, 28; 15:7, 22; 16:5, 11, 14, 18; 17:2, 5, 8;
18:6; 20:12; 24:14; 26:12; 28:57; 31:12). On the one hand, Ibn Ezra suggests that
the pilgrims first return to their tents, which they have erected in the environs of
Jerusalem, where they have spent the first night celebrating the *pesaḥ*, and from
there return to their homes. On the other hand, as Scott (1993: 70–71, n. 85) has
pointed out, the idiom "go to your tent" is a proclamation dismissing an assembly (1 Kgs 12:16), a description of the loss of a battle (2 Kgs 14:12), and a formula
for dismissing soldiers (Judg 7:8; 1 Sam 13:2; 2 Sam 20:22) or a guest (Judg 19:9;
note that its speaker actually lived in a house, v. 29). Thus it is clear that this idiom, despite its uniqueness in Deuteronomy, implies that from the sanctuary Israelites went straight home (see NOTE on "seven sabbath-weeks," v. 15).

The prohibition to abstain from leaven in D continues for another six days
while the erstwhile pilgrims are working in their fields. But on the seventh day,
no work is done. Instead, an *'ăṣeret* 'solemn assembly' is held during which, presumably, spiritual instruction takes place as well as prayers for the welfare of the
crops (see above, and NOTE on v. 36). The fact that D takes pains to state the
work prohibition for the seventh day, which it does not do for any other festival, is irrefutable evidence that the people are at home, where the temptation
(and need) to work the fields is strong.

As further evidence of D's awareness that the spring is a time when the farmer
is concerned less about holiday observance and more about his ripening crops
is demonstrated by the fact that the *pesaḥ* pericope contains no mention of aliens,
widows, orphans, Levites, or even sons and daughters rejoicing in the festival,
as is found in the texts dealing with the Festivals of Weeks and Booths (Deut
16:11, 14). The reason is not that on "the festival which remembers their founding history . . . it is not appropriate to invite those who do not share this common history, i.e., aliens . . . nor is it appropriate to make a point of including
everyone" (van Houten 1991: 90). The reason is rooted in agricultural reality.
The spring is a time of anxiety and trepidation lest an unseasonable rain or another blight wipe out the ripening crops. The Israelite farmer has no mind for
celebration until the crops are in (see NOTE on "seven sabbath-weeks," v. 15).

Vv. 9–22. The Firstfruits of the Grain Harvest

As pointed out by Ginsberg (1982: 72), the absence of the term *ḥag* implies that
the grain harvest pilgrimage-festival (Exod 23:16a) has been abolished. But as
will be shown (see COMMENT A), the specification of the sacrificial offerings is

not "remarkable"; it is the logical decision of the H redactor to specify them whenever he differs with the text of Num 28–29.

The fact that a series of practical measures is attached to the grain festival prescription (see below)—which occupies the largest bloc in this chapter—undermines Gerstenberger's (1996: 353) claim, based on his need to justify a post-exilic provenance for P (and H), that "the priestly tradition has emancipated itself from agricultural society . . . [it] no longer took harvest activities into consideration."

Vv. 9–10aα. Introductory Formula

These verses compose the introduction to the firstfruits offering of both the barley and the wheat harvest. They are included under one heading because the date of the wheat offering is dependent on the date of the barley offering (v. 15; Ramban). Ramban also notes that each pericope set off by an introduction (vv. 1–2, 9–10aα, 23–24a, 33–34a) contains some novelty. He is right. The novelty, I submit, is that it adds to or disagrees with the parallel prescription in Num 28–29 (see below).

Vv. 10aβ–14. The First Barley Offering

That this pericope and the following, vv. 15–22, consist of three contributions of the school of H, see the INTRODUCTION to vv. 15–22, and COMMENT A.

10. *When you enter the land.* ʾimkî-tābōʾû ʾel-hāʾāreṣ. The same heading is found in Exod 12:25; Lev 14:34; 19:23; 25:2; Num 14:30; 15:2. The one in Lev 19:23 is most instructive: it also introduces new material describing how an offering to the sanctuary frees new produce for profane use (Kochman 1987). The fact that this heading is missing in the previous sabbath and *pesaḥ/maṣṣôt* pericopes indicates that they were already observed in the wilderness, as confirmed by Exod 16:29–30; Num 9:2 (Ibn Ezra).

the land I am giving to you. This refers to cis-Jordan (Num 34:12; *Sipra* Emor, par. 10:2). This clause, which appears so frequently in this formula (14:34; 25:2; Exod 12:25; 13:11; Num 15:2, 18; Deut 17:14; 18:9; 26:1) bears added force in this pericope: precisely because YHWH has given you this land, he is entitled to the firstfruits of its soil (see NOTE on 25:2).

and you reap its harvest. ûqĕṣartem ʾet-qĕṣîrāh. The verb qāṣar means "bind, collect" (as does its Akk. cognate kaṣāru); it assumes that the grain has been cut. Indeed, the Babylonians called harvest time ṣibit nigallim 'grasping of the sickle'. The first grain is barley, as proved by the comment on the plague of hail: "Now the flax and barley were ruined, for **barley was in the ear** and the flax was in bud; but **the wheat** and the emmer were not hurt, for they **ripen late** [my emphasis]" (Exod 9:31–32). Also note that Ruth (and Naomi) "arrived in Bethlehem at the beginning of the barley harvest" (Ruth 1:22b), and "she gleaned until the barley harvest and wheat harvest were finished" (Ruth 2:23aβ; see also Philo, *Laws* 2.175; Jos. *Ant.* 3.250–51; *b. Menaḥ.* 68b). Furthermore, if the first grain were wheat, the two loaves brought seven weeks later could not be called *bikkûrîm* 'firstfruits' (vv. 17, 20; *Sipra* Wayiqra, par. 13:4)!

sheaf. ʿōmer. The LXX renders *dragma* 'handful' (also Philo, *Dream* 2.75). Others render "armful"—that is, whatever is swathed with a sickle and swooped under the arm (Dalman 1933: 3.18, 46–52, 48–60, 62–66; Ginsberg 1979–80: 142). The former is preferable, to judge by an Egyptian painting. Either meaning is attested in Deut 24:19; Job 24:10; Ruth 2:7, 15. The rabbis, however, on the basis of Exod 16:16–32, 36, claim that the ʿōmer is a specific dry measure, namely, one-tenth of an ephah of flour made from the grain and then offered up on the altar (*m. Menaḥ.* 10:4).

In general, the barley was not ripe by Nisan 16 (the date of the ʿōmer rite set by the rabbis) or by either of the two following sabbaths (the dates chosen by the sectarians; see COMMENT B) particularly if they fall at the end of March or the beginning of April. Only in low-lying areas (the coast and the Jordan and Jezreel valleys) does the barley ripen in mid-April (Dalman 1928: 1.415). Therefore, the ʿōmer is not ripe barley, but the color of ripe barley (Dalman 1928: 1.456–57). This fact corroborates Ginsberg's (1980) rendering of ʾābîb (see also Feliks 1990: 157), the condition of the ʿōmer, as "milky grain" (see NOTES on v. 14; 2:14).

The ʿōmer rite, as practiced at the end of Second Temple times, merits quotation in full:

> The prescribed rite for the ʿōmer is that it should be brought from [barley growing] near by. If [the crop] near Jerusalem was not yet ripe, it could be brought from any place. . . . How was it made ready? The messengers of the court used to go out on the eve of the festival-day and tie the grain in bunches while it was yet unreaped to make it easier to reap; and the towns nearby all assembled there together that it might be reaped with much pomp. When it grew dark, he (the reaper) called out, "Is the sun set?" and they answered, "Yea!" "Is the sun set?" and they answered, "Yea!" "Is this a sickle?" and they answered, "Yea!" "Is this a sickle?" and they answered, "Yea!" "Is this a basket?" and they answered, "Yea!" "Is this a basket?" and they answered, "Yea!" On the sabbath he called out, "On this sabbath?" and they answered "Yea!" "On this sabbath?" and they answered "Yea!" "Shall I reap?" and they answered, "Reap!" "Shall I reap?" and they answered "Reap!" He used to call out three times for every matter, and they answered, "Yea!" "Yea!" "Yea!" Wherefore was all this? Because of the Boethusians [*BYTWSYM*, possibly to be read as *BYT ʾSYM* 'The Essene School'] who used to say: The ʿōmer may not be reaped at the close of a festival-day. (*m. Menaḥ.* 10:2–3)

The rabbinic polemic against sectarian belief is transparent even without its being identified as such (see COMMENT B on "from the day after the sabbath-week," v. 11). Here, too, is a reflection of Second Temple practice when this rite was a public offering of a single ʿōmer of barley grain rather than the individual offering of each farmer who would offer it (together with a lamb as a burnt offering; Noth 1977) at the local sanctuary whenever his grain ripened, akin to the individual firstfruits offering preserved in Deut 26:1–11. For the conjectured development of this firstfruits rite, see the INTRODUCTION to vv. 15–22, and COMMENT A.

the first sheaf of your harvest. rē'šît qĕṣîrĕkem. "First" has a temporal connotation (Gen 1:1)—that is, when you first begin to harvest. Elsewhere in priestly texts, it usually bears a quantitative sense (2:12; Num 15:20, 21; 18:12); that is, the 'ōmer is not to be selected from the many sheaves that make up the first harvest, but must be the very first sheaf. As Deuteronomy puts it, *mēhāḥēl ḥermēš baqqāmâ* 'when the sickle is first put to the standing grain' (Deut 16:9).

Indirect evidence supports this interpretation. The priestly texts distinguish very clearly between *bikkûrîm* and *rē'šît* (Num 18:12–13; cf. Ezek 44:30; Neh 10:36, 38). The former is designated as first-ripened fruits; the latter, as first-processed fruits. Thus the first of the grain kernels, wine, and oil (Num 18:12) as well as fruit syrup (Lev 2:11–12; 2 Chr 31:5), leaven (Lev 2:11–12), and dough (Num 15:20–21; Neh 10:38) are termed *rē'šît* (Milgrom 1976e; 1990a: 427–28). Hence this term could not be applied to standing grain. Since it also cannot denote first-ripe fruits, a meaning reserved for *bikkûrîm* (but see NOTE on v. 17), it takes on the connotation "first" in a temporal sense—the very first 'ōmer to be harvested.

The first of the ripened and processed fruits belong to the Deity (Exod 22:28; 23:19a; 34:26a; Deut 26:1–11) so that "a blessing may rest on your home" (Ezek 44:30; cf. Lev 19:24–25). Note also the pragmatic advice of wisdom: "Honor YHWH with your substance and with the firstfruits of all your produce; then your barns will be filled with plenty, and your vats will be bursting with wine" (Prov 3:9–10). Avoiding this quid pro quo language, the Bekhor Shor focuses on etiquette: "It is not good manners to eat of the new (crop) until you bring a gift before the Holy One Blessed Be He." In the case of the (public) 'ōmer rite, the rabbis found cause to celebrate the magnanimity of YHWH: "When I (the Lord) gave you the manna I provided an 'ōmer for every person (Exod 16:16); now that you give me an 'ōmer, I require only one 'ōmer from all of you" (*Lev. Rab.* 28:3).

11. *He shall elevate the sheaf. wĕhēnîp 'et-hā'ōmer.* That the verb *hēnîp* means "elevate, lift" and its nominal derivative *tĕnûpâ* means "elevation offering," see vol. 1.461–73. There it is demonstrated that there are two principles for determining the need for the *tĕnûpâ* rite: either the offering is still in its owner's possession before it is sacrificed on the altar (e.g., the breast of the *šĕlāmîm*, 7:30; the two loaves of bread on the Festival of Weeks, vv. 17, 20), thereby transferring the offering to the domain of God, or most sacred gifts whose composition or mode of offering is different from the norm require additional sanctification by means of the *tĕnûpâ*.

The 'ōmer falls into the second category. It is a cereal offering, and, therefore, its status is automatically most sacred. True, the 'ōmer is not explicitly called a cereal offering, but because the loaves made from the following wheat harvest are called *minḥâ ḥădāšâ* 'a **new** cereal offering' (v. 17; cf. Num 28:26), it may be inferred that the previously mentioned 'ōmer is also a type of cereal offering; and the rabbis so designate it (*m. Menaḥ.* 6:1). According to the scheme of Lev 2, the cereal offering is composed of semolina (v. 1; cf. Exod 29:2), or wheat, and oil and incense are added to it (v. 1). But the *ʿōmer* is barley, not wheat, and it lacks oil and incense. Thus its exceptional composition makes it subject to the *těnûpâ*.

What was done with it? There are only two possibilities: giving it to the priest as his prebend or having him offer the flour prepared from its grains (*m. Menaḥ.* 10:4) as a cereal offering on the altar. The analogous offering of the firstfruits of the wheat (v. 20b) indicates that it is a priestly prebend. If the objection is raised that the wheat loaves are leavened (v. 17) and, therefore, banned from the altar (2:11), the cereal offering described in 2:14–16, which I claim is identifiable with the firstfruits barley sheaf (vol. 1.192–94), proves that only a token was burned on the altar, but that the remainder "parched with fire, groats of the fresh ear, as a cereal offering of your first-ripe fruits" (2:14) became the property of the officiating priest (7:9). If my case that the cereal offering of 2:14–16 refers to the *ʿōmer* is sustained, it will explain why it is not explicitly told in Lev 23 that the *ʿōmer* of barley is not entirely burned in its raw state on the altar; these facts have already been stated in 2:14 and 7:9 (P), another indication that H takes P's texts for granted and, therefore, must be chronologically later. Furthermore, the conditional wording of 2:14–16 *wĕ'im taqrîb* 'If you bring . . .' would also prove that originally the *ʿōmer* was a voluntary offering (vol. 1.192–93).

before YHWH. lipnê YHWH. This modifier nearly always accompanies the phrase *hēnîp těnûpâ* (Exod 29:24–25; Lev 7:30; 8:27, 29; 9:21; 10:15; 14:12, 24; 23:20; Num 6:20; 8:11, 21), implying that it is a sanctuary ritual. Only in Exod 35:22 and Num 8:13 is the *těnûpâ* "to YHWH." But in the former verse, the *Tgs.* read *těrûmâ* (cf. Exod 35:5), and in the latter verse, many MSS and the Old Greek read *lipnê YHWH*.

For acceptance on your behalf. lirṣōnêkem. Thus the cereal offering of the barley (and of the wheat) not only functions as a sign of thanks for the new crop, but also expresses the hope that God, in turn, will bless the new crop (Ezek 44:30; Prov 3:9–10; see NOTE on 19:25). The rabbis were unambiguously frank concerning this purpose: "The Holy One Blessed Be He has said: Bring before me an *ʿōmer* on the Festival of Protection [*pesaḥ*] so that you will be blessed with grain in the fields" (*t. Suk.* 3:18; for a possible Hittite analogy, see COMMENT F).

That *rāṣôn* with the object *lipnê YHWH* implies seeking the Deity's favor is confirmed by Mal 1:8: "When you offer a blind animal in sacrifice, is that not wrong? And when you offer one that is lame or sick, is that not wrong? Try presenting it to your governor; will he accept you [*hăyirṣĕkā*] or show you favor [*hăyiśśā' pānêkā*]?—says YHWH of Hosts." Thus *rāṣâ* and *nāśā' pānîm* are functionally equivalent, and the purpose of the *ʿōmer*—as is the case for all firstfruit offerings—is to offer thanks for and solicit favor on the forthcoming harvest. It can hardly be an accident that this term appears with the *ʿōlâ* and *šělāmîm* when they function as thanksgiving (19:5; 22:19, 20, 21, 29), but it never appears with the purification and reparation offerings. These two sacrifices are strictly expiatory (chaps. 4–5). Their offerers approach God under the burden of sin; they seek his pardon, not his blessing.

The noun *rāṣôn* is also found in connection with the inscribed plate (*ṣîṣ*) on the high priest's turban on behalf of the people in case their sacrifices are (inadvertently; cf. *m. Zebaḥ.* 8:12) defective. Finally, in the priestly texts it occurs in the opening statement on the *'ōlâ*. It, too, emphasizes that the sacrifice must be unblemished (1:3; vol. 1. 149–50), again implying that its purpose is to elicit favor. This final citation indisputably stems from P, and it is one more reason why I cannot accept Knohl's (1995: 163) categorical statement that P's cultic system "concentrates on the essential numinous dimension of God, which is completely divorced from the image of God as providential creator." For the other reasons, see the Introduction II Q.

Note that the day of the *'ōmer* rite is not "a sacred occasion" when "laborious work" is prohibited. It thus does not qualify as a *mô'ēd* 'festival' and, hence, does not technically belong under the heading of v. 4. This fact lends support to Ramban's suggestion that vv. 9–22 describe a single event: the two grain harvests tied by the counting of the intervening days, culminating in the fiftieth day, "a sacred occasion" on which "laborious work" is proscribed (v. 21). Qumran, on the contrary, explicitly calls the day when the *'ōmer* is brought to the sanctuary a *mô'ēd* 'festival', as evidenced by two Cave 4 fragments: *MW'D Ś['RYM]* (4Q326, l. 4) and *[MW']D ŚRYM* (4Q325, col. 2, l. 3).

from the day after the sabbath-week. haššabāt. See COMMENT B.

the priest shall elevate it. yěnîpennû hakkōhēn. In an ordinary prose sentence, these two words would be entirely superfluous. However, as pointed out by Paran (1989: 69), as an exclusive feature of priestly style (some twenty times), the first part of a circular inclusio uses the accusative particle *'et* and in the second part, it is bonded directly to the verb (e.g., Exod 12:8, 11; 25:11; Lev 6:9; 10:12).

12. Levine (1989: 63) suggests that vv. 12–13 were added later to convert a nonsacrificial elevation offering of the barley into a sacrifice. The contrast between the requirement of one lamb for the *'ōmer* and that of two bulls, one ram, and seven lambs for the wheat offering (vv. 18–19), however, suggests that the former was, indeed, brought by the individual farmer. This would explain the unique requirement of two-tenths of an ephah of semolina for the cereal offering (see NOTE on v. 13). Furthermore, if the sacrificial requirements of vv. 12–13 were part of the public cult, one would expect the addition of a purification offering, as in v. 19. It should be kept in mind that the sacrificial adjuncts were mandated for burnt and well-being offerings in individual as well as public sacrifices (Num 15:1–16), and it is highly probable that these requirements were not innovated by the Jerusalem Temple, but were the practice in regional sanctuaries throughout the land. I differ further with Levine in that the barley (i.e., a token thereof; 2:16) indeed was sacrificed (see NOTE on "He shall elevate the sheaf," v. 11).

To recapitulate: each landowner initially brought the firstfruits of the barley ('*ōmer*) to his local sanctuary (H₂). Subsequently, the words "from the day after the sabbath-week" were inserted so that the *'ōmer* should be brought to the sanctuary on the nearest Sunday (H₁). The Sabbath date was deliberately not fixed (contrary to the Festivalian argument, no. 1, above) because in the land the harvest varied from region to region. The *'ōmer* was a priestly prebend and was probably accompanied by a burnt offering lamb and its sacrificial adjuncts for reasons cited above. The final metamorphosis of the ʿōmer reflects the ideology of the Jerusalem Temple (H). H continued to uphold the same sacrificial requirements: the ʿōmer prebend for the priests and a lamb with its adjuncts for the altar, but with one radical change. These offerings no longer came from the people, but from the Temple. The landowner was now free to remain at home, where all able hands were needed for the harvest (see COMMENT A). This innovation corresponds with H's abolition of the pilgrimage for the Festival of First Wheat (see NOTE on v. 21). Thus the landowner was released from journeying to his sanctuary during the barley and wheat harvests. Or, conversely, H was making the best of the situation: since relatively few landowners were showing up at the sanctuaries, H legislated that their presence was no longer required.

A more practical motivation may also have been at work. The Sunday of the ʿōmer fell close to the fifteenth day of Nisan, the date of the pilgrimage (ḥag) to the sanctuary to celebrate the Feast of Unleavened Bread. As long as the ʿōmer was brought to the local sanctuary (H_1 and H_2), no pilgrimage was required. But once a journey had to be undertaken to a regional sanctuary (H), it automatically would have eliminated a second journey during the nearby ʿōmer. Thus henceforth the sanctuary would be responsible for the ʿōmer and its sacrifices in order not to compete with the increasing number of people who journeyed to it for the required Festivals of Unleavened Bread.

you elevate. hănîpĕkem. Leqaḥ ṭob recognizes the problem: "This teaches us representation by agency, since the text states 'the priest shall elevate it' (v. 11b). Perhaps, the elevation rite was carried out by both the priest and the offerer (see NOTES on 7:30; 8:27). Alternatively, it can be rendered as "you have [the sheaf] elevated."

Ḥazzequni comments: "Because these sacrifices (in vv. 12–13) will not be recorded in the parasha of Phineas (i.e., in Num 28), they were written here. So too (some of the sacrifices of the Festival of Weeks, v. 18) . . . because they will not be recorded in the parasha of Phineas. However, the other festival sacrifices are mentioned here by the term *'iššeh*, since they and their accompanying cereal and libation offerings will be recorded in the parasha of Phineas." Ḥazzequni has hit on the relationship between Lev 23 and Num 28–29, tacitly admitting that the former is dependent on the latter.

of the first year. ben-šĕnātô. This expression must be differentiated from *ben-šānâ* 'yearling' as first recognized, to my knowledge, by the Karaite David the Prince, followed by Ehrlich (1908) and Joüon (1923: 129), namely, that the suffixed form should be rendered "within/of the first year." That is to say, the animal is less than one year old. However, this distinction is not rigorously followed and must be qualified (see NOTE on "yearling," 12:6; vol. 1.757).

as a burnt offering. Its purpose is to propitiate YHWH so that the grain harvest will be bountiful (1 Sam 13:12; 1 Kgs 18:36–38; Jer 14:12; cf. *Lev. Rab.* 28:3, 5 and vol. 1.175–76).

13. *The accompanying cereal offering shall be two-tenths of an ephah of semolina. (ûminḥātô) šĕnê ʿeśrōnîm sōlet.* This is twice the required amount

(Num 15:4; 28:13, 29; *Sipra* Emor, par. 10:7). The Bekhor Shor suggests that the cereal offering combines both the requisite one-tenth and the *'ōmer*, probably basing his solution on the fact that the rabbis also state that one-tenth of (an ephah of) the sheaf is actually sacrificed (*m. Menaḥ.* 10:4; cf. Jos. *Ant.* 3.251). He is decisively refuted by Ḥazzequni, who points out that the cereal offering is composed of semolina—that is, it is wheat and not barley—and, therefore, cannot be the *'ōmer*. In defense of the rabbis (and of Josephus), it must also be stated that although they ordain that the *'ōmer* offering is one-tenth of an ephah, they do not identify it with the cereal accompaniment of the burnt offering.

Why, then, the double portion for the cereal offering? A midrash MS (cited in *TS* 33.182) states that the cereal offering is enlarged, since it accompanies the *'ōmer* as well as the lamb. Ḥazzequni proposes that it represents the farmer's hope that his forthcoming harvest will similarly be blessed. Dillmann and Ryssel (1897) echo the same sentiment when they write that harvest time generates greater gifts to the sanctuary. For this reason, it is probable that the burnt offering to which the cereal offering is an adjunct was brought by the individual farmer and is, therefore, attributable to Pre-H$_1$ (see the translation).

of pleasing aroma. rēaḥ nîḥōaḥ. The LXX adds "to the Lord," as it is usually found in the MT (e.g., 1:9; Hartley 1992), but not after *'iššeh laYHWH*, to avoid the double mention of the divine name.

and its accompanying libation shall be one-fourth of a hin of wine. The tandem of wine and cereal accompanies the burnt and well-being offerings (e.g., Num 15:1–16) in preexilic times (2 Kgs 16:13, 15). It was not offered by itself in the official cult (it is missing in the discussion of the sacrifices in chaps. 1–7), but elsewhere a discrete wine offering is attested (Gen 35:14; cf. Hos 2:10–11; 9:4). The word *wĕniskōh* (K.) is read *wĕniskô* (Q.; Sam.). The measure *hîn* is probably an Egyptian loanword (Lambdin 1953: 149); for its quantity (about a quart), see vol. 1.896–900.

The oil needed to moisten the semolina is taken for granted either because it is the regular amount (one-quarter of a hin; e.g., Num 28:5; S. Rattray) or because it is twice the required amount (*Seper Hamibḥar*), implied by the mention of wine even though its amount (one-quarter of a hin) is the required amount for a lamb (Num 15:5; 28:7).

Rendtorff (1996: 30) postulates that in view of the absence of the wine offering (*nesek*) in chaps. 1–7, "Lev 23 contains an addition and expansion of the earlier sacrificial laws." This assumption is unnecessary and invalid once it is realized that Lev 23 (H) bases itself on P's sacrificial laws in Num 28–29, which do not overlook the *nesek* requirement (cf. Num 28:7, 14, 24, 31; 29:6, 11, 16, 18, 19, etc.).

14. *bread. wĕleḥem.* This refers to barley that has been milled into flour and baked.

or parched or fresh grain. wĕqālî wĕkarmel. Grain undergoes three stages in ripening:

1. *'ābîb* 'milky grain' (see NOTE on 2:14), a wet, green stage. To be edible, it must be *qālî* 'parched with fire' (2:14), or "roasted" (LXX). The word occurs in

1 Sam 17:17; 25:18; 2 Sam 17:28; Ruth 2:14, where it refers solely to barley. To this day, Arab peasants roast barley, but not wheat, because of the latter's flat taste (Y. Feliks, personal communication; cf. Dalman 1928: 1.457).

2. *karmel* 'fresh grain', which is waxy and yellow. It is a step before the dry, fully ripe kernel. "It is neither soft [i.e., wet] nor dry but in between" (y. *Šabb.* 1:2). It is eaten fresh off the stalk (Matt 12:1; cf. Mark 2:23) or after it is crushed (2:14; *Tgs.*), or is made into porridge (Aram., Syr. *daysaʾ*; cf. *b. Ber.* 36b; *b. Taʿan.* 24b). That it was eaten fresh is implied by an erstwhile crux that was resolved on the basis of Ugaritic: "bread of the first reaping—twenty loaves of barley bread [*wĕkarmel bĕṣiqlōnô*] and some fresh ears on the stalk" (2 Kgs 4:42; Ug. *bṣql*, *KTU* 1.19 II:13; cf. Albright 1950: 392; Cassuto 1954b; Cohen 1978: 112). For details see Qimron (1989: 308–10) and Feliks (1990: 158). The Temple Scroll describes the firstfruits of wheat in the Festival of Weeks as *LḤM ḤDŠ ʾBYBWT WMLYLWT* 'new bread (made of) fresh ripe ears' (11QT 19:7), where *MLYLWT*, found only in Deut 23:26, is synonymous with *karmel* (see Yadin 1983: 1.106–7; correcting vol. 1.194).

3. *dagan*, 'fully dried kernels', which are edible after they are baked into *leḥem* 'bread'.

until the very day. ʿad-ʿeṣem hayyôm hazzeh. Compare Josh 10:27; Ezek 2:3; with *ʾet*: Ezek 24:2; *bĕʿeṣem*: Gen 7:13; 17:23, 26; Exod 12:17, 41, 51; Lev 23:21, 28, 29, 30; Deut 32:48; Josh 5:11; Ezek 24:2; 40:1.

you have brought your God's offering. ʿad hăbîʾăkem ʾet-qorban ʾĕlōhêkem. Either this refers to only the *ʿōmer* (*Sipra* Emor, par. 10:10; cf. *m. Menaḥ.* 10:5: only the *ʿōmer* is indispensable) or the singular *qorban* is a collective (as in Num 7:3, 10, 12, 17, etc.), which could also include the burnt offering and its adjuncts (the LXX renders *dōra* 'gifts, sacrifices').

This verse proves that the unleavened bread consumed with the paschal sacrifice (Exod 12:8) and on the next day is made from old grain. Thus regardless of whether the *ʿōmer* is brought on the second day (the Pharisees), the following Sunday (Samaritans), the Sunday after the festival (Qumran) (see COMMENT B), or whenever the grain ripens (conjectured original practice), *it is independent of the Festival of Unleavened Bread.* And conversely, the Festival of Unleavened Bread has nothing to do with the firstfruits. The mistake has frequently been made setting up the following ratio: *pesaḥ* is to the firstlings as *maṣṣôt* is to firstfruits. But just as the *pesaḥ* has nothing to do with firstlings (mistaken because of the tenth plague; cf. Nikolsky 1927; Loewenstamm 1965), so the unleavened bread is unrelated to firstfruits.

in all your settlements. bĕkōl môšĕbōtêkem. When this phrase accompanies *ḥuqqat ʿōlām lĕdōrōtêkem* 'a law for all time' (Exod 12:17, 20; Lev 3:17; 23:14, 21, 31), the focus shifts from the sanctuary to the home (cf. Exod 27:21; Lev 7:35; 10:9; 17:7; 23:41; 24:3; Num 10:8; 15:15; 18:23; J. Ludlow). The tannaitic rabbis claim that the diaspora communities are included (*Sipra* Emor, par. 10:11; *m. ʿOr.* 3:9; *m. Qidd.* 1:9; but see the controversy, *b. Qidd.* 37a). However, this would hold only if the Temple is functioning (see NOTE on v. 3). Moreover, as pointed out by Joosten (1996: 161–62), it is controverted by Num 15:2; Ezek

6:6. The plain sense of this verse is that without the offering of the ʿōmer, the new crop may not be eaten. Of course, this law and all others dependent on the sacrificial system had to be suspended once the Temple was destroyed.

Vv. 15–22. The First Wheat Offering

This name, ḥag šābūʿōt, first appears in the deuteronomic sources (Deut 16:10, 16; Exod 34:22; cf. Jer 5:24). In the earliest calendar, it is called ḥag haqqāṣîr 'The Pilgrimage-Festival of the Harvest' (Exod 23:16). In P, it is referred to as yôm habbikkûrîm 'The Day of the Firstfruits' (Num 28:26), though the name šābūʿōt is adumbrated in the same verse, bĕšābūʿōtêkem 'your Festival of Weeks'. H alludes to both of P's names in the seven-week counting (though it uses the term šabbātôt, not šābūʿōt, for "weeks," vv. 15–16) and expressly as bikkûrîm 'firstfruits' (vv. 17, 20). The word "Pentecost" from the Greek pentekost 'fifty' first appears in Tob 2:1 and 2 Macc 12:31–32 (books for which we do not have the original Hebrew). The rabbis prefer the name ʿaṣeret (Aram. ʿaṣartāʾ; e.g., m. Bik. 1:3, 6; 9:5; m. Šebi. 1:1; m. Ḥal. 4:10; Sipra Emor 13:12; cf. Jos. Ant. 3:252), the name given to the seventh day of the Festival of Unleavened Bread (Deut 16:8) and to the day following the Festival of Booths (Lev 23:36; Num 29:35), thereby affirming their conviction that the Festivals of Unleavened Bread and Weeks mark the termini of the grain harvest. Indeed, the fact that the Festival of Weeks is given no discrete introduction indicates that the authors of this chapter felt likewise. Since ʿaṣeret means "assembly" (see NOTE on v. 36), the possibility exists that the rabbis employed this term because the people assembled to hear the word of YHWH on yôm haqqāhāl 'the day of the assembly' at Sinai (Deut 9:10; 10:4; 18:16) and thereafter during the Festival of Booths every seventh year (cf. Deut 31:10–12; Hoffmann 1953:2.160–61; Weinfeld 1991: 267).

In Jubilees, apparently, šābūʿōt was read as šĕbūʿōt 'oaths', since it dates all covenants on this day (Jub 6:17; cf. 17:1; 22:1; 29:7; 44:4; cf. Zeitlin 1939–40: 6). Jubilees is also the first—and until the Babylonian Talmud, the only—source to unambiguously identify this festival with the Sinaitic revelation (Jub 6:17–19; b. Meg. 31a). It has been suggested that the festival in the third month mentioned in 2 Chr 15:10–14, which features a covenant oath, may also reflect this idea (so understood by the Tg., which, however, being a late work, presumably was influenced by the Babylonian Talmud). According to 4Q266 (Milik 1972: 135), the sectaries of Qumran celebrated an annual covenant renewal rite during the third month. But neither Philo nor Josephus mentions this rite. Furthermore, rabbinic tradition is unsure about the exact date when either the Festival of Weeks was celebrated or the Sinaitic revelation occurred. It is thus not until the Babylonian Talmud that the two are linked in rabbinic tradition, though the evidence in Jubilees points to this linkage in sectarian movements as early as 200 B.C.E. (D. Cohen, personal communication). The need to root the Festival of Weeks in the Sinaitic revelation may have been prompted by the steady commercialization and urbanization of the Jewish community, thereby removing the grounds for observing this agricultural festival. In any event, the historical grounding traceable for the Paschal Offering and the Festival of Unleavened Bread to its beginning and improvised for the Festival of Booths during the exile (see NOTE on v. 43) is totally absent for the Festival of Weeks in biblical times.

It is significant that in the priestly texts describing this festival, the word ḥag 'pilgrimage' is missing (note *yôm habbikkûrîm*, Num 28:26 [P], not ḥag *habbikkûrîm*). Indeed, the fact that H ordains that the day be marked by an absence of work "in all your settlements" (v. 21) implies that the people are at home, not at the sanctuary. This speaks for the realism of this priestly source: a pilgrimage to the sanctuary cannot be expected in the midst of the grain harvest. This fact may also account for its absence in the festival list of Ezek 45:21–25, which is concerned solely with Temple celebrations (Haran 1978: 297). Indeed, as pointed out by Merras (1995: 23, n. 17), the Festival of First Wheat (Shabuʿot) continued to be a minor pilgrimage festival in Second Temple times, to judge by the rabbinic statement that an overnight stay at the Temple was required on the Festivals of Passover and Booths, but not on Shabuʿot (*b. Roš. Haš.* 5a).

Many scholars presume that this festival marks the end of the wheat harvest (e.g., Dillmann and Ryssel 1897; Bertholet 1901; Kalisch 1867–72; Licht 1976: 492; Haran 1978: 295; Ginsberg 1982: 59; Levine 1989a: 265). Indeed, some scholars have relied solely on the statement in the Gezer calendar (tenth century B.C.E.; for the text, see NOTE on 26:5) that the barley and wheat harvest lasted for two months, ending with the Festival of First Wheat (Borowski 1987: 36–38; Tigay 1996: 156). However, this evidence holds for only the Gezer region, located in the southern Shephelah, where grain could ripen early. The agricultural reality of the rest of the land, however, prove otherwise:

1. As noted by the rabbis, "The beginning of the barley harvest till the end of the wheat harvest is three months" (*Ruth Rab.* 5). But three months after Nisan 16 is Tammuz 16, not any date in Sivan.

2. The rabbis knew of years when no wheat had ripened by the festival, and they were compelled to sanction the use of the old wheat for the "firstfruits" offering (*t. Menaḥ.* 10:33). Indeed, Dalman (1928: 1.417) reports that on May 26, 1926, when the Festival of Weeks was celebrated in Jerusalem, the wheat harvest had not yet begun.

3. The rabbis cite *exceptionally* warm areas where wheat might ripen before the festival (*m. Ḥal.* 4:10; *m. Bik.* 1:3). Thus most wheat ripened after the festival (cf. Feliks 1990: 183–86).

4. "R. Akiba said, The Torah has required to bring the ʿōmer of barley on Passover because it is the season of barley, so that the wheat-harvest would be blessed on its account. It required bringing firstfruits (of wheat) on Pentecost because it is the season of wheat [MSS], so that on its account the produce of fruit-bearing trees will be blessed" (*t. Suk.* 3:18). Thus the ʿōmer of barley and the firstfruits of wheat are to be brought at the *beginning* of their respective seasons.

Besides, if the festival marked the terminations of the harvest, the farmer was free to celebrate at the sanctuary. Why, then, did the priestly texts cancel the *ḥag*? Moreover, why would the firstfruits offering be delayed until the end of the harvest when their primary purpose was to beseech the Deity for a bountiful harvest? Finally, would the farmer really wait until the entire harvest was in before he could partake of the new crop? For my tentative, conjectured reconstruction of the development of the grain festivals in other cultic calendars, see COMMENT D. Here, however, I limit the discussion to its development within the two priestly schools, P and H.

As we have observed, H's citation of P's text on the paschal sacrifice and the Festival of Unleavened Bread is virtually the same (cf. Num 28:16–18, 25 and Lev 23:5–8). However, in their respective treatments of the barley and wheat firstfruit offerings, this situation changes radically: there is no barley (*ʿōmer*) pericope in P, and H's firstfruit of wheat differs sharply from that of its P counterpart (cf. Lev 23:15–21 and Num 28:26–31 —the precise reason why they are included in H [see below]). The opening words of the P pericope (v. 26a) are pregnant with historical implications. Four words stand out (in boldface):

ûbĕyôm habbikkûrîm bĕhaqrîbĕkem minḥâ ḥădāšâ laYHWH bĕšābūʿōtêkem

On the **day** of firstfruits, when **you** present a **new** cereal offering to YHWH, on **your** Festival of Weeks (Num 28:26a)

1. The Festival of Weeks, uniquely, is called a *yôm* 'day', not a *ḥag* 'pilgrimage' (contrast the Festivals of Unleavened Bread and Booths, Num 28:17; 29:12). The implication is clear. For P (as for H; see NOTE on "in all your settlements, v. 21), the beginning of the wheat harvest is no time to ask the harried farmer to undertake a family celebration at the sanctuary.

2. The subject of *bĕhaqrîbĕkem* 'when you present' is the same as that of *wĕhiqrabtem* 'you shall present' (Lev 23:16) namely, the sanctuary. That is, on the same day that the sanctuary offers up the new grain offering, it shall also offer up the following sacrifices (Num 28:27–31). The individual's first wheat offering has been replaced by the public offering of the first wheat by the sanctuary.

3. That the firstfruits consists of "a new cereal offering" implies that there was a prior offering of grain, which can only be barley. Thus P alludes to the *ʿōmer* rite. Why was it omitted? The answer can only be that it was a private offering of each individual farmer, whereas P's cultic calendar consists of only *public* offerings by the sanctuary (see further below). P, therefore, harks back to an earlier time before firstfruit offerings became standardized in the cultic calendar of the sanctuary.

4. Finally, the unique expression *bĕšābūʿōtêkem*, a suffixed "*your* Festival of Weeks," betrays the existence of more than one date for the festival. Since, as I have proposed (vol. 1.29–34), P reflects the law code of a central but not single sanctuary (i.e., Shilo), the likelihood exists that each regional sanctuary cele-

brated the festival whenever the wheat ripened in its area. Since we know that the ripening of grain, both barley and wheat, varied as much as a month from region to region, it makes sense that their respective firstfruit offerings were subject to a similar time differential. Thus, again, P alludes to the existence of a barley offering brought by the individual farmer to his regional sanctuary. P also adds the information that, seven weeks later, on a day set by the sanctuary, the sanctuary would offer up the sacrifices enumerated in 28:27–31.

Indirect proof that originally the farmer brought his firstfruits to the sanctuary whenever they ripened is provided by D's *undated* injunction: "You shall take some of every firstfruit of the soil . . . " (Deut 26:2).

Thus H reflects the conversion of the firstfruit offerings from a private, individual rite to a public, collective rite. But the text of H (the present MT) is not a unitary composition. By examining its editorial seams and comparing it with its P prototype, a three-layered text emerges:

The Firstfruits of the Grain Harvests (vv. 10aβ–21)

[10] . . . *kî-tābō'û 'el-hā'āreṣ 'ăšer 'ănî nōtēn lākem ûqĕṣartem 'et-qĕṣîrāh wahăbē'tem 'et-ʿōmer rēʾšît qĕṣîrĕkem 'el-hakkōhēn* [11]*wĕhēnîp 'et-hāʿōmer lipnê YHWH lirṣōnĕkem* **mimmāḥŏrat haššabbāt** *yĕnîpennû hakkōhēn* [12]*wa ʿăśîtem bĕyôm hănîpĕkem 'et-hāʿōmer kebeś tāmîm ben-šĕnatô lĕʿōlâ laYHWH.* [13]*ûminḥātô šĕnê ʿeśrōnîm sōlet bĕlûlâ baššemen 'iššeh laYHWH rêaḥ nîḥōaḥ wĕniskōh[ôQ] yayin rĕbiʿît hahîn* [14]*wĕlehem wĕqālî wĕkarmel lōʾ tōʾkĕlû ʿad-ʿeṣem hayyôm hazzeh ʿad hăbîʾăkem 'et-qorban 'ĕlōhêkem ḥuqqat ʿōlām lĕdōrōtêkem bĕkol mōšĕbōtêkem.*

[15]*ûsĕpartem lākem* **mimmāḥŏrat haššabbāt** *miyyôm hăbîʾăkem 'et-ʿōmer hattĕnûpâ šebaʿ šabbātôt tĕmîmōt tihyênâ* [16]*ʿad* **mimmāḥŏrat haššabbāt** **haššĕbîʿît** *tispĕrû ḥămiššîm yôm wĕhiqrabtem minḥâ ḥădāšâ laYHWH.* [17]*mimmôšĕbōtêkem tabîʾû lehem tĕnûpâ štayim šnê ʿeśrōnîm sōlet tihyênâ ḥāmēṣ tēʾāpênâ bikkûrîm laYHWH.* [18]*wehiqrabtem ʿal-halehem šibʿat kĕbāśîm tĕmîmîm bĕnê šānâ ûpar ben-bāqār 'ehād wĕʾēlîm šnāyim yihyû ʿōlâ laYHWH ûminḥātām wĕniskêkem 'iššēh rêaḥ-nihōaḥ laYHWH.* [19]*waʿăśîtem sĕʿîr ʿizzîm 'ehād lĕḥaṭṭāʾt ûšĕnê kĕbāśîm bĕnê šānâ lĕzebaḥ šĕlāmîm.* [20]*wĕhēnîp hakkōhēn 'ōtām ʿal lehem habbikkûrîm tĕnûpâ lipnê YHWH ʿal-šĕnê kĕbāśîm qōdeš yihyû laYHWH lakkōhēn.* [21]*ûqĕrāʿtem bĕʿeṣem hayyôm hazzeh miqrāʾ-qōdeš yihyeh lākem kol-mĕleʾket ʿăbōdâ lōʾ taʿăśû ḥuqqat ʿōlām bĕkol-môšĕbōtêkem lĕdōrōtêkem.*

When you enter the land I am giving to you and you reap its harvest, you shall bring the first sheaf of your harvest to the priest. [11]He shall elevate the sheaf before YHWH. For acceptance on your behalf **from the day after the sabbath-week** the priest shall elevate it. [12]On the day that you elevate the sheaf, you shall sacrifice an unblemished male lamb in its first year as a burnt offering to YHWH. [13]Its accompanying cereal offering shall be two-tenths of an ephah of semolina mixed with oil, a food gift of pleasing aroma to YHWH; and its accompanying libation shall be one-fourth of a hin of wine. [14]Do not partake (from the new crop) of any bread or parched or fresh grain until the very day you have brought your God's offering—a law for all time, throughout your generations, in all your settlements.

[15]And **from the day after the sabbath-week,** from the day on which you bring the elevation offering of the sheaf, you shall count for yourselves **seven sabbath-weeks. They must be complete:** [16]**You shall count until the day after the seventh sabbath-week** fifty days. Then you shall present a new cereal offering to **YHWH**. [17]You shall bring from your settlements as an elevation offering of two bread (loaves), comprising two-tenths (of an ephah) of semolina and baked after leavening, as firstfruits for **YHWH**. [18]With the bread you shall offer seven unblemished yearly lambs, one bull of the herd, and two rams; (they) shall be a burnt offering to YHWH, and with their cereal offerings and libations, a food gift of pleasant aroma to YHWH. [19]You shall sacrifice one he-goat as a purification offering and two yearling lambs as a sacrifice of well-being. [20]And the priest shall elevate them *with the bread of firstfruits* as an elevation offering to YHWH *with the two lambs*; they shall be holy to YHWH for the priest. [21]On that very day, you shall proclaim: It shall be for you a sacred occasion; you must do no laborious work—a law for all time, in all your settlements, throughout your generations.

This pericope is composed of three layers, each representing a distinct contribution of the Holiness School.

The earliest, Pre-H_1 (regular type), ordains that each farmer shall bring to his local sanctuary his firstfruits of barley (*ʿōmer*) and wheat (two loaves), fifty days apart, as an elevation offering. This offering entails neither a pilgrimage (*ḥag*) nor a fixed date nor a rest day. This text represents the pre-Hezekian firstfruits offering of the grain, on which H, the main H strand, is based.

An interpolator, Pre-H_2 (boldface), sets the barley offering for the first Sunday after the week (ending with the sabbath) during which the harvest has begun. His purpose was to provide a collective offering for farmers in a localized area (where the grain ripened at approximately the same time) and, thereby, create a celebratory event, a mini-*ḥag* (in the spirit of Exod 23:16a), at the local sanctuary. The selection of Sunday was inevitable: it was an extension of the sabbath. While in the celebratory mode of the sabbath, the farmer and his family might make the short trip to his sanctuary, before donning the clothes and woes of the work week. It also should be apparent that this firstfruits offering had nothing to do with the approximately concurrent Festival of Unleavened Bread. Later interpreters, however, made this connection because they understood the word *šabbāt* to mean the sabbath day or the first day of the festival (see COMMENT B). However, it is of significant relevance to note that some Jewish sects (the Mesuri of Baalbeck and Boktan) began their pentecontal count on the first Sunday after the harvest began (Haran 1978: 518). For other views, see Tigay, 1978b: 111–12: Simon 1985: 122–23; Nach 1992: 427–35; Schwartz 1995b: 189–94.

Independently, and perhaps coevally, P (Num 28:26a), while presuming a barley offering (note "a *new* cereal offering" [v. 8]), prescribes a *public* (sanctuary) firstfruits wheat offering (quantity unspecified) fifty days later ("in your Festival of *Weeks*") at the *regional* sanctuary ("in *your* Festival of Weeks"), integrated into a series of fixed sacrifices (Num 28:27–30). As mentioned, the presumed barley offering is omitted from the list of public sacrifices in the calendar of Num 28–29 because it was brought by the individual farmer (cf. Exod 23:16a; Lev 2:14; vol. 1.192–93). Possibly, each sanctuary may have dedicated (*tĕnûpâ*) the collected sheaves on a fixed day, unaccompanied by other sacrifices, which became the first day of the seven-week counting. No date is given because the grain may have ripened at different times among the various regional sanctuaries. Neither offering was declared an official *ḥag* (note *ûbĕyôm*, not *ûbĕḥag*). The offerers remained at home to tend to their harvest, while the sanctuary offered the requisite sacrifices on their behalf. Pre-H₂, however, by his interpolation of *mimmāḥŏrat haššabbāt*, tries to turn both grain festivals into mini-pilgrimages to the local sanctuaries, an attempt that is vitiated by H, as explained below.

H (sans-serif italic), reflecting the viewpoint of the sanctuary in Jerusalem, supplements the text by converting the individual's barley and wheat offerings into collective public sacrifices and integrating them into an array of fixed sacrifices, borrowed mostly from Num 28–29 (P). This time, however, it cannot employ its customary "compare" notation *wĕhiqrabtem 'iššeh* (as in vv. 8, 25, 27, 36) because it prescribes a slightly different series of sacrifices for the wheat offering (vv. 18–19). It also drops P's term for the pentecontal *bĕšābu 'ōtēkem* 'in your Festival of *Weeks*' since it has no choice but to accept the (interpolated) text's term for weeks, *šabbātôt*. But it does borrow P's declaration that the day of the wheat offering must be observed as a sacred occasion requiring rest from laborious work (v. 21aβ; Num 28:26b), adding—rather awkwardly (see NOTE on "On that very day you shall proclaim," v. 21aα)—that the Israelites remain at home ("in all your settlements," v. 21b), thereby implying that this day is not a *ḥag*. Furthermore, H totally abolishes the individual farmer's offerings, as predicated by Pre-H₁ and Pre-H₂, on purely pragmatic grounds. Surely, farmers cannot be expected to make a pilgrimage to this central sanctuary together with their families and dependents (cf. Deut 16:11, 14). Instead, it ordains that, henceforth, it is the sanctuary's responsibility to supply both the barley and wheat offerings. The emphasis by both priestly texts, P and H, that the wheat offering is not a pilgrimage day may also be an undisguised polemic opposing the inclusion of this day among the required pilgrimage-festivals (contrast Exod 34:22a, 23; Deut 16:10, 16; see COMMENT A).

To recapitulate: it has been proposed that chap. 23 shows a three-layered development of the firstfruits offering of the barley and the wheat (vv. 9–21):

1. The earliest text (Pre-H₁) prescribes that each landowner bring his offering, fifty days apart, to his individual sanctuary (for a possible explanation of the counting, see NOTE on "seven sabbath weeks," v. 15).

2. An interpolator (Pre-H₂), attempting to coordinate these offerings for a joint sanctuary rite on the same day at each sanctuary, fixed the date of the barley offering on the first Sunday following the week (ending in sabbath) during which

the harvest began, thereby ensuring that the wheat offering (by tradition) fifty days later will also fall on Sunday.

3. The final stage (H) represents the Hezekian period. In the throes of the harvest season, most Israelites could not take the time to present their firstfruits in person. Therefore, following the precedent of the cultic calendar of public sacrifices endorsed by prior regional sanctuaries (Num 28–29), H converts the hitherto individual grain offerings into public sacrifices operated by the regional sanctuary, which are given in detail because they either differ with P (concerning the wheat) or fill in a lacuna of P (concerning the barley). Interestingly, Qumran retains the individual wheat offering, equating it with the mandatory loaf of the first-ripe wheat (Num 15:17–21; 4Q270; cf. Baumgarten 1985).

The parallel development of the grain offerings in the other cultic calendars of the Bible has been illumined by Ginsberg (1982). He postulates that the oldest rite is reflected in Exod 23:16a, 19a (E), which presumes that there was a ḥag for the firstfruits *of barley* at the local sanctuary. Thus E would anticipate Pre-H$_2$'s ʿōmer offering. Deut 16:9–11 (D) postpones the ḥag for seven weeks to the end (*sic!*) of the wheat harvest. No firstfruits are required (they can be brought anytime, Deut 26:1–11), only the generous bounty of each landowner that he and his family are willing to share with the underprivileged.

Ginsberg's reconstruction is problematic, since, as indicated (see INTRODUCTION to vv. 15–22), seven weeks after the beginning of the barley harvest marks only the *beginning* of the wheat harvest. One could object that it would hardly be a propitious time for a farmer to make a pilgrimage with his family and servants to the central sanctuary. But my student D. Stewart, an erstwhile farmer, on the basis of his experience and research (citing Peterson 1965 and Kirby 1984), informs me that of the final two stages of ripeness, the "fully ripe" and the "dead-ripe," the early "fully ripe" must be the firstfruits and that "while waiting for the entire crop to be ready, i.e., waiting for 'dead-ripeness,' one could take a break from farmer chores, take a pilgrimage bearing firstfruits to a nearby sanctuary and not miss the ideal moment to begin the harvest in earnest." Thus D's establishment of the Festival of Weeks as a national ḥag (Deut 16:10; cf. Exod 34:22a) is not as irrational as it sounds.

Ginsberg (1982) convincingly demonstrates that the calendar of Exod 34 is a deuteronomic revision of the calendar of Exod 23, which he labels E^d. Differing with its D prototype, Exod 34:22a restores the firstfruits offering of wheat (an indication that E^d is aware of Pre-H$_1$; see COMMENT D).

Vv. 15–16a. The opening sentences of the pericope on the Festival of First Wheat take the form of an AXA' construction:

A   a   *ûsĕpartem lākem*
    b   *mimmāḥŏrat haššabbāt*
      [c   *miyyôm hăbîʾăkem ʾet-ʿōmer hattĕnûpâ*]
    X   *šebaʿ šabbātôt tĕmîmōt tihyênâ*
A'   b'   *ʿad mimmāḥŏrat haššabbāt haššĕbîʿît*
    a'   *tispĕrû ḥămiššîm yôm*

A a And you shall count
   b from the day after the sabbath-week
     [c from the day on which you bring the elevation offering of the sheaf]
     X seven sabbath-weeks. They must be complete:
A′   b′ Until the day after the seventh sabbath-week
   a′ you shall count fifty days

AA′ are chiastically related not only to X but also to each other by means of their inner structure, as ab[c] ‖ b′a′. Clause c (v. 15aβ) is thus projected as an excrescence, but an essential one, that indicates when the fifty-day counting is to start. The word *šabbāt* is common to, and thereby unifies, all three sections. X and A′ are further linked by the common word *šeba* 'seven' as a modifier of *šabbāt*. The number seven abounds in this chapter (seven times). Its occurrence in X, the fulcrum of this twofold chiasm, is highlighted by its unique appearance in this chapter as 7 × 7 (M. Hildenbrand). Since this structure includes the interpolatory material (Pre-H$_2$), it is the work of the main H School (H), and it is consonant with other structural contributions of this school (see Introduction I A and, as an example, chap. 21, COMMENTS A and B).

In contrast, it is interesting to see Qumran's rewriting of this passage:

A *wĕsāpartā* [*lĕkâ*]
  B *šebaʿ šabbātôt tĕmîmôt*
    X *miyyôm hăbiʾăkemmâ ʾet hāʿômer* [*hattĕnûpâ* **tis**]*pôrû*
  B′ *ʿad mimmahŏrat* **haššabbāt haššĕbîʿît**
A′ **tispôrû** [*hămiššîm*] *yôm*

A You shall count [for yourself]
  B seven complete sabbaths.
    X From the day you bring the elevation offering of the sheaf, you shall
    count
  B′ until the day after the seventh sabbath.
A′ You shall count fifty days

In this structure, the unifying root is *spr*, occurring at the ends (AA′) and the center (X), the latter being the author's own addition. Also the terms *šebaʿ* (*haššĕbîʿît*) / *šabbātôt* (*haššabbāt*) 'seven (seventh) / sabbaths (sabbath)' occur in matching lines (BB′). In comparison with the MT, the singular *wĕsāpartā* [*lĕkâ*] is borrowed from 25:8 (Sweeny 1983: 62, contra Yadin 1983: 2.78), and the first *mimmāhŏrat hašššabbāt* is eliminated to improve the style and clarify the meaning (Milgrom 1978: 25–27, contra Levine 1978). This enabled the author to eliminate a hanging *tihyênâ*, and move up *šebaʿ šabbātôt tĕmîmôt* (Sweeny 1983: 62). Doing so, however, did not improve the introverted structure of the MT and, in fact, proves inferior to it.

15. *from the day after the sabbath-week. mimmāhŏrat haššabbāt.* This is a gloss (see INTRODUCTION to vv. 11–15 and COMMENT B).

you shall count for yourselves. ûsĕpartem lākem (i.e., each of you). The rabbis hold that the counting should be oral, both the days and the weeks (*b. Menaḥ.* 66a), but Ehrlich (1899–1900) makes a cogent case for claiming that the counting was done by writing. He does so by citing the derivative nouns *sēper* 'document' and *sōpēr* 'scribe', to which can be added the Akkadian cognates *šapāru* 'write' and *šipru* 'document' and Ugaritic *spr* (I AB, vi 53*; IIK,VI Colophon). Ehrlich also argues that when God asked Abraham *ûsĕpōr hakkôkābîm 'im-tûkal lispōr 'ōtām* 'count the stars, if you are able to count them' (Gen 15:5), he surely did not expect him to execute the count in his head.

The answer may lie in the one other ritual that prescribes counting: the seven days until a person who suffered a chronic genital flux undergoes purification (15:13, 28). For this short period, it is doubtful that the counting was in writing. Relevantly, the Hittite religion requires counting in the case of a parturient, who has to count until her purification. Even though that period is long—three months for a male child, four for a female (KBo XVII 65, ll. 31–36, rev. 40–44; Beckman 1983: 135–37, 142–43)—there is no indication that the counting was in writing.

It should be noted in passing that the corresponding Israelite ritual for a parturient does not require counting, even though the waiting period is also long: forty days for a male, fifty for a female. This is surprising, since at the end of this period the parturient brings her prescribed sacrifices "to the priest at the entrance of the Tent of Meeting" (12:6). If her counting is short, she will have defiled the sacred precinct! The Hittite text offers a possible solution. There the parturient does not do the counting, but "they count off" (lit. "let them count off," l. 31, rev. 40). It then may be surmised that in Israel the parturient's long count was performed by others, probably the priest at the local sanctuary (subsequently, a regional sanctuary). That is, a birth was a noteworthy event in the community, and it would be registered at the sanctuary. There and then, the counting would take place and the priest would inform the husband (or family) precisely when the purificatory sacrifices were due. For this reason, the counting is not mentioned in the parturient text (chap. 12). The case of the person healed of genital flux is different. The waiting period is short (seven days) and private; only the afflicted person would know when he or she was healed. Therefore, that person alone was responsible for the counting.

To carry my conjecture further, since the barley crop ripened at different times in different areas, each farmer was responsible for the counting. The fifty-day count would not be difficult: the day after seven complete sabbath-weeks. That is, the farmer need not count daily, but seven sabbaths plus one—unlike in Second Temple times to the present, when a calendar-pegged *ʿōmer* rite (Nisan 16) made a daily count necessary.

seven sabbath-weeks. šeba ʿšabbātôt. The term *šabbāt* here clearly means weeks (*šĕbûʿan*, Tgs.; cf. Matt 28:1; Luke 18:12; Mark 16:2, 9) and is distinguished from the usual term *šābuaʿ* by the fact that it ends with the sabbath (Dillmann and Ryssel 1897, citing Hitzig and Knobel). Whereas D (Deut 16:9), E[d] (Exod 34:22a), and P (Num 28:26a) call this festival *šābuʿōt*, implying that the counted weeks may start or end on any day, H (rather Pre-H$_2$; see INTRODUCTION to vv. 11–15) insists that the weeks end on the sabbath. Similarly, *šabbĕtôt šānīm* 'seven septenaries' (25:8) refers to seven cycles of seven years, each of which ends with a sabbatical year.

Whereas the LXX renders *šabbāt* as *sabbatōn*, it renders *šabbātôt* here as *hebdomadas* (and *šabbāt* in v. 16 as *hebdomados*). Since the Septuagint translators already operated on a Sunday-to-Saturday week, they therefore concur that each counted week must end on Saturday (Levine 1989a: 58–59), confirming Ginsberg (1979–80; cf. Milgrom 1978c: 25–27). However, Ginsberg's inference that P's use of *šābu ʿôt* (Num 28:26) is subsequent to Lev 23 is unwarranted. P, like Deut 16:9–10, uses *šābu ʿôt* to mean a seven-day period. H, however, rejects this tradition and introduces the new terms: sabbath-ending week and sabbath-ending year.

I admit that I cannot fathom the purpose of the fifty-day counting, and the literature I have consulted is of no help. But I have a visceral intuition that, originally, there was some incantation recited each day to ward off the demons of the weather, but with the triumph of Israelite monotheism, the magical incantations were excised and all that survived was the counting. Moshe Greenberg (personal communication) plausibly suggests that the counting by itself is purposeful and reflects not apprehension, but blessing. He points to the priestly blessing (Num 6:24–26), which comprised an arithmetic progression of consonants (15, 20, 25), syllables (12, 14, 16), and words (3, 5, 7; cf. Freedman 1975; Milgrom 1990a: 51). So, too, the farmer counts fifty days, forty-nine (a number of perfection, 7×7) plus one. Thus the fiftieth day is, as it were, perfection enhanced. I have already observed that the number fifty ($7 \times 7 + 1$) is an enhanced number eight ($7 + 1$), which is frequently encountered in the cult (vol. 1.571). Similarly, the jubilee cycle of fifty years constitutes forty-nine complete sabbath-weeks of years plus the jubilee-sabbath year (25:10–12). In both counts of fifty, the number forty-nine is a sabbath (day or year), and the number fifty is a "sabbath" (festival day or jubilee year).

Nonetheless, the question remains: Why is the request for blessing limited to the approaching wheat harvest? Why wasn't it mandated before the earlier barley harvest or in advance of the forthcoming grape and olive harvests? (Interestingly, Qumran requires a fifty-day count for the latter, 11QT 19:11–25:1; see COMMENT E.) Thus the conclusion is inescapable: blessing is inextricably tied to apprehension. In this case, the counting (for blessing) is necessitated in order to neutralize any cause for apprehension. But what could be the cause of the fear that would grip the farmer during these days?

It is no accident that the sirocco, the hot, dry Egyptian east wind, is called in Arabic *el-ḥamsîn* (*el-ḥamāsīn*), a word related to Arabic *ḥamsûn* and Hebrew *ḥămiššîm* 'fifty' (Hareuveni 1980: 60). The fifty-day period when the sirocco blows occurs between April and June, when these winds suddenly cause the temperature to rise and the humidity to plummet, resulting in the withering and killing of plants (Gen 41:6, 23; Isa 27:8; Ezek 17:10; 19:12; Hos 13:15; Jon 4:8) and weakness, heat stroke, and death to humans (2 Kgs 4:18–20, during the grain harvest! cf. Dalman 1928.1/2: 318–29, 460–61; Keel 1972).

An oblique reference to the danger posed by the weather during harvesttime is found in Jeremiah: *YHWH 'ĕlōhênu hannōtēn gešem wĕyōreh ûmalqōš bĕ'ittô šĕbū'ōt ḥuqqôt qāṣîr yišmōr-lānû* 'YHWH our God who gives rain, the early and late rain, in its season, who keeps the appointed weeks of harvest for our bene-fit' (Jer 5:24). That is, Israel is dependent on YHWH to provide adequate rain during the growing season, but during the *fixed weeks* of harvest (a probable ref-erence to the fifty-day period), he is asked to guard the crop against rain and other dangers, presumably the sirocco-*ḥamsîn*. (There's no need to delete *ḥuqqôt* [McKane 1986] as a deuteronomistic gloss.) A more explicit reference is the in-cident recorded in 1 Sam 12:17–19, when at Samuel's behest God brings rain on a day of harvest and thereby frightens the people.

A silent but striking witness to the perilousness of this season is the fact that Deuteronomy stresses the motif of rejoicing for the Festivals of Weeks and Booths (Deut 16:11, 14–15), but omits it for the Festival of Unleavened Bread (vv. 1–8), even though the gathering of the nation at the central sanctuary—Deuteron-omy's innovation—would, presumably, be a prime occasion for family celebra-tion (cf. *Yal.* 654). The beginning of a fifty-day period of unstable and precari-ous weather, which could possibly fatally damage the year's crop, not to speak of human health, is no time for rejoicing (cf. *Yal.* 654). Hence Deuteronomy recommends: "in the morning (following the *pesaḥ* sacrifice) you may start back on your journey home" (Deut 16:7b NJPS).

This distinction among the three pilgrimage festivals is also reflected in the distribution of the verb *śāmaḥ* 'rejoice', caught by the following midrash:

> You find three (expressions of) rejoicing written for the Festival of Booths: "You shall rejoice in your festival" (Deut 16:14); "so that you shall become completely joyful" (Deut 16:15); "You shall rejoice before YHWH your God seven days" (Lev 23:40). But on Passover you do not find written in it (the Bible) even one (expression of) rejoicing! Why? Because on Passover the grain is being judged, and no man knows whether there will be grain this year or not. . . . And on the Festival of Weeks (you find) only one (expression of) re-joicing, as written, "You shall keep the Festival of Weeks to YHWH Your God . . . and you shall rejoice before YHWH your God" (Deut 16:10–11). And why is there only one (expression of) rejoicing there? Because the fruit of trees is being judged. . . . But on the Festival of Booths . . . the grain and the fruit of the trees are inside [i.e., have been harvested and stored]; therefore three (expressions of) rejoicing are written. (*Yal.* Emor 23:654)

Thus one cannot be but struck by the stark differences in the deuteronomic calendar (Deut 16:1–17) between the Pilgrimage-Festival of Unleavened Bread and the Pilgrimage-Festivals of Weeks and Booths. In the latter, the legist takes pains to emphasize that everyone in the household, including the slaves, and even the underprivileged in the community—Levite, orphan, and widow—should accompany the head of the household in a pilgrimage to the central sanctuary (vv. 11, 14). But in the prescription for the Pilgrimage-Festival of Unleavened Bread, this stipulation is conspicuous by its absence. The only possible explanation is that the householder is eager to return to his fields. The text therefore states *ûpānîtā babbōqer wĕhālaktā lĕ'ōhālêkā* 'in the morning you may start back on your journey home' (v. 7b NJPS; on the meaning of *'ōhālĕkā*, see NOTE on "the seventh day is a sacred occasion," v. 8, and Driver 1895). At first blush, a totally superfluous statement! It reveals, however, the legist's assurance that the *pesaḥ* sacrifice and the *maṣṣôt* pilgrimage can be fulfilled by a one-night and one-person stand. The householder's family and retainers can stay home. He need but offer the sacrifice, eat it, and see the light of day at the sanctuary, thereby fulfilling the ancient commandment to observe the Festival of Unleavened Bread beginning that morning (v. 16a; cf. Exod 23:17; 34:23)—and then hasten home (see also Bekhor Shor on Deut 16:11, 16).

To be sure, during Second Temple times, particularly at the end of this period, large-scale family pilgrimages to the Temple took place for the *pesaḥ* sacrifice (cf. 2 Chr 30; Jos. *Ant* 17.214). By then, however, political and economic circumstances had changed. The economy of the large diaspora and of many in the land was no longer agricultural, but mercantile. Celebrating the seven-day *maṣṣôt* festival, paralleling the required seven-day *Booths* festival, in Jerusalem was now possible. Nonetheless, echoes of this anxiety and trepidation during the fifty days following the spring festival continue to resound. They are reflected in the medieval prayerbook *Abudarham haššālēm* (Jerusalem 1959: 241, a reference I owe to Greenberg 1979: 297, n. 22): "Some explain it . . . on the ground that the world is anxious between Passover and Weeks about the crops and the fruit trees. . . . Therefore God commanded to count these days, to keep the anxiety of the world in mind and to turn to him in wholehearted repentance, to plead with him to have mercy upon us, on mankind and on the land, so that the crops should turn out well, for they are our life." They burgeon in the rabbinic laws of semimourning during these fifty days, which prohibit the solemnizing of marriages, the cutting of hair, and the playing of musical instruments, and, for justification, allude to a plague that decimated the disciples of R. Akiba during this period (*b. Yeb.* 62b [bar.]; *Shulḥan 'Arukh, 'Oraḥ Ḥayyim* 493:1–3; cf. Silberman 1949).

They must be complete. *tĕmîmōt tihyênâ.* This rendering is achieved by transposing the *'atnaḥ* from *hattĕnûpâ* to *šabbātôt* (Ehrlich 1908), making the latter the object of "count." The LXX does the same by more radical means, deleting (or ignoring) *tihyênâ.* The Sam. adds *lākem* at the end of the verse, thereby preserving the Masoretic reading.

The rabbis suggest that the adjective "complete" implies that the counting must be done in the evening in order that the counting be "complete," assuming that the fiftieth day, the Festival of Weeks, begins in the evening (R. Eliezer in *b. Qidd.* 37a). The likelihood, however, is that the week's completeness is stressed to make sure that the week ends with the sabbath. This is also a deduction of R. Hiyya (*Lev. Rab.* 28:22; cf. *m. Ḥag.* 2:4).

16. *until the day after the seventh sabbath-week.* *'ad mimmāḥŏrat haššabāt haššĕbî'ît.* This is the end of the interpolation (by Pre-H₂), which begins after

lākem (v. 15; see INTRODUCTION to vv. 15–22). Here *mimmāḥorat*, literally "*from the morrow of*," betrays its petrified nature. (*Seper Hamibḥar* cites as an example *mitṭerem*, Hag 2:15.)

count . . . fifty days. The Ṭipḥa under *tispĕrû* 'count' reflects the rabbinic view that the counting should be for only forty-nine days (Abravanel). This view, however, cannot be accepted, since the major division is the *zāqēp parvum* on *haššĕbî'īt*, reflecting a fifty-day count (B. J. Schwartz, personal communication).

The parallel to the jubilee is noteworthy. Both year 49 (a sabbatical) and year 50 (the jubilee) are holy (25:10). So day 49 (a sabbath) and day 50 (the Feast of Weeks) are holy (v. 21).

a new cereal offering. minḥâ ḥădāšâ. This offering is from wheat, in contrast to the "old" cereal offering from barley. This phrase occurs independently in Num 28:26a. This is evidence that P is aware of the barley offering but has omitted it, possibly because it was brought by individual farmers and offered at their regional sanctuary on a fixed date unaccompanied by public sacrifices (for its background, see INTRODUCTION to vv. 15–22).

The rabbis interpret this phrase differently: *šettĕhē' ḥădāšâ lĕkōl hammĕnāḥôt* 'it should be the first cereal offering from the new crop' (*b. Menaḥ.* 83b; *Sipra* Emor 12:9). That is, even the barley offering for the suspected adulteress (Num 5:15) must be of the past year's barley if it is offered before the firstfruits of the wheat.

The rabbis also hold that there is no prohibition against eating of the new wheat before its first fruits offering (cf. *m. Menaḥ* 10:3)—and, indeed, there is no such prohibition in the biblical text. Since the two grain offerings appear as a single festival (fifty days apart but united by the counting), only in the case of the first offering (barley) would such a prohibition make sense. But Qumran does not accept scriptural silence as license. An unpublished fragment states 'L Y'KL '[Y]Š ḤTYM ḤDŠYM . . . 'D YWM B' LḤM HBKWRYM 'The new wheat may not be eaten . . . until the day the firstfruit loaves arrive (at the Temple)' (4Q274, frag. 5:5–6)

Actually, both Qumran and the rabbis are correct. Their reasoning is impeccable. But they come to opposite conclusions by virtue of their differing premises. Qumran bases itself on its tradition of a series of four firstfruits festivals (barley, wheat, grapes, and olives), fifty days apart. The firstfruits offering releases (*hillel* 'desanctify', Deut 20:6; 28:30) the use of the crops to the entire people (11QT 1:26–6:23) and betokens the hope that God will bless all of Israel with an abundant crop (Ezek 34:29).

The rabbis, however, drew their conclusion on the basis of the changes that had occurred in the observance of the Festival of Wheat. It had become known as *'ăṣeret*, a term designating the conclusion of a festival (cf. Lev 23:36; Deut 16:8). It was the conclusion of the two grain festivals, tied to the first (the *'ōmer*) by a fifty-day count. Moreover, its agricultural nature had faded, replaced by a religio-historical meaning—the anniversary of the Sinaitic revelation and covenant (cf. Exod 19:1–2). The people no longer brought the firstfruits of the wheat (already replaced in H; see NOTE on 23:21). This offering was brought by the priests and for the priests. It released the new crop for sacrifices, but it had no effect outside the Temple. The people, therefore, having observed the '*ōmer* as the firstfruits *grain* offering, were free to eat of the wheat whenever it ripened.

17. *You shall bring.* *tābî'û.* The *mappiq* in the *aleph* converts it into a vocal consonant (see also Gen 43:26; Job 33:21; Ezra 8:18; GKC § 14d). Noth (1977) postulates, correctly I believe, that originally every landowner was required to bring the offering of two loaves (see INTRODUCTION to vv. 11–15).

from your settlements. *mimmôšĕbōtêkem* (i.e., from each of your settlements). The rabbis, however, hold that this means from wherever it ripened first. Both opinions are correct: the former is the original custom; the latter, the revised law (see INTRODUCTION to vv. 15–22).

as an elevation offering of . . . bread. *leḥem tĕnûpâ.* The loaves have neither oil nor frankincense, and they are leavened (*m. Menaḥ.* 5:3). Therefore, they controvert the scheme of cereal offerings detailed in chap. 2. It is their different composition that determines their special need for dedication called "the elevation offering." Ordinarily, most holy offerings, such as the cereal offering, automatically belong to God. But leaven is banned from the divine presence, the altar (2:11). Therefore, the loaves continue to belong to the offerer until they undergo the dedication rite of the *tĕnûpâ* (details in Milgrom 1983c: 149). Noordtzij's (1982) explanation that as a public offering it requires this rite is contradicted by the breast of the well-being offering brought by an individual, which also requires it (7:34).

Nonetheless, it is surprising that the entire offering is banned from the altar because it is leavened. Could it be that nothing from the new wheat crop is offered to YHWH (in distinction to the barley offering, vv. 13–14)? After all, it is a firstfruits offering (*bikkûrîm*)! Therefore, there is room for conjecturing that *originally* leavened bread was offered on the altar. A possible indication that such was the practice is *wĕqaṭṭēr mēḥāmēṣ tôdâ* 'Burn a thanksgiving offering of leaven' (Amos 4:5). That the prophet is not castigating his audience for violating the priestly prohibition of leaven on the altar (Ibn Ezra) is shown by the immediately following statement *wĕqir'û nĕdābôt hašmî'û* 'call loudly for free will offerings', which is perfectly legitimate. Moreover, the repeated warning not to sacrifice leaven (Exod 23:18; 34:25; Lev 2:11; 6:10) may, indeed, reflect a polemic against popular practice. (Was D's limitation of the ban, in its rewording of Exod 23:18 in Exod 34:25 [see COMMENT D], a concession to popular demand?)

Perhaps, then, the offering of the two bread loaves is a vestige of an earlier nonpriestly practice that was so entrenched in the populace that it could not be changed by H. Instead, it prescribed that these loaves should not be sacrificed, but handed over to the priests as their prebend (v. 20).

two . . . (loaves). *štayim.* The *Tgs.*, LXX, Sam., and Pesh. add *ḥallôt* 'loaves' (as in 24:5), supported by the feminine plural verbs *tihyênâ, tē'āpênâ* (cf. the view of Ben Nanos, *b. Menaḥ.* 45b). Surprisingly, Josephus (*Ant.* 3.352) calls for the making of one loaf.

Deuteronomy, which mandates a single sanctuary, permits money gifts instead of the two loaves (Deut 16:10). This change is a further indication that H presupposes multiple sanctuaries so that the loaves, a priestly prebend (v. 20), will be fresh on arrival.

two-tenths. Two interpretations are possible. First, each loaf is two-tenths, which would make them comparable to the *'ōmer* (v. 10) and Bread of Presence (24:5). Qumran concurs: ŠNY] 'ŚRNYM SWLT TH[YH] HḤLH H'ḤT 'each loaf [will] comprise [two] tenths of semolina' (11QT 18:15). Second, both loaves add up to two-tenths, and each is one-tenth (*m. Menaḥ.* 6:6; *Sipra* Emor 13:2; *b. Menaḥ.* 76b, 77a). The LXX concurs, since it reads *miššĕnê* 'of two tenths'; that is, it is the total for both loaves. The Karaites interpret similarly, but they mistakenly grade the loaves as lesser sacred offerings eaten by the entire priestly family.

semolina. sōlet. This constitutes proof that it is a wheat offering (see NOTE on 2:1). The Qumranites, however, are not content with this inferential deduction: they insert this identification into their version of the biblical text *LḤM ḤYM* 'loaves of wheat' (11QT 18:14).

baked after leavening. ḥāmēṣ tē'āpênâ. The loaves are leavened because they are a thanksgiving offering (Ramban; Knohl 1995: 25). The analogy is inexact, since only one of the required thanksgiving loaves is leavened (7:13–14). Moreover, it would hardly make sense to bring a thanksgiving offering at the beginning of the harvest rather than at its end. The reason may be more practical: roasted wheat, in comparison with roasted barley, tastes flat (see NOTE on "parched," v. 14). Leavened bread qualifies as a *qorban rē'šît* 'a first-processed offering' (2:11–12; Knohl 1987: 82; 1995: 24).

If, however, as conjectured above, the two loaves were originally brought as a firstfruits offering, it would make sense that they were leavened as a sign of being a thanksgiving offering. This offering, as argued above (see INTRODUCTION to vv. 11–22), was brought at the end of the wheat harvest—that is, when the entire barley and wheat crop had been reaped. Then, as with the fully baked loaves brought as a firstfruit offering to the prophet (2 Kgs 4:42), the Israelite farmer would have brought a similar offering as his gratitude to his Deity (alluded in Amos 4:5).

as firstfruits. bikkûrîm. In the priestly texts, this term is found in 2:14 (twice); 23:17, 20; Num 18:13; 28:26; compare *leḥem habbikkûrîm* 'firstfruit loaves' (v. 20; 2 Kgs 4:42). The Feast of Weeks is known as *yôm habbikkûrîm* 'the day of firstfruits' (Num 28:26) and in Second Temple days as *ḤG HBKWRYM* 'the Festival of Firstfruits' (11QT 19:9). That is, the fixed day of the wheat offering is the day of firstfruits, par excellence. However, firstfruits from products other than grain can be brought at any time (Num 18:13; Deut 26:1–11). In actuality, the terms *bikkûrîm* for baked bread and *rē'šît* for the raw barley (v. 10b) contravene P's terminological distinction, where, contrariwise, *bikkûrîm* stands for the raw product and *re'šît*, the processed product (details in Milgrom 1976e)— another example of how H blurs and, at times, reverses P's precise definitions (see Introduction I C; vol. 1.35–38; but cf. NOTE on "the first sheaf of your harvest," v. 10, where *rē'šît* may have a temporal meaning).

Kaufmann (1937: 1.124) correctly points to 2 Kgs 4:42 as evidence that the individual was wont to bring his firstfruits of grain in the form of loaves.

Vv. 18–19. Interpolation

An interpolation by H (see INTRODUCTION to vv. 15–22); it converts the erstwhile individual offering of the firstfruits of wheat into a public offering in the sanctuary (Kalisch 1867–72 and early critics; Knohl 1987: 84; 1995: 26; Levine 1989a: 63). Kuenen (1886: 99, n. 39) admits that in this case Num 28:27–31 has been interpolated into Lev 23: that P is earlier than H. He attributes it to "a very natural mistake" (309, n. 28), not realizing the basic principle of Lev 23: H gives sacrificial details only when it differs from Num 28 (P). Otherwise, it refers to Num 28 by the formula *wĕhiqrabtem ʾiššeh* (see NOTE on v. 8). Baentsch (1903) also argues that Lev 23 copies from Num 28, but attributes the difference to a copyist's error. On the contrary, it is the difference that accounts for its inclusion. Besides, as pointed out by Hoffmann (1954: 2.155, n. 141), error is unlikely since the proportion of two bulls and one ram is again found in the sacrificial prescriptions for the new moon and the Festival of Unleavened Bread (Num 28:11, 19). Gerstenberger's (1996: 346) claim that this prescribed sacrificial quota was imposed on households (from Jerusalem) is far-fetched: it would bankrupt most of them.

The series "seven lambs, one bull . . . one goat . . . cereal and (wine) libations" and its source in Num 28 is not arbitrary, but is based on a pattern attested elsewhere. Thus the Hittite Karahna festival rereads the same series, "one bull, seven lambs and one goat with groats and wine libation" (Dinçol and Darga 1969–70: 100).

In Second Temple times, both sacrificial lists—Lev 23 and Num 28—were considered mandatory, and their combined total was offered (*m. Menaḥ.* 4:2–3; Jos. *Ant* 3.253 [note the error: two rams instead of three]). Qumran also combined them (e.g., fourteen lambs, 11QT 20:12). The rabbis, however, do not combine them, but regard them as distinct offerings—those of Num 28 as *mûsāpîn* 'additional sacrifices' and those of Lev 23 as altar sacrifices for the sake of the bread loaves (*Sipra* Emor 13:6). Ibn Ezra, though, suggests that the priests had the option of offering either list.

18. *seven . . . lambs. šibʿat kĕbāśîm.* Based on Num 28:27, but the lambs are first in this list, whereas the normal sequence, observed throughout Num 28–29, is bulls, rams, and lambs. A number of explanations have been offered for this exception:

1. It contrasts with the one lamb required for the barley offering (v. 12; Hoffmann 1953; Boleh 1991–92).
2. Beginning with the number calls attention to the difference between the two lists; since one cannot say *ʾeḥād par* (the real difference), the text begins with the number that can precede the noun (Paran 1983: 100). However, the text could have said *šĕnê ʾēlîm*.
3. A corrected variation of the preceding reason is that the term *šibʿâ kĕbāśîm*, wherein the number comes first, does occur in Num 28:17 (cf. v. 19).

None of these explanations is satisfying.

one bull of the herd, and two rams. The difference. Numbers prescribes two bulls and one ram (v. 27). The LXX and Sam. add the adjective *tĕmîmîm* 'unblemished'.

(they) shall be a burnt offering. yihyû 'ōlâ. Why didn't H follow its model *wĕhiqrabtem 'ōlâ* (Num 28:27)? That is, why was it necessary to add the verb *yihyû*? The answer is obvious: *'ōlâ* as the object of *wĕhiqrabtem* here would lead one to deduce that the bread loaves were also included. By making *'ōlâ* the object of *yihyû*, the sense now is: added to the loaves, shall be the following burnt offerings.

and with their cereal offerings and libations. ûminḥātām wĕniskêhem. The singular form for the cereal offerings and the plural for the libations betray their Numbers original, where these forms make sense (Num 28:28aα, 31bβ). The rabbis, too, recognize that *dibbēr hakkātûb biqṣārâ* 'This text is abbreviated' (*Sipra Emor* 13:5). Thus Lev 23 has borrowed text from Num 28: [16b](*ûbĕyyôm habbikkûrîm*) *wĕhiqrabtem minḥâ ḥădāšâ laYHWH* (*bĕšābu 'ōtêkem*). [21]*miqrā' qōdeš yihyeh lākem kol-mĕle'ket 'ăbōdâ lō' ta'ăśû.* H adds the text of the original, individual firstfruits offering (the two loaves), which it converts into a public offering consisting of seven lambs, one bull, and two rams as burnt offerings with their cereal offerings and libations, one he-goat as a purification offering, and two lambs as a well-being offering (cf. Kochman 1987: 166).

a food gift of pleasant aroma to YHWH. 'iššeh lĕrêaḥ-nîḥōah laYHWH. These terms cannot be applied to the purification offering, which follows in a separate sentence (v. 19; vol. 1.161–62). The phrase *'iššeh laYHWH* 'a food gift to YHWH' occurs seven times in the festival calendar (vv. 8, 13, 18, 25, 27, 36 [twice]). Perhaps that is the reason it is broken up in v. 18, an indication that vv. 18–19 are an interpolation and its author was aware of its seven-time occurrence in the calendar (M. Hildenbrand).

19. *as a purification offering.* H replaces the function of the sacrifice *lĕkappēr 'ălêkem* 'to effect purgation on your behalf' (Lev 8:34) with its name, *lĕḥaṭṭā't* 'as a purification offering', proving that the function is ensconced in the name (details in vol. 1.253–58).

and two yearling lambs as a sacrifice of well-being. ûšĕnê kĕbāśîm bĕnê šānâ lĕzebaḥ šĕlāmîm. Weinfeld (1980: 76, n. 61; see also Knohl 1995: 25) holds that originally the two lambs were brought by each farmer, but when the firstfruits rite was converted into a public offering, vv. 18–19a were added and the two lambs became a public well-being offering (*šalmê ṣibbûr*, the rabbinic term) — the only such sacrifice in the Torah. This may well be the case, and the rabbis who posit that the lambs were subject to an elevation offering (see NOTE on "them," v. 20) may be preserving an ancient tradition. Abetting this interpretation is the fact that in every series of P's prescribed public sacrifices in the calendar year, the purification offering is the last to be specified, except for allusions to other previously scheduled sacrifices (Num 28:15, 22–23, 30–31; 29:4–5, 11, 16, 22, 25, 28, 31, 34, 38). Thus the two lambs that follow cannot be part of the list of public sacrifices (H), but belong to the earlier text (Pre-H₁) addressed to the farmer. These lambs would parallel the lamb prescribed for the barley firstfruits offering (v. 12), which, as argued above, was also brought by the individual.

The objection may be raised, however, that this text speaks of a public offering, presumably on a fixed date, when the people are not commanded to be present (it is not a *ḥag*; see NOTE on "all your settlements," v. 21). If it were a required private offering, incumbent on each farmer, what would the priest do with all the meat? Even assuming that it was considered a lesser sacred offering eligible to be eaten by the families of the priestly cadre, most of the meat piling up at the sanctuary could not possibly be eaten during its permitted forty-eight-hour time frame and would have to be destroyed (7:17)! Thus it would have to be concluded that the two lambs were not originally given over to the priest, but were the private well-being offering of each farmer as he and his family celebrated this day a short distance from his home *at his local sanctuary*. Subsequently, H (the MT) innovates this public well-being offering and ordains (as recognized by the rabbis, *m. Zebaḥ.* 5:5) that the two lambs are most holy offerings, eaten solely by the priests on the same day.

This, in itself, provides a further reason to suspect that originally the two lambs were nothing else but an ordinary, private well-being offering. Nowhere else is a well-being offering a public sacrifice! Finally, it should be pointed out that in the calendar of *public* sacrifices in Num 28–29, the two well-being lambs are omitted from the sacrifices for the Festival of New Wheat. This, too, provides evidence that in the regional sanctuary reflected in these chapters, the two lambs were a private offering. The motivation for creating this unique public offering is not difficult to fathom. Once the firstfruits wheat pilgrimage was no longer required (see NOTE on "all your settlements," v. 21), the Jerusalem (and regional) sanctuary took over the responsibility of the well-being offering of the two lambs, adding it to the roster of public sacrifices for the day.

In either case, whether a public or a private offering, the reason for the joy, which motivates a well-being offering (vol. 1.217–25), can be surmised. Although this day marks the beginning of the wheat harvest, it anticipates the end of the grain harvest. The months of anxiety and fear are nearly over. The crop is ripening, and in a few weeks it will be harvested.

The LXX adds *metà tōn ártōn tou prōtogenématos*, reading *ʿal leḥem hab-bikkûrîm* 'in addition to the bread of firstfruits', but it is superfluous in view of its mention in v. 20.

20. *them.* *ʾōtām.* Theoretically, there are three possible antecedents: the two loaves, the two lambs, or the other public sacrifices. According to the present MT of v. 20, which mentions the loaves and lambs separately, only one possibility remains—the other sacrifices. But public sacrifices never undergo the elevation offering; being taken from sanctuary stock, they do not have to be transferred to the realm of the Deity—the purpose of the elevation offering (vol. 1.462). The two lambs, as mentioned, cannot be a public sacrifice. That is probably why the LXX adds at the end of v. 19 that the two lambs should be sacrificed "with the loaves of the firstfruits," in order to convert the two lambs into a private sacrifice and dissociate them from the lambs assigned to the priest in

v. 20 (Swanson 1995: 40–41). Even as a private sacrifice, however, only their breasts would be subject to the elevation rite (7:30), not the entire animals. Thus it must be deduced that only the loaves were elevated (in conformance with the second principle expounded in vol. 1.465–67). Supporting this deduction is the fact that the firstfruits wheat loaves would exactly parallel the firstfruits barley sheaf, which was also elevated (v. 11)—but not its accompanying lamb (v. 12). The loaves, the main subject of the original passage (after removing the interpolated public sacrifices, vv. 18–19a), would therefore be the sole antecedent of *'ōtām*. The confusion created by the immediately preceding two lambs would then be accountable for the insertion of the two clauses—the loaves and the lambs—into this verse. The interpolator responsible for the two lambs held that they too should be elevated, and the one responsible for the two loaves was apprehensive lest "them" be understood as referring to the lambs.

The rabbis, however, claim that the antecedent is the lambs (*Sipra* Emor 13:8; *b. Menaḥ.* 62a [the text of *Sipra* Emor 13:7 has to be corrected to the reading of *b. Zebaḥ.* 6b; cf. Rabad]). Presumably, the purpose of the otherwise superfluous lambs clause would have to be for emphasis. Saadiah suggests that only the breasts and right thighs of the two lambs were elevated (in keeping with the rabbinic interpretation of 7:34) because the whole animal would be too difficult to lift. However, the lamb of the healed scale-diseased person was elevated (14:12, 24), as, indeed, the entire male population of the Levites (Num 8:11)—obviously, through a symbolic "elevation" (vol. 1.851–52; Milgrom 1990a: 62).

with the two lambs. *'al šnê kĕbāśîm.* The lack of the article (which the LXX and Sam. remedy) is a further indication of its interpolative character.

they shall be holy. The referent, once again, is the two loaves. R. Akiba declares these breads as most holy offerings. Ben Nanos, on the contrary, claims that only the lambs are most holy offerings. As explained by Rashi: since an individual's well-being offerings are lesser holy offerings, the text had to state that these (lambs are holy; that is, they) are most holy offerings. Rashi (and Ben Nanos) is right, but his justification is wrong. R. Akiba has given the correct interpretation of the subject: it refers to the two loaves. Both the breads and the lambs are most holy because of a more direct reason: they are consumed totally by the priests. The lambs are therefore akin to the meat of the most holy purification and reparation offerings, which also are eaten by the priests (cf. 6:22; 7:6). In contradiction to priestly prebends of well-being offerings (7:31–33), which, falling under the category of lesser holy offerings (*qōdeš*), may be eaten by the priest's family and servants (22:11–13; Num 18:11), the rabbis ordain that public well-being offerings, being totally assigned to the priests, are to be eaten solely by them within the Temple's inner court (cf. *m. Zebaḥ.* 5:5). In other words, the lambs and loaves are treated as most holy offerings (*qodšê qodāšim*). Interestingly, the Qumranians concur, if the reconstruction of their text is correct: *L]KWHNYM YH[YU] W'KLWM BḤṢ[R/ HPNYMIT]* 'They belong to the priests, and they shall eat them in the inner court' (11QT 19:5–6)—where only most holy offerings are eaten (6:9; cf. *m. Zebaḥ.* 5:5).

to YHWH for the priest. *laYHWH lakkōhēn.* First they are dedicated to God, who then transfers them to the priest (*Sipre* Num 4; Ehrlich 1908). Individual well-being offerings are eaten by the worshiper (7:15–16), and only their breasts and right thighs are priestly prebends (7:34). Firstlings experience the opposite development: initially, they belonged to YHWH, i.e., the priests (Exod 13:2, 15; Lev 27:26; Num 18:15), but the deuteronomic reform restored them to their owners (Deut 15:19–23).

The LXX adds *tōi propthéronti autà autōi èstai* 'it will be for him (the priest) who offers them', in keeping with the regulation of 7:8–9, assuming that the text is referring to the lambs, and forgetting that the lambs were a public, not an individual, offering.

21. *On that very day.* *bĕʿeṣem hayyôm hazzeh.* This is a typical priestly phrase: vv. 14, 21, 29, 30; Gen 7:13; 17:23, 26; Exod 12:17, 41, 51; Deut 32:48. Elsewhere, see Josh 5:11; 10:27; Ezek 2:3; 24:2 (twice); 40:1.

you shall proclaim. *ûqĕrāʾtem.* Since the verb indisputably means "proclaim," its cognate accusative *miqrāʾ* has to mean "proclamation" (see NOTE on v. 2).

It shall be for you a sacred occasion. The best way of making syntactical sense of this otherwise gauche construction is to regard these words as the beginning of the actual message of the proclamation (accepted for the sake of clarity in the translation). Ehrlich (1908) would even include *bĕʿeṣem hayyôm hazzeh* 'on this very day'. The Sam., recognizing the syntactic awkwardness, omits *yihyeh lākem*, yielding "On that very day you shall proclaim a sacred occasion . . . " (followed by NJPS). The LXX reads *kaì kalésete tautēn tēn hēméron klētēn hagia éstai humin* 'And you shall call this day a convocation; it shall be holy to you', which, however, wrongly renders *miqrāʾ* as "convocation." The insertion of the word *šābbatôn* 'a rest' before *yihyeh lākem*, yielding "you shall observe a rest," gives v. 21a a smooth reading (see NOTE on v. 24). In the long run, however, there may be no alternative but to accept the awkwardness as a consequence of H borrowing the phrase *miqrāʾ-qōdeš yihyeh lākem kol-mēleʾket ʿăbōdâ lōʾ tāʿăśû* from its prototype (Num 28:26b) and ineptly adding the incomplete beginning as well as a proper ending (Knohl 1987: 70; 1995: 12). The fact that this statement makes the firstfruits of the wheat into a sacred occasion implies that it is now a fixed day—the product of H.

in all your settlements. *bĕkol-môšĕbōtêkem.* The implication is clear: the day of the wheat offering is not *ḥag*; the sanctuary makes the requisite offerings, and the people stay at home.

This clause is added wherever the context demands it (*ṣôrek hāʿinyān*; b. *Qidd.* 37b). Thus it occurs in the pericope on the Day of Purgation (v. 31) and the sabbath (v. 3) so that it is understood that the ban on all work applies everywhere; it is found in the blood and fat prohibition (3:17), lest one think that it does not apply outside the sanctuary (Ramban). Similarly, one may not eat of the new grain *anywhere* before it is offered (v. 14). The prohibition against eating leaven during the week-long Festival of Unleavened Bread also applies everywhere. To be sure, it is not found in Lev 23, but it is expressly mentioned in Exod 12:20, which is—together with the detailed observations of the paschal offering of 12:1–14—taken for granted in vv. 5–8 (see NOTE on v. 5). Note that this phrase is applied to the prohibition against eating any leaven, but not to the statements on unleavened bread since there is no requirement to eat unleavened bread except with the paschal sacrifice (Exod 12:8). Only its absence in the Festival of Alarm Blasts (vv. 23–25) and the Festival of Booths has to be accounted for. The latter omission makes sense: the people are not at home; they are at the sanctuary for the entire seven-day festival (vv. 34b, 39–41; but see NOTE on v. 42). The omission of this phrase from the Festival of Warning Blasts is difficult to explain, since the shofar, by implication, must be blown everywhere (see NOTE on v. 24). Nonetheless, one might argue that the latter eventuality would have been expressed explicitly (as in 25:9b) and that, therefore, the shofar blowing would have been confined to the sanctuary. However, if that were the case, it would contradict rabbinic law, which may actually reflect the end of the Second Temple period (*m. Roš. Haš.* 4:1). I have no answer.

It is hardly surprising that the Qumranians omit this phrase from their rendition of this verse (11QT 19:8). For them, no textual ambiguity could be allowed: the Festival of New Wheat [*ḤG Š*]*BW 'WT HW' WḤG BKWR 'M* 'is [the festival of the W]eeks, a festival of Firstfruits' (11QT 19:9), which is celebrated at only the central sanctuary (Deut 16:10–11).

throughout your generations. lĕdōrōtêkem. This term follows *bĕkol-môšĕbōtêkem* in this verse, whereas it precedes it in vv. 14 and 31, thereby creating an ab, ba, ab chiasm (M. Hildenbrand).

22. This verse should be compared with its prototype (19:9–10), from which it is clearly copied:

ûbĕquṣrĕkem 'et-qĕṣîr 'arṣĕkem lō' tĕkalleh pĕ'at śādĕkā liqṣōr wĕleqeṭ qĕṣîrĕkā lō' tĕlaqqēṭ (wĕkarmĕkā lō' tĕ'ōlēl ûpereṭ karmĕkā lō' tĕlaqqēṭ) le'ănî wĕlaggēr ta'ăzōb 'ōtām 'ănî YHWH 'ĕlōhêkem

[9]When you reap the harvest of your land, you shall not reap to the edges of your field, or gather the gleanings of your harvest. [10](You shall not pick your vineyard bare, or gather the fallen fruit of your vineyard), you shall leave them for the poor and for the alien: I am YHWH your God. (19:9–10)

The most obvious change is the omission of 19:10a, since it includes the grape harvest, an event that does not occur until mid-summer; hence its omission is logical (Wenham 1979: 305). The direction of the borrowing is also indicated by the same switch in numbers from the first plural clause to the singular, which dominates thereafter (Noth 1977). As demonstrated by Knohl (1995: 52–53), the addition of a verse ending with "I am YHWH your God" (v. 22) following a passage ending with "an eternal law throughout your generations" (v. 21) is indicative of H's legal style (e.g., in Num 10:1–10 [H], see vv. 1–8, 9–10, and in Lev 23:39–43, see vv. 39–41, 42–43; but for my reservations, see NOTES on vv. 39–43).

What purpose did H have in mind in repeating an injunction that it already ordained? Greenberg (1985: 115) argues cogently that this verse was deliberately appended to the pericope on the firstfruits of the grain (vv. 9–21) in order to underline God's sovereignty over the land: Israel may farm God's land (25:23) only if it brings its firstfruits to YHWH and provides these specified gifts to the poor. H may have had a larger purpose in mind. As will be pointed out in the NOTE on 25:6, in order to induce the landowner to observe the sabbatical prescriptions, H alters the old (reigning?) law of Exod 23:10–11 (JE), which assigns the entire produce of the sabbatical to the poor (and the beasts), so that the sole beneficiaries are the landowner and all those under his control. The poor, however, are thereby excluded. Hence H repeats the injunction to help the poor (19:9–10) in the festival calendar as a reminder to the landowner that sharing the grain harvest with the poor and the alien is not just an ethical desideration, but a specific, time-bound, yearly obligation even on the sabbatical.

That this command originally referred to "a votary offering to chthonic spirits in the hope of their beneficence during harvest time" (Fishbane 1985: 279, n. 21) is pure conjecture. But here its goal is unambiguous and direct: do not forget your obligation to the poor during harvest time (Ibn Ezra).

you shall not complete (it). lō'-tĕkalleh . . . bĕquṣrekā, literally "you shall not complete in your reaping." This provides a slight stylistic improvement over *lō'-tĕkalleh . . . liqṣōr*, literally "you shall not complete to reap" (19:9a). Both are grammatically correct, but the latter represents the more difficult reading and is, therefore, more probably original. The Sam., though, reads *liqṣōr* here in order to harmonize with 19:9.

edge of . . . gleanings of. pĕ'at . . . leqeṭ. These terms are discussed in the NOTE on 19:9.

I am YHWH your God. 'ănî YHWH 'ĕlōhêkem. This closing formula serves a dual function: to complete the citation from 19:9–10 and to serve as a marker ending the first half of the chapter and, thereby, forming an inclusio with v. 43b, which effectively ends the second half of the chapter (see INTRODUCTION to vv. 4–38).

Vv. 23–25. The Festival of Alarm Blasts

As pointed out in the NOTE on "the fixed times of YHWH," v. 2, although the new moon was observed as a special day in the cult (calling for additional sacrifices, Num 28:11–15) and by the people (as a day of rest, Amos 8:5; joy, Hos 2:13; feasting, 1 Sam 20:5; family sacrifice, 1 Sam 20:6; receiving spiritual guidance from the prophet, 2 Kgs 4:23), it is neither a *mô'ēd* 'fixed time' nor a *miqrā' qōdeš* 'sacred occasion' and, hence, is omitted from the holiday calendar of Lev 23. This exclusion, however, does not apply to the new moon of the seventh month. That the number seven bears special and, perhaps, sacred significance in the calendar (and in progeny) has long been recognized (for the earliest source, see *Lev. Rab.* 29:11). The seventh month is set apart just as the seventh day, the seventh year, and the jubilee (the end of the seventh week of years). Moreover, note that the offerings listed for the first day of the seventh month almost duplicate and are in addition to the offerings of a normal new moon (cf.

Num 28:11–15; 29:1–6). Thus the seventh new moon is to the ordinary new moon as the seventh day is to the ordinary day (Num 28:3–10), thereby preserving the sabbatical cycle in the lunar calendar. However, this can be accredited as only an ancillary factor. More central is the reality that it is inextricably associated with the other festivals of the seventh month—the Day of Purgation and the Festival of Booths (see below). That this month is replete with festivals (ten days, fully one-third of the month) should not surprise. It is the only month that follows the harvests and precedes the rains. Still the common denominator that binds these festivals into a single unit is something else, as will be explained below.

It cannot be the proposition that, as a unit, these festivals celebrate the New Year. The voluminous bibliography on this theory is witness to the fact that there are nearly as many interpretations as interpreters: for example, there was no New Year festival (Pap 1933: 33, 92); New Year was the autumn festival (de Moor 1972: 1.11); the year began after the autumn festival (Wellhausen 1963: 108); the New Year began in the spring (as early as the eighth century B.C.E.; Kraus 1966: 45); it was at one time in the spring and the other in the autumn (Morgenstern 1962: 3.544–45); there were simultaneously two New Years each year, one in the spring and the other in the autumn (Kaufmann 1960: 306; Segal 1961: 78; Engnell 1969); and every harvest is essentially a New Year (Businck 1970: 1.122).

To be sure, the oldest biblical calendars set the autumn festival *běṣē't haššānâ* (Exod 23:16) or *těqûpat haššānâ* (Exod 34:22b), but the former has been rendered as "the beginning of the year" (e.g., Gray 1925: 300; Ginsberg 1982: 49) or "the end of the year" (Kutzch 1971) and the latter as "the turn (i.e., the midpoint) of the year (cf. Myers 1965: 136, on 2 Chr 24:23), based on a spring calendar. Clines (1974) has assembled many of the arguments that favor either an autumnal or a vernal New Year during the preexilic period and has judiciously concluded that there is no conclusive evidence for either position. Perhaps, the rabbinic view that there were several New Years during the year reflecting the agricultural, cultic, and civil needs of the people (*m. Roš. Haš.* 1:1; *Mek. Bo'* 1; cf. Jos. *Ant.* 1.81; *b. Roš. Haš.* 11b) is closer to the mark. So, indeed, the apparent autumnal calendars of Exod 23 and 34 (cf. Lev 25:9–12) as well as the Gezer (tenth-century B.C.E.) calendar, which begins with *yrḥw 'sp* (see NOTE on "threshing," 26:5), focus on the agricultural year, whereas the spring calendars of Lev 23, Num 28–29, and Deut 16 represent the official, cultic year set by the Temple, which would correspond with the civil year set by the palace (cf. Jer 36:22; 40:10; 41:8). It should not be forgotten that in first-millennium Uruk, two New Year festivals were celebrated, one in Nisan (the first month) and the other in Tashritu (the seventh month), and that both months qualified as "the beginning of the year" (*sag mu-an-na*). In addition, third- to second-millennium Ur also held two New Years annually (Klein 1992; M. Cohen 1993: 400–406) that can only be explained as the beginning of the agricultural year (the seventh month) and the beginning of the civil year (the first month; cf. van der Toorn 1989b: 331). Also, chronological considerations can lead to the conclusion that the royal year in Judah began in the spring, whereas the royal year in North Israel began in the autumn (Tadmor 1962: 267). Nor should it be forgotten that rather recently, in our time, multiple New Years (civil, legal, and fiscal) were normative in the Western world. Finally, it must frankly be stated that there exists not a single hint in all of Scripture that the first day of Tishri, the seventh month, was New Year's Day. Ezekiel calls for a semiannual purification of the Temple on Nisan 1 (Ezek 45:18–19) and, probably, on Tishri 1 (Ezek 45:20 LXX), but these are preparatory rites for the major festivals beginning on the fifteenth day of each month (Unleavened Bread and Booths, respectively; see below). In sum, the text must be taken as it is: it prescribes the rites for the first day of the seventh month, which falls at the end of the harvests (the old agricultural year) and before the onset of the rainy season (the beginning of the new agricultural year).

The pericope on the Festival of Alarm Blasts is brief (vv. 23–25) due to its derivation from Num 29:1–6:

Lev 23:23–25	Num 29:1–6
[*wayyĕdabbēr YHWH ʾel-mōšeh lē ʾmōr dabbēr ʾel-bĕnê yiśrāʾēl lē ʾmōr*] *bahōdeš haššĕbîʿî bĕ ʾehād lahōdeš yihyeh lākem* [*šabbātôn zikrôn*]*tĕrû ʿâ miqrāʾ qōdeš kol-mĕle ʾket ʿăbōdâ lōʾ ta ʿăśû* [*wĕhiqrabtem*] *ʾiššeh laYHWH*	(*û*)*bahōdeš haššĕbîʿî bĕ ʾehād lahōdeš miqrāʾ-qōdeš yihyeh lākem kol-mĕle ʾket ʿăbōdâ lōʾta ʿăśû (yôm) tĕrû ʿâ (yihyeh lākem wa ʿăśîtem ʿōlâ . . . lĕrêah nîhōah) ʾiššeh laYHWH*
[23][YHWH spoke to Moses saying: [24]Speak to the Israelites thus:] In the seventh month, on the first day of the month, you shall observe a rest, a sacred occasion, commemorated with alarm blasts. [25]You shall do no laborious work, and you shall present a food-gift to YHWH.	[1](And) in the seventh month, on the first day of the month, you shall observe a sacred occasion; you shall do no laborious work (You shall observe a day of) alarm blasts. [2](You shall sacrifice a burnt offering . . . [6b]of pleasant aroma) a food gift to YHWH.

The parentheses in the Numbers passage enclose the words deleted in Leviticus, and the brackets in Leviticus enclose its additions to the Numbers passage. The changes will be discussed in the commentary below. Lev 23 (H) takes for granted the character and rites of Num 29 (P), and its innovations rest with two new (for H) concepts: *sabbātôn* and *zikkārôn*.

24. *a rest. šabbātôn.* This term occurs in Exod 16:23; 35:2; 37:15; Lev 16:31; 23:3, 32; 25:4—all H (see Introduction I E). It stands alone, not in construct with the word *šabbāt*, only here and in v. 39, where it refers to the first and eighth days of the Festival of Booths. The absolute form also occurs in the pericope on the sabbatical year (25:5; cf. v. 4) but for structural, not semantic, reasons (see its NOTE), and it stands in reverse order with *šabbāt* in Exod 16:23, where, however, it has the same meaning as the normal construct chain.

Clearly, *šabbātôn* is an H creation. It is no accident that it is associated with those festivals on which *mĕleʾket ʿăbōdâ* 'laborious work' is prohibited, but not *kol-mĕlāʾkâ* 'all work'. In other words, *šabbātôn* implies a less stringent work prohibition than that which is enjoined for the sabbath (v. 3). I find it remarkable that the Targums preserve this distinction. For *šabbātôn*, *Tg. Onk.* reads *nĕyāḥāʾ* 'rest' (vv. 24, 39); *Tg. Ps.-J.*, *yômâʾ tābāʾ* 'holiday' (v. 24), *nĕyāḥāʾ* 'rest' (v. 39). However, a Genizah MS reads *šbt šbtn* 'complete rest' for the same verses (vv. 24, 39). In my judgment, *Tgs. Onk.* and *Ps.-J.* reflect an earlier practice that allowed lesser labors on this day, but the Genizah fragments, being mainly medieval in origin (Klein 1986: 1.xxxvii), reflect a later (and present) halakha, which rules that all festivals are as stringent as the sabbath except for the concession of food preparation (cf. Exod 12:16). True, it is missing in the prescriptions for two other "laborious work" festivals: Unleavened Bread (vv. 7–8) and First Wheat Offering (vv. 15–22). But its omission from the former may be deliberate, since its work prohibition may be severer than that of other "laborious work" festivals (Exod 12:16b; see NOTE on "laborious work," v. 7).

Its omission from the Festival of the Wheat Offering is, admittedly, inexplicable. Possibly, it may have fallen out of v. 21a. Its restoration would relieve the awkward syntax, which, as observed, is so uncharacteristic of H. The text would then read *ûqĕrāʾtem bĕ'eṣem hayyôm hazzeh miqrāʾ-qōdeš* [*šabbātôn*] *yihyeh lākem kol-mĕleʾket ʿăbōdâ lōʾ taʿăśû.* Thus v. 21a would consist of three coherent statements: "On that very day, you shall proclaim a sacred occasion; you shall observe [a rest]; you shall do no laborious work." For then, *miqrāʾ qōdeš* would be the cognate accusative of the verb *qārā* (as in vv. 2, 4, 37), restored *šabbātôn* would be the subject (stated or implied) of the verb *hāyâ* "be" (as in vv. 24, 39 [twice]), and it would be associated with the ban on *mĕleʾket ʿăbōdâ* 'laborious work' (vv. 25, 35, 36). Admittedly, there is no textual warrant for this conjecture in the Versions. At best, it can receive the rating of only attractive speculation.

commemorated with short blasts. zikrôn tĕrûʿâ. H changes its P *Vorlage* from *yôm tĕrûʿâ* to *zikrôn tĕrûʿâ*, literally "a reminder [by means of] of alarm blasts." For whom is the reminder, Israel or God?

The obvious clue to the answer is the one other verse that also associates the alarm blasts with a *zikkārôn* reminder:

ûbĕyôm śimḥatkem ûbĕmôʿădêkem ûbĕrāʾšê ḥodšêkem ûtĕqaʿtem baḥăṣōṣĕrōt ʿal ʿōlōtêkem wĕʿal zibḥê šalmêkem wĕhāyû lākem lĕzikkārôn lipnê ʾĕlōhêkem ʾănî YHWH ʾĕlōhêkem

And on your joyous occasions, your fixed festivals, and new moon days, you shall sound the trumpets over your burnt offerings and your sacrifices of well-being. They shall be a reminder of you before YHWH your God: I, YHWH, am your God. (Num 10:10)

Thus it is clear that on every **new moon** day (not just on the first day of the seventh month), **trumpets** should be blown as a **reminder**. Indeed, Philo (*Laws*

2.188), following the LXX, fuses both the *šôpar* and the *ḥăṣōṣĕrâ* (contra Belkin 1940: 212–13), renders both as *salpigx* 'trumpet', and calls the first day of Tishri *salpiggōn* 'trumpet feast'. In a lengthy essay, Finesinger (1931–32: 210) also concludes that this *tĕrû'â* was blown by the *ḥăṣōṣĕrâ*, conjecturing that this priestly instrument displaced the original, popular *šôpār*.

Before this parallel is uncritically accepted, however, caution is advised. This Numbers verse differs from our pericope in three significant ways:

1. The *zikkārôn* is "before YHWH," which, in this case, indubitably signifies that the reminder is to God, not to Israel (Dillmann and Ryssel 1897).
2. The instruments of blowing are specified as *ḥăṣōṣĕrôt*, whereas there is at least one other wind instrument, the *šôpār* (Ps 150:2) or *yôbēl* (Exod 19:13; cf. v. 16).
3. The word rendered "sound," *ûtĕqa'tem*, stems from a different root (*tq'*) than *tĕrû'â* (*rw'*).

The discussion of these differences follows.

As mentioned, a *zikkārôn lipnê YHWH* manifestly implies a reminder to God: the inscribed precious stones on the high priest's shoulders (Exod 28:12) and breast plate (Exod 28:29); the monetary contribution of Israel's soldiers to the Tabernacle (Exod 30:16; Num 31:54); and the trumpet sounds on Israel's new moons, festivals, and festive occasions (Num 10:10). Also, since the cereal offering of the suspected adulteress is presented to God (Num 5:15, 18), it, too, is a reminder to God of its sinful nature.

However, the incense pans of the Korahite rebels that form the outer plating of the altar are manifestly a reminder to the Israelites of the consequences of unauthorized access to the Deity (Num 17:5), and the stele set up by the Israelites after the miraculous fording of the Jordan as well as the annual celebration of the paschal rite by the descendants of the generation of the Exodus are a reminder to them and their progeny of YHWH's salvific acts (Exod 12:14; Josh 4:7).

Yet ambiguity remains concerning the goal of other reminders. The frontlets placed on the forehead, to be sure, are reinterpreted as a reminder to Israel of its redemption from Egypt (Exod 13:9, 16) or of YHWH's teachings (Deut 6:7–8; 11:18–19). But was not, perhaps, their original—and, for the people, their ongoing—function to act as amulets invoking divine protection (Weinfeld 1991: 341–43)? This ambiguity is indeed expressly demonstrable in the biblical text. In Deuteronomy, Israel is commanded: "Remember [*zĕkôr*] what Amalek did to you . . . you shall blot out the memory [*zēker*] of Amalek from under heaven" (Deut 25:17–19)—a *zikkārôn* unambiguously addressed to Israel. However, the earlier version of this command is entirely different: "Then YHWH said to Moses, 'Inscribe this in a document as a reminder [*zikkārôn*], and read it aloud to Joshua: I will utterly blot out the memory [*zēker*] of Amalek from under the heaven!' And Moses built an altar and named it Adonai-nissi. He said: 'Hand upon the throne of YHWH!' (presumably, a divine oath). YHWH will be at war with

Amalek throughout the ages" (Exod 17:14–16). There is no escaping the conclusion that in this version, the written reminder is meant for God. There is no indication that YHWH's victory over Amalek is dependent on Israel's initiative and action.

To judge by later Jewish liturgy for the first day of the seventh month (called Roʾš Haššānâ, New Year's Day in the religious calendar), the zikkārôn is a reminder to God of Israel (m. Roš. Haš. 4:5–6), "so that your remembrance may rise favorably before me; and through what? Through the šôpār" (b. Roš. Haš. 16a). For a further discussion of zikkārôn, see Fox (1974).

The second difference between Num 10:10 and Lev 23:24 is that the former mentions a specific instrument, ḥăṣōṣĕrâ, and mandates that it be employed solely by the priests (Num 10:8). Our pericope, however, mentions neither qualification (contra Knohl [1995: 36], who claims that the shofar was blown by priests). The matter would rest there were it not for the additional evidence supplied by the Psalms: tiqʿû baḥōdeš šôpār bakkeseh lĕyôm ḥaggēnû 'Blow the shofar on the new moon, on the full moon for our pilgrimage day' (Ps 81:4). At once it can be noted that the command is addressed to all of Israel, not to the priests (similarly, harnînû 'sing joyously', hārîʿû 'raise a shout', v. 2; śĕʾû-zimrâ 'take up the song', ûtĕnû-ṭōp 'sound the timbrel', v. 3). Furthermore, the horn is specified as the šôpār, not the ḥăṣōṣĕrâ. Finally, the new moon is followed by a pilgrimage day at full moon—that is, the fifteenth of the month. Theoretically, this psalm could be referring to the first month, Nisan, which also celebrates a pilgrimage day (the Festival of Unleavened Bread) at the full moon. However, the fact that the new moon of Nisan is not a special day, and the unspecified ḥaggēnû 'our pilgrimage' more likely fits the description of the Festival of Booths and not the Festival of Unleavened Bread (see INTRODUCTION to vv. 33–36), tips the scales in favor of the seventh month.

The rabbis (Sipra Emor, par. 11:6) come to the same conclusion on the basis of another verse: wĕhaʿăbartā šôpar tĕrûʿâ baḥōdeš haššĕbîʿî bĕʿāśôr laḥōdeš bĕyôm hakkippurîm taʿăbîrû šôpār bekol-ʾarṣĕkem 'You shall sound the shofar loud; in the seventh month, on the tenth day of the month—the Day of Purgation—you shall have the horn sounded throughout your land' (25:9; for the rendering of tĕrûʿâ as "loud," see its NOTE). The fact that on the tenth day of the seventh month, it is explicitly mandated that the shofar be blown throughout the land makes it highly plausible that the rabbis are right—the shofar is the instrument that must be used for all the festivals of the seventh month, on the first, tenth, and fifteenth days. Wessely (1846) adds a final consideration: the ḥăṣōṣĕrâ is sounded by the priests during the sacrificial service (Num 10:9), whereas the "alarm blasts" of our verse precede and are separated from any mention of sacrifices. For the identification and function of both the ḥăṣōṣĕrâ and the šôpār, see Milgrom (1990a: 372–73).

The third and final difference between Num 10:10 and Lev 23:24 is their different words for "blast": ûtĕqaʿtem (verbal noun tĕqîʿâ) and tĕrûʿâ, respectively. The pericope of Num 10:1–10 makes it absolutely clear that there is a sharp distinction between them. The Israelite camp is assembled by the tĕqîʿâ (vv. 3–4);

indeed, the priests are warned that for this purpose the *těrû ʿâ* is not to be used (v. 7). The *těrû ʿâ*, however, is used for breaking camp (vv. 5–6; see also LXX on v. 6). But especially relevant is v. 9: "When you are at war in your land against an aggressor who attacks you, you shall sound alarm blasts [*wahărē ʿōtem*] on the trumpets, that you may be remembered [*wěnizkartem*] before YHWH your God and be delivered from your enemies." Thus the *těrû ʿâ* functions as a battle cry (cf. Jer 4:19; Amos 1:14). It both rouses the people to move from an encamped peaceful position into a mobile battle formation and functions as a call for divine help. Indeed, the trumpets taken into the Midianite war are actually called "the trumpets of *těrû ʿâ*" (Num 31:6; cf. 2 Chr 13:12). On the basis of this biblical precedent, the Dead Sea War Scroll prescribes trumpets to be used *BHPTḤ ŠʿRY HMLḤMH LṢʾT* 'when the battle intervals open (for skirmishers) to go forth', which bear the inscription *ZKRWN NQM BMWʿD ʾL* 'vengeful remembrance at the appointed time of God' (1QM 3:1–11; cf. Num 31:3). Rabbinic tradition may, therefore, be correct in defining the *těqî ʿâ* as equivalent in length to three *těrû ʿâ* sounds (*m. Roš. Haš.* 4:9), thereby justifying the translation "long blasts" for the former and "short blasts" for the latter (see also 1QM 8:7, 12). In sum, the *terû ʿâ* is a signal of alarm. Indeed, the *Tgs.* faithfully echo this meaning when they render *těrû ʿâ* in this verse (and in Num 29:1) as *yabbābāʾ* 'wailing' (cf. *m. Roš. Haš.* 4:9; Judg 5:28). The question then remains: Why is the call of alarm sounded on the first day of the seventh month? Rabbinic tradition cites a number of reasons:

1. As instanced by the use of the shofar in royal coronations (e.g., 1 Kgs 1:39), it is a reminder of the kingdom of God (*Sipra* Emor, par. 11:2–6; *b. Roš. Haš.* 16a; Ibn Ezra, Sforno, Abravanel). This theory undoubtedly influenced Mowinckel (1962: 1.120–92) to advance the (unsubstantiated) suggestion that there existed in preexilic Israel an autumn festival on which God was "enthroned." However, the shofar call in Solomon's coronation, cited above, is the *teqî ʿâ*, not the *těrû ʿâ*, and the verb *hēriaʿ* and its nominal form *těrû ʿâ* cited by Mowinckel from the psalms means "shout" by humans, not by a horn (Pss 47:2, 6; 95:2; 98:6; Num 23:21; cf. Josh 6:5, 10, 16, 20). Incidentally, Ehrlich's (1908) claim that the verb used with the shofar is *tāqaʿ* not *hēriaʿ*, based on *bitěrû ʿâ ûběqôl šôpār* (2 Sam 6:15; Amos 2:2; Zeph 1:16), is erroneous since *těrû ʿâ* in this expression means "*vocal* shouting."

2. On Rosh Hashana, the fate of the world is decided (*m. Roš. Haš.* 1:2; cf. Ramban). This view was certainly maintained in the ancient Near East. A Hittite text reads, "For the Weather-god, the mighty festival of the beginning of the year. . . . Pronounce (the life of) the king and the queen. Pronounce (the life of) heaven and earth, (pronounce the life of) the crops" (Otten 1956). A neo-Babylonian text is more explicit: "In Ubšukina the Dais of the Fates [*parak šimāti*] at the beginning of the year . . . the fate of my life they decree there" (Langdon 1912: 126, cited in Weinfeld 1983a: 117). Nonetheless, Rosh Hashana is not a dour day. Nehemiah enjoins his people: "Go, eat choice foods and drink sweet drinks and send portions to whoever has nothing prepared, for the day is holy to YHWH. Do not be sad, for your rejoicing in YHWH is the source of your

strength" (Neh 8:10). Besides, neither Philo nor Josephus mentions this day as a time of judgment. Philo (*Laws* 2.188, 192) recommends extending gratitude to God for endowing Israel with Torah, prosperity, and peace, and for Josephus (*Ant.* 3.d239), it seems, Rosh Hashana holds no special significance except for its prescribed sacrifices. Thus it must be concluded that in biblical times, despite the Mesopotamian antecedents, the first day of the seventh month was not commemorated as a day of judgment. (The subsequent celebration in the Jewish New Year liturgy as commemorating the birthday of the world and the annual determination of the fate of every human being may have been influenced by the Babylonian New Year festival [Klein 1992], but not before the Babylonian Exile.)

3. The purpose of the *terû'â* is to arouse the deity's attention: "R. Josiah said: It is written, 'Happy is the people that know the sound of *terû'â*.' (Ps 89:16). But do not the nations of the world know how to sound the *terû'â*? What a host of horns they have! What a host of *bucinae* (horns) they have! What a host of trumpets they have! Yet you say, 'Happy is the people that know the sound of *terû'â*!' It can only mean that they know to win over their Creator with the *terû'â*" (*Lev. Rab.* 29:4). Thus the rabbis credit the shofar as an instrument of prayer, one that alerts God to Israel's needs. But what are Israel's pressing needs that surface on the first day of the seventh month? The mishna Ta'anit, in my opinion, strikes the mark. The twenty mishnayot that compose *m. Ta'an.* 1:1–3:3 deal with the sounding of the shofar at the assembly of a community engaged in a fast to implore God for rain. This will be discussed in detail in the NOTE on "you shall rejoice before YHWH your God," v. 40. Here suffice it to say that all three festivals of the seventh month—the *terû'â* call on the first day, the fast day on the tenth, and the circumambulation of the altar with waving fronds and other vegetation for seven days, from the fifteenth through the twenty-second—as well as the tradition of a water libation offered during these days combine into a single-minded goal: to beseech God for adequate and timely rain in the forthcoming agricultural year.

The "alarm blasts" for rain do not imply a somber celebration. For example, the Feast of Booths is the most joyous festival of all despite its central focus on rituals for rain. Thus Ezra and Nehemiah urge the people: "Go, eat choice foods and drink sweet drinks and send portions to whoever has nothing prepared, for the (New Year) day is holy to YHWH. Do not be sad, for your rejoicing in YHWH is the source of your strength" (Neh 8:10). These instructions echo those issued for the New Year celebration among the Hittites (Otten 1956), an indication that the joyous nature of the New Year was nigh universal. It was uniquely in Israel, however, that the anticipatory note for the forthcoming rains was added. The alarm blasts, then, served to warn the people that in the midst of their rejoicing over the conclusion of the agricultural season just passed they should not forget that in the days ahead they should implore God's mercy for adequate rain for the new season.

you shall observe a rest, a sacred occasion. yihyeh lākem šabbātôn . . . miqrāʾ-qōdeš. The linkage of *yihyeh lākem* with *šabbātôn* rather than with *miqrāʾ-qōdeš* provides grounds for the conjectured restoration of *šabbātôn* between *miqrā'- qōdeš* and *yihyeh lākem* in v. 21a.

25. *and you shall present a food gift to YHWH. wĕhiqrabtem 'iššeh laYHWH.* Once again, the text resorts to H's "compare," referring to the sacrifices enumerated in Num 29:1–6. It rightfully occasions surprise that the *mûsāp*, the additional burnt sacrifices specified for this day—one bull, one ram, and seven lambs—are fewer in number than those required for an ordinary new moon— *two bulls*, one ram, and seven lambs (Num 28:11). It should be noted that the same minimal series is also mandated for the Day of Purgation (Num 29:8) and the *'ăṣeret* day following the Festival of Booths (Num 29:36). This coincidence leaves room for speculating that these three festival days are directed toward a common goal, which will be discussed in the NOTE on "you shall rejoice before YHWH," v. 40.

Vv. 26–32. The Day of Purgation

Once again, H constructs its text on the basis of its Numbers prototype, but this time it appends a large section of its own:

<table>
<tr><td>

Num 29:7–11

^{7}*(û)be 'āśôr lahōdeš haššĕbî'î hazzeh miqrā'- qōdeš yihyeh lākem wĕ'innîtem 'et-napšōtêkem kol-mĕ'lā'kâ lō' ta'ăśû* ^{8}*wĕhiqrabtem ('ōlâ) laYHWH (. . .)*^{12}

</td><td>

Lev 23:26–32

^{26}[*wayyĕdabbēr YHWH 'el-mōšeh lē'mōr* ^{27}'*ak*]*be 'āśôr lahōdeš haššĕbî'î hazzeh* [*yôm hakkippurîm hû'*] *miqrā'- qōdeš yihyeh lākem wĕ 'innîtem 'et-napšōtêkem wĕhiqrabtem* ['iššeh] *laYHWH* ^{28}[wĕ] *kol-mĕlā'kâ lō' ta'ăśû* [. . .]^{33}

</td></tr>
<tr><td>

^{7}(And) the tenth day of this seventh month shall be a sacred occasion for you; you shall practice self-denial; you shall do no work; ^{8}and you shall offer (a burnt offering) to YHWH (. . .)^{12}

</td><td>

^{26}[YHWH spoke to Moses, saying: ^{27}Mark,] the tenth day of this seventh month [is the Day of Purgation.] It shall be a sacred occasion for you; you shall practice self-denial; and you shall offer [a food gift] to YHWH; ^{28}[and] you shall do no work [. . .]^{33}

</td></tr>
</table>

The parentheses in the Numbers passage enclose the words deleted in Leviticus, and the brackets in Leviticus enclose its additions to the Numbers passage. The long passage detailing the sacrifices (Num 29:8–11) is characteristically encapsulated by the word *'iššeh* 'food gift'. The long and unique addition (vv. 28aβ–32), however, makes sense only when it is realized that Lev 23 is also interested in summarizing the day-long purgation rites for the sanctuary detailed in Lev chap. 16. In particular, as will be shown below, it wishes to supplement its own appendix to Lev 16 (vv. 29–34a). First, it should be noted that H's summary of Num 29 (vv. 26–28aα) is blended with its comment of Lev 16 (vv.

28aβ–32) to form an artfully constructed introversion (Galbiati 1956: 53–54; di Marco 1975: 41):

A ʾak beʿāśôr laḥōdeš haššěbîʿî hazzeh yôm hakkippurîm hûʾ miqrāʾ-qōdeš
   yihyeh lākem
   B wěʿinnîtem ʾet-napšōtêkem wěhiqrabtem ʾiššeh laYHWH (v. 27)
      C wěkol-mělāʾkâ lōʾ taʿăśû běʿeṣem hayyôm hazzeh kî yôm kippurîm
         hûʾ lěkappēr ʿălêkem lipnê YHWH ʾělōhêkem (v. 28)
         D kî kol-hannepeš ʾăšer lōʾ-těʿunneh běʿeṣem hayyôm hazzeh
            wěnikrětā mēʿammêhā (v. 29)
         D′ wěkol-hannepeš ʾăšer taʿăśeh kol-mělāʾkâ běʿeṣem hayyôm hazzeh
            wěhaʾăbadtî ʾet-hannepeš hahûʾ miqqereb ʿammâ (v. 30)
      C′ kol-mělāʾkâ lōʾ taʿăśû ḥuqqat ʿōlām lědōrōtêkem běkol-môšěbōtêkem
         (v. 31)
   B′ šabbat šabbātôn hûʾ lākem wěʿinnîtem ʾet-napšōtêkem
A′ bětišʿâ laḥōdeš bāʿereb mēʿereb ʿad-ʿereb tišbětû šabbatkem (v. 32)

The key injunctions for the Day of Purgation, fasting and total abstention from work, are contained both in the center (DD′) and in its flanks (BB′ and CC′). Thus the threefold mention of fasting and working is not haphazard, but essential to this consummately designed structure. However, there are several oddities:

1. The date is given twice (AA′), but A′ qualifies A.
2. The emphasis of the center (DD′) is on the mortal penalty for violating the injunctions to fast and abstain from work, whereas the function of the day, to effect purgation on behalf of the people, appears only as a casual comment (C).
3. Even the penalties (DD′) are not equivalent: working (D) appears as a graver violation than not fasting (D′).

On the surface, these differences seem inconsequential. But a comparison of this structure with a similar one that H devised in its supplement to chap. 16 (vv. 29–31) will project their significance. I shall limit myself to the key phrases:

A wěhāyětā lākem lěḥuqqat ʿōlām . . .
   B těʿannû . . . ʾet-napšōtêkem
      C wěkol-mělāʾkâ lōʾ taʿăśû . . . (v. 29)
         X kî bayyôm hazzeh yěkappēr ʿălêkem lěṭahēr ʾetkem mikkōl
            ḥaṭṭōʾtêkem lipnê YHWH tiṭhārû (v. 30)
      C′ šabbat šabbātôn hîʾ lākem
   B′ wěʿinnîtem ʾet-napšōtêkem
A′ ḥuqqat ʿōlām (v. 31)

The full implication of this introversion is discussed in vol. 1.1057–58. That it is the handiwork of H is demonstrated in vol. 1.62, 1064–65. Here I wish to discuss only the differences between 23:26–32 and 16:29–31.

1. The date given for the Day of Purgation in 16:29, the tenth of the seventh month, is repeated in 23:27 (A), but has to be qualified as no ordinary day (i.e., from sunrise to sunrise) but from the evening before, which is still part of the ninth day until the evening of the tenth—that is, up to half of the tenth day (23:32 [A']). See the discussion in the NOTE on v. 32.

2. The function of the day has already been dealt with at length in chap. 16, and duly emphasized by the center of the structure in 16:29–31: to effect purgation for the people (v. 30 [X]). Hence it can be relegated as an aside in the structure of 23:27–32, in which the center is occupied by the penalties for non-compliance (vv. 29–30 [DD']), a subject that is absent from all of chap. 16.

3. The punishment for working on this day is indeed severer than that decreed for not fasting. See the discussion in the NOTE on v. 30.

Thus it can be seen that H's extraordinary expansion of its summation of Num 29:7–11 is a refinement of and supplementation to 16:29–31. For detailed discussion of the purgation rites and their significance, see vol. 1.1009–84.

The ballooning of P is clearly due to the threefold repetition of the command to fast and abstain from work. Why was it necessary? The answer lies in H's premise that sins pollute not only the sanctuary (P's thesis), but also the sinners themselves, and simultaneously with the purgation of the sanctuary, they must purge themselves. P's theology of sin, it will be recalled (vol. 1.254–61), postulates that the sinner is unpolluted by his sin, but he pollutes the sanctuary. H disagrees with P and shifts the emphasis on the Day of Purgation from Israel's sanctuary to Israel itself: the quintessence of this day is self-purgation.

Knohl (1995: 32–34, 195–96), on the basis of Num 29:7, maintains that the tenth day of the seventh month initially was a fast day, which subsequently was incorporated by H into the sanctuary purgation rite. I disagree. As I have argued from both biblical and rabbinic evidence (vol. 1.1066–67), the fast day was originally dissociated from the tenth day of the seventh month, which was a day of unbridled joy. H, however, added to this day the purgation rite of the Temple and its attendant requirement of fasting (16:31) so that the high priest's confession of the sins of *all of Israel* would be efficacious.

26. **YHWH** *spoke to Moses, saying.* This introductory formula lacks the customary ending: *dabbēr 'el-bĕnê yiśrā'ēl lē'mōr* 'speak to the Israelites thus' to limit the name "Israel" to seven times (vv. 2, 10, 24, 34, 42, 43, 44) in this chapter (M. Hildenbrand).

27. *However. 'ak.* A particle favored by H (Exod 12:15, 16; 31:13; Lev 21:23; 23:27, 39; 27:26, 28), it (contra Knohl 1987: 91, n. 77) is also frequently attested in P (Gen 9:4; Lev 11:4, 21, 36; Num 1:49; 18:3, 15, 17; 26:55; 31:22, 23; 36:6). According to the rabbis, its function is to exclude (*Gen. Rab.* 1:14). Thus the Targums render it "however," justified by its contrast with the preceding Festival of Alarm Blasts, which is a day of rejoicing (cf. Neh. 8:10; Ibn Ezra).

Other renderings are "indeed" (Ramban), "moreover" (Levine 1989), "mark" (*NJPS*), and "now" (*NRSV*). All can be justified because of the protean range of this particle. The Targums' rendering, I believe, is the most accurate.

the tenth day. It was New Year's Day for the jubilee (25:9–10: Ezek 40:1, according to the Karaites). Its connection with the festivals of the first and fifteenth to the twenty-second days of the month will be discussed in the NOTE on "You shall rejoice before YHWH," v. 40.

the Day of Purgation. yôm hakkippūrîm. This name is found only here and in 25:9. Knohl (1987: 91) suggests that the plural refers to both the purgation and the fasting aspects of this day. However, the plural is also used in *ḥaṭṭaʾt hakkippurîm* in H's *Vorlage*, Num 29:11 (P), as well as in Exod 29:36; 30:10, referring to the sacrificial purgation of the sanctuary. Thus the plural should be understood as a superlative "full atonement" (Snaith 1967) or "complete purgation" (the plural of intensification, GKC § 124e). Note its use in *kesep hakkippūrîm* 'ransom money' (Exod 30:16) and *ʾēl hakkippūrîm* 'the atonement ram', or *ʾāšām* (Num 5:8).

for you. lākem. For you alone (Ibn Ezra). Ostensibly, Ibn Ezra's rendering is correct, since this phrase is followed by the fasting injunction, and, as discussed in the NOTE on 16:29 (vol. 1.1055–56), a cogent argument can be built for exempting the *gēr*, the resident alien, from the requirement to fast (a performative commandment), but not from the prohibition against working (a prohibitive commandment; for the distinction, see Milgrom 1982b). However, *lākem* 'for you' occurs again in this pericope attached to *šabbat šabbātôn* 'complete rest' (v. 32)—that is, no work is allowed—and surely the *gēr* falls under the injunction to abstain from work. Thus it must be concluded that H simply did not transfer its concern for the *gēr* from 16:29 to Lev 23.

This apparent ambivalence toward the *gēr* is reflected in the larger question of whether the Yom Kippur sanctuary rites effect purgation for the *gēr* as well as for the Israelite. Judging by H's many statements on this subject, the answer is mainly in the negative. Note that the object of *kippēr* is *běnê yiśrāʾēl* 'the Israelites' (16:34a), *ʿălêkem* 'on your (Israel's) behalf' (16:30), *ʿam haqqāhāl* 'the people of the congregation' (16:33), and *qěhal ʿădat yiśrāʾēl* 'the Israelite community' (Num 14:5; that the *gēr* is not included in the *qāhāl*, see Num 15:15). And if this argument is countered by the inclusion of the *gēr* in communal forgiveness granted by God for inadvertent violations (Num 15:26), it should be pointed out that the verb there is *sālaḥ*, not *kippēr*; that is, God extends forgiveness (rather, "reconciliation"; see Milgrom 1981a) to the *gēr*, but he does not purge the sanctuary on his behalf.

However, this conclusion is flatly contradicted by H's insistence that the individual *gēr*, no differently from the Israelite, who commits an inadvertent violation must bring a purification offering to the sanctuary *lěkappēr ʿālāyw* 'to effect purgation on his behalf' (Num 15:28–29), and the advertent violator is punished with *kārēt*, again no differently from the Israelite (Num 15:30). Hence the question remains: Doesn't the sanctuary require that its annual purgation by the high priest also be for the advertent sins of the *gēr*? Or do these H texts imply that whereas the *inadvertent* violations of the individual *gēr* do pollute the sanctuary (requiring its purgation by the violation), his *advertent* violations do not affect the sanctuary, and, hence, Yom Kippur is not relevant to the *gēr*.

The latter distinction receives support from the case of the corpse-contaminated person: the affected *gēr* must undergo purification (Num 19:10), but only the Israelite who fails to purify himself pollutes the sanctuary (Num 19:13, 20; that these verses have been edited by H, see Knohl 1993: 89). Thus the *gēr* who is an advertent violator—he deliberately neglects to purify himself—has no impact on the sanctuary. This confirms the conclusions drawn from H's texts on Yom Kippur (Lev 16:29–34; 23:27–32): this day's rites purge the sanctuary of the advertent sins of Israel but not those of the *gēr* because they have no impact on the sanctuary. If so, I must admit that I am at a loss to explain the theology behind this distinction: the inadvertent violations of the *gēr* pollute the sanctuary, but his advertent violations do not. Or, as a last resort, shall we say that H is just as imprecise and inconsistent in theology as in terminology?

you shall afflict yourselves. wě'innîtem 'et-napšōtêkem, literally "you shall deprive your throats" (16:29, 31; 23:27, 29; Num 30:14; Isa 58:3). This refers to the injunction that you shall fast, as shown by its antonym *hiśbîaʿ nepeš* 'feed', literally "satisfy the throat" (Isa 58:10–11; Ps 107:9; Schwartz 1991: 41, n. 3). But this idiom means more than fasting, as indicated by its occurrence in Num 30:14; Ps 35:13; Dan 10:12 (see vol. 1.1054).

That vv. 27–28a are copied from their P *Vorlage* (Num 29:7) is evidenced by the insertion of this clause in both texts between the standard formula *miqrā'-qōdeš yihyeh lākem* 'it shall be a sacred occasion for you' and *kol-mělā'kâ / -mēle'ket ʿăbōdâ lō' taʿăśû* 'you shall do no work / laborious work' (for the unbroken formula, see vv. 8a, 21, 24bγ–25a; Num 28:18, 26b; 29:1, 12). Once the formula was broken, the clause *wěhiqrabtem 'iššeh laYHWH* was also inserted, as in v. 36, so as not to leave it hanging by itself, as in v. 25. Note that in the cases where the latter clause follows the formula, it is connected to multiple days (e.g., vv. 8, 36) or a list of sacrifices (Num 28:19, 27; 29:2, 36).

and you shall offer a food gift to YHWH. wěhiqrabtem 'iššeh laYHWH. As recognized by Hoffmann (1953), this phrase refers solely to Num 29, whereas v. 28b refers to Lev 16. It should be noted, however, that in Num 29, the prohibition against working precedes the list of sacrifices (v. 7b); here, it follows (v. 28a) because it will be expanded (v. 28b) and repeated (vv. 30, 31). Thus combining the sacrifices of Num 29 and Lev 16 yields the following totals: burnt offerings: one bull, three rams, and nine lambs; purification offerings: one bull and two he-goats (not counting the scapegoat).

28. *you shall do no work. wěkol-mělā'kâ lō' taʿăśû.* This is precisely the same wording as in the sabbath pericope (v. 3aβ), proving that the Day of Purgation ranks equally with the sabbath in importance (but see NOTES on vv. 29–30). The full formula (e.g., v. 7) is split (cf. v. 27aβ) so that this (second half) can form an inclusion with v. 31a (cf. CC′ in the diagram [above]).

on that very day. bě'eṣem hayyôm hazzeh. Ramban provides two meanings for *bě'eṣem: gûp* 'body, essence' (Exod 24:10) and, following *Tg. Onq., běqeren yômā' hādên* 'by the strength of the day' (*Sipra* Emor 14:1; Y. Deut. 5:17; Ps 68:36; Job 21:23), related to *'eṣem* 'bone' (cf. Beyse 1987).

This expression is found with only the *ʿōmer* offering (v. 14), the Feast of Weeks (v. 21), and the Day of Purgation (v. 28), which leads Ramban to deduce that it implies the extra power of these days: the *ʿōmer* releases the barley crop for profane use even without the required sacrifices (vv. 12–13); the Feast of Weeks does the same for the wheat crop independently of the mandated counting (vv. 15–16) and sacrifices (vv. 17–19); and the Day of Purgation itself effects atonement separately from the sanctuary rites (cf. *m. Yoma* 8:8–9; *m. Šebu.* 1:2–6). This halakhic interpretation, however, appears forced. The chances are that if the other festivals—Unleavened Bread, Warning Blasts, and Booths—had reason to use the words *hayyôm hazzeh* 'this day', it would also have added *bĕ'eṣem*. In other words, the expression is idiomatic, a stylistic flourish of H.

a purgation day. *yôm kippūrîm.* The lack of the definite article (contrast v. 27 and 25:9) is not accidental. Its function is to have the reader focus on what follows: "to effect purgation on your behalf before YHWH your God." Herein H provides the rationale for the fast day absent in its P's *Vorlage* (Num 29:7–11). Undoubtedly, the purgation of the sanctuary is presumed, but H's emphasis is on the purgation of the people through its exercise of self-denial and abstention from total work, as explicitly and repeatedly stated in the following verses.

29. *afflict himself.* *tĕ'unneh.* This is the only occurrence of the passive of *'nh.* Perhaps the *Pu'al* has reflexive force (unrecognized by the grammars, but see Siebesma 1991), indicating "afflict himself." Or alternatively, it may be a vestige of an ancient imperfect passive *Qal* (e.g., 11:35, 38; Isa 1:20).

will be cut off from his kin. *wĕnikrĕtâ mē'ammêhā.* The punishment of *kārēt* for not practicing self-denial (and for working, v. 30) is not mentioned in chap. 16. Conversely, the *kārēt* penalty for eating leavened bread during the Festival of Unleavened Bread is not mentioned in chap. 23 because it is given earlier in Exod 12:15. In this respect, the pericopes on the Day of Purgation resemble those of illicit sexual unions: chap. 20 states the penalty for violating the prohibitions of chap. 18. The absence of penalties from the sabbath pericope, however, can be explained on other grounds (see INTRODUCTION to vv. 1–3).

The presumed parity between the severity of the sabbath and that of the Day of Purgation breaks down at this juncture. It is true that both are called *šabbat šabbātôn,* days of "complete rest," when absolutely no work is permitted (cf. v. 3 with vv. 31–32), and, ostensibly, the Day of Purgation has a slight edge on the degree of severity because of its requirement to practice self-denial. It, however, turns out that the sabbath is severer because of the differential in penalties: although both days invoke the *kārēt* for their violation, the sabbath violator also incurs the death penalty by man, carried out by the court (*môt yûmat,* Exod 31:14–15; Num 15:32–36), which means that he is immediately put to death as well as being punished with the excision of his line (see NOTE on "and cut him off," 20:3, and vol. 1.460). Thus since the severity of a law is determined by the penalty for its violation, the sabbath must be adjudged severer than the Day of Purgation. For another reason, see the NOTE on "your sabbath," v. 32, and for the discussion on the probable meaning of *kārēt,* see vol. 1.457–61.

30. *I will cause that person to perish.* *wĕha'ăbadtî.* In priestly texts, the verb *'ābad* is found in the *Qal* (26:38; Num 17:27 [twice]), in the *Pi'el* (Num 33:52), and in the *Hip'il* (Lev 23:30). The LXX renders *apoleîtai* '(that soul) will perish', using a passive to avoid an anthropomorphism, though it has no such qualms

in rendering *wěhikratti* 'I (God) will cut off' (e.g., 17:10; 20:3, 5, 6) or in rendering *wěha'ăbadti* 'I will destroy' elsewhere (e.g., Ezek 25:7, 16; 30:13; 32:13; Ob 8; Zeph 2:5; cf. Deut 9:3). Perhaps, the LXX is reluctant to use the verb *he'ĕbîd*, which implies *physical* destruction for the *psychē* 'soul'.

There is a subtle difference in the penalties for violating the injunctions of the Day of Purgation. "I will cause that person to perish" (*wěha'ăbadtî*) implies the Deity's immediate intervention (Ibn Ezra), perhaps because working is a public violation, whereas not fasting (i.e., eating) is done in the privacy of one's home. This is another reason (in addition to the fact that working violates a prohibitive commandment) why the *gēr* may be liable for punishment only for working, but not for eating (vol. 1.1054–56).

among his people. miqqereb 'ammah. The Sam. correctly reads *mē'ammêhā* 'his kinspeople'. As explained in the NOTE on 17:10, H constantly fudges the precision of the terminology of P, which never uses the singular *'am* 'people' for the *kārēt* penalty. It would seem that H's frequent use of the preposition *miqqereb* 'from among' was responsible for the reduction of *'ammîm* to *'am* 'people' (cf. 17:4, 10; 18:29; 20:3, 5, 6, 18; 23:30; Num 15:30), but even here H is inconsistent (cf. Exod 31:15).

31. *in all your settlements. bekōl mōšbōtêkem.* The self-denial and work injunctions apply everywhere. It is not a *ḥag*: people are at home, not at the sanctuary (J. Ludlow). On the omission of this phrase in some of the festival pericopes, see the the NOTE on v. 22.

32. *and you shall afflict yourselves.* According to *Tgs. Ps.-J.* and *Yer.,* the purpose of this third mention of the self-denial injunction is to stress that it commences the previous evening. However, as we have seen (see INTRODUCTION to vv. 26–32), it is needed because it is an essential element in the pericope's structure. Thus it cannot be "an editorial addition" (Knohl 1995: 20). Besides the Masoretic *'atnaḥ* under *napšōtêkem* correctly separates this injunction from the time designation.

Gerstenberger's (1996: 353) assertion that "work-free days of penitential rites in the midst of harvest activities, possibly even under the threat of death . . . [proves that the writer] is no longer earning his own keep through agriculture" is undermined by the fact that on this one day, the tenth of the seventh month, the harvest season is virtually over.

on the ninth day of the month at evening. This is proof that the biblical day continued through the night until the following morning (see below).

from evening to evening. As discussed in the NOTE on "the fourteenth day of the month," v. 5—and as recognized by Rashbam on this verse—the biblical day began at dawn. Thus the Day of Purgation, like the Festival of Unleavened Bread (see NOTE on "the fourteenth day of the month, v. 5), is a pointed exception—one that is not difficult to fathom. I find unconvincing Knohl's (1995: 20) rationale that it "intended to guard the proper observance of the holy day by specifying the time of its onset." Rather, its more practical, hence obvious, purpose is to limit the fast to twenty-four hours. Otherwise, the Israelite would begin to fast on the ninth day at bedtime and not break his or her fast until the morning of the eleventh—a period of thirty-six hours.

V. 32 clearly amends v. 27, which prescribes the fast day for the tenth day of the month. V. 32, however, should not be considered a change introduced by a later H tradent. Rather, since v. 27 is built on its P prototype (Num 29:7; see INTRODUCTION to vv. 26–32), v. 32 reflects an alteration of P, not of H. V. 32, therefore, is not an addition to the pericope, but is an integral part of it.

Talmon (1994) has put forth the claim that this verse is the addition of a late H tradent and reflects the changeover from a solar day, beginning at sunrise, to a lunar day, beginning at nightfall. He holds a similar verdict for Exod 12:18, which states that the Festival of Unleavened Bread begins and ends at nightfall (see NOTE on v. 5). His proposal should be dismissed out of hand. On structural grounds alone, it can be seen that v. 32 is an integral part of the pericope, vv. 26–32; remove it, and the structure collapses (see also above). As demonstrated (see INTRODUCTION to vv. 26–32), this pericope is entirely the handiwork of H, which constructs its text by basing it on Num 29:7–11 (P) and by taking into account an earlier H passage, Lev 16:29–34a.

Moreover, Talmon's (1994) claim is illogical. He correctly criticizes the established rabbinic position that reasons analogically that since the Festivals of Unleavened Bread and Day of Purgation are specified to begin in the evening, all other festivals (and days) also begin in the evening. Then, however, he follows the same analogous reasoning, only slightly altered: the change to the day beginning in the evening, reflected by the addition of this statement to the Festivals of Unleavened Bread and Day of Purgation, holds for the rest of festivals (and days). But the glaring question remains unanswered: Why didn't this alleged H tradent also insert this change into the other festival pericopes or, rather, why were the pericopes on the Unleavened Bread and Day of Purgation chosen and not any other festival to mark this change? At least, according to the reasoning presented above, unique circumstances attended these two festivals that warranted their beginning on the preceding evening. But according to Talmon's proposal, the choice was entirely haphazard, and without any supporting evidence, we must presume that the change in the day's beginning holds equally for every day in the year.

Unfortunately, there is no evidence that can pinpoint the time when the transition from a sunrise day to a sunset day took place (see NOTE on "the fourteenth day of the month," v. 5).

your sabbath. šabbatkem. But not the Lord's sabbath (Ibn Ezra). This distinction explains why the Day of Purgation can be shifted to begin the previous evening: it is not YHWH's sabbath (v. 3), which begins at daybreak. This distinction provides another reason why the sabbath day is superior to the Day of Purgation: it inheres in creation (Gen 2:1–3) because it became sanctified as YHWH's day of rest (Exod 20:11), whereas the "complete rest" of the Day of Purgation was ordained subsequently, for Israel's benefit, to purge the people and its sanctuary from their sins that YHWH might continue to abide in their midst.

Tg. Ps.-J. and a Genizah MS (Klein 1986) add the sentence "and celebrate the times of your fixed festivals in joy." I would suggest that its motivation stems from the injunction for the Festival of Booths "and you shall rejoice before YHWH your God seven days" (v. 40b). Lest one think that the other festivals are not joyous occasions, the Palestinian Targums insert this reminder at the close of their enumeration.

Vv. 33–36a. The Festival of Booths

This H text, as all the others in this chapter, presumes the existence and authority of the equivalent prescriptions in the P text of Num 28–29, namely, 29:12–38. Note the similarity of the opening lines (the parallel words are in bold-face).

Num 29

²⁹:¹²*ûbaḥămiššâ ʿāśār yôm laḥōdeš haššĕbîʿî miqrāʾ-qōdeš yihyeh lākem kol-mĕleʾket ʿăbōdâ lōʾ taʿăśû wĕhaggōtem* **ḥag laYHWH** *šibʿat yāmîm* ¹³*wĕhiqrabtem ʿōlâ ʾiššeh rēaḥ nîḥōaḥ laYHWH . . .*

Lev 23

²³:³⁴ᵇ*baḥămiššâ ʿāśār yôm laḥōdeš haššĕbîʿî hazzeh* **ḥag** *hassukkôt šibʿat yāmîm laYHWH.* ³⁵*bayyôm hāriʾšôn miqrāʾ-qōdeš kol-mĕleʾket ʿăbōdâ lōʾ taʿăśû* ³⁶*šibʿat yāmîm taqrîbû ʾiššeh laYHWH . . .*

For the sake of conciseness, H has deleted *yihyeh lākem, wĕhaggōtem, ʿōlâ,* and *rēaḥ nîḥōaḥ.* It retains *ʾiššeh,* as is its wont (vv. 8, 25, 27), for its "compare," embracing all the sacrifices enumerated in Num 29:13–38, including the purification offerings (and for that reason, it must delete the words *ʿōlâ* and *rēaḥ nîḥōaḥ;* see NOTE on v. 18). It adds the word *hazzeh* for stylistic consistency (cf. vv. 6aα, 27aα) and *bayyôm hāriʾšôn,* since the work prohibition will apply to only the first day (and the eighth, v. 36b; note the similar construction in vv. 6–8). The major addition is the name of the festival *sukkôt,* which H emphasizes by making it the predicate of its opening nominative sentence. This change by itself suffices to indicate that this pericope stems from H (contra Knohl 1987: 94). The significance of this name will be discussed in the NOTES on vv. 34, 42.

34. *the Pilgrimage-Festival of Booths. ḥag hassukkôt.* The only other penta-teuchal code that calls this festival by this name is Deuteronomy (16:13, 16; 31:10). Afterward, this name occurs only in postexilic sources (Zech 14:16, 18, 19; Ezra 3:4; 2 Chr 8:13). The significance of this distribution cannot be over-estimated. It indicates that the name became preferable at the Jerusalem Temple (H; see chap. 17, COMMENT D) and subsequently became mandatory there (D). It is missing in the precentralization calendars of Exodus (E) and Numbers (P)—another piece of evidence that P does not presuppose a single sanctuary. The importance of this fact in understanding the origin and meaning of the festival's name is discussed in the NOTE on v. 42.

It could not have been long after deuteronomic centralization when this festival became known as *heḥag* "the Festival" (1 Kgs 8:2, 65; 12:32; Ezek 45:25; Neh 8:14; 2 Chr 7:8, 9). It is most natural that only after the ingathering of all the crops and before the advent of the rainy and sowing season that the Israelite farmer had the leisure to make a pilgrimage to Jerusalem for the seven days of the festival.

During Second Temple days, due to the decreasing farming population and growing diaspora, the Passover pilgrimage began to outstrip that of the Festival of Booths in popularity (Jos. *Ant.* 17.213–18; cf. 15:50–52). Moreover, the scholarly consensus that had assumed that the observance of Booths did not continue in the early church has been effectively refuted by Merras (1995), who has demonstrated that the festival of Epiphany in the triad Passover, Pentecost, and Epiphany cited in the *Didascalia Apostolorum* (early third century C.E.) refers to the Festival of Booths and that the statement by Ephraem of Syria (C.E. 306–373) that the Epiphany was the greatest of all the festivals (cf. McVey 1989: 4.20, 23, 28, 59) relates to the continuation of a Festival of Booths, but in a radically spiritualized form.

seven days to YHWH. šib'at yāmîm laYHWH. The order of the words in the presumed P original is (*ḥag*) *laYHWH šib'at yāmîm* (Num 29:12). The change allows for greater stress on the seven-day duration of the festival, a fact that will be given staccato emphasis by its fourfold repetition in the addendum of vv. 39–43.

As noted by Scolnic (1995: 40), the command that all males appear at the (regional) sanctuary on the three pilgrimage festivals (Exod 23:17 [JE]) is expanded in Deuteronomy to include the landowner's entire family and his dependents for the Festivals of Weeks and Booths (Deut 16:11–14; the omission of the Festival of Unleavened Bread is explained in the NOTE on v. 15). Thus, for the Festival of Booths, the injunction reads: "You shall rejoice in your festival with your son and daughter, your male and female slave, the Levite, the alien, the orphan [Renkema 1995], and the widow in your communities" (Deut 16:14).

It should be noted that the wife is not excluded, but is subsumed under *'attâ* 'You'. The same holds for *'attâ* in the sabbath commandment of the Decalogue (Exod 20:10b; Deut 5:14b); surely, the wife is not permitted to work! And H goes even further in allowing *lĕkā* 'for you' (25:6) to include the entire family (see its NOTE).

On the matter of family participation at the sanctuary during the Festival of Booths, the priestly texts (P and H) are silent. But since this festival lasts for seven days *at the sanctuary* (*laYHWH, lipnê YHWH*, vv. 34, 36, 39, 40, 41; Num 29:12), the entire family's presence is taken for granted. The (chattel) slave would naturally be included, and to judge from v. 22, so would the Levite, the alien, and the other underprivileged.

V. 36b. The Eighth Day

As all sources agree that the Festival of Booths lasts for seven days (vv. 34, 39, 40, 41, 42; Num 9:12; Deut 16:13; 1 Kgs 8:65–66; Ezek 45:25; Neh 8:18; 2 Chr 7:8, 9), the eighth day mentioned here is clearly an added day. This is conspicuously apparent in the P calendar. Whereas the listing of sacrifices for the seven days of the Festival of Booths begins each day with the phrase "and on the X day" (Num 29:17, 20, 23, 26, 29, 32), the introductory phrase for the eighth day lacks the *waw* (Num 29:35), indicating that it is an independent celebration. Its significance is discussed in the NOTES.

The standard formulas ". . . shall be for you a sacred occasion; you shall do no (laborious) work" (cf. vv. 7, 8, 21, 24b–25a, 35) are broken by the insertion of *wĕhiqrabtem 'iššeh laYHWH 'ăṣeret hi'* (K: *hw'*), just as this formula is broken in the Day of Purgation pericope by *wĕ'innitem 'et-napšōtêkem wĕhiqrabtem 'iššeh laYHWH* (v. 27). In both cases, the additions state the main characteristic of the day, a solemn assembly and fasting, respectively; they are related to each other chiastically ab ‖ b'c.

present a food gift to YHWH. taqrîbû 'iššeh laYHWH. Note that this clause is missing in the prescription for the concluding (seventh) day of the Festival of Unleavened Bread, whose wording otherwise is exactly the same (v. 8b). The reason for this added clause can be explained as a recognition (or vestige) of the fact that this day is an independent holiday with its own set of observances. Indeed, the sacrifices for each day of the Festival of Booths are uniform in their prescription for two rams and fourteen lambs, and even the differing numbers for bulls are ordered by their descending progression from thirteen to seven bulls (Num 29:13–34). But the sacrifices for the eighth day break sharply from those of the preceding days: one bull, one ram, and seven lambs (v. 36). The sacrifices prescribed for this day are precisely those prescribed for the Festival of Warning Blasts (Num 29:2) and the Day of Purgation (Num 29:8). That this is not a coincidence will be discussed in the NOTE on "you shall rejoice before YHWH," v. 40.

a solemn assembly. 'ăṣeret. There are three main interpretations of the noun (and its by-form 'ăṣārâ).

1. Since the verb 'āṣar is mostly attested with the meaning "hold back, refrain" (e.g., Gen 20:18; Num 17:13, 15; Deut 11:17; Judg 13:15–16; 1 Sam 21:6; 1 Kgs 18:44; Jer 36:5), its nominal form has been interpreted as a reference to abstention from work, an injunction that in the cultic calendars is always associated with it (v. 36bβ; Num 29:35; Deut 16:8; Ibn Ezra, Rashbam, Sforno).

2. It signifies the "final or closing celebration," implied by the LXX *exódion* 'recessional, release' (cf. Philo, *Laws* 2.211; MacRae 1960: 258). This rendering is supported by the fact that in the cultic calendars it describes the final day of the festival: the seventh day of the Feast of Unleavened Bread (Deut 16:8) and the final (rather, added) day of the Festival of Booths (v. 36; Num 29:35). It is this meaning that underlies the rabbinic designation of the Festival of the First Wheat Offering as 'ăṣeret (e.g., *m. Ḥal.* 4:10) because it completes the 'ōmer count (v. 16) and celebrates the end of the grain harvest. Its Aramaic form 'ăṣartā' (e.g., Num 29:35, *Tgs*) is attested for this festival in Josephus (*Ant* 3.252): *asarthà*. For a possible Hittite analogy, see COMMENT F.

3. The most likely meaning of 'ăṣeret is "solemn assembly" (*kĕnîšîn, Tgs.*). Jeremiah's condemnation of his people as an 'ăṣeret bōgĕdîm can only mean "a

band of traitors" (Jer 9:1). However, this meaning comes to the fore more strikingly in actual calls for an assembly:

tiq'û šôpār běṣiyyôn qadděšû-ṣôm **qir'û 'ăṣārâ** *'ispû-'am qadděšû qāhāl qibṣû zěqēnîm 'ispû 'ôlālîm . . .*

Blow a horn in Zion, solemnize a fast, **proclaim a solemn assembly, gather** the people, bid the congregation purify themselves. **Bring together** the old, gather the babes . . . (Joel 2:15–16; cf. 1:14)

Note the synonyms for "gather" (*'āsap* [twice], *qābaṣ*), the parallelism between *qāhāl* 'congregation' and *'ăṣārâ*, and the result of proclaiming (*qāra'*) an assembly: the people, old and young, gather together. The context indicates that the inhabitants of Jerusalem are summoned to the Temple (cf. Joel 1:14; 2:17) because of an emergency—not for one of the appointed festivals—and the emergency is a drought compounded by a locust invasion (1:4–12; 2:23–25). The shofar blowing and the fasting that precede the assembly is of utmost significance for understanding the common theme uniting the three festivals of the seventh month. It will be developed in the NOTES on v. 40.

A supporting passage is 2 Kgs 10:20–21:

. . . *qadděšû 'ăṣārâ labba'al* **wayyiqrā'û** *wayyišlaḥ yēhû' běkol-yiśra'ēl* **wayyābô'û** *kol-'ōbědê habba'al*

" . . . **solemnize an assembly** to Baal." Jehu sent word throughout Israel, and all the worshipers of Baal **came**

Jehu summons all the Baal worshipers for an *'ăṣārâ* at his temple. Here there is neither shofar blowing nor fasting; the purpose of the assembly is rejoicing (2 Kgs 10:18–19). Once again, this is an ad hoc celebration, not a fixed festival. Hence it is called *'ăṣārâ*. Finally, note that Isaiah concludes his litany of the sacrifices and fixed holidays that YHWH repudiates by adding *'āwen* (which the LXX renders *hēmeran megalēn* 'great day', equivalent to *yāma' rabbā'*, Aram. for Yom Kippur, hence, probably reading *ṣôm*) *wa'ăṣārâ* 'fast and assemblies' (Isa 1:13)—that is, the specially proclaimed occasions of fasting and assembly (see also Amos 5:21).

Thus far, the assemblies seem to have taken place at a sanctuary. However, this need not be the case, as attested by Deut 16:8. The people return home from the Temple on the day following their offering of the paschal sacrifice (v. 7b), and on the seventh day they hold an "*'ăṣeret* for YHWH" (v. 8). They were not expected to make a pilgrimage a second time to the Temple for this occasion—certainly not during the taxing harvest season. Thus the *'ăṣeret* must have been held in their hometowns. What could have been the purpose of those town assemblies? An answer, albeit a surmise, immediately comes to mind: to pray for a successful harvest. As has been pointed out (see NOTE on "you shall count off," v. 15), the spring season was fraught with hazards for the crops: unseasonable rain (and even hail) storms, locust invasions, and the dreaded sirocco. (Is it possible that the origins of the synagogue actually lie in these special convocations of *ʿăṣeret?*)

To be sure, the *ʿăṣeret* that marked the end of the Festival of Booths would have been celebrated at the Temple, and on that day the pilgrims were free to return to their homes (cf. 1 Kgs 8:66). But would it be far afield to suggest that those who did remain also gathered for prayer—but this time exclusively for rain? That the theme of rain is dominant in nearly all the rites of the Festival of Booths (as well as in those of the other festivals of the seventh month) will be demonstrated in the NOTES on v. 40. Here, however, let it be considered that on the last day before the Israelite landowner returns home (or while he is doing so), his thoughts and concerns would be focused on the prospects of his forthcoming plowing and sowing being blessed with an adequate supply of rain. Prayer would have been in his heart and verbalized communally at the *ʿăṣeret*. It is surely significant that *Tg. Ps.-J.* affirms that the assembly was for supplication for rain (cf. *Koh. Rab.* 7:14) and that the synagogue has preserved an ancient prayer for rain—marked by the solemnity that matches that of Yom Kippur—for this eighth and final day.

That this eighth day became a festival in its own right is obliquely witnessed in Scripture. Whereas King Solomon sent the celebrants of the Temple dedication home on this eighth day (1 Kgs 8:66), the book of Chronicles lets it be known that the king observed the eighth day as a festival and released the people only on the following day (2 Chr 7:9–10). The book of Nehemiah records that Ezra had the people observe the eighth day *kammišpāṭ* (Neh 8:18bβ). This term should not be rendered "as prescribed" (e.g., *NJPS*), since the only prescription for this day is its sacrificial requirement, a Temple matter wholly outside the activities and concerns of the laity. Rather, it should be rendered "as practiced" (e.g., Exod 21:9), and most likely refers to the agenda of the assembly—supplication for the rain (see NOTE on "you shall rejoice before YHWH," v. 40, and Kochman 1985: 159).

However, the uniqueness of this day did not have to await popular assent or royal decree. The sharp contrast in the number of sacrificed bulls, seventy during the seven days and only one on the eighth day, should suffice to indicate that the Temple early on recognized this sacrificial distinction, in line, perhaps, with the following midrash (*Num. Rab.* 21:24):

> You find that on the Booths Festival, Israel offers to Him seventy bulls as an atonement for the seventy nations. Israel says: "Sovereign of the worlds! Behold, we offer for them seventy bulls and they ought to love us, yet they hate us! As it says, 'In return for my love they are my adversaries' " (Ps 109:4). The Holy One Blessed Be He, in consequence, said to them: "Now, therefore, offer a sacrifice on your own behalf: 'On the eighth day . . . one bull' " (Num 29:35–36).

That the total number of bulls amounts to seventy, not by mandating ten bulls for each of the seven days but by an arithmetically reduced progression (n − 1) beginning at the arbitrary number thirteen, can only mean that the total of seventy was aimed for at the outset. It also can be no accident that the number seventy corresponds—in biblical times—to the assumed number of nations in the world (Gen 10; Deut 32:8–9 LXX, Sam., 4QDeut 32; Dan 10:13, 20; cf. Fensham 1977). After all, the Festival of Booths, focusing on man's needs and desire to give thanks to God for the year's harvest, is of universal appeal. It is small wonder that Zechariah prophesies that this festival would become observed universally (Zech 14:16). The eighth day, by contrast, prescribes only one bull—for Israel. Israel, in its rain-dependent land—contrast Egypt—has need for a separate dialogue with its God. The midrash continues:

> This may be compared to the case of a king who made a banquet for seven days and invited all the people in the province during the seven days of the feast. When the seven days of the feast were over he said to his friend: "We have already done our duty to all the people of the province, let us now make shift, you and I, with whatever you can find —a pound of meat, or of fish, or vegetables." In like manner the Holy One Blessed Be He said to Israel: " 'On the eighth day, you shall hold a solemn assembly'; make shift with whatever you can find; with 'one bull . . . ' " (Num 29:35–36).

Scholars as early as Kuenen (1886: 282, n. 8) and as recent as Scott (1993: 110–11) have held that the prescriptions for the eighth day (vv. 36b, 39b) are postexilic insertions. Kuenen points to the evidence, mentioned above, that Solomon dismissed the people on the eighth day (1 Kgs 8:66) and it was not until the Chronicler's time that it was incorporated into the festival (2 Chr 7:8–10). Kuenen's data are correct, but incorrectly interpreted. All of 1 Kgs 8 is a deuteronomistic composition, which follows D's prescription for a seven-day pilgrimage-festival (ḥag) in the autumn (Deut 16:13–15). Lev 23, however, incorporates the equally old tradition of P prescribing an ʿăṣeret on the eighth day. That Dtr may have had Lev 23 before it, including the supplement, vv. 39–43, is possibly demonstrated by its claim that Solomon celebrated the Festival of Booths for fourteen days (1 Kgs 8:65b), which Auerbach (1958) plausibly explains as Dtr's mistake in regarding the second mention of a seven-day Festival of Booths (v. 39) as an additional period. (True, the mention of fourteen days in 1 Kgs 8:65 is missing in the old Greek, but its presence is confirmed by Jos. Ant. 8.123.) Scott stakes his claim for the lateness of the eighth day on his general assumption of the lateness of the priestly texts. He asks: If P (and H) preceded D, why didn't the latter include the ʿăṣeret of the Festival of Booths, as it did for the ʿăṣeret of the Festival of Unleavened Bread (Deut 16:8)? The answer has been given above: the eighth day is not a ḥag; hence D does not mention it, whereas D's ʿăṣeret for the seventh day of the Festival of Unleavened Bread is its replacement for the ḥag of its source (Exod 13:6b [E]; see Note on "The seventh day," v. 8).

Vv. 37–38. The Summary

The close of the original calendar (vv. 4–38) in this chapter (Pre-H₁; see COMMENT A) forms a chiastically structured inclusio with the opening verse, v. 4. The explicit mention of the sabbath as not included among "the fixed times of YHWH" proves unquestionably that the inclusio is with v. 4 and not with vv. 1–2.

37. *which you shall proclaim as sacred occasions.* ʾăšer-tiqrĕʾû ʾōtām miqrāʾê qōdeš. The order of these words is reversed in v. 4 miqrāʾê qōdeš ʾăšer-tiqrĕʾû ʾōtām 'the sacred occasions which you shall proclaim', thereby locking in vv. 4–38 by means of a chiastically related inclusio.

sacrifices. zebaḥ. Knohl (1987: 95, n. 97; 1995: 37, n. 83), who holds that H here summarizes an original P stratum (disputed in COMMENT A), also maintains that the term *zebaḥ* is in the wrong place; it should precede *minḥâ* so that the blood sacrifices *ʿōlâ* and *zebaḥ* would be followed by their adjuncts, *minḥâ* and *nĕsākîm*. The LXX solves this problem by omitting the *minḥâ*. However, the order of the MT is justified: it follows the order in chaps. 1–3, namely, most sacred offerings *ʿōlâ* and *minḥâ* preceding *zebaḥ*, a lesser sacred offering.

The *zebaḥ* is generally understood as referring to the two lambs prescribed for the Festival of First Wheat as a *zebaḥ šĕlāmîm* (v. 19b). Wessely (1846) maintains that it also includes the paschal sacrifice (v. 5). I submit that he is right. His suggestion would explain the use of *zebaḥ* instead of the given expression *zebaḥ šĕlāmîm*, since the *pesaḥ* is indeed a *zebaḥ* — it is eaten by the offerer (and his company) — but it is not considered a *šĕlāmîm* (cf. 7:11–18): It is sui generis, consumed in one day (rather, one evening) with unleavened bread and bitter herbs (Exod 12:8).

A more difficult problem is the absence of the *ḥaṭṭāʾt* from this summary even though it is expressly mentioned in v. 19a and for every festival in the P *Vorlage*, Num 28–29. There are three proposed solutions:

1. Since the *ḥaṭṭāṭ* is not an *ʾiššeh* 'a gift', it automatically had to be excluded. Note that in the sacrificial order for the Festival of First Wheat, it is listed separately, after the *ʾiššeh* offerings (vv. 18–19; see NOTE).
2. The *ḥaṭṭāʾt* clauses in Num 28–29 are not original (except in 28:15), but are H additions, as indicated by their opening word *milbad*, an H term (Knohl 1995: 31, n. 68; cf. Fisher 1970: 499–500).
3. Ḥazzequni, Wessely (1846), and, McConville (1984: 52) maintain that *zebaḥ* is an inclusive term covering not only the *zebaḥ šĕlāmîm* and the *pesaḥ*, but also the *ḥaṭṭāʾt*. This would account for its absence not only in Deut 12:6, 11, but also in H itself (e.g., 17:8).

Thus the *ḥaṭṭāʾt* (1) does not belong in this verse, (2) is not original in the P text (Num 28–29), or (3) is subsumed under the term *zebaḥ* in H (and D). Each of these explanations has its strengths and weaknesses. The first claims that the *ḥaṭṭāʾt* is not an *ʾiššeh*, but admits that the *ʾiššeh*, as the generic term for all sacrifices (vv. 8, 25, 27, 36), must include the *ḥaṭṭāʾt* (see NOTE on v. 8). The second neatly eliminates the contradiction between *ʾiššeh* and *ḥaṭṭāʾt* by presuming that the *ḥaṭṭāʾt* passages in Num 28–29 (except for 28:15) are H additions and that the original text of Lev 23 is a P text—without any reference to a *ḥaṭṭāʾt*. However, once the H additions were inserted into both Lev 23 and Num 28–29, the anomaly that H's *ʾiššeh* in Lev 23 includes the *ḥaṭṭāʾt* again resurfaces, unless one would presume that the calendar of Num 28–29, which lay before H, did not contain the *ḥaṭṭāʾt* additions. The third solution is the simplest, though the most radical in its implications. It presumes that in the expression *ʿōlâ wāzebaḥ*, the *zebaḥ* stands for all the blood offerings, including the *ḥaṭṭāʾt*. This explanation would serve well for H (17:8), and perhaps for D (Deut 12:6, 11) which presumably would be aware of the *ḥaṭṭāʾt*. It could also receive support from Josh 22:23, 27. The chapter in Joshua exhibits priestly influence; it distinguishes between the *zebaḥ* and the *šĕlāmîm* (further evidence that *zebaḥ* of v. 37 could embrace the *pesaḥ*; see above), but there are a number of passages that state that the *zebaḥ* in this tandem expression was eaten *by the worshiper* (Exod 18:12; Jer 7:21–22), which eliminates the *ḥaṭṭāʾt*. Thus the probability rests that the tandem *ʿōlâ wāzebaḥ*, at least in most of its occurrences, refers to the time when the *ʿōlâ* was the all-purpose sacrifice, including that of expiation, before the creation of the *ḥaṭṭāʾt* by the priestly legists (vol. 1.176). The *ḥaṭṭāʾt* problem has yet to be satisfactorily resolved.

and libations. ûnĕsākîm. This is written in the plural because they accompany all the previously mentioned offerings (Elliger 1966). There is a more logical reason for the plural. The clue is that all four sacrificial terms are found in vv. 18–19, where, indeed, only the word "libations" occurs in the plural. Plainly, this summary is scrupulously accurate.

the daily protocol on each day. dĕbar-yôm bĕyômô. This idiom is found in Exod 5:13, 19; 16:4; 1 Kgs 8:59; 2 Kgs 25:30 (= Jer 52:34), Dan 1:5; Ezra 3:4, etc. A reference, once again, to the P calendar of public sacrifices, which specifies the offerings for each festival day.

38. *apart from. milbad* (cf. 9:17; 23:38 [thrice]; Num 5:8; 6:21; 17:14; 28–29 [twelve times]). For the argument that this word (and the clause it controls) stems from the pen of H, see Knohl (1987: 115–17; 1995: 56–58). He attributes this verse to a late H tradent to account for the lack of sacrifices in the sabbath interpolation (v. 3). A simpler and preferable explanation is that this verse continues the work of H, which wishes to account for the absence of the sabbath (and personal) sacrifices *in the festival calendar*.

the sabbath-offerings of YHWH. šabbĕtōt YHWH, literally "the sabbaths of YHWH." This phrase, however, clearly refers to the sacrifices prescribed for the sabbath (Num 28:9–10), just as *šabbat hāʾāreṣ* (25:6), lit. "the sabbath of YHWH," refers to its produce (see its NOTE). It proves that for H (as for all other sources), the sabbath is not a *môʿēd*, and, hence, vv. 2b–3 are the product of the latest (exilic) H stratum (Hr), which wanted to incorporate the sabbath into the calendar of the *môʿădê YHWH* 'the appointed times of YHWH' (see INTRODUCTION to vv. 1–3). This phrase is unique in the Bible.

The mention of the sabbath sacrifices here only accentuates their omission in v. 3, indicating that the latter stems from a time when sacrifices could not be offered, namely, the Babylonian Exile.

The sectaries of Qumran use this clause to derive a new ruling *'L Y'L 'YŠ LMZBḤ BŠBT KY 'M 'WLT HŠBT KY KN KTWB MLBD ŠBTWTYKM* 'Let no man offer on the altar on the sabbath except the burnt offering of the sabbath; for thus it is written "apart from your sabbath (offerings)" ' (CD 11:17–18). This interpretation ostensibly contradicts the plain meaning of Num 28:10, which prescribes that the sabbath sacrifices be offered *'al* 'in addition', to the daily *tāmîd*. This difficulty is explained by Schiffman (1975: 128) by positing that "one can only assume that the sect interpreted the word *'al* in Num 28:10 to mean 'instead of'." This is hardly likely because (1) there exists no such meaning for *'al*; (2) it is unlikely that this literalist sect would flatly contradict explicit Scripture; and (3) rather, Qumran's exegesis of vv. 37–38a is as follows: these are the sacrifices for the appointed days of YHWH except for (*milbad*) YHWH's sabbaths *when only the prescribed 'ōlâ and its adjuncts* are offered up — that is, the sacrifices for the *tāmîd* (Num 28:11–15) and the sabbath (Num 28:9–10).

(*apart from*) *your gifts. mattěnôtêkem.* Dillmann and Ryssel (1897) claim that the reference is to the firstlings and tithes. To be sure, tithes are referred to as "gifts" in Num 18:29. However, the term *mattānâ* 'gift' is applied, in the same chapter, to all the *required* offerings that fall under the category of *qŏdāšîm* 'lesser sacred offerings' (Num 18:11, 19; cf. Exod 28:38), namely, firstfruits (ripe and processed); firstlings, *ḥērem* (see NOTES on 27:26–31); and redemption money for the firstborn (vv. 10–18). Elliger (1966) proposes that this term has an even wider meaning than the prescribed *qŏdāšîm*. Any additional "gifts," however, would be subsumed under the category "freewill offerings."

The difference between the offerings mentioned in vv. 37–38a and those in v. 38b is not that the former are obligatory and the latter, voluntary (*mattānôt* 'gifts' are obligatory), but public versus private offerings (the *pesaḥ*, though brought by the individual, is a public offering since it is required of every Israelite family). Cartledge (1992: 33) plausibly suggests that these private offerings were brought during the pilgrimage festivals (cf. Num 29:39).

It is instructive to observe the conflational technique of Qumran as it fuses this verse and its analogous summary of the P calendar *lěbad minnidrêkem wěnidbōtêkem* (Num 29:39):

LBD MNDBWTMH LKWL 'ŠR YQRYBW LKWL NDRYHMH WLKWL MTNWTMH 'ŠR YBY'W LY

besides their freewill offerings — all they will offer — all their votive offerings, and all their gifts which they will bring to me. 11QT 29:5–6

The Qumran text uses the *lěbad* of Numbers (P) but includes the *mattānôt* of Leviticus. More interestingly, it uses a synonym *yābî'û* 'bring' for Leviticus's *tittĕnû* 'give', but only for votive offerings and gifts, whereas it adds its own word *yaqrîbû* 'sacrifice, offer' for freewill offerings. I believe that it has in mind that votive offerings as well as gifts need not be limited to sacrifices, whereas freewill offerings can refer to only the well-being offering prescribed in Lev 7:11–16. Note also that the sabbath offerings of v. 38a are deleted so as not to give the impression that the sacrificial offerings of v. 38b may be sacrificed on the sabbath (contra Rabin 1954: 59; Yadin 1983: 1.131).

you give. *tittĕnû*. This verb controls all the preceding objects in v. 38b. H, therefore, is not as precise as Qumran (above), which clearly recognizes that the *nĕdābâ*, the freewill offering, is not "given," but sacrificed.

Vv. 39–43. Addendum on the Festival of Booths

This pericope is a later addition. As Hartley (1992: 372–73) points out, the dating of the festival (v. 39) is so similar to that of v. 35 that it must have had an independent existence. Abetting this hypothesis are the differences between this pericope on the Festival of Booths and the preceding one (vv. 34–36):

1. The festival is called *ḥag-YHWH* 'the Festival of YHWH' (v. 39), not *ḥag hassukkôt* 'the Festival of Booths' (v. 34).
2. The first and eighth days in this pericope are called *šabbātôn* 'rest' (v. 39), not *miqrā' qōdeš* 'sacred occasion' (vv. 35–36).
3. This pericope provides a historic rationale for the festival (v. 43), whereas the prior one confines itself to the word *'ăṣeret* 'assembly' regarding the eighth day—a functional term, not a rationale (v. 36).
4. This pericope prescribes the use of branches and the building of booths by all Israelites (vv. 40, 42), on which the prior pericope is silent.

The original provenance of these added prescriptions is obscure, but as will be demonstrated in the NOTES, their aim, as now incorporated into the pericope, is directed to the Babylonian Exiles.

This is not to say that the entire pericope was *composed* in the exile. The command "you shall rejoice before YHWH your God" (v. 40b) clearly implies a celebration at a sanctuary, as do the expressions *ḥag YHWH* (v. 39aα) and *ḥag laYHWH* (v. 41a). Moreover, the setting "when you have ingathered the produce of the land" (v. 39aβ) presumes that Israel is in *its* land. Therefore, I must conclude that the pericope has three strata: Pre-H$_1$ a preexilic document, which prescribes seven days of rejoicing at a nearby sanctuary (vv. 39a [minus *'ak*], 40); H, a statement of closure (v. 41a, bα); and Hr, an exilic expansion (see COMMENT A), which ordains that all Israel must dwell in booths and also provides a rationale (vv. 39b [plus *'ak*], 42, 43).

The earlier, preexilic stratum bears all the earmarks of Pre-H$_1$. This precentralization (hence, pre-Hezekian) layer, on which the school of H constructed its text on the grain offering (vv. 9–22), posits multiple sanctuaries, each of which received grain offerings from Israelite landowners in its area (see INTRODUCTION to vv. 15–22). Ostensibly, the two pericopes clash because the autumn festival is expressly called a *ḥag* (v. 39a), mandating a sanctuary celebration, whereas the grain offerings, by silence and implication (see NOTES on "in all your settlements," vv. 14, 21), are not a *ḥag*. But this discrepancy is chimerical: it is only when the year's harvest has been ingathered that the farmer can spend seven consecutive days away from his fields. Indeed, the term for the national celebration of this festival, *ḥag YHWH*, and its analogue *heḥag* 'The Festival', attested in the historical sources (see NOTES on "the Festival of Booths," v. 34, and "the Festival of YHWH," v. 39), probably trace their origin to the earlier practice of the individual farmer making his one, annual visit to his local or regional sanctuary, at which he would celebrate the *ḥag* with his family and clan.

V. 41a,bα is a brief statement of closure in the characteristic style of H (see below). It functions the same way as vv. 14 and 21, which mark the closure of the barley and wheat pericopes, respectively, by H. However, the addition of v. 41bβ transforms v. 41 into a larger inclusio, also typical of H style, which furthermore serves a sharp polemical purpose (see below). V. 41 now functions to permit the altar circumambulation at the Temple and to envelop vv. 39–41a,bα in a larger inclusio. The absence of the term *běkol-môšěbōtêkem* 'in all your settlements' (cf. vv. 14, 21) is an indication that the focus is on observances at the Temple.

The exilic stratum could well have been the work of the author of vv. 2aβ–3, who realized that the only "fixed times" of Israel's calendar that could be observed in the exile were the sabbath and the people's nonsacrificial-related rites: the Festival of Unleavened Bread, the fast on the Day of Purgation (previously prescribed), and the use of plants and booths on the Festival of Booths.

To be sure, the term *ḥag* had to undergo a transformation. No longer was it a communal pilgrimage to and celebration at a sanctuary; it became a general term meaning "holiday." Indirect support for this change is provided by the attested transformation of the term *ḥag hammaṣṣôt* from a preexilic single-day observance at the Temple to a postexilic seven-day holiday (Ezek 45:21; Ezra 6:22; 2 Chr 8:12–13; 30:13, 21; 35:17; see NOTE on "the Pilgrimage-Festival of Unleavened Bread to YHWH," v. 6). In the latter case, the Temple celebration took place on the first day, but the remaining six days of the festival were spent at home (Deut 16:7). Thus the term *ḥag*, covering all seven days of the festival, took on the meaning "holiday." By the same token, the *ḥag YHWH* describing the seven-day fall festival at the sanctuary became, in the exile, a seven-day holiday celebrated with booths and plants.

Similarly, *sukkôt* was no longer an incidental feature of the preexilic festival, namely, the shelters erected by *some* of the celebrants—those who journeyed to the sanctuary from afar—but a divine imperative to *all* Israelites to construct them and dwell in them *at home*. I submit that it was this *exilic* custom that prompted Ezra to demand of his compatriots to build *booths* not just on the Temple grounds, but at their homes (Neh 8:16; see NOTES on v. 42, and COMMENT C).

Regarding the use of the prescribed plants (v. 40a), the matter is more complex. The case will be made that these plants were used in processions round the altar (see NOTE on "you shall rejoice before YHWH," v. 40b). If so, how could it viably be reinterpreted in the exile? To be sure, later Judaism had no difficulty in doing so. The circumambulations were resumed in the synagogue, and the central platform from which the Torah scroll was read substituted for the altar. But we have no evidence that there was either a synagogue or a Torah scroll in the Babylonian Exile; at most, the *ʿăṣeret* tradition survived—praying (Temple Psalms) and teaching from portions of the Torah that were accepted as divinely revealed (e.g., deuteronomic law). I surmise, therefore, that the altar circumambulations fell into desuetude, for there was no way of reviving them in the exile. Thus we can plausibly explain Ezra's apparent bewilderment of how to interpret v. 40 during his reading of the Torah to the assembled Jerusalem throngs on the second day of the seventh month (Neh 8:13). Without an exilic precedent and separated from Temple observance by a century and a half, he made the understandable error of interpreting the command *ûlĕqaḥtem* 'And you shall take' the enumerated branches as construction materials for the booths (Neh 8:14–15).

Finally, since the Festival of Unleavened Bread is also independent of the sacrificial cult, why is its observance not commanded in the purported exilic stratum of Lev 23? First, some clarification: there is no requirement to eat unleavened bread during the seven-day festival, except for that which accompanies the paschal sacrifice (Exod 12:8; see NOTE on "in all your settlements," v. 21); hence it is irrelevant to the exiles. Besides there is no indication that the paschal unleavened bread could not contain a leavening substance (see NOTE on "unleavened bread," v. 6). As for the unambiguous prohibition against eating leavened bread (Exod 12:20), this text—which was in Ezra's Torah—also contains the relevant phrase "in all your settlements." The exilic writer, therefore, had no need to repeat this prohibition in his text of Lev 23; he had it in Exod 12:20.

A reprise of the entire chapter in its suggested historical unfolding is in COMMENT A.

39. *However.* ʾak. In priestly texts, this particle is found in 11:4, 36; 21:23; 23:27, 39; 27:26, 28; Gen 9:4–5; 23:13; Exod 12:15, 16; 31:13; Num 1:49; 18:3, 15, 17; 26:55; 31:22, 23; 36:6. It is used when new material is introduced (Kalisch 1867–72). It differs in function from the *ʾak* that introduces the pericope on the Day of Purgation (v. 27). There it is a contrastive particle (see NOTE); here it marks a supplement that informs us how and why the festival should be celebrated—information found in the prescriptions for the festivals for the firstfruits of grain (vv. 9–22), *pesaḥ-maṣṣôt* (Exod 12:1–20), and Yom Kippur (Lev 16; Dillmann and Ryssel 1897). Although this reason may be true, I submit that this particle does carry a contrastive nuance. It intimates that the sacrificial prescriptions (v. 36) are no longer operable, and what remains of the festival that can be observed is the rite with the branches (v. 40) and the building of booths (v. 42). I, therefore (as in v. 27), prefer the rendering "However."

when you have ingathered the yield of the land. bĕ'ospĕkem 'et-tĕbû'at hā'āreṣ. The use of the verb *ʾāsap* 'ingather' alludes to the earliest name of the festival *ḥag hā'āsîp* (Exod 23:16; 34:22). The purpose of the ingathering is for storage, as the deuteronomic prescription mandates: *bĕ'ospĕkā miggornĕkā ûmiyyiqbekā* 'when you gather in from your threshing floor and your vat' (Deut 16:13). The grain kernels and the grapes and olives pressed into wine and oil, respectively (Jer 40:10, 12), including, presumably, the summer fruit, are brought into storage. The difference between the use of this verb in D and in H should not be overlooked. D's festival is not fixed at a specific date. Probably originating as a North Israelite document, it reflects the later agricultural season of the north, which prompted Jereboam I to set this festival for the fifteenth day of the eighth month (1 Kgs 12:33)—fully one month after the corresponding one in Judah (Eerdmans 1912: 115–16).

the Pilgrimage-Festival of YHWH. ḥag YHWH. The rendering is capitalized because that is its name. It probably reflects the period toward the end of the monarchy, characterized by a mass pilgrimage to the Temple at the most propitious time of the year when all the crops were in and before the rainy season had begun. That is, it was popularly called by two names: the Festival of Booths (see NOTE on v. 42) and *heḥag* 'The Festival' (1 Kgs 8:2, 65; 12:32; Ezek 45:25; Neh 8:14; 2 Chr 5:3; 7:8, 9; cf. *ḥaggēnu* 'our Festival', Ps 81:4; and in rabbinic literature, see *m. Roš. Haš.* 1:2; *m. Suk.* 3:13, 14, etc.). Its significance as *The* Festival is corroborated by Deuteronomy's call for a septennial reading of the Torah (i.e., a rite of covenant renewal) to be held at this festival (Deut 31:10–13)—obviously, at a time when everyone might be expected to be present.

The Mishna and Tosefta have preserved details of how this rite was carried out in Second Temple times (*m. Sot.* 7:8; *t. Sot.* 7:13–17). A wooden platform was placed in the outermost (women's) court (cf. *b. Sot.* 41b) and the king (Agrippa) was seated on it. The scroll of the Torah was then passed from hand to hand, starting with the head of the synagogue, until it reached the high priest, who presented it to the king. The king received it standing and then sat. He read out the following portions: Deut 1:1–6:9; 11:13–21; 14:22–29; 26:12–15; 28.

The portions 14:22–29; 26:12–15, dealing with the tithes, were added presumably because it was customary then to bring the second (deuteronomic) tithe to Jerusalem on the Festival of Booths (Albeck 1954: 3.389). Otherwise, the reading was confined to the exhortatory passages of Deuteronomy, concluding with the blessings and curses. Thus rabbinic tradition confirms that the command to read "this Torah" (Deut 31:11, 12) does not extend beyond the book of Deuteronomy, which coincides with the plain meaning of the text. The Tosefta records an even shorter reading and some MSS include Deut 17:14–20. Although the Torah does not specify the reader, it is interesting that this honor was bestowed on the king. Josephus (*Ant.* 4.209–11) states that the high priest was the reader, not because the king might absent himself from this duty (Albeck 1954: 3.389), but most likely because for most of the Second Temple period there was no king (Safrai 1976: 2.89b).

The name *ḥag YHWH*, appearing in the reference to the wine festival at Shilo (Judg 21:19), has frequently been identified as the Festival of Booths (e.g., de Vaux 1961: 495). But this supposition is in error, since the wine harvest occurs in the middle of the summer. (In the calendar of Qumran, it falls on the third day of the fifth month, more than two months before the Festival of Booths; see COMMENT E.) Most likely, the Shilonic festival reflects the mores of the central highlands, which gave special prominence to the major crop of that area, the grape harvest (for nearby Shechem, see Judg 9:27).

rest. šabbātôn. Missing are the words *yihyeh lākem lā'areṣ* 'you the land shall observe a (rest)', found everywhere else with this word (cf. 16:31; 23:24; 25:4, 5; Exod 35:2; Ibn Ezra). In the prior pericope on this festival (H), the term *miqrā' qōdeš* is used (vv. 35–36; cf. vv. 7–8), evidence that this addendum stems from a different, and later, hand (Hr; see COMMENT A). However, since *šabbātôn* appears as an H idiom in the Festival of Alarm Blasts (v. 24), its use may be old. Perhaps because *šabbātôn* 'rest' implies a prohibition against work, the injunction *kol-mĕle'ket 'ăbōdâ lō' ta'ăśû* 'you shall do no laborious work' (v. 36b) need not be repeated. That the term *šabbātôn* implies a minor sabbath (except in the compound *šabbat šabbātôn*) when minor, nonoccupational work is permitted, see the NOTE on v. 24.

40. (*On the first day*) *you shall take for yourselves. ûlĕqaḥtem lākem.* But how shall this "taking" be accomplished? Shall it be in accordance with *ûlĕqaḥtem 'ăguddat 'ēzôb* 'you shall take a bunch of hyssop' (Exod 12:22)—that is, in your hand (*Sipra* Emor 16:1)—or in accordance with *wĕyiqḥû lāhem 'îš śeh* 'each of them shall take a lamb' (Exod 12:3)—that is, for another purpose, mentioned three verses later: the paschal sacrifice (v. 6; *Seper Hamibḥar*)? On this question hangs a major controversy between the rabbis and the Karaites. The latter argue that if the branches are to be used only in the hand (the rabbinic interpretation), the text should state that they should be taken for seven days, not just on the first day. The Karaites therefore conclude that the purpose of the branches is to build the prescribed booths (v. 42). The rabbis, however, counter their argument by claiming that the purpose of the "taking" on the first day is to rejoice in the Temple for seven days (v. 40b; *Sipra* Emor 16:9). Besides, one is forbidden to do laborious work (i.e., build a booth) on the first day. Ehrlich, who sides with the Karaites but who is sensitive to the rabbis' counterargument, wants to emend *bayyôm hāri'šôn* 'on the first day' to *layyôm hāri'šôn* 'for the first day', (i.e., the booth is built in advance of the festival), an emendation for which there is no warrant in the Versions. Presumably, both the Karaites and Ehrlich are influenced by the narration of Neh 8:15, which explicitly states that the people built booths with these branches (see COMMENT C).

Interestingly, the Hittite king and queen "take" the AN.TAH.ŠUM plant on the ninth day of its festival. As noted by Weinfeld (1983a: 129, n. 135), whereas the king takes the plant into the temple, the queen does so in her palace—indicating the possibility that the ritual use of the vegetation is not limited to the sanctuary. However, the AN.TAH.ŠUM festival occurs in the spring. This as well as other discrepancies between Hittite and Israelite cult practices give pause concerning the extent to which intercultural parallelisms may be helpful (see COMMENT F).

the boughs of majestic trees. pĕrî 'ēṣ hādār. The identification of this species has long been debated. Under the assumption that the *pĕrî* has to be given its usual rendering as "fruit," the following solutions have been offered:

1. The fruit has been identified as the citron (*Citrus medica*), rabbinic *'etrôg* (Jos. *Ant.* 13.372; *Tgs.*; Pesh.), as explained by the rabbis: both the tree and its fruit are majestic (*y. Suk.* 3:5); the aroma is in both the fruit and the tree (*Sipra* Emor 16:4); "whose fruit lives [*haddār*; play on *hādār* 'majestic'] in its tree annually" (i.e., the tree always bears fruit; Ben Azzai in *Sipra* Emor 16:4). Ramban bases the citron identification on the presumed root of *'etrôg* as *rgg* by which the *Tgs.* render the verb *ḥāmad* 'desire'—that is, "the desirable fruit."

There is no doubt that this identification was adopted in Hellenistic times. The *'etrôg* is described for the first time by Theophrastus in the fourth century B.C.E.. It appears on Hasmonean coins and on early mosaics. By then, it must have grown in abundance since the aberrant Sadducean priest was pelted with them (*m. Suk.* 4:9; *t. Suk.* 3:16). And it must have been cheap: a large one cost two pennies (*m. Meʿil.* 6:4; *t. Meʿil.* 2:10); children possessed them (*m. Suk.* 4:7), but during difficult times (possibly the Hadrianic persecutions) they had to be imported (*t. Dem.* 3:4; Feliks 1968: 66–67). However, the fact that *'etrôg* is a Persian loanword (Josephus (*Ant.* 3.245) calls it "the Persian apple," and Skt. *soronga* means "having a beautiful color") leads scholars to postulate that the *'etrôg* seeds may have been brought to the land of Israel no earlier than the sixth century with the return of the Babylonian Exiles; others claim that the *'etrôg* already appears in Egyptian iconography of the fifteenth century B.C.E. (Feliks 1968: 66–67; 1986). Moreover, as demonstrated by Bieger and Lipschitz (1996–97), the identification of the *'etrôg* with the *Citrus medica* did not occur before the tenth century C.E. In sum, the midrashic interpretations of the rabbis notwithstanding, the identification of this "fruit" with the citron is doubtful.

2. On the basis of the olive branches prescribed for the booths in Neh 8:15, the fruit has been identified with the olive. Rofé (1986: 12) points to Jer 11:16, where the olive tree is called *yĕpēh pĕrî-tō'ar* 'fair, with choice fruit', and Hos 14:7, which extols its *hôd* 'splendor' (noted earlier by the twelfth-century Karaite R. Yehuda Hadasi; cf. Eshkol Hakofer 1836: 866, par. 246).

3. Vocalizing *hādār* as *haddār* 'the dar tree', Tolkovsky (1928) claims that *dar* is the name of a tree in Sanskrit, short for *divdar* 'tree of *div* (genii)', which refers to the Himalayan cedar, whose fruit is its cone. The cone's rugged skin is much like that of the citron, hence the confusion between the two.

4. Tur-Sinai (1962: 143) and Elliger (1966) agree with the LXX that the fruit of any majestic tree is intended.

An entirely different and preferable solution is that in this verse the word *pĕrî* does not mean "fruit," but "branches." As Ginsberg (1963: 167–70) has demonstrated, the word pair *pĕrî* and *šōreš* (e.g., 2 Kgs 19:30; Isa 14:29; 37:31; Ezek 17:9; Hos 9:16; Amos 2:9) is a synecdoche for the tree, where *šōreš* means "stock" and *pĕrî* means "branches." Already Ehrlich 1908, following the Karaites (see *Seper Hamibhar; Keter Torah*), had speculated that *pĕrî* should be read *pōrê* / *pō'ărê* from *pō'ar* / *pō'ărâ* 'branch' (e.g., Ezek 31:5–6; note that in fifty MSS, related *pu'râ* [Isa 10:33] is spelled *pûrâ*). Aiding this interpretation is the fact that the next species in the list *kappōt tĕmārîm* is not introduced by a *waw*. Thus *pĕrî ʿēṣ hādār* is the general term "boughs of majestic trees," followed by the specification of branches of three majestic trees. It is therefore no wonder that in the list of Neh 8:15 there is no mention of fruit (for the implications, see COMMENT C). This rendering is adopted in the translation.

fronds of palms. kappōt tĕmārîm. Ehrlich reads *kippōt* on the presumption that the singular is *kippâ.* However, the singular is *kap* 'palm', and the MT vocalization is correct. The plural is used probably because one frond has many branches. The leaves would have been thought as branches because of their stiffness and sharpness. The rabbinic requirement to close and bind the leaves (*b. Suk.* 32a) may stem from their prickly nature, rendered especially hazardous during festival processions.

branches of leafy trees. waʿănap ʿēṣ-ʿābōt. The tree is unspecified. The rabbis identify it with the *hădās* 'myrtle', (*Myrtus communis*) (Isa 41:19): "The branches of its tree that resemble a braid—this is the myrtle" (*Sipra* Emor 16:6); "a braid resembles a chain—this is the myrtle" (*b. Suk.* 32b). The myrtle grows in damp plains such as the banks of the Jordan River, in the Dan Valley in the Golan, in upper Galilee, and, rarely, on Mount Carmel (Zohary 1982). This interpretation is supported by *maʿăśēh ʿăbōt* 'cordage work' (Exod 28:14; *Tg. Onq. gĕdîl* 'rope'; cf. Judg 15:13–14; 16:11–12; Isa 5:18).

Alternatively, and preferably, *ʿăbōt* can be rendered "leafy." (The usual rendering "thick" is unsupported in Biblical Hebrew.) It surely has this meaning in *wĕtaḥat kol-ʿēṣ raʿănān wĕtaḥat kol-ʾēlâ ʿăbuttâ* 'under every green tree and under every leafy oak' (Ezek 6:13; cf. 1 Kgs 14:23; Jer 2:20; Ezek 20:28; Greenberg 1983a: 136). Nehemiah mentions both *ʿălê hădās* 'myrtle leaves' and *ʿălê ʿēṣ ʿābōt* 'leaves of a leafy tree' (Neh 8:15), which indicates the possibility that both interpretations were already current in the fifth century.

and willows of the brook. This is identified as a poplar (*Populus euphratica*). There are two types of willow: *Salix fragilis* and *Salix alba* (Snaith 1967, both recorded by R. Hisda in *b. Šab.* 36a; *b. Suk.* 34a). They must have been tall, even longer than palm fronds, for according to the rabbis: "There was a place below Jerusalem called Motsa. They (the gatherers) went down thither and collected thence young willow-branches, and they came and set them upright along the sides of the altar with their tops bent over the top of the altar" (*m. Suk.* 4:5). The purpose of taking these species of vegetation will be discussed below.

and you shall rejoice before YHWH your God seven days. ûśĕmaḥtem lipnê YHWH ʾĕlōhêkem šibʿat yāmîm. The theme of rejoicing predominates in D's description of visits to the Temple during the pilgrimage Festivals of Weeks (Deut 16:11) and, especially, Booths (Deut 16:14, 15). As observed earlier (see NOTES on "the seventh day is a sacred occasion," v. 8, and "you shall count off," v. 15), the theme of rejoicing is totally absent in D's description of the Festival of Unleavened Bread (16:1–8). The midrash casts light on this distinction: "The expression of rejoicing occurs three times in connection with Sukkot, 'You shall rejoice in your festival' (Deut 16:14); 'You shall only rejoice' (Deut 16:15); 'And you shall rejoice before the Lord your God seven days' (Lev 23:40). But no such expression occurs even once regarding *Pesaḥ.* This is because the fate of man's crops is still in balance on *Pesaḥ,* and he does not know whether there will be a yield or not" (*Yal.* 654).

To "rejoice before YHWH" always means in the sanctuary. But how should one rejoice? It is too late for bringing firstfruits (as in the case of the earlier grain harvests, the *ʿomer* of barley and the two loaves of wheat). Of course, feasting is always implied (cf. Deut 14:26). But the command to rejoice follows and must result from the command to take the enumerated plants. What seems to be taken for granted in Scripture is made explicit by the rabbis:

> Each day they walked in procession (with the branches) round the altar and recited, "We beseech you, O Eternal, save we pray; we beseech you, O Eternal, send prosperity, we pray. . . . " But on that day (the seventh) they walked in procession round the altar seven times. . . . When would they wave (the branches)? At "Praise the Lord," at the beginning and at the end and at "We beseech you, O Lord, save us" (Ps 118:25a), the words of the school of Hillel. The school of Shammai says: also at "We beseech you, O Lord, prosper us." (Ps 118:25b; *m. Suk.* 4:5; 3:9)

That the circumambulation of the altar with these plants was an ancient rite is attested by *Jubilees*, which attributes it to Abraham: "And Abraham took branches of palm trees and fruit of good trees and each of the days (of the Festival of Booths) he used to go around the altar with branches" (*Jub* 16:31; cf. 2 Macc 10:7; Jos. *Ant.* 3.245).

Thus the dual purpose of the branches follows the order of Ps 118. One chants first "Praise YHWH" (v. 1), presumably thanksgiving for the completed agricultural cycle, and then "We beseech you, O Lord" (v. 25) for a purpose that we now shall examine. It can be ascertained by examining some of the other non-biblical rites recorded for this festival:

> They used to bring palm twigs and beat them on the ground at the sides of the altar, and that day (the seventh) was called "The day of beating the palm twigs." (*m. Suk.* 4:6)

> *The water-libation:* How so? A golden flagon holding three logs was filled from the pool of Shiloah. When they arrived at the Water Gate they sounded a prolonged blast, (and) a quavering note, and a prolonged blast. He went up the ramp and turned to his left where there were two silver bowls. . . . And they each had a hole like a narrow spout, one wide and the other narrow, so that both were emptied out together, the one to the west was for water and that to the east for wine. . . . R. Judah says, with one log they would carry out the libations all eight days. (*m. Suk.* 4:9)

The rabbis were fully cognizant that the theme that unites all these rituals is a supplication for rain. The waving of the branches in all directions is a summons to the four winds to bring rain or "to hinder the bad winds and the bad dews" (*b. Suk.* 37b–38a). The blowing of the shofar is mandated for the production of rain:" A city upon which no rain has fallen . . . blows (the shofar) and fasts" (*m. Taʿan.* 3:3; cf. *t. Taʿan.* 2:8). The water libation unique to this festival speaks for itself: water brought from the Pool of Shiloah through the Water Gate "because through it the water pitcher was brought for the libation on the Festival of Booths" (*t. Suk.* 3:3) could be for only one purpose: "so that the rain would be blessed on its account" (*t. Suk.* 3:18); "Why did the Torah enjoin on us to pour out water on the Booths Festival? The Holy One, Blessed Be He, said: Pour out water before me on the Booths Festival, so that your rains this year may be blessed" (*b. Roš. Haš.* 16a; cf. *t. Roš. Haš.* 1:12–13); "By these four kinds which grow near water; therefore they serve as pleaders for water" (*y. Taʿan.* 1:1). And the Mishna states categorically: "in the days of the Festival (Booths), the sentence on the waters will be passed" (*m. Roš. Haš.* 1:2). For further sources, rabbinic and modern, see Milgrom (1983c: 170, n. 38).

The rabbis acknowledged that the water libation rite had been performed from earliest times: "The laws . . . of the willow branch and the water libation were given to Moses at Mt. Sinai" (*b. Suk.* 44a; *t. Suk.* 3:2). They, of course, had Samuel's emergency water libation before them (1 Sam 7:6). They also had the more explicit eschatological statement of the prophet: "All who survive of all those nations that came up against Jerusalem shall make a pilgrimage year by year to bow low to the King Lord of Hosts and to *observe the Festival of Booths.* Any of the earth's communities that does not make the pilgrimage to Jerusalem to bow low to the King Lord of Hosts *shall receive no rain* [my emphasis]" (Zech 14:16–17).

The streams of "living waters" (Zech 14:8) that will flow out of Jerusalem during this eschatological Festival of Booths is reinterpreted by Jesus in his sermon in the Temple during this festival: "On the last day of the festival (the seventh), the great day (when the altar was circumambulated seven times), while Jesus was standing there, he cried out, 'Let anyone who is thirsty come to me, and let the one who believes in me drink. As the scripture has said, "Out of his (Jesus') belly shall flow rivers of living water" ' " (John 7:37–38)

There is little doubt that these rites have a magical origin: setting up the branches on the altar (Ps 118:27), beating them at the altar, circumambulating of the altar, pouring the water libation on the altar, all accompanied by shofar blowing, can in each case be traced to equivalent rites of sympathetic magic. A revealing example is cited by Patai (1939: 281, n. 152): the rabbis' claim that all kinds of danger can be averted by blowing the shofar, except too heavy rains (*m. Taʿan.* 3:8), can be explained by the belief that the shofar blasts resemble thunder, which produces rain but does not stop it. However, the magical origins had been expunged in biblical times (Milgrom 1990a: 353, 438–56, 71–73), all the more so in the rabbinic period. Let us take the instance of the circumambulation of the altar each day and seven times on the seventh day. The parallel of the story of the conquest of Jericho immediately comes to mind. That, too, involved a daily circumambulation, seven times on the seventh day (Josh 6:3–4, 14–18), accompanied by blasts of the shofar (vv. 8–9, 16, 20). However, the magical circle augmented seven times on the seventh day notwithstanding, the rite was executed at the command of YHWH (vv. 2–5). Similarly, it can be assumed that all the nonbiblical rites of the Festival of Booths, though undoubtedly originating in popular worship and rooted in magical practices, were ultimately assimilated into Israel's official monotheism so that the rabbis could say with confidence that they were revealed to Moses at Sinai.

Another example, which is illuminating in many other respects, is Elijah's sacrifice on Mount Carmel (1 Kgs 18). Patai (1939: 254–58) sees symbolism in everything Elijah does—all related to rain. Above all, the pouring of water on the altar (vv. 34–35) was not to heighten the miracle of fire consuming the drenched sacrifice (the usual interpretation), but was a quintessential water libation for rain. The incineration of the sacrifice was therefore only a prelude to the real test: Which God would end the three-year drought (v. 1)? Elijah, indeed, expects his successful sacrifice to produce rain at once (v. 41). But only after he sends out his attendant to search for signs of approaching rain for the seventh time does a small cloud appear in the western horizon followed by a great rain (vv. 43–45). Nonetheless, notwithstanding all the uncontestable magical elements in the narrative, the rainmaking is attributed not to Elijah, but only to YHWH (vv. 1, 24, 36–38, 46).

Perhaps the most instructive passage of all is *tiq'û šôpār běṣiyyôn qadděšû-ṣôm qir'û 'ăṣārâ* 'Blow a horn in Zion, solemnize a fast, proclaim an assembly' (Joel 2:15; cf. 1:14). The purpose of these three actions is to supplicate God for rain: "O children of Zion, be glad, rejoice in YHWH your God. For he has given you the early rain in kindness, now he makes the rain—the early rain and the late— fall as formerly" (2:23). As astutely noted by Knohl (1987: 95; 1995: 37), all three actions—horn blowing, fasting, and assembling—characterize, respectively, the three festivals of the seventh month: the first day, "commemorated with short blasts" (Lev 23:24); the tenth day, "you shall practice self-denial" (vv. 27, 32), and the twenty-second day, the "solemn assembly" (v. 36), following the seven-day Festival of Booths. These three days are further united by their sacrificial service: only on these three days are the following burnt offerings required: one bull, one ram, and seven lambs (Num 29:2, 8, 36). This interpretation was already given by *Tg. Ps.-J.*: *kěnîšîn tehěwôn lěṣalā'â qŏdām YY 'al miṭrā'* 'You shall hold an assembly to pray to YHWH for rain' (see NOTE on "a solemn assembly," v. 36).

My student R. Gane has noticed that the Hittite Telepinu festival, observed in both the fall and the spring, included all the elements that characterize Israel's autumn festivals—solemnity and joy, communal feast and cultic purification—lending credence to the possibility that all three festivals compose a single unit. The myth and ritual school, particularly Mowinckel (1967: 106–92), has also posited that these three festival were once united by a theme, the annual enthronement rite of YHWH, but this school also assumes that an original long festival subsequently split into the three prescribed in the MT. The enthronement motif, based on purported evidence from the Psalms, has not been accepted by the scholarly world (see NOTE on "commemorated with short blasts," v. 24). But the close proximity of the festivals, the fact that they alone require the same number of burnt offerings, and the strong possibility, just argued, that they celebrate the same theme give ample reason to reflect that perhaps originally they were one festival whose manifold rites were directed toward the purpose of supplicating God for adequate rain. Neither should we be surprised by its putative twenty-two-day length. The Hittite AN-TAH.ŠUM festival is at least thirty-eight days long. A closer analogy at hand is LB Emar in Syria, which can boast of three long festivals composed of seven-day units (Fleming 1995: 144). In any event, the common bond—the supplication for ample rain—has been demonstrated: shofar blowing, fasting, followed by a seven-day festival marked by rites with water and to produce water, climaxed by a solemn assembly whose total focus is supplication for rain (see NOTE on "a solemn assembly," v. 36).

To convey some impression of the unprescribed, nonsacrificial festivities indulged in by laity and clergy alike during the water-libation rites, I conclude with this probable eyewitness description:

> Anyone who had not witnessed the rejoicing at the Libation Water-Well had never seen rejoicing in his life.

At the close of the first Holyday of the Festival of Booths they went down to the court of the Women where they had made an important rearrangement. And golden candlesticks were there with four golden bowls at their tops and four ladders to each one, and four youths from the young priests with pitchers of oil, holding a hundred and twenty *logs*, in their hands, which they used to pour into every bowl. From the worn-out drawers and girdles of the priests they made wicks and with them they set alight; and there was no courtyard in Jerusalem that was not lit up with the light of the Libation Water-Well ceremony.

Pious men and men of good deeds used to dance before them with burning torches in their hands and sang before them songs and praises. [Rabban Simeon b. Gamaliel danced with eight flaming torches, and not one of them fell to the ground. Now he would prostrate himself, he would put his finger on the ground, bow low, kiss (the ground), and forthwith straighten up (*t. Suk.* 4:4)]. And the Levites on harps, and on lyres, and with cymbals, and with trumpets and with other instruments of music without number upon the fifteen steps leading down from the court of the Israelites to the Women's Court, corresponding to The Fifteen Songs of Ascent in the Psalms; upon them the Levites used to stand with musical instruments and sing hymns. And two priests stood at the Upper Gate which led down from the Israelites' Court to the Court of the Women with two trumpets in their hands. At cockcrow they sounded a prolonged blast, (and) a quavering note, and a prolonged blast. When they arrived at the tenth step they sounded a prolonged blast, (and) a quavering note, and a prolonged blast. When they reached the Forecourt they blew a prolonged blast, (and) a quavering note, and a prolonged blast. They kept up prolonged blasts and proceeded until they reached the gate that led out to the east; when they arrived at the gate that led forth to the East they turned their faces to the West and said, "Our ancestors when they were in this place turned 'with their backs unto the Temple and their faces towards the East and they prostrated themselves eastward towards the sun' (Ezek 8:16), but as for us our eyes are turned to the Eternal." (*m. Suk.* 5:1–4)

Finally, it must to be stated that some segments of the Jewish community were unhappy with these folk rites in the Temple, particularly the processions around the altar. In Ezekiel's visionary Temple, this could never have taken place because the inner court was the private reserve of the priests (Ezek 46:1–3). The Qumran sectaries accept this restriction in their visionary Temple, and because its breach would take place mainly on the Festival of Booths, they ordained that booths be built on the roofs of the buildings girding the outer courtyard wall (11QT 42:12–17). Their probable purpose was to allow the people's elders to observe the priestly rites and, thereby, prevent the populace from entering the inner court and circumambulating the altar (Knohl 1992: 605–7; cf. Rabad on *Sipra* Emor 12:13). Sussman (1990: 67, n. 220) adds the enlightening point that most of the subsequent Sadducean–Pharisaic controversies fall in the sphere of the public cult: the *'ōmer* (*m. Menah.* 10:3; *m. Ḥag.* 2:4), the Red Cow (*m. Para* 3:7; cf. 3:3); and, especially during the Festival of Booths, the water libation (*m. Suk* 4:9), the beating of the willows (*t. Suk.* 3:1; cf. Lieberman 1962: 4.869), the immersion of the candelabrum (*t. Ḥag.* 3:35), and the processions around the altar (*t. Suk.* 4:1).

41. *You shall celebrate it as a pilgrimage-festival to YHWH for seven days.* *wĕhaggōtem 'ōtô ḥag laYHWH šibʿat yāmîm.* This sentence is modeled on P's *wĕhaggōtem ḥag laYHWH šibʿat yāmîm* (Num 29:12b), as frequently attested in H (see COMMENT A), followed by a statement of closure (v. 41bα), typical of H (vv. 14b, 21b). Note that the injunction to observe a seven-day *ḥag* occurs four times in this appendix (vv. 39aα, 40b, 41a, 42a).

What, however, is the antecedent of "it"? One would have to reach back to *ḥag* (v. 3a) for the nearest (but unlikely) choice. As shown by Hoffmann (1953: 2.95), this verse is modeled on Exod 12:14aβ,b (H; Knohl 1995: 52) *wĕhaggōtem 'ōtô ḥag laYHWH lĕdōrōtêkem ḥuqqat 'ôlām tĕḥagguhû* 'you shall celebrate it as a pilgrimage-festival to YHWH throughout your generations; you shall celebrate it as an eternal law' where "it" refers to the immediately preceding *hayyôm hazzeh* 'this day' (v. 14aα). Nonetheless, it should be noticed that H does not completely repeat its Exodus pattern, but alters the second half of the verse in order to insert (for the third time) the injunction that the festival should fall in the seventh month (see below).

as a law for all time, throughout your generations. *ḥuqqat 'ôlām lĕdōrōtêkem.* Missing is *bĕkol-môšĕbōtêkem* 'in all your settlements' (cf. vv. 14, 21), which indicates that the "law" refers to the seven-day observance at the sanctuary—proof that v. 41a,bα does not stem from H$_R$ (contra Knohl 1987: 96).

You shall celebrate it in the seventh month. *baḥōdeš haššĕbîʿî tāḥōggû 'ōtô.* The seventh month has already been stated twice (vv. 34, 39). Moreover, the original pericope probably closed with v. 41a (see NOTE on "a law for all time," v. 21), further emphasizing the redundancy. Indeed, would anyone doubt that the festival was to be celebrated in the seventh month? Merely to ask the question is to provide the answer: Jeroboam I did change the date from the seventh to the eighth month (1 Kgs 12:33). Even though the seasons and, hence, the harvests occur as much as one month later in North Israel than in Judah, this text is emphatic in insisting on keeping it everywhere in the seventh month (Hoffmann 1953; Scott 1993: 112). This admonition most likely reflects the fear that this calendrical aberration would contaminate Judahite practice. When is the most obvious time for such fear to have been realized? Nothing comes to mind so readily as the reign of Hezekiah, when Judah was flooded by refugees from North Israel, who brought their traditions and observances with them. Thus this repetitive sentence should be attributed to H that operated during Hezekiah's reign. The style of the entire verse might indicate that it was composed by a single author: imperfect *taḥōggû* creates a circular inclusio with *wĕḥaggōtem*, through a change of verb pattern—a typical H maneuver (Paran 1983: 35). But it is more likely that H contributed only the clause under discussion (v. 41bβ) and inverted the verb pattern to create the circular inclusio. That this alternative is preferable is demonstrated by the previous clause *ḥuqqot 'ōlam lĕdōrōtēkem*, which most likely concludes the pericope vv. 38–41a. Accordingly, it was H that added and appended the addition vv. 39–41, to which H_R is responsible for the appendices to chap. 23 (vv. 2aβ, b–3 and vv. 42–43). If my contention is correct, it will prove that the deuteronomistic author of 1 Kgs 12:32 was polemicizing not only against Jereboam I, but also against North Israelite practice that may have continued into the exile from the time of North Israel's destruction in the reign of Hezekiah.

42. *In booths you shall live seven days. bassukōt tēšĕbû šib'at yāmîm.* The object "booths" (lit. "the booths") begins the verse for the sake of emphasis. The definite article implies that their use and purpose are well known (GKC § 126n). All Israelites, but not resident aliens (see below), are commanded to live in booths for seven continuous days. These facts offer, in my opinion, strong evidence that this injunction was written in and for the exile, as will be substantiated below.

The word *sukkâ* 'booth' occurs in a variety of contexts. It is a stall for animals (Gen 33:17), a dwelling for guards or harvesters of vineyards (Isa 1:8), a temporary shelter against the sun (Jon 4:5), and a dwelling for besieging soldiers (1 Kgs 20:16) and even for the encamped holy Ark (2 Sam 11:11). It is a metaphor for Jerusalem (Isa 4:6; Amos 9:1), for the Temple (Ps 27:5), for the heavens (Ps 18:12; Job 36:29), and for divine protection (Ps 31:21), and it serves as a double entendre for Israel's first station in the wilderness (Exod 12:37; Num 33:5) as well as a type of dwelling (v. 43; Levine 1989). In any case, in this verse, the prescribed booth clearly describes a temporary shelter. What is its function? The proposed answers fall into three main categories:

1. The most cited explanation, from Wellhausen (1963: 83) to the present, is that it served as a temporary dwelling for the farmer during the harvest, by day for exploiting every minute for harvesting and by night for guarding his crops. The flaw in this argument is readily apparent from the NOTE on "when you have ingathered the yield of the land," v. 39: the Festival of Booths took place when all

the crops had been harvested and the farmer had no need to be in his field, much less live on it (cf. Tur-Sinai 1957: 3.81). Other objections stem from the text: there are no firstfruit offerings (Dillmann and Ryssel 1897); *ʾāsîp*, the original name of the festival (Exod 23:16b), does not refer to the harvest, but to the processing and storage of the entire yield (Deut 16:13); and the purpose of this festival is both thanksgiving and hope for continuous blessing (Deut 16:15b; cf. Scott 1993: 23–25)—that is, for adequate seasonal rain (see NOTE on v. 40). Note specifically the text of Deut 16:13: "You shall observe the Festival of Booths for seven days when you ingather *from* your threshing floor [*miggornĕkā*] and *from* your vat [*ûmiyy-iqbekā*]"—that is, after the grain has been threshed and the wine and grapes have been pressed. Thus the produce has been not only harvested, but even processed. Tigay (1996: 538a, n. 8) suggests that these objections are obviated if the booth were a celebration of the harvest just passed. However, the booth symbolism would then be weak. It could symbolize only the grape harvest (and possibly that of other summer fruits). What would it have meant to the grain farmer who did not live in booths? Rather, a symbol for all farmers would be required.

2. The rabbis maintain that the etiology enunciated in v. 43 is correct. Some of them hold that it refers to the Israelites' first station in the wilderness (Exod 12:37), where God literally provided them with *sukkôt*, adequate shelter and shade, and, thereby, assured them with his ongoing protection in the wilderness (R. Akiba in *b. Suk.* 11b; R. Eliezer in *Sipra* Emor 17:11; cf. *Mek. RŠbY* to Exod 13:20; Wessely 1846; most recently, Elgabish 1994; Knohl 1995: 39). That the etiology of a place-name is popularly assigned to a past event is substantiated by the very name of Sukkoth given by Jacob to the place where he erected *sukkôt* for his livestock (Gen 33:17).

A slightly variant approach is taken by the rabbis who aver that *sukkôt* of v. 43 is a metaphor for God's protecting cloud, which shielded Israel from the dangers both natural (sunstroke) and physical (enemies) from the moment they left Egypt (*Tgs.*; R. Akiba in *Sipra* Emor 17:11; *Mek.* Bo' 14; for a thorough discussion of the symbolism of the *sukkâ* in rabbinic Judaism, see Rubinstein 1994). This interpretation has been revived most recently by Scott (1993: 166–74) and will be discussed below. At this juncture, I shall state my (admittedly biased) view that post hoc historical etiologies and allegorical interpretations of customs and practices, though unquestionably valuable to the believing community, do not penetrate to their origins. The probable rationale for the meaning of v. 43 is expounded in its NOTE.

3. The most natural and logical explanation, I submit (vol. 1.27–28), is that the *sukkâ* refers to the shelter built by pilgrims to the Jerusalem Temple for the one festival during which there were too many of them to be accommodated in the city (Ehrlich 1908; Licht 1968: 1042; Ginsberg 1982: 60). To be sure, after centralization, the imperative to offer the paschal sacrifice would have brought large numbers to Jerusalem, but this occasion was limited to a one-night observance. If booths were erected, they would have been dismantled by the morning. The booths of the autumn festival, however, had to last for seven (and probably eight) days. Strewn on the hillsides that surrounded Jerusalem, they would

have been the distinctive visual characteristic of the festival. Jerusalem was not unique in this regard. In ancient Greece, at the Carnea festival, the Spartans "dwelt in tentlike bowers after the fashion of a military camp" (Kedar-Kopfstein 1980: 205). It is, therefore, of ultimate significance that the name *ḥag hassukkôt* 'the Festival of the Booths', occurs solely in Lev 23:36 and Deut 16:13, 16, the only pentateuchal legal corpora in the Pentateuch that presume regional preference or national centralization. But when the festivals became national celebrations at the capital, the booths erected by pilgrims probably would match and outnumber the residences in the city.

Scott (1993: 72) objects to this interpretation on the basis of Neh 8, which commands all Israelites to build booths, not just in Jerusalem. However, this is precisely Ezra's innovation. In preexilic, postcentralization Judah, the booths were, indeed, clustered around Jerusalem. Ezra insists, on the basis of Lev 23:42, that all Israelites must build booths at their residences (Neh 8:16a), *precisely as they did in the Babylonian exile*. Scott (1993: 73) raises another objection: On the presumption that pilgrims would have erected any kind of shelter, including tents, why did Ezra insist on branches? The answer is evident: Ezra based himself on his (mis)understanding of Lev 23:40 of the canonized Torah (see COMMENT C). Finally, the question is asked why the injunction to build booths does not appear in Ezekiel and Numbers. Here, too, the answer is at hand: Ezekiels' brief enumeration of the festivals (Ezek 45:18–25) focuses solely on the services in his visionary Temple. The absence of the word *sukkôt* in Num 29:12–38 is specially significant: this pericope reflects the precentralization era, when the festival was celebrated at local or regional sanctuaries within commuting distance of the worshipers' homes. Naturally, some families may have chosen to "camp out" in *sukkôt*. But they were not so distinguished a feature of the festival for it be called by the name *sukkôt*.

At the outset of this discussion, it has been proposed that this verse and the following one (vv. 42–43) were composed in the exile. Note these facts:

1. The word *sukkôt*, though an object, is placed in the emphatic position at the beginning of the verse. Its emphasis is augmented by its repetition in the verse using the same verb *yāšab* 'live'. This staccato demand on living in booths makes best sense as an address to the Babylonian Exiles (see below).

2. Only Israelites are commanded to build booths, but not the *gēr*, the resident alien. To be sure, this requirement, a performative commandment, is not incumbent on the *gēr* (see chap. 17, COMMENT B; vol. 1.1055–56). However, he certainly is permitted to worship at the sanctuary (22:25)! But there is no indication that he is required to construct a booth while he is there. His omission from the injunction is explicable on the basis of historical reality: in the exile, there were no "resident aliens"! Interestingly and corroboratively, non-Israelites who were attracted to the exiles (especially to their sabbath, Isa 56:1–3) are not called *gērîm*, but *bĕnê-hannēkār* 'foreigners' (Isa 56:3, 6; cf. *ʿēreb*, Exod 12:38; *ʾăsapsūp*, Num 11:4 designating those who left Egypt with Israel). The clearest example is the blasphemer in the wilderness who, though his mother is an Israelite, is called "the son of an Egyptian father" (Lev 24:10), not a *gēr*. It is only

when the exiles return to their homeland and can resume complete control of their political, social, and religious life can those *resident* non-Israelites be called *gērîm* (Isa 14:1–2). (The ostensible exception, Josh 8:33, 35, is a deuteronomistic anachronism; note the absence of the *gēr* from the prototype, Deut 27.)

3. Only now can the historical rationale for building booths (v. 43) be projected into full significance. Its illusiveness has already been alluded to and will be further examined in the NOTE on v. 43. I believe it to be an act of desperation, but one fully explicable: without the Temple and its attendant rites — the circumambulations of the altar, the water libation, the participation of the Levitic choir and orchestra, the water-well festivities (see NOTE on v. 40) — what of the festival could be observed? Hence the emphasis on building booths and justifying them on historical grounds, as well as taking the ceremonial plants (v. 40), presumably accompanied by some of the prayers preserved in the Mishna, cited above. No wonder, then, that the original festival calendar (vv. 4–38) became flanked by two exilic additions — the observance of the sabbath (vv. 1–3) and the celebration of the Festival of Booths by building booths and taking (and supplicating God with) leafy branches — both of which could be observed in the exile without recourse to the Temple. That rationale of v. 43 fits best an exilic provenance (see NOTE on "I made the Israelites . . . ," v. 43).

4. For me, the clinching evidence for the exilic provenance of this injunction is its insistence that it is incumbent on all Israelites. Allegorical explanations, such as those given by Scott (1993: 166–72), citing Volz (1912) and Riesenfeld (1947), that booths symbolized the dwelling of God among his people or that booths put all Israelites, rich and poor, on the same level do not resonate with authenticity. Logic, at least for me, points to one answer: whereas in the homeland only pilgrims coming from afar built booths, in the exile — if the festival was to survive — all Israelites were commanded to build them. After all, what sense did it make for a Jerusalemite to leave the comforts of his home to endure the inconveniences of living in an improvised shelter? However, once the exiles returned and rebuilt the Temple, pilgrimages were resumed. Presumably, since most of the postexilic settlements were clustered around and within commuting distance of Jerusalem, fewer booths were visible on Jerusalem's outskirts during the Festival of Booths. But when Ezra read to the returned exiles Lev 23:42 at that momentous assembly on the first day of the seventh month (Neh 8:2), he thereby informed them that every Israelite had to construct a booth. The crowded Israelite city, as can be determined from archaeological excavations (Herzog 1992: 1037–43, esp. 1040), would have allowed only a minority (in the royal and aristocratic quarter) the space to build booths adequate in size to accommodate an entire family. However, roofs were flat, allowing for the possibility that if *ḥaṣrōtêhem* 'their courtyards' were lacking, they could construct the booth *ʾîš ʿal-gaggô* 'everyone on his roof' (Neh 8:16; see COMMENT C). Thus the booth, a convenience for pilgrims, became a divine imperative for all Israel — a reminder of YHWH's salvific providence during the wilderness sojourn.

all citizens in Israel. kol-hāʾezrāḥ bĕyiśrāʾēl. Everywhere else in H, the *ʾezrāḥ* 'the Israelite' is equated with the *gēr* 'the resident alien' (16:29; 17:15; 18:26;

19:34; 24:16, 22; Exod 12:19, 48, 49; Num 9:14; 15:13, 29, 30; for the source attributions, see Introduction II O) as well as elsewhere (Josh 8:33; Ezek 47:22). Rather than allow for this sole exception, many critics insert the *gēr*. The rabbis deduce the presence of the *gēr* from the apparent superfluous *běyiśrā'ēl* (*Sipra* Emor 17:9). Elliger (1966) suggests that the omission is deliberate, to show the inferiority of the *gēr*, a sentiment combated by Isa 56:3. Ehrlich 1908 (H), I believe, strikes close to the mark by stating that the *gēr* is exempt from building booths (at the sanctuary), since he is not required to worship YHWH. However, it can be stated as a general principle that the *gēr* is not required to observe a performative commandment, such as slaughtering his sacrificeable animal at the authorized altar (17:3–5; see chap. 17, COMMENT B). Also, as stated above, this injunction is unique in that it was promulgated in the exile, where there were no "resident" aliens.

Since the term *'ezrāḥ* originally meant "native" (see NOTE on 19:34), explanatory "in Israel" had to be added, since the "natives" in the exile were Babylonians; similarly, *ke'ezrāḥ bibnê yiśrā'ēl* (Ezek 47:22)—additional evidence that this verse too was written in exile.

Uniquely, but predictably, the Dead Sea sectaries restrict the same phrase *LKWL H'ZRḤ BYŚR'L* to its own membership (1QSa 1:6).

shall live in booths. yēšěbû bassukkōt. The singular *yēšěb* is attested in 4Q365, frag. 25, l. 1; LXX; Sam. The verse pattern abcdb'a' (Hartley 1992) is typical of H. The switch from second to third (impersonal) person is characteristic of both priestly sources, P and H (e.g., Exod 25:2; Num 5:2–3; 18:10; 35:8; Paran 1983: 45–46). The change of person is usually accompanied by a change in verb pattern, the suffixed to the prefixed form. But instead of the anticipated *wiyěšabtem bassukkōt*, the sentence begins with *bassukkōt tēšěbû* in order to emphasize the object, *sukkōt* (Paran 1983: 42; see above).

43. *I made the Israelites live in booths when I brought them out of the land of Egypt. bassukkôt hôšabtî 'et- běnê yiśrā'ēl běhôṣî'î 'ōtām mē'ereṣ miṣrāyim.* The various and, admittedly, far-fetched explanations for this rationale are cited in point no. 2 in the NOTE on "In booths you shall live seven days," v. 42. As soon as I (1994c) had expounded my theory of an exilic provenance for this addendum, Moshe Greenberg suggested, most plausibly, that an exilic setting would best explain the motivation of this rationale: since God provided Israel with booths in an earlier "exile," the wilderness, Israel should recall this event by living in booths during the Festival of Booths in the new exile, Babylonia.

According to Yehuda Feliks (personal communication), 95 percent of the peasants in Egypt live in virtual booths to this very day: the roofs of their huts consist of nothing but palm fronds. This, Feliks claims, logically, is how Israel lived in Egypt. YHWH promised Israel that when he took Israel out of Egypt, it would again be provided with booths, which took place at the first wilderness station, Succoth (= Booths; Exod 12:37). Thus the booth is the symbol of Israel's exile in and redemption from Babylonia.

Indeed, this explanation dovetails with the sabbath interpolation at the head of this chapter (v. 3), which also is attributable to an exilic author (see NOTE on "fixed times of YHWH," v. 2). The sabbath, according to priestly tradition, was not only legislated but actually observed in the wilderness, before Israel entered its land

(Exod 16:22–30 [P]). Also, it can hardly be an accident that Ezekiel, the prophet to the exilic community, constantly emphasizes the sabbath (cf. Ezek 20:12, 13, 16, 20, 21, 24; 22:8; 26; 23:28; 44:24; 45:17; 46:1, 3, 4, 12), particularly that its observance was commanded in the wilderness (Ezek 20:10–12). As noted by Ramban (Num 30:1; also Joosten 1996: 79), the priestly calendars are distinguished from most of the other laws commanded to Moses in that they have a concluding passage of compliance (23:44; Num 30:1). The reason for this singularity escapes me.

Thus there is no reason to speculate further on the historical reality of the alleged wilderness booths. It makes no difference whether the reference is to a place-name, God's protecting cloud, or actual booths. A vague recollection of Israel's booths in the wilderness sufficed to engender the command to build booths during the Festival of Booths in the new wilderness, the Babylonian Exile.

the Israelites. běnê yiśrā'el. Instead, 4Q365, frag. 25, reads *'ăbôtêkem* 'your ancestors' in a transparent attempt to exclude the *gēr*, a term that by the end of Second Temple times meant "the proselyte." The book of *Jubilees* holds a similar view, since it relates that when Abraham celebrated the Festival of Booths "there was no alien with him or any who were not circumcised" (*Jub* 16:25). As indicated above, this sectarian position was categorically opposed by the rabbis who include the *gēr* (i.e., the proselyte) among those required to construct booths (*Sipra* Emor 17:9).

in order that . . . when I brought them out of the land of Egypt. lěma'an . . . běhôṣî'î 'ōtām mē'ereṣ miṣrāyim. The style is identical with that of the rationale for preserving the flask of manna (Exod 16:32b). On the basis of the poetic parallelism *'ōhel / sukkâ* (e.g., Ps 27:5), Noth (1977: 176) avers that this rationale is correct, "a reminder of the tents improvised with staves and tent-cloth by the nomadic shepherd" (but see above).

The attempt to anchor the Deity's salvific acts in the cult is not unique to Israel (cf. Albrektson 1967: 115–16; Hammershaimb 1971). In Greece, "cultic actions were explained on the basis of quasi-historical etiologies: the Thargelia, for example, were associated with the Athenian tribute to Minos and Theseus' voyage of deliverance. At the Carnea, the Spartans gave thanks to Apollo for bringing them into the land as conquerors" (Kedar-Kopfstein 1980: 205).

I am YHWH your God. 'ănî YHWH 'ĕlōhêkem. This formula (or in its shortened form *'ănî YHWH*) frequently is associated with the deliverance from Egypt (e.g., 22:33; 25:55). Perhaps its H author was also responsible for its insertion in v. 22 in order to divide the chapter into two: the spring and autumn festivals (Wenham 1979). Alternatively, it may be the work of an exilic tradent (Hr) who wished to authenticate his additions (vv. 22, 42–43; see NOTE on v. 22).

44. *Thus Moses declared the fixed times of YHWH to the Israelites. wayyědabbēr Mōšeh 'et-mō'ădê YHWH 'el-běnê yiśrā'el.* Tg. Ps.-J. glosses correctly *wě'alpěnûn liběnê yiśrā'el* 'and he taught them to the Israelites'. The same compliance is attributed to Moses in 21:24 (also *wayyědabbēr*) and at the end of P's festival calendar (Num 30:1).

the fixed times of YHWH. mō'ădê YHWH. One can argue that this expression forms an inclusio with its counterpart in v. 2, thereby including the sabbath among the *mô'ădîm*, but it is more likely a closure for the original calendar (vv. 4–38), forming an inclusio with the same expression in v. 4.

COMMENTS

A. The Composition of Chapter 23

In recapitulating the arguments dispersed throughout this chapter, it becomes clearly apparent that they are based on the assumption, convincingly established, in my opinion, by Knohl (1995) that H is both a later stratum and a redaction of P. If any doubt remains, it should be dispelled by the sacrificial notices in Lev 23.

The formula *wĕhiqrabtem 'iššeh la YHWH* 'you shall present the food gift to the Lord' appears frequently throughout this chapter (vv. 25, 27, 36 [bis], 37). It is H's "compare." But what is its referent? Since the formula refers to public sacrifices for festivals at the sanctuary, its referent can be only Num 28–29 (P). Of course, it can be argued that the antecedent source may not be in Scripture. However, that the public sacrifices alluded to in Lev 23 must be those of Num 28–29 can be demonstrated on other grounds. It should be noticed that the only festivals in Lev 23 that do list public sacrifices are the grain offerings: the barley in vv. 12–13 and the wheat in vv. 18–19. The first, however, is entirely omitted in Numbers, and the second is in Numbers but it differs in the quantities (cf. Lev 23:18 with Num 28:29). This chapter uses the formula *wĕhiqrabtem 'iššeh laYHWH* whenever it agrees with Num 28–29 (P), but enumerates the sacrifices when it differs.

A logical consideration should clinch the argument. Nearly every critic has held (under the assumption that P is later than H) than the calendar of Num 28–29 (P) was composed subsequent to that of Lev 23 (H). Since in this earlier calendar, H takes pains to specify the sacrifices for the grain offerings, we would have to conclude that the category, species, and numbers of sacrifices unmentioned for the remaining festivals (Unleavened Bread, v. 8; Warning Blasts, v. 25; Purgation, v. 27, and Booths, v. 36 [bis]) would be left to the discretion (or whim) of the sanctuary! The absurdity of this deduction suffices, in itself, to demonstrate that Lev 23 is wholly dependent on an antecedent source, which can be only Num 28–29 (P). Thus Num 28–29 (P) must be earlier than and the basis of Lev 23 (H), implying the possibility that not only in this chapter, but in general, H is the heir and redactor of P.

Readers are referred to the chapter's translation, which is composed of four typefaces corresponding to its presumed four strata: Pre-H₁ is represented by regular type; Pre-H₂, by boldface; H, by italic block type; and H_R, by bold block type.

Pre-H₁ stands for the pre-Hezekian stratum. It consists of three injunctions:

1. A first sheaf of the barley crop must be brought to the local sanctuary as an elevation offering (vv. 10aβ–11), accompanied by a lamb as burnt offering (v. 12), before partaking of the new crop (v. 14a).
2. Fifty days later, the firstfruits of the wheat crop in the form of two leavened loaves are brought to the local sanctuary as an elevation offering, accompanied by two lambs as well-being offerings (v. 19b), which become a priestly prebend (vv. 15a*, 16aβa*, 20*).

3. On the fifteenth day of the seventh month, the Israelite landowner is enjoined to celebrate a seven-day festival at his sanctuary with the use of branches (vv. 39a*, 40), presumably in processions round the altar (see NOTES).

Pre-H$_1$, therefore, reflects a flexible agricultural calendar, depending on the Israelite's place of residence. He brings a firstfruit offering of his crops to his local sanctuary whenever they ripen. But *ḥag hā'āsîp* 'the Festival of Ingathering' (Exod 23:16) he celebrates at the same time as the rest of the nation. Its purpose is both to rejoice over the past year's yield and to supplicate God for adequate and timely rain for the following year's crop. To achieve the latter end, he circumambulates the altar with specified branches (see NOTE on v. 40).

Pre-H$_2$ is the "Sunday Pentacostalist." Its purpose is to establish a *ḥag* at each local sanctuary for its devotees by declaring that the barley offering be brought on the first Sunday after the harvesting has begun. The wheat offering, fifty days later, also falls on a Sunday, thereby creating another communally celebrated event at the sanctuary. It is Pre-H$_2$ that introduces the notion of *šabbāt* as the sabbath-week, which later Jewish groups mistook for the sabbath day, giving rise to schismatic differences on the relation between this sabbath and the proximate Feast of Unleavened Bread (see NOTE on "another day after the sabbath-week," v. 15).

H comprises the main strand of this chapter. It is the true H, the founder of the school reflecting the worship of God at the Jerusalem Temple. The individual firstfruits offerings are abolished and are offered, instead, by the Temple on a Sunday fixed by the Temple authorities. The individual farmer is spared a pilgrimage to the Temple (or to his regional sanctuary; see chap. 17, COMMENT D) and can remain at home to tend to the harvest.

H is also responsible for the main text on the calendar year (vv. 4–38). It adopts the catalogue of public sacrifices followed by (a) regional sanctuary(ies) (Num 28–29 [P]) and indulges in detail when it is either innovative (barley) or different (wheat; see NOTE on v. 8, and INTRODUCTION to vv. 15–22). In describing the Day of Purgation (vv. 26–32), it supplements Lev 16 by supplying the penalties for working or eating on this day (vv. 29–30). That it calls the autumn festival "the Festival of Booths" reflects the Temple when the environs of Jerusalem abounded in pilgrims' booths (see NOTE on v. 36). It also transfers from the regional sanctuaries to the Temple this festival's rite of circumambulating the altar with specified branches—a tradition that persisted in the Second Temple until its destruction (see NOTE on v. 40) and has been continued in the synagogue. The staccato emphasis on the seventh month (vv. 39aα, 41a, following 34b) may be attributed to the practice of the North Israelite refugees who flooded the land of Judah during the reign of Hezekiah to observe the festival on the eighth month.

H$_R$ represents the final stratum of this chapter. It is the end product of the H Source composed in the Babylonian Exile. Its purpose is to salvage as much of the cultic calendar so that Israel might retain its ethnic and religious identity in the exile. It assumes that all observances mentioned in H that are practiced independently of the cult would be followed, namely, the consumption of unleavened bread during the Festival of Unleavened Bread and the abstention from (laborious) work during the festivals. It focuses expressly on the sabbath and the Festival of Booths, since the former's inclusion as a "fixed time" and the latter's mandatory prescription to live in booths are H's innovation. The observance of Booths is now enjoined on all Israelites, and a rationale is supplied, rooting it in Israel's exodus tradition (vv. 42–43). Also, the first and eighth days of the Festival of Booths continue to be observed as rest days (*šabbātôn*, v. 39b; cf. *miqrāʾ qōdeš*, vv. 35a, 36bα).

In sum, Lev 23 is totally the product of the H Source. Contra Haran (1978: 298, n. 17) and Knohl (1987; 1995: 8–52), there is not a trace of P in this entire chapter (cf. Scott 1993: 105–8). To be sure, it relies on P's cultic calendar (Num 28–29) and, hence, takes for granted the required public sacrifices except in two cases, one of which is lacking in P (the barley offering, vv. 12–13), and the other of which differs from P (the wheat offering, vv. 18–19).

Also, the designation of this calendar as "priestly-popular" (Knohl 1987: 104–6; 1995: 45) must be modified. When we look at the stratum of H (the true H, the founder of the H School), there are practically no folk elements. On the contrary, H has, in effect, abolished them by turning them over to the authority of the Temple. Thus the individual's barley and wheat offerings are now the responsibility of the Temple. As for other popular observances, such as the paschal sacrifice and the abstention from leaven during the following seven days (vv. 5–6) and the blowing of the shofar (v. 24), these are enjoined in previous calendars (cf. Exod 12:1–20; Num 29:1). Ostensibly, the only exception is the Day of Purgation, which emphasizes the people's role in effecting divine forgiveness by abstaining from work and food (vv. 26–32). And if the objection is raised that this, too, already has been prescribed (16:29–33), it need only be mentioned that this passage, too, is the product of H (vol. 1.62, 1064–65). But this is precisely the point: all that H adds are the penalties for disobeying these injunctions—a far cry from endorsing popular religion. To be sure, H_R focuses on a folk rite when it enjoins all Israel to dwell in booths during the autumn festival (v. 42), but this is an act of desperation born out of the necessity to survive in a cultless diaspora.

The enduring value of this chapter is that it has preserved the pre-Hezekian strata, which truly reveal a vibrant folk tradition: firstfruit grain offerings and, according to the testimony of Second Temple sources, circumambulations of the altar to supplicate God for rain. These rites may reflect an incipient but inchoate H contribution (and on that possibility, I have labeled them Pre-H_1 and Pre-H_2), but they were obliterated—rather, preempted—by the Temple with the blessing of the H Source, represented by H.

B. The Sabbath-Week: A Resolution of a Heavy Crux

The expression *mimmāḥŏrat haššabbāt* 'on the day after the sabbath-week' occurs three times in this chapter (vv. 11b, 15b, 16a). All three cases present syntactic and semantic problems in their contexts. The prefixed preposition *min* can mean "on" and is interchangeable with *beth* (Sarna 1959). Alternatively, this expression became petrified—it fits only in v. 15b, an indication of its interpolative nature (see NOTE on v. 16).

There are four interpretations of this expression, which gave rise to arguably the most long-lasting schism in the history of the Jewish people: those who hold that the word "sabbath" refers to the weekly sabbath—either the one falling during the week of the Festival of Unleavened Bread (Samaritans, Karaites) or the one falling after the festival (Boethusians, Qumran)—and those who hold that the sabbath means the day of rest from laborious work prescribed for this festival, either the first day (the Pharisees; cf. LXX on v. 11; Philo, *Laws* 2.162; Jos. *Ant.* 3.250) or the seventh day (Pesh., modern Falashas; Gerstenberger 1996: 344). To give some inkling of the ensuing polemic, I shall present some of the arguments that each side mustered *against its opposition*, countered point by point.

Against the Sabbatarian Position

1. If *haššabbāt* refers to the weekly sabbath, an ambiguity arises: we do not know which one it is (*Sipra* Emor 12:4; *b. Menaḥ.* 66a).

2. Since H applies the term *šabbāt* wherever a period of rest is intended—the seventh week (v. 15), the seventh year (25:2), the land's sabbath (25:6), a cycle of seven years (25:8)—it can apply also to a festival rest day (Paran 1989: 270). And the festival is, indeed, called *šabbāt* (vv. 24, 32, 39, Ibn Ezra; cf. Abravanel).

3. When the Israelites entered the land, they ate parched grain from the new crop *mimmāḥŏrat happesaḥ* 'on the day following the *pesaḥ* offering' (Josh 5:11; Meshullam b. Kalonymus, cited by Ibn Ezra; Maimonides *ʿĀbōdâ*, Temidin 7:11; Ralbag).

4. If the sabbath does not fall on a fixed day of the month, the Festival of Weeks will never fall on a fixed day of the month (*b. Menaḥ.* 66a).

5. Deut 16:8 states, "You shall eat unleavened bread for six days." This implies that the first day is from the old grain, and the six remaining days is from the new grain (*Sipre* Deut. 134), further implying that the *ʿōmer* was offered on the second day of the Festival of Unleavened Bread, the sixteenth day of Nisan (*b. Menaḥ.* 66a). I could not find a counterargument in the literature, but it is obvious: Deuteronomy's "six days" refers to the time when the Israelites are at home; it bears no implication concerning the source of the grain. Besides, this argument would imply that the unleavened bread would have to be barley, but no such requirement exists. Just the same, the rabbis claimed that this argument and no. 1 are irrefutable (*b. Menaḥ.* 66a).

Against the Festivalian Position

1. If *šabbāt* is the festival day, the same ambiguity prevails in interpreting it as the weekly sabbath: Which day of the festival, the first or the seventh (cf. Raba in *b. Menaḥ.* 66a)? Wessely (1846), wishing to eliminate the last day from consideration in favor of the first, argues that if *šabbāt* refers to the seventh day, the expression would read *mimmāḥŏrat hahag* 'the day after the festival'. However,

Wessely has actually argued against his own (Pharisaic) position. The *ḥag* in this chapter is not for the entire seven-day festival (its later meaning; see NOTE on "All seven days," v. 3), but for the first day! Indeed, if the *ʿōmer* was offered on the sixteenth day of Nisan, why was this date not given in the text (as were the fourteenth and fifteenth days, vv. 5, 6)?

2. Paran's (1989: 270) and Ibn Ezra's point cannot be sustained. Paran has overlooked H's penchant to diffuse P's precise language (see NOTE on v. 32). Nonetheless, H's extended use of the word *šabbāt* is always tied to the number seven and its multiples (on Paran's misunderstanding of the sabbath-week, see NOTE on v. 15). All of Ibn Ezra's festival citations do not use the term *šabbāt*, but *šabbātôn*, implying a less severe sabbath (see NOTE on v. 24), or they use the term *šabbat šabbātôn* (vv. 3, 32), giving it superlative force (see NOTE on v. 3). If, indeed, the *ʿōmer* was to be offered on the day after the pesaḥ, the text— to be precise—should have read *mimmāḥŏrat haššabbātôn*.

3. That the Israelites ate parched grain "on the day following the *pesaḥ* offering" is refuted by Ibn Ezra on the basis of "the Israelites left [Egypt] on the day following the pesaḥ" (Num 33:3b). Thus "the day following the *pesaḥ*," observed on the fourteenth day of Nisan must be the fifteenth (and is so explicitly stated in the first part of this verse), not the sixteenth, the day held by the rabbis for the *ʿōmer* offering. Saadiah's harmonization of these two verses, that the Israelite *pesaḥ* was on the fourteenth day but YHWH's *pesaḥ* was on the fifteenth must be rejected, since the fifteenth day is not *pesaḥ*, but a *ḥag*. For similarly flawed reasoning, see Albeck's (5.1956: 369–71) long note on *m. Menaḥ.* 10:3.

4. The fixed-day argument is irrelevant and invalid since it will be shown that, originally, before the centralization of the cult, the Festival of the First Wheat Offering was not observed on a fixed date. Indeed, the rabbis themselves were unsure about the fixed date (the sixth, or seventh day of Sivan; *b. Sabb.* 86b).

5. An additional argument in favor of the weekly sabbath hypothesis is achieved by comparing the parallel structures of the firstfruits offerings and that of the sabbatical and jubilee years. Just as the jubilee, the fiftieth year, is hallowed (25:10), and it follows upon a sabbatical year (the forty-ninth), thereby creating two successive years during which working the land is forbidden (25:20–22), so the fiftieth day is both hallowed (23:21) and follows a sabbath day, thereby creating two successive days during which work is forbidden (Ramban on v. 15; Ben-Shaḥar 1979).

Fishbane (1985: 149–51) has attempted to justify the Pharisaic view by postulating that the word *šabbat*, both originally and in this expression, designates neither the weekly sabbath nor the festival day but the full moon, on the basis of Akkadian *šapattu*, the Mesopotamian term for the full moon at mid-month. Thus the "day after the sabbath" would denote the sixteenth day, in keeping with Pharisaic tradition. However, Albright (1945: 290), commenting on Lewy and Lewy (1942–43: 47–75), agrees with them that *šapattu* originally meant "half-month" (old Assyrian), referring to a sixteen-day intercalation, and only in later Babylonian texts does it come to mean "full moon." Albright concludes:

"There is no real basis for the now almost universally accepted hypothesis that Heb. *šabbāt* . . . meant 'full moon' and not 'week'."

Fishbane (1985) also attempts to adduce proof from Josh 5:10–12 and Num 33:3 that "the day after the *pesaḥ*" must be the fifteenth day of the month. But as pointed out, Ibn Ezra refuted this "proof" that in the Pharisaic view Israel may eat of the new produce on the sixteenth of the month, when the *ʿōmer* rite takes place, not on the fifteenth. All the same, this evidence from Joshua also refutes the opposing sabbatarian hypothesis, since Israel ate of the new grain the day after the *pesaḥ*, not the day after the sabbath. Thus the chances are that the expression *mimmāḥŏrat happesaḥ* (Josh 5:11) stems from the pen of a proto-Pharisaic interpolator to equate it with *mimmāḥŏrat haššabbāt* in Lev 23, just as the latter expression probably can be ascribed to a "Sunday Pentacostalist" (to use Ginsberg's [1982] apt description), as will be argued below.

The alternative to the flawed sabbatarian and festivalian hypotheses is to regard *mimmāḥŏrat haššabbāt* as a gloss (also in vv. 15–16) and to posit that originally the *ʿōmer* was brought to the (local) sanctuary by the individual farmer whenever his barley crop ripened (a thesis already proposed by Shadal). This would imply that the firstfruits of the wheat harvest, coming fifty days later, originally also did not fall on the same date (an eventuality labeled by Ramban as "nonsense"). Support for this supposition is discussed in the INTRODUCTION to vv. 15–22. It is summarized and supplemented as follows:

1. Deuteronomy states explicitly that the seven-week counting begins *mēhāḥēl ḥermēš baqqāmâ* 'when the sickle is first put to the standing grain' (Deut 16:9). Admittedly, the ensuing *ḥag* mandated for the national sanctuary probably occurred on a fixed date each year, so that it would be a national pilgrimage. However, the language of the clause betrays the *origin* of this *ḥag* as a private celebration, dependent on the day when the individual farmer began to harvest his grain.

Indeed, if the firstfruit rite of 2:14 (P) reflects the *ʿōmer* offering, as I have maintained (see its NOTE), then P ordains that it is a voluntary offering (reversing vol. 1.193), allowing the individual to offer the first handful of his barley harvest at his (regional) sanctuary, presumably whenever it ripens. (The sanctuary, however, presumably celebrates a public offering on a fixed date; see INTRODUCTION to vv. 15–22.)

2. Ramban (on v. 15) unintentionally put his finger on this solution by admitting that the phrase "seven sabbaths" (v. 15) cannot refer to the festival day, but must be rendered, with *Tg. Onq.*, as "seven weeks." He was certainly aware of the rabbinic use of *šabbāt* as referring to a week ending with the sabbath day (*m. Ned.* 8:1–2; *b. Men.* 65b). Thus two different meanings for the word "sabbath" occur in the same verse (see also Ginsberg 1982: 74). In any case, whether one interprets *šabbāt* as the weekly sabbath or the festival day, the incongruity remains: two different meanings for *šabbāt* in the same verse (but see below).

3. The most telling evidence, I submit, stems from syntax and style. In H, the term *lirṣōnĕkem* always occurs in the apodosis (19:5; 22:9 [see NOTE], 29)—except in our verse. If, however, the phrase *mimmāḥŏrat haššabbāt* is removed, the usual H structure emerges: *wĕhēnîp ʾet-hāʿōmer lipnê YHWH lirṣōnĕkem yĕnîpennû*

hakkōhēn 'He shall elevate the handful before YHWH; on your behalf the priest shall elevate it.' The *'atnāḥ* moved to YHWH allows for *lirṣōněkem* to become part of the second sentence. Moreover, typical priestly style also emerges: the verb appears in both halves, the first time prefixed and the second suffixed (e.g., vv. 11, 15, 41; 25:22, 29; Exod 12:14; 30:19; Num 6:9; 9:10–11; Paran 1989: 56–73).

Kuenen (1886: 282, n. 8) attempts to save the Sabbatarian interpretation of *mimmāḥŏrat haššabbāt* by conjecturing that the individual farmer would offer the *'ōmer* on the morrow of the first sabbath after he began the harvest. I believe he is right, but for the wrong reason. First, there is the need to parry the objection that can be raised to Kuenen and all other Sabbatarians that it is difficult to conceive that the author or interpolator would use *šabbāt* in the same pericope in two different senses: the sabbath day (vv. 11, 15a) and the sabbath week (vv. 15b, 16). That is, the same objection voiced against the Festivalians who interpreted the sabbath as a festival day can boomerang against the Sabbatarians. The resolution, I submit, is that *šabbāt has been wrongly translated. In vv. 11–16, it bears only one meaning, the sabbath-week, not the sabbath day.*

This new interpretation allows us a glimpse into the purpose of fixing the barley offering on the day after the sabbath-week. It would allow the farmers in a particular area, devotees of the same regional sanctuary, to begin the grain harvest during the same week and, collectively, celebrate the firstfruits festival together on the same day. To be sure, the present MT text, which presumes the viewpoint of Jerusalem (H), prescribes that the Temple is responsible for the firstfruits offering and, thereby, the harvest-burdened farmer is released from the obligation of a pilgrimage. Nonetheless, *mimmāḥŏrat haššabāt* may well be an old gloss, dating back to the time when a firstfruits pilgrimage was mandated (see Exod 23:16a, and INTRODUCTION to vv. 11–15).

Finally, the question of rationale must be addressed. None is given or adumbrated either in the Bible or in subsequent polemics. The clearest rationale can be deduced from the Dead Sea Scrolls. The Qumran calendar follows that of 1 Enoch and *Jubilees* and is based on a solar year of 364 days beginning on a Wednesday, since it was on the fourth day that the solar light was created (cf. Talmon 1958: 169–76; VanderKam 1992: 818–20). The year is divided into four seasons, each containing three months of 30, 30, and 31 days, respectively. Each date falls on the same day of the week every year, since 364 is exactly divisible

TABLE 1. Qumran Calendar

MONTHS	1	4	7	10		2	5	8	11		3	6	9	12
Wednesday	1	8	15	22	29		6	13	20	27		4	11	18	25
Thursday	2	9	16	23	30		7	14	21	28		5	12	19	26
Friday	3	10	17	24		1	8	15	22	29		6	13	20	27
Shabbat	4	11	18	25		2	9	16	23	30		7	14	21	28
Sunday	5	12	19	26		3	10	17	24		1	8	15	22	29
Monday	6	13	20	27		4	11	18	25		2	9	16	23	30
Tuesday	7	14	21	28		5	12	19	26		3	10	17	24	31

by 7 (Table 1). The numbers in boldface represent the festivals appearing in the priestly calendar. These dates are confirmed in a Qumran document (4Q Mishmarot; tentatively, see Milik 1957b), which gives the name of the priestly family (corresponding to the list in 1 Chr 24:7–18) serving in the Temple on the festival and the number of the day of the week on which each festival occurred. The available part of the text reads:

On the third (day) in Maoziah: pesaḥ	1/14
[On the first (day)] in Jeda [19h]: the ['ōmer] elevation	1/26
On the fifth (day) in Seorim: the [second] *pesaḥ*	2/14
On the first (day) in Jeshua: the Festival of the First Wheat	3/15
[On] the fourth (day) in Maoziah: the Day of Remembrance	7/1
[On] the sixth (day) in Joiarib: the Day of Purgation	7/10
[On the fourth (day) in Jeda]iah: The Festival of Booths	7/15

Since *Jubilees* fixes the date of the Festival of the First Wheat on Sunday, 3/15 (*Jub* 15:1; 44:4–5, followed by Qumran), it follows that the 'ōmer offering, occurring seven weeks earlier, would fall on Sunday, 1/26—the morrow of the sabbath following the Festival of Unleavened Bread. When and in what circles this calendar originated cannot as yet be determined. But a number of scholars, largely on the basis of the Flood narrative, have recently championed the theory that the *Jubilees* calendar is not a wild-eyed, utopian scheme, but is an actual vestige of preexilic practice (Jaubert 1957: 33; Davies 1983; Wenham 1987: 180–81; but cf. Baumgarten 1982). Perhaps, some proto-*Jubilees* adherent(s) may have been responsible for the interpolation of *mimmāhŏrat haššabbāt*. Later Sabbatarians, reflected in the Samaritan and Karaite traditions, would have opted, instead, to interpret the MT text as referring to the sabbath occurring during the seven-day festival. A more likely explanation, however, is that given above—a vestige of the first attempt to prescribe a pilgrimage festival for the firstfruit of the grain heretofore brought by individual farmers whenever their grain ripened (see INTRODUCTION to vv. 11–15).

But what may account for the Festivalian tradition adopted by the Pharisees? There is not the slightest hint in the sources. I can only allow myself an unalloyed conjecture: the Pharisees and their predecessors had adopted the lunar calendar, thereby making it impossible to observe the Festival of the First Wheat on the fifteenth day of the third month. Even assuming that both the first and the second month (Nisan and Iyar) had thirty days (though twenty-nine and thirty days is more likely), seven weeks before 3/15 brings us to 1/24 for the day of the 'ōmer offering, and not 1/26. Moreover, had the Pharisees accepted the Sabbatarian viewpoint, then in their calendar the Festival of the First Wheat would not always fall on the same date (see *b. Menaḥ.* 66a, and nos. 4). And a fixed date was essential to their system because they held that this festival coincided with God's revelation at Sinai, which followed upon their arrival at the mountain *bayyôm hazzeh* 'on this day' (Exod 19:1). Finally, a lunar calendar vitiates any attempt to fix the Festival of the First Wheat (and hence, the 'ōmer offering) so that it always falls on a Sunday. It would have been the lunar calendar, therefore, that coerced the Pharisees to seek a meaning of *mimmāḥŏrat haššabbāt* so that it could be tied to the festival and, therefore, be independent of the days of the week. (It should also be noted, in passing, that it was the possibility that the first and second months could be thirty days in length [instead of the normal twenty-nine and thirty days] that would have allowed R. Jose to declare [according to his calculation of the date of the Sinaitic revelation] that the Festival of the First Wheat falls on the seventh day of the third month, and not the sixth—the accepted rabbinic date; see *b. Šabb.* 86b–87a).

The (pre-)Pharisaic solution, the *'ōmer* offering on a fixed day of the lunar calendar, was not without cost. A farmer in the mountainous area near Jerusalem, where cooler weather prevailed, harvested his grain three to four weeks later than a farmer in the Jordan Valley. No wonder the tradition is recorded by the rabbis, "One does not bring the *'ōmer* except from fields on those slopes over which the sun rises and sets" (*b. Menaḥ.* 85a)—in order to get the earliest ripened grain from the mountains. In the Jericho region, though, the crops ripen so early that farmers were found to harvest and stack their barley *before* the fixed day for the *'ōmer* offering. Despite the general prohibition against this practice, the rabbis had no choice but to ignore its violation (*m. Pesaḥ.* 4:8).

The book of *Jubilees* contains the earliest known evidence for linking the Festival of the First Wheat with the Sinaitic revelation. In brief, the covenant with Noah had taken place at this conjunction, and it was renewed by Moses on the same date (*Jub* 6:1–19). Indeed, the Feast of Weeks, as the Festival of the First Wheat is called in Deuteronomy (Deut 16:16; cf. Exod 34:22 [reworked by D]), is interpreted by *Jubilees* as "The Feast of Oaths," implying that the covenant sworn by Noah and Moses took place annually on the Feast of the First Wheat. D. L. Cohen (personal communication) demonstrates convincingly that this linkage was known neither to Philo nor to the authors of the New Testament, but can firmly be placed only in late-second-century rabbinic texts (*t. Meg.* 3:3) and subsequently in the Babylonian Talmud (*b. Meg.* 31a; see also Herr 1987: 860).

In sum, all the differences in the interpretation of *mimmāḥŏrat haššabbāt* boil down to one cause—the calendar. The firstfruit grain offerings, initially an individual rite performed by the Israelite farmer whenever his grain ripened, became fixed dates on a presumed solar calendar at the hands of a "Sunday Pentacostalist" who ordained that a handful of barley be brought on the Sunday during or after the Festival of Unleavened Bread (Nisan 21 or 26) and two loaves of wheat seven weeks later on Sunday, Sivan 8 or 15. Later, those who espoused a lunar calendar, finding *mimmāḥŏrat haššabbāt* in the canonized Torah text, had no choice but to interpret *šabbāt* as signifying the first day of the Festival of Unleavened Bread, which also allowed the Festival of the First Wheat to fall on a fixed date.

Levine (1978; 1990) has cast doubt on whether Qumran followed the *Jubilees* calendar at all. He does so, in particular, by pointing to the omission of *mimmāḥŏrat haššābbat* from the rewording of vv. 15–16a in the Temple Scroll. I cite the two passages in full, rendering them literally:

Lev 23:15–16	11QT 18:10–13
ûsĕpartem lākem mimmāhŏrat	WSPRT [LKMH] ŠB' ŠBTWT
haššabbāt miyyôm hăbî'ăkem 'et-'ōmer	TMYMWT MYWM HB'KMH 'T
hattĕnûpâ šeba' šabbātôt tĕmîmōt	H'MR [HTNWPH TS]PWRW
tihyenâ 'ad mimmāhŏrat haššabbāt	'D MMHRT HŠBT HŠBY'YT
haššĕbî'ît tispĕrû hămiššîm yôm	TSPWRW [HMŠYM] YWM

you shall count for yourselves, on the day after the sabbath-week, on the day on which you bring the elevation offering of the sheaf, seven complete weeks. They must be complete. Until the day after the seventh sabbath-week you must count.

You shall count seven complete sabbaths; on the day on which you bring the sheaf of the elevation offering you shall count; until the day after the seventh sabbath you shall count fifty days.

Regarding the meaning of ŠBT in this passage, an alternative to Levine's interpretation suggests itself at once: ŠBT means only the "sabbath day," the same as it means everywhere else in the scroll, whereas ŠBTWT TMYMWT 'complete sabbaths', refers to weeks, but weeks that terminate on the sabbath. If so, then MMHRT HŠBT HŠBY'YT 'the day after the seventh sabbath', is Sunday. This interpretation would also explain the threefold use of the verb SPR (against two in the MT): the first, so that seven weeks should be counted; the second, so that the counting begins on the 'ōmer festival; and the third, so that the counting ends on Sunday.

Still the question remains: Why did the Temple Scroll omit MMHRT HŠBT, a phrase that underscores that the counting begins on Sunday? A comparison of the two texts is now in order. First, it should be noted that the author of the scroll has moved up ŠB' ŠBTWT TMYMWT to be the object of WSPRT, thereby making it even clearer than the MT that seven complete weeks are counted. Now if he had kept MMHRT HŠBT in its original place, what would be the meaning of "You shall count from the day after the sabbath"? Which sabbath is meant? The MT is no problem, since the following phrase identifies the sabbath as the one *before* the bringing of the 'ōmer. However, now that the phrase ŠB' ŠBTWT TMYMWT has been interposed, the identification of this sabbath is no longer certain. In fact, since the previous pericope ends with the words BYWM HNYPT H'WMR 'on the day of the 'ōmer elevation', the sabbath in question might well be taken to be the one that *follows* the 'ōmer festival! To avoid this ambiguity, the term would have been deleted. Thus the omission of *mimmāhŏrat haššabbāt* can be explained on purely stylistic grounds: it adds nothing but confusion (details in Milgrom 1978; cf. Yadin 1980; Sweeny 1983; Swanson 1995: 31–33).

C. The Festival of Booths in Nehemiah 8

[14]*wayyimsĕ'û kātûb battôrâ 'ăšer siwwâ YHWH bĕyad-mōšeh 'ăšer yēšĕbû bĕnê-yiśrā'ēl bassukkôt behāg bahōdeš haššĕbî'î* [15]*wa'ăšer yašmî'û wĕya'ăbîrû qôl*

bĕkol-ʿārêhem ûbîrûšāla[y]im lēʾmōr ṣĕʾû hāhār wĕhābîʾû ʿălê-zayit waʿălê-ʿēṣ šemen waʿălê hădas waʿălê tĕmārîm waʿălê ʿēṣ ʿābōt laʿăśōt sukkōt kakkātûb. ¹⁶wayyēṣĕʾû hāʿām wayyābîʾû wayyaʿăśû lāhem sukkôt ʾîš ʿal-gaggô ûbĕhaṣrōtêhem ûbĕhaṣrôt bêt hāʾĕlōhîm ûbirĕḥôb šaʿar hammayim ûbirḥôb šaʿar ʾeprāyim. ¹⁷wayyaʿăśû kol-haqqāhāl haššābîm min-haššĕbê sukkôt wayyēšĕbû bassukkôt kî lōʾ-ʿāśû mîmê yēšûaʿ bin-nûn kēn bĕnê-yiśrāʾēl ʿad hayyôm hahûʾ wattĕhî śimḥâ gĕdōlâ mĕʾōd ¹⁸wayyiqrāʾ bĕsēper tôrat hāʾĕlōhîm yôm bĕyôm min-hayyôm hāriʾšôn ʿad hayyôm hāʾaḥărôn wayyaʿăśû-ḥāg šibʿat yāmîm ûbayyôm haššĕmînî ʿăṣeret kammišpāṭ.

¹⁴They found in the Torah that YHWH had commanded Moses that the Is-raelites should dwell in booths during the festival of the seventh month, ¹⁵and that they should announce and proclaim throughout their towns as follows: "Go out to the mountains and bring leafy branches of olive trees, pine trees, myrtles, palms, and [other] leafy trees to make booths as it is written." ¹⁶So the people went out and brought them, and made for themselves booths on their roofs, in their courtyards, in the courtyards of the House of God, in the square of the Water Gate, and in the square of the Ephraim Gate. ¹⁷The whole community that returned from the captivity made booths and dwelt in the booths—the Israelites had not done so since the days of Joshua son of Nun to that day—and there was great rejoicing. ¹⁸He read from the scroll of the Torah of God each day, from the first to the last day. They celebrated the festival seven days, and there was a solemn assembly on the eighth, as prac-ticed. (Neh 8:14–18)

First, a number of exegetical explanations of Neh 8:15 are in order:

1. The proclamation to build booths is perhaps influenced by the general re-quirement to proclaim all the festivals, as stated in the heading and sum-mary of the festival calendar in Leviticus (23:4, 37; Williamson 1988: 30; see NOTE on "sacred occasions," v. 2).
2. The plural *ʿălîm*, literally "leaves," refers to foliage, including the branches to which the leaves are attached (for the sing., see Prov 11:28).
3. The *ʿēṣ šemen*, literally "the oil-tree," is best identified with the Jerusalem pine (*Pinus halepensis*); its sap yields turpentine, and it abounds in the central highlands (called by the Kurdistani Jews *ʾāʿāʾ dĕmišḥāʾ* 'an oil-tree'; Feliks 1985; 1992: 377–79). As for tree sap being called *šemen* 'oil', I am reminded by Avigdor Hurowitz that in Akkadian the sap of the cedar tree is called *šaman erēni* 'cedar oil' (*CAD* E 4.277–78).
4. The branches of the myrtle (*ʿălê hădas*), being a shrub, were probably cho-sen as a roof cover for the booths.

As will be shown, the returning Babylonian Exiles clearly modeled themselves on the text of Lev 23:40, but they interpreted it in the light of v. 42, namely, that the prescribed species of vegetation referred to the building materials of the booths. As I have maintained, this is not the plain meaning of the text: the object of taking these species is "you shall rejoice before YHWH" (v. 40b) and refers to processions around the altar, as part of a larger ritual complex, to supplicate God for adequate and timely rains during the coming agricultural year (see NOTES on v. 40).

We know that the exiles' interpretation was followed by many Karaites, and earlier by the Samaritans. That the controversy—processions or booths—raged for a long time is reflected among the rabbis, for though the majority favored processions, R. Judah maintained that "the booth is made with the same four species of the *lûlāb*" (*b. Suk.* 36b [bar.]; cf. *Sipra* Emor 17:10)—that is, the species specified in Lev 23:40 (but see Albeck 1952: 2.253, n. 2, concerning manuscript inconsistencies). In any event, all the rabbis are in agreement that one of the branches collected by the exiles, that of the myrtle, was indeed for the purpose of constructing the booths. This myrtle, the rabbis claimed, was a wild variety—thereby avoiding the contradiction in their own interpretation that the *ʿēṣ ʿābōt* of Lev 23 was also a myrtle (*b. Suk.* 12a; *y. Suk.* 3:4). Interestingly, the sectaries of Qumran follow the majority view of the rabbis (4Q409; see COMMENT E) even though the only explicit text in Scripture mandates that the branches be used in the construction of booths (Neh 8).

The fundamental question, however, is: Is there any relationship between the lists in Lev 23 and Neh 8? Ostensibly, the differences are irreconcilable:

1. In Nehemiah, there are five species; in Leviticus, four.
2. Olive branches and pine branches (lit. "leafy branches of an oil tree") are not in Leviticus.
3. Conversely, the fruit of the majestic tree and the willows of the brook are not in Nehemiah.

These discrepancies lead most scholars to conclude that the two lists are independent; that is, Ezra's Torah was not equivalent to the MT and, hence, the canonization of the latter was a subsequent development.

These seemingly irreconcilable differences, I submit, are surmountable, once we reckon with the rendering of the first species *pĕrî ʿēṣ hādār* as "the boughs of majestic trees." With one stroke, we eliminate the incongruity of constructing booths with fruits and, at the same time, allow for this term to be a generalization, which can include more than the three enumerated plants. (Indeed, the *ʿănap ʿēṣ-ʿābōt* 'the branches of a leafy tree' is also a nonspecific category, and is therefore not limited to one species!)

Supporting evidence may possibly be gleaned from 2 Macc 10:6–7 (Harrington 1993: 1711): "They celebrate for eight days with rejoicing in the manner of the Festival of Booths, remembering how not long before, during the Festival of Booths, they had been wandering in the mountains and caves like wild animals. Therefore, carrying ivy-wreathed wands and beautiful branches and also fronds of palm, they offered hymns of thanksgiving to him who had given success to the purifying of the holy place."

The author of this second-century B.C.E. work relates that Judah the Maccabee and his followers celebrated the purification of the Temple for eight days "in the manner of the Festival of Booths" by carrying in procession wands, branches, and palm fronds—but no fruit. Perhaps the *kladous hōraious* 'beautiful branches' is a rendering of *pĕrî 'ēṣ hādār*. But it is equally possible that fruit indeed was brought but not used in the processions, as testified in *Jubilees* (see below). In any case, it is clear that the processions "in the manner of the Festival of Booths" left the choice of branches to the decision of each participant. The same view is reflected in the even earlier second-century book of *Jubilees* (16:29–30): "it is ordained forever concerning Israel so that they should observe it (the Festival of Booths) and they should dwell in tents and that they should place crowns on their heads and so that they should take branches of leaves and willows from the stream. And Abraham took branches [emendation of Wintermute 1985: 89] of palm trees and fruit of good trees and each of the (seven) days he used to go around the altar with branches."

In this passage is the earliest attestation of the traditional interpretation of *pĕrî* as fruit. Nonetheless, the text states that the procession took place with just branches, which are unspecified. Additional relevant information can be gleaned from these two pseudegraphical works: the processions are associated with joyous celebrations (in accordance with v. 41b) and the exodus from Egypt (in accordance with v. 43), the purpose of the processions is to circumambulate the altar (see NOTE on "you shall rejoice before YHWH your God seven days," v. 40), and the branches are carried in the hand, but not used for the building of booths (contrary to Neh 8). The absence of willows in 2 Macc 10:6–7, as in Neh 8:14–18, should occasion no surprise, since the choice of branches was left to each participant. Finally, the separation of the species in *Jub* 16:29–30—two for Abraham and two for his progeny—may testify to the recognition that the identification of the traditional species developed over time.

The only remaining problem is the absence of the willows of the brook from Nehemiah's list. In this case, I believe, Ezra had no choice but to omit it. Identified as the poplar (see NOTE on v. 40), it is tall and stately, but the fact that its top "is bent over the altar" (*m. Suk.* 4:5) is sufficient evidence that it is incapable of supporting any weight. Besides, it is not found in the mountains (Neh 8:15; see illustrations in VBW 1.196; Feliks 1968: 115). The same objection may ostensibly be levied against palm fronds, but as demonstrated by Meshel (1982: 20), booths made exclusively of palm fronds are widespread among the bedouin of the Sinai oases. Also to be kept in mind is that the list in Lev 23:40 cites only examples, implying that each person is free to make his own choice of branches for the regional procession (Leviticus) or the booth (Nehemiah).

Therefore, when the text of Neh 8 states that these five-plus species of vegetation are found in Scripture *kakkātûb* 'as it is written' (v. 15), it can be believed. There is no need to conjecture that it "does not necessarily indicate that the Torah was being quoted exactly since the label *kakkātûb battôrâ* is also applied to the wood offering (Neh 10:35)" (Knohl 1995: 39, n. 88). The alleged exception of the wood offering is erroneous, since *kakkātûb battôrâ* refers to the previous words *lěba 'ēr 'al-mizbaḥ* YHWH *'ĕlōhênû* 'to burn upon the altar of YHWH our God', which obviously is a requirement of the priestly *tôrâ* (cf. 6:1–6; Williamson 1988: 27–28). Therefore, it can be assumed that Ezra had the MT of Lev 23 before him. See, however, Qumran's *tôrâ*, discussed in COMMENT E.

Thus once it is recognized that Ezra interpreted the four species of Leviticus to designate all sorts of branches, he had no difficulty in connecting v. 40 with v. 42 and interpreting the former as prescribing the materials with which to construct the booths prescribed in the latter. The likelihood is that this interpretation had already been devised in the Babylonian Exile, since there was no altar around which these species could be carried. The command "you shall rejoice before YHWH" (v. 40b) was therefore restricted to constructing and dwelling in booths for all seven days of the festival. To be sure, Ezra's interpretation was subsequently overruled, since all sources agree that processions with the four species were resumed in the Second Temple. Indeed, it is even possible that this contrary opinion was even voiced in Ezra's time.

Finally, the novelty in the claim that "the Israelites had not done so since the days of Joshua son of Nun" (Neh 8:17) was not that the Israelites constructed booths in the living quarters of Jerusalem (de Vaux 1961: 497; Kaufmann 1977: 4.382), or that booths were an innovation (Knohl 1995: 39, n. 88), or that it was now done everywhere by all Israelites (Licht 1968: 1042). It may be that the booths were also built by Jerusalemites, not only by pilgrims, as practiced heretofore at the end of First Temple days (see NOTE on v. 42). A more plausible answer has been proposed by Feliks (1992: 378), who points out that there are three scriptural references to a command to fetch building material from the mountains: in the times of the conquest (Josh 17:15–18) and the return of the Babylonian Exiles (Hag 1:8; Neh 8:15). Only during these two periods were the mountains covered by forests; in the exilic period, the mountain slopes, which had been extensively cultivated, returned to their pristine forested condition (cf. Hos 2:14). Thus the reference in our text to Joshua is not a metaphor for the distant past, but must be taken literally: in the mountainous area, the exiles found an abundance of building material unequaled "since the days of Joshua son of Nun" (Neh 8:17).

D. Exodus 23:18–19; 34:25–26 and the Paschal Sacrifice

The first half of these verses reads as follows:

lō' tizbaḥ 'al-ḥāmēṣ dam-zibḥî wělō' yālîn ḥeleb-ḥaggî 'ad-bōqer
lō' tišḥaṭ 'al-ḥāmēṣ dam-zibḥî wělō' yālîn labbōqer zebaḥ ḥag happāsaḥ

You shall not offer the blood of my sacrifice with anything leavened; and the suet of my pilgrimage offering shall not remain until morning. (Exod 23:18)

You shall not slaughter [the blood of] my sacrifice with anything leavened; and the sacrifice of the Pilgrimage-Festival of *pesaḥ* shall not remain until morning. (Exod 34:25)

The prevailing interpretation of Exod 23:18–19 is that these two verses encode a general rule applying to all three pilgrimage festivals (vv. 14–17; Dillmann and Ryssel 1897; Driver and White 1894–98; Cassuto 1951a; Noth 1977; Childs 1974). That is, the sacrifices mandated for these festivals should not be offered up with leaven (forbidden by Lev 2:11), and their suet must be consumed on the altar by morning.

This interpretation has been rejected by two eminent scholars. The first, Haran (1979: 328–32), raises two objections:

1. If this text meant to prohibit the use of leavened cereal offering as a sacrificial adjunct, the text would have read "You shall not burn (or put, or bring) unleavened [sic!] bread *on* [the blood of] my sacrifice"; that is, the cereal offering would have to be secondary to the blood offering.
2. The requirement to incinerate the suet by morning flies in the face of the priestly law that the šĕlāmîm intended as a votive or freewill offering may be consumed over two days (Lev 7:16–18).

Haran, therefore, concludes that this verse speaks solely about the paschal sacrifice, an interpretation that the parallel text (Exod 34:25) makes explicit, namely, that no leaven must remain in the home after the paschal sacrifice has been slaughtered.

Haran's objections cannot pass muster. The preposition ʿal does not mean "upon" (Haran 1979), but "with," thus removing the alleged secondary position of the blood sacrifice. As for the contradiction offered by the rules governing the šĕlāmîm, the following must be said:

1. These two verses are not P, and may therefore reflect other sacrificial rules (cf. Driver and White 1894–98).

2. Even if Lev 7:16–18 were not disallowed, it should be noticed that it allows only the meat to be eaten over a two-day period. It says nothing about suet. There can be no question, given the high flammability of suet, that when the priest lays the suet on the altar (Lev 7:31a), it is completely incinerated within twelve to twenty-four hours. Finally, and decisively, every morning the altar must be cleared of all its ashes (Lev 6:3–4). When the morning tāmîd begins the daily service (Exod 29:39), it does so on an ash- and sacrifice-free altar. Thus there may be no contradiction between this verse and Lev 7 (P) at all: the meat may, indeed, be eaten over two days, but the suet must not remain until the following morning—hence, its emphasis here.

3. If this verse dealt exclusively with the Paschal Offering, why is its concern limited to the suet? After all, the altar fire, as mentioned, would take care of the suet. But would there not be a greater concern that the meat be consumed by the following morning, as explicitly enjoined by Exod 12:10?

4. Finally, the ḥag, as demonstrated, occurs on the Festival of Unleavened Bread and not on the preceding paschal sacrifice (see NOTE on v. 6). To be sure, Exod 34:25 explicitly labels the *pesaḥ* as *ḥag*—a fact that requires its own explanation—but it gives no license for assuming analogously that *ḥaggî* in the parallel verse, Exod 23:18, also refers to the *pesaḥ*.

The second scholar, Ginsberg (1982: 51–52), avoids the last-mentioned pitfall by postulating that *ḥaggî* refers to the seventh day (Exod 13:6) and that the suet is not allowed to burn into the morning lest it come into contact with newly permitted leavened bread. This interpretation is ingenious, since it allows for both the festal calendar of Exod 23 and the seventh-day *ḥag* (Exod 13:6) to be the product of the same source, E. However, it is weighed down by its own bag of difficulties:

1. All the objections offered against Haran's (1979: 328–32) interpretation of Exod 23:18a—that it refers to the paschal sacrifice—remain in force.

2. The phrase *ʿal-ḥāmēṣ* is rendered "while leavened bread still exists" (so, too, the rabbis; cf. *Mek.* Mishpatim, par. 20; *b. Pesaḥ.* 63a). Haran, who maintains a similar interpretation, is at a disadvantage because he holds that it refers to the *ḥag* when the Israelite and his family are gathered at the sanctuary and, hence, there is no apprehension that they have brought along some leavened bread. Ginsberg, on the contrary, argues that the paschal rite is a home observance, and the fear that some leaven still remains in the house is a realistic one. Nonetheless, the identification of the paschal offering as a *zebaḥ* belies its putative, nonsacrificial character. There are only two verses that refer to the *pesaḥ* as a *zebaḥ* (Exod 12:27; 34:25), and both betray the influence of Deuteronomy (see below).

3. The second half of the verse, referring to the seventh day, is also not free of objections. If the legist's apprehension is that the paschal suet may contact newly permitted leaven, the text should have read *ʿad-ʿereb* 'until evening' not *ʿad-bōqer* 'until morning' since, according to Exod 12:18, the prohibition against eating leaven ends in the evening, not the following morning. To be sure, this argument can be parried by maintaining that the two verses in question, Exod 12:18 and 23:18, stem from different sources (the former H and the latter E), but the interpretation is weakened nonetheless. And here, too, even after positing that the *ḥag* falls on the seventh day, there exists the inexplicable lack of concern that the paschal meat should also be consumed by morning.

The supposition that the two verses Exod 23:18–19 form a general rule governing all sacrifices also makes sense of the second verse Exod 23:19 (and 34:26). But Ginsberg (1982) argues that the verse's first half "You shall bring the choice firstfruits of your soil to the house of YHWH your God" refers to the Festival of Weeks because *bikkûrîm* 'firstfruits' is the main identifier of this festival (e.g., Exod 23:16; Lev 23:17, 20; Num 28:26), and its second half "You shall not boil a kid in its mother's milk" refers to the Festival of Booths because dams drop their young in the autumn.

This, too, is freighted with difficulties. The calendar of Exod 23 in fact calls the second pilgrimage festival *wĕḥag haqqāṣîr bikkûrê maʿăśekā* 'the (grain) harvest pilgrimage of the firstfruits of your work', an identification made certain by its qualifying clause *ʾăšer tizraʿ baśśādeh* 'of what you sow in the field' (v. 16a). However, the wording of v. 19a *rēʾšît bikkûrê ʾadmātĕkā* 'the choice firstfruits of your soil' precludes the limitation of the firstfruits to the grain harvest. These *bikkûrîm* are more in line with those of Num 18:13 *bikkûrê kol-ʾăšer bĕʾarṣām* 'the firstfruits of everything in their land', which surely must include the new must and olive oil (Num 18:12) as well as other fruits (Deut 26:1–11; note the use of *rēšît*, vv. 2, 10). Thus the firstfruit injunction of Exod 23:19a cannot be limited to any particular crop or festival, but must apply to all firstfruits whenever they ripen.

There is also an objection to pinpointing the prohibition "You shall not boil a kid in its mother's milk" (Exod 23:19b; 34:26b; cf. Milgrom 1985b) to the Festival of Booths. Dams also drop their young through the winter (Ahituv 1971: 648). Dalman (1939: 6.188–89) even declares that there is no specific season, but they give birth all year round.

Thus, in conclusion, there is no solid reason for assigning Exod 23:18–19 to the three festivals of the calendar year. These are *general sacrificial requirements*, befitting the last line of a cultic calendar that lays its emphasis on the offerer's responsibility at the sanctuary.

The culprit for confusing Exod 23:18 with the Paschal Offering is clearly Exod 34:25b, which explicitly identifies the *ḥēleb-ḥaggî* 'the suet of my pilgrimage offering' with *zebaḥ ḥag happāsaḥ* 'the sacrifice of the Pilgrimage-Festival of *pesaḥ*.' A lasting contribution of Ginsberg's (1982: 64–65) treatment of the pentateuchal calendars is his demonstration that the culprit is, in reality, the deuteronomic redactor of Exod 34:15–26. Here is his evidence with a few items of my own:

1. Exod 34:15–16 is modeled on Deut 7:3–5, but the former's *hiznû* 'whored' is not as appropriate as the latter's *tiqqaḥ* and *tittēn*, denoting "marriage." In addition, Exod 34 drops the phrase "do not give your daughters to their sons" (Deut 7:3; e.g., Gen 34), a less frequent occurrence than intermarriage with their daughters.

2. Exod 34:18 (the Pilgrimage-Festival of Unleavened Bread) and 34:21 (the sabbath) are compatible with D. The Festival of Weeks (Exod 34:22a) veers from its Exod 23:16a prototype to adopt deuteronomic terminology. Thus *ḥag šābū'ōt sukkōt* (cf. Deut 16:10); *wĕ'āśîtā, ta'ăśeh lĕkā* (cf. Deut 16:10, 13). Ginsberg (1982) also suggests that the specification *qĕṣîr ḥiṭṭîm* 'wheat harvest' (Exod 34:22) is due to the fact that D is responsible for moving the harvest festival seven weeks later in order to coincide with the conclusion of the grain harvest, thereby allowing the Israelite farmer the leisure for a second pilgrimage to the central sanctuary. Here I differ with him: the Festival of Weeks occurs *at the beginning* of the wheat harvest, not at its end (see INTRODUCTION to vv. 15–22).

3. Exod 34:25 alters Exod 23:18 in two ways. The word *tišḥaṭ* 'slaughter' replaces *tizbaḥ* 'sacrifices'. Even with the centralization of worship, D follows the normative sacrificial procedure of allowing (and in the case of the *pesaḥ*, requiring) the slaughter to be performed by the offerer (cf. Exod 12: 6, 21; Lev 1:5; 2 Chr 35:11; 2 Chr 30:17 is an apology for the exception). But lest *tizbaḥ* be misconstrued as authorizing the laity to offer their paschal animals on the altar, the verb is changed to *tišḥaṭ*, to denote that only slaughter is permitted to the offerer. The major change is *ḥēleb ḥaggî* 'the suet of my pilgrimage offering' to *zebaḥ ḥag happāsaḥ* 'the sacrifice of the Pilgrimage-Festival of the *pesaḥ*'. D is totally unconcerned about the suet. (It is missing from the central-

ization injunctions, Deut 12, implying that offering up the suet elsewhere than the central sanctuary is not prohibited! The same holds true for the cereal offering; see Milgrom 1979a; 1979b.) The offering of the suet is the responsibility of the priests, who, D assumes, know what to do. D, however, is very much concerned lest the offerers and their families neglect to consume or incinerate the animal's meat until the morning, and thereby directly violate the primary injunction of Exod 12:10.

In sum, D rewords the prescription of Exod 23:18 (which, as explained, has nothing to do with the *pesaḥ*) so that it not only applies to the *pesaḥ*, but, directed solely at the offerer, demands that he rid himself of any leaven before he slaughters the paschal animal and not allow the meat to remain into the morning. As Ginsberg (1982) has shown, D is responsible for converting the seventh-day *ḥag* (Exod 13:6 [E]) into the first-day *ḥag*, thus allowing for the previous evening's *pesaḥ* to be observed by the pilgrims at the central sanctuary.

E. The Firstfruits Festivals of Qumran

The sectaries of Qumran prescribe additional firstfruit festivals that, following the pattern of the grain festivals, also fall on a Sunday. The pentateuchal festivals on the Qumran calendar have been discussed (see COMMENT B). It remains only to tabulate its innovative, nonpentateuchal festivals:

Priestly Consecration (eight days)	Begins 1/1 Wednesday
New Barley	1/26 Sunday
New Wheat	3/15 Sunday
New Wine	5/3 Sunday
New Oil	6/22 Sunday
Wood (six days)	Begins 6/23 Monday (?)

Following the example of the pentacontad, Qumran ordains that the firstfruits (*rēʾšît*) of must (*tîrôš*) and olive oil (*yiṣhār*) must also follow this pentacontad pattern (Num 18:12). By making the fiftieth day of the old cycle also the first day of the new cycle, they are able to follow the pentateuchal requirement that the festival day fall on Sunday. The Festival of New Oil (11QT 21–22) leads into the six-day Festival of Wood (11QT 23–25), during which the twelve tribes of Israel bring their (presumably, assigned) quota of wood for the altar and other sanctuary needs. The tribes are required to double up (two tribes per day) so that the festival will not run into the Day of Remembrance, 7/1 (Lev 23:23–25; details in Yadin 1983: 1.89–162).

But how did Qumran have the audacity to innovate new firstfruits and a wood festival that were not explicitly prescribed in the Torah? A published scroll fragment (4Q365, frag. 23 [White 1992: 225–28]) provides the answer:

1. [BSW]KWT TŠBW SBʿT YMYM KWL HʾZRḤ BYŚRʾL YSB BSWKWT
   LM[ʿN YDʿ]W DW[RWTYKM]

2. *KY* [*BS*]*WKWT HWŠBTY 'T 'ABWTYKM BHWṢY'Y 'WTM M'RṢ MṢRYM 'NY YHWH 'LWHYK*[*M*]

3. vacat *WYDBR MWŠH 'T MW'DY YHWH 'L BNY YŚR'L* vacat

4. *WYDBR YHWH 'L MWŠH L'MWR ṢW 'T BNY YŚR'L L'MWR BBW'KMH 'L H'RṢ 'ŠR*

5. [*'*]*NWKY NWTN LKMH LNḤLH WYŠBTM 'LYH LBTḤ TAQRYBW 'SᶜYM L'WLH WLKWL ML*[*'*]*K*[*T*]

6. [*HB*]*YT 'ŠR TBNW LY B'RṢ L'RWK 'WTM 'L MIZBḤ H'WLH* [*W*]*'T H'GL*[*YM*

7. [ ]*M LPSḤM WLŠLMYM WLTWDWT WLNDBWT WL'LWLT DBR YWM* [*BYWMW*

8.]*L*° [ ]*L*° [ ] *MYM WLD*[*L*]*TWT WLKWL ML'KT HBYT YQRY*[*BW*

9.   *M*]*W'D HYṢHR YQRYBW 'T H'ṢYM ŠNYM* [

10.   ] ° *Y HMQRYBYM BYWM HRYŠ*[*WN*]*LWY*[

11.   *R'W*]*BN WŠM'WN*[*WB*]*YWM HRB*[*Y'Y*

12.   ]*L*[

The translation of the additional text (ll. 4–11) to Lev 23:42–44:

[4]And YHWH spoke to Moses, saying, command the Israelites, saying: When you come to the land which [5]I am giving to you for an inheritance, and you dwell upon it securely, you will present wood for burnt offerings and for all the wo[r]k of [6][the Ho]use which you will build for me in the land, to arrange them on the altar of burnt offering, and the calv[es] . . . [7] . . . for paschal offerings, and for well-being offerings, and for thanksgiving offerings, and for freewill offerings, and for da[ily] burnt offerings . . . [8] . . . and for the doors and for all the work of the House the[y] will pres[ent . . . [9] . . . the fe]stival of oil, they will present the wood two [by two . . . [10] . . . those who present on the firs[t] day, Levi . . . [11] . . . Reuben and Simeon [and on] the four[th] day [. . .

The introduction (l. 4) begins with 24:1–2α, followed by a conditional clause, composed mainly of phrases from Num 15:18; Lev 14:34a; 23:10a; 25:19b. The main clause (ll. 5–7) states the general purpose of the wood offering: to provide the annual fuel for the burnt offerings and Temple repairs. Specifically, the wood is to be laid out on the altar (see 1:7) for the offerings of paschal calves (Deut 16:2; 2 Chr 35:7–9), well-being (perhaps the two lambs on the Festival of Weeks [23:19], called *zebaḥ* in 23:37), thanksgiving (7:11–25), freewill (7:16), and daily burnt offerings (23:37bβ; Num 28:3–8). The following badly broken text (ll. 8–12) mentions the Temple doors as an example of potential repair work; probably mentions (in the lacuna) the Festival of New Wine before mentioning the Festival of New Oil; and finally cites, day by day, the wood offering of the twelve tribes. It should be pointed out, however, that the absence of the Festivals of New Wine, New Oil, and Wood from the recently published Qumran calendar of priestly courses (*Mišmarot* Bᵃ, 4Q321) probably indicates that these nonbiblical festivals were not accorded the same status as the biblical festivals (Talmon and Knohl 1995: 294).

The startling fact is that this fragment has appended Qumran's Festival of Wood to Lev 23 or, to be more precise, to the beginning of chap. 24, thereby attributing it to the Sinaitic revelation of God to Moses. Moreover, since the Festival of New Oil (and Festival of New Wine, which probably should be restored in the preceding lacuna) is explicitly mentioned as a recipient of the wood offering, it is plausible to conclude that Qumran's additional firstfruits festivals of wine and oil also were believed to have been an integral part of YHWH's command to Moses. Indeed, it may well be the case that these festivals were prescribed in the missing beginning of this fragment in their proper chronological place after the Festivals of New Barley and New Wheat and before the prescribed festivals of the seventh month (i.e., after Lev 23:22). To be sure, all three festivals are commanded by God in the Temple Scroll (11QT 19:11–25:1). But the scroll is a discrete, sectarian document, and scholars have long debated whether it was Qumran's sixth book of the Torah or a "torah" at all. All doubts can now be laid to rest, at least regarding these additional festivals: they are Torah, not as a supplement to the Pentateuch, but incorporated into and inseparable from the book of Leviticus.

However, a problem arises concerning this appendix on the wood offering. It is chronologically out of place: it, too, belongs before the festivals of the seventh month (i.e., before 23:23)! The clue that can resolve this problem lies in the placement of the wood offering. It is not an appendix to the Festival of Booths, which concludes chap. 23, but an insertion into the opening pericope of the following chapter (24:1–9), which begins with *ṣaw 'et-bĕnê yiśrā'ēl* 'Command the Israelites' (v. 2) and concludes *mē'ēt bĕnê yiśrā'ēl* '(a commitment) of the Israelites' (v. 8).

Here, I submit, rests a Qumranic polemic against the prevailing practice. The wood offering is first recorded in Nehemiah *wĕhaggōrālôt hippalnû 'al-qurban hā'ēṣîm hakkōhănîm halĕwiyyim wĕ'hā'ām lĕhābî' lĕbêt 'ĕlōhênu lĕbêt-'ăbōtênû lĕ'ittîm mĕzummānîm šānâ bĕšānâ lĕba'ēr 'al- mizbaḥ YHWH 'ĕlōhênu kakkātûb bāttôrâ* 'We—the priests, Levites and the people—cast lots concerning the wood offering, to bring (it) to the House of our God—the House of our ancestors—during fixed times each year to burn on the altar of YHWH our God as written in the Torah' (Neh 10:35; cf. 13:31). The rabbis provide a rationale: "When the exiles ascended (from Babylonia) they did not find wood in the (Temple) storeroom, and these (families) [enumerated in *m. Ta'an.* 4:5] voluntarily contributed (the supply). Therefore the prophets among them decreed that even if the storeroom is full of wood, these (families) will (continue to) contribute and every sacrifice will be offered first with their wood" (*b. Ta'an.* 28a [bar.]).

Yadin (1983: 1.125) was perfectly correct in claiming that the sect objected to the tradition that the wood supply is maintained by certain families from the tribes of Levi, Judah, and Benjamin (*m. Ta'an.* 4:5) and, instead, made this an obligation for all the tribes (11QT 24:10–25:2). Qumran's polemic, however, strikes much deeper ground. It is objecting not just to the restriction of the wood offering to the priests, Levites, and Judean (Judah and Benjamin) exiles, but to the very notion that only certain families have been granted the everlasting privilege of contributing it to the Temple. Hence although the Temple Scroll models the ceremonial of the wood offering on the precedent of the inaugural offering of the tribal chieftains to the Tabernacle (Num 7; cf. Yadin 1983: 1.127), the scroll deliberately omits the mention of the chieftains (or any other group or family) and speaks solely and unqualifiedly of each tribe.

The published fragment (4Q365, frag. 23 [White 1992: 225–28]) confirms this observation. By its insertion into the initial pericope of Lev 24, the sectaries fulfill three objectives:

1. The requirement to contribute the wood supply for the Temple is subsumed under the rubric "Command the Israelites" (24:2) and is "(a commitment) of the Israelites as a covenant for all time" (24:8)—all the Israelites and not just a few privileged families.

2. As will be demonstrated in the INTRODUCTION to 24:1–9, this pericope is in itself a polemic (of H) against P's declaration that the oil and the spices (including the frankincense for the Bread of Presence) were contributed by the tribal chieftains (Exod 35:28 [P]). Thus H qualifies P by stating that the chieftains were indeed responsible for these gifts, but only for the initial supply of the Tabernacle; henceforth, this responsibility is incumbent on all the people.

3. This fragment resolves the search for the biblical support for the wood offering. Its publication demonstrates that in *Qumran's* Torah—and not just in the Temple Scroll—the command to bring a regular wood offering to the Tabernacle / Temple indeed exists. Presumably, Nehemiah's *'ittîm mĕzummānîm/ôt* 'fixed periods' (Neh 10:35; 13:31) was condensed into a single period, the six days following on the Festival of New Oil, 6/23–29 (but not on the intervening sabbath; cf. Yadin 1983: 1.130), and Nehemiah's "We casted lots" (10:35) would have been interpreted as referring to the order of the twelve tribes or to the order of the nine North Israelite tribes, assuming that Levi, Judah, and Benjamin would have been given priority because they composed the original returnees from the Babylonian Exile. Qumran's ruling may not only have been a product of its biblical hermeneutics. Josephus (*Wars* 2.425) informs us that such indeed was the practice during his time: on a *single* festival (probably the fifteenth day of Ab), *all the people* brought wood for the altar.

It is clear from the early rabbinic sources that the days designated for the wood offering were festive occasions (*m. Taʿan.* 4:4), resembling in some respects the firstfruit festivals (*t. Bik.* 2:9). Maimonides (*Temple Service,* "Temple Vessels" 6:9) sums up: "What is the Wood Offering? There was a fixed time for certain families to go out to the forests in order to bring wood for the (altar) hearth. And on a day that fell to members of a family to bring wood, they would sacrifice voluntary burnt offerings; this is the Wood Offering. It was like a festival for them, and it was forbidden to engage in mourning, fasting, or labor. This is (not a law but) a custom."

By the same token, it is not implausible to deduce that Qumran's additional firstfruit Festivals of New Wine and New Oil were not its theoretical innovations, but were codifications of existing practice. This certainly holds true for the Festival of New Wine, which is recorded for the ancient regional sanctuary at Shilo (Judg 21:19–20). Furthermore, the possibility exists that Hosea's *wĕlāqaḥtî . . . wĕtîrôšî bĕmô ʿădô* (2:11) should be rendered "and seize my musk at its festival"; that is, on the day the firstfruits of the vats (musk) are offered to God, he will seize all of it, leaving nothing for its producers. This rendering, I believe, is correct, since *mô ʿed* in Hosea always means "festival" (2:13 [the same pericope]; 9:5 [|| *ḥag YHWH*]; 12:10). Moreover, such a festival apparently was observed throughout the ancient Near East. In the Greek world, the Anthesteria and the older Mycenaean Festival of the Thirsty (Dead) were annual three-day festivals of new wine. The first day was called "the opening of the casks (of the new wine)," followed by a day of drinking and revelry (Palmer 1963: 250–55). Indeed, such a festival name appears in ancient Mari on the Euphrates (*ARM* 1.52.9–11). The Temple Scroll, however, makes certain that the unbridled revelry, characteristic of such bacchanals, is put under strict controls (11QT 21:8). This being the attested case for the Festival of New Wine, it may be plausibly conjectured that a similar celebration attended the Festival of New Oil.

Scholars have long held that Qumran held an annual covenant renewal rite during the Feast of Weeks (or "Oaths"; see INTRODUCTION to vv. 15–22), which, in its calendar, fell on the fifteenth day of the third month, on the basis of the book of *Jubilees*—a document closely associated with the Qumran community: "That is why it is ordained and written on the heavenly tablets that they should celebrate Shebuot this month [i.e., the third month] once a year—so as to renew the covenant each year" (*Jub* 6:17). To be sure, early Jewish tradition commemorated the Sinaitic revelation on the Festival of Weeks (*b. Pesaḥ*. 68b). Newly available 4Q documents have now made the identification of the Feast of Weeks with covenant renewal at Qumran virtually certain. Thus a CD fragment (4QD^b 18V:16–18) states:

BNY LWY [W'NŠY] ḤMḤNWT YQHLW BḤWDŠ ḤŠLYŠY W'RRW 'T ḤNṬH YMYN [UŚM'L MN H]TWRH

The Levites and the men of [the camps] will assemble in the third month and curse those who stray right [or left from the] Torah.

Although this fragment mentions only the month (the third) and not the day, it seems virtually certain that it corresponds to the Feast of Weeks at Qumran, which commemorated the annual renewal of the covenant, and when the curses of Deut 27:11–26 were recited by the Levites (v. 14) and the assembled camps (of tribes, vv. 12–13; cf. 1QS 2:11–12; CD 2:5–10).

There is no indication in the Bible that prayer accompanied the sacrificial service. Except for the priestly blessing (Num 6:24–26) at the *end* of the service (vol. 1.586–88), the priests were silent *during* the service (Kaufmann 1947: 2.476–77; 1960: 303–4). But, surely, a liturgy of words and music was sung and played (instrumentally) by the Levites (vol. 1.60–61) at appropriate points during the sacrificial ritual (cf. *m. Mid.* 2:5–6). The QL corroborates this conclusion (although nothing extant indicates the liturgical role of the Levites). Praises to God are mandated for new moons and festivals (1QS 9:26–10; 17), and one published fragment specifies prayer explicitly for the firstfruits festivals and the Day of Purgation (4Q508, 509; Baillet 1982: 175–215). Another published fragment (4Q409, col. I [Qimron 1990]) ordains the festivals, following their order in Lev 23, as time for praising God:

1. [. . . Praise and bless] on the days of the Firstfruits (Festival)
2. [of Wheat, of New Wine, and of New Oil with] New Cereal Offering
3. [and bless his holy name, Praise and bless] in the days
4. [of the Wood Festival with offering of] wood for the burnt offering
5. [and bless his name. Praise and bless] on the Day of Commemoration with Loud Blasts
6. [. . . and bless] the Master of the Universe. Praise
7. [and bless . . . and bless] his holy name
8. [. . . and bless] the Master of the Universe
9. [. . . Praise and bless] on these days
10. [. . .] Praise and bless and thank
11. [. . . Praise and bless] and thank with branches of a [leafy] tree

The festivals explicitly mentioned are Firstfruits (Wheat, Wine, and Oil [reconstructed], expressly designated as such in 11QT 21:16; 43), the Wood Offering (11QT 23–25), the First Day of the Seventh Month (v. 24), and the Feast of Booths (23:40). Because these festivals are listed in their calendric order, the Paschal, Unleavened Bread, and Sheaf Offerings would have been mentioned at the beginning of the list (cf. vv. 5–14) and, hence, were probably lost. Qimron (1990) surmises that the Day of Purgation would have been located in the missing parts of ll. 6–10 (cf. vv. 26–32). However, the somber nature of this day (see NOTE on v. 27, and vol. 1.1065–67) precludes any mention of praise and thanks.

F. A Brief Comparison of the Israelite and Hittite Festival Calendars (David T. Stewart)

Güterbock (1970: 175) observes that "among the peoples of the Ancient Near East the Hittites are those who left the richest literature concerning festivals." Their festival texts "are the most numerous category among the tablets and fragments" found at Boğazköy. These festivals are designated by the ideogram *EZEN*, Akkadian *isinnu*, meaning "feast, meal, party" in mythical texts and "cult festival" in cultic texts (175). The Hittite correspondence to the ideogram remains unknown. The "Instructions for Temple Officials" (*KUB* XIII 4 i 39–45) lists eighteen festivals for the capital city, Hattusa (Güterbock 1970: 177). Outside the capital, regional centers such as Nerik (Haas 1970: 43–61), Karaḫna

(Dinçol and Darga 1969–70), Ḫanḫana, and Kašḫa (Haas and Jakob-Rost 1984; Taracha 1986; Gane 1992a) hosted special festivals or were stopping points in festival circuits. Local sites usually had at least two festivals for the local gods, one in the autumn and the other in the spring.

Four of these festivals are of special importance (Haas 1988: 284), two in the spring and two in the autumn. In the center of the country, both the autumn festival **EZEN** *nuntarriyašḫaš* (Güterbock 1964; 1970; Haas 1970; Košak 1976) and the spring festival that takes its name from the crocus or saffron (Cornelius 1970: 171), **EZEN AN.TAH.ŠUM**ᔆᴬᴿ (Güterbock 1960; Houwink ten Cate 1966; Cornelius 1970; Hoffner 1974; Ardzinba 1982; Gonnet 1982; Haas 1982; Weinfeld 1983a; Popko and Taracha 1988), involve trips from the capital to other cult centers. The two festivals are agrarian. They focus on closing the grain jar in the fall and opening it in the spring (Archi 1973; Gonnet 1992: 226). The **EZEN KI.LAM** (Güterbock 1970; Hoffner 1974; Singer 1983; Weinfeld 1990c), possibly celebrated in the autumn, and the **EZEN** *purulliyaš* (Gaster 1961; Güterbock 1964; Lesky 1966; Haas 1970, 1982, 1988; Kellerman 1981), in the spring, fill out the picture of the important Hittite festivals.

Surveying the Hittite calendar and its attendant rituals, one must do more than simply observe that Israel also has spring and autumn festivals. One must do more than beachcomb among the cult inventories for isolated numerical co-incidences (Weinfeld 1983a). Rather, one must ask: To what degree will a comparison of the whole organism of Hittite festival to Israelite festival yield information about their functions?

To my eye, three things become visible in attempting to organize the current state of knowledge about the Hittite festival calendar. First, the Hittite calendar exhibits a complex pattern of coalescence. Multiday festivals contain overlays of local festivals borrowed from multiple cultures, Hattic and Hurrian, to name two. Second, the integration of the multiple festivals into festival complexes is accomplished by the tour of participants through multiple cultic sites where "great assemblies" are often held. Third, the manipulation of cereal grain provides cohesion in time between the autumn and spring celebration complexes.

In light of the thirty-eight or more days of the AN.TAH.ŠUM festival in the spring and the twenty-one to twenty-four days of the *nuntarriyašḫaš* in the fall, the fifty days of the Israelite Festival of Weeks is not surprising, or the twenty-two days of the festival-cluster in the fall. Festivals of many days were within the repertoire of both peoples. Moreover, the coalescence of *maṣṣôt* and *pesaḥ* in Deut 16:3–8, or the possible intermingling of Weeks with *maṣṣôt*, depending on the date of first ripening barley (Deut 16:9), also seem less strange. The numerous festivals integrated into the AN.TAH.ŠUM and the possible confusion of KI.LAM and *purulli* with elements of each other attest a developmental process that involves the accretion of festivals one to another. Another possible evidence of this is the multiple names attached to certain Israelite festivals. Besides the tendency in later tradition to refer to the entire complex of *maṣṣôt* and *pesaḥ* as Pesach, multiple names appear for the Festivals of Weeks, Alarm Blasts, and Booths, and the Day of Purgation. The Festival of Weeks, *ḥag šābu ʿōt* (Exod

34:22), also goes by the expression *yôm habbikkûrîm* (Num 28:26). The Festival of Alarm Blasts is *zikrôn tĕrû'â* (Lev 23:24b), *yôm tĕrû'â* (Num 29:1b), and Rosh Hashanah in late tradition. The Day of Purgation, *yôm hakkippurîm* (Lev 23:27aβ, 28; 25:9), is called *rō'š haššānâ* in Ezek 40:1a. Finally, *ḥag hassukkôt* (Lev 23:34b) takes the name *ḥag hā-'āsîp* in Exod 23:16; 34:22, and *he-ḥāg* in 1 Kgs 8:2, 65; 2 Chr 7:8. Goldstein and Cooper (1990), for example, take these naming differences as part of the evidence for the merger of a North Israelite calendar with a Judaean one.

Second, cultic tours are not unknown in Israel. Samuel, for instance made an annual circuit through Bethel, Gilgal, and Mizpeh with a final return to Ramah (1 Sam 7:16). Indeed, he is perhaps on that circuit when he meets Saul searching for the asses of Kish (1 Sam 9:12–13). The latter passage makes it clear that there were sacrifices at the local *bāmâ* along with a communal meal. The people are unable to eat the festal meal until Samuel blesses the *zebaḥ*. Likewise, a seer was also part of the king's entourage in Hatti-land. Part of the seer's role was to deliver bread loaves to the sacred stelae. Furthermore, the main celebrant, a member of the royal family, traveled from locale to locale, as did Samuel in his circuit.

One might envision the *ḥag*, or pilgrimage, as the inverse image of the seer's circuit. As the cult became progressively centralized, the people, rather than the leader of the celebration, traveled. Already at Hattusa during the EZEN KI.LAM, the *abarakku*-officials present produce to the royal couple brought from their respective towns. Although the couple travels from building to building within Hattusa, they do *not* go to other towns. This centralization for one festival in Hatti-land suggests intermediate steps in the process of cult centralization in Israel: under the auspices of the king, first one festival and then another are centralized.

Leviticus commands that during the seven-day *ḥag* of the Booths (23:39a, 41), the people actually dwell in a *sukkâ* (v. 42). The writer justifies this command with an appeal to the wilderness march (v. 43), where the Israelites dwelt in *sukkôt*. One *sukkâ* of that *ḥag* was the *'ōhel mô'ēd*, the tent under which the Ark was set when the entourage came to a stopping point. The forty-two stopping points are all duly noted in Num 33, including a famous mountain. Again, both the Hittite and the Israelite peoples had in their cultic repertoire (1) the tour of cultic celebrants (2) to open-air sites (some near mountains) (3) with a cult object. At the stopping sites (4), a tent was pitched for the cult object, and (5) celebrations were held. The sketch of these circuits in Israel may reveal developmental stages: (1) the mass march of a whole people with their cult objects; (2) the circuit of a seer between cult sites; (3) the centralization of some cult festivals at particular sites under the authority of the king; and (4) the mass pilgimmage of a whole people to one cult site three times a year. Thus the *ḥag* seems to be the mirror image of the wilderness march, the inversion of a traveling *cultus*. In Hatti-land, we see examples of steps (2) and (3).

One also notes the many "great assemblies" that occur throughout all four principle festivals of the Hittite cycle. Similarly, we find an *'ăṣeret* during the Israelite *ḥaggîm* of Booths (Lev 23:36b, 39a; Num 29:35; cf. 2 Chr 7:9; Neh 8:18) and *maṣṣôt* (Deut 16:8b). However, the Israelite assemblies both are markedly fewer in number and differ in attendees. All males (Deut 16:16) or perhaps all the people (Deut 16:11) come in Israel, while Hittite assemblies seem to accommodate only the royal family, cult and state officials, and entertainers.

The cultic manipulation of grain also provides cohesion in both cultic systems. In Israel, the autumn festival is *ḥag hā-'āsîp*, the garnering or ingathering festival. While this particular usage of *'āsîp* is a *dys legomenon* (Exod 23:16; 34:22), other usages of the root make its sense clear. One may *'sp* people, animals, eggs, money, ashes of the red cow, and chariots. But among things, the produce of the earth is most commonly collected (Lev 23:39; 25:3, 20; Deut 11:14; 16:13; 28:38, etc.). In Lev 23:39, the use of the infinitive construct *bĕ'ospĕkem* 'when you have gathered in' points to the completion of harvesting. The threshed and winnowed grain is garnered from the threshing floor. We read in Job 39:12 *hăta'ămîn bô kî-yāšîb zar'ekā wĕgornĕkā ye'ĕsōp* 'will you trust him that will bring home your seed and garner your threshing floor', and in Deut 16:13 one celebrates *ḥag hassukkôt . . . bĕ'ospĕkā miggornĕkā ûmiyyiqbekā* 'when you have garnered from your threshing floor and from your winepress'.

Cultic supplies of grain were garnered at the First Temple in the *bêt hā'ăsuppîm* near the southern gate of the Temple complex (1 Chr 26:15). The tithes of grain were brought and laid in heaps (2 Chr 31:6b; cf. Jer 50:26; Ruth 3:7; Song 7:3) starting in the third month and finishing in the seventh month (2 Chr 31:7). (Likewise, on the fifteenth day of the *nuntarriyašḫaš*, mounds were piled up for the Hittite priests.) Thus by the time of the Festival of Booths, the garnering of grains and other produce must be near completion. We read in Hag 2:19 that on the twenty-fourth day of the seventh month, *hazzera' bammĕgûrâ* 'the seed is in the granary'. Booths is thus *not* a harvest festival, but a festival of storage. In the northern kingdom, Jeroboam actually institutes a festival *kehāg 'āšer bîhûdâ* at Bethel in the eighth month (1 Kgs 12:32), the same month as the Hittite *nuntarriyašḫaš*, the festival when grain is poured into the grain jar.

Unfortunately, there is no record of any attendant ritual of storage or unstorage in Israel. However, we do have rituals associated with the old and new grain in the spring. During *maṣṣôt*, presumably before the new barley harvest has begun, *tō'kal-'ālāyw maṣṣôt leḥem 'ōnî* 'you will eat maṣṣot, bread of affliction' (Deut 16:3)—that is, bread made without leaven. On the verge of the barley harvest, the Israelites eat with the paschal sacrifice a lesser bread made from the old crop. Only after the *'ōmer* of the new barley crop is presented can *leḥem*, *qālî*, and *karmel* (three degrees of ripeness of the new barley) be eaten (Lev 23:14). Thus in some sense, the *tĕnûpâ* of the barley *'ōmer* (Lev 23:11) *releases* the new crop, just as the Hittite king's "taking" wheat bread does on the fourth day of the *nuntarriyašḫaš*. From the elevation of the *'ōmer*, the Israelite counts seven weeks (Lev 23:15). This is the only "cultic" activity listed for the intervening period until the fiftieth day. On that day, *wĕhiqrabtem minḥâ ḥădāšâ laYHWH* 'you will offer a new cereal offering to YHWH' (Lev 23:16). Until then, old wheat is used in the cereal offering. With the beginning of the wheat harvest, the new crop becomes available. On that day, *mimmôšĕbōtêkem tābî'û leḥem tĕnûpâ štayim* 'from your dwelling places bring two elevation loaves [of wheat]' (Lev 23:17) made with leaven. We meet something akin to these two loaves at two points in the AN.TAH.SUM festival. During the high days (seven to nine), the king sacrifices two loaves of sweetbread at Arinna. On the twenty-ninth day, two loaves of sourdough bread are presented to the goddess Ea.

This careful waiting to "release" the new crop for common use after the presentation of samples of the new crop to the deity is part of both the grain-jar cycle in Hatti-land and the Feast of Weeks in Israel. More than fecundity of the earth, or thanksgiving for harvest, these efforts seem to betray, as Archi (1973: 24) noted, a fear that the gods would abandon the land (cf. Hoffner 1974: 215). In Israelite tradition, the curse that the land would not produce (Lev 26:20) is part of a schema of intensifying trouble for disobedience to *miṣwōt hā-'ēlleh* (Lev 26:14). The antecedent to *hā-'ēlleh* is the positive commands of Lev 25 concerning the land, the *šabbāt*, and the *yōbēl*. Their nonobservance violates YHWH's residual property rights (Lev 25:23). Similarly, in the Hittite Anitta Inscription, the weather-god reasserts his property rights over the city of Harkiuma after the king curses it and forbids resettlement (Stewart 1992: 11). Thus the festival cycles of both cultures, with their attendant grain rituals, may serve the purpose of acknowledging divine ownership of the land and the crop rights of the deity.

In sum, the manipulation of cereal grain, the tour of festival celebrants through various cultic sites that host "great assemblies," and the development of multi-day festival complexes offer three points of comparison between the entire complex of Hittite and Israelite festivals.

24. Tabernacle Oil and Bread; The Case of Blasphemy

TRANSLATION

Oil for the Tabernacle Lamps

[1]YHWH spoke to Moses, saying:
[2]Command the Israelites to bring you clear oil of beaten olives for lighting, for kindling a flame regularly. [3]Aaron shall set it up in the Tent of Meeting outside the veil of the Pact [to burn] from evening to morning before YHWH regularly; it is a law for all times, throughout your generations. [4]On the pure (golden) lampstand shall be set up the lamps before YHWH [to burn] regularly.

Bread for the Tabernacle Table

[5]You shall take semolina and bake it (into) twelve loaves; two-tenths of an ephah shall be in each loaf. [6]You shall place them (in) two piles, six to a pile, on the table of pure (gold) before YHWH. [7]With each pile you shall place pure frankincense, which shall be a token offering for the bread, a food gift for YHWH. [8]Every sabbath day it shall be set up before YHWH regularly, (a commitment)

of the Israelites as a covenant for all time. [9]It shall belong to Aaron and his descendants; and they shall eat it in a holy place; it is a most sacred portion for him from the food gifts of YHWH, a due for all time.

The Case of the Blasphemer

[10]There came out among the Israelites a man whose mother was Israelite and whose father was Egyptian. And a fight broke out in the camp between the son of an Israelite woman and a certain Israelite. [11]The son of the Israelite woman pronounced the Name, cursing it, and he was brought to Moses—now his mother's name was Shelomith, daughter of Dibri, of the tribe of Dan—[12]and he was put in custody, (until) the decision of YHWH should be made clear to them.

[13]And YHWH spoke to Moses, saying: [14]Take the blasphemer outside the camp; and have all who were within hearing lean their hands on his head; then have the whole community stone him. [15]And to the Israelites speak thus: Anyone who curses his God shall bear his punishment; [16]but if he (also) pronounces the name of YHWH he must be put to death. The whole community shall stone him; alien as well as citizen, if he has (thus) pronounced the Name, he must be put to death.

The Talion Laws

[17]If anyone kills any human being, he must be put to death. [18]But anyone who kills an animal shall make restitution for it, life for life. [19]If anyone maims another, as he has done so shall it be done to him: [20]fracture for fracture, eye for eye, tooth for tooth. The injury he has inflicted on the person shall be inflicted on him. [21]One who kills an animal shall make restitution for it; but one who kills a human being shall be put to death. [22]You shall have one law for the alien and citizen alike: for I YHWH your God (have spoken).

The Compliance Report

[23]Moses spoke (thus) to the Israelites. And they took the blasphemer outside the camp and pelted him with stones. The Israelites did as YHWH had commanded Moses.

Comments

The structure of Lev 24:13–23, COMMENT A; and *lex talionis* in the Bible, ancient Near East and rabbinic literature, COMMENTS B and C; an alternative structural exegesis of 24:10–23 in COMMENT D.

NOTES

Lev 24 presents two nettling questions: the placement of this anomalous chapter, and the relationship between its two parts, vv. 1–9 and vv. 10–23. The latest to attempt a solution is Warning (1999: 92–96), who suggests that the double mention of the sabbath (v. 8) bridges its sevenfold occurrence in chaps. 23 and 25–26. On the second problem, Warning (1999: 94, n. 80) follows Gains (1992: 90) that chaps. 19–24 exhibit an ascending progression of holiness terminating with the outer sanctum (24:1–9) and the inner sanctum (i.e., the name of God; 24:10–23). These answers, and those that preceded them, are shots in the dark. I have a preference for Douglas's (1993a: 11) ring structure for *all* of Leviticus, whereby 24:10–23 balances 10:1–5, the only narrative in Leviticus, which I have supported by claiming that chap. 24's deliberate desecration of YHWH's name complements its (reinterpretive) inadvertent violation in 5:20–26 (see INTRODUCTION to vv. 10–23; Introduction I E and I L). As for the second problem, I point out (see INTRODUCTIONS to vv. 1–9, 5–9) that the oil and bread for the sanctuary's menorah and table, respectively, are assigned to Israel as its permanent responsibility. This assignment follows logically chap. 23, which emphasizes Israel's responsibility in the cultic calendar.

Vv. 1–9. Introduction

Israel's responsibility for observing the festival calendar and its required sacrifices and offerings (chap. 23) continues here in vv. 1–9 with Israel's responsibility to supply the daily oil for the Tabernacle lamps and the weekly bread for the Tabernacle table—both located in the shrine. This forms the main reason why the passage on the oil (vv. 1–4) is not included in Exod 40, which describes the installation of the candelabrum (vv. 24–25), and why the passage on the bread (vv. 5–9) is not inserted into Exod 40, which describes the installation of the table and bread (vv. 22–23) or into Lev 2, which details the composition of all other cereal (*minḥâ*) offerings. Lev 23:1–24:9 focus on the public sacrifices, whereas chaps. 1–7 deal exclusively with private, individual offerings (Levine 1989; Douglas 1993a: 14). Exod 25–40, in turn, concentrate on the construction of the Tabernacle, but not on the function of the people to maintain it (the exception of Exod 27:20–21 is explained in the INTRODUCTION to vv. 1–4). The responsibility of *the people* to maintain *the public* cult is the burden of 23:1–24:9 (see INTRODUCTION to chap. 23). Perhaps it is this singular emphasis of Lev 23 that is responsible for Qumran's insistence that all of Israel be represented in the sacrificial offerings of the firstfruits and wood festivals (11QT 19:16; 21:6–10; 21:14–15; 23:1–25:16).

Since this pericope prescribes the people's obligation in maintaining the sacrificial rites in the shrine, why are they not also obligated to supply the needs for the remaining sanctum in the shrine, the daily incense offered on the inner, gold altar (as implied by Exod 35:8)? If the answer is ventured that the incense was provided by the chieftains and not by the entire people (Exod 35:27–28), these verses prescribe—ostensibly, in contradiction to our pericope—that the chieftains also supplied the lighting oil! The resolution of this apparent contradiction is that the chieftains contributed the initial supply, but thereafter the responsibility falls on the entire nation, and this permanent arrangement is reflected in 24:1–9. This being so, the question still remains: Why is the incense omitted from Israel's obligations in this pericope?

Meyers (1996) argues that the incense altar occupies an anomalous position among the inner sancta: its vessels are missing from the prescriptive account of the Tabernacle (Exod 25–27) because, in her opinion, they were made of bronze, not the requisite gold, in order to bring in incense, coals, and blood from the outer altar. This is not correct. Incense was brought in a gold ladle (Num 7:14), coals in a gold firepan, and blood in a gold bowl (1 Kgs 7:50; cf. *m. Yoma* 4:4; 11QT 3:12–13; Hurowitz 1995). Besides, it is inconceivable that the purgation blood and incense brought inside the Holy of Holies were in anything but gold vessels (16:12–15). It must be kept in mind that Exod 25–27 describe the sacred objects according to their location, moving from the Holy of Holies (the inner sanctuary), to the outer sanctuary, to the court. Since the incense altar's vessels were located in the court, it is quite understandable why they are omitted from Exod 25–27: they were not attached to the incense altar (contrast the utensils of the table and the candelabrum, Exod 25:29, 38; 37:16, 23) and, hence, do not belong with the objects located in the outer sanctuary. However, being made of gold, they are included with the incense altar while the Tabernacle is in transit (Num 4:12). As for the absence as well of prescriptions for the altar itself, a different logic prevails (vol. 1.236–37). In any case, the omission of the incense in our pericope has to be grounded in some other explanation.

An answer can be only conjectured. Perhaps this pericope reflects reality. Olive oil, even the best quality (see NOTE on "clear," v. 2), was relatively cheap; the land of Canaan abounded in olive groves (Deut 6:11; 8:8; 28:40; Josh 24:13; 2 Kgs 18:32). Excavations at Tel Miqne-Ekron and nearby Timnah and at other locations reveal that in the seventh century B.C.E., this region was the center of a vast olive-oil industry. At Ekron, for example, over 100 oil presses were discovered in surface surveys. At all these sites, the oil presses were "inside ordinary houses, indicating that the manufacture of olive oil was a cottage industry practiced by families at their homes" (Mazar 1990: 491; cf. Eitam and Shomroni 1987). Not so with spices, which were imported and therefore costly. It is no wonder, then, that the list of gifts of the tribal chieftains to the Tabernacle expressly (and consistently) singles out spices (Num 7:14).

Support for this conjecture may lie in the fact that the anointment oil, initially brought by the chieftains (Exod 35:27–28), is also missing from this inventory. Here, too, the answer may be that the anointment oil contained spices (Exod 30: 22–25), thus effectively putting it out of people's reach. If this surmise has merit, then the incense for the Temple would have fallen into the same category as the wood for the altar, which Scripture relates was supplied by a few families at fixed times during the year (Neh 10:35; 13:31; *m. Ta'an.* 4:5)—a practice that was opposed by the sectaries of Qumran (cf. 11QT 23–25; see chap. 23, COMMENT E).

The structure of vv. 1–9 can be outlined as follows:

I. Introductory formula (v. 1)
II. Speech (vv. 2–9)
   A. Oil for the Tabernacle lamps (vv. 2–4)
      1. Commission formula (v. 2aα)
      2. Speech proper (vv. 2aβ–4)
         a. Israelites commanded to supply the oil (v. 2aβ,b)
         b. Aaron commanded to tend the lamp (v. 3)
        [c. Aaron commanded to tend the lamps (v. 4)]
   B. Bread for the Tabernacle table (vv. 5–9)
      1. Instructions to Moses (vv. 5–7)
         a. On baking the bread (v. 5)
         b. On displaying the bread (v. 6)
         c. Accompanied by pure frankincense (v. 7)
      2. Replaced every sabbath (v. 8)
      3. Old bread consumed by the priests (v. 9)

Vv. 1–4. Oil for the Tabernacle Lamps

Exod 27:20–21 contains a nearly similar prescription. Are we confronting a doublet? Rashi, I submit, supplies the correct answer: "The pericope 'You shall command' [wĕ'attâ tĕṣawweh; Exod 27:20] is stated (in the imperative) implying that *in the future* Moses will command the Israelites concerning it [my emphasis]." That is, Lev 24:1–4 is the fulfillment of the command given in Exod 27:20–21. So, too, wĕzeh 'ăšer ta 'ăśeh 'al-hammizbēaḥ 'Now this is what you *shall* offer on the altar . . . [my emphasis]' (Exod 29:38–42) anticipates the altar's future use (Haran 1978: 209, n. 6). Thus as the latter passage is integral to its text, so the two passages concerning the lighting oil are to theirs.

Lev 24:2–3 duplicates Exod 27:20–21 with slight variations: Lev 24:3 adds tāmîd 'regularly', and Exod 27:21 adds 'ăšer 'al (-hā'ēdūt) 'which is over the Pact'; ('ahĕrōn) ûbānāyw '(Aaron) and his sons'; and lĕdōrōtām (not lĕdōrōtêkem) mē'ēt bĕnê yiśrā'ēl 'for their generations from the Israelites'. The only change of any ideological consequence is that, in Exodus, Aaron and his sons (i.e., the entire priestly cadre), rather than Aaron alone, bear the responsibility for setting up the lamps (see NOTE on "Aaron," v. 3).

Also, the addition of mē'ēt bĕnê yiśrā'ēl in Exod 27:21 is patently an attempt to equate the Exodus passage with that of Leviticus (using the language of v. 8bα), which imposes the obligation of supplying the lighting oil on all the Israelites (v. 2aα). If so, then the addition stems from a later H tradent. This explanation would also clarify the strange placement of Exod 27:20–21, ostensibly where it does not belong: on the one hand, it seems superfluous after Exod 25:31–39; on the other hand, it is followed by the presumably irrelevant account of the priestly vestments and their consecration (chaps. 28–29). According to Ibn Ezra, Exod 25:1–27:19 prescribes the composition and dimensions of the sacred objects, but Exod 27:20–21 begins a new section whose theme is the function and operation of these objects. Indeed, his explanation satisfyingly accounts for the removal of the altar of incense from its logical place in Exod 25 (cf. Exod 37:25–29; 40:26; Num 4:11–12; vol. 1. 236–37), but it does not solve our problem. Why begin this new section with the (repetition of the) menorah? Why not open with the "missing" golden altar (30:1–10) or the basin (30:17–21)?

The answer, I submit, is that it is not the menorah that is featured in Exod 27:20–21, but its oil, and distinguished from all the sancta and their two functioning ingredients, the anointment oil and the incense (30:22–38)—both of which are or contain spices and could be afforded by only the presumably wealthy chieftains (Num 7:14 and passim)—the oil for the menorah is the obligation of all the people. It is therefore H, the editor and redactor, who reworked Exod 27:20–21 and inserted it at the head of the sancta-in-action section to emphasize that the oil used by the priests must stem from the people-at-large. (That olive oil was plentiful and affordable, see NOTE on "Command the Israelites," v. 2.) Finally, if Paximadi (forthcoming) is proved right that Exod 25–31 comprises a giant ABA'B' structure in which Exod 27:20–21 stands at the very center, then H's championing of the people of Israel is projected into even greater prominence.

In Leviticus, the prescription for the lampstand comes before that for the Bread of Presence, but in Exodus the bread is mentioned first (Exod 25:30, 31–37), as it is in the prescriptions for the Hittite temple of Nerik (Beckman 1982b). Clearly, the table and its bread are more sacred, to judge by their respective order and coverings during the wilderness trek (Exod 40:22–23, 24–25; Num 4:7–8, 9–10; cf. Milgrom 1990a: 25). Why, then, is the order reversed here? The clue to the answer is provided by the context. Lev 24 speaks of the actual performance of these rites: whereas the bread is offered weekly, the lamps must be tended daily, and the rule in ritual descriptions (not in prescriptions), is—as formulated by the rabbis—*kol- hattādîr qôdēm* 'The more frequent (use) precedes' (*m. Zebaḥ.* 10:1).

The Pharisees apparently allowed the menorah (and the table with the bread loaves on it) to be taken out of the Temple during the festivals and displayed to the pilgrims. The result was that it became defiled by their touch (*m. Ḥag.* 3:8) and had to be purified by immersion. The Sadducees, vehemently opposing the removal of the menorah, would taunt the Pharisees, "Come and see the Pharisees immersing the light of the moon" (*t. Ḥag.* 3:35; cf. Sussman 1990: 59, 66–68; Maimonides on *m. Ḥag.* 7:5; Albeck 1952: 3.515; Lieberman 1967: 5.1935, n. 72). The sectaries of Qumran clearly were in accord with the Sadducees, and they (rather, they averred that God) ordained: *MZBḤ] QṬWRT HSMYM WˀT HŠLḤ[N . . .] LWˀ YMWŠ MN HMQDŠ* 'the altar] of the fragrant incense and the tabl[e . . .] shall not move from the temple' (11QT 3:10–11; cf. Knohl 1992: 605).

This pericope gives every impression of being mainly a P text:

1. The standardization of cultic practice is a characteristic of P, not H.
2. Moses as the active subject and not just the passive transmitter of God's

commands is also a P characteristic (e.g., Exod 25:10–29:46; 30:1–6, 18, 23–30 (Cholewinski 1976).

3. Above all, an H text would have YHWH speaking in the first person (not *lipnê YHWH*, vv. 3, 4, 8 or *'iššê[eh]* [*lĕ]YHWH*, vv. 7, 9, but *lĕpānay*, 22:3; *'iššay*, Num 28:2).

Perhaps, Noth (1977: 177) may be correct in concluding that this pericope "presupposes as in nowhere else the case in the Law of Holiness—the P-narrative." However, it can also be argued that this pericope stems from the school of H (see NOTE on "a flame," v. 2).

2. *Command the Israelites. ṣaw 'et-bĕnê yiśrā'ēl* (cf. 6:2; Num 5:2; 34:2; 35:2). The ostensible contradiction that the oil was brought by the chieftains (Exod 35:28) is resolved by limiting their contribution to the initial supply of oil, after which the responsibility falls on the nation (see above). The unusual command *ṣaw* instead of the customary *dabbēr* may be a structural device to form an inclusio with *ṣiwwâ* (v. 23; M. Hildenbrand).

to bring you. wĕyiqḥû 'ēleka. The Israelites have to provide the oil (Exod 27:20) and the bread (v. 8). The LXX reads *lî* 'me'. If correct, it would indicate an H revision of a P text. However, the consistent reference to the Deity throughout this pericope in the third person argues for the MT.

you. 'ēleka. This refers to Moses, "but not me [*'ēlay*], for I am not in need of light" (*b. Menaḥ.* 86b).

clear. zak. For this meaning, see Job 11:4 (‖ bar. 'pure'); *Sipra* Emor, par. 13:6; *b. Menaḥ.* 86b (bar.). This adjective is also applied to the bread (v. 7) and the incense (Exod 30:34). It is no coincidence that all these uses refer to the sancta inside the shrine; it is a mark of their superior holiness (Haran 1978: 166, n. 30). The rabbis asseverate that this attribute refers to only the first pressed oil:

> There are three kinds of oil. The first is when . . . the olives are pounded (in a mortar) and put into the basket (and the oil oozes out and filters through the basket into the vessel below). R. Judah says, around the basket (around its sides so that the oil does not mix with any solid matter but runs down the sides and filters through the bottom of the basket); this gives the first oil. They (the pounded olives) are then pressed with the beam; R. Judah says with stones; this gives the second oil. They are then ground and pressed again; this gives the third oil. The first oil is fit for the lampstand and the others for cereal offerings. (*m. Menaḥ.* 8:4; cf. *Sipra* Emor, par. 13:1)

The requirement of pure oil within the shrine has a practical rationale: the walls and curtains are less likely to become darkened with soot (Stager and Wolff 1981: 97).

Haran (1978: 208) claims that the *zak* is "a stipulation not made concerning either the anointing oil or the oil added to the grain offering, both of which are mainly used in the court." He is not entirely correct. The anointing oil was used to consecrate all the inner sancta (Exod 30:26–27) and *continued* to be used in consecrating the high priest. This latter fact may provide the answer: in contrast to the oil for the menorah, used exclusively in the shrine, the high priest, bearing the anointing oil, officiated on the outer altar in the courtyard, rendering that oil of lesser sanctity.

beaten. kātît (Deut 9:21; see NOTE on "crushed," 22:24). That is, the olives are pounded in a mortar, (*m. Tah.* 9:5) and not by a beam (*m. Menah.* 8:4), and then passed through a strainer. This term is attested in only the priestly texts (Exod 27:20; 29:40; Lev 24:2; Num 28:5) and in the Solomonic archival account (1 Kgs 5:25), always in a description of olive oil.

olives. The source of the oil had to be specified, since kindling oil was also available from sesame seed, flax, and animal fats (Sarna 1992: 175).

for lighting. lammā'ôr. There are two possible renderings for this word. The first is that it is a noun, referring to the instrument for lighting. The sun and moon are called mĕ'ōrōt (Gen 1:16; Ezek 32:8) because they are the implements to transmit on the fourth day the light created on the first day. Hence this word would be a synonym for mĕnōrâ 'lampstand' (v. 4; cf. Wessely 1846).

Alternatively, and preferably, this word can be construed as an infinitive construct (as in Aramaic) to be rendered "for lighting," as lĕ'anhārā' 'for lighting' (Tgs.; cf. *luxnon* 'light' LXX). This rendering is confirmed by the expression mĕnôrat hammā'ôr, literally "the lampstand of the light" (Exod 35:14a; Num 4:9), which vitiates the previous suggestion that mā'ôr can mean "lampstand." Thus the expression šemen hammā'ôr in the same verse (Exod 35:14b; cf. 39:37; Num 4:9) must be translated "the lighting oil," and all other priestly attestations to this phrase in reference to the oil for the lampstand must be rendered similarly (Exod 25:6; 27:20; 35:8, 28).

for kindling. lĕha'ălōt. For this rendering, see lĕ'adlāqâ (Tgs.); *kausai* (LXX; cf. Saadiah, Bekhor Shor, *Sipra* Emor 17:7). It is confirmed by other attestations of this verb in connection with the lampstand. In the account of the erection of the Tabernacle, we read wayya'al 'ālāyw 'et-hā'ōlâ wĕ'et-hamminḥâ 'He (Moses) offered [note the same verb] on it (the bronze altar) the burnt offering and the cereal offering' (Exod 40:29b). We would therefore expect that the lampstand, in the same pericope, would also be put into operation. Hence wayya'al hannērōt (v. 25) must mean "he kindled the lamps." Furthermore, Aaron's task was to prepare the lamps in the morning and *kindle* the lamps (ûbĕha'ălōt 'et-hannērōt) in the evening (Exod 30:7–8). Thus in our pericope, since the verb 'ārak 'set up' (v. 4) indicates that the lamps have been prepared for lighting, the only possible meaning for lĕha'ălōt (here and in Exod 27:20) is "for kindling" (vol. 1.173–74). (Perhaps this is its meaning also in Exod 25:37 and Num 8:2–3.)

a flame. nēr. The rabbis hold that the lamps burned out by the end of the night, except the westernmost lamp, which, although it was the first to be lit, continued to burn through the following day (*b. Šabb.* 22b; *b. Menaḥ.* 86b). Josephus (*Ant.* 3.199; cf. *Apion* 1.22) reports that three of the lamps burned during the day.

A possible support for this view is the use of the singular nēr and 'ōtô (v. 3; cf. Holzinger [1922], who, however, mistakenly adds mā'ôr, taking it as a sing.

noun "light"; see above). If so, then vv. 1–3 (and Exod 27:20–21, which employs the same sing. words) would be assigned to H, in contrast to P, which uses the plural *nērôt* (Eerdmans 1912). V. 4, containing *nērôt*, would then be assigned to a redactor who harmonized P and H and also left his mark in Exod 27:20–21 (see NOTE on v. 4). Even though *nēr* may be a collective (Elliger 1966; Haran 1978: 208, n. 4), as in 1 Sam 3:3 (and cf. sing. *wĕhē'îr*, despite pl. *nērôtêhā*, Exod 25:37), the possibility that it refers to a single lamp cannot be dismissed.

Meyers (1976) has shown that the ur-form of the menorah is a simple stand and that the branches are a secondary development. As for the extant, early seven-spouted Palestinian lamps and seven-pointed flames of Assyrian incense stands, they are associated with a central bowl. Nonetheless, Meyers (1976: 57–84) avers that the seven-branched candelabrum is old. Her view has recently been challenged by Hachlili and Merhav (1985), who argue that texts, iconography, and artifacts point to a Second Temple origin for the seven-branched candelabrum and that the First Temple form probably was a conical base decorated with a floral capital, surmounted by a lamp or bowl (plate 51). Indeed, such a seven-spouted pedestal oil lamp was found at Tell Dan (see also Zech 4:2). Thus the singular *nēr* (Exod 27:20; Lev 24:2) may, indeed, represent the original.

Without further evidence, this debate cannot be resolved: both parties argue out of silence. But they agree on the chronological sequence: the seven-branched menorah represents a later stage. As to whether this development took place in First or Second Temple times has yet to be determined.

The presence of the menorah, the incense altar, and the Bread of Presence inside the sanctuary originally may have represented, respectively, the light, aroma, and food offered to the resident Deity. A deeper symbolism, however, may have been understood. One such possibility for the menorah is suggested by Gerstenberger (1996: 356): "God forfeits none of his power, even if the sun itself 'goes down'. The lamp before the holy of holies extends this daylight symbolically through the darkness, signalling thus God's unbroken life: in this sense it is an 'eternal light'." For the symbolism of the bread of presence, see the INTRODUCTION to vv. 5–9.

regularly. tāmîd. The lamp(s) were lit every evening (Exod 30:8); the bread was set on the table every sabbath (v. 8); the altar fire was rekindled before it died (6:6; see further vol. 1.388–89). Thus *tāmîd* must be rendered "regularly," not "perpetually." For other occurrences of *tāmîd* in P, see Exod 25:30; 27:20; 28:29, 30, 38; 29:38; Num 9:16.

3. *Aaron.* The LXX, Sam., and thirteen MSS add *ûbānāyw* 'and his sons', an ostensible harmonization with *'ahărōn ûbānāyw* (Exod 27:21). Both texts speak of the same priestly role of *preparing* the lamps (*'ārak*). Note, however, that the function of *kindling* the lamps is assigned to only Aaron (Exod 30:8; Num 8:2–3). That is, Aaron alone may *officiate* in the shrine, but priests may enter the shrine (*bĕbō'ām 'el- 'ōhel mô'ēd*; Exod 28:43; 30:20; Lev 10:9), presumably to assist Aaron in noncultic tasks such as the preparation of the lamp(s). Thus rather than striking *ûbānāyw* from Exod 27:21 (Haran 1978: 209, n. 6), this word should be added to Lev 24:3, in conformance with the LXX and the other sources.

To be sure, 2 Chr 13:10–11 speak of the priests' role regarding the cande-labrum: *ûmĕnôrat hazzāhāb wĕnērōtêhā lĕbāʿer bāʿereb bāʿereb*, literally "and the golden lampstand and its lamps to burn each evening." However, this statement is ambiguous; the infinitive "to burn" may imply that the priests only enable "the lamps to burn," but do not actually kindle them. Perhaps the Second Tem-ple practice had changed. In any event, this text would have sufficed as biblical precedent for the rabbinic ruling that all priests may participate even in the kin-dling (*m. Tam.* 3:9).

The Qumran sectaries conflated these two texts, favoring the Exodus reading: *WʿRKW HKWHNYM BNY [ʾHRWN ʾT HNRWT LPNY YHWH TMY]D ḤWQWT ʿWL[M LDWRW]TMH* 'and the priests the sons of [Aaron] shall set up [the lamps before YHWH regular]ly; it is a law for all tim[e throughout] their [generations]' (11QT 9:13–14 [Yadin 1983: 2.39]). Of the two pentateuchal pas-sages, Exodus would appear to be a later interpolation, since Aaron's appoint-ment to the priesthood (in P) occurs in only the following chapter (Exod 28).

shall set . . . up. yaʿărōk. In the priestly texts, this verb always bears this cul-tic connotation (1:7, 8, 12; 6:5; 24:3, 4, 8; cf. Exod 27:21; 40:4, 23). Durham (1987: 379, n. 21a) claims that this verb also refers to fueling, trimming, and lighting the lamp(s), but these acts are expressed by different verbs: *hēṭîb* and *heʿĕlâ* (Exod 30:7–8).

it. ʾōtô. The referent of this singular suffix is *nēr*, indicating the possibility that the original candelabrum was a single branchless stem (see above).

the veil of the Pact. pārōket hāʿēdūt. This is a condensation of *pārōket ʾăšer ʿal-hāʿēdūt* 'veil that is over the Pact' (Exod 27:21); *happārōket ʾăšer ʿal- ʾărōn hāʾēdūt* 'the veil that is over the ark of the Pact' (Exod 30:6a). The Pact refers to the Decalogue, as indicated by *lūḥōt hāʾēdūt* 'the tablets of the Pact' (Exod 31:18; 32:15; 34:29).

from evening to morning. mēʿereb ʿad-bōqer. This phrase cannot modify the verb *yaʿărōk* 'shall set up', since this task occurs once a day. Wessely's (1846) suggestion that it modifies the following phrase "before YHWH regularly" must be rejected on grammatical grounds (a verb or an adjective is required). The verb *lĕbāʿer* 'to burn' (cf. 2 Chr 13:11) must be supplied or understood, since the light had to burn until dawn (LXX; cf. 1 Sam 3:3). The instructions for the Hittite temple in Nerik read, "When it becomes dark they (the priests) will kin-dle the lamp and close the gate."

Philo (*Laws* 1.297) maintains that the lit lampstand illuminates "some rites of the same kith and kin as those of the day-time." He is probably thinking of the *tāmîd* and incense offering, which in addition to their morning offering are also performed *bên hāʿarbayim* 'at twilight' (Exod 29:41; 30:8). Thereafter, the sanctuary shuts down for the night.

regularly. tāmîd. This word is repeated here (but not in Exod 27:21), perhaps to emphasize that the supply and kindling of the oil must never cease (see NOTE on "regularly," v. 2).

throughout your generations. lĕdōrōtêkem. Exod 27:21 reads *lĕdōrōtām* 'throughout their generations', which the LXX harmonizes with Leviticus by reading *lĕdōrōtêkem*. However, MT Exodus is clearly preferable, since a second-person plural is out of place in vv. 1–9. (Was it possibly an attempt to create an inclusio with the one other second-person-plural suffix in this chapter, *'ĕlōhêkem*, v. 22?)

Exodus 27:21 adds *mē'ēt bĕnê yiśrā'ēl* 'from the Israelites'. Its purpose, presumably, is to emphasize Israel's permanent role in supplying the oil (see IN-TRODUCTION to vv. 1–4). But to get this reading, a loose translation must be improvised for *ḥuqqat* (Exod 27:21bα): "It shall be due (from the Israelites)" (*NJPS*). In any event, the subject of both v. 3 and v. 4 is Aaron's role in the sanctuary. Thus *mē'ēt bĕnê yiśrā'ēl* 'from the Israelites', if original to Exod 27:21 (though probably the addition of an H tradent; see INTRODUCTION to vv. 1–4), would be out of place here.

4. *the pure (golden) lampstand. hammĕnōrâ haṭṭĕhōrâ.* This phrase is found again in Exod 31:8; 39:37. The definite article indicates that there was no other lampstand (Ibn Ezra; *Abod. Z.* 43a). It is an ellipsis of *mĕnōrâ(t) zāhāb ṭāhôr* 'a pure golden lampstand' (Exod 25:31; 37:17; Zech 4:2)—that is, a lampstand made of pure gold. Meyers (1976: 27–31) refers to the metallurgical process of washing gold and renders this expression "washed gold." The absence of the vital specification "gold" presumes a knowledge of Exod 25:31, one of the many indications that H is dependent on P. The same holds true in the specifications for the table (see NOTE on "the table of [pure] gold," v. 6).

Sforno suggests that the candelabrum and table (v. 6b) were "pure" because they could never be contaminated and, hence, never received the blood of the purification offering. However, the rabbis aver that the candelabrum and the table could be contaminated because they were displayed before (and possibly touched by) the festival pilgrims (*m. Ḥag.* 3:8). Moreover, the incense altar, which also contained "pure gold," did indeed require purification-offering blood (4:7, 18). And as was theorized in vol. 1.255–58, the sevenfold sprinkling of the purification blood before the Veil (4:6, 17) was intended to purify the entire room, including the candelabrum and table. As to why the incense altar requires special purification by blood daubing, I have posited that the two altars, the incense in the shrine and the sacrificial altar in the courtyard, require sevenfold aspersion and daubing (cf. 16:18–19) because they are the funnel of the people's prayer to God, symbolically represented by the ascending smoke of the incense and sacrifice and, hence, necessitate stronger prophylaxis against the "demonic" forces of impurity (vol. 1.258–61).

The rabbis render *ṭĕhōrâ* as "clean," by which they mean that there was no material intervening between the lamps and the lampstand (*Sipra* Emor 13:12). The reason for this bizarre explanation, as suggested by Knohl (1992: 605, n. 8), is that the candelabrum (and the table) was displayed before pilgrims and, hence, could not always be guaranteed to be "pure."

This verse, as will be summarized below, is a reprise of vv. 2–3. Its purpose is immediately betrayed by this opening phrase: *mĕnōrâ* replaces *mā'ôr* (v. 2aβ), thereby clarifying that the latter refers not to a single light source (lamp), but to the entire candelabrum (see further below).

shall be set up the lamps. ya ʿărōk ʾet-hannērôt. The subject and object are repeated to emphasize that *nēr* (v. 2bα) must be understood as a collective for *nērôt* and, hence, refers to the seven-branched candelabrum (Elliger 1966; Noth 1977). Alternatively, it can be argued that this verse does not reprise the preceding but adds the information that the lamps, not being an integral part of the lampstand, must be added separately atop its branches. However, this obvious fact hardly requires repetition (cf. Exod 25:37).

regularly. tāmîd. The third and final occurrence of this word in this brief pericope (vv. 1–4) stresses once again that the rite of preparing and lighting the lamps must never cease. The LXX and Sam. read, instead, *ʿad bōqer* 'until the morning', which, as the object of *ya ʿărōk* 'shall set up', makes no sense. Perhaps these two ancient versions, in repeating only part of the phrase *mē ʿereb ʿad-bōqer* (v. 3aβ), had in mind that the candelabrum burned until the morning.

In sum, v. 4 is clearly a redactional supplement to vv. 2–3, to clarify that the lampstand did not consist of a single lamp. That this verse is an addendum is indicated by the phrase "it is a law for all time, throughout your [their] generations" (v. 3bβ), which normally ends a pericope (e.g., 3:17; 10:9; 17:7; 23:14, 21, 31), except when it is followed by a redactoral addition (e.g., 3:17b; 10:10–11)—precisely the case here—or when it is composed by the author himself (23:22, 32). For this reason, it could not be a stylistic device known as a "repetitive summary" (Paran 1989: 57–58), frequently attested in P (e.g., Exod 12:3–4; 25:2; 30:1; Lev 1:2). Regarding the authorship of these verses, the verdict is difficult. The impersonal style and Moses as an active subject lean toward P (see INTRODUCTION to v. 1–4), while the singular *nēr* and *ʾōtô* point to a tradition that is at variance with P, namely, the basic H stratum (called H in chap. 23), which an H tradent corrects in v. 4 and Exod 27:21 (see NOTE on "a flame," v. 2).

Vv. 5–9. Bread for the Tabernacle Table

In P, the term for this bread is *leḥem (hap)pānîm* '(the) bread of presence' (Exod 25:30; 35:13, 39:36), but once it is called *leḥem hattāmîd* 'the regular bread' (Num 4:7), an ellipsis from *leḥem pānîm lĕpānay tāmîd* 'bread of presence before one regularly' (Exod 25:30). In postexilic literature, *leḥem happānîm* appears once (2 Chr 4:19) as a quotation from an earlier source, the archival account of the building of the Solomonic Temple (1 Kgs 7:48). Otherwise, it has been altered to *leḥem hamma ʿăreket* 'pile bread' (Neh 10:34; 1 Chr 9:32; 33:29); *ma ʿăreket leḥem* 'pile(s) of the bread' (2 Chr 13:11); or simply *ma ʿăreket* '(bread) pile(s)' (2 Chr 2:3). This terminology is probably borrowed from our pericope (vv. 6–7), *wĕ ʾāraktā ʾet- ʿerkô* 'you shall set up its order' (Exod 40:4) and *ʿerek leḥem* 'an order of bread' (Exod 40:23; cf. Dillmann and Ryssel 1897; Paran 1989: 281). The change in terminology, I suggest, is not because the earlier term fell out of use, but because, in official circles, there arose aversion to its anthropomorphic implications (see below).

The table on which the bread was always present—even when the table was transported (Num 4:7b)—was, perhaps for that reason, the most important sanctum except for the Ark. It follows the Ark in all accounts (prescription, Exod 25:29–30; construction, Exod 37:10–16; installation, Exod 40:4, 22; and transport, Num 4:7–8). Its relative importance is further underscored by its being covered during transport. It joins the Ark in meriting three coverings, whereas the other sancta—the menorah and the two altars—rate only two coverings (cf. Num 4:5–8 with vv. 9–14).

There can be no doubt that the display of bread before a deity is an ancient practice. In Egypt, the offerings are placed on the outer altar, but only the fresh bread and cakes are brought into the sanctuary and laid on mats (together with incense and *Ma'at*) before the god's table (Saueron 1960: 84), where they are burned and sprinkled with wine, as surety for the eternal duration of the sacrificial worship (*RAB* 557; cf. Dommershausen 1984; Blackman 1918–19; Erman 1907: 44; see NOTE on "a covenant for all time," v. 8).

Hittite religion also evidences the centrality of a bread offering laid out on a table before the deity (Hoffner 1974: 216). The Hittite king Muršili II attests that "the offerers of sacrificial loaves and the offerers of libations were giving bread and making libations to the gods, my lords" (Hoffner 1974: 216). Ritual bread-laying was an early custom in Mesopotamia, appearing in a Sumerian inscription of Urukagina of Lagash (ca. 2340 B.C.E.; Cooper 1983: 60). Babylonians laid sweet unleavened bread before various deities, in twelves or multiples of twelve (Zimmern 1905: 600; cf. Blome 1934: 247–50, and NOTE on v. 6). A table for the bread is also attested in the Greek temple at Delphi that, according to Josephus (*Ant.* 3.139), was precisely of the same dimensions as that prescribed for the Tabernacle.

Thus there can be no doubt that the bread display was integral to Israelite worship from earliest times. It is first attested for the Nob sanctuary, where the bread was given to David and his soldiers (nonpriests!), apparently as an emergency measure to prevent starvation (cf. *b. Menaḥ.* 95b–96a).

It is important, however, to recognize the wide gulf that separates the bread rite prescribed for the Tabernacle from its counterparts in the neighboring cultures. Whereas the latter baked bread for the god's table daily, Israel prepared it once weekly—clearly a token offering whose purpose was exposure, not food (Barr 1963). Indeed, even the term *leḥem happānîm*, literally "bread of the face" or "personal bread" (Johnson 1947; de Vaux 1964: 39, n. 35)—a gross anthropomorphism—is missing in this pericope, probably deliberately (Kalisch 1867–72). The classic polemic against the pagan notion that the sacrifices and food offerings actually fed the deity was penned by the Psalmist: "If I were hungry I would not tell you, for mine are the world and its fullness. Do I eat the flesh of strong bulls, or is the blood of goats my drink?" (Ps 50:12–13).

Nonetheless, vestiges—though only fossils—of such earlier beliefs in ancient Israel are evident from the cultic apparatus of the table, which included *qĕśôt hannesek* 'libation bowls' (Num 4:7). Since they were made of gold (Exod 25:29; 37:16), they were not originally intended for the wine libations on the outer altar (Num 15:5, 7, 10), for its vessels were exclusively bronze (Exod 27:3; 28:3).

Being of gold, they could be used only *inside* the shrine. Only there—and nowhere else—was gold used on the cult objects (candelabrum table, incense altar) and structure (inner curtains, planks, pillars, bars, hooks, and rings). Where this libation was offered is not clear. The obvious place, the inner altar—to correspond with the libation on the outer altar—is strictly forbidden by Exod 30:9 (which perhaps betrays that it originally was done there). Another verse, however, furnishes stronger evidence that a libation on the inner altar originally did take place: *baqqōdeš hassēk nesek šēkār laYHWH* 'in the sanctuary the pouring a libation of beer to YHWH' (Num 28:7b).

Akkadian *šikaru, šikru* means "beer, ale." Although the beer and ale industry is attested from early on in the predominantly grain-growing countries of Egypt and Mesopotamia, whereas Canaan was celebrated for its wine as among its chief exports in every age, archaeology reveals that undoubtedly beer was also manufactured in Canaan. Typical of Philistine pottery is a jug "usually provided with a strainer spout . . . in order to strain out the beer without swallowing barley husks. It is not difficult to infer from the ubiquity of these . . . beer jugs that the Philistines were mighty carousers. In this respect, archaeology is in full agreement with biblical tradition, as we see from the story of Samson, where drinking bouts are mentioned several times in connection with the Philistines (Judg 14:10, 12, 17), though it is said emphatically of Samson that he drank neither wine nor beer" (Judg 13:14; Albright 1949: 115).

Where would a beer libation have been made? All the biblical texts asseverate unambiguously that wine alone was poured on the outer altar. Num 28:7b, however, testifies that beer was poured *baqqōdeš*. The protean term *qōdeš* means "holy place" and can thus refer to all or part of the Tabernacle compound (cf. Milgrom 1976a: 35–37; vol. 1.322–24). Ibn Ezra (on Lev 6:23) suggests that it is used in relative comparisons: the Tabernacle enclosure is sacred (*qōdeš*) in relation to the camp, the shrine in relation to the court, and the adytum in relation to the shrine (cf. Haran 1965: 213, n. 17). Yet the fluidity of this term is more apparent than real. In P, when *qōdeš* refers to a place, it stands for the shrine in contrast to the *qōdeš qodāšîm*, the adytum (e.g., Exod 26:33), or the area in the court between the altar and the tent (Lev 10:4, 17, 18), or both (Exod 28:43; for its discrete use in Lev 16, see NOTE on 16:2).

Thus the beer libation *baqqōdeš* must have taken place inside the shrine on the inner altar. However, after it was forbidden as a gross anthropomorphism, lest one think that YHWH—in his private chambers—actually imbibed the brew, the libation was set on the table together with its loaves of bread, and neither was offered on the altar. And just as the bread was assigned to the priests, one may assume that, originally, the beer also became a priestly prebend. Perhaps at some subsequent juncture, the beer was altogether eliminated, since it did not fit with the priestly sacrificial system: the bread, being a *minḥâ*, could be assigned to the priests, but the beer, being a unique liquid offering that never is a priestly prebend, was eliminated. The golden cups on the table remained, but were empty.

It can be no accident that in contrast to all other bread offerings, at least part of which is consumed on the altar (2:2, 9, 16; 6:8), only the frankincense placed alongside (but not on) the table is burned on the altar, but none of the bread. In sum, the bread and the beer are displayed to the Deity and not "consumed" by the Deity. The bread (and, originally, the beer) is given to the priests in its entirety, but only after being displayed before YHWH for an entire week.

This altered ritual inside the shrine is clearly rife with symbolism. What could it be? According to an ancient interpretation, the table is an instrument not of sacrifice, but of nourishment—not for God but for persons. As God destined the plant kingdom for human nourishment, so did he require a table for the Tabernacle (*Midrash Agada* on Exod 38:21; Philo, *Moses* 2.104; cf. Chinitz 1993: 52).

A more productive line of inquiry begins with the observation that the Bread of Presence is changed every sabbath (v. 8), corresponding to the change of the priestly courses and Temple guards, which also took place on the sabbath (2 Kgs 11:4–9; 2 Chr 23:4–6; cf. *m. Ta'an.* 4:2; *b. Ta'an.* 27a,b). Thus the sabbath, the resting place of God in time, is matched by the Tabernacle, the resting place of God in space (R. Gane). It is hardly a coincidence that both the Bread of Presence and the sabbath are designated as a *bĕrît 'ôlām* 'an eternal covenant' (v. 8b; Exod 31:16b [H]). Joosten (1994: 166–67; 1996: 119–20) makes the attractive suggestion that just as the sabbath (for H) is both a sign (*'ôt*) and a covenant (Exod 31:16–17), so the bread loaves, by implication are also a sign. They also function as a *zikkārôn* 'a reminder' (see NOTE on 23:24), so that, lying continuously in God's presence, the loaves will always remind God of his covenant with Israel. Also, the verbs used in this pericope, *śîm* 'set' (v. 6), *nātan* 'place' (v. 7), and *'ārak* 'arrange' (v. 8), are precisely those describing the making of a covenant (*śîm*, 2 Sam 23:5; *nātan*, Gen 17:2; Num 25:12; *'ārak*, 2 Sam 23:5). Moreover, Akkadian *riksa rākāsu* means literally "arranging a covenant" (Weinfeld 1975: 255; 1977: 249). A final clue is that the bread loaves are twelve in number. Thus I can only concur with the opinion that the bread offering is a "pledge of the covenant between the twelve tribes and the Lord" (de Vaux 1961: 422).

According to Second Temple sources, the frankincense brought with the new loaves was burned, thereby permitting the partaking of the old loaves, which were distributed equally between the entering and the departing priestly courses; and it is recorded that "once one (priest) grabbed his portion as well as that of his fellow, wherefore they would call him 'grasper' until his dying day" (*t. Menaḥ.* 11:12–13; *b. Yurma* 39a). According to one tradition, the outgoing course blessed the incoming one: "Let him who dwells in this house cause to dwell amongst you love and fraternity, peace and comradeship" (*m. Tamid* 5:1; *b. Ber.* 12a; *y. Ber.* I, 3a).

But on which altar was the frankincense burned? The biblical text is silent. The rabbis opt for the outer altar (*t. Menaḥ.* 11:13; cf. *Jos. Ant.* 3.256); the Qumran sectaries, for the golden, inner altar (11QT 8:11–12). Qumran, I submit, has it just right. It must be kept in mind that all sancta and appurtenances in the shrine were made of or plated with pure gold (Exod 25:23–39; 30:3). The frankincense was pure (Lev 24:7), in distinction to that burned on the outer altar (6:8), and it was placed in gold bowls. Only incense was burned on the gold altar; the single stipulation was that it should not be *zārâ* 'alien' (Exod 30:9)— that is, anything but the prescribed incense (which also contained *pure* frankincense, Exod 30:34–35). Thus it stands to reason that the pure frankincense displayed in gold vessels on the gold table was also burned on the gold altar.

If this is correct, how can we account for the change? The answer can only be surmised. As mentioned earlier (see INTRODUCTION to vv. 1–4), the table with its bread loaves (and the candelabrum) was removed from the inner shrine during pilgrimage festivals and displayed to the public (*m. Ḥag.* 3:8). The reason for this concession may have been to demythologize them—that is, to remove any lingering notion that, other than the bread consumed by the priests, the table contained food for the Deity. The bread had to be displayed inside the shrine, since it was prescribed by Scripture. The Bible's silence about the disposal of the frankincense accompanying the bread, however, allowed the Temple authorities (perhaps, under the influence of proto-Pharisaic teaching) to have it burned, as any other cereal offering, on the outer altar.

In sum, the twelve loaves displayed on the table in the inner shrine probably had the same function as the two onyx stones attached to the two shoulder-pieces of the high priest's ephod and, most likely, as the twelve stones mounted in his breastpiece of decision as a "remembrance of the Israelites . . . before YHWH" (Exod 28:12; cf. v. 21). This interpretation is reinforced by the association of the loaves with the covenant (v. 8b). They are a constant reminder to YHWH of his *běrît 'ôlām*, his "eternal covenant" with his people. Finally, the two pericopes on the oil and bread (vv. 1–9) emphasize Israel's everlasting obligation to supply the requisite oil (v. 2) and bread (v. 8b) for the inner sancta (see INTRODUCTION to vv. 1–9 concerning the incense altar).

5. *You shall take . . . and bake. . . . You shall place. wĕlāqaḥtā . . . wĕ'āpîtā . . . wĕsamtā.* Moses is the active subject. He not only transmits YHWH's words, but initiates their fulfillment. According to Ezek 45:17, it was the obligation of the king (*nāśî'*) to supply the offerings on sabbaths, new moons, and festivals. In Mesopotamia, the king also furnished the god's table (Bel and Dragon, v. 14). The LXX voices these verbs in the plural, perhaps laying the responsibility for the bread supply on the priests. However, the text is explicit: Moses contributed the initial supply; thereafter, it was the responsibility of the people (v. 8b).

semolina. sōlet. Cognates are Akkadian *siltu*, Arabic *sult.* That it was wheat is proved by its contrast with barley (2 Kgs 7:16), and that it was not fine flour (the usual understanding), but the coarse part of the grain (grits), see *m. 'Abot* 5:15; *Sipra* Nedaba 10:1; *m. Menaḥ.* 12:3, and the more extensive discussion in the NOTE on 2:1.

and bake. wĕ'āpîtā. The cantillation mark has been irregularly placed on the final syllable for phonetic reasons: the following word begins with an *aleph* (GKC § 49l). This verb may take a double accusative: to bake something into something (GKC § 117ii).

twelve. The verb *'āpâ* 'bake' takes a double accusative: bake something (into) something (GKC § 117ii). The twelve loaves in the Babylonian cult had astral (zodiacal) significance (Zimmern 1901: 94–95; Philo, *Laws* 1.172). In Israel, however, it probably stood for the twelve tribes of Israel (*b. Menaḥ.* 94b; see above).

loaves. ḥallôt. In the priestly texts, see Exod 29:23; Lev 2:4; 7:12 (bis), 13; 8:26 (bis); 24:5 (bis); Num 6:15, 19; 15:20; elsewhere 2 Sam 6:19. Tradition holds that they are unleavened (*m. Menaḥ.* 5:1; *b. Menaḥ.* 57a; Jos. *Ant.* 3.142; Philo, *Laws* 2.161). This stands to reason: if leaven was forbidden on the outer altar (2:11), all the more so should it be forbidden in the shrine, the more sacred part of the sanctuary. Besides, on practical grounds, would the bread have been edible one week later if it were leavened? Perhaps. Amos rebukes the North Israelites precisely because they are offering leavened bread on the altar to God (Amos 4:5). The loaves brought to the Bethel sanctuary, however, probably were leavened since two of them were consumed by Saul (1 Sam 10:3–4), the assumption being that they were given directly to the officiating priest and/or eaten by the worshipers (cf. Lev 7:14), but none was offered on the altar.

two-tenths of an ephah shall be in each loaf. One loaf, one-tenth (0.10) of an ephah (6–8 liters of flour; Dalman 1935: 4.122), suffices for a person per day (Exod 16:16, 36). Correspondingly, YHWH's portion per day would be two-tenths divided by seven, which yields about three-hundredths (0.03) of an ephah, or 30 percent less than the required ration for a person! Nothing more is needed to prove that the bread offering was not intended as nourishment. The verb "shall be" is masculine (*yihyeh*), though its subject is feminine (*haḥallâ*), a frequent occurrence when the subject follows the verb (GKC § 145).

6. *them. 'ōtām.* The antecedent is *ḥallôt* 'loaves' despite the fact that there is no agreement in gender. The same phenomenon, however, a feminine plural noun followed by *'ōtām* (masc.), is encountered in 20:8 and 22:31.

two. štayim. If this number were shortened from *šĕnātayim** (fem. of *šnayim*), then the *dagesh* in the *taw* would be *forte*. But in that case, the word would have been vocalized as *šittayim* (GKC § 97b, n.1).

piles. ma'ărākôt. The related word *ma'ărākâ* refers to a row (Exod 39:37), an arrangement having both a vertical and a horizontal aspect (Judg 6:26) or an arrangement in ranks (1 Sam 4:2, 16). This rendering, however, is impossible in this context. The dimensions of the table surface are 2 × 1 cubits (3 × 1.5 ft. or 90 × 45 cm). The loaves, each containing 6 to 8 liters of flour, are too large to fit on this small table in two rows (Mitchel 1982: 447). Indeed, if the loaves were flat—a likely possibility since they were unleavened—they would need even more room than ordinary, leavened loaves. Thus the rendering "piles" becomes a logistic necessity.

six to a pile. šēš hamma'ăraket. This interpretation is followed by Philo (*Laws* 1.172, on the basis of LXX*) and the rabbis. The Talmud (*b. Menaḥ.* 94–95) speaks of a tiered, divided utensil into which six loaves are stacked on each side. The two piles of loaves would be arranged lengthwise on the breadth of the table. The dimensions of the table's surface was 2 cubits long and 1 cubit wide (Exod 25:23), a cubit equaling six handbreadths. As the loaves, according to the rabbis, were ten handbreadths long and the table six handbreadths wide, the loaves would have projected two handbreadths on each side (*m. Menaḥ.* 11:5). Two arrangements become possible, as sketched in figure 1.

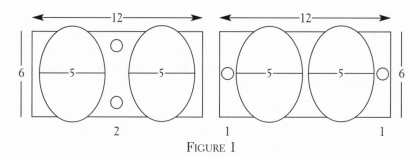

FIGURE 1

In the postexilic books, *ma'āreket* became the fixed term for the *leḥem happānîm* 'the bread of presence' (most likely to avoid the latter's anthropomorphic connotations). Thus we find *leḥem hammǎ'āreket* 'pile bread' (Neh 10:34; 1 Chr 9:32; 23:29); *šulḥan hamm'āreket* 'table of the pile (bread)' (1 Chr 28:16; 2 Chr 29:18), *ma'āreket leḥem* 'pile bread' (2 Chr 13:11); *ma'āreket tāmîd* 'pile (bread laid out) regularly' (2 Chr 2:3).

Conversely, the expression describing the display bread in the Nob sanctuary *leḥem happānîm hammûsārîm millipnê YHWH*, literally "the bread of presence removed [pl.] from the presence of YHWH" (1 Sam 21:7), indicates the possibility that before the bread offering was institutionalized by the priestly legist, there were many—more than two—loaves set before the Deity (the sing. *leḥem* is a collective). If this proves to be the case, then the limitation of the offering to two loaves a week would have been the innovation of the priestly legists.

the table of pure (gold). haššulḥān haṭṭāhōr. This is an ellipsis of *šulḥan hazzāhāb haṭṭāhōr.* That the table was plated with gold of the highest purity, see Exod 25:24 and the NOTE on "the pure [golden] lampstand," v. 4. The absence of the word "gold" and the indispensable term "presence" clearly indicates that this H passage takes for granted a knowledge of Exod 25:30 (P).

The rabbis, however, render this phrase midrashically *'al ṭohǎrô šel šulḥān* 'on top of the table' (*m. Yoma* 5:6), taking the adjective *ṭāhōr* to be equivalent to the noun *ṭōhar* and understanding the latter to be equivalent to Aramaic *ṣōhar* 'top' (*t. Yoma* 4:2; cf. Rashi on this verse). These philological gymnastics can be attributed to the reluctance of the rabbis to ascribe purity to the table, which had to be purified by immersion after each pilgrimage festival, during which the table (and the candelabrum; see above) was removed from the shrine and displayed to the masses of pilgrims—a concession that made the table susceptible to contamination by touch (see NOTE on "the pure [golden] lampstand," v. 4; cf. Knohl 1992: 605, n. 8).

before YHWH. lipnê YHWH, literally "in the presence of YHWH." Hence the table is called *šulḥan happānîm* 'the table of (the bread of) presence' (e.g., Num 4:7), and the bread is called *leḥem happānîm* 'the bread of presence' (e.g., Exod 25:30; 35:13; 39:36). The LXX also provides the literal rendering "face to face with YHWH."

7. *With each pile. 'al-hamma'āreket.* This rendering follows the view of 'Abba Sha'ul that *'al* here means "besides, alongside," offering as proof *wě'ālāyw maṭṭēh*

měnaššeh 'Next to it the tribe of Manasseh' (Num 2:20; *m. Menaḥ.* 11:5; cf. *Baraita de-Meleket Hamishkan*; see NOTES on 2:1; 23:20). His view has to be correct: the frankincense had to be in two containers, separable from the bread; the containers had to be of solid gold (see above); and gold vessels placed on top of the piles would have smashed the bread. Hence they were set on the table at the side of the piles.

But where exactly were the vessels placed? The rabbis record two opinions. The majority hold that they were set at the two ends of the table in order not to break the loaves. R. Meir, however, maintains that they were placed in between the bread piles so the bread would be cooled by the intervening air (*m. Menaḥ.* 11:5). Both solutions are represented in figure 1.

Josephus (*Ant.* 3.143, 256) holds that the frankincense containers were placed on top of the piles. So, too, Philo (*Laws* 1.175), based on the LXX *èpi* 'on'. My student R. Gane suggests that the Temple Scroll is of a similar opinion (taking *'al* to mean "on," 11QT 8:9–10). However, the scroll is quoting only this Scripture, where its meaning is ambiguous. Josephus's view remains a puzzle, unless we assume that by his time, the loaves were placed inside a tiered vessel (see NOTE on "six to a pile," v. 6), thus permitting the frankincense containers to be placed on top of the vessel and not on the loaves.

pure frankincense. lěbōnâ zakkâ. As the incense burned on the inner altar had to be pure (Exod 30:34), so the frankincense, placed on the inner table and probably burned on the inner altar (see INTRODUCTION to vv. 5–9), was required to be pure. According to the LXX, followed by Philo (*Moses* 2.104), salt was added to the frankincense, probably in accordance with Lev 2:13.

a token offering for the bread. lallehem lě'azkārâ. The token (*'azkārâ*) was always offered up with part of the *minḥâ*, the cereal offering (e.g., 2:9), but in this instance, since none of the bread is burned on the altar, the text has to state explicitly that the frankincense is offered in place of the bread. The reason for this exception is that it is prohibited to offer food to God inside the shrine—that is, in his "house" (cf. Exod 30:9; see INTRODUCTION to vv. 5–9). For more details on the *'akārâ*, see the NOTE on 2:2.

8. *Every sabbath day. běyôm haššabbāt běyôm haššabbāt.* As the Temple guards rotated each sabbath (2 Kgs 11:5) and as, later, the priestly courses rotated each sabbath (2 Chr 23:4–6), so the bread loaves were changed each sabbath (*Sipra Emor* 18:8; *m. Menaḥ.* 11:7; cf. 11QT 8:11). The old loaves were eaten, half by the incoming priests and half by the outgoing priests (*b. Suk.* 56a).

Noth (1977) suggests that one prescription concerning the bread loaves implies that at an earlier time they were changed daily. It reads *wěnātattā 'al-haššulḥān lehem pānîm lěpānay tāmîd*, literally "You shall set on the table the bread of presence in my presence always" (Exod 25:30). Abetting Noth is the description of the practice prevailing in the Nob sanctuary: *lehem happānîm hammûsārîm millipnê YHWH lāśûm lehem ḥōm běyôm hillāqěḥô* 'the bread of presence, which had been taken from the presence of YHWH to be replaced by fresh bread on the day (the old) was removed' (1 Sam 21:7). This verse also seems to imply that there was always freshly baked bread on display before

YHWH. If my theory concerning the provenance of P is correct, namely, that its core is traceable to the regional sanctuary of Shilo, then both verses just cited reflect the pre-Jerusalemite practice of changing the bread loaves frequently.

It should not be forgotten that outside Israel, the bread, indeed, was probably changed daily. For example, in the Hittite temple of Nerik, "*daily* bread . . . when the priests and the seer come before the god they will remove the (old) bread . . . and will arrange the (new) bread [my emphasis]" (Haas 1970: 131–33). In Babylonia, the bread was changed even four times daily (*ANET* 343; cf. Weinfeld 1990b: 109). Thus the unique change from daily bread for the deity, attested in the ancient Near East and, possibly, early Israel (Shilo [P] and Nob), to weekly bread in the Jerusalem Temple (H) may be attributed to the trend of the Jerusalemite priesthood to eviscerate Israelite ritual from anthropomorphic concepts of the Deity (see also INTRODUCTION to vv. 5–9).

it shall be set up. ya ʿărkennû. The subject and object of this verb are not identified. The masculine object could be either *leḥem* 'the bread' (v. 7bα) or, more likely, the immediately preceding *ʾiššeh* 'a food gift' (v. 7bβ), composed of the bread and the frankincense, since both are permanent commitments of the Israelites (v. 8b). The subject could be either the high priest (LXX), who alone may officiate in the shrine, or, more likely, by taking the verb as a passive, any priest, since the task here is to arrange the bread loaves, not to officiate (i.e., burn the incense). Then, the setting up (*ʿārak*) of the loaves would parallel the setting up of the lamp(s), which also may be performed by any priest (Exod 27:21; see NOTE on "Aaron," v. 3).

In the Second Temple, the Kohathite Levites are given the responsibility of preparing the sacred bread loaves "every sabbath" (1 Chr 9:32). These duties fall in line with the other sancta that are attributed to the Kohathites as their portage responsibility in the wilderness (Num 4:1–16). Gerstenberger (1996: 358) rationalizes the ostensible violation of the sabbath by suggesting that the bread preparation was "not occupational work." On the sabbath, however, *kol-mĕlaʾkâ* 'all work' (23:3) is prohibited. Furthermore, the anointed, assistant high priest prepares the daily cereal offering even on the sabbath (6:15)! These purported aberrations are resolved once it is realized that a Temple offering was also required each sabbath, which included the daily Tamid, the content of which was doubled on the sabbath (Num 28:3–10). In other words, the sabbath prohibitions were suspended within YHWH's sphere (for another explanation, see Knohl 1995: 18–19). An analogy is provided by *šaʿaṭnēz*, mixtures of linen and wool, which are forbidden to Israelites (19:19; Deut 22:11), but are worn by priests in the sanctuary (Exod 28:6, 37, 39; 39:29) and woven into the inner curtains of the sanctuary (Exod 26:1). God's realm is governed by laws different from those of man's realm (see Introduction II P).

regularly. tāmîd. This adverb modifies the verb *ʿārak* 'set up', an action that occurs each sabbath. The rabbis, however, understood it as "always," implying that the table may not be bare of bread even for an instant. Hence they pre-scribe (perhaps, describe) the following dramatic choreography:

> Four priests entered, two bearing the two piles (of loaves) in their hands and two bearing the two bowls (of frankincense) in their hands; and four went in before them, two to take away the two piles (of loaves) and two to take away the two bowls (of frankincense). Those who brought them in stood at the north side with their faces to the south, and those who took them away stood at the south side with their faces to the north (separated only by the breadth of the table, since the table stood lengthwise from east to west). These (the latter priests) withdrew (the old bread) and the other (the former priests) laid down (the new bread), the handbreadth of the one being by the side of the handbreadth of the other (so that the removal of the old and the placing of the new was simultaneous). (*m. Menah.* 11:7)

of the Israelites. mē'ēt běnê-yiśrā'ēl. During Second Temple times, the Is-raelites provided the cost of the bread (*m. Šek.* 4:1). Nonetheless, we read *ûmin-běnê haqěhātî min-'ăhêhem 'al-lehem hamma'ărāket lěhākîn šabbat šabbāt* 'Some of their Kohathite kinspeople were in charge of the pile bread every sabbath' (1 Chr 9:32). This verse, however, speaks of only the preparation of the bread; the people were responsible for bringing (or paying for) the grain. (The Ko-hathite role was probably defined by Num 4:7b, which states that the Kohathites carried the sancta during the wilderness trek, including the table with the bread still on it; R. Gane.) Thus both the oil and the bread (vv. 1–9) are added to the festival offerings of chap. 23 to indicate that all public offerings are the respon-sibility of the Israelite people.

The LXX reads *enōpion* 'in the presence of' the Israelites. The rabbis allude to this rendering: "There were two tables inside the porch at the entrance of the Temple, the one of marble and the other of gold. On the marble table they laid the bread of presence when it was brought in, and on the gold table they laid the bread of presence when it was brought out, since what is holy we must el-evate (in honor) and not bring down" (*m. Menah.* 11:7). Thus before the in-coming bread was brought into the Temple and before the outgoing bread was distributed to the priests, it was displayed on two tables located at the entrance, in view of the people assembled in the court (Pelletier 1967).

a covenant for all time. běrît 'ôlām. This term is attested in the priestly texts (Gen 9:16; 17:7, 13, 19; Exod 31:16; Num 25:13). The most significant verse is Exod 31:16, which deals with the sabbath and is also the product of H (see NOTE on v. 26:45a). Wessely (1846) is probably correct in suggesting that it is this phrase *běrît 'ôlām*, held in common, that is responsible for the change of bread taking place on the sabbath. Moreover, Israel's everlasting obligation to supply the grain for the bread becomes a ritual demonstration that it eternally pledges itself anew to uphold the covenant (see INTRODUCTION to vv. 5–9).

9. *It shall. wěhāyětâ.* What is the antecedent feminine subject? Five answers have been proposed: (1) the unstated subject, *minhâ,* "since every offering of

grain is a *minḥā"* (Rashi); (2) *ma ʿăreket* (v. 7a), each of the piles (Ramban); (3) *haḥallā* (v. 5b), each of the loaves (*Seper Hamibḥar*; Noth 1977); (4) *běrît* (v. 8b), the implications of the covenant; and (5) *wěhāyětā* (v. 7b), a stylistic imitation. Perhaps, the answer is—all the above.

belong to Aaron and his descendants. Of the bread, nothing is burned on the altar, lest it be taken as food for the Deity (see INTRODUCTION to vv. 5–9). This transfer from Deity to priest (and, in emergency situations, to ritually pure lay persons) took place early in Israel, to judge by 1 Sam 21:6.

and they shall eat it. wa'ăkālūhû. The Sam. reads *W'KLWH* (fem.) to harmonize with the feminine form of the verb, *wěhāyětā*. Here, however, the antecedent is clearly the bread (*lallehem*, v. 7; Rashi; note the masc. suffix *yaʿărkennû*, v. 8).

in a holy place. bĕmāqôm qādōš, namely, as glossed the first time this expression occurs, *baḥăṣar 'ōhel-mô ʿēd* 'in the court of the Tent of Meeting' (see NOTE on 6:9). The Hittite "Instructions" also specify that the priestly prebends must be consumed within the sacred precincts (*ANET* 208).

most sacred portion. qōdeš qŏdāšîm. All the offerings eaten solely by the priests fall into the category of most sacred, including the *minḥâ* (2:3), the *ḥaṭṭā't* (6:22), the *'āšām* (7:1)—all the more so the bread of presence, which not only is a *minḥâ*, but, uniquely, is offered inside the shrine.

food gifts of YHWH. This is the seventh occurrence of the Tetragrammaton in vv. 1–9, possibly a hint that the following pericope will deal with an attempt to impair (i.e., blaspheme) the perfection (prefigured by the number seven) of the divine name (M. Hildenbrand).

a due for all time. hoq-ʿôlām. H preserves the P distinction between *ḥoq* 'due' and *ḥuqqâ* 'law' (v. 3b; see NOTE on 10:13).

Vv. 10–16, 23. The Case of the Blasphemer

This pericope subdivides into four parts: the crime (vv. 10–11), the confinement (v. 12), the oracular decisions (vv. 13–22), and the compliance (v. 23). It exhibits the same literary pattern as that of three other cases: the second *pesaḥ* (Num 9:1–14), the wood-gatherer (Num 15:32–36), and the ability of women to inherit (Num 27:1–11; Fishbane 1985: 102). In this passage, however, the third element—"oracular decisions"—appears to have been expanded more than in the other three. This pericope can be outlined as follows:

   I. The case of the blasphemer (vv. 10–11)
  II. Confinement awaiting an oracle (v. 12)
 III. The oracular decisions (vv. 13–22)
      A. Introductory formula (v. 13)
      B. The blasphemer's sentence (v. 14)
      C. The promulgation of seven laws (vv. 15–22)
         1. Commission to Moses formula (v. 15a)
         2. The laws (vv. 15b–21)

     a. Regarding cursing God (vv. 15b–16)   LAW
       (1) Cursing God(s) (v. 15b)   1
       (2) While pronouncing his name (v. 16a)   2
       (3) Applies to alien and citizen alike (v. 16bα)
       (4) While pronouncing his name (v. 16bβ)
     b. Regarding killing and personal injury (vv. 17–21)
       (1) Killing a human (v. 17)   3
       (2) Killing a beast (v. 18)   4
       (3) Injury to a human (vv. 19–20)   5
         (a) Case (v. 19a)
         (b) Regulation: *lex talionis* (vv. 19b–20)
       (4) Killing a beast (v. 21a)   6
       (5) Killing a human (v. 21b)   7
   3. Applies to alien and citizen alike (v. 22a)
   4. As commanded by YHWH (v. 22b)
IV. The compliance report (v. 23)
   A. Moses delivers YHWH's message (v. 23aα)
   B. The Israelites comply (v. 23aβ,b)

This pericope is one of only two narratives in the book of Leviticus. According to Hartley (1992: 406), the first, the story of Nadab and Abihu (10:1–11), bears a similar structure, a narrative (10:1–7) followed by a law (10:8–11). However, it can be shown that 10:8–11 is a heterogeneous insert by a later hand that has no ideological connection with the narrative (vol. 1.611–17). But, this pericope is of a piece with the major priestly blocs containing law and narrative, which utilize narrative to provide a specific case for the promulgation of a general law (see Introduction I G).

Law is inextricably bound to narrative—that is, the set of circumstances that engender it. Thus, as will be demonstrated, all seven laws that emanate from this single case of blasphemy (vv. 15–22), even though they are general in form, can never be dissociated from the narrative framework in which they are embedded (vv. 10–14, 23). Even the generalization "You shall have one law for the alien and citizen alike" (v. 22a), which is frequently repeated in the H corpus (19:34; 24:22; Exod 12:49; Num 15:15–16; cf. Exod 12:19, 48; Lev 16:29; 18:26; 17:15; Num 9:14; 15:29–30; cf. Josh 8:33; Ezek 47:22), always applies to the case under discussion (see chap. 17, COMMENT B).

A distinction must be made between law and narrative that deal with the same event (e.g., 24:10–23) and law and narrative that are discrete but related (e.g., Lev 1:1 and 1:2–7:38; chaps. 8–10; 16:1 and chaps. 11–15). In the last case, as held by the consensus, the legal sections were inserted into the narrative.

1. The view of the consensus is nowhere better upheld than in the text of P based on lexical and cultic evidence: Chaps. 8 and 9 prescribe a different sacrificial procedure for the *ḥaṭṭāʾt* (vol. 1.580–81).
2. The vocabulary and procedure of the ritual to purge entirely the sanctu-

ary (chap. 16) indicates that their uniqueness represents an earlier stratum of P (see NOTE on 16:9, and COMMENT A).

This indissoluble connection between law and narrative is eloquently described by the legal theorist Robert Cover (1983: 4–5): "Every prescription is insistent in its demand to be located in discourse—to be supplied with history and destiny, beginning and end, explanation and purpose. And every narrative is insistent in its demand for its prescriptive point, its moral. History and literature cannot escape this location in a normative universe, nor can prescription, even when embodied in a legal text, escape its origin and its end in experience, in the narratives that are the trajectories plotted upon material reality by our imagination." As pointed out by Tucker (1993: 4), Cover was long anticipated by the equally eloquent Hebrew poet Bialik (1947: 207): "The halakha and *'ăgādâ* (equivalent to law and narrative, respectively) are but two that are one, two faces of a single creature. The relationship between them is like the relationship between the act and concrete form and between the word. . . . The dream hastens to be drawn to solution, the desire to the deed, the thought to the word, the flower to the fruit . . . the *'ăgādâ* to the halakha. However, within the fruit the seed is already ensconced from which a new flower is destined to emerge."

Cover exemplifies his axiom by pointing to the comment of Joseph Caro, the sixteenth-century codifier, on the difference between two similarly structured rabbinic aphorisms recorded in the same context: "Simon the Just [ca. 200 B.C.E.] said, Upon three things the world stands: upon Torah, upon the temple service, and upon deeds of kindness" (*m. 'Abot* 1:2); "Rabbi Simeon b. Gamaliel [ca. C.E. 100] said: Upon three things the world continues to exist: upon justice, upon truth, and upon peace" (*m. 'Abot* 1:18). Caro writes:

> "Simeon the Just spoke in the context of his generation in which the Temple stood, and R. Simeon b. Gamaliel spoke in the context of his generation after the destruction of Jerusalem. . . . For there is a difference between the (force needed for the) preservation of that which already exists and the (force needed for the) initial realization of that which had not earlier existed at all. . . . And so, in this instance, it would have been impossible to have created the world on the basis of R. Simeon b. Gamaliel. But after the world had been created on the three things of Simeon the Just it can continue to exist on the basis of R. Simeon b. Gamaliel's three" (Bet Yosef at Tur: *Ḥoshen Mishpat*, 1 [trans. Cover 1983]).

Caro teaches us two things concerning jurisgenesis: law arises synchronically from its *Sitz im Leben* (its narrative) against the backdrop of the reality—socioeconomic, political, and religious—of its time. Law also develops diachronically, building on past precedents that form new realia for succeeding ages. The law is incomprehensible without its framing narrative, which illustrates both the application and the limit of the law. Thus not only casuistic (case) law of which Scripture abounds describes the parameters of a law's application, but even apodictic law, despite its imperative nature, can be traceable to particular circumstances from which it arose. Fortunately, both legal forms attested in Lev 24 are attached to narratives that assist in defining their parameters.

Watts (1995a) has demonstrated the bond between narrative and law ("lists" in his terminology) exemplifying the rhetorical strategy of the pentateuchal writers and editors. He points to the prologues to the law codes, itemizing God's beneficence to Israel, and to their appendices, depicting the sanctions in the wake of nonfulfillment; he also mentions the "intrusion" into the laws of the stories describing the breakdown in compliance by the people (Exod 32–34) and priests (Lev 10:1–3). Presumably, because of space limitations, his article would have added the striking alternation between law and narrative in the book of Numbers (Milgrom 1990a: XV–XVI; Douglas 1993b: 102–4). He also omits the one story in the Holiness Source—in Lev 24. His rhetorical analysis, nonetheless, applies equally well in offering another explanation of why the story of the blasphemer was affixed to the laws of talion: the story informs us that the punishment for blasphemy is inexorable and precise, just as codified in the talion formulas (see INTRODUCTION to vv. 17–22).

Cover (1983) and Watts (1995a) differ fundamentally, however, in their assumptions, which should not be overlooked. Cover holds that narrative *generates* law, whereas Watts maintains that narrative *justifies* law. The logical deduction from these differing assumptions is that Cover would argue the antiquity of the narrative, whereas Watts would champion the antiquity of the law. Nonetheless, both would strongly defend the indissolubility of the tandem.

Cover and Watt's telling arguments concerning the bond between law and narrative do not, however, apply to Carmichael's frequent attempts to associate pentateuchal law with the patriarchal narratives. For example, in his most recent publications, Carmichael (1994; 1995) attributes the choice and wording of the diverse laws of Lev 19 to episodes in the lives of Jacob and Joseph, especially the latter. However, that Lev 19 censures Joseph's interpretation of his dream that his parents will bow to him (19:3), that *'ĕlîlîm* (v. 4) plays on *'ălummîm* (Gen 37:7), or that Joseph's "exile" to Egypt lurks behind 19:8 (a mistaken rendering of *wĕnikrĕtâ*, vol. 1.457–61) does not demonstrate that laws are "embodied in a narrative history" (Carmichael 1994: 245–56). Carmichael, in effect, has created modern midrash, which, like its rabbinic predecessors, also finds allusions to the lives of its patriarchal protagonists in subsequent biblical literature, including the law. If Carmichael were right, the relationship between the Genesis narratives and the laws of Lev 19 would not necessitate the tortuous word plays and obscure allusions he attributes to the legist. As in the case before us in chap. 24, the law would follow logically and unambiguously from the narrative. The working of the law would not be fraught with so many possible allusions as to render its alleged narrative background mercurially elusive.

As indicated in the outline, seven laws emerge out of this single case of blasphemy. Rather, there are seven statements of laws, since several of them are repeated (e.g., cf. laws 6 and 7 with laws 3 and 4). In COMMENT A, it will be shown that the entire pericope is structured as a giant introversion, thus proving that the law section (vv. 15–22) is inextricable from the surrounding narrative (vv. 10–14, 23).

It is therefore difficult to accept Knohl's verdict on this pericope (1995: 121, n. 38) and on Num 9:1–14 (1995: 90) that the narratives (vv. 10–14; Num 9:1–8) were composed at a later stage than the legal units (vv. 15–22; Num 9:9–14; see Gerstenberger 1996: 364). In fact, the chronological relationship should be reversed. The law cites two criteria for postponing the *pesaḥ* offering: distance and impurity. The narrative, however, speaks of only impurity. Thus the formulation of the law must have been subsequent to that of the narrative. Focusing on the narrative, however, generates a deeper question. If a Mosaic precedent were needed for justifying the law, why the story of Moses' indecision? Indeed, why a story altogether? Why did the law not begin with the usual introduction "YHWH spoke to Moses"?

Exactly the same questions arise out of our text. If the narrative were subsequent to the law, why does it not provide some background for the otherwise irrelevant laws of talion (vv. 17–22)? The answer cannot be that the talion laws were a later insertion into the law unit, since it is clear, as demonstrated in COMMENT A, that the H author inherited the entire pericope—narrative, law, and talion—which he reworked into a masterful construction. Furthermore, if the law had to be the product of divine revelation, why the need for an oracle? Why was it not handed down as the direct command of God to Moses?

Thus one cannot escape the conclusion that there was an ancient narrative tradition of Moses' indecision concerning this and three other points of law (Num 9:1–14; 15:32–36; 27:1–11). It can hardly be a coincidence that all four cases are said to have arisen in the wilderness. Although the historicity of the Mosaic attribution can justifiably be suspected, there can be no doubt that the cases themselves must have arisen early in Israel's history. This certainly must be true, considering the questions involved: cursing God (cf. Exod 22:27), impure persons at the *pesaḥ*, inheritance rights of daughters in the absence of sons, and perhaps the sabbath violator (cf. Exod 16:29b).

But here we are dealing not with the antiquity of a law, which demonstrably is old, but with the antiquity of its narrative. Thus I must conclude that the law and the narrative share a simultaneous origin. They were inextricably woven into each other not just in the present introverted structure of the text, but also from the beginning.

Besides 24:10–23, the only other narrative in Leviticus is 10:1–7. There can be no doubt that the latter illustrates the efficacy of teaching law by means of a story (vol. 1.638–33, cf. David Wright's comments). By the same token, this pedagogic function is duplicated in 24:10–23 (see below). On this point we witness a convergence of views from the perspectives of a jurist (Cover 1983), biblicist (Watts 1995a), and structural anthropologist (Douglas 1993a; see also below, and Introduction I G).

Douglas (1993a: 18–20) argues—cogently, in my opinion—that the term *mûm* '(physical) blemish', central to both the qualification of priests/sacrifices (chaps. 21–22) and the talion laws (vv. 19–20), also suggests the figurative notion of injustice done to another "taking away something that is his by right, leaving him with too little. Or, by oppression, giving him a heavy load to bear" (20), thereby connecting chaps. 20, 21, 22, dealing with physical blemishes, with the "moral" blemishes detailed in chap. 19, arguably the very center of the book of Leviticus (see COMMENT A). She also argues—again persuasively—that structurally, chap. 24 is, in Leviticus, the counterpart to chap. 10: the Name defiled balancing the Holy Place defiled (see her ring diagram in Douglas 1993a: 11, and in Introduction I L). The placement of chap. 24 is a conundrum that even uncharacteristically baffled Ibn Ezra. Douglas, I submit, is on the right track. Her solution, however, is more promising than she has realized. First, it is no accident that her parallels are not chapters but only some verses, those that compose a narrative (10:1–7; 24:10–23)—the only two narratives in Leviticus. Thus it may be surmised that the redactor, in creating the giant introversion (or ring) of Leviticus around the fulcrum of chap. 19, balanced the two stories of defilement—of YHWH's sanctuary and his name—in his structure of Leviticus. Moreover, these two stories artfully supplement (and expand) the basic postulate undergirding P's pericope on the reparation offering: whereas *inadvertent* or *unwitting* desecration of YHWH's sancta (5:14–16, 17–19) or YHWH's name (5:20–26) may be expiated by sacrifice (vol. 1.319–78), *advertent, brazen* desecration of YHWH's sancta (10:1–4) or YHWH's name (24:10–16) is punishable by death. Thus the H redactor realized that P's law of desecration was incomplete, since it dealt with inadvertent and unwitting desecration of YHWH's sanctuary and name and contained *a story* about the deliberate desecration of his sanctuary, but said nothing about the deliberate desecration of his name. Thereupon, the redactor added *his story* of the deliberate desecration of the divine name and placed it within Leviticus to balance structurally the corresponding story of the deliberate desecration of the sanctuary (see Introduction I L). In so doing, however, he fulfilled another objective—to indicate that injury to a person is a *mûm* 'blemish'; it is unacceptable to YHWH, as though it were borne by his sacrifices and priests (chaps. 21–22), and it is equivalent to and symbolic of depriving a person of his dignity (chap. 19) and property (chap. 25).

Jackson (1996: 120–21) has astutely recognized that the thematic parallels with the Covenant Code are numerous and significant: the regulation of cursing (Exod 22:27), concern for the legal position of aliens (Exod 22:20; 23:9), homicide (21:12–14), fatal and nonfatal injuries arising from a quarrel (Exod 21:18–19, 22–25), fatal injuries to animals (Exod 21:33–36; neither the Covenant Code nor Lev 24 deals with nonfatal injuries to animals), and the talionic formula, the center of the introversion (Lev 24:20a; see COMMENT A), which "is the closest *verbal* parallel to the Covenant Code. In short, the Levitical passage gains immensely in coherence if viewed as a literary reworking of themes from the Covenant Code."

There are many other conclusions that can be derived from the structure of this pericope. These will be detailed in the NOTES and in COMMENT A.

10. *There came out among. wayyēṣēʾ . . . bĕtôk.* The term *wayyēṣēʾ* 'There came out', implies the object "from his tent," as expressly stated in *wĕdātān waʾăbîrām yāṣĕʾû niṣṣābîm petaḥ ʾohălêhem* literally "And Dathan and Abiram

had gone out (of their tents), standing at the entrance of their tents" (Num 16:27; Ibn Ezra). Keil and Delitzsch (1874) suggest that this phrase implies that the blasphemer came from a place other than the Israelite camp. A possible support is that the priestly account of the Israelite camp was aligned according to the patrilinear system, *'îš lĕmišpĕḥōtāyw 'al-bēt 'ăbōtāyw* 'each with his clan according to his *father's* house' (Num 2:34). The blasphemer, son of an Egyptian father, would therefore have to take residence with the *'ēreb rab* 'mixed multitude' (also termed *hā'sapsup* 'the riffraff', Num 11:4) who would have been excluded from the camp.

Alternatively and preferably, the addition of the preposition *bĕtôk* 'among' renders the entire expression equivalent to "make a public appearance" (cf. Exod 11:4; Jer 37:4; Ezek 3:25; Est 4:1). Thus there is no need to postulate that the half-Israelite was excluded from the camp of Israel. To the contrary, he probably would be attached permanently to his mother's clan. Indeed, Cohen (1985: 7) plausibly suggests that "the offspring of Israelite women and foreign men were judged matrilineally only if the marriage was matrilocal, that is, only if the foreign husband joined the wife's domicile or clan." By this criterion, the children of the half-Israelite would become members of the clan (for cogent examples, see 1 Chr 2:17, 34–35). But one qualification needs be added: The children would not be considered full-fledged Israelites (see chap. 17, COMMENT B).

whose mother was Israelite. ben-'iššâ yiśrĕ'ēlît. Even though the rabbis rule that the offspring of an Israelite mother is an Israelite (*b. Yeb.* 45a), he could not be counted among those who would inherit the land, since that right descends patrilinearly: "The Israelites shall camp each with his unit, under the banners of their *father's* [lit.] house" (Num 2:2; *Sipra* Emor, par. 14:1), and, especially, "and the allotment shall be made according to the listings of their *fathers'* tribes" (Num 26:55; Ramban). The fact that the blasphemer's father is not mentioned in v. 11 means that the father remained in Egypt (Ginsburg) or that he had joined the *'ēreb rab* 'mixed multitude' (Exod 12:38)—ignominiously called *hā'sapsup* 'the riffraff' (Num 11:4; Bertholet 1901)—or "that one who has the audacity to curse the name of God is not worthy of having his own name articulated in the Torah" (Honigwachs 1991: 136).

whose (father). wĕhû' (ben 'îš), literally "and he (was the son of)." The pronoun is added lest the impression be given that two discrete persons are involved.

And a fight broke out. wayyinnāṣû. The verb *nāṣâ* 'struggle, fight with' (BDB 663) occurs in *Nip'al* (Exod 2:13; 21:22; Deut 25:11; 2 Sam 14:6) and *Hip'il* (Num 26:9 [twice]; Ps 60:2), instances that connote fierce physical fighting.

a certain Israelite. wĕ'îš hayyiśrĕ'ēlî. That is, a known Israelite. The definite article may have been influenced by previous *hayyiśrĕ'ēlît* 'Israelite woman'. A similar construction, a definite article after indefinite *'îš,* is attested in *lĕ'îš he'āšîr* 'to the rich man' (2 Sam 12:4; GKC § 126r,w). The Sam. simply reads *yiśrĕ'ēlî.* The form *hayyiśrĕ'ēlî* occurs only once more (2 Sam 17:25; cf. Joüon 1923: § 88 Mg).

11. *pronounced. wayyiqqōb.* The verb *nāqab* is often found construed with *šēm* (Isa 62:2, *Qal*) or with *bĕšēmôt* (Num 1:17; Ezra 8:20; 1 Chr 12:32; 16:41;

2 Chr 28:15; 31:19, *Nip'al*), where it means "pronounce, designate" (LXX; *Tg. Onq.*; *m. Sanh.* 7:5; Rashbam; Weingreen 1972; Gabel and Wheeler 1980: 229; Livingston 1986). It does not denote "treat derogatorily" (Scharbert 1986), as indicated by its favorable meaning in Num 1:17; Isa 62:2, etc. A similar usage is attested in Nabatean *nqwbyn bšmhn* (Rabinowitz 1957). If, indeed, the writer had intended to say that God's name was treated negatively, he would have added a qualifier such as *laššāw'* 'in vain, falsely' (Exod 20:7; Deut 5:11). Westbrook (1992: 549) renders *nāqab* as "slander," for which, however, there is neither scriptural nor etymological support.

Some scholars hold that the root is *qbb*, *Nip'al* (e.g., Schottroff 1969: 28), an example of Aramaic imperfect doubling (GKC § 67g), which bears the meaning "curse" (e.g., Num 23:8; Prov 11:26; 24:24; Job 3:8). However, this root never occurs with the object *šēm* 'name', and moreover it cannot be construed with the participle *nōqēb* (v. 16). *Tg. Ps.-J.* translates this verb as *pěrēš wěḥārîp*, noncommittingly employing both possibilities.

the Name. haššēm. The name YHWH (cf. v. 16aα); *haššēm* is also a circumlocution for YHWH, which occurs in *lěyir'â 'et-haššēm* 'to revere the name' (Deut 28:58; cf. Deut 6:24; 10:12; 14:23), frequently attested in Rabbinic Hebrew (e.g., *m. Yoma* 3:8). Another circumlocution is *'ōyěbê YHWH* 'the enemies of YHWH' (2 Sam 12:14; Ibn Ezra, Dillmann and Ryssel 1897; Driver and White 1894–98). Baentsch (1903) suggests that the reason for its use here was to avoid the juxtaposition of YHWH and the following word *wayyěqallēl*, thereby associating it with cursing.

The suggestion has been made that *haššēm* here should be rendered "the Lofty One," derived from Arabic *šamā' / šamawa*, meaning "lofty, elevated." Thus the theophoric names *šěmû'ēl* means "lofty is El" and *šem'ēber* (Gen 14:2) would be rendered "the Mighty One is lofty" (Rin-Rin 1967). Perhaps, the Eblaite names *ṭù-bí-da-mu* 'my god is Damu' and *ṭù-bí-šum* imply that "Šum is the divine element in the names *ṭù-bí-šum* and *iš-mà-šum*" (Pettinato 1981: 283). However, if *šum / šem* is a proper name, why would it take the definite article?

cursing (it). wayyěqallēl, literally "and he cursed." The absolute use of the *Pi'el* of *qll* (with no object) is attested in the Bible only in a participial form (24:14, 23; 2 Sam 16:5, 7, 10, 11, 13; Isa 8:21; Pss 62:5; 109: 28). Why the hanging verb? Again, reasons of piety prevail: the object YHWH is understood. Contrast the law (vv. 15b–16), which is more explicit than the narrative: the name YHWH is indeed pronounced (v. 16aα), but a euphemism is still employed for the object of *qillēl* 'curse'— *'ělōhāyw* (v. 15b; cf. Exod 22:27a).

Some commentators claim that two discrete acts are implied: *hizkîr 'et haššēm wě'aḥar kak bērăkô* 'He pronounced the Name and afterwards cursed it' (Rashbam; cf. Rashi; Ibn Janaḥ, *Hariqmah* 1.287); that is, "he uttered a curse in the name of God" (Snaith 1967). Thus pronouncing the divine name in a curse would be required for blasphemy to be treated as a punishable crime: *hamměgaddēp 'ênô ḥayyāb 'ad šeyyěpārēš 'et haššēm* 'The blasphemer is not liable (in a human court) until he pronounces the name' (*m. Sanh.* 7:5). Strikingly, Mesopotamian law requires a similar condition: *zakāru šum (ili / šarri) ana masikte* 'invoke the name of (a god / king) blasphemously' (for examples from the MA harem edicts, see *AfO* 17 279:57; 280:61; 287:103, cited in *ṣaltu*, *CAD* 86–87, and *zakāru* A, 18).

The crime, however, is not clear: Did the blasphemer use the divine name in cursing his opponent or in cursing God? In the Akkadian expression, cited above, it would seem that the former is the case. For example, *ina ṣaltišina šu[m i]li ana masikte tazakrūni* '(when the wives of the king and other women fight among themselves) and one (of them) utters the name of the god in a curse during their quarreling' (*AfO* 17 297:58). However, in biblical (and later rabbinic) jurisprudence, it would seem that God himself is being cursed (cf. Exod 22:27a; 1 Kgs 21:10), termed by the rabbis "he 'blesses' the Name by the Name" (*b. Sanh.* 56a; cf. *m. Sanh.* 7:5), whereas cursing an enemy in YHWH's name is normative (e.g., Josh 6:26a; 2 Sam 16:8; 2 Kgs 2:24). Thus the only reason the blasphemer was condemned was that he cursed God.

Why was cursing God such a heinous offense? D. N. Freedman (personal communication), I believe, is on the right track: "How is it possible, first of all, to bless God when he himself is the source of all blessing? . . . Perhaps it is a hangover from primitive views that indeed human beings could confer blessings on God, just as he could confer them on human beings. [It betokens] a certain reciprocity, corresponding to the sacrificial system, which somewhere in its roots had the idea of providing the God with nourishment." Conversely, a curse was believed to be so powerful that it was conceived to be efficacious against a deity. How does one curse God? Presumably, the name of God would be used, and one would say something like "may God be damned."

Another problem is the precise meaning of *qillel* 'curse', which also denotes "revile, dishonor" (cf. Akk. *qullulu* 'discredit', *CAD* 13.57–58), a meaning attested in H in the case of parents (20:9) and the deaf (19:14; see their NOTES). Another unambiguous example is *mĕqallĕlîm lāhem* (1, [']*lhm* [Tiq. Soph., LXX] *wĕlō' kihâ bām* "they [Eli's sons] dishonored God [by taking their share of the sacrifice before God, 1 Sam 2:29 LXX], but he [Eli] did not rebuke them" [1 Sam 3:13; Ehrlich 1910; Brichto 1963]). This meaning is also verified by its antonym *kibbed* 'honor' (e.g., 1 Sam 2:30; Isa 8:23; cf. Akk. *kubbutu*, *CAD* 8.17–18).

What is the difference between cursing and reviling? Presumably, the former, but not the latter, would employ the name of God. Nonetheless, the meaning of "curse" for *qillēl* is well attested (e.g., Balaam, Num 22:6, 12; 23:7; 24:9 ['*rr*]; Deut 23:5; Jos 24:9 [*qll*]; Shimei; 2 Sam 16:5–8; 19:22; 1 Kgs 2:8; God/earth, Gen 8:21; cf. Gen 12:3; Pss 62:5; 109:28 [‖ *brk*]; Elisha/children, note *wayyĕqallĕlēm bĕšēm YHWH* 'he cursed them in the name of YHWH', 2 Kgs 2:24). This meaning is corroborated by its antonym *bērēk* 'bless' (e.g., Gen 27:12; Deut 11:26–28; 23:6; 30:1, 19). However, the equivalent law *'ĕlōhîm lō' tĕqallēl wĕnāśî' bĕ'ammĕkā lō' tā'ōr* 'You shall not curse God, nor curse a chieftain of your people' (Exod 22:27, where *qll* is paralleled by '*rr* 'curse') tips the balance in favor of the view that cursing God, not reviling him, is the case under discussion.

of the tribe of Dan. It may not be an accident that Dan subsequently developed a reputation for intermarriage and illicit worship. Note Samson the Danite's easy relationships and intermarriages with Philistines (Judg 14:1–20; 16:1–4) and the Danite craftsman Hiram (Huram-abi), whose father was a Tyrian (2 Chr 2:12–13; but contrast 1 Kgs 7:13–14). Moreover, Dan would have been considered by the authorities of the Jerusalem Temple as an apostate tribe because it set up a graven image (Judg 18:30). Perhaps since Dan's priesthood claimed descent from Moses (Judg 18:30), a tradition developed, reflected in the story of the blasphemer, that Moses himself condemned the Danites. In any event, the mention of Dan was clearly intended as a slur against the tribe. As recognized by the rabbis, the names given in the text are signs of opprobrium: "a disgrace for him (the blasphemer), a disgrace for his mother, a disgrace for his family, and a disgrace for his tribe" (*Sipra* Emor, par. 14:4).

Douglas (1999: 207) argues, however, that the three proper names in this verse, by their meaning, direct the reader's attention to the case and the punishment. As a story told to children it would read like this: "Once there was a man (with no name), son of Compensation (preferably "Requital," cf. Deut 7:10; JM), grandson of Law-suit, from the house of Judgment and he cursed the Name . . . and the Lord said 'He shall die, he reviled my name, he shall be reviled to death'." There are no further details about the blasphemer. The midrash fills in the gaps:

> A wicked man (also) rebels against God in heaven. (Thus) there departed from Egypt the son of an Egyptian, who had killed an Israelite in Egypt and impregnated his wife. She bore a son, who wanted to set up his tent in the tribe of Dan when the Israelites encamped in the wilderness. They (the Danites) did not permit him because the Israelite units encamped by their banners according to their fathers' clans (Num 2:2). They quarreled in camp. Then the son of the Israelite woman and a (certain) son of an Israelite man from the tribe of Dan brought (their dispute) to court. When the former emerged guilty from the court, he pronounced and cursed the Name. (*Tg. Ps.-J.*; cf. *Sipra* Emor, par. 14:1; *Tanḥ* Exod. 9, Emor 24)

12. *in custody. bammišmār.* The definite article implies a specific place (Ibn Ezra). The verb *hinnîaḥ bĕ* is also used in the case of the wood-gatherer (Num 15:34 [H]), an indication that it is a priestly term (contrast *nātan bĕ*, Gen 40:3, and *'āsap 'el*, Gen 42:17 [both JE]). Prisons were seldom used for punishment of crimes in the ancient Near East. They existed for debtors and slaves, on the estates of kings and landowners. They were at most nonexistent in small countries and tribal groups. Here (and in Num 15:34) the word connotes a temporary holding place until God would render judgment on the transgressor (Levine 1989).

the decision of YHWH. 'al-pî YHWH, literally "by the mouth of YHWH" (Exod 17:1; Num 3:16, 39, 51; 4:37, 41, 45, 49; 9:18, 20, 23 [twice]; 10:13; 13:3; 33:2, 38; 36:5; Deut 34:5; Josh 19:50; 22:9; 2 Kgs 24:3).

should be made clear. liprōš. The verb *pāraš* (*Qal* here) also occurs in the *Pu'al* with this meaning (Num 15:34; Neh 8:8), though in the latter verse it probably has the more specific connotation "paragraph by paragraph" (i.e., verbatim; Driver 1931a: 251–53; Falk 1969: 42–43). In the *Nip'al* it means "separated, scattered" (Ezek 34:12). Not surprisingly, Akkadian and Aramaic cognates also denote "separate" and "declare, clarify" (cf. *parāsu, AHw* 830–31; cf. Heinemann 1947). And not by accident the root *psq* in Rabbinic Hebrew means both "separate, divide" and "decide." Both the expression *pāṣaq dîn* and Akkadian *purussû dīnu* (*AHw* 831b) denote "render a verdict," and this is probably the sense of the verb both here and in Num 15:34 (cf. Fishbane 1985: 108, n. 9). Should, perhaps, this verb be vocalized *lĕpārēš, Pi'el?*

Fishbane (1985: 245) aptly compares the development of our term with that of the contextually allied word *dāraš* 'inquire'. Whereas older texts speak of *dāraš 'et- 'ĕlōhîm / YHWH* 'inquire of God / YHWH' (Exod 18:15; 1 Kgs 22:8), referring to oracular consultation (Weber's [1954] "formally irrational," the first stage in lawmaking; see below), it becomes a term for rational, legal investigation in later texts (e.g., Deut 13:15; 17:4, 9; 19:18), and in postexilic texts is attested as *lidrôš 'et-tôrat YHWH* 'to inquire of the torah of YHWH' (Ezra 7:10), where the text of the divine words serves as the oracle. The term *pāraš* also undergoes a development, since in postexilic literature it is found as *mĕpōrāš* (Neh 8:8), a participle used as an adverbial accus (GKC § 118p; Williamson 1985: 278–79) in the same context, "the torah of God." Here it translates "paragraph by paragraph," an offshoot of the root meaning "separate," a forerunner of the rabbinic term *pārāšâ*, a subdivision of the Pentateuch.

In the case of the wood-gatherer (Num 15:32–36), the punishment is clear: he brazenly violated the sabbath (Exod 31:14). Clarification was needed, however, either in regard to the mode of execution (*Sipre* Num. 114) or, more likely, whether his execution was by God or man (Milgrom 1990a: 408–10; note the ambiguity in Exod 31:14). In this case, however, Moses clearly did not know the punishment (Philo, *Moses* 2.201; *Sipra* Emor, par. 14:5). Indeed, the prohibition against blasphemy (Exod 22:27) contains no penalty, but the death sentence must be assumed: if it is prescribed for cursing (or reviling) parents (Exod 21:17), all the more so for God. Besides, the case of Naboth, who was (falsely) condemned and executed for cursing God (1 Kgs 21:13), demonstrates that the death penalty for blasphemy was well known.

The legal question that required resolution was this: Does the death penalty apply to a non-Israelite (or half-Israelite) blasphemer? The midrash is puzzled about the inability of Moses to decide the issue on his own, which it explains as follows:

This was one of four legal cases that came up before Moses, and he decided them in accordance with the understanding from above; in two of them (Num 9:1–14; 27:1–11) Moses was quick, and in two of them (Lev 24:10–23; Num 15:32–36) Moses was slow. In the latter two (cases) he said: "I have not heard (the like)." In (the judgment of) impure persons (who were not able to perform the *pesaḥ* [sacrifice; Num 9:1–14]), and in the judgment of the daughters of Zelophehad (Num 27:1–11) Moses was quick, because their cases were civil cases. (In the judgment) of him who gathered wood (and thereby) desecrated the sabbath willfully (Num 15:32–36), and (in the judgment) of the blasphemer who expressed his Holy Name with blasphemies Moses was slow, because their cases were capital cases, so that those would not be killed quickly, who were worthy before him in judgment to be killed, lest acquittal be found for him from another angle in the trial. And lest they be ashamed to say "we have not heard (a similar case)," Moses their master said "I have not heard (a similar case)." And they shall guard him in prison until it is declared to them from before the Lord with which judgment they shall have to kill him. (*Tg. Neof.* [trans. M. McNamara 1994: 197]

The midrash is certainly correct, despite its patent harmonization, in grouping these four cases into a single category. According to Weber (1954: 63–64), they exemplify the earliest stage of lawmaking, which he terms "formally irrational." That is, the procedures for adjuration are formal, fixed, but the conclusions are irrational because through these formal procedures divine intervention is sought. The common denominator in these four cases is that Moses cannot resolve the legal problem either on precedent or on his own, so he seeks divine—hence, irrational—intervention by the sanctioned formal means of an oracle. Fishbane (1985: 238) is surely correct in deducing that the appearance of these four cases "in the context of narrative of Israel's desert sojourn may actually bear precious historical witness to the diversity of 'formal irrationality' in ancient Israelite praxis." Fishbane (1985: 234–65) offers a lucid and illuminating biblical application of Weber's four-staged development of lawmaking.

13. *And YHWH spoke to Moses.* This indicates that the decision was received by Moses by means of an oracle. In the priestly tradition, the only legitimate oracle is the Urim and Thummim, handled exclusively by the high priest (vol. 1. 507–11). Even though he is not mentioned in all four cases (see above), his presence might be assumed since his name occurs in another verse ascribed to H (Num 27:21; Deut 33:8). However, even if we allow for the possibility that the laconic and enigmatic answer of the Urim and Thummim required exposition by the high priest, it is difficult to conceive of an answer like this one: removal of the blasphemer, hand leaning by the hearers, stoning by the *'ēdâ* (vv. 13–18) and, above all, the detailed and lengthy laws of the blasphemer and talion (vv. 15–22). Thus it can be assumed that the high priest is absent because he is, and YHWH's answer is lengthy because it is. One must keep in mind that in the priestly tradition YHWH speaks directly to Moses. As for Num 27:21, this verse speaks of Joshua. He and all who follow him must consult the Deity first through the medium of the oracular pronouncement of the Urim and Thummim, solely controlled by the high priest. But not so Moses: "With him I speak mouth to mouth, plainly and not in riddles" (Num 12:8).

14. *outside the camp. miḥûṣ lammaḥăneh.* This expression always signifies "close by, in the vicinity of the camp" (Aloni 1984; see NOTE on 17:3).

The death sentence and burials took place outside the settled area lest corpse-contamination befall the entire community (cf. 1 Kgs 21:13).

and have all who were within hearing lean their hands. wĕšāmĕkû kol-haššōmĕʿîm ʾet-yĕdêhem. The rendering "lean the hand(s)" for *šāmak yād/ yādayîm* is expounded in the NOTE on 1:4. Here the hand-leaning rite is performed with both hands. It serves a transference function: to convey the pollution generated by the blasphemy back to its producer (vol. 1.1041). Similar interpretations, mutatis mutandis, are conveyed by "to remove the guilt from themselves, they (the witnesses) say: Your blood is upon your head and not on ours" (Abravanel); "in order that they (the witnesses) will be forgiven for having heard the Name 'blessed'" (Bekhor Shor; cf. Wessely 1846; Elliger 1966).

Wright (1986: 435–36, supported by *Sipra* Emor 19:2; Rashi; Ibn Ezra; Dillmann and Ryssel 1897; Noordtzij (1982); Gerstenberger (1996) and based on Sus 34 [= Dan 13:34]) offers two other rationales: the hand leaning is "a means whereby the witnesses designate the blasphemer as guilty of the crime and worthy of death. By it the witnesses symbolically confirm their testimony to the community and also acknowledge their responsibility in the death of the criminal." Gerstenberger (1996: 364) adds this consideration: if the testimony is false, then the curse will revert to the perjurious witnesses (assuming H's acceptance of the rule expressed by Deut 19:16–19). My major objection to this interpretation is that in the analogous case of the wood-gatherer (Num 15:32–36), those who witnessed the violation are not required to perform the hand-leaning rite. Thus there is a need neither to designate the culprit nor to assume responsibility for his death. The difference between the two cases rests in their respective crimes: sabbath violation has no effect on its witnesses, whereas cursing God generates pollution that impinges on all who hear it.

Wright (1986: 435) questions this position, as the Bible gives no indication that blasphemy causes pollution. In response (vol. 1.1041), I have pointed out that H attributes pollution to violations for which there is no remedial sacrifice, such as illicit unions (18:24–28) and Molek worship (20:3). If it is objected (as did M. Segal in a seminar) that in these cases, but not in the case of the blasphemer, pollution (*ṭumʾâ*) is expressly mentioned, it need only be stated that for many transgressions the term *ṭumʾâ*, though not explicit, has to be assumed. This holds true in P itself for the pollution-remover par excellence, the purification offering of chap. 4, which never resorts to the root *ṭmʾ*.

Even more striking evidence is the case of one who *hears* an imprecation to testify but witholds his testimony (5:1), for which the priestly legists (again P, not H) prescribe a *ḥaṭṭāʾt* (other examples and details in vol. 1.314–15), and again the root *ṭmʾ* does not occur. Thus if P holds that an imprecation is binding merely by hearing it so that its violation generates pollution, it is only logical that P would hold that a blasphemous imprecation also affects those who hear it, by polluting them.

What is true for P is all the more valid for H, whose concept of impurity is more figurative and metaphoric. For example, Israel's repeated violation of the sabbatical—working the land instead of giving it rest—results in the pollution of the land, which can be cleansed not by an appropriate sacrifice (this would have been P's solution), but by the exile of its inhabitants (see INTRODUCTION to 26:43–44). In all of 26:14–45, however, the word for pollution *ṭum'â* does not occur, though for another case of expulsion (18:24–26)—which strengthens our case—the word surfaces.

An echo of this primordial tradition concerning the polluting effect of blasphemy is still detectable in rabbinic treatments of this topic: "They (the judges) send out all the people (in the court) and ask the chief among the witnesses and say to him 'Say expressly what you heard,' and he says it. Then the judges stand up and rend their garments (cf. 2 Kgs 18:37), and they may not mend them again. And the second witness says, 'I also heard the like,' and the third says, 'I also heard the like' (without repeating the curse)" (*m. Sanh.* 7:5; cf. *b. Sanh.* 60a).

Admittedly, the case of Susanna (Dan 13:34 LXX) presents a problem (vol. 1.1041–42), and I now concur (on the basis of Deut 13:10; 17:7) that witnesses in capital crimes take responsibility for the death of the persons they condemn. Perhaps this constitutes an additional (perhaps, subsequent) function of hand leaning. However, the transference of pollution/guilt back to the miscreant remains primary.

the whole community. kol-hā'ēdâ. Are all adults intended (Rashi) or only their leaders (Ibn Ezra)? The Hittite equivalent, the *panku tuliya,* can shed some light. It is defined as "all present, congregation, totality (of those present on a given occasion)"—in other words, the assembly. Its powers are illustrated by the Proclamation of Telepinu, which stipulates that a prince who shed blood within his own family was responsible to the assembly (KB₀ III 1 II 50–53); the assembly condemned to death plotters against the throne, but the king commuted their sentence to exile (KB₀ I 27; Beckman 1982b).

In the Hittite instance, the assembly was composed of the members of the high state bureaucracy, not exclusively of the nobility. Hebrew *'ēdâ,* however, is a more protean term (see NOTE on 19:2). In this instance, it probably referred to clan and tribal leaders (Saadiah). Apparently, the *'ēdâ,* when it meant "national assembly," did not include either women or *gērîm* 'aliens'. The latter are specifically excluded by the expressed statement that Moses' instructions were carried out by Israelites (v. 23b).

stone him. wěrāgěmû 'ōtô. The object of *rāgam* is generally expressed directly, as here (see also 20:2, 27; 24:23; Num 14:10; 15:35, 36; Deut 21:21; Josh 7:25; Ezek 16:40; 2 Chr 24:21). Occasionally, it is expressed indirectly with the preposition *bě* (24:16; 1 Kgs 12:18; 2 Chr 10:18). For a discussion of the means by which this punishment was executed, see the NOTE on 20:2. Douglas (1999: 207) suggests that the measure for measure principle is being invoked: "he has hurled insults at the Name, let him die by things hurled at him."

15. *And to the Israelites speak thus. wě'el-běnê yiśrā'ēl tědabbēr lē'mōr.* The reversal of object and verb in the usual address formula to Israel is an aspect of emphatic word order, indicating that the previous words (vv. 13–14) were addressed to Moses alone (Muraoka 1985: 38–39; see NOTE on 17:8).

(curses) his God. (yĕqallēl) 'ĕlōhāyw. Brichto (1963: 143–47), in the course of discussing the root *qll,* erroneously assumes that the target of abuse is not the Deity but the full Israelite, which leads him to conclude that there is a total absence of blasphemy in the Bible—a conclusion flatly contradicted by this verse and Exod 22:27 (see also Weinfeld 1972d: 241, n. 2; Paul 1990: 348, n. 64).

Some hold that the use of *'ĕlōhāyw* 'his God' rather than YHWH indicates that a surrogate name was used (e.g., Rashbam); hence his punishment is by God, not man—*wĕnāśā' ḥeṭ'ô* (see below). But if he expressly uses the Tetragrammaton, he is stoned to death (v. 16). A surrogate name, however, would have been expressed by *'ĕlōhîm,* without the pronominal suffix. Interestingly, the principal LXX witnesses do read *theos* (= *'ĕlōhîm*).

A more widely held view is that the pronominal suffix emphasizes that he curses his own god (Philo, *Moses* 2.204; *Zohar* Emor 1066; Abravanel; Ginsburg; Dillmann and Ryssel 1897; Schult 1974: 31, Joost 1994: 96–97; 1996: 68–69; cf. Fishbane 1985: 101). That is to say, the blasphemer of any *other* god will be subject to that god's wrath, but the blasphemer of Israel's God must be put to death (v. 16). However, the use of *'ĕlōhîm* with a pronominal suffix is typical H style (e.g., 21:6, 7, 8, 12, 17, 21 [mostly third person!]). Besides, it is doubtful if H believed in the autonomous powers of other gods (see Introduction II D). Thus it must be concluded that *'ĕlōhāyw* is used as a euphemism, so that YHWH would not become the object of *qillēl* 'curse' (see NOTE on "in a curse," v. 11). Alternatively, the H legist restated the older prohibition *'ĕlōhîm lō' tĕqallēl* 'You shall not curse God' (Exod 22:27) in order to add the element missing in Exodus—the punishment (M. Segal). The introverted structure of the entire pericope explains the placement of this verse here (see COMMENT A). The word *'ĕlōhāyw* in this verse (D) balances *'ĕlōhêkem* in v. 22 (D').

A radical solution has been proposed by Halevi (1975): *'ĕlōhāyw* should be translated "his ancestral spirits"; that is, if one curses (or offends) his ancestral spirits, they will punish him. Halevi reaches this conclusion on the basis of his analysis of the prohibition *'ĕlōhîm lō' tĕqallēl wĕnāśî' bĕ'ammĕkā lō' tā'ōr* (Exod 22:27), which he renders "Do not curse (your) ancestral spirits nor curse your (living) clan head." His evidence is an Arabic curse directed against both the father and the great-great-grandfather (five generations)—that is, the ancestral spirits. The problem with this interpretation is that *'ĕlōhîm* occurs again in the same pericope: *zōbēaḥ lā'ĕlōhîm yoḥărām biltî laYHWH lĕbaddô* 'Whoever sacrifices to a god other than YHWH alone shall be proscribed' (Exod 22:19), where *'ĕlōhîm* cannot refer to ancestral spirits for the obvious reason that the prohibition against sacrificing to other gods would be missing, unless one were to assume that such worship was permitted! Moreover, in the large blocs of prohibitions against worship of other deities in Deut 13–18, ancestor worship is specified as *dōrēš 'el-hammētîm* (18:11b), and other gods are labeled *'ĕlōhîm 'ăḥērîm* (13:3, 7, 14; 17:3; cf. Bloch-Smith 1992a: 227). In Exod 22:19, the LXX and Sam. add *'ăḥērîm,* which D. N. Freedman (personal communication) suggests may be the original reading. By simple homoeoteleuton, the scribe's eye jumped from the first *-ym* to the next one, and thus elided the word *'ăḥērîm.* Indeed, the fact that the next word *yḥrm* has several of the same letters as the missing *'ḥrym* only strengthens the case for a scribal oversight.

shall bear his punishment. wĕnāśā' ḥeṭ'ô. Assumed is that the blasphemer cursed God in secret; hence God alone can punish him (Ibn Ezra[1]; Wessely 1846). Thus this verse does not repeat the case cited in v. 11, which presumes that the pronunciation (and cursing) of God's name was done in public.

Possibly supporting this interpretation is the reference to cursing God in the Job narrative. Job fears that his sons *bērĕkû 'ĕlōhîm bilbābām* 'cursed (or belittled) God in their hearts' (Job 1:5aγ), which indicates that cursing God in one's thoughts is a sin that can be expiated only by sacrifice (Job 1:5aβ). Job's wife reacts to his afflictions by counseling him *bārek 'ĕlōhîm wāmūt* 'curse God and die' (Job 2:9b). The *Qal* formation of *wāmūt* implies that his death will be executed by God (Milgrom 1970: 5–8). Furthermore, we learn that Job "did not sin with his lips" (Job 2:10b), confirming that a curse must be articulated for it to warrant the death sentence. This would correspond precisely with the case presumed for Lev 24:15b: if one curses God in private (without witnesses), he is liable to death by divine agency.

There is one severe objection, however, to this interpretation. It requires eisegesis: in v. 15b, the curse was uttered privately; in v. 16a, publicly. Nothing in the text warrants such a distinction. Thus an alternative solution must be sought. Perhaps *both cases presuppose public acts.* That is, even if one curses God without pronouncing his name (v. 15b), he is not subject to the jurisdiction of the court. He is liable for punishment, but only at the hands of God. The implication of this interpretation is that the powers of the court are not unlimited. Witnesses would have to step forward and testify that they heard God's name pronounced as he was being cursed. If, however, the witnesses admitted that the curse omitted God's name, their testimony would be rejected. The court would reply that it had no authority to encroach on God's domain. It was for him to punish the miscreant who cursed him.

The demarcation between the two jurisdictions depends on whether the sin is committed against God or against man (see Milgrom 1970: 6–7), and in the latter case, whether the alleged sinner was apprehended. A parade example is the suspected adulteress of Num 5:11–31. An irate husband suspects that his wife has been unfaithful. Having no proof, his only recourse is to bring her to the sanctuary, where she undergoes an ordeal. The priest makes her drink a potion of sacred water to which dust from the sanctuary floor and a parchment containing a curse have been added. The curse spells out the consequences: if she is guilty, her genital area will distend and she will no longer be able to conceive; if, however, the water has no effect on her, she is declared innocent and she will be blessed with seed.

The key to unlocking this trial by ordeal is the fact that her alleged adultery was unapprehended. Had there been witnesses, there would be no need to cite this case: she would summarily have been put to death. Instead, her case is transferred to divine jurisdiction. But why this unique (in biblical jurisprudence) ordeal? And why consult God at all? Since he will decide the case, let him decide her judgment and, if she is guilty, let him put her to death.

To pose these questions is to answer them. Since the purported adulteress has not been apprehended—as the text repeats with staccato emphasis (Num 5:13)—then the community and, especially, the overwrought husband may not give way to their passions and *lynch her*. Indeed, even if she is proved guilty by the ordeal, they may not put her to death. Unapprehended adultery remains punishable only by God, and there is no need or warrant for human mediation (for a detailed analysis of this extraordinary trial, see Milgrom 1990a: 346–54). Thus a cardinal principle of biblical jurisprudence is that the unapprehended criminal is not subject to the jurisdiction of the human court.

In the long run, however, it makes little difference in our case whether the curse was uttered in private or public: there are no witnesses who can testify that the curse was hurled against God while pronouncing his name. Whether one curses God in private, even if he pronounces the divine name, or in public, but without pronouncing the name, he is punishable—but only by God. Nonetheless, the second alternative is preferable because, as indicated above, it does not require the assumption of a switch from a private to a public setting in vv. 15b–16a.

The question arises as to why the text uses the vague expression *wĕnāśā' ḥet'ô* instead of the unambiguous *wĕnikrĕtâ napšô miqqereb 'ammô*. The former makes sense in 20:19 when it forms the bridge and shares the characteristics of *kārēt* (vv. 17–18) and *'ărîrî* (vv. 20–21). But why is it used here? The answer, I suggest, is that the text is citing the entire law of blasphemy: cursing God by using a surrogate or using his name. However, only the latter blasphemy is relevant here. It is as though the text were saying, in the former case, God will take care of him in due time, but, in our case, the blasphemer must be put to death.

MAL A § 2 states, "If a woman . . . has uttered blasphemy or spoken sedition/insolence that woman shall bear her punishment; they shall not touch her husband, children, or daughters." Paul (1990: 350) correctly identifies *aranša tanašši* 'shall bear her punishment' with *nāśā' ḥet'ô* of this verse. In the light of MAL A § 32, which prescribes punishment of a wife for the malfeasance of her husband, the second half of MAL A § 2 means that "there is no vicarious liability for the acts of a woman" (Yaron 1970: 551), though the added statement implies that originally collective retribution was enacted on the entire family (Driver and Miles 1935: 20–21). Westbrook (1992: 549) applies this insight to our verse by interpreting it: the blasphemer alone will bear his punishment "i.e., his family shall not be touched, as in the Assyrian Laws." There is nothing in this pericope, however, that would imply otherwise. Moreover, the dichotomy between *yĕqallēl* (v. 15) and *nōqēb* (v. 16) would be left unexplained (Westbrook's rendering of *nōqēb* as "slander" is baseless; see NOTE on "cursing [it]," v. 11).

16. *but if he (also) pronounces the name of YHWH, he must be put to death.* *wĕnōqēb šēm YHWH môt yûmāt.* Weingreen (1972) holds that this verse is a later addition prohibiting the use of the divine name indiscriminately (cf. the LXX and Philo, *Moses* 3.25–26). Gabel and Wheeler (1980) go even further and declare that pronouncing the Name for any purpose is punishable by death. Rashi (followed by most moderns, most recently Joosten 1994: 96; 1996: 69) claims that *nōqēb* here should be rendered "curse," as in Num 23:8. This view must sum-

marily be rejected. As pointed out in the NOTE on "cursing (it)" (v. 11), the verb with the proximate root meaning "curse" is *qbb*, Nip'al, which, however, does not have a participle *nōqēb*. Gerstenberger (1996: 364) concludes that vv. 15–16 represent two parallel versions. In the first, the curser is given over to the God he has cursed; in the second, his punishment is death at the hands of the authorities. As will be explained, the two cases are entirely unlike in both the act and the punishment. For an entirely different exegesis of vv. 15–16, see COMMENT D.

Tg. Ps.-J. glosses *dimĕpārēš ûmĕḥarēp* 'who pronounces and curses'. Indeed, the rabbis insist that the mere pronunciation of the Tetragrammaton incurs no penalty (*m. Sanh.* 7:5; *Sipra* Emor, par. 14:2; *b. Sanh.* 55b–56a; Dillmann and Ryssel 1897, following Dalman 1889).

Saadiah, in my opinion, offers the correct reason: "Scripture's manner is to mention something without completing it if it already completed it in another place. For example, *wayyiqqōb ben hā'iššâ hayyiśrĕ'ēlît 'et-haššēm wayyĕqallēl* (v. 11aα) (means) he pronounced and then cursed. Thus, when Scripture later mentions the punishment it states *wĕnōqēb* (v. 16aα), implying he pronounced and cursed, for it is known to us that pronouncing the Name without cursing (it) incurs no punishment" (Kapach 1963: 112, n. 3; cf. Zucker 1959: 397; 1989: 370). Conversely, the compliance report (v. 23) mentions only *hammĕqallēl*, literally "the curser," under the assumption that blasphemy was committed; that is, the curse in the name of God (*nōqēb*) was actually a curse against the name of God (*mĕqallēl*; see NOTE on "cursing [it]," v. 11).

This interpretation can also be derived by considering vv. 15b–16 as a single unit, namely, "He who curses his God will bear his sin, but he who (also [with NJPS]) pronounces the name of God will be put to death."

One should also take note that law is more precise than narrative; narrative resorts to the circumlocution *haššēm* 'the Name', but law must specify the exact nature of the crime. Nonetheless, both avoid using the Tetragrammaton as the object of *qillēl* 'curse' (vv. 11, 15).

he must be put to death. môt yûmāt. Although the death penalty has not been stated before (no punishment is contained in the prohibition against blasphemy in Exod 22:27), it can be derived a fortiori from the death penalty prescribed for cursing parents, Exod 21:17 (see NOTE on "should be made clear," v. 12), is implied by Job 2:9 (but its meaning there may be death by God), and is taken for granted in the suit against Naboth (1 Kgs 21:13).

An illuminating parallel to the case of the blasphemer is found in the Assyrian harem edicts from the time of King Ninurta-apal-ekur (1192/91–1180/79 B.C.E.).

luašša šarri lu sinnišāti mādātu [ša . . . itti] aḫā'iš iddukāni ina ṣaltišina šu[m il]i ana maškite tazzakrūni napšāte ša Aššur it[-] inakkisu (ll. 56–58)

[Should] either the wives of the king or the other women [of the harem] fight with each other, and during their quarrel utter/invoke the name of the/a god blasphemously, they will cut the throat of the one who has [reviled] the god Aššur.

As pointed out by Paul (1990: 346–50), here too we have a case of a brawl, during which the name of a/the god is uttered blasphemously (cf. *maskītu, CAD* 10/1.323–24), and the prescribed punishment is death—an indication that the biblical case is based on old ancient Near Eastern precedents. There is a difference, however, between the two punishments: *mōt yūmāt* implies a trial; Akkadian *dâku*, in this case, connotes a summary execution (see NOTE on 20:16, and Levinson 1995).

alien as well as citizen. kaggēr kā'ezraḥ. ka . . . ka denotes the same level (*IBHS* § 11.2.9b; cf. *kāmôkā kĕparʿōh* 'you are the equal of Pharoah', Gen 44:18). For the meaning of *'ezrāḥ*, see the NOTES on 16:29 and 17:15, and for its possible etymology, see the NOTE on 19:34.

Fishbane (1985: 103, n. 46) claims that this provision is "not necessarily broad-minded . . . extending the law to strangers would be one way to regulate their behavior and guarantee that no ritually impure person was resident in the land" (cf. Weber 1952: 337–38; Smith 1971: 178–82). He (and his cited predecessors) are right, but their reasoning is itself founded on a deeper fear, one that is ensconced in a fundamental legal postulate of the priestly system: the *gēr* is subject to all the prohibitive commandments, the violation of which can pollute the land and exile its inhabitants (see chap. 17, COMMENT B). Indeed, the inclusion of the *gēr* in the talion laws (vv. 17–22, cf. v. 22) is one of the main reasons for attaching to them the narrative about the *gēr* (see COMMENT A).

if he has (thus) pronounced the Name. bĕnoqbô šem. This is an infinitive construct prefixed by *beth* (e.g., Exod 16:7; 34:29). Alternatively, it could be rendered "by (also) pronouncing the Name." The LXX adds *YHWH* to correspond with the beginning of the verse. Following the suggestion of D. N. Freedman (personal communication), haplography (rather homoeoarcton) may have occurred: the scribe's eye skipped from the *Y* at the beginning of a fully written *YHWH* to the *Y* at the beginning of *YWMT*. If so, it would account for the lack of a definite article on *šēm* (supplied by the Sam.). It would be a construct, the same form it takes at the beginning of the verse.

But the major omission is once again the verb *qillēl* 'curse', leaving the impression that merely to pronounce the divine name is subject to the death penalty. However, all the ellipses here (and in the following verses) can be explained by Saadiah's stylistic law: in the repetition of a statement, omissions may occur. To cite two examples, v. 21 omits *nepeš* (found in vv. 17–18), implying that merely striking an animal or a human is a capital crime, and hand leaning (v. 14), omitted in the compliance statement (v. 23), must be assumed. Thus a verse may never be pulled out of the context of the entire structure in which it is embedded. As will be demonstrated in the analysis of this pericope's structure (see COMMENT A), all its puzzling stylistic problems can be satisfactorily resolved.

Vv. 17–22. The Talion Laws

According to Sun (1990), the self-contained nature of the talion laws of vv. 17–22 implies that its connection with the law on blasphemy (vv. 15–16) is secondary.

Ibn Ezra connects the two legal sections by surmising that talion is introduced here because injury or death resulted from the quarrel (vv. 10–11), and although the laws on injuries, which include talion, are cited earlier (Exod 21:12–27), the novelty here is that one participant was a non-Israelite. Schwartz (forthcoming) suggests that they were conjoined because they both equate the alien and the citizen (vv. 16b, 22a)—though this would not explain why one law (talion) was inserted *into* the narrative depicting the circumstances of the citizen (blasphemy).

Nonetheless, it can be shown that vv. 15–22 form a unified bloc (Noth 1977) and that the entire pericope (vv. 10–23) comprises a single structure embodying an old talion law, which has been reworked by H within a narrative framework (see COMMENT A). A number of expressions are unmistakable signs of H's handiwork:

1. The use of *'ĕlōhāyw* (e.g., 21:7, 12, 17, 21, 22; see NOTE on "his God," v. 15).
2. The use of *nepeš 'ādām/bĕhēmâ* in the talion laws (vv. 17–18; see NOTE on "Anyone who kills an animal," v. 18).
3. The juxtaposition of the penalties *nāśā' ḥēṭ'* and *môt yûmāt* (vv. 15–16; cf. 20:2–3 and Exod 31:14 [H], *môt yûmāt* and *kārēt* juxtaposed).
4. The insertion of v. 21 for the sake of the introverted structure (see COMMENT A).
5. The term *šeber* (v. 20a) replacing JE's *yād* and *regel* (Exod 21:24; see its NOTE).
6. The use of *mûm* (vv. 19–20), connecting this pericope with chaps. 21–22 and, metaphorically, with chap. 19 (see INTRODUCTION to vv. 10–23, and COMMENT A).

The import of the uniform application of talion to injuries is eloquently expressed by Hartley (1992: LXII): "This principle does not imply that punishment was carried out by inflicting bodily injury in kind, but that punishment for harm to a person is to be commemorate with the harm done, not greater as revenge dictates, nor less as indulgence desires. This principle was a great advance in law codes, for it raised personal injury from a civil tort to criminal law, increasing the social worth of a citizen."

The point was raised by my student R. Pinchover that talion in the story of the blasphemer is inexact: the punishment, stoning, does not correspond to the crime, cursing! Moreover, God, the object of the curse, but not the community, should have punished the blasphemer. Finally, talion, the law applied to the blasphemer, does not even allude to his crime. As a reply to all these points, Pinchover has brought to my attention a fascinating passage from the Vassal Treaties of Esarhaddon: "Just as one cuts off the hands and feet and blinds the eyes of those who blaspheme against the god or the lord, so may they bring about your end" (*ANET* 540, par. 95). Thus the talion law, which begins "fracture for fracture, eye for eye" (v. 20), where *šeber* 'fracture' replaces *yad* 'hand' and *regel* 'foot', actually corresponds to the punishment meted out by the god to a blasphemer. Perhaps this reference would even resolve the problem of why the legist felt impelled to remove the inapplicable *nepeš taḥat nepeš* 'life for life', which usually heads the talion list (Exod 21:23b–25; Deut 19:21b; see NOTE on v. 18b).

Nonetheless, these points remain unanswered. The blasphemer does not have his limbs broken or his eyes blinded. He is stoned to death: *nepeš taḥat nepeš* 'life for life' is, indeed, applied to him.

The questions that must be addressed can be summed up as follows: What is it about cursing God that corresponds to and warrants death, and why is the talion law employed to specify the penalty? The answer is: if the community had not put the blasphemer to death, the inexpiable impurity generated by the curse (see NOTE on "lean their hands," v. 14) would have caused the destruction of the community (vol. 1.254–61). Thus one might even say that the community had to kill the blasphemer in self-defense. Another approach is taken by Douglas (forthcoming), who opts for true talion: "the blasphemer has hurled insults at the Name of God, let him die by stones hurled at him." The advantage of both suggestions is that the insertion of the talion laws into the narrative is explained. Nonetheless, as discussed in COMMENT B, the more likely answer is that YHWH's talion need not always be precise. He punishes collectively (note Moses' complaint, Num 16:22), and his punishment, unless it is graded as a series of warnings (26:14–38; cf. Isa 9:7–10:4; Amos 4:6–11), causes death. Thus talion is frequently but a literary figure for the purpose of vividly emphasizing that God's justice is uncompromisingly inexorable.

17. *kills any human being. yakkeh kol-nepeš 'ādām.* The term *nepeš 'ādām* can mean either "a corpse" (e.g., Num 19:11) or "a person" (e.g., Num 31:35, 40, 46). Here, however, the term is not tautological (Hartley 1992). As the object of *hikkâ* 'strike', its function is to indicate that the blow resulted in death, as in *kol-makkēh-nepeš* 'whoever kills a person' (Num 35:30) and *wĕhikkāhû nepeš* 'struck him mortally' (Deut 19:6, 11). Otherwise, H would have borrowed P's term *šōpēk dām* 'spills blood' (Gen 9:6; 17:4). The LXX adds *kai apothanē* 'and he dies' (influenced by Exod 21:12?) but, as indicated, the text presumes it.

The use of *'ādām* 'human being' and especially the seemingly superfluous *kol* 'any' is deliberate, to include the non-Israelite under Israelite jurisdiction, namely, the *gēr* (correctly, Ibn Ezra; contra Rashi and the *Mekilta* on Exod 21:12).

he must be put to death. This is the first case of talion: *nepeš taḥat nepeš* 'life for life' (v. 18b; Exod 21:23b). Actual juridical practice derives from the narratives, not the codes, which, like those in Mesopotamia, may be utopian. For example, *šĕmōr 'et-hā'îš hazzeh 'im-hippāqēd yippāqēd wĕhāyĕtā napšĕkā taḥat napšô 'ô kikkar-kesep tišqôl* 'Guard this man! If he is missing, it will be **your life for his,** or you will have to pay a talent of silver' (1 Kgs 20:39). Thus the talion formula (in boldface) is employed in actual circumstances. Daube (1947: 118), however, claims that compensation rather than talion is exemplified here, namely, that the alternative, following the escape of the prisoner, is either monetary payment or incarceration (replacing the prisoner). This cannot be correct, since this incident is applied by the prophet to the king of Aram, who is *'îš-ḥermî* 'the man whom I (YHWH) doomed' (1 Kgs 20:42a), and the decree *wĕhāyĕtā napšĕkā taḥat* *napšô wĕ'ammĕkā taḥat 'ammô* 'your life shall be forfeit for his life and your peo-ple for his people' (v. 42b) is a death sentence. Indeed, Ahab subsequently dies in battle (1 Kgs 22:37), presumably, together with many of his people.

This talion formula appears again in similar circumstances: *hā'îš 'ăšer-yimmālēṭ min-hā'ănāšîm 'ăšer 'ănî mēbî' 'al- yĕdêkem **napšô taḥat napšô*** 'Who-ever permits the escape of any of the men (the Baal prophets) I commit to your charge shall forfeit **life for life**' (2 Kgs 10:24). Again, Daube (1947: 118) denies that death is intended by the talion formula, but the fact that the Baal devotees are about to be put to death (v. 25) can only mean that the exaction of talion implies the death of the negligent Israelite guards.

18. *But anyone who kills an animal. ûmakkēh nepeš-bĕhēmâ.* "Only in a priestly system would the role of *noepoeš* (= *nepeš*) be emphasized in this fashion; only a priestly system would make the slaying of the *noepaeš* and the penalty for it be the one governing idea of the two cases" (Daube 1947: 112). Gerstenberger (1996: 366) postulates a case in which a thief slays an animal from someone else's herd. Considering that according to the Covenant Code, a thief is fined double the amount he has stolen (Exod 22:3), and if he has killed the stolen an-imal he must return four or five times the worth of the animal (Exod 21:37), is it possible that according to H the thief is not fined at all, but simply makes good his theft? The only possible solution is that this case presumes that the an-imal was killed accidentally.

shall make restitution for it. yĕšallĕmennâ. Wessely's (1846) and Daube's (1947: 134–44) claim that restitution in kind is intended can be disproved by pointing to the fact that *šullumu*, the exact Akkadian cognate, means "to make good, re-store," but it will not mean payment in kind unless it is so specified. This also holds for Hebrew *šillēm*: payment in kind must be specified (e.g., Exod 21:36, 37; 22:4). But where specifics are absent, restitution can take any form, includ-ing money (details in Milgrom 1976b).

life for life. nepeš taḥat nepeš. Doron (1969), and Mikliszanski (1947) before him, argue that this formula (Exod 21:23–25; Lev 24:18–20; cf. Deut 19:21) refers to monetary compensation (see also Weismann 1972). Doron rests his case mainly on parallels in the Mesopotamian law codes, in which, he claims, death sentences are explicit, but talion formulas are used solely for compensation:

1. *šumma ša libbišu ṣuḫartu napšātema umalla*
   If the fruit of her womb is a girl, he nonetheless **pays** a life. (MAL A § 50)

2. *šumma awīlum īn mār awīlam úḫtappid īnšu úḫappadū*
   If an *awīlum* has destroyed the eye of a son of an *awīlum*, **they shall destroy his eye**. (CH § 196)

3. *šumma sinništum šî imtūt mārassu ídukku*
   If that woman has died, they shall put **his daughter** to death. (CH § 210)

contrast 4. *sûmma [alpam] u lū immeram innadnûšum uḫtalliq alpam kīna*
alpum immeram kīma immerim ana kēlišunu iri"ab
If he has lost the **ox or sheep** that was entrusted to him, he shall
make good **ox for ox, sheep for sheep** to their owner. (CH § 263)

Of these four examples, nos. 2 and 3 are true cases of talion (note boldface).
Example no. 2 is complete in itself and is self-explanatory. Example no. 3 deals
with a case of an *awīlum* striking the pregnant daughter of another *awīlum* and
causing her to miscarry. Note that in neither case is a talion formula used. Example no. 1 also deals with a case of miscarriage. If an *awīlum* strikes the wife
of another *awīlum* and causes her to miscarry but the embryo is a girl, then he
"pays a life." This case deals with compensation (see *umullu, CAD* 10/2.189).
It may be argued that the expression *napišta umallu* is an ellipsis of "a life (for
a life)." However, as shown by Westbrook (1986: 63–64), it is not a talion formula at all; it merely states that the payment must be the full value of the dead
girl. Example no. 4 concerns a hired shepherd. Here, too, it can be observed
that "ox for ox, sheep for sheep" is not a formula, but refers to the specific animals mentioned in the case. Thus there is no basis in Mesopotamian law for
claiming that the talion formula is limited to cases of compensation. What about
biblical law?

Westbrook (1986) has argued that the talion law in Exod 21:22–25 refers to
the miscarriage case to which it is appended—a matter of accidental death. All
the cases in Lev 24:17–21, however, being opposed in principle to any compensation for homicide (in agreement with Num 35:31–32), prescribe death for
any premeditatedly inflicted death. Lev 24, therefore, removes the (Exodus-
tainted) formula from the talion law (v. 20) and places it with the case of the
animal, thereby saying that compensation for death applies only to animals.
Westbrook's proposal is subject to a major objection. All scholars concur that
the legislation of D (not H) was influenced by the Covenant Code. However,
the talion law of Deuteronomy *nepeš běnepeš* 'life for life' (Deut 19:21), embedded in the case of perjuring witnesses (whose testimony may have put someone to death), must mean what it says—literally, life for life (see COMMENT B).

Other, even less convincing, proposals have been advanced:

1. This talion law covers both v. 17 (homicide) and v. 18a (Ibn Ezra; Daube
   1947: 113). However, the previous word *yěšallěmennâ* 'shall make restitution for it' remains unresolved.
2. The restitution is not by money, but one animal for the other (Dillmann
   and Ryssel 1897; Ehrlich 1908; Gerstenberger 1996: 367). But it can be
   shown that the legal term *šillēm* always means "monetary payment," not
   "payment in kind" (contra Saadiah; Daube 1947; see Milgrom 1976b).
3. The same objection can be leveled against the view that *šillēm* refers to
   payment of the animal's worth (*b. B. Qam.* 83b; cf. the Mesopotamian
   laws, cited above).

4. Jackson's (1996: 114) suggestion that "life for life" literally means a live animal for the slain one is based on his questionable assumption that this phrase in Exod 21:23 originally meant a live person for the lost fetus (1972: 97–98, 104–5).

In admitted desperation, I can propose only a radical solution. The phrase *nepeš taḥat nepeš* indeed does not belong here. Its extraneousness is graphically displayed by the introverted structure of the entire pericope (vv. 10–23; see COMMENT A). Glaringly, this phrase is missing in the repetition of the verse (v. 21b). Clearly, it would have been totally illogical to insert it here. It must have fallen into this verse accidentally. But from where? I tentatively suggest that it belongs at the head of the talion law (v. 20). However, it makes no sense following immediately on the previous verse (v. 19), which states a general principle concerning injury (*mûm*). There is a more cogent reason. As expounded in the NOTE on "he has inflicted on," v. 20, the legist of Lev 24 applies talion literally to injury (*mûm*) as well as to life (*nepeš*). It is inconceivable, however, that a sitting judge would have found it possible to carry out talion in injury cases (see COMMENT C). Literal talion could have been executed only by the god through its earthly representative, the king (see NOTE on "he must be put to death," v. 17). Perhaps, when Hammurapi decreed the talion principle (he may even have invented it; see COMMENT B), he had his own situation in mind. But we know that his code remained a dead letter; it is nowhere reflected in the voluminous jurisprudence of Mesopotamia. In contrast to the absolute (god-like) powers of the monarch, the ordinary jurist would inevitably have had to decide in favor of monetary compensation. Thus it can be conjectured, plausibly I believe, that a subsequent H tradent, fully aware of the juridical practices in the land, deliberately would have broken the nexus between *nepeš* and *mûm* in the talion formula, lest the impression be given that the latter, like the former, prescribes literal talion. It was then mistakenly placed before v. 19 instead of its more logical location after v. 17. However, I am reluctant to attribute such a gross error to the redactor (who, subsequently, would surely have become aware of his mistake) and must admit that the solution escapes me.

Recently, I stumbled across Goldberg (1977: 55–56), who resolves the problem of v. 18b by a much more radical reconstruction: vv. 21b, 18b, 17, 22, 19, 20, 21a, 18a. He moves v. 18b after v. 21b and has it begin the talion laws, since v. 17, in his opinion, is not a general statement on homicide but one specifically directed to include the *gēr*. Hence v. 22, also directed to the *gēr*, follows. The remaining passages deal with injuries. The two equivalent passages on restitution for killing an animal, vv. 21a and 18a, are juxtaposed on the grounds (with Rashbam) that only v. 18a, containing *nepeš*, refers to killing, but v. 21a refers to injury. This reconstruction is pockmarked with faults: v. 17 clearly includes the *gēr*, not only because of its expression *kol-nepeš 'ādām*, literally "the life of every man," but also because it follows the expression *kaggēr kā'ezrāḥ* 'alien as well as citizen' (v. 16bα); v. 22, the equality of the *gēr*, serves better as the conclusion of the talion laws because it is a generalization covering all civil law; vv. 21a and 18a are legally equivalent (despite the addition of *nepeš* in v. 18a), since *makkeh*, in v. 21b, refers to a death blow (see also Exod 2:12; Num 21:35; 1 Sam 17:9 [bis], 3b); above all, the intricate introversion of vv. 13–23 (see COMMENT A) is destroyed. Nonetheless, Goldberg's suggestion to have v. 18b follow v. 21b is commendable, if for no other reason that it actually improves the structure of vv. 13–23. Note that FF′ are exactly equivalent, and EE′ are equivalent in the number of accented words (seven).

19. *maims. yittēn mûm bĕ,* literally "puts a blemish upon." It may be no accident that a similarly constructed idiom is *nātan nĕqāmâ bĕ* 'wreaks vengeance upon' (Num 31:3; Ezek 25:14, 17), since vengeance is a form of talion. The *beth* may have been chosen because it is the preposition of hostility. Assumed is that the maiming was done deliberately (contra Ibn Ezra). The centrality of this term in the structure of this pericope is discussed in COMMENT A.

another. ba ʿamîtô. This term usually refers to one who is known and with whom there is a relationship (see NOTE on 18:20). However, the corresponding verse in the pericope's structure uses *bāʾādām* (v. 20b); hence any person is intended (contra Saadiah).

so shall it be done to him. kēn yēʿaśeh lô. It may be that literal talion is intended (see NOTE on v. 20b). Doron (1969) claims that this phrase occurs in the story of Samson (*kēn ʿaśîtî lāhem,* Judg 15:11), where literal talion was not exacted—Samson burned the Philistines' grain stacks because they had deprived him of his wife (see also Ibn Ezra). The loose wording of the narrative, however, should not be taken as a legal pronouncement. All it may mean is that Samson is boasting: "I gave it right back to them." Jackson (1996: 42) makes the attractive suggestion that literal talion was imposed twice in the Bible: to Adoni-Bezek (Judg 1:6–7) and, here, to the blasphemer.

A semantically equivalent expression in Akkadian offers support: *kî epušušini epušuši* 'she (the wife of the striker) shall be treated as he treated her (the pregnant woman)' (MAL A §50)—an unambiguous talion formula (cf. Driver and Miles 1935: 418; Dillmann and Ryssel 1897; Elliger 1966; Westbrook 1986).

20. *fracture. šeber.* On the one hand, H does not seem to reckon with the milder injuries detailed in the fuller talion law of Exod 21:23–25, such as *kĕwîyâ* 'burn' and *ḥăbûrâ* 'bruise' (v. 25). On the other hand, the same Covenant Code contains a law stipulating that a bailiff is responsible for an animal only if it was *nišbâ* or *nišbar* (Exod 22:9). The former term means "carried off," leaving *nišbar* to cover all forms of impairment. Perhaps, then, its nominal form *šeber* should be rendered "injury" (Hoffmann 1953).

Daube (1947: 113) argues that "the author of the formula of retaliation in 24:20 has replaced the two clauses present in Exodus and Deuteronomy, 'hand for hand, foot for foot' by the one 'breach (*scil.* of hand or foot) for breach (of hand or foot)'. . . . The formula in Leviticus is concerned solely with the causing of a deformity in the priestly sense." However, H's list of priestly deformities includes the phrase *šeber regel ʾô šeber yād* 'a broken foot or a broken hand' (21:19a), implying that the term *šeber,* by itself, is not limited to a fractured limb. What of an injury to another part of the body (e.g., the neck, cf. CH § 246) such as a wound (*peṣaʿ,* as specified in Exod 21:25)?

Since v. 20b appears to be a generalization (otherwise, it would be superfluous), the chances are that the items listed in v. 20a are meant to be examples, with no intention to cover every kind of injury (L. Chelnov).

for. taḥat. That is, instead of (cf. Gen 4:25; 22:13; 44:33; 2 Sam 19:1).

eye, tooth. 'ayin šēn. CH §§ 245–48 list the same sequence of injuries (to an ox): life, fracture (leg or neck), eye, horn (= tooth?) (Westbrook 1986: 69, n. 71).

he has inflicted on . . . shall be inflicted on him. yittēn . . . ba . . . kēn yinnāten bô. The rabbis interpret the second *nātan bĕ* to mean "compensation," since the verb *nātan* frequently means "pay" (e.g., Exod 21:19, 22, 23, 30, 32; *b. B. Qam.* 84a). Saadiah (on Exod 21:22) and Ibn Ezra (first explanation) derive the same ruling from *wĕyāšît 'ālāyw . . . wĕnātan bi . . .* (Exod 21:22): *bĕ = al* and, hence, *yinnāten bô* means "shall be imposed upon him," namely, compensation. This is an indication of the tortuous exegesis indulged in by the rabbinic expositors to avoid the application of talion to injuries (see their humane reasoning detailed in COMMENT C). Indeed, Saadiah's interpretation (as reported by Ibn Ezra on Exod 21:24) is countered by ben Zuta', whose sharp questions only produce the lamest of answers. For the precise (and literal) sense of *nātan be* 'put on' in H, see 19:28 (R. Pinchover).

Clearly, there cannot be two different renderings for *nātan bĕ* in the same verse, the first meaning "inflict" and the second, "compensate." Moreover, the fact that the text uses *nātan bĕ* rather than *šillēm*, the precise word for "compensate," which it employs elsewhere in the talion laws (vv. 18, 21), implies that literal talion is intended (Westbrook 1986: 69, n. 72; see COMMENT A).

on the person. bā'ādām. As perceptively observed by Joosten (1994: 110–11; 1996: 78), the use of this term here (and in the rule concerning manslaughter, v. 17) may be H's way of polemicizing against JE's *'îš* in similar legislation (Exod 21:12, 20–21). That JE's term is restricted to the meaning "free citizen" is shown by the exclusion of slaves from this rule (Exod 21:21, 32). Thus for H, the life and body of all human beings is sacred.

21. There can be no doubt that this verse is a precise summary of vv. 17–18 (laws 6 = 4 and 7 = 3; see COMMENT A) with nothing else added. What is its purpose? The rabbis, noting the absence of the term *nepeš*, reason that the text here is speaking of injury, not death (*b. Sanh.* 84b; cf. Rashi). Ibn Ezra suggests that this verse must be read with the following one (v. 22), which applies talion to the alien. Westbrook (1986: 68) argues that it emphasizes that *nepeš taḥat nepeš* (v. 18b) does not mean "compensation" (as it does in Exod 21:23b), but must be understood as talion.

The answer, I submit, is none of the above. This verse is here for stylistic reasons: to complete the giant introversion of this pericope. Furthermore, it provides the seventh law in this pericope, thereby artfully perfecting its structure (see COMMENT A).

but one who kills a human being shall be put to death. Another reason for this repetition (cf. v. 17) is to emphasize the basic biblical postulate: no compensation for homicide—a leniency allowed in ancient Near Eastern law (and practice) to those of a higher social status. Note this Hittite example: "They seize the killer of such a person and hand him over to the brothers of the murdered man. His brothers take the monetary compensation for the murdered man and they perform the expiatory ritual on the murderers, through whose act a life was taken. But if the brothers do not want to accept a monetary compensation, they execute the man who has taken a life" (Oppenheim 1967: 144).

22. *one law. mišpaṭ 'eḥād.* The absolute form *mišpāṭ* should be read (as in Num 15:16; GKC § 134α). This term refers to civil law (*jus*), not religious law (*fas*). The latter category is expressed by *tôrâ* (the *pesaḥ*, Exod 12:49a) and *ḥuqqâ* (sacrificial supplements, Num 15:15; the second *pesaḥ*, Num 9:14). H insists that both religious, or cultic, and civil law are binding on the alien (Num 15:16); the former, however, is qualified by being limited to prohibitions (see chap. 17, COMMENT B). That the observance of both religious and civil law is incumbent on the alien is vividly expressed in this pericope, which expressly mentions the alien in regard to both the law of blasphemy (v. 16) and the talion laws for injuries (v. 22; Knohl 1995: 175).

The egalitarian treatment of the *gēr* stems from H's theology. Since YHWH is the owner of the land (see NOTE on 25:23), all who settle on it—provided they obey his laws mutatis mutandis—are entitled to his protection (see chap. 17, COMMENT B).

"The stranger was to be protected, although he was not a member of one's family, clan, religion, community or people, simply because he was a human being. In the stranger, therefore, man discovered the idea of humanity" (Hermann Cohen, cited in Telushkin 1997: 467).

I, YHWH your God. 'ănî YHWH 'ĕlōhêkem. The addition of this concluding formula enables the entire verse to balance vv. 15b–16a (DD′ in COMMENT A), which include both divine names: YHWH and *'ĕlōhîm*. The plural suffix (-*kem*, rather than sing. -*kā*, which would correspond to sing. -*āyw*, v. 15b) is employed to embrace both citizen and alien (Rashi, Ibn Ezra).

V. 23. The Compliance Report

23. *Moses spoke (thus) to the Israelites. wayyĕdabbēr mōšeh 'el-bĕnê yiśrā'ēl.* Why is this sentence necessary? It would have sufficed to have the normal compliance report (beginning with v. 23aβ) without this obvious—and syntactically difficult (what did Moses speak?)—introduction. Again, the stylistic demands of the structure are responsible: it balances the introduction of Moses' speech to the Israelites (v. 15a; CC′ in COMMENT A).

Indirect confirmation of this tactic can be found in the similarly structured story of the wood-gatherer (Num 15:32–36; see INTRODUCTION to vv. 10–23). Note that the *absence* of *wayyĕdabbēr* (v. 36b) is due to its *absence* in the introduction to Moses' speech (v. 35aα). Schwartz (personal communication) adds: "In the priestly narrative, the laws compelled by God at *His own* initiative are *assumed* to be reported to the people subsequently. In this case, however, the initiative came from below, and Moses committed himself explicitly to report back to the people. Thus the narrator must indicate what he normally just implies: that Moses took the message and repeated it."

And they took the blasphemer . . . The compliance report omits the hand leaning (v. 14aβ), since the focus is on the people who perform the stoning (v. 14b), not the witnesses who perform the hand leaning.

The Israelites did. This refers to the stoning. The execution of Naboth (1 Kgs 21:13) provides an actual case (cf. Deut 17:5).

as YHWH had commanded Moses. This is the counterpart to v. 13 (AA' in COMMENT A).

COMMENTS

A. The Structure of Lev 24:13–23 and Its Significance

Chap. 24 contains a sophisticated mega-introversion outlined and explicated below. The numbers on the left refer to seven laws contained within the structure.

A   *wayyĕdabbēr* YHWH *'el-mōšeh lē'mōr*
    B   *hôṣē' 'et- hammĕqallēl miḥûṣ lammaḥăneh (wĕsāmĕkû kol-*
        haššōmĕ'îm 'et-yĕdêhem 'al-rō'šô) **wĕrāgĕmû** *'ōtô kol-hā'ēdâ*
        C   *wĕ'el-bĕnê yiśrā'ēl tĕdabbēr lē'mōr*
1.   D   *'îš 'îš kî-yĕqallēl* **'ĕlōhāyw**   *wĕnāśā' ḥeṭ'ô*
2.   a   *wĕnōqēb šem-***YHWH**   *môt yûmāt*
                  x   **rāgôm yirgĕmû**-*bô kol-hā'ēdâ*
                     kaggēr *kā'ezrāḥ*
                 a'   *bĕnoqbô šem*   *yûmāt*
3.   E   *wĕ'îš kî yakkeh kol-nepeš 'ādām*   *môt yûmāt*
4.   F   *ûmakkēh nepeš bĕhēmâ*   *yĕšallĕmennâ*
               nepeš taḥat nāpeš
5.   G   *wĕ'îš kî-yittēn mûm ba'ămîtô*   *ka'ăšer*
                 'āśâ kēn yē'āśeh lô
                 X   *šeber taḥat šeber 'ayin taḥat 'ayin*
                    šēn taḥat šēn
               G'   *ka'ăšer yittēn mûm bā'ādām*   *kēn*
                 yinnātēn bô
6.   F'   *ûmakkēh nepeš bĕhēmâ*   *yĕšallĕmennâ*
7.   E'   *ûmmakkēh 'ādām*   *yûmāt*
          D'   *mišpāṭ 'eḥād yihyeh lākem* **kaggēr** *kā'ezrāḥ yihyeh kî*
            'ănî **YHWH** *'ĕlōhêkem*
        C'   *wayyĕdabbēr mōšeh 'el-bĕnê yiśrā'ēl lē'mōr*
    B'   *wayyôṣî'û 'et-hammĕqallēl 'el-miḥûṣ lammaḥăneh* **wayyirgĕmû** *'ōtô*
    'āben
A'   *ûbĕnê- yiśrā'ēl 'āśû ka'ăšer ṣiwwâ* YHWH *'et-mōšeh*

A   And YHWH spoke to Moses, saying: (v. 13)

     B   Take the blasphemer outside the camp; and have all who were within hearing lean their hands on his head; then have the whole community **stone** him. (v. 14)

          C   And to the Israelites speak thus: (v. 15a)

1.   D   Anyone who curses **his God** shall bear his punishment; (v. 15b)

2.   a   but if he (also) pronounces the name of **YHWH,** he must be put to death. (v. 16aα)

                                      x   The whole community shall **stone** him; alien as well as citizen, (v. 16aβ,bα)

                                a' if he has (thus) pronounced the Name, he must be put to death. (v. 16bβ)

3.   E   If anyone kills any human being, he must be put to death (v. 17)

4.   F   But anyone who kills an animal shall make restitution for it, life for life (v. 18)

5.   G   If anyone maims another, as he has done so shall it be done to him: (v. 19)

                             X   fracture for fracture, eye for eye, tooth for tooth. (v. 20a)

                     G' The injury he has inflicted on the person shall be inflicted on him. (v. 20b)

               F' One who kills an animal shall make restitution for it; (v. 21a)

7.   E' but one who kills a human being shall be put to death. (v. 21b)

          D' **You** shall have one law for the alien and citizen alike; for **I, YHWH your God** (have spoken). (v. 22)

          C' Moses spoke (thus) to the Israelites. (v. 23aα)

     B' And they took the blasphemer outside the camp and **pelted** him with stones. (v. 23aβ)

A' The Israelites did as YHWH had commanded Moses. (v. 23b)

Lund's *Chiasmus in the New Testament* (1942), with examples from the Hebrew Bible, was the first major work that seriously treated Scripture's large, widely attested chiastic structures, alternately called introversions (Kikawada 1974) or palistrophes (McEvenue 1971: 29, n. 18), as one of the preeminent organizational devices employed by the biblical authors. They have proved to be more than literary artifices. By the use of repeated words and inner chiasms, and, above all, by the choice of the center or fulcrum around which the introversion is structured, the ideological thrust of each author is revealed. In a word, structure is theology. I have demonstrated that this theological device prevails through-out Numbers (1990a: xxiii–xxix, 359–60, 368–69, 376–80, 387–90, 437–38, 463–67, 491–94, 500–501), which can be attributed to the redactional activity of the school of H (see Introduction I A). It also is dominant in H's contribu-tions to Leviticus (e.g., 11:43–44; 16:29–31; see esp. chap. 21, COMMENTS A and B). The palistrophic nature of 24:10–23 has been recognized in part (Boys 1825: 41, cited by Welch 1990: 7–9; Wenham 1979a: 312; Galil 1987: 177; Jackson 1996: 119–20) and in whole (Fishbane 1985: 101, n. 4; Paran 1989: 171). But the full ideological implications of this structure have yet to be explored.

First, this structure proves that the case of the blasphemer and the laws of tal-ion have been completely integrated. It makes no difference if, for example, H drew each from a different source. The fact is that it fused them into a single, organic structure. Interestingly, and supportively, the sentence issued against the wood-gatherer (Num 15: 35–36), also the work of H, forms a perfect introver-sion in miniature:

A   wayyō'mer YHWH 'el-mōšeh
  B   môt yûmat hā'îš
    C   rāgôm 'ōtô bā'ăbānîm
      D   kol-hā'ēdâ miḥûṣ lammaḥăneh
        X   wayyōṣî'û 'ōtô
      D'   kol-hā'ēdâ 'el-miḥûṣ lammaḥăneh
    C'   wayyirgĕmû 'ōtô bā'ăbānîm
  B'   wayyāmōt
A'   ka'ăšer ṣiwwâ YHWH et-mōšeh

A   Then YHWH said to Moses: (v. 35)
  B   The man must be put to death
    C   Shall pelt him with stones
      D   the entire community outside the camp
        X   They took him out (v. 36)
      D'   the entire community outside the camp
    C'   They pelted him with stones
  B'   and he died—
A'   as YHWH commanded Moses

This brief pericope is translated literally (and awkwardly) to illustrate its per-fect chiastic structure. Note that its author was forced to add the superfluous word wayyāmōt 'and he died' (B') in order to balance môt yûmat hā'îš 'the man must be put to death' (B). The relevance of this pericope to ours is that it, too, reveals that the case and the sentence are an organic unit. And since the talion laws form an inextricable part of the structure of 24:10–23, it must follow that its author reworked the case of the blasphemer and the talion laws into his com-position because he felt that both were indispensable to his message.

The heart of H's message must be contained within the talion laws, particu-larly in law no. 5 (GXG'), the heart of the structure. It states that any injury inflicted (presumably, maliciously) on another is subject to talion. Here the priestly author (H) purposely uses the word *mûm* 'blemish' to describe the effect of the injury (contrast the classic statements of the talion laws, Exod 21:23b–25; Deut 19:21b). It is hardly coincidental that it is the same term *mûm*, the physical defects of persons and animals, that disqualifies them from entering the service of and to God (21:16–23; 22:19–25). A theological message emerges here: he who injures a person has disfigured *ṣelem ʾĕlōhîm* 'the image of God' (Gen 1:27; 9:6b). For the priestly legist, this is blasphemy, and so he applies the law of talion to the case of the blasphemer. Thus the law of talion is operative because, in effect, the crime was committed not only against the person and, hence, adjudicable in the human court, but also against God and, hence, subject to his law of talion (e.g., Deut 32:21; Isa 5:8–9; Jer 32:19; Prov 26:27, and see the curses, 26:14–39, which largely reverse the blessings of vv. 3–13). Westbrook (1986) has raised the possibility that the talion laws of Exod 21:23b–25, being tied to the case of an accidentally inflicted miscarriage (vv. 22–23a), allow for compensation. But there can be no question—at least in my mind—that in the talion laws of Leviticus (and Deuteronomy) literal talion is intended. (Note that the rabbis, who always opt for compensation, are nonetheless ambivalent regarding Lev 24; cf. *b. B. Qam.* 83b–84, cited in COMMENT C.)

Douglas (1993a: 20) pursues the choice of *mûm* even further:

> So causing a blemish in a neighbor is doing him a damage according to the elementary principles of justice: taking away something that is his by right, leaving him with too little. Or by oppression, giving him a heavy load to bear. Causing a blemish is giving a laborer excessive burdens. The interesting thing is that the neighbor who has suffered outrage in the case of the blasphemer is YHWH himself, and we soon see, in ch. 26, that YHWH is included squarely in the law of talion with the rest of his creation. The statements on blemish connect it with inequitable dealings.

She makes two points. The first is that *mûm* associates chap. 24 not only with chaps. 21–22 (priestly and sacrificial defects), where the term *mûm* is actually employed, but also with chap. 19 (and, presumably, chap. 25), where figuratively a *mûm* occurs each time a person is unjustly deprived of his due. Her second point (implied rather than stated) is that the case of blasphemy against God, who punishes by talion, provides both the background and the rationale for exacting talion in all cases of (permanent) injuries and death. Douglas's intuitions are eminently worth considering (see Introduction II P).

I was justifiably asked by a seminar student (B.-Z. Horowitz) why talion is at the center of the structure (GXG′), rather than the law about the blasphemy of the *gēr* (DD′), which, after all, is the subject of the story, and conversely why a story about a *gēr*, rather than a story about injury, was chosen to match the law of talion.

It must be kept in mind that H is obsessed with the problem of the *gēr* both legally and theologically. Since H has expanded P's holiness horizon from the sanctuary to the promised land, it must ipso facto be concerned with the *gēr* because, as a resident of the land, he is capable of polluting it. Thus the *gēr* must heed all the prohibitions incumbent on the Israelite (but not the nonpollutable permissive commandments; see chap. 17, COMMENT B) against blasphemy. This prohibition, however, lies in a marginal area. Since the *gēr* is not bound by a covenant to worship YHWH, is it truly a crime if the *gēr* cursed him, pronouncing his name? The structure provides the answer in the juxtaposition of D and E and of E′ and D′. Blasphemy is equivalent to murder; both are capital crimes requiring the death penalty. This equation in D (including its internal chiasm axa′) E is completed in E′D′, which adds the *gēr* to the equation. Since blasphemy is the novel law in biblical jurisprudence, it is only logical that it, rather than the case about murder, be cited.

It also should be added, parenthetically, that in the theology of H, the *gēr* simulates the life of holiness demanded of the Israelite. This theological postulate perhaps justifies and motivates H's general ruling that for violations of all prohibitions, civil and religious alike, the *gēr* is subject to the same penalty as the Israelite.

The second question is not legitimate. It assumes a chronological inaccuracy, namely, that the story was brought to illustrate talion. The reverse is true. The story of the blasphemer survived as an ancient tradition, and the talion law "life for life" was brought in to explain why the blasphemer was served the death penalty (see INTRODUCTIONS to vv. 10–23, 17–22) and, as mentioned above, applied secondarily to the *gēr*.

Another theological lesson lies implicit in the structure, rather, in its glaring deviation: the rule on blasphemy (D) is expanded by an internal chiasm (axa′). Thus axa′ provides the center for ABCDD′C′B′A′, which also deals with the case of blasphemy. It introduces the term *rāgôm yirgĕmû* in its center (x), making it the only term to be cited three times in this pericope (vv. 14b, 16aβ, 23aγ [boldface]), thereby creating a new center for the structure. Its purpose cannot be missed: to apply the law of blasphemy to an alien (also included in X). That this is the plain (but not deepest) intention of this structure is buttressed by its counterpart (v. 22 [D′]), which switches to second-person plural (*lākem*, *'ĕlōhêkem* [boldface]), in order to emphasize that the alien (*gēr* [boldface]) as well as the Israelite is subject to the prohibition against blasphemy. H, however, placed the talion law as applied to injury at the center of his message (GXG′) and not the law against blasphemy as applied to the *gēr* (DD′). The latter is made the center of a minor introversion (axa′), but center stage is occupied by talion.

Other stylistic points should be noted:

1. The need to summarize effectively bloated D is effectively accomplished in D′ by its phrase YHWH *'ĕlōhêkem* (v. 22b), which thereby refers to both parts of the blasphemy law (the *nōqēb* and the *mĕqallēl*, vv. 15b-16a), the first using *'ĕlōhāyw* (v. 15b) and the second, YHWH (v. 16aα). This artifice also provides another reason (in addition to the need for a euphemism)

for choosing the general term *'ĕlōhîm* 'deity' instead of the Tetragrammaton.

2. Seven laws are contained in this pericope (enumerated in the outline; Galil 1987). Moreover, as noted by Hartley (1992), the laws come in pairs: 1–2, 3–4, 6–7. Law no. 5 stands on its own: it is the center of the structure.

3. V. 21 (F'E') adds absolutely nothing to its counterpart (EF), F' demonstrating, however, that the phrase *nepeš taḥat nāpeš* in F is superfluous (see NOTE on v. 15). The author had no choice: H needed it to complete the structure.

To recapitulate: on one level, the structure emphasizes that the blasphemy prohibition applies to the alien. But on a deeper level, indicated by the true center of the structure (X), H makes the point that talion for permanent injuries is justified theologically because just as blasphemy is an offense against God, so are injuries that disfigure God's image—the human being. Thus we see that the episode of the blasphemer bears a secondary role. The talion laws for blemishes are H's primary objective; it attaches the case of blasphemy only to provide a *Sitz im Leben* for the legislation. Once again, narrative is proved to be an ancillary tool for illustrating the law. For an alternative structure and exegesis, see COMMENT D.

B. Lex Talionis *in the Bible and the Ancient Near East*

This subject is so vast that I must confine myself to a few salient points. *Lex talionis* is defined as "a law of retaliation by which the guilty party suffers the same harm as that experienced by the injured party" (Huffmon 1992: 321), which is a rephrasing of the rabbinic definition, "With what measure a man metes; with it one will mete to him," where "one" is a circumlocution for God (*m. Soṭ.* 1:7; cf. *b. Ned.* 52a; Matt 7:2; Mark 4:24; Luke 6:38; Wis 11:16). Its literal meaning is that God will punish the criminal with the same instrument with which the latter committed his crime (e.g., Num 5:27–28; see NOTE on "shall bear his punish" v. 15; Prov 30:17; 1 Sam 15:33; Est 7:9–10) and is found in the legislation but once (Deut 25:11–12; cf. Loewenstamm 1962b). Also in the case of false testimony, the penalty for the allegation is carried out on the perjuring party (Deut 19:19; see below). Precise formulations of talion are found in our pericope *ka'ăšer 'āśâ kēn yē'āśeh lô* 'as he has done so shall it be done to him' (v. 19b); *ka'ăšer yittēn mûm bā'ādām kēn yinnātēn bô* 'the injury he has inflicted on the person shall be inflicted on him' (v. 20b). As noted in COMMENT A, Israel's God always prefers to act by talion (Deut 32:21; Isa 5:8–9; Jer 32:19; Prov 26:27; see esp. NOTES on 26:23–24; Boleh 1991–92: 175–76).

It is important, however, to recognize that the talion attributed to YHWH is not always precise. For example, Israel is punished for panicking at the negative report of the scouts and rebelling against Moses, Aaron, and God (Num 14:4, 9a) by being condemned to forty years in the wilderness. If one wanted to concoct a true talionic punishment, one would expect some disinformation disseminated by YHWH, via Moses, that would cause the Israelites to panic and flee back to Egypt (cf. vv. 3–4). The figure of forty is seemingly derived by a tal-ionic principle: "You shall bear your punishment for forty years, corresponding to the number of days—forty days—that you scouted the land, a year for each day" (v. 34a). Besides the inexactness of the punishment, year for day, a more troubling imprecision remains. Talion also implies that the instrument of both the sin and the punishment is identical. But the forty-day reconnaissance by the scouts was no sin at all!

Thus, as recognized by Heinemann (1950: 64–70; cf. Loewenstamm 1962b: 845–46), talion as operated by God is frequently a literary device to indicate the inevitability and irreversability of divine retribution—a similar illustration of God's uncompromising justice.

The oldest ancient Near Eastern laws provide for compensation (Sumer, Ur Nammu, Eshnunna, Hatti), but later Mesopotamian laws prescribe talion (LH and CH; MAL). Extant evidence indicates that talion is an innovation of the laws of Hammurabi. Finkelstein (personal communication) writes:

> The institution of talionic punishment in LH was a conscious departure from what was plainly the established custom. Nor can this innovation be charged to Hammurapi's Amorite antecedents—and ostensibly "primitive" traditions of the western desert as compared with the more "civilized" traditions of Sumero-Akkadian civilization. For it cannot be shown that Amorite customs—whatever they may have been—influenced Hammurapi's legislation in other areas; in all major respects . . . LH represents the same legal tradition appar-ent in the earlier Mesopotamian corpora.

Goetze (1956: 122, n. 9) regards talion in CH as "archaism." But, as pointed out by Diamond (1957: 151), it is strange that later MAL not only archaized to the same degree, but added a category of corporal punishment—forced labor. Moreover, since an archaism must go back to something, where is there any ear-lier evidence for talion (R. Gane)? Diamond (1957: 153) has plausibly con-cluded that talion reflects a more organized state. It gives maximum protection for its free citizens and serves to lessen differences between rich and poor citi-zens. That is, wealthy citizens cannot buy their way out by compensating the victim or his family. Moreover, talion guards against excessive punishment (e.g., Gen 4:23–24) or multiple punishments (e.g., MAL A § 50) for a crime. Philo's (*Laws* 3.181–82) spirited defense of talion merits quotation in full:

> The legislators deserve censure who prescribe for malefactors punishments which do not resemble the crime, such as monetary fines for **assaults**, dis-franchisement for **wounding** or **maiming** another, expulsion from the coun-try and perpetual banishment for **wilful** murder or imprisonment for **theft**. Our law exhorts us to equality when it ordains that the penalties inflicted on offenders should correspond to their actions, that their property should suffer if the wrongdoing affected their neighbor's property, and their bodies if the offense was a bodily injury, the penalty being determined according to the

limb, part or sense affected, while if his malice extended to taking another's life his own life should be forfeit. For to tolerate a system in which the crime and the punishment do not correspond, have no common ground and belong to different categories, is to subvert rather than uphold legality.

From Philo's understanding of talion, it is to be (1) taken literally, (2) applicable to property (which includes animals) as well as to persons, and (3) restricted to willful acts (boldface). Points 1 and 3, I submit, correspond with the plain meaning of the text; point 2, only partially, since damage to animals (and other property) is assessed monetarily.

The ancient Near East is a cultural continuum, particularly in the field of law, as exemplified by the major similarities in the law of talion:

1. The specific loci of talion in Mesopotamian law, assault and, especially, that which causes miscarriage, are remarkably paralleled in biblical law. Huffmon (1992: 4.321) argues that since mutilation in biblical law is restricted to one case (Deut 25:11–12) and one incident (Judg 1:6–7), the law of false witnesses (Deut 19:16–21) must be "a statement of equivalent compensatory punishment . . . compensation or fine." However, the fact that this latter law begins its talion declaration with the words wĕlōʾ tāḥōs ênekā 'Your eye shall not pity' (Deut 19:21a) indicates that corporal and not financial punishment is prescribed (R. Gane). Moreover, since the perjury may have been uncovered before the penalty was imposed, there could be no compensation — only talion (Enker 1991: 54–55).

2. Many losses enumerated are similar: eyes, tooth, and so on.

3. Talion is primarily for permanent physical loss (exclusively in CH, Lev 24, and Deut 19; but possibly not in MAL A §§ 50 and 52 or in Exod 21:25, R. Gane). Paul (1970a: 77) finds CH to be inconsistent for not prescribing talion for all physical invasions against the awīlum (e.g., smiting the cheek, CH §§ 202–3). He states that "this inconsistency is not to be found in the biblical collections of law." However, once it is recognized that talion is applied for physical loss rather than for any physical invasion, CH is found to be consistent (R. Gane). As for the Bible, the phrases "burn for burn, wound for wound, blow for blow" (Exod 21:25) may prove an exception, since they would include injuries that may heal. However, the possibility must be considered, with Westbrook (1986: 62–67), that Exod 21:22–25, where an innocent passerby is injured as a result of a brawl, declares that the community must pay a monetary penalty in case the perpetrator is not caught; in other words, the talionic principle is not involved.

There are, nonetheless, differences between biblical talion and that of its environment:

1. In Mesopotamian law, talion is applied if the victim is an a-wi-lum me-iḫ-ri-šu 'an awīlum "gentleman" [CAD 1/2.55–56] of his own rank', but if the victim is a muškēnum 'commoner' (CAD 10/2.272–75) there is monetary payment (CH §§ 196–201). This corresponds with Exod 21:12, 20–21 (JE), which, however, enjoins humanitarian provisions for injuries to slaves, even if they are not Israelites. H, though, prescribes talion for all human beings, including non-Israelites under its jurisdiction, namely, the gēr (Lev 24:21; see above).

2. In ancient Near Eastern talion, intention is essentially irrelevant. In other words, there is no excuse for the loss of limb or life since it is so costly (R. Gane). To be sure, the abstract formulation of biblical talion also omits any concession for inadvertence. However, since the principle of intention operates in all statements of the law of homicide (Exod 21:12–13; Num 35:11–12, 22–25; Deut 19:2–10), it must presume to prevail in the laws of talion. Nonetheless, it is hardly an accident that the priestly laws for homicide apply the talion principle to unintentional homicide—not by the death of the offender, but by the natural death of the high priest (Num 35:25)—a symbolic talion that exacts "life for life." The question remains: If talion is applicable for only intentional homicide, is it also applicable for only intentional injuries? Although the text is silent, it must be presumed. It would be hard to believe that the priestly legists, who go to great lengths to establish that inadvertence operates in wrongs committed against God (see discussion on šĕgāgâ and the 'āšām sacrifice for fraud, NOTES on 4:2; 5:20–26, and vol. 1.373–78)—the same God who exacts punishment by talion—would not also insist on limiting talion to cases of deliberate injuries and allow for monetary compensation in cases of accidental injuries. However, with textual evidence lacking, my argument remains a hypothesis.

3. Biblical law rejects vicarious talion. For example, in Mesopotamia someone responsible for the death of a citizen's son or daughter has his son or daughter put to death (CH §§ 116, 210, 230; MAL §§ 50–52; contrast Exod 21:31; Deut 24:16). The death of the high priest, however, which releases unintentional homicides from their respective city asylums (Num 35:25), is not vicarious talion. The high priest is not executed but dies a natural death, and his death provides amnesty for all unintentional homicides in the land.

The upshot is that the talion formula in the ancient Near East is to be understood literally. Was it ever carried out? The Bible cites one incident: when Adoni-bezek had his thumbs and big toes cut off by his Judahite captors, he said "As I have done, so God has requited me" (Judg 1:6–7). But this act was a consequence of war. Was it also carried out by the court? It is hardly likely, to judge by the rabbinic discussion on this subject (see COMMENT C).

For additional treatments of talion, see Daube (1947: 102–53); Alt (1972), Jackson (1973), Brauner (1974), Loewenstamm (1977), Frymer-Kensky (1980), Fisher (1982), and Hayes (1982: 8–13).

C. Lex Talionis *and the Rabbis*

The rabbis, who unanimously declare that all injuries (but not death) inflicted on persons are subject to compensation, are clearly troubled by Lev 24, as the following talmudic discussions illustrate (translations mainly by Ackerman [1992] and Zohar [1991]; boldface is biblical verse; italic, baraita):

Why [monetary compensation]? God said "**An eye for an eye**" (Exod 21:24). Why not take this literally? Not so, since it has been taught: *Is it the case that where he put out his (another's) eye, we put out his (the offender's) eye, or where* *he cut off his arm, we cut off his arm, or where he broke his leg, we break his leg? [Not so, for] Torah states:* **One who strikes a human being . . . but one who strikes an animal . . .** (Lev 24:18, 21) *[teaching that] just as in the case of striking an animal compensation is to be paid, so in the case of striking a man compensation is to be paid. And should this [source] not satisfy you, note that the Torah states:* **You may not accept ransom for the life of a murderer who is guilty of a capital crime; he must be put to death** (Num 35:31) *[teaching that] it is only for the life of a murderer that you may not take ransom, whereas you may take ransom for principal limbs that do not restore themselves.*

To what [two textual instances of] **strikes** does it (the baraita) refer? Should you say [that it refers] to **One who strikes an animal shall make restitution for it, but one who strikes a human being shall be put to death** (Lev 24:21), this verse refers [not to injury] but to murder. The reference must therefore be to this text **Anyone who strikes a beast shall make restitution for it, life for life** (Lev 24:18), which is immediately followed by **If anyone maims another, as he has done so shall it be done to him** (v. 19). But [the term] **strikes** is not used [in the latter text]? The baraita is comparing [not the term but the] juxtaposition of striking: Just as the "striking" mentioned in the case of an animal entails monetary payment, so too does the striking of a man entail monetary payment.

But surely is it not written **If anyone kills a human being, he shall be put to death** (v. 17)? This refers to monetary compensation. On what grounds [do you take it to refer] to monetary compensation? Why not say that it really means capital punishment? Not so; first, because it is immediately followed by **Anyone who kills an animal shall make restitution for it** (v. 18), which refers to monetary payment; and furthermore, because soon after it is written **as he has done so shall it be done to him** (v. 19), thus proving that it (**so shall it be done**) means monetary compensation. (*b. B. Qam.* 83b)

The exegetical convolutions exhibited in this exposition, whereby *yakkeh* 'kills' is forced to mean "strikes," though the death penalty is invoked (v. 21) and death in v. 21 is forced to mean compensation, betray the troubled rabbinic conscience concerning talion. This is a true case where "the halakha supplants Scripture" (*b. Sota* 16a) or, in Rashi's more vivid metaphor, "the halakha crushes the scriptural text under heel and overthrows it" (*b. Sota* 16a; cf. *y. Qid.* 1:2, 59α)—and the rabbis were well aware of it.

In an engaging symposium on rabbinic talion, Zohar (1991: 51) is probably right in stating that the rabbis "tended toward a dualistic picture, identifying the Divine Image in humans as pertaining to the soul or spirit. . . . 'Mere' bodily-injuries are categorized with damages to animals, not involving an affront to human but as valuable by market standards." Enker (1991: 55), however, goes too far in claiming that the roots of the rabbinic view lie in biblical terminology, namely, that "the primary text calling for talion for physical injuries (*'ayin tachat 'ayin*) has deliberately chosen a phrasing that is susceptible of more than one meaning . . . the biblical corpus . . . is not a modern legal text. It is a literary document that conveys multiple levels of meaning and application." True, the word *tahat* may possess other meanings (BDB), but in no way can it be construed to refer to compensation. More important, a legal term cannot be ambiguous. Imagine leaving the law to the subjective exegesis of every judge!

Nonetheless, it is hard to believe that strict talion (except for murder) was anything but legal theory. It is plainly impossible to execute talion with absolute equality. This is precisely how the rabbis reason:

> R. Simeon b. Yohai says: **Eye for eye** means monetary compensation. You say monetary compensation, but perhaps it is not so, but actual talion is meant? What then will you say where a blind man put out the eye of another man, or where a cripple cut off the hand of another, or where a lame person broke the leg of another? How can I carry out in this case **eye for eye**, seeing that the Torah says, **You shall have one law** (Lev 24:22), implying that the manner of law should be the same in all cases? . . .
>
> The school of Hizkiah taught: **Eye for eye, life for life** (Exod 21:24) but not "life and eye for eye." Now if you assume that actual talion is meant, it could sometimes happen that while the offender is being blinded, his life might depart from him. (*b. B. Qam.* 84a)

The rabbis' logic is better than their exegesis. Nor did they have to wait for Shakespeare's Portia to concoct their argument. (The irony is that Shylock would have been well aware of the rabbis' views.) Moreover, they surely did not originate it. It must have been the primary experience of jurists (not legists!) over the ages that talion in cases of personal injury was not only impracticable, but unjust. In other words, in such cases the very retributive equality that forms the basis of talion is totally vitiated. Indeed, since compensation was actually practiced in the ancient Near East from earliest times, it is likely that it was practiced in the courts of Israel also from earliest times.

In sum, what we have represented in the biblical formulation of the talion law is theory not practice, the work of legists not jurists. Nonetheless, the plain meaning of the text cannot be altered: literal talion is intended, but it probably did not take long, especially in the centralized government of Israel's monarchy, for talion to be interpreted as compensation. Why, then, was the talion formula retained? Perhaps the answer lies with Rabbi A. Karelitz (known as Hazon 'Ish) who is reputed to have said: "The intention is to teach the punishment [i.e., talion] in order to instill in the hearts of the people appreciation of the evil, and to this end it is proper to adopt a strong phrasing" (cited in S. Cohen 1970: 139, n. 30).

Thus it turns out that the pentateuchal codes prescribe talion in only three cases: the woman who, intervening in a brawl, seizes a man's private parts (Deut 25:11–12), the perjured witness (Deut 19:16–21), and murder (Deut 19:21). The last is also stipulated in Gen 9:6; Exod 21:23–25; Lev 24:19–20; and Num 35:33, but I have singled out the deuteronomic citation to indicate that all three cases are found in a single source: D.

This fact only accentuates a long-standing crux: Why doesn't D also apply talion in the case of the bride accused of infidelity (Deut 22:13–21)? Note the circumstances: if the husband's charge is validated, his bride is put to death; if his
charge is proved false, he pays a fine (to his father-in-law) and may never divorce
his wife. Is this not a case where talion should be applied? He has been proved to
be a false "witness" whose testimony, if validated, would have resulted in her execution. Why, then, is not talion exacted against him, calling for his execution?

The answer, I suggest, lies in the respectively different background of each
case. The unfaithful bride is judged at the town gate by the community's elders;
the false witness testifies in a court. Only the court can impose an oath; no oath
is taken in the proceedings against the accused bride. The result is that the false
witness has committed not only perjury, but also blasphemy. He has sinned
against God, and God exacts his punishment measure for measure—his law of
talion.

One must deal separately with the cases of the suspected adulteress (see also
Num 5:11–31) and the woman who grasps a man's genitals, on the one hand.
Domestic issues such as these belong in the domain of customary law handled
by communal elders. False witness and murder, on the other hand, fall in the
province of the court. Since in Deuteronomy, the court is a federally regulated
institution (Deut 16:18; 17:8–12), the same legal postulate must undergird both
cases; it can only be that they are sins against God. In the instance of murder,
the image of YHWH has been destroyed, and YHWH has decreed:

*ûmiyyad hā'ādām miyyad 'îš 'āḥîw 'edrōš 'et-nepeš hā'ādām šōpēk dam
hā'ādām bā'ādām dāmô yiššāpēk kî běṣelem 'ělōhîm bārā' 'et-hā'ādām*

Of man, too, of every man his fellow man, will I require a reckoning for human life. Whoever sheds the blood of man for that man shall his blood be
shed; for in the image of God he created man. (Gen 9:5b–6)

This passage is part of the P corpus, but its postulate informs all of biblical law
(vol. 1.705). In the instance of the false witness, as explained, he has testified
under oath, the penalty for which is death (vol. 1.368). In each case, the court
acts as the divine agent to carry out the punishment.

One objection has to be faced. There is no evidence in the Bible that a witness was adjured. Where evidence was lacking, the litigants themselves were
subjected to an oath: *šěbu'at YHWH tihyeh bên šěnêhem* 'an oath to YHWH
shall decide between the two of them' (Exod 22:10; cf. v. 8; Lev 5:22, 24). Conflicting witnesses are, in a real sense, no different from conflicting litigants. To
be sure, the court thoroughly investigated the matter (Deut 19:18), but it is only
logical to assume that it employed the exculpatory oath as part of its investiga-
tory arsenal. Moreover, if a court could impose an imprecation on an entire
community to force reluctant witnesses to testify (see NOTE on 5:1), does it not
stand to reason that it had equal power to impose an oath on reluctant witnesses
in order to force them to tell the truth?

Furthermore, Mesopotamian law does cite cases where witnesses were adjured. The one case involving witnesses in CH (§ 9) reads: "the witnesses in whose presence the purchase was made, along with the witnesses attesting to the lost (property), shall declare what they know in the presence of god." Here, too, we have a case of conflicting witnesses, and the text states explicitly that their testimony is given "in the presence of god"—that is, under oath. That witnesses were expected to testify under oath seems to be taken for granted in Mesopotamian jurisprudence, to judge by this statement from the laws of Ur-nammu, thus far the oldest Mesopotamian code: "If a man appeared as a witness (in a lawsuit), but declined to testify on oath, he must make good as much as is involved in that lawsuit" (B § 35). What is of additional interest is that here, too, we presumably have a case of a false witness, who, as in the Bible, is punished by talion.

To recapitulate: it must be assumed that conflicting witnesses—if not every witness—were put under oath. Thus a perjured witness was punished by talion because he had sinned against God. Domestic cases, such as the suspected unfaithful bride, involved no oath, and hence talion could not be exacted against her husband.

Finally, I append the rabbis' definition of compensation, which reveals their sensitivity to the psychological as well as material damage caused by injury (translation mainly by Ackerman and Zohar).

> One who injures his fellow becomes liable to him for five items: for depreciation, for pain, for healing, for loss of time, and for degradation. How is it with "depreciation"? If he put out his eye, cut off his arm, or broke his leg, we consider him (the injured person) as if he were a slave being sold in the market place, and valuation is made as to how much he was worth [previously], and how much he is worth [now]. "Pain"—if he burned him either with a spit or with a nail, even though on his [finger]nail, which is a place no bruise forms, we estimate how much a man similar to him would want to be paid to undergo such pain. "Healing"—if he has struck him, he is under obligation to heal him. Should ulcers [meanwhile] arise, if as a result of the wound, he (the offender) is liable, but if not as a result of the wound, he is exempt. When the wound was healed and reopened, he is still under obligation to heal him. If, however, it had completely healed, [and subsequently reopened], he is not obligated to heal him. "Loss of time"—we consider him (the injured person] as if he were a watchman of cucumbers (a simple task), for he (the offender) has already given the value of his hand or the value of his leg (under "depreciation"). "Degradation"—is figured entirely according to who is offended and who causes the offense. (m. B. Qam. 8:1)

D. Lev 24:10–23: Apostasy in H (Simeon Chavel)

The pericope conforms to the literary motif found in all the pentateuchal sources, that Israel commits apostasy during the Sinai/Horeb theophany. In each source, the apostasy depicted reflects the definitive aspect of that source's theology (Chavel 1998: 16–21). Although not a narrative source, H, too, felt impelled to offer a paradigmatic tale of apostasy. In line with H's larger program of supplementation and re-emphasis with regard to P, H presents a counterpart to P's story of Nadab and Abihu (9:23–10:2).

The average Israelite has at his disposal essentially two ways of approaching YHWH: sacrifice, in the tight professional grip of the trained priests, and prayer, available to anyone and everyone, in any place, at any time (see Greenberg 1983). Against P's technical cultic story about the holiest priests violating the holiest sacrifice in the holy center of the camp, H depicts a marginal, anonymous Israelite of questionable pedigree and dubious religious culture, let alone lack of genuine training, attacking YHWH in some unspecified part of the camp with the power of his human voice alone (cf. Netziv 1959: 207). Whereas paradigmatic apostasy in P requires specific circumstances to reflect the camp hierarchy that defines P's viewpoint, in H, which re-emphasizes the religious significance of life outside the cult proper, paradigmatic apostasy requires no special circumstances at all—anyone, anywhere, anytime, with the most prosaic of religious mediums and paraphernalia (see further Chavel 1998: 21–26).

The legal bloc in vv. 17–21 gives poignant expression to the extreme nature of the apostasy: the criminal cursing YHWH intends not merely to insult him, "blasphemy", but to kill him (cf. OED 1971: 1.904, s.v. blasphemy; 1.1273, s.v. curse). The bloc constitutes a palistrophe: 17 = A, 18 = B, 19 = C, 20a = D, 20b = C', 21a = B', 21b = A'. Emphasizing especially the first, middle, and last stichoi, the palistrophe points to the principle of talion as the determinative factor in the punishment for murder. The invaluable nature of human life and the cosmic imbalance ensuing upon its unjust loss demand extreme redress: measure for measure, life for life (Diamond 1957; Greenberg 1960; Finkelstein 1961; 1981; cf. Chavel 1998: 28–9). One cannot pin down the specific author's role in formulating and shaping the bloc, but the *'îš kî* formulations (vv. 17, 19) and the abbreviated repetitions (vv. 20b–21) bear the distinctive priestly imprint; the palistrophic structure and seven-eight scheme (17–21 + 22) conform to H's stylistic predilections; and the equality of the *gēr* likewise marks a typical H concern. In any event, juxtaposing this bloc with the laws against cursing YHWH depicts such venting as attempted deicide and comments on its capital punishment as most fitting; if attacking the *ṣelem 'ĕlōhîm* brings retribution in kind, so must attacking *'ĕlōhîm* himself.

The proper diagram of the legal half of the pericope (vv. 13–23), then, should not present the simple, but extended palistrophe commonly drawn (ABCDEFGHG'F'E'D'C'B'A'), which in any case has a major flaw in that it correlates the all-important laws against cursing YHWH (vv. 15–16, D), because of their curt nod at the equality of the *gēr* (*kaggēr kā'ezrāh*, v. 16), with the fuller expression of that thematically marginal principle (v. 22, D'). Instead, the diagram should align the palistrophic damage laws (vv. 17–21 + 22a) and the linearly ordered laws against cursing YHWH (vv. 15–16) *alongside* each other as twin foci—human and divine—in the pericope (cf. Netziv 1959: 207). Each of these blocs closes with a formula regarding the equality of the *gēr* (on v. 16, see below), as in so many other laws throughout the priestly writings, and both share a single coda, H's signature to the entire set of laws, "for I YHWH your god (have spoken)" (v. 22b). This complex unit—structurally parallel and thematically analogous blocs of laws + signature coda (vv. 15b–22)—constitutes the structural and thematic center of the palistrophic narrative frame comprised of vv. 13–15a and 23 (ABCC'B'A').

    A. And YHWH spoke to Moses, saying (13):
        B. Take the blasphemer outside the camp, and have all who heard lean their hands on his head; then have the whole community pelt him with stones (14).
        C. And to the Israelites speak thus (15a):

I. If any man curse <his> God, he shall bear his sin (15b).	α. If anyone kill a human being, he shall surely be put to death (17);
II. a. Whoever pronounces the name YHWH shall surely be put to death;	β. Whoever kills an animal shall make restitution for it, life for life (18);
b. The whole community shall stone him, alien as well as citizen;	γ. If anyone maims his fellow, as he has done so shall be done to him (19):
a'. For pronouncing the name [YHWH], he shall be put to death (16).	δ. Fracture for fracture, eye for eye, tooth for tooth (20a);
	γ' As the injury he has inflicted on the person so shall be inflicted upon him (20b);
	β'. Whoever kills an animal shall make restitution for it (21a);
	a'. Whoever kills a human being shall be put to death (21b).

                              You shall have one law for the alien and citizen alike (22a)
                FOR I YHWH your God (have spoken) (22b).

        C'. Moses spoke (thus) to the Israelites (23aα);
      B'. So they took the blasphemer outside the camp and pelted him with stones (23aβ);
    A'. The Israelites did as YHWH had commanded Moses (23b).

The complicated structure and the way its various parts interact to give meaning to each other and to the pericope as a whole exemplify H's consummate skill as a manipulator of diverse materials in the shaping of a literary unit, as a composer of text. It does have one fault, though, not having formulated the two laws against cursing God in some symmetric or parallel manner. In fact, a number of indications signal that H has taken two laws originally from two different contexts and brought them together on account of their thematic similarity (cf. Gerstenberger 1996: 362–65).

The law of cursing God depends on its predecessor in the Covenant Code (Exod 22:27; Bertholet 1901: 84; Paran 1989: 29–40 brings additional examples), where the parallelism between '*rr* and *qll* (Noth 1962: 187) settles it that *qll* there and here means "curse," not "insult." H recast the classical apodictic form in the casuistic form unique to priestly drafting, '*îš* '*îš kî* + imperfect (Lev 15:2; Num 5:12; 9:10; cf. Lev 17:3, 8, 10, 13; 18:6; 20:2, 9; 22:18; Ezek 14:4, 7), and added the priestly expression of general responsibility, *wĕnāśā' ḥeṭ'ô*. Precisely because the previous, apodictic law did not specify a punishment, the priestly author added only a broad expression, even though it normally has a specific meaning (on which see Schwartz 1995a); contrast the law of cursing one's parents (Lev 20:9) which can specify capital punishment because its predecessor did (Exod 21:17). Other examples of the general expression serving to fill this lacuna caused by the reuse of texts that did not specify consequence include Lev 5:1 (cf. Prov 29:24; vol. 1.293–297, esp. 1.314–315); 17:15–16 (a reaction to 11:39–40, but see also 22:8 and Deut 14:21); and 19:17 (cf. Prov 10:18; 26:26; 27:5).

The chiastic shape of the law against pronouncing YHWH's name indicates that it, too, has undergone revision. The original form, whose provenance remains buried in the past, stated simply, *wĕnōqēb šēm YHWH môt yûmāt* (16aα; cf. Exod 21:12, 15–17; 22:17–18) 'Whoever pronounces the name YHWH shall surely be put to death' (*nqb* = 'pronounce, designate'; see Num 1:17; Isa 62:2; Amos 6:1; Ezra 8:20; 1 Chr 12:32; 16:41; 2 Chr 28:15; 31:19). To this original law against pronouncing YHWH's name, H added communal stoning (16aβ), the equality of the *gēr* (16bα), and an enclosing repetitive resumption that stresses the responsibility of the sinner for his punishment, *bĕnoqbô šēm [YHWH] yûmāt* 'for pronouncing the name [YHWH] he shall be put to death' (16bβ, with causal *bet*; chiastic repetition works to similar effect in 20:9, which, too, revises a previous law [Exod 21:17], and in Gen 9:6, which, too, employs causal *bet* as the syntactic hinge of the chiasm).

In its original provenance, the bald form of the law against pronouncing YHWH's name most likely referred neither, at one pole, to cursing YHWH proper, nor, at the other, simply to pronouncing his name; it probably envisioned a specific set of circumstances somewhere in between. It is impossible to reconstruct with certainty the presumed context, but the situation in ancient Sumer may provide a lead. Sumerians believed in the power of the name of Utu, the sun-god and the god of justice, such that a person caught in a hopeless predicament would utter the name, which would magically bring deliverance. However, such utterances were fraught with danger; with deliverance often came disaster. Subsequent law, therefore, prohibited them (Jacobsen 1976: 134, 212).

A story about Elisha points to a similar, biblical conception of YHWH's name as magical and dangerous. Elisha curses youths insulting him (LXX: pelting him with stones) over his baldness *bĕšēm YHWH* 'with the name YHWH' (2 Kgs 2:23–24). The common explanation that Elisha prayed to YHWH to avenge his honor and YHWH responded with children-eating bears to teach unruly youths some respect for their elders is simply untenable. Rather, out of sheer frustration born of his sensitivity to the fact that prophets and saviors such as Samson (Judg 13:5; 16:4–30), Samuel (1 Sam 1:11), and especially his mentor Elijah (2 Kgs 1:8) sported the telltale wild mane of hair while he goes bald, Elisha lashes out with a magical utterance. A later incarnation of the cursing and utterance laws in the Community Rule found at Qumran poses, "And if he cursed or *pronounced out of alarm* . . . " (sheet 7 lines 1–2; Licht 1965: 160; cf. other possible examples in Chavel 1998: 39–40).

Although, practically and theologically, cursing and pronouncing as described here differ from each other, phenomenologically and sociologically, they resemble each other quite closely. For this reason, presumably, the author of the pericope brought them together. The different styles of revision signal that the author received them already in their recast forms.

Overshadowing the stylistic asymmetry, the juxtaposition of the laws amounts to an editorial, hermeneutic tour de force in which the two laws depend on each other for clarification and meaning. On one hand, the context of the law against cursing God supersedes and redefines its counterpart, the deleterious use of YHWH's name; on the other, the law of pronunciation delimits the vague law of cursing. The effect, manifest in the framing narrative, takes the two laws together as one unit envisioning only one case: cursing YHWH while pronouncing his name for which one incurs the death penalty. In this view, "bearing sin" anticipates death by stoning (Snaith 1969: 110; Weingreen 1972: 121 n. 2; cf. Ehrlich 1968: 2.88; note the contradictory Sabbath laws similarly juxtaposed in Exod 31:14bα and 14bβ and resolved in v. 15 through conflated reformulation; cf. Lev 20:2–3). Having accepted the implications of the pericope in Lev 24, the later Naboth story (1 Kgs 21) employs only the root *qll* and takes for granted the punishment of stoning (cf. Rofé 1988: 300–302).

The climactic role of the laws in the pericope aims at providing an additional dimension to H's version of the theophany and apostasy pattern. Apostasy in each source raises a crucial problem: how can Israel survive in close proximity to YHWH's demanding presence? Infraction brings swift and broad, even indiscriminate punishment, but human beings are doomed to sin. P offers YHWH's patience as a solution (like J and E; details in Chavel 1998: 18), but expresses it, characteristically, through the cult (note the narrative causality asserted by 16:1). Impressions of impurity and sin, blemishes in essence, will accrue in the Tabernacle for the duration of a year without drawing fire; at year's end, the high priest will perform a ritual that will wipe away the impressions and heal the blemishes, sustaining YHWH's presence (Lev 16). H, too, addresses this issue, indicating that by stoning the sinner in fulfillment of YHWH's word, by the human administration of religious as well as secular justice, even to the ultimate degree of capital punishment (contrast Num 35 H with Gen 9:5–6 P; cf. Fokkelman 1975: 35; vol. 1.705), Israel can ensure YHWH's forebearance, sympathy, and perpetual residence. Again, H reacts particularly to P. P's ritual solution clears the blemishes from the Tabernacle by removing them to the scapegoat through hand leaning and sending the animal out of the camp to the wilderness, where presumably it will die at the hands of nature, i.e., YHWH (16:21–22). H's judicial solution clears the air through hand leaning and taking the sinner out of the camp, where, at the hands of the community, he will surely die (24:14, 23).

Only H lays this much stress on the place of law and its human execution in Israel's relationship with YHWH, exemplifying H's appreciation for the active role human beings have in their relationship with God. Indeed, the analogy between homicide and cursing YHWH established by the juxtaposition of the two blocs of law in vv. 15–21 and by the consequent application of talion conceives of YHWH, legally speaking, in human terms, namely, as subject to human conception of law and justice.

This understanding of H's conception and use of law in the pericope illuminates the unique cross-generic weave of the pericope. Not only does H establish the administration of law as the medium sustaining YHWH's close relationship with Israel where the other versions had not (P offers a ritual solution not a legal, judicial one), but law plays a critical role structurally and interpretively. Remove the law and the story hangs in abeyance robbed of climax, conclusion, and coherence; strip the law of its narrative and the law loses its drama, vitality, and much of its conceptual power. This interdependence ultimately expresses H's conception of the constitution and sustenance of Israel's identity on several levels. In terms of Israel's proximity to YHWH, without the law—without YHWH's law—and so without fulfillment of that law, there can be no permanent, safe relationship between Israel and YHWH. Sociologically speaking, without a hallowed tradition no judge can properly decide cases, leaving the community without the self-definition and affirmation that justice normally brings. In the pericope's terms, without YHWH's law, the story—Israel's story— stop dead in tracks, no resolution, no identity, no future. Only through the ongoing, dynamic interweaving of YHWH's law with Israel's story can Israel assure itself of a meaningful future.

25. JUBILEE, THE PRIESTLY SOLUTION FOR ECONOMIC INJUSTICE

TRANSLATION

Introduction

[1]YHWH spoke to Moses at Mount Sinai: [2]Speak to the Israelites and say to them:

The Sabbatical Year

When you enter the land that I give you, the land shall observe a sabbath to YHWH. [3]Six years you may sow your field, and six years you may prune your vineyard and gather in its produce. [4]But in the seventh year there shall be a sabbath of complete rest for the land, a sabbath to YHWH; you may neither sow your field nor prune your vineyard. [5]The aftergrowth of your harvest you shall not reap, nor the grapes of your untrimmed vines shall you pick; it shall be (a year of) complete rest for the land. [6]But the sabbath (-yield) of the land will be for you to eat: for you, for your male and female slaves, your resident hirelings, who live under your authority, [7]your livestock and the wild animals in your land—all of its yield will be (available for you) to eat.

The Jubilee Year

[8]You shall count for yourself seven weeks of years—seven times seven years— so that the period of seven weeks of years gives you (a total of) forty-nine years. [9]Then you shall sound the horn loud; in the seventh month, on the tenth day of the month—the Day of Purgation—you shall have the horn sounded throughout your land, [10]and you shall sanctify the fiftieth year, proclaiming release throughout the land for all its inhabitants. It shall be a jubilee for you, when each of you shall return to his holding and each of you shall return to his kin group. [11]That fiftieth year shall be a jubilee for you; you shall not sow, nor shall you reap its aftergrowth or pick its untrimmed vines. [12]Since it is a jubilee, sacred it shall be to you; you may only eat its produce (direct) from the field. [13]In this year of jubilee, each of you shall return to his holding.

[14]When you sell property to your fellow, or buy (any) from your fellow, you shall not cheat one another. [15]On the basis of the number of years since the jubilee shall you buy from your fellow; on the basis of the number of (remaining) crop years shall he sell to you; [16]the more such years, the more its purchase price; the fewer such years, the less its purchase price; for it is the number of crops that he is selling you. [17]Do not cheat one another, but fear your God; for I YHWH am your God.

[18]You shall perform my laws, and my rules you shall heed and you shall perform them, that you may dwell on the land in security. [19]The land shall yield its fruit and you shall eat your fill, and you shall dwell upon it in security. [20]And should you say, "What are we to eat in the seventh year, if we may not sow or gather in our crops?" [21]I will ordain my blessing for you in the sixth year, so that it will yield a crop (sufficient) for three years. [22]When you sow (in) the eighth year, you will (continue to) eat from the old crop; until the ninth year, until its crop comes in, you shall eat the old.

Redemption of Property: The Basic Principle

[23]Furthermore, the land must not be sold beyond reclaim, for the land is mine; you are but resident aliens under my authority. [24]Therefore, throughout the land you hold, you must provide redemption for the land.

The Three Stages of Destitution

Stage One: Sold Land and Houses and Their Redemption

²⁵When your brother (Israelite) becomes impoverished and has to sell part of his holding, his closest redeemer shall come and redeem the sold property of his brother. ²⁶If a man has no redeemer but prospers and acquires enough for his redemption, ²⁷he shall compute the years since its sale, refund the difference to the man to whom he sold it, and return to his holding. ²⁸If he does not acquire sufficient means to recover it, his sold property shall remain with its buyer until the jubilee year; it shall be released in the jubilee, and he shall return to his holding.

²⁹If a man sells a dwelling house (in) a walled city, it may be redeemed until the end of a year of its sale; its redemption period shall be a year. ³⁰If it is not redeemed before the completion of one full year, the house in the walled city shall belong to its purchaser beyond reclaim throughout the ages; it shall not be released in the jubilee. ³¹However, houses in hamlets that have no encircling walls shall be classed as open country; they may be redeemed, and in the jubilee they shall be released. ³²As for the Levitic cities—the houses in the cities they hold—the Levites shall forever have the right of redemption. ³³Whoever of the Levites redeems (should know that) the house sold (in) the city of his possession shall be released in the jubilee; for the houses in the cities of the Levites are their holding among the Israelites. ³⁴But the field of the livestock enclosures (about) their cities may not be sold, for that is their holding forever.

Stage Two: Lost Land

³⁵If your brother, being (further) impoverished, falls under your authority, and you (would) hold him (as though he were) a resident alien, let him subsist under your authority. ³⁶Do not exact from him advance or accrued interest. Fear your God, and let your brother subsist under your authority. ³⁷Do not lend him money at advance interest, or lend him food at accrued interest. ³⁸I, YHWH, am your God, who freed you from the land of Egypt, to give you the land of Canaan, to be your God.

Stage Three: "Slavery"

³⁹If your brother, being (further) impoverished under your authority, is sold to you, do not make him work as a slave. ⁴⁰He shall remain under you as a resident hireling; he shall work under you until the jubilee year. ⁴¹Then he and his children with him shall be released from your authority; he shall return to his kin group and return to his ancestral holding.—⁴²For they are my slaves, whom I freed from the land of Egypt; they shall not be sold as slaves are sold.—⁴³You shall not rule over him with harshness; you shall fear your God.

⁴⁴Male and female slaves as you may have—(it is) from the nations around about you, from them that you may buy male and female slaves. ⁴⁵Also from among the children of residents (aliens) who live under your sway, from them

you may buy (slaves), or from their kin groups that are under your sway, whom they begot in your land. These shall become your property; [46]you may keep them as a possession for your children after you, for them to inherit as property for all time. These you may treat as slaves, but as for your Israelite brothers, no one shall rule over the other with harshness.

[47]If a resident alien under you has prospered, and your brother, being (further) impoverished, comes under his authority and is sold to the resident alien under you, or to a branch of the alien's kin group, [48]after he is sold he shall have the right of redemption. One of his brothers shall redeem him, [49]or his uncle or his uncle's son shall redeem him, or anyone of his kin group who is of his own flesh shall redeem him; or if he prospers, he may redeem himself. [50]He shall compute with his buyer the total from the year he was sold to him until the jubilee year: the price of his sale shall be applied to the number of years, as the term of a hired laborer he shall be under the other's authority. [51]If many years remain, he shall pay back (for) his redemption in proportion to his purchase price; [52]and if few years remain until the jubilee year, he shall so compute; according to the years involved, he shall pay back (for) his redemption. [53]As a worker hired by the year shall he be under his (the alien's) authority, who (however) shall not rule over him with harshness in your sight. [54]If he has not been redeemed in any of these ways, he and his children with him shall go free in the jubilee year. [55]For it is to me the Israelites are slaves. They are my slaves whom I freed from the land of Egypt. I am YHWH your God.

Comments

The background of the jubilee, COMMENT A; the observance of the sabbatical and jubilee, COMMENTS B and C; the slave laws of Lev 25, Exod 21, and Deut 15, COMMENTS D and E; evidence for the observance of the jubilee, COMMENT F; and the contemporary relevance of the jubilee, COMMENT G.

NOTES

Lev 25 can be outlined as follows:

Introduction (vv. 1–2aα)
A. The laws of the sabbatical and jubilee years (vv. 2aβ–22)
   1. The sabbatical year (vv. 2aβ–7)
      a. The basic regulation (v. 2aβ, b)
      b. Explication of the regulation (vv. 3–7)
         (1) Normal agricultural activity for six years (v. 3)
         (2) Rest from agricultural activity during the seventh year (vv. 4–7)
   2. The jubilee year (vv. 8–22)
      a. The basic regulation (vv. 8–13)
         (1) The calendar (v. 8)

(2) The proclamation (vv. 9–10)
(3) The explication (vv. 11–13)
  b. Leasing of land and the jubilee (vv. 14–19)
    (1) Regulations about leasing of land (vv. 14–17)
    (2) Prohibition and exhortation (vv. 18–19)
  c. Assuaging the people's concerns (vv. 20–22)
B. The laws of redeeming property (vv. 23–34)
  1. The basic principle (vv. 23–24)
  2. Explication of the principle (vv. 25–34)
    a. Redemption of a patrimony (vv. 25–28)
    b. The sale of houses (vv. 29–31)
      (1) Permitted in a walled city (vv. 29–30)
      (2) Prohibited in an unwalled city (v. 31)
    c. The sale of the property of Levites (vv. 32–34)
C. The indebted Israelite who lost his land (vv. 35–38)
  1. The basic principle (v. 35)
  2. The prohibition against charging interest (vv. 36–37)
  3. The rationale (v. 38)
D. The Israelite debt-slave (vv. 39–55)
  1. The basic principle (vv. 39–43)
    a. A resident hireling, not a slave (vv. 39–40a)
    b. Release at the jubilee (vv. 40b–41)
    c. The rationale (vv. 42–43)
  2. Aside on Israelites' holding of slaves (vv. 44–46)
  3. An Israelite debt-slave held by a resident alien (vv. 47–54)
    a. Must be redeemed (vv. 47–49)
    b. Setting the redemption price (vv. 50–52)
    c. Standard of treatment (v. 53)
    d. Guaranteed release at the jubilee (v. 54)
  4. The rationale (v. 55)

Scholars disagree widely on the development of Lev 25. For example, Reventlow (1961: 347–49) holds that originally independent units have been combined; Kilian (1963: 130ff) finds four chronological stages of development; and Elliger (1966: 347–49) argues that there are as many as eight. Fager (1987: 88–89) atomizes this chapter into five strata: an independent sabbath law, a debt-sale law, a redaction of the jubilee law, an initial priestly redaction, and a later priestly redaction (reconstruction in Fager 1993: 123–25), and Sun (1990: 439–559) claims to have unearthed three discernible layers: the oldest cast in 2ms form (vv. *3–7, 15–16, 25–34, 35–37, 39–43, 47–54), probably of post-deuteronomic date; the second cast in 2mp form; and tertiary additions (in vv. 11–13). Noth (1977: 181–93), conceding that Lev 25 is composed of heterogeneous materials, is of the opinion that it is no longer possible to identify the separable stages of growth. Among the commentaries, neither Wenham (1979) nor Levine (1989) even attempts a compositional analysis.

I shall follow the last position, not because the identification of the literary strata is too difficult, but because the search for them—if they exist at all—is meaningless. The chapter, as is, flows logically and coherently. Even if the redactor had different sources before him, he welded them together in such an artistic and cogent sequence that it suffices to determine what he had in mind. This view is echoed in rabbinic literature:

> R. Samuel the son of Gedaliah said: There is no unit in the Torah whose opening subject is not followed by its substantiation. How does it (chap. 25) begin? "The Lord spoke to Moses . . . the Land shall rest . . ." (vv. 1–7). It is followed by the subject of the jubilee, "You shall count for yourself seven weeks of years . . ." (vv. 8–13). If he has not observed the sabbaticals and jubilees, he ultimately will sell his movables, "when you sell [i.e. lease] your property . . ." (vv. 14–23). If he repents [i.e. changes his ways], fine; if not, he ultimately will sell his land, "When your brother (Israelite) becomes impoverished and has to sell part of his holding . . ." (vv. 25–28). If he repents, fine; if not, he ultimately will sell his house, "If a man sells a dwelling house . . ." (vv. 29–34). If he repents, fine; if not, he ultimately will go begging, "If your brother, being (further) impoverished, falls under your authority . . ." (vv. 35–38). If he repents, fine; if not, he ultimately will sell himself to you, "If your brother being (further) impoverished under your authority, is sold to you . . ." (vv. 39–46). If he repents, fine; if not, he will ultimately sell himself to the gentile, "If the resident alien under your authority has prospered, and your brother, being (further) impoverished, comes under his authority and is sold over to the resident alien . . ." (vv. 47–55), not only he himself but (ultimately) all of Israel. (*Midr. Tanḥ.* B.2).

What makes this sequence so compelling is that it reveals both the logic of the chapter's order and its underlying theology. For example, with one stroke, it solves the problem of why the pericope on houses was placed in its present spot (vv. 29–34), and it settles the question of why the series of successive impoverishments *wĕkî-yāmûk* (vv. 25–55) follows the jubilee law (vv. 8–24), which is applied in case a landowner is forced to sell his property. Indeed, this midrash perceptively recognizes that the selling here is, in fact, leasing, since he is selling only his movables—that is, his usufruct. The proof text for the final stage, affecting "all of Israel," is 2 Chr 36:21 (not cited here) attributing the seventy-year Babylonian Exile *'ad-rāṣĕtâ hā'āreṣ 'et-šabtôtêhā kol-yĕmê hoššammâ šābātâ* 'until the land paid back its sabbaths; during all the time it lay waste it rested'. This verse, however, is clearly modeled after Lev 26:34a; perhaps the midrash had Lev 26 in mind. For then it would also explain the juxtaposition of chaps. 25 and 26, unified as they are by the mention of the sabbatical year and their attribution to the revelation on Mount Sinai (25:1; 26:46). The inclusio formed by these verses is reinforced by their almost perfect chiastic relation: *'el-mōšeh bĕhar sînay* (25:1) and *bĕhar sînay bĕyad-mōšeh* (26:46; D. N. Freedman, personal communication). Simply put, the enslavement of the individual Israelite to the non-Israelite leads, in the wake of the neglect of the land's sabbath, to the enslavement of the entire nation in exile.

The attribution of chaps. 25–26 to Mount Sinai leads R. Ishmael (*Mekh* Jethro Baḥodesh, 3) to conjecture that they were originally part of the Covenant Code, which was ratified at Sinai (Exod 24:8). Ehrlich (1908 on 25:1) senses that chaps. 25–26 have the character of a *Bundesrede*, and C. Wright (1991: 149–50) concludes that chaps. 25–26 were intentionally juxtaposed to form the climax to the Holiness Source by pointing to the fact that chap. 26 is not prefaced by "YHWH said to Moses," as are all the other chapters in the code, and that the deliverance from Egypt is the refrain running through both chapters (25:38, 42, 53; 26:13, 45) but is infrequent elsewhere in the code (19:36; 23:43).

The common denominator of all the sections of chap. 25 (except the interpolation on houses, vv. 29–33) is land, a word that occurs twenty times. The associated words *'ăḥuzzâ* 'holding' appears twelve times; *gā'al* 'redeem', fifteen times; *yōbēl* 'jubilee', ten times; *šabbāt* 'sabbath (of land)', nine times. Land, therefore, which is held (i.e., inherited), rests and, if sold, is redeemed on the jubilee.

Vv. 1–2aα. Introduction

1. *at Mount Sinai.* In Leviticus, this designation is found in 7:38; 25:1; 26:46; 27:34. As noted by R. Ishmael, this chapter (and the next) is an exception: all other laws were generalized to Moses at Mount Sinai, but were detailed in the Tent of Meeting (*b. Zebaḥ.* 115b). The medieval commentaries explain this "exception" in different ways. Some, recognizing that chronologically chaps. 25–26 belong together with the Decalogue and Book of the Covenant revealed to Moses on Mount Sinai (Exod 20–24), aver that they were transposed here to be included among the laws (like sexual prohibitions, 18:28), the violation of which are expressly mentioned as a cause for expulsion (26:35–38; Ibn Ezra, Abravanel). Others (e.g., Ramban) speculate that initially chaps. 25–26 were included in the second covenant struck by God with Moses on Mount Sinai (Exod 34:10–26), whereas only a generalization of the sabbatical was given in the first covenant (Exod 23:11); this second covenant was not ratified by a blood ceremony (Exod 24:4–11), but by a series of imprecations (26:14–34) concerning which all of Israel took an oath (cf. Deut 27:9–26).

Moderns, of course, adopt a more critical stance. According to Dillmann and Ryssel (1897), this heading was necessitated by the intrusion of the narrative of 24:10–23, a post-Sinaitic event, into H, all of which was promulgated at Mount Sinai (27:34; but they leave the mention of Mount Sinai in 26:46 unexplained!). Ehrlich (1908) states dogmatically that *wayĕdabbēr* must be rendered as a pluperfect, "(YHWH) had spoken," since Moses never reascended Mount Sinai after the time attested in Exod 34:28. More compelling is the view of Muffs (1965b: 4.10–11; Robinson 1991) that, like the Mesopotamian kings who freed indentured slaves (see NOTE on "proclaiming release," v. 10) by issuing an *andurāru* when they ascended the throne, the divine king of kings freed the Israelites from the Egyptian bondage at Sinai. This view is expanded independently by Tsevat (1970), who points to specific scriptural references connecting the sabbatical law to the Sinaitic covenant, such as "I made a covenant with your fathers in the day I brought them out of the land of Egypt. . . . After seven years you shall release . . . " (Jer 34:13–14; cf. Deut 15:1) and "After seven years, the year set for remission, at the Feast of Booths . . . you shall read this Teaching aloud in the presence of all Israel" (Deut 31:10–11)—that is, for a ceremony of covenant renewal (cf. Deut 28:69; 29:13–14). Thus since these two chapters deal primarily with the edicts releasing persons and property, as well as the covenant imprecations in the wake of their violation, they were attributed to Sinai. The possibility must also be considered that the placement of these chapters here implies that Moses relayed YHWH's Sinaitic instructions to Israel at this juncture in the wilderness.

Vv. 2aβ-7. The Sabbatical Year

2. *When you enter the land.* This phrase is found also in 19:23; 23:10; 25:2; 14:34 (+ "Canaan"); Num 15:2 (+ "your settlements")—all probably H! M. Hildenbrand suggests that because this decree concerning the sabbatical and jubilee is effective in the first regnal year of Israel's sovereign Lord *in his land*, it resembles the practice of the *mīšarum* issued by the Babylonian kings during the year of their accession to the throne.

that I give you. The special force of this clause in this verse has been noticed by Joosten (1994: 237; 1996: 173): YHWH, as the owner of the land, can demand restraint in its use: it has to rest every seventh year (see NOTE on 23:10).

the land shall observe. wĕšābĕtâ hā'āreṣ, literally "the land shall rest." The notion of the land resting, šābat, occurs in only these two chapters (25:3, 4, 6; 26:34, 35) and in their reflex (2 Chr 36:21). Otherwise, the subject is man (e.g., 23:32; Exod 16:30) or God (e.g., Gen 2:2, 3; Exod 31:17). The Aramaic translations use the verb šĕmaṭ 'release, loosen' (based on Exod 23:11), leading to the rabbinic expression šĕmîṭat qarqaʿ 'release (or rest) of the land' for the agricultural aspect of the sabbatical year (b. Giṭ. 36a; b. Moʿed Qaṭ. 2b; cf. Exod 23:11) and šĕmîṭat kĕsāpîm 'release of cash debts' for the monetary aspect of the sabbatical year (b. Giṭ. 36a; b. Moʿed Qaṭ. 2b; cf. Deut 15:1–2).

Ibn Ezra makes the prescient comment that since the text does not say tašbîtû 'you (the Israelites) shall impose rest (on the land)' but "the *land* shall rest," this injunction applies also to the alien. The reverse situation holds true for the jubilee. Since its observance is incumbent on only the Israelites (*lākem*, v. 11), its requirements of rest for the land and release of persons do not apply to aliens. For this reason, the jubilee is not a sabbatical, and, indeed, the term *šabbāt* is assiduously avoided in the entire jubilee pericope (see NOTE on "for you," v. 11).

a sabbath to YHWH. šabbāt laYHWH. This phrase occurs in Exod 16:25; 20:10; 31:15 (šabbāt šabbātôn); Lev 23:3; 25:2, 4; Deut 5:14. The Aramaic translations render it qādām YHWH 'before YHWH' (Tgs. Onk., Ps.-J.), lišmâ dĕYHWH 'for the honor of YHWH' (Tg. Neof.), and, as the rabbis emphasize, *kĕšēm šene'ĕmar bĕšabbat bĕrē'šît šabbāt laYHWH* 'as it is stated regarding the sabbath of creation (Exod 20:10) "a sabbath to the Lord" ' (*Sipra* Behar 1:2); that is, just as it was not God (but Israel) who was to rest every sabbath day, so here too on the sabbatical year, it was not God (but the land) that was to rest. However, this sophisticated rabbinic reasoning notwithstanding, the priestly texts clearly state that God personally rested on the seventh day:

> "The writer is so certain of this point that he repeats it *wayyišbōt bayyôm haššĕbî'î . . . bô šābbat mikkol-mĕla'ktô* (Gen 2:2–3). There is also a modest chiasm to show that the repetition is not only deliberate but conclusive. As though this emphatic statement were not enough (and by using the same word for work that occurs in the Decalogue), the writer wants to emphasize that the motivation for observing the sabbath is precisely to follow the precedent of God himself, a true example of *imitatio dei*. As if this were not enough, P (rather H–JM) again adverts to the subject in Exod 31:16–17, where sabbath-observance is made an eternal sign of the covenant concluded between God and Israel at Mt. Sinai. Here we are told that: *ûbayyôm haššĕbî'î šābat* to which is added the concluding note: *wayyinnāpaš*, and he revived himself, i.e., he was refreshed by resting. Basically, it means he got his *nepeš* back, after being exhausted by all that work through the first six days." (D. N. Freedman, personal communication)

Indeed, in support of the rendering "of YHWH," one might point to the crucial differences between the sabbatical and the jubilee. The jubilee has to be sanctified by Israel *wĕqiddaštem* 'and *you* shall sanctify' (v. 10), a prescription absent in regard to the sabbatical. It must therefore be assumed that just like the sabbath of creation (Gen 2:3), the sabbatical is sanctified by God. Moreover, the jubilee is not called a "sabbath," and its restrictions apply to only the Israelite, but not to the resident alien, in contrast to the sabbatical (see NOTES on "a jubilee" and "for you," v. 10). Thus, it can be argued, the severer prohibitions of the sabbatical warrants its similitude to the sabbath day, namely, that it too is "of YHWH."

Nonetheless, the expression *šabbat laYHWH* in this verse is more an objective than a subjective genitive; not that YHWH is observing the sabbath, but that the land's sabbath is imbued with his presence (J. Wyrick). The land is to be returned to its condition on the sabbath of creation (Kochman 1987). D's *šĕmittâ laYHWH* 'a remission to/ in honor of/ YHWH' (Deut 15:2 NAB) is equivalent, since it reserves *šabbat laYHWH* for the sabbath (Dillmann 1886: 306–7; Paran 1983: 259).

As will be discussed in COMMENT C, the periodic fallowness of agricultural land is indispensable to its continued fertility. But not a word of this practical consideration is voiced in the text. Its requirement is justified theologically, not economically—the sabbath.

Tsevat (1970) claims that this phrase further implies that all the inhabitants of the land are equal before God (as also implied by *qārā' šĕmittâ laYHWH*,

Deut 15:2). This is not true. As will be pointed out below (see NOTES on v. 6), Leviticus prescribes that the aftergrowth of the sabbatical year may benefit only those living on landowners' land, but not unattached persons such as the poor and the alien (contrast Exod 23:11). Moreover, the rabbis posit that the actual location of the landowner makes a difference in the force of the sabbatical law: those lands occupied for a shorter period in Israel's history are subject to fewer restrictions (*m. Šebi* 6:1). In contrast to Leviticus, where the entire land is of equal sanctity since it belongs to God, the Mishna endorses the bold concept that Israel plays a role in sanctifying the land (Newman 1983: 19, 21). Maimonides (*Code* 3.39) offers an agricultural rationale: the sabbatical year is essential for the land to renew its strength (see COMMENT B).

Lev 25 models its text on Exod 23:10–11, which links it to the immediately following verse dealing with the sabbath day (Exod 23:12) and therefore prescribes that the land, too, is required to observe a fixed sabbatical. As shown by Paran (1983: 15–19, 259–61), the text of Lev 25:2aβ,b–7 is based on Exod 23:10–11:

Lev 25:2–7	Exod 23:10–11
²*kî tābō'û 'el- hā'āreṣ 'ăšer 'ănî nōtēn lākem*	
wĕšābĕtâ hā'āreṣ šabbāt laYHWH	
³*šēš šānîm tizra' śādekā*	¹⁰*wĕšēš šānîm tizra' 'et-'arṣekā*
wĕšēš šānîm tizmōr karmekā	
wĕ'āsaptā 'et-tĕbû'ātāh	*wĕ'āsaptā 'et-tĕbû'ātāh*
⁴*ûbaššānâ haššĕbî'ît*	¹¹*wĕhaššĕbî'ît*
šabbat šabbātôn yihyeh lā'āreṣ šabbat laYHWH	*tišmĕṭennâ ûnĕṭaštāh*
śādĕkā lō' tizrā'	
wĕkarmĕkā lō' tizmōr	
⁵*'et sĕpiaḥ qĕṣîrĕkā lō' tiqṣôr*	
wĕ'et-'inbê nĕzîrekā lō' tibṣōr	
šĕnat šabbātôn yihyeh lā'āreṣ	
⁶*wĕhāyĕtâ* **šabbat** *hā'āreṣ lākem lĕ'oklâ*	*wĕ'ākĕlû*
lĕkā	
ûlĕ'abdĕkâ	
wĕla'ămātekā	
wĕliśĕkîrĕkā	
ûlĕtôšābĕkā haggārîm 'immāk	*'ebyōnê 'ammekā*
⁷*wĕlibhemtĕkā*	
wĕlaḥayyâ 'ăšer bĕ'arṣekā	*wĕyitrām tō'kal ḥayyat haśśādeh*
tihyeh kol-tĕbû'ātāh le'ĕkōl	
	kēn-ta'ăseh lĕkarmĕkā lĕzêtekā

²When you enter the land that I give you,
the land shall observe a sabbath to YHWH

³Six years you may sow your field,	¹⁰Six years you may sow your land
and six years you may prune your vineyard	
and gather in its produce.	and gather in its produce;

Lev 25:2–7	Exod 23:10–11
[4]But in the seventh year	But in the seventh (year)
There shall be a sabbath of complete	you shall let it rest and lie
rest for the land, a sabbath to YHWH;	fallow.
you may neither sow your field	
nor prune your vineyard.	
[5]The aftergrowth of your harvest you shall not	
reap, nor the grapes of your untrimmed vines	
shall you pick; **it shall be (a year of) complete**	
rest for the land.	
[6]But the sabbath (-yield) of the land will be for	[11]Eat of it may
you to eat; for you, for your male and female	
slaves, your resident hirelings, who live under your	the needy of your people,
authority, [7]your livestock	
and the wild animals in your land—	and what they leave the wild
will be (available for you) to eat	beasts may eat.
	You shall do the same with your
	vineyards and your olive groves

As indicated by Paran (1989: 29–34), the author of this Leviticus text had the Exodus counterpart before him, as evident from the following:

1. The antecedent of *tĕbû 'ātāh*, literally "its produce" (Lev 25:3) is not *'arṣekā* 'your land' (Exod 23:10; cf. Ibn Ezra) but, ungrammatically, *śādekā* 'your field' and *karmekā* 'your vineyard' (Lev 25:3).

2. The shift from the plural to the singular, v. 2 > vv. 3–5, is due to the Exodus version; this also holds true in reverse for vv. 6–7 (*lākem . . . haggārîm 'immāk*, to correspond with *'ebyōnê 'ammekā*, Exod 23:11aβ).

3. The use in Exodus of both *'arṣekā* (v. 10) and *haśśādeh* (v. 11b) is probably what caused the Leviticus writer to adopt the same sequence, in reverse (vv. 3, 7) causing a lack of agreement (in gender) in v. 3.

4. The expansion of the Exodus text in Leviticus (boldface) is due to the unique H style: (a) the absence of the particle *'et* in the two couplets (vv. 3–4, noted by Ramban), an indication of a poetic style (but not of a poetic substratum), as is the word pair *kerem* and *śādeh* (*śādeh wĕkarem*, Num 16:14; 20:17; *śādeh 'ô kerem*, Exod 22:4; and, in parallelism, Mic 1:6; Ps 107:37; Prov 24:30; Job 24:6; Song 7:12); (b) the use of the refrain (vv. 2b, 4aβ, 5b), but with variation; (c) the bracketing of the concluding passage (vv. 6–7) with *l'kl/h*, with seven items in between, all beginning with *lamed*.

Others have noted the following differences:

1. Exodus speaks of only inherited, but not acquired land, while Leviticus imposes the sabbatical on the entire land (Falk 1964: 90).

2. Whereas in Exodus it is the produce, *tĕbû 'ātāh*, that is allowed to rest (v. 10b), in Leviticus it is the land (Wellhausen 1963: 164).

3. The poor and the wild beasts would derive little benefit from the Exodus law if it ordained a fixed sabbatical year, an indication that Exodus presupposes

that there always was some fallow land (C. Wright 1991: 145). This is further supported by the difference in the texts: in Exodus it is "*your* land" (v. 10a) that observes the sabbatical, but in Leviticus it is "*the* land" (vv. 2, 4). Also, in Exodus the beasts of the field (*haśśādeh*), presumably wild animals that are nearby, may benefit from the aftergrowth (v. 11aβ), but in Leviticus it is the beasts of the land (*hā'āreṣ*), those of the entire land. Thus, according to Exodus, each farmer determines the seventh year he will observe; in Leviticus, it is fixed for the entire land (Wright 1984: 131; cf. Chirichigno 1993: 310–11, n. 1).

4. Slaves and domestic animals, categories absent from Exodus, would have been cared for by their owner (Phillips 1970: 75, n. 49).

Additional differences should also be noted:

5. The word *ûnĕṭaštāh*, literally "abandon it" (Exod 23:11aα) is dropped in Leviticus in order that the owner and his retainers may benefit.

6. As argued by Cohen (1979: 45–49), the sabbatical was rarely observed, necessitating that the priestly legist decree that its neglect would be punished by exile (26:34; 2 Chr 36:21). The abandonment of a vineyard for one year would result in severe damage, including a crop loss of two years from lack of pruning, weakened vines from wild growth, untended terraces broken by the weather, hardened ground that is difficult to loosen (see, however, COMMENT C), and damage done by outsiders (persons and animals). However, it is clear that the clause on the vineyard in Exodus (and the olive growth) is a subsequent appendix (v. 11b). Initially, the sabbatical applied to only grains, which could be stored in the years before the sabbatical, making it easier to observe. Furthermore, the cultivation of the vine is a later development in Israel's economy, a factor that Leviticus, but not Exodus, had to reckon with.

7. Vv. 6–7, allowing the landowner and all those living with him to benefit from the aftergrowth, patently contradicts vv. 4b, 5a. The obvious solution is that the latter follows the law of the *Vorlage* in Exod 23, while the former constitutes H's innovation.

8. Finally, as the chart clarifies, the conversion of the Exodus passage into the Leviticus sabbath—a fixed year for the entire land—is marked by interpolations into the text (boldface). Another difference is implied herein: the sabbatical of Exod 23 was unfixed (rotational), but became fixed for all landowners on the same year (see COMMENT C). Thus the cumulative effect of the evidence makes it highly probable that the H legist expanded the provisions for the sabbatical in Exodus in order to compose his own law.

This structural comparison between vv. 2–7 and Exod 23:10–11, showing the former as demonstrably an expansion of the latter, puts to rest the claim of many scholars (most recently Fager 1993: 101) that vv. 3–5 and 6–7 represent two levels of tradition whereby the absolute prohibitions of the former are amended.

3. *Six years you may sow.* *šēš šānîm tizra'* (= Exod 23:10). Structurally this phrase corresponds with the sabbath commandment: *šēšet yāmîm ta'ăbōd* 'six days you may work' (Exod 20:9; Ramban). There is also an ideological similarity between the sabbatical year and the weekday sabbath of the Decalogue: both place the land under the lordship of God (Tsevat 1972: 452–54).

It should be kept in mind that these six years (as well as the seventh year, v. 4) refer to the agricultural year, not the civil year, which begins in the spring (cf. Exod 12:2).

prune. tizmōr, rendered *tiksaḥ* (*Tg. Onk.*); compare *qôṣîm kĕsûḥîm* 'cut down thorns' (Isa 33:12); *śĕrûpâ bā'ēš kĕsûḥâ* 'it is burned by fire, cut down' (Ps 80:17); *tigzĕrûn* 'you shall cut down' (*Tg. Ps.-J.*). The time for pruning the vineyard is clearly indicated: "For before the vintage, yet after the budding / when the blossom has hardened into berries / He will trim away the twigs with pruning hooks (*mazmērôt*) / and lop off the trailing branches" (Isa 18:5). For *mazmērâ* as "pruning hook," see Isa 2:4. Note that *'ēt hazzāmîr* 'the time of pruning' (Song 2:12), refers to the period after the rainy season when the fig and grape blossoms have appeared (Song 2:13); that is, the time for pruning is at the beginning of summer. This is confirmed by the Gezer calendar, which places *yrḥw zmr* 'months of pruning' between *yrḥ qṣr wkl* 'month of wheat harvest and measuring' and *yrḥ qṣ* 'a month of summer fruit' (ll. 5–7; cf. Gibson 1971: 1–4).

your vineyard. karmekā. What of the olive grove explicitly mentioned in Exod 23:11b? The question is resolved once it is realized that an olive grove is also called a *kerem* (cf. Judg 15:5).

gather in. wĕ'āsaptā. This refers to collecting from the threshing floor and the vats for purposes of storage (Deut 11:14). This period falls in the autumn before the Feast of Tabernacles (*bĕ'ospĕkem*, 23:39; *bĕ'ospĕkā*, Exod 23:16; Deut 16:13). After the produce has been ingathered (i.e., stored), the work on the land has ended.

its produce. tĕbû'ātāh. The nearest antecedent that agrees in gender is *hā'āreṣ* (v. 2; Ibn Ezra). However, it betrays its *Vorlage* (Exod 23:10b; Fishbane 1985: 180; cf. Paran 1983; 1959). The term *tĕbû'â* encompasses the entire yield of the field: the threshing floor (grain), the vat (grapes, olives; Num 18:30), and the fruit (Lev 19:25).

4. The wording of the sabbatical law (25:4) is strikingly similar to H's law of the sabbath:

ûbayyôm haššĕbî'î šabbat šabbātôn miqrā'-qōdeš kol-mĕlā'kâ lō' ta'ăśû šabbāt hi(w)' laYHWH . . .

But on the seventh day (there shall be) a sabbath of complete rest, a sacred occasion. You shall not do any work; it shall be a sabbath of YHWH (23:3a$\beta\gamma$,b)

ûbaššānâ haššĕbî'īt šabbat sabbātôn yihyeh lā'āreṣ šabbāt laYHWH śādĕkā lō' . . .

But in the seventh year there shall be a sabbath of complete rest for the land, a sabbath to YHWH; you shall not . . . (25:4)

The majority of the words in each law are the same (boldface); they are also in the same syntactical relationship. Also, note that the dissimilar words are also related to one another: *šabbat laYHWH* 'a sabbath of YHWH' (25:4) and *miqrā' qōdeš* 'a sacred occasion' (23:3) are apposite objects, and the former stands in chiastic relation with *šabbat hi(w)' laYHWH* 'it shall be a sabbath of YHWH' (23:3b). Thus structure as well as content prove that the sabbatical year is modeled after the weekly sabbath.

seventh (year). haššěbî'ît. The number seven occurs seven times in this chapter (vv. 4, 8 [four times], 9, 20).

a sabbath of complete rest. šabbat sabbātôn. This expression occurs with only the sabbath (23:3) and the Day of Purgation (23:32), which are the only days when abstention from *kol-mělā'kâ* 'all labor' is prescribed (23:3, 28; Wessely 1846). "It must have implied a suspension of all debts during the Fallow Year, as no debtor could have been expected to repay his loans while he was prohibited from tilling or reaping his land" (Neufeld 1958: 68). Chirichigno (1993: 272–75) even claims that this sabbatical law implies a full remission. If that were the case, however, the jubilee provisions would be largely superfluous. Even if the debtor had descended to a "slave" status (vv. 39–43), the cancellation of his loan would have resulted in the return of his land. Under these circumstances, what creditor would ever extend credit?

a sabbath to YHWH. šabbāt laYHWH. Compare *šěmiṭṭâ laYHWH* 'a remission to YHWH' (Deut 15:2), but not "a sabbath / remission to the king," as prevailed in Mesopotamia (see COMMENT A, and NOTE on "you shall proclaim release," v. 10). Even when Zedekiah proclaims a *děrôr* 'release' (Jer 34:12–22), he does so in the name of YHWH. Contrast the sabbath day, which probably should be rendered not "to YHWH," but "of YHWH" (see NOTE on 23:3).

sow . . . prune. Are only these labors on the land prohibited (R. Yohanan in *b. Mo'ed Qaṭ.* 3a), or is this a merism for all labors (R. Eliezer in *Sipra* Behar 1:2)? Josephus (*Ant.* 3.281) apparently holds the latter view, stating that plowing and planting (not in the text!) are only examples.

nor prune your vineyard. This would cause a loss for the following year (see NOTE on "sabbath on the land," v. 2).

5. *aftergrowth. sěpîaḥ.* The root *sph* in all its verb patterns denotes "add" (1 Sam 2:36 *Qal*; Isa 14:1 *Nip'al*; Hab 2:15 *Pi'el*; Job 30:7 *Pu'al*; 1 Sam 26:19 *Hitpa'el*). The possibility exists that the term *šāḥîs* (Isa 37:30), *sāḥîš* (2 Kgs 19:29), or *ša'îs* (1QIs[a]) refers to the second year's aftergrowth. If so, then this aftergrowth would supply Israel's needs during the jubilee, the fiftieth year, which would be a second fallow year following the forty-ninth year, a sabbatical (see NOTES on v. 21). There is ample evidence that the aftergrowth during the first fallow year is so abundant that at times two or three harvests are obtained from one sowing in the Galilee highlands and in Wadi Artas, near Bethlehem (Kalisch 1867–72).

the grapes of. 'inněbê. The purpose of the dageshed *nun* is to make the *šěwâ* more audible (GKC § 20h).

untrimmed vines. nězîrěkā. Read the singular *nězîrěkā*, as accompanying *qěṣîrěkā* (Ehrlich 1908). However, since there is no *yod* before the final *kaph* (the sign of the pl.), this word may represent the pausal form of the singular (Schwartz, personal communication). The root *nzr* means "withhold, abstain, separate from" (see NOTE on 22:2). The interpretations of the application of this term in this context are various: (1) the grapes from which you have kept people away (Rashi) or from which you will now keep away (cf. *šibqāk, Tg.Onk.*; Bekhor Shor; Ramban₁, as in 22:2); (2) "grapes of your consecration" (LXX), as the Nazirite is consecrated to God (cf. Num 6:6); (3) "untrimmed" (i.e., grapes allowed to grow wild), as the Nazirite's hair (Jer 7:29; Ramban₂; Mendelssohn 1846). Note the metaphoric use of other body language: *ʿorlâ* 'uncircumcised' fruit (19:23), *bětûlat šiqmâ* 'virgin (unclipped) sycamore' (*b. Ned.* 8b). The vine (and fruit trees) furnished ample produce during the fallow year, since they did not require labor.

(a year of) complete rest. šĕnat šabbātôn. The term *šabbāt* occurs seven times in vv. 1–7, as noted by Abravanel. Perhaps that is the reason for this changed expression (its only occurrence), rather than *šabbat šabbātôn* (to accord with its wording in v. 4, an emendation needlessly adopted by Ehrlich 1908).

The significance of identifying the seventh-year fallow (Exod 23:11) with the sabbath was perceptively caught by Moltmann (1985: 31, 296): "the crown of creation is not the human being; it is the sabbath. It is true that as the image of God, the human being has his special position in creation. But he stands together with all other earthly and heavenly beings in the same hymn of praise of God's glory, and in enjoyment of God's Sabbath pleasure over creation."

6. *the sabbath (-yield) of the land. šabbat hā'āreṣ,* literally "the land's sabbath," an ellipsis of *tĕbû'at šabbat hā'āreṣ* (i.e., sabbatical produce; Ramban). The missing word *tebu'at* is supplied at the end of v. 7, which in true H style repeats the beginning of v. 6, in order to create the chiasm ABB'A':

A ⁶*wĕhāyĕtâ šabbat hā'āreṣ lākem lĕ'oklâ*

  B *lĕkā ûlĕʿabdĕkā wĕla'ămātĕkā wĕliśkîrĕkā ûlĕtôšābĕkā haggārîm ʿimmāk*

  B' ⁷*wĕlibhemtĕkā wĕlaḥayyâ 'ăšer bĕ'arṣekā*

A' *tihyeh kol-tĕbû'ātāh le'ĕkōl*

A ⁶The sabbath (-yield) of the land shall be for you to eat:

  B for you, for your male and female slaves, your resident hirelings, who live under your authority,

  B' ⁷your livestock and the wild animals in your land—

A' all of its yield shall be (available) to eat.

The eligible recipients of the sabbatical aftergrowth (BB') are seven in number, all preceded by the preposition *lĕ.* The alliterative *lamed* also occurs twice in A and once in A'. Note the repetition in AA' of the infinitive *le'ĕkōl / lĕ'oklâ* and the repetition of the verb *tihyeh / wĕhāyĕtâ,* both in the prefixed and suffixed form, as is customary in H. But the term *šabbat hā'āreṣ* is paralleled by *tĕbû'ātāh,* which provides the meaning. The expression (its only occurrence) emphasizes that the land is enjoined to observe the sabbath (cf. "the land shall observe a sabbath," v. 2b), as distinct from the jubilee, which is not a sabbatical year but a holy year (see NOTE on "sacred it shall be to you," v. 12).

for you. lākem. The switch to the plural (contrast the context, vv. 3–7) is probably an indication that a list of eligible beneficiaries will follow. This parallels the similar change in number in vv. 2–5, where the plural is used to emphasize that all the land occupied by Israel must rest (v. 2). The singular follows, indicating the sabbatical responsibilities of each landowner. Not everyone may benefit (Ibn Ezra), but only those listed in this verse, thereby excluding the poor and the aliens (Exod 23:11).

to eat. lĕ'oklâ. The yield can be used only as food, but not for cereal and libation offerings (*Sipra* Behar 1:6) or for storage (Driver and White 1894–98). This word in the translation is followed by a colon, listing those who may benefit from the aftergrowth. For a similar construction, see *ḥelbô* 'its suet': (3:9). Vv. 6–7 ostensibly contradict v. 5a, which forbids the landowner to harvest his field and vineyard (contra Ginzberg 1932: 353). Gerstenberger (1996) suggests that even if the aftergrowth of the field (*śādeh*) is forbidden (v. 4), the aftergrowth of the open, uncultivated land (*'ereṣ*) is permitted. His solution must be rejected. A hypothetical construct *šabbat haśśādeh* is incongruous, since the entire land is subject to the sabbatical (vv. 2, 4, 5). Besides, are the landowner, his family, and his animals to subsist for more than a year on wild berries and roots? Rather, the answer is that the landowner is not free to harvest as in normal years, when he can do with his produce as he wills: to store and sell in addition to eat. Its point is that the harvest may satisfy only the hunger of those listed. Indeed, the verb *lĕ'oklâ / le'ĕkol* 'to eat' is needlessly repeated in v. 6b in order to emphasize the point.

for you. lĕkā. Although singular, this word refers to the landowner's resident family. Vv. 6–7 are based on Exod 23:10–11, but they alter it to allow the landowner and his entire household, including his animals, and to exclude the poor. Thus Lev 25 does not supplement Exod 23 (as maintained by Fishbane 1985: 180) but patently opposes it. Leviticus is thus a corrective to Exodus, which, in depriving the landowner and his household from the aftergrowth is harsh and, indeed, utopian. It is Leviticus that makes the sabbatical law workable (cf. Ginzberg 1932: 355–56). This realistic aspect of Lev 25 will again be demonstrated by its adjustment for urban centers (vv. 29–34) and its extension of the sabbatical from seven to fifty years, thereby providing greater inducement for creditors to lend (see NOTE on "and each of you shall return to his kin group," v. 10).

The exclusion of the poor is not that they are "not their [P and H's] primary concern" (van Houten 1991: 121), but that, on the contrary, H has provided for them elsewhere (19:9–10; 23:22), laws that apply to the sabbatical as well as all other years. Interestingly, Josephus (*Ant.* 3.281) and the rabbis (with the exception of R. Judah in *m. Šebi* 9:8) combine the permitted beneficiaries of Exod 23 and Lev 25 by allowing everyone to partake of the sabbatical aftergrowth. The rabbis, however, ban the sabbatical aftergrowth, with the exception of R. Simeon b. Yohai, who permits it (*m. Šebi* 9:1; cf. *Pirqe R. Kah.* 11:17; on the rabbinic prohibition, see Feliks 1973: 235–49). I submit that both views are rooted in Scripture. The rabbis are influenced by Exod 23:11, which forbids the farmer and his relatives to benefit from the sabbatical aftergrowth, whereas R. Simeon anchors his view in Lev 25:6–7, which benefits them (correcting Newman 1983: 215, n. 1). For a discussion of the possible *Sitz im Leben* and historical date of the sabbatical, see COMMENT B.

for your male and female slaves. ûlĕ'abdĕkā wĕla 'ămātekā. The reference here is to chattel-slaves (i.e, non-Israelites; also in vv. 44–46), whereas the other occurrences of 'ebed in this chapter (vv. 39–43, 55) refer to debt-slaves (i.e., Israelites).

resident hirelings. ûlĕśĕkîrĕkā ûlĕtôśābĕkā. This phrase also appears in 22:10; 25:40; Exod 12:45. A hendiadys, discussed in the NOTE on v. 40, it refers to a laborer resident on the person's land. The rabbis' opine that he is a non-Israelite (*Sipra* Behar 1:7), presumably on the basis of the preceding mention of non-Israelite slaves.

who live. The plural *haggārîm* applies to all the previously listed: family, slaves, and hirelings, provided that they live with and are under the authority of the landowner. Thus the married daughter (cf. 22:12), the divorced wife, or the married son, not to speak of brothers and sisters, who live independently or who live under someone else's authority are not eligible for the aftergrowth. This condition also explains the otherwise inexplicable absence of the *gēr*, the alien, from the list. The alien does not live on the landowner's property. For that reason, he is grouped with the poor (19:10; 23:22) as recipients of charity. Both are outsiders, and their support is not one of patriarchal obligation, but of individual generosity. That the *gēr* is an autonomous person can be demonstrated by the following considerations:

1. He is punishable by God for violating any of the divine prohibitions (e.g., 16:29; 17:8–10, 12, 13; 18:26; cf. Num 15:26, 30–31).
2. He can become independently wealthy (25:47).
3. The word *gēr* and its verb *gār* take the preposition *'et* 'with' (19:33, Exod 12:48; Num 9:14; 15:14) or *bĕtôk* (17:8, 10, 12, 13; 18:26), followed by the word *yiśrā'ēl*, implicitly or explicitly (20:2; 22:18; Ezek 14:7). They never take the preposition *'im* (except here and in v. 47, which bears the singular meaning "under the authority of"; see NOTE on "under your authority," v. 35). True, the word *gēr* also appears with a personal suffix *gērĕkā* (Deut 5:14 [= Exod 20:10]; 24:14; 29:10; 31:12) and *gērô* (Deut 1:16), but all these citations are of deuteronomic origin, and they reflect an urban background—that is, the *gēr* in your/his city.
4. The sentence *himmôl lô kol-zākār* 'let all his (the alien's) males be circumcised' (Exod 12:48) implies that he had his own household over which he had exclusive control (contra van Houten 1991: 58, 67).

One might argue that H is quite niggardly with the poor, never giving a thought to them except at the harvest (19:9–10; 23:22; see its NOTE). Yet when one examines the prescriptions of humanitarian D, again it is only harvesttime that is mentioned (14:29; 16:11, 14; 24:17–21; 26:12–13). Should not one presume that the obligation to care for the poor continues through the year? H ostensibly would deny it. On the basis of this verse, one might conclude that the landowner is responsible for only those under his direct care—but not the community's poor. The aftergrowth, however, may be an exception based on pragmatic considerations: the aftergrowth is so skimpy that it would feed only those for whom the landowner is directly responsible so not feeding poor is understandable.

under your authority. '*immak.* For the substantiation of this rendering, see the NOTE on v. 35. The use of the singular in vv. 3–7 may be responsible for its continuation in vv. 8–9a (contrast 23:15).

7. *your livestock and the wild animals.* This verse is connected with the preceding one. Leviticus supplements the beneficiaries of the aftergrowth in Exodus with "your livestock," in consonance with the principle that the aftergrowth is limited to those on the landowner's land and under his authority, including his animals. From the equation of these two kinds of animal, the rabbis derive the following rule: "As long as the wild animals eat (the aftergrowth) in the field, the domesticated animals eat (it) at home; if it ceases in the field it ceases at home" (*Sipra* Behar 1:8; 3:4). That is, the aftergrowth may be eaten at home as long as there is some in the field; if it ceases in the field, the landowner is required to move some of it from the house to the field. Here the rabbis tacitly recognize that whereas Exodus gives humans priority over animals (*wêyitrām,* 23:11), Leviticus equates them (see also Elliger 1966).

all of its yield will be (available) to eat. tihyeh kol-těbû'ātâ le'ěkōl. A near repetition of the first sentence *wěhāyětâ šabbat hā'āreṣ lākem lě'oklâ* (v. 6aα), this is an example of H's style, attested also in v. 9: *wěhaʿăbartā sôpar . . . taʿăbîrû šôpār.* Some scholars claim that H is repetitive because it is hortatory (Ehrlich 1908 [H]; Elliger 1966). However, H's purpose may be purely aesthetic. Note that both citations exemplify the chiastic form of ABB'A': 6aα, 6aβ,b, 7a, 7b and 9aα, 9aβ, 9bα, 9bβ (J. Wyrick).

to eat. lě'ěkōl. The repetition here may also serve a heuristic purpose: the aftergrowth may be used only as food, not for any other purpose, "not even for (purchasing) medication" (*Sipra* Behar 1:12).

Vv. 8–22. The Jubilee Year

8. This verse exhibits a panel construction ABC A'B'C' (J. Wyrick):

A	*wêsāpartā lěkā*	A'	*wěhāyû lěkā*
B	*šebaʿ šabbětōt šānîm*	B'	*yěmê šebaʿ šabbětōt haššānîm*
C	*šebaʿ šānîm šebaʿ pê'āmîm*	C'	*tēšaʿ wěʿarbāʿîm šānâ*

The literal translation shows the words in common (boldface):

A	You shall count off **for you**	A'	and it shall be **for you**
B	**seven weeks of years**	B'	the period of **seven weeks of years**
C	seven **years** seven times	C'	nine and forty **years**

weeks of years. šabbĕtōt šānîm; šemîṭîn dišnîn, "sabbaticals of years" (*Tgs*). That *šabbāt* can stand for a week, see the NOTE on 23:15. In fact, this verse is clearly modeled on 23:15: *ûsĕpartem lākem . . . šeba' sabbātôt . . . tihyênâ.* Thus it is one of the indications that the period of the jubilee cycle (49 + 1 years) is based on the pentecontal calendar, the fifty days (49 + 1) between the barley and wheat offerings (23:15–16; Kottackal 1983). The jubilee of years is structured on the "jubilee" of weeks. Shadal also notices a correspondence between the jubilee and the festival calendar: just as there are seven festivals (*miqrā'ê qōdeš*) in the year (*pesah, maṣṣôt* [seventh day], *šābû'ôt, rō'š haššānâ, yôm kippûr, sukkôt* [first day], *'āṣeret*), so there are seven sabbaticals in the jubilee.

—*seven times seven years*—. This parenthetical clause is required lest one think that the sabbatical years are consecutive (*Sipra* Behar, par. 2:1). Perhaps it also evidences that in contrast to general amnesties in the ancient Near East, which occurred irregularly according to the decision of the ruler, in Israel the jubilee was fixed, a divinely ordained institution that was independent of any human sovereign.

period of. yĕmê. For this usage—that is, the total time—see Gen 25:7; 47:8, 9.

gives you. wĕhāyû lĕkā. You refers to the Israelite, but not the *gēr*, the alien, even though he resides in your land (see NOTE on "for you," v. 10).

9. This verse bears a chiastic construction (M. Hildenbrand):

A   *wĕha'ăbartā šôfar tĕrû'â*
   B   *bahōdĕs haššĕbī'î be'āśôr lahōdeš*
   B'   *bĕyōm hakkippurîm*
A'   *ta'ăbîrû šôfār bĕkol- 'arṣĕkem*

This verse sets the date of the announcement of the jubilee, specifying that it is signaled by horn blowing throughout the land (AA'), and that it occurs on the annual Day of Purgation (BB'). That the shift to plural *ta'ăbîrû* (A') does not mean that v. 9b is a later addition (Noth 1977) is demonstrated by its essential place in the chiasm. For other stylistic reasons, see the NOTE on "you shall have the horn sounded," below).

Then you shall sound. wĕha'ăbartā, literally "you shall cause to pass through" (i.e., "sound"), as *he'ĕbîr qôl* (Exod 36:6; Ezra 1:1; 10:7; Neh 8:15; 2 Chr 30:5; 36:22). This verse contains the only two instances of *šôpār* as the object of this verb. The usual verb with *šôpār* is *tāqa'* 'blow' (Josh 6:9; Judg 7:22; Isa 18:3; Jer 4:5; 6:1). The last cited verse also mentions that the horn blowing was accompanied by the setting of a *maś'ēt* 'a fire-signal', by means of a torch. This word is used with the same connotation in the Lachish letters (4:10: *ANET* 322). On the use of fire-signals in Mesopotamia, see Dossin (1938). More relevantly, the Mesopotamian *andurāru* (see NOTE on "proclaiming release," v. 10) was proclaimed by "the raising of a torch" (Finkelstein 1968: 236; Weinfeld 1980: 89; 1990a: 44; Bar-Maoz 1980: 73, n. 99). Perhaps the jubilee, too, was promulgated throughout the land by lighted torches.

the horn. The word *šôpar* is accurately translated as "horn" (*keratinēs* 'horn trumpet', LXX) because it was made from the horn of an animal. In the Bible, the *šôpār* serves to muster an army (Judg 3:27; 6:34), to frighten the enemy (Judg 7:8, 16, 22), to proclaim victory (1 Sam 13:3), to terminate a battle (2 Sam 18:16; 20:22), to warn of an approaching enemy (Jer 4:21; Hos 5:8), to install the Ark in David's tent (2 Sam 6:15), and to crown kings (2 Sam 15:10; 2 Kgs 9:13). In modern Israel, the *šôpār* announces the advent of sabbaths and festivals, and its blast, in keeping with its jubilee function and that stated in Isa 27:13, proclaims the restoration of the exiles and their emancipation. For the difference between the *šôpār* and the *ḥăṣōṣĕrâ* 'trumpet', see Milgrom (1990a: 372–73).

loud. tĕrû'â, literally "(horn of) loudness." This term and corresponding verb *hērîa'* refer to a loud shout by warriors (e.g., Josh 6:5, 10, 16, 20) and worshipers (e.g., Pss 47:2; 95:1). If it takes the verb *tāqa'*, the expression then signifies the blowing of a specific military signal (e.g., Num 10:5, 6; contrast v. 7). This is probably the reason why this verse uses the hapax *he'ĕbîr*, so that the *teru'â* would not be identified with a *tĕqîâ'* signal.

in the seventh month, on the tenth day of the month. Since the jubilee is a sacred year (vv. 10, 12), it cannot begin until the purgation of the Temple and the people is complete (Gaster 1952: 183–84). This date proves that the jubilee (and probably the sabbatical year) is based on the agricultural year, namely, a fall calendar (cf. *m. Roš Haš.* 1:1). Interestingly, Josephus (*Ant.* 1.80–81) acknowledges that originally Israel followed an autumn calendar (cf. Exod 23:16; 34:22b; *Mekh.* Bo 1). Shalit (1967: 15) adds that Josephus may also have been aware that the Macedonian solar calendar was preceded by a lunar one.

the Day of Purgation. bĕyôm hakkippūrîm. For this rendering, see vol. 1.1079–84, and for a discussion of this day and its ritual, see vol. 1.1009–78. This specification of both date and name may also be needed, in addition to the needs of the chiastic structure, mentioned above (see NOTE on "all of its yield will be [available for you] to eat," v. 7), lest one think that the *šôpār* is blown on the eve of Yom Kippur, which is still the ninth day of the month (Lev 23:32). The day, however, always begins at sunrise (see vol. 1.420, and NOTE on 23:32).

Why did the jubilee begin on the tenth day of the seventh month (*yôm hakkippurim*), rather than at the beginning of the agricultural year, the first day of the month? One can suggest a number of reasons:

1. The shofar call would not be confused with that on the first day (23:24b).
2. A "holy" year (*wĕqiddaštem*, v. 10) would be initiated only after the sanctuary and, symbolically, the people and land have been purged of their impurities (see chap. 16, esp. v. 33 [H]).
3. Philo (*de Congressu* 107–8), as usual, adopts a more allegorical view: Yom Kippur celebrates the liberation (*dĕrôr*) of the body and soul.

Originally, the tenth day of the seventh month was the climax of a New Year festival that began on the first day (vol. 1.1067–70). This may be adumbrated in the dating of Ezekiel's futuristic Temple vision: "In the twenty-fifth year of our exile, at the beginning of the year [*bĕrōš haššānâ*] on the tenth day of the month [*be'āśôr laḥōdeš*]" (Ezek 40:1). On the basis of this dating, Meṣudat David (eighteenth century) concludes that the jubilee year begins on the tenth day. Morgenstern (1958), among others, has speculated that originally Yom Kippur was New Year's Day. I have partially supported this view, first, by demonstrating that the instructions to fast on Yom Kippur are based on an H supplement (16:29–34a) and, second, by citing from the Mishna that into rabbinic times Yom Kippur was celebrated as a joyous day (*m. Ta'an.* 4:8; cf. Loewenstamm 1958b: 599). A hint about the original character of the first day of the seventh month indicates that it, too, was a festive day: "Go eat choice foods and drink sweet drinks and send portions to whoever has nothing prepared, for the day is holy to our Lord" (Neh 8:10; cf. vv. 11–12).

That New Year's Day could simultaneously fall on the first and the tenth day of the month is suggested by Safren (1999), who renders *běrōš haššānâ* (Ezek 40:1) as "during the New Year Festival period." He points to prolonged New Year festivals in ancient Mesopotamia. He might have added that these festivals are bound up in temple purgations (vol. 1.1067–70). This correspondence with Yom Kippur has led me to conclude (vol. 1.1069; cf. *b. Roš Haš.* 8b):

[I]f the tenth of Tishri can be seen as the culmination of Israel's New Year festival, then it was the tenth and climactic day of Israel's ten-day New Year festival. The first ten days of Tishri are, in Jewish tradition, its penitential period during which man, through his repentance, can alter the divine decree (*b. Roš. Haš.* 18a). Its roots could then be traced back to a putative ten-day New Year festival, ending in the joyous celebration of the sanctuary's purgation on the tenth and last day.

Further support may be adduced from two Nuzi texts containing the formula *tuppi arki šudūti ešši kīme qibitti* (*ša šarri*) *ša arḫi kinunāti ša āl ilāni ina arḫi* [month name] *ina ali* [city name] *šater* 'This tablet was written after the new *šudūtu* in the month [name] in the city [name] according to the order of the king in the month Kinunatim in the City of the Gods'. Since Nuzi Kinunatim, the first month of the Nuzi calendar (equivalent to Baby. *nissanu* / Heb. *nīsān*), is the New Year festival month on which the *šudūtu* (equivalent to Baby. *andurāru* / Heb. *děrōr*) was proclaimed, it is reasonable to conclude with Müller (1971, cited in Weinfeld 1995: 93–94) and followed by Safren (forthcoming) that originally the tenth day of Tishri, the first month of the Hebrew calendar, was the last day of the ancient New Year festival.

you shall have the horn sounded. ta'ăbîrû šōpâr. This is a repetition of *wěha'ăbartā šōpar* (v. 9aα); for another example of H's repetitive style and its aesthetic purpose, see the NOTE on "all of its yield will be [available for you] to eat" (v. 7). As noted by S. Chavel, the verb change from singular to plural may be due to the influence of the contiguous plural noun *kippurîm*. An equally plausible stylistic reason is that when the verb expresses the impersonal passive, H frequently uses the plural (e.g., 27:9, 11). Moreover, frequent shifts in number are attested in H (e.g., 19:9, 12, 15, 19, 27, 33; 23:22; 25:14, 17, 46; cf. Schwartz 1987: 48, 53, 59, 70, 103).

throughout your land. běkol-'arṣěkem. This essential addition informs that the fixed jubilee is nationwide, serving a similar purpose as *bē'arṣekā* 'in your land' (v. 7a) regarding H's sabbatical.

10. *and you shall sanctify. wěqiddaštem.* A hapax; the only other unit of time that Israel is commanded to sanctify (*qdš Pi'el*) is the sabbath (Exod 20:8, 11; Deut 5:12; Jer 17:22, 24, 27; Ezek 20:20; 44:24; Neh 13:22). However, in these citations the verb *qiddeš* is not to be rendered "sanctify," but "treat as holy" (cf. 21:8), as shown by Jeremiah's exposition of the term, namely, that Israel should treat the sabbath as holy by neither working nor bearing a burden on this day (17:22, 24). In contrast, the jubilee is sanctified by the positive act of a proclamation heralded by the blowing of a shofar—a rite of sanctification.

This rendering of the *Pi'el* is exemplified in P's *ṭihēr* 'pronounce / proclaim pure' (13:6, 13, 17, 23, 28, 37) and *ṭimmē'* 'pronounce impure' (13:8, 15, 20, 25, 27, 44). Abetting this rendering is the context. It is preceded by the *šôpār* sounding throughout the land (v. 9) and followed by *ûqěrā'tem* announcing release. The sequence of *šôpār, qiddeš,* and *qārā'* is, tellingly, found in *tiq'û šôpār . . . qadděšû-ṣôm qir'û 'āṣārâ,* which, I submit, should be translated "Blow a horn . . . proclaim the sanctity of a fast, call an assembly" (Joel 2:15–16; cf. 1:14; 2 Kgs 10:20–21). Indeed, should not P's declaration of God's sanctification of the sabbath *wayyěqaddēš 'ôtô* (Gen 2:3) be rendered "and he proclaimed it holy"?

The implication is clear: just as Israel sanctifies the sabbath by abstaining from all work, so the call to sanctify the jubilee year means that Israel should abstain from working the land (vv. 11–12). However, the jubilee is not called a sabbath, as is the seventh year (vv. 2, 4, 5, 6), for reasons discussed in the NOTE on *lākem,* below.

the fiftieth year. šěnat haḥămiššîm šānâ, literally "the year of the fifty years" (cf. GKC § 128k; 1340N). The year must begin with Tishri, the seventh month (siding with R. Eleazar against R. Joshua, *b. Roš Haš.* 10b), reflecting an agricultural calendar since sowing (in the fall) as well as reaping (in the spring) are forbidden (v. 11; Ibn Ezra). The rabbis are also ambivalent about whether the jubilee year begins on the first day or on the tenth day when the shofar is blown. Their compromise: "R. Yochanan b. Beroqah said: Slaves did not leave for their homes and fields were not returned to their owners (on the first day) but they ate, drank, and rejoiced with crowns on their heads until the Day of Purgation. When the Day of Purgation arrived the shofar was blown and fields were returned to their owners and slaves left for their homes" (*Sipra* Behar 2:1).

There can be little doubt that the choice of the number fifty is based on the pentecontal structure of the calendar in chap. 23. That is, just as the seven weeks terminate in a fiftieth day, so the seven septennates terminate in a fiftieth year (see NOTE on "weeks of years," v. 8).

proclaiming release. ûqěrā'tem děrôr. The same expression *liqrō' děrôr* is found in Isa 61:1 and Jer 34:8 (cf. *šěnat hadděrôr,* Ezek 46:17). Three interpretations are extant for the meaning of *děrôr:* (1) "release" (LXX; Jos. *Ant.* 12.3; Ibn Ezra);

(2) "flow," as in *mōr* / *môr děrôr* 'free flowing myrrh' (Exod 30:23; Song 5:5, 13), supported by Arabic "flowing streams" (Snaith 1967; see also Lewy 1958: 21–22); and (3) "freedom" (*Tgs*; *Sipra* Behar 2:2; Ibn Ezra, "free as the swallow," *děrôr*, Ps 84:4; Prov 26:2; *b. Beṣa* 24a). One can easily see that the three meanings are related: whatever is released, flows and gains freedom. The first meaning, "release," would be primary, with "flow" and "freedom" as its natural but secondary extension.

This intuitive analysis is confirmed by the precise Akkadian cognate *durāru* / *andurāru*. Its Sumerian equivalent is *amargi* 'return to the mother', a meaning that fits precisely Leviticus's definition of *děrôr*: "when each of you shall return to his holding [i.e., mother earth] and each of you shall return to his kin group [i.e., mother family]" (v. 10b; cf. v. 41). The meaning of Sumerian *amargi* is explicitly stated in an early Mesopotamian release: "to the mother he returned her children, and to the children he returned the mother "(Entemena, ca. 2430 B.C.E., III:10–IV:5, cited by Edzard 1974: 146, n. 7; Lambert 1972). The proclamation of *andurāru* 'release' is part of the larger edict of *mīšarum* (lit. a "straightening out"), the socioeconomic reform enacted by Mesopotamian kings on their ascension to the throne or for emergencies. "While *andurāru* was the specific state of 'release,' the misharum act was a general decree by the king which included as its major component acts of release, but of course of classes rather than individuals" (Westbrook 1991b: 45). One of the earliest *mīšarum* enacters, Urukagina (2370 B.C.E.), details the reason: officials stole property and land from citizens, forced them to sell their houses, demanded exorbitant rates for essential services (e.g., sheepshearing), and imposed unjust taxes for any economic activity, even for burial. Impoverished farmers and artisans became indentured servants; the blind, the widow, and the orphan were exploited. Nigirsu, the god of Lagash, commanded Urukagina to correct these evils: "He (Urukagina) amnestied the 'citizens' [lit. "the sons"] of Lagash who (were imprisoned because of) the debts (which they) had incurred (or because of) the amounts (of grain claimed by the palace as its) due (or because of) the barley (claimed by the palace for its) stores, (or because of) theft (or) murder, and set them free" (Urukagina of Lagash, XII, 13–22; Kramer 1963: 319). As summarized by Edzard (1965: 225), the *mīšarum* "has a twofold aim: to prevent the collapse of the economy under too great a weight of private indebtedness (the normal interest rate for barley was $33^1/_3$ percent, for silver 20 percent); and to prevent excessive accumulation of private wealth in too few hands" (see also Olivier 1984). Westbrook (1995: 159), however, doubts that economic stability was the motive behind the reforms. Rather, he favors social factors, particularly latifundia. He points to an edict of debt release promulgated by Tudhaliya IV as a result of social unrest, which took the form of a petition by a group of citizens (cf. Westbrook and Woodard 1990: 642). Military needs provided another motivating factor: "Soldiers were often settled on royal lands. When creditors attempted to take the crops from their fields, they threatened to strip the ruler of the ability to fill the military draft in an age when war was endemic and mercenary armies were still largely unknown" (Hudson 1999: 31). For a comprehensive account of the *andurāru / mīšarim* in Mesopotamia, see Weinfeld (1990a: 45–56) and see further the NOTE on "redemption" (v. 24). For a recent survey, see Hudson (1999).

It is now clear that the *andurāru / mīšarum* was not limited to Mesopotamia, but had also spread northward to the Hittites (cf. Westbrook and Woodward 1990) and westward into the territory of present-day Syria, up to the Mediterranean Sea. Of special significance is that in Mari at the beginning of the second millennium, during the reigns of Yahdun-Lim, Išar-Lim, Samsî-Addu, and Zimri-Lim, and contemporaneously in the neighboring states of Alep and Kurdâ not only is the *andurāru / mīšarum* a theoretical construct—that is, a promise held out by the monarch—but there exists incontrovertible evidence that it was put into practice, particularly at the accession of a new monarch to the throne (cf. Charpin 1990). For example, the very fact that creditors could and would insert a clause into the loan document stipulating that the *andurāru / mīšarum* would have no effect on their loans can only be interpreted that the proclamation was a living, efficacious instrument. It was regularly instituted on a monarch's accession to the throne and sporadically thereafter, and like the edict of Ammiṣaduqa (*ANET* 520–25), it proclaimed a remission of debts, a return of immovable properties to their original owners, and the manumission of debt-slaves.

In Ptolemaic Egypt as well, freedom proclamations are attested that continue ancient Pharaonic tradition (Smith 1968: 209–12). As pointed out by Weinfeld (1995: 168–74), when Ptolemy V Epiphanes reached his majority he bestowed the following boons on his people: remission of debts to the Crown, release of persons in prison and under indictment, and release of rebels and return of their property (Rosetta Stone, II.19–20). Weinfeld then demonstrates that the freedom declaration of Ptolemy VIII resembles Nehemiah's reform (Neh 5), Ammiṣaduqa's edict, and Solon's *seisachtheia*:

Ptolemy VIII	1. Those forced out of their homes shall recover their property
	2. Arrears in grain and money will be remitted
	3. Citizens shall not be dunned for taxes and corvee
Ammiṣaduqa	1. Remission of debts in grain and money
	2. Manumission of indentured men and children
	3. Cancellation of debts to the Crown
Nehemiah	1. Remission of debts in grain and money (5:10)
	2. Manumission of indentured children (5:2, 5)
	3. Return of mortgaged fields and vineyards because of debts to the Crown (5:11)
Solon	1. Remission of debts
	2. Manumission of indentured persons
	3. Release of land

In sharp contrast with all ancient Near Eastern *andurāru / mīšarum* proc-lamations, the biblical jubilee was cyclical—ordained by God and not by an earthly ruler according to his whim or need—and could not be revoked or circumvented.

throughout the land for all its inhabitants. bā'āreṣ lĕkol-yōšĕbêhā. In contrast, the Mesopotamian *andurāru / mīšarim* affected different districts and subjects at different times. However, this clause excludes the non-Israelites (e.g., the *gērîm* 'aliens'), who it assumes are landless and, hence, unaffected by the jubilee (see NOTE on "for you", v. 6).

a jubilee. yôbēl. The etymology is unclear. R. Akiba claims that in Arabic *yûblā* means "ram" (*b. Roš Haš.* 26a), a meaning that is supported by the Marseilles Tariff, *bybl 'm b'z* 'concerning a *ybl* or a goat' (AKAI 69). *Tg. Ps.-J.* renders *šôpĕrôt hayyôbĕlîm* (Josh 6:4) as *šûprā' dĕqeren dîkra'* 'a shofar (made) of the horn of a ram'. Thus it would be some form of horn that gave its name to the *yôbēl*-year because it was blown at its onset. Another rabbinic source claims it is a mountain goat (*m. Roš Haš.* 3:5). Others claim that it is a nominal forma-tion from the root *ybl*, which is frequently attested in the *Hip'il / Hop'al* de-noting "bring / brought" (e.g., Isa 55:12; Jer 31:9; Zeph 3:10; Pss 60:11; 68:30; Job 10:19), from which stem the following derivatives: *yābāl* 'stream' (Isa 30:25), *yĕbûl* 'produce of the earth' (Lev 26:4), and probably *tēbēl* 'earth' (1 Sam 2:8). This basic meaning is supported by its Akkadian cognate *abālu/ wabālu* 'bring' and its use in Aramaic, such as *wĕ'ôbîl* for *wĕhôlēk* 'bring' (Num 17:11). A third, slightly different, rendering is LXX *apheseōs* 'send away' (i.e., freeing), inde-pendently adopted by Ibn Ezra: "*yôbēl* is like sending forth." The LXX conflates two words *apheseōs sēmasia*, literally "a release proclamation" (vv. 10–13; in v. 15 only *sēmesia* 'proclamation' appears, thereby adding a second interpretation referring to the blowing of a ram's horn). Fox (1995) renders "Homebringing" on the grounds that sheep were "brought in" by horn blowing, a rendering ex-plicated by the rest of the verse. For other notions, see North 1990: 2–3. The likelihood of the first interpretation is supported by the fact that outside this source *yôbēl* only occurs with the meaning of "horn" (Exod 19:13; Josh 6:4, 5, 6, 13; cf. Loewenstamm 1958a). As the name of the fiftieth year, it never reappears in Scrip-ture: Ezekiel calls it *šĕnat haddĕrôr* 'the year of release' (Ezek 46:17).

As explained in the NOTE on "weeks of years," v. 8, the jubilee is based on the pentecontad calendar, whereby 49 + 1 days become 49 + 1 years, or seven sabbaths (weeks ending with the sabbath) plus one day become seven sabbaths (years ending with the sabbatical) plus one year. Abravanel cites another model, which, even if it cannot be substantiated, contains interesting similarities. The Torah was revealed to Israel fifty days after the Exodus (assuming that Pentecost coincided with the date of the Sinaitic revelation); the divine revelation was ac-companied by shofar blasts (Exod 19:16, 19), it required the sanctification of Mount Sinai (19:23), and it made use of a *yôbēl* (v. 13).

The jubilee release is extended to dedicated property (27:14–25) and, in Ezek 46:16–18, to property given by the prince to his servants.

The following verses (10aγ–13) are arranged chiastically (I. Kislev) in order to reveal the intent of the author:

A   *yôbēl hî'* (K: *hw'*) *tihyeh lākem*
    wĕšabtem 'îš 'el-'ăhuzzātô
    wĕ'îš 'el-mišpahtô tāšūbû
    B   *yôbēl hî'* (K: *hw'*) *šĕnat hahămiššîm šānâ tihyeh lākem*
      lō' tizrā'û
      wĕlō' tiqṣĕrû 'et-sĕpîhêhā
      wĕ'lō' tibṣĕrû 'et-nĕzīrêhā
    B'   *kî yôbēl hî'* (K: *hw'*) *qōdeš tihyeh lākem*
      min-haśśādeh tō'kĕlû 'et-tĕbû'ātāh
A'   *bišnat hayyôbēl hazzō't*
   tāšūbû 'îš 'el-ăhuzzātô

A   A jubilee it shall be for you (v. 10aγ)
    when you return, each one, to his holding (v. 10bα)
    and each of you to his kin group shall return (v. 10bβ)
    B   A jubilee it, the fiftieth year, shall be for you (v. 11a)
      You shall not sow
      You shall not reap the aftergrowth
      You shall not pick the untrimmed vines (v. 11b)
    B'   Since it is a jubilee, sacred it shall be for you. (v. 12a)
      From the field you may eat its produce (v. 12b)
A'   In this year of the jubilee, (v. 13a)
   You shall return, each one, to his holding (v. 13b)

The clause *yôbēl hî' tihyeh lākem* 'jubilee it shall be for you' is stated three times (the opening statements ABB'), thereby emphasizing the added words in BB' *šĕnat hahămiššim*, *qōdeš*, the fiftieth year is sacred, as well as repeating the first three words of v. 10. The purpose of emphasizing the sanctity of the jubilee is to associate it with the sabbath (cf. Exod 35:2), particularly the work prohibitions of the sabbatical year (cf. vv. 4b–5a with v. 11b), but at the same time to refrain from using the term "sabbath" because of the dissimilarity between these two institutions. AA' is obviously imbalanced. Either *wĕ'îš 'el-mišpāhtô tāšūbû* 'And each of you to his kin group shall return' fell out of A', or it was purposely added in A. There is no textual warrant for the former, and it must be ruled out of court. A close look at the latter alternative reveals the author's purpose. The full law of the jubilee is stated in v. 10b, an intimation that the details of the law will also include a pericope canceling the loan on the ancestral land owed to the creditor (vv. 23–55), thereby also indicating that the entire chapter is a unity. This clause is missing in A', showing that the immediately following verses (vv. 14–19) concentrate on the land and the means of computing its sale, which also sets the stage for the most likely case of this happening, namely, its owner has fallen into debt. Bβ‖B'β states the law concerning the land itself during the jubilee year: three staccato prohibitions regarding working the land and a concession concerning its aftergrowth.

It shall be a jubilee. yôbēl hi'(K: hw') tihyeh. The first of three uses of this clause in vv. 10–11 maintains that the jubilee celebrates the release of property and persons. The otherwise superfluous *hi'* is necessary to keep the clause the same in all three occurrences. The subject of *tihyeh* (fem.) is assumed to be previous *šĕnat*, as attested in v. 13a.

for you. But not for the alien! As the jubilee does not release the alien slave (vv. 45–46), it allows the *gēr* to continue to work the land. This is the reason why the term "sabbath" is assiduously avoided in describing the jubilee. In contrast to the sabbatical year, which falls uniformly on the land (vv. 4–5), the jubilee observance is only "for you," the Israelites (repeated in vv. 11–12). Thus one cannot presuppose with many moderns (most recently Schenker 1998: 25) that the fiftieth year (jubilee) collapses into the forty-ninth (sabbatical).

when each of you shall return to his holding. wĕšabtem 'îš 'el-'ăhuzzātô. Nothing better illustrates the permanent inalienability of inherited land than the story of Naboth (1 Kgs 21), which clearly demonstrates that this principle was long entrenched in Israel before the advent of kingship. The rabbis wonder whether this principle "includes a man who sold his field, which was then redeemed by his son? It shall be returned to his father in the jubilee" (*Sipra* Behar 3:6), on which Rabad remarks: "We do not know if it will even leave the hand of the one who redeems it, so for this reason it is said that in the jubilee year 'each of you shall return to his holding'" (noted by Japhet 1986: 79, n. 45). This comment is important for its two assumptions: if the original owner dies, his heir(s) would take possession, and, more significantly, if the land is redeemed by the gō'ēl, he keeps it, but only until the jubilee (see NOTE on v. 25). For the importance of this provision in the manumission of Israelite debt-slaves, see also the NOTE on v. 41.

his holding. 'ăhuzzātô (cf. 25:13, 27, 28, 41; Josh 22:9; Neh 11:3; 2 Chr 31:1). Two words are usually considered as synonyms and defined as "possession": 'ăhuzzâ and naḥălâ, with the latter being more narrowly defined as "inheritance" (LXX; Tgs.). Gerlemann (1977: 313–25, followed by Fager 1993: 89) proposes that the two terms differ sharply, 'ăhuzzâ as "arable land put at someone's disposal" and naḥălâ as "dwelling place." He argues that these words cannot mean "property" because Lev 25:23 states that the land is God's and Israelites are its resident aliens and, thus, do not possess it. Gerlemann's view cannot be sustained.

As pointed out by my student S. Rattray, the land of Canaan is also Israel's yĕruššâ 'possession', and repeatedly (especially in deuteronomistic literature) Israelites are spoken of as "entering the land to take possession of it [lĕrištāh]." Moreover, the root yrš is not limited to the Deuteronomist, but is found throughout the Pentateuch, including P and H (e.g., Gen 28:4; Exod 6:8; Lev 20:24; Num 33:53). Furthermore, 'ăhuzzâ can refer to property that is owned, not just rented. Non-Israelite slaves are 'ăhuzzâ lĕ'ōlām 'property for all time' (Lev 25:46): they can be bequeathed. Furthermore, houses (also 'ăhuzzâ), a year after their sale, become the permanent possession of their purchasers, a matter expressed by *qām laṣṣĕmîtūt laqqōneh* 'belong to the purchaser beyond reclaim' (v. 30). Also the verb *qām* followed by *lamed*, as corroborated by their use for Abraham's *'ăḥuzzâ* (Gen 23:20), testify that Abraham's property is his forever, and neither Ephron nor anyone else has further claims to it.

Rattray's solution is that *'ăḥuzzâ* is inalienable property derived from a sovereign (i.e., a fief), whereas *naḥălâ* is inalienable property obtained by virtue of belonging to a family (i.e., inheritance), as is Mari's *niḥlatum* (cf. Malamat 1988: 172–76). However, there are many instances where this distinction or, for that matter, any distinction will not hold. Num 32, because of its repeated speeches, provides excellent testing ground. One merely has to compare v. 5 with v. 19 and v. 18 with v. 30 to see that *'ăḥuzzâ* and *naḥălâ* interchange with no change of meaning. The same holds true for one verse, Num 35:8, in which both words occur. Ezek 46:16–18 provides another instance of this confusion: the land of the *nāśî'* is both *'ăḥuzzātô* and *naḥălātô*, and the peoples' land is both *'ăḥuzzātām* and *naḥălat hā'ām*. Finally, to compound the confusion, the two terms are found in construct, *'ăḥuzzat naḥălâ* (Num 27:7; 32:32) and *naḥălat 'ăḥuzzâ* (Num 35:2). What are we to make of this ostensible babel? The two must be largely similar in meaning; otherwise, they would not interchange. However, they could not be synonymous; otherwise, they could not be combined in a construct chain.

The term *'ăḥuzzâ* provides the key to the answer. First, it should be noted that *'ăḥuzzâ* in P is clearly preexilic. This was adequately demonstrated by Paran (1989: 303), who pointed out that whereas in P this word carries a rural, agricultural connotation, accompanied by either *'ereṣ* or *śādeh* (except in the case of the Levites [vv. 32–34], who are not landed), in the postexilic literature it is associated exclusively with *'îr* 'city' (Neh 11:3; 1 Chr 9:2; 2 Chr 31:1). Thus the claim that *'ăḥuzzâ* is a postexilic term (Levine 1983) must be dismissed (see also Hurvitz 1988: 95–96).

Second, contrary to Rattray, it does not denote "inalienable property." It stands for a permanent acquisition only when it is modified by the words (*'ăbōtāyw*, v. 41), *'ôlām* (Gen 17:8), *naḥălâ* (Num 27:7; 32:32), or *qeber* (Gen 23:9, 20; 49:30; 50:13). Thus *'ăḥuzzâ* by itself should be rendered as "holding or tenure." The land that the Israelites conquer, take, or seize (the root meaning of the verb *'āḥaz*) or the land given to them temporarily (cf. Gen 47:11) is an *'ăḥuzzâ*, but only God grants it to them as a *naḥălâ*. The latter term never has to be modified by an explanatory word, since, as "inheritance," it automatically conveys the notion of permanence. Our verse, of course, does not imply *any* previous holding. As indicated by the parallel verse (v. 41), *'ăḥuzzātô* is an ellipsis of *'ăḥuzzat 'ăbōtāyw* 'his ancestral holding' (Paran 1989: 105), and is clearly synonymous with *naḥălâ*.

The distribution of these two words in the Torah discloses a striking phenomenon. Israel's land is always called *naḥălâ* in D, always called *'ăḥuzzâ* in H, and called both *'ăḥuzzâ* and *naḥălâ* in P. One can explain D's insistence in calling Israel's land *naḥălâ* by its dogma, in contrast to the other conquest traditions, that Transjordan was also bequeathed to Israel by God (cf. Deut 2:24

with Num 34:12; Jos 22:19; see INTRODUCTION to Num 21:33–35 in Milgrom 1990a: 183–84). In this brief comment, however, I can focus only on H.

The term *'ăhuzzâ* clusters in Lev 25 and 27. In addition, it is found in 14:34 (demonstrated as H in vol. 1) and Deut 32:49. In Gen 17 and 23, where it also refers to the promised land, it is modified (as indicated above) by the terms *'ôlām* or *qeber*. How can one explain H's obsession to call Israel's land exclusively by the word *'ăhuzzâ?* The answer is evident when it is noticed (and here Gerlemann [1977] is right) that H, alone of all the sources, insists on referring to Israel's land as God's land and Israel's tenure on it as resident aliens (25:23). What God has granted to Israel is therefore an endowment, a fief (Rattray), but with conditions. If Israel does not fulfill them, it will be expelled from the land (18:26–30; 20:22–23; 26:14–38). Strikingly, here we have manifested a reversal in the terminological distinctions between H and P. Whereas H generally fudges and expands P's precise definitions (vol. 1.36–38; Knohl 1988: 95–100), here we find the reverse. Because of H's specific theology of Israel's land, it is constrained to reject the term *nahălâ* '(permanent) inheritance' and resort to the term *'ăhuzzâ* '(conditional) holding'.

and each of you shall return to his kin group. *wĕ'îš 'el-mišpahtô tāšūbû.* The Ugaritic verbal parallel *w tb l untֹ hm* 'they will return to their *untֹ* (16.191 + 272; *PRU* 2.18–19) is most attractive (first suggested by Yaron 1959: 167), but until the enigmatic term *untֹ* is clarified, the parallel remains a conjecture. Dybdahl (1981: 73) suggests that on the jubilee, each kin group redistributes the land it possesses to its component families (*bātê 'āb*). He assumes that even non-debtor families, those who did not lose this land, participate in the redistribution. This cannot be true because the text states repeatedly that each person returns to his (i.e., ancestral) holding (*'ăhuzzātô*, vv. 10bβ, 13b, 28b; cf. 41bβ).

The text clearly assumes that in order for the landholder to be restored to his land and his kin group, he no longer remains indebted or indentured to his creditor (see NOTES on vv. 25–49). Neh 10:32b indeed combines the two requirements for the seventh year: *wĕnittֹōš et-haššānâ haššĕbî'ît* 'We will forgo (the produce of) the seventh year' based on *ûnĕtֹaštāh* (Exod 23:11aα), and *ûmaššā' kol-yād* 'and the exaction of every debt' based on *maššēh yādô* (Deut 15:2). There is reason to assume that Nehemiah was the first to merge the two (cf. Kaufmann 1977: 424–25, n. 45; Williamson 1985). One cannot work without the other, a postulate that must have been taken for granted in the *dĕrôr* 'release' of the jubilee (pace Tigay 1996: 467). Indeed, what good is land burdened by the same debt, which caused its loss in the first place? Moreover, the tandem, simultaneous land restoration and debt remission could have been deduced from the prevalent and antecedent edicts of (*an*) *durāru* in Mesopotamia (see above, and COMMENT B).

Scholars have routinely wondered about the absence of debt-release provisions in Lev 25 (e.g., Kaufman 1984: 283), some claiming that H had none (Tigay 1996: 467). In my opinion, they fail to distinguish between the release laws of D, focusing on debt release (Deut 15:1–11), and those of H, focusing on land release (Lev 25:8–19). Since D is silent on land release, it has no choice but to mention debt release. However, since H emphasizes land release, it has no need to mention debt release but can take it for granted. The reverse (in D), however, is probably not true. As argued by Kaufman (1984: 282), if alienated lands were also returned to their former owners, why does the creditor need, in addition, to provide his debtor with a largesse? In H, however, land release without simultaneous debt release would be meaningless.

Later corroboration can be found in rabbinic texts: *y. Roš Haš.* 3:5; *y. Šebi.* 10:2; *b. Roš Haš.* 29a; *b. ʿArak.* 3b–4a (oldest MSS, versus *Sipra* Behar 3:6; *Sipre* Deut. 112; cf. Gilat 1995). Josephus's (*Ant.* 3.280) claim that the debtor's loan was remitted at the jubilee is probably correct, despite the assertion of his translators-annotators (Thackeray 1986: 4.454, n. b; Shalit 1967: 2.74, n. 207) that he confused the jubilee with Deut 15:1–6.

Neither can Robinson (1991) be right in claiming that the jubilee contains no new provisions other than those already found in the seventh-year release of Exod 21 and Deut 15. The latter (or the sabbatical of Lev 25) did not provide for the return of the alienated property to the original owner. This, indeed, constituted D's major failing. The landowner remains landless, and without any means of support is most likely to fall back into debt.

I suggest that another pragmatic basis for the jubilee (in addition to postponing Exodus' manumission of slaves from seven to fifty years) is the recognition that a fifty-year period would also give the creditor ample time to recoup his loan, except if it were contracted in the last years of the jubilee. Thereby, he would avoid the problem acknowledged by the Deuteronomist that within a seven-year period many loans could not be repaid by the debtor's labor (Deut 15:9). Rather than holding out D's promise of heavenly reward (Deut 15:10), H extends the period of the loan until the jubilee.

That this divine promise did not convince many creditors is demonstrated by R. Hillel's edict of Prosbul (*m. Šebi.* 10:3–4), a Greek legal device that circumvented the sabbatical by empowering the court, in place of the creditor, to collect the debt from the real property of the creditor (*m. Šebi.* 10:6) if the bond were delivered to it in advance of the sabbatical year.

Was R. Hillel anticipated in some way in the jubilee provisions? The text is silent. Perhaps just as divine blessing is vouchsafed to those who observe the sabbatical / jubilee fallow (vv. 20–22), so it awaits those who do not refrain from lending just before the jubilee. I would, however, suggest a more likely scenario: on the model of Mesopotamian *ṣmt* (see NOTE on "beyond reclaim," v. 23), a proviso would have been inserted into the bond that the loan would not be affected by the jubilee.

In any case, the silence of the text on this matter indicates, for me, that the legist did not think through all the implications of the jubilee—a clear sign that it was never implemented (see COMMENTS B and F).

return. tāšūbû. The change of person and the doubling is typical of H's style (cf. vv. 41, 48–49; Hoffmann 1953). The doubling is also essential for the chiastic structure of v. 10b.

his kin group. mišpaḥtô. The usual renderings for *mišpāḥâ* 'family' or 'clan', are not sociologically valid. The term "family" is apt for the *bêt 'āb*, comprising "all the living descendants of a single living ancestor . . . with their families, servants, and so forth" (Wright 1990: 53). The word "clan" designates the exogamous group, whose marriages *must* be outside the group, a requirement totally foreign to Israel's social structure. Gottwald (1979: 301–5) defines the *mišpāḥâ* as a "protective association of extended families." The same notion is conveyed by the less cumbersome expression "kin group" (Wright 1990: 49). The terms *bêt 'āb* and *mišpāḥâ* are not interchangeable (pace Weinfeld 1972b; Rogerson 1978: 93–95; Mendenhall 1983: 93; Chirichigno 1993: 131–36). The precise equivalents are *bêt 'ābôt* and *mišpāḥâ* (Milgrom 1978).

The *mišpāḥâ* "is the primary social unit as far as the territorial holding is concerned" (Johnstone 1969). In Scripture, it is identified with villages (e.g., Mic 5:1; 1 Chr 2:50–51; 4:5) and erstwhile Canaanite towns (e.g., Shechem, Tirzah, Hepher; cf. Gen 34; Josh 12:17, 24 with Josh 17:2–6). The Samaria ostraca, where seven districts correspond to kin groups of Manasseh (cf. Num 26:30–33; Josh 17:2–3; 1 Chr 7:14–19) dating from the first half of the eighth century, offer valuable evidence that the ancient kin-group divisions retained their identity and importance in the administrative structure of the nation well into the monarchy (Wright 1990: 48–53; Milgrom 1990a: 224).

11. *That fiftieth year shall be a jubilee for you. yôbēl hi'* (K: *hw'*) *šĕnat haḥămiššîm šānâ tihyeh lākem,* literally "A jubilee it, the fiftieth year, a year it shall become for you." The same structure is attested in Ezek 11:15; 21:16 (Dillmann and Ryssel 1897), as well as Isa 10:5 (Driver 1892: 272, § 201). Driver and White (1894) regard the words *šĕnat haḥămiššîm šānâ* as a gloss on the demonstrative pronoun *hi'* (K: *hw'*). However, as demonstrated, the purpose of this "gloss" and that in v. 12a is to emphasize the sacredness of the fiftieth year by repeating the key words *qōdeš / wĕqiddaštem* and *šĕnat haḥămiššîm* (see INTRODUCTION to vv. 10aγ–13).

for you. The second occurrence of *lākem* in vv. 10–13, this time it emphasizes that the negative commands that follow apply to Israelites, but not to aliens. This constitutes an exception to the rule that resident aliens are subject to all prohibitive commandments. Hence the need to stress "for you."

a jubilee. The second of three occurrences of *yôbēl hi'* (K: *hw'*) in vv. 10–13, this time it stresses the prohibition of any field work. Structurally, it ends the introversion ABB'A' and begins the series of negative commands (see INTRODUCTION to vv. 10–13).

its aftergrowth . . . its untrimmed vines. sĕpîḥēhā . . . nĕzîrêhā. But what is the antecedent of "its" (fem.)? It is either "the land" (v. 10a) or "year" (fem.), as in v. 11.

you shall not sow. Why is there no balancing "you shall not prune," as in v. 4b? If one answers that the expression "untrimmed vines" implies that no pruning is done (Wessely 1846), a counter-argument can be offered: so does "the aftergrowth" imply that no sowing is done, and yet sowing is expressly prohibited!

Moreover, as is visible from the structure of vv. 10–13, the brevity of this prohibition is out of kilter with the size of the following two, and rather than adding "you shall not prune," the structure would be more symmetrical (two positive commands [v. 10a] balanced by two negative commands [v. 11b]) if this prohibition "do not sow" were deleted. I have no answer.

12. *it is a jubilee.* This is the third of three occurrences of *yôbēl hi'* (K: *hw'*) in vv. 10–13. Its purpose is to stress that the aftergrowth may be eaten if it is taken directly from the field (Rashbam), not that the farmer may store it in his house (Ramban). Structurally, it also binds the two halves of vv. 10aγ–13.

sacred it shall be to you. qōdeš tihyeh lākem. Repeating the injunction "you shall sanctify the fiftieth year" (v. 10aα), this phrase unites the two halves of the structure of vv. 10aγ–13. It should not be overlooked that the verb *qārā'* 'announce, proclaim' occurs in this unit (v. 10a). Thus in effect the jubilee, no differently from the sabbath and festivals, is a *miqrā' qōdeš* 'a sacred occasion' (see NOTE on 23:2). In this case, however, it is the land that rests. Perhaps this idiom is deliberately avoided in order not to give the impression that the Israelites also must rest. Nonetheless, the notion of sacred time so prominent in chap. 23 is echoed here, despite the interruption of chap. 24 (see Introduction I M).

to you. The third occurrence of *lakem* implies that, in contrast to the aftergrowth of the sabbatical year, which is available *lĕkā,* the landowner and his relatives, the aftergrowth of the jubilee is available to all Israelites, including the poor.

its produce. tĕbû'ātāh. The feminine suffix once again refers either to "the land" (v. 10aα) or, preferably, to the year (*hi'*) as its antecedent. V. 12b does not contradict v. 11, which is alleged to be an absolute prohibition (Fager 1993: 101). See the NOTE on "a sabbath to YHWH," v. 2.

from the field. min-haśśādeh. "if it (the aftergrowth) disappears from the field it must disappear from the house" (*Sipra* Behar 3:14). Here, the rabbis claim that this jubilee injunction prohibits storing the aftergrowth.

13. The entire verse A' repeats and, thereby, locks in key words and phrases of A, the entire introversion contained in the first half of the structure (see INTRODUCTION to vv. 10aγ–13).

Vv. 14–17. These verses, dealing with the calculation of the price one may put forward in buying or selling land, also form an organic structure (J. Wyrick):

A   *wĕkî-timkĕrû mimkār la'ămîtekā 'ô qānōh miyyad 'ămîtekā*
  B   *'al-tônû 'iš 'et-'āhîw*
    C   *bĕmispar šānîm 'aḥar hayyôbēl tiqneh mē'ēt 'ămîtekā*
      D   *bĕmispar šĕnê-tĕbû'ōt yimkor-lāk*
        E   *lĕpî rōb haššānîm tarbeh miqnātô*
        E'   *ûlĕpî mĕ'ōṭ haššānîm tam'îṭ miqnātô*
      D'   *kî mispar tĕbû'ōt hû' mōkēr lāk*
  B'   *wĕlō' tônû 'iš 'et-'ămîtô*
A'   *wĕyārē'tā mē'ĕlōhêkā kî 'ănî YHWH 'ĕlōhêkem*

A   When you sell property to your fellow, or buy (any) from your fellow,
   B   you shall not cheat one another. (v. 14)
      C   On the basis of the number of years since the jubilee shall you
         buy from your fellow;
         D   on the basis of the number of (remaining) crop years shall
            he sell to you; (v. 15)
            E   the more such years, the more its purchase price;
            E'   the fewer such years, the less its purchase price;
         D'   for it is the number of crops that he is selling you. (v. 16)
   B'   Do not cheat one another,
A'   but fear your God; for I YHWH am your God. (v. 17)

EE' are identical in syntax, each using the same root (antonyms) to express both the verb and the substantive adjective. Since EE' speak exclusively of the buyer (note *miqnātô*, lit. "the purchase price"; the subject has already shifted to the buyer in C, v. 15a; contrast A, v. 14a) and the remaining jubilee years, they cover the case of C, which therefore explains the omission of C' from the structure. BB' are identical, but for the negative particles. AA' have nothing in common, A setting up the hypothetical case and A' the motive clauses.

14. *sell. timkĕrû.* The context implies "lease," but there is no word for it in Biblical Hebrew (Dybdahl 1981: 71). So it was understood by the rabbis who speak of selling the movables—that is, the usufruct of the land (cf. *Midr. Tanḥ. B* 2, cited in INTRODUCTION).

property. mimkār, literally "sold things" (Ezek 7:13). Perhaps this term was deliberately chosen throughout this chapter (vv. 14, 25, 27, 28, 29, 33, 50) to avoid the impression that real estate was being sold. Note that in Neh 13:20, *mimkār* specifically connotes movables, merchandise. Alternatively, H may have chosen the form *mimkār* to match *miqnâ* (v. 16): as *miqnâ* is a noun formation from *qānâ* 'purchase', so *mimkār* is a noun formation from *mākar* 'sell'.

to your fellow. The term *'amît* always refers to an Israelite, as indicated in such passages as 18:20 and 19:17 (parallel with *'aḥ*). Also note that Ezek 18:6, 11, 15 replace *'āmît* of Lev 18:20 with *rēaʿ*, a term that is also strictly confined to an Israelite (see NOTE on "your fellow," 19:15). For the corroboration of the Akkadian cognate *emūtu*, see the NOTE on 18:20. The use of the singular *'āmîtekā*, here and throughout (vv. 14, 15, 17; cf. 19:11), is distributive, a common stylistic phenomenon (e.g., Jer 16:7; Hos 4:8).

buy. qānôh. An infinitive absolute may be used as a continuation of a finite verb (GKC § 113z).

cheat. tônû. This verb is used frequently by Ezekiel regarding property (45:8; 46:18) and the poor (18:7, 12, 16; 22:7, 29), where, however, the verb takes on its general meaning "oppress" (see NOTE on 19:33). The context (v. 14a) manifests that the object of the cheating is the purchase price (contrast v. 17a).

another. 'āḥîw, literally "his brother." This injunction does not imply that one may cheat a non-Israelite. The context deals exclusively with Israelites because Israelites alone possess inherited land.

15. *On the basis of the number of years since the jubilee shall you buy.* The years that have elapsed after the previous jubilee must be counted to ascertain the remaining years until the next jubilee (Kalisch 1867–72). Perhaps this statement is based on the required counting of each day between the *ʿōmer* offering until the fiftieth day (23:15–16), as recited by traditional Jewry to this day: "This is the [number] day of the *ʿōmer.*" Surely, it is much easier knowing how many years have elapsed since the previous jubilee than keeping in mind how many years remain until the next jubilee.

In Mesopotamian documents, it was possible to affix a clause whereby the *andurāru / durāru* would not affect the sale of property or the loan of money—for example, *šumma durāru šakin* PN *kasapšu idaggal* 'If the release is declared the (creditor) person will see his money' (cf. Weinfeld 1985a: 55, n. 67). Note that the order of the buyer and seller in this verse is in chiastic relation with that in v. 14 (Hoffmann 1953).

crop years. šĕnê tĕbûʾōt. All of v. 15b seems superfluous. Indeed, the same redundancy surfaces in v. 16b, containing *mispar tĕbûʾōt* 'number of crops'. It seems to me that the legist wishes to emphasize that what counts in determining the price of the land is not its size, but its productive capacity. Surely, that is what any potential buyer would have in mind. The principle holds in evaluating the price of a dedicated field (see NOTE on 27:16, and chap. 27, COMMENT K), and it is confirmed by the rabbis (*Sipre* Num. 132; *b. B. Batra* 122a [bar.]) Jos. *Ant.* 5.76–79), and earlier in Greece (e.g., Plato, *Laws* 5.745b–c; Ahiṭuv 1992).

sell. Neither the term "sell" nor even the word "lease" is accurate, since the seller or renter can always redeem his land (Muffs 1965b: 4.10).

16. *its purchase price. miqnātô.* The term *miqnâ* means "purchase price" or "purchase" (e.g., *sēper hammiqnâ* 'the deed of purchase', Jer 32:11), which motivates Ehrlich's (1908) comment that this word is an ellipsis for *kesep miqnātô* 'its purchase price', as *gĕʾullātô* (v. 51) is an ellipsis for *kesep gĕʾullātô* 'its redemption price'. The antecedent of the suffix is *mimkār* 'property' (v. 14a), but addressed to the buyer (Shadal).

the more . . . the less. This is an instance of the increase–decrease formula (cf. Ezek 16:17–18; 30:15; Num 11:32–33; 33:54).

for . . . selling. This rationale is not repeated for buying, since this subject is fully covered in v. 16a (see structural outline in INTRODUCTION to vv. 14–17).

the number of crops. Minus the intervening sabbaticals and the years of natural disasters (*Sipra* Behar, par 3:10). The former, being fixed, can be deducted in advance; the latter, being unpredictable, would be the buyer's loss.

17. *Do not cheat one another.* This phrase is repeated for the sake of the introverted structure. The context, though (vv. 15–16), indicates that the subject is the price at the time of redemption, whereas the first time this injunction is used (v. 14b), the reference is to the price at the time of the sale. The rabbis find the repetition an opportunity for an ethical teaching: it is sinful to remind a man who has repented of his former misdeeds (*Sipra* Behar 4:1–2). Here, *tônû* takes on the extended meaning "oppress." This injunction is also found in Exod

22:20–23; Lev 19:33–34; Deut 23:16–17; Jer 22:3; cf. Ezek 18:7–8, 12–13, 16–17; 22:7, 29; 45:8; 46:16–18. It is designed to protect the underprivileged and unprotected in society and "to deter any form of economic exploitation arising from the dichotomy of rich and poor" (Gerstenberger 1996: 381). The same injunction is found in the Qumran writings: 4QD^c 1 I:5.

but fear your God. wěyārē'tâ mē'ĕlōhêkā. This rationale is cited for an ethical and, hence, unenforceable law (see NOTE on 19:14). The preposition *min* is equivalent to *lipnê* 'before', giving the sense "You shall be afraid in the presence of your God" (cf. vv. 36, 43; Gruber 1990a: 419, n. 29).

your God. 'ĕlōhêkem. The pronominal suffix attached to the word "God" switches from the singular *mē'ĕlōhêkā* to the plural *'ĕlōhêkem* as a warning to both buyer and seller (Ibn Ezra). The simple reason, however, is that YHWH *'ĕlōhêkā* (sing.) does not occur with *'ănî* as its subject, but with *'ānōkî* (Exod 20:2, 5; Deut 5:6, 9). This is the first of eight occurrences of the formula *'ănî* YHWH in chaps. 25–26, three in chap. 25 (vv. 17, 38, 55), three in the blessings and curses of chap. 26 (vv. 13, 44, 45), and twice in the theological bridge in the center of these chapters (26:1, 2), hence comprising one formula occurrence (M. Hildenbrand).

18. *You shall perform my laws, and my rules you shall heed and you shall perform them. wa'ăśitem 'et-huqqōtay wě'et-mišpāṭay tišměrû wa'ăśitem 'ōtām.* As pointed out by Gerstenberger (1996: 381), v. 18a is found in 18:4–5, 26; 19:19, 37; 20:8, 22, and it always concludes a unit. Possibly, it ended the original form of this chapter in which the jubilee is spoken of in general, abstract terms. Such a division would also resolve the awkwardness of two similar outcomes (vv. 18b, 19b) in the same unit (but see the possible structural analysis, below). The verbs and nouns are exchanged in 18:4, 5; 19:37, perhaps an indication that these verses are being cited here (Seidel's [1955–56] law; see NOTE on 26:42). For the distinction between laws and rules, see the NOTE on 18:4. The verb *šāmar* generally serves as an auxiliary, in this case with the following *wa'ăśitem* 'and you shall perform'. Both verbs are attached to *mišpāṭay* 'my rules'. D. N. Freedman (personal communication) notes the aesthetic chiasm.

that you may dwell on the land in security. wîšabtem 'al-hā'āreṣ lābetaḥ. In security from your enemies (*Sipra* Behar 4:3; cf. Deut 12:10; Judg 18:7–8). For the opposite effect resulting from nonobservance of the sabbatical years, see 26:34b, 43a (Sforno). If this proves to be the case, it forms a strong argument on behalf of the suggestion that, initially, vv. 18–22 dealt with the sabbatical year.

Doubts are expressed and allayed lest two successive fallow years, the jubilee and the preceding sabbatical (the forty-ninth) year, bring starvation. Similarly, doubts were expressed about the observance of the pilgrimage festivals, which, requiring the presence of all Israelite males, would cause their defenseless homes and villages to become attractive prey for the enemy (Exod 34:24).

19. *its fruit. piryāh.* Although *pěrî* normally is used with trees, it can also denote "produce": *pěrî hā'āreṣ* (Num 13:20, 26, 27; Deut 1:25; Jer 2:7); *pěrî hā'ădāmâ* (Deut 7:13; 26:2, 10; 28:4, 11).

eat your fill. wa ʾăkaltem lāśōbaʿ. This expression is also found in 26:5, 26, one of the indications that chaps. 25–26 form a single unit. See also Exod 16:3; Prov 13:25.

and you shall dwell upon it in security. wîšabtem lābeṭaḥ ʿālêhā. This is a repetition of v. 18b; whereas the latter speaks of political security, here the emphasis is on economic security, as indicated by the following verses (Ramban). It should also be noticed that the chiasm presented by these duplicate clauses is balanced by another chiasm (v. 22aβ, bβ) as part of a larger structure (J. Wyrick):

> a *wîšabtem ʿal-hā ʾāreṣ lābeṭaḥ*
> 　x *wĕnātĕnâ hā ʾāreṣ piryāh wā ʿăkaltem lāśōbaʿ*
> a′ *wîšabtem lābeṭaḥ ʿālêhā*
>
> A *wĕkî tō ʾmĕrû mah-nō ʾkal baššānâ haššĕbî ʿît hēn lō ʾ nizraʿ*
> 　B *wĕlō ʾ ne ʾĕsōp ʾet-tĕbû ʾātēnû*
> 　　X *wĕṣiwwîtî ʾet-birkātî lākem baššānâ haššiššît*
> 　B′ *wĕ ʿāśāt ʾet-hattĕbû ʾâ lišlōš haššānîm*
>
> A′ *ûzĕra ʿtem ʾēt haššānâ haššĕmînīt*
> 　b *wa ʾăkaltem min-hattĕbû ʾâ yāšān*
> 　　x *ʿad haššānâ hattĕšî ʿît ʿad bô ʾ tĕbû ʾātāh*
> 　b′ *tō ʾkĕlû yāšān*
> 　a you may dwell on the land in security. (v. 18b)
> 　　x The land shall yield its fruit and you shall eat your fill,
> 　a′ and you shall dwell upon it in security. (v. 19)
>
> A And should you say, "What are we to eat in the seventh year, if we may not sow
> 　B or gather in our crops?" (v. 20)
> 　　X I will ordain my blessing for you in the sixth year,
> 　B′ so that it will yield a crop (sufficient) for three years. (v. 21)
>
> A′ When you sow (in) the eighth year,
> 　b you will (continue to) eat from the old crop;
> 　　x until the ninth year, until its crop comes in,
> 　b′ you shall eat the old. (v. 22)

This structure "could be likened to a mountain with two smaller foothills on either side" (J. Wyrick). The main pivot (X) contains the answer to the question posed by two successive fallow years—God's blessing. It is preceded by the question (AB), which emphasizes the lack of grain due to the prohibition against sowing, and is followed by the answer (B′A′) that God will provide grain for three years so that sowing can be postponed to the eighth year. The foothills are alike in form more than in content: axa′ sets up the question by asserting that Israel shall dwell in economic security on its land; bxb′ details the answer (B′) that Israel's sixth year crop will last for three years.

Admittedly, this structure is conjectural because the "foothill," v. 18b (a), is an integral part of v. 18a, which is omitted from the structure; and the repetition of *wa'ăkaltem yāšān . . . tō'kĕlû yāšān* (bb') is not due to structural needs, but is a characteristic of H's style (see NOTE on v. 22). The "mountain" is more convincing, since it puts the center of the entire pericope (X) where it logically belongs—on God's blessing. For a more precise example of the same compound structure, see Num 11–12, which succeeds in uniting three independent narratives (Milgrom 1990a: 376–80).

20. *And should you say. wĕkî tō'mĕrû.* The verb *'āmar* is frequently used as a sign of a quotation (Kochman 1987); compare *wa'ămartem, lāmmāh tō'mĕrû, 'ēk tō'mĕrû* (e.g., Isa 40:27; Jer 5:19; 8:8; 48:14; Ezek 18:19, 25; Mal 1:4, 6–7).

if. hēn. This word corresponds with Ugaritic *hm*; Aramaic *hn, 'n*; Arabic *'innah* (e.g., Exod 4:1; 8:22; Jer 2:10; 3:1; Hag 2:12; Job 9:11, 12; cf. GKC § 159w).

sow. In the sixth year (see table 4).

gather in. In the seventh year (see tables 2–4).

21. *I will ordain my blessing. wĕṣiwwîtî 'et-birĕkātî.* The same language recurs in Deut 28:8 and the same thought in Deut 15:9–10.

in the sixth year. This is comparable to the double portion of manna on the sixth day (Exod 16:22–23).

so that it will yield a crop. wĕ'āśāt 'et-hattĕbû'â. For *'āśâ* meaning "produce," see Ps 107:37. The older form of the third-person feminine singular *'āśāt* is found preceding an aleph (GKC § 75n). Its subject may be *bĕ'arṣekā* (v. 7); if so, then vv. 18–22 originally belonged after it.

22. *you will eat . . . you shall eat. wa'ăkaltem . . . tō'kēlû.* This circular inclusio with change of verb pattern is typical of H's style (Paran 1983: 35).

the old. yāšān. For a similar usage, see 26:10. The major crops, as frequently indicated in Scripture, are grain, wine, and oil (Num 18:12; Deut 7:13; 11:14; Hos 2:8, 22; Neh 5:11; 10:40). Grain can be stored for long periods (Gen 41:47–48), as can wine (*m. B. Bat.* 6:3). The shelf life of olive oil, however, is a year. But if it is mixed with flour, it can last a very long time; as demonstrated by an experiment conducted by student S. Rattray, an unrefrigerated batch tested after three and a half years contained no trace of spoilage (Milgrom 1990a: 364).

The question is: How can the harvest of the sixth year last for three years, particularly if the sabbatical and jubilee years are consecutive? Of the many solutions suggested for resolving the chronological difficulties in vv. 20–22, three are worthy of consideration: two posit only the sabbatical (Rashi; Morgenstern 1935: 86–88), and one posits both the sabbatical and the jubilee (Ramban; independently R. Gane and J. Wyrick).

As seen in table 2, *Rashi* presumes a total fall calendar (religious and agricultural). The major defect is that the harvest of the sixth year does not last for three more years (v. 21), unless it is assumed that the harvest of the eighth year is not eaten until the ninth year. However *bô' tĕbû'ātāh* 'its crop comes in' (v. 22b) connotes the spring, when the grain harvest "comes in." Thus the harvest becomes available for the remainder of the eighth year, in contradiction to

TABLE 2

FALL		SPRING
6 Sow		6 Reap
7 ——	sabbatical	7 ——
8 Sow		8 Reap
9 Sow		9 Reap

the text, which states explicitly that during the eighth year only the *yāšān* 'old crop' is eaten (v. 22a), as well as for most of the ninth year, again in contradiction to the text, which states that the *yāšān* lasts until the ninth-year harvest is in. Blasser (1981: 130–31), who also opts for Rashi's system, cannot be correct: the sixth-year harvest lasts for only two years.

Morgenstern (1935: 86–88) presumes a total spring calendar, as depicted in table 3. The major defect in this reconstruction is the inaccuracy regarding the sabbatical. True, reaping is forbidden in the seventh year, but the landowner, his family, and, indeed, all Israelites may benefit from whatever is growing on the fields (vv. 11–12). Hence there is no reason not to sow in the sixth year (B. Scott) and tend the entire crop until the beginning of the seventh year, when the crop is nearly ripe. The harvesting of that full crop would surely supply enough food "(directly) from the field" (v. 12b) during the sabbatical and, perhaps, into the eighth year. Moreover, as shown by v. 9 (see its NOTE), the beginning of the jubilee year in the seventh month proves that the jubilee (and probably the sabbatical) followed the agricultural, or fall, calendar.

As seen in table 4, Ramban presumes a spring calendar, except for the sabbatical and jubilee. This system works the best. The harvest of the sixth year lasts for three years (v. 21); what is sown in the eighth year is reaped in the ninth; and vv. 10–22 are in place, as part of the jubilee pericope. There is one defect, however. The years should read not 6, 7, 8, and 9, but 48, 49, 50, and 51. Perhaps the latter notation was considered too cumbersome. (Also, there is no year 51 in the pentecontad system.) Alternatively, the possibility must be considered that originally vv. 20–22 were attached to v. 7 as part of the sabbatical pericope (see NOTES on "that you may dwell in the land in security," v. 18, and "so that

TABLE 3

SPRING		FALL
6 Reap		6 ——
7 ——	sabbatical	7 ——
8 ——		8 Sow
9 Reap		9 Sow

TABLE 4

FALL		SPRING
5 Sow		6 Reap
6 —	sabbatical	7 —
7 —	jubilee	8 —
8 Sow		9 Reap

it will yield a crop," v. 21) and subsequently were reformulated and moved into its present place as an appendix to the jubilee pericope. Hartley (1992: 437) prefers the latter solution because "the text says that they will sow in the eighth year, which would be forbidden in the year of the Jubilee if it is the fiftieth year, but not if it was the eighth year of a sabbatical-year cycle." Ramban, however avoids this pitfall by positing that the sabbatical and jubilee years are fixed according to the agricultural, or fall, calendar.

Is it possible that Scripture actually ordains that for two successive years the farmer is barred from working his fields? Does this not throw the sabbatical cycle out of kilter, since eight years will elapse between the last sabbatical of one cycle (the forty-ninth) and the first sabbatical of the next cycle? If, however, one should posit that the seven-year count should be maintained, then the first sabbatical will fall on the sixth year of the new cycle, allowing only five years for farming the fields. This possibility must be ruled out of court because Scripture specifically demands "Six years you may sow . . . and you may prune" (v. 3). Thus the jubilee cannot enter into the sabbatical count (M. Siegel). Does this not prove that the jubilee system is sheer utopia? The questions of the feasibility of two successive fallow years as well as the historic evidence for the observance of the sabbatical and jubilee are discussed in COMMENTS B and F.

Vv. 23–24. Redemption of Property: The Basic Principle

The introduction to a new subject, the laws of property redemption, takes the form of a general postulate (Kalisch 1967–72). These two verses also form an inclusio with v. 38, enveloping the pericope on property redemption (Cholewinski 1976).

23. *Furthermore, the land. wĕhā'āreṣ.* Not only does ownership of the land require you to observe the sabbatical and jubilee years, but it also implies that the land may not be sold without reclaim (B. S. Schwartz, personal communication).

must not be sold. lō' timmākēr. This apodictic and permanent (*lō'*) prohibition is a reminder to the buyer that his ownership of the land does not extend beyond the jubilee (Ramban).

beyond reclaim. lišěmītut, rendered *laḥǎlûṭîn* "in perpetuity" (Tgs.; cf. *lěḥûlṭānît*, *Sipra* Behar 4:8). Two meanings are ascertainable for the root *ṣmt* in Biblical Hebrew: 'destroy' and 'silence' (e.g., Lam 3:53 *Qal*; Job 6:17; 23:17 *Nipʿal*; Ps. 88:17 *Piʿel*; Pss 18:41; 54:7; 69:5; 73:27; 94:23; 101:5, 8; 143:12 *Hipʿil*). One cannot but compare similar connotations in the related roots *dmh* 'destroy' (Isa 15:1; Jer 47:5) and *dmm* 'silence' (Exod 15:16; 1 Sam 2:9; Jer 8:14; 47:6; Amos 5:13; Pss 30:13; 131:2). Both these meanings are present in *ṣěmītût*: the seller's claim is "ended / destroyed," or the seller is constrained to silence. In either case, the seller cannot revoke the sale. Another suggestion relates this root to *ṣmd* 'tie, bind'; the property, henceforth, is bound to the buyer and his progeny (Weinfeld 1990a: 59).

Of greater relevance is Akkadian *ṣamātu* 'finally hand over (real estate)', first noticed by Rabinowitz (1958) in a Ugaritic document and supported by Loretz (1962: 269–79) and Boyd (1978: 350–58) in the expression *ṣamit adi dāriti* 'finally hand over to all generations' (PRU 3.15:136; 16:131, 137), which is the precise semantic equivalent of *laṣṣěmîtut . . . lědōrōtāyw* (v. 30; cf. CAD 16.94). In Mesopotamia (and Ugarit), "only real-estate at the ultimate disposal of the crown seems to be at issue in these cases . . . the implication is clear that normal real-estate transactions were subject to royal annulment unless specifically declared to be a *ṣmt*, a practice prohibited by Leviticus" (Kaufman 1984: 280).

The terms *ṣamat* and *ṣummit* are also found as glosses to the Sumerogram ŠÁM.TIL.LA.BI.ŠÈ, 'at its full price' (CAD 16.94–95). The chances are that the purchaser did not pay the full price of the field; otherwise, it could *not* have been subject to the *děrôr* / jubilee; it would have been *lišěmîtut* 'in perpetuity' (Muffs 1965b: 2.1965). The *děrôr* did not affect property bought at *kesep mālē'* 'full price' (Gen 23:9), *ana šīm gamer* (Lewy 1958: 26, n. 48), *dāmîn gamrîn* (Milik 1954; 1957a: 264, l. 6); compare *Muraba'at* document 30:18–19 (Muffs 1969: 20, n. 4).

for the land is mine. kî-lî hā'āreṣ. The "land" is the promised land (cf. 18:25–27), not the earth, a notion developed in later times (e.g. Ps 24:1). Neither is this doctrine a priestly—indeed, nor an Israelite—innovation. It stems from an old Semitic, perhaps a universal, belief. Mesha, king of Moab, acknowledges that the god Chemosh "was angry with his land" (*'rṣh*; Mesha Stone, ll. 5–6). Enlil is titled *bēl mātāti* 'lord [lit. "owner"] of the lands'. Marduk also bears this title. Similarly, the soil of Canaan belongs to the local divinities, the *bě'ālîm*. When YHWH, like Marduk, dispossesses the *bě'ālîm*, he absorbs their function and takes on their role (cf. Schaeffer 1915: 165–171). This, surely, is the basis of the contest between YHWH and the Baal on Mount Carmel (1 Kgs 18). The Greeks espoused a similar doctrine: "The land is holy to the gods . . . whoever shall sell the property of his family or his land shall be overtaken by the punishment suitable for such deeds" (Plato, *Laws* 6.741b).

Canaan is called *'ereṣ YHWH* (Hos 9:3) and, with suffixes, "my / your / his land" (Isa 14:25; Jer 2:7; 16:18; Ezek 36:5, 20; 38:16; Joel 1:6; 2:18; 4:2; Pss 10:16; 85:2). YHWH's ownership is already adumbrated in the Song of the Sea (Exod 15:17), where it is called *har naḥǎlātěkā* 'the mountain of your inheritance'. That the expression "inheritance of YHWH" can refer to the land, see Jer 2:7; 50:11; Ps 79:1 (the term *naḥălâ* in 1 Sam 26:19; 2 Sam 14:16, however, probably refers to the people Israel, as do most of its attestations [e.g., Deut 4:20; 9:26–29; 1 Kgs 8:50–51; Jer 10:15–16; Pss 78:62, 71; 106:39–40; Joel 4:2]).

Thus the right of redemption is theologically grounded. The Israelites received their property by lot (Num 33:50–56; Josh 14–19)—that is, from God. Given by God it is revocable only by God (cf. Philo, *Laws* 2.113).

Further buttressing YHWH's claim to the land is a precedent found in Middle Assyrian law: "All privately 'owned' land was originally conceded by the crown to its 'owners' and it therefore reverts to the crown for concession (to others) when the direct line of succession fails" (Postgate 1971: 512). Thus if all land in Mesopotamia theoretically belongs to the king, all the more so in Israel, where YHWH is the king. In Mesopotamia, the king grants land in return for *ilku* 'services' (cf. *CAD ilku* A), whereas Israel receives and retains land in return for keeping YHWH's covenant.

The larger implication of "the land is mine" is that the land is holy. In the priestly system whatever belongs to God is sacred. Whereas P restricts the sacred sphere to the sanctuary, H extends its borders to embrace the entire land. Thus the doctrine of the "holy land," though not explicitly stated, is implied (cf. Exod 15:13; Isa 11:9; 57:13; Jer 31:23; Ps 78:54; cf. Loewenstamm [1984: 162, 169], who points to the antiquity of the concept in the description of Baal's heritage *bqdš bġr nḥlty* 'in the sacred mount of my heritage' [*KTU* 1.3 III:29–30; IV:19–20]). But H never calls the land holy. When the land is polluted, it cleanses itself by regurgitating its inhabitants. If the entire earth is polluted, the cleansing is done by a flood (Gen 6:13–17). Employing the terms of the purity scale, impure changes back to pure. In neither case, therefore, need the status of holy be involved (see INTRODUCTION to 18:24–30).

H had two basic theological reasons for refraining from calling the land holy. The first was its apprehension that such a notion implied that holiness inheres in the land—indeed, in nature. It would not be a far remove from the theology of the pagan world, which hypostatized nature as representing, even embodying, various deities, who were members of the divine assembly, or independent and even malevolent forces (e.g., Ug. *Yamm* 'Sea'). Second, YHWH's ownership of the land implied Israel's obligation as its residents to obey the owner's rules (particularly, if he is also their redeemer, v. 24). The so-called holiness of the land is only YHWH's holiness when it is palpable on the land, a condition that is met if Israel fulfills his commandments (see COMMENT on chap. 19, and NOTES on 26:11–12).

The notion of God's ownership of the land is found throughout Scripture (e.g., Exod 15:17; Isa 14:2, 25; Jer 2:7; Ezek 36:5; 38:16; Hos 9:3; Pss 10:16; 85:2). Divine ownership of the land of Canaan does not, however, delimit the boundaries of his control. The God who created the world by his fiat (Gen 1 [P]) and whose glory is the fullness of the earth (Isa 6:3; for the translation, see Levenson 1988: 141, 170–71) is also, of certainty, the ruler of the earth (cf. Halpern 1987: 96). An unbridgeable distinction between the two spaces is manifest: the land of Canaan / Israel occupies a special place in the divine schema. It is set apart from all other earth-bound territory; it is holy and, hence, imposes special requirements on its inhabitants.

Joosten (1994: 243; 1996: 177) has brought to my attention Clements's article (1961–62; cf. Clements 1965: 73–76), which demonstrates that certain psalms presuppose that the Temple is coextensive with the land. The request to dwell in YHWH's house *for a lifetime* (e.g., Pss 23:6; 27:4; 61:5) indeed implies the right to dwell in his land. Moreover, that the land is but an extension of the Temple Mount / God's house is presumed by other texts (Exod 15:17; Isa 11:9; 57:13; Hos 9:15; Ps 78:54). Hence YHWH can be conceived as residing in the entire land (e.g., Num 35:34; Josh 22:19).

It seems to me, however, that Joosten (1994: 247; 1996: 182) goes too far in conceiving the Temple as a "place of refuge and asylum [and] the *gēr* becomes a metaphor for the asylant seeking refuge in the temple." Here Joosten bases himself on the comprehensive study of asylum cities in the ancient Near East by Weinfeld (1985a: 57–78). However, the parallels drawn for Israel's institution of asylum cities (Num 35:9–15; Deut 4:41–43; 19:1–9) are flawed and misleading. As I have demonstrated (1981c: 299–310), Israel's priests introduce a major change (but not innovation, as I originally proposed) in their nature: the asylum cities must be *devoid of sanctuaries*. It was in the primary, indeed urgent, interest of the priesthood to abolish sanctuary asylum and thus prevent the altar from being seized and, hence, contaminated by murderers and thieves. And it is remarkable that D did not specify that the Temple-city, "the place where YHWH has chosen," should be an asylum city. Moreover, the metaphor of Israel as asylants distorts the image conveyed by our text: Israel is not a group of refugees seeking asylum (from whom?), but God's people whom he assigns to dwell in his territory (for pertinent examples from the ancient Near East of other peoples claiming that they have been chosen by their god to settle in his territory, see Weinfeld 1985a: 133–39).

I also differ with Joosten on a more fundamental issue. He claims that "the land is YHWH's because his sanctuary is located there" (1996: 189; cf. 176–78), which he supports by pointing out that "before the occupation of the land by the Israelites (18:24–28; 20:22–24), YHWH does not dwell in the land but in the camp. And after the expulsion of the Israelites (26:33–45), YHWH will no longer dwell in the land, for the sanctuaries will have been destroyed (26:31)" (92). If so, by what right did YHWH expel the Canaanites for polluting the land (18:24–30)—unless the land was already his! Moreover, that YHWH owned the land from time immemorial in the consciousness of Israel is expressly stated in the ancient Song of Miriam: *tĕbī'ēmô wĕtiṭṭā'ēmô bĕhar naḥălātĕkā* 'You brought them and planted them in the mountain of *your* inheritance' (Exod 15:17a; Ps 78:54). That is, the land was YHWH's even before Israel's arrival. Regarding the exile, Joosten (1996; 189, n. 73) has to admit that the land remains in YHWH's possession (26:42). Furthermore, Joosten has overlooked H's incipient monotheism. H's *miškān* is not YHWH's sanctuary, but his presence (26:11): YHWH is a transcendent, universal God capable of being both beneficently present in the land and punitively present outside the land (26:33a, 36–38). Thus before and after Israel's residence in the land, it is YHWH's.

Thus the land must be distinguished from the sanctuary. The former enables Israel to dwell there; the latter obligates Israel to achieve a life of holiness. Joosten (1996: 176) asks: "If there is no natural relationship between YHWH and his land and if his power is not limited to a particular domain, what is the sense of the statement that the land is his?" The answer, I submit, is that the land of Canaan was preordained by YHWH as the *future* site of Israel's residence, as concretized in the priestly account of the covenant with Abraham (Gen 17:8). This divine grant would not be abrogated even if Israel were expelled from it as long as Israel would contritely confess its sins and adhere to its covenantal obligations (26:3, 40).

resident aliens. gērîm wĕtôšābîm. As first recognized by Melamed (1944–45), this compound is a hendiadys. Its nature is indicated not only by its context, but even more decisively by the fact that the term *tôšāb* never occurs in isolation (except in 1 Kgs 17:1, where *mittôšābê* is probably a dittography following *hattišbî*; cf. LXX). It is either compounded with *gēr* (vv. 35, 45, 47 [twice]; Gen 23:4; Num 35:15) or broken into two parallel poetic *stichoi* (Ps 39:13; 1 Chr 29:15)—a characteristic of the hendiadys (e.g., *hesed wĕ'emet*, Isa 16:5; Mic 7:20; Pss. 57:11, 69:14; cf. Melamed)—as well as compounded with *šākîr* (vv. 6, 40; Exod 12:45; Lev 22:10; see NOTES on v. 6 and 22:10). To be sure, the term *gēr* exists independently, which indicates only that the person is alien, whereas *gēr wĕtôšāb* emphasizes that the alien has taken root and settled in a community. Indeed, since he has probably settled on land belonging to an Israelite, he is totally dependent on the latter for his sustenance (Levi-Feldblum 1986: 35). Moreover, as a *gēr* he may never own land in perpetuity. This rule apparently held true among the ancient peoples of Canaan. When Abram had taken up residence as a *gēr wĕtôšāb* among the Hittite occupants of Hebron, he not only had to turn to the owner of his desired burial cave, but had to receive the permission of the ruling council of the entire city in order to buy the lot in perpetuity (Gen 23:3–16).

That Israel presumably owns its land (*'ăhuzzātô*, vv. 10b, 25, 41b) does not contradict the primacy of divine ownership. Israel's hold (*'ăhuzzâ*) is provisional (see NOTE on "when each of you shall return to his holding," v. 10). It depends on Israel's fulfillment of its covenantal obligations. Failing that, YHWH will expel Israel (26:33, 38–41). Indeed, to use H's impurity terminology, the land itself will disgorge Israel (18:25, 28; 20:22; see NOTE on 26:34).

The status of Israel's land may be illuminated by the comparable status of the *kidinnūtu* cities of Mesopotamia, which were sacred to the gods. As shown by Dandamaev (1965), in the Achaemenid period in Mesopotamia, the sacred cities were considered to be the property of the relevant god (Weinberg 1992: 103). Entmetena (2430 B.C.E.) frees the Sumerian cities Lagash, Erech, Larsa, and Bad-Tibira and dedicates them to the gods. Manishtusu (ca. 2230–2292 B.C.E.) frees thirty-eight cities from *ilku* duties and transfers them to Šamaš. (For Hittite and Egyptian parallels, see Weinfeld 1995: 120, 233–35.) So, too, YHWH has redeemed Israel from bondage (redemption implies ownership; see below) and planted them in his territory (*nāḥălâ*, Exod 15:17; Ps 78:54–55). They are obligated to obey the terms of his covenant and, according to one tradition, are consecrated to him as his priests (Exod 19:6; Isa 61:6). Thus by their covenantal (and sacral) status, they are freed of *ilku* duties to any other people; they belong solely and totally to YHWH. Still, residing in his land, their status before YHWH is as his *gērîm wĕtôšābîm* 'resident aliens'. The notion that Israel or the Israelite is a *gēr* before YHWH is stated elsewhere in Scripture (Pss 39:13; 119:19; 1 Chr 29:15).

Muffs (1965b: 4.7) offers an alternative model for understanding the relationship between Israel and its land, namely, family law. The marriage-adoption formula found in Exod 6:7 and Lev 26:12, both H (see also Hos 1:9; 2:4), implies that YHWH has legally "adopted" Israel as his family-nation. Through this adoption pact, Israelites have received the right to hold (*'āḥaz*, but not inherit, *nāḥal*; see NOTE on v. 10) land. According to this pact, Israel's hold on the land is dependent on its behavior, spelled out in the blessings and comminations of Lev 26.

under my authority. 'immādî. A form equivalent to *'immî*, it is found only in the first person; perhaps it is an ellipsis of *'im yādî* (Joüon 1923: § 103i).

With *gēr* as its object, *'im* does not mean "with," but "under the authority, in the service of." For a substantiation of this rendering and extra-biblical cognates, see the NOTE on v. 35. It cannot mean "under the protection of," as claimed by Wright (1990: 64; see also Preuss 1977: 450), on the basis of the rendering of Clements (1961–62: 23, in a garbled line that Wright misconstrues).

24. *the land you hold. 'ereṣ 'ăḥuzzatkem.* Ramban offers two explanations. The first is that this verse contrasts with the previous one—that is, the whole earth belonging to God rather than the land on which Israel is settled. As discussed in v. 23, however, God's land is not the earth, but only the land he has assigned to Israel. These two verses, therefore, are complementary, not contrastive. How, then, can we explain the change of terminology, from "land" to "the land you hold"? What is the significance of the qualification *'ăḥuzzatkem* '(the land) you hold'?

Ramban, in his second reply, follows Ibn Ezra in suggesting that Israel's land (the priestly tradition) had the Jordan River as its eastern boundary, thus excluding the territory of Reuben and Gad (Num 34; Josh 22:19; see INTRODUCTION to Num 21:33–35 in Milgrom 1990a: 183–84). Thus the use of the term *'ăḥuzzâ*, derived from the verb *'āḥaz* 'seize', is deliberate: all the land that Israel has conquered, including Transjordan, whether God's land or not, is subject to redemption. For a full discussion of *'ăḥuzzâ* and its distinction from the near-synonymous term *nāḥălâ*, see the NOTE on "his holding," v. 10.

redemption. gĕ'ullâ. This term indicates the transitional position of the verse. On the one hand, it connects with the previous one: Israel not only does not possess its land *liṣĕmitut* 'beyond reclaim', but must allow it to be reclaimed through *gĕ'ullâ* 'redemption'. The process of redemption, on the other hand, does not refer to the automatic release of the land at the jubilee year, the subject of the previous pericope (vv. 8–22), but to monetary redemption (Isa 52:3) during the period between jubilees. Thus v. 24 also heads up a series of cases that exemplify redemption (cf. Shadal).

The *gĕ'ullâ* institution is invoked in other situations, all of which predicate a clan-structured society, and, hence, it must be of early preexilic provenance (Cardellini 1981: 280–86). Redemption denotes the restoration of the status quo, a responsibility that rests on the next of kin, called the *gō'ēl* 'the redeemer'. He is variously (1) the levir who, as in Ruth 3:13, provides his deceased kinsperson with a survivor by marrying his childless widow; (2) the receiver of reparation due the deceased (Num 5:8); (3) the "blood redeemer," *gō'ēl haddām*, who is obligated to put to death the (unlawful) slayer of his kinsperson (Num 35:9–34; cf. Milgrom 1990a: 504–11); and (4) the one who, as in the cases dealt with here, is obligated to buy back the inherited field of his indebted kinsperson (vv. 25–28) and to bring him out of slavery (vv. 47–55). The jubilee guarantees redemption in case the *gĕ'ullâ* institution does not work. Indeed, this is probably the reason why the jubilee was instituted in the first place (cf. Schaeffer 1915: 165–171), as an extension of no. 4. Scripture records two optional redeemers. The first is the owner of the field, house, animal, or tithe who dedicated it to the sanctuary (27:15, 19, 27, 31). The second is YHWH, who by his grace redeemed Israel from the Egyptian bondage (Exod 6:6; 15:13) and the Babylonian Exile (Isa 43:1; 44:22, 23; 48:20; 51:10; 52:3, 9; 62:12). As indicated by the refrain in Moses' addresses to Pharaoh, *šallaḥ 'et-ammî* 'Let my people go' (Exod 5:1; 7:16, 26; 8:16; 9:1, 13; 10:3), YHWH is the "owner" of Israel; hence Israel's deliverance constitutes redemption (S. Nikaido).

Throughout the ancient Near East, the principle is maintained that divine lands may not be sold. Fields, gardens, and vineyards of the Hittite "Stone House" (i.e., mausoleum) as well as its personnel may not be sold (Otten 1958: 106, ll. 15–16). In ancient Greece, whoever sells sacred land is subject to punishment (Plato, *Laws* 741). Colophon inscriptions in Lydia testify that sanctuary cities were initially given by the gods (Weinfeld 1985a: 136). Israel, too, bore the tradition from old that its land belonged to its God. The land is called, in one of earliest texts, *har naḥălātkā* 'your own mountain', *mākôn lĕšibtĕka* 'the place of your residence', *miqdāš 'ădōnāy* 'the sanctuary, O Lord' (Exod 15:17; cf. Ps 78:54). It is not by accident that in the Ugaritic texts, Baal's residence on Mount Zaphon bears similar terminology: *bqdš bǧr nḥlty* 'in the sanctuary in the mountain I own' (CTA 3, III: 27–28). No wonder, then, that Israel is forbidden to sell its land in perpetuity.

The right of the original owner to redeem his land in certain circumstances seems to be taken for granted in ancient Near Eastern jurisprudence, as exemplified in an Eshnunna law: "If a man became impoverished and sold his house, the day the buyer will sell, the owner of the house may redeem" (LE § 39); that is, the original owner has the first rights to reclaim his property. Nothing is said about the redemption price. For Szlechter (1954: 56) and Westbrook (1985: 97–102), this means that the land is redeemed at the price at which it was sold by the owner. The purpose of this redemption clause would then be "to allow a person who has been forced to sell his ancestral land at *undervalue* to buy it back at the same low price" (Westbrook 1985: 110). Interestingly, later mish-naic law, in the single passage it deals with land redemption (*m. 'Arak.* 9:2), favors the original owner even more by stating that the redeemer is entitled to pay the lowest price obtained for the property since its original sale. Szlechter (1954: 96) and Westbrook (1985: 105–8) cite CH § 119, 281, and a *kudurru* from the reign of Meli-shishu as direct evidence of the original price being the price for the redemption of the land (questioned, however, by Yaron 1988: 234). In any case, there is evidence in the legal systems of the ancient Near East of traces of a universal right to redeem family land (cf. *ipṭirū, CAD* 7.171–72). Nonetheless, the difference between redemption rights in Mesopotamia and Israel must be noted. According to the Eshnunna law, "the occasion to exercise the power (to redeem) depends on the buyer's intention to alienate the property. As long as the buyer holds on to it, *he is secure in his possession*" [my emphasis] (Yaron 1988: 233). The Leviticus law, however, indicates that the buyer has no right to refuse redemption.

Babylonian sale documents often contain a statement that excludes the seller from making a claim on his former property (a further indication that "the right of buying back such property must have existed on the seller's side" [Schaeffer 1915: 165]). Moreover, Westbrook (1988: 111–16) argues that the sale documents imply that land sold at "full price" (i.e., *not* undervalued) is irredeemable; it passes into the hands of the buyer and his heirs forever. (Westbrook, however, has been anticipated by Ehrlich [1908] and Muffs [1965b: 2.6–7] on Gen 23.) He cites the following formula occurring frequently in Susa sale contracts: *ul ipṭirū ul manzazānu šīmu gamru* 'it is not (a case of) redemption, it is not (a case of) pledge, it is (a case of) the full purchase price' (e.g., MDP 22 44: 20–21, 45:15–17 and passim). This formula has important reflexes in biblical narratives dealing with the sale of property. Abraham resists Ephron's attempt to give him the cave, but insists on paying *kesep mālē'* 'full price' (Gen 23:9) for the field (vv. 11, 13) in order to acquire an inheritable estate. David asks Arauna / Ornan to sell his threshing floor at full price, saying, "I will not bear that which is yours to YHWH" (1 Chr 21:22, 24). Finally, Jer 32:11–15 stipulates that the deed, which has recorded the low price Jeremiah paid for the field, is to be carefully preserved (Jer 32:11–15) so that "when the external danger is past, Hanamel or his heirs may exercise their right to redeem the field at Anatot for the same low price" (Westbrook 1985: 127).

The theological underpinning of the biblical law of redemption only reinforces its obligations for Israel: as God has redeemed the land from those who, having forfeited the land, now hold on to it illegally (18:24–25), so must Israel redeem the land from those of its own people who, not being its rightful inheritors, possess it illegally. To be sure, nowhere in Scripture is God called the redeemer (*gō'ēl*) of his land. But such is the implication of the institution of the jubilee: if the human redeemer fails to intervene, then the divine redeemer acts—by his law of the jubilee. By virtue of redeeming Israel from Egyptian bondage, God has become Israel's owner. If any Israelite is enslaved by any non-Israelite, the human redeemer is God's agent to restore his enslaved kinsman to the service of God (see INTRODUCTION to vv. 47–55). Divine intervention also lies behind the other cases where redemption is required: *wĕ'ak 'et-dimkem lĕnapšōtêkem 'edrōš . . . ûmiyyad hā'ādām miyyad 'îš 'aḥîw 'edrōš 'et-nepeš hā'ādām* 'But for your own life-blood, I will require a reckoning . . . of man will I require a reckoning for human life, of every man for that of his fellow man' (Gen 9:5b). That is, if the blood redeemer (*gō'ēl haddām*) fails to slay the murderer, God himself will do so. This principle apparently lies behind the folk tradition of the levirate: because the *gō'ēl* Onan refused to produce an offspring from his deceased brother's widow, God slew him (Gen 38:8–10).

Here the redeemer acts as God's agent on and for the land that God has declared as his own. YHWH has established Israel as the lawful tenants (his "resident aliens," v. 23) on the land, which should be subdivided equitably among Israel's tribal families as their permanent inheritance. If through indebtedness any of the land is sold, the nearest kinsperson is obligated to redeem it and return it to its owner on or before the jubilee. If, however, the family fails or forfeits its redemptive responsibility, then God intervenes by the unilateral action of his jubilee, which automatically cancels the debt and restores the land to its original possessor. The same procedure is invoked in the case of an Israelite enslaved by a non-Israelite creditor (see NOTE on vv. 47–55). For the wider theological implications, see the Introduction II K.

Vv. 25–55. The Three Stages of Destitution

A likely scenario can be reconstructed:

1. An Israelite farmer is forced to sell part of his land to cover his debt. If he cannot redeem the land, his redeemer does, and the latter retains it until the jubilee (vv. 25–28).

2. In the event of crop failure on his reduced land, the farmer takes out a loan to purchase seed for the next year's crop. It is estimated that the present-day peasant of Iraq breaks even if no more than every fourth harvest fails. If crop failures occur more frequently, the peasant has to make use of credit (Wirth 1962: 20–21). The probability is higher in areas such as Israel, which experiences lower rainfall and less irrigation. Thus the farmer may default and lose his land (but not the title) to his creditor. If he still owes on his loan, he works his land as a tenant farmer. Although he has lost the land, its usufruct is still his. It amortizes the loan (on which he pays no interest), or the land reverts to him at the jubilee (vv. 35–38).

3. If the farmer still cannot pay off his loan, he forfeits not only his land but also its usufruct. He and his family enter the household of the creditor (vv. 41a, 54b): "The rich rule the poor, and the borrower is a slave to the lender" (Prov 22:7). That indebtedness could end in enslavement, see 2 Kgs 4:1; Amos 2:6; Neh 5:5. However, in Lev 25, the debtor's status is that of a resident hireling, not a debt-slave. He receives wages that amortize his debt (vv. 39–43). In stages 2 and 3, the redeemer does not intervene (see INTRODUCTION to vv. 39–55). But if the farmer sells himself to a non-Israelite, he must be redeemed, and until the jubilee he works for his redeemer (vv. 47–55).

Chirichigno (1993: 323–43) proposes a slightly altered series. In stages 2 and 3, there is no antecedent debt; that is, each stage of destitution is incurred independently. The main difference in our interpretations lies in stage 2. He presumes that the farmer still owns the remaining land, but it is not able to provide sufficient support for him and his family. His family refuses to redeem him, and he has to rely on charitable, interest-free loans (Chirichigno 1993: 327–29). It is only in stage 3 that he loses his land (see NOTE on "a resident alien," v. 35, and INTRODUCTION to vv. 39–55). Schenker (1998: 27) gives the impression that Chirichigno presumes a prior stage of destitution when the paterfamilias sells his children into slavery. I could not find such a statement in Chirichigno. It rather fits Schenker's own theory that Lev 25 does not differ with Exod 21:2–7, but completes it. That the biblical codes could contemplate and approve any situation whereby a father would sell off his children, even for a six-year period, before selling any part of his land, is beyond my comprehension.

The worsening stages of indebtedness may be compared with a similar account told in the Joseph story (Gen 47:13–26). The Egyptians sold all they owned to Pharaoh in order to buy food: first their mobile possessions, then their land, and finally their persons; and thus they were reduced to serfdom. Who was the author of this policy—Joseph. And who became its main victims—Joseph's descendants (a subtle critique of "Joseph the Wise; Joseph the Provider"). Our text's message is loud and clear: in Israel, this must not happen!

The preventive force is the institution of redemption: "The centre of gravity passes from him (the original owner) to a relative; he loses in importance what the relative gains, but the family, as a family, loses nothing. The property is not left to chance, but remains in the kindred with which it is familiar" (Pedersen 1926: 1.84). This simultaneously answers the question: If, according to H, the property reverts to its owner only at the jubilee whether or not it is redeemed, what, indeed, is the purpose of redemption? The fundamental principle (with Pedersen 1926: 1.81–85) is that ancestral lands should never be alienated from the (kin) family. At the moment the land is sold, the obligation falls on the redeemer to reclaim it. Ostensibly, this is supported by the assumption throughout the hexateuchal sources that the kin group, not the individual, was the unit for land allotment (cf. Num 26:1–56; 33:54; Josh 13–17). But contrary to general practice, as attested by Jer 32 (see below, and contra Pedersen), H ordains that the property does not even belong to the redeemer. He retains it only so its usufruct will repay him his redemption costs—technically, until the jubilee—when it must revert to its owner (i.e., bêt 'āb 'the father's house'). This, then, is the innovation of Lev 25: the redeemer does not keep the property forever. He must return it to the original owner, at the latest, at the jubilee (Loewenstamm 1958a: 578–82; see below). Thus Lev 25 breaks the age-old, time-honored institution of clan ownership of property (contra Tigay 1966: 467). Henceforth, the concern of the law is to preserve the property rights of the individual.

Wright (1992: 3.1027) has caught the precise significance of the jubilee:

The main aim of redemption was the preservation of the land and persons of the clan, whereas the main beneficiary of the jubilee was the extended family, or "father's house." The jubilee therefore functioned as a necessary override to the practice of redemption. The regular operation of redemption over a period could result in the whole territory of a clan coming into the hands of a few wealthier families, with the rest of the families in the clan in a kind of debt servitude, living as dependent tenants of the wealthy. . . . The jubilee was thus a mechanism to prevent this.

Vv. 25–34. Stage One: Sold Land and Houses and Their Redemption

The impoverished landowner presumably took out a loan for the purchase of seed. In the event of crop failure, he is forced to sell part of his family land. The intervention of the redeemer (v. 25) is treated ahead of the possibility of self-redemption (v. 26) because the latter occurrence is less likely than the former.

25. *your brother (Israelite).* '*āḥîkā.* Gerstenberger (1996: 394) aptly remarks that H breaks the barriers of clan solidarity and blood relationships, but with the term '*āḥ* kinship is extended to the entire Israelite nation, contra Cross 1998: 4–6 (see NOTE on 19:17). Interestingly, a late-eighth-century bowl with the same consonants '*ḥk*, incised just below the rim on the inside, was discovered in an excavation at Beth Shemesh. If this word is vocalized '*āḥîkā* 'your brother', the bowl may have been placed at a local shrine by its priests for contributions to the poor (Barkay 1991; 1992).

becomes impoverished. yāmûk. Speiser (1960: 39) opts for the rendering "declines" on the basis of the law of Eshnunna (LE § 39), which uses the verb *enēšu* 'to grow weak'. However, impoverishment is the natural extension of "weakness," a meaning it clearly has not only in the cited Eshnunna law, but also in the following: 1 GÍN KÙ.BABBAR *lišābilam la e-ni-iš appūtum* 'please let him send me one shekel of silver (so that) I shall not be destitute' (*BIN* 7 53:29, cited in *CAD* 4.167). Tg. Onk. also renders it *yitmaskan* 'becomes impoverished'.

This verb appears in only this chapter, at the head of the first three cases (vv. 25, 35, 39) and in 27:8. Its root is the subject of dispute among the medieval grammarians and exegetes: *mwk* (Ibn Janah), *mk,* a bi-radical (Ibn Ezra), or *mkk* (Radak). The last root is, indeed, attested elsewhere (e.g., Ps 106:43; Koh 10:18), where it means "buckle, sink," but the second radical *waw* determines conclusively that the root is *mwk.*

sell. The buyer is someone outside the kin group. Otherwise, there would be no need for the intervention of a redeemer.

part of his holding. "But not all of his holding" (*Sipra* Behar 5:1). This constitutes vivid proof that only under the direst circumstances will an Israelite sell his land (note the case of Naboth, 1 Kgs 21:1–6). And if he does, it will be minimal, just enough to cover his debt. Moreover, the dead were buried "with their fathers" in the inherited land (cf. Judg 8:32; 2 Sam 2:32; 19:38; 21:14); if the family parted with the land, it would abandon its dead: "The land was more than an economic asset; it represented the family, joining the ancestors with their progeny and objectifying the irreducible bonds of friendship and descent upon which the early Israelite society was founded" (van der Toorn 1996b: 199).

Resistance to the alienation of patrimonial land is attested in anterior Mesopotamia. As cogently posited by Greenberg (1971c: 14.577), all land theoretically "belonged to the king, and was held only as a grant or fief by his subjects. They had possession, but not ownership, of the property entrusted to them. In return, each subject owed some service to the king, but he had no right to dispose of or transfer his property to any person other than a male relative of his immediate family" (cf. CD §§ 36–39). In Mesopotamia, the seller was able, under certain conditions, to redeem his property at the original price. This equitable principle applied, as in Israel, only to members of the family sold as slaves and to ancestral land (Westbrook 1991a). The sale of patrimonial land was banned outright at Nuzi (*ana* ^{lú}na-ka₄-ri; cf. Lacheman 1976: 135), but the law could be circumvented by the fiction of adoption, whereby the seller "adopted the buyer as his 'son,'" in consideration of the buyer's gift—the purchase price (Steele 1943: 14–15).

With these precedents, it is readily comprehensible, on the one hand, that the jubilee provision for the return of land to the original owner was not a revolutionary idea. The God of Israel had replaced the earthly monarch: all land was his; he parceled it out to Israel's clans, and it could never be alienated. But, on the other hand, all loopholes such as the fiction of adoption were hermetically sealed: the prohibition against land alienation was enshrined in the jubilee—cyclical, universal, and immutable.

his closest redeemer. gōʾălô haqqārōb ʾēlāyw, equivalent to šĕʾērô haqqārōb ʾēlāyw (21:2), which assumes that the redeemer is a šĕʾēr, a kin relative (i.e. by blood). The succession would be the same as in inheritance (Num 27:9–11), cited partially in the case of redemption from slavery of an Israelite sold to his non-Israelite creditor (v. 49).

The centrality of this clause is borne out by the verse's chiastic construction (M. Hildenbrand):

kî-yāmûk
A   ʾāḥîkā
    B   ûmākar mēʾăḥuzzātô
        C   ûbāʾ gōʾălô
            X   haqqārōb ʾēlāyw
        C'   wĕgāʾal ʾēt
    B'   mimkar
A'   ʾāḥîw

If impoverished becomes
A   your brother
    B   and has to sell part of his holding
        C   then shall come his redeemer
            X   who is closest to him
        C'   and he shall redeem
    B'   the sold property of
A'   his brother

The parallel phrases (BB') clarify why *mimkār* is employed. Another aesthetic reason is to bring the attestations of this term in this unit up to seven. For an ideological reason, see below.

A further assumption is that the indigent Israelite will first offer his land to his redeemer (Ehrlich 1908), as Hanamel did to his first cousin Jeremiah: "Buy my land . . . *kî lĕkā mišpaṭ haggĕʾullâ liqnôt*, literally "for yours is the procedure of redemption by purchase" (Jer 32:7). Note that nothing is said about the land reverting to Hanamel or his descendants in the jubilee. The basic postulate there is that the land remains in possession of the kin group. This postulate is only partially maintained in Lev 25. The redeemer, acting on behalf of the kin group, indeed maintains control of the redeemed land, but only until the jubilee, when he must transfer the land to its original owner.

Levine (1983a: 100–101; 1989a) argues that because the verb *qānâ* 'purchase' occurs in Jeremiah (and in a similar case in Ruth 4:4–9), but not in our case, the redeemer does not acquire the land, but must return it immediately to the original owner. Levine is correct, but only partially. The presence or absence of *qānâ* does, indeed, indicate a difference between Jeremiah and Ruth, on the one hand, and Leviticus, on the other. This, however, is due, in my opinion, to the absence of the jubilee institution in the former, which implies that the redeemer possesses the land for himself. And unless the original owner or his heirs exercise their rights of redemption and repurchase the property, it remains with the redeemer in perpetuity. In Leviticus, however, the onset of the jubilee year blocks such an acquisition. But that can hardly mean that the redeemer must return it at once. Isn't he entitled to get his money back? If not, what incentive does he have to redeem the field? Since the indebted owner is in no position to repay the redeemer, the only solution is that the redeemer retains and uses the field until the jubilee. In a sense, he leases, not acquires, the field—just as the buyer did—until he regains his costs at the jubilee. Finally, that the redeemer retains possession of the property until the jubilee is explicitly stated in v. 33 regardless of how that verse is interpreted (see below). That this principle obtained elsewhere is shown by the ancient law of Gortyn, which states that a ransomed captive belongs to the ransomer until reimbursement (Daube 1963: 42).

shall come. ûbāʾ. This technical, juridical term implies that the redeemer must intervene. In some societies (e.g., Indonesia, Tswana), the indebtedness of an individual becomes the liability of the clan (Neufeld 1958: 76). In Israel, however, the custom prevailed that the redeemer had the right of preemption or the right of refusal (i.e., to renounce his duty) before the land was offered on the open market (Ruth 4:1–7), as well as the right to renounce his duty (Ruth 3:13; Neufeld 1958: 77).

and redeem. The redemption price is not mentioned, but it is assumed to be that of vv. 27, 50–52, and therefore calculated on the basis of the sale price (see NOTE on "redemption," v. 24). As indicated, the property is retained by the redeemer until the jubilee (with Hoffmann 1953; Pedersen 1926: 1.272–73; McKane 1961–62; Daube 1956: 272–73; Loewenstamm 1958a; de Vaux 1961: 167; Westbrook 1971; Wright 1990: 120–21). Others hold, with Levine (1983:

100–101; 1989), that the property is returned at once to the original owner (Wessely 1846; Noth 1977; Leggett 1974: 95, Nordtzji 1982). Daube cites interesting support for the former contention: God redeemed Israel from Egypt; therefore, Israel is his permanently (see NOTES on vv. 42, 55). The implication of this theological axiom, buttressed by the evidence of Jer 32:11–15 and Ruth 4:4–9, is that the jubilee constituted a revolution in the laws of landed property: even in the absence of self-redemption by the owner, the redeemer still may not retain permanent possession of the land.

Westbrook (1985) has observed that all three cases in this pericope on redemption begin with the condition *yāmûk* 'becomes impoverished' (vv. 25, 35, 39) and that the one comparable case in Mesopotamian law (LE § 39) also predicates destitution. This leads him to the conclusion that the law of the redeemer applies to only cases of destitution. This makes sense. The law would not be interested in a commercial transaction. The rabbis also concur, for they state explicitly that ancestral land may be sold under economic duress. This, however, is for them the biblical principle, for they added that *in practice* "if the land was sold, it is sold" (*t. 'Arak.* 5:6–8). Consider now the case that the land would in the meantime increase in value. The redeemer would buy back the property for a profit! Westbrook would have to assume that the redemption price is the sale price. This, too, makes sense. The hard-pressed owner would probably sell his property at below market value. The law would certainly not be interested, in this case, that the buyer make a profit.

Unfortunately, Westbrook's (1985) support for his assumption from the Bible cannot be sustained. There is no way of determining whether the redemption price of consecrated land (27:14–24; minus the one-fifth penalty) is the value of the land at the time of its consecration. The sanctuary is perfectly at liberty to set the price according to the market value. Similarly, there is no way of determining whether the nearest kinsperson was eager to redeem Naomi's ancestral land because of its low sale price. And the case of Jeremiah (Jer 32:11–15), I believe, is misinterpreted. Since Jeremiah is the redeemer, Hanamel or his heirs have lost their rights of redemption. If Jeremiah wishes, at some future date, to return the land to them at his cost, he does so as a family favor and not as a legal requirement.

the sold property of his brother. mimkar 'āḥîw. Whereas the owner has sold *mē'āḥuzzātô* 'from his holding', the redeemer no longer redeems *mē'āḥuzzātô*, but from his *mimkār*. The land, in the hands of the buyer, is not his holding, but only what its true owner has sold him. He has, in effect, purchased not the land, but only its usufruct (Wessely 1846). Perhaps the fact that the term *mimkār*, a nominal form of *mākar* 'sell', occurs seven times in this chapter (vv. 14, 25, 27, 28, 29 33, 50) is deliberate, to indicate its significance. Ezek 7:13a is probably an allusion to this law (see chap. 26, COMMENT D). The choice of this term is also conditioned by this verse's chiastic construction (see above).

26. *but prospers. wĕ'hiśśîga 'yādô,* literally "his hand attains" (5:11; 14:21, 22, 30, 31, 32; 25:26, 47, 49; 27:8; Num 6:21; Ezek 46:7). Less frequently, the synonymous expressions *higgîa' yādô,* literally "his hand reaches" (5:7), and *māṣā' yādô,* literally "his hand finds" (v. 28; 12:8), are used.

and acquires. ûmāṣā'. The verb is not superfluous; it is required for the idiom *māṣā' (kē)dê* 'acquire enough' (v. 28). The *Sipra* (Behar 5:2) adds, correctly, that the redeemer may not acquire only part of the sold land because his redemption must result in the return of the owner's entire property (v. 27b).

27. *the years since its sale. šĕnê mimkārô.* This phrase is equivalent in form to *šĕnê-tĕbû'ōt* 'crop years' (v. 15). The preposition *min* "from" is omitted (it would have to be expressed as *haššānîm mimmimkārô*), probably because of the awkwardness of having four consecutive occurrences of the *mem*. First, a computation must be made as to how many crop years have elapsed since the sale. Then that sum is subtracted from the sale price. The expression cannot mean "the years *until* the jubilee," the clause used in the computation given in v. 50. That verse expresses a different goal; it refers to the total sum, from the sale to the jubilee.

the difference. hā'ōdēp. This occurs as a *Qal* participle (Exod 16:23; 26:12, 13; Num 3:46, 48, 49) and in *Hip'il* (Exod 16:18).

and return to his holding. wĕšāb la'ăḥuzzātô. This clause occurs in vv. 10, 13, 27, 28, 41 always in connection with the jubilee. Its absence in v. 25 is, therefore, all the more glaring. This constitutes strong evidence that the property remains in control of the redeemer until the jubilee (Hoffmann 1953).

28. *If. wĕ'im.* This word is used rather than *wĕkî*—the sign of sub-unit.

not acquire sufficient means to recover it. lō'-māṣĕ'â yādô dê hāšîb lô. That is, if the original owner is not able to come up with the difference. This expression is equivalent in meaning to *ûmāṣā' kĕdê gĕ'ullātô* (v. 26). The verb *māṣā'* is preferred over the synonym *hiśśîg* whenever it is conditioned by the noun *dê* (as in 12:8; Prov 25:16; Sun 1990: 464).

until the jubilee year. 'ad šĕnat hayyôbēl. The return of the land, according to *Sipra* (Behar 5:6), therefore takes place at the onset of the jubilee, in contrast to the debt annulment, which takes place at the end of the seventh year (*miqqēṣ*, based on Deut 15:1; 31:10).

it shall be released in the jubilee. wĕyāṣā' bayyôbēl. This juridical, technical term (vv. 28, 30, 31, 33, 41, 54; 27:21; cf. Exod 21:2, 5, 11) is precisely equivalent to Akkadian *ina durāri uṣû* (Weinfeld 1983a: 128). In Mesopotamia, the contract, written on clay tablets, was literally broken: *ša ina mišari waṣia uḫeppû* '(and) ordered broken those (in which the land was) to be released by (the terms of) the *misharum*' (Finkelstein 1968: 234, l. 9).

Vv. 29–34. This supplementary pericope on the sale of houses reflects the attempt of the H legist to update the agricultural holdings of the tribes to the reality of the subsequent occupation and development of urban communities. It is true that antecedent Mesopotamian *mišarum* edicts were also directed to the agrarian population and exempted urban houses and other objects in the commercial sphere. However, the fact that this pericope assumes the existence of Levitic cities, whose number, location, and dimensions are not detailed until Num 35:1–8, indicates that it probably is the work of a later H tradent. This is reminiscent of the rites of purification prescribed for the healed scale-diseased person in the retrojected wilderness camp (14:1–32), to which are added the changes in the ritual for urban centers (14:33–53), also attributable to an H tradent (vol. 1.864–67). Also, the fact that Levites here encompasses both priests and Levites (see NOTE on v. 32), which is a deuteronomic usage, whereas the priestly texts never fuse the two, also indicates the lateness of this passage (see Introduction I F).

Vv. 29–31. City Property

City property follows ancient Canaanite law (Noth 1977). Similarly, "the legislator cannot eradicate traditional law, he can only add to it" (Westbrook 1991b: 53). "Walled towns, typical of Canaanite city culture, were a novelty to the Israelite farming population and their customary family law did not provide for them. So a house in such a town was considered more an individual than a family possession" (Porter 1976). Since the jubilee was intended to preserve the economic viability of the peasant farmer, there was no need to protect urban property from alienation (Bess 1963: 121–22). This is confirmed indirectly by the absence of the *yāmûk* clause in the case of city property. In other words, destitution plays no role; the sale of a home is considered a business transaction (contra *t. 'Arak.* 5:7). Thus one may not conclude that "private ownership supersedes Yahweh's law" and "the elite placed economic security before Yahweh's commandments" (Gerstenberger 1996: 385, 396). The jubilee provisions are directed solely to the land, since God owns the land, not the cities, which are a human achievement (Muffs 1965b: 4.11). An urban culture is a later phenomenon in Israelite society. Patently, vv. 29–31 represent a judicial attempt to introduce a jubilee concept where it has neither historical nor theological grounding. All these factors point to the same conclusion: the jubilee law is not purely utopian, but must have a historical basis (Elliger 1966; cf. Loewenstamm 1958a).

29. *a dwelling house (in) a walled city. bēt-môšab 'îr ḥômâ.* This is a triple construct, though a quadruple already has been encountered (13:59a; Abravanel); *bēt-môšab* is a hapax, but not *môšab 'îr* (2 Kgs 2:19; cf. *môšab qîr*, 1 Sam 20:25).

may be . . . shall be. wĕhāyĕtâ . . . tihyeh. A circular inclusio, this uses a suffixed and prefixed form of the verb (Paran 1983: 36).

a year. yāmîm. A full year is meant, as specified in the previous phrase "the end of a year of its sale" and in the following verse *šānâ tĕmîmâ* 'one full year' (v. 30), and precisely translated by the Aramaic idiom *min 'îdān lĕ'îdān* (Tg. Ps-J. = Rabbinic Hebrew *mē'ēt lĕ'ēt*, b. *'Arak.* 319)—that is, a full year and not to the end of the calendar year. Thus after one year the purchaser could begin to make home improvements, which he would not do if the house were subject to redemption year after year.

The ancient Mesopotamian (Sumerian) law of Eshnunna (LE § 39; see NOTE on "redemption," v. 24) allows the buyer of a house to be secure in its possession as long as he holds on to it (cf. Yaron 1988: 232–34). Leviticus, however, grants him that security only after the first year. The redemption price of purchased land is determined by the usufruct earned by the purchaser (vv. 14–16).

No such provision is attached to the redemption price of a walled-city house. Thus the redemption price must be the purchase price. The difference between land and house rests on the jubilee principle; it is operative for land, not a house.

The question arises: Considering all the factors mentioned above—the jubilee protects the farmer not the urbanite, ancestral land not city property, and so on (see INTRODUCTION to vv. 29–31)—why allow redemption altogether, even for one year? Herein, I submit, we touch on the merciful foundations of the jubilee legislation. Just as demonstrated in the case of the destitute farmer described in v. 25, so this person may have been driven by economic constraints to sell his city holding. Hence for a short period of time, one year—but no more—the opportunity is granted to him and his kin group to regain his possession.

30. *shall belong to. wĕqām . . . l,* literally "rises to." As pointed out by Muffs (1965b: 2.9), "the transfer of ownership is described metaphorically: the land gets up from one owner and goes over to the second one"; that is, it is incontestably transferred. The procedure is explicitly detailed in the sale of the cave of Machpelah to Abraham in Gen 23:17–20 (note the twofold use of *qām l*). This idiom is also attested in the transfer of property to and from the sanctuary (27:14, 17, 19) and is applied to the validity of vows (Num 30:5[twice], 6, 8[twice], 10, 12[twice], 13.

in the walled city. ʾăšer-lōʾ(ôQ) ḥōmâ. Perhaps the masculine *lô* (also Sam.) was intended to preserve the same vocalization as the Ketib (as *kullaʾ,* K [*kullâ,* Q], Ezek 36:5). According to Rashi, since *ʿîr* is feminine (with exception of 2 Sam 17:13), the preposition should read *lâ.* Rashi's conclusion cannot be sustained because *ʿîr* is elsewhere construed as masculine: with *yihyû* (26:33; Josh 15:21; Isa 17:9), *ḥaṣērêhem* (Josh 13:28; Neh 11:30), *migrĕšêhem* (Josh 14:4; 1 Chr 6:49), *bāhem* (Josh 24:13; Judg 21:23; Jer 44:2; 1 Chr 10:7; 2 Chr 14:13), *wayyitpĕśēm* (2 Kgs 18:13 = Isa 36:1), *lĕbiqĕʿām* (2 Chr 32:1), as well as *šām* (2 Sam 17:13). The Qriʾ *lô* is therefore clearly preferred.

beyond reclaim throughout the ages. laṣṣĕmîtūt . . . lĕdōrōtāyw. The precise Akkadian equivalent *ṣamit ana/adi dārīti* was first recognized by Rabinowitz (1958) in a Ugaritic sale document (see NOTE on "beyond reclaim," v. 23). Weinfeld (1993: 259, n. 154) adds that *lĕdōrōtāyw,* literally "throughout his generations" is attested in *eqlam ana duriš u idna* 'give the field throughout his generations' (TCL 7, 16:13), which can only mean "for his permanent property."

it shall not be released in the jubilee. lōʾ yēṣēʾ bayyōbēl. Note the exact Akkadian equivalent *ina andarārum inandar* (Wiseman 1953: 65.6–7).

31. *hamlets. haḥăṣērîm.* Compare *paṣhayāʾ* (Tg. Onk.), *kupĕrnayyāʾ* (Tgs. Ps.-J., Neof.; cf. Tg. Neof. margin *prwwylyyh* [= Greek *peribolaion*]); *epaúlesin* (LXX). The term is attested in Gen 25:16; Deut 2:23; Isa 42:11; Neh 12:29, and in Joshua, where the cities allotted to the tribes include *ḥaṣērêhem* 'their villages' (Josh 15:32–62; 16:9; 18:24, 28; 19:6–8, 15–16, etc.). The Levitic cities, however, do not extend beyond their borders except for the livestock enclosures in the surrounding field (*śĕdēh migrāš;* cf. v. 34). The one exception is Hebron,

which, though assigned to the Aaronids by lot (Josh 21:10, 11), had also been promised on oath by Moses to Caleb (Josh 14:6–14; Judg 1:20) and corroborated by God (Josh 15:13; Haran 1978: 117, n. 9). A compromise is effected: the city and its livestock enclosures are assigned to the Aaronids, and its agricultural fields (śĕdēh hāʿîr) and hamlets go to the Calebites (Josh 21:10–12; Portugali 1984: 282–84). It should be noted that Levitic cities own only the adjoining migrāšîm, whereas other cities have no migrāšîm but possess agricultural fields and hamlets. On the term migrāš, see the NOTE on "field of the livestock enclosures," v. 34.

The word derives from a primitive Semitic root "surround." Old Babylonian ḫaṣāru 'fold, pen' can include a human enclosure; compare Ugaritic ḫzr 'enclosure' and Old South Arabic ḥḍr 'dwelling' (Orlinsky 1939; Malamat 1962: 146–47; Hamp 1986). The most extensive archaeological excavation of villages — settlements outside urban centers — has been done in the region of Samaria (Finkelstein 1988).

that have no encircling walls. An explicative clause, it was written at a time when the term ḥăṣērîm meant only "courts," at least in this legislator's circle.

shall be classed as open country. ʿal-śĕdēh hāʾāreṣ yēḥāšēb. These houses "are farm buildings" (Philo, *Laws* 2.116). Philo is probably right. The villages are the residences of farmers and are inseparable from the land they work (Mendelssohn 1846). However, the śādeh is not limited to "arable land" (Levine 1989) because pastoral lands (e.g., those of Reuben and Gad, Num 32), are also included. Neither does it refer to a grain-producing field (Dybdahl 1981: 77) on the grounds that orchards were allegedly exempt from the jubilee laws. As orchards also had to remain fallow (v. 11bβ; cf. v. 4bβ), it is hard to believe that the law of release did not apply to them. One could employ his holding any way he wanted, but it was always subject to the jubilee.

ʿal here is equivalent to ʾim (cf. Exod 35:22; Ibn Ezra). The text did not use the comparative kĕ (e.g., Num 18:27) precisely in order to avoid comparison: the houses and fields form an integral unit. śĕdēh hāʾāreṣ is a hapax; it is synonymous with śĕdēh ʾăḥuzzātô 'the land of his holding' (27:16, 22, 28). yēḥāšēb and the rest of the verse (sing.) are used in a distributive sense (cf. v. 14b); there is no need to read yēḥāšĕbû (pl.), with Sam. The verb ḥāšab, among its various meanings, is also a legal term when employed in the Nipʿal, meaning "classed, reckoned" (see NOTE on "imputed," 17:4; see also 7:18; Num 18:27, 30). For the idiom hēḥāšēb ʿal 'be reckoned with', see 2 Sam 4:2.

in the jubilee they shall be released. ubayyōbēl yēṣēʾ. Presumably, the sale price must have been the rental value of the house until the jubilee. Note the chiasm with v. 30b (D. N. Freedman, personal communication). It effectively unites vv. 30–31, the redemption of a lay Israelite's city dwelling, into a single unit. One might expect the addition of wĕšāb laʾăḥuzzātô 'and he shall return to his holding', as in v. 28bβ. However, houses, in contrast to land, are not ʾăḥuzzâ. Hence this term does not appear at all in this unit (vv. 29–31). Contrast the houses of Levites, which are their only inheritance (Num 35:1–8): this term appears four times in their brief unit (vv. 32–34).

Vv. 32–34. Levitic Property

The houses of Levites in the assigned Levitic cities are always subject to the laws of redemption and jubilee. Their homes are thus juridically equivalent to the Israelites' fields (Shadal). The pastureland surrounding each Levitic city, however, may not even be sold.

This constitutes the only reference to the Levites in all of Leviticus (note Gerstenberger's [1996: 308] perplexity). There is no enigma. The discussion of the Levitic profile is postponed to the movement of Israel away from Sinai, which requires a total census, describing the camp and detailing the transport of the dismantled sanctuary (Num 1–4), an indication that this text stems from the redactorial work of H (see Introduction I M). Here, however, H had no choice: the discussion of the redeemability of Israelite homes could not but include the Levitic homes within their own cities.

32. *As for the Levitic cities. wĕ 'ārê halĕwiyyim.* Although the Levites are to receive no permanent property in the promised land (Num 18:23; 26:62), this restriction applies solely to farmland. They are provided permanent residences for themselves and pasturage for their livestock in the form of forty-eight towns and their surrounding fields, the measurements of which take into account variations in the size of the towns and the possibility of their future growth (Num 35:1–8; cf. Milgrom 1982a). The execution of these prescriptions is recorded in Josh 21, where the Aaronids are awarded thirteen towns in Judah, Simeon, and Benjamin; the Kohathites, ten towns in Ephraim, Dan, and western Manasseh; the Gershonites, thirteen towns in Issachar, Asher, Naphtali, and eastern Manasseh; and the Merarites, twelve towns in Reuben, Gad, and Zebulun. To be sure, since many of these towns are attested urban centers occupied by other Israelites, this can only mean that the Levites received dwelling rights within them (Noth 1977).

At Ugarit, entire cities were granted to royal servants by the king as part of their tithes (*PRU* 3.69–70, 146–47) as their permanent possession (*ana dāriš*; cf. Heltzer 1976: 48–51). In truth, all this means is that the grantees were given the perpetual right to collect the tithes of the inhabitants. Weinfeld (1983a: 126) has proposed that the Levitic cities must be understood in a similar manner. Accepting the suggestion of Mazar (1960) that these cities were settled by the Levites who served the king in the period of the United Kingdom, he postulates that the Levites did not acquire these cities as their permanent possession (*nahălâ*), but only to collect their tithes. However, as argued in the NOTE on "his holding," v. 10, H's term *'ăhuzzâ* is only theologically different from P's word *nahălâ*—to forestall the belief that Israel's land is an unconditional endowment—but juridically, it is exactly equivalent. The Levites, then, did acquire holdings, either as entire towns or within the assigned cities, that were subject to the laws of redemption and were, therefore, their permanent possession.

Nonetheless, as the text reminds us, the cities of the Levites are only their *'ăhuzzâ* 'holding', not their *nahălâ* 'inheritance'. The cities, no differently from the fields of their fellow Israelites, belong to YHWH, and they occupy them as his tenants. This point is driven home by the suffixed form of *'āḥuzzâ*, which occurs seven times in referring to the total land of Israel (farms plus cities) in vv. 25–34. Thus both the lay Israelites and the priestly class are equal in this regard: neither are owners of their real estate. What YHWH has granted them by grace of his covenant with the forefathers, he can at any time rescind if Israel violates its tenancy requirements, namely, obedience to the commandments (details in chap. 26).

One can also point to the sacred cities of Mesopotamia as a possible parallel to the Levitic cities. Since the inhabitants of the former were viewed as being "slaves to the deity," they were exempt from human jurisdiction. These cities or groups of persons received the status of *zakûtu* 'freedom, exemption' or *kidinnūtu* 'privileged status'—"in order that they may return to the hands of the gods" (Entmetena, 2430 B.C.E.; Weinfeld 1985a: 134). The parallel exists; however, it is applied by H to the entire land and nation. Because Israel is YHWH's possession, it is exempt from human jurisdiction over ownership and servitude.

The rationale for the distinction between Israelite and Levitic cities is obvious: whereas city property "was not the means of economic support for a family in the same way as rural property" (Bess 1963: 82), this did not hold true for the Levites. Their city homes were their only residences (except for the pastureland held in common, see at v. 34, below). To permit their irrevocable acquisition by outsiders would render the impoverished Levites homeless.

the Levites shall forever have the right of redemption. This is true even after the first year (contrast v. 30): *'ôlām* 'forever' as opposed to *yāmîm* 'a year' (v. 29; Dillmann and Ryssel 1897). This rule would apply to only the Levitic cities, not to Israelite homes purchased by a Levite.

33. *Whoever of the Levites redeems. wa'ăšer yig'al min-halĕwiyyim.* The exegesis of this long-standing crux hinges on the interpretation of *min*. It can mean either "from," thus making "the Levites" the object, or "of," which makes "the Levites" the subject.

For the meaning "from," three interpretations have been suggested, each of which is subject to question:

1. The verb *gā'al* takes on the meaning "purchase" (Saadiah, Rashi, Ibn Ezra [first explanation], Ḥazzequni; cf. *b. 'Arak.* 33b) or "appropriate" (Levine 1989). Unfortunately, neither meaning is attested anywhere.
2. Whereas v. 32 cites the case of a Levite redeeming from an Israelite, v. 33 adds the case of an Israelite redeeming from a Levite: just as an Israelite cannot possess a Levitic house forever (v. 32), since Levites have permanent rights of redemption, so a Levite may not possess an Israelite house forever, since the Israelites have the same redemption rights (Bekhor Shor). This interpretation runs into the snag of v. 33b, the rationale for v. 33a, which speaks of Levitic, not Israelite, houses.
3. Whether a Levite redeems a Levite's house from an Israelite (v. 32) or even a Levite's from a Levite (v. 33a), the house must revert to the original Levite owner (*Sipra* Behar 6:6; *m. 'Arak.* 9:8; Wright 1990: 123–24).

The last is the best of the three "from" interpretations. However, it, too, can be challenged. First, on what grounds would a Levite redeeming from a Levite think that his case is different from a Levite redeeming from an Israelite (v. 32)? Second, if the emphasis is on the thought process of the Levite redeemer, he should be the subject of the sentence. And, indeed, that is the case if *min* means "of."

Three interpretations have also been proposed in support of *min* as "of":

1. Reading with the Vulgate *wā'ăšer lō' yigāēl* 'Whatever is not redeemed (of Levite property)', but this requires the insertion of the negative particle *lō'* and pointing *yg'l* as a passive (Shadal [second explanation]; Dillmann and Ryssel 1897; Bertholet 1901; Ehrlich 1908; Killian 1963: 337; Elliger 1966; Levine 1989: 177 n. 34). This radical solution, for which there is no warrant in the MS traditions or Versions, is one of desperation.

2. Connect v. 33a to v. 32b and render "The Levites shall forever have the right of redemption; either one of the Levites shall redeem or . . . shall be released in the jubilee" (Möller 1976: 412). The problem is to justify rendering the two *waw*s of *wa'ăšer* and *wĕyāṣā'* as "either . . . or." Besides, *wā'ăšer* meaning "what/whoever" is ignored.

3. "Whoever of the Levites redeems (should know that) . . ."

The last is the translation I have adopted (cf. TN; Rashi[2]; Rashbam; Saalschütz 1853: 150; Ginsburg 1966 [first explanation]). The Levite redeemer might think that because the house remains a Levitic property, he can hold onto it forever (Ramban, Shadal [first explanation]). Or he reasons that the Levitic house is likened to an Israelite house, which does not revert to the original owner in the jubilee (v. 30). Such reasoning is categorically rejected: the property must return to the original Levite owner in the jubilee. That is, the Levite homeowner has sold it for only its rental value until the jubilee. In effect, the Levite's city house is equivalent to the Israelite's village house (v. 31): both are subject to the law of the jubilee.

the house sold (in) the city of his possession. mimkar-bayit wĕ'îr 'ăhuzzātô. Drop the *waw of wĕ'îr*, reading *bêt 'îr* (BHS), regard the compound *bayit wĕ'îr* as a hendiadys (Kalisch 1867–72), or understand the *waw* as explicative (i.e., "which is in"; Mendelssohn 1846, Shadal). In favor of the first option is the attestation of this compound (without the *waw*) in the previous verse: *bātê 'ārê 'ăhuzzātām* 'the houses in the cities they hold' (v. 32).

the houses . . . are their holding. bātê . . . hî'(K:hw') 'ăhuzzātām. The pronoun *hî'(K:hw')*, resuming the subject, is nonetheless attracted in number to the predicate (e.g., Josh 13:14; Jer 10:13; cf. GKC § 145 nN). The masculine Ketib follows the subject; the feminine Qere, the predicate.

34. *But the field. ûśādēh.* Note the similar vocalization of *ûzăhab* (Gen 2:12), a phenomenon occurring with sibilants to emphasize the vocal *šĕwa*, giving it a distinct pronunciation (GKC § 10g).

field of the livestock enclosures. śĕdēh migrāš. The *migrāš* has been defined as "a demarcated area extending outside the city walls and actual inhabited region of a city" (Barr 1986: 25). This definition is too general. The term clearly refers to the outskirts of a settled area that is designated neither for agriculture (usually called *śādeh* 'field', v. 3; 27:16, 17) nor for human habitation (*môšāb*, v. 29; Ezek 48:15–17), but for livestock pens (Portugali 1984: 283; cf. Num 35:3; Josh 14:4; 21:2). The possessors of the *migrāš* are always the Levites, except for the Gadites who dwell *běkol-migrěšê šārôn* (1 Chr 5:16). But whether one regards *šārôn* as an unidentified area of Transjordan or emends it to *śiryôn* (e.g., Braun 1986: 76), there is no problem in attributing livestock to the Gadites, who, with the Reubenites, were pastoralists (Num 32). Levites could not engage in agriculture, since they possessed no landed property (Num 18:20; 23bβ, 24b) except their habitations. Their only means of livelihood, besides their theoretical tithe (Num 18:21, 24a), was their livestock. Hence the land immediately surrounding their cities was allotted to them to house their animals, their heavy equipment (Portugali 1984: 283), and perhaps their collected tithes (Faust 1996: 25, n. 6). Faust (1996: 24–25) claims that the *migrāš* also contained storehouses for agricultural implements, wine vats, and quarries. Undoubtedly true. But this area was not called *migrāš* (from *grš*, a place into which animals are driven [i.e., pens]). This would account for the otherwise puzzling absence of this term in regard to the cities of other tribes. The *migrāš* was legally part of a city (Josh 21). Hence the property law of the *migrāš* would be tied to the law of the city. That *migrāš* is in construct with preceding *śādeh* 'field' proves that the customary rendering "pastureland" for *migrāš* is wrong.

may not be sold. lōʾ yimmākēr. Another characteristic of pastureland is that it is common property, such as obtained in ancient Ugarit; farmland, by contrast, is owned by individuals. Besides, if the *migrāš* were parceled out to individual Levites, it would violate the basic, oft-repeated ban on Levites owning any *land* (Num 18:20, 23b, 24b; 26:62, etc.; contra Gerstenberger 1996: 385). According to Ezek 48:14, the same prohibition is invoked against the sale of priestly or Levitic lands, but for a different reason: they are "sacred to YHWH."

holding forever. ʾăḥuzzat ʿôlām. For the expression, see also v. 46; Gen 17:8; 48:4. There is no equivalent expression for *naḥălâ*, since it implies permanence. That is why H consistently uses *ʾăḥuzzâ* to emphasize that the land is only a "holding" granted to the Israelites by the grace of God (Gen 17:8 and possibly Gen 48:4 are also H). Hence those who purchase it or redeem it must return it to their original possessors—that is, those whom God has specified as their authorized possessors. Ezek 48:14 as pointed out in the NOTE on "may not be sold," goes one step further: clerical land is sacred and may never be sold.

for them. hûʾ lāhem. These words are placed at the end of the verse for emphasis, perhaps to stress that *migrāš* property is held in common by *all* the Levites.

Vv. 35–38. Stage Two: Lost Land

Assumed is that the sold property was not redeemed. The owner again incurred a crop failure on his reduced property (which, to begin with, probably supplied only a subsistence level) and was forced to take out a new loan. This time when he defaults on his loan, he forfeits all his land, but still owing on his loan, he becomes a "tenant farmer" for the creditor. Technically, he has lost his land, but the produce is still his. It amortizes his loan since he pays no interest. In a sense, he rents the land from the creditor. "Landless agricultural workers typically earn smaller incomes than landowning peasants. In addition, the landless are much more vulnerable to destitution in periods of crisis than those who farm their own land" (Fager 1993: 88, citing studies by Collier 1983 and Sen 1977). Note that the *gō'ēl* 'redeemer' makes no appearance in this case. But neither does he in the third case (vv. 39–43), where this problem will be discussed.

35. *falls. ûmāṭâ yādô.* From the root *mwṭ* 'totter, slip', this is used with natural objects (Isa 24:19; 54:10; Pss 46:3; 82:5; 93:1) and with "foot" (Deut 32:35; Pss 17:5; 38:17; 66:9; 94:18; 121:3). Only here is it used with *yād* 'hand', probably to contrast with the expression previously used in the chapter, *hiśśîg / māṣā' yād* 'prosper, acquire' (vv. 26, 28: cf. v. 47). For another example of the apposition of *māṭâ* and *māṣā' yād*, see Ps 21:8b–9. Thus the antonym *māṭâ yād* would mean "fail" (*adunatēsē̦*, LXX), an extended connotation of *māṭâ* attested elsewhere (e.g., Pss 15:5; 21:8; 55:23; Prov 10:30). Adding *yād* 'power' to *māṭâ* further implies failing in one's financial power, becoming bankrupt, a meaning supported by its modifying preposition *'immāk* (see below).

under your authority. 'immāk. Speiser (1960: 38–39) points to *'immô* (v. 47), which is meaningless if rendered "with him," but can only refer to an Israelite falling under the authority of an alien. In truth, it can be demonstrated that all instances of *'im* referring to the creditor in this chapter have this meaning (as well as in Gen 29:25, 30; Deut 15:16; 23:17; 1 Sam 2:21b; and all the verses cited and incorrectly rendered in BDB 768a, 3a).

This meaning is clearest in vv. 6, 23 (argued in their NOTES) and in vv. 40–41, 47 (thrice). To be sure, the indentured Israelite labors not "with" but "under" your (the creditor's) authority"; *wĕyāṣā' mē'immāk* must be rendered "and shall be released from your authority" by the jubilee together with his sons (vv. 40–41), a rendering adopted by recent translations, including "from your service" (NAB); "from your authority" (NRSV). The resident alien who is *'immāk* 'under your authority' (v. 47 [twice]), or rule, since he lives in your land, must obey the law if one of you Israelites falls *'immô* 'under his authority' (v. 47). The same holds true for Abraham, who is a resident alien "under your (Hittites') authority" (Gen 23:4), and for the Israelites, who hold an alien status "under your (God's) authority" (Ps 39:13). So also Jacob, who worked not "with" but "under" Laban (Gen 29:14, 25, 30; 31:38); Samuel, who grew up not "with" but "in the service of the Lord" (1 Sam 2:21b NJPS); and the Israelite who wishes to continue his slave status and proclaims "I do not want to be released *mē'immāk*, from your authority" because he is happy *'immāk* 'under your authority' (Deut 15:16).

Extra-biblical evidence is what led Speiser (1932; 1933) to his deduction, in particular, the clause *ina / ana bit C wašābum*, literally "to stay in the creditor's household," or remain under his authority. His finding has been corroborated by texts from Alalakh (20.5–10; Wiseman 1953) and the Diyala Region (70 No. 3, l. 3; Harris 1955), which leads Eichler (1973: 57, n. 18) to conclude that "KI (= *itti*) 'with' . . . seems to denote a subordination to the creditor's authority."

Finally, proof of this meaning for ʿim can be adduced from this chapter. Note that it is present in the protasis of stages 2, 3, and 4 (vv. 35, 39, 47), but is totally absent in stage 1 (vv. 25–28). Why? Your brother is "with you" in v. 25 as much as he is in the following stages! However, in this initial stage of impoverishment, when he sells only *part* of his land, he remains an independent farmer; he is as yet not "under the authority" of the creditor. Also, that is why the phrase *ûmāṭâ yādô* occurs only in this stage: when, for the first time, the debtor "slips, falls" under the creditor's control.

and you (would) hold him. wĕheḥĕzaqtā bô. Two renderings are possible. The usual one is "support, maintain" (*antilēmpsę̄*, LXX; *wĕtatqêp*, Tgs. Onk., Ps.-J.; cf. *TN*; note also that the Akkadian cognate *ṣabātu qātam*, literally "seize the hand," means only "help, support [a person]," and the causative *šuṣbutu* [= *heḥĕzîq*] can denote "provide [someone with income, food, etc.]" [*CAD* 16:31–32, 38]). This rendering incurs two main objections. First, implied is that you should support him as "a resident alien" (the term that follows) who, however, is only a recipient of charity but is not entitled to free loans (vv. 36–37; see NOTE on "who live," v. 6). Indeed, Deuteronomy explicitly permits taking interest from a non-Israelite (Deut 23:21; *nokrî*, contrasted with *ʾāḥîkā*, v. 20, includes the alien, but not in 14:21, where he is expressly excluded). One cannot counter with "no alien [*gēr*] spent the night in the open: I opened my doors to the passer-by" (Job 31:32). Only temporary shelter is intended here, to serve the emergency needs of the alien or passerby, but not long-range food and shelter, much less free loans. Neither can one counter with the Hittite instruction "A foreigner who settles (finds shelter) in the land, provide him fully with seeds, cattle, and sheep" (von Schuler 1957: 47, III A, 36–37). This, too, is an exception; foreigners are encouraged to settle in a remote area, and border guards are encouraged to assist them. Second, in the *Hipʿil*, this meaning can be expressed only by *heḥĕzîq yād* (Ezek 16:49), *heḥĕzîq bĕyād* (2 Kgs 15:19; Isa 42:6; 51:18), or *heḥĕzîq bĕyāmîn* (Isa 41:13; 45:1; contra Levi 1981: 158).

However, if the object is a person (Gen 21:18; Exod 9:2; Deut 22:25; Judg 19:25, 29; 2 Sam 13:11; Isa 4:1; Jer 50:33; Prov 7:13; Job 8:15; 2 Chr 28:15), his limbs, but not his hands (Deut 25:11; 1 Sam 17:35; 2 Sam 2:16; 2 Kgs 4:27; Zech 8:23; Prov 26:17), his clothing (1 Sam 15:27; 2 Sam 1:11; 2 Kgs 2:12; Zech 8:23), or his things (Judg 7:20; 1 Sam 15:27; 2 Sam 1:11; 3:29; 1 Kgs 1:50; 2:28; Neh 4:15), *heḥĕzîq* means "seize, take control of" (cf. Ehrlich 1899–1900). And so I have rendered.

Finally, this understanding *heḥĕzîq* as "seize" vitiates the proposal that a kinsperson has exercised the rights of preemption in the first stage (v. 25) and that, in the second stage (vv. 35–38), the kinsperson is maintaining the debtor as a dependent laborer with interest-free loans (C. Wright 1991: 121–22). A kinsperson would neither "seize" him nor treat him as an alien.

(as though he were) a resident alien. gēr wĕtôšāb. Ibn Ezra suggests that a new sentence begins here: "(If he is) a resident alien, let him live with you"; that is, whether he is an Israelite or an alien, you must support him (cf. *b. Pesaḥ.* 21b) because he is one of the underprivileged requiring support (19:10; 23:22). This

interpretation, however, has rightly been challenged, since (1) the *'atnaḥ* would then have to be under *bô*, and (2) *gēr wĕtôšāb* should bear the same cantillation as *'āḥîkā* (*Qarne 'Or* on Ibn Ezra).

The only possible rendering is "as a resident alien" (LXX). That the term *gēr wĕtôšāb* is a hendiadys, see the NOTE on v. 23. Some have understood this metaphorically; for example, Saadiah renders it "let him reside with you" (following *yĕdûr wĕyittôtab*, Tgs. *Onk., Ps.-J.*). Most others interpret more literally; for example, "he should be taken into a home . . . and be given the same hospitality as an alien or a stranger [*sic*] would be" (Porter 1976; cf. LXX). This interpretation falls victim to the erroneous interpretation of *wĕheḥĕzaqtā* as "sustain," namely, that the resident alien must be treated as a ward of the Israelite.

Muffs (1965b: 4.5), who, following Ehrlich 1899–1900 and Speiser (1932; 1933), champions the rendering of *wĕheḥĕzaqtā* as "seize," interprets as follows: the debtor "is now seized by his creditor, not as a slave, but as a *ditennu / manzazānu* = Hebrew *gēr wetôšāb*; he enters the household of the creditor where his service pays off the interest on the loan." The importance of this interpretation is its recognition that a debtor can be seized (and enslaved, vv. 45–46) for defaulting on a debt. I would, however, modify Muff's insight in this regard: the debtor does not "enter the household of the creditor"; that happens in stage 3 (vv. 39–43), when he is reduced to a slave status. Note that in the latter case, the debtor is considered *kĕśākîr kĕtôšāb* 'a resident hireling', not a resident alien. Only a resident hireling, but not an alien receives maintenance. At stage 2, however, the creditor is not obligated to support him and his family (see below). Those who hold that the creditor is responsible for the debtor's room and board have been led astray by their misinterpretation of the next term: *wāḥay*. In sum, the text is warning the creditor not to treat the debtor, who has forfeited his land and presumably still owes on his loan, as a resident alien, who in the case of default can be seized as a slave (cf. vv. 45–46).

Seeligmann (1978: 200, n. 51) suggests that the attempt of H to equalize the civil status of the resident alien and that of the Israelite (cf. 24:22) betrays H's relative lateness in comparison with D, where the *gēr* is one of the underprivileged dependent on Israelite charity (contrast Deut 14:21 with Lev 17:15). Our passage, however, offers a glimpse of H's complete awareness of the alien's true status. He can be "seized" as a debt-slave and, if he cannot repay his loan, as a permanent chattel-slave, a status predicated in vv. 44–46a. And, as illuminated by vv. 45–46, his progeny also continue to be retained as slaves. One should not confuse H's utopian ideals, which are far ahead of their time, with the socio-economic problems that H is attempting to solve. The fact that H is more constructive than D is an indication of only H's loftier vision, not its alleged lateness.

Chirichigno (1993: 327–28) presumes that in this second stage of destitution (vv. 35–38), the Israelite farmer still owns his land, but finding that it cannot support him and his family, he must rely on charitable, interest-free loans. This interpretation, however, founders on the shoals of the term "resident alien." The assumption of Lev 25 and, indeed, of all other biblical sources is that the *gēr*, the resident alien, may not and does not possess Israelite land in perpetuity (see NOTE on "resident aliens," v. 23). Thus if the creditor is warned not to treat the debtor as a resident alien, it can only mean that the debtor no longer owns his land, which has fallen into the possession of the creditor.

Schenker (1998: 29–31) renders this verse, in consonance with the Versions, "And if your brother becomes poor, and cannot maintain himself with you, then you shall relieve him: a stranger and a sojourner, he will live with you." Schenker, however, provides this rendering with an original interpretation: "if impoverishment constrains somebody to emigrate within the land of Israel, then you must let him immigrate to your area and lend him the support he needs." The immigrant (*gēr*) would work for his hosts in return for some capital and food (v. 37). For my critique, see APPENDIX D.

let him subsist under your authority. wāḥay ʿimmāk. The usual rendering is "let him live with you" (LXX, Tg. Onk., etc.), which Speiser (1960: 39) refines as "and he lives in your household"; that is, the debtor is forced into the creditor's service. Speiser considers this term, as the rest of the verse, as part of the protasis. He compares it with Akkadian *ina / ana bīt C wašābu / erēbu* 'to stay/enter the house of C', which "signifies that the *tidennu* [see NOTE on "as a resident hireling," v. 40] enters into a subservient relationship by becoming part of the creditor's household, and, in all likelihood, by receiving support from him" (Eichler 1973: 43).

Muffs (1965b: 4.6–7) objects forcefully and cogently:

1. *ḥay* does not mean "dwell." The Hebrew equivalent of *wašābu* is its cognate *yāšab*.
2. *ḥay* means "be healthy, stay alive." The true Akkadian equivalent is *balāṭu* 'obtain food (keep alive)' (CAD 2.57–58). The intensive (D) form of the verb *bulluṭu* means "provide food" (CAD 2.61), "sustain, keep alive" (CAD 2.59–60). Indeed, the creditor is sometimes called the *muballiṭānu* 'the sustainer'. So, too, the *Piʿel ḥiyyâ* (e.g., Deut 6:24; Jer 49:11; Pss 33:19; 41:3; Koh 7:12; Neh 9:6; cf. Lohfink 1992).
3. The creditor sustains the debtor by providing him with room and board.

I take exception to only the last statement. It is certainly true that in Mesopotamia, being "kept alive" provided sufficient grounds for enslavement: "Bunamuwadi, in distress, gave Aluluwa and his wife to Walkuwa. In (time of) distress he kept them alive [*ina danati ubalisunu*]. Aluluwa (is) his slave: his wife (is) his maid-servant" (cited in Yaron 1959: 160). However, this need not be true for Israel. Nothing in our text is said about room and board. The debtor gets a loan only so he can continue to support himself and his family. Presumably, he continues to work on his land, not as its owner—he sold it—but as a tenant. How, then, does the creditor sustain him? By not charging him interest (Levi 1981: 165). This constitutes a total reversal of the antichretic arrangement practiced in Mesopotamia. In Israel, whatever the debtor earned as a tenant farmer amortizes the principal and supports his family. He does not become a ward of the creditor, but continues to live in his own home. That the sustenance provided him is not room and board but his exemption from paying interest is emphasized by the text: *ḥay ʿimmāk* is cited twice, at the end of vv. 35 and 36, thus forming an envelope about the prohibition against taking interest. The text is thus saying: This is the way you should sustain him: Do not charge him interest as if he were a resident alien (cf. Levi-Feldblum 1986: 41, and see NOTE on "as a resident hireling," v. 40).

under your authority. ʿ*immāk.* The renderings "with you" (LXX), "beside you" (NAB), "in dealing with you" (Ehrlich 1908) all fail in confronting v. 47 *ûmāk* ʾ*āḥîkā* ʿ*immô* 'and your brother being (further) impoverished falls ʿimmô' where the suffix refers to the alien. Speiser (1960: 39), although I disagree with his interpretation, is surely correct that some form of subservience is intended. The rendering "falls under his authority" (NJPS), I submit, is apt for all uses of ʿ*im* in this chapter (and in Exod 22:24; cf. NJPS and in the verses examined above).

36. *advance or accrued interest.* *nešek wĕtarbît.* Rendered *ḥibûlyāʾ wĕribbîtāʾ* (*Tg. Onk.*; cf. Akk. *ḥubullu* and *ribbetu*); *šaʿārîn wĕribyān* (*Tgs. Ps.-J., Neof.*); *tókon . . . plēthei* (LXX), all denote "advance or accrued interest"—that is, interest taken off the top when the loan is made or collected at the end of the loan period. This combination is attested again in v. 37; Ezek 18:8, 13, 17; 22:12; Prov 28:8.

What is clear from all biblical sources is that interest from an Israelite is prohibited (Exod 22:24; Deut 23:20–21) and condemned (Ezek 18:8, 13, 17; 22:12; Ps 15:5; Prov 28:8), whereas elsewhere it was permitted without limits (LE §§ 18 A-21; CH §§ 48–51, 88–101), as high as 60 percent at Elephantine (Cowley 10, 11; cf. Neufeld 1955). Even in Syria during the 1960s, interest was as high as 40 to 60 percent for six months and 5 to 8 percent a month (Wirth 1971).

As the Covenant Code mandates that the creditor may not distrain (not "pawn"; Milgrom 1976a: 95–98) the debtor's cloak (Exod 22:25), Gerstenberger (1966) wonders whether the same rule held for a distrained field. The two situations are not analogous. The cloak stands for basic means of survival. The lost field, however, is available to the debtor as a tenant farmer (stage 2). And even if he is reduced to "slavery" (stage 3), he farms the land as a hired laborer for which he receives a daily wage (see NOTE on "as a resident hireling," v. 40).

Gerstenberger (1996: 387) suspects that the jubilee and redemption remedies proposed in Lev 25 border on being utopian, artificial, and inoperative because "a total prohibition against taking interest, of course, would prevent indebtedness and bankruptcy declarations from ever arising in the first place." He overlooks, however, the possibility of two or more successive years of drought, not an uncommon phenomenon in the ancient Near East (cf. Gen 41:25–57; 1 Kgs 17:1; 18:1), in which case the debtor, though exempted from interest, has difficulty in repaying the principal.

There is no consensus, however, concerning the different kinds of interest represented by these two terms. Ramban holds that *nešek* is yearly interest and *tarbît*, interest paid at the end (i.e., accrued). Eliezer of Beaugency (on Ezek 18:8; cf. Poznanski 1913) derives *nešek* from *nāšak* 'bite off' (cf. *m. B. Meṣ.* 5:1), hence advance interest (also Buhl 1899: 98, n. 2; Neufeld 1955: 355–57; Speiser 1960: 44). The tannaitic sages, though, register the view that *nešek* is interest paid at the end, whereas *tarbît* refers to food that has increased in price (based on v. 37b; *m. B. Meṣ.* 5:1). However, Deut 23:20 relates *nešek* also to foodstuffs! To deepen the confusion, the amoritic sages disagree with the Mishna and, in apparent agreement with Deut 23:20, conclude that both terms mean "interest," without any distinction between them (*b. B. Meṣ.* 60b), a view apparently held by the Masoretes, whose cantillation marks indicate that these two words should be read together as if they were a hendiadys.

Loewenstamm (1969: 79) detects order in this semantic chaos by postulating a chronological development: originally, the terms were distinguished (as in v. 37), *nešek* for money, and *m/tarbît* for victuals; subsequently, as a money economy became predominant, *nešek* became the exclusive term for "interest," even when it referred to victuals (Deut 23:20): "the tendency to an abstract and comprehensive formulation is evident (cf. Deut 17:6–7; 19:15 [against Num 35:30]; 22:1–3 [against Exod 23:4] . . . in this style the more dominant term for interest became the designation for interest in general" (cf. Gamoran 1971).

If Loewenstamm (1969) is correct, then Deuteronomy reflects a later period than Leviticus. This is clearly the implication of Seeligmann's (1978) study of biblical interest and of Fishbane's (1985: 175–76) stylistic analysis of the two laws, namely, that Deut 23:20–21 expands Lev 25:36–37 to include any commodity and exclude the foreigner.

Whether one holds that *m/tarbît* refers to money or to victuals, all agree that the interest is taken at the end of the loan. Both the verb *rābâ* and its Akkadian cognate *rabû* mean "grow, increase," and Akkadian *ribbetu, ribbātu (AHw)* means "back payment, arrears," or "the additional payment one owed *from the time he borrowed* [my emphasis]" (Levine 1989). Thus it makes sense to assume that *nešek* refers to another—indeed, the only other—attested interest, one that has been implied by the Versions and averred by Eliezer of Beaugency and others: advance interest.

Fear your God. wĕyārē'tā mē'ĕlōhêkā. The same motive clause appears in Deuteronomy under similar circumstances: if the debtor is refused a presumably interest-free (cf. Deut 23:20–21) loan (because of the approaching sabbatical cancellation of debts), "he will cry out to YHWH against you, and you will incur guilt" (Deut 15:9b). This phrase implies that taking interest was not illegal and, hence, unenforceable by man, but immoral and, hence, punishable by God. The rabbis sensitively remark that this phrase refers to *dĕbārîm hammĕsûrîm lallēb* 'words that are directed to the heart' (*b. Qidd.* 32b). The money lender (for interest) was accordingly condemned by the prophets (Jer 15:10); his profits were attributed to his exploitation of the poor (Ezek 22:12; cf. Prov 28:8); he was the reverse of the righteous man (Ezek 18:8, 17; cf. Ps 15:5); his dealings were regarded as an abomination (Ezek 18:13). In wisdom literature, nonrepayment of debt was condemned

(Ps 37:21); however, loans made without interest were regarded as ideal and gracious acts (Pss 15:5; 37:21, 26; 112:5; Prov 19:17).

let your brother subsist under your authority. wĕḥê 'āḥîkā immāk. For a discussion of this unique H expression, see the NOTE on v. 35. The form *ḥê* is a construct of the noun *ḥay* (Ehrlich 1908 on Gen 42:15 [H]; Greenberg 1957), which has no place here. Repoint *wāḥay* (as in v. 35; 18:5) or *wĕḥay* (2 Sam 12:22) (Driver and White 1894–98; cf. GKC § 76i), alternatively, render it as a purpose clause "and/so that your brother may subsist."

37. This verse is almost a verbatim repetition of the previous one. Why was it necessary? The slight change in one of the objects and in their placement may provide the answer. V. 36 focuses on the interest; v. 37, on the principal and on the fact that it does not have to be money. V. 37 envisages that if the principal is money, the same amount will be paid back; if it is victuals—and here is the main point—its monetary value at the *end of the loan* will be returned. Thus the creditor may not gain accrued interest either by charging interest or, if the price of the food has dropped, by demanding its monetary value at the time the loan was made. What, however, if the price of food has risen? The answer is not clear. The rabbis rule that the original price is repaid—in order to obviate any *monetary* interest accruing to the creditor (*m. B. Meṣ.* 5:1). But, then, if the creditor purchases the same amount of victuals that he lent the borrower, he will incur a loss, and it will appear that the debtor has now accrued interest—a situation that is prohibited by the rabbis (*m. B. Meṣ* 5:11; *b. B. Meṣ.* 75b)! Furthermore, it is hardly likely that the creditor would have lent under those circumstances, and it was probably stipulated in advance that the creditor would sustain no loss.

The impasse envisioned by the rabbis could not occur if the creditor stipulated that he be repaid in kind (e.g., grain), in which case the *marbît* would be taken from the grain harvest. That principal and interest could be taken directly from the new crop can be deduced from grain taxes in Israel (*maś'at-bar*, Amos 5:11; cf. Paul 1991) and Mesopotamian *biltul* (CAD 2.232–34) and *nusāḫū* (CAD 11/2.351–52).

This verse is constructed chiastically (Paran 1983: 26–27, 89):

> 'et-kaspĕkā   lō'-tittēn   lô   bĕnešek
> ûbĕmarbît   lō'-tittēn   'oklekā

This is quintessential H style: expansive, poetic, with metric balance, word pairs, and refrains. The alternative term for *tarbît, marbît,* in its meaning "increase," is found once more: *wĕkol-marbît bêtĕkā yāmûtû 'ănāšîm* 'all the increase of your house shall die [by the sword of (adding *bĕḥereb* with LXX, 4QSam[a])] men' (1 Sam 2:33b). In later attestations, its meaning is "most (1 Chr 12:30; 2 Chr 9:6; 30:18), as in Rabbinic Hebrew—another indication that H is preexilic (Paran 1983: 212). Both halves of the verse use the same verb *nātan,* probably to intensify the chiasm. Ordinarily, the verb pair is *lāqaḥ* and *nātan* (cf. Ezek 18:8, 13), as in v. 36.

38. This verse is structured chiastically:

A   *'ănî' YHWH 'ĕlōhêkem*
    B   *'ăšer- hôṣē'tî 'etkem mē'ereṣ miṣrayim*
    B'   *lātēt lākem 'et- 'ereṣ kĕna'an*
A'   *lihyôt lākem lē'lōhîm*

The purpose of YHWH's salvific act freeing Israel from Egypt was to give it the land of Canaan (BB') and to be its God (AA'). This can only mean that Israel's occupation of the land is contingent on its observance of YHWH's commandments, a point already emphasized in the exhortations appended to chap. 18 (vv. 1–5, 24–30; cf. 20:22–24).

who freed you from the land of Egypt. '*ăšer-hôṣē'tî 'etkem mē'ereṣ miṣrāyîm.* This clause is repeated (with third-person object) at the middle and the end of the law prohibiting slavery (vv. 42, 55), serving the same binding function as the thrice-repeated *ḥuqqat 'ôlām* (16:29a, 31b, 34a). This formula is again found in 19:36; 26:13, 45; Exod 20:2 (= Deut 5:6); 29:46; Num 15:41. The participle used nominally *hammôṣî'* is attested (22:33) as well as the verb *hamma'āleh* (11:45). The nuanced meaning of *hôṣē'tî* as equivalent to *gā'altî* 'I redeemed' is discussed in the NOTE on v. 55 (see also next NOTE).

to give you the land of Canaan. This purpose for God's redemption of Israel is found only here. It stresses that the land is God's, and in ceding it to Israel, God makes it incumbent on all the people to obey all the laws relating to the land, especially the sabbatical and jubilee. Moreover, it should be noted that in contrast to the four other pericopes on the loss of property or person (vv. 25–54) that close with the law of the jubilee (vv. 28, 31–33, 40, 54), this one closes with this verse. There can be no doubt, however, that the jubilee is implied. Indeed, it is a restatement of the opening rationale (vv. 23–24). It is a reminder that since the lost land is God's land, it must be redeemed at the jubilee. Also, as YHWH has redeemed Israel from Egypt, and the land from the immoral Canaanites, Israel must redeem the land from rapacious creditors (cf. Ibn Ezra).

to be your God. *lihyôt lākem lē'lōhîm.* This clause forms an inclusio with the first part of the verse and with v. 55b, enclosing the entire slave law as a single unit. V. 38 is therefore a transitional verse; it points in both directions, connecting with vv. 39–55 as well as serving as a reminder of the opening statement of the Decalogue, adumbrated in the opening verse of this chapter: "on Mount Sinai." The combination of God's land gift to Israel and his being its God is found again in Gen 17:8 (H) and Ezek 36:28.

Vv. 39–55. Stage Three: "Slavery"

If, as a tenant (vv. 35–38), the debtor still cannot repay his loan and otherwise cannot support himself and his family, they enter the household of the creditor (vv. 41a, 54b). He no longer enjoys the usufruct of his forfeited land. Nonetheless, his status is not that of a slave, but of a resident hireling; he receives wages, all of which pay off his debt. However, non-Israelites may become bona fide slaves.

According to Chirichigno (1993: 145–46),

> In the ancient Near East debt-slaves were not identified with chattel-slaves. For example, according to LH (= CH) §117 if a loan was foreclosed and dependents were sold or surrendered to a creditor . . . as debt-slaves, they were released after three years' service. These laws demonstrate that citizens who became debt-slaves were not to be regarded as the property of their creditors—viz., the creditor has only purchased the service or capacity for work (*Arbeitskraft*) of his debt-slaves. While certain rights pertaining to debt-slaves were also extended to chattel-slaves (e.g., LH [= CH] §119), the latter were always the property of their owners. This attitude is also reflected in the *mēšarum* acts, which proclaimed the release of debt-slaves and their estranged property but not the release of chattel-slaves . . . it is likely that the compilers of LH (= CH) and MAL did not employ the term *wardum* "slave" of debt-slaves in order to make it clear that a debt-slave was not to be identified with or treated like a chattel-slave.

The pentateuchal slave-laws, in contrast, do not distinguish between the debt-slave and the chattel-slave: both are called *'ebed*. Chirichigno (1993: 182–85) presents a strong case for regarding the adjective *'ibrî* in Exodus and Deuteronomy (e.g., Exod 21:2 [contrast vv. 20, 26, 27]; Deut 15:12 [contrast v. 15]) as designating a debt-slave (over against the foreign chattel-slave). It must be admitted, however, that in Lev 25 there is no such terminological distinction, though ostensibly both kinds of slavery are mentioned (contrast vv. 39, 42b with vv. 42a, 44, 46, 55). The reason, as will be demonstrated, is of utmost significance. For Israelites, both kinds of slavery, chattel and debt, are prohibited: chattel-slavery is abolished, and debt-slavery is transformed into work for hire. The two terms, therefore, coalesce.

Slavery was widespread in the ancient Near East, including Israel: "The basic supply source for slaves was the freeborn native defaulting debtor. Mesopotamian law (CH §§ 114–19; MAL A § 48) recognizes the right of the creditor to seize the defaulting debtor and force him to perform compulsory service" (Mendelsohn 1962: 385). "To stave off his own enslavement, the debtor handed over to the creditor as hostages his slave, concubine, wife, and children. Theoretically, they were kept in bondage until the debt has been worked off. In practice, however, unless they were redeemed, they remained in the possession of the creditor as long as they lived" (Mendelsohn 1949: 7, 14). In Rome, according to the Twelve Tables (fifth century B.C.E.), the *praetor* could ultimately assign the debtor to the creditor, who was authorized to seize him and keep him bound with rope or fetters. If at the end of sixty days the debt could still not be repaid, the debtor could be sold abroad as a permanent slave to a foreigner (Aulus Gellius, *Attic Nights*, 20.1.41–46, cited in Jackson 1988: 89).

In Israel, slaves were supplied by war captives (Num 31:7–12; Deut 21:10–14; 2 Chr 28:8) and by native population: by sale of minors (2 Kgs 4:1; Neh 5:5), by self-sale due to hunger or debt (Exod 21:5–6; Lev 25:39–43; Deut 15:16–17), or by enslavement of defaulting debtors, including the thief who could not pay his fines (Exod 21:37–22:3), the widow who could not pay her late husband's debts (2 Kgs 4:1), and, in general, impoverished Israelites who were unable to repay their loans (Neh 5:1–13; cf. 1 Sam 22:2; Isa 50:1; Amos 2:6; 8:6). That Israel knew from past (and exilic?) experience the meaning of slavery is attested by the terminology employed by Second Isaiah (Baltzer 1987). "A borrower is a slave of the man who lends" (Prov 22:7) was, most often, the bitter reality (cf. Lang 1983: 114–27). However, if the historical references (or lack of them) are reliable, there seem to have been certain self-imposed limits on the extent of slave practice. No captive during Israel's internecine wars was ever forced into slavery; the one ostensible exception, North Israel's treatment of Judean prisoners, was terminated by the prophet Obed (2 Chr 28:7–15). And Jeremiah, who relies on the debt-slave law of Deut 15:12, nonetheless, adds that "no one should keep his fellow Judean enslaved" (Jer 34:9b), a clause probably based on Lev 25:40 (see its NOTE).

As demonstrated in NOTE on "tattoos," 19:28, indirect evidence that H abolishes the slavery of Israelites can be derived from the prohibition against tattooing. The other pentateuchal law codes, which accede to the institution of slavery, allow a permanent slave to be marked (i.e., tattooed; Exod 21:6 [JE]; Deut 15:17 [D]), a practice attested in Babylonia (CH §§ 226–27) and in Elephantine (Cowley 28). That is, if H had accepted the slavery of Israelites, it would have allowed the indentured servant to remain in servitude beyond the jubilee. Perhaps just as Mesopotamian land and slave contracts could stipulate that the king's mīšarum would have no effect in the sale, so Israelite contracts might have stipulated that the slave willingly waived his jubilee rights if his debt had not been repaid. In any event, rather than searching (in vain) for a funerary practice, as in the adjoining prohibition against laceration (19:28αβ), tattooing may be a discrete prohibition aimed at preventing the enslavement of Israelites.

Prophetic remonstrances and Israelite law against the excesses of slavery and, especially, our pericope (vv. 39–43), which virtually abolishes the institution of slavery, may, however, never have been put into practice. Exod 21, followed by Deut 15, demands the release of Israelite slaves after six years of service. However, Jer 34 testifies that this law was not observed. In Mesopotamia, CH § 117 proclaims that three years of enslavement suffice to work off any debt. But not a single Mesopotamian document, whose number is legion, testifies that this law was ever enforced (cf. Finkelstein 1961; Leemans 1991: 414–20). On the contrary, Hammurabi's son Samsuiluna and his successors effectively circumvented CH § 117 by limiting release from debt-slavery to the first year of the king's reign and special occasions (Hallo 1995). The same, of course, holds true for Israel. The jubilee laws remain utopian; at least there is no hard evidence that they were ever enacted (for a more sanguine view, see COMMENT F). In either case, the theoretical principles that undergird them are radically different. For example, as mentioned above, Israel alone does not distinguish between chattel-slaves and debt-slaves. Moreover, both kinds of slavery are abolished by H.

The pernicious hold of slavery in modern societies, even democratic ones, is best illustrated in the case of India:

> Bonded labor—the practice of engaging laborers without wages to pay off real or imagined debts—is against the law. But it persists despite court rulings [and] occasional police intervention. . . . We estimate a very conservative estimate, that there are five million adults and ten million children in bonded labor in India. . . . Virtually all of India's bonded laborers are untouchable, who are at the bottom of the caste hierarchy. Some were born into this condition because their parents or grandparents were sold long before they were born. Others were lured into servitude by agents for quarry owners or brick kiln managers with promises of higher paying jobs than those they had. Still others fell into their position from the need to repay loans that were already given, but that can never be fully repaid. Once indentured, it is almost impossible to escape. (*New York Times*, 4 June 1992)

If, in a democracy, despite its laws and enforcement agencies, slavery of the most invidious kind—not of a few, but of millions—exists in the twenty-first century, how can we expect the slave laws of the Torah to have taken root in Israelite society except in the minds of idealists and prophets?

Scant few passages in Scripture attest to this idealism, but they indicate its existence. The prophets, for example, rail against the brutalities of slavery, but they do not advocate its abolition. Yet "I will even pour out my spirit on male and female slaves" (Joel 3:2 [2:29 English]) surely evinces an egalitarian tendency, and "Did not he who made me in my mother's belly make him" (Job 31:15) argues for it. That these were not isolated voices in the wilderness but represent an entire branch of Israel's spiritual leadership will be demonstrated in this pericope, which openly, univocally, and unambiguously looks forward to the dissolution of slavery. How else can we explain the sharp contrast between the intellectual leaders of Israel and those of the Hellenistic world except by the legacy provided by prophecy and law. As noted by Kalisch (1867–72), Philo (*Laws* 2.123) admits that "the law does permit the acquisition of slaves from other nations . . . that most indispensable possession, domestic service, should not be absolutely excluded from his commonwealth." But he adds, "For servants are free by nature, no man being naturally a slave" (*Laws* 2.69; cf. also Colson 1968: 624–25, refuting the contention that Stoics harbored a similar doctrine). Contrast Aristotle's view that "a slave is an animated tool, and a tool is an inanimate slave, whence there is nothing in common" between master and slave (*Ethic. Nic.* 8.11; cf. *Polit.* 1.3–6), and Plato's advice to the master "to treat his slaves well, not for their sake but for his own; but it would be foolish to treat them as free men for it would make them arrogant" (*Laws* 6.19) with a contemporary Israelite statement: "If you have one slave treat him like yourself . . . deal with him as a brother" (Sir 33:31–32). Philo (*Quod Omnis* 79; cf. *de Vita* 70) also testifies, "Not a single slave is to be found among them (the Essenes), but all are free . . . and they denounce the owners of slaves, not merely for their injustice in outraging the law of equality, but also for their impiety in annulling the statute of Nature, who mother-like has born and reared all men alike, and created them genuine brothers."

Stage 3 is startlingly conspicuous by the absence of the provision for redemption, which the rabbis confirm when they declare that relatives are under no obligation to redeem their indentured kinsperson (*b. Qidd.* 15b). Yet redemption of debt-slaves was obtained in Mesopotamia. In Sippar, during the reign of Rim-Sin, a female slave regained her freedom by paying 10 shekels to her owner. As for redemption by a relative: "17 shekels of silver for the redemption of Hagaliga, his father, Zagagan has received (as a loan). (But) he had no silver (so) he sold himself to the *enum* priest" (Khafajah 88, cited in Leggett 1974: 63–83). Here the son borrows money to redeem his father, but being unable to repay the loan, he sells himself into bondage. In CH § 117, we find the clause "has sold his wife, his son or his daughter, or gives (them) into servitude." Its two verbs translate, respectively, *ana kaspim nadānu* and *ana kiššātim nadānu*, where the latter implies the power of redemption (Driver and Miles 1952: 212–14). The edict of Ammisaduqa confirms CH § 117 and adds the further option *ana manzazānim ezēbu* 'to leave as a pledge', by which the creditor has no power of alienation (cf. Yaron 1959: 158–59). Thus redemption of debt-slaves prevails in Mesopotamia. Why, then, is it missing in Israel? Similarly, there is surprisingly no allowance for self-redemption (contrast vv. 26, 48–49).

The answer is that the Israelite slave is not a slave (pace Weinfeld 1990a); he is *śākîr*, a "hireling" (see NOTE on "as a resident hireling," v. 40), whose work amortizes the principal—a status to which redemption does not apply. The wages he earns may even provide him a surplus with which to free himself of his debt and status (see NOTE on "or if he prospers," v. 49). Thus it is preposterous to deduce categorically from the absence of a redemption provision that "the one who sold himself into debt bondage remains in service until the jubilee" (Fager 1993: 102, following Horst 1961: 219). To be sure, his family has no obligation to redeem him. Only if neither he nor his family can supply the means for his redemption, as we shall see, will the jubilee free him, cancel his debt, and give him back his land. Thus he (or his inheritor) will be able to start out afresh as a debt-free landowner who will be independent of his family.

The redemption and self-redemption clauses are also missing in the second stage (vv. 35–38), again for the same reason: the term "redemption" does not apply. Redemption is applicable to only sold land and sold (i.e., enslaved) Israelites (to a non-Israelite owner, vv. 47–52), but not to a loan. Perhaps because his loan is interest-free, his labor (as a tenant farmer) can repay the loan. Also, the *gō'ēl* (or anyone else) may lend him money to pay off his debt. But that person does not, as a consequence, come into possession of the land or the enslaved kinsperson; his act does not constitute redemption. Similarly, the term "self-redemption" also does not apply; the debtor's income as a tenant farmer may produce a surplus (in nonfamine years) that can fully amortize his loan.

Chirichigno (1993: 329) suggests that the redeemer in stages 2 and 3 is absent, presumably, because he refuses to help: "if there were someone who could help the debtor he would have done so when the debtor was forced to sell part of his land." First, it should be noted, his statements to the contrary notwithstanding (see INTRODUCTION to vv. 25–55), Chirichigno makes stage 2 dependent on stage 1. Furthermore, there is no indication in the text that the redeemer is reluctant to redeem. The required intervention of the redeemer when his kinsperson sells himself to a non-Israelite (vv. 48–49) indicates that the text's silence concerning the redeemer in stages 2 and 3 is intended to mean that he is not required to redeem. A possible reason for his exemption has been presented above. It is based on a principle of law, not on the redeemer's whim: redemption, which allows the redeemer to retain possession to the jubilee, applies to only sold land and enslaved Israelites, not to monetary debt.

Japhet (1996: 43) has noted that the slave law is the mirror image of the land law. As only the usufruct of the land, but not the land itself, may be sold, so only the labor of the Israelite, but not the Israelite himself, may be sold. Although, technically, the creditor has bought the land or the person, he cannot own either of them. Hence, in effect, he leases the land or the person until the jubilee. The Israelite can, therefore, never become a slave; if he is reduced to indebtedness, his status is that of a *śākîr*, a wage-earning day laborer.

The slave pericope, vv. 39–46, is composed of two parallel panels:

<table>
<tr><td colspan="2" align="center">Israelite slave</td><td colspan="2" align="center">Non-Israelite slave</td></tr>
<tr><td>A</td><td>³⁹wĕkî-yāmûk 'āhîkā 'immāk wĕnimkar- lāk lō-tā'ăbōd bô 'ăvōdat 'ābed ⁴⁰kĕśākîr kĕtôšāb yihyeh immāk 'ad-šĕnat hayyōbēl ya'ăbōd immāk</td><td>A'</td><td>⁴⁴wĕ'abdĕkā wa'ămātkā 'ăšer yihyû-lāk mē'ēt haggôyim 'ăšer sĕbîbōtêkem mēhem tiqnû 'ebed wĕ'āmâ</td></tr>
<tr><td>B</td><td>⁴¹wĕyāṣā' mē'immāk hû' ûbānāyw 'immô wĕšāb 'el-mišpaḥtô wĕ'el 'ăhuzzat 'ăbōtāyw yāšûb</td><td>B'</td><td>⁴⁵wĕgam mibbĕnê hattôšābîm haggārîm 'immākem mēhem tiqnu ûmimmišpaḥtām 'ăšer 'immākem 'ăšer hôlîdû bĕ'arṣĕkem wĕhāyû lākem la'ăhuzzâ</td></tr>
<tr><td>C</td><td>⁴²kî-'ăbāday hēm 'ăšer hôṣē'tî 'ōtām mē'ereṣ miṣrāyim lō' yimmākĕrû mimkeret 'ābed</td><td>C'</td><td>⁴⁶wĕhitnahaltem 'ōtām libĕnēkem 'ahărêkem larešet 'ăhuzzâ lĕ'ōlâm bāhem tā'ăbōdû</td></tr>
<tr><td>D</td><td>⁴³lō'-tirdeh bô bĕpārek wĕyārē'tā mē'ĕlōhêkā</td><td>D'</td><td>ûbĕ'aḥêkem bĕnê-yiśrā'ēl 'îš bĕ'āḥîw lō'-tirdeh bô bĕpārek</td></tr>
<tr><td colspan="2" align="center">Israelite slave</td><td colspan="2" align="center">Non-Israelite slave</td></tr>
<tr><td>A</td><td>³⁹If your brother, being (further) impoverished under your authority, is sold to you, do not make him work as a slave. ⁴⁰He shall remain under you as a resident hireling; he shall work under you until the jubilee year.</td><td>A'</td><td>⁴⁴Male and female slaves as you may have—(it is) from the nations round about you, from them that you may buy male and female slaves.</td></tr>
</table>

	Israelite slave		Non-Israelite slave
B	[41]Then he and his children with him shall be released from your authority; he shall return to his kin group and return to his ancestral holding.	B′	[45]Also from among the children of residents (aliens) who live under your sway, from them you may buy (slaves), or from their kin groups that are under your sway, whom they begot in your land. These shall become your property;
C	[42]For they are my slaves, whom I freed from the land of Egypt; they shall not be sold as slaves are sold.—	C′	[46]you may keep them as a possession for your children after you, for them to inherit as property for all time. These you may treat as slaves,
D	[43]You shall not rule over him with harshness; you shall fear your God.	D′	but as for your Israelite brothers, no one shall rule over the other with harshness.

ABCD deals with the indentured Israelite who may not be treated as a slave and must be released at the jubilee; A′B′C′ deals with the non-Israelite who may be acquired as a permanent slave and bequeathed to one's descendants. The exception is D′, which repeats the injunction of D not to treat the Israelite harshly, implying that the non-Israelite slave may receive harsh treatment. This conclusion can only be drawn by comparing the two panels. Apparently, there was some uneasiness in stating this explicitly, and it has to be inferred from the pericope's structure. AA′ contrasts the Israelite who sells himself (*nimkar*), but not as a slave, with the non-Israelite who may be bought (*tiqnû*) as a slave. BB′ again contrasts the two: the Israelite who is released at the jubilee with his children and returns to his family and restored property compared with the non-Israelite whose family and children are permitted to become Israelite property. Finally, CC′ contrasts the rationale for the prohibition against enslaving Israelites—they are enslaved to God—with the non-Israelites who may become permanent, inheritable slaves. D′, however, leaves the topic of the non-Israelite slave and repeats the injunction to the Israelite creditor not to treat the Israelite "slave" harshly. In view of the panel structure, parallelism should have required a statement like "You may rule over him with harshness." Instead, this concession is implied indirectly.

My student J. Wyrick has discerned an introverted structure that overlaps the two pericopes dealing with the Israelite debtor (vv. 36–43):

A   [36]*al-tiqqaḥ mē'ittô nešek wĕtarbît wĕyārē'tā mē'ĕlōhêkā wĕḥay 'āḥîkā 'immāk*
        [37]*'et-kaspĕkā lō'-tittēn lô benešek ûbĕmarbît lō'-tittēn 'oklekā*
     B   [38]*'ănî YHWH 'ĕlōhēkem 'ăšer-hôṣē'tî 'etkem mē'ereṣ miṣrayim lātēt lākem 'et-'ereṣ kĕna'an lihyot lākem lē'lōhîm*

X ^{39}wĕkî-yāmûk ʾāḥîkā ʿimmāk wĕnimkar-lāk lōʾ-taʿăbôd bô ʿăbōdat
    ʿebed
    ^{40}kĕśākîr kĕtôšāb yihyeh ʿimmāk ʿad-šĕnat hayyōbēl yaʿăbōd
    ʿimmāk
    ^{41}wĕyāṣāʾ mēʿimmāk hûʾ ûbānāyw ʿimmô wĕšāb ʾel-mišpaḥtô
    wĕʾel-ʾăḥuzzātô yāšûb

B′ ^{42}kî-ʿăbāday hēm ʾăšer-hôṣēʾtî ʾōtām mēʾereṣ miṣrayim lōʾ yimmākĕrû
    mimkeret ʿebed

A′ ^{43}lōʾ-tirdeh bô bĕpārek wĕyārēʾtā mēʾĕlōhêkā

A ^{36}Do not exact from him advance or accrued interest. Fear your God,
    and let your brother subsist under your authority. ^{37}Do not lend him
    money at advance interest, or lend him food at accrued interest.

B ^{38}I, YHWH, am your God, who freed you from the land of Egypt,
    to give you the land of Canaan, to be your God.

    X ^{39}If your brother, being (further) impoverished under your au-
        thority, is sold to you, do not make him work as a slave. ^{40}He
        shall remain under you as a resident hireling; he shall work un-
        der you until the jubilee year. ^{41}Then he and his children with
        him shall be released from your authority; he shall return to his
        kin group and return to his ancestral holding.

B′   —^{42}For they are my slaves, whom I freed from the land of Egypt;
    they shall not be sold as slaves are sold.—

A′ ^{43}You shall not rule over him with harshness; you shall fear your God.

AA′ are divine injunctions, the first a deprecation with *ʾal* and the second a prohibition with *lōʾ* (similar to BB′ in the introversion of vv. 14–17). Both contain
the motive clause "fear your God." BB′ are motive clauses that contain the Exodus motif: "I freed you from the land of Egypt." The pivot X states the basic
law that indebted Israelites may never be treated as slaves.

The advantage of combining the two stages of impoverishment, indebtedness,
and slavery (for an Israelite) into a single structure is that it permits the prohibitions contained in one to apply to the other. Thus we are certain that the prohibition against taking interest (stage 2, vv. 35–38) is also in force in stage 3 (vv.
39–43) and, conversely, that the prohibition against treating the Israelite "slave"
harshly (A′) also applies in stage 2 (vv. 35–38). Finally, if this conjectural structure is correct, it would explain the repetition and positioning of the motive
clauses (BB′)—to create the introversion pattern.

39. *is sold to you. wĕnimkar lāk.* The temptation to render the verb as a reflexive (e.g., *Tgs.*, *NJPS*, *NRSV*), implying that the sale is voluntary (e.g., Eichler 1985) and even that the debtor has the right to sell himself to another employer, must be resisted. All eighteen occurrences of *mkr*, *Nip ʿal* have a passive
meaning. If a reflexive meaning had been intended, the *Hitpaʿel* would have
been used, as is attested in Deut 28:68 (A. Schenker, personal communication).
In Lev 25, the case detailed in vv. 47–48 corroborates this conclusion. If an Is-

raelite had the option to sell himself to a non-Israelite, then stage 3, where redemption is not required (see INTRODUCTION to vv. 39–55), would never occur. Every Israelite debtor would naturally seek a non-Israelite master who would be obligated to release him when "repurchased" by his relative. This is also the situation predicated in Neh 5:8: *ʾaḥênû hayyĕhûdîm hannimkārîm laggôyim* 'our Jewish brothers who have been sold to the nations'. Surely, they have not voluntarily sold themselves (see also Deut 15:12; Isa 50:1; 52:3; Jer 34:14; Est 7:4 [bis]).

Thus it must be assumed that the debtor has no choice. If he sinks further into debt to his creditor, the latter can seize him as though he were a resident alien, an act prohibited in stage 2 (v. 35) but permitted here. However, his status is not that of a slave, as made explicit by the continuation of the verse.

I must presume that the debtor's sale does not mean he is the recipient of the sale price—the amount he would fetch in the slave market. If that were the case, the creditor would be burdened by two payments: the cost of his debtor and the cost of his work. Would not the owner rather purchase a true slave who would not receive wages? Moreover, a literal sale would undermine the basic premise of the Israelite slave law as formulated in this chapter: the person of the Israelite is not for sale, only his work. Thus the root *mkr* in this context must be understood figuratively. It is used because it is the terminology of the slave market. But in reality, his sale amounts to his hire (see NOTES on v. 40).

Paran (1989: 35, 36, n. 27) claims that H (vv. 39–40a, 43) fully accepts the earlier slave law (Exod 21:2–6) in its stipulation that the slave is released in the seventh year, and only a subsequent insertion of P (vv. 40b–42, 44–46) polemicizes with H and the Exodus law by introducing the later concepts of jubilee and redemption. His proposal must be rejected out of hand, not only because H has been demonstrated to be subsequent to and the redactor of P (see Introduction I H), but also because the concepts of jubilee and redemption are demonstrably old (see NOTES to vv. 10, 24).

do not make him work as a slave. lōʾ-taʿăbōd bô ʿăbōdat ʿābed, literally "do not enslave him with the enslavement of a slave." The threefold use of the root *ʿbd* indicates the revulsion at the institution of slavery in the mind of the writer. The *Qal* of *ʿbd*, having the transitive meaning "make/put to work," requires the *beth* of means (e.g., v. 46; Exod 1:14; Deut 15:19). If, however, the *Hipʿil* is used (Exod 1:13), the *beth* is unnecessary (cf. McConville 1984: 95). The rationale for this prohibition is given at the end of this pericope: the Israelite cannot be the slave of any person because he is God's slave (v. 42; cf. v. 55).

Philo (*Laws* 2.83) expounds: "Do not harness him like an unreasoning animal, nor oppress him with weights too heavy and too numerous for his capacity, nor heap insults upon him, nor drag him down by threats and nuances into cruel despondency." The rabbis prefer to specify: "He should not have to carry his (the master's) things before him when going to the bath house, nor support him by his hips when ascending steps, nor wash his feet, nor tie his shoes, nor carry him in a litter, chair or sedan chair as slaves do (*Mekh.* Mishpatim, Nezikin 1; *Sipra* Behar 7:2).

Nonetheless, this prohibition, as well as those prohibiting the creditor from confiscating the defaulting debtor's clothing (Exod 22:25; Deut 24:12–13), taking his tools of food production (Deut 24:6), and even entering his house in order to seize his property (Deut 24:10–11), indicate, only too starkly, that this is precisely what was done: the indentured Israelite would end as a slave with all his property lost.

40. *as a resident hireling. kĕśākîr kĕtôšāb.* As demonstrated in the NOTE on "(as though he were) a resident alien," v. 35, the word *tôšāb* is never attested independently, but only in tandem with either *gēr* 'alien' or *śākîr* 'hireling'. Furthermore, this term takes a singular verb (Exod. 12:45; Lev 22:10). Thus Melamed (1944–45: 176) is correct in regarding it as a hendiadys. The addition of the word *tôšāb* 'resident' is significant. The resident hireling is not a *śākîr*, a day laborer who returns to his home and family each evening (19:13; Deut 24:14–15; Job 14:6), but a long-term employee who lives with his family on the landowner's property (*haggārîm 'immāk*, v. 6). In this respect, he resembles the California migrant farm worker who receives room and board from his employer. An examination of the three other contexts in which the resident hireling is attested will clarify his status:

1. *tôšāb wĕśākîr lō'-yō'kal bô* 'the resident hireling may not partake of it (the *pesaḥ* sacrifice)' (Exod 12:45). This is a categorical prohibition, like that affecting the foreigner (v. 43b), as distinct from the landowner's slave (v. 44) and the alien (v. 48), who may eat of the *pesaḥ* if they are circumcised. At first glance, this prohibition seems to be directed solely to the non-Israelite because, according to Exod 12:4, an Israelite neighbor may be invited to the paschal feast. The two verses, however, are not analogous. Lev 25, on the one hand, speaks of an *individual* who, presumably, is a member of another family. Exod 12, on the other hand, presumes that the invitation is extended to the neighbor's entire *family*, in which case the household unity, so essential to the *pesaḥ*, is not broken. Thus a resident hireling can be either Israelite (contra Reviv 1982: 285) or non-Israelite (in conformance with Deut 24:14). If the former, he joins his own family for the *pesaḥ* observance; he is a free-born Israelite and not a member of the landowner's household (see 22:10b), even though he and his family may be living on the owner's property. If the latter, he is *ben-nēkār*, a migrant foreigner contracted by the Israelite for a limited period, probably the harvest season. If, however, he were a permanent resident in the land, then the status of *gēr* would apply (v. 48).

2. *tôšab kōhēn wĕśākîr lō'-yō'kal qōdeš* 'A priest's resident hireling may not eat sacred food' (22:10b). That this sentence contains the same hendiadys even though it is broken by *kōhēn*, an absolute noun, which forms part of the construct chain, including the construct, *tôšab*, see the NOTE on 22:10b. Its context indicates that the *zār* 'the stranger' (i.e., the nonpriest) is also forbidden (vv. 10a, 13b), whereas the priest's slave (v. 11) and his single, childless daughter qualify (vv. 12–13a). Since the hireling presumably is also a nonpriest, why mention him separately? The answer probably is that being resident (*tôšāb*) on the priest's property, like the slave, he too might be assumed to be eligible for the priest's

sacred food. Without the master's food, how do the hireling and his family sub-sist? The hireling receives wages, presumably enough to buy unconsecrated food and the rest of his family's needs. Clearly, this law applies to both an Israelite and a non-Israelite hireling.

3. *wĕhāyĕtâ šabbat hā'āreṣ lākem lĕ'oklâ . . . wĕlišĕkîrĕkā ûlĕtôšābĕkā* 'But the sabbath (-yield) of the land will be for you to eat: for . . . your resident hirelings' (25:6). This law applies to both Israelites and non-Israelite hirelings living un-der the authority of the landowner (*'immāk*). Consult the details in the NOTES on v. 6.

At once, one can see why the term "hireling" is qualified by "resident." In the laws, the single term *šākîr* refers to a day laborer (19:13; Deut 24:14–15; cf. Job 14:6; Matt 20:8). The one ostensible exception is Deut 15:18 (see also at vv. 50b, 53a), where *mišneh* has been rendered "the equivalent of (the hire of a hired ser-vant six years)" (Tsevat 1958: 125–26; cf. NRSV). However, as cogently argued by Lindenberger (1991: 479–82), the biblical and extra-biblical evidence adduced by Tsevat will not stand muster, Tsevat's (1994) rebuttal notwithstanding. Focusing on only the plain meaning of the text, it cannot be argued that since "double" is an exaggeration, it would lead the cynical owner to ignore the entire law. In that case, all of D's laws would be abandoned since they are replete with exaggerations (e.g., 12:31b; 15:4a; 16:19b; 20:4 [also the promises of vv. 5–8]; 23:15; 24:19b). It should be noted that these citations are mainly motive clauses, just as the clause containing *mišneh*. In this respect, D borrows the language of wisdom literature, where hyperbole is the norm (Weinfeld 1972d: 307–19).

Moreover, Tsevat's (1994: 593) claim that in a premarket economy "if the maximum is procured by slaves, owners will expect and ordinarily get about the same result from hired workers" is incorrect. The owner can torment the hireling only by holding back his wages (19:13b; Job 7:2b), but he cannot compel him to increase his productivity. The hireling is a free person and can find another owner. Not so the slave. The owner is in full control of the slave's productivity, and toward that end he can treat him harshly (vv. 43a, 46b). Thus the traditional rendering "double" is preferable. That is, the text merely states that the slave works twice as hard as a hireling.

The resident hireling may be either Israelite (contra Levi 1981: 143–49; Re-viv 1982: 285; Bultmann 1992: 187, n. 56) or non-Israelite. The exception is the verse under discussion: it would apply to only Israelites; non-Israelites may be treated as slaves (vv. 44–46), and the jubilee law does not pertain to them. The length of service is relative to the landowner's needs—for example, one year (v. 53; Isa 21:16 [three years in 1QIs^a]), three years (Isa 16:14; cf. CH § 17), or seven years (Gen 29:18).

Nothing is stated concerning the exact wages of the *šākîr*. Those of his Mesopotamian counterpart were fixed by law. If he worked with the crops or the flocks, he received his wages from the produce (e.g., barley, wheat, or wool), and if at other occupations, in silver (LE § 7–9; CH §§ 257–58, 273–77; HL §§ 150–51, 157–58). Mesopotamian documents supplement our knowledge of working conditions; for example, hired laborers could be paid in wool, receive a monthly wage, be hired for eight or forty days, hire a substitute, or have their wages posted on royal stela (cf. *agru, CAD* 1/1: 151–53).

The major difference between the *bonded* laborer (i.e., the laborer who pays off his debts) in Mesopotamia and Israel is that the former (*d/tid/tennu*) works off only the interest of his loan (personal antichresis), whereas the latter, having no interest to pay (vv. 36–37), works off the principal; that is, he can apply all his wages to amortize his debt: "The institution of personal *tidennūtu* represents not only an antichretic security transaction but also a type of indentured servitude. As long as the debt remains unpaid, the *tidennu* loses his freedom of movement. He and his children are bound to the creditor by an obligation of service" (Eichler 1973: 45). Considering the high rates of interest that prevailed in Mesopotamia, as noted above, it must have been rare for a *tidennu* to redeem himself. The Israelite *'ebed–śākîr*, on the contrary, unburdened by any interest whatsoever, frequently could meet this goal. If not, the safety net of the jubilee would rescue him.

In this respect, Lev 25 (H) provides a clear advance over the slave laws of Exod 21 (JE) and Deut 15 (D). Both JE and D stipulate six years of servitude, with no indication that this term can be reduced by early redemption, whereas H implies that the maximum period is the jubilee, which can be curtailed through redemption by self or others (Levi 1981: 180). If so, why then is the possibility of redemption omitted in the text both here, vv. 39–43, and in vv. 35–38 (stages 2 and 3)? The answer is that redemption applies to only property (vv. 25–33) and true slavery (vv. 47–55). Land, house, and slaves are owned by the purchaser. The hireling, however, is a free person. He is a *śākîr*, not an *'ebed*. Of course, he could be redeemed by a relative. The right of redemption existed in the ancient Near East (e.g., CH § 119; MAL A § 48), even for a female slave (Schorr 1913: 52–53, no. 28). It surely, then, existed in Israel (Levi 1981: 190, n. 11). However, it is omitted from the slave law of Lev 25 because it is an option, not an obligation (see INTRODUCTION to vv. 39–55). Furthermore, it would not be true redemption. As noted above, the relative would only be lending the hireling the required money. The terms for repayment would be worked out by the two parties. Alternatively, the relative might give him a free loan, an act of charity. The relative could not hold him until the jubilee, which he could do were it a case of redemption.

The superior status of the hireling over the slave is manifest not only in his economic advantages, but also in his working conditions. This is implied by the repeated admonition *lō'-tirdeh bô bĕpārek* 'do not treat him harshly' (vv. 43, 46b) in contrast with the non-Israelite slave, concerning whom the text states *bāhem taʿăbōdû* 'These you may treat as slaves' (v. 46aγ). After all, the terms of the hireling's labor are stipulated in advance; the slave, in contrast, is subject to the demands and whims of his master. This difference is subtly acknowledged by D in its admission that the slave works twice as hard as the hireling (Deut 15:18; for *mišneh* 'double', see no. 3, above). Considering that the hireling is a free person, it may very well be that if he finds the creditor's conditions too harsh or the wages too low, he can seek another employer.

under you . . . under you. 'immāk . . . 'immāk. See the NOTE on "under your authority," v. 35.

until the jubilee year. The rabbis harmonized the seventh- and fiftieth-year manumissions (Exod 21; Lev 25) by interpreting this clause as signifying that if the jubilee interrupts the seven-year indenture, the debtor goes free (*m. Qidd.* 1:2) and by interpreting the word 'ōlām (Exod 21:6; Deut 15:17) as "until the jubilee" (*b. Qidd.* 14b). Also, they suggest that two different kinds of enslavement are intended: seven years if he is sold by the court (Exod 21), and fifty years if he sells himself (Lev 25).

Interestingly, fifty years seems to be the maximum period for mortgaging a man for debt (*tidennūtu*) both in Nuzi (Eichler 1973: 34) and in Seleucid Babylonia (McEvan 1982, cited in Weinfeld 1990a: 61, n. 98).

41. *he and his children.* hû' 'ûbānāyw. "As his master is responsible for his food so is the master responsible for the food of his wife and children" (*Sipra* Behar 7:3). Why is the wife not explicitly mentioned? The problem may not be brushed aside by presuming that the wife is taken for granted. Note that when the subject switches to the non-Israelite slave, the text makes certain, not once but twice, that the female slave is specified (v. 44). But, again, when the subject reverts to the Israelite slave (bonded to a non-Israelite), only he and his children are released by the jubilee, with the wife missing once more (v. 54b). In Mesopotamia, the creditor had the right to seize the wife and the children (e.g., CH §§ 116, 117, 119, 151–52; MAL A §§ 39, 44, 48). The Bible, too, attests to the indenture of children as a means of paying off the debt (2 Kgs 4:1–7; Neh 5:5; cf. the implication of Isa 50:1; Wessely 1846).

I submit that one has to consider seriously the possibility that Leviticus deliberately omits any mention of the Israelite's wife in order to make a legal statement: she does not leave the creditor's service because she does not enter it. Here, Leviticus is conducting a tacit polemic against Exod 21:7–11 (and Deut 15:12, 17): the wife may not be indentured! What, then, is the meaning of the emphasis provided by the repeated mention of the release of the children (vv. 41, 54)? There, again, Leviticus is waging a polemic against the earlier slave law, but this time verbally. Exod 21:4 states that if the master provides the slave with a wife, "the wife and her children belong to the master and he (the slave) is released alone" (wěhû' yēṣē' běgappô). No, says Leviticus. Even if the master provides him with a wife, she is entirely free of the master's control, *and her children* are released with the hireling at the jubilee (see COMMENT D).

with him. 'immô (i.e., under *his* authority). Compare mē'immāk 'from your authority'.

Then he . . . shall be released. wěyāṣā'. The adverb ḥopšî 'free', found in the other slave laws (Exod 21:2b; Deut 15:12b), is deliberately omitted here because the debtor is not a slave (Lohfink 1986: 118), but *Tg. Ps.-J.* adds ḥôrîm 'free', overlooking this subtlety. Crüsemann's (1996: 285) reverse argument that the "slave" does not actually go free but is transferred to the control of the redeemer is refuted by the fact that here no redeemer appears or is allowed (see INTRODUCTION to vv. 39–43) and that both here and in v. 50, where a redeemer is allowed, indeed urged (vv. 48–49), the same verb *yāṣā'* refers to the time of the jubilee. Akkadian *waṣû* 'leave (one's authority)' is the etymological and functional equivalent of Biblical Hebrew *yāṣā'* (cf. Paul 1970a: 47–48). The *Hip'îl hôṣî'* 'free' is discussed in the NOTE on v. 55.

shall return . . . return. wĕšāb . . . yāšûb. This is a quintessential example of H's style. For the same technique with the same verb, see NOTE on "return," v. 10.

to his kin group. 'el-mišpaḥtô. Clearly, then, the debtor has bonded himself to someone outside his kin group. The text assumes that if he sold himself to a relative, the admonitions concerning his treatment would be superfluous; a relative would not treat him as a slave (see NOTE on v. 10). Furthermore, this proves beyond doubt that the principle of the *gō'ēl*, obviously a member of his kin group, is nonoperative in this case. Otherwise, the *gō'ēl* would have intervened before the advent of the jubilee, an act that would have rendered this clause redundant and meaningless.

to his ancestral holding. 'el-'ăhuzzat 'ăbōtāyw. The text assumes that the debtor sold all his land before he sold himself (*Keter Torah*; Hoffmann 1953). It offers firm support for the supposition that vv. 25–55 form a single cohesive unit of successive stages of impoverishment. At the jubilee, he receives the land either from the relative who redeemed it earlier (v. 25) or from the buyer (v. 28). The significance of this clause rests in the supposition that the restored land will provide him with subsistence so he need not fall immediately into debt and, ultimately, have to be sold once more into servitude, as probably would have happened after his manumission without any means of support in the seventh year (Exod 21). The weakness of Exodus is recognized by Deuteronomy, which urges a largesse of gifts at the time of manumission (Deut 15:13–15). Our clause also explains why there is no provision for voluntary life servitude, as in Exod 21:5–6; Deut 15:16–17; the erstwhile "slave" now has the means to support himself (see COMMENT D, and Loewenstamm 1971b: 13).

Three stylistic elements are also significant. The exact phraseology appears twice earlier in the chapter *wĕšabtem/tāšûbû 'îš 'el-'ăhuzzātô* (vv. 10, 13), providing another bit of evidence for linking the two pericopes, the redemption of land (by the jubilee) and persons into a cohesive unity. Also, the phraseology *'ăhuzzat 'ăbōtāyw* appears as *nahălat 'ăbōtāyw* in Num 36:8 (cf. vv. 3–4), another link in the chain of evidence that *'ăhuzzâ* and *nahălâ* are H and P terms, respectively (see NOTE on "his holding," v. 10).

Finally, it will be noted that the order of the phraseology in this verse is the reverse of that in v. 10bβ. The reason, I submit, is eminently logical. V. 10bβ anticipates the sequence of the topics discussed in the remainder of the chapter. The immediate topic is the redemption of the land (see INTRODUCTION to vv. 10b–13): first the determination of the land's value (vv. 14–19), and then its redemption and return to the original owner (vv. 25–34). Afterward, the subject is the redemption of persons at the jubilee: their release from indebtedness to the creditor (stages 2 and 3 of destitution, vv. 35–43, 47–55). V. 41, however, deals with the chronological sequence occurring at the jubilee: the debtor returns first to his kin group and then to his private land. This order is remarkably confirmed by Judg 21:24, describing the return of the Israelite soldiers from the internecine wars with Benjamin: "Thereupon the Israelites dispersed from there (Bethel, v. 2), each to his tribe [*lĕšibṭô*] and to his kin group [*ûlĕmišpaḥtô*]; everyone departed from there (his kin group) to his inherited land [*ûlĕnaḥălātô*]."

42. *For they are my slaves. kî-ʿăbāday hēm.* As shown by Daube (1963: 27–29, 42–45), the legal aspect of redemption operates in the Exodus: God owns Israel because he is their *gōʾēl.* Freedom means solely a change of masters; henceforth, the Israelites are slaves of God. Daube, however, was long anticipated by the rabbis: "My deed (of ownership) has first priority" (*Sipra* Behar, par. 6:1) because God redeemed them from the "house of slaves" (Exod. 20:2; Ibn Ezra; cf. Exod 6:6)—and the redeemer becomes the new owner (see NOTE on "his closest redeemer," v. 25). The rabbis expound this theme at length by means of a parable:

Why at every performance of a commandment must we have the Exodus in our thoughts? Here is a parable: It may be likened to a king whose friend's son was taken prisoner. The king redeemed him but expressly upon the understanding that he should become a slave, so that at any time, if he should disobey the king, the latter would say: "You are my slave!" As soon as they entered the country, the king said to him: "Put on my sandals! Take my clothes to the bathhouse!" When the son began to protest the king pulled out the bill of sale and said to him: "You are my slave!" So when the Holy One redeemed the descendants of Abraham, his "friend" (Isa 41:8), he did not redeem them so that they should be his sons but his slaves, so that when he commands and they do not obey he could say to them: "You are my slaves." And as soon as they went out into the wilderness, he began to issue some light commandments and some weighty ones, for instance: the laws concerning the sabbath and incest (weighty ones) and fringes and phylacteries (light ones). When Israel began to protest, he said to them: "You are my slaves! For this reason have I redeemed you, that I might issue decrees and you should keep them." (*Sipre* Num. 115)

Israel's enslavement to God is not an innovation of Leviticus; it is found in the earliest levels of Scripture: "For YHWH will vindicate his people, and take revenge for [*ʿăbādāyw*] his servants/slaves" (Deut 32:36; Hurowitz 1992: 66). Moreover, since a slave's children are the master's property, which he also bequeaths to his children (v. 46), so the Israelites are God's slaves throughout their generations. Furthermore, since the term *ʿebed* means "servant" as well as "slaves," Israel is obligated to serve YHWH by worshiping him; he becomes not only their master but also their God (Joosten 1994: 137–38; 1996: 98).

Implied is that Israel owes no obligations to any other power but God. This concept also prevailed in the ancient Near East. The caretakers of a Hittite mausoleum are exempted from villeinage or compulsory labor (Otten 1956: 104–7), and residents of sacred cities are considered servants of the gods and the release (*amargi* = *anduraru*) returns them to their respective gods (cf. Weinfeld 1995: 79). They have been freed from all outside jurisdictions and impositions (e.g., taxes) so they may serve their respective gods (Weinfeld 1995: 133–39). Each sacred city, not just its sanctuary, belongs to the resident god (cf. Weinberg 1992: 103). As Joosten (1994: 140; 1996: 99) independently deduces: "the underlying idea of H seems to be much the same: if YHWH took the Israelites for his slaves so that they might serve him, he must also provide them with a dwelling-place; he therefore settles them on his land around the sanctuary" (see NOTE on "resident aliens," v. 23, and Introduction II I). However, a fundamental difference should not be overlooked: Israel serves its God by obeying his commandments; in the ancient Near East, the gods are served just in their sanctuaries (Weinfeld 1995: 16).

whom I freed from the land of Egypt. *ʾăšer-hôṣēʾtî ʾōtām mēʾereṣ miṣrayim.* The precise nuance of *hôṣēʾtî* is deferred to the NOTE on v. 55. Contrast this motive with that given in Deut 15:15. Both cite the exodus from Egypt, but each with a different emphasis. Deuteronomy sanctions the enslavement of Israelites; it only wishes to ameliorate their conditions on humanitarian grounds: all Israelites were slaves in Egypt. Leviticus, to the contrary, unconditionally prohibits the enslavement of Israelites since all are the slaves of their God. The alien, however, was not redeemed by God; he is not God's slave, and thus he can be charged interest and enslaved by others.

they shall not be sold as slaves are sold. *lōʾ yimmākĕrû mimkeret ʿabed*; "according to the laws of slaves" (*TN*). In this apodictic prohibition, the negative particle *lōʾ* implies permanence (Bright 1973). Slavery of Israelites is out! The rabbis interpret this prohibition in terms of the slave markets of their time: "They should not make them stand in the marketplace upon the slave block" (*Sipra* Behar, par. 6:1).

43. *You shall not rule over him with harshness.* *lōʾ-tirdeh bô bĕpārek.* According to this follow-up apodictic prohibition, not only may you not enslave an Israelite (but have to treat him as a resident hireling, v. 40), but you may not treat him harshly. "An Israelite could sell only his capacity for work, but not his body" (Noordzji 1982). Not by accident, as noted by Greenstein (1984a: 97), this word is purposefully chosen because of its occurrence in Exod 1:13, 14. That is, you shall not follow the practice of the Egyptians, who imposed hard labor "with harshness" on the Israelites. The prohibition includes not only hard work, but exploitation (Kochman). The rabbis prefer specificity: "Do not tell him to heat your cup when you don't want it (or) hoe under the grape vine until I arrive" (*Sipra* Behar, par. 6:2)—that is, just to keep him busy.

rule over him. *tirdeh bô.* Limiting ourselves to priestly texts, the verb *rādâ Qal* is found in the following passages: 25:43, 46, 53; 26:17; Gen 1:26, 28—all with an object governed by the preposition *be*, with the exception of 25:53, which takes an accusative. It uniformly denotes absolute control: over the animal kingdom (Gen 1:26, 28), a neutral meaning, but over persons, a pejorative connotation. In other biblical books, however, the connotation frequently becomes neutral (e.g., the rule of the Davidic dynasty, 1 Kgs 5:4, 30; Isa 14:2; Pss 72:8; 110:2). Concerning the complication of a purported second root *rdh* and the confusion caused by the closely related *rdd*, see Zobel (1990).

with harshness. *bĕpārek, bĕqašyô,* "ruthlessly" (*Tgs.*). This verb has Semitic cognates that are closely related in meaning: Aramaic *pĕrak* 'rub, pulverize'; Arabic: *paraka* 'rub, press, hate strongly'; Akkadian *parāku* 'block, hinder, oppress'. The Akkadian *ina parikti* 'with force' corresponds precisely with biblical *bĕpārek* (cf. *AHw* 828–29). Ezek 34:4b both borrows and interprets v. 43a: *ûbĕḥozqâ rĕdîtem ʿōtām ûbĕpārek*; the text explains *bĕpārek* by the adverb *bĕḥozqâ* 'with force'. Leviticus uses this phrase three times in this chapter (vv. 43, 46, 53), probably as a reminder of the Egyptian bondage, when the travail of the enslaved Israelites is described by the same phrase (Exod 1:13–14 [P]). The message is clear: do not treat your Israelite "slaves" as the Egyptians treated you. If behind the stages of destitution (vv. 25–28, 35–55) lies a condemnation of Joseph's manipulation of the years of famine to enslave the Egyptians (see INTRODUCTION to vv. 25–55), this text commands the opposite behavior: what Joseph did to the Egyptians do not do to your fellow Israelites.

Gerstenberger (1996: 397) aptly remarks that "this is not the individualistic and optimistic argument that a brother will surely treat another brother as an equal. Rather, the view here is realistic and institutional. Wherever human beings are subject to other human beings for better or for worse (even if they are 'brothers'), one will encounter 'harsh rule.'"

you shall fear your God. wĕyārē'tā mē'ĕlōhekā. As elsewhere in H (see NOTES on 19:14; 25:17), this admonition is attested in private, nonpublic acts, where no human eye can witness them (see NOTE on "in your sight," v. 53), or in ethical injunctions that are not adjudicatible (see NOTE on v. 17). Was Neh 5:9b influenced by this context and phrase?

44. This verse is structured chiastically:

A   *wĕ ʿabdĕkā wa ʾāmātĕkā*
　　B   *ʾăšer yihyû-lāk*
　　　　X   *mē ʾēt haggôyim*
　　B'   *ʾăšer sĕbîbōlêkam*
A'   *mēhem tiqnû ʿebed ʾwĕ ʾāmâ*

A   And the male and female slaves
　　B   that you will possess
　　　　X   from the nations
　　B'   that surround you
A'   from them you should purchase male and female slaves

The center of this small introversion emphasizes that from the nations (X) surrounding Israel it can acquire (BB') male and female slaves (AA'). The otherwise unbalancing and superfluous *mēhem tiqnû* lays stress on "from them" (the non-Israelites), implying but not from Israelites.

Male and female slaves. wĕ ʿabdĕkā wa ʾāmātkā. This terminology of Exod 21:2, 7 is employed in order to contradict it: slaves, yes, but not Israelites! Note its use in the sabbath commandment of the Decalogue (Exod 20:10), where it also refers, as does the *gēr*, to non-Israelites (due to a priestly expansion?).

you may have. yihyû-lāk. There is a change in vocabulary: not *ʾimmak*, but *yihyû-lāk*, a sign that non-Israelite slaves will be *permanent* slaves. There is also a change in number. Only *lāk* is singular, which leads some critics to read *lk[m] m't*, a haplography. However, switch of number is prevalent in H—for example, in the similar passage, v. 46b. The chiastic structure of this verse is, as often noted, typical of H's style, which requires, however, shifting the *'atnah* from *lāk* to *sĕbîbōtêkem*. But the sense remains with the MT.

nations round about you. "But not from the Canaanites in your land" (*Sipra* Behar, par. 6:3), an apparent attempt by the rabbis to harmonize this provision with the deuteronomic command to annihilate the Canaanites (Deut 20:16) and the priestly command to drive them out (Num 33:52). It is clearly refuted by the following verse.

from them that. mēhem, literally "it is from them." This otherwise superfluous word emphasizes that slaves can be taken from foreigners, not from Israelites. It is also required for the chiastic structure (see its layout, and NOTE on "you may have").

45. *the children of residents (aliens) who live under your sway. wĕgam mibbĕnê hattôšābîm haggārîm 'immākem.* These are children of mixed marriages between Canaanites and foreigners (*Sipra* Behar, par. 6:4; cf. *Tg. Ps.-J.*)—another attempt by the rabbis to disallow any progeny both of whose parents are Canaanites since theoretically the Canaanites were driven out of the land (see NOTE on "nations round about you," v. 44). This interpretation also betrays the realistic admission by the rabbis that Canaanite enclaves remained in the land (cf. Judg 3:5–6; 1 Kgs 9:20). The clear intention of this verse, indeed, is to add indigenous non-Israelites of whatever origin to foreigners (v. 44) as a source of slaves.

This is the only case where *tôšāb(im)* stands alone. But it has the hendiadys *gēr wĕtôšāb* in mind (see NOTE on v. 35). The latter is not used probably because it would result in the awkward, overloaded phrasing *haggērîm wĕhattôšabîm haggārîm.* Hence the participle *haggārîm* absorbs the subject *haggērîm.* This phenomenon does not occur, however, in v. 6, where the plural participle *haggārîm* applies to all the *singular* subjects that precede it.

These two *haggārîm* participles (vv. 6, 45) must also be carefully distinguished from those that originally were most likely intended to read *gēr(îm)*, but were repointed by the Masoretes because they referred to uprooted Israelites. Five such instances can be cited:

1. "If a Levite would go, from any of the settlements throughout Israel [*'ăšer-hû' gār šām*] where he had been residing" (Deut 18:6).
2. "He was a Levite, and he [*gār-šām*] resided there" (Judg 17:7b).
3. "This man hailed from the hill country of Ephraim, [*wĕhû'-gār*] and he resided at Gibeah, where the townspeople were Benjaminites" (Judg 19:16).
4. "They (Israelites) were then few in number, of little account, [*wĕgārîm bāh*] residing there (in Egypt)" (Ps 105:12 = 1 Chr 16:19).
5. "He assembled all the people of Judah and Benjamin [*wĕhāgārîm 'immāhem*] and those who sojourned among them of Ephraim, Manasseh, and Simeon" (2 Chr 15:9a).

It is no coincidence that each of these cases involves a member of a tribe that either has no territory of his own (i.e., a Levite) or, having it, finds residence in some other tribe. To be sure, the Versions do not support any textual change. But even if the MT is correct, the intent of the verb is to imply an alien status (Smith 1927: 75–81, 531).

from them you may buy (slaves). mēhem tiqnû, literally "from them you may buy." The direct object, "male and female slaves," is inferred from v. 44b. The emphasis connoted by *mēhem* 'from them', as in v. 44b, implies—but not from Israelites.

The assumption here is that the alien is a chattel-slave, not a debt-slave. This is confirmed by the verb *qānā* 'purchase'. A non-Israelite chattel-slave is defined as a *miqneh kesep* 'purchased' (Gen 17:12–13, 23, 27; Exod 12:44) or simply as *kaspô* 'his property' (Exod 21:21). It is hardly an accident that *miqneh* also denotes "livestock", and that in *śĕdēh miqnātô,* the former designates bought land and the latter, inherited land (Kochman 1987). For the (tangential) reference to an alien debt-slave, see the NOTE on "a resident alien," v. 35.

or from their kin groups. ûmimmišpaḥtām, ûmizzar'ayatĕhôn (Tg. Onk.) 'offspring'. Does this imply offspring of mixed marriages? If so, then H is ethnocentric, just as D, with the exception that it does not impose a ban on the Canaanites. There is no explicit ban on intermarriage in the priestly texts (contrast Exod 34:15–16; Deut 7:2–4). However, signs of disapproval are visible throughout: intermarriage leads to incest (Lev 18, 20), blasphemy (Lev 24:10–12), and idolatry (Num 25:10–18), and Canaanites who are not expelled will be "thorns in your side" (Num 33:55), probably through intermarriage and their cult (Milgrom 1990a: 500–501). This verse seems to imply that in H's time there were still Canaanite enclaves and that the pedigree of offspring of mixed marriages was well known.

property. la'ăhuzzâ. This is the one place where this term is applied to persons. Canaanite slaves, like Israel's land, are permanent possessions. This law merely indicates that the jubilee does not apply to non-Israelite slaves: "it does not imply that the slave is a piece of property at the mercy of his master" (Mendelsohn 1962: 388).

This practice prevailed throughout the ancient Near East. Those born in slavery (Akk. *wilid bitim;* Heb. *yĕlîd bayit,* Gen 17:13, 23) remained slaves.

46. *you may keep them as a possession. wĕhitnaḥăltem.* Some take the *Hitpa'el* as transitive: *wĕtaḥsĕnûn* 'You will bequeath them' (Tgs.), exemplified by *wĕhit'awwîtem* 'you shall draw a line' (Num 34:10; Ibn Ezra); *tithaṭṭā'û* 'you shall purify' (Num 31:20). However, *hitnaḥēl* occurs elsewhere as a reflexive (Num 32:18; 33:54; Isa 14:2). Therefore, Rashi is probably correct in rendering "Take (them) for yourselves (for the benefit of your children)." Indeed, the verse *wĕhitnaḥălûm bēt-yiśrā'ēl 'al 'admat YHWH la'ăbādîm wĕlišĕpāḥôt* 'And the house of Israel will take them upon the land of YHWH as male and female slaves' (Isa 14:2) may have been influenced by this passage.

as property for all time. 'ăhuzzâ lĕ'ōlām. In v. 45, the slaves are *'ăhuzzâ,* since the subject is limited to one, the acquiring, generation. Here the subject is the succeeding, inheriting generations; hence, *lĕ'ōlām.* This phrase is not equivalent to *'ăhuzzat 'ōlām* regarding the prohibition to sell the Levites' pastureland (v. 34). This land, as explained, is the common property of the Levites and may never be alienated. Here slaves belong to individual Israelites and, hence, may be sold. The status of a non-Israelite slave, as pointed out by Japhet (1992: 79–81), is exemplified in the plan conceived by Shesha (1 Chr 2:34–41), which could only be executed by a non-Israelite slave. If he were an Israelite, his children would be manumitted, at the latest, in the jubilee, and they would belong to him (vv. 46, 49–50), not to the master, Shesha.

The expression *'ăḥuzzâ lĕ'ōlām* 'property for all time' as well as the wording of the supply source for permanent slaves in the contiguous verses—"children" (v. 45), "from their kin groups" (v. 45), "a branch" (v. 47)—clearly demonstrates that the *gēr* was not admitted into the peoplehood of Israel for generations. Here the law is completely in accord with reality. The *gēr* might become rich (e.g., Ziba, the slave of Saul, 2 Sam 9:10b; 16:4) and achieve high social status (e.g., Doeg the Edomite, 1 Sam 21:8; Zelek the Ammonite, 2 Sam 23:37; Uriah the Hittite, 2 Sam 11:3, all high officers in the royal court or army). Although he may have totally assimilated into Israelite society, even to the point of being a zealous worshiper of Israel's God (a matter emphasized in the Doeg and Uriah accounts), he retained his ethnic label and was not reckoned an Israelite.

The parade example is Ruth the Moabite. When she entered Israel's land with her mother-in-law, Naomi, she declared herself a *nokriyyâ* 'foreigner' (Ruth 2:10). Eventually, she became a resident alien, a *gēr*, but not an Israelite. Even after her marriage to Boaz, an Israelite "of substance" (Ruth 2:1), she probably retained her alien status (Ruth 4:10). In the long run, marriage was the only way for the *gēr* to become an Israelite: not the *gēr* himself or herself, but only his or her progeny—the fourth generation of limited ethnic stock, according to the rigid scruples of Deuteronomy (23:2–9). Ironically, it is Deuteronomy that deliberately denies that privilege to the descendants of Ruth the Moabite (Deut 23:4–7), presumably in order to invalidate the legitimacy of the Davidic line (details in Milgrom 1982b; 1989b).

As noted by Gerstenberger (1996: 390), the distinction between natives and resident aliens—rather, the outright discrimination against the latter—flies in the face of 19:33–34. In effect, the institutions of redemption and jubilee are unavailable to the resident alien. Indeed, it is ironic that the absolute equality (in civil matters) between native and alien is unambiguously proclaimed in the previous chapter (24:22). Surely, the H redactor must have been fully aware of this blatant contradiction. It must, therefore, be presumed that the axiom that YHWH's bestowal of inheritable land exclusively on the Israelites—to the exclusion of the resident alien (see NOTE on v. 23)—takes priority, in H's theological system, over the egalitarian ideal of the alien's equality before the law. The purpose of the jubilee and its attendant redemption is to restore the land to its original owner. Since the alien has no land to lose to a creditor, these remedies are of no meaning. Thus the discrimination against the alien rests not on the absence of jubilee, but on his inaccessibility to land. Even Ezekiel, who rectifies the discrimination against the alien in regard to possessing and bequeathing land (Ezek 47:21–23), remains silent about the remedies of redemption and jubilee for the alien.

These. bāhem. But not Israelites! Each of the verses in the pericope dealing with non-Israelite slaves contains this emphasis, see *mēhem* (vv. 44, 45) and *bāhem* (v. 46), indicating a clear polemic with the other slave laws (Exod 21:2–11; Deut 15:12–18), which permit the enslavement of Israelites (Paran 1983: 20). This word clearly begins v. 46b, requiring that the *'Atnāḥ* be moved back to *lĕ'ōlām*.

over the other. ʾîš bĕʾāḥîw. For this expression, see Gen 9:5; 13:11; Exod 32:29; Zech 7:10; etc.

no one shall rule . . . with harshness. lōʾ-tirdeh bô bĕpārek. The verb switches from the plural to the singular because the sentence is an exact quotation of v. 43a (S. Chavel). Not only may an Israelite not be enslaved, but he may not be treated harshly. This injunction was ostensibly observed by Solomon: "But he did not reduce any Israelites to slavery" (1 Kgs 9:22a, cited in Wessely 1846), a statement that, however, is flatly contradicted by 1 Kgs 5:27–30; 9:23; 11:28; 12:4 (note the use of hārôdîm, 5:30; 9:23). The former claim is nothing but deuteronomistic propaganda. It was influenced by Deut 15:12–15, which refers to the indentured Israelite as ʾāḥîkā hāʿibrî 'Your Hebrew brother' (v. 12) and assiduously avoids the use of ʿebed (except for voluntary life-long slavery, v. 17).

Implied is that the alien slave may be treated harshly, but according to Job 31:13, 15, such treatment is not acceptable to YHWH (cf. van der Ploeg 1972: 82).

Vv. 47–55. Alternatively, the Israelite may fall into the hands of a non-Israelite creditor with the attendant risks of unobserved harsh treatment (see NOTE on "shall not rule over him with harshness," v. 53). The pericope on an Israelite sold to a non-Israelite constitutes a parallel panel with many verses in the pericope on sold land (vv. 15–28), as noted by Levi (1981: 189–90), but which I have amended and expanded. The boldfaced words are (nearly) exactly the same; the parallel passages are similarly structured using semantically equivalent vocabulary:

Sold Israelite (to a non-Israelite)		*Sold Land*	
A	⁴⁸ʾaḥărê nimkar **gĕʾullâ** tihyeh-lô	A'	²⁴ᵇ**gĕʾullâ** tittĕnû lāʾāreṣ
B	ʾeḥād mēʾeḥāyw **yigʾalennû** ⁴⁹ʾô-dōdô ʾô ben-dōdô **yigʾalennû** ʾô-miššĕʾēr bĕśārô mimmišpaḥtô **yigʾalennû**	B'	²⁵ᵇᵅʾûbāʾ haqqārōb ʾēlāyw **wĕgāʾal**
C	ʾô-hiśśîgâ yādô wĕnigʾal	C'	²⁶ᵇ**wĕhiśśîgâ yādô** ûmāṣāʾ kĕdê **gĕʾullātô**
D	⁵⁰**wĕḥiššab** ʿim-qōnēhû **miśśĕnat himmākĕrô** lô wĕhāyâ kesep **mimkārô**	D'	²⁷ᵃᵅ**wĕḥiššab ʾet-šĕnê mimkārô**
E	**bĕmispar šānîm** kiyēmê śākîr yihyeh ʿimmô	E'	¹⁵ᵃᵅ**bĕmispar šānîm**
F	⁵¹ʾim- ʾôd **rabbôt baššānîm** lĕpîhen yāšîb gĕʾullātô mikkesep **miqnātô**	F'	¹⁶ᵃᵅ**lĕpî rōb haššānîm** tarbeh **miqnātô**
G	⁵²wĕʾim-mĕʿaṭ nišʾar **baššānîm** ʿad-šĕnat hayyōbēl	G'	¹⁶ᵃᵝ**ûlĕpî mĕʿaṭ haššānîm**
H	**wĕḥiššab-lô** kĕpî šānāyw yāšîbʾ et-gĕʾullātô	H'	²⁷ᵃᵅ**wĕḥiššab ʾet-šĕnê mimkārô wĕhēšîb** ʾet-hāʾōdep
I	⁵³kĕśākîr šānâ bĕšānâ yihyeh ʿimmô lōʾ yirdennû bĕperek lĕʾênêkā	I'	¹⁶ᵇ⁻¹⁷ᵃkî mispar tĕbûʾōt hûʾ mōkēr lāk wĕlōʾ tônû ʾîš ʾet-ʿămîtô

J ^{54}*wĕ'im-lō' yiggā'ēl bĕ'ēlleh*   J' ^{28}*wĕ'im lō' . . . wĕyāṣā'*
   wĕyāṣā' bišĕnat hayyōbēl hû'   *bayyōbēl*
   ûbānāyw 'immô
K $^{55a\alpha}$***kî-lî** bĕnê-yiśrā'ēl 'ăbādîm*   K' $^{23a\alpha}$***kî-lî** hā'āreṣ*

An Israelite who is sold as a slave to a non-Israelite is likened to an Israelite who sells his ancestral land. The parallels are evident not only by the same or synonymous vocabulary (boldface) but, more important, by the same underlying premises. Since both Israelites and their land belong to God (KK'), they are subject to the laws of the jubilee (JJ') and redemption (AA') by the nearest relative (BB') or by the person (slave or landowner) himself (CC'). The redemption price is calculated according to the years remaining until the jubilee (D–H, D'–H'). Accordingly, the land and the slave have not been sold, but, in reality, they have been only leased. That is, the buyer benefits from only the usufruct of the land, and the creditor benefits from only the labor of the slave calculated as a yearly wage. The buyer or creditor is therefore admonished that he may not exceed these limitations by oppressing the seller or debtor by cheating on the redemption price or imposing harsh labor (II'). In sum, the people Israel and its land belong solely to God; neither can be owned in perpetuity. Absolute ownership of natural property and Israelites is thereby abolished; persons and land may be leased, not sold. The question cannot be resisted: Has a more sublime safeguard against the pauperization of society ever been found?

The pericope itself (vv. 47–53) is composed of two inner introversions:

Redemption is Required, vv. 47–49 (J. Wyrick)

A ^{47}*wĕkî taśśîg yad gēr wĕtôšāb*   A   If a resident alien under you has
   'immāk   prospered,
  B   *wĕmāk 'āḥîkā 'immô*   B   and your brother, being (further)
    wĕnimkar lĕgēr tôšāb 'immāk   impoverished, comes under his
    'ô lĕ'ēqer mišpaḥat gēr   authority and is sold to the
                                           resident alien under you, or to a
                                           branch of the alien's kin group,

    X ^{48}*'aḥărê nimkar gĕ'ullâ*   X ^{48}after he is sold he shall
     tihyeh lô   have the right of redemption.
  B'   *'eḥad mē'eḥāyw yig'ălennû*   B'   One of his brothers shall redeem
    ^{49}*'ô dōdô 'ô ben-dōdô*   him, ^{49}or his uncle or his uncle's
    yig'ălennû 'ô-miššĕ'ēr bĕśārô   son shall redeem him, or anyone
    mimmišpaḥtô yig'ălennû   of his kin group who is of his
                                           own flesh shall redeem him;

A'   *'ô-hiśśîgâ yādô wĕnig'āl*   A'   or if he prospers, he may redeem
                                          himself.

The idiomatic expression *hiśśîg yād* 'prosper' is found in AA'. BB' contrasts the members of the alien's family who may be enslaved with the members of the Israelite family on whom the obligation of redemption falls. There is no distinction, however, between an enslaved Israelite (B) and his free kinsperson (B′); both are designated as *'āḥ*. The pivot of the introversion (X) states the underlying postulate: in contrast to the Israelite who is enslaved by an Israelite creditor, for whom there is no redemption (vv. 39–43), an Israelite enslaved by a non-Israelite creditor must be redeemed.

The underlying theology needs to be underscored. YHWH redeems on both a national and an individual scale. YHWH is the redeemer of the people of Israel whenever it is subjected to (i.e., enslaved by) a foreign nation. This was the case in the Egyptian bondage (Exod 6:6; 15:13; cf. Isa 63:9; Ps 106:10). And according to Second Isaiah, such will be the case in the Babylonian Exile (Isa 35:4, 9; 43:1; 44:22, 23; 48:20; 51:10; 52:3; 63:9; cf. Mic 4:10). Thus the example of divine intervention whenever any part of his land is lost (i.e., the jubilee) is to be duplicated whenever any of his people is lost (i.e., enslaved). Just as the nearest relative is obligated to redeem the land of his kinsperson sold (or forfeited) to another, so is he obligated to redeem the person of his kinsperson sold to (i.e. enslaved by) a non-Israelite. As explained earlier (see NOTE on vv. 39–55), no such obligation rests on the redeemer if his kinsperson is sold to an Israelite, since such a sale does not constitute enslavement. The principle of *imitatio dei* applies only when the loss of land (stage 1) or person stands in jeopardy, but not in situations where, in addition, the repayment of a loan is required (stages 2 and 3), which can be accomplished by using the debtor's wages.

Computing the Redemption, vv. 50–53

A ^{50}*wĕḥiššab 'im-qōnēhû miššĕnat himmākĕrô lô 'ad šĕnat ḥayyōbēl wĕhāyâ kesep mimkārô bĕmispar šānîm kiyĕmê śākîr yihyeh 'immô*

A ^{50}He shall compute with his buyer the total from the year he was sold to him until the jubilee year: the price of his sale shall be be applied to the number of years, as the term of a hired laborer he shall be under the other's authority.

B ^{51}*'im-'od rabbôt bāššānîm lĕpîhen yāšîb gĕ'ullātô mikkesep miqnātô*

B ^{51}If many years remain, he shall pay back (for) his redemption in proportion to his purchase price;

B′ ^{52}*wĕ'im mĕ'aṭ nîs'ar baššānîm 'ad šĕnat hayyōbēl wĕḥiššab- lô kĕpî šānāyw yāšîb 'et-gĕ'ullātô*

B′ ^{52}and if few years remains until the jubilee year, he shall so compute; according to the years involved, he shall pay back (for) his redemption.

A′ ^{53}*kiśĕkîr šānâ bĕšānâ yihyeh 'immô lō'-yirdennû bĕperek lĕ'ênêkā* A

A′ ^{53}As a worker hired by the year shall he be under his (the alien's) authority, who (however) shall not rule over him with harshness in your sight.

BB' is a computational formula akin to that of v. 16, and similarly at the heart of an introverted structure. A, repeated by A', emphasizes that, no differently from an Israelite enslaved by an Israelite, the Israelite enslaved by a non-Israelite must be treated like a hireling so his labor amortizes his debt. Indeed, the fact that the hireling status is here mentioned twice (vv. 50, 53), whereas in the case of an Israelite creditor it is stated once (v. 40), indicates the stress that the legist is laying on the non-Israelite creditor, who must be meticulous in carrying out the law. Also, the provision that the latter may not treat his Israelite "slave" harshly (v. 53b) is similar to the one incumbent on the Israelite creditor (v. 43), with the qualification that the authorities have no right to disturb the non-Israelite's privacy in order to investigate (see NOTE on "in your sight," v. 53).

The debtor who falls into the hands of a non-Israelite creditor is considered a captive. Hence redemption is required. The obligation to redeem captive Israelites is traceable back to Abraham and Lot (Gen 14), and it persists in biblical and rabbinic tradition (cf. Neh 5:5–12; *m. Ket.* 4:8–9; *m. Giṭ.* 4:6, 9) as a *miṣwâ rābbâ* 'a paramount duty' (*b. B. Bat.* 8a–b). Indeed, when King Herod wanted to sell Jewish criminals, who had been punished with slavery, to a foreign nation, he was warned that this policy would only increase the people's hatred of him (Jos. *Ant.* 16.1–4), an indication that the repugnance of selling Jews — even criminals — to Gentiles was not a theoretical, halakhic desideratum but a tradition practiced by the people at large.

To be sure, the redemption of captives is also attested in Mesopotamian law:

> If either a runner or a fisher, who is taken captive on a mission of the king (and) a merchant has ransomed him and so has enabled him to regain his city, has the means for ransoming (himself) in his house, he shall ransom himself; if there are not the means of ransoming in his house, he shall be ransomed out of (the resources of) the temple of his city; if there are not the means of ransoming him in the temple of his city, the palace shall ransom him. His field, his plantation and his house shall not be given for ransom." (CH § 32).

However, a significant difference between the redemption of captives in Mesopotamia and in Israel should not be overlooked: in Israel all captives must be redeemed, not just those on the king's mission. They are God's slaves (vv. 42, 55) and must be returned to that status. In effect, they are on a "mission" of the king of kings to fulfill his covenantal commands.

Presumably, on the basis of this Mesopotamian law, Yaron (1959: 155, 167–74) suggests that the redemption of persons in the ancient Near East, including the case of Lev 25:47–54, was a charitable act. In Israel, the certainty holds true in legal texts whenever the verb *pādâ* 'ransom' occurs. Thus whether the person ransoms himself (Exod 21:30) or others provide the ransom (Exod 21:8), "the act of ransoming as reflected in the term *pādâ* depends on the voluntary act and financial capacity of the ransomer, as well as in some cases upon the willingness of the party who must accept the ransom in exchange for the release of the

subject" (Nikaido personal communication). Moreover, one should not analo-
gize redemption by the state or temple (CH § 32 and later redemption of captives by the community) with redemption by relatives. Just as redeemed land remained in the possession of the redeemer until the jubilee (see NOTES on "his
closest redeemer," v. 25, and "Whoever of the Levites redeems," v. 33), so
it must be assumed that the redeemed person passes into the hands of his re-
deemer-relative, for whom he works until the jubilee (Chirichigno 1993: 340–41;
cf. Daube 1963: 42). That is, the redeemer enjoys the usufruct of the debtor's
land, which has been redeemed with him (see NOTE on "his closest redeemer,"
v. 25), and the redeemed debtor works for the redeemer as a resident hireling,
in keeping with v. 40, until the jubilee (see NOTE on "shall redeem him," v. 48).

47. *resident alien. gēr wĕtôšāb.* Rendered as *ʿaral wĕtôtāb* 'an uncircumcised resident' *(Tgs. Onk., Ps.-J.),* it is an admission that the expression is a hendiadys, but
reflecting the rabbinic view that *gēr* (unqualified by *tôšāb*) is a convert. *Tg. Neof.,*
though, continues to render *gēr* as "alien" (Ohana 1974; Grossfeld 1988: 59, n. 10).

under you . . . under you. ʿimmak . . . ʿimmak. Since the *resident* alien is "under you," you have the power to enforce the law.

has prospered. taśśîg yad. As the alien is entitled to full and equal rights (24:22),
the possibility exists that he will acquire wealth and slaves, as well as uninher-
ited (presumably unarable) land. Note that Abraham, the *gēr,* was able to purchase a permanent burial place (Gen 23), and Jacob bought a camping ground
(Gen 33:19). Isaac, the farmer, probably rented his land (Gen 26:12). (Is it possible that the same rule concerning arable land prevailed among the other inhabitants of Canaan?) Note as well the high social status of other *gērîm:* Doeg
the Edomite (1 Sam 21:8), Zelek the Ammonite (2 Sam 23:37), and Uriah the
Hittite (2 Sam 11:3) were high officials in the royal court or army, and Ziba,
technically a slave (2 Sam 9:2, 12), owned slaves and fields (2 Sam 9:10; 19:30).
These facts call into question Levine's (1989a: 274) assertion that the only time
when Israelites were likely to be indentured to non-Israelites was the postexilic
period, during which Judah contained a mixed population (see also Schenker
1998: 39–40).

Moreover, as argued cogently by Kaufmann (1956: 4.171–76; 1977: 197–203)
the returnees went back to the cities of their origin (Ezra 2:1), where they encountered no entrenched aliens. That they could have returned to their former
cities and lands is clearly shown in the case of the Tobiads (Mazar 1957). The
Persian province of Judea consisted of Jerusalem and its surrounding area, Lod,
Hadid, and Ono to the north (Ezra 2:33; cf. Neh 6:2) and Bethlehem (Ezra
2:21) or Beth-zur (Neh 3:16) to the south. Nebuchadnezzar had exiled its original inhabitants but, in distinction to Assyrian policy, did not replace them with
an alien population. For purely strategic reasons, he kept this area void of any
population. The Edomites, Philistines, and Samaritans, clearly with Babylonia's
consent, penetrated deeply into areas of Judah, but not into "the province."

Thus it is precisely in the monarchic period that we read of aliens rising to
status and wealth, but not in early postexilic times. According to Deut
28:43–44 — of preexilic vintage — aliens prospering is the sign of a curse.

under his authority. *'immô.* The singular suffix proves that the expression *gēr wĕtôšāb* is a hendiadys.

and is sold. *wĕnimkar.* The term must be understood figuratively (see NOTE on "is sold to you," v. 39).

to a branch. *lĕʿeqer.* A term in Old Aramaic (Dan 4:12, 20, 23; *Sefire* 1 A: 2–3) [*ʿm ʿqr* 'with the offspring']; II C: 15; III 1, 3, 15, 25 [*ʿqrk, ʿqrh*]; Degen 1969: 47; Gibson 1975: 54, n. 13) and in Ethiopic (*eqre*, Leslau 1976: 40). Rabbinic tradition holds—under the assumption that the *gēr* is a proselyte—that the offspring became heathens (*'armaʾy, Tg. Onk.*), or, as *Tg. Ps.-J.* expatiates, "the stock [*šĕrîš*, based on Deut 29:17] of a strange religion, to serve him or to worship with him who is of the generation of aliens" (cf. *b. Qidd.* 20a). The rabbis were fearful that servitude under an alien would lead to assimilation (*Sipra* Behar 8:2). Ibn Ezra prefers to derive the meaning from the verb *ʿāqar* 'uproot'—that is, one who uprooted himself from the status of an alien. Ehrlich (1899–1900) reaches deep into his imagination by proposing that the Israelite was sold to a "branch" (i.e., family) of the *gēr* who live in his former home; they would assuredly treat the Israelite according to Israelite law (e.g., allow redemption) lest their relative, the *gēr*, suffer at the hands of his Israelite neighbors.

48. *after he is sold.* *'aḥărê nimkar.* The finite verbal form functions as a noun phrase following a construct form (GKC § 130d). As soon as the Israelite is sold, the redemption requirement goes into effect (Bekhor Shor).

he shall have the right of redemption. In contrast to the Israelite slave bonded to an Israelite creditor who has no such right, only a privilege (see INTRODUCTION to vv. 39–46).

One of his brothers. *'eḥād mē'eḥāyw.* Cardellini (1981: 286–305) claims that *'āḥ* (as in v. 47) is a technical term for an Israelite citizen. This cannot be true, certainly in this context; only a relative is obligated to redeem, as specified in the following verse (v. 49). Here, then, his brothers of the same parents are intended, whose omission would conflict with the line of succession as explicitly stated in Num 27:1–11, where sibling brothers also head the list. The absence of the son or father as a required redeemer is explained in v. 49.

shall redeem him. "Redemption by a close relative . . . will probably in most cases be charitable, though this is not necessarily so" (Yaron 1959: 174). CH § 32, which forms Yaron's basis for this statement, is not analogous because it is limited to those taken captive on "the king's mission." The Israelite redeemer could and probably would hold on to the redeemed relative until the jubilee so that, analogously to redeemed land, he would be fully reimbursed for his expenses (see NOTE on "his closest redeemer," v. 25). The redeemer would enjoy the usufruct of the redeemed land worked by the redeemed kinsman, who would receive wages for his work as a hired laborer (v. 40).

49. *uncle . . . uncle's son . . . his own flesh.* *dōdô . . . ben-dōdô . . . miššĕ'ēr bĕśārô.* This is the *gō'ēl* chain, as is brothers, father's brothers, nearest flesh relative (*šĕ'ērô haqqārōb 'ēlāyw*) (Num 27:9–11). On the basis of the inheritance laws, it can be assumed that just as a daughter may inherit if there are no sons (Num 27:1–11), so an *independent* woman kinsperson could redeem. Such in-

deed was the case in Ugarit, where a woman (who probably had no brothers) had the privilege to buy back her late father's property ahead of all purchasers (*Ugaritica* V, 6, cited in Heltzer 1976: 100–101). Gottwald (1979: 264) asks whether this *goʾel* chain includes the maternal as well as the paternal side. The answer is unambiguously provided by *mimmišpaḥtô* 'his kin group' and underscored by the explanatory *miššěʾēr běśārô* 'his own flesh', or the paternal side only. The only other attestation of this idiom is in 18:6. The six other occurrences of *šěʾēr* as "relative" (18:12, 13, 17; 20:19; 21:2; Num 27:11) are H (see Knohl 1995: 100, and NOTE on 18:6). Why is the son missing from the list of redeemers? The answer is that if the father is impoverished, so is the son; if the father has to sell himself as a hireling to the creditor (v. 53), the son accompanies him as the creditor's ward (vv. 41, 54b), but not as his slave (see NOTE on "he and his children with him," v. 41). By the same token, the omission of the father as a required redeemer can also be accounted for. Assumed is that the son adheres to the ancestral land and is not a tradesman or a merchant, which speaks for the antiquity of this text.

The duty to redeem captives was admirably fulfilled in the time of Nehemiah: "We have done our best to buy back our Jewish brothers who were sold to the nations" (Neh 5:8a). "This verse preserves a heartwarming insight into the humanitarian concerns of the Judean community stretching over a considerable period" (Williamson 1985: 240). The evidence of Nehemiah goes beyond that of Leviticus; the redemption obligation encompasses the entire nation, not just the kin group. This is the first recorded instance of the paramount Jewish duty of *pidyôn šěbûyīm* 'the ransom of captives'.

Furthermore, Nehemiah uses his personal example of ransoming Jews sold to foreigners to shame the creditors who are likely to sell their indentured fellow Jews. It should be noted that the root *gʾl* is assiduously avoided. The redemption, rather than the ransom, of Jews would imply that the redeemed person would remain in the hands of his redeemer until the jubilee (see NOTE on "his closest redeemer," v. 25). Perhaps that is why Nehemiah was able to prick the conscience of the creditors. He would have no personal gain in buying back his (and their) indentured fellows, whom they might sell as slaves. It was a novel approach that went beyond the sharply defined limitations of Lev 25. Redemption of Jews from non-Jews was mandated, but not their ransom. However, as observed, redemption from Jews was not even required (see INTRODUCTION to vv. 39–43). Perhaps that is why Nehemiah made a request, not a demand, which he phrased as a nonbinding (but embarrassing) question: "What you are doing is not good. Will you not walk in the fear of our God in order to avoid the reproach of our Gentile enemies?" (5:9).

or if he prospers. How is this possible? Through inheritance (Ibn Ezra) or by marrying someone with a rich dowry (CH § 176). A Sumerian text states that in Sippar, during the reign of Rim-Sin, a female regained her freedom by paying 10 shekels to her owner. The source of her income is not stated. We know, however, that in Neo-Babylonian times, slaves would be permitted to work on their own, provided the master shared in the profits. Some "were engaged as craftsmen, agents and tenant farmers; they owned houses and land, and even possessed their own slaves" (Mendelsohn 1962: 387). So, too, in Israel: Kish's slave carried with him one-quarter of a silver shekel (1 Sam 9:8), and Ziba, Saul's slave, is recorded as having had fifteen sons and twenty slaves (2 Sam 9:10), though "the legal owner of the slave's peculium was his master" (Mendelsohn 1962: 387; cf. 2 Sam 9:12).

he may redeem himself. wěnigʾāl, a *Nipʿal* reflexive. He hardly can do so by means of the wages he earns as a hired laborer (Elliger 1966). He would need every bit of it to pay off his debt, except in the probably rare case where his yearly earnings exceed the fixed (according to the remaining jubilee years, v. 50) yearly portion of his debt.

50. *He shall compute.* The subject is the redeemer or the slave.

until the jubilee year. His sale, like that to an Israelite creditor (v. 40), is a terminal lease, as explicated below.

as the term of a hired laborer. kiymê śākîr, literally "as the days of a hired laborer," which perhaps implies that his wages are calculated on a daily basis (Kalisch 1867–72; Noth 1977). That is, the value of his work is figured on the bases of the current wages and conditions of a day laborer.

51–52. See NOTES on v. 16.

53. *As a worker hired by the year. kěśěkîr šānâ běšānâ.* This is an explication of *kiymê śākîr* (v. 50). Why is it needed? It compares the yearly labor of an Israelite "slave" with the yearly yield of land. As only the usufruct of the land is sold, so also the usufruct (i.e., the labor) of the slave. But neither the land nor the man is sold. They are not free to be sold; they are the possessions of YHWH (cf. Japhet 1986: 86). Note that in this case, *śākîr* is not qualified by *tôšāb* 'resident' for the obvious reason that the worker's long-term residence is expressly stated: "by the year."

shall not rule over him with harshness. lōʾ-yirdennû běperek. Not only by an Israelite (vv. 43, 46bβ), but also by a non-Israelite (53b). This threefold repetition emphasizes this prohibition's significance and, perhaps, the fact that its continual violation required repeated admonition.

in your sight. lěʿênêkā. "The injunction only applies to what you can see" (*Sipra* Behar 8:8; cf. *Tg. Ps.-J.*). It partially calls to mind the deuteronomic rule in the case of distraints: "you must not enter to seize his pledge. You must remain outside" (Deut 24:10b–11a). But H goes further: even an alien's privacy is to be respected. This qualification is omitted in regard to an Israelite creditor probably because the injunction is only a moral admonition for the Israelite, subject to only divine punishment (v. 43b). But it has punitive implications. The alien creditor's behavior toward his indentured Israelite can be investigated.

54. *in any of these ways. běʾēlleh.* This refers to the means of redemption specified in vv. 48–49 (Ibn Ezra).

he and his children with him shall go free. The absence of any mention that his land is also restored to him, as is land sold to an Israelite (v. 41b), suggests to Gerstenberger (1996: 392) that a non-Israelite may not possess Israelite land even temporarily.

55. *For it is to me the Israelites (are slaves). kî-lî běnê-yiśrā'ēl.* The structure of this clause, by the double use of the *maqqeph*, corresponds with the clause *kî-lî hā'āreṣ* (v. 23). Just as the latter opens the unit on redemption of property (vv. 23–38), so the former closes the unit on the redemption of slaves (vv. 39–55, M. Hildenbrand).

They are my slaves whom I freed from the land of Egypt. This word-for-word repetition of v. 42a is essential to the logic of this verse: it forms the rationale for the initial statement: "For it is to me the Israelites are slaves." As pointed out by Wright (1990: 182, n. 2), that redemption results in ownership is attested in the Bible itself: "I will redeem you [*gā'altîk*]; I have singled you out by name; you are mine [*lî- 'attâ*]" (Isa 43:1); "Remember the community you acquired [*qānîtā*] long ago, your very own tribe that you redeemed [*gā'alta*]" (Ps 74:2).

The final three verses, dealing with the alien master (vv. 53–55), match the final two verses dealing with the Israelite master (vv. 42–43):

A   *kî-'ăbāday hēm 'ăšer-hôṣē'tî 'ōtām*   C'   *lo 'yirdennû běperek lě'ēnêkā*
     mē'ereṣ miṣrayim
B   *lō' yimmākěrû mimkeret 'ābed*   B'   *wěyāṣā' bišěnat hayyōbēl*
C   *lo'-tirdeh bô běpārek*   A'   *'ăbāday hēm 'ăšer-hôṣē'tî 'ōtām*
                                                        mē'ereṣ miṣrayim
D   *wěyārē'tā mē'ělōhêkā*   D'   *'ănî YHWH 'ělōhêkem*

A   For they are my slaves, whom I   C'   shall not rule over him with
     freed from the land of Egypt;   harshness in your sight. (v. 53b)
     (v. 42a)
B   they shall not be sold as slaves   B'   he . . . shall go free in the
     are sold. (v. 42b)   jubilee year. (v. 54aβ)
C   You shall not rule over him with   A'   They are my slaves whom I
     harshness; (v. 43a)   freed from the land of Egypt.
                                                   (v. 55aβ)
D   You shall fear your God. (v. 43b)   D'   I am YHWH your God. (v. 55b)

ABC is inverted by C'B'A', and inversion is a stylist sign of quotation (Seidel 1978). However, B and B', the axis, though entirely different in language, complement and complete each other in meaning: the essence of the prohibition against treating the Israelite debtor as a slave (B) is that he is freed by the jubilee (B'). DD', which supplement both inversions, are also different in language but complementary in meaning: the bottom-line rationale for fearing God (D) is that he is Israel's God, the God of the covenant, to which Israel is pledged (D').

I freed. hôṣē'tî. Tg. Neof. adds *prîqîn* 'redeemed' (as does Tg. Ps.-J. in vv. 38, 42), which is precisely what we find in the H source itself: "I will free [*wěhôṣē'tî*] you from the burdens [i.e., *corvée*] of the Egyptians, deliver you from their bondage, and redeem [*wěgā'altî*] you . . . " (Exod 6:6). As pointed out by Daube (1963: 31–34), *hôṣî' min* is a technical legal term denoting the release of slaves or property, which was borrowed from its sociolegal setting by the narrator of the Exodus story to convey the importance of God's saving activity. Note also "YHWH your God, who freed [*hammôṣî'*] you from the land of Egypt and who ransomed [*wĕhappōdĕkā*] you from the house of bondage" (Deut 13:6). The exact Akkadian cognate *sûṣû* 'take out' also means "redeem." For example, "he (the owner) shall take out (*ušeṣa*) from their acquirer" (lit. "life giver," see NOTE on "let him subsist," v. 35); "shall he redeem the man" (*amelu ušeṣa*); "shall he free the wife" (*sinništu ušeṣa*) (Kohler and Ungnad 1913: 188, 189).

The rabbis saw the Exodus as an act of *mīšarum*: "Rabbi Levi said: It is like a *dux* (commander) before whom the legions cast the purple cloak (proclaim him as emperor). He remits the arrears (of taxes), burns the bond, and leads the legions out (in parade), and this dates the beginning of his rule (Exod 15:3)" (*Midr. Exod. Rab.* on Exod 12:1, noted by Weinfeld 1982b: 505).

I am YHWH your God. *'ănî YHWH 'ĕlōhêkem*. This is a reminder of God's self-declaration that opens the Decalogue (Exod 20:2), thus anchoring the entire chapter in the Sinaitic covenant and forming an inclusio with the opening verse "on Mount Sinai" (25:1). Its implication is clear: as God redeemed you from Egypt in the time of your national need, should you not do the same when your brothers find themselves in slavery in the time of their individual need? (Elliger 1966: 360).

COMMENTS

A. The Jubilee: Its Date and Background

That the jubilee has many antecedents in the ancient Near East, especially in Mesopotamia, has been briefly described in the NOTE on "You shall proclaim release," v. 10. Of certainty, the Mesopotamia *mīšarum* touches on all aspects of its biblical counterpart: lands and houses (immovable property) returning to their original owners, cancellation of debts, and release from slavery; see, for example, the Edict of King Ammisaduqa (*ANET* 526–28). However, they exhibit differences that are not insignificant. As pointed out by Bar-Maoz (1980: 56, 66, 68, n. 82), the *mīšarum* was, in the main, limited to the king's retainers and to loans given by the palace. Also, there is no basis for Finkelstein's (1965: 243–46) claim that there was periodicity in the *mīšarum*. The jubilee, however, was both universal (for Israelites) and cyclical. Scholars have wondered whether the jubilee may not have canceled debts, but only have postponed them. On this matter, the Bible is silent. However, the Mesopotamian material speaks explicitly *tuppam ḫeppû* 'break a tablet' (cf. Finkelstein 1968: 236, ll. 8–9, 36–37). Thus there is no reason to assume that the jubilee merely claimed a moratorium on the outstanding debts (cf. Weinfeld 1982b: 498). As it restored the debtor to his family land, it irrevocably canceled his debts.

According to Westbrook (1991b: 50–51), it is the very periodicity of the jubilee, in contrast to the sporadic and unpredictable *mīšarum*, that renders the biblical legislation "academic and theoretical": "loss of the means of security would lead to a drying-up of credit before the Jubilee or to conditions being inserted into contracts to make the debt fall due after the Jubilee year. If the law were really effective the size of the loans available would decrease as the Jubilee approached and the value of security available accordingly shrank" (see also Westbrook 1995: 160–61). However, this is precisely the condition stipulated by the biblical legist. The land was not transferred to the creditor as security, but as the very means to repay the loan. And the creditor would demand sufficient land to yield enough usufruct to cover the entire loan *until the jubilee*.

The Greek world, as demonstrated by Weinfeld (1985a: 87–89), also possessed *mišārum* equivalents. To cite two examples, Solon declared in his reform "I also restored to freedom those who here at home had been subjected to shameful servitude, and trembled before the moods of their masters" (frag. 24.13–15 West 1972, vol. 2 = Aristotle *Ath. Pol.* 12), and Diodorus Siculus (5:9, 4–5), drawing on ancient sources, informs us that men of Lipar divided the land of the islands into holdings, which could be transferred for a period of twenty years; thereafter, these holdings returned to their former status (cf. Buck 1959: 35–39). Here, too, one must be careful to note the differences. It will not do to make a blanket judgment that "neither in Amos, Micah, or 1 Isaiah, neither in Hesiod or Solon, do we find any concern about the lot of serfs or privately-held or state slaves, other than the former landowners who have been newly enslaved" (Brown 1983: 396–97). The assumption of the jubilee law is that all Israelites are landowners and "privately-held or state slaves" are aliens (see NOTES on vv. 42, 44). To be sure, as will be shown in COMMENT B, there was a wide discrepancy between law and practice, but it was precisely these same eighth-century prophets of Israel who exposed the gap and railed against its perpetrators.

In any event, these parallels in the ancient Near East contemporary with or prior to Israel's settlement on its land tip the scales in favor of a preexilic and, probably, premonarchic date for the inception of the jubilee concept, a time when family membership and land ownership had "critical weight in the matter of one's own standing in the religious community" (Wright 1980: 126). To claim that Lev 25 was enacted in the Persian period in order "to prevent the loss of land by Israelites and their families" (Levine 1989a: 274) only turns one's back on the early evidences of the ancient Near East and the requisite societal structure for a land in the possession of kin groups. Moreover, not only does such a late date undermine the existence of Deuteronomy's law of debt remission (15:1–3), which surely would have been invoked by the returning exilics (admitted by Levine) but it also leaves unanswered this question: What comfort would the jubilee law have brought to indentured Israelites knowing that they would have to wait as long as fifty years before they would be restored to their lands?

Finally, as pointed out to me by N. Gottwald (personal communication), the restoration period cannot possibly have produced the jubilee legislation for the following reasons:

1. It is not evident that the Aaronid priests gained undisputed leadership in Yehud at once. Although their cultic program may have won the day in

the rebuilt Temple, their economic proposals would have encountered fierce "secular" opposition.

2. The holdings of Israelites at the fall of Jerusalem in 586 B.C.E. were very unevenly distributed. Restoration of lands to their previous owners would incorporate gross inequities and ensure the vulnerability of small landowners to indebtedness.

3. The very slow economic recovery of Yehud would not have provided optimal conditions for enforcing the jubilee, which depended so much on high productivity.

4. Above all, the jubilee program provides no way to settle jurisdictional disputes over land ownership. What would be done about land formerly owned by exiles, but occupied for the past fifty years by other Israelites? Returning exiles would press their case as a "purified" remnant entitled to recover their former lands. Nonexiled Israelites would counter that the exiles had forfeited their rights because their disastrous policies had led to the fall of the nation in 586.

A number of scholars have acknowledged the early provenance of the jubilee laws (bibliography in Wright 1980: 125, n. 8). But the first one, to my knowledge, who pinpointed the eighth century and its prophetic spokesman as the most likely time for its origin was Neufeld (1958; most recently, Knohl 1995: 204–16). During the second half of the ninth century, money became the accepted medium of public exchange. The small farmer could no longer borrow wheat or barley, which he could repay in better years. Instead, he had to borrow money, which he could not repay, and often he fell into debt—bondage. Also, trade and commerce replaced the old ideal of tilling the soil as activities of high prestige. Land lost its earlier significance and became a form of capital. Land was transformed from a condition of status to one of contract.

Initially, in contrast to the "Canaanization of the city" (Neufeld 1958: 102), a wealthy man like Boaz (Ruth 2:4) and a rich farmer of Shunem (2 Kgs 4:18) are found in the field among the reapers. Even Saul, already a king, is seen returning from his day at the plow (1 Sam 9:5), and Elisha works with his father's oxen (1 Kgs 19:19). During the first half of the eighth century, with the economic boom and political stability under Jeroboam II (787–47) in North Israel and under Uzziah (783–42) in Judah, a prosperous stratum of landowners far outstripped the small farmers, intent only on self-sufficiency, with marked-orientated surplus production (Pemmath 1988). The institution of absentee landlords becomes rampant. Those who acquire new lands by debt default live in the cities, removed in distance and in kinship from the plight of the impoverished, landless farmers and indulging in licentious living (cf. Isa 3:16–26; 5:11, 22; 22:13; 28:1, 3, 7; Amos 4:1; 6:4–6; 8:3). Farming loses its high prestige and is confined to mainly the poor masses. Land becomes a form of capital, belonging to the king and his nobility rather than to the kin group—indeed, to be seized by the king and granted to his loyal officials as a boon (1 Sam 8:14; 2 Sam 13:23; 14:30; 1 Kgs 2:26; 1 Chr 27:25–31), not hesitating to include the smallest estate of the orphan (cf. Prov 23:10). Reversion to the Canaanite system of land tenure, according to which land was owned by the king and a few nobles, which Samuel feared when he warned the people of the dangers of the monarch (1 Sam 8:10–17), was realized by the land-accumulating activity of the kings of Israel (Halpern 1981a). Ahab's dispossession of Naboth from his vineyard (1 Kgs 21) was not unique; note David's usurpation of Meribaal's lawful inheritance (2 Sam 16:4; 19:30). The nobility was often accused of dishonesty, oppression, and living in luxury while the masses were starving (Isa 1:23; 3:12–15; 10:1–2; Jer 12:11–12). Ezekiel places emphasis on fixed boundaries for Crown land around Jerusalem so that "my princes shall no longer oppress my people" (Ezek 45:7–8; cf. 48:21).

Archaeology bears silent but effective witness to this economic transformation: "At Tirsah, the modern Tell el-Farah near Nablus, the houses of the tenth century B.C. are all of the same size and arrangements. Each represents the dwelling of a family which lived in the same way as its neighbors. The contrast is striking when we pass to the eighth century houses on the same site: the rich houses are bigger and better built and in a different quarter from that where the prior houses are huddled together" (de Vaux 1961: 72–73; cf. Chambon 1984: 43–44; disputed by McClellan 1987: 86).

The eighth-century prophets railed against these social injustices (Isa 1:15, 17, 23; 3:13–15; 5:8–10; 10:1–2; 33:15; Hos 5:10; 12:7–8; Amos 2:6–7; 3:10; 4:1; 5:7, 10–12; 6:4–7; 8:4–6; Mic 2:1–3, 8–9; 3:1–3, 9–11; cf., most comprehensively and profoundly, Kaufmann 1948: 3.1–292; 1960: 363–98; Dearman 1988: 18–61). Earlier, Jehu's rebellion, probably "an uprising of the provincial peasantry against 'metropolitan' life in Samaria" (Baron 1952: 89), had received the prophetic support of Elisha. But most of the prophets and, certainly, the priestly legists of the Holiness Source espoused a peaceful reform. Other voices interpreted the acquisitions of the wealthy as a sign of divine blessing, however. This certainly was the supposition of the earliest sources (Gen 26:12; 27:28; 33:11) as well as Deuteronomy, which, as pointed out by Albertz (1994: 324, n. 31), promised further riches to the wealthy if they provided for the underprivileged (Deut 14:24, 29; 15:14; 23:21; 24:19).

Neufeld (1958: 118) comes to the conclusion (citing Jirku 1929: 178) that the sabbatical and jubilee were the priestly response to the prophetic accusations, "a counter-attack against the new economic and social conditions, and aimed at the abolition of the urban economy which produced so much evil . . . . Being recurrent institutions at fixed periods, [they] fundamentally embraced much more; in addition to relieving victims of economic distress, they tended to prevent the development of city economic life and to suppress the growth of economic differentiation by a system which would force the community to live within simple economic conditions" (cf. Knohl 1995: 217–18). Here I must enter a slight demurrer: H shows no signs of being opposed to urban life (note, to the contrary, its prescriptions, without a trace of opposition, for houses in walled cities, vv. 29–34); it is concerned with only latifundia. Its solution, the jubilee, as recent investigations have concluded, is not only socially feasible, but also economically advantageous: there is greater productivity in small farms than in large estates (Lappé and Collins 1986: 67–76). Moreover, H had another aim in mind: "A wealthy kinsman could use the perfectly legal and indeed 'charitable' procedure of land redemption to acquire the land of poverty stricken families. The Jubilee checks such expansionism" (C. Wright 1991: 177–78) by providing the debtor with interest-free loans (vv. 36–37), if necessary, until the jubilee, which cancels his debt and restores him to his land. Finally, the jubilee effectively makes the buyer's risk greater than the seller's because the seller can renege at any time by paying the prorated amount, or he can amass the required amount by hiring himself out (cf. Soss 1973). The jubilee thus assumes that, even before its occurrence, the land will revert to its original owner.

The probability that the jubilee and, indeed, most of H's laws were motivated by the economic stress of the eighth century, as forcefully punctuated by the prophets, is discussed in the Introduction II R.

B. The Sabbatical and Jubilee: Their Observance

Scripture records two different sabbaticals, aptly titled by the rabbis (*b. Giṭ.* 36a; *b. Moʿed Qaṭ.* 2b) *šĕmiṭṭat qarqāʿôt* 'release of lands' (Exod 23:10–11; Lev 25:2–7) and *šĕmiṭṭat kĕsāpîm / ḥôbôt* 'release of monetary claims' (Deut 15:1–3). Are they complementary (the rabbinic view) or contradictory? I opt for the former for two reasons. First, "no debtor could be expected to repay his loans while prohibited from tilling or reaping his land" (Neufeld 1958: 68; cf. Driver 1895: 178). The land sabbatical of Exod 23 and Deut 15 presumes at least a *suspension* of debt payments during that year. (Whether a cancellation is also presumed will be discussed below.) Second, in my judgment, the text itself points to their being complementary. Deuteronomy prescribes a debt release *kî qārāʾ šĕmiṭṭâ laYWHW* 'because YHWH's release has been proclaimed' (Deut 15:2). This is not deuteronomic language; not a single one of its laws, institutions, or festivals is described by such terminology. Whence, then, its origin? A hint by Ibn Ezra supplies the answer: the phrase is modeled on *šabbat laYWHW* 'YHWH's sabbath' (25:2b, 4a; cf. also 23:3; Exod 16:25; 20:10 [= Deut 5:14]; 31:15), a priestly expression for the sabbatical of the land. Moreover, the use of *qārāʾ* 'proclaim' is also unique in Deuteronomy. Whence its origin? Again, it is priestly terminology, employed in regard to the sabbath (23:3) and the festivals (23:4–37; cf. Exod 12:16; Num 28–29). Deuteronomy, then, is aware of and agreeing with H's sabbatical, and it issues this command: observe the release of debts *in addition to* the release of the land because both have been proclaimed as YHWH's. In any event, once the Pentateuch was canonized, both laws had to be considered as complementary and, in early postexilic times, were observed together (Neh 10:32).

The question of whether D enjoined a remission of debts or just their suspension is, admittedly, more difficult to answer (see Driver 1895: 178–80). Unfortunately, the text of Deut 15:2a *šāmôṭ kol-baʿal maššēh yādô* 'every creditor shall release the debt' is ambivalent. And its echo in Nehemiah *wĕniṭṭōš ʾet-haššānâ haššĕbîʿît ûmaššāʾ kol-yād* 'We will forgo (the produce of) the seventh year and every debt' (10:32b) only confounds the issue because, it can be argued, they cancel each other. Deuteronomy's verb šāmaṭ 'release' seems to imply remission (Weinfeld 1990a: 47–51), whereas Nehemiah's verb nāṭaš (the verb used with the land sabbatical in Exod 23:11) implies that the prohibition against collecting the interest on one's debt, like the prohibition against collecting one's produce, is limited to the sabbatical year (Rofé 1986).

To be sure, the earliest rabbinic sources are unanimous in upholding the remission option (e.g., m. Šebi. 10:1), a view also supported by Philo (Laws 2.71). That such, indeed, was the practice is verified by its legal circumvention, the Prosbol (prosbolē) instituted by Hillel (first century C.E.). In order to overcome a creditor's reluctance to grant loans as the sabbatical approached (precisely the fear of Deut 15:9), this decree granted him exemption from the sabbatical year by transferring his bond documents to a court (m. Šebi. 10:3–4; m. Giṭ. 4:3). Moreover, a purchase document from the Murabba'at caves actually contains such a provision: 'epra'ānāk . . . ûšěnat šěmiṭṭâ dāh 'I will pay you . . . in this year of release' (DJD 2.101; cf. Wacholder 1976: 17–18). All the evidence, however, can be culled from only late Second Temple sources, and the question of the nature of the debt release in the preexilic period and if it was observed at all must be left open.

The nature of the land sabbatical, however, is, in theory, unambivalent, except in details. Its two laws (Exod 23:10–11 and Lev 25:1–7) differ on only the beneficiaries of its produce, the extent of the land affected, and the question of whether sabbatical was a fixed year (see NOTE on "a sabbath to YHWH," v. 2). On whether it was actually observed, however, there is ample room for doubt. There is no textual evidence that it was observed in prexilic times. To the contrary, the admonitions of Lev 26:34–35 (cf. 2 Chr 36:21) testify that the law was observed only in the breach. (The claim that Zedekiah's release occurred in an actual sabbatical year [Sarna 1973] has been disputed [Lemche 1976: 51–53, 59]; see COMMENT F). In any event, this text—whether it stems from preexilic or exilic times is inconsequential—proves that the law itself is older (Alt [1968: 165, n. 118] dates it to Israel's settlement in Canaan). From earliest times, farmers would have realized that fertility was a coefficient of periodic fallowness (cf. Philo, Laws 2.97–98). Also, there was an economic advantage to accumulate a surplus during the first six years to be consumed in the seventh and thereby obviate the need to engage in a money economy (Soss 1973). And as demonstrated by M. Hildenbrand and Hopkins (1985; see COMMENT C), leaving the entire land fallow for the seventh year, provided there had been judicious rotation during the previous six, need not have resulted in economic stress.

The absence of data for the preexilic period stands in sharp contrast to the plethora of data for the Second Temple period (Neh 10:32; 1 Macc 6:49, 53; Philo, cited in Eusebius praep. ev. 8:7; Jos. Ant. 12.378; 23.234; 14.202–6, 475; 15.7; Wars 1.60; Tacitus, Historiae 5.4). Wacholder (1973; cf. also Blosser 1981) has made a plausible case for attaching specific dates to some of these data: 163/62 (1 Macc 6:49, 53); 135/34 (Jos. Ant. 13.234); 37/36 (Jos. Ant. 14.475); 41/42 C.E. (M. Soṭ. 7:8); 55/56 (Mur. 18); 69/70 (Seder Olam 30); 132/33 (Mur. 24).

The land sabbatical was also observed in the era after the destruction of the Temple. During the sabbatical year, Jews were supported by gentile enclaves and diaspora Jews, on whom the prohibition did not fall. Concessions were made by the rabbis (cf. R. Yannai's proclamation, *b. Sanh.* 26a) to work the land in order to pay the Roman taxes (the exemption of taxes during the sabbatical year since the days of Caesar [Jos. *Ant.* 14.202–6] was abrogated in 261 C.E.). There also exists evidence that pious Jews would tear down the fences of their farms and vineyards in order to literally fulfill the command *ûnĕṭaštāh* 'abandon it' (Exod 23:11a)

In contrast to the land sabbatical, there is no evidence at all that the jubilee was ever observed. There is no doubt that the obligation of land redemption existed. Certainly, Jeremiah observed it (Jer 32:6–12), but Naomi's *gō'ēl* opted to ignore it (Ruth 4:6). As pointed out by Amit (1992: 58), Nehemiah's written pledge (*'ămānâ*) mentions the sabbatical (Neh 10:32b), but not the jubilee (but see COMMENT F). Indeed, on the basis of the text that the jubilee is proclaimed *lĕkol-yōšĕbêhā* 'for all its inhabitants' (v. 10), the rabbis conclude that the jubilee was suspended after the first recorded exile at the fall of Samaria (*Sipra* Behar 2:3; *b. 'Arak.* 32b; *y. Šebi.* 10:3). Was it, then, "a utopian law [that] remained a dead letter" (de Vaux 1961: 177) or "is it far-fetched to suppose that the entire Jubilee system was an artificial invention" (Driver and White 1894–98)?

To be sure, the main postulate of the jubilee, that ancestral land is inalienable, is attested in many societies contemporary with and prior to Israel. Such is the case in old village communities (Maine 1890: 81–88). The evidence is particularly abundant for ancient Greece. For example, in the foundation of a new community at Kerkyra Melaina, it was decreed that a portion of the original allotments to the first settlers belonged permanently to them and their descendants. In 228/227 B.C.E., Miletus gave land to some Cretan refugees, specifying that it was inalienable. The Gortyn Code (6:2–12) distinguished between property acquired by inheritance and that obtained in other ways. The decree of the Arcadian league mandated that "none of those receiving a *kleros* (land allotment) or house . . . may alienate them for twenty years" (details in Finley 1968).

The Bible itself bears hints to the effect that the jubilee law was enacted, even if attempts at its enforcement may have failed. Patrick (1985: 5–6) correctly observes that one must distinguish between moral law, governed by social mores, and judicial law, which is enforceable by the use of sanctions. Thus since the jubilee legislation is devoid of sanctions, "obedience must be elicited by appeal to the theological and moral sensibilities of the community" (Fager 1993: 106).

That the jubilee was not completely utopian is, in my opinion, proved by the insertion into the law of the section on houses in walled cities (vv. 29–34); had the jubilee been a utopian statute, there would have been no need to alter or add to it (Elliger 1966; Loewenstamm 1958a). Moreover, Ezek 46:17 takes the concept of *dĕrôr* for granted—that is, when allotted or inherited property returned to its original owner (Eerdmans 1912: 123–28). Thus just as the law of slave release existed but was not practiced (Jer 34:8–11), so too the jubilee.

Finally, I would like to cite a modern, if exotic, example where some of the jubilee provisions, mutatis mutandis, are operative and effective. As reported by Dommen (1972), in the kingdom of Tonga, an island in the South Pacific, some 90,000 people live under laws reminiscent of those in Lev 25.

"All the land of the Kingdom is the property of the Crown." Every Tongan male, on reaching the age of sixteen (law of 1839), is entitled to a farm plot sufficient to support himself and his family. The payment of an annual tax guarantees tenure on the land and the right to bequeath it to his heir. Sales (even most leases) between Tongans are forbidden. On the approval of the cabinet, foreigners may lease land, provided that they keep it productive (and pay their taxes), but, even after renewals, they may hold it for a maximum of only ninety-nine years. Otherwise, foreigners are restricted to trading.

Note the parallels:

1. Land belongs to the Crown / YHWH.
2. The Crown / YHWH has granted the land to his (chosen) people and divided it equitably among them.
3. Each landowner is subject to an annual tax / tithe.
4. Sales of land, whether to citizens or foreigners, are forbidden. Land may be leased to foreigners, but for only a number of years.

These laws were passed in the nineteenth century. They have prevented the development of latifundia among the Tongans and takeovers by foreigners. The kingdom of Tonga has for more than a century succeeded in preserving its independence and has guaranteed, until recently, economic security for its citizens.

Differences should not be overlooked, but they are readily explicable. There is no necessity to sell (or lease) land because destitution is nonexistent. The land is perpetually fertile. Copra and other coconut products, the main export, never fail. The land's produce is always self-sustaining. The termination of a lease is not at a fixed year.

Overpopulation has forced many Tongans off the land. Today, the landless amount to about 25 percent of the population. But they do not lack for employment. The slack is filled by jobs in government, tourism, handicrafts, church, and commerce related to agriculture.

To be sure, this island paradise is so far unaffected by racial or religious conflict or by global economics. Yet, at the least, it shows that the jubilee laws were, for their time, practical and workable. And as more and more Third World countries have discovered, they provide a model for solving their own economic distress (see COMMENT G).

C. The Sabbatical and Jubilee: Are They Consecutive?

How can a farmer afford to leave his entire land fallow for an entire year (Elliger 1966, among others, claim that the fixed year is utopian), much less two successive years (if the sabbatical is followed by the jubilee)? First, this question must be put into the perspective of the ancient, Israelite farmer, not his modern counterpart. My student M. Hildenbrand contributes from his ample farming background the following observation:

> There is an often expressed objection to the practice demanded in chapter 25 of leaving the land fallow for one, and even two years (assuming a separate, consecutive jubilee year). One might think that the land would be left a jumbled mess of weeds by leaving it fallow, and that farmers would face great difficulty, and even hardship preparing the soil for planting following the fallow year(s) with only oxen and plow to do the job. In reality, these objections have no basis in the reality of agriculture. Soil, under the duress of modern farming practice, becomes so difficult to work after remaining fallow for any length of time because of the heavy machinery used to work the land. This heavy machinery causes the soil only a few inches below the surface to compact and become *very* hard. Any weeds and aftergrowth make it *necessary* to reuse the same heavy machinery to again work the land, compacting the soil more and more with each reworking of the land. Additionally, as the subsurface soil hardens, erosion of the topsoil begins, eventually rendering the land nearly useless for agricultural purposes. On the other hand, ground which is worked by single plowing with animals *never* develops this hard packed subsurface soil, leaving the ground quite soft and usable, even after being allowed to lie fallow. It is true that the ground would need to be ploughed twice (or even three times) to eliminate any weed–seeds that would have dropped during the fallow year, but ground that has only been plowed by single plows with animals will remain quite soft for the first plowing after a fallow year and a second plowing of ground is never very difficult. Additionally, after completing his final harvesting before the fallow year a wise farmer could spread a leguminous ground cover like beans, or somesuch, which would benefit the soil by restoring its nitrogen content and cut down on weed growth.

Moreover, according to Hopkins (1985), the Israelite farmer probably fallowed his land more frequently than one year out of seven, most likely biennially, on a rotational basis. Such an arrangement could be incorporated into a sabbatical system (fig. 2). In the year before the sabbatical, the farmer could increase production by eliminating the fallow (F) of an area (P) just cropped (C). In order to compensate for this heavy use, this area would then be rested not only for the sabbatical year (S), but also for the subsequent year as the other half of the farm-

P	C	F	C	F	C	C	S	F	C	F	C	F	C	S
Q	F	C	F	C	F	C	S	C	F	C	F	C	C	S
	1	2	3	4	5	6	7	1	2	3	4	5	6	7

FIGURE 2

land (Q) continued in its regular biennial rotation (Hopkins 1985: 201; Borowski 1987: 8, 15–18, 143–48).

Thus the transition from Exod 23:10–11, which probably prescribes an unfixed (perhaps, rotational) sabbatical, to the fixed sabbatical of Lev 25 could have been easily accomplished. The succession of two fallow years—the sabbatical of the forty-ninth year followed by the jubilee of the fiftieth year—is beset with problems, however. First is the arithmetic problems generated by the sequence. When is the next sabbatical following the jubilee? The rabbis hold that the year after the jubilee (year 51) is the first of a new cycle. The next sabbatical would then fall on year 57 (b. Roš Haš. 9a [bar.; cf. Tosafot for a superior reading]; b. Ned. 61a [bar.]). This solution, however, breaks the sabbatical cycle: the first sabbatical of the new jubilee period would fall eight years after the previous one! One sage, R. Judah, differs with his colleagues in proposing that the jubilee year itself (the fiftieth) is the first of a new cycle. Then the next cycle falls in the fifty-sixth year, and the sabbatical cycle (years 49–56) is preserved. This solution, too, faces the objection that there are only five work years in the first sabbatical. However, this difficulty evaporates as soon as it is realized that the weekly cycle on which the sabbatical cycle is based is not interrupted by additional rest days that fall during the week (R. Gane).

Many moderns follow North (1954: 51, 54; most recently Schenker 1998: 25) in postulating that the jubilee (the fiftieth year) coincided with the forty-ninth year—the first to suggest this, according to Kalisch (1867–72), was Bishop Isidorus Hispalensis—a procedure that would correspond to the inclusive chronology of North Israel (the year of ascension is the king's first year and the last year of the preceding king). This system may have been followed by the sectaries of Qumran, whose seven-week cycle of firstfruit festivals always ended on a Sunday (11QT 18–23; see also Jub 4:29; 10:16; passim). Nonetheless, it cannot be sustained for the problem at hand, if for no other reason that one cannot explain the biblical text if the jubilee collapses into the sabbatical year (see NOTE on v. 22). Moreover, the prohibitions prescribed by these two institutions are not congruent: the jubilee is not a sabbatical year. Hence the non-Israelite may work his land on the jubilee, but not on the sabbatical (see NOTE on "for you," v. 10). Besides, the oldest witnesses (Jos. Ant. 3.281–82; Philo, Laws 2.287–90) uniformly speak of two successive years.

Other solutions have been proposed, such as the jubilee is not a year but a proclamation and, although it is called the fiftieth year, it is the first of a new cycle (Kaufman 1984: 280, n. 1). Or the jubilee is a forty-nine-day intercalation (following Zeitlin 1962: 216) required because of a solar calendar of 364 days that fell short 1 day each year (Hoenig 1969). These proposals also fail because they ignore the biblical evidence: first, the jubilee is independent of and sequential to the sabbatical year and, second, the fertility required for the land to produce crops that will feed the nation for three years is not answered by a rationalistic compromise, but is due solely to divine grace (Kochman).

Thus, as stated in my conclusion to COMMENT B, the jubilee law existed, was intended to be implemented, and would have been implemented were it not for the typical and expected resistance from those who might be adversely effected: the rich and the political leaders in control.

D. The Slave Laws of Exodus 21 (and Deuteronomy 15) versus Leviticus 25

The relationship of the slave laws of Lev 25:39–55 to those of Exod 21:1–11 (and Deut 15:12–18) is beset with many difficulties. Here I wish to focus on the one that I consider to be the main problem. Lev 25 posits that in the seventh year there will be only "release" of land from cultivation, but not release of Israelites from slavery. How, then, can Lev 25, the repository of such idealistic, humanitarian legislation as the sabbatical and jubilee, have devised a law that postpones the manumission of slaves from seven years (Exodus and Deuteronomy) to fifty years? Gerstenberger (1996: 398) issues a condemnatory judgment: the fifty-year release "was conceived as a compromise with money lenders at that time. That would constitute an extremely questionable dilution of Yahweh's will with regard to social justice in Israel." One cannot argue (with Loewenstamm 1958a and others) that Leviticus has to be pragmatically hard-hearted in order to induce creditors to be willing to offer loans. Neither can one parry this question by answering, as does Neufield (1958: 60), that the termination of all bondage by the jubilee is an advance over lifelong bondage (Exod 21:5–6). The question still remains: Why did H drop the provision for seven-year manumission? Of course, in phrasing the problem this way, I am assuming two things: that Leviticus is later than Exodus, a proposition on which all scholars agree, and that H, the author of Lev 25:39–55, is cognizant of Exod 21:1–11 (and even polemicizes against it; see NOTES on vv. 39–41, 46).

The rabbis, fully aware of this and other discrepancies, offer two solutions. One is that Exodus and Leviticus envisage two different circumstances: in Exodus, the slave is sold by the court; in Leviticus, he sells himself (b. Qidd. 14b [bar.]). The other is that both termini, the septennate and the jubilee, are of equal validity; the slave is freed by whichever comes first (m. Qidd. 1:2; y. Qidd. 1:2; Sipra Behar 7:4), a solution already recorded by Philo (Laws 2.122). However, there is no evidence to support either solution; they are clearly the product of harmonization. The rabbis, however, also record the view that the jubilee, but not the sabbatical (of Exod 21 and Deut 15), manumits the slave (Sipra Behar 3:6); in other words, the jubilee supersedes the sabbatical. The notion that different circumstances lie behind these slave laws does find an echo in the modern proposal that they are the products of different locales, such as North Israel and Judah (Elliger 1966), or two tribes (Loewenstamm 1971b: 13).

The most accepted solution is that these laws deal with different persons. Only Leviticus speaks of Israelites ('āḥ), whereas Exodus concerns itself with a non-Israelite, the 'ibrî. The rabbis, to be sure, never doubted the equation of 'ibrî with Israelite (cf. *Mekh* Mishpatim on Exod 21:2). However, the first to sever this identity, to my knowledge, were the Karaites (cf. *Seper Hamibḥar* and *Keter Torah* on Exod 21:2), who aver, on the basis of the fact that Abram is called ʿibrî (Gen 14:13), that this designation applies to all his progeny, including the Edomites (Esau, Gen 36) and the Arabian tribes (Ishmael and Keturah, Gen 25:1–6, 12–18). Ibn Ezra (on Exod 21:2) counters their contention:

1. The ʿibrî is called ʾāḥîkā 'your brother', which indicates that he is an Israelite (but see C. Wright 1991).
2. In Moses' dialogue with Pharaoh, he refers to his God as both ʾĕlōhê yiśrāʾēl and ʾĕlōhê hāʿibrîm (Exod 5:1, 3).
3. Everywhere else in Scripture, the ʿibrî is an Israelite (e.g., Gen 41:12; 43:32; Exod 2:11; Jer 34:9; Jonah 1:9).
4. It is inconceivable that an Edomite or Ishmaelite would be released after six years, but an Israelite would have to wait until the jubilee (see also Levi 1981: 40–42).

Ibn Ezra, however, does concede that the phrase "Abram the ʿibrî" (Gen 14:13) reflects his geographic origin (from across [ʿēber], Gen 10:21), but not his nationality, thus opening the possibility that *originally*, ʿibrî had a totally different meaning than "Israelite."

And this possibility, in our time, became a probability when Akkadian documents from Tell El-Amarna and Nuzi revealed the existence of a group called ḥapiru and those from Ugarit, the designation ʿprm (e.g., Alt 1968: 122; Cazelles 1946: 44–45; Cassuto 1951a: 184–85; Noth 1962: 177; Clements 1972; Ellison 1973; Lemche 1975; Noordzji 1982: 259). However, on philological as well as semantic grounds (the ḥapiru is not an ethnic unit, but a motley group of social outcasts), the identification has been vigorously denied (e.g., Kaufmann 1942: 2.333; Mendelsohn 1949: 87; Rainey 1967: 93–94; Naʿaman 1986, partially; Jackson 1988).

Most recently, C. Wright (1991: 253–59) has proposed a new solution: the ʿibrî (Exodus) is a landless Israelite, and the ʾāḥ (Leviticus) is a landed Israelite. The former, having lost his land and with no means for supporting himself, is quite willing to become a slave, even a lifelong one. The latter, having land to return to, must be redeemed or allowed to redeem himself. Wright avers that Deuteronomy's expanded designation ʾāḥîkā hāʿibrî (also cited in Jer 34:14) would be a tautology if ʿibrî had the same meaning as ʾāḥ, and, therefore, it cannot denote the same Israelite.

Wright's proposal, at first blush, is seductive, but, upon examination, it cannot be sustained. First, D's expression is not a tautology. Being based on the Exodus text, it merely states that the ʿibrî of Exodus is also an ʾāḥ, a brother Israelite. One must keep in mind D's persistent use of ʾāḥ for an Israelite (note how the ʾāḥ is meticulously distinguished from the gēr and nokrî, Deut 1:16; 15:3; 17:15) as its constant reminder that every Israelite must be treated as a brother (e.g., 15:2, 12; 19:19; 22:1, 2 (twice), 3, 4; 25:3, 5, 6, 7, 9, 11; 28:54).

Furthermore, that a landless Israelite would retain the title *'ibrî* into the seventh century, the age of Deuteronomy (a date verified by finding it in Jer 34:14), is incomprehensible.

As for Lev 25, the immediate question that comes to mind is: if the *'ibrî* constituted a distinct social class in Israel, why is there no mention of him in Lev 25 or, for that matter, anywhere in H (e.g., 19:10)? Furthermore, Wright is wrong in his attribution of redemption to the Israelite slave. The reverse is true. Total silence reigns in H's slave law regarding redemption, except in the case where the debtor sold himself to a non-Israelite. This can only mean that his status has changed to a point where the concept of redemption is no longer applicable—which leads me to my own proposal.

H rejects the septennate manumission of Exodus because it abolishes the slave status for an Israelite outright. It insists that an Israelite who has to indenture himself must be treated as a *śākîr tôšāb* 'resident hireling' (vv. 40a, 53a). Moreover, since he pays no interest on his debt (reversing the Babylonian practice of personal antichresis), all his earnings can be directed toward amortizing his debt. His family, therefore, is under no obligation to redeem him. (Of course, his family can *lend* him the money to cover his debt, but this is no longer "redemption.") And if by chance he still cannot pay back his debt—under these favorable conditions, an unlikely eventuality—the escape hatch of the jubilee will release him (see NOTES on vv. 39–42).

H, therefore, is a marked improvement on Exod 21 (and Deut 15). In the seventh year, having no resources, it will not be too long before the erstwhile slave reenters indenture—a dire consequence that D (vainly) tries to obviate by encouraging his master to shower him with parting gifts (Deut 15:13–15). H, therefore, legislates that when he pays off his debt or when the jubilee occurs—whichever is earlier—he "returns to his ancestral land" (v. 41). The status quo is reestablished; he is on a par with his fellow Israelites—this time, hopefully, never again to sink into debt. Thus there exists no discrepancy between the slave laws of Exodus/Deuteronomy and those of Leviticus regarding the identity of the enslaved person. They both speak of undifferentiated Israelites. The use of *'ibrî* in Exodus, imitated by Deuteronomy, may indeed reflect an earlier connotation of the term (as attested in Gen 14:13) when it had wider social or ethnic parameters, but by the time of the Covenant Code it had lost the earlier designation and denoted only the Israelite.

As a final remark, I wish to respond to a serious question posed by my student S. Nikaido. He asks: Since Exodus presumes the existence of blood redemption (see Exod 21:13), why does it not "address any kin group responsibilities in slavery laws which are supposed to be dealing exclusively with 'Hebrew' slaves"? The absence of personal redemption in Exodus is a problem. The answer may lie in chronology: either blood redemption, undoubtedly present from earliest times, had not yet evolved into personal redemption or, more likely, considering that bondage was limited to six years, there was no burning need for family intervention.

E. The Slave Laws of D and H Compared

The relationship between the slave laws of D (Deut 15:12–18) and H (Lev 25:39–55) is difficult to determine. There are three possibilities and all three have their protagonists:

1. H is later than D, the regnant theory, promulgated initially by the Graf-Kuenen (1886)-Wellhausen (1963) school (most recently, see Cholewinski 1976; Cardellini 1981: 280–86; Gnuse 1985; Kaufmann 1984, 1985; Sun 1990; Bultmann 1992: 175–96).
2. D is later than H (Japhet 1986; cf. Wright 1984).
3. D and H are independent compositions (Kaufmann 1937: 1.64), but are related in content (Weinfeld 1972d: 223, n. 3).

We begin our investigation with the prevailing theory that H is later than D. The arguments usually offered, unfortunately, are not based on bona fide evidence, but only on a series of suppositions. The recent treatment by Sun (1990) provides a parade example. He gives five reasons:

1. The phrase *šabbat laYHWH* is late P (Exod 31:15; 35:2; Lev 25:2; cf. Exod 16:23, 25); hence its application to the idea of the sabbatical is also late. But all the cited verses are H, not P (see Introduction II R), and there are no verifiable grounds for labeling them late (which for Sun means post-exilic; see Introduction I K).
2. *děrôr* is a loanword from Akkadian *andurāru* in its late form *durāru*. It is indeed later than *andurāru*, and is attested only in NA and NB. Note that the so-called late period covers most of the first millenium. For example, *durāru* appears in BM 132001 (cited by Lewy 1958: 31*), a Sargonid document, of the eighth century, the very period that saw the inception of the H School.
3. There are references to the jubilee in postexilic literature, but none in pre-exilic literature. Arguments from silence are specious. The silence may simply mean that the jubilee was not *enacted* until later (see COMMENT B).
4. "Plural texts constitute a secondary redactional hand" (Sun 1990: 549; cf. 503, 548–50, 558–59). The widespread presence of the singular and plural in homogeneous biblical and ancient Near Eastern texts permanently vitiates this distinction as a valid compositional criterion (see Weinfeld 1991: 15–16).
5. "The coincidence of fifty years of exile and fifty years of jubilee is best explained by the supposition that this law justified the reappropriation of Palestinian land by returning exilees," supported by 2 Chr 36:21, according to which the years of the exile substitute for the unobserved sabbatical years (Weinfeld 1990a). This assertion is erroneous because the jubilee is not a sabbath (see NOTE on "the land shall observe" v. 2).

There are other objections to making H later than D. The one that, for me, is irrefutable has been posed by Weinfeld (1972d: 223, n. 3). On the one hand, why would Lev 25 omit the law of debt remission if it were an established D tradition? (Note how [Gruse 1985: 45] and Levine [1989a: 273] are stumped by this question.) On the other hand, it can readily be seen that D's doctrine of debt cancelation (*šĕmîṭṭâ*, Deut 15:1–3) was influenced by H's presupposition of this doctrine. That the freed debtor is restored to his land (vv. 10, 13, 41) implies that the creditor's loan on it is simultaneously canceled, or he could have impounded his erstwhile slave as soon as he was released.

Cardellini (1981: 342, 350) uses the textual approach to prove the later date of H. For example, he avers that Deut 15:12 aα and 18aβ lie behind Lev 25:39a and 40a. The brackets indicate where H purportedly supplemented D:

kî-yimmākēr lĕkā 'āhîkā hā'ibrî	If a Hebrew brother is sold to you (Deut 15:12aα)
wĕkî-[yāmûk] 'āhîkā ['immāk] *wĕnimkar-lāk*	If your brother [being (further) impoverished under your authority,] is sold you (Lev 25:39a)
mē'immāk kî mišneh śĕkar śākîr	from under your authority, double the wage of a hireling (Deut 15:18aβ)
kĕśākîr [kĕtôšāb yiyeh] 'immāk	He [shall remain] under you as [a resident] hireling (Lev 25:40a)

Japhet (1986) has investigated these verses, and her findings point entirely in the opposite direction. First, she argues that D has changed its *Vorlage*, Exod 21:2, by converting its opening clause *kî tiqneh* to *kî-yimmākēr lĕkā*—that is, changing not just the verb (to *mākar*) but its form: second to third person and *Qal* to *Nip'al*, precisely as we find in H. Second, D changes Exodus's *'îš* to *'āhîkā*, again as we find in H. This argument, however, must be discounted because, as shown by Hoffmann (1980: 23), D frequently refers to the Israelite as *'āhîkā* (a point that Japhet admits). Her contention that this word is not integral to D's slave law because, unlike H, D is not contrasting the Israelite and non-Israelite is refuted by Deut 1:16; 15:3; 17:15. Besides, all D is saying is that Exodus's *'ibrî* is "your brother" and should be treated accordingly. Third, the reference to a *śākîr* 'a hireling', is essential to the theology and argumentation of H (see NOTES on v. 40), whereas in D it is totally irrelevant.

More recently, Amit (1992: 55–56) has argued that the slave laws of Lev 25 are later than those of Deut 15. She seems aware of Weinfeld's (1985a: 94–95) strong case for the antecedence of Mesopotamian *mīšarum* and *andurāru*, but not of his other counterarguments (mentioned above). In any event, she offers no point-by-point response (1992: 56, n. 1), except a single, unsubstantiated claim that Jehoiachin's release from his captivity by Evil-merodach in the year of his accession (2 Kgs 25:27) "is one of the proofs [sic] to the existence of the *anduraru(m)* in the first millennium and not only in earlier periods" (58, n. 3). If this statement in Kings is reliable, it shows only that Jehoiachin, who had been granted favorable conditions at the beginning of his exile (cf. *ANET* 308a), may have fallen into disfavor and been thrown into prison. Thus his release was, most likely, an act of personal amnesty, not part of a general *andurāru*. Similarly, all Amit can say concerning Japhet's (1986) close reading of both texts, again without substantiation, is that the evidence can point to borrowing in the opposite direction. There are also additional arguments.

To Japhet's evidence, I would add the following. Fourth, *'immāk/mē'immāk* occurs five times in Deut 15:12–18, four times in Lev 25:39–43, but is totally absent in Exod 21:1–11. Whence did D draw this term? One can argue that it appears nineteen times in the rest of Deuteronomy; hence it is a normal D usage. However, all its five occurrences in D's slave law denote "under your authority," the same as in H, whereas in the rest of Deuteronomy, it never bears this ramified meaning, but only its usual connotation "with." What alternative remains except to admit that D must have drawn it from the slave law of H. Fifth, a major difference between Deuteronomy and Exodus is that the term *'ebed* does not appear in D except in the passage dealing with the lifelong slave (Deut 15:16–17). Neither does it appear in H. In the latter source, its absence makes sense, since the indentured Israelite is no longer a slave, but a *śākîr tôšāb* 'resident hireling'. D, however, implores the master to shower his manumitted slave with gifts, and reminds him that he has benefited from the slave twice as much as from a *śākîr* (Deut 15:18). Thus for D, he is not a *śākîr*, as in H, but an *'ebed*. I submit that the best explanation of this paradoxical situation is that D has been influenced by H to ameliorate its *attitude* toward the slave; but without H's theological postulate that all Israelites are slaves of God (25:42, 55), it has no basis for abolishing Israelite slavery. Sixth, as argued in COMMENT B, D devised its law for debt release (Deut 15:1–3) as a supplement to H's law for land release (25:1–7). It has done the same in the contiguous law for slave release.

Finally, seventh, I have demonstrated elsewhere (1976: 9–13) that D's formula *ka'ăšer ṣiwwâ / nišbā' / dibbēr*, by which it indicates its sources, cites a priestly source in three instances: (1) scale disease (Deut 24:8; cf. Lev 13); (2) the covenanted relationship (Deut 29:12; cf. Gen 17:7–8; Exod 6:7; Lev 26:12 [all H]), which D reworks (Muffs 1965a); (3) the Levitic prebends (Deut 10:9; 18:2; cf. Num 18:20, 24). To be sure, one can argue that D may have been aware of the content of the priestly law, but not of the formulation. This argument will not hold, however, in the case of the impure birds. It can be demonstrated, conclusively, I believe, that D abridged the entire text of Leviticus as it presently exists in the MT (vol. 1.698–704). To be sure, the impure-bird text of Lev 11 stems from the hand of P, and D may have been familiar with only an earlier form of Leviticus, before H added its supplement and insertions (which I dispute, vol. 1.703). But the possibility must be reckoned with that D was familiar with other *written* laws of P and, perhaps, also of H.

In any event, a comparison between the slave laws of D and H, as shown by the evidence adduced above, leads to the conclusion that D was cognizant of the very *language* of H. That is why I feel constrained to reject, as well, the third possibility that the slave laws of D and H are totally independent compositions.

Nonetheless, it should not be forgotten that the postulates underlying the two and, hence, their content (enumerated above) are at total variance with each other. They are well contrasted by Joosten (1994: 221; 1996: 159): "Whereas Deuteronomy accentuates the independent value of personal freedom, the conception of H is that without land no man is entirely free, since he will not be able to support himself."

F. Was the Jubilee Year Observed in Preexilic Judah?
(Lisbeth S. Fried and David N. Freedman)

It was suggested in COMMENT A that the eighth century was the most likely period for the inception of the jubilee laws. The question remains as to whether they were ever actually observed. We begin our investigation into this question with the reign of Zedekiah and the mass manumission of Hebrew slaves. We read in Jer 34:8–9a that Zedekiah made a covenant with all the people in Jerusalem "to proclaim to them liberty [*līqrō' lāhem děrôr*] that everyone should send his Hebrew male and female slave away free." This is also the language of Lev 25:10, the language of the jubilee year, so that we see that both this general release of Hebrew slaves and the language used to promulgate it are in conformity with the law of the jubilee year.

Many scholars argue, however, that this release of slaves was an effort to observe the sabbatical year, not the jubilee (e.g., Bright 1965; Sarna 1973; Wright 1992). The assumption that Jeremiah refers to the sabbatical laws may have arisen from the statement in Jer 34:14–15a in which we read: "[Thus says YHWH], 'By the end of seven years each of you must set free the fellow Hebrew who has been sold to you and has served you six years; you must set him free from your service.' But your fathers did not listen to me or incline their ears to me. You recently did what was right in my eyes by proclaiming liberty [*līqrō' děrôr*], each to his neighbor." Most scholars assume that the six years referred to are the general six years that end with the *šěmīṭṭāh*, and when Jeremiah talks about doing what is right he is talking about the *šěmīṭṭāh*. But the *šěmīṭṭāh* does not require a universal manumission of slaves, only the remission of debts (Deut 15:1–11). The confusion arises from the fact that Deuteronomy follows its discussion of the laws of the sabbatical year with a discussion of the laws of the release of slaves (Deut 15:12). In actuality, this is simply because they share the number seven. Deuteronomy does not provide for a general manumission of slaves in the sabbatical year, and no general manumission of slaves in the sabbatical year is assumed by the laws of Leviticus either, for in Lev 25:6 we read that "the sabbath of the land shall provide food for you, for you, your male and female slave, and your resident hirelings who live under your authority." Thus the assumption by both D and P is that there is no universal manumission during the sabbatical year and no universal return to one's own property. This is mandated for only the jubilee year. All that Jeremiah says is that even though the fathers had not released their slaves after their individual six years of servitude in the past, as they ought to have (Exod 21:2; Deut 15:12), they still did what was right this time and had released their slaves during the year of the *děrōr*, the only occasion demanding universal manumission.

This language of the jubilee is also played out in Jeremiah's scathing denunciation of the people when they recaptured their slaves: " 'Because you did not heed me and proclaim release [*līqrō' děrôr*] each to his brother and each to his neighbor, behold I am proclaiming release to you [*qōrē' lākem děrôr*],' says YHWH, 'to the sword, to pestilence, to famine, and I shall give you as a frightened quaking thing to all the kingdoms of the earth' " (Jer 34:17). The play on the word *děrôr* evokes the language of Lev 25:10 and links the release of slaves commanded there with YHWH's action in releasing Israel from himself, the sole legitimate owner of the Israelite people, to all the kingdoms of the earth. Further, the statement that "you did not heed me" with reference to the release of slaves suggests that the release was in response to a long-standing law or tradition, and was not simply a hasty maneuver to gain YHWH's good graces in a time of national emergency. It is not likely, furthermore, that YHWH was viewed as the sort of god who responded to hasty maneuvers. It seems more likely that he would be swayed the most by obedience to ancient tradition. It is not likely, therefore, that a release of slaves would effect a victory over the Chaldeans if Zedekiah was seen as introducing an innovation; rather, the universal release of slaves had to be viewed as being in conformity with ancient law. This suggests that there must have been a long-standing tradition of a jubilee year and that it was in conformity with the laws of this tradition that the release was made. This suggests that Zedekiah released the slaves at the start of a jubilee year in Judah [see, however, the objections by Ehpʻal 1996: 149–50 — J.M.].

To test the hypothesis that the release of slaves was a response to the start of a jubilee year, we have to know what other events occurred that year and determine if those events were also in response to the laws of the jubilee. We know that Zedekiah's edict to grant release to all the slaves occurred during the siege of Jerusalem by the Chaldeans (Jer 34:6–7). We also know that the people of Jerusalem attempted to recapture their released slaves and bring them back into servitude during the withdrawal of the Babylonians and the lifting of the siege (Jer 34:16–17a, 21). We know that the Babylonians withdrew from Jerusalem in response to the approach of the Egyptian army (Jer 37:5–11) and that it was at this time, during the lifting of the siege, that Jeremiah attempted to leave Jerusalem to go to Anathoth, but was arrested at the gate of the city and thrown into the court of the guard, where he remained until the capture of Jerusalem and the end of the war (Jer 37:11–21). We know that it was while Babylon was besieging Jerusalem that Jeremiah was visited in the court of the guard by his cousin Hanamel (Jer 32:1–15). Thus we see that the slaves were released during the siege and recaptured when the siege was lifted, that it was while the siege was lifted that Jeremiah was imprisoned, and that it was when the siege had resumed that he was visited by his cousin Hanamel. During that visit, Jeremiah buys a field from his cousin, because he had the right of inheritance as the *gō'ēl* 'redeemer'. Thus to test the hypothesis that the manumission of slaves was in response to the jubilee year, we must determine whether or not this transaction between Jeremiah and his cousin occurred during the same liturgical year and, if so, whether it also was in conformity with the laws of the jubilee. We will begin with the date.

The Date

Nebuchadnezzar began his siege of Jerusalem on the tenth day of the tenth month of the ninth year both of the reign of Zedekiah (2 Kgs 25:1; Jer 52:4) and of the captivity of King Jehoiachin (Ezek 24:1–2). To determine when this was, we have to know when both the reign and the captivity began. According to the cuneiform tablet of the Babylonian Chronicles, Jehoiachin, Zedekiah's predecessor, was captured by the Babylonians on the second of Adar, at the end of the seventh year of Nebuchadnezzar (ANET³ 564), and, thanks to the calculations of Parker and Dubberstein (1956), we know exactly when this was: March 16, 597 B.C.E. The counting of the years of the Babylonian Exile began officially the next month on the first day of the Babylonian year, the first day of Nisan, or April 13, 597, the beginning of the eighth year of Nebuchadnezzar. It was on this date that Zedekiah would have been placed on the throne by Nebuchadnezzar (Jer 37:1; Babylonian Chronicle, ANET³ 564), so whether Zedekiah's first regnal year began that Nisan, at the beginning of the Babylonian calendrical year, or the following Tishri, at the beginning of the Jewish liturgical year, the beginning of the final siege of Jerusalem would have occurred on the tenth day of the tenth month of both Zedekiah's ninth regnal year and of the ninth year of the captivity—January 15, 588 (2 Kgs 25:1 [= Jer 52:4; Ezek 24:1–2]).

The city was besieged almost continuously until it fell in the eleventh year of King Zedekiah (2 Kgs 25:2 [= Jer 52:5]). Since we know that the manumission of the slaves occurred during the siege (Jer 34:6–10), it must have occurred sometime after its start on January 15, 588. If the slaves were, as speculated, released in response to the laws of the jubilee year, then they would have been released in the autumn, on the tenth day of the seventh month, the month of Tishri (Lev 25:9). If it was the first autumn after the siege began, it would have been October 8, 588, and we may hypothesize that the Jewish liturgical year from Tishri 588 to Tishri 587 was a jubilee year. Accordingly, whether Zedekiah began his official reign in Nisan 597 or in the following Tishri, the year that we hypothesize as the jubilee year would overlap with both the tenth year of his reign and the tenth year of the captivity. If the release of slaves occurred in the second autumn after the siege began, it would have begun in the fall of 587, and the eleventh liturgical year of Zedekiah, the final year of his reign, would have been the jubilee year.

Fortunately, the oracles of Ezekiel enable us to determine the precise year when the siege was lifted in response to the approach of the Egyptians, so we may ascertain precisely when the slaves were released, when they were recaptured, and when the transaction between Jeremiah and his cousin occurred. Three oracles of Ezekiel, all dated to the tenth year of the captivity, and all directed against

Egypt, condemn Egypt for its hubris in attempting to relieve Babylon's siege of Jerusalem. The first of these is dated to the tenth year of the captivity, the tenth month, the twelfth day, thus the twelfth day of Tebeth, or January 7, 587 (Ezek 29:1–16). In this oracle, Ezekiel condemns Egypt for raising false hopes in Israel and for being a broken staff of reed that makes unsteady all who lean on it (29:6–7). Egypt will be made small so that it never again will be a staff for the house of Israel (29:14–15). The precipitating event in this first oracle therefore would have been the news that Pharaoh Hophra had left Egypt to come to the aid of Jerusalem. Freedy and Redford (1985) suggest subtracting four months from the date of each oracle, however, to allow time for the news to reach Ezekiel, who is living in Babylon. This would give us the twelfth day of Elul, or September 10, 588, for the time when the army of Pharaoh Hophra left Egypt.

The second oracle against Egypt (Ezek 30:20–26) is dated to the eleventh year of the captivity, the first month, the seventh day of the month, or the seventh day of Nisan 587. Subtracting the requisite four Hebrew months, we have the seventh day of Tebeth, or December 29, 588. In this oracle, Ezekiel quotes YHWH as saying, "I will strengthen the arms of the king of Babylon and put my sword in his hand, and I will break the arm of Pharaoh" (30:24). This precipitating event would have been the lifting of the Babylonian siege in response to the approach of the Egyptian army. Thus the siege was not lifted until the end of December, so Jerusalem still would have been under siege three months earlier, on the tenth day of Tishri, or October 8, the date we hypothesize for the manumission of the slaves.

The third oracle of Ezekiel (Ezek 31:1–18) is dated to the eleventh year of the captivity, the third month, the first day of the month. In this oracle, Ezekiel comments on how the mighty have fallen: " 'Who is like this in glory and greatness among the trees of Eden, but you shall be brought down with the trees of Eden to the land below, among the uncircumcised you will lie with all those who perished by the sword. This is Pharaoh, and all his horde,' says my Lord YHWH" (31:18). Thus the precipitating event would have been the defeat of the Egyptians and the resumption of the siege of Jerusalem by the Babylonians. Subtracting the requisite four months, we see that this would have occurred in the twelfth month of the tenth year of the captivity, the first day of I Adar (there being two months of Adar that year, since it was a leap year), or February 24, 587. Thus the siege was lifted between December 29, 588 and February 24, 587. It was during those two months that the slaves were recaptured (Jer 34:16) and during those two months that Jeremiah attempted to go to Anathoth and was instead thrown into the court of the guard (Jer 37:11–38:28), where he remained until Jerusalem was taken (Jer 38:28).

While imprisoned in the court of the guard, and after the resumption of the siege on February 24, 587, Jeremiah was visited by his cousin Hanamel (Jer 32:28). We read that he was visited during the eighteenth year of Nebuchadnezzar, but still in the tenth year of Zedekiah. It is well known that Nebuchadnezzar's regnal years began on the first day of Nisan, so that the eighteenth year of Nebuchadnezzar began on April 23, 587, but the dating of the regnal years of the kings of Judah has been disputed, with some arguing for a year beginning in the spring on the first day of Nisan, like those the Babylonian kings, and others arguing that it began in the fall, on the first day of Tishri, the beginning of the Jewish liturgical year. It is clear, however, that the eighteenth year of Nebuchadnezzar, which began on the first day of Nisan 587, could overlap with the tenth year of Zedekiah only if Zedekiah's regnal years began in the fall, in Tishri; otherwise, Zedekiah would be beginning his eleventh year at the same time that Nebuchadnezzar was beginning his eighteenth. The tenth year of Zedekiah and the eighteenth year of Nebuchadnezzar could only co-occur, therefore, between the first of Nisan, or April 23, 587, and the first of Tishri, or October 18, 587, when Zedekiah's eleventh year began. Thus it was during the summer of 587 that Hanamel risked his life to cross the siege lines to visit his cousin Jeremiah, who was imprisoned at the court of the guard. Therefore, both the manumission of the slaves and the transaction between Jeremiah and his cousin Hanamel occurred during the same liturgical year, the tenth year of Zedekiah, between Tishri 588 and Tishri 587—September 29, 588 and October 18, 587. To determine if this was in fact a jubilee year, we must learn if the transaction between Jeremiah and his cousin is indicative of a jubilee year, is simply consistent with it, or, in fact, militates against the hypothesis of a jubilee year in Judah.

The Goal of the Transaction Between Jeremiah and His Cousin

During the lifting of the siege, Jeremiah attempted to go to Anathoth, at which point he was arrested, beaten, imprisoned, and sentenced to death (Jer 37:11–38:28). We conclude that he must have known that he was risking his life to go there, so the question is why he took this risk. According to the Hebrew, "Jeremiah goes out of Jerusalem to go to the land of Benjamin *laḥălīq mīšām* among the people" (Jer 37:12). In Jer 37:12, no object for the verb *laḥălīq* is explicitly mentioned, but since we do not have a context in which spoils of war would accrue to the citizens of Anathoth, "the land as an inheritance" can safely be supplied as the most likely referent. We may conclude, therefore, that Jeremiah attempted to go to Anathoth to participate in an allocation of land in order to receive his share of an inheritance. In fact, since the verb is in the *Hiphil* here, denoting causation, we may infer, more importantly, that Jeremiah went to Anathoth to *arrange* for a redistribution of the land. We also conclude that arranging for this redistribution was important enough for him to risk his life, even though he knew that all the land was shortly to fall into the hands of the Chaldeans.

We know that this event occurred during the tenth year of Zedekiah, while the siege had lifted, and we have hypothesized that this was a jubilee year. If our hypothesis is correct, then this redistribution may not have been an ordinary redistribution, but occasioned by the laws of the jubilee. We hypothesize, therefore, that Jeremiah was going to Anathoth to arrange for the land to be redistributed to its original owners.

A few months later, sometime after April 23, 587, Hanamel visits his cousin Jeremiah in the court of the guard. Because Hanamel visits his cousin so that

Jeremiah will buy his field in Anathoth, we hypothesize that the purpose of the visit is to consummate the transaction that was aborted when Jeremiah was arrested a few months earlier. If it is indeed the jubilee year, then the goal of both Jeremiah's aborted trip to Anathoth and Hanamel's visit to the court of the guard may be the same: to return the land to its original owner, as required by the jubilee laws (Lev 25:10). Now since the original owner of any plot of land would be the owner of fifty years earlier, who may now be deceased, it may be that the land can be returned to only the nearest relative of that owner. If the original owner is not alive, one can assume that the right to receive that land by any individual must be adjudicated in a court of law, or by the proper authorities, for while such a return to the descendent would be automatic in principle, the specificities of the transaction, and the determination of the proper recipient, would have to be approved, certified, and documented in each case.

We hypothesize that such is the case with Jeremiah. Jeremiah is told (by YHWH) that he has "the right of redemption by purchase" (*mišpaṭ haggĕ'ullāh līqnōt*) of Hanamel's field in Anathoth (Jer 32:7). We will examine each of the terms in this phrase in turn. The word *mišpaṭ* most often denotes a legal decision, a legal ordinance, a sentence resulting from a legal trial (Exod 21:1; Deut 1:17). It can also connote the site itself where the legal dispute is adjudicated (Deut 25:1) or the whole case is brought to trial (Num 27:5; Isa 3:13–14). It may also denote the sentence resulting from the adjudication of the legal dispute (Exod 21:31). In every case, however, it has a legal connotation. Thus we may conclude that Jeremiah's "right" had been determined in a court of law. The process of that determination may have been similar to that described in Ruth 4:1–12.

But what is meant by "redemption" (*haggĕ'ullāh*) of land, and can land be redeemed during a jubilee year? The return of land to its original owner during the jubilee year is, indeed, termed a "redemption," for we read in Lev 25:23–24: "The land shall not be sold in perpetuity, because the land is mine, for you are but resident aliens under my authority. In all the land of your possessions you shall grant a redemption [*gĕ'ullāh*] of the land." A redemption of the land, therefore, is mandated for the jubilee year. The redemption process consists of the payment of the superfluity—that is, the difference between the number of years that were paid for and the number of years that were used, because the price of a field is always the number of years until the next jubilee (Lev 25:16). When this superfluity reaches zero, the land simply goes out to the legitimate owner, it is not redeemed.

The fact that redemption always involves a payment of the value of the object redeemed is also stressed in Lev 27. There it states that if a person dedicates an animal to YHWH, it may be redeemed, "but if a redeemer shall redeem it, he shall add a fifth to its valuation" (27:13). This is also true for a house (v. 15). Redemption thus always implies the payment of a sum of money; only if an object had been dedicated to YHWH; then an extra fifth must be paid to redeem it. Redemption, we learn, is simply "buying back." This also applies to fields, which are dedicated to YHWH—if the person wants to redeem a field, one-fifth of its value shall be added to it (27:19).

The text also states that a field is to be valued according to the number of homers of barley that can be sowed on it; an area on which exactly 1 homer of barley can be sowed is valued at 50 shekels of silver (27:16). "And if he dedicates his field from the jubilee year, it shall stand at full valuation [i.e., at 50 shekels]. But if he dedicates his field after the jubilee year, the priest shall compute the silver according to the years remaining to the year of jubilee, and he shall deduct it from its valuation" (27:17–18). During the jubilee year, then, an area of land that can be sown by 1 homer of barley would be valued at 1 shekel throughout the year and presumably would be pro-rated further as the year drew to a close. In fact, the evaluation of the land never reaches precisely zero since it has real value, albeit a diminishing one, throughout the jubilee cycle until the very end of the jubilee year. The first day after the jubilee year ends, the next cycle begins and the field is at full valuation again. Thus we may conclude that all redemption must involve an exchange of money, for a field will always have value, even during the jubilee year. It would presumably reach zero only on the last minute of the last day of that year. Only at that moment, presumably, would it go out to its owner without charge and without a purchase fee, and because this would be unachievable in practice, we may assume that in practice all redemption involves a fee.

The text states who may redeem the land: "After it is sold there may be a redemption for it. One of his kinspeople may redeem it, either an uncle or the son of an uncle may redeem it, or anyone else of his flesh from his own family may redeem it, or if he is able he may redeem it himself" (Lev 25:48–49). Thus if a person is able to redeem the land himself, he would have the first priority, and then his direct descendants; following that, the right of redemption would go to the uncle or the son (or another direct descendant) of the uncle of the original owner. Although not specified, presumably the uncle would be the uncle on the father's side of the original owner, so that the land is retained in the male line. Finally, any family member on the male line could redeem it.

We may now understand the transaction described in Jer 32. Jeremiah is described as having "the right of redemption by purchase." Since in practice *all* redemption is by purchase, perhaps it is more accurately translated as "the right to purchase the redemption." Jeremiah is the *gōʾēl*. Since it is termed a redemption, not an ordinary sale, we conclude that the land is being transferred from a non-rightful owner to a rightful one, from Hanamel to Jeremiah. Jeremiah is redeeming the land, not simply purchasing it, and he does so by paying his cousin the superfluity, the overpayment, which in this case is 17 shekels of silver. We are hypothesizing that this is the jubilee year, so we suppose this payment to cover the six months or less remaining to the close of the year. We must consider if it is possible for Hanamel to be a non-rightful owner, and Jeremiah a rightful one, when Hanamel is the son of Jeremiah's uncle. Each should be the *gōʾēl* for the other. We should realize, however, that if they are cousins through Jeremiah's mother, then they would not be considered to be members of the same family, and thus Hanamel would not be the rightful owner. The fact that buyer and seller are related would then be irrelevant to the transaction; it would be only Jeremiah's relationship to the original owner that is relevant, and we are told that he is the gō'ēl.

It should be recalled, moreover, that Jeremiah's prayer upon purchase of the land (Jer 32:16–25) is a statement of faith that the Israelites who are about to go into exile will, like the land, also be redeemed by their Redeemer. The jubilee year, with its mandated redemption of land, provides an analogy and gives rise to a faith that the people, too, will be redeemed in their turn. Redemption of land in the context of a jubilee year, a mandated year of release, is a far more powerful statement than simply redemption of land to provide a cousin with 17 shekels of silver. YHWH had said that because of the sins of the people they, too, would be released to the sword, to pestilence, and to famine in a perversion of the usual meaning of the term (Jer 24:17). YHWH has sold his people to a non-rightful owner. The regular cycle of jubilee years, and the regular cycle of being sold and redeemed as played out again and again in the book of Judges, yields a faith that the time will come when YHWH will redeem his people again. In his prayer, Jeremiah may be interpreting YHWH's law of the jubilee year virtually as a promise that it will be so.

Thus we see that both Jeremiah and Hanamel risked their lives to ensure that this redemption of the land could take place. The extreme urgency exhibited by both of them suggests that they may have believed it necessary to make the transference before the year ended and to transfer an actual deed from one to the other. It is reasonable to suppose that the land originally had belonged to Jeremiah or, more probably, his father. If Hanamel had purchased the land for the price of a certain number of seasons until the end of the jubilee year, then the 17 shekels of silver paid by Jeremiah may represent the overpayment for the few months remaining until the end of the year (Lev 25:13–16, 26–27). Because both the mass manumission of the slaves—proclaimed in the language of the jubilee—and Jeremiah's redemption of his land occurred during the same year, the tenth year of Zedekiah, it seems plausible that this liturgical year, the year 588/587, was a jubilee year in Judah.

The Jubilee

There is evidence that a jubilee year seems to have been a well-known institution during the exile. The prophet Ezekiel, in stating the laws of the prince (hannāśî'), requires that if the prince makes a gift of his inheritance to his sons, it shall belong to his sons, but if he makes such a gift to one of his servants, it shall belong to the servant only until the year of the release ('ad šĕnat haddĕrōr), at which time it must revert to the family of the nāśî' (Ezek 46:16–17). The purpose of Ezekiel in restating the law is to ensure that the king be prevented from ever again rewarding his retainers with hereditary fiefdoms as a way of building up his own power, as must have occurred before the exile. We see that Ezekiel does not proclaim something new in stating the law of the jubilee; rather, this text implies that the jubilee was an institution well known to his audience.

If we have established at least the plausibility that the liturgical year 588/587 was a jubilee year in Judah, then it may be instructive to examine intervals of fifty years from this date to determine if there is evidence of other jubilee years in Judah. Fifty years after Zedekiah's release of the slaves is the year 538/537, which was the first regnal year of Cyrus as king of Babylon. According to the so-called Nabonidus Chronicle, Cyrus entered Babylon without a struggle in the seventeenth year of Nabonidus, on the third day of Heshvan, or October 29, 539 (Parker and Dubberstein 1956), and would have begun his first regnal year as king of Babylon on the first day of Nisan, or March 24, 538. Shortly after his accession, he issued an edict ordering the return of captive peoples, an edict recorded in the Cyrus Cylinder (*ANET*[3] 315–16). This edict does not mention the Jews. The MT records two additional edicts of Cyrus, however, and they do pertain specifically to the return of the Judeans, one in Hebrew (Ezra 1:2–4) and the other in Aramaic (Ezra 6:3–5), both dated to the first year of Cyrus as king of Babylon (538/537). The Aramaic document evidently had been stored in Ecbatana (Hagmatana) (Ezra 6:1, 2), the summer palace of the Persian kings, so we may reasonably suppose that it was issued in the summer of 538, the summer of Cyrus's first regnal year. That autumn, then, would have marked the beginning of the Jewish liturgical year 538/537, and would be exactly fifty years after the date we posit for Zedekiah's mass manumission of the slaves. Coincidentally, we read in Isa 61:1–2a that "the spirit of my lord, YHWH, is upon me, because YHWH has anointed me. He sent me . . . to proclaim liberty to captives [*lĕqrō' deror*]." The prophet is using the language of the jubilee year. Perhaps in this oracle, Isaiah is speaking for Cyrus, the only non-Jew ever to be surnamed "anointed" (Isa 45:1–4), and announces the miraculous confluence of the jubilee year and the release of captive Jews to their own land, both of these events commencing in the fall of 538.

If we admit the plausibility of the hypothesis that the Jews took note of a jubilee year in 588/587, and again in 538/537, we may reasonably ask how far back the institution went in the history of Judah. One hundred years before Zedekiah's mass manumission of slaves was 688/687. If we are correct, this year would also have been a jubilee year. To discover whether the jubilee actually took place we need to know who was king in Judah at the time.

Unfortunately, the dating of the reigns of the Judean kings in this period is disputed. According to one method of dating, this two-year fallow period would have occurred during the reign of Hezekiah, whereas according to a second method of dating, it would have occurred during the reign of his son Manasseh. Is it possible to distinguish between these two alternatives? Surprisingly, we find the following words of Isaiah to Hezekiah on learning that Sennacherib is threatening to attack Judah and Jerusalem: "And this for you will be the sign, eat this year the aftergrowth [*sāpîaḥ*], and in the second year that which comes up by itself [*sāḥîš*], and in the third year plant and harvest, and plant vineyards and eat their fruit" (2 Kgs 19:29 [= Isa 37:30]). Thus "this year" there was to be no planting and no harvesting, and the following year there was to be no planting or harvesting; only in the third year would planting and harvesting be permitted. We read here a clear notice of two fallow years in a row during the reign of Hezekiah. In fact, this is one of only four passages in the Bible where this specific word *sāpîaḥ* occurs (cf. Lev 25:5, 11; Job 14:19). Coincidentally, "this year," the first of the two fallow years, the year we posit to be 689/688, is the very year that has long been suggested independently as the beginning of a second campaign by Sennacherib against Judah, the first having been in 701. This may be independent support for the late dating of the reign of Hezekiah and for the second-campaign theory as well as an indication that the agricultural component of the jubilee year—a second fallow year—goes back at least to the age of Hezekiah.

Parenthetically, this statement of Isaiah provides some information on the nature of the calendar that he has in mind. Isaiah states that "in the third year plant and harvest, and plant vineyards and eat their fruit" so he is referring to a year that begins with planting, which is followed by harvesting, by planting vineyards, and, finally, by harvesting the vineyards and eating the fruit. In a detailed examination of agricultural practices in Iron Age Israel, Borowski (1987) has shown that the agricultural year began in the fall with planting wheat and barley in November and December, followed by harvesting these grains in April and May, and, finally, by harvesting grapes and other fruit from June through September. Thus Isaiah clearly has in mind a year beginning and ending in the autumn.

Moreover, it seems that Isaiah is making his speech before the time of the spring harvest of that first fallow year and after an autumn when there had been no planting, for he states that they will have only the aftergrowth to eat—that there will be no spring harvest this year. Thus he seems to have made his speech between December and April, and, coincidentally, these are the months in which Sennacherib's second campaign against Judah was most likely to have occurred. In a comprehensive study of Sennacherib's campaigns on his southern front, Levine (1985) concludes that Babylon fell to Sennacherib on the first day of Kislev 689, or early December of that year, and he would have been free to march on Judah any time after that. Indeed, early 688 is the exact period proposed independently by those who advocate the theory of a second campaign. It seems, moreover, that a two-year fallow period in Judah would have been the most auspicious time for a military campaign against it.

An additional question is whether the institution of the jubilee was recognized in postexilic times. Was Nehemiah reacting to the jubilee year, for example? We read that during the time of Nehemiah, there was a great outcry among the people, for they had mortgaged their fields, vineyards, and houses and had sold their sons and daughters into slavery in order to have money to pay the royal tax and buy food (Neh 5:1–5). Nehemiah responds by ordering the wealthy nobles and priests of Jerusalem to return to the impoverished peasants their small landholdings, their fields, their vineyards, their olive groves, their houses, as well as the interest on the silver, grain, new wine, and new oil that they had lent them (Neh 5:11). Thus we read here of a simultaneous remission of debts and return of land to these small landholders, so we would like to know if this was in response to the sabbatical or jubilee year. A universal remission of debts is mandated every seventh year in the laws of the sabbatical year, or *šĕmīṭṭāh*, as specified in Deut 15:1–12. The universal release of slaves and the release of landholders to their land, however, is mandated only by the laws of the jubilee (Lev 25:8–13, 39–41). The end of the šĕmĭṭṭāh year and the beginning of the jubilee year that followed would be the expected time for the pronouncement of Nehemiah, if, indeed, he were responding to both these sets of laws in a single declaration. It is of interest, then, to determine the date of Nehemiah's release of land and slaves.

According to Nehemiah's memoirs, in the twentieth year of the reign of Artaxerxes, Nehemiah appealed to the Persian king for permission to go to Jerusalem to rebuild the fortress, the walls of the city, and his own house, and it was granted him (Neh 2:1–8). We also know that Nehemiah served in Jerusalem as governor for twelve years—that is, until the thirty-second year of the reign of Artaxerxes—and that it was during this twelve-year period that the wall was built and the debts were remitted (Neh 5:14; 13:16). Since the publication of the Elephantine papyri it has been well accepted that the king in question is Artaxerxes I (*AramP.* 30). Thus Nehemiah was in Jerusalem from 445 to the beginning months of 432, a period that included the jubilee year of 438/437 and two sabbatical years: 446/445 and 439/438. The edicts of Nehemiah are consonant with the laws of the two-year period of the sabbatical and jubilee years, rather than the sabbatical alone, so that we would predict a priori that it would be during this period that the edicts were announced.

We do not know the precise date of the pronouncement, but its placement in the book of Nehemiah suggests that the outcry occurred at some point during the period when the wall was being built. According to the text, the wall was finished in fifty-two days, on the twenty-fifth day of Elul, a few days before the beginning of the month of Tishri, the beginning of the Jewish liturgical year (Neh 6:15). If this was during the twentieth year of the reign of Artaxerxes, as the text suggests, then the wall would have been completed four days before the end of the sabbatical year of 546/545. The edict canceling debts could have occurred shortly thereafter, right before the sabbatical year ended. This analysis would be consistent with the literal rendering of Deut 15:1, mīqēṣ šebaʿ šānîm, at the end of *seven* years. Indeed, Wellhausen (1963 [1885]:117), interestingly enough, suggests that release of debts "does not embrace the whole seventh year, it does not come at the end of six years as in Exodus, but at the end of seven; the surrender of the harvest demands the whole year, the remission of debts, comparatively speaking, only a moment." Thus Nehemiah's edict could have been a response to the sabbatical year, rather than to the jubilee year, but as we have pointed out, the sabbatical year does not mandate a release of slaves or a return of landholders to their land. These acts are in conformity with the laws of the jubilee, so the end of the sabbatical year and the beginning of the jubilee year that follows it would have been the most likely time for these edicts.

Interestingly, according to Josephus (*Ant.* 11.5, 7, 8), Nehemiah did not arrive until the twenty-fifth year of the king's reign, and the walls took two years and four months to build, being completed in the twenty-eighth year of the king's reign, in the ninth month. Josephus gives the king's name as Xerxes, rather than Artaxerxes, however, but Myers (1965: 92) suggests that this may be because he is reserving Artaxerxes for the time of Esther. It could not have been Xerxes, in any case, since Xerxes reigned for only twenty-one years. According to the reckoning of Josephus (and assuming Artaxerxes I), Nehemiah would have begun the wall in the month of Ab, August 439, and completed it in the month of Kislev, early January 436. This includes precisely the two-year period of a sabbatical year followed by a jubilee year, starting two months before the beginning of the sabbatical year and finishing two months after the end of the jubilee year. It is reasonable to suppose that Nehemiah would have wanted to provide work for people at a time when they could no longer find sustenance on their land. It is also reasonable that dire straits would arise if the royal tax was due in this period of two fallow years in a row. The difficulty is that we are given two entirely different dates for the building of the wall, one from the text of Nehemiah's memoirs and one from Josephus, and no date at all for the promulgation of the edict of release. The dating of Josephus seems a credible time for the building of the wall, however, and the promulgation of the edict would then have occurred in the middle of the wall building, toward the close of the sabbatical year and the beginning of the jubilee.

It is interesting to note that, according to Nehemiah's memoirs, rebuilding the wall took fifty-two days, finishing on the twenty-fifth day of Elul. Fifty-two days is almost two months on the Hebrew calendar, and, indeed, if five more days were added to the fifty-two, the wall would have been finished, according to Nehemiah, on the thirtieth day of Elul, or the last day of the liturgical year. Thus both Nehemiah and Josephus begin the building of the wall at the same time, two months before the start of the Jewish liturgical year—the late-summer months of Ab and Elul. Furthermore, according to Nehemiah it would have been the last two months of the sabbatical year, whereas according to Josephus these would have been the two months before the start of a sabbatical year—for Nehemiah, an ordinary sabbatical year; for Josephus, the sabbatical year prior to a jubilee year. One might wonder if workers can be pulled from the land during the two summer months before a two-year fallow period. In an ordinary year, this would be the time for harvesting of the fruit of the vine and the tree: grapes, figs, pomegranates, and olives (Borowski 1987: 37). The grain would have been harvested by late May, and there would have been time to plow it under and leave the suggested leguminous ground cover, which also would have been harvested by then. It is only the harvest of the fruit of the vine and the tree that they would be missing, and it may be that before the sabbatical year the fruit was not harvested, but left on the branches to be gathered at will.

In conclusion, we have seen that in 588, Zedekiah used the language of the jubilee (līqrō' děrôr) to proclaim a mass manumission of the slaves, Jeremiah and Hanamel risked their lives to ensure that Jeremiah could redeem his ancestral lands. That both these acts occurred during the same year, the tenth year of the reign of Zedekiah, the year 588/587, permits us to suggest that this was a jubilee year in Judah. Exactly fifty years later, 538/537, was the first year of the reign of Cyrus as king of Babylon and the time of his edict giving permission for the Jews to return to their homeland. We have suggested that it may have been this remarkable confluence of the jubilee year and the release of captive Jews that prompted Deutero-Isaiah to use the language of the jubilee (*līqrō' děrôr*) in his oracle on the return of captives (61:1–2a). Moreover, we see that during the reign of Hezekiah, there was a period of two fallow years in a row at the time when Sennacherib was campaigning against Judah. We suggest that this occurred exactly 101 and 100 years before the mass manumission of the slaves, beginning in the sabbatical year of 689/688, the year many suppose to be the time of Sennacherib's second military campaign against Judah. Finally, we see that Nehemiah issued an edict promulgating the release of slaves, debts, and peasants to their landholdings at a time that may have been, if we accept the dating of Josephus, during the two-year period of 439 to 437, the sabbatical and jubilee years, respectively. This series of events, occurring, as it does, at precise fifty-year intervals, provides support for the hypothesis that the jubilee year and the sabbatical year that preceded it were historic institutions in biblical Judah.

Table of Major Dates

FROM	TO			EVENT
HEZEKIAH				
Tishri 715–	Elul 714			First regnal year of Hezekiah
Tishri 702–	Elul 701			Fourteenth year of Hezekiah: Sennacherib attacks Judah after Nisan 701
Tishri 689–	Elul 688			Sabbatical year
Kislev 689–	Nisan 688			Sennacherib attacks Judah in a second campaign
Tishri 688–	Elul 687			Jubilee year in Judah
ZEDEKIAH				
Adar 2, March 16	597			Nebuchadnezzar captures Jerusalem; Jehoiakin taken captive
Nisan 1, April 13,	597			Beginning of the Babylonian Exile; accession of Zedekiah to the throne
Tishri 1, October 9,	597			First regnal year of Zedekiah
Tishri 1, October 10,	589	Elul 29, September 28,	} 588	Sabbatical year
Tebeth 10, January 15,	588			Final siege of Jerusalem by Nebuchadnezzar
Tishri 1, September 29	588	Elul 29, October 17,	} 587	Jubilee year; tenth regnal year of Zedekiah
Elul 12, September 10,	588			The army of Pharaoh Hophra leaves Egypt to help defend Jerusalem

FROM	TO			EVENT
Tishri 10, October 8,	588			General manumission of the slaves on Yom Kippur
Tebeth 7, December 29,	588			The siege is lifted
I Adar 1, February 24,	587			The siege is resumed
Tebeth 7, December 29,	588	I Adar 1, February 24,	} 587	Slaves are recaptured; Jeremiah attempts to go to Anatoth
Nisan 1, April 23,	587	Elul 29, October 17,	} 587	Jeremiah is visited by his cousin Hanamel
Ab 7, August 14,	586			Jerusalem captured; Temple destroyed
CYRUS				
Heshvan 8, October 29,	539			Cyrus enters Babylon without a struggle
Nisan 1, March 24,	538			Cyrus becomes king of Babylon; first regnal year begins
Nisan 1, March 24,	538	Elul 29, September 16,	} 538	Edict of Cyrus
Tishri 1, September 17,	538			Jubilee year begins; return of captive Jews to Judea
NEHEMIAH				
Tishri 1, September 20,	446	Elul 30, October 7,	} 445	Sabbatical year in Judah (leap year, with II Adar)
Ab 3, August 11,	445	Elul 25, October 2,	} 445	The time of the building of the wall according to the memoirs of Nehemiah
Ab 1, August 15,	439	Kislev 30, January 5,	} 436	The time of the building of the wall according to Josephus
Tishri 1, October 2,	439	Elul 29, September 20,	} 438	Sabbatical year in Judah
Tishri 1, September 21,	438	Elul 30 October 8,	} 437	Jubilee year in Judah (leap year, with II Adar)

G. Jubilee: A Rallying Cry for Today's Oppressed

I was invited to participate in a "Jewish–Christian Symposium on the Jubilee," sponsored by the World Council of Churches at the Ecumenical Institute, Bossey, Switzerland, May 19–23, 1996. Present were thirty-two representatives from fifteen countries, including India, Uganda, Brazil, the Philippines, and Indonesia. I single out the Third World nations because, first, I was able to feel, even vicariously, their people's pain and suffering, and, second, I was witness to a vivid demonstration that their hopes for remedial action are expressed by the biblical jubilee.

The jubilee has become the rallying cry for oppressed peoples today, as was the exodus theme for their counterparts in previous decades. This time, however, they are not enslaved politically (except where colonial rulers have been replaced by their own), but shackled economically. The global market economy has generated unprecedented growth and prosperity, but not for them. The fact is that 20 percent of the world's people possess 83 percent of the wealth (*UN Human Development Report*, 1993, 37). Moreover, "three quarters of adjusting countries in Sub-Sahara Africa have suffered declining per capita incomes and in Latin America the declines were at least as bad" (*Development Report*, 45).

The impoverishment of the Third World has brought attendant injustices. Relevant to the jubilee (and sabbatical) theme is the issue of global pollution, especially in the developing nations. The depletion of the rain forests in the interest of the timber and mining industries, for example, has caused irremedial losses to Costa Rica. Although it, singularly among Latin American countries, experienced significant economic growth between 1970 and 1990, the concomitant environmental decay of its soils and forests produced the loss of natural capital totaling 6 percent of the gross domestic product of that period; in Indonesia, the loss was 9 percent (*Development Report*, 30).

As a result, the debtor world has issued the following demands to the creditor nations (which operate through the International Monetary Fund and similar agencies): (1) cancellation of their debts; (2) restitution of land and resources to their original owners; (3) cessation from pilfering natural resources and polluting them (one symposium paper cited Gen 2:15b: God leased us the earth "to fill it and tend it," but not to despoil it); and (4) termination of economic slavery (e.g., the atrocious case in *democratic* India, cited in INTRODUCTION to vv. 39–55) by universally raising wages to a subsistence level.

The jubilee prescribing remission of debts, restoration of land, sabbath rest for land and people, and release from economic servitude corresponds to all four demands. Obviously, their implementation would be met by large-scale resistance. Some demands would have to be modified. For example, as one symposium paper pointedly asked: Wouldn't the simultaneous remission of all debts inhibit creditors from lending at all (shades of R. Hillel's Prosbul; see NOTE on "each of you shall return to his kin group" v. 10)? Yet evidence can be adduced that countries employing some of the jubilee provisions have experienced spectacular economic growth rather than precipitous decline. For example, in just the two years from 1952 to 1954, the percent of South Korean farmers who owned their land instead of working as tenants jumped from 50 to 94 percent. Something similar happened in Taiwan, another "Asian Tiger." Thus the jubilee laws, mutatis mutandis, offer a realistic blueprint for bridging the economic gap between the have and have-not nations, which otherwise portends political uprisings that can engulf the entire world.

In May 1996, in Bossey, Switzerland, I witnessed the unfurling of the flag of the jubilee.

26. BLESSINGS, CURSES, AND THE RECALL OF THE COVENANT

TRANSLATION

The Essence of God's Commandments

¹You shall not make idols for yourselves, and a carved image or pillar you shall not set up for yourselves, and a figured pavement you shall not place in your land to worship upon it, for I YHWH am your God. ²You shall keep my sabbaths and venerate my sanctuary: I YHWH (have spoken).*

The Blessings

³If you follow my laws and keep my commandments and observe them, ⁴I will grant you rains in their season, so that the earth will yield its produce, and the trees of the field will yield their fruit. ⁵Your threshing shall overtake the vintage, and the vintage will overtake the sowing; you shall eat your fill of food and dwell securely in your land.

⁶I will grant peace in the land, so that you shall lie down, and no one shall make you afraid; I will eliminate vicious beasts from the land, and no sword shall traverse your land. ⁷You shall give chase to your enemies, and they shall fall before you by the sword. ⁸Five of you shall give chase to a hundred, and a hundred of you shall give chase to ten thousand; your enemies shall fall before you by the sword.

⁹I will look with favor upon you, and make you fruitful and multiply you; and I will uphold my covenant with you. ¹⁰You shall eat old grain long stored, and you shall have to clear out the old to make room for the new. ¹¹I will establish my presence in your midst, and I will not expel you. ¹²I will walk about in your midst: I will (*continue to*) be your God, and you shall be my people. ¹³I YHWH am your God who freed you from the land of Egypt from being their slaves; I broke the bars of your yoke and made you walk erect.

The Curses

¹⁴But if you do not obey me and do not observe all these commandments, ¹⁵if you despise my laws and loathe my rules, so that you do not observe all my commandments, thereby breaking my covenant, ¹⁶I in turn will do this to you: I will bring panic upon you—consumption and fever wearing out the eyes and drying out the throat; you shall sow your seed to no purpose, for your enemies shall eat it. ¹⁷I will set my face against you: you shall be routed by your enemies, and your foes shall dominate you. You shall flee though nobody pursues you.

---

*Boldface block type (vv. 1–2, 33b–35, and 43–45) stands for H_R. For details see NOTES E.

¹⁸And if, for all of that, you do not obey me, I will go on to discipline you sevenfold for your sins, ¹⁹and I will break your proud strength. I will make your skies like iron and your earth like copper, ²⁰so that your strength shall be spent to no purpose. Your land shall not yield its produce, nor shall the trees of your land yield their fruit.

²¹And if you continue in opposition to me and refuse to obey me, I will go on smiting you sevenfold in measure for your sins. ²²I will let loose wild beasts against you, and they shall bereave you of your children and wipe out your cattle. They shall make you few (in number), and your roads shall be deserted.

²³And if, in spite of these (things), you are not disciplined for me, and you continue in opposition to me, ²⁴I too will continue in opposition to you: Yes, I myself will smite you sevenfold for your sins. ²⁵I will bring a sword against you, executing vengeance for the covenant; and if you withdraw into your cities, I will send pestilence among you, and you shall be delivered into enemy hands. ²⁶When I break your staff of bread, ten women shall bake your bread in a single oven; they shall dole out your bread by weight, and though you eat, you shall not be satisfied.

²⁷But if, despite this, you disobey me and continue in opposition to me, ²⁸I will continue in wrathful opposition to you; Yes, I myself will discipline you sevenfold for your sins. ²⁹You shall eat the flesh of your sons, and the flesh of your daughters you shall eat. ³⁰I will destroy your cult places and cut down your incense stands, and I will heap your carcasses upon your lifeless fetishes.

I will expel you. ³¹I will lay your cities in ruin and make your sanctuaries desolate, and I will not smell your pleasant odors. ³²I myself will make your land desolate, so that your enemies who settle in it shall be appalled by it. ³³You, however, I will scatter among the nations, and I will unsheath the sword after you.

When your land will be a desolation and your cities a ruin, ³⁴then the land shall be paid its sabbath years throughout the time that it is desolate. When you are in the land of your enemies, then the land shall rest and pay off its sabbath years. ³⁵Throughout the time it is desolate, it shall have the rest it did not have on your sabbaths when you were living on it.

³⁶As for those of you who survive, I will bring faintness in their hearts in the land of their enemies. The sound of a driven leaf will put them to flight. They shall flee as though from the sword, and they shall fall though nobody is pursuing. ³⁷They shall stumble over one another, as if (to escape) a sword, though pursuing is nobody. You shall not be able to stand (your ground) before your enemies. ³⁸You shall be lost among the nations, and the land of your enemies shall devour you. ³⁹And those of you who survive shall rot because of their iniquities in the land of your enemies; also they shall rot because of the iniquities of their ancestors (adhering) to them.

Remorse and the Recall of the Covenant

⁴⁰But if they confess their iniquity and the iniquity of their ancestors, in that they committed sacrilege against me and, moreover, that they continued in op-

position to me—[41]so that I, in turn, had to continue in opposition to them and disperse them in the land of their enemies—if, then, their uncircumcised heart is humbled and they accept their punishment in full, [42]then I will remember my covenant with Jacob; also my covenant with Isaac and also my covenant with Abraham I will remember, namely, I will remember the land. **[43]For the land shall be deserted by them that it may be paid its sabbath years by being desolate without them, as they accept their punishment in full for the very reason that my rules they spurned and my laws they loathed. [44]Yet, for all that, while they are in the land of their enemies I have not spurned them or loathed them so as to destroy them, annulling my covenant with them: for I YHWH am their God.** [45]But I will remember in their favor the covenant with the ancients whom I freed from the land of Egypt in the sight of the nations to be their God: I YHWH (have spoken).

Summation

[46]These are the laws, rules, and the rituals that YHWH established between himself and the Israelites on Mount Sinai through Moses.

Comments

The nature of the covenants, COMMENT A; the linguistic relationship of chap. 26 to Deuteronomy and Ezekiel, COMMENTS B and C; the linguistic relationship of the rest of H to the other pentateuchal sources and Ezekiel, COMMENT D; and the date of Lev 26, COMMENT E.

NOTES

In the INTRODUCTION to chap. 25, it was argued that chaps. 25 and 26 form a continuous unit because:

1. Chap. 26 lacks the preface "YHWH spoke to Moses," found in the previous chapters.
2. They are enveloped by the inclusio (unique in Leviticus): *běhar sinay* (25:1; 26:46).
3. The deliverance from Egypt is a refrain running through both chapters (25:38, 42, 55; 26:13, 45).
4. Both chapters (uniquely in Leviticus) refer to the sabbatical year (25:1–7; 26:34–35, 43a).
5. Together they have a single theme: Israel's violation of YHWH's commandments, especially of the sabbatical, leads inexorably to its exile.

A sixth unifying factor, a countervailing positive one, can now be discerned: the concept of redemption. Israel is granted the power to redeem its land and those brethren enslaved to non-Israelites (chap. 25). And if it demonstrates contrition for its sinful past, YHWH will redeem it from exile (26:39–45). The theme of redemption is also carried forward into chap. 27 (see its INTRODUCTION).

Vv. 1–2 The Essence of God's Commandments

According to the Masoretes' parashiot division, these verses conclude chap. 25. Abetting their decision is the fact that these verses, ostensibly a new subject, do not begin with the expected introductory formula: "YHWH spoke to Moses, saying: Speak to the Israelites saying" (cf. 25:1; 27:1). The assignment of these verses to chap. 25 is in keeping with an interpretation taken by the rabbis:

> Said R. Yose bar Hanina: Come and see how severe are the consequences of (violating the provisions of) the sabbatical year. How so? If a man does work on the produce of the sabbatical year, he begins to sell his movables, as it is said, "When you sell property to your neighbor" (25:14). If he disregards this (bad omen) he begins to sell off his estate, as it is said, "when your brother becomes impoverished and has to seel part of his holding" (25:25). It (the proceeds) scarcely reaches his domain before he has sold his house, as it is said, "If a man sells a dwelling house in a walled city" (25:29). It scarcely reaches his domain, before he has sold his daughter, as it is said, "when a man sells his daughter as a slave" (Exod 21:7). It scarcely reaches his domain, before he has borrowed in interest, as it is said, "If your brother being (further) impoverished, falls under your authority. . . . Do not exact from him advance or accrued interest" (25:35–36). It scarcely reaches his domain, before he has sold himself, as it is said, "If your brother, being (further) impoverished, must sell himself" (25:39). And not to you, but to a proselyte, as it is said, "and sells himself to the *gēr*" (25:47). And not to a righteous proselyte but to a resident alien, as it is said, "and sells himself to a *gēr tôšāb*" (v. 47). Even to an idolater, as it is said, "or to a branch of the alien's kin group" (v. 47)—he becomes an acolyte in the service of idolatry (26:1). (t. *'Arak.* 5:9, cf. *b. Qidd.* 20a)

The gradations of impoverishment recorded in 25:25–55 are extended by the rabbis into chap. 26 so that apostasy (and ultimately exile, 26:33) becomes the end result of a process of economic deterioration initiated by violating the sabbatical prohibitions (25:1–7). Although, as shown, there are cogent reasons for regarding chaps. 25–26 as a unified bloc, the most likely function and purpose of 26:1–2 can be elucidated when viewed from a totally different perspective.

First, it should be noted that these two verses consist of five commands, three negative and two positive separated by the Deity's self-declaration formula (v. 2b). Then, when these commands are compared with corresponding ones in chap. 19, they will adumbrate some of the commands in the Decalogue (table 5).

A mere glance at table 5 suffices to realize that 26:1–2, though using typical H formulae (e.g., "idols," 1aα; "keep my sabbaths," 2a; cf. 19:4aα, 3aβ), is rephrasing the introduction and first, second, and fourth commands of the Deca-

TABLE 5

	EXOD 20	LEV 26	LEV 19
	'ānōkî YHWH 'ĕlōhêkā . . . (v. 2)	*'ănî YHWH 'ĕlōhēkem* (v. 1b; 25:55b)	*'ănî YHWH 'ĕlōhêkem* (v. 3b)
[1]	*lō'-yihyeh lĕkā 'ĕlōhîm 'ăhērîm* (v. 3)	*lō-ta'ăśû lākem 'ĕlîlîm* (v. 1aα)	*'al-tipnû 'el-hā 'ĕlîlîm* (v. 4aα)
[2]	*lō' ta'ăśeh lĕkā pesel wĕkol-tĕmûnâ . . . lō'-tišahăweh lāhem wĕlō' to'obdĕm* (vv. 4–5a)	*ûpesel ûmaṣṣbâ lō'-tāqîmû lākem wĕ'eben maśkit lō'titĕnû bĕ'arṣĕkem lĕhištahăwōt 'ālêhā* (v. 1aβγ)	*wĕ'lōhê massēkâ lō' ta'ăśû lākem* (v. 4aβ)
[3]	*lō' tiśśā' 'et-šēm YHWH 'ĕlōhêkā laššāw'* (v. 7a)		*wĕlō'-tiššābĕ'û bišĕmî laššeqer* (v. 12a)
[4]	*zākôr 'et-yŏm haššabbāt lĕqaddĕšô* (v. 8)	*'et-šabbĕtōtay tišmōrû ûmiqdāšî tîrā'û* (v. 2a)	*wĕ'et-šabbĕtōtay tišmōrû* (vv. 3aβ, 30a)
[5]	*kabbēd 'et-'ābîkā wĕ'et-'immekā* (v. 12a)		*îš 'immō wĕ'ābîw tîrā'û* (v. 3a)
	I YHWH am your God . . . (v. 2)	I YHWH am your God (v. 1b; 25:55b)	I YHWH am your God (v. 3b)
[1]	You shall have no other gods beside me (v. 3)	You shall not make idols for yourselves (v. 1aα)	Do not turn to idols (v. 4aα)
[2]	You shall not make for yourself a sculptured image, or any likeness. Do not bow to them or serve them (vv. 4–5a)	or set up for yourselves carved images or pillars, or place figured pavement in your land to worship upon it (v. 1aβ)	or make molten gods for yourselves (v. 4aβ)
[3]	You shall not swear falsely by the name of YHWH . . . (v. 7a)		You shall not swear falsely by my name (v. 12a)
[4]	Remember the sabbath day and keep it holy (v. 8)	You shall keep my sabbaths and venerate my sanctuary (v. 2a)	and keep my sabbaths (v. 3aβ, 30a)
[5]	Honor your father and mother (v. 12a)		You shall each revere his mother and his father (v. 3aα)

logue. One exegetical advantage of this synoptic table is that light will be thrown on the meaning of the abstruse terms *'eben maskît* (see NOTE on "a figured pavement," v. 1aγ). Here, it need only be stated that the purpose and function of these verses are unveiled. They are, in the mind of the author/redactor, a pithy summary of God's commandments given heretofore in H's laws (chaps. 17–25), which are reflected in the Decalogue and its elaboration in chap. 19 (see INTRODUCTION to chap. 19). Thus these verses may be an incipit of all the ritual and *ethical* injunctions contained in chap. 19, implying that YHWH's blessings

and curses that follow (vv. 3–45) are invoked on Israel for its obedience or disobedience of all of God's commands.

That this priestly legist has in mind this entire law corpus can be demonstrated by pointing to Nehemiah's pact (*'ămānâ*), which also, in its specific regulations (Neh 10:31–40), virtually covers the same ground as 26:1–2: intermarriage (v. 31, the classic coefficient of idolatry; cf. Exod 34:15–17; Deut 7:3–5),
the weekly and septennial sabbath (v. 32), and the duties to the sanctuary (vv.
33–40; cf. Witman 1987: 20).

The tabular comparison also discloses a major question: Why are only three
commandments of the Decalogue singled out? One can readily understand the
omission of the Decalogue's second half on the grounds that the priestly legist
may be for some reason (explicated below) deleting the duties to one's fellow
(i.e., ethics). But why are the third and fifth commandments, duties between
man and God (regarding parents; see NOTE on "You shall each revere his father
and his mother," v. 19:3), also omitted? Indeed, not only is commandment 5
(parents) in chap. 19 (v. 3a), but commandment 3 (false oath) is accounted for—
further down in the chapter, v. 12a (see its NOTE).

My student M. Hildenbrand observed (followed by Joosten 1998: 160) that
vv. 1–2 form an inclusio with vv. 44–45, the closing verses of chap. 26. The first
verse in each set begins with the long formula of YHWH's self-presentation *'ănî
YHWH 'ĕlōhêkem* preceded by the particle *kî*, and the second verse ends with
the short formula *'ănî YHWH*. This combination of the formulas is not strange
to H. It occurs at the conclusion of the opening exhortation in chap. 18 (vv.
4–5) and at the end of chap. 19 (vv. 31–32, 36–37). The latter is helpful in un-
packing the formation of chap. 19. As argued in the INTRODUCTION to chap. 19,
vv. 31–32 formed the original ending to chap. 19, and when vv. 33–37 were
added they, too, were given this structure. Thus it can be seen that the combination of long and short formulas is a stylistic mark signifying the end of a unit.

Since vv. 1–2 are assigned to exilic H_R (see below), the same verdict must be
rendered for vv. 44–45. Moreover, just as vv. 1–2 emphasize the sabbath, so does
the verse that precedes vv. 44–45, thereby demonstrating that chap. 26 begins
and ends (vv. 1–2, 43–45) with a reference to the sabbath, both of which are the
product of exilic H_R (see their NOTES). Thus the structure of chap. 26 resembles that of chap. 23, which also closes and ends with additions by H_R (see NOTES
on vv. 1–3, 34–43). The question, however, still remains: Why did H_R select
commandments 1, 2, and 4 and omit commandments 3 and 5?

As perceptively seen by Kochman (1987), commandments 3 and 5 relate to
individual behavior, whereas commandments 1, 2, and 4 relate to the state of
the nation—that is, those factors that in the opinion of H determine the destiny
of Israel in its land. Thus 26:1–2 forms a transitional unit that functions as both
summary and prolepsis: a capsule containing the essence of God's commandments, which are determinative for the survival or destruction of Israel's national
existence, the subject of the following verses, 26:3–46. It also serves as a prolepsis of the notion of covenant, a leitmotif in the entire chapter (vv. 9, 15, 25,
42–45).

One of the many lasting contributions of Kaufmann is his distinction between the prophetic indictments of the eighth and seventh centuries (1947: 3.8–10, 70–79, 369–92; 1960: 365–67, 401–2, 417–20), namely, that social injustices, stressed in the former, are missing in the latter. Rather, the seventh-century prophets, notably Jeremiah and Ezekiel, in concordance with the deuteronomistic edition of the book of Kings, point their accusing finger at idolatry (see Introduction II D) as the cause of Israel's national destruction. It is, therefore, of no small significance that idolatry, specified in three of its forms—carved images, pillars, and figured pavements—stands at the head of this triad of commands that constitutes the essence of the divine will for Israel (see further below).

The other two commands (v. 2) are a verbatim quotation of 19:30 (its significance will be explained below). It will suffice here to indicate that only in the prophecies of the seventh century and thereafter does the sabbath become a national factor (e.g., Jer 17:27; for the likely preexilic date of Jer 17:19–27, see Greenberg 1971b). In Ezekiel, it achieves an importance equivalent to that of the rest of the commandments (e.g., Ezek 20:13, 21), alongside idolatry (Ezek 20:16, 24) and, in one verse (23:38), it is conjoined with the sanctuary, just as in 26:2. The projection of the sabbath into singular importance in the exile is also attested in Isa 56:2, 4, 6; 58:13; Neh 13:18 (see Introduction I F, and NOTE on 23:1–3). In all the instances cited above, the sabbath is the weekly sabbath. In our verse, however, one can hardly escape the suspicion that the septennial sabbath is also intended, or at least adumbrated (note its inclusion in Nehemiah's pledge, Neh 10:32). In any case, the placement here of the weekly sabbath is significant. It indicates proleptically that the sabbath, the neglect of which is the cause of Israel's national destruction and exile (26:34–35, 43), is not limited to the septennate, but must include the weekly sabbath.

The continuation of Israel on its land is predicated on its fulfillment of all of God's commandments (vv. 3, 14, 15, 43). However, as will be argued in the IN-TRODUCTION to vv. 43–44 (and in COMMENT E), an exilic interpolator (called H_R in my discussion of Lev 23) consoled his people in regard to the delay in redemption by pointing to the requirement that the land first make up its neglected sabbaticals. The provenance of vv. 1–2 is also to be found in the exile (see below). That is, after the rest of the chapter had attained its present (Masoretic) form, an H tradent (perhaps the same H_R) did not want to limit Israel's sabbath neglect to the septennate. He therefore added the neglected weekly sabbaths to the extent of Israel's required exile. Thereby, however, the original calculation of the exilic period turned completely askew. A simple calculation indicates that Israel's exile would have to last nearly twice as long: there are 364 sabbaths, an entire year of sabbaths, in a septennial cycle (52 sabbaths in a year, and 7 times that many, or 364 in 7 years). To use round figures, if Israel as a people had existed for 630 years (1216–586 B.C.E.), 90 years of sabbaths would have elapsed—nearly twice the 50 years of Israel's actual exile.

Thus this H legist sums up in a condensed form the divine laws determinative for Israel's continuous presence on its land by selecting three commandments of the Decalogue: the worship of one God, but not with images, and the observance of the sabbath. He adds reverence for the sanctuary as a generic encompassing all the duties incumbent on the Israelites for the maintenance of the (now suspended) cult. Since he is interested in only those national factors that decide Israel's destiny, he cites 19:30 as his proof text for the sabbath (instead of 19:3) because it contains an additional national factor: reverence for the sanctuary (i.e., the cult).

It can now readily be seen that the author of these two verses is not the same as the one who composed chaps. 18 and 20, which expressly specify sexual violations as factors leading to exile (18:24–30; 20:22). That we may be viewing the work of the H School at the end of the monarchy or during the exile is supported by a number of facts:

1. The stress on idolatry as the main cause of Israel's exile is a feature of the deuteronomic historian.
2. The term *maśkît* in a cultic context is found in only Num 33:52 and Ezek 8:12a (cf. v. 10). That Num 33:50–56 stems from H, see the Introduction I E. That it is an editorial insert by Hr and, hence, exilic, is shown by its use of *'bd, Pi'el* (v. 52), found in a cultic context in only deuteronomistic texts (Deut 11:4; 12:2; 2 Kgs 19:18; 21:3) and Ezek 6:3.
3. The sabbath rises to singular prominence in 23:1–3, which, I have argued, is exilic. On the provenance of this pericope, see the Introduction I F.

1. *idols.* *'ĕlîlîm*. See the NOTE on "Do not turn to idols," v. 19:4. This prohibition corresponds to the first commandment of the Decalogue, forbidding not only the worship of other gods, but also their possession—their images (cf. Exod 20:3; Ps 81:10)—or even, as this verse specifies, their manufacture (*'āśâ*), thereby combining the first and second commandments. According to D. N. Freedman (personal communication),

The writer of Leviticus . . . has done this in two ways: he changed *'ĕlōhîm* to *'ĕlîlîm* which may be a play on words; and he has replaced (not expanded on) *hāyâ le* with *'āśâ*. I think there is a significant shift of emphasis, and this is where the chiasm comes in. The author is rephrasing and shaping the commandments, not to separate them but to bring them together, just as the Deuteronomist does, and subsequently both Jewish and Catholic tradition, which combine the first two commandments in one commandment. Thus in Judaism these two commandments constitute the second commandment (the first being the opening declaration, which isn't a commandment at all), while for Catholics and Lutherans, and some other groups, the first two commandments are the first commandment.

That the term *'ĕlîlîm* occurs in the Torah only here and in 19:4 is but another indication that the H editor wished to associate the blessing and curses of Lev 26 with the fulfillment of the commandments of Lev 19 (R. Gane).

The question is whether these prohibitions were to be taken literally (e.g., *Mekh. RSbY* on Exod 20:3) or metaphorically. That one is not permitted to own or make idols *for worship* (e.g., the view of Ramban on Exod 20:3) was fiercely debated throughout the tannaitic period, especially in view of the necessity of many Jewish artisans to earn their livelihood by making idols for gentiles (see the detailed discussion in Urbach 1959). Notwithstanding the rabbinic attempts to mitigate the severity of these prohibitions, they must be taken literally. The rabbis lived in a time when they could testify: "For there has not arisen among us in recent generations, nor does there exist today, any tribe, or clan, or town, or city of ours that worships gods made by hands, as happened in former days" (Jdt 8:18). However, seventh-century D (but not eighth-century H) could hardly be expected to adopt a tolerant line regarding any contact with idols.

and a carved image. *ûpesel*, rendered *glyptà* 'graven, carved' (LXX). This word is always singular, with the verb *hēqîm* 'set up, erect' (Judg 18:30); it is also found with *'āśâ* make (Exod 20:4 [= Deut 5:8]; Deut 27:15; Judg 17:4; 18:31; Isa 44:15) and *yāsar* 'fashion' (Isa 44:9, 10; Hab 2:18).

The figure can be sculpted out of wood (e.g., Isa 40:20) or stone (cf. Exod 34:1). However, all the attestations of *pesel* in Scripture refer to wooden objects. Kaufmann (1962: 269) believes that the *pesel* of Isa 40:19; 44:10; Jer 10:14 is molten, but the verb *nāsak* 'melt' probably refers to the plating, which may or may not be overlaid metal (e.g., Isa 30:22, a process described in Isa 40:19–20). A distinction, however, must be made between *pesel* 'sculpted image' and *massēkâ* 'molten image', both in combination (Deut 27:15; Judg 17:3, 4; 18:14; Isa 48:5; Nah 1:14; see esp. Judg 18:17–18) and in parallelism (Isa 30:22; 42:17; Jer 10:14; 51:17; Hab 2:18). The prohibition directed solely against molten images occurs in early passages (Exod 34:17; Lev 19:4), which may reflect a period when sculpted images, such as teraphim (e.g., 1 Sam 19:13), were acceptable in the Israelite cult (Porter 1976).

In any event, *pesel* is not to be equated with *'ĕlîlîm* (Ibn Ezra). The *pesel* and the *massēbâ* (see below) were meant to represent Israel's God, and their manufacture was, therefore, a violation of, not the first commandment of the Decalogue, but the second. This can be deduced not just from the synoptic table (above) but also from Deuteronomy's elaborate rephrasing of the second commandment. The commandment reads: "You shall not make for yourself an idol [*pesel*], any likeness of what is in the heaven above, or on the earth below, or in the waters below the earth" (Exod 20:4; Deut 5:8). Deuteronomy's comment reads: " . . . be most careful—*since you saw no shape when YHWH your God spoke to you* at Horeb out of the fire—not to act wickedly and make for yourselves an idol [*pesel*] in any likeness whatever: the form of a man or woman, the form of any beast on earth, the form of any winged bird that flies in the sky, the form of anything that creeps on the ground, the form of any fish that is in the waters below the earth" (Deut 4:15–18).

The common denominator of *pesel* suffices to identify v. 1a$\beta\gamma$ with the second commandment, and the explicit statement in Deuteronomy's comment that these forms are purportedly likenesses of Israel's God makes it abundantly clear that the second commandment and its reflex in chap. 26 (v. 1aβγ) refer to the use of images to worship Israel's God.

or pillar. ûmaṣṣēbâ, rendered *stēlēn* 'stele' (LXX). This is the only occurrence of this word in P or H. It is found with *hiṣṣîb* (Gen 35:14, 20 [JE]), *hērîm* (Gen 31:45 [JE]), and *hēqîm* (Josh 4:9 [D])—all meaning "erect, set up," implying that this was a standing object. It is found in a memorial for the dead (Gen 35:20; 2 Sam 18:18), a boundary stone (Gen 31:41–52; Isa 19:18–23), a memorial for an important event (Josh 4:4–9, 20–24), and a memorial for a covenant (Exod 24:4; Josh 24:27).

Pillars were also a regular feature in Israel's early sanctuaries (Gen 28:18; 35:14; Hos 3:4), evidence of which are those unearthed in the Israelite sanctuary of Arad. They were placed beside the altar (Exod 34:13; Deut 16:22; Hos 3:4; 10:1–2). In the Arad sanctuary, a pillar was located inside the adytum. Originally, they were considered to be equivalent to idols and revered as gods (cf. Paus. 7.22:4) or endowed with divine power (Noordtzij 1982). According to van der Toorn (1997; cf. Mettinger 1995; Lewis 1998), they were deified and worshiped. However, this verse cannot be used as evidence, since the referent for the verb "worship," literally "bow down" is the immediately preceding flat "pavement," the only object in this verse that can take the preposition "on" (contra Lewis 1998: 22–23, n. 24). Pillars were forbidden in Israel only if they were idolatrous (Exod 23:24; 34:13), but beginning with the period of Hezekiah–Josiah they were also prohibited in the Israelite cult (Lev 26:1; Deut 16:22), even in worship of Israel's God (Wessely 1846). However, for noncultic purposes, they were always permitted (*Tg. Ps.-J.* specifies *mĕṭôl sĕgôda'* 'for worship'). The rabbis were fully aware of the disqualification of the pillar at a subsequent period of Israel's history when they declared "although the pillar was beloved as a means of worship by the patriarchs, it was objectionable in the time of their descendants" (*Sifre* Deut. 146).

In the NOTE on 19:4, I suggested that the absence of pillars from the absolute prohibition against any representations of the deity may indicate (with Mettinger 1995) that during the eighth century and earlier, the use of pillars in worshiping YHWH was tolerated as long as they were imageless. Thus the *maṣṣēbâ* 'standing-stone' was fully a part of Israel's cult (cf. Gen 28:18, 22; 31:51–52; Exod 24:4; Isa 19:19; Hos 3:4; 10:1; the Arad Temple).

a figured pavement. wĕ'eben maśkît. As a cultic term, *maśkît* occurs in only Num 33:52 and Ezek 8:12 (cf. Ps 73:7; Prov 18:11; 25:11), but not with *'eben* as its construct. The Versions render it in different ways: *líthon skopòn* 'guardian stone(?)' (LXX); *'eben sigdā'* 'a stone for worship' (*Tg. Onk.*); *'eben mĕṣayyêr* 'figured stone' (*Tg. Ps.-J.*; cf. Ibn Ezra), probably a mosaic, which *Tg. Ps.-J.* expands as follows: "However, a pavement inscribed with figures and pictures you may place into the ground of your sanctuaries but not to prostrate upon it." The etymology is equally disputed, with Rashi opting for *śkk* 'cover' (Exod 33:22), that is, "covering the floor with a mosaic," and Rashbam choosing *śkh* 'look' (citing

Isa 2:16; Ps 73:7), that is, a figured stone appealing to the eye. Some moderns would have it refer to boundary stones on which various emblems of gods and demons have been engraved. However, one would expect the accompanying verb to be *hēqîm* 'erect' or its synonyms, and not *nātan* 'place.' Indeed, the Pana-mua inscription contains the phrase *whqm lh maśky* (KAI 2. no. 215, 1:18), which may refer to an erected stone bearing an inscription with an image in bas-relief, but this reading has recently been challenged by Hoftijzer and Jongeling (DNSI 1995:II 701, s.v. *msky*).

Mansur (1959–60), simply on the basis of the preposition *'ālêhā*, surmised that the *'eben maśkît* was not an object or worship, but a stone placed in front of an idol on which the worshiper placed his hands and head. Hurowitz (1999: 201–208) argues, on the basis of an Akkadian text (K4732 + Sm 1081; cf. George 1986: 144–45)—which shows that on the *šiknu* 'representation / picture' (?) in the temple of Assur the king stands (and) kisses—that the *'eben maśkît* was a decorated threshold (for a similar act of prostration on the Temple threshold, but minus the decoration, see Ezek 46:2).

The rendering of the *Tg. Ps.-J.*, followed by Ibn Ezra, "figured pavement," seems preferable for three reasons:

1. the verb *hištaḥāwâ* followed by *'al* means "prostrate oneself upon" (Gen 47:31; 1 Kgs 1:47; Isa 60:14; Ezek 46:2; Zeph 1:5).
2. The synoptic table, above, indicates that this expression is paralleled by *tĕmûnâ* 'picture, likeness' (Exod 20:4).
3. The *ḥadrê maśkît* (Ezek 8:12a) explicitly were decorated with pictures (Ezek 8:10).

The Dead Sea sectaries, in writing the Temple Scroll, follow their customary harmonistic hermeneutics and weave together the closely related material, mainly from Lev 26:1 and Deut 16:21–22, as follows: "You shall not do within your land as the na[t]ions do: sacrifice, and plant Asheroth, and erect pillars, and set up [rather, "place"] figured stones to bow down to them and build" (11QT 51:19–21). An even closer resemblance is found in 11QT 52:2–3: "and you shall not set up a pillar [which I hate, and a fi]gured sto[ne] you shall [no]t make in all your land to [b]ow down to [rather "upon"] it" (Yadin 1983: 2.232).

in your land, bĕ'arṣĕkem. M. Hildenbrand suggests that the pronoun in this word means more like "the land you are on" rather than ownership, for the laws of jubilee make it clear that God, not Israel, owns the land (cf. 25:23). On the basis of this qualification, the rabbis (illogically) exempt the Temple from this prohibition (*b. Meg.* 22b [bar.]), presumably a reference to the Herodian Temple. However, the pavement on the Temple Mount to this day and, probably, within the Temple building itself, though split, was not figured. Maimonides ("Alien worship," 6:7) adds that synagogues of his own day covered their mosaic floors with rugs, mats, or straws, though they (logically), not being in the "land," would be exempt from this prohibition.

to worship. lěhištăhăwōt. The etymology and, hence, the meaning are moot. It seems likely that the verb is a vestige of an obsolete *št* form from the root *ḥwh* rather than a *Hitpaʿel* from *šḥh.* The most compelling evidence is that the forms *hištaḥăwû, wayyištahû, wayyištaḥăwû* can take a singular subject (e.g., Gen 18:2; 19:1; 23:7, 12; 24:26; Exod 12:27; 33:10; 34:8), thereby indicating that the *waw* is a radical of the root. On the recent debate, see Preuss (1980), Emerton (1977), Davies (1979), and Kreuzer (1985).

This verb is not found in priestly texts, which, instead, use the expression *nāpal ʿal-pānîm*, literally "fall on (one's) face" (9:24; Gen 17:3, 17; Num 14:5; 16:4, 22; 17:10; 20:6). Its use here may be based on Exod 20:5, and may be another indication that 26:1–2 has the Decalogue as its model.

The precise meaning of *hištaḥăwâ* is equally in doubt. The rabbis, preferring a finely nuanced meaning, distinguish it from near synonyms: "*Qîdâ* means falling upon the face, as it says *wattiqqōd bat-šebaʿ ʾappayim ʾereṣ.* 'Bathsheba bowed low with her face to the ground' (1 Kgs 1:31); *kěrîyʿâ* means going down upon the knees, and so it says *mikkěrōaʿ ʿal-birkayw* 'from kneeling on his knees' (1 Kgs 8:54); *hištaḥăwāʾâ* is spreading out the hands and feet, as it says *lěhištaḥăwōt lěkā ʾarṣâ* 'to bow low to you on the ground' (Gen 37:10)" (*b. Meg.* 22b [bar.]), a statement that the rabbis qualify, however, in their statement that this posture of worship is permitted on the pavement of the Temple (*Sipra* Behar 9:5). There is no way to determine whether the rabbis' fine-tuning is correct. To the contrary, given H's flair for imprecision (see Introduction I C), it is more likely that this term simply means "worship," and so it has been translated. This rendering may be derived from the synoptic table (above). If Lev 26:1aβ is indeed redolent of the second commandment, then the H tradent intended to express the two verbs *tišhtaḥăweh* and *to ʿobdēm* 'bow down' and 'serve' (Exod 20:4, 5a) by the one verb *lěhištahăwōt* 'worship'.

upon. ʿal. As indicated above, this preposition proves that the *ʾeben maśkît* cannot be a standing stone, but one that is horizontal and flat; hence the verb changes from *tāqîmû* 'erect, setup' to *tittēnû* 'place' (Ehrlich 1908). The use of the prepositions is crucial to the meaning: *hištaḥăwâ*, the usual expression, is generally metaphoric for "pay homage," but *hištaḥăwâ ʿal* implies a specific physical act, namely, fall down in worship or homage (e.g., Gen 47:31; Isa 60:14; Ezek 46:2; Zeph 1:5; cf. Mansur 1959–60). Thus Paran (1989: 218) cannot be right when he claims that this final verb *lěhištaḥăwōt* could apply to the previous two acts. However, he correctly points to a stylistic nuance, that instead of listing the three prohibitions with the negative particle first (as in 19:11, 26), H prefers a chiastic structure for the first two and a lengthened statement for the third (as in 21:1–3; 26:9). As noted, the three examples of images, *pesel* 'carved image', *maṣṣeba* 'pillar', *eben maśkît* 'figured pavement' fall under the rubric of the second commandment. Similar examples are Exod 20:20 (cf. 20:4) and Deut 4:15–18 (cf. 5:8). It is noteworthy that Exod 20:23 is the first interpretation not only of the second commandment, but of the entire Decalogue.

Exod 20:23 "with me . . . you shall not make for yourselves any gods of gold" anticipates the story of the golden calf (Exod 32:1–6). As long as Moses was visible, the freshly emancipated Israelite slaves could believe in Moses' invisible God. But once Moses disappeared from sight on Sinai's shrouded peak—without prior notice—Israel panicked. They needed assurance that this god was still with them. Hence, they built a golden calf, (a young bull), a visible sign of God's presence. In the Ancient Near East, the bull served as the pedestal on which the God stood or rode (cf. *ANEP*, nos. 470–74, 479, 486, 522, 525–26, 531, 534, 537, 830, 835). In many respects it was equivalent to the Ark flanked by two winged *kerubim* which served as YHWH's throne. However, it was ensconced in the adytum of the Tabernacle, invisible to priests and laypersons alike.

The danger of a visible image is best illustrated by the *nĕḥaš nĕḥašet* 'the copper serpent' (Num. 21:4–9). As a relic of the Mosaic age, venerated because it saved Israel (homeopathically) from the plague of serpents, it was enshrined in the Temple court where Israel *mĕqaṭṭĕrîm lo* 'offered incense to it' and was ultimately destroyed (2 Kgs 18:4b).

The copper serpent and the three objects of Lev 26:1, enumerated above make it clear why the image was prohibited. The distinction between the deity and its iconic representative is easily blurred. The invisible god fuses with its visible symbol. His transcendance over nature is reduced to an object of nature. The image is imagined to have divine, magical properties; it becomes a fetish.

Moshe Greenberg (personal communication) has pointed out to me that the authorized images associated with YHWH are explicitly dissociated from him in the theophany to Elijah at Horeb/Sinai (1 Kgs 19:11–12): The wind, quake, and fire which Israel had witnessed during YHWH's earlier revelation at Sinai (Exod 19:16–18; cf. Deut 4:11–12). Elijah is expressly shown and informed that YHWH is distinct from manifestations of nature. They are just his outrunners.

This lesson needed to be impressed because these outrunners of YHWH, especially the fire, were by tradition, the earthly manifestation of the divine presence. YHWH spoke to Moses from within the burning bush (Exod 3); YHWH's presence resided with the Tabernacle and emerged from it in a pillar of fire (Exod 40:38). The earlier view is retained in the deuteronomic tradition of the Sinaitic revelation *vayyedabbēr YHWH 'ălêkem mittôk ha'es* "YHWH spoke to you out of the fire" (Deut 4:12a).

Elijah's vision is the inevitable ultimate consequence of the second commandment. All images are distinct from God; hence they may not be worshiped.

for I YHWH am your God. kî 'ănî YHWH 'ĕlōhēkem. This is H's customary motive clause in regard to violations that are committed secretly and, hence, go unpunished by a human court. In chap. 19, it appears sixteen times. The LXX moves it from the end of 25:55 to the head of 26:1–2. In this position, it is parallel to the self-declaration of the Deity at the opening of the Decalogue (see the synoptic table, above). In the MT, there are seven occurrences of this formula (either long or short) in chaps. 25 and 26, thereby indicating their unity: three in chap. 25 (vv. 17, 38, 55), three in the blessings and curses of chap. 26 (vv. 13, 44, 45), and two in the bridge between these chapters (26:1, 2), which in effect makes them one. A possible reason for placing both a long and a short formula in vv. 1–2 is to form an inclusio with the same combination at the end of the chapter (vv. 44–45). The only other occurrence of the formula is in v. 13, which demarcates the boundary between the blessings and the curses (M. Hildenbrand).

2. *You shall keep my sabbaths.* 'et-šabbĕtōtay tišmŏrû. The entire verse is a repetition of 19:30, where the sabbath of creation is intended. Its purpose here, as indicated above, is to allude to the fourth commandment (see INTRODUCTION to 26:1–2). However, it is also possible that it was added at the head of 26:3–46 as indicating the legist's view that working the land on the weekly sabbath as well as on the septennial sabbath is a violation that incurs and prolongs the exile (see INTRODUCTION to 26:1–2).

and venerate my sanctuary. ûmiqdāšî tîrā'û. The more precise rendering of miqdāš is "sacred precincts"—that is, the divine spatial domain. Thus it provides a complementary balance to the previously mentioned sabbaths: both the temporal and spatial spheres of YHWH must be respected. See the more detailed discussion in the NOTE on 19:30.

Joosten (1998: 154) claims that YHWH redeemed Israel from Egypt "in order to be served by them in his sanctuary which he planned to establish for them." I disagree. There is no indication in H that God even wanted a sanctuary. This holds true for P (Exod 25:8) as for H (Exod 29:42–46), which state explicitly that the purpose of the sanctuary is for Israel, not for God, namely, for sacrifice and consultation (see NOTE on v. 11). As for the other attestations of miqqdāš 'sanctuary' in H (20:3; 21:12, 23), they are objects of the verbs ḥillēl 'desecration' and šāmar 'guard' (19:30; 26:2), implying that since Israel (not YHWH) has constructed a sanctuary, it should guard it from desecration. Joosten bases his remark on miškānî (v. 11a), which, with most commentators, he interprets as "my tabernacle" (for my basic disagreement, see NOTE on "my presence," v. 11).

To be sure, in the mythology of the ancient Near East, the god wants a temple. In fact, the climax of the Babylonian creation epic is that the gods build a temple for Marduk (*ANET* 68b). In the priestly story of creation, however, the climax of creation is the sabbath, the divine Temple in time, not space, that God builds (i.e., creates) by himself, without any assistance above or below (Gen 2:1–3).

As for the term miqdāšî 'my sanctuary' in this verse, it is there because the verse is a verbatim quotation of 19:30, and the purpose of this verse is to emphasize the sabbath. Note that the mention of the sabbath is at the virtual end of the holiness requirements in chap. 19. Neither can one object that if 26:2 wished to emphasize the sabbath, it could have cited its first occurrence in 19:3. The author (Hr) wished to cite the *national* causes for Israel's potential destruction in case it defected from God, and the mention of parental fidelity (v. 3a), dealing with relations between *individuals*, would not have suited (see below).

Joosten (1998: 163) also states that "YHWH intended from the start to settle his servants on land surrounding the sanctuary so as to create the concrete economic and political frame rendering the whole undertaking feasible. Similar schemes are attested in a wide variety of ancient Near Eastern texts." Joosten has been influenced by Weinfeld's (1995: 97–132) superb account of the sacred cities. H, however, is describing a sacred land with multiple sanctuaries (see chap. 17, COMMENT D, and Introduction II M). Jerusalem, however, is not a sacred city in priestly tradition (neither is it in D), but only in prophetic eschatology (e.g., Isa 35:8; 48:2; 52:1; Joel 4:7). In fact, in the priestly lists of asylum cities—which in many ways correspond to their ancient Near Eastern counterparts—Jerusalem is never listed among them (cf. Josh 20–21). Thus there is no analogy between Jerusalem and ancient Near Eastern sacred cities—at least, not in preexilic times.

Vv. 3–39. The Blessings and Curses

This pericope is about the power of the word in blessings, curses, vows, and oaths when spoken in God's name and with his approval. Ostensibly, Isaac's blessing (stolen by Jacob) is autonomous and, hence, irreversible (Gen 27:37). It is conditioned, however, by *lipnê YHWH* 'with YHWH's approval' (v. 7; for other examples of this idiom, cf. Gen 10:9; 27:7; Num 14:37). Thus all blessings and curses, even when nonexplicit, are optatives.

Nonetheless, belief persisted in the magical power of the spoken word. An example is provided by the story of Micah's mother, who is able to cancel her previously uttered curse with a blessing (Judg 17:1–2). Note, however, that here too the blessing is recited in YHWH's name. Again, it is an optative *bārûk běnî la YHWH* 'blessed be my son of YHWH'. (Presumably, the curse, though not explicit, was also uttered in YHWH's name.) For an extensive survey of this subject, see Scharbert (1975), Richards (1992), and Urbrock (1992).

Thus it is understandable why a collection of blessings and curses is frequently found at the end of major legal documents both in Israel (Exod 23:25–33; Lev 26:3–39; Deut 28; Josh 24:20) and throughout the ancient Near East (the law codes of Ur-Nammu, Lipit-Ishtar, Hammurabi; the Hittite, Assyrian, and Aramaic treaties [predicted by Dillmann 1886: 674!]; and the boundary stones). A pithy example of such an epilogue, one that resembles Lev 26, is attested in the Code of Hammurabi:

> If that man [i.e., the king who shall be raised up in the land] has heeded my words, which I have inscribed on my monument, has not made light of my commandments . . . may Shamash enlarge the man's empire like mine, the just king, and may he lead his people in justice. If that man has not heeded my words which I have inscribed on my monument . . . may the great god, Anum, father of the gods, deprive that man . . . of royal splendor, break his scepter, curse his destiny. . . .

The number and length of curses generally exceed those of blessings both in the law codes (e.g., CH concludes with 16 lines of blessings but some 280 lines of curses [*ANET* 178–80]) and in the extrabiblical treaties (e.g., Esarhaddon: ll. 414–493, 515–665 [*ANET* 534–41]). Ramban's sharp observation deserves to be mentioned: "the empty-headed who remarked (in puzzlement) that the curses are more numerous than the blessings, have not told the truth. The blessings are stated as generalizations whereas the curses are stated in detail in order to frighten the hearers." That is why Gerstenberger (1996: 410–12) cannot be correct in declaring that the blessings and curses pericopes (vv. 14–33) are independent documents. His reasons, the lopsided size and different formulations of the curses are not compelling. Had the author of the curses limited himself to a point-by-point refutation (as in Deut 28:3–5, 16–19), both the Leviticus and Deuteronomy curses would have monotonously fallen on deaf ears. Indeed, just as the blessings and curses in the CH epilogue differ in number, as noted above, they differ in formulation.

A cursory examination of these formulas will reveal the major distinction between the epilogues in the Bible and those of its environment: "Whereas the biblical texts are straightforward promises that God will respond to his people's behavior, the nonbiblical texts are prayers to the gods to act" (Wenham 1979). To be sure, the terms *běrākâ* 'blessing' and *qělālâ* 'curse' do not appear in these verses. Nor is there any requirement that they be invoked at some solemn gathering(s) of the people. Nevertheless, the possibility exists that a biblical law code, containing the provisions of God's covenant with his people, was read out in public ceremony at regular intervals (cf. Deut 31:10–13; 2 Kgs 23:2; Neh 8:1–8), followed by the intoning (Deut 27:14) of blessings and curses to secure its observance (Josh 8:34; cf. Deut 27:15–28; 28; Porter 1976).

I use the accepted designation blessings and curses for the context of Lev 26 (and the epilogues of Mesopotamian treaties and codes), though more precisely they are promises and comminations. There is much disagreement among scholars regarding the grouping of its blessings and curses (or promises and comminations). For example, Wenham (1979) finds that the blessings fall into three subsections, each beginning with *wěnātattî* (vv. 4, 6, 11): gift of rain and good harvests (vv. 4–5), gift of peace (vv. 6–10), gift of God's grace (vv. 11–13). He divides the curses into six subsections by the introductory clauses "If you will not listen to me (vv. 14, 18, 21, 23, 27, 40 [converse]), I shall punish you (seven times for your sins)" (vv. 16, 18, 21, 24, 28; v. 40 states the converse): general curses (vv. 14–17); drought and bad harvests (vv. 18–20); wild animals (vv. 21–22); war, leading to plague and famine (vv. 23–26); war, leading to cannibalism, devastation, and deportation from the land (vv. 27–39); restoration (vv. 40–45). Hoffmann (1953) finds five units of blessing and five of curses, which, he claims, are intended to correspond in number to the Decalogue. Kochman (1987) also favors this division on the following grounds: four sections introduced by *wěnātattî* (vv. 4, 6, 11) and *ŭpānîtî* (v. 9), and dividing vv. 4–12 into two sections, yielding rain and fertility (vv. 4–5); peace inside the land (v. 6); victory over enemies outside the land (vv. 7–8); fertility of womb and land (vv. 9–10); God's presence in Israel (vv. 11–12). The five curse subsections are vv. 16–17, 18–20, 21–22, 27–39, all but the first beginning with *wě'im*, and the first, though beginning with "I in turn will do this to you" (v. 16), connects with *we'im* (v. 14). Kochman also points to a typology of five curses in Job (1:13–15; 2:7) and Amos (4:6–11), on which see below.

Wessely (1846) sees four sets of blessing matched by four sets of curses: famine, wild beasts, sword, and plague, which are also found in Deut 32:24–25 and Ezek 14:13–21. Lev 26, however, adds a fifth set of blessings and curses that are not typological because they are uniquely limited to Israel: God's beneficent presence (vv. 11–12) and God's destruction of Israel's cult places and his pursuit of Israel in exile (vv. 27–33).

There can be no doubt that the curses can be broken into five units of increasing severity, indicated by the opening words (vv. 16, 18, 21, 23–24, 27–28), which describe illness, famine, and defeat (vv. 16–17); drought and poor harvests (vv. 18–20); wild animals causing a reduced population and deserted roads (vv. 21–22); war resulting in plague and famine (vv. 23–26); and war leading to cannibalism, destruction of cultic sites, deportation from the land, and psychological breakdown of the exiles (vv. 27–39).

My student M. Hildenbrand has observed that the number of curses falls into a definite pattern, indicated by the verbs beginning with a *waw*. The five subsections reveal the following numbers: 7, 5, 5, 7, 14. The importance of the number seven is well attested, enhanced by the fact that some of the key terms also occur seven times: *'ākal* (vv. 5, 10, 16, 26, 29 [twice], 38); *šābat* (vv. 34–35); *šeba'* (25:8 [thrice]; 26:18, 21, 24, 28, tying together chaps. 25–26); and *qerî* (vv. 21, 23, 24, 27, 28, 40, 41, tying vv. 40–45 to the curses). The number five is a negative, foreboding number (e.g. Judg 18:2; 19:8; 2 Kgs 25:8; Jer 1:3). Perhaps, the number *šeba'* is missing in v. 16, though the first unit (vv. 16–17) actually contains seven curses, in order to restrict the use of *šeba'* to seven times in chaps. 25–26, thereby tying the two chapters together.

The first set of curses is marked by the measure-for-measure principle: "I in turn will do this to you" (v. 16). The following sets utilize the refrain "sevenfold for your sins" (a metaphoric number; see the NOTES) in crescendo intensity (see the NOTES). There are clear echoes of the blessings in the curses: "covenant" (vv. 9, 15, 25, 42, 44); "commandments" (vv. 3, 14–15); "become their (your) God" (vv. 12, 45); "brought you out of the land of Egypt" (vv. 13, 45); "loathe" (vv. 11, 15, 30, 43); "and I shall give" (vv. 4, 6, 11, 17, 19, 30–31; Wenham 1979).

Levine (1989: 276) aptly refers to the distinctions between the rewards and punishments as an "asymmetry of contrasts": the fertile land (vv. 4–5, 10) will become unproductive (vv. 16, 19–20, 26); God will turn with favor toward his people (v. 8) or will set his face against them (v. 17); Israel will repulse its enemies (v. 9) or be battered by them (vv. 17, 25); wild beasts will disappear from (v. 6) or devour the people (v. 22); the sword will not traverse the land (v. 6) or will bring destruction (v. 25); obedience brings secure settlement (v. 5), whereas disobedience brings exile (v. 33a). See further the INTRODUCTION to vv. 14–39.

As mentioned earlier, the curses of Amos 4:6–11 are also divided into five sections (vv. 6, 8, 9, 10, 11). Each ends with "yet you did not turn back to me," implying that Israel's punishments will only worsen. Brueggemann (1965: 2) claims that this is "a liturgical formula of preparation for covenant-making or renewal which includes both threat and repentance . . . the climax of curse recital (v. 12) is not destruction, but an invitation to Israel that she may repent . . . and thereby confront the God of Sinai and remake the covenant which she has dissolved by disobedience." His view has been strongly opposed by Paul (1991: 151, n. 119) on the grounds that all but the last chapter of Amos end on a dire note and that the doxologies (e.g., v. 13) always follow directly on verses describing punishment. Isa 9:7–10:4 also consists of a series of curses that end with the refrain "Yet his anger has not turned back and his arm is outstretched still" (9:11, 16, 20; 10:4). The refrains in Amos and Isaiah clearly indicate that the purpose of the calamities sent by God is to bring Israel back to obedience. In Lev 26, the repetition of the phrase "I, in turn" (vv. 16; cf. 24, 28, 32) also show that God unleashes his punishment on Israel, but only with reluctance (Noordtzji 1982). This chapter, however, ends with consolation and hope that the punishment and confession will atone, based on the assumption that the covenant is eternal (vv. 40–45). On the question of whether this appendix is secondary, see COMMENT E.

The contents of the blessings and curses can be outlined:

A. The blessings: obedience is rewarded (vv. 3–13)
  1. Condition (v. 3)
  2. Enumeration (vv. 3–12)
    a. First blessing: plenty (vv. 4–5)
    b. Second blessing: peace inside the land (v. 6)
      x. Third blessing: victory over the enemy outside the land (vv. 7–8)
    b'. Fourth blessing: abundant life, fulfillment of the covenant (vv. 9–10)
    a'. Fifth blessing: God's presence in Israel (vv. 11–12)
  3. YHWH's self-declaration (v. 13)
B. The curses: disobedience is punished (vv. 14–39)
  1. First curse: illness, famine, defeat (vv. 14–17)
    a. Condition (vv. 14–15)
    b. Curse (vv. 16–17)
  2. Second curse: drought and poor harvests (vv. 18–20)
    a. Condition (v. 18a)
    b. Curse (vv. 18b–20)
  3. Third curse: harmful beasts (vv. 21–22)
    a. Condition (v. 21a)
    b. Curse (vv. 21b–22)
  4. Fourth curse: war, pestilence, famine (vv. 23–26)
    a. Condition (v. 23)
    b. Curse (vv. 24–26)

  5. Fifth curse: destruction and exile (vv. 27–39)
    a. Condition (v. 27)
    b. Curses (vv. 28–39)
       (1) Cannibalism (vv. 28–29)
       (2) Destruction of cult places (vv. 30–31)
       (3) Desolation of land (v. 32)
       (4) Exile (v. 33a)
       (5) The land will be fallow (vv. 33b–35)
       (6) Psychological disintegration (vv. 36–39)
C. Remorse and the recall of the covenant: restoration implied (vv. 40–45)
  1. Confession (v. 40)
  2. Remorse (v. 41)
  3. God will remember the Patriarchal Covenant (v. 42)
  4. The land must make up the neglected sabbaticals (vv. 43–44)
  5. God will remember the Sinaitic covenant (v. 45)

Vv. 3–13. The Blessings: Obedience Is Rewarded

"Reverence begets favour; sacrifice [p]rolongs life; and prayer [at]ones for guilt" (*BWL* 104–5, ll. 143–45); ". . . and know before whom you are exerting yourself; moreover, your Employer is reliable in that he will pay you wages due for your work" (*m.* '*Abot* 2:14).

The entire blessing section (vv. 1–13) is constructed as a giant introversion (M. Hildenbrand, with adaptations):

A   '*im-bĕḥuqqōtay* **tēlēkû** *wĕ'et-miṣwōtay tišmĕrû wa'ăśîtem 'ōtam*

  B **wĕnātattî** *gišmêkem bĕ'ittô* **wĕnātĕnâ** *hā'āreṣ yĕbûlāh wĕ'ēṣ haśśādeh* **yittēn** *piryô*

    C *wĕhiśśîg lākem dayiš 'et-bāṣîr ûbāṣir yaśśîg 'et-zera'* **wa'ăkaltem** *laḥmĕkem lāśōba'wîśabtem lābeṭaḥ bĕ'arṣĕkem*

      D *wĕnātattî* **šālôm** *bā'āreṣ ûśĕkabtem wĕ'ên maḥărîd wĕhišbattî ḥayyâ rā'â min-hā'āreṣ wĕḥereb lō'-ta'ăbōr bĕ'arṣĕkem*

        E$_1$ *ûrĕdaptem 'et-'ōyĕbêkem* **wĕnapĕlû** *lipnêkem leḥāreb*

          E$_2$ **wĕrādĕpû mikkem** *ḥămiśśâ* **mē'â**

          E$_2$' **ûmē'â mikkem** *rĕbābâ* **yirdōpû**

        E$_1$' **wĕnapĕlû 'ōyĕbêkem lipnêkem leḥāreb**

      D' *ûpānîtî 'ălêkem wĕhiprêtî 'etkem wĕhirbêtî 'etkem wāhăqîmōtî 'et-***brîtî*** 'ittĕkem*

    C' **wa'ăkaltem** *yāšān nôšān wĕyāšān mippĕnê* **ḥādāš** *tôṣî'û*

  B' **wĕnātattî** *miškānî bĕtôkĕkem wĕlō'-tig'al napšî 'etĕkem*

A' **wĕhithallaktî** *bĕtôkĕkem wĕhāyîtî lākem lē'lōhîm wĕ'attem tihyû-lî lĕ'ām*

The parallel words are indicated in boldface. The major themes of the structure are identified in the following outline:

A   "walks" (Israel, v. 3)
    B   "give" rain and fertility (v. 4)
        C   superabundant food (v. 5)
            D   peace in the land (v. 6)
                E   victory over the enemy (v. 7)
                E'   victory over the enemy (v. 8)
            D'   covenant (v. 9)
        C'   superabundant food (v. 10)
    B'   "give" presence (v. 11)
A'   "walks" (God, v. 12)

AA' emphasizes the complementary relation between Israel's behavior and God's response: if Israel "walks" with God's commandments, God will "walk" among Israel. BB' begins the itemization of the divine blessing: God's "giving" presence "gives" rain and fertility, which yield abundant nourishment (CC'). Peace in the land is the essence of God's covenant (DD'), as attested elsewhere; note the construct *bĕrît (bĕrîtî) šālôm* (Num 25:12; Ezek 34:25; 37:26, on which see below). The pivot and center of the entire construction (EE') is the absolute prerequisite for the effectiveness of God's blessing of material welfare: victory over threatening armies poised to invade the land. EE' itself is a minor introversion of continuous chiasms:

E₁   *ûrĕdaptem ʾet-ōyĕbêkem* **wĕnāpĕlû lipnêkem leḥāreb**
E₂   *wĕrādĕpû* mikkem *ḥămiššâ mēʾâ*
E₂'   *ûmēʾâ mikkem rĕbābâ yirdōpû*
E₁'   **wĕnāpĕlû** *ōyĕbêkem* **lipnêkem leḥāreb**

E₂E₂' is a chiasm at the ends, whereas E₁E₁' is a chiasm (note the words in boldface) with the subject and verb, resulting in an E₁ (ab) E₂ (cd) E₂' (dc) E₁' (ba) construction. Another derivative of this structure is that the last verse in the blessing pericope (v. 13) falls outside the structure, adding emphasis to its function as a rationale, namely, God's providential care in the past by freeing the Israelites from Egypt and bringing them to the land.

Here is the appropriate place to point out how Ezekiel twice uses the vocabulary of Lev 26:1–13 to construct his own version of God's blessing for Israel. Again, the parallel words and phrases are in boldface.

[25]*wĕkārattî lāhem* **bĕrît šālôm** *wĕhišbattî ḥayyâ-rāʿâ min-hāʾāreṣ wĕyāšĕbû* **bammidbār lābetaḥ** . . .   [26]*wĕhôradtî* **haggešem** *bĕʿittô* . . .   [27]*wĕnātan ʿēṣ haśśādeh ʾet-piryô wĕhāʾāreṣ tittēn yĕbûlāh wĕhāyû ʿal-ʾadmātām* **lābetaḥ** . . . *ʾănî YHWH bĕšibrî ʾet-mōṭôt ʿullām* . . .   [28]*wĕhayyat hāʾāreṣ lōʾ tōʾkĕlēm wĕyāšĕbû lābetah wĕʾēn maḥărîd* (Ezek 34:25–28)

It will be immediately apparent that Ezek 34:25 is modeled on Lev 26:6; Ezek 34:26–27a, on Lev 26:4; and Ezek 34:27b, on Lev 26:13. That Ezekiel is the borrower has already been pointed out by the fact that he kneads together DD′ into his construct *bĕrît šālôm* (see above) and that he explicates *haggešem bĕ'ittô* by his addition *gišmê bĕrākâ yihyû* (see NOTE on v. 4).

²⁶*wĕkāratî lāhem* **bĕrît šālôm . . . wĕhirbêtî** *'ôtām* **wĕnātattî** *'et-miqdāšî bĕtôkām lĕ'lām* ²⁷*wĕhāyâ* **miškānî** *'ălêhem* **wĕhāyîtî lāhem lē'lōhîm wĕhēmmâ yihyû-lî lĕ'ām** (Ezek 37:26–27)

In this passage, Ezekiel bases himself on different verses of the blessing pericope, Lev 26:9, 11, 12, but again kneading together 26:6, 9 (DD′) into his construct *bĕrît šālôm*. He also adds the installation of God's everlasting sanctuary, *miqdāšî* 'my sanctuary,' an apparent contrast with the curse of Lev 26:31 where God avers that he will destroy *miqdĕšêkem* 'your sanctuaries' (Ezekiel continues his midrash on the blessing pericope in 37:28; see NOTE on "my presence," v. 11).

Thus Ezekiel has utilized entire phrases of Lev 26:4, 6, 9, 11, 12, and 13 in a creative way, which, in addition to the evidence adduced in COMMENT C, demonstrates that Lev 26:1–39, in its present MT form, lay before the prophet.

3. *my laws . . . my commandments. huqqōtay . . . miṣwōtay.* Which? Two referents have been suggested:

1. They allude to the sabbatical and jubilee laws of chap. 25, the observance of which will guarantee the blessings announced in the next verse (v. 4); the rain will come in their seasons, and the land will produce its crops in abundance (Abravanel).
2. As *huqqōtay* and *miṣwōtay* (as well as *mišpāṭay*, v. 15) are terms describing other laws in H (e.g., 18:4–5, 26; 19:37; 20:22; 22:31), their referents are the entire Holiness Source (cf. Hoffmann 1953, who, however, would include the rest of Leviticus because of *tôrōt*, v. 46).

The first view is acceptable if chaps. 25–26 are regarded as a closed unit; the second makes even better sense if chap. 26 is seen as the epilogue to the entire H Code and v. 46 as an editorial closure for the entire book, before the addition of chap. 27 (see NOTE on v. 46). There can be no doubt that the second view is correct. As will be argued in the INTRODUCTION to vv. 43–44, an exilic tradent of the H School added the neglect of the septennate to the rest of Israel's sins. Thus from the literary perspective, H as the *author* of Lev 17–26 structured these chapters so that they would begin with the law of sacrifices and end with blessings and curses (as the law codes of the Book of the Covenant, Exod 20:22–23:33, and Deuteronomy, Deut 12–28). However, H as the *redactor* attached these chapters to chaps. 1–16 (P) so that "my laws . . . commandments" would apply to the entire book. For the distinction among *huqqōt, mišpāṭîm,* and *miṣwōt,* see the NOTES on v. 15, 18:4–5.

Note that these two objects precede their verbs (a phenomenon repeated in v. 15), thereby placing emphasis on "my"; that is, it is YHWH's commandments.

and observe them. waʿăśîtem ʾōtam. This clause is not superfluous. The verb *šāmar*, rendered here as "keep," involves no activity. It means "keep in mind." It must *always* be balanced by a positive, performative verb, usually *ʿăśâ* 'do, observe, perform' (19:37; 20:22; Ezek 11:20; 20:19) and (rarely) *hālak* (18:4). Since *ʿăśâ* and *hālak* in this text are synonymous (also in 18:4), the former takes as its object only *miṣwōtay* 'my commandments'. Therefore, the *ʾAtnaḥ* placed by the Masoretes under *tēlēkû* is correct.

Vv. 4–5. The First Blessing: Plenty

Note that Ezekiel's order of curses: famine, wild beasts, sword, and plague (Ezek 14:13–21) is precisely matched by their opposites in these blessings: plenty (vv. 4–5), security and peace from wild beasts and sword (vv. 6–8), and abundant life (vv. 9–10), leading to the possibility that Ezekiel modeled himself on this section (see COMMENT C). The content and language of 26:3–5 are precisely the same as that of 25:18–19, which, however, are more concise because they are legalistic, whereas Lev 26, being hortatory, is more expansive and indulges in literary embellishment (S. Nikaido).

4. This verse exhibits the pattern ABC‖A′DB′‖D′A′′B in which the verb *nātan* is conjugated three ways in a circular inclusio (D. Stewart).

your rains in their season. gišmêkem bĕʿittām. The plural (also in Ezek 34:26; Ps 105:32; Ezra 10:9, 13) refers mainly to the two distinctive downpours at the beginning and end of the rainy seasons, known as the *yôreh* and *malqôš* (Deut 11:14; Jer 5:24; Joel 2:23; cf. Zech 10:1; Prov 16:15), each essential in its time (Abravanel): "Gentle early rains would fall in October and November to make the land ready for plowing and sowing; strong winter storms would come in mid-December to mid-March in order to saturate the ground, filling the wells and making the springs overflow; and the later rains of April would cause the ears of grain and the fruit to swell and enable the fields to endure the heat of the summer" (Noordtzij 1982). Ezekiel's comment says it all: *wĕhôradtî haggešem bĕʿittô gišmê bĕrākâ yihyû* 'I will send down rain in its season, rains of blessing they will be' (Ezek 34:26b), where *gešem* is a collective and *beʿittô* 'in its time' is explained as "rains of blessing."

Of course, lack of rain is a terrible curse (Amos 4:7), but an unseasonable rain can be equally devastating: "a destructive rain that leaves no food" (Prov 28:3b). When Samuel's prayer brings rain during the wheat harvest, it is a curse and the people react accordingly (1 Sam 12:15–19). As explained by Ḥazzequni, if the rains fall out of season (e.g., as in Samuel's case during the harvest), the crops will rot (cf. *b. B. Bat.* 91b [bar.]).

its produce. yĕbûlāh. Here and in v. 20 are the word's only occurrences in priestly texts (cf. Deut 11:17; 32:22; Ezek 34:27; Hab 3:17; Pss 67:7; 85:13). While some conjecture that it derives from the root *bwl* (Ibn Ezra, Abravanel), as *yĕqûm* does from *qwm*, it is more likely that its root is *ybl* (Radak). The contrast with fruit makes it clear that produce here refers to grain (also in v. 20). It is synonymous with *tĕbûʾâ*, except that *yĕbûl* refers to grain before it is stored and *tĕbûʾâ* afterward (*Hôʾîl mōšeh*, cited by *Qarnê ʾôr* on Ibn Ezra).

The reversal of subject and object, usually effected by writing one verb with a *waw* conversive, and thereby producing a chiasm, is particularly attested in H (e.g., vv. 4, 5, 8, 20, 29, 33; 16:29–31; 25:10, 41; Paran 1989: 64–65, 116).

5. *threshing. dayiš.* This is a hapax (cf. inf. const. *bĕdiyšô*, Deut 25:4). Grain was usually gathered in late spring; then there was a gap of two months until the grapes were ready for harvesting. But in good years, the seasons are contiguous. Thus divine intervention is required only for abundant and timely rains, not for continual harvests. As recognized by the rabbis: "Are not all the days of the year (characterized) by harvest? With the end of the barley harvest, the wheat harvest begins; the wheat harvest ends, the grape harvest begins; the grape harvest ends, the olive harvest begins. Thus, there is harvest every day of the year" (*t. 'Ed.* 1:6). Adding to the harvesting of grain and grapes the sowing time in the winter and the harvesting of flax in early spring, there is no "dead" season (Kochman 1987).

Eloquent testimony to this fact is the earliest Hebrew inscription, the tenth-century Gezer tablet:

1. *ẙrḥw 'sp yrḥw ẑ*	1. months of ingathering; months of
2. *r'yrḥw lqš*	2. sowing; months of late planting;
3. *yrḥ 'ṣd pšt*	3. month of flax pulling;
4. *yrḥ qṣr ś'rm*	4. month of barley harvest;
5. *yrḥ qṣr wkl*	5. month of wheat harvesting and measuring;
6. *yrḥw zṁr*	6. months of pruning
7. *yrḥ qṣ*	7. month of summer fruit

For *lqš* referring to late planting, see Paul (1991: 227, n. 7) on Amos 7:1; for *kl* meaning "measuring," see Isa 40:12. Since *yrḥw* can no longer be understood as a dual, but as a plural, it is no longer possible to regard this inscription as describing a twelve-month calendar (details in Gibson 1971: 1–4, esp. n. 1; see also Young 1992: 363–66). In fact, the overlapping accords precisely with the testimony of this verse. A similar promise is made by the prophet:

A time is coming—declares YHWH—
When the plowman shall meet the reaper,
And the treader of grapes
Him that holds the (bag of) seed;
When the mountains shall drip wine
And all the hills shall wave (with grain). (Amos 9:13)

Why three species: grain (barley and wheat) and grapes? What of the other four fruits attested as products of the land: figs, pomegranates, olives, and dates (Deut 8:8)? There is a broad distinction between these two groups. The former symbolize the agricultural produce of the *entire* land: the grain, all the plains; the grape, all the hills. The latter are grown in limited areas, and their output is much less. Also, the harvest season of the former is lengthy: more than two months for grain and nearly two months for grapes (Kochman 1987). That Canaan's staples are chiefly grain and grapes can be learned from the Rab-shakeh's promise of "a land like your own, a land of bread and wine, of grain (fields) and vineyards" (Isa 36:17). It can also be derived from the annual cul-tic dues: grain, grape juice (must), and olive oil (Num 18:12; Deut 14:23). Nonetheless, precisely because grain and grapes are the dominant crops, the others probably are implied, just as in the sabbatical laws where they probably constitute a merism for the land's entire produce (25:3, 5; see NOTE on "food").

eat. The verb *'ākal* occurs seven times in the combined blessings and curses (vv. 5, 10, 16, 26, 29[twice], 38). The presence or absence of nourishment is the chief determinant for a blessing or a curse.

fill. lāśōba', literally "to the full." A full stomach is the prerequisite of *economic* security (see below).

food. The word *leḥem* here denotes "food," a meaning it clearly has in P (e.g., 3:11, 16; Num 28:24) and H (21:8, 17, 21, 22; 22:25) as well as elsewhere (e.g., Gen 3:19; 31:54; 37:25; 43:32). Rather than limit its connotation to bread, it refers here to all of the land's produce and supports the merism of grain–grapes.

and dwell securely in your land. wīšabtem lābeṭaḥ bĕ'arṣĕkem. This clause oc-curs twice in 25:18–19, where it stands for military and economic security. It surely has the latter meaning here. Ibn Ezra connects it with "eat your fill," im-plying that when the land does not produce enough, its ihabitants must leave (cf. Gen 4:12; 12:10; 26:1; Ruth 1:1). Interestingly, Ezekiel uses this phrase in three contexts: military and economic security and protection from beasts (Ezek 34:25, 27, 28).

V. 6. The Second Blessing: Peace Inside the Land

Economic security (vv. 4–5) is now followed by political security (vv. 6–8); the former is worthless without the latter (*Sipra* Beḥuqotay 1:8; Rashi; Bekhor Shor).

peace in the land. šālôm bā'āreṣ (i.e., *within* the land). This means no civil strife (Ibn Ezra, Ramban), in distinction to the incursion of wild beasts and armies within Israel's borders, dangers that follow. A similar blessing is predi-cated in Ezek 34:25, which has been amplified by the term *bĕrît šālôm*, bor-rowed from Num 25:12. If this verse were directed to threats from the outside, it would be expressed by *šālôm lā'āreṣ* 'peace *for* the land'. For this reason, Oded (1993) cannot be right in claiming that *šālôm* here implies all-embracing secu-rity, both within and without. He is most illuminating, however, in illustrating in exhausting detail that the Assyrian imperial concept of *salīmu* (= BH *šālôm*) was bound up with *tašmu* 'obedience', namely, that vassal states would achieve peace only by their total submission to the will of the Assyrian king. Not sur-prisingly, this concept is echoed in vv. 3–13, namely, that Israel's prosperity and security are also bound up in obedience—not to an early monarch, however, but to the divine will (v. 3). Tellingly, both the Assyrian ruler and Israel's God imposed their will through an oath, which took the form of the vassal treaty and the Sinaitic covenant, respectively. The difference between the two concepts was in the manner in which the suzerainty was imposed: Assyrian ruthless force versus YHWH's invitation and Israel's willing compliance (cf. Exod 19:8; 24:3), though the rabbis also transmit the graphic midrashic tradition that God would have dropped Mount Sinai on the Israelite's heads had they refused (*Mekh.* Haḥodesh and parallels).

and no one shall make you afraid. wĕ'ên mahărîd. This is the reward of peace (Ezek 34:28; 39:26).

I will eliminate (vicious beasts from the land). wĕhišbattî, literally "cause to cease." According to the rabbis (*Sipra* Beḥuqotay 2:1), this can be done in two ways: by removing them (R. Judah; cf. Ezek 34:25) or neutralizing them (R. Simeon)—that is, by changing their nature (Isa 11:9a; Ramban; Job 5:23; Hoffmann 1953). Philo (*Praem.* 88) connects the two halves of verse: "that when the wild beasts within us are fully tamed, the animals too will become tame and gentle."

In biblical times, lions and bears inhabited Canaan (Judg 14:5; 2 Kgs 2:24; Isa 11:6–7; cf. Gen 9:5; 37:33; 1 Kgs 13:24–25; Sefire I A: 30–32). Lions reappeared after the destruction of North Israel and preyed on the new settlers (2 Kgs 17:24–28; cf. Exod 23:29). One can thus comprehend the implication of this blessing that man alone is incapable of coping with this menace: its resolution can stem only from YHWH (see also Hos 2:20; Job 5:23).

and no sword shall traverse your land. wĕhereb lō'tā'ăbōr bĕ'arṣĕkem. There is no point in having an abundant harvest if the enemy will snatch it away, as did the Midianites: "After the Israelites had done their sowing . . . they would attack them, destroy all the produce of the land all the way to Gaza, and leave no means of sustenance in Israel" (Judg 6:3–4). The enemy will not enter your borders because, without the need to assemble an opposing force, a few of your soldiers *at the border* will put the enemy to rout (vv. 7–8; Wessely 1846) or the enemy "will dissolve and fall to pieces of itself" (Philo, *Praem.* 93). The LXX moves this sentence to the end of v. 5, presumably to get *šālôm* to mean "(military) peace."

Ezekiel combines this clause with its equivalent in the curses *wĕhābē'tî 'ălêkem hereb* (v. 25aα): *'ô hereb 'ābî' 'al-hā'āreṣ hahî' wĕ'āmartî hereb tā'ăbōr bā'āreṣ* [Or, if I were to **bring the sword upon** the land and say, "**Let a sword pass through the land . . .**"] (Ezek 14:17). Ezekiel borrows the verbal phrase from the curse (v. 25) and adds the negation of the blessing (indicated in boldface). Apparently, he knew Lev 26 as it exists in the MT (see COMMENT C).

Lohfink (1994: 212, n. 87) notes that *hereb* 'sword' occurs seven times in chap. 26 (vv. 6, 7, 8, 25, 33, 36, 37) in contrast to its absence from Deut 28 (read *ûbaḥereb* in Deut 28:22 V), another indication that they are independent documents (see chap. 26, COMMENT B).

Vv. 7–8. The Third Blessing: Victory over the Enemy Outside the Land

Victory will be accomplished without mobilizing the manpower and disrupting the economy. How is this possible? Because a few (presumably stationed at the border) will be empowered by God to do it.

7. *fall . . . by the sword.* The expression *nāpal laḥereb* is found only in Lev 26:7, 8. The *lamed* is equivalent to *beth, baḥereb* (Radak).

8. *Five . . . hundred || hundred . . . ten thousand.* Usually we find multiples of ten (e.g., Judg 20:10; Amos 5:3), but here we are confronted with two different proportions: 1:20 and 1:100. Various answers have been suggested:

1. Groups of five are more powerful together than separately (Ibn Ezra); that is, when the attacking force grows in arithmetic proportions, the rout of the vanquished grows in geometric proportions.
2. The proportions are, in their psychological effect, equivalent; the victory of five will be valued as more of a miracle than a victory of a hundred (Ralbag).
3. A group of five will be considered by the enemy as the vanguard of a larger army (Bekhor Shor).
4. Other ratios are attested elsewhere in Scripture (Deut 32:30; Josh 23:10; Isa 30:17), among which Deut 32:30 also attests to an imbalance: 1:1000 and 1:5000.

This verse has a chiastic structure ABCD || DBC'A; a quintessential example of H's style (Paran 1983, Kselman 1978).

your enemies shall fall before you by the sword. This is a repetition of v. 7 for the sake of forming the minor introversion (E_1, E_1') and the axis of the larger one (EE'). See the INTRODUCTION to vv. 3–13.

Vv. 9–10. The Fourth Blessing: Abundant Life and the Fulfillment of the Covenant

The covenant promised Israel progeny and land. The progeny, however, cannot survive unless the land, too, is fruitful. For the complementary passage in the blessing of peace (v. 5), see the discussion on CC' of the introverted structure of the blessing pericope in the INTRODUCTION to vv. 3–13.

9. *I will look with favor upon you.* *ûpānîtî 'ălêkem,* literally "I will turn to you," to which the rabbis add "with favor" (*Sipra* Beḥuqotay 2:5). This favorable nuance is determined by the preposition *'el* (e.g., Num 6:26; 16:15; 1 Kgs 8:28; 2 Kgs 13:23; Ezek 36:9; Pss 25:16; 69:17; 86:16), whereas *pānâ b* means "turn against" (the *beth* of hostility; see NOTE on "I will set my face against you," v. 17).

and make you fruitful and multiply you. *wĕhiprêtî 'etkem wĕhirbêtî 'etkem.* Both elements are essential for ample progeny: fruitfulness (*prh*), or fertility yielding an increase, and a multitude (*rbb*), implying that the progeny will survive; that is, Israel will not lose anyone in childbirth (Ramban). Perhaps these two verbs are separated from each other in order to comprise two blessings that will be reversed by two curses (see NOTE on v. 22). This idiom abounds in the Torah, but only in the priestly (P/H) texts. It is the blessing given to marine and sky life (Gen 1:22) and to all humanity (Gen 1:28; 9:1, 7). It is a concomitant of the covenant with Abraham (Gen 17:6, 7) and of the promise to Ishmael (Gen 17:20), Isaac (Gen 26:4, 24), and Jacob (Gen 28:3; 35:11; 48:4), fulfilled for Israel in Egypt (Gen 47:27; Exod 1:7; see also Jer 3:16; 23:3; Ezek 36:11).

It should be noted that 26:9 is structured similarly to Gen 17:6–7; in both passages, the promise of progeny is linked to the covenant, in the identical language *wahăqīmōtî 'et-běrîtî* 'I will maintain my covenant'. Knohl (1995: 102, n. 145) detects H's vocabulary in Gen 17:7–8, but rightly hesitates to attribute this passage to H on the grounds that the promise of land (v. 8) is found elsewhere in P. He might also have noted that Gen 28:3–4 (P) mentions both progeny and land, as does Gen 17:6, 8, thereby demonstrating that the entire passage (Gen 17:6–8) belongs to P. Thus the identical linkage of promise and covenant in Gen 17:6–7 (P) and in Lev 26:9 (H) indicates that H borrowed P, omitting the promise of multiple nations and kings (Gen 17:6aβ, b). Indeed, it should not go unnoticed that in the entire blessings pericope (26:1–13), the focus is exclusively on the fertility of the land and its security from civil strife and external enemies.

Lohfink (1973) notes the parallels 26:9b ‖ Gen 17:4a, 7a (and 12aβ ‖ Gen 17:8b; Exod 29:45), but overlooks the P passages. Moreover, he is in error in claiming that in vv. 9, 11–13, H synthesizes the priestly and deuteronomic theologies of Israelite history (cf. Joosten 1996: 117–18, 200–203). However, he correctly observes the parallels between 26:9–13 and Exod 6:4–7 (partially):

	Lev 26:9–13			Exod 6:4–7 (H)
A	*wahăqīmōtî 'et-běrîtî 'ittĕkem* (v. 9b)		A'	*hăqīmōtî 'et-běrîtî 'ittām* (v. 4aα)
B	*wěhāyîtî lākem lē'lōhîm* (v. 12aβ)		C'	*wělāqahtî 'etkem lî lě'ām* (v. 7aα)
C	*wě'attem tihyû-lî lě'ām* (v. 12b)		B'	*wěhāyîtî lākem lē'lōhîm* (v. 7aβ)
D	*'ănî YHWH 'ĕlōhêkem 'ăšer* *hōṣē'tî. 'etkem mē'ereṣ miṣrayim* *mihyōt lāhem 'ăbādîm* (v. 13a)		D'	*wîda'tem kî 'ănî YHWH* *ĕlōhêkem hammōṣî' 'etkem* *mittaḥat siblōt miṣrayim* (v. 7b).

The chiastic switch in the order of the two middle members of a panel construction (BC to C'B') ensures the linkage of the two panels. (For an excellent example, see the structure of Num 20–21 in Milgrom 1990a: 463–67; see also Gen 1:6–10, 20–22). However, its purpose here is more logical than aesthetic: in Exod 6, the peoplehood of Israel comes first because they are not yet a people; in Lev 26, the continuity of God's providence for Israel is the more important element.

and I will uphold my covenant with you. wehăqîmōtî 'et-běrîtî 'ittěkem. For the significance of this rendering of *hēqîm,* see COMMENT A.

10. *You shall eat. wa'ăkaltem.* This verse constitutes with the preceding one a single (fourth) blessing: even though you will be numerous, there will be food in abundance (Ibn Ezra). It thus adds to a similar statement in v. 5, where the abundance is natural; here, however, in prospect of the teeming population, the

abundance is supernatural (Hoffmann 1953). Thus there is no need to transpose this verse after v. 5 (Baentsch 1903). Besides, to do so would be wrong: the
introversion characteristic of the blessing pericope depends on positioning v. 10
exactly where it is (CC′ in the structure; see INTRODUCTION to vv. 3–13). To be
sure, Ezek 37:26–28 is modeled on 26:9, 11, 12. This, however, is not evidence
that Ezekiel did not find v. 10 in his Lev 26 *Vorlage*. All it means is that he
found v. 10 irrelevant—which it is in the context of Ezek 37.

   long stored. yāšān nôšān. There are two main interpretations of this idiom.
First, it connotes older than old (Ibn Ezra): "Better to eat three-year-old than
two-year-old grain" (Rashi; cf. Radak; based on *Sipra* Behuqotay 3:1) or nine-
year-old rather than eight-year-old grain (Bekhor Shor, Abravanel, Wessely 1846;
cf. Dillmann and Ryssel 1897), probably based on 25:20–22. This interpretation
is already adumbrated in the LXX *palaià kaì palaià palaiŵn* 'old and very old'
(see also Philo, *Sac.* 7a). Second, the word *nôšān* also denotes "of long-standing,
inveterate" (Lev 13:11; Deut 4:25). In this interpretation, accepted in the translation, the entire idiom means "very old," as *hăkāmîm měhukkāmîm* designates
"the very wise, the wisest of the wise" (Prov 30:24; Ehrlich 1899–1900 [H]).

   clear out. tôṣî'û. That is, take it from the granaries and sell it (Rashbam). Similarly, "you shall clear out [*tôṣî'*] the full tithe of your yield [i.e., from your gra-
naries] and leave it in your towns" (Deut 14:28).

V. 11–12. The Fifth Blessing: God's Presence in Israel

Just as the traditional typology of plague, famine, sword, and wild beasts will be
supplemented by a unique fifth set, God's punishing curses will pursue Israel
in its exile, so the fourfold set of typological blessings of abundant food, peace,
victory, and abundant life is now supplemented by a special blessing for Israel—
YHWH's continuous presence.

   11. *establish. wenatatti,* as opposed to *hāqîmōtî* 'uphold'. Whereas God's
covenant with Israel is never abrogated, his presence is not guaranteed unless
Israel is deserving of it—if it follows God's commandments (v. 3). For the full
discussion of the difference between these two seminal terms, see COMMENT A.

   my presence. miškānî. The usual translation "Tabernacle" (*skēnen,* LXX; *NEB*;
Kochman 1987, citing Num 5:3; 35:34; Exod 25:8; 29:45–46; Lev 15:31, but
only the last verse uses *miškān*) cannot be correct. To be sure, this is its meaning elsewhere in H (15:31; 17:4), but not here. The verb *wěnātattî* would testify
that there is no sanctuary building at the moment, which patently is not the
case; the blessings and curses, promises and admonitions, directed to the future,
presume that the sanctuary exists (contra Joosten, 1994: 174; 1996: 125). Thus
miškānî cannot refer to the Tabernacle or any other sanctuary building. The
other current renderings, "abode" (*NJPS*), "dwelling" (*NRSV*), and "Dwelling"
(*NAB*) are, perhaps deliberately, ambiguous.

   In keeping with H's tendency to render P's technical vocabulary metaphorically and figuratively (see Introduction I C), H has here transformed P's Tabernacle into an expression connoting the divine presence (Wessely 1846; Hoff-

mann 1953; Levine 1989; Sun 1990; Haran 1978: 14, n. 3). Manifestly, Ezekiel, the earliest interpreter of this verse, understood it this way:

> *wĕhāyâ miškānî ʾălêhem wĕhāyîtî lāhem lēʾlōhîm wĕhēmmâ yihyû-lî lĕʿām wĕyādĕʿû haggôyim kî ʾănî YHWH mĕqaddēš ʾet-yiśrāʾēl bihyôt miqdāšî bĕtôkām lĕʿôlām.*

My presence shall rest over them; I will be their God and they shall be my people. And when my sanctuary abides among them forever, the nations shall know that I the Lord do sanctify Israel. (Ezek 37:27–28 NJPS)

Note that in speaking of God's *miškan*, Ezekiel uses the preposition *ʿal* 'over' (v. 27), but in referring to God's *miqdāš*, the "sanctuary," or the physical build-ing (cf. Exod 25:8), he uses the preposition *bĕtôk* 'among' (v. 28; also v. 26). Clearly, the two nouns are not synonymous, and the former, the *miškan*, can connote only an ethereal, spatially unbounded presence. Hurvitz (1982: 109–13) is surely correct in concluding that Ezekiel's *miškān* is equivalent to and pro-leptic of rabbinic *šĕkînâ*, which also takes the preposition *ʿal* (cf. *šĕkînat yĕqārî*, Tg. Ps.-J.; *ʾîqar šĕkînātî*, Tg. Yer. to Lev 26:11). This also holds true, I maintain, for H, on which Ezekiel depends (see COMMENT B). Also supporting my inter-pretation is the verb used in the following verse *wĕhithallaktî* 'walk, move about' (v. 12), again implying that God's presence is not condensed into a building, but is present everywhere among the Israelites.

My interpretation is ostensibly contradicted by another H passage, Exod 29:42–46 (for its consignment of H, see Introduction I E). Its key phrases can be contrasted with 26:11a, 12.

Lev 26:11–12		Exod 29:42–46	
wĕnātattî miškānî bĕtôkĕkem	(v. 11a)	*ʾăšer ʾiwwāʿēd lākem (lĕkā, LXX, Sam.) šāmmâ*	(v. 42bα)
wĕhithallaktî bĕtôkĕkem	(v. 12aγ)	*lĕdabbēr ʾēlêkā šām*	(v. 42bβ)
		wĕnôʿadtî šāmmâ libnê yiśrāʾēl	(v. 43a)
		wĕšākantî bĕtôk bĕnê yiśrāʾēl	(v. 45aβ)
		lĕšoknî bĕtôkām	(v. 46aγ)

Both passages are similarly constructed, since they contain (not illustrated) the covenant formula (Exod 29:45b–46aα; Lev 26:12aβ,b) and the redemption from Egypt (Exod 29:46aβ; Lev 26:13a). But otherwise, they differ. Exod 29 speaks not of the *miškān* 'Tabernacle', but of the *ʾōhel môʿēd* 'the Tent of Meeting'. Of course, the terms refer to the same structure, but the differing choice of names is significant. The latter name is cited in its etymological quintessence. The pur-pose of *môʿēd* is that "I YHWH" *ʾiwwāʿēd lĕkā* (LXX, Sam.) *šāmmâ* 'will *meet* you (Moses) there' (Exod 29:42bα), and *wĕnôʿadtî šāmmâ libnê yiśrāʾēl* 'I

(YHWH) will *meet* the Israelites there' (Exod 29:43a). The reading of the Versions *lākem* > *lĕkā* makes sense in view of the rest of v. 42: *lĕdabbēr 'ēlêkā šām* 'to speak to you [sing.] there', a clear reference to Moses' exclusive mediation of the divine message to Israel. Also, one should note the near resemblance of *š* and *m* in the ancient Hebrew script (ש and מ). Thus the purpose of the Tent of Meeting is *communication*. The Tent is Israel's *oracular center*. In the priestly schema, the mediation of Moses is replaced by the Urim and Thummim administered by the high priest. This is why the sanctuary is indispensable. The difference between the two passages is highlighted by the word preceding the preposition *bĕtôk*. In Exod 29:45–46, it is the verb *šākan* 'rest' (see also Exod 25:8); in Lev 26:11–12, it is first *miškānî* 'presence' followed by *wĕhithallakî* 'walk about, circulate'. YHWH's presence is not limited to *one* sanctuary, but is present throughout the land in *many* sanctuaries. This precisely is the message of YHWH to the prophet Nathan: *lō' yāšabtî bĕbayit . . . wā'ehyeh* **mithallēk** *bĕ'ōhel ûbĕmiškān* '(From the day I brought the people of Israel out of Egypt to this day) I have not dwelt in a house, but have **moved about** in Tent and Tabernacle' (2 Sam 7:6). This, in my opinion, is an explicit statement that the Ark and its paraphernalia housed with a (the?) tented Tabernacle *moved about* Israel's major settlements before (and even after) the Temple was built (cf. Judg 20:1, 18, 23, esp. 27). Where else would the Ark and its Tent be housed if not within the sacred compound (*temenos*) of Mizpah, Bethel, Shilo, Gilgal, and other sanctuaries of Israel's settlements (see chap. 17, COMMENT D, no. 2). This usage is also a literary allusion to the Garden of Eden (Gen 3:8), an indication that paradisiacal conditions can be restored.

Alternatively, one should reckon with the possibility that we are dealing with a literary allusion. God's voice **moved about** (**mithallēk** *baggān*) the Garden (Gen 3:8); it will again happen in the paradisiacal conditions of the blessed land when God himself (not his voice) will move about. In this case, the image of YHWH's movements is metaphoric, not literal. Perhaps both interpretive options are viable.

The clear implication is that, in contrast to his location in P, YHWH is not confined to a sanctuary but is present everywhere in the land (see also Num 5:3 [H]). Perhaps this theology betrays the influence of the eighth-century prophets, who also posit that YHWH is dissociated from any sanctuary (e.g., Hos 5:6, 15; 9:15) and, moreover, that his sanctuary (*hêkāl*) is actually located in the heavens (Isa 6:1; Mic 1:2–3). However, the theology of the P School also postulated that though YHWH is to be sought in the sanctuary, he was at any time capable of leaving it (vol. 1.258–61).

and I will not expel you. wĕlō'tig'al napšî 'etkem. Literally and picturesquely, this is rendered "and my gullet will not expel you." The word *gā'al | gō'al* (mostly with *nepeš*) is found, in the Torah, only in this chapter (vv. 11, 15, 30, 43–44); elsewhere, in Jer 14:19 and Ezek 16:5, 45; and in the QL, where it is spelled *gā'al* (cf. 1QM 9:8; CD 12:16). It conveys the notion of "nausea, loathing." The primary meaning of *gā'al* is "abandon, spill, drop" (2 Sam 1:21b; Job 21:10). The idiom *gā'ălâ nepeš* means "gullet expels" and is the poetic synonym of *mā'as* 'reject' (vv. 15, 43; cf. Galatzer-Levy and Gruber 1992: 81–82). Here, however, *nepeš* denotes the essence of the divine being. The same idiom occurs in the list of curses (v. 30), where its meaning is reversed. However, the sequence in reverse order recurs in the appendix to the curses (vv. 43, 44, the latter verse without *nepeš*).

Rambam questions its propriety here: Can a negative statement be a blessing? Indeed, some regard it as an interpolation that breaks up the flow of 11a, 12a (Kochman 1987). However, it should be seen as serving a binding function, connecting the blessings with the curses (vv. 15, 30, 43, 44) and, thereby, it carries a powerful theological message: even if Israel loathes God's commandments (vv. 15, 43), God is ever ready *not* to loathe Israel (v. 44) and only awaits Israel's repentance (vv. 40–42).

Ehrlich (1908) connects this sentence (v. 11b) with the previous one (v. 11a), logically and psychologically: "When an earthly ruler condescends to dwell with persons who are beneath his status, he cannot allow those in his surroundings to feel that his relationship with them is beneath his dignity."

12. *I will walk about in your midst. wĕhithallaktî bĕtôkĕkem.* This is found again only in Ezek 19:6; 28:14. The *Qal hālak* means "walk" to a specific destination; the *Hitpaʿel hithallēk* also means "walk," but to move about, to and from (cf. 2 Sam 7:6–7). The choice of the *Hitpaʿel* is theologically significant: God will walk with his people, as he walked with Adam and Eve in the Garden of Eden (Gen 3:8; cf. Deut 23:15; *Sipra* Behuqotai 3:3; Wenham 1979). That is, God's blessings can bring a return of paradisiacal conditions. For the tradition that the Garden of Eden was a sanctuary, see *Jub* 3:8–14, *PRK* 1:1 (see NOTE on 12:4). The *Hitpaʿel* is also used of the patriarch's "walk" with God (Gen 5:24; 6:9; 17:1; 24:40; 48:15), implying a certain intimacy with the Deity gained, presumably, by moral rectitude (Skinner 1910: 131; Driver 1906: 77; cf. Helfmeyer 1978: 392–95). And as pointed out by Blum (1990: 326), in this idyllic setting God's *hithallēk* inverts the patriarchs' *hithallēk*, an indication that paradise has been regained.

I will (continue to) be your God, and you shall be my people. According to the priestly texts, this is the binding formula of the covenant: not the Abrahamic covenant (Gen 17:8), in which the second half of this formula is missing (the patriarchs are not an *ʿam*), but the Mosaic / Sinaitic covenant (Exod 6:7; cf. Buis 1974; note the inversion, stressing the innovation: Israel is about to become God's people). Blum (1990: 328) is certainly correct in noting the close association of vv. 9–13 with Exod 6:2–8 (especially by this full covenant formula), but he fails to realize that the latter as much as the former is the composition of the H School (see Introduction I E). The formula may be rooted in marriage and adoption terminology (Muffs 1965a; Weinfeld 1972d: 80–81; Joosten 1994: 142–47; 1996: 101–5). It is taken up by Ezekiel (11:20; 36:28) and reflected in 11QT 59:13.

As pointed out by Joosten (1994: 149–50; 1996: 106–7), the future setting of the covenant formula does not imply that the old covenant has been broken and must be established anew. Just as YHWH will remain Israel's God despite its disobedience, so his covenant with the fathers (v. 42) and with Moses (v. 45) will continue to remain in force (see COMMENT A). This is the only blessing not reversed in the curses.

13. *I YHWH am your God. ʾănî YHWH ʾĕlōhêkem.* The self-declaration formula of the Decalogue, but addressed to the people Israel (hence, the pl.). It is not a blessing in itself and, thus, is outside the introversion scheme (see INTRODUCTION to vv. 3–13). It is the Deity's assurance that the blessings will take place if Israel deserves them, a fitting closure to the blessings pericope. An index of this verse's independence of the structure (vv. 3–13) is that it and v. 3 are the only ones that do not begin with a *waw*. Also, they are not blessings in themselves, but function as an envelope for the entire structure (M. Hildenbrand). As a result, this verse is not reversed in the curses.

who freed you from the land of Egypt. This is continuation of the Decalogue self-declaration (see Exod 20:2). There, however, its purpose is to claim God's ownership of Israel (so, too, in Lev 25:42, 55). Here, it assures Israel that the one who performed the miraculous exodus from Egypt is, therefore, capable of performing all the enumerated blessings (*Sipra* Beḥuqotay 3:4).

from being their slaves. mihyōt lāhem ʾăbādîm. The *mem* with an infinitive can express a negative consequence (Gen 27:1; Exod 14:5; Deut 28:55; 1 Sam 15:26; Joüon 1923: 169h). Perhaps the model for this verse was Exod 6:7b, which also stems from the School of H: "And you shall know that I, YHWH, am your God who freed you from [*mittaḥat*, lit. "from under," the same *mem*] the burdens of Egypt."

The LXX omits *lāhem* 'their', presumably because it has no antecedent. Perhaps it was deliberately inserted in MT to contrast with *ʿăbāday hēm* (25:55) — that is, not their slaves, but "my slaves" (M. Hildenbrand). Smith (1996: 29) also noted this connection between chaps. 25 and 26: "Just as the individual Israelite was not to be enslaved, so the nation was meant to live freely."

I broke the bars of your yoke. wā ʾešbōr mōṭōt ʾullĕkem. This clause is repeated in Ezek 34:27b. "The ancient 'yoke' was a pole of wood, resting horizontally on the neck of an animal, or on the necks of a pair of animals; and the . . . 'bars' consisted of pieces of wood passing perpendicularly through the yoke, and fixed on each side of the neck by 'thongs' (*môsērôt*; Jer 2:20; 27:2)" (Driver and White 1894–98). Resting on the hump of the animal, the yoke appears to hold the animal down. Israel is here pictured as a beast of burden (cf. Isa 9:3; 10:27; 14:25). Therefore, when its yoke is removed, Israel can stand upright.

erect. qômĕmiyyût. This hapax is rendered *bĕqômā ʾ zêqûpā ʾ* 'in an upright posture' (*Tg. Ps.-J.*); that is, "so that they will not be afraid of any creature" (*Sipra* Beḥuqotay 3:7), as opposed to "your tormentors who have commanded you, 'Get down, that we may walk over you' — so that you made your back like the ground, like a street for passersby" (Isa 51:23; Sforno). An equivalent expression is *rômâ* 'erect' (from *rwm*, cf. Mic 2:3), and from the same root, but with a different nuance, *bĕyād rāmâ*, literally "with upraised hand," or defiantly (Exod 14:8).

Vv. 14–39. The Curses: Disobedience Is Punished

Five sets of curses (vv. 16–17; 18–20, 21–22, 23–26, 27–39) match the five sets of blessing (see INTRODUCTION to vv. 3–39). The increasing severity of the punishments can be seen in the introduction to the curses:

v. 16 *'ap- 'ănî 'e'ĕśeh-zō't*	*lākem*
v. 18 *wĕyāsaptî lĕyassĕrâ 'etkem*	*šeba' 'al-haṭṭĕ'ōtêkem*
v. 21 *wĕyāsaptî 'ălêkem makkâ*	*šeba' kĕhaṭṭĕ'ōtêkem*
v. 24 *wĕhālaktî 'ap-'ănî 'immākem*	
bĕqerî wĕhikkētî 'etkem gam 'ănî	*šeba' 'al-haṭṭĕ'ōtêkem*
v. 28 *wĕhālaktî 'immākem baḥămat-qerî*	
wĕyissartî 'etkem 'ap-'ănî	*šeba' 'al-haṭṭĕ'ōtêkem*

v. 16 I in turn will do this	to you
v. 18 I will go on to discipline you	sevenfold for your sins
v. 21 I will go on smiting you	sevenfold in measure for your sins
v. 24 I will continue in opposition to you:	
Yes, I myself will smite you	sevenfold for your sins
v. 28 I will continue in wrathful opposition to you;	
Yes, I myself will discipline you	sevenfold for your sins

Vv. 14–15. The Introduction to the Curses (vv. 16–39)

This introduction is twice the length of the introduction to the blessings (v. 3): three *'im* clauses against one *'im* clause.

14. *obey . . . observe all these commandments. tišmĕ'û . . . ta'ăśû 'ēt kol-ham-miṣwôt.* This is a repetition in the negative of the heading to the blessing pericope: *miṣwōtay tišmĕrû wa'ăśîtem* (v. 3), *šāma'* being equivalent to *šāmar*. Both these verbs require the additional verb *'āśâ* 'observe' since commandments are not violated by "keeping [*šāmar*]" or "obeying [*šāma'*]," connoting passivity, but by doing (*'āśâ*; see NOTE on v. 3).

these. hā'ēlleh. Which? "Those written" (i.e., previously in Leviticus; Ibn Ezra), which *Yahel 'Or* identifies as chaps. 18–20, 25–26, but which Witman (1987: 13) limits to chaps. 25–26. As chap. 26 is the epilogue to the entire H Code, probably all of chaps. 17–26 is intended.

15. *despise my laws. bĕḥuqqōtay tim'āsû,* the reverse of *bĕḥuqqōtay tēlēkû* (v. 3).

loathe. tig'al napšĕkem. Had you obeyed God's commandments, he would not have vomited you out (v. 11). The combination of *ga'al nepeš* and *mā'as* is found again in v. 43, Jer 14:19, and 1QS 2:26–3:1; note the influence of this entire verse on 11QT 59:8–9. These two verbs, as *tišmĕ'û*, in v. 14, are emotions, which in themselves are not violations (hence, unpunishable). Therefore, the specification that they lead to the violation of God's commandments and covenant.

my rules. mišpāṭay. This legal category is missing in v. 3. However, it is essential for completing the entire inventory of Israel's jurisprudence. It embraces case law, enforceable in a human court, which is civil law in the main (e.g., Exod 21:1–23:19; cf. Ramban).

observe all my commandments. ʿăśôt ʾet-kol-miṣwōtay. Repeating v. 14b and forming an inclusio with it, this is a typical instance of H style. Its effect is semantic as well as aesthetic: Israel spurns God's commandments twice over.

thereby breaking my covenant (with Ginsburg 1966). *lĕhaprĕkem ʾet-bĕrîtî.* This refers to rejection of God's promise to "uphold my covenant with you" (v. 9). Implied is that the observance of "all my commandments" was stipulated in the covenant. The referent is unmistakably the Sinaitic covenant, which according to H, included Leviticus (see NOTE on "my laws," v. 3, and the detailed discussion in NOTE on v. 45). The phrase *ʾet-bĕrîtî hēpēr* does occur in connection with the patriarchal covenant (Gen 17:14b), but it refers solely to the nonobservance of circumcision, the sign of the covenant.

The nearly equivalent phrase in Mesopotamian law codes is *awatiya uštepēl* 'revoked my commandments' (CH § 26b.29–30), where the referent of "my" is the king. Herein lies the contrast: it is the king's law, not God's; the idea of covenant between the deity and the people is absent.

Schwartz (1996), who claims that P (including H) does not contain a Sinaitic covenant ceremony or any recognition of it, can set aside the specific mention of *bĕrît* in vv. 9, 44, 45 as referring to the Abrahamic covenant on the grounds that its subject is uniformly the land promise (cf. Gen 17:7, 8). However, he has to rationalize *bĕrît* in this verse, where the subject is punishment for violating the commandments—a major Sinaitic agenda—as "a rhetorical reflex" (1996: 171). Besides, he overlooks *bĕrît* in v. 25 reflecting a similar theme (see NOTE on v. 45, and Introduction II F).

Vv. 16–17. The First Set of Curses: Illness, Famine, and Defeat

16. *I in turn* (with NJPS). *ʾap ʾănî.* The divine response to Israel's defection follows the principle of talion, which is a recurring motif in H. As pointed out by Douglas (1995: 252), righteousness that should prevail in the human realm, both positively (chap. 19, esp. vv. 11–18, 35–36) and negatively (24:17–22), is modeled by righteousness in the divine realm: if Israel will fulfill its covenantal obligations, God will bless it (26:3–13), but if it violates them, God will punish it commensurately (vv. 14–39).

will do. ʾeʿĕśeh. In response to Israel's *lōʾ taʿăśû* (v. 14), *biltî ʿăśôt* (v. 15)—that is, Israel's *double* rejection of God's laws.

I will bring . . . upon you. wĕhipqadtî ʾalêkem. The list of divine punishments in Jer 15:3–4 begins with the same phrase (in the *Qal*). It is a figurative extension of *pāqad* (*Hipʿîl*) 'appoint over' (see Gen 39:4; Jer 1:10).

panic. bĕhālâ. The absence of the definite article indicates that it is not the name of an affliction (Shadal), but a general term, the specifics of which follow. Perhaps for this reason, TN renders *bibĕhîlû* 'suddenly', making it an adverb (as does Ibn Ezra [second explanation]; Mendelssohn). The noun denotes "confusion, panic" (Isa 65:23; Jer 15:8; Ps 78:33). It stands in contrast to the blessing "you shall lie down, and no one shall make you afraid" (v. 6aβ).

consumption. haššaḥepet. This word is found only here and in Deut 28:22. In Arabic, *śuḥāp* means "consumption" (Saadiah, Ibn Janaḥ, Parḥon); therefore, this is an educated guess.

fever. haqqaddaḥat. The etymology of this word stands on firmer ground. The verb *qādaḥ Qal* means "be kindled" (Deut 32:22; Jer 15:14; 17:4) and "kindle" (Isa 50:11; 64:1). The noun occurs only here and in Deut 28:22.

Possibly these are plagues affecting the grain, as in "I scourged you with blight and mildew" (Amos 4:9), thereby explaining "You shall sow your seed to no purpose" (v. 16bα) and "the eyes that pine"—for grain (Shadal). But this interpretation is rejected by Ibn Ezra, since the enemy does take possession of the grain (v. 16bβ). Thus the diseases are intended to weaken the farmers so that they cannot oppose the invaders.

wearing out the eyes. mêkallôt ʿênayim, hoping that the body will be healed; *mĕhaššĕkān ʿênîn* 'obscuring the eyes' (*Tg. Onk*; cf. Ibn Ezra). "Any desire that does not come to fulfillment and any hope deferred is called *kîlyôn ʿênayim*" (Rashi); compare "Even now our eyes pine away [*tiklênâ ʿênênu*] in vain for our deliverance" (Lam 4:17). The same joint idioms are again found in Deut 28:65 and 1 Sam 2:33 (cf. Job 11:20; 17:5; 31:16).

and drying out the throat. ûmĕdîbōt nāpeš. The etymology is disputed and, hence, so are the interpretations: (1) from the root *d'b* (cf. Jer 31:12, also with *nepeš*; Ps 88:10, with "eye") or *'db*, a variant or corruption of *d'b*, meaning "languish" (Syr. and Arab.; cf. Greenspahn 1984: 109); thus a text similar to this one, *lekallôt 'et- ʿênêkā wĕlaʾădîb ʾet-napšekā* (1 Sam 2:33aβ), leads to the translation "causing the body to languish (*NJPS*); (2) from the root *dwb/zwb*, yielding "causing the life to pine away" (KB[3]); (3) *ûmappĕḥān nĕpaš* 'emotional exhaustion' (*Tg. Onk.*; cf. Rashi); (4) "causing your throat to dry" (Gruber 1987a), namely, a languishing and depression that lead to a medically verified drying of saliva. That *nepeš* originally denotes throat, a meaning it also has in Scripture, see Isa 5:14; 29:8; 32:6b; Jon 2:6; Ps 63:6; Prov 10:3, and the NOTES on 11:43 and 17:10 as well as Akkadian *napištu* (*CAD* 11, I:303–4). Note the parallelism *nepeš ʿăyēpâ* 'parched throat' and *nepeš dāʾăbâ* 'dry throat' (Jer 31:25), and that in this verse, it is juxtaposed with another bodily organ, *mĕkellôt ʿênayim* 'wearing out the eyes' (see also Deut 28:65; 1 Sam 2:33). This rendering is etymologically sound, contextually plausible, and, therefore, adopted here.

you shall sow your seed to no purpose. In contrast to the blessing of v. 5a (Bekhor Shor). This curse is spelled out by Micah: "You have been sowing, but have nothing to reap / You have trod olives, but have no oil for rubbing / And grapes, but have no wine to drink" (Mic 6:15). From the reverse, see Isa 62:8; 65:22–23 (note the parallelism of *bĕhālâ* and *lārîq*, as in this verse).

for your enemies shall eat it. In contrast to the blessing of v. 5bα (Bekhor Shor). The curse of Deut 28:33 is more terrifying: "A people *you do not know* shall eat up the produce of your soil and all your gains" (cf. Judg 6:2–4; Jer 5:17).

17. *I will set my face against you. wĕnātattî pānay bākem.* In contrast to the blessing *ûpānîtî ʾălêkem* 'I will look with favor upon you' (v. 9; *Sipra Beḥuqo-*

tay 4:4). For *pānâ b* 'turn against', see 17:10; 20:3, 5, 6; 26:17; Jer 44:11; Ezek 14:8; 15:7 (twice), and, especially, Lev 20:6, which uses both *pānâ 'et* and *pānâ b*. The addition of *lĕrā'â* in Jer 44:11 is for emphasis.

you shall be routed by your enemies. wĕniggaptem lipnê 'ōyĕbêkem. Reversing the blessing of v. 7a. This is the only attestation of the verb *nāgap* in the priestly texts, and neither it nor its nominal forms *negep, maggēpâ* is found meaning "defeat (in war)." Rather, they describe sickness and plague (e.g., Num 17:12–13). Paran (1989: 257) aptly cites the episode of the wilderness scouts, where the JE account warns Israel that it will be "routed [*tinnāgĕpû*] by its enemies" (Num 14:42), whereas P (or H) describes the death of the calumniating scouts in "a plague [*maggēpâ*] at the will of God" (Num 14:37). Military defeat in the curses of Lev 26 is always attributed to God (cf. vv. 25, 31, 32) and, indeed, the use of *ngp Nip'al* in this verse also points to its divine causer.

dominate you. wĕrādû bākem (cf. Akk. *redû* 'lead, direct, manage'). Note the synonymous phrase *wayyimšĕlû bāhem śōnĕ'êhem* 'their enemies ruled over them' (Ps 106:41). The LXX reading *wĕrādĕpû* 'pursue' is unacceptable because this verb must be followed either by *'aḥărê*, the direct object, or by the *beth* of means, and because it is contradicted by what immediately follows.

You shall flee though nobody pursues. In contrast to the blessing of v. 8. This theme returns in more poignant detail in vv. 36–37 (cf. Deut 28:25; Ps 53:6; Prov 28:1 LXX, noted by Sun 1990: 482). A punishment for disobedience is anxiety (cf. Gruber 1990a: 419, n. 30). It is the final and climactic result of "panic" (v. 16).

Vv. 18–20. The Second Set of Curses: Drought and Poor Harvests

18. *for all of that. 'ad-ēlleh* (with Ḥazzequni, who cites Gen 7:16; Job 2:4). Tg. Ps-J. renders *bĕtar 'îlên* 'after all this'. Note as well *bê'ēlleh* (v. 23) and *bezo't* (v. 27).

I will go on. wĕyāsāptî, from *yāsap* 'continue' (cf. Deut 5:19; Ibn Ezra).

to discipline. lĕyassĕrâ, an infinitive construct. Pi'el with a feminine ending (e.g., *zammĕrâ,* Ps 147:1; GKC § 52p; Joüon 1923: § 52c). YHWH utilizes corrective discipline to motivate repentance, either through the preaching of a prophet (Jer 7:28; Zeph 3:2) or, more likely, through suffering (vv. 18, 23; Isa 26:16; Jer 2:30; 5:3; 6:8; 10:24; 31:18; see Wessely 1846, on v. 28). In wisdom literature, it is executed through the rod (Prov 13:24; 22:15) and corporal punishment (Prov 23:13). God himself punishes redemptively "as a father disciplines his child" (Deut 8:5; cf. 21:18; cf. Branson and Botterweck 1990: 130). This chapter must have been a formative influence on the author of 2 Macc, who prays that if the people of Israel "should ever sin, they might be disciplined by him with forbearance" (2 Macc 10:4; cf. 6:12–17). The same theology, according to the Deuteronomist, graces the Davidic dynasty: God will punish its sinful descendants with "the rod of men and the affliction of mortals" (2 Sam 7:14; cf. Ps 89:33) without removing them from the throne.

sevenfold. šeba'. The word means "manyfold," although Ḥazzequni suggests that it alludes to the neglected sabbatical (v. 34) as a form of divine measure-for-measure punishment. However, it cannot be literal. First, there are only six punishments in vv. 16–17 (Ibn Ezra, contra Rashi, following *Sipra* Behuqotay 5:2, who has to count "You shall flee though none pursues" as two punishments). Then, if it were literal, it would be expressed by *šib'ātayim* (Gen 4:15, 24; Isa 30:26; Pss 12:7; 79:12; Prov 6:31; Dillmann and Ryssel 1897). Hence *šeba'* must be regarded as a round number (as in 1 Sam 2:5; Isa 4:1; Ps 119:164; Prov 24:16; Job 5:19; Luke 17:4). "When it comes to restitution or reimbursement, seven times seems to be the maximum, so it becomes a staple of speech or writing about such subjects" (D. N. Freedman, personal communication). More likely, however, the number seven has been chosen, regardless of the exact enumeration, because it was thought to possess a magical capacity of threat. As suggested by Gerstenberger (1996: 414), the verb *nišba'* 'swear' etymologically meant "be-seven oneself."

19. *I will break your proud strength. wěšābartî 'et-gě'ôn 'uzzěkem.* In contrast to "I broke the bars of your yoke" (v. 13bα). Ehrlich (1908) wants to emend the verb to *wěhišbattî* in accordance with the attested usage of the idiom (e.g., Ezek 7:24; 33:28; see below), but he overlooks the writer's artful intention to contrast it with *wā'ešbōr* in the blessing of v. 13bα.

your proud strength. gě'ôn uzzěkem. This refers to abundant harvests (Ibn Ezra) or the Temple (*Sipra* Behuqotay 5:2; cf. *Tgs. Neof., Ps.-J.*), the latter on the basis of "I am going to desecrate my sanctuary, the pride of your strength" (*gě'ôn uzzěkem*, Ezek 24:21).

Both interpretations, however, are negated by the other attestations of this idiom in Ezekiel: "*wěhišbattî gě'ôn 'azzîm* and their sanctuaries (LXX) shall be defiled" (Ezek 7:24); "those who support Egypt shall fall *wěyārad gě'ôn 'uzzāh'* (Ezek 30:6); "I will make the land a desolate waste *wěnišbat gě'ôn 'uzzāh*" (Ezek 33:28). Therefore, both in Ezekiel and here, I submit, the idiom should be rendered "the pride of your strength," referring to Israel's resistance, stubbornness, in its refusal to heed the punishment. God will break Israel's strength and resistance through the new punishment, famine (Mendelssohn 1846).

It is First Isaiah, however, who emphasizes that man's basic sin is his hubris (e.g., Isa 10:12–15). Often does he resort to the root *g'h* (Isa 2:12; 9:8; 13:3, 11, 19; 14:11; 16:6; 23:9; 28:1, 3, 11). He condemns towers and large ships and even natural heights (Isa 2:12–16) as being affronts to YHWH, the only legitimate source of *gā'ôn* (Isa 2:10, 19, 21; cf. 2:11; 5:15).

I will make your skies like iron and your earth like copper. In contrast to the blessing of v. 4a (Bekhor Shor). *Tg. Onq.* glosses correctly, "from letting the rain fall . . . from producing fruit" (cf. *Tgs. Neof., Ps.-J.*). The definitive article, *kab-barzel . . . kanněhūšâ*, is used with the genus, not with individual members; compare *bammišqāl* 'in scales', (v. 26) and the French *la femme* (Ehrlich 1908 [H]).

The entire statement occurs once more in Deut 28:23, but in reverse order: "The skies above your head shall be copper and the earth under you iron." It occurs again in expanded form, in an ancient Near Eastern treaty curse (the parallel in boldface): "May all the gods who are named in this treaty tablet reduce your soil in size to be narrow as a brick, **turn your soil into iron,** so that no one may cut a furrow in it. Just as **rain does not fall from a copper sky,** so may there

come neither rain nor dew upon your fields and meadows, but let it rain burning coals in your land instead of dew" (*VTE,* ll. 526–33; *ANET* 539).

Lev 26 is not influenced by either Deut 28 or *VTE* because of (1) the singular (Lev 26) versus the plural (Deut 28); (2) the rhythm: 3 + 2 (Lev 26), 3 + 3
(Deut 28); (3) the reverse order in Deut 28; (4) *VTE* is in prose. Perhaps all three
curses are dependent on an oral curse tradition (Hillers 1964: 42; 1984: 54–56).

copper. nĕḥûšâ. Rather than nĕḥōšet (Deut 28:23; cf. *hārê* nĕḥōšet, Zech 6:1),
a form found in poetry (Isa 45:2; Job 28:2; 40:18), perhaps in order to place the
stress at the end (R. Meridor). Also, it provides "gender matched parallelism"
(Watson 1986: 53): v. 19bα, masculine ‖ v. 19bβ, feminine.

20. *shall be spent.* wĕtam, from *tmm* (cf. Ezek 24:11).

to no purpose. lārîq. This is the same word used in v. 16, but there Israel's efforts produced grain (plundered by the enemies). In this verse, they will not even
do that because the land and its trees shall not yield (Bekhor Shor).

Your land shall not yield its produce. Reversing the blessing "the earth will
yield its produce" (v. 4bα; Bekhor Shor; cf. Deut 11:17).

nor shall the trees of your land yield their fruit. Reversing the blessing "the
trees of the field will yield their fruit" (v. 4bβ).

Vv. 21–22. The Third Set of Curses: Harmful Beasts

The same curse appears in Ezek 5:17; 14:15, 21 (attested in 2 Kgs 17:22–26).

21. *And if you continue in opposition to me* (with NRSV). wĕ'im-tēlĕkû 'immî
qerî. The contrastive goal is responsible for the choice of each word: wĕ'im tēlĕkû
balances *'im* (bĕḥuqqōtay) tēlĕkû (v. 3); (tēlĕkû) 'immî balances (wĕhithallaktî)
bĕtôkĕkem (v. 12); that is, God chose to be with Israel, but Israel rejected him. The
negation of the blessing is collapsed into one word qerî, bĕqerî. It appears seven
times (vv. 21, 23, 24, 27, 28, 40, 41), which indicates its significance as a key stylistic and semantic element in the entire list of curses. Its general meaning, derived
from the context, is clear, but its etymology (and precise meaning) is disputed:

1. *Tgs. Onk.* and *Neof.* render qerî as bĕqašyû 'stubbornly'; the LXX, *plágioi*
'perversely'; *Sam. Tg.* and Syr., *mar'ay* 'rebelliously'. All three translations render the Hebrew term from qārar 'be cold': qārâ 'cold wave' (Nah 3:17); mĕqērâ
'cool chamber' (Judg 3:24; Levine 1989), in which case qĕrî would be the nominal form of qārar as kĕlî 'tool' from kālal (R. Meridor). The sense here would
be "you treat me coldly." However, this interpretation would render baḥămat-
qerî 'in wrathful fury', a "meaningless oxymoron" (B. S. Schwartz, personal
communication).

2. *Tg. Ps.-J.* renders it bĕ'ar'ay 'incidentally, nonchalantly' (cf. *m. Ta'an.* 1:3;
Sipra Beḥuqotay 11:5) from miqreh 'chance, accident'. That is, Israel denies
God's providence and regards its deprivations as the result of chance; God will,
therefore, remove his presence and let "chance"—the forces of chaos—prevail
over Israel (Ibn Ezra; Radak; Maimoides, *Guide,* chap. 36; *Letter to Yemen*).

3. In Ugaritic, the root qry means "encounter, meet with" (*KTU* 1.3 II:4–5).
It and its byform qr' with the preposition *lamed* yield liqrat (e.g., *'îš* liqrat rē'ô
'one [gang] toward the other'; Siloam inscription, *KAI* 189, 4) or liqra't 'toward'

and 'against, contrary to' (e.g., Num 21:23; 1 Sam 4:2; 17:2; 2 Sam 10:9, 10, 17). Therefore, *hālak qerî* means literally "walk against, contrariwise" (e.g., *bĕlektēnû qerî bĕhuggê habbĕrît*, lit. "walking contrariwise against the ordinances of the covenant," (CD 20:29). Thus if Israel walks contrary to God (vv. 21, 23, 27, 40), God, in turn, will walk contrary to Israel (vv. 24, 48, 41) in reciprocal opposition (adopted in the translation).

for your sins. kĕḥaṭṭō'tĕkem. Here Ibn Ezra must be rendering literally "in accordance with your sins" because he remarks "and not more." Indeed, Abravanel (citing *Seder 'Olam*) claims that it refers to the neglected sabbaticals. However, the comparative *kap* need not refer to number (quantity) but to gravity (quality), and, as discussed in v. 18, *šebā* need not be rendered its precise number, but as "manifold."

22. *I will let loose wild beasts against you.* Reversing "I will eliminate vicious beasts from the land" (v. 6bα; Bekhor Shor). The *Hip'îl wĕhišlaḥtî bĕkā* with the *beth* of hostility is attested elsewhere, such as *hinĕnî mašlîaḥ bĕkā* 'behold, I am sending against you' (Exod 8:17; cf. 2 Kgs 15:37; Ezek 14:13; Amos 8:11 [also punishments]). The outbreak of wild beasts is frequently regarded as a punishment for sin (Deut 32:24; 2 Kgs 2:24; 17:25; Isa 13:21, 22; Ezek 5:17; 14:15; cf. Hillers 1964: 54–56). Weinfeld (1993: 191, n. 17) aptly points to a similar series of punishments of drought, wasteland, and wild animals (vv. 20–22) that appears in the Sefire treaty 1A 27–28 (eighth century B.C.E.).

Gerstenberger (1996: 417) aptly points to the story of the bears that mauled the forty-two children who were cursed by Elisha for having teased him by calling him "baldy" (2 Kgs 2:23–24) as playing the same role in Israel as the "bogey bear" in our tradition, namely, if you children do not behave, you will be eaten by the bears. Here, too, the adults are warned that if they do not heed YHWH's commandments, predatory beasts will devour them.

they shall bereave you. Reversing "and (I) shall make you fruitful" (v. 9aβ); note the emphasis on *pĕrî* 'fruit, offspring'. Ezekiel repeats this verse almost verbatim (Ezek 5:17; cf. 14:15).

make you few. wĕhim'îṭâ 'etkem (cf. Ezek 29:15b). This statement is not redundant in view of the previous "they shall bereave you," since its purpose is to reverse the blessing *wĕhirbêtî 'etekem* 'multiply you' (v. 9aγ; Ḥazzequni). Perhaps, this explains why *hirbêtî* is separated from *hiprêtî* in v. 9 in order to be matched by two distinct curses.

and your roads shall be deserted. The same sequence, wild beasts and deserted roads, is found in Ezekiel: "Or, if I were to send wild beasts to roam the land and they depopulated it, and it became a desolation with none passing through it because of the beasts" (Ezek 14:15; cf. Judg 5:6; Isa 33:8; Lam 1:4). This is a standard curse in the ancient Near East: "That no one tread the highways, that no one seek out the roads" (*ANET* 612, l. 39).

Vv. 23–26. The Fourth Set of Curses: War, Pestilence, and Famine

23. *in spite of these (things). bĕ'elleh*, explicated by *Tgs. Ps.-J.* and *Neof.* as "by these chastisements."

you are not disciplined for me. tiwwāsĕrû lî. Rashi explicates "to turn to me (in repentance)." For *lamed* as "for," see *kōhēn lĕ'ēl 'elyôn* 'a priest of God Most High' (Gen 14:18); *yē'āśeh lākem* 'prepared for you' (Exod 12:16). For the *Nip'al* of *yāsar,* see Jer 6:8; Ps 2:10; Prov 29:19.

24. *I too. 'ap-'ānî.* Or "even I" (BDB; cf. Andersen 1974: 166); "I myself" (Sun 1990: 452, citing 2 Kgs 2:14, where the LXX, however, reads *'ēpō'*). God will match Israel's *qerî* with *qerî,* but will punish "seven times over"; that is, the manifold punishments will be more severe than those enumerated in v. 22. The series plague, famine, and sword is not just a hypothetical formula; it was experienced by Israel, as attested by Jeremiah (14:12; 21:7, 9; 24:10; 27:8, 13; 29:17; Elliger 1966).

25. *I will bring a sword against you.* Reversing "no sword shall traverse your land" (v. 6bβ; but see NOTE on "and I will unsheath the sword after you," v. 33). Also, the same sword that "cuts a covenant" to establish a relationship between the parties will now be used to punish the party or parties violating the covenant (N. Shaked). *Tg. Onk.* explicated "sword" by *bĕqāṭlîn bĕḥarbā'* 'those who kill by the sword' (cf. *Tg. Ps.-J.*). For the expression, see Ezek 5:17; 6:3; 14:17; 29:8.

executing vengeance. nōqemet. Mendenhall (1973: 96) renders our verse "redressing (the redress of the covenant)" by deriving this verb from Amarna Akkadian *naqāmu,* which, he claims, is "either based upon some sense of legitimacy or is actually the prerogative of the divine world." This definition has been rebutted by Pitard (1982) as a faulty understanding of Amarna Akkadian, which justifies in many instances the customary rendering "revenge" and in others "just recompense."

Instead, Westbrook (1988: 94) focuses on the juridical parameters of this term: "*nqm* is exacted not upon the wrongdoer himself but either upon the whole group that he represents or upon selected members of that group, especially children of the wrongdoer." As examples, he cites God's revenge on foreign nations (Isa 34:5–12), on Israel (Ezek 24:6–8, 21–23; note "your sons and daughters whom you left behind," v. 21), on oppressors within Israel (Isa 1:22–31), on men of Anathoth (Jer 11:21–23), on Saul's household (1 Sam 24:12; 2 Sam 4:8), and on Ahab's household (2 Kgs 9:7; Westbrook 1988: 92–94).

vengeance for the covenant. This refers to the Sinaitic covenant (Exod 24:8), which Israel has broken (v. 15b). Elements of rewards and punishments are absent in the patriarchal covenant (cf. Knohl 1995: 141–45). The triad of punishments—sword, plague, and famine—explicitly follows in the wake of the breaking of a covenant (Jer 34:17; cf. Isa 33:8; Ezek 17:11–21). The entire expression surfaces in the QL (CD 1:17–18; 19:1). Peels (1994: 84–89), cited by Joosten (1994: 159, n. 70; 1996: 114, n. 78), claims that this expression refers to the punitive rights of the suzerain in case the vassal proves treasonous. Such, indeed, is the use of the root *nqm* in its two occurrences in the Aramaic treaty from Sefire (Sefire II, 11–12; III, 22).

if you withdraw into your cities. wĕne'ĕsaptem 'el-'ārêkem. This rendering would require shifting the *'atnāḥ* from *'ārêkem* to *bĕrît.* The meaning is elucidated in Jeremiah: *hē'āsĕpû wĕnābô'â 'el- 'ārê hammibṣār* 'Assemble, and let us go into the fortified cities' (Jer 4:5; cf. 35:11; *Sipra* Beḥuqotay 6:1). The purpose is explicitly elucidated in 2 Chr 11:11–12a: "He (Rehoboam) strengthened the fortified towns and put commanders in them, along with stores of food, oil, and wine, and shields and spears in every town." That is, fortified cities prepared for the eventuality of a siege by stocking ample supplies of food and weapons.

I will send. wĕšillaḥtî deber, literally "I will release pestilence." The language betrays the original notion of personified forces of the divine assembly acting as agent of YHWH, such as *hammašḥît* 'the Destroyer' (Exod 12:23), *hammal'āk* 'the Messenger' (Zech 4:1), *haśśāṭān* 'the Accuser' (Job 2:1). The natural forces are also personified as members, such as "the Wind / Spirit" (1 Kgs 22:21–23; cf. Isa 31:3; Ps 148:8; Job 4:15–16) and the astral bodies (Josh 5:13–15; 10:12b–13a; Judg 5:20; Ps 148:2–3; Job 38:7). Even more striking is that the Semitic god *rešep*, who is illustrated as a flame of fire in Egyptian paintings, is attested in the Bible as YHWH's agent of plagues (Hab 3:5) also in the form of fire (Song 5:6; Sir 16:8; cf. Loewenstamm 1976: 437–41). It is therefore not unexpected that *šlḥ Pi'el* is consistently used for fire released by YHWH as his agent of destruction (e.g., Ezek 39:6; Hos 8:14; Amos 1:4, 7, 10, 12; 2:2, 5). The same holds for other divine agents of destruction, such as *deber* 'pestilence' (Lev 26:25; Ezek 14:19; 28:23; Amos 4:10; 2 Chr 7:13).

It is not by accident that *šlḥ Pi'el* is deliberately avoided in regard to the agency of wild beasts, and instead *wĕhišlaḥtî Hip'îl* (v. 22) is used for the obvious reason that the earth's wild beasts were never members of the divine assembly (the poetry of Deut 32:24 is not that discriminating). The same nuance marks the other attestations of *šlḥ Hip'îl*. Note that in Ezek 5:17 it is again applied to animals. The human enemy (2 Kgs 15:37) is surely not part of the heavenly hosts. Famine (*rā'āb* 'famine', Amos 8:11) ostensibly is an exception, but as the rest of the verse explains, the "famine" is for the word of God. Ezekiel's use of *šlḥ Hip'îl* in regard to *rā'āb* (14:13) is truly an anomaly. But elsewhere, Ezekiel consistently employs the *Pi'el* with *rā'āb* (5:17; 14:21); indeed, it appears *in the same chapter* (14:19, 21), which arouses the suspicion that in 14:13 *wĕhišlaḥtî* should be emended to *wĕšillaḥtî*.

In any event, the caveat must be added, this verb betrays the personification of the subject from an earlier period. In the Bible, however, it serves to reify, not to personify, a literary means of vivifying the activity of God.

among you. bĕtôkĕkem. Perhaps this is a play on the same word in v. 12. Instead of God himself moving about the land "among you," he will send his pestilence. Also, *bĕtôkĕkem* contrasts with *bākem* 'against you' (v. 22). That is, your cities will not help you, "for death will strike you within while sword bearers will surround you without" (*Sipra* Beḥuqotay 6:1). Crowding together will make the besieged vulnerable to pestilence, killing both humans and animals (Exod 9:3; Deut 32:25; Jer 24:10; Lam 1:20; Noordtzij 1982). Ezekiel spells it out in detail: "one-third of you shall die of pestilence or perish in your midst by famine" (Ezek 5:12); "The sword is outside and pestilence and famine are inside; he who is in the open shall die by the sword, he who is in the city shall be devoured by famine and pestilence" (Ezek 7:15; cf. Jer 21:6–9; 34:17). *Seper Hamibḥar* suggests that the text is speaking of a past occurrence because of the cantillation mark on the penultimate, instead of the ultimate, syllable *wĕšillaḥti*; however, there is no consistency in the tone shift (GKC § 49k, l). Moreover, the principle of *nāsôg ʾāḥôr* operates here because of the penultimate accent on the following word (GKC § 29e).

Pestilence (*deber*) is surely one of the forms personified by "the Destroyer" (*hammašḥît*). Once God sets loose (*Piʿel* rather than *wĕhišlaktî*, Hip̄ʿil, v. 22) the Destroyer, it mows down everything in its path, as forcefully expressed by the rabbis; *miššennittĕnâ rĕšût lammašḥît lĕhabbēl ʾênô mabḥîn bên ṣaddîq lĕrāšāʿ* 'Once the destroyer is given permission to injure it does not discriminate between the righteous and the wicked' (*Mekh*. Bo on Exod 12:23). In this way, the rabbis rationalize theologically the amorality of natural disasters, putting the blame on the agent rather than on God himself. In this regard, they take their cue from Scripture. The verse dealing with the activity of the Destroyer reads as follows: *ûpāsaḥ YHWH ʿal-happetaḥ wĕlōʾ yittēn hammašḥît lābōʾ ʾel-bāttêkem lingōp* 'and YHWH will protect the doors and not let the Destroyer enter your homes' (Exod 12:23b). Thus were it not for YHWH's personal intervention to protect the Israelite homes, the Destroyer indiscriminately would also kill Israel's firstborn. (For the verb *pāsaḥ* 'protect', see the NOTE on "a paschal offering," 23:5.)

and you shall be delivered. wĕnittattem. That is, you will be too weak to resist. Alternatively, this *Nipʿal* may be rendered as a reflexive, "you shall deliver yourselves"; that is, you will want to surrender (Ibn Ezra; Kilian 1963).

26. The triad of sword, pestilence, and hunger is found in this order only in Jer 34:17 (but substituting *rāʿāb* for the metaphoric "when I break your staff of bread"). The most common order is sword, hunger, and pestilence (Jer 14:12; 21:9; 24:10; 27:8, 13; 29:17–18; 32:24, 36; 38:2; 42:17, 22: 44:13; Ezek 6:11; 7:15; 12:16). Alternative orders are pestilence, sword, hunger (Jer 21:7); hunger, pestilence, sword (Ezek 5:17). Ezekiel adds a fourth calamity: wild beasts (Ezek 14:21).

When I break. bĕšībrî. For a similar vocalization, see *bĕšikbāh* (Gen 19:33). This verb was chosen because of "staff," but its use is metaphoric, like *mišʿān* 'prop' (Isa 3:1; Ibn Ezra); *maṭṭēh ʿōz* 'strong rod' (Jer 48:17; Rashi). This curse reverses the blessing *wāʾešbōr mōṭōt ʿullĕkem* 'I broke the bars of your yoke' (v. 13bα; B. Begleiter); that is, whereas God once broke the bars of your bondage, he will now break the staff of your existence (*mût* and *maṭṭeh* [from *nṭh*] may be related; cf. Ug. *mṭ*, pl. *mṭm*). Gerstenberger (1996: 419), however, points out that the metaphor of broken bread staff has a literal basis. It refers to the pole on which the cakes of bread in the form of rings were hung to protect them from mice. Figuratively, this means that there will be no more stores of bread.

staff of bread. maṭṭēh-leḥem, that is, *sĕʿēd mêklāʾ* 'your supply of food' (*Tg. Onq*.; cf. *Tg. Ps-J*.). The same metaphor is found in Ezek 4:16; 5:16; 14:13; cf. Isa 3:1; Ps 105:16. Lev 26:25–26a has replaced hunger with this metaphor and placed it last, after sword and pestilence (D. Stewart). Ezekiel adopts this metaphor twice and feels constrained both times to explain that it means hunger (Ezek 5:16; 14:13)—a clear sign of borrowing (see COMMENT C)—placing it first in the order and adding a fourth calamity, wild beasts (5:16–17; 14:13–20), but altering the order in his summary for chiastic effect (Ezek 14:21).

That besieged cities were frequently reduced to starvation is expressly admitted in Jer 37:21: "So King Zedekiah gave instructions to lodge Jeremiah in the person compound and to supply him daily with a loaf of bread from the Bakers' Street—*until all the bread in the city was gone*" (Eph'al 1996: 59, n. 62).

ten women. That is, "many" (Saadiah, Ramban), another round number (cf. Gen 31:7; Zech 8:23; Job 19:3). This image is a popular one in ancient Near Eastern curses: *wm ʾh: nswn: l'pn btnwr: lḥm: w'l: yml'mh* 'May 100 women bake bread in an oven and not fill it' (Tell Fekhariyeh Assyrian–Aramaic Bilingual, l. 22; see Millard and Bordreuil 1982; Greenfield and Shaffer 1983; Sasson 1985; Grapp and Lewis 1985). Sefire prefers the seven typology: *wsbʿ bnth y'pn b[]ʿ lḥm w'l yml'n* 'And may his seven daughters bake bread in an oven(?) but not fill it' (Sefire I, A:24, as restored by Kaufman 1982). Note also "Let there be no sound of the grinding stone or the oven in your houses, let barley rations to be ground disappear for you, so that they grind your bones, (the bones of) your sons and daughters instead of barley rations, and not even the (first) joint of your finger should be able to dip into the dough, may the [. . .] eat the dough from your troughs" (*VTE,* ll. 444–49; *ANET* 538).

in a single oven. For lack of wood (Rashi, Ehrlich 1899–1900 [H]) or for lack of bread dough (Rashbam), one oven can suffice. The simple oven was a pit about 2.5 feet in diameter. The dough was slapped against its sides or placed in a vessel. Branches, rape, or dung (Mal 3:15) served as fuel. To prevent fires or smoke, ovens were sometimes built not in private courtyards, but in public places, such as "the Tower of Ovens" (Neh 3:11; Stern and Gilboa 1987).

they shall dole out your bread. wĕhēšîbû laḥmĕkem. That is, to those who gave them the flour; otherwise, the text would have read *laḥmān* 'their (the women's) bread' (Ehrlich 1899–1900; and is so interpreted by Ezekiel, below). For this meaning of *hēšîb,* see *wĕhăšîbēhû* 'turn it over' (1 Kgs 22:26) and *yāšûbû rĕšāʿîm lišĕʾōlâ* 'the wicked shall depart to sheol' (Ps 9:18 NRSV). Ehrlich (1899–1900) also cites *hēšîb ʿāšām* 'make reparation / restitution' (e.g., Num 5:7, 8; 18:9). Here, however, *hēšîb* means "return"; it is based on *wĕhēšîb ʾet-haggĕzēlâ* 'he shall return that which was stolen' (Lev 5:23). It is as though, in committing desecration, a person had illicitly taken something from God that he now returns (cf. Milgrom 1976a: 13–14). Not all the bread is removed to induce Israel to repent; v. 29, however, implies total starvation (Wessely 1846).

Ezekiel expands this verse: *hinĕnî šōbēr maṭṭēh-leḥem biyrušālayim* (Qere perpetum) *wĕʾākĕlû-leḥem bĕmišqāl ûbidĕʾāgâ ûmayim bimĕśûrâ ûbĕšimmāmôn yištû* 'I am going to break the staff bread in Jerusalem, and they shall eat bread by weight, in anxiety, and drink water by measure, in horror' (Ezek 4:16).

and though you eat, you shall not be satisfied. waʾăkaltem wĕlōʾ tiśbāʿû. Reversing *waʾăkaltem laḥmĕkem lāśōbāʿ* (v. 5bα). A similar theme prevails elsewhere in Scripture (e.g., Hos 4:10a; Amos 4:6–8; Mic 6:14) and in the ancient

Near East: "seven nurses shall anoint [their breasts, and] suckle a child, but let him not be satisfied; [seven] cows shall suckle a calf, but let it not be satisfied; seven sheep shall suckle a lamb, but [let it not be] satisfied" (Sefire I, A:21–24).

Vv. 27–39. The Fifth Set of Curses: God Abandons His Cult Places and Land and Pursues Israel in Exile

These verses constitute a reversal of the fifth blessing (vv. 11–12).

27. *despite this. bĕzō't.* This is the same *beth* as in *bĕkōl hā'ōtōt* 'despite all the signs' (Num 14:11; Ehrlich 1899–1900 [H]); that is, if after these four sets of punishments, Israel has still not changed its ways.

28. *in wrathful opposition. baḥămat-qerî.* Whereas in the previous (fourth) set of curses, God's and Israel's hostility (*qerî*) to each other have been in balance, here God's *qerî* is intensified. Note that Ezekiel also uses the term *ḥēmâ* to express God's increased anger: *bĕ'ap ûbĕḥēmâ ûbĕtōkĕḥōt ḥēmâ*, literally "in anger, in fury and in fury of chastisements" (Ezek 5:15). According to Gerstenberger (1996: 420), "This is the intensification that makes the person of antiquity genuinely quake. 'Do not rebuke me in your anger, or discipline me in your wrath,' pleads the Psalmist (cf. Pss. 6:2; 38:2). What they do not want is to be subject to impulsively imposed—albeit justified—punishment; rather, they would prefer to wait. All this is conceived in a very human fashion until God has calmed down and allow his milder disposition to reign. In this text, however, God's full wrath is turned loose."

Because of God's wrath, he no longer applies the measure-for-measure principle, but exacts punishments that find no counterpart in Israel's behavior: cannibalism, destruction, exile (for the ostensible exception of vv. 34–35, see their NOTES).

I myself (with Sun 1990).

will discipline you. wĕyissartî 'etkem. It is significant that the final and most severe set of curses is designated as "discipline." This is the first of a series of hints that YHWH does not intend to abandon Israel (see NOTES on "desolate," v. 31; "lost," v. 38; and vv. 34–35).

29. *You shall eat. wa'ăkaltem.* God is not the subject; hence this curse is a continuation. Such, indeed, it must be since cannibalism is likely only when there is a shortage of food (see v. 26).

An ABCB'C'A' chiastic construction, this repeats the noun *bĕśar* (BB') and the verb *'ākal* (AA'), the latter in typical perfect–imperfect H style.

Cannibalism is a frequent theme in ancient Near Eastern curses. For example, "May you eat in your hunger the flesh of your children, may, through want and famine, one man eat the other's flesh, clothe himself in the other's skin" (*VTE*, ll. 449–51; *ANET* 538). According to the prophetic story in 2 Kgs 6:28–29, Israel actually experienced cannibalism during the Aramean wars (Dillmann and Ryssel 1897; Noth 1977). As noted by Greenberg (1985: 113–14), Ezekiel borrows this theme and expands it: "Assuredly, parents shall eat their children in your midst, and children shall eat their parents" (Ezek 5:10a; cf. Jer 19:9; Mic 3:2–3; Lam 2:20; 4:10). However, the most appalling description of cannibalism is found toward the end of the deuteronomic series of curses:

He who is most tender and fastidious among you shall be too mean to his brother and the wife of his bosom and the children he has spared to share with one of them any of the flesh of the children that he eats, because he has nothing left as a result of the desperate straits to which your enemy shall reduce you in all your towns. And she who is most tender and dainty among you, so tender and dainty that she would never venture to set a foot on the ground, shall begrudge the husband of her bosom, and her son and her daughter, the afterbirth that issues from between her legs and the babies she bears; she shall eat them secretly, because of utter want, in the desperate straits to which your enemy shall reduce you in your towns. (Deut 28:54–57)

30. *your cult places. bāmōtēkem.* Comprehensive discussions of the *bāmâ* are found in Vaughan (1974), Haran (1978: 18–25; 1981a), and Emerton (1997). Two points made by Vaughan merit mention here. First, the funerary origin of *bāmâ*, advocated by Albright (1957), must be rejected (see also Barrick 1975). Second, the accepted rendering "high place," first advanced by the LXX (cf. Macalister 1912), must also be abandoned, since the *bāmâ* could be a valley shrine, such as the *bāmâ* in the Valley of Ben Hinnom outside Jerusalem (Jer 32:35; cf. Ezek 6:3). Moreover, Ezekiel states explicitly: "Thus said the Lord YHWH to the mountains and to the hills, to the gullies [*lā'ăpîqîm*] and to the valleys [*wĕlaggē'āyōt* (*-'ēyôt* Q)]: I am going to bring a sword upon you and destroy your cult places [*bāmôtêkem*]" (Ezek 6:3b). Possibly, Greek *bōmós* 'altar' (i.e., "place of sacrifice," ("base of statue," or "platform for a chariot") became contaminated with Ugaritic *bmt* 'back', imposed its Greek phonology on Hebrew *bāmâ*, and led to LXX "high place" (Brown 1980: 1–7; cf. *bāmāsêkôn, Tg. Neof.*).

It is now certain that the *bāmâ* was not an open-air altar (cf. Barrick 1980; 1992; 1996; Nakhai 1994; Catron 1995; contra Haran 1978: 23–25). The *liškâ* 'chamber' (1 Sam 9:22), where Samuel and his invited guests ate the sacrificial meal, most likely lay within the *temenos*, the sacred compound (see also 1 Sam 1:18b LXX). More compelling is Solomon's dream at the great *bāmâ* of Gibeon, where he not only sacrificed but spent the night in the hope of a divine revelation (1 Kgs 3:4–5). This is the well-attested *incubatio*, which had to take place *within* the sacred compound, if not *inside the temple* itself (cf. 1 Sam 3:3–4), as attested in other ancient Near Eastern cultures: Egyptian (Bergmann 1980: 423), Hittite (Ottosson 1980: 424), Mesopotamian (Oppenheim 1956: 188), Mari (Botterweck 1980), West Semitic (Ottosson 1980: 426). These rooms for sacrificial meals and incubations, therefore, most likely were located in chambers that adjoined the the sanctuary, such as those found in the Arad temple complex (Aharoni 1968; Herzog et al. 1984; cf. Barrick 1992: 199). More decisive evidence is provided by the language itself, namely, the prepositions and verbs used with *bāmâ*. The preposition is routinely *be* (twenty times), not *'al* (for the ostensible exception, Isa 16:12, see Barrick 1992: 199). The difference in cultic usage is decisively demonstrated by their juxtaposition in 2 Kgs 16:4: *wayĕzabbēaḥ wayĕqaṭṭēr babbāmôt wĕ'al-haggĕbā'ôt* 'And he sacrificed (animals) and made (cereal) offerings [a non-P usage; cf. Haran 1978: 233–34] *in* the *bāmôt* and *on* the hills' (cf. Barrick 1996: 641, n. 93). Moreover, that 1 Kgs 3:4 and 2 Kgs 23:15 juxtapose *bāmâ* and *mizbēaḥ* (also 2 Kgs 18:22; Isa 36:7) indicate that they refer to "two different phenomena" (Barrick 1996: 641; contra Vaughan 1974: 32–33; Haran 1978: 24–25, n. 21). Thus the prepositional evidence demonstrates that the *bāmâ* cannot be an open-air altar or a raised platform, such as that found at Tel Dan (Biran 1998), but must be an installation within which cultic acts take place (Tur-Sinai 1938: 30; Barrick 1992: 197).

This conclusion is reinforced by the utilized verbs. The description of the *bāmâ* in 1 Sam 9 makes it certain that since eating (*'ākal*) takes place inside a *liškâ* 'chamber' (v. 22), then *ya'āleh habbāmātāh le'ĕkōl* (v. 13) must be rendered "would go up *to* the *bāmâ* [note the locative *heh*] to eat" (see also v. 19). Finally, the verb *bā'* 'enter' in *habbā'îm* with preceding *hābbāmāh* (Ezek 20:29; a mocking pun; cf. Greenberg 1983a: 370–71) clinches the case that *bāmâ* is a structure within which cultic acts are performed.

What, then, is the difference between *miqdāš* and *bāmâ*? They are not equivalent (cf. Amos 7:9; Isa 16:12). I have long maintained (Milgrom 1970: 23–24, n. 78) that *miqdāš* never means a sanctuary building, but refers to the sacred precincts, the *temenos*, in which the building and its cultic installations are located. The building would be called *bêt hammiqdāš*, literally "the house of the sacred area" (2 Chr 36:17). It would be roughly equivalent to *bêt / bātê-bāmôt*, possibly a derisive term used for a non-Judahite *miqdāš* (tentatively, see Barrick 1996).

Idolatrous *bāmôt* are banned in H (Num 33:52 is probably H). The identity of the *bāmôt* referred in this verse, unfortunately, cannot be determined. It must be kept in mind that the pre-deuteronomistic sources of the Former Prophets do not display negative attitudes toward the *bāmâ* (1 Sam 9:12–25; 10:5; 1 Kgs 3:4). Neither do the eighth-century prophets regarding the cultic sites of other people (Isa 15:2; 16:12) or those of the Israelites decreed for destruction (Amos 7:9; cf. Haran 1978: 20). These latter *bāmôt* were centers for YHWH worship, whereas in our verse, to judge by its remainder, they were idolatrous (contra Nakhrai 1994: 29, n. 10).

Thus to judge by the distinction between *bāmôt* and *miqdāšîm* in vv. 30–31, we may be witnessing, for the only time, a new differentiation between them: *bāmôt* is a house for the worship of pagan gods; *miqdāš*, a house for the worship of YHWH. This distinction certainly was not adopted by the Deuteronomist, since he maintains that YHWH's worship also prevailed at the *bāmôt* (cf. 2 Kgs 23:8; Isa 36:7 [=2 Kgs 18:22]. Also his recurrent comment *wĕlō' hēsîr 'et-habbāmôt* [1 Kgs 15:14; 22:44; 2 Kgs 12:4; 14:4; 15:4, 35] refers to cult sites dedicated to YHWH). Thus the Deuteronomist distinguishes between only legitimate and illegitimate cult sites—that is, the Jerusalem Temple to all others, though they may also practice the worship of YHWH. The book of Deuteronomy is silent on these matters, mentioning neither *bāmôt* nor *miqdāšim*. A possible reason, suggested by M. Weinfeld (personal communication), is that Deuteronomy is anachronistically ascribed to wilderness-bound Moses, who would not have known of the existence of such institutions in Canaan. Ezekiel, it should be noted, follows the Deuteronomist, not H. If *mĕqadšēhem* (MT of Ezek 7:24) is revocalized *miqdĕšēhem*, a reference to pagan sanctuaries (see NOTE on 26:31), then it may be claimed that Ezekiel also did not accept H's distinction between *bāmôt* and *miqdāšîm*.

your incense stands. ḥammānêkem. This cultic object is mentioned again in Isa 17:8; 27:9; Ezek 6:4, 6; 2 Chr 14:4; 34:4, 7, but its nature and function are shrouded in darkness. The following suggestions have been proposed:

1. Cultic objects for astral worship were set on roofs under the sun (Rashi; "sun images," *Tg. Onq.*). The word is derived from *ḥammâ* 'sun', with an added *nun*, as in *nāšîm raḥmāniyôt* 'merciful women' (Lam 4:10; cf. Ibn Ezra).

2. "These are magical practices in Israel' (*Sipra* Beḥuqotay 6:4). The *Sipra* is forced to render it this way because what sort of punishment is it to destroy *idolatrous* objects? The assumption must therefore be that *legitimate* worship is destroyed.

3. These were "incense altars" (Albright 1942: 215, n. 58; Orlinsky 1969: 221, citing Galling 1962). An inscription on an altar from Palmyra reads in part *ḥmn w'lt' dnh* 'this *ḥammān* and this altar'. The reverse side of the altar contains a relief depicting two standing men with an incense stand or altar between them.

4. Galling (1973), followed by Levine (1989), who focuses on Ugaritic ritual texts, suggest a connection with the god Baal-Ḥammôn, implying the meaning "an altar of Ḥammôn." Fritz (1981), however, rejects this connection and proposes, instead, that the *ḥammān* was a building where foreign gods were worshiped.

The testimony of 2 Chr 34:4a, I submit, is crucial: "At his bidding, they demolished the altars of the Baals, and he had the *ḥammānîm that were upon them* cut down." Thus the *ḥammān* was not itself an altar, but a cult object set on the altar. This verse together with the evidence of the Palmyran inscription, which differentiates between the *ḥmn* and the altar, tips the scales in favor of "incense stand."

your corpses. pigrêkem. (Maiberger (1987) cites Obermann (1941) that Hebrew *peger* is a denominative from Semitic *pgr* 'lifeless mass', which became "corpse" (in Hebrew, Aramaic, and Akkadian) and "a stone, heap of stones, altar" (in Ugaritic). Akkadian *pagru* means "body," both living and dead, human as well as animal. Hebrew *peger* designated only human corpses, chiefly in the context of war, but it also denotes memorial stele or stone heaps (Obermann 1941: 39). This double entendre was developed by Neiman (1948), who renders here "your funerary steles," and accepted by Albright (1957) and de Vaux (1961: 287; see also Noth 1977). Alternatively, it has been rendered as "your funerary offerings" (Malamat 1956: 77–78; 1989: 97, n. 91; cf. Moran 1969: 43, n. 1). However, this view is contradicted by the first interpreter of Lev 26, Ezekiel:

I will bring a sword against you and destroy your cult places [*bāmôtêkem*]. Your altars shall be wrecked and your incense stands [*ḥammānêkem*] smashed, and I will hurl down your slain [*ḥălĕlêkem*] before your fetishes [*gillûlêkem*]. I will set the corpses of the people of Israel [*pigrê bĕnê yiśrā'ēl*] in front of their fetishes [*gillûlêhem*], and scatter your bones around your altars in all your settlements. The towns shall be laid waste [*he'ārîm teḥĕrabnâ*] and the shrines [*habbāmôt*] shall be devastated [*tî̌sāmnâ*]). Thus your altars shall be laid waste [*yeḥerĕbû*] and bear their punishment; your fetishes [*gillûlĕkem*] shall be smashed and annihilated, your incense stands [*ḥammānêkem*] cut down. (Ezek 6:3–6)

The terms rendered in the Hebrew make it evident that Ezekiel was modeling himself on Lev 26:30–31. However, he alters *pigrêkem* of our verse to *ḥălĕlêkem* (Ezek 6:4b), which unambiguously means "your (slain) corpses." This explanation is original with Ezekiel, as it is buttressed by v. 5a, which repeats v. 4b, substituting *pigrê bĕnê yiśrā'ēl*. That this is a gloss is suggested not only by its absence in the LXX, but by its being cast in the third person, thereby interrupting the flow between v. 4b and v. 5b (see Greenberg 1983a: 132). The glossator's purpose is clear: to restore the original Leviticus term. However, Ezekiel's understanding of our verse is also clear: *peger* means "corpse" (see also below).

upon your lifeless (fetishes). 'al-pigrê (gillûlêkem). That *peger* by itself means "corpse" is further supported by this clause, in which, to connote metaphorically an idol, *peger* cannot stand alone but must be in construct with "fetishes." Note the Sefire curse *wpgr 'rb 'm 'l pgr* 'I shall multiply [i.e., heap] corpse upon corpse' (Sefire I, B:30). The entire clause simply states that Israelites will be slain at their idolatrous cult places (Ibn Ezra, Rashbam). Thus *peger* here has nothing to do with the Akkadian *pagru*-offering and the cult of the dead (Heider 1985: 393; Block 1992: 131). It has also been argued that *peger* has this meaning in Ezek 43:7, 9 (Ebach 1971). In any event, there is no great difference between "corpse" and "offering to a corpse," since the latter could take place at the site of the former.

The connotation of idols as corpses is attested elsewhere: *niblat šiqqûṣêhem* 'the carcasses of your abominations' (Jer 16:18); *zibḥê mētîm* 'sacrifices of (= to) the dead' (Ps 106:28). Ehrlich (1908, following Klostermann 1893) emends *'al* to *'al-pĕnê* to conform to Ezekiel's *lipnê* (6:4); it is rightly rejected by Dillmann and Ryssel 1897: the borrowing is in the reverse direction.

Contacting sancta with corpses constitutes their ultimate pollution; they can no longer be decontaminated and reused (cf. 2 Kgs 23:14–16; Ezek 6:4–5).

your . . . fetishes. gillûlêkem. This word derives from *gālāl* 'dung, dung balls' (*'Abot R. Nat.*² 38; Ibn Janaḥ; Radak; cf. 1 Kgs 14:10; Ezek 4:12, 15; Zeph 1:17) and the denominative *gālal* 'be dirty' (2 Sam 20:12; Isa 9:4). The vocalization has been assimilated to *šiqqûṣîm* 'detested objects', with which it is occasionally paired (Deut 29:16; 2 Kgs 23:24; Ezek 7:20). It appears thirty-nine times in Ezekiel where it is frequently associated with the word *ṭāmē'* 'impure' (20:7, 18, 31; 22:3–4; 23:7, 30; 36:18, 25; 37:23). That it is Ezekiel's favorite term for idols is shown, in contrast, by his use of *'ĕlîlîm* only once (30:13, for another people) and the other derisive term *šiqqûṣîm*, seven times (5:11; 7:20; 11:18; 20:7, 8, 30; 37:23). See the discussion in Haran (1978: 104–6).

Greenberg (1983a: 132, on Ezek 6:4) attributes to Baudissin (cited in BDB 1122a) the suggestion, on the basis of a Palmyrene bilingual inscription in which *gĕlālāʾ* is rendered as "stela" in Greek, that originally *gillûlîm* referred to pillars (*maṣṣēbôt*), explicitly forbidden in H (v. 1). Tigay (1996: 398, n. 32) adds that in Akkadian, *galālu* refers to a large type of stone (cf. Babylonian Aramaic *gĕlāl* 'stone') on which inscriptions and pictures were carved (cf. *CAD* 5.11).

I will expel you. wĕgāʿālâ napšî ʾetkem. This is a negation, expressed in the first person, of God's blessing *wĕlōʾ-tigʿal napšî ʾetkem* (v. 11b). The fact that the latter follows the blessing "I will establish my presence in your midst" leads the *Sipra*, correctly, to deduce that this curse refers to *sîlûq haššĕkînâ* 'the departure of the divine presence' (Beḥuqotay 6:4; see below). This deduction, admittedly abstract, follows logically from the etymological meaning of this idiom: the sense of God's gullet expelling Israel (see NOTE on "and I will not expel you," v. 11) is that he abandons his people.

31. *your sanctuaries. miqdĕšêkem.* The plural is unsettling. In contrast to v. 30, which speaks of idolatrous cult sites, this verse focuses on the legitimate cult. "I will not smell your pleasant odors" (v. 31b) implies that if Israel were obedient, God would, indeed, look with favor on his people's sacrifices at their "sanctuaries." The same word in Ezek 7:24 (revocalizing MT *mêqadšêhem*; cf. Zimmerli 1979; Greenberg 1983; note the absence of doubling expected in the *Piʿel*), however, in view of its context (vv. 20–23), can only refer to sanctuaries erected to other gods.

The plural has been explained "away" by pointing to fifty-three MSS, Sam. and *Syr.*, which read the singular, or by claiming that this term was influenced by the other plurals in vv. 30–31 (Kochman 1987). Another possible explanation is that this term should be rendered "your sancta" (see NOTE on 21:23), thereby obviating the necessity of attributing a notion of multiple legitimate sanctuaries to Israel. However, all difficulties melt away once it is realized that H acknowledges the existence and legitimacy of multiple sanctuaries (see chap. 17, COMMENT D).

make . . . desolate. wahăšimmôtî. As astutely noted by Ehrlich (1908), when the direct object of *šmm Hipʿil* is a locality, it implies not so much destroying it as emptying it of its inhabitants (also as in vv. 22, 43). The prophet Amos, however, has no compunctions about predicting the destruction of North Israelite sanctuaries (Amos 7:9).

not smell your pleasant odors. wĕlōʾ ʾārîaḥ bĕrēaḥ nîḥōḥăkem. For this expression, see Gen 8:21; 1 Sam 26:19; Amos 5:21–22. This clause resurfaces in the QL (D^b18V:4). The meaning of this fossilized expression is correctly ascertained by *Tg. Onq*: "I will not accept with favor the offering of your congregation" (cf. *Tgs. Ps.-J.* and *Neof.*; see NOTE on 1:9). The positive statement *wayyāraḥ YHWH ʾet-rēaḥ hannîḥōaḥ* 'and YHWH smelled the pleasant odor' (Gen 8:21aα) indicates that he was favorably disposed to Noah, for thereupon he resolves, despite the human inclination to sin, that he will not again destroy all life (v. 21b), a doctrine that he enshrines in a covenant with Noah and his sons (9:8–17). The negative "I will not smell your pleasant odors" therefore implies that YHWH rejects not only the sacrifices but also the sacrificer, who now realizes that, having lost divine protector, he faces an ominous future. In the priestly system, sacrifices are said to produce "a pleasant odor" (but not the expiatory sacrifices, see vol. 1.160–63, 252) in the hope (but not the assurance, contra Knohl 1995, see vol. 1.17–18, 245) that they will find acceptance with YHWH. Kaufmann (1937: 1.133; 1960: 183) plausibly suggests that this clause indicates the divine (hence H's) approval of multiple sanctuaries (see COMMENT D). However, his claim that its absence from Ezekiel's expansion on this verse (Ezek 6:3–6) proves that the deuteronomic reform has intervened cannot be taken seriously. That Ezekiel speaks of cult places (*bāmôt*), incense stands (*ḥammānîm*), and multiple altars is, rather, evidence that he is referring to predeuteronomic times. Another possibility is that Ezekiel is speaking of his own time, when, despite the deuteronomic reform, surreptitious cult places reappeared with their appurtenances (incense stands and altars). But destroyed sanctuary *buildings*, always in public view, could not be restored.

Another reason why this chapter cannot be referring to the debacle of Judah in 586 B.C.E.—in addition to the fact that multiple sanctuaries, rather than a single Temple, are contemplated—is the total absence of the priestly theology concerning the conditions and process by which the Jerusalem Temple would be destroyed. As vividly portrayed by Ezekiel, YHWH's *kābôd*-presence would depart the sanctuary (Ezek 10), thereby leaving it and the city defenseless against the enemy. This calamity would result from the pollution in the Temple affected by the accumulation of Israel's sins upon the sancta (vol. 1.254–61). Thus the exilic priests would have been able to rationalize the Temple's destruction as due not to YHWH's inability to protect it (and his people) against the ostensibly superior foreign forces and their gods, but exclusively to Israel's refusal or negligence to uphold its covenantal obligations. This theology is responsible, together with other factors (Kaufmann 1977: 11–34), for the virtual eradication of polytheistic worship among the Israelites. But it makes sense only when applied to a single, authorized sanctuary, where the presence of YHWH is totally (though symbolically) condensed, not dissipated in multiple sanctuaries throughout the land. Moreover, according to our verse, these sanctuaries are not even destroyed, but only vacated (cf. *m. Meg.* 3:3).

32. *'ănî. myself*. After God's agents—wild beasts, plagues, and enemies—will have done their destructive acts, God will now do his: send Israel into exile.

make your land desolate. The desolation of the land by emptying it of the people of Israel (v. 33) follows the destruction of the sanctuaries (Ibn Ezra). The threat of exile is commonplace in the curses appended to Near Eastern treaties (e.g., "the scattering of his people," CH, col. 26.74 [see NOTE on "I will scatter among the nations," v. 33]). Joosten's (1994: 261; 1996: 192) assertion that "if the Israelites are not living in the land, YHWH's ownership and lordship over it are rendered problematic," is itself problematic. YHWH settles in his land whomever he pleases or ejects them if he is displeased. He alone determines the laws whose violation pollutes the land, and the personifying metaphor of the land vomiting out its inhabitants (18:28) picturesquely describes the result of YHWH's decision, not that of the land.

who settle in it. hayyōšĕbîm bāh. If the enemies who settle in the land are "appalled" because they cannot farm it, this verse would be proleptic of vv. 34–35. However, if they are appalled at only the extent of the desolation and destruction of the land (cf. 1 Kgs 9:8; Jer 18:16; 19:8; Ezek 5:15a; 33:28a), there would be reason to doubt that, uniquely in this passage, the enemies have displaced the exiled Israelites. Perhaps, it is a gloss, for the added reason that it breaks the rhythm (Elliger 1966).

The settlement of enemies on the conquered land implies an exchange of populations, a policy enforced by the Assyrians (2 Kgs 17:24). This statement would, then, support the view that Lev 26 had the conquest of North Israel and the exile of its inhabitants in mind (with Heinisch 1935; see COMMENT E). 11QT 59:5–6, following the MT, avers *wĕhāyû ʾōyĕbēhemmâ šōmĕmîm bāmmâ* 'And their enemies will be appalled in them (while they, in their enemies' lands, will groan and cry out)'. This rendering is contra Yadin's (1983: 2.267) "their enemies will devastate them" and an improvement on Milgrom (1980: 101–2).

33. *You, however. wĕʾetkem.* The word order of subject–object is here the reverse of that in v. 32a. The land will be made desolate; you, however, will not have even that "peace," but will be uprooted and scattered (B. S. Schwartz, personal communication).

I will scatter (among the nations). ʾĕzāreh (baggôyîm). This is a favorite term of Ezekiel (5:2, 10, 12; 6:8; 12:14–15; 20:23; 22:15; 29:12; 30:23, 26), but always with *bāʾărāṣôt* (see also Jer 31:10; 49:32, 36; Ps 44:12). Similarly, the subsequent ruler who does not heed the Code of Hammurabi is threatened with *naspuḫ nišīšu* 'the scattering of his people' (CH § 26b.174; cf. *VTE* 297; "Lamentation over the Destruction of Sumer and Ur," *ANET* 611–21). But here the parallel stops. In ancient Near Eastern curses, the punishing deity does not pursue his people in exile. He cannot, since it is the territory of another god; contrast the next NOTE and vv. 36–39.

and I will unsheath the sword after you. wahărîqōtî ʾaḥărêkem ḥāreb. That is, in exile (*NEB*, correctly), in order to prevent anyone from returning. Contrast the blessing "no sword shall traverse your land" (v. 6b). For this expression, another favorite of Ezekiel, see Ezek 5:2, 12; 12:14, and compare 21:8–10. In the Esarhaddon inscriptions, an exile is described in some detail (Epis.a, Fass.c; cf. § 11, Bab A–G in Borger 1956: 12–15, cited by Weinfeld [1972d: 116]), not as the result of a pursuing deity, but as historical fact.

Jeremiah makes this unique aspect of Israel's God quite explicit: "I will scatter them among the nations which they and their fathers never knew; and I will dispatch the sword after them [*wĕšillaḥtî ʾaḥărêhem ʾet-haḥereb*] until I have consumed them" (Jer 9:15; cf. Amos 9:4). The same sequence and vocabulary of v. 33a is found in Ezekiel (5:2, 12; 12:14).

When your land will be a desolation and your cities a ruin (with Ibn Ezra and Abravanel). If v. 33b is translated as a separate punishment (in all translations, to my knowledge), it is a redundancy (see vv. 31a, 32a); it is out of place—the action has moved into exile (v. 33a). Moreover, it breaks the thought; Israel is being punished in exile, and there is no reason to mention again the condition of its land. Thus if vv. 34–35 are an interpolation (see below), so is v. 33b. The fact that it repeats vv. 31a, 32a reveals its function: it is a presumptive repetition, used as an indicator of a new theme.

your cities (a ruin). *ʿārêkem yihyû* (*ḥorbâ*). Because there is no distinctive third-person-plural feminine form in the suffixed verbs (perfect), there frequently is none in the prefixed verbs (imperfect) (e.g., Judg 21:21, 1 Kgs 11:3b; 2 Chr 6:40; Joüon 1923: § 150c).

Vv. 34–35. These verses constitute a parenthetical statement that interrupts the flow of vv. 33, 36 (admitted by Hoffmann 1953). Probably an interpolation (Baentsch 1903), this interpolation, however, includes v. 33b. The root *šbt* occurs seven times in these two verses, thereby linking the entire curse section to the neglect of the sabbatical year detailed in chap. 25, a point made emphatic by the particle *ʾāz* 'then' (M. Hildenbrand). This passage therefore records that the sabbatical has long before been established as a national institution (already required on an individual basis in Exod 23:11; see chap. 25, COMMENT C). Thus the jubilee is the sole innovation of Lev 25, which furnishes evidence that the jubilee is not a sabbatical year (see NOTE on "for you," 25:11).

34. *shall be paid. tirṣeh*. Scholars are at their wits' end to render this word. The search for its etymology or cognates is in vain. One can only guess by context: (1) "appease" God's anger for neglecting the sabbatical years (Rashi); (2) "appease" the land, which, figuratively, is incensed against the Israelites for neglecting the sabbatical years (Wessely 1846); (3) "complete," as in "until, as a hireling, he completes [*yirṣeh*] his day" (Job 14:6) or "her punishment is *nirṣâ* ‖ *mālěʾâ* completed" (Isa 40:2, Ibn Ezra, to which he adds "and pay," on v. 41; cf. Abravanel); (4) "accept" in payment (Driver and White 1894–98). Note *nirṣâ* (1:4) *yêrāṣeh* (7:18; 22:23) *lirṣônô / lěrāṣōn / lirṣōněkem* (1:3; 22:20, 29) ʿbe acceptable' (P/H) and Rabbinic Hebrew *rāṣâ* Piʿel 'pay' (cf. *b. Šabb.* 22a; *b. ʿErub.* 18b).

That payment is involved with this use of *rāṣâ* is demonstrated by the following: "I will repay [*wěšillamtî*] you for years consumed by (a variety of locusts)" (Joel 2:25). Here we see that God will use the very medium by which he punished Israel—in this case the land, as in our verse—as the means of blessing it, in a precise measure-for-measure repayment. There is a difference, however. In our verse, the *justice* of God decrees that Israel must repay the land for its lost sabbaticals. For the prophet, the *mercy* of God motivates God himself to repay Israel for its lost harvests. For the discussion on the measure-for-measure principle operating throughout the chapter, see the NOTE on v. 16.

I would suggest that H also sought a synonym for *kipper* 'atone', a P term, however, that implied a cultic rite, which Israel—in exile—obviously could not perform. That the land requires atonement, see Num 35:33; Deut 32:43. One wonders why Num 35:33, a priestly passage (probably H), did not also use the verb *rāṣâ*. The answer may be that what has to be atoned in that verse is spilled blood (*šāpak dām*, mentioned twice), a reminiscence of H's cardinal rule that spilled blood (of sacrificial animals) requires atonement (*kippēr*, Lev 17:11). See also the NOTE on "and they accept their punishment in full," v. 41.

its sabbath years. šabbĕtōtêhā. According to Rashi, Ibn Ezra, and the moderns (most recently, Wacholder 1975 [on Dan 9]; C. Wright 1991: 150), this term includes both sabbaticals and jubilees. The exceptions are the rabbis recorded in *Tg. Ps.-J.; m. ʾAbot* 5:8, *Sipra* Behuqotay 7:2; *y. Taʿan.* 66c (also Ramban on v. 16), who maintain that it refers to only the sabbaticals, perhaps because the jubilee had long ceased—rather, been suspended—before their time. Whatever their reasoning, they are correct (see the substantiation in the NOTE on "for you," 25:11).

it is desolate. hoššammâ. A suffixed infinitive without the *mappiq* (see NOTE on 6:2, and GKC §§ 62y, 91e).

When you are. wĕʾattem ‖ *wĕhāyĕtâ* (v. 33b). Thus we have two similarly structured sentences: a conditional clause followed by a main clause beginning with *ʾāz.*

shall rest. tišbat. The pausal form of the imperfect is *tišbōt* (as in v. 35a; Exod 34:21, note the *ʾAtnaḥ*); otherwise, it has a *pataḥ* (e.g., Neh 6:3; Rashbam), as one might suspect in an intransitive verb (GKC § 47h). But there are exceptions (e.g., Gen 2:2; Hos 7:4; Prov 22:10; see also GKC § 47i). That the land is at total rest implies that the enemy dwelling there (v. 32b) will either not farm it (i.e., just occupy it militarily) or have to abandon it (Wessely 1846; but see NOTE on "who settle in it," v. 32b).

and pay off (with Driver and White 1894–98). *wĕhirṣāt.* An older form of the third-person-singular form were perfect (GKC § 75m). For the rendering, see the NOTE on "shall be paid," v. 34a. Why the repetition, and why the *Hipʿil*? Both questions have one answer: H's style. Note the same phenomenon in reverse: *wahăšimmôtî . . . wĕšāmēmû* (v. 32; S. Nikaido). In addition to creating a circular inclusio by altering the verbal aspect (e.g., v. 4), H changes the verbal pattern (D. Stewart). The *Hipʿil* also serves a semantic function: "The land is conceived as a debtor . . . the rest, which is paid by the exile of its inhabitants, it owes" to God (Driver and White, 1894–98).

The Chronicler comments on this verse: "in fulfillment of the word of YHWH spoken by Jeremiah, until the land be paid back its sabbaths [*ʿad rāṣĕtâ hāʾāreṣ ʾet-šabbĕtôtehā*]; as long as it lay desolate [*kol-yĕmê hoššammô*] it kept sabbath, till seventy years were completed" (2 Chr 36:21). The Chronicler fused this verse (including its hapax *haššammâ*) with Jeremiah's prophecy of a seventy-year exile (Jer 25:11; 29:10). Most likely, the Chronicler, in whose time the Torah was already canon, assumes that Jeremiah utilized this verse in molding his prophecy. D. N. Freedman, personal communication asks:

How do you reckon the Chronicler reckoned the number of years involved? If it took 70 consecutive years of sabbaticals to make up the difference, would that mean that the Chronicler thought that the Israelites had been in default for a total of 490 years, i.e., from the time they arrived in the land until they went into exile? . . . One of the reasons I mention this point is that Daniel uses a similar calculation forwards to get his famous 490-year prediction. If my suggestion is correct, then first of all, the number 490 was already in the picture long before Daniel came up with his ingenious scheme, and secondly, it implies an important symmetry in biblical history, from 490 years before the exile to 490 years after the exile for the eschaton, which is the way Daniel calculates the end-time.

35. *the rest it did not have.* *ʾēt ʾăšer lōʾšābĕtâ.* This clause is construed as an accusative of the previous verb *tišbōt* (cf. 25:2), and, hence, its object (e.g., Gen 30:29; Deut 9:7; 29:15; Dillmann and Ryssel 1897; Sun 1990).

This is another example of divine measure-for-measure retribution rampant throughout this chapter.

Vv. 36–39. The continuation of v. 33a describes the final stage of punishment: psychological disintegration and total demoralization.

36. *As for those of you who survive.* *wĕhanniš'ārîm bakem.* That is, those who have not been cut down by the pursuing sword (v. 33a; Ibn Ezra). The change from second- to third-person suffixes is necessitated by this subject. But there is a subtler reason: God is distancing himself from the remnant.

faintness. *mōrek.* This word is a hapax, from *rkk* (Ibn Janaḥ, Rashi). The idiom *mōrek bilbābām* 'faintness in their heart' would correspond with *rak hallēbāb* 'faint hearted' (Deut 20:8; cf. v. 3; Job 23:16). Ibn Ezra's analogy *mōʿal yĕdêhem* (Neh 8:6) is flawed, since it clearly means "(with hands) upraised," a by-form of *maʿal*, from the root *ʿlh*. Perhaps it developed from *mĕrōk*, as *mĕtōm* 'soundness of body' from *tmm* (GKC § 85k; Ehrlich). Alternatively, one might regard it as a nominal of *mrk*, as *ʾōhel*, *ʾōkel*, and it appears in Rabbinic Hebrew as the verb *nitmārēk* (b. Ḥul. 45b; Rashbam, Wessely 1846), but this is clearly a later development.

in their hearts. *billĕlābām.* This is an H term (19:17; 26:36, 41; Num 15:39) as opposed to P's *lēb* (e.g., Exod 25:2; 28:3, 30; 35:5, 21; 36:2).

The sound of a driven leaf. For similar imagery (using the same verb *nādap*), see Pss 1:4; 68:3; Job 13:25.

they shall fall though nobody is pursuing. *wĕnāpĕlû wĕ'ên rōdēp.* This accelerated punishment of "You shall flee though nobody pursues you" (v. 17b) totally reverses the blessing of v. 7, *ûrĕdaptem ʾet-ʾōyĕbêkem wĕnāpĕlû lipnêkem* **lehāreb** 'they shall fall before you by the sword' (words in boldface are also in this verse). For a similar description of irrational fears, see Deut 28:66–67.

37. As a result of their panic, they not only will flee with none pursuing, but also will stumble on one another. For a similar notion, see Isa 59:10.

as though from. *kĕmippĕnê.* The double preposition can be explained as if the first preposition and its attached substantive have become one word before the *kap* was affixed (e.g., *kĕbāri ʿšōnâ*, Isa 1:26; GKC § 118sN₂).

though pursuing is nobody. *wĕrōdēp ʾāyin.* This is repetition of v. 36b in reverse order, emphasizing the psychological collapse.

to stand (your ground). *tĕqûmâ,* literally "a stand," a hapax. For the verb in this sense, see Josh 7:12–13. Similarly, "may you not stand [*la tazazāni*] before your enemies" (VTE 1.535; ANET 539). This word reverses the blessing *qômĕmiyyût* 'upright' (v. 13; Levine 1989: 276). Not coincidentally, both occur at the end of each series of blessings and curses, respectively.

38. *You shall be lost. wa'ăbadtem.* The LXX, *NJPS*, NEB, NRSV, among others, render "perish." Rashi renders "lost, strayed, dispersed"; compare *hā'ôbĕdîm*, Isa 27:13, which *NJPS* renders as "strayed" and *NAB*, "lost among" (see also R. Akiba in *Sipra* Behuqotay 8:1). The difference between the two renderings is not inconsequential. Rendering "perish" would contradict the following verses, which speak of survivors (cf. Deut 26:5; Ezek 34:4, 16; Job 31:19).

devour. wě'ākĕlâ. Reversing the blessing of vv. 5, 10: not only will you not eat, but you will be eaten. It is the final appearance of the verb *'ākal* (twice in the blessings, five times in the curses). The remnant in exile will be "eaten" by wars and conquest (not by climate, Ibn Ezra; or by plague, *Tg. Ps.-J.*), as attested in Num 13:32; Jer 2:3; 30:16, among others.

39. This verse is a perfect ABXB'A' construction (M. Hildenbrand):

wĕhannišārîm bākem

A   *yimmaqqû*
    B   *ba'ăwônām*
       X   *bĕ'arṣōt 'ôyĕbêkem*
    B'   *wě'ap ba'ăwônōt 'ăbôtām 'ittām*
A'   *yimmāqqû*

And those of you who survive

A   **shall rot**
    B   because of their **iniquities**
       X   in the land of your enemies;
    B'   also because of the **iniquities** of their ancestors (adhering) to them
A'   they **shall rot**

The first two words *wĕhannišārîm bākem* are introductory and stand outside the structure. The parallel words *'ăwônām/ōt* (BB') and *yimmāqqû* (AA') indicate the cause, "iniquities," and the punishment, "rot." The center "land of your enemies" (X) refocuses on the locus "exile" (as in v. 36a).

And those of you who survive. wĕhanniš'ārîm bākem. The same phrase as in v. 36a, this indicates the progressive decimation of those in exile. Note the close analogy in the First Isaiah, who also speaks of multiple purges before the survivors are permitted to repent (e.g., Isa 6:13). The meter (3+3) is broken (Elliger 1966). Clearly, it is a transitional verse. However, it does not begin a new section because of a shift to third-person speech (Elliger 1966). Such a shift is already in evidence in v. 36, as pointed out by Buis (1974).

shall rot. yimmaqqû. The meaning of this term is critical for the understanding of the following verses. Three interpretations are current: (1) "melt" (*yitmĕsûn*, *Tgs.*; *Sipra* Behuqotay 8:2, followed by Rashi), suggesting that *mqq* is synonymous with *mss* (cf. Zech 14:12; Ps 38:6); (2) "rot" (Ibn Janaḥ), pointing to Rabbinic Hebrew *mqq* (said of books; *m. Šabb* 9:6) as well as to Isa 3:24; 34:4; Zech 14:12; Ps 38:6 (*hib'îšû nāmaqqû* 'stink and rot'); and (3) "be heartsick" (Ginsberg 1982: 80; Levine 1989), indicating remorse and, hence, the beginning of Israel's repentance.

This last interpretation cannot be substantiated etymologically. Ginsberg justifies his rendering on contextual grounds: because the survivors are blameless, they need no longer suffer. However, as indicated by the Isaianic parallel (see above), the survivors (v. 36) still must undergo purging (v. 39) before they may repent. Ginsberg (1982: 80, n. 96), pointing to Ezek 24:23–24, also states that "Ezekiel does not tell his fellow exiles—the very remnant destined for survival and restoration (Ezek 11:15–20; 36:16ff.)—to pine away for their iniquities but to be contrite because of them." However, contrition is expressed in Ezekiel by another root *qwṭ*, whereas *mqq* in all its other Ezekielian attestations never expresses this notion, but, to the contrary, is a negative term, connoting suffering and punishment. Note "Our transgressions and our sins weigh upon us, and we waste away because of them [*ûbam 'ănaḥnû nêmaqqîm*]; how then can we live?" (33:10, with NRSV; see also 4:17; 24:23). The despair of the exiles is due not to their repentance, but to their suffering.

because of their iniquities. ba'ăwōnām. The LXX reads "your iniquities," patently to harmonize with "your enemies." This is wrong: the survivors must suffer for *their* own sins.

your enemies. The reading in many Versions and in many Sam. MSS *'ōyĕbêhem*, "their enemies," is not compelling. This is the final second person in this chapter, referring to all the exiles, including those who will not survive.

because of the iniquities of their ancestors. ba'ăwōnōt 'ăbōtām. This is in keeping with the "visiting the sins of the fathers on the children" theology (cf. Exod 34:7b; Num 14:18b), exemplified in the lament of the generation of the destruction: "Our fathers sinned and are no more; and we must bear their guilt" (Lam 5:7; Ibn Ezra). The *Sipra*, however, qualifies this text with "whenever they adhere to their fathers' deeds" (Beḥuqotay 8:2; and Rashi), following the deuteronomic amelioration of this retribution doctrine as found in the Decalogue (Exod 20:5–6; Deut 5:9–10; cf. 7:9–10; see Milgrom 1981a).

Tigay (1996: 437) distinguishes between cross-generational (i.e., vertical) retribution (e.g., Exod 34:7b) and compound retribution (e.g., Exod 20:5–6), the former connoting the transfer of the fathers' sins, and the latter the addition of the fathers' sins to those of the children. According to the doctrine of compound retribution, if the children are virtuous, vertical retribution is suspended; the children do not suffer for their fathers' sins. As Tigay (1996: 437) perceptively observes: "This qualification avoids the demoralizing effect that the principle of cross-generational retribution has in its unconditional form ('Why obey if our fate has already been determined by our ancestors' conduct?')."

Tigay, however, includes Lev 26:39–40 under the rubric of compound retribution. I cannot agree. True, the fathers' sins are added to those of the children. But there is nothing in these verses or in all of Leviticus that implies the cancellation of vertical retribution if the children are virtuous. The existence of the *kārēt* penalty, endorsed by H as well as P, implies the reverse: the line of the sinner will be cut off, even if his descendants remain steadfastly virtuous. Moreover, H's vertical retribution also functions horizontally. Note that in H, not only do descendants suffer, but also the extended family (e.g., the family of the Molek worshiper, 20:5) and, at times, even the entire nation (e.g., its exile, though not all have sinned, 18:25; 26:14–39). Returning to our verse, H is so intent on inserting the doctrine of vertical retribution that it has to abandon the fiction of the wilderness setting (Joosten 1994: 7–8, n. 28; 1996: 9, n. 28).

Can H's harsh retributive theology be justified? Given H's premise, it can. The world, breached by sin, must be restored—if not by the father, then by the son. In the exile, expiation cannot be by sacrifice. Remorse and confession alone are required, a harbinger of prophetic repentance.

It must, therefore, be concluded that H retains the full, unattenuated formula of vertical retribution, in contrast to D, Jeremiah, and Ezekiel. D not only expounds compound retribution, as exemplified in the two versions of the Decalogue (Exod 20:5–6; Deut 5:9–10), but, in accordance with the principle of individual retribution it sets in Deut 24:16, emphasizes, in Deut 7:9–10, that "God punishes sinners personally and instantly, and not a word is said of this extending the punishment to sinners' descendants" (Tigay 1996: 437).

In Jeremiah, the two doctrines are actually juxtaposed: "You show kindness to the thousandth generation, but visit the guilt of the fathers upon their children after them . . . so as to repay every man according to his ways, and with the proper fruit of his deed" (Jer 32:18–19). The deuteronomic modification effectively harmonizes the opposing views. For in the same chapter, Jeremiah explains that "the people of Israel and Judah have done nothing but evil in my sight *since their youth*. . . . This city has aroused my anger and my wrath *from the day it was built until this day* [my emphasis]" (vv. 30–31). Thus, according to Jeremiah (and Deuteronomy), God punishes the wicked together with their children only if the children continue in their fathers' ways or, as the rabbis express it, "if they hold the deeds of their fathers in their hands" (*b. Sanh.* 27b). For Jeremiah, then, collective (vertical and horizontal) and individual retribution coexist simultaneously in the divine sphere (see also Jer 15:4; 31:29–31).

Ezekiel is the only biblical personage to deny absolutely the existence of collective (both vertical and horizontal) retribution (chaps. 18 and 33). As astutely pointed out by Greenberg (1985: 340), whereas Jeremiah postpones the abolition of collective retribution until the distant future (Jer 31: 29–30), Ezekiel proclaims its abolition immediately. As explicitly (and boldly) acknowledged by R. Jose b. Ḥanina (third century C.E.), "Moses said, 'visiting the iniquity of fathers upon the sons,' but Ezekiel came and annulled it: 'It is the person who sins that shall die'" (*b. Mak.* 24a). It is not by accident that when Ezekiel uses the verb *kārat*, he cites it only in the *Hipʿil* in a general context, where it means "destroy" (Ezek 14:17, 19, 21; 17:17; 21:8, 9; 25:7). Only once does he apply the *kāret* penalty to the individual (Ezek 14:8), but the context (vv. 4–8) makes it clear that he is applying the sin, and hence the language, of Molek worship (Lev 20:3) to all forms of idolatry (see NOTE on 20:3). Even more instructive is that when Ezekiel recasts our verse, he cites only part of it, "You shall rot because of your iniquities" (Ezek 24:23), but omits the remainder (Wellhausen 1963: 169). This, I submit, is clinching evidence that Ezekiel abolishes, once and for all, the doctrine of vertical retribution.

(adhering) to them. '*ittām*, literally "with them." Some claim that, following the cantilations, the antecedent is the ancestors; that is they will rot *as* the ancestors ('*im*, normally "with," can also mean "as"; cf. Job 9:26; 37:18; Dillmann and Ryssel 1897). However, in addition to this dubious rendering of '*ēt*, it is contradicted by both the context and the historical reality: except for the generation that went into exile, the ancestors went unpunished! Rather, it refers to the ancestors' sins: *da'ăhîdîn kĕyadhôn* 'that adhere to them' (*Tgs. Onq* and *Ps.-J.*). This reading of '*ittām* should require a disjunctive cantillation.

Vv. 40–45. Remorse and the Recall of the Covenant: Return from Exile Implied

This appendix to the section of curses functions much like Deut 30:1–10 for the curses of Deut 28:15–68 (see COMMENT B). Vv. 40–41a constitute Israel's confession that it committed sacrilege and stubbornly resisted God, and consequently God brought them into exile. Vv. 41b–45 constitute God's response: if Israel truly humbles itself and accepts (the justice of) its punishment, then God will remember the covenant and, as soon as the land has made up its neglected sabbaticals, will restore Israel to the land.

Weinfeld (1993: 250) associates the end of Lev 26 with the grant deeds of the ancient Near East. In my opinion, they are not analogous. These deeds indicate only that the grant remains permanent even if a descendant "sins" (see the Hittite land grants cited in Weinfeld 1993: 237–38). However, they contain no provision for the sinner to repent (or in some manner make amends) and be restored to the donor's favor.

The possibility of the restoration of divine favor by the acknowledgment and remorse of sin (also Deut 30:1–10) is unique to the Bible. Knohl (1995: 206–7, n. 22) claims that "Amos and Isaiah foresaw the revival that would take place after the exile; so too the idea of revival arose in the writings of the members of HS." However, the authorship of Amos 9:14–15 is disputed, and Isaiah does not predict exile for those who survive God's purge of the wicked. Indeed, Isaiah's prophecy of exile is confined to one verse (5:13), in which, as Ginsberg pointed out (oral teaching), *gālâ* may be an error for *kālâ* (a favorite Isaianic verb; cf. 1:28; 10:18, 25; 15:6; 16:4; 21:16; 29:20; 31:3; 32:10). An ostensible precedent may exist in the Sumerian "Lament over the Destruction of Sumer and Ur" (*ANET* 612–19). Nanna-Sin, the god of Ur, pleads with his father, Enlil, for the restoration of Ur and its temple. Finally, Enlil's response is favorable, and the people throng to the city from all over the land (ll. 457–79). However, the analogy to Lev 26 is illusory. To be sure, the inhabitants of Ur and Sumer (and their priests and sancta) have been carried off into captivity (ll. 195, 208, 243, 253, 347, 416), but there is no indication that the exiles themselves returned. Even assuming that they did, it was not due to their own efforts, but to the intervention of their god. Thus the idea that restoration and renewal are conditioned on *repentance in exile* is novel and can be attributed to H. Deut 4:29–30; 30:1–2, 8, adopting the *later* terminology of *šûb*, are demonstrably later (vol. 1.377–78).

Furthermore, these passages were probably exilic interpolations ameliorating the disasters predicted by Deut 28 (Tigay 1996: 432).

40. *But if they.* Saadiah renders "until they," forming the beginning of the apodosis. He is correct in that it signals the beginning of a new pericope. I would, however, regard vv. 40–41 as the protasis of the new pericope and vv. 42–45, its apodosis.

confess. wehitwaddû. H adopts P's legal formula that confession transforms an advertent act into an inadvertent one, rendering it eligible for expiation (5:5; 16:21; cf. Num 5:6–7), but with one main difference: P requires an appropriate sacrifice, whereas H waives the sacrificial requirement. To be sure, sacrifices to YHWH are prohibited outside the authorized sanctuary (17:8–9), all the more so in exile—in impure land (cf. Josh 22:19; Hos 9:3). Perhaps this is the reason that the divine response of forgiveness is missing in this pericope (see NOTE on "namely, I will remember the land," v. 42). Gerstenberger (1996: 429–30) argues that, in view of Neh 9, the confession took the form of a historical discourse recounting the sins of the past as well as the present, and it was recited by an individual on behalf of the collective. His conjecture is contradicted by Neh 9:2–3, which indicates that first each individual was obligated to confess. The group confession (vv. 6–37), on the contrary, speaks exclusively of past sins (except for the nondescript "and we have been wicked," v. 33bβ). All we can infer from the statement that God remembers his covenant is that Israel will be returned from exile. H's assumption may well be—it should always be kept in mind that H is a priestly source—that once Israel is restored and the authorized cult reestablished, the appropriate expiatory sacrifices will be offered (although the first *recorded* sacrifices were those of the reconstituted cultic calendar, Ezra 3:2–6). Nonetheless, the importance of this concession should not be underestimated. It approximates, and perhaps influences, the prophetic doctrine of repentance, which not only suspends the sacrificial requirement, but eliminates it entirely. For a full discussion of the role of confession in Israel and the ancient Near East, see Milgrom (1976a: 106–10, supplemented by vol. 1. 101–3).

Interestingly, Ezekiel denies any role to Israel in the redemptive process. God will restore Israel to its land unconditionally: "Say to the House of Israel: Thus said YHWH God: Not for your sake will I act, O House of Israel, but for my holy name, which you have caused to be profaned among the nations to which you have come" (Ezek 36:22). Ezekiel, like Jeremiah before him, despairs of Israel's ability to change its ways and, as a consequence, predicts that God will perform a "heart transplant," which will guarantee that Israel will sin no more (Ezek 36:25–27; Jer 31:31–34; see Milgrom 1990b).

Note how the QL echoes this verse (parallel words in Hebrew): "and confess [*wayitwaddû*] before God saying: Indeed we have acted wickedly, both we and our fathers, by walking contrariwise [*gam ʾănaḥnû gam ʾăbôtênû bĕlektēnû qerî*]" (CD 20:28–29; cf. 1QS1:24–26).

iniquity of their ancestors. ʿăwōn ʾăbōtām. Herewith H sets a precedent for all *subsequent* confessions: "We have sinned with [not "like," NJPS] our ancestors" (Ps 106:6); ". . . for because of our sins and the iniquities of our fathers, Jerusalem and your people have become a mockery among all who are around us" (Dan 9:16b; cf. vv. 8, 11, 20); as well as the verse from, *QL* (CD 20:28–29). This view, an offshoot of the doctrine of collective responsibility—a cardinal plank in the structure of priestly theology (e.g., vol. 1.254–61)—is vehemently rejected by Jeremiah for the future (Jer 31:29) and by Ezekiel for the present (Ezek 18, esp. vv. 2–3, 30–33). Thus Ezekiel, following the lead of Jeremiah, doffs once more his priestly vestments to drape himself in the prophetic mantle of repentance, which denies both sacrifices (see previous NOTE) and collective responsibility as requisites for divine expiation.

in that they committed sacrilege against me. běmaʿălām ʾăšer māʿălû-bî. Which group committed the sacrilege, and what precisely did it do? Ibn Ezra simply states "the ancestors" without further specification. Presumably, he means that all past violations were responsible for the destruction of the land and Temple. Alternatively, one might think that the sacrilege is restricted to the violation of the sabbatical and jubilee laws of chap. 25, in which case *maʿal* would preserve its purely cultic connotation of sancta violation (see the discussion of *maʿal* and its nuances in vol. 1.345–56). However, the probability rests with Ibn Ezra's (implicit) view. We are dealing with H, which is notorious for converting the precise terminology of P into wide-ranging metaphors (Knohl 1995; Milgrom 1992b). Ginsberg (1982: 82–83) goes so far as to render *limʿōl maʿal baYHWH* 'to break faith with YHWH,' a meaning also attested in Ezek 17:20; 18:24; 39:23 (Levine 1989). A clear example of this extended connotation is "if a land were to sin against me" (*limʿāl-maʿal,* Ezek 14:13), which clearly refers to a broad spectrum of moral as well as cultic violations (Ezek 15:8; 18:24; 20:27; 39:26–27).

Knohl (1995: 109, n. 165) suggests that I erred (1976a: 86) in claiming that this is the only instance of *maʿal* in H, citing Num 5:6; 31:16; Deut 32:51 which he also assigns to H. Note, however, that even if these verses stem from H, they share with our verse a characteristic that distinguishes them from P: *maʿal* is used in a figurative sense, whereas in P it is limited to sancta desecration.

Nonetheless, it must be borne in mind that one of God's sancta, the violation of which P vociferously condemns, is *his name* taken in a false oath (5:20–26; vol. 1.365–73). It must equally be borne in mind that the commandments alluded to in this chapter are those contained in and stemming from the covenant (vv. 9, 15, and, especially in this pericope, vv. 42 [thrice], 45), concerning which Israel swore a solemn oath of obedience. Assumed is that a covenant accepted by one generation is binding on future generations (Deut 29:14; cf. *Tanḥ. Niṣabim* 3), a stipulation explicitly written into ancient Near Eastern treaties (*VTE* § 1, 57 [*ANET* 534c, 539b]; Sefire 1A [*ANET* 659c]). In that sense, Israel throughout its generations has indeed committed sacrilege: it has trespassed against the most precious sanctum of all—God's holy name. Such an explanation would also explain why H has avoided its own coinage for *maʿal,* namely, *lĕhallel šēm YHWH* 'desecrate YHWH's name' (18:21; 19:12; 20:3; 22:2, 32) and reverts to the older P term. Here, H wishes to emphasize that in regard to the covenant, its violation constitutes true sacrilege, the consequences of which will amply be realized in Israel's impending destruction. For an alternative explanation, see the NOTE on 19:12.

that they continued in opposition to me. wĕʾap ʾăšer-hālĕkû ʿimmî bĕqerî. Ibn Ezra comments that "'they' refers to the children." He may well be right. According to the imprecations, it is the generation of the destruction that receives the punitive warning notices, to which it responds with cold aloofness. In that case, it must be part of the confessional.

41. *had to continue.* ʾēlēk. The precise nuance of this prefixed verb is moot. The imperfect sense—"going to" (Wessely 1846) or "will" (*NEB*) continue hostile and bring Israel into exile—cannot be correct because Israel already is in exile. Conversely, the rendering "continued" (*NRSV*) is equally difficult to derive from a prefixed (imperfect) verb (one would have expected *hālaktî*, or the verse would have begun with *wāʾēlēk*). Driver (1892: 39B, cited in Bertholet 1901) makes better sense by rendering "would" (see also below), attributing to the verb a subjunctive force in past time. The most acceptable rendering, in my opinion, is "had to." That is, it is a modal verb (Driver and White 1897; Baentsch 1903), according to the rule that prefixed verbs may be deonitic modals (Rattray 1992: 26–27, citing Foley and Van Valin 1984: 231). The importance of this rendering (following Driver or Baentsch) is that it makes v. 41a a continuation of the confessional: God would or had to match Israel's hostility with his own.

and disperse. wĕhēbēʾtî, literally "bring." The LXX reflects wĕhaʾăbadtî 'and I will destroy them', a tacit recognition of the problem with the MT—God has already brought them into exile. An answer, as indicated above, is to understand the verb modally. God *had to* bring them. It is the conclusion and an indispensable part of the confessional: it is important that Israel confess that God (and not the enemy) is responsible for its plight.

The rabbis read into this statement a note of consolation: YHWH does not "send" them but "brings" them into exile, indicating that he will not abandon them (Bekhor Shor, based on *Sipra* Behuqotay 8:5); the text hints that the God who personally brings them into exile will also bring them back (Rambam). Clearly, the absence of any explicit promise of a return bothers the medievalists (see COMMENT E). Another problem is the preposition *bĕ* in *bāʾāreṣ*, which is incomprehensible as modifying wĕhēbētî (B. Horowitz).

Alternatively and preferably, as aptly suggested by Levine (1995), the LXX *Vorlage* wĕhaʾăbadtî is original. As evidence, he brings to bear Akkadian *abātu* B 'be lost' and Hebrew ʾibbēd (*Piʿel*) 'banish, deport, disperse' as the meaning of wĕhaʾăbadtî, which the LXX misconstrued. Thus the verb can be rendered "and disperse (them in the land of their enemies)."

if, then. ʾô-ʾāz. Rashi renders ʾô as ʾim 'if', citing Exod 21:36 (see also 1 Sam 20:10; GKC § 150c). Rashi, in a second explanation, renders it šemā 'perhaps' (followed by Wessely 1846; Driver and White 1894–98; cf. *Tg. Neof.*). The LXX and Syr. read wĕʾāz 'then' (beginning the apodosis). However, it reads better as part of the protasis: Israel's confession cannot be lip service, but must derive from pangs of conscience and the acceptance of the punishment—that is, taking responsibility for its deeds.

uncircumcised heart. lĕbābām heʿārēl. A metaphor denoting the dull insensitive heart (Deut 10:16; 30:6; Jer 4:4; 9:25), it is also utilized by Ezekiel (44:7,

9). Perhaps it also denotes "thickened": "The thickened heart cannot feel or think; one whose earlobe is too thick cannot hear God's words" (Jer 6:10); Moses' thickened lips made it difficult for him to speak articulately (Exod 6:12)" (Levine 1989). See also the NOTE on 19:23.

is humbled. yikkāna ʿ. This verb appears here for the first time in a religious sense. Elsewhere it is used by the Deuteronomist: 1 Kgs 21:29; 2 Kgs 22:19; see also Ps 107:12; 2 Chr 7:14, etc. (noted by Japhet 1968: 359, n. 7). Ezekiel is more specific: *wĕnāqōṭû bipnêhem* 'they will loathe themselves' (Ezek 6:9; 36:31; cf. 16:63). It should not go unnoticed that this verb coupled with *hitwaddâ* 'confess' approximates H's concept of repentance and constitutes a stage prior to prophetic *šwb* (Milgrom 1976a: 119–27; see COMMENT F).

and they accept their punishment in full (with NEB). *wĕʾāz yirṣû ʾet-ʿăwōnām.* The renderings "and they make amends for their guilt" (NAB), "and they make amends for their iniquity" (NRSV), and "and they shall atone for their iniquity" (NJPS) cannot be correct because they impute to Israel a further activity in order to secure its redemption. This cannot be. One should not confuse Israel's confession and remorse with the prophetic doctrine of repentance. Here Israel is required to change only its heart, but not its ways. From this point on, all the activity stems from God: once the land has made up its neglected sabbaticals, God will recall the covenant and, presumably (it is not stated explicitly), restore Israel to its land.

Furthermore, the verb *rāṣâ, Qal* (see NOTE on v. 34) is intransitive and belies any activity; it implies receiving, not doing, and the notion of "accept, acquiesce" (see NOTE on v. 34) is well documented. Finally, the consequential meaning of *ʿāwōn* 'punishment' is best suited here (vol. 1.339). Thus Israel is called on to accept its punishment. (For a similar thought, see Mic 7:9; C. D. Ginzburg 1966.)

Alternatively, the verb *rāṣâ* may be a substitute for *kipper* 'atone', and this clause would then be rendered "while they atone for their iniquity" (NJPS, similarly in v. 43aγ). The choice of this unusual verb might then be justified on the grounds that *kipper* refers to the subject, YHWH, who grants atonement by sacrifice (P's notion), whereas H wants to stress that Israel, deprived of its sacrificial cult, would express its atonement by contritely and patiently accepting its punishment of exile until the land made up its neglected sabbath years (see NOTE on v. 34).

In either case, the implication is that Israel, in a state of remorse, must wait *passively* until its punishment is paid in full (with Driver and White 1894–98)— that is, until its land has been paid back its neglected sabbaticals—and then God will act by virtue of his commitment to the covenant. This thought, I submit, is fully echoed by Second Isaiah, using the same vocabulary: "Speak tenderly to Jerusalem and declare to her that her term of service [i.e., the exile] is completed, that her punishment is accepted [*kî nirṣâ ʿăwōnāh*]" (Isa 40:2). Levine (1989: 279) claims that the borrowing is reversed, from Isa 40:2 to Lev 26:41, 43. But in view of my demonstration that Ezekiel is consistently the borrower from Lev 26 (see COMMENT C), the probability is that Isaiah of the exile, who prophesied at least a generation after Ezekiel, is the actual borrower.

42. *then I will remember. wĕzākartî*. This marks the beginning of the apodosis. "Remember" here means more than to recollect, but also to take action on what is recalled (Schottroff 1966: 201; Porter 1976). For this sense, especially in regard to the covenant, see Gen 9:15; Exod 2:24; 6:5; Jer 14:21; Ezek 16:60; Pss 105:8; 106:45 (see also Gen 8:1; 19:29; Jer 2:2).

Vv. 42–45 are constructed as an introversion (M. Hildenbrand):

A　　*wĕzākartî 'et- bĕrîtî wĕ'ap 'et- bĕrîtî yiṣḥāq wĕ'ap 'et-bĕrîtî 'abrāhām 'ezkōr wĕhā'āreṣ 'ezkōr* (v. 42)

　　B　　*wĕhā'āreṣ tē'āzēb mēhem wĕtireṣ 'et-šabbĕtōtêhā bohšammš mēhem wĕhēm yirṣû 'et- 'awônām ya'an ûbĕya'an bĕmišpāṭay mā'āsû wĕ'et-ḥuqqōtay gā'ālâ napšām* (v. 43)

　　B'　　*wĕ'ap-gam-zō't bihyôtām bĕ'ereṣ 'ōyĕbêhem to'-mĕ'astîm wĕlō'-gĕ'altîm lĕkallōtām lĕhāpēr bĕrîtî 'ittām kî 'ănî YHWH 'ĕlōhêkem* (v. 44)

A'　　*wĕzākartî lāhem bĕrît ri'šōnîm 'ăšer hôṣē'tî- 'ōtām mē'ereṣ miṣrayîm lĕ'ênê haggôyim lihyōt lāhem lē'lōhîm 'ănî YHWH* (v. 45)

The key term *bĕrît* occurs five times (AB'A'). Although Israel has spurned (*mā'as*) and loathed (*gā'al*) God's laws, God has not spurned and loathed Israel (BB'). YHWH's self-declaration is written chiastically (B'A') in order to form an inclusio with vv. 1–2.

my covenant with Jacob. 'et-bĕrîtî ya'ăqôb. This peculiar construction is variously explained:

1. A metathesis yields *bĕrîtî 'et-ya'ăqôb* (Joüon 1923: § 129aN; but, as Zimmerli [1980: 510, n. 49] trenchantly asks, three times?). The MT is attested in *'et-bĕrîtî 'ôtāk* (Ezek 16:60, 62; cf. Exod 2:24; Jer 14:21; Elliger 1966). However, the medial *waw* in *'ôtāk* indicates that it is a *nota accusativa*, not a preposition.

2. It is an ellipsis for *bĕrîtî brît ya'ăqôb* (Ibn Ezra), or it contains a dittography of the *yod* (GKC § 128d; cf. LXX).

3. The previous explanation is correct, but without having to assume a dittography.

The construction, with *bĕrît*, occurs elsewhere: *bĕrîtî hayyôm wĕ'et-bĕrîtî hallaylâ* (Jer 33:20); *bĕrîtî šālôm* (Num 25:12). It is a survival of an original genitive case ending, such as *rabbātî 'ām* (Lam 1:1); *mĕlē'ātî mišpāṭ* (Isa 1:21); *šōkĕnî sĕneh* (Deut 33:16), found in constructs and participles (GKC § 90l–n).

What are the three covenants struck between God and the patriarchs? The answer of *Tgs. Ps.-J.* and *Neof.*, with my bracketed corrections, follows: Jacob "at Bethel" (Gen 35:9–15), Isaac "at Mount Moriah" (Gen 22:16–18? [Gen 17:19]), and Abraham "between the divided parts" (Gen 15:18–21 [17:7–8]). All these (corrected) scriptural citations stem from a priestly (P or H) source and were, therefore, familiar to the author of this verse. However, it should be emphasized that, in effect, there was only one covenant with Abraham, *renewed* with Isaac, and *presumably* renewed with Jacob (the term "Abraham's blessing" is used, Gen 28:4). See COMMENT A.

But why was the writer so insistent on emphasizing the patriarchal covenants, singling out each of them for mention? On the basis of Weinfeld's (1970) thesis that the patriarchal covenant is unconditional and, hence, indestructible (but see NOTE on n. 45, and Waltke 1988), Ginsberg (1982: 6–15) postulates that the patriarchal covenants, a priestly innovation (cf. also Exod 2:24; 6:2–8), must be late, a product of the exilic period, formulated as an assurance to the exiles that God was obligated to redeem them. He offers challenging proof of the lateness of this passage by pointing to the inverse order of the patriarchs (exhibited nowhere else), in keeping with Seidel's (1955–56: 148) demonstration that "later biblical versifiers reversed some *a* and *b* synonyms of their models" (Ginsburg 1982: 107, n. 36).

I am prepared to accept this observation, but all it proves is that the writer of 26:42 was aware of *earlier* citations of the covenant with all three patriarchs (Exod 2:24; 6:2–8)—indeed, he might even have been their author—but this does not make him necessarily exilic. There is a more cogent reason for particularizing the patriarchal covenant: it alone specifies the promise of *land* and *seed*. The Sinaitic covenant bound Israel and God together—Israel became his people—but, even if the Sinaitic covenant implied the eternity of Israel and its inheritance of the land, it derived these doctrines from the earlier patriarchal covenant, in which they were made explicit.

Gerstenberger (1996: 431) surmises that since the H tradent presupposed a Sinaitic setting for this chapter (vv. 1, 46), he had no choice but to refer back to the patriarchal covenant. Overlooked, however, is that the chapter is couched in the future and that this pericope (vv. 39–45), in particular, is projected into a *future* exile. Hence the tradent could just as well have referred to the Sinaitic covenant, which he indeed does in v. 45 (see below). For the discussion of the possible date of this passage, see COMMENT E.

I will remember (also). *'ezkōr.* This verb refers to both Isaac and Abraham (note the placement of the *'atnaḥ*). The repetition of the verb is quintessential H style; see the similar syntax in 25:10b, 41b, 48, 49.

namely, I will remember the land. The *waw* on *wĕhā'āreṣ* is explanatory. This is to say, the essence of the covenant with the patriarchs is the promise of land (Brettler 1978–89: XI). This personification of the land is brought to its most poignant expression in Second Isaiah's comforting words (e.g., Isa 49:17–23).

Keter Torah astutely observes, with surprise, that God neither grants the exiles forgiveness nor promises to restore them to their land. Because of this latter fact, Gerstenberger (1996: 429) postulates that vv. 40–45 constitute an independent document. However, as indicated earlier, the patriarchal covenant clearly implies Israel's return; nonetheless, *Keter Torah* is surely correct in noting that the concept of forgiveness is absent. One has to keep in mind at all times that this is a priestly document, the product of a theology, one of whose dogmas is that there is no full expiation—especially for sins of *ma'al* (v. 40)—without the requisite sacrifices. Thus total reconciliation with God (*sālaḥ*) will occur only after Israel returns and rebuilds its sanctuary. Another omission, already alluded to (see NOTE on "accept their punishment," v. 41), is the requirement of repentance, for which confession and remorse (vv. 40–41) are only the initial steps. Again, it must be kept in mind that this is a priestly, not a prophetic, document, and as I have argued in explicating Lev 5:20–26 (vol. 1.373–78), the priestly doctrine, as exemplified here, laid the foundation for prophetic repentance.

vv. 43–44. There are three prefixed (imperfect) verbs in v. 43a because the sabbaticals have yet to be made up. That is, not only does Israel have to repent of its sins and thereby motivate God to recall his covenant, but it also has to atone to the land for neglecting its sabbaticals. It is almost as if there are two independent agencies requiring reparation—God and the land. This may be an indication that vv. 43–44 are a parenthetical remark (Hoffmann 1953; Noth 1977; Noordtzij 1982) written in exile, together with vv. 33b–35, as a consolation for the delay of redemption (see COMMENT E).

The theological postulate underlying this doctrine needs to be underscored. It recalls the primeval Flood, which was not a punishment but a necessary consequence, to cleanse the earth, which had become polluted by human corruption (Gen 6:11–12 [P]; cf. Frymer-Kensky 1977).

Once again, earth (of Israel) is polluted by its residents, by depriving it of its sabbatical rest to recoup its depleted energies. The remedy is identical. The land must be rid of its inhabitants. This time, however, the purifying agency is not the flood—nor can it be, since God swore never again to flood the earth (Gen 9:15; Isa 54:9)—but exile. Moreover, in the priestly view the Flood was the only way to purify the earth (and, hence, had to entail the almost total loss of human and animal life), since the cleansing of pollution (*ṭum'â*) in every case (for P) requires ablution. The sin of working the land on the sabbath, however, does not generate pollution. The earth has been violated nonetheless, and since it is God's land (25:23) and the sabbath is his time (25:2, 4), they are sanctums and their violation constitutes desecration (*ma'al*, 26:40). Desecrated sanctums must be compensated and a fine exacted (5:14–16)—neglected sabbaticals repaid by exile. (Is Israel's suffering in exile, 26:36–39, its reparation offering?)

In either case, flood or exile, the result is the same: the restoration of the status quo. Noah's earth is returned to the days of creation so that the human race may be constituted afresh, and Israel's earth is returned to its pristine status so that it may be repopulated by a repentant Israel.

43. V. 43aβγ repeats most of v. 34a, and v. 34aδ repeats v. 41bβ.

that it may be paid. wĕtireṣ. This is a conjunctive *waw*; the sense is jussive (Baentsch 1903).

by being desolate. bohšammâ. This is an irregular syncope for *bĕhoššammâ* (cf. v. 34; GKC § 67y, 91e). B. S. Schwartz (personal communication) explains the grammatical development:

1. The *Hop'al* for *šmm* is:
   perfect *hûšammâ* or *hoššammâ*
   imperfect *tûšam* or *toššām*
   infinitive construct *hoššam*

2. Adding the feminine suffix to the infinitive construct yields *bĕhoššammāh*.
3. The pattern ⊡XX (of the first three letters) metamorphoses into □XX (sv = short vowel). That is, there is a switch and a loss of Dageš forte. Thus *bĕhošša* > *bohša*. For example, *bĕ'aśśôt* > *ba'śot*.
4. The loss of the *Mappiq*, while uncommon, is not irregular per se (e.g., Num 32:42) and is unrelated to the form of the infinitive construct here.
5. GKC, 519, Paradigm g, requires correction. The infinitive construct is *hoššam* not *hoššammâ*, since the final *Hē* is the pronominal suffix (cf. GKC § 67y).

for the very reason that. ya'an ûbĕya'an. The doubling of the word has been explained as anticipating the two reasons that follow (Rashi [MSS]; Qara; Ibn Ezra; Ḥazzequni) or as an indication of multiple reasons (Radak). However, it should be noted that Ezekiel (and no one else) uses this expression for single sins (Ezek 13:10; 36:3). Thus its purpose is probably for emphasis, "for the very reason that."

my rules they despised and my laws they loathed. bĕmišpāṭay mā'āsû wĕ'et-ḥuqqōtay gā'ālâ napšām. This is a chiastic reordering of v. 15a.

44. *Yet, for all that. wĕ'ap gam-zō't.* The Targums render this as *we'ap bĕram dā'* (Onq.); *wĕ'ap 'al kol dā* (Ps.-J.); *wĕ'ap bahădâ* (?). They all mean "Yet in spite of this," implying the reading *bĕzō't*, as in v. 27 (cf. Driver and White 1894–98; Bertholet 1901).

I have not despised them or loathed them. lō'-mĕ'astîm wĕlō'-gĕ'altîm. Without the subject *nepeš* 'gullet,' *gā'al* connotes more abstractly "loathe." This indicates a reversal of what Israel had done (v. 43b; cf. v. 15a). It is not, however, a reversal of God's statement "I will loathe you" (v. 30b), which refers to God's reaction to Israel's misbehavior, not to God's fidelity to his covenant.

The suffixed verbs (perfects) betray the exilic provenance for the composition of vv. 43–44. I would, however, reject Ginsberg's (1982: 80–81) claim that v. 43 was composed after v. 44 because both verses form a cohesive unit (v. 44 reversing v. 43) typical of the structure of the entire chapter, which is built on the principle of reversals.

As Gerstenberger (1996: 432) points out, the measure-for-measure principle that God employs in dispensing divine justice (vv. 21, 23–24, 27–28), in response to Israel's despising and loathing of the covenantal commandments (v. 15), is herewith broken: Israel will continue as his people, and the covenantal promises will remain in force. This statement belies the claim that divine mercy is absent in priestly theology (Friedman 1981b: 27–28).

annulling my covenant with them. lĕhāpēr bĕrîtî 'ittām. This indicates reversal of Israel's act *lĕhaprĕhem 'et-bĕrîtî* 'your annulling my covenant' (v. 15). The placement of v. 44 in the seventh and penultimate use of *bĕrîtî* underscores the significance of YHWH's fidelity to his covenant (Warning 1999: 119). This is a clear, unambiguous statement that the Sinaitic covenant remains in force (see NOTES on vv. 9, 15, 25, and 45). It complements the patriarchal covenant (v. 42): the patriarchal covenant guarantees Israel's return to the land, and the Sinaitic covenant guarantees (following Israel's punishment and remorse) God's "return" to Israel, "for I YHWH am their God." "The rejection of Israel for defection, although demanded by logic, is precluded by divine love" (Muffs 1965a: 5).

45. This verse is a continuation of the promise of v. 42. God will take account of both his covenants.

But I will remember in their favor. wĕzākartî lāhem. The expression *zākar le,* as its Aramaic equivalent *'št l* (Elephantine, no. 9; Kraeling 1953: 16–17), means "remember favorably" (e.g., Jer 2:2; Ginsberg 1967: 81–82).

the covenant with the ancients. bĕrît rī'šōnîm. Some scholars hold that the patriarchal covenant is intended:

1. This verse argues that just as God remembered the patriarchal covenant for the exiles in Egypt (Exod 2:24; 6:2–8), so will he remember the covenant for the present exiles (Wessely 1846).
2. In all of P and H, *bĕrît* 'covenant' never refers to Sinai (Bertholet 1901; Buis 1974).

These reasons are flawed. The Egyptian experience is not analogous. In Egypt, Israel had only the patriarchal covenant to rely on; those in later exiles could also be sustained by the promise of the Sinaitic covenant. The argument of silence concerning *bĕrît* is equally invalid. The only text that matters is chap. 26, and the covenant containing laws, rules, commandments, and the consequences for their nonobservance, which can be only the Sinaitic covenant, is alluded to three times: vv. 15, 25a, 44a. Moreover, as observed by Gerstenberger (1996: 432), the polaric behavior in chap. 26, imposing obligations on each side, is characteristic solely of the Siniatic covenant.

Ezekiel refers to the Sinaitic covenant in his condemnation of Israel: "Truly, thus said YHWH God: I will deal with you as you have dealt, for you have spurned the pact and violated the covenant" (16:59). Then, following the sequence of our chapter (vv. 40–42, 45), he reaffirms the validity of this covenant: "nevertheless, I will remember the covenant I made with you in the days of your youth" (*bîmê nĕ'ûrayik*; note the reference to Jer 2:2, another indication that the subject is the Sinaitic covenant), and makes explicit what is only implicit in our verse: "and I will maintain an everlasting covenant with you [*wahăqīmôtî lāk bĕrît 'ôlām*]" (Ezek 16:60). For the exclusive meaning of *hēqîm bĕrît* as "maintain a covenant," see COMMENT A.

A decisive answer, however, can be given only by the terminology, beginning with the immediately following ambiguous clause *'ăšer hôṣē'tî-'ōtām.* On the one hand, it is possible to argue that it refers back to the patriarchal covenant in the pre-Sinaitic declaration *wā'ezkōr 'et-bĕrîtî lāken . . . wĕhôṣē'tî 'etkem* 'and I remembered my covenant. Therefore . . . I shall free them' (Exod 6:5b–6aα). In that case, *'ăšer* would have to be emended to *ba'ăšer*—that is, preceded by the *beth* of means. Then, our clause could be rendered "the covenant with the ancients by which I freed them." But in the few cases where *ba'ăšer* is attested, the *beth* of means never occurs (cf. BDB 84a). Alternatively, v. 45a could be rendered as "I *who* took them out from the land of Egypt will remember their first covenant" (Propp 1996: 475, n. 69). However, this reading would require a transposition of v. 45aα and v.aβ. Besides, what in the MT corresponds with "I (who)," which requires the use of the pronoun *'ănî*? If, on the other hand, the referent is the Sinaitic covenant, neither emendation nor transposition is required. The clause means "whom I freed" or "for whose sake I freed" (Rashbam), which can refer to only the generation of the Exodus. (The writer, of course, has had to abandon the fiction that he is a member of that generation.)

The term *rī'šōnîm* also requires investigation. If the author had the patriarchal covenant in mind, he could have written *bĕrît 'ăbōtêkā* 'the covenant with your fathers' as in Deut 4:31, which clearly refers to the patriarchs (cf. Weinfeld 1991: 210). Moreover, where *rīšōnîm* does not take the article (Deut 19:14; Isa 61:4; Ps 79:8), it carries the plural sense of "previous generations" (Joüon 1923 § 137i). In fact, one of its three attestations *lō' tassîg gĕbûl rē'ăkā 'ăšer gābĕlû rī'šōnîm* 'You shall not move your neighbor's landmark, set up by previous generations' (Deut 19:14a) is wisdom instruction duplicated in Prov 22:28 *'al-tasség gĕbûl 'ôlām 'ăšer 'ăśû 'ăbôtêkā* 'Move not the ancient landmark set up by your fathers', where *rī'šōnîm* is paralleled by *'ăbôtêka*, referring to the fathers of many prior generations. Moreover, Joosten (1998: 152), citing Elliger (1966: 379), correctly remarks that *rī'šōnîm* exhibits the "well-known tendency of the Holiness Code occasionally to step out of its fictional framework so as to address its real addressees directly" (see NOTE on "vomited out," 18:25). Since v. 45, in my opinion, was composed by exilic H$_R$ (see INTRODUCTION to vv. 1–2), the use of *rī'šōnîm* 'ancients' so many generations later is apt.

Therefore, the verdict must be in favor of the Sinaitic covenant. One question, however, still remains to be resolved. Just as the patriarchal covenant should have been termed *bĕrît 'ăbōtêka*, so the Sinaitic covenant should have been called by the more obvious term *bĕrît sînay*, particularly since it occurs in the envelope of chaps. 25–26 (25:1; 26:46). Why, then, the rare and enigmatic *rī'šōnîm*? I would suggest that the author of this verse wanted to refer to both covenants simultaneously. First, as noted, this term implies multiple generations. Then, the author must have had the patriarchal covenant also in mind, since he refers to it (v. 42). Thus he had to connect the two covenants by a single word. He may even have regarded the two as a single covenant. Since the universal demands of morality inherent in the patriarchal covenant (cf. Knohl 1995: 147) remain in effect, it is possible to speak of the Sinaitic covenant as an extension of its patriarchal forerunner. Above all, H was telling his audience (and us) that God will restore Israel to its land both on the basis of the patriarchal covenant, the promise of progeny and land (v. 42), and on the basis of the Sinaitic covenant, Israel's observance of the revealed commandments (vv. 3, 14–15). The tacit assumption derivable from this conclusion is that with the Sinaitic covenant continuing in force, the gruesome consequences detailed in this chapter also remain in force. How different is H's implicit warning from the subsequent picture of the return from exile envisaged by the prophets (Jer 31:31–33; Ezek 36:24–30)?

Finally, the reference to the Sinaitic covenant in this verse (and allusions to it in 19:2–4; 26:1–2, 15a, 25a) should put an end to the question that has plagued theologians since the beginning of modern scholarship: Why is the Sinaitic covenant absent from P? Zimmerli (1960) holds that it was deliberately excised from P (and H) so that the relationship between YHWH and Israel would no longer be conditioned by Israel's obedience to the commandments. Instead, it is the covenant with Abraham that is given prominence, a covenant of promise (*Verheissungsbund*) and grace (*Gnadenbund*). Thus Israel is enabled to survive in the exile without its Temple and state, not by obedience to God's law, but by his eternal grace.

That God's covenant with Abraham was one of pure grace is totally refuted by the P source itself: *hithallēk lĕpānay wehyēh tāmîm wĕ'ettĕnâ bĕrîtî bênî ûbênekā* 'Walk before me, and be blameless and I will make a covenant between me and you' (Gen 17:1b–2a). Therefore, the covenant with Abraham is conditioned on Abraham's blameless behavior, not on God's grace (details in Waltke 1988; Joosten 1994: 154–57; 1996: 110–12). Moreover, his descendants are equally bound by this condition: "I have chosen him (Abraham) that he may charge his children and his household after him to keep the way of YHWH by doing righteousness and justice" (Gen 18:19a [JE]). Thus the Abrahamic covenant is not one of grace; it is not even unconditional (which requires a revision of Weinfeld's [1970] covenant of grant hypothesis, followed by many, most recently Otto 1995b: 390). This verse can hardly be called "an expectation" (Weinfeld 1993: 249, n. 118) rather than a condition. Similarly, Gen 17:1b *hithallēk lĕpānay wehyēh tāmîm* is not equivalent to Akkadian *ittalak maḫriya* and *(ittalak) šalmiš* (Weinfeld: 1993: 230), since the latter verbs are perfects, while the former are imperatives so that the covenant (v. 2a) is clearly conditioned on Abraham's moral rectitude.

Weinfeld's (1993) contention that royal grants were unconditional has been challenged. As shown by Knoppers (1996), available evidence in the ancient Near East from Mari, Ugarit, Ḫatti (but cf. Weinfeld 1990c), Babylonia, Assyria, and Elephantine shows that such grants, either explicitly or implicitly, are conditional. The recipient and his progeny are expected to provide obligatory service in the form of military service, land cultivation, and/or payment of dues (cf. Gen 18:19).

Crüsemann (1996: 305–6) has argued that YHWH's explicit statement that he never repudiates the covenant (v. 44a) can refer to only the Abrahamic covenant, which "is independent of failure on Israel's part." However, as explicated in vv. 40–41, the divine willingness to fulfill the covenant is dependent on Israel's penitence. Moreover, even the Abrahamic covenant is contingent on the behavior of his progeny "in order that YHWH may bring about for Abraham what he has promised him" (Gen 18:19b). YHWH need not change; his promise remains unbroken. But for it to be realized, Israel must change. Otherwise, Israel remains in exile (the ultimate national punishment) forever. Indeed, as pointed out above, the laws and commandments (vv. 3, 15) that Israel is obligated to obey most easily point to Sinai as their source. In truth, however, as explicated in COMMENT A, it turns out in the long run that there is little difference between the covenants of Sinai and Abraham in regard to their fulfillment. The difference lies in their content, but their realization is dependent on Israel's behavior.

Even more recently, Cross (1998: 13–19, n. 41) has argued that both the Abrahamic and Davidic covenants are unconditional. His evidence is the thirteenth-century Hittite covenant between Tudkhaliyas IV and Ulmi-Teshep (Weinfeld 1970: 189–90), which states that rebellious sovereigns may be removed, but they must be succeeded by members of the same dynasty. This policy holds for the Davidic covenant, but breaks down when applied to the seed of Abraham. YHWH will remember the covenant with the patriarchs only if Israel repents (26:41, 42).

This view accords with other pentateuchal sources that aver that Israel will occupy the land or remain on it if it is obedient to the covenant (Exod 23:20–25 [JE]; Lev 18:26–28; 26:14–15, 32–33 [H]; Deut 4:1; 8:1; 11:8 [D]). Thus despite the Abrahamic promise, the eventuality can occur that a sinful Israel will be removed from its land, never to return.

The prophets maintain that God purges the wicked, but not the entire people. Yet his fidelity to Israel is always contingent on the existence of a righteous remnant (e.g., eighth-century Isa 1:18–20; 10:20–22; 17:4–6). Thus God's covenant with Israel is conditional. To be sure, this view changes in the exile. As indicated in the *exilic* additions to chap. 26 (vv. 33b–35, 43), the return to the land will take place only after the barren land makes up the number of its violated sabbatical years. Isaiah of the exile transfers the determining factor from the land to the people: Israel must pine sufficiently in the exile (Isa 40:2). However, H and the other preexilic sources maintain that God's fidelity to his covenant is *conditional* on the observance of the covenant.

Thus the reciprocal obligations implied by H's covenant (vv. 15, 25a, 44a), the explicit association of H's covenant with the Exodus generation (v. 45a), and the possibility that H's sabbath is a covenantal sign (Exod 31:16–17) can only lead to the conclusion that the priestly school of H presumed the existence of the Sinaitic covenant. How, then, can we explain its absence in the H Source? One must therefore conclude that the H redactor either removed P's Sinaitic tradition when he merged JE and P (von Rad 1962: 1, 135) or, preferably, relied on E's account of such a ceremony (Exod 24:1–8; Cross 1973: 320). Moreover, the redactor's hand is clearly visible in the placement of priestly texts as the encasement of the Sinaitic pericope (Exod 19:1–2; 24:15b–18), further indicating that he adopted the entire epic tradition of the Sinaitic event (see Introduction II F).

This eventuality still leaves open the question about the absence of such a tradition in P itself. To be sure, P speaks of a Sinaitic theophany in the Tabernacle on the day following the week-long consecration rites for the priesthood when YHWH's *kābôd*-fire incinerates the sacrifices at the inaugural service (9:23–24). However, a ceremonial binding the people to God's laws would still be lacking. The problem is discussed further in the Introduction II F. Here, I briefly state my conclusion. P does not know the Sinaitic revelation and covenant; it relates only that YHWH's cloud (presence) condescended into the completed Tabernacle (Exod 40:34–35) and, by means of incinerating the altar's sacrifices with the divine fire *emanating from the adytum* (indicating his presence there; Lev 9:24), YHWH indicates his acceptance of the priestly service. That is, he demonstrates his willingness to abide among Israel. But H, as shown by its polemics with the laws of JE (see Introduction I I), is as much aware of JE as it is of P. Therefore, H can and does absorb the Sinaitic revelation and covenant. And as exemplified by this chapter, H has incorporated both of JE's covenants (patriarchal and Sinaitic) and both revelations (P's Tabernacle and JE's Sinai).

whom I freed from the land of Egypt. 'ăšer hôṣē'tî-'ōtām mē'ereṣ miṣrayîm. This phrase balances *'ăšer hôṣē'tî 'etkem mē'ereṣ miṣrayîm* (v. 13). Thus the curses (vv. 14–39) end on the same note as the blessings (vv. 3–13), subtly indicating that Israel's remorse will not only cancel the curses and return it to its land, but also restore the fullness of blessing if Israel will adhere to the divine commandments (E. Tawil).

in the sight of the nations. lĕ'ênê haggôyim. This is a favorite phrase of Ezekiel (5:8; 20:9, 14, 22; 22:16; 25:28; 38:23; 39:27).

V. 46. The Summation

the laws, rules. haḥuqqîm wĕhammišpāṭîm. These refer to the Covenant Code (Exod 20–23) whatever was revealed at Sinai (Ibn Ezra); to the sabbatical and jubilee laws of chap. 25 (Rashbam); and to all of Leviticus (Wessely 1846). This question can be settled by the next term "the rituals" (see next NOTE). The term *ḥuqqîm* for "laws" occurs in Leviticus only once again, in 10:11 (as noted by Elliger 1966), a verse stemming from H, another example of the breakdown of P's technical terms when handled by H (vol. 1.617–20). The term *mišpāṭîm* occurs frequently in H (18:4, 5, 26; 19:37; 20:22; 25:18; 26:15, 43) but never in P (Joosten 1996: 81).

and the rituals. wĕhattôrōt. This term refers to all the rituals mentioned in Leviticus—that is, all of P—because it does not occur in H (6:2, 7, 18; 7:1, 11; 13:59; 14:57; 15:32; Num 19:14; R. Akiba in *Sipra* Beḥuqotay 8:13, followed by Hoffmann 1953; cf. Elliger 1966: 371; Hartley 1992: XXXIII).

at Mount Sinai. bĕhar sînay. Forming an inclusio with 25:1, this phrase implies that chaps. 25–26 form a separate scroll within Leviticus. This location is found twice more, first in 27:34, an attempt to attribute all of Leviticus to the Sinaitic revelation to Moses, and then in 7:38, a gloss (probably traceable to H) claiming that the sacrificial laws transmitted to Israel by Moses from the Tabernacle were initially revealed to him on Mount Sinai (vol. 1.438–39). Thus whereas 26:1–39 (with the addition of vv. 40–45) forms the epilogue to the Holiness Source, v. 46 is the closure to the entire book (prior to the addition of chap. 27). See the NOTE on v. 3, and the Introduction I M.

The key words in this verse form a significant inclusion with key words in 25:1–2 (M. Hildenbrand):

A   *wayyĕdabbēr YHWH ʾel-mōšeh*
   B   *bĕhar sînay* (25:1)
      C   *bĕnê yiśrāʾēl*
         D   *ʾel-hāʾāreṣ ʾăšer ʾănî nōtēn lākem* (25:2)
         D'   *ʾēlleh haḥuqqîm wĕhammišpāṭîm wĕhattôrōt ʾăšer nātan*
            YHWH
      C'   *bĕnê yiśrāʾēl*
   B'   *bĕhar sînay*
A'   *bĕyad-mōšeh*

The inclusion attributes the composition of chaps. 25–26 to Moses at Mount Sinai (AA'). B and C are identical with C'B'. The center of this introversion has in common the verb *nātan* 'give' and the subject, the Deity, stating that both the land and the laws stem from YHWH and thereby implying that Israel's tenure on God's land is dependent on its obedience of God's laws.

COMMENTS

A. The Unbroken Covenant

The thesis of this COMMENT was developed in a term paper written by my son, Jeremy J. Milgrom (in 1978) (for Moshe Greenberg) that the expression *hēqîm bĕrît* means "maintain / fulfill a covenant," but never "establish a covenant" (see also Dumbrell 1984: 25–26). His focus was on Ezek 16:60, 62, but his findings are relevant throughout Scripture, especially in the priestly texts. It is well known that *hēqîm* can mean "fulfill," as in *hēqîm dābār* 'fulfill a word / promise' (e.g., Deut 9:5; 27:26; 1 Kgs 2:4; 12:15); *hēqîm neder / šĕbûʿâ* 'fulfill a vow / oath' (Gen 26:3; Num 30:14–15; Jer 11:5; cf. Gruber 1978–79); and *hēqîm bĕrît* 'fulfill a covenant' (Deut 8:18). The last expression, however, can, and frequently does, mean "maintain a / uphold a covenant"; that is, the fulfillment is postponed. God will "maintain" the Abrahamic covenant with his offspring (Gen 17:7, 9), specifically with Isaac (Gen 17:21), with Israel in Egypt (Exod 6:4), and in the future (Babylonian) exile (Lev 26: 9, 42). According to Ezekiel, the Sinaitic covenant also continues to sustain its validity because God promised the exiles: "I will remember the covenant I made in your youth [*bîmê nĕʿûrāyik;* see Jer 2:2, and NOTE on "covenant with the ancients," v. 45], and I will *maintain* [*wahăqîmōtî*] an eternal covenant with you" (Ezek 16:60).

Thus *hēqîm bĕrît* implies a prior covenant, not the establishment of a new one. The latter notion is expressed by the verb *kārat* 'cut' (e.g., Gen 15:18; 21:27, 32; 26:28; 31:44; Exod 23:32; 24:8; 34:10, 12, 15, 27). Those sources that use both *kārat* and *hēqîm* carefully distinguish between them. Deuteronomy, for example, regularly uses *kārat* for cutting, establishing a covenant (Deut 5:2, 3; 7:2; 28:69; 29:13), but it will resort to *hēqîm* when it wishes to denote fulfilling a covenant (Deut 8:18). Similarly, when Jeremiah refers to the covenant that the slave owners made with God to release their slaves, he uses *kārat* (Jer 34:8, 13, 15), but for the notion of fulfilling the covenant, he must switch to *hēqîm* (v. 18). Ezekiel, too, must employ *kārat* in describing the covenant struck between Zedekiah and Nebuchadrezzar (Ezek 17:13) and between Israel and God concerning the new order that will prevail when Israel is returned to its land (Ezek 34:25; 37:26). However, in referring to the Sinaitic covenant, as shown above, Ezekiel resorts to *hēqîm* (Ezek 16:60, 62).

The priestly terminology is even more instructive. To describe the making of a covenant, it eschews the verb *kārat*. (Is it because this word originated in the ceremony of passing between the "cut" halves of animals [cf. Gen 15:17; Jer 34:18], implying an illegitimate sacrificial rite?) Instead, we find the neutral *nātan* 'give, grant, establish' (Gen 17:2; Num 25:12). What is particularly impressive is the sequence of verbs in Gen 17, concerning the covenant between God and Abraham. The establishment of the covenant, as mentioned, employs *nātan* (v. 2); thereafter, the verb is *hēqîm* (vv. 7, 19, 21). The context reveals the reason for the change: the object has switched from Abraham to his progeny. The covenant that God made with Abraham will be *maintained* with his offspring.

Another proven method of determining the precise meaning of a term is to examine its semantic field and, in particular, to identify its antonym. In the case of priestly *hēqîm*, this search is both simple and rewarding: "Every vow and sworn obligation of self-denial *'iššāh yĕqîmennû wĕ'iššāh yĕpērennû* may be upheld by her husband or annulled by her husband" (Num 30:14; cf. vv. 15–16). Thus the opposite of *hēqîm* is *hēpēr* 'annul'. One can only annul what was previously in force. It is, therefore, conclusive that when the curses of Lev 26 speak of Israel annulling the covenant (*lĕhaprĕkem 'et-bĕrîtî*, v. 15), whereas God refuses to do so (*lĕhāpēr bĕrîtî*, v. 44), they reverse *wahăqîmōtî 'et-bĕrîtî* of the blessings (v. 9), and, therefore, the latter can only mean "and I will uphold my covenant." Thus one can no longer hold that "in *hēqîm* the idea of establishing is dominant" (Weinfeld 1975a: 260) or that on the basis of Ginsberg's (1982: 107) reading of Lev 26:9b "I will establish [*sic*] my covenant with you . . . ," he writes: "There is not a word here about YHWH's having already been 'the God of your fathers' and about his having already established a covenant with them." To the contrary, Lev 26 is stating clearly and unambiguously that the covenant God established with the fathers, renewed and expanded at Sinai, will be upheld and not be annulled.

Finally, to complete my case, it is crucial to examine the passages that, ostensibly, give the appearance of exceptions. The first is the Noahide covenant. Thrice in Gen 9:8–17, God informs Noah concerning the covenant: *hinĕnî mēqîm* (v. 9) and *hăqīmōtî* (vv. 11, 17). Is this a new covenant that God makes with Noah? The terminology belies it. It should be noted that whereas the text consistently uses *hēqîm* with the covenant, it just as consistently uses *nātan* in regard to the *'ôt*, the rainbow-sign (vv. 12–13). As indicated above, when the priestly source wishes to say "establish," it will use *nātan*. And the rainbow-sign, indeed, is new and the use of *nātan* is appropriate. Thus if the covenant is described by *hēqîm*, the assumption must be that it is not new. Alternatively, one can argue that just as the covenant with Abraham is explicitly intended for his subsequent progeny (Gen 17; see above), so God's covenant with Noah is explicitly directed to subsequent generations. Note "your seed after you" (v. 9) and "all flesh" (vv. 11, 17), in which case the rendering "maintain" would be appropriate.

Moreover, the possibility must be considered, especially in view of the use of *hēqîm* and not of *nātan*, that the text is referring to an earlier covenant, which has not been abrogated and is renewed with Noah—the covenant with Adam. True, the term "covenant" is absent in the passages dealing with Adam, but I suggest that it may be implied. Note that the text immediately preceding the Noahide covenant is the Noahide law (Gen 9:1–7), which repeats verbatim God's blessing "Be fruitful and multiply and fill the earth" (Gen 1:28; 9:1; cf. v. 9) and grants Noah control over the animal kingdom (Gen 9:2), but with new concessions and restrictions (vv. 3–6). And just as the Abrahamic covenant is renewed and expanded in the Sinaitic covenant, so the tacit, but limited, pact with Adam is reaffirmed and expanded with Noah. In the Bible, there is no covenant without obligations. In other words, there is no such thing as an unconditional covenant (see NOTE on v. 45). To be sure, God's covenant with Abraham in Gen 15 (JE) imposes no obligations on Abraham. But the same JE tradition subsequently states that Abraham's promise of seed and soil is explicitly dependent on his posterity, "to keep the way of YHWH by doing what is just and right, in order that YHWH may bring about for Abraham what he has promised him" (Gen 18:19). Mutatis mutandis, God's covenant with Noah includes obligations for Noah and his progeny as laid out in the contiguous passage.

Finally, a fourth passage in the Noah story contains this idiom, in the initial annunciation scene (Gen 6:18). Here, also, the two explanations proposed above are possible. Either God's covenant is intended for Noah's posterity, or he is reaffirming the covenant with Adam. In either case, God is "maintaining" his covenant to keep the human race alive.

The last problematic occurrence of *hēqîm běrît*, Exod 6:4, speaks of the covenant with the forefathers. The verb clearly cannot mean "establish," since it is only with Abraham that God established a covenant. On the contrary, another text explicitly testifies *wahăqīmōtî 'et-haššěbû'â 'ăšer nišba'tî lě'abrāhām 'ābîkā* 'I shall fulfill the oath I swore to Abraham your father' (Gen 26:3b), implying that none was sworn to Isaac (note that *hēqîm* here means "fulfill"). The Exodus text simply means that the covenant that God *maintained* with the forefathers is still in force and is operative for the redemption of Israel from Egypt.

The significance of whether God's covenant with Israel is maintained or established for determining the antiquity and age of Lev 26 is discussed in COMMENT E. On the theological plane, however, the significance can be ascertained here. For the priestly legists (P and H), God has never broken his covenants with Israel—even though it languishes in exile. There are basically two covenants: one with the forefathers and the other at Sinai, which P and H would uphold. But each covenant has its own interest and purpose, and they move in opposite directions: one from God to Israel, and the other from Israel to God. And the anchor is the divine commitment that YHWH will never desert or abandon Israel, however much Israel violates its terms under the covenant and is destroyed in the process.

B. *Leviticus 26 and Deuteronomy 28*

This COMMENT analyzes the parallels and differences between Lev 26 and Deut 28 compiled by Driver (1895: 304), Hoffmann (1953), Hillers (1964: 30–42), Cholewinski (1976), and Kochman (1987). They have *some* vocabulary in common:

Lev 26	Deut 28
ʾet-haššahepet wĕʾet-haqqaddahat (v. 16)	baššahepet ûbaqqaddahat (v. 22)
šĕmêkem kabbarzel wĕʾet-ʾ arṣĕkem kannĕhušā (v. 19)	šāmêkā . . . nĕhōšet wĕhāʾāreṣ barzel (v. 23)
wĕniggaptem lipnê ʾōyĕbêkem (v. 17)	niggap lipnê ʾōyĕbêkā (v. 25)
mĕkallôt ʿênayim ûmĕdîbōt nāpeš (v. 16)	wĕʿênêkā . . . wĕkālôt . . . wĕkilyôn ʿênayim wĕdaʾăbôn nāpeš (vv. 32, 65)
waʾăkaltem bĕśar bĕnêkem ûbĕśar bĕnōtêkem (v. 29)	wĕʾākaltā . . . bĕśar bānêkā ûbĕnōtêkā (v. 53)
wĕʾên mahărîd (v. 6)	wĕʾên mahărîd (v. 26)

Not much can or should be deduced from these parallels, since they represent typological curse vocabulary in ancient Near Eastern treaties (for a parade example, see NOTE on v. 19). The differences, however, are more significant:

1. "In the former (Lev 26), Israel is addressed in the plural and Moses uttered them (the blessings and curses) on behalf of the Almighty; in the latter (Deut 28), Israel is addressed in the singular, and Moses uttered them in his own name" (*b. Meṣ.* 31b)—"since the Almighty made Moses his agent" (Ramban; cf. *Zohar* Ethanan 265a). Specifically, in Lev 26, God speaks in the first person to Israel in the second person, and to the exilic remnant (vv. 36–45) in the third person, whereas in Deut 28, Moses speaks in the first person to Israel and refers to God in the third person.

2. The blessings unique to Lev 26 are removing wild beasts (v. 6bα), turning favorably to Israel (v. 9aα), establishing the divine presence and walking among Israel (vv. 11a, 12aα), and no loathing of Israel (v. 11b); unique to Deut 28 are Israel's superiority among the nations (vv. 1b, 10, 13), Israel's blessed existence in its settlements (v. 3), fertility (vv. 4, 11aβ), produce (v. 5), affairs (vv. 6, 8aβ, 12aγ), and banking (v. 12b).

The curses unique to Lev 26 are wild beasts (v. 22), destruction of cult places (vv. 30, 31aβ, b), cities and land (vv. 31aα, 32, 33); those unique to Deut 28 are: within Israel's settlements (v. 16), produce (v. 17), fertility (v. 18), affairs (v. 19), rainfall (v. 24), skin diseases (vv. 27, 35), madness (vv. 28aα, 34), blindness (vv. 28aβ, 29a), theft of wives and property (vv. 30–31), children taken captive (vv. 32, 41), crops devoured by insects (vv. 38–39, 42), superiority of aliens (vv. 43–44), fatal slavery conditions (v. 48), extraordinary diseases (vv. 59–61), and Egyptian bondage (v. 68).

Especially notable in Lev 26 is the destruction of the cult, the disciplinary function of the exile, and the explicit reference to the covenant (vv. 9b, 15b, 25a, 31aβ,b, 41b; cf. the oblique reference in Deut 28:9).

3. The short tight phrases of Lev 26 are repeated and lengthened in Deut 28. Compare:

- Disease: Lev 26:16 and Deut 28:22, 27–28, 59–61
- Enemy: Lev 26:17 and Deut 28:25–26, 30–33, 48–52
- Drought: Lev 26:19–20 and Deut 28:23–24, 40

4. The schema of increasing torment in Lev 26 has no analogue in Deut 28. It is grouped in five sets, each beginning with the same refrain (vv. 16–17, 18–20, 21–22, 23–26, 27–39), a typology that is found in Amos and Isaiah (see INTRODUCTION to vv. 3–39).

5. The curses of Lev 26 are provincial in character, whereas those of Deut 28, except for a few verses (vv. 38–42), derive from the punitive imagery of the Assyrian suzerainty treaties. In this respect, Lev 26 resembles the older Sefire treaty (details in Weinfeld 1972d: 123–26). A particularly striking contrast is offered by Lev 26:25, which implies that Israelites normally reside in rural areas and gather in cities only for protection against invading armies, in comparison with Deut 28:3, 16, which juxtaposes the city and the countryside (Joosten 1994: 221–22; 1996: 159–60, though Lev 26:32 as well as Deut 28:30–32 presume foreign occupation).

6. Deut 28 is an unrelenting litany of punishments, whereas the punishments in Lev 26 are chastisements. Their fivefold grouping is an undercurrent of hope that Israel will change its ways. Even after Israel is exiled, hope is not lost; the covenant remains unbroken (v. 44), and it needs only Israel's remorse to be reactivated.

My net deduction from this comparison is that Lev 26 is the older text (a conclusion reached by Dillmann and Ryssel [1897] on the basis of just no. 3). I cannot prove, nor do I claim, that Lev 26 was the *Vorlage* of Deut 28. But all the signs, indicated in nos. 3, 4, and 5—the lengthy and repetitive phrases of Deut 28, and the typology of the form and locale of Lev 26, resembling the earlier models in Amos, Isaiah, and Sefire—argue strongly for the conclusion that Lev 26 reflects an older form than Deut 28.

I would add only one additional argument, which for me is decisive. Deut 28 has no consolatory epilogue comparable to Lev 26:40–45. For that, one must turn to Deut 30:1–10, a passage that may originally have served as the epilogue to Deut 28:1–68 (Wolff 1961: 181; Rofé 1985: 311–12). Indeed, Deut 30:1–10 and its verbal and contextual counterpart, Deut 4:27–31, may be regarded as an inclusio for the original book of Deuteronomy (Weinfeld 1991: 216). This fact is sufficient for most scholars to decide that Deut 28 is the later text (at least its epilogue) because purportedly it reflects the despair of the Babylonian Exiles.

Unfortunately, insufficient attention has been paid to the difference between the two consolatory additions. Deut 30:1–10 stresses that God will restore Israel only on condition that Israel repents (wĕšabtā, v. 2; tāšûb, v. 10, an inclusio enveloping the entire pericope, implying that Israel's repentance is the sine qua non for redemption). The verb šwb is an unambiguous reference to *prophetic* repentance, which calls for a radical change in behavior (e.g., Isa 1:16–17). This root, however, is missing from Lev 26. Israel is called on only to confess, feel remorse, accept the divine punishment, but nothing else. This is only embryonic repentance; it is a far cry from the subsequent demands of Israel's prophets. I cannot conceive that any exilic text exhorting Israel to repent could have ignored the prophetic demands and, instead, substituted an older, inchoate—and, for the prophets, inadequate—form of repentance (vol. 1.373–78). Lev 26, to be sure, suspends the priestly demand for sacrificial expiation and, thus, sets the stage for the prophetic repentance, which drops it entirely. But the qualitative and, hence, chronological gap between the two remains.

C. Leviticus 26 and Ezekiel

All commentators have noted the extraordinary correspondence between the language of Ezekiel and that of the Holiness Source, in general, and Lev 26, in particular. There is no consensus, however, on the chronological relationship: Who borrowed from whom? Or did both Ezekiel and H borrow from a third source? (For a summary of past views, see Burrows 1925: 28–30). The issue, I submit, can be settled only by examining those passages where there is irrefutable evidence that one source has clearly altered the other. I shall devote this COMMENT to Lev 26, where the parallels are abundant, and discuss the rest of the Holiness Source in COMMENT D.

1. A glaring example of borrowing is Ezek 34:24–28 (parallels in boldface):

[24]wa'ănî **YHWH** 'ehyeh lāhem lē'lōhîm wĕ'abdî dāwid nāśî' bĕtôkām 'ănî **YHWH** dibbartî. [25]wĕkāratti lāhem bĕrît šālôm wĕhišbattî ḥayyâ-rā'â minhā'āreṣ wĕyāšĕbû bammidbār lābetaḥ wĕyāšĕnû bayyĕ'ārîm [26]wĕnātattî 'ōtām ûsĕbîbôt gib'ātî bĕrākâ wĕhôradtî **haggešem** bĕ'ittô gišmê bĕrākâ yihyû [27]wĕnātan 'ēṣ haśśādeh 'et-piryô wĕhā'āreṣ tittēn yĕbûlāh wĕhāyû 'al-'admātām lābetaḥ wĕyādĕ'û kî-'ănî YHWH bĕšibrî 'et-mōṭôt 'ullām wĕhiṣṣaltîm miyyād hā'ōbĕdîm bāhem [28]wĕlō'-yihyû 'ôd baz laggôyim wĕḥayyat hā'āreṣ lō' tō'kĕlēm wĕyāšĕbû lābetaḥ wĕ'ên maḥărîd

[24]**I YHWH will be their God,** and my servant David shall be a ruler among them—**I YHWH** have spoken. [25]And I will strike with them a covenant of **friendship. I will banish vicious beasts from** their **land, and they shall live**

secure in the wasteland, they shall even sleep in the woodland. [26]I will make these and the environs of my hill (?) a blessing: I will send down **the rain in its season,** rains that bring blessing. [27]**The trees of the field shall yield their fruit and the land shall yield its produce.** And they (Israel) shall continue secure on their own soil. They shall know that **I am YHWH when I break the bars of their yoke** and rescue them from those **who enslave them.** [28]they shall no longer be a spoil for the nations, and the beasts of the earth shall not devour them: **they shall dwell secure and untroubled.**

In general, it can be seen that in chap. 34, Ezekiel has transferred the blessings of Lev 26 into the image of sheep (already noted by Hoffmann 1928: 23) and the blessings are now linked with the idealized Davidic king (the shepherd of vv. 23–24; Porter 1976). The details are even more revealing.

V. 24 has selected from Lev 26:12aβ, 13aα *wĕhayîtî lākem lē'lōhîm . . . 'ănî YHWH* and added the Davidic ruler as part of the divine ordinance (Hoffmann 1953). V. 25a has reworked 26:6a, bα; *šālôm* of the latter has been strengthened by the term *bĕrît* 'covenant' (borrowed from Num 25:12), necessitating the change from *wĕnātatti* 'grant' to *wĕkārattî* 'strike'. In Lev 26, *šālôm* is granted to the land; in Ezek 34, to the sheep/Israel 'with them.' In the former, its meaning is peace (i.e., absence of violence); in the latter, it refers to a relationship with Israel and, hence, the rendering "friendship." The image of the sheep in Ezek 34 necessitates that Israel dwell (and sleep) securely not in the land (Lev 26:5b), but in the wasteland and woodland (Ezek 34:25b).

V. 26a is, unfortunately, obscure. V 26b, however, is clearly an explication of Lev 26:4a: Ezekiel explains that what is meant by "rain" (sing.) denotes "rains" (pl.), and if they fall in their proper season, "they bring blessing." The subject, however, has been switched from the people (v. 25) to the land. Paran (1989: 111, n. 66) points out that nowhere else but in Ezekiel do we find that the action of God or the skies bringing rain is described by the verb *yārad* (rather than *nātan*). V. 27 is a combination of Lev 26:4b, 5bβ, and 13aγ-bα, and consists of two inversions (cf. v. 27aα with Lev 26:4b and v. 27bβγ with Lev 26:13aγ–bα) and a change from the past Egyptian enslavers, a frequent H expression (e.g., Lev 25:38, 42, 55), to the present but unnamed enslavers. The subject, once again, has been altered from the land (v. 27a) to the people (v. 27b). Finally, v. 28aβ, b inverts (and rephrases) Lev 26:6bα with 6aβ. Again, the rephrasing is essential, since the subject is no longer the land (Lev 26:6b), but the people. Thus the mixed metaphors, changes of subject, stylistic inversions, and explanatory expansions make it amply clear that Ezekiel has reworked the blessings of Lev 26:3–13. Some of the other verses from Leviticus' blessings reworked by Ezekiel are, as follows:

2. Ezek 11:12, "Then you shall know that I am YHWH, whose laws you did not follow and whose rules you did not obey, acting instead according to rules of the nations around you," is modeled on Lev 26:3, 15, 43b (a favorite Ezekielian condemnation; e.g., Ezek 5:6, 7; 11:20; 20:13, 16, 19, 21, 24). What betrays the direction of the borrowing is the second half of the verse, which is an adapta-

tion of Lev 18:3–4, changing the specific mention of Egyptians and the long-defunct Canaanites to the unspecified but all-embracing nations surrounding Israel (see also Ezek 5:5–7).

3. Ezekiel uses the verb *'ābaral bā'āreṣ* 'traverse the land' (Lev 26:6) in reference to the calamities of pestilence, bloodshed, wild beasts, and sword (Ezek 5:17; 14:15, 17). But in the last verse the context is revealing: *'ô ḥereb 'ābî' 'al-hā'āreṣ hahî' wĕ'āmartî ḥereb ta'ăbōr bā'āreṣ wĕhikrattî mimmennâ 'ādām ûbĕhēmâ* 'Or, if I were to bring a sword upon the land and decree **"Let a sword traverse the land** so that I may cut off from it man and beast"' (Ezek 14:17). Only here to we find an inner quotation. The boldfaced words betray the source: Lev 26:6bβ. The rest of the divine decree, however, is a borrowing and reworking of the wild-beast curse (Lev 26:22aβ), in which, one must concede, the wording is more logical: one would expect predatory beasts and not the sword to cut down (*hikrît*) domestic animals.

4. Ezek 36:9–11 is an expansion and reworking of Lev 26:9. Note the parallels (boldface): ... *ûpānîtî 'ălêkem ... wĕhirbêtî 'ălêkem 'ādām ... wĕhirbêtî 'ălêkem 'ādām ûbĕhēmâ wĕrābû ûpārû '* ... I will **turn to you** ... **and multiply** upon you persons ... **and multiply** upon you persons and livestock'. This is the only place in Ezekiel where God says *ûpānîtî* 'I will turn to you'. The twice-cited verb *wĕhirbêtî* 'I will multiply' also points to Lev 26:9 as the source. That the borrowing cannot have gone in the reverse direction, from Ezekiel to Leviticus, is evident not only by contrasting the tightness of the latter with the expansiveness of the former, but by comparing the contexts: Ezekiel is addressing the mountains and, as a result, has to change Leviticus's direct object *'etkem* to *'ălêkem* 'upon you'. In other words, Ezekiel takes the natural promise of God to multiply Israel and turns it into the forced image of God performing Israel's multiplication on the mountains.

5. Ezek 37:26–27 is an expansion and reworking of Lev 26:9, 11a, 12, underscored by the boldface:

²⁶*wĕkārattî lāhem **bĕrît** šālôm **bĕrît** 'ôlām yihyeh 'ôtām ûnĕtattîm **wĕhirbêtî** 'ôtām wĕnātattî 'et-miqdāšî bĕtôkām lĕ'ôlām* ²⁷*wĕhāyâ **miškānî** 'ălêhem wĕhāyîtî lāhem lāhem lĕ'lōhîm wĕhēmmâ yihyû-lî lĕ'ām*

²⁶I will make **a covenant** of friendship with them—it shall be an everlasting **covenant** with them—I will establish (?) them and **multiply them, and I will place** my sanctuary among them forever. ²⁷**My presence** shall rest over them; **I will be their God** and they **shall be my people.**

Since Ezekiel is speaking of a new covenant, he alters *wĕhăqîmōtî* 'I will maintain' (Lev 26:9b) to *wĕkārattî* 'I will make, establish' (see COMMENT A), adding "it shall be an eternal covenant." It is followed by "and I will multiply them" (Lev 26:9a); this reversal of the two halves of Lev 26:9 is another indication of borrowing. The next sentence *wĕnātattî 'et-miqdāšî bĕtôkām lĕ'ôlām* is a reworking of *wĕnātattî miškānî bĕtôkĕkem* (Lev 26:11a), first emphasizing the eternity of the new sanctuary, which is then followed by Leviticus's *miškānî* 'my presence' and its clar-ifying preposition *ʿălêhem* 'over them' (for the significance of this change, see NOTE on "my presence," v. 11). Strikingly, Ezekiel has passed over Lev 26:10, which, as has been pointed out (see its NOTE), is irrelevant, contextually belonging with v. 5, and put there only for the sake of the structure of vv. 3–12. Ezekiel also rejects v. 11b, which—because of its negativity—creates problems for the commentators (see NOTE on "and I will not expel you," v. 11) and is irrelevant to Ezekiel's pur-pose. Ezekiel follows with the adoption formula of Lev 26:12, but as pointed out by Hurvitz (1982: 102–3), he drops the anthropomorphic verb *wĕhithallaktî* 'and I will walk about' (v. 12a) for YHWH. Similarly, Ezekiel omits the anthropomor-phic *wĕlōʾ-tigʿal napšî ʾetkem* 'I will not expel you', literally "my soul will not ab-hor you" (v. 11b). (Cf. Lev 26:30 with Ezek 6:3–5 and Lev 26:43 with Ezek 5:6; Hurvitz 1982: 104.) In conclusion, Ezekiel repeats his mention of the new sanc-tuary, emphasizing its significance for Israel and the nations (Ezek 37:28).

6. Turning to the curses, we note first that in Lev 26:22, vicious beasts de-stroy the livestock. Ezekiel, however, in one of his chapters, attributes a similar destruction of livestock (using the same verb *hikrît*) to famine (14:13), sword (14:17), and pestilence (14:19); but surprisingly in the section dealing with vi-cious beasts (14:15), he omits mention of the livestock, where it logically be-longs (though he lists it in his summary, v. 21; cf. 25:13; 29:8; Baudissin, cited in Hoffmann 1928: 246, n. 6).

7. Ezek 4:16, *hinĕnî šōbēr maṭṭeh-leḥem bîrûšālēm wĕʾākĕlû-leḥem bĕmišqāl* 'I am going to break the staff of bread in Jerusalem, and they shall eat bread by weight (in anxiety, and drink water by measure, in honor)' is almost a verbatim quotation from Lev 26:26, except for its application to Jerusalem and its expan-sion in the rest of the verse. That Ezekiel is the borrower (and not the reverse, as claimed by Levine 1989: 281) is confirmed by two other citations of this quo-tation (Ezek 5:16; 14:13) where the metaphor "break the staff of bread" is ac-companied by a gloss explaining that it refers to famine.

8. As recognized by Wellhausen (1963: 169), Ezekiel replaces the older for-mula of vertical retribution with his doctrine of individual retribution and, there-fore, is compelled in 24:23 (see also 4:17; 33:10) to omit *baʿăwōnōt ʾăbōtām* 'be-cause of the iniquities of their ancestors' from his citation of Lev 26:39 (see its NOTE).

9. Finally, as observed in the NOTE on 26:29, Ezekiel borrows this verse and then expands it into a reciprocal curse: "parents shall eat their children, and children shall eat their parents" (Ezek 5:10a).

These nine examples (and there are others) indicate signs of borrowing, and they all point in one direction: from Lev 26 to Ezekiel. It is Ezekiel who ex-hibits expansions, omissions, and reformulations, all of which lead to the con-clusion that Ezekiel is the borrower. That he probably had the entire MT of Lev 26:3–39 before him is further supported by the host of other parallels between them, including Lev 26:17aα (cf. 17:10; 20:3, 5, 6) and Ezek 14:8; 15:7; Lev 26:19a and Ezek 26:19; 30:6, 18; 33:28; Lev 26:25aα and Ezek 5:17; 6:3; 11:8; 14:17; 33:2; Lev 26:25aβ and Ezek 24:8; 25:12, 15; Lev 26:25bα and Ezek 5:17;

14:19, 21; 28:23; Lev 26:28a and Ezek 5:15b (*ḥēmâ* for increased hostility); Lev 26:31a and Ezek 5:14; 6:6; 25:13; 29:10; 30:12; 35:4; Lev 26:32 and Ezek 30:12, 14; 26:16; Lev 26:33a and Ezek 5:2, 12; 12:14; Lev 26:38b and Ezek 36:13; Lev 26:40aγ and Ezek 14:13; 15:8; 17:20; 18:24; 20:27; 39:26; Lev 26:43bα and Ezek 26:43; 36:3; and Lev 26:45bα and Ezek 20:9, 14, 22 (note the inversion!).

Thus there can be no doubt that Ezekiel had Lev 26 before him, at least vv. 3–39 (minus vv. 33b–35), where evidence of borrowing by Ezekiel has been demonstrated. As for vv. 40–45, no conclusion can be drawn. Clearly, borrowing has taken place, but without the kind of evidence demonstrated by the nine examples, the direction of the borrowing remains indeterminable (see COMMENT E).

D. H (Except Leviticus 26), the Other Pentateuchal Sources, and Ezekiel

The procedure adopted in COMMENT C will also be followed here: only those citations of one source that have been altered by the other will be included. Thus the elaborate listing given by Paton (1896: 101) of ninety cases where H expressions are found in Ezekiel (thirteen of which are found in only these two sources) will be discounted until the direction of the borrowing, if any, can be determined. Similarly, the cases cited by Burrows (1925: 28–36, 47–67) where Ezekiel ostensibly reworks priestly sources must also be set aside until it can be demonstrated with more compelling evidence that Ezekiel is truly the borrower. All parallels are in boldface.

1. **wěnātattî pānay** bannepeš . . . **wěhikrattî** 'ōtāh miqqereb 'ammāh

   I will set my face against the person . . . and I will cut him off from among his kinspeople (Lev 17:10; 20:3)

   wěnātattî pānay bā'is hahû [wahăšīmōtîhû lě'ôt wělimēšālîm] **wěhikrattîw mittôk ammî**

   I will set my face against that man [and make him a sign and a byword] and I will cut him off from the midst of my people (Ezek 14:8)

The bracketed passage in Ezekiel, as noted by Hoffmann (1904: 25, n. 2), is a reworking of Deut 28:37a. The change from *miqqereb* to *mittôk* is typical of Ezekiel, who uses *mittôk* only in similar contexts (cf. Ezek 14:9; 28:16) and, indeed, always uses it to the exclusion of *miqqereb* (Ezek 1:4, 5; 11:7, 9; 28:18; 29:4; 32:21).

2. **wěšāpak** 'et-dāmô **wěkissāhû bě'āpār**
   he shall pour out its blood and cover it with earth (Lev 17:13b)

   lō' **šepākathû** 'al-hā'āreṣ **lěkassôt** 'ālāyw 'āpār
   She did not pour it out on the ground to cover it with earth (Ezek 24:7b)

Ezekiel applies H's law of game to human blood. Indeed, Greenberg (1983a: 252) has aptly noted that the structure (as well as much of the vocabulary) of Ezek 14:4–10 is modeled on Lev 17:

Ezek 14	Lev 17
speak . . . and say. . . . (v. 4a)	speak . . . and say . . . (v. 2)
The illegitimate inquirer:	*The illegitimate sacrificer:*
anyone of the house of Israel (v. 4a)	anyone of the house of Israel (v. 3)
punishment (v. 4b)	punishment (v. 4b)
purpose (*lĕmaʿan*, v. 5)	purpose (*lĕmaʿan . . . wĕlōʾ . . . ʿôd* (vv. 5–7; cf. Ezek 14:11)
The illegitimate inquirer:	*The illegitimate sacrificer:*
anyone . . . or of the aliens . . . (v. 7)	anyone . . . or of the aliens (v. 8)
I will set my face against . . . and cut him off from the midst of my people (v. 8)	. . . I will set my face against that person . . . and I will cut him off from among his kinsman (v. 10)
The unauthorized prophet:	*He who eats forbidden meat:*
They shall bear their punishment (v. 10)	he shall bear his punishment (v. 16)

What makes the borrowing especially convincing is that Ezekiel repeats the double prohibition against the same act (17:3–8) with a double accusation of his own (Ezek 4:4–8).

3. *ûšĕmartem ʾet-huqqōtay wĕʾet-mišpātay ʾăšer yaʿăśeh ʾōtām hāʾādām wāḥay bāhem*
   You shall keep my laws and my rules, by the pursuit of which man shall live (Lev 18:5)

   wāʾettēn lāhem ʾet-huqqôtay wĕʾet-mišpātay [hôdaʿtî ʾôtām] ʾăšer yaʿăśeh ʾōtām hāʾādām wāḥay bāhem
   I gave them my laws and [informed them of] my rules, by the pursuit of which man shall live (Ezek 20:11; cf. vv. 13, 21)

The similarity is striking, especially in view of the complex sentence structure. Ezekiel, however, makes "laws" and "rules" into A and B words in parallel *stichoi* by adding the verb and suffix "informed them." That it is Ezekiel who is the borrower is demonstrated by comparing two other parallel passages:

4. *ûlĕhabdîl bên haqqōdeš ûbên haḥōl ûbên haṭṭāmēʾ ûbên haṭṭāhōr ûlĕhôrōt ʾet-bĕnê yiśrāʾēl*

   (You must) distinguish between the sacred and the common, and between the impure and the pure. (And you must) teach the Israelites (Lev 10:10–11a) *wĕ'et-'ammî yôrû* **bên qōdeš lĕḥōl ûbên-ṭāmē' lĕṭāhôr yôdî'ûm**

And they shall teach my people what is sacred and what is common and inform them what is impure and what is pure (Ezek 44:23)

Ezekiel, who once again wishes to create parallel *stichoi*, discards H's verb *hibdîl* (for which there is no exact synonym) in favor of the next verb *hôrâ* and a synonymous object, "my people," adding a new verb *hôdîa'* 'inform', the same verb that he appended in 20:11. Another indication that Ezekiel is the borrower is the change between H's *bên . . . ûbên* to *bên . . . lĕ* (Hannemann 1975–76; Hurvitz 1982: 113–14; for the argument that Lev 10:10–11 stems from H, see vol. 1.616–17). The same phenomenon is exhibited in Ezek 22:26, where, however, he retains *hibdîl* and adds *hôdîa'* in order to create the two *stichoi*. Finally, that Ezekiel is the borrower is demonstrated by the two other attestations in chap. 20 of this quotation from H (20:13, 21), to which Ezekiel attaches a specific sin: the desecration of the sabbath (see also 22:26).

5. *'erwat 'ābîkā wĕ'erwat 'immĕkā lō' tĕgalleh*

The nakedness of your father, that is, the nakedness of your mother, you shall not uncover (Lev 18:7a)

'erwat-'āb gillâ-bāk

In you he has uncovered (their) father's nakedness (Ezek 22:10a)

Ezekiel assumes that this prohibition is well known, to the extent that he can chop off Leviticus's explanatory gloss. To be sure, this does not constitute proof that Ezekiel drew the prohibition from H, but the precise idiom without explanation renders the borrowing highly probable.

6. *wĕ'el-'iššâ bĕniddat ṭum'ātāh lō' tiqrab lĕgallôt 'erwātāh wĕ'el-'ēšet 'ămîtĕkā lō'-tittēn šĕkobtĕkā lĕzāra' lĕṭāmĕ'â-bāh*

You shall not approach a woman during her menstrual impurity to uncover her nakedness. Do not have carnal relations with your neighbor's **wife** and **defile yourself** with her (Lev 18:19–20)

wĕ'et-'ēšet rē'ēhû lō' ṭimmē' wĕ'el-'iššâ niddâ lō' yiqrab

he has not defiled another man's **wife or approached a menstruous woman** (Ezek 18:6b)

According to Seidel's (1978) law, inversion indicates a later quotation. What makes the direction of the borrowing certain is the change from *'ămît* to *rē'a* (the one word in Ezekiel *not* in boldface). As demonstrated by Hurvitz (1982: 74–78), by the time of Ezekiel, *'ămît* had fallen out of use and been replaced by one of its synonyms.

7. *lō'-tēlēk rākîl bĕ'ammekā lō' ta'ămōd 'al-dam rē'ekā*

> You shall not go about as a slanderer (?) among your people; you shall not stand aloof beside the blood of your fellow (Lev 19:16a)

'ănšê rākîl hāyû bāk lĕma'an šĕpāk-dām

> In you are those who slander (?) to shed blood (Ezek 22:9a)

Lev 19:16a is intractable, but it cannot be denied that it consists of two discrete prohibitions. Ezekiel offers his interpretation by combining the two sentences into a single prohibition: the ultimate result of slander is bloodshed (for an evaluation of his exegesis, see NOTE on 19:16).

8. *et-šabbĕtōtay tišmōrû ûmiqdāšî tîrā'û*

> You shall keep **my sabbaths** and revere **my sanctuary** (Lev 19:30a; 26:2a)

ṭimmĕ'û 'et-miqdāšî bayyôm hahû' wĕ'et šabbĕtōtay hillēlû

> on the same day they defiled **my sanctuary** and desecrated **my sabbaths** (Ezek 23:38b)

Instead of keeping **my sabbaths** and revering **my sanctuary** (Lev), Israel has defiled **my sanctuary** and desecrated **my sabbaths** (Ezek). Further evidence that Ezekiel is the borrower is his insertion of *bayyôm hahû* 'on the same day', thereby tracing the source of Israel's compound sin to its worship of Molek (see NOTE on 20:3).

9. *kĕ'ezrāḥ mikkem yihyeh lākem haggēr haggār 'ittĕkem*

> The alien who resides with you shall be to you as one of your citizens (Lev 19:34aα)

ûlĕhaggērîm haggārîm bĕtôkĕkem . . . wĕhāyû lākem kĕ'ezrāḥ bibĕnê yiśrā'ēl 'ittĕkem yippĕlû bĕnaḥălā

> and for the aliens who reside among you . . . You shall treat them as Israelite citizens; they shall receive allotments along with you among the tribes of Israel (Ezek 47:22)

Ezekiel applies the general rule affording equal civil rights and certain religious obligations to the resident alien (an H innovation; vol. 1.1065) to an entirely new law—the right to receive and bequeath land allotments in Ezekiel's redivision of the promised land.

10. *yĕqallēl 'et-'ābîw wĕ'et- 'immô . . . 'ābîw wĕ'immô qillēl*

> (If any man) humiliates his father or his mother (he shall be put to death;) he has humiliated his father and his mother (Lev 20:9)

'āb wā'ēm hēqallû bāk

Fathers and mothers have been humiliated with you (Ezek 22:7aα)

Ezekiel refers to an existing prohibition. True, a *Hip'il* formation, *maqleh*, occurs in Deut 27:16, but it derives from the root *qlh*, not *qll*. In any event, as Rashi has noted (on Ezek 22:7), Ezek 22 is largely based on Lev 19.

11. *lĕnepeš lō'yiṭṭammā' bĕ'ammāyw*

No (priest) shall defile himself for any (dead) person among his kin (Lev 21:1bβ)

wĕ'el mēt 'ādām lō'yābô' lĕṭāmĕ'â

(A priest) shall not defile himself by entering (a house) where there is a dead person (Ezek 44:25a)

The rephrasing of Lev 21:1b–3 in Ezek 44:25 involves three changes. First, and foremost, Ezekiel explicates the rare usage of *nepeš* meaning "corpse" (cf. Num 5:2; 6:11; 19:11, 13) by *mēt 'ādām*. (Note that in Num 19:11, 13, a tautology is created by adding *mēt* to explicate *nepeš* 'corpse'.) Then Ezekiel drops *bĕ'ammāyw* 'among his kin' (also an abstruse term) as superfluous, since the kin is specified in the remainder of the verse. Finally, adopting the terminology of Num 6:6b, Ezekiel adds the verb *yābô'* 'enter (a house)'. Although, obviously a priest will not advertently touch a corpse, he may inadvertently enter a house containing a corpse and become defiled because of overhang (Num 19:14; cf. Milgrom 1990a: 161). The contingency of corpse-contamination by a Nazirite is also predicated on the same circumstance, *'al nepeš mēt lō' yābô'* 'he shall not go in (a house) where there is a dead person' (Num 6:6b).

12. *nĕbēlâ ûṭĕrēpâ lō yō'kal lĕṭāmĕ'â-bāh*

He shall not eat anything that died or was torn by beasts, thereby becoming impure (Lev 22:8a)

kol-nĕbēlâ ûṭĕrēpâ min-hā'ôp ûmin-habbĕhēmâ lō' yō'kĕlû hakkōhănîm

Priests shall not eat anything, whether bird or animal, that died or was torn by beasts (Ezek 44:31)

Ezekiel expands the Leviticus law to make certain that all carcasses, including those of birds, are designated as sources of defilement.

13. *lō'-tirdeh bô bĕpārek*

You shall rule over him with harshness (Lev 25:43a [46bβ, 53b])

ûbĕḥozkâ rĕdîtem 'ōtām ûbĕpārek

and with force you have ruled over them and with harshness (Ezek 34:4b)

Ezekiel not only indicates that the prohibition thrice stated in Lev 25 has been violated, but also explicates the uncommon term *bĕpārek* by its synonym *bĕḥozkâ* 'with force'. More precisely, he begins with the well-understood *bĕḥozkâ* and appends the less-known *bĕpārek* in order to cite the exact wording of the prohibition of Lev 25.

These twelve examples from Leviticus can be supplemented by H passages in Exodus and Numbers. That these passages are to be assigned to H, see the Introduction I E.

14. *wā'ērā' 'el-'abrāhām 'el-yiṣḥāq wĕ'el ya'ăqōb bĕ'ēl šadday ûšĕmî YHWH lō' nôdā'tî lāhem . . . lākēn 'ĕmōr libnê-yiśrā'ēl* **'ănî YHWH** *wĕhôṣē'tî 'etkem. . . . wĕhēbē'tî 'etkem 'el-hā'āreṣ 'ăšer* **nāśā'tî** *'et-yādî lātēt 'ōtāh lĕ'abrāhām lĕyiṣḥāq ûlĕya'ăqōb*

I appeared to Abraham, Isaac, and Jacob as El Shaddai, but I did not **make myself known to them** by my name **YHWH**. . . . Say, therefore, to the Israelites: I am YHWH and I shall **bring** you **out** . . . . I will bring you into the land which **I solemnly swore** to give to Abraham, Isaac, and Jacob (Exod 6:3, 6aα, 8a)

bĕyôm bohŏrî bĕyiśrā'el wā'eśśā' yādî lĕzera' bêt ya'ăqob wā'iwwada' lāhem bĕ'ereṣ miṣrayim wā'eśśā' yādî lē'mōr **'ănî YHWH** *'ĕlōhêkem. bayyôm hahû'* **nāśā'tî** *yādî lāhem lĕhôṣî'ām mē'ereṣ miṣrayim 'el-'ereṣ 'ăšer tartî lāhem*

On the day I chose Israel—when **I solemnly swore** to the progeny of the house of Jacob, **and made myself known to them** in the land of Egypt, when **I solemnly swore to them**, saying, **I YHWH** am your God—on that same day **I solemnly swore to them** to **bring** them **out** of the land of Egypt to a land I had searched out for them (Ezek 20:5–6bα [28, esp. 42])

The boldfaced words indicate the parallels. Ezekiel's choice of the verb *yāda'* in the *Nip'al* mirrors precisely the same use of the verb in Exodus, both being in a reflexive stance, to indicate the self-presentation of YHWH to the generation of the Exodus. Ezekiel's three mentions of God taking an oath in a series of expanded statements indicates how important the oath is to Ezekiel: YHWH, on this one occasion, took an oath to bring Israel to its land (see also Num 14:30), but wayward Israel (Ezek 20:28) did not keep its covenantal pledge and rebelled against YHWH's commandments. What is surprising, however, is that Ezekiel makes the Exodus generation, not the patriarchs, the recipients of the oath: "Ezekiel's disregard of the patriarchs is perhaps deliberate. . . . Ezekiel could not well have started Israel's career of apostasy with the patriarchs, the archetypical pious recipients of God's blessings" (Greenberg 1983a: 364; cf. Propp 1996: 475–76, n. 69). The use of deuteronomic terminology *bāḥar* (Weinfeld 1972d: 327) indicates further how Ezekiel intertwined another source with his revamping of Exod 6.

15. *ûbĕkol-'ĕlōhê miṣrayim 'e 'ĕśeh šĕpāṭîm 'ănî YHWH*

> and against the gods of Egypt I will execute punishments, I YHWH (Exod 12:12b)

Ezekiel adopts the same phrase *'āśâ šĕpāṭîm* 'execute judgments' and applies it to Sidon (28:22), once again to Egypt (30:14, 19), and, especially, as a boomerang, to Israel (5:10, 15; 11:9; 16:41; 25:11).

16. *'ak 'et-šabbĕtōtay tišmĕrû kî 'ôt hî' (K: hw') bênî ûbênêkem lĕdōrōtēkem lāda'at kî 'ănî YHWH mĕqaddiškem*

> Nevertheless, you must keep **my sabbaths**, for this is **a sign between me and you** throughout the ages, that you **may know that I YHWH have sanctified you** (Exod 31:13)

> *wĕgam 'et-šabbĕtôtay nātattî lāhem lihyot lĕ 'ôt bênî ûnbênêkem lāda'at kî 'ănî YHWH mĕqaddĕsām . . . .wĕ 'et-šabbĕtôtay qaddĕśû wĕhayu lĕ 'ôt bênî ûbênêkem lāda'at kî 'ănî YHWH 'ĕlōhêkem*

> Moreover, I gave them **my sabbaths** to serve as a **sign between me and them, that they might know that is I YHWH who sanctify them. . . .** And sanctify **my sabbaths**, that they may be a **sign between me and you, that you may know that I YHWH** am your God (Ezek 20:12, 20)

Ezekiel uses the sabbath commandment of Exod 31:13 twice in chap. 20 (boldface), to indicate that by the sabbath, YHWH has sanctified Israel and YHWH is Israel's God (the latter Ezekiel's addition). He also adds that Israel must "sanctify my sabbaths" (cf. Ezek 44:24), an injunction found previously only in the Decalogue (Exod 20:8 [= Deut 5:12]; cf. Jer 17:22, 24, 27).

17. *ûzĕkartem 'et-kol miṣwōt YHWH wa 'ăśîtem 'ōtām wĕlō'-tātûrû 'aḥărê lĕbabkem wĕ 'aḥărê 'ênêkem 'ăšer-'attem zōnîm 'aḥărêhem*

> **And remember** all the commandments of YHWH and observe them, so that you do not follow **the whoring of your heart and your eyes** (Num 15:39)

> *wĕzakĕrû pĕlêṭêhem 'ôtî . . . 'et-**libbām hazzôneh** 'ăšer sār mē 'ălay wĕ 'ēt 'ênêhem hazzōnôt 'aḥărê gillûlêhem*

> And your survivors **will remember** me . . . **their whoring heart** that turned away from me and **their eyes that whored after** their idols (Ezek 6:9a)

Ezekiel combines *zānâ mē 'al*, literally "to play the whore away from (one's husband)," used elsewhere only in Hos 9:1, and *sār mē 'al* 'turn away from', used elsewhere only in Jer 32:40 (Greenberg 1983a: 134), with Num 15:39 (parallels in boldface) so that Israel's whoring heart and eyes, which in the Numbers passage *presumably* abandon God's commandments (for what is not mentioned), turn (hence the change from *tār* to *sār*), in Ezekiel's phrasing, specifically from God to idols.

18. *pārah maṭṭēh-'ahărōn . . . wayyōṣē' perah wayyāṣēṣ ṣîṣ*

The rod of Aaron had flowered; it had brought forth flowers, produced sprouts (Num 17:23)

yaṣě'a haṣṣěpîrâ ṣaṣ hammaṭṭeh pārah hazzādôn

doom **has gone forth, the rod has sprouted,** insolence **has flowered** (Ezek 7:10b)

Ezekiel's parody of Num 17:23 (boldface, noted by Yellin 1939: 118–19) also extends to the word *maṭṭeh* 'rod', which, in view of *muṭṭeh* 'perversion of the law' (‖ *dāmîm* 'bloodshed', Ezek 9:9), is defined here by Ibn Janah as injustice (Greenberg 1983a: 149).

19. *wěšāměrû mišmeret 'ōhel mô'ed . . . ûšěmartem 'ēt mišmeret haqqōdeš wě'ēt mišmeret hammizbēah*

and **they (the Levites) shall perform the guard duties** of the Tent of Meeting . . . and **you (the priests) shall perform the guard duties** of the shrine **and the guard duties of the altar** (Num 18:4aβ, 5a)

lakkōhănîm šōměrê mišmeret habbayit . . . lakkōhănîm šoměrê mišmeret hammizbeah

for the priests **who perform the guard duties** of the Temple . . . for the priests **who perform the guard duties** of the altar (Ezek 40:45b, 46aβ)

Ezekiel transfers the vocabulary of Num 18 (boldface), changing "Tent of Meeting" to "Temple" and the Levites to a lower order (non-Zadokite) of priests (Milgrom 1970: 8–16, esp. n. 47).

20. *kol-qorbānām lěkol-**minhātām** ûlěkol-**hattā'tām** ûlěkol-**'ăšāmām** 'ăšer yāšîbû lî qōdeš qŏdāšîm lěkā hû' ûlěbānêkā. . . . **kol-herem běyiśrā'ēl lěkā yihyeh***

every offering, namely, **all their cereal offerings, all their purification offerings, and all their reparation offerings** that they restore to me are most sacred; they belong to you and your sons. . . . **Everything proscribed in Israel shall be yours** (Num 18:9b, 14)

hamminhâ wěhahattā't wěhā'āšām hēmmâ yō'kělûm wěkol-hērem běyiśrā'ēl lāhem yihyeh

The cereal offerings, purification offerings, and reparation offerings shall be consumed by them. Everything proscribed in Israel shall be theirs. (Ezek 44:29)

Ezekiel strips Num 18:9b to its essentials, but follows the same sacrificial order (as found in Lev 2–5, 6–7). Num 18:14, except for the change of person, is quoted verbatim. Ezekiel's major change is that he attaches the *ḥerem* (v. 14) to the most sacred offerings, ahead of the lesser sacred offerings (Ezek 44:30), probably under the influence of Lev 27:28 (see the NOTE), whereas Num 18 lists the *ḥerem* among the lesser sacred offerings (vv. 11–19). Concerning the anomalous status of the *ḥerem*, see Milgrom (1990a: 429).

21. *wĕzeh-lĕkā tĕrûmat mattānātām.* . . . *kōl ḥēleb yiṣhār wĕkol-ḥēleb tîrôš wĕdāgān rē'šîtām 'ăšer-yittĕnû laYHWH lĕkā nĕtattîm bikkurê kol-'ăšer bê'arṣām 'ăšer yābî'û laYHWH lĕkā yihyeh*

This too shall be **yours: the gift offerings of their contributions** . . . . The best of the new oil and the best of new wine and grain—**the first processed** that they present to YHWH—**I give to you.** The first ripe of everything in their land, that they bring to YHWH, **shall be yours** (Num 18:11–13)

wĕrē'šît kol (kōl LXX) bikkûrê kōl wĕkol-tĕrûmat kōl mikkōl tĕrûmôtêkem lakkohănîm yihyeh

The first processed of every kind, the first ripe of every kind, and all the gifts of every kind—of all your contributions—shall belong to the priests. (Ezek 44:30a)

Ezekiel has neatly condensed Num 18:11–13 (boldface) into a single statement so that the reader must rely on the Numbers passage to know exactly which are "the first processed of every kind" (see the discussion of these renderings in Milgrom 1990a: 427–28).

22. *'mê niddâ lo'-zōraq 'ālāyw ṭāmē' hû'*

The water of lustration was not **dashed upon him;** he is impure (Num 19:20bβ)

wĕzāraqtî 'ălêkem mayim ṭĕhôrîm ûṭĕhartem mikkōl ṭum'ôtêkem ûmikkol-gillûlêkem 'ăṭahēr 'etkem

I will dash pure **water upon you,** and you shall be pure: I will purify you from all your impurities and fetishes (Ezek 36:25)

In this celebrated passage, Ezekiel utilizes the rite of dashing lustral waters (prepared from the ashes of a red cow) to purify a corpse-contaminated person as a symbol of God's future activity to purify Israel. Interestingly, in this verse, Ezekiel distinguishes between *ṭum'ōt* 'impurities' and "fetishes," though elsewhere he regards idolatry as a source of impurity (e.g., Ezek 22:3, 4), in order to remain true to the Numbers original, in which impurity is always of a ritual nature. That *ṭāmē'* 'impure' and *ṭāhôr* 'pure' are employed by H in a metaphoric sense, see the NOTES on 16:30 (vol. 1.1056–57) and 18:24–30.

Since these twenty-two examples indicate that Ezekiel borrowed from H, it can safely be assumed that the other parallels between these two works also point to Ezekiel as the borrower. Compare Lev 11:44; 22:8 with Ezek 4:14; Lev 17:8 with Ezek 14:7; Lev 19:35 with Ezek 4:16; Lev 19:36 with Ezek 45:10; Lev 20:25 (10:10–11; 19:8) with Ezek 22:26; 44:23; Lev 22:32 with Ezek 36:20 (cf. Hoffmann 1928: 28, n. 1); Lev 25:10 with Ezek 46:17; Lev 25:13–14 with Ezek 7:13; Lev 25:14 with Ezek 18:7; Lev 25:18 with Ezek 28:26; Lev 25:37 with Ezek 18:8; Lev 25:41 with Ezek 46:18; Lev 25:48 with Ezek 11:15; Lev 26:1 with Ezek 18:12; Lev 26:2 with Ezek 23:38 (Hoffmann 1953).

More compellingly, Paton (1896: 111–13) points to instances where Ezekiel amplifies H:

1. *'ănî YHWH* (*'ĕlōhêkā*) is accompanied by an apposite expression.
2. *hālak bĕḥuqqôt wĕšāmar miṣwôt la 'ăśôtām* (Lev 18:3, 4; 20:23; 26:3) is accompanied by a hortatory phrase (e.g., Ezek 11:20; cf. 5:7; 11:12; 18:9).
3. *dāmāyw bô* (Lev 20:9), to which Ezekiel adds *yihyeh* (Ezek 18:13).
4. The sin of *hillēl šēm 'ĕlōhêkā* (Lev 18:21; 19:12; 20:3) is specified and paraphrased (Ezek 20:39; 36:20, 22).
5. Lev 18:3 is applied in Ezek 20:5–26 to Egypt and vv. 27–44, to Canaan.
6. Ezekiel adds the desecration of the sabbath to his condemnation of Israel for following the mores of Egypt and Canaan in chap. 20.
7. The *ḥuqqôt* and *mišpāṭîm* in Ezek 20:11, 13, 21 must refer to Lev 18:5 (cf. 19:37; 20:23; 26:3).

Burrows (1925: 35) remarks that Ezekiel rarely quotes his sources verbatim, but reworks them. In the case of P (H?), he compares Exod 12:12 (Lev 10:3) with Ezek 28:22; Exod 24:17 with Ezek 8:4; Lev 15:26 with Ezek 36:17; Lev 27:32 with Ezek 20:37; Num 16:9 with Ezek 44:8, 11 (cf. Milgrom 1970: 83–86, nn. 226, 272).

Although Ezekiel favors the language of H, he by no means neglects P. Compare *rāqîa', kol-nepeš haḥayyâ . . . 'ăšer šārĕṣû, lĕmînah . . . bidĕgat hayyām, 'adam kidĕmûtēnû* (Gen 1:6, 21, 25–26 with Ezek 1:22, 47:9; 47:10; 1:26) and especially *ûlĕkol-ḥayyat hā'āreṣ ûlĕkol- 'ôp haššāmayim . . . lĕ'oklâ* (Gen 1:30 with Ezek 29:5; cf. 33:27; 34:5; 39:4); *bĕyôm hibbārĕ'ām* (Gen 5:2 with Ezek 28:15); *wattimmālē' hā'āreṣ ḥāmās* (Gen 6:11 with Ezek 8:17; cf. 7:23; Hoffmann, 1954: 2.260–62); Gen 7:14; esp. 9:12; 9:14; 36:7; 34:23 with Ezek 17:23; esp. 38:20; 1:28; 20:18; 38:12, 13; Exod 25:4–5; 25:20; esp. 26:3; 28:17–18, 20; 30:13 with Ezek 16:10; 28:16; esp. 1:9; 28:13; 45:12; Lev 1:6; 1:9; 4:2; 4:25; esp. 5:21; 7:24; esp. 10:3; 10:9; 13:45; 14:22; 14:45; 16:4; 16:12; 27:9–10; 27:32 with Ezek 24:6; 6:13; 18:10; 45:19; esp. 14:13; 15:5; esp. 28:22; 44:21, 24:17; 46:7; 26:12; 10:2, 7; 10:2; 48:14; 20:37; Num 5:15; 19:13; 28:3; 33:54; 34:2; 34:5; 34:6; 34:8 with Ezek 21:28; 36:25; 16:13; 47:13; 47:14; 47:19; 47:20; 48:30 (see also Burrows 1925: 47–68).

An illuminating example, pinpointed by Zimmerli (1979: 1.445), in Ezekiel's transformation of P's technical terminology in the case of a suspected adulteress (Num 5:12–31):

wĕhī(w)' lō' nitpāśâ . . . wehebi' 'et-qorbānāh . . . mazkeret 'āwōn

(If) she is not apprehended . . . he (the husband) shall bring her offering . . . (which) recalls (her) wrongdoing (Num 5:13, 15)

wĕhû'-mazkîr 'āwōn lĕhittāpēś

and it (the divination) recalls (their) wrongdoing bringing about (their) capture (Ezek 21:28b [cf. NRSV])

The unapprehended adulteress would be apprehended by a sacrifice and divinely approved ordeal. So, too Nebuchadrezzar's divinatory techniques, though patently false, would receive YHWH's approval by which to apprehend (i.e., capture) Israel. The direction of the borrowing is unmistakable. Ezekiel employs P's precise legal terminology to support his contention analogously that Nebuchadrezzar's attack against Jerusalem was divinely approved.

Ezekiel fuses the priestly sources (P and H) with JE. Burrows (1925: 67) supplies the following instances: J and P of the Flood story: Gen 6:11, 13 and Ezek 7:23; 8:17; 9:9 (the earth filled with violence); Gen 6:13 and Ezek 7:2–3, 6 (the end is come); Gen 9:5 and Ezek 3:18, 20; 33:6, 8 (requite blood at the hands of); Gen 9:6 and Ezek 18:10 (spill blood); Gen 9:14 and Ezek 1:28 (the only references to the rainbow); Gen 10 and Ezek 27 (J and P names of countries); Exod 3:8, 17 (J); 6:3–8 (H) and Ezek 20:5–6. Hoffmann (1954: 266–67) adds the following: Ezek 18:20 fuses Deut 24:16 with idioms of Lev 4:2; 19:8; *zārâ* (Lev 26:33) and *hēpîṣ* (Deut 4:27; 28:64) used in Ezek 12:15; 20:23; 22:15; 29:12; 30:23, 26; 36:19; *ḥayyat hā'āreṣ* (P) and *ḥayyat haśśādeh* (JE) in Ezek 34:28; 38:20; *lĕmāšāl*, Deut 28:37 and Ezek 14:8 (rest of the verse is H); Ezek 22:6–8 is replete with idioms of Lev 19, 20 (H), but for *'āb wā'ēm hēqallû bāk* (v. 7aα), see Deut 27:16. Ezek 8:10a adumbrates elements from P, H, and D (Milgrom 1992b). See also the additional cases cited by Burrows (1925: 67).

Ezekiel also differs from the priestly sources in small details, such as the purification of priests (44:20–26; cf. Lev 21:1–9) and the inadmissibility of their marriage with widows (44:22; cf. Lev 21:14, only the high priest). Chronological priority is difficult to determine in these cases. But one major theological difference leaves no doubt as to which is older. Ezekiel assigns the sole responsibility for sin to the individual (chap. 18), whereas H continues the doctrine of collective responsibility, involving the family (Lev 20:5) and previous generations (Lev 26:39; Elliot-Binns 1955: 34).

The conclusion, I submit, is inescapable: Ezekiel had all of P and nearly all of H (see COMMENT E) before him, the language and ideas of which he refashioned in novel ways. One can fully agree with the comment of Eliezer of Beaugency (twelfth century): "You will not find a prophet besides him who reproves his generation by the standard of the Torah; his idiom is for the most part that of the Torah, and he comes close to repeating the whole Torah for them" (introduction to his commentary on Ezekiel, cited in Greenberg 1993: 29, n. 4).

E. The Date of Leviticus 26

There is consensus that Lev 26:3–33a is a preexilic composition, whereas the remainder of the chapter is exilic or postexilic. The most recent treatment is that of Ginsberg (1982: 79–80, 100–101, n. 136), followed by Levine (1987; 1989a: 275–81), who aver that vv. 3–45 comprise three compositional levels: (1) vv. 3–33a, 37b–38, the primary epilogue, written in the exilic period or just before; (2) vv. 39–40a, 44–45, the first postcatastrophic interpolation, added in the late sixth century, and (3) vv. 33b–37a, 40b–43, a second interpolation, composed in the last years of the exile or at the beginning of the return.

They cite four reasons:

1. The primary epilogue is paralleled by Amos 4:6–11; Deut 28:1–48, classical admonitions that end in doom.
2. The patriarchal (unconditional) covenant is an exilic creation.
3. The idiom *rāṣâ 'āwōn* was originated by Isaiah of the exile (Isa 40:1–2).
4. As Deut 30:1–10 supplements Deut 28, so Lev 26:33b–37a, 39–45 supplements Lev 26:1–33a, 37b–38.

These arguments will be parried point by point:

1. Even if we admit that the appendix to Lev 26 had doom (i.e., exile) in mind, need it be the Babylonian Exile? It could just as well have been referring to the exile of North Israel in the eighth century (see below). Alternatively, it could even have in mind the exile of Judeans in 701 B.C.E. Despite the silence of such an exile throughout the Bible, particularly in the book of Kings, a compelling case has been mounted by Stohlmann (1983) that Sennacharib's account of large-scale exiles of Judeans (despite its exaggerated numbers) is eminently credible.

2. That the patriarchal covenant is an exilic creation is based on the facile assumption that it is unconditional (see NOTE on "my covenant with Jacob," v. 42), which therefore assures the exiles that God *cannot* abrogate it. First, I have grave doubts about the presumed unconditional character of the patriarchal covenant (e.g., Gen 18:19). Then, as pointed out in the NOTE on v. 42, the thrust of this covenant is to guarantee Israel land and progeny—rather than unconditionality—which the Sinaitic covenant does not do.

3. The idiom *rāṣâ 'āwōn* is undeniably a Deutero-Isaiah usage, but it is just as arguable—and for me more compelling—that Isaiah borrowed this expression from Lev 26 (see NOTE on "pay off," v. 34).

4. Deut 30:1–10 may actually have formed the close of Deut 28, and it was moved to its present position to accommodate the additional curses of Deut 29 (see Rofé 1985: 311–12, and COMMENT B).

Finally, an independent terminological argument must be entered. As Weinfeld (1991: 218) has demonstrated, D's doctrine of repentance, in both idiom and thought, is recognizable in Hosea (cf. Deut 4:29–30 with Hos 5:15–6:1). The fact that D and all the writing prophets utilize a single verb *šûb* to denote "repent," whereas H must resort to *nikna'* 'be humbled' and *hitwaddâ* 'confess' (and P to *'āšām* 'feel guilt') to approximate the same concept, which disappears from usage after the Babylonian Exile, indicates that H (and P) stem from a time before *šwb* became the exclusive term for repentance (Milgrom 1976a: 119–27). In any event, it is hardly conceivable that after the refugees from North Israel brought with them the writings of Amos and Hosea and the Judahite prophets Isaiah and Micah promulgated their kerygma of repentance, their term *šŵb* would not at least have penetrated, if not dominated, the priestly doctrine of repentance.

Rather, I follow Dillmann and Ryssel (1897: 674–72)—but not in details— that the core of Lev 26 was composed in the eighth century, interpolated and expanded during the captivity. In particular, I agree with Eerdmans (1912: 135–36) and Heinisch (1935: 121–22), who hit on specific details that, instead, point to the destruction of North Israel—in particular, the fact that the enemies settled on its depopulated territory (2 Kgs 17:24; cf. Lev 26:32b) and that wild animals ravaged the land (2 Kgs 17:26; cf. Lev 26:22).

The same reasoning, I submit, holds for vv. 40–42, 45. It stands to reason that the Judeans, let alone their northern brethren who were not exiled, remained in contact with the exiled Israelites and offered them the solace that the God of the covenants (both patriarchial and Sinaitic) had not forsaken them, and that if they would but repent he would restore them to their land. Indeed, if the Chronicler's account of Hezekiah's attempt to reach out to his Israelite brethren (2 Chr 30:1–11) is credible (Milgrom 1970; 1985b; most recently, Dillard 1987), why would not the official circles of Jerusalem, especially the priesthood, have sent out messages of consolation and hope to the exiles, which would have been imbued with at least the same yearning and passion of Jeremiah's early (Josianic) prophecies to the north delivered fully a hundred years later (cf. Jer 3:6–17; 31:1–26)? Of course, it can be postulated that vv. 40–42, 45 may also have been intended for the Babylonian Exiles, but, as argued throughout this COMMENTARY, the Holiness document is, in the main, a product of the Hezekian period (see Introduction I F): chap. 26, in particular, influenced the metaphoric language of Ezekiel (COMMENTS B–D); its verses reflect the Hezekian atmosphere (see NOTES on "cult places," v. 30, and "your sanctuaries," v. 31); descriptions of exile need not reflect the historical past but can be a prediction both in the Bible (Amos 5:27; 6:7) and in the treaties of the ancient Near East (cf. Weinfeld 1972d: 133); and, above all, the absence of any reference to prophetic repentance in vv. 40–45 betrays its preexilic provenance (see COMMENT B). For all these reasons, vv. 40–42, 45 constitute an integral part of the same eight-century composition of the main text of this chapter (vv. 3–33a, 36–42, 45–46).

The same verdict, however, cannot be rendered for vv. 33b–35, 43–44, which feature the sabbatical theme. As argued in the NOTES on these verses, the neglect of the sabbatical year is introduced to account for the delay in the redemption of the exiles. To be sure, it can be contended that this rationale might also have comforted the exiles of North Israel for their long-postponed return to their land. But it is hard to believe that the Judeans, who clearly violated or ignored the sabbatical laws in their own country (see chap. 25, COMMENT B), would have hypocritically forged this rationale to "console" their exiled brethren.

It is, therefore, herewith submitted that 26:3–45 comprises two strata: vv. 3–33a, 36–42, 45, composed during the reign of Hezekiah, and vv. 33b–35, 43–44, an exilic interpolation.

27. CONSECRATIONS AND THEIR REDEMPTION

TRANSLATION

Vows of Persons and Animals

[1]YHWH spoke to Moses, saying: [2]Speak to the Israelites and say to them: When a person makes an extraordinary vow to YHWH concerning the (fixed) valuation of a human being, [3]these shall be the valuations: If it is a male from twenty to sixty years of age, the valuation is fifty shekels of silver by the sanctuary weight. [4]If it is a female, the valuation is thirty shekels. [5]If the age is from five years to twenty years, the valuation is twenty shekels for a male and ten shekels for a female. [6]If the age is from one month to five years, the valuation for a male is five shekels of silver, and the valuation for a female is three shekels of silver. [7]If the age is from sixty years and over, the valuation is fifteen shekels in the case of a male and ten shekels for a female. [8]But if he is too poor (to pay) a valuation, he shall be presented before the priest, and the priest shall assess him; the priest shall assess him according to what the vower can afford.

[9]If [the vow concerns] any quadruped that may be brought as an offering to YHWH, any such that may be dedicated to YHWH shall be holy. [10]One may not exchange it or substitute it—a healthy with an emaciated one or emaciated with a healthy one; if one does substitute one animal for another, it (the vowed one) and its substitute shall be holy. [11]If [the vow concerns] any impure quadruped that may not be brought as an offering to YHWH, the quadruped shall be presented before the priest, [12]and the priest shall assess it. Whether high or low, whatever is the valuation of the priest, so it shall stand; [13]and if he wishes to redeem it, he must add one-fifth to its valuation.

Consecrations of Houses and Fields

[14]If a man consecrates his house to YHWH, the priest shall assess it. Whether high or low, as the priest assesses it, so it shall stand; [15]and if he who consecrated his house wishes to redeem it, he must add one-fifth to the sum at which it was assessed, and it shall be his.

[16]If a man consecrates to YHWH any part of his tenured field, its valuation shall be according to its seed requirement: fifty shekels of silver to a homer of barley seed. [17]If he consecrates his field as of the jubilee year, its valuation stands. [18]But if he consecrates his field after the jubilee, the priest shall compute the price according to the years that are left until the jubilee year, and its valuation shall be so reduced; [19]and if he who consecrated the field wishes to redeem it, he must add one-fifth to the sum at which it was assessed, and it shall pass to him. [20]But if he does not redeem the field but has sold the field to another, it shall no longer be redeemable; [21]when the field is released in the jubilee, it shall be holy to YHWH, as a proscribed field; it belongs to the priest.

[22]If he consecrates to YHWH a field that he purchased, which is not of his tenured field, [23]the priest shall compute for him the proportionate valuation up to the jubilee year, and he shall pay the valuation as of that day, a sacred donation to YHWH. [24]In the jubilee year the field shall revert to him from whom it was bought, to whom the tenured land belongs. [25]All valuations shall be by sanctuary weight, the shekel being twenty gerahs.

Firstlings

[26]However, a firstling of quadrupeds—designated as a firstling to YHWH—cannot be consecrated by anyone; whether bovine or ovine, it is YHWH's. [27]But if it is of impure quadrupeds, it may be ransomed at its valuation, with one-fifth added; if it is not redeemed, it may be sold at its valuation.

Proscriptions

[28]However, anything a man proscribes to YHWH of what he owns, be it persons, quadrupeds, or his tenured land, may not be sold or redeemed; every proscribed thing is totally consecrated to YHWH. [29]No human being who has been proscribed can be ransomed: he must be put to death.

Tithes

[30]All tithes from the land, whether seed from the ground or fruit from the tree, are YHWH's; they are holy to YHWH. [31]If a man wishes to redeem any of his tithes, he must add one-fifth to them. [32]All tithes of the herd or flock—of all that passes under the shepherd's staff, every tenth one—shall be holy to YHWH. [33]He must not seek out the healthy as against the emaciated and substitute (the

latter) for it (the former). If he does provide a substitute for it, then it and its substitute shall be holy: they cannot be redeemed.

Summary

³⁴These are the commandments that YHWH commanded Moses for the Israelites on Mount Sinai.

Comments

The construction, date, and function of chap. 27, COMMENTS A and B; the distinction between vows and consecrations, COMMENT C; sanctifications, COMMENT D; the firstborn, COMMENT E; proscriptions, COMMENT F; tithes, COMMENTS G–I; and the problem of seed mensuration, COMMENT J.

NOTES

This chapter concerns gifts to the sanctuary: vows of persons and animals (vv. 1–13), consecrations of houses and fields (vv. 14–25), firstlings, proscriptions, and tithes (vv. 26–33). The outline of the chapter is as follows:

Introduction (vv. 1–2aα)
A. Vows of persons and animals (vv. 2aβ–13)
    1. Of persons (vv. 2aβ–8)
    2. Of animals (vv. 9–13)
B. Consecrations of houses and fields (vv. 14–25)
    1. Of a house (vv. 14–15)
    2. Of a field (vv. 16–24)
        a. Tenured land (vv. 16–21)
        b. Purchased land (vv. 22–24)
    3. The value of the shekel (v. 25)
C. Restrictions on consecrated objects (vv. 26–33)
    1. Firstlings (vv. 26–27)
    2. Proscriptions (vv. 28–29)
    3. Tithes (vv. 30–33)
        a. Of crops (vv. 30–31)
        b. Of animals (vv. 32–33)
D. Summary (v. 34)

This tripartate division is substantiated by the opening particles:

A. *'îš kî* (v. 2), followed by a series of *wě'im*
B. *'îš kî* (v. 14), followed by a series of *wě'im*
C. *'ak* (v. 26; also v. 28), a restrictive particle

Some consecrations are redeemable; others are not. The laws of redemption fit into the following graded system:

1. *ḥērem* is "most sacred" and irredeemable
2. *Offerable* animals—be they firstborn, tithes, or consecrations—are irredeemable
3. *Nonofferable* consecrations—such as impure animals, land, houses, and crops (except when they are *ḥērem*)—are redeemable.

One postulate explains the gradations: offerable animals are irredeemable because they must be sacrificed on the altar, and nonofferable animals and other consecrations are always redeemable unless they are *ḥērem* (see COMMENT A).

Vv. 1–13. Vows of Persons and Animals

Philo (*Laws* 2.32–34) sums up the import of this pericope succinctly and accurately:

> . . . the law laid down a scale of valuation in which no regard is paid to beauty or stature or anything of the kind, but all are assessed equally, the sole distinctions made being between men and women and between children and adults . . . that all males and all females should be assessed equally at every age was made for three cogent reasons. First, because the worth of one person's vow is equal and similar to that of another, whether it is made by a person of great importance or one of mean estate; secondly, because it was not seemly that the votaries should be subject to the vicissitudes of slaves who are valued at a high price or on the other hand are rated low accordingly as they have or have not a time condition of body and comeliness; thirdly, and this is the most convincing of all, that in the sight of men inequality, in the sight of God equality, is held in honor.

2. *a person*. *ʾîš*. That is, including women. That women had the right to make a vow is attested in law (Num 6, 30) and in practice (1 Sam 1:11–12). Thus vv. 3–8, which include the valuations of women, are not limited to men who vow the valuation of women, but also include women who vow their own valuation.

makes an extraordinary vow. *yaplîʾ neder*. The traditional rendering of this idiom is "verbalizes or articulates a vow" (*Tgs.*; Rashi, Ibn Ezra, Rashbam; see NOTE on 22:21). That is, the vow must be distinctly pronounced in words, not merely conceived in the mind, a point that is emphasized in other biblical attestations of the vow, such as *môṣaʾ śĕpōtêkā*, literally "what emerges from your lips" (Deut 23:24); *kĕkol-hayyōṣēʾ mippîw*, literally "according to all that emerges from his mouth" (Num 30:3; cf. Judg 11:35–36; Jer 44:25; Ps 66:14).

The LXX renders this idiom as a cognate accusative, "vow a vow," but in Num 6:2 it takes the form of a cognate accusative; yet it adds *hiplîʾ*: *yaplîʾ lindōr neder*. Therefore, *hiplîʾ* cannot mean "vow." A rabbinic interpretation renders it "(vows) rashly" (*Num. R.* 10:7; for other rabbinic views, see Milgrom 1990a: 44). However, this notion is expressed by *biṭṭē'* (5:4; Ps 106:33). A modern interpreter suggests "set aside a votary offering" where the root *pl'* is a variant of *plh* 'set apart' (Levine 1989; cf. Rashbam). However, nothing is "set aside"; the vow at this point is only a verbal statement.

Ehrlich (1908) suggests that the *Hip'il* of *pl'* means "make (a vow)," whereas the *Pi'el* means "fulfill (a vow)." His suggestion is most attractive, since it actually fits the four contexts in which these forms occur (*Hip'il*, 27:2; Num 6:2; *Pi'el*, Lev 22:21; Num 15:3, 8; see NOTE on 22:21), but philological evidence is lacking.

Wessely (1846) makes the insightful suggestion that there is a different distinction between *pillē'* (*Pi'el*) and *hiplî'* (*Hip'il*), the latter (attested only in this verse and in Num 6:2) being limited to persons (noted by Cartledge 1992: 142), and the former being used with only animal sacrifices (22:21; Num 15:3). The *Pi'el*, then, denotes "express, articulate," whereas the *Hip'il* means "make an extraordinary (vow)," as in *wĕhiplā' 'et-makkōtĕkā* 'and he will inflict extraordinary plagues' (Deut 28:59). Wessely's distinction is accepted in the translation.

The reason why this vow is extraordinary—"special," according to Ehrlich (1908)—is that it is unconditional. That is, whereas all other vows are conditional, dependent on the fulfillment of an expressed wish (e.g., Jacob in Gen 28:20–22), this vow (and, presumably, the Nazirite vow, Num 6:2) is not attached to any prior condition. The silence of the text concerning the circumstances of the vow, however, does not allow for this inference (see COMMENT C). A more plausible answer is that this verb is a vestige of the earlier practice of vowing persons, who were intended either as human sacrifices (e.g., Jephthah's daughter, Judg 11:35–36) or as lifelong servants of the sanctuary (e.g., Samuel, 1 Sam 1:11). This "extraordinary" vow by the time of Lev 27 had been reduced to fixed monetary valuations (contra Cartledge 1992: 142). Schapiro (1909) makes the interesting suggestion that in case of nonpayment of the vow of Lev 27, the person belonged to the sanctuary. However, his surmise lacks evidence.

to YHWH. laYHWH. Ehrlich (1908) would transpose this word after v. 2a. This certainly is the sense of this verse, and so it has been translated. However, structural considerations have determined its position; note that the protasis of v. 9, which begins the second pericope of the section on vows, vv. 9–13, also ends with "to YHWH." Thus the two beginning protases are in balance.

concerning the (fixed) valuation. bĕ'erkĕkā. The qualifier "fixed" is implied (Berlinerblau 1996: 116, n. 4, citing Gianto's [1987: 400] analysis of the Mulk inscription of Nebi Yunis). There are four current explanations for the final *kap*:

1. It is "a pronominal suffix that became fossilized and thus absorbed in the nominal stem" (Speiser 1960: 30), as in *bō'ăkā* (Gen 10:19, 30; 13:10; 25:18; 1 Kgs 18:46), which originally may have meant "your coming" (Malul 1987a). Speiser (1960: 30–31) cites the transformation of Akkadian *mimma šumšu* 'whatever be its name' > 'what's-its-name' > a noun that can take a (second) pronominal suffix: *mimmušunšu-ya* 'my what's-its-name' (i.e., "anything of mine"). Unfortunately, there is no analogous suffixed form in BH.

2. The suffix indicates that originally the valuation was determined by a priest, as in vv. 8, 17, 14, and thereafter it became a fixed value (Porter 1976).

3. It is not a suffix, but part of the root (Ibn Ezra) because the word occurs as a construct (vv. 3, 5) and takes the definite article (v. 23 [twice]). Ibn Ezra's insight is developed by Rashbam.

4. The word should be vocalized *'erkāk*, namely, as a doubled third radical (Rashbam), like *ra'ănān* 'fresh'; *ša'ănān* 'tranquil' (Shadal); *nahălāl* (a site in Zebulun, Josh 19:15); *pirḥaḥ* 'striplings'? (Job 30:12). Zorell (1945) adds further that the Tiberian Masoretes, in their zeal to replace the older, well-attested second-person-singular masculine pronominal suffixes *āk* with *kā*, mistook the substantive *'erkāk* as a suffixed form of *'ērek*. Zorell's theory was supported (independently) by Gumpertz (1963), who, on grammatical grounds, deduced that the absence of accent marks (called *meteg* or *maqel*) preceding *wĕkol* (v. 25) can be explained only by reducing the syllables of the word formed by the quadriliteral *'rkk* from three to two: from *'erkĕkā* to *'erkāk*. The Rashbam–Zorell theory makes sense.

a human being. nĕpāšōt. Any human being, including minors (cf. vv. 5–6), is meant. Ibn Ezra, followed by Ehrlich (1908), claims that animals are also included because they, too, possess a *nepeš* (Gen 1:20, 24, 30; 9:10, 16; see NOTES on 11:10, 46; 17:11, 14), and, therefore, this verse is also the heading for vv. 9–13. However, as pointed out by Kalisch (1867–72), sacrificeable animals are not subject to valuation (vv. 9–10) and, hence, cannot be subsumed under this verse.

The reversal of these terms (*kesep*) *napšôt 'erkô* (2 Kgs 12:5) is comparable to *kesep-'erkĕkā* (vv. 15, 19) and *'erkĕkā kesep* (5:15; Num 18:16), and is attested in other compound expressions (Paran 1983: 227).

In the realm of vowing persons to YHWH, it became necessary to put a price on the different categories of humans, which is exactly what vv. 3–7 specify. The valuation of persons is fixed, as indicated in table 6. The rationale behind these sums is disputed. Many claim that they vary according to a person's productive capacity (see the NOTES below). Wenham (1978) surmises that they are the prices that these persons would fetch in the slave market, and he points to the 50 shekels per landowner levied on Menahem, king of North Israel (2 Kgs 15:20), and the 20 shekels, the sale price of young Joseph (Gen 37:28). The sale price for slaves attested in many Mesopotamian documents seem to confirm that 50 shekels is a reasonable sum for a male adult (Mendelsohn 1949: 117–27).

TABLE 6

AGE (IN YEARS)	MALE (IN SHEKELS)	FEMALE (IN SHEKELS)
1 month–5	5	3
5–20	20	10
20–60	50	30
60+	15	10

Noting that 30 shekels is a fixed sum for the value of a slave (Exod 21:32), Dillmann and Ryssel (1897) suggest that the figures cited in these verses do not correspond to the actual capacity of the person, but represent an average. Thus when these sums are totaled, they yield the average of 37 shekels for a man and 22 shekels for a woman, or 30 shekels for both—the established average market value of a slave.

All these theories are unconvincing. In his commentary, Wenham (1979) admits that since the average wage for a laborer was about 1 shekel a month, few people could have afforded to make the vow, and he suggests that these prices were deliberately set high in order to discourage people from making these vows. Abravanel proposes, to the contrary, that these sums *distinguish* Israelite persons from slaves: all, regardless of productive capacity, bear a fixed price (see also Philo, *Laws* 2.34). The rabbis stress this very point in their statement: "Whether a man vowed the valuation of the fairest (adult) in Israel or of the most unseemly in Israel, he must pay 50 selas" (*m. 'Arak.* 3:1; cf. Philo, *Laws* 2.32). Levine (1989: 193) postulates that the differentiation between the valuations of men and women is due to the relative greater productive capacity of men, a suggestion that is refuted by Wegner (1992: 43), who points out that the priority of care for home and children left little time for the spindle and the loom. Moreover, as convincingly demonstrated by Meyers (1983: 584–87) the relatively high value for female valuations indicates the reverse, that the woman was an indispensable part of the labor force, nearly equivalent to that of the male (see below). For additional theories, see Firmage and Milgrom (1987).

In passing, one should note that the Hittites (and other ancient peoples) viewed the vow of persons more literally: the vower paid the sanctuary the form of the vowed in gold and silver. Thus "I will go (and) make for Lelwanis, my lady, a silver statue of Hattusilis—as tall as Hattusilis himself, with its head, its hands (and) its feet of gold—moreover, I will hang it (with ornaments)" (*ANET* 394, ll. 36–42). At Ugarit, vows were made according to the vowed person's weight. For example,

ṯm yd[r. k]rt. ṯˤ ʾiṯt ʾaṯrt. ṣrm w'ilt.	There, Kret of Thaʾ vows a gift
ṣdynm	O, Asherah of the Tyrians, even the
	goddess of the Sidonians:
hm. ḥry. bty ʾiqḥ ʾaš ˤrb. ǵlmt ḥẓry	If Hurrai into my house I take,
tnh w[k]spm ʾatn wṯlṯh ḥrṣm	(or if) I cause the girl to enter my court,
	twice her (weight) in silver I will give,
	even thrice her (weight) in gold
	(*Krt* 199–206 [CTA 14 IV; cf. Fisher 1975: 47])

This practice of vows by weight continued into late antiquity and is reflected in rabbinic literature: "If a man said, 'I vow my weight,' he must give his weight in silver if (he had said) 'in silver,' or in gold if (he had said) 'in gold.' Once the mother of Domitia said, 'I vow my daughter's weight,' and she went up to Jerusalem and weighed her and paid her weight in gold" (*m. 'Arak.* 5:1).

The rabbis distinguish between vows (*nĕdārîm*) and valuations (*ʿărākîm*): vows, whether by weight (*mišqāl*) or worth (*dāmîm*), are conditional; valuations are unconditional (cf. *m. ʿArak.* 1:1). This distinction would lend support to Ehrlich's (1908) view that the valuation vow was "special" because it was unconditional. However, the rabbinic position is not validated by the biblical text: the valuations of vv. 3–8 explicitly are vows, and the conditionality characteristic of vows probably prevails in this pericope as well (see COMMENT C). Nonetheless, the rabbinic view is surely correct that in contrast to a person's worth (*dāmîm*), which is assessed in the slave market (cf. *m. ʿArak.* 3:1), the biblical valuations are predetermined and fixed and thus are independent of the slave market.

Speiser (1960: 30–33) has observed that in certain Nuzi cases, fines were imposed in terms of fixed animal ratios that were commutable to stipulated amounts of currency, a datum that throws light on the biblical reparation offering (vol. 1.328, on 5:15). The biblical analogy is even stronger. The reparation animal remains the same regardless of the extent of the damage to the desecrated sanctum (see NOTES on 5:15–16). Chap. 27 is its parallel counterpart: whereas 5:14–26 deals with illegitimate desecration, chap. 27 deals with legitimate desanctification (see COMMENT A). Both require the same fixed fine: one-fifth (20 percent) for property (animals, houses, and lands) and a fixed, but high, valuation for persons. Thus the contrast between the prices for (Israelite) persons and for property is of prime significance. Whereas the latter always represents the market value, the former does not. It is this contrast between persons and property regarding the same fine imposed for desecration (chap. 5) and desanctification (chap. 27) that determines the distinctiveness of the fixed sums for the valuation of person: they differ from property in that they are not assessed according to each one's economic value (details in Firmage and Milgrom 1987).

However, when male and female valuations are compared, the results show that women, as a class, must have been considered an indispensable and powerful element in the Israelite labor force (table 7). Meyers cogently argues (1983: 584–87) that the variation in the female percentage of the combined value of a male and a female in each age group reflects realistically the value of the woman's productivity relative to the male's. Obviously, children below the age of five would contribute little to the labor force; and especially in view of their high mortality rate, their valuations would be low. In the next age group, five to twenty years, the percentage of the woman's value is at its lowest, which would

TABLE 7

AGE (IN YEARS)	MALE (IN SHEKELS)	FEMALE (IN SHEKELS)	COMBINED VALUE	FEMALE PERCENTAGE OF COMBINED VALUE
0–5	5	3	8	38
5–20	20	10	30	33
20–60	50	30	80	38
60+	15	10	25	40

be expected since it coincides with her highest child-bearing years (cf. de Vaux 1961: 29), with their attendant mortality risks. In the following years, the woman's relative worth increases, reaching its maximum in the senior years when male efficiency declines, whereas the female is able to continue her domestic responsibilities and register a minimal decrease in productivity. Above all, the high relative percentage of women, at or near 40 percent, demonstrates without a doubt that they achieved a high status in Israelite society.

3. *by the sanctuary weight. bĕšeqel haqqōdeš*, literally "by sacred weight." Why is this term not expressed as *šeqel hammiqdāš* if the institution of the Temple is intended? First, *miqdāš* does not mean Temple, but "sacred area" or "sacred objects" (Milgrom 1970: 23–24, n. 78). The Temple (i.e., the sanctuary building) is expressed by the compound *bêt hammiqdāš* (1 Chr 28:10; 2 Chr 36:17). Second, this phrase may have originated from a time when there was no central sanctuary that regulated the official currency. The most likely answer, however, is that this term, literally "sacred shekel," was coined to contrast it with the "secular" shekel, which was *ʿōbēr lassōḥēr* 'the going merchant's rate' (Gen 23:16), or the one employed by the Crown, *ʾeben hammelek* 'the royal weight' (2 Sam 14:26).

5. *twenty years*. This was the age of conscription in Israel (Num 1:3). The census taken by King Amaziah in the early eighth century B.C.E. also began with those aged twenty (2 Chr 25:5). In the classical world, the age for entering military service was twenty in Sparta, eighteen in Athens, and seventeen in Rome.

6. *one month to five years . . . five shekels*. Five shekels is also (and primarily) the ransom price for the firstborn male (Num 18:15, 16; cf. 3:15, 39, 40, 43) paid at the age of one month (based on Num 3:44–51). An infant younger than thirty days old was not considered a person (cf. *t. Šabb.* 15 [16]:7), presumably because of the high rate of infant mortality (cf. *Tanḥ* Num 21), a situation that probably continued, though not as severely, until age five; hence the lower valuation, five shekels, for this age category. The inclusion of infants clearly demonstrates that others (presumably, in the main, parents) could vow them. The rabbis deduce logically: "A deaf-mute, an imbecile, or a minor (under thirteen years of age) may have their worth or their valuation vowed by others, but they may not vow another's worth or valuation, since they lack understanding" (*m. ʿArak.* 1:1).

7. "Why is a female when she is old valued only at one third, whereas a man not even a third (30 > 10 versus 50 > 15 shekels)? Said Hizkiah: People say, an old man in the house is a burden in the house; an old woman in the house is a treasure in the house" (*b. ʿArak.* 19a); that is, she can be useful in household chores.

from sixty years. mibben-šiššîm šānâ. The rabbis interpret the preposition as implying that the starting age is sixty-one and that, correspondingly, the upper age limits in all the other categories are inclusive, i.e., belong to the same category (*m. ʿArak.* 4:4). Sixty apparently was considered the "retirement" age, though for Levites, the change between their job profile from sanctuary transport to the less arduous sanctuary custody took place at age fifty (Num 8:25).

8. *too poor (to pay) a valuation. māk hûʾ mēʿerkā*, literally "sinks from a valuation" (for *māk*, see NOTE on 25:25). The participle is used here rather than

the imperfect as in chap. 25 to convey the sense of immediacy. Does it also indicate that this vow, differently from all the others, is not conditional? Not at all. All it means is that the priest's determination of the amount (i.e., his estimation of the extent of the vower's penury) is made at the same time that the vow is made; the payment stipulated in the vow still depends on its condition being met (see NOTE on "may be dedicated," v. 9).

The ethical and theological significance of this concession needs to be emphasized. Concessions to the indigent are also granted in the sacrificial system (e.g., for the burnt offering, 1:14–17; the graduated purification offering, 5:1–13; the parturient, 12:6–8; the scale-diseased person, 14:21–32). Here, however, although a vow is made in the name of God, and a specific person, whose worth is fixed in the holy writ, is stipulated in the vow, the priest is allowed to lower the valuation of the vowed person according to the financial ability of the vower. The rabbis extend this concession even further (see NOTE on "what the vower can afford," below). Clearly, we are dealing with a legal fiction on a par with the concession made to the repentant defrauder before he is apprehended (see NOTES on 5:20–26, and vol. 1.365–78).

he shall be presented. wĕheʿĕmîdô, literally "and he shall present him." Four interpretations of the subject and the pronominal suffix have been cited:

1. The object is the vowed person, and the subject is the priest, as in "The priest shall take . . . his own left hand," literally "the priest's left hand" (14:15; Ibn Ezra₁).
2. The subject is the vower (Ibn Ezra; Wessely 1846; Dillmann and Ryssel 1897).
3. The subject is the vowed person, and the object is the vowed thing (Strack, cited by Bertholet 1901)!
4. Preferably, the verb must be treated as an impersonal passive, a common feature in priestly texts and, particularly, in this chapter (see NOTES on "may be brought," vv. 9, 11; Dillmann and Ryssel 1897; Baentsch 1903; Bertholet 1901).

assess. wĕheʿĕrîk (cf. 2 Kgs 23:35). According to the rabbis, the price is set so that the vower will have enough to live on, including a bed, a mattress, a cushion, and the tools needed for his trade (b. ʿArak. 23b). Neither may he deprive his dependents of their basic needs to pay his vow: "He has no claim on his wife's raiment or his children's raiment, or to dyed clothes which he had dyed for their need, or to new sandals which he had bought for their need" (m. ʿArak. 6:5).

(assess) him. ʾōtô (i.e., the vowed person). If one neglects to pay, his goods may be confiscated, but officials must leave him sustenance for thirty days, bedding for twelve months, his sandals and phylacteries, two sets of tools if he is a mechanic, a yoke of oxen if he is a farmer, and his animal if he is a donkey driver (m. ʿArak. 6:3). The biblical text's concession to the indigent is matched by the rabbis in their severity to the rich, in blatant contradiction to the text: "If a poor man vowed the valuation of a rich man, he need pay only the valuation of

a poor man; but if a rich man vowed the valuation of a poor man, he must pay the valuation of a rich man" (*m. 'Arak.* 4:1; cf. *t. 'Arak.* 2:12). The biblical text clearly has in mind the situation where the indigent person vows his own valuation. The rabbis, however, seize on the phrase "what the vower can afford" to penalize the rich man who had planned to offer a lesser sum to the sanctuary by vowing the valuation of a poor man.

the priest shall assess him. The repetition of this phrase is characteristic of H's style (see COMMENT B). The explicit mention of the priest as the assessor is correctly understood by the rabbis as an example of the hermeneutic principle of *binyan 'āb,* literally "a structure (emerging out) of the father," which in this case implies that the priest must be the assessor in all valuations. (For the antecedent and, perhaps, original use of this principle in Qumran's Temple Scroll, see Milgrom 1989a; 1990b.)

what the vower can afford. Compare the Greek Cyrene law (ca. 330 B.C.E.), which stipulates that a vowed (tithed) man is "sold in the market-place for the most that he is worth" (A ll. 33–35). Presumably, his value is determined in the slave market according to the going price of a fully healthy, able-bodied man in order to determine how much he owes to the sanctuary. Palmer (1963: 343) suspects that this kind of sale is fictional. But rabbinic provisions for estimating a permanent injury inflicted on a person indicate otherwise: "One who injures his fellow becomes liable to him for five items: for depreciation, for pain, for healing, for loss of time, and for degradation. How is it with 'depreciation'? If he put out his eye, cut off his arm, or broke his leg, we consider him (the injured person) as if he were a slave sold in the market place, and valuation is made as to how much he was worth [previously], and how much he is worth [now]" (*m. B. Qama* 8:1 [full translation in chap. 24, COMMENT C]).

9. *If [the vow concerns]. wĕ'im.* Dillmann and Ryssel (1897), followed by Noth (1977) and, most recently, by Cartledge (1992: 53, 137), claim that vv. 9–13 deal with consecrations, not vows. However, the particle *'im* is a telltale sign that what follows is a subunit of the previous pericope introduced by *kî* (v. 2). Moreover, the pericope on consecrations, vv. 14–25, indeed, opens with *kî* (v. 14), indicating the beginning of a new unit.

quadruped. bĕhēmâ. Perhaps this term, as in all extant translations, should be rendered "animal," implying that H has (once again) broadened P's limited, more precise meaning "quadruped" (1:2; cf. *Sipra* Behuqotay 9:7); that is, it now includes sacrificeable birds. However, birds are not permitted as *šĕlāmîm,* well-being offerings, both in P (see chap. 3, COMMENT) and in H (17:3; 22:19, 21), and vows can be—and usually are—fulfilled by *šĕlāmîm* (7:16; 22:21; cf. Ps 116:17–18; Prov 7:14). Moreover, H itself limits *bĕhēmâ* to quadrupeds (18:23; 20:15, 16; esp. 20:25). Hence H, no differently from P, limits *bĕhēmâ* to quadrupeds.

may be brought. yaqrîbû. Fourteen MSS and Sam. (again in v. 11) read the singular *yaqrîb.* The variant must be rejected both here and in v. 11; an impersonal passive need not be expressed in the singular. Thus there is no need to harmonize with the other singulars in this pericope.

may be dedicated. yittēn mimmennu. Again, an impersonal passive. *Tg. Neof.* renders correctly *yprš* 'separates, sets apart'. The meaning of "dedicate" for *nātan* is especially clear in the description of the job profile of the Levites (Num 3:9; 8:16–18; see Speiser 1963).

The question arises about why the priestly writer has chosen this rare usage of *nātan* when he customarily, and throughout the next pericope (vv. 14–25), uses the normal term for dedication and consecration, *hiqdîš*. Here we see the scrupulousness of the priestly legists to deny the use of the root *qdš* to all lay persons, even to Levites, in order not to imply in any way that nonpriests are holy.

The antecedent of the masculine suffix of *mimmennû* (untranslated) is *qorbān*. It is one of six places where the Masora expects *mimmennâ* (Exod 25:15; Lev 6:8; 7:18; 27:9; Josh 1:7; Judg 11:34; see the extensive NOTE on 6:8) on the assumption that the antecedent is the feminine *běhēmâ*. Indeed, some Hebrew MSS, Sam. MSS, LXX, and Pesh. read *mimmennâ*. The emendation is unnecessary. Note the switch between masculine and feminine elsewhere in this chapter (vv. 10, 13; cf. 22:6). The repetition of *'ăšer yaqrîbû* (*yittēn*) *mimmennâ(û) laYHWH* is, again, indicative of H's style (see COMMENT B).

shall be holy. yihyeh-qōdeš. How the quadrupeds were offered up is not stated. On the analogy of firstlings (Num 18:17–18), their flesh would belong to the priests. Even more relevant is the parallel with consecrated and proscribed property (vv. 14–25, 28). Just as it belonged to and could be utilized by the sanctuary priests, so it may logically be argued that the priesthood benefited from the vowed animal, unless it was expressly specified as a burnt offering (22:18). The rabbis claim that the vowed animal could be sold as a burnt or well-being offering to other Israelites, and the currency derived from their sale would be added to the Temple treasury for maintaining the building or for purchasing public burnt offerings (*m. Šek.* 4:7; *m. Tem.* 7:2).

10. *One may not exchange it or substitute it. lō' yaḥălîpennû wělō'-yāmîr 'ōtô*. Some claim that the two verbs are synonymous (LXX, *Tg. Neof.*, *m. Tem.* 5:5; Maimonides, *Sacrifices* 1:1). However, on the principle that synonymity is eschewed in law, these two consecutive verbs must differ with each other. Their most likely meaning is that *heḥĕlîp* refers to another kind (cf. Isa 9:9), or "exchange," while *hēmîr* refers to the same kind (cf. Jer 2:11), or "substitute" (Abravanel, Wessely 1846; Ehrlich 1908; Elliger 1966). This distinction is supported by v. 33: an animal tithe might (illegally) undergo substitution (i.e., of the same species [hence *hēmîr*], but not exchange (i.e., of a different species). This distinction is also supported by the Hittite "Instructions to Temple Officials," which includes as criminal acts both exchange and substitution (with an emaciated animal): "(if) we have given it (the animal) to ourselves, or (if) we have sold it for ourselves, or if we have exchanged it, made a deal and substituted in its place an emaciated (animal), then do thou, O god, pursue us together with our wives (and) our children on account of thy most valued possessions" (IV, 72–78 [cf. II, 14; IV, 61–66; ANET, 207–10]).

That such deception occurred in the Jerusalem Temple is attested by the prophet: "You bring the stolen, the lame, and the sick; and you offer such an oblation. Will I accept it from you?—said YHWH. A curse on the cheat who has an (unblemished) male in his flock, but for his vow sacrifices a blemished animal to YHWH" (Mal 1:13b–14a)!

a healthy with an emaciated one. tôb bĕrāʿ. The Hittite analogy, cited above, vindicates the Masoretic cantillation: this clause modifies "substitute," not "exchange." The rendering accepted here is supported by the two kinds of cows in Pharaoh's dream: *habbĕrîʾôt* and *hārāʿôt* (Gen 41:4, 27; Wessely 1846), as well as by the expressed mention of emaciated sacrificial animals in the Hittite "Instructions to Temple Officials."

Alternatively, *raʿ* can be interpreted as a blemished animal (*Sipra* Beḥuqotay 9:6; *Tg. Ps.-J.*; cf. 22:19–25), as stated explicitly by *mûm kōl dābār rāʿ* 'any defect of a serious kind' (Deut 17:1). Note that a blemished animal may be offered as a free-will offering, but banned for votary purposes (22:23), which would explain its prohibition here. The antonym *ṭôb* would, then, mean "unblemished" (*tāmîm*, 22:19, 21).

Both interpretations are possible, since both kinds of deception were practiced in the Temple (Mal 1:13b–14a). I prefer the contrast "healthy" and "emaciated" for *ṭôb* and *rāʿ* because of the recurrence of the two terms in v. 33 in connection with the animal tithe. If the tenth animal "that passes under the shepherd's staff" is blemished, it is automatically barred as a sacrifice, but not if it is emaciated. However, at least according to Malachi's indictment, deception with blemished animals was actually practiced. Thus either translation is acceptable. Perhaps one might conclude that not only are blemished animals intended by the term *raʿ*, but even emaciated ones that may pass as a sacrifice.

and its substitute. ûtĕmûrātô. The noun is attested in Job 15:31 and Ruth 4:7.

(substitute) shall be holy. Wessely (1846) logically deduces that if the vower exchanges (instead of substituting) the animal, the exchanged thing does not become holy.

11. *impure quadruped. bĕhēmâ ṭĕmēʾâ.* The rabbis claim that this refers to blemished animals (*Sipra* Beḥuqotay, par. 4:1; *Tg. Ps.-J.*; *b. Menaḥ.* 101a) whose value is contributed to the sanctuary (*b. Tem.* 33a). The *Sipra's* proof text is *mûm . . . raʿ* (Deut 17:1); however, D's usage is no proof for priestly terminology. On the contrary, Deut 17:1 actually demonstrates that blemished animals are covered by *raʿ* (as shown above; Abravanel) or by another verse, 22:21 (*Seper Hamibḥar*), not by the word *ṭāmēʾ*. Above all, a blemished sacrificial animal is not *ṭāmēʾ* 'impure', since it may be eaten (*Seper Hamibḥar, Kefer Torah*), even by the priests.

The carcass of a *ṭāmēʾ* animal defiles by touch; eating or carrying it requires laundering as well as bathing for purification. (Animals that are not *ṭāmēʾ* but *šeqeṣ* are forbidden as food, but do not defile. Quadrupeds, however, are never *šeqeṣ*; see NOTE on 11:10; Milgrom 1992a; 1992b; 1993.) The rabbis certainly knew that this was the true meaning of *ṭāmēʾ* (see Ramban on v. 27). Why, then, did they alter its meaning here? One can only speculate that perhaps it reflects their incredulity that a Jew would ever consider offering an impure animal (e.g., a pig) as a sacrifice. Therefore, they restricted the meaning of the term to the other category of ineligible sacrifices—blemished animals.

that may not be brought as an offering. Levine (1989) presumes that from the outset the offerer meant to contribute only its monetary value. Not necessarily. The offerer intended the animal (e.g., a donkey) for sanctuary maintenance (Rabbinic Heb. *bedeq habbayit*). The question arises: An impure animal obviously is ineligible as a sacrifice, so why the redundancy? The answer is that it is a matter of style peculiar to H: the same structure is kept, as in v. 10, to contrast sacrificial and nonsacrificial animals (see COMMENT B).

shall be presented. *wĕhe'ĕmîd,* literally "and he shall present." The subject is the vower (Wessely 1846). However, this verb is probably an impersonal passive (as in v. 8), and the subject is anyone.

12. *Whether high or low.* *bên ṭôb ûbên rāʿ.* Since these masculine adjectives are construed with the feminine *'ōtāh,* some render this expression not as two adjectives, but as the single prepositional phrase "midway between high and low," or a median price (Ehrlich 1908, citing Knobel 1857; Keil and Delitzsch 1874, followed by Gispen 1961).

Speiser (1960: 40–41), however, brilliantly transfers the *'atnaḥ* from *raʿ* back to *'ōtāh,* thereby allowing the phrase under discussion to become the protasis of what follows, which he renders "high or low, whatever the priest's assessment, it shall be so," and which is supported by Nuzi *lū mād lū ṣeḥer* 'whether it be large or small'; that is, the priest's assessment is final. Speiser did not realize that much earlier, Ralbag (cited by Hoffmann 1953)—without the help of the Akkadian parallel—came to exactly the same conclusion.

whatever is the valuation of the priest, so it shall stand. This is true for others who wish to purchase the animal from the sanctuary (see NOTE on "it may be ransomed," v. 27), but not for the owner, who has to add one-fifth to the sale price (v. 13; Rashi), in keeping with the rabbinic dictum: "The owner adds a fifth, but no other person" (*Sipra* Beḥuqotay, par. 4:7).

13. Many moderns believe that the antecedent of this verse must be the offerable animal of v. 10. Their arguments are weighty. First, if offerable animals were irredeemable, the text would say so, as it does with animal tithes (*lōʾ yiggāʾēl,* v. 33). The distinction between the redeemable dedicated animal and the irredeemable tithe animal is then readily understandable: "Indeed, offerable animals, which are vowed of one's free will, are redeemable, not those which lo ipso belong to YHWH" (Elliger 1966: 392). Second, the alternative, that v. 13 speaks of the redemption of an impure animal, is impossible, since "there is no mention of a state of holiness" (Elliger 1966: 387). Third, the assessment of the nonofferable animal (vv. 11–12) would coincide in procedure and style with the assessment of persons in the previous section (vv. 1–8), the entire pericope (vv. 1–13) averring that the assessment of the votive *nepeš* of persons or impure animals must be contributed to the sanctuary. Fourth, the *ḥērem* is called "most sacred" by virtue of its irredeemability (v. 28). Ordinary dedication, being of lesser sanctity, should therefore be redeemable. Fifth, the otherwise superfluous

v. 12 can now be explained. It prescribes that impure animals dedicated to the sanctuary may be released upon the payment of their assessed value. The impure firstborn requiring an additional fifth for its redemption (v. 27) is inherently different, since it belongs to God from birth (Num 3:13; 8:17).

The alternative interpretation also does not lack compelling arguments. The redemption, v. 13, must refer to nonofferable animals (vv. 11, 12). First, it follows v. 12 sequentially, and no transposition is required. Second, the following section, the redemption of houses (vv. 14–15), exhibits a similar structure and procedure: neither the animal nor the house can be redeemed until it is assessed. Third, the special statement on assessment (v. 12; cf. v. 14) is not superfluous, but brings the vital information that the sanctuary may put the dedicated property up for sale at its assessed value. This is confirmed by the stated provision for the impure firstborn: "if it is not redeemed [*wĕnimkar bĕ'erkekā*], it may be sold at its assessed value" (v. 27b). To this analogy, an argument a fortiori can be added: if the impure firstborn—the Deity's property from birth— can be sold at face value, all the more so an impure animal that had a profane status until vowed to the sanctuary. Fourth, this correspondence with the impure firstborn sets up a consistent criterion for the redemption of sancta: offerable animals are irredeemable; nonofferable sancta, if sold by the sanctuary, are redeemable at their assessed value, but if redeemed by the owner require the payment of an additional fifth. Fifth, that now both impure animals and impure firstborn require the additional one-fifth for redemption is not surprising. It is not the time of their dedication that matters (the firstborn being dedicated from birth), but their status at the time of dedication. Both are nonofferable and, hence, redeemable.

Brin (1994: 46, n. 48) claims that the law of vv. 11–13 *exceptionally* begins with nonredemption and subsequently with the option of redemption. However, this sequence is attested with the consecration of a house (vv. 14–15) and, as indicated by the verb *pādâ* 'ransom', the nonredemption of an impure firstling precedes its redemption (v. 27). On the contrary, the single case in this chapter is where redemption comes first (vv. 19–20) due to the exceptional condition stipulated in v. 20 (see its NOTE).

Thus he who redeems his own property from the sanctuary pays a 20 percent fine, but if it is purchased by someone else no fine is involved. The distinction between redeemer and purchaser is perhaps based on the premise that the owner might be so attached to his property that he will have second thoughts about having dedicated it. Endless and fruitless bookkeeping would devolve on the temple staff, not to speak of the slight to God implied by such frivolity. The purchaser, though, has no emotional attachment to the property (it belonged to another); his purchase is a pure business transaction, which is precisely what the Temple intended when it put up the property for sale (I was partially anticipated by Maimonides, *Code, Sacrifices*, Tem. 4:13; cf. also Bekhor Shor).

The arguments of the first interpretation will be answered point by point. First, the contrast with animal tithes fails, since they are not YHWH's from birth, but only after tithing. To the contrary, the reasoning should be that both dedicated animals and tithe animals are similar in that they are profane until their dedication or tithing. Therefore, if the tithe animal is declared irredeemable (v. 33), so is the dedicated animal, and the absence of an explicit *lō' yiggā'ēl* (v. 10) can only be accidental (see NOTE on v. 33). Second, the assumption that an unoferable animal cannot be dedicated is false. How, then, are patently unofferable houses or land dedicated? Thus impure animals are subject to the same law as all other unofferables: they may be dedicated, sold, or redeemed. Third, vv. 1–13 now conform better to the plain meaning of the text. Humans and impure animals are not to be regarded as similar votive categories, since, from the outset, it is the fixed value of the human that is vowed, whereas, as maintained by the text (v. 11), it is the animal and not its assessment that is vowed by the owner. Fourth, the reason that the *ḥērem* is called "most sacred" is to emphasize that nonofferable objects like land (vv. 21, 28) and impure animals, though ordinarily redeemable, may, however, not be redeemed if they are *ḥērem*. Pure animals that are offered up as *šĕlāmîm*, just like *ḥērem*-animals (cf. Num 18:14, 18), would also be irredeemable (see NOTES on v. 28).

one-fifth. Namely, 20 percent of the value (Gen 47:24). The rabbis, however, compute it to be 25 percent (*m. 'Arak.* 8:2–3; *Sipra* Ḥobah 20:8; see discussion in *b. B. Meṣ.* 53b–54a). Thus if the sale price is 20 shekels, the owner-redeemer would pay 5, not 4, shekels more; the 20 percent would be taken on the total price, 25 shekels.

One is inclined to associate the institution of the one-fifth with the 20 percent levied by Joseph on all Egyptian produce (Gen 47:24). Jackson (1972: 179) objects on the grounds that "the fifth amounted to a fifth of virtually all their possessions, whereas the priestly texts imply a fifth of only that (consecrated) property involved." However, since the Egyptians had sold all their lands to Pharaoh (Gen 47:23, the preceding verse), they were now seeking to benefit from sacred property (Pharaoh being a god), and Joseph could legally impose on them the desanctification penalty of one-fifth. The analogy is suggestive, but without further evidence, the purported non-Israelite origin of this desanctification penalty remains obscure.

Vv. 14–25. Consecrations of Houses and Fields

The jubilee institution is mentioned, and its laws (chap. 25) are assumed (cf. vv. 17, 21a). Vows (vv. 1–13) are, in the main, for animate things; consecrations, for inanimate things (vv. 14–25). Presumably, one can also vow inanimate things (e.g., Jacob's vow to pay crop tithes to a temple that he will build, Gen 28:22), and animate things, such as impure animals for temple maintenance (e.g., Num 7:3–8), but one cannot, in the priestly view, consecrate animate things such as persons (see NOTE on "may be dedicated," v. 9). Consecrations differ from vows in that they take effect the moment they are verbalized (see COMMENT D).

Vv. 14–15. Consecrated Houses
14. *If. kî.* This word introduces a new unit.

consecrates. yaqdîš. Consecration can be defined as a transfer from the realm of the profane to the realm of the holy (Milgrom 1976d: 782). Examples include sacrifices (22:2–3), dedications to the sanctuary (Exod 28:38), and the firstborn (Num 3:13, God is the subject. However, the Levites who replace the firstborn are not consecrated [*qdš*] but dedicated [*ntn*]; cf. Num 3:9, 13; 8:18–19). God, too, is "sanctified" when he is treated as holy (Num 20:12; 27:14).

his house. Two questions arise: Are both field houses and town houses included in this law (25:29–31)? Why is the jubilee provision missing: is it taken for granted (but not in the following fields pericope, vv. 17, 21a) or just inoperative and, if the latter, are redemption rights unlimited in time? There are three possible answers covering both questions:

1. All houses are included, even town houses, which remain the buyer's inalienable property if they are not redeemed within the first year following their sale (25:29–30). The absence of the jubilee provision is not accidental: the owner may always redeem his house unless the sanctuary has sold it.
2. All consecrated houses are released by the jubilee (cf. *t. ʿArak.* 5:11; *m. ʿArak.* 9:7). The priests' valuation is based on the house's worth until the jubilee.
3. All houses become the permanent property of the sanctuary after the jubilee.

Since consecrated fields return to their owners at the jubilee (vv. 16–19), one would expect a similar rule to prevail for consecrated field houses. There is no indication that the word "house," being unqualified, is limited to town houses. So the third option is not satisfactory. The second option is the least plausible, since no method is given—or is even possible—for determining the annual worth of a house. Thus the first proposed solution seems the most satisfactory. The original owner may always redeem his consecrated house once it is in the hands of the priests. Hence even a town house, which is the inalienable property of the buyer, becomes eligible for redemption by its original owner if the buyer consecrates it.

to YHWH. qōdeš laYHWH, literally "a sacred thing to YHWH." The word *qōdeš,* the cognate accusative of *hiqdîš,* matches *yaqrîbû . . . qorbān laYHWH* (v. 9) and thus allows this pericope to begin the same way as the pericope on animal vows. It is therefore not superfluous, but is required for stylistic reasons.

the priest shall assess it. The house is valuated for the purpose of sale (see NOTE on "it may be ransomed," v. 27 and Philo, *Laws* 20.37) and redemption (v. 15). This must mean that the priest has to inspect the house and, to establish its market value, consult the equivalent of a real-estate agent.

Whether high or low. bên tôb ûbên rāʿ. The protasis of a new sentence, this necessitates the transfer of the *ʾatnaḥ* from *rāʿ* to *hakkōhēn* (for a similar occurrence, see NOTE on "Whether high or low," v. 12).

so it shall stand. kēn yāqûm. This technical term implies that the priests' valuation is final (for the usage, see Gen 23:17, 20; Lev 25:30; Num 30:5, 8, 10, 12, 13). It is equivalent to *kēn yihyeh* (v. 12b), but possess greater legal force.

15. *one-fifth.* Only the previous owner pays this surtax. Philo (*Laws* 2.37) regards it as a penalty for his "thoughtlessness, in making the dedication, and lust of possession, in his desire to regain what he had surrendered." Worded differently, "It diminishes the sacredness of the consecration if he can keep changing his mind" (J. Sheldon).

Vv. 16–25. The Consecration of Fields

16. *If. wĕ'im.* This word signals the beginning of a subunit.

any part of his tenured field. miśśēdēh 'ăhuzzātô. This construction is similar to (*mākar*) *mē'ăhuzzato* '(he sells) part of his tenured field' (25:25). Just as he can sell only the usufruct of his ancestral property (see NOTE on "what [his brother] has sold," 25:25), so he can consecrate only the land's usufruct: in effect, he leases the land to the sanctuary until it is redeemed or released by the jubilee.

(according to) its seed requirement. lĕpî zar'ô. Wenham (1979a) and de Vaux (1961: 48) hold that this phrase refers to a field *producing* a homer of seed, citing *mizzera' hā'āreṣ* (v. 30), which can refer to only the land's productive capacity. However, this latter phrase, literally "from seed of the ground," does not specify the products of the land, but their source, the seed (see NOTE on v. 30). As correctly understood by the rabbis: "This is the decree of the king: Whether a man consecrated (a field) in the desert of Machoz or in the gardens of Sebaste, he pays the fifty shekels of silver" (*Sipra* Behuqotay 10:3; *m. 'Arak.* 3:2), which Rashi interprets: "Whether it is a good field or bad field, the money for redeeming it from its consecrated state is the same." Compare "an area for seed" (*Tg. Onk.;* Pesh.); "an area suitable for sowing" (*Tg. Ps.-J.*). Thus the field is assessed not by its yield, but by its seed requirement—that is, its size.

Common sense dictates this solution. Who can foretell what a land will produce? "The estimate by the quantity of seed used affords an easier and more uniform standard than uncertain and fluctuating harvests" (Kalisch 1867–72). Indeed, a fixed price means that investment costs (the seed) are the same irrespective of the yield (D. Stewart). Moreover, as Eden (1987) points out, land measurement required special tools (Ezek 47:3; Amos 7:17) that were unavailable to the ordinary farmer, who therefore measured his land, after years of experience, by the amount of its seed requirement. Mensuration by seed requirements is well attested in ancient Mesopotamia, as demonstrated by Sheldon in COMMENT J. Note as well the absence of the phrase "whether high or low," present with animals and houses (vv. 12, 14). There is no guesswork, as would be the case in estimating the crop yield: the price is fixed by its seed requirement.

homer. This quantitative measure was equivalent to a *kûr* (*Tgs.*; Pesh.; cf. *kurru* A, CAD 8:564–65) and comprising 10 baths (Ezek 45:14) or 30 seahs. It contains between 29 and 53 gallons, or 134 to 241 liters (de Vaux 161: 202), or, according to S. Rattray's calculations (vol. 1.895), 117.5 liters (about 3.5 bushels).

The word is probably derived from *hămôr* 'donkey' and originally probably meant "donkey load." Significantly, Akkadian *imēru* means both "donkey" and "homer," the measure of area computed by the quantity of grain necessary for seeding; (*CAD* 7:114; see COMMENT J).

fifty shekels. Does this sum represent the estimated value set on a single crop (i.e., an annual sum) or on all the crops for the entire jubilee period? Ostensibly, the biblical data point to the former option: if in a good season 2 *seahs* of barley were sold for 1 shekel (2 Kgs 7:1), then crops resulting from 30 *seahs* (1 homer) would sell for 15 shekels, and in a poor season the price would even be higher. Therefore, the price of 50 shekels would represent the price per year (Kalisch 1867–72). However, Jeremiah buys Hanamel's field for 17 shekels (Jer 32:9) and David gives Araunah 50 shekels for his threshing floor (2 Sam 24:24). Thus 50 shekels stands for the value of the entire field or, in chap. 27, the estimated value of the crops for the whole jubilee period (Driver and White 1894–98, in agreement *m. 'Arak.* 7:1). This deduction is supported by the Mesopotamian evidence that the standard price of barley was 1 shekel per homer (Maloney 1974: 4–20). Thus the annual valuation of 1 shekel per year on 50 shekels for the jubilee period is appropriate (Wenham 1979).

Vv. 17–19. The same principles prevail as those pertaining to the redemption of sold fields (25:25–28). Redemption rights of family members are not mentioned, but they must be assumed. Redeemers, however, would be exempt from the one-fifth surtax (see NOTE on "may be ransomed," v. 27), and presumably this is why they are not mentioned: in reality, they are not redeemers but purchasers (who pay no surtax). They would keep the land (rather, the usufruct) until the jubilee in order to recoup their "redemption" costs (see NOTE on "his closest redeemer," 25:25). It also must be assumed that the authorities would have to watch out for collusion: the owner might have the redeemer purchase the field to avoid paying the surtax.

The frequent mention of the jubilee (vv. 17, 18 [bis], 21, 23, 24) and redemption (vv. 13, 19, 20 [bis], 27, 28, 31, 33) indicates that this chapter is the logical continuation of chap. 25 and must, therefore, stem from the hand of H.

This similarity of the procedures for the consecrated land (vv. 17–19) and sold land (25:25–28) proves that the owner has consecrated only the usufruct. Presumably, the priests or their hirelings would work the land (just as its purchaser would)—not the owner, even though, in theory, he still owns it—in order to ensure its maximum productivity.

18. *reduced. wĕnigra'* This mathematical term means "be subtracted" (Exod 5:8, 19; 21:10; Num 36:3–4; for its metaphoric use "be barred, lost," see Num 9:7; 27:4). What is subtracted are the years that the land was held by the sanctuary from the *previous* jubilee.

20. *but has sold. wĕ'im-mākar.* Three problems with this phrase coalesce to make this verse a notorious crux:

   1. Does the *waw* mean "or," implying two conditions, either of which forfeits the land to the sanctuary: if the land is not redeemed *or* the land is sold. Or does the *waw* mean "and" or "but," implying the need for two conditions to forfeit the land: the land is not redeemed, *and* the land is sold.

2. Who is the subject (i.e., who sells the land), the owner or the sanctuary.

3. What is the exact tense of the verb *mākar*: is it perfect or pluperfect.

1. The *waw*. Those who hold that it means "or" (Ibn Ezra; Ḥazzequni; West-brook 1991b: 225; Hartley 1992; Brin 1994: 45–46) maintain that if the owner does not redeem the land, it belongs to the sanctuary permanently. That is, even though the owner consecrated only the usufruct until the jubilee, his failure to redeem it forfeits the land. This case thus differs from that of a sold field, which must revert to the owner at the jubilee, and is more like that of a sold town house, which is retained permanently by the purchaser if the owner does not (within one year of the sale) redeem it. If, however, the *waw* is rendered "and" or "but" (Kalisch 1867–72; Dillmann and Ryssel 1897; *NJPS*; *NEB*), the owner's failure to redeem the land is a necessary but not sufficient condition for forfei-ture: the land must be both unredeemed *and* sold.

An a priori consideration tends to favor the second option. Inherited land al-ways returns to its owner at the jubilee (25:10, 28). The only case where the sanctuary retains the land is when it is declared *ḥērem* (v. 28) or equivalent to *ḥērem* (vv. 20–21). This case is, therefore, cited only because it is an exception; it does not constitute a general rule. The exceptional nature of this verse ex-plains the order of the options: redemption followed by nonredemption. In other cases (vv. 11–13, 14–15, 27), the order is reversed (contra Brin 1994: 45, n. 48; see NOTE on v. 13). The option of nonredemption (i.e., sold by the sanctuary) is omitted in the case of the tithe (see NOTE on v. 31).

2. The subject. The rabbis hold that the seller is the sanctuary (*Sipra* Beḥuqo-tay 10:12, followed, among others, by Abravanel; Hoffmann 1953; and, most re-cently, Levine 1989). Hoffmann bases his decision on v. 27, where the right to sell (*wĕnimkar*) consecrated property is explicitly given to the sanctuary. How-ever, the two forms of the verb are not identical: it is *Nipʿal* in the latter pas-sage. Abravanel states outright that if the owner fails to redeem the land before the sanctuary sells it, the land automatically becomes *ḥērem* and reverts to the sanctuary at the jubilee. But if the owner cannot afford to redeem it, does he lose his patrimony? Moreover, if the sanctuary sells it immediately on acquiring it, the owner is given no chance to redeem it (Shadal contra Abravanel). It is Shadal, however, who, in my opinion, delivers the coup de grâce: *ma'n dĕkar šĕmêh*, literally "who mentioned its (the sanctuary's) name?" The intrusion of the sanctuary is textually unwarranted.

This leaves the owner as the subject. But this option is also beset with diffi-culties. If the owner sells his land *after* he has consecrated it, he has engaged in deception. And this is precisely the reason cited by Shadal, Kalisch (1867–72), Dillmann and Ryssel (1897), Noth (1977), Porter (1976), and Westbrook (1991b: 225) why the land is forfeited to the sanctuary—he is penalized for his chicanery! There is, however, no trace of censure in the text. According to priestly law, the owner would have been guilty of *maʿal* 'sacrilege' and subject to divine pun-ishment (e.g., 2 Chr 26:16–18). Ehrlich (1899–1900 [Heb]) is aware of the prob-lem, but rationalizes the owner's action by suggesting that he sold the land in order to obtain the money to redeem it. But regardless of his motive, he has committed sacrilege! The answer will be provided in the discussion.

3. The verb tense. One would expect the prefixed (imperfect verb) *yimkor*, in keeping with the other verbs in this verse! Lambert (1901) already noticed the morphological change, but attributed it to the change of subject, from seller to sanctuary—an assumption that has no grammatical justification. It is Haran (1971) who, to my knowledge, is the first to suggest that the verb is a pluperfect: the owner of the land consecrated it *after having sold it*. In order to reclaim it, he would have to pay more than twice its value: repurchase it from the buyer and redeem it from the sanctuary. Thus it is clear that from the outset, when he consecrated his sold property, he intended it as a permanent gift to the sanctuary. To this can be added an even more compelling argument: the sanctuary cannot benefit from the consecration, since the land is in the buyer's hands until the jubilee. Therefore, the owner's purpose in consecrating the land is that the sanctuary should take it over after the jubilee. Thus in consecrating the land, the owner wishes to forfeit his jubilee rights. Now the explanatory clause comes into full light: "The field shall be holy to YHWH, as *ḥērem*-field." It is put into the most sacred category (v. 28) in order to justify its irredeemability.

In sum, the *'ăhuzzâ*, inherited land, must revert to its owner at the jubilee. He consecrates (or sells) its usufruct, that is, he only leases the land until the jubilee. However, if he consecrates the land after selling it, he thereby indicates that he does not want the land back, and the land becomes sanctuary property after the jubilee, as if it had not been consecrated (*hiqdîš*, v. 16) but proscribed (*heḥĕrîm*, see NOTES on v. 28). Lev 27:20–21, 28, permitting the sanctuary to own tenured property permanently, is not contradicted by Num 18:20, which prohibits only *individual* priests, but not the sanctuary, from privately owning land.

It is thus not correct to state that "the claim that Yahweh owned the land gave the priests even greater power since they were the logical 'caretakers' of Yahweh's interests" (Fager 1993: 62; see also Ringe 1985: 26–27). The basic postulate behind this law is that the sanctuary takes no priority over the landowner. The priestly legists have made an amendment to "the land is mine" principle. Inherited land always reverts to the owner, except when by word (v. 28) or act (vv. 20–21) he consecrates his land (and not just its usufruct) to the sanctuary. Why this alteration of the divine (i.e., sanctuary) principle of ownership? Perhaps it is the priestly response to the condemnation of the eighth-century prophets of the growing latifundia of their time: indentured land being swallowed up by avaricious creditors (e.g., Isa 5:8–10; Mic 2:1–2). On the one hand, they devised the jubilee system, whereby the status quo ante concerning land ownership would be restored and indentured Israelites would be released (25:8–43). And on the other hand, they insisted that consecrated land was also subject to the jubilee (vv. 20–21) so that the priests could not participate in the land-grabbing practices that prevailed all about them. It must be remembered that in the neighboring high civilizations of Egypt and Mesopotamia, the temples acquired vast tracts of land. This example as well as the temptation always lay before Israel's priesthood.

21. *released in the jubilee*. A consecrated (or sold) field would normally revert to the owner at the jubilee. For this technical meaning of *yāṣā'*, see the NOTE on "released," 25:28.

holy to YHWH. But not before the jubilee! This statement proves that the field was not the sanctuary's property (except for its usufruct) before the jubilee.

as a proscribed field. kiśdēh haḥērem. The field belongs to the priesthood (see the next NOTE), as does any other proscribed object (Num 18:14). This entitlement does not contradict the basic rule that priests (and Levites) may not possess inherited land (Num 18:20, 23). This rule must be properly understood: Israel's priesthood may not be *allotted* any land, but is permitted land that has been *voluntarily* proscribed—that is, intended by the owner to be transferred to the sanctuary.

Proscribed property is unsalable and irredeemable (v. 28a); it is not transferable. The consecration or sale of tenured land is never final; the land returns to its owner at the jubilee. This verse continues and spells out the apodosis "it shall no longer be redeemable" (v. 20b). Consecrated land that had been sold does not revert to the owner at the jubilee. The implication is clear: land that is consecrated while in its owner's possession does revert to him at the jubilee, even if he does not redeem it (see NOTE on "but has sold," v. 20).

it belongs to the priest. lakkōhēn tihyeh. The rabbis deduce from this phraseology that the field does not belong to the sanctuary (for maintenance, *bedeq habbayit*) that is, transferred to the Temple treasurer's office—but to the priestly course in service on Yom Kippur (*Sipra* Beḥuqotay 11:3; *m. 'Arak.* 8:6; *b. 'Arak.* 28b). The rabbis consistently distinguish between priestly and sanctuary entitlements: consecrations may be specified to one or the other. Perhaps this was the practice at the end of the Second Temple period. However, there seems to be no such distinction in the priestly laws of the Bible: for all purposes, priesthood and sanctuary were one and the same. The rabbis' case is particularly vulnerable in proscriptions. V. 28b does not designate the priest as beneficiary (see its NOTE). Moreover, how could any tenured field belong to a priest, when Scripture repeatedly forbids it (e.g., Num 18:20a; Ezek 44:28b)? The answer, of course, is that the field belongs to the sanctuary, but the priest may benefit from its produce.

22. *a field that he purchased. śdēh miqnātô*, as contrasted with *miśśdēh 'ăhuzzātô* 'part of his tenured field' (v. 16). This phrase presumes that whereas a person will consecrate only part of his ancestral holding (or sell part of it, 25:25), he is more likely to consecrate all of his bought field. Here, too, he can consecrate only the usufruct, not the field, which does not belong to him.

which is not of his tenured field. 'ăšer lō' miśśdēh 'ăhuzzātô. Why is this clause needed? The rabbis put forward the case of a son purchasing part of his father's tenured field and consecrating it while the father is alive. Does the field follow the law of tenure or of purchase? This clause decides for the latter option. Although eventually it will be the son's tenured land, it is not so at present. The rule is that the status of the property at the time of the consecration determines its law. This is the majority view. However, R. Judah and R. Simeon render this clause to mean "a field that is ineligible to become his tenured field." But in this case, even if the property at present is not his, eventually it will be; hence it is treated as his tenured field (*m. ʾArak.* 7:5).

23. *proportionate. miksat.* Some derive this noun from the root *kss* (Ibn Janaḥ, Ibn Ezra, Radak). However, the expected nominal form should then be *mĕkissâ* (Sarna 1991: 244, n. 12). Rather, the root is *mks*, and the noun is the feminine form of *mekes*, demonstrated by its Akkadian cognate *miksu* 'a share of crops due to another, customs, dues' (*CAD* 10.2:63) and its denominative *makāsu*, which means "to collect a share from a rented field."

valuation. hāʿerkĕkā. The definite article is one of the several indications that the root is quadriliteral (see NOTE on v. 2). The "proportionate valuation" is computed on the basis of the estimated usufruct of the remaining crop years until the jubilee, as in the case of a sold field (25:15; *Sipra* Beḥuqotay 11:4). Another view holds that the calculation of the remaining years is by the standard given in this chapter—50 shekels per seeded homer (v. 16; *b. ʾArak.* 14a; R. Eliezer in *Sipra* Beḥuqotay 11:5).

he shall pay. wĕnātan. For this meaning of *nātan*, see Exod 21:22, 30, 32; 30:12.

the valuation. ʿet-hāʿerkĕkā. This constitutes the difference between the cost of redeeming consecrated and sold land: the latter involves only the valuation; the former, an additional one-fifth (*m. ʾArak.* 3:2).

as of that day. bayyôm hahûʾ. Some render the phrase "on the day"; that is, the buyer must pay the sanctuary the valuation on the very day it is made so that the owner may redeem his property whenever he wishes. For as long as the buyer owes the sanctuary, the owner cannot redeem his field (Driver and White 1894–98). Also, the field, not being his patrimony, cannot be used as collateral (Levine 1989; cf. Kalisch 1967–72). Alternatively, one may argue that the buyer may pay the valuation in installments on the basis of the principle *ʾămîrātô laggābôah kimĕsîrātô lahedyôṭ* 'a (dedicatory) statement to the Temple (lit., "the Most High," i.e., God) is equivalent to (the act of) delivery to a common person' (*m. Qidd.* 1:6; *t. Qidd.* 1:9). This interpretation is supported by taking the verb *nātan* in another of its attested meanings "assign" (see NOTE on 17:11). The *NJPS* embraces both solutions satisfactorily by rendering "pay as of that day," the translation adopted here.

24. *land. hāʾāreṣ.* The switch from *śādeh*, a cultivatable field to the general term *ʾereṣ* "land" may be deliberate—to include any purchased land, even one that is not arable.

25. *gerah.* A coin, attested in Exod 30:13; Num 3:47; 18:16; Ezek 45:12, rendered *māʿā* (Tgs.); *ʾobolós* (LXX). The word *gērâ*, root *grr*, stems from *gargār* 'seed', and the coin *māʿâ* also means "grain" (Isa 48:19), as the word "karat" derives from *koret* (grain). The name implies that it is the smallest of coins. In Talmudic coinage, it is one-twenty-fourth of a *sela*. It must be assumed that the gerah is one-twentieth of not only the sanctuary shekel (Exod 30:13; Num 18:16), but also the commercial shekel (Gen 23:16) and the royal shekel (2 Sam 14:26).

The gerah appears among a list of weights in a Hebrew ostracon, dated in the sixth century B.C.E., found in Kadesh-Barnea (Barkay 1987).

Vv. 26–27. Firstlings

The conflicting laws on the firstling reflect historical development. Originally sacrificeable firstlings were entirely incinerated on the altar as burnt offerings: "Therefore I sacrifice to YHWH every first male issue of the womb" (Exod 13:15 [JE]). The priestly laws, however, prescribe that the meat of the sacrificed firstling is a priestly perquisite: "But their meat shall be yours" (Num 18:18a [P]). Finally, Deuteronomy revokes both laws, by declaring that the meat of the sacrificed firstling belongs to its owner: "You and your household shall eat it annually before YHWH your God" (Deut 15:20a). For details, see the NOTES on v. 26, and COMMENT E.

26. *However.* '*ak.* The firstling can be neither vowed (vv. 1–13) nor consecrated (vv. 14–25; Hoffmann 1953). For the use of contrastive '*ak* in biblical law, see Exod 21:21; Lev 21:23; Num 18:15b.

designated as a firstling to YHWH. yĕbukkar laYHWH. This rendering of the intensive stem of *bkr* (*Pi'el* and *Pu'al*) is supported by *yĕbakkēr* 'treat as a first-born' (Deut 21:16). This clause indicates that the owner must set aside the firstling as a sacrifice. However, he should not think that he will be rewarded in heaven for consecrating it as he would for consecrating any other sacrificeable animal (vv. 9–10)—the firstling is God's from birth.

cannot be consecrated by anyone. lō'-yaqdîš 'îš 'ōtô. A similar phrase also appears in Num 18:17. One may not use the ploy of paying a vow with a firstling (Hartley 1992).

The contradiction with the firstling law of Deut 15:19—*taqdîš* 'You shall consecrate'—is blatant. It clearly states that the firstling is not innately holy. R. Ishmael attempts to harmonize the two laws by suggesting that one may consecrate *the value* of the firstling, but not the animal itself (*m. 'Arak.* 8:7; *Sipra* Behuqotay, par 5:3; *b. 'Arak.* 29a). Another rabbinic resolution is that "consecrate" can also mean *declare* that the animal is holy to the Lord "to receive the award for doing so" (*Mekh.* Bo 16). The contradiction stands.

Another problem is the law of Exod 13:2 *qaddĕš-lî kol-bĕkôr* 'Consecrate to me every firstborn', which is assigned by the critics to P. Ostensibly, this law, like its D counterpart, assumes that the firstling does not belong to God from birth, but must be consecrated to him. One can resort to the rabbinic harmonizations or, preferably, rethink the underlying—and unsubstantiable—assumption that Exod 13:2 is part of the priestly corpus. Since the following verses (vv. 3–16), by all accounts, belong to JE, this verse too, I submit, should be attributed to JE. It then would form the precedent for Deuteronomy's law and be in consonance with the fact that nearly all of Deuteronomy's derived laws stem from JE (Milgrom 1976b). Supporting this attribution is Exod 22:29, indisputably JE, where *bayyôm haššĕmînî tittĕnô-lî* must be rendered "on the eighth day you shall dedicate it to me," also implying (contra P and H) that the firstling is not innately holy. For *nātan* meaning "dedicate," see Exod 30:16; Num 3:9; 8:16, 19; 18:6; Speiser (1963), and the NOTE on v. 9.

it is YHWH's. That is, it must be sacrificed; that is, its blood and suet will be offered on the altar, before its meat is transferred to the priests (Num 18:18a).

27. This priestly law of the impure firstling is also contradicted in Exodus: "But every firstling ass you shall redeem with a sheep or goat; if you do not redeem it, you must break its neck" (Exod 13:13a; cf. 34:20a). Three harmonizing solutions have been attempted:

1. The rabbis aver that Lev 27:27 does not refer to an impure firstling, but to any impure animal. Hence v. 11 refers to a blemished animal, and the law of Exod 13:13 is limited to an ass, but all other impure firstlings are for the sanctuary's maintenance (cf. Saadiah, Rashi, Radak, Rashbam, Bekhor Shor). This interpretation, however, flies in the face of the plain meaning of vv. 11 and 27: v. 27 is clearly connected with v. 26. Not only does v. 27 begin with *'im*, indicating that what follows is a subunit of the preceding, but the next word begins with the telltale preposition *be, babbĕhēmâ*, compelling the rendering "If it is *of* impure quadrupeds," which clearly marks the subject as the firstling. Moreover, only the firstling (*bĕkôr*) explains the masculine form of *wenimkar* (see below). Furthermore, v. 11 cannot possibly refer to a blemished animal (see the reasons cited in the NOTE on v. 11). A twist on the rabbinic interpretation is provided by Bertholet (1901), who proposes that this verse (not v. 11) speaks of a blemished animal. The objections cited in v. 11 also hold here, especially the fact that an impure (*ṭāmē'*) animal is not a blemished one: the latter may be eaten; the former defiles.

2. Ibn Ezra (followed by Wessely 1846; Shadal; Kalisch 1867–72) suggests that, in contrast to a sacrificeable firstling, which cannot be consecrated (v. 26), an impure firstling must be consecrated (v. 27). If, however, the owner wishes to redeem it, he adds a flock animal (Exod 13:13) as well as a surtax of one-fifth (Lev 27:27). But if the firstling is an ass, then, following the law of Exod 13:13, the animal's neck is broken if it is not redeemed. This interpretation, too, does not fit the facts. According to both the Exodus and Leviticus laws, all firstlings, pure and impure alike, are innately holy, as implied by the requirement to ransom them from the sanctuary (v. 27; Exod 13:13). If the impure firstling is neither sold nor redeemed, it remains sanctuary property, used presumably for maintenance (*bedeq habbayit*). Finally, the imposition of the flock animal of Exodus onto the law of Leviticus is without warrant.

3. Ramban and Abravanel, like Ibn Ezra, aver that v. 27 deals with an impure firstling, and it is not God's from birth. Only if it is consecrated is it ransomed by the priests' valuation (v. 27). Thus these exegetes disconnect the Leviticus and Exodus laws and eliminate the contradiction between them by presuming that Exodus refers to only an ass, whereas Leviticus deals with all other animals. Here, my objection is limited to their assumptions that Lev 27 neither deals with an automatically consecrated animal nor includes the ass among its firstlings. Neither assumption is warranted, and the contradiction remains. The conclusion is inescapable: the laws of impure firstling reflect historical development (see COMMENT E).

it may be ransomed. ûpādâ. The verb *pādâ* is found in the following priestly texts: *Qal*, 27:27; Num 18:15 (thrice), 16, 17; *Nipʿal*, Lev 19:20 (+ *Hopʿal*); 27:29, and the noun *pĕduyyim / pĕdûyîm* in Num 3:46; 49, 51; 18:16. It is used with only animate beings as its objects (Driver 1895: 101, on Deut 7:8), which would account for its absence in vv. 14–25, addressed to houses and lands. Levine (1989) is surely correct in pointing out that this provision is a radical departure from the firstling law of Exod 13:13; 34:20, which does not allow the sanctuary to benefit from firstlings, whereas Lev 27:27 permits the sanctuary to dispose of firstlings profitably. However, his suggestion that Leviticus reflects the Exodus legislation, except for its use of *gāʾal* (v. 27b) instead of *pādâ*, must be rejected since in the priestly vocabulary *pādâ* and *gāʾal* are not synonymous: *pādâ* refers to the price set by the sanctuary, which others but not the owner pays; *gaʾal* refers to the price paid by the owner, which includes the one-fifth surtax (see further below). To be sure, *pādâ* and *gāʾal* are employed synonymously (and metaphorically) in poetic texts by the prophets (Isa 35:9b–10a; 51:10b–11; Jer 31:11; Hos 13:14; see NOTE on 25:24), but not in legal texts where synonyms are eschewed.

As to why the term *pādâ* 'ransom' rather than *gāʾal* 'redeem' is appropriate here, my student S. Nikaido offers the plausible explanation that since all first-born belong to the Deity, the offerer is not the "original owner." He, therefore, cannot "redeem" his property, but only, as a third party, ransom it.

Budd (1996: 387) opines that on the basis of Num 18:15, the firstling of impure animals must be redeemed. He has overlooked the fine distinction that his cited verse makes between the firstborn and the impure firstling: the ransom of the former (not redemption) is exposed by the emphatic *pādōh tipdeh*; that of the latter by the simple imperfect *tipdeh*, which therefore should be rendered "you may have ransomed" and, here, "it may be ransomed" (Milgrom 1990a: 152).

at its valuation. bĕʿerkĕkā. For an analysis of this term, see the NOTE on v. 2. The fact that the priests (i.e., the sanctuary) determine the valuation (vv. 11–12) proves that the impure firstling, no differently from the pure firstling, innately is holy and is, therefore, sanctuary property at birth. This fact undermines the interpretations suggested by Ibn Ezra, Ramban, and their followers (nos. 2 and 3, above).

No method is given for determining the valuation; the process described in vv. 11–13 is assumed. Neither is any method cited in the other priestly text dealing with the ransom of firstlings (Num 18:15b); a knowledge of Lev 27 must again be presumed. Kalisch (1867–72) and, independently, Ehrlich (1908) claim that the redemption price is uniformly 5 shekels, which is explicitly stated in the following verse, Num 18:16. However, they misread this verse, which refers to only human firstborn. The sum of 5 shekels is paid to the sanctuary when the human firstborn male is one month old (cf. Num 3:40, 47). No date is mentioned for the redemption of the impure firstling. Moreover, if the redemption price for impure firstlings was always 5 shekels, then one would rightly have expected the surtax to read "1 shekel" instead of "one-fifth" (see COMMENT E).

with one-fifth added. wĕyāsap hᵃmīšitô ʿālāyw. Kalisch (1867–72) claims that the masculine suffixes refer to the unmentioned fact that the animals are male. On the contrary, the antecedent, indeed, is mentioned—the *bĕkôr*, the firstling of v. 26. What is the rationale for the surtax? One is readily understandable for consecrated property: to prevent a cycle of consecration and redemption by an owner who regrets losing his field or animal (see NOTE on v. 15). But the firstling is not his to begin with; it belongs to God from birth. Since there can be no suspicion of fickleness on the part of the owner, why not let him ransom the firstling by paying its valuation price as may any other purchaser! I have no answer. Perhaps the priestly legist insisted on consistency in the five redemption procedures of Lev 27: for the impure vowed animal (v. 13), the consecrated house (v. 15), the consecrated tenured field (v. 19), the impure firstling (v. 27), and the crop tithe (v. 31).

it may be sold. wĕnimkar. Wessely (1846) claims that the implied subject is the owner. If that were the case, the verb would read *ûmākar* 'he shall sell' (not Nip ʿal, but Qal as *ûpādâ* and *wĕyāsap*), and the direct object would have to be inserted. Moreover, the owner would have no right to sell it—it is not his!

This verb is crucial in reaching the conclusion that the purpose of the valuation is for the sale of the animal by the sanctuary (but not to the owner), a procedure described by the verb *pādâ* (see NOTE on "whatever is the valuation of the priest," v. 12).

Vv. 28–29. Proscriptions

The word "proscription" is succinctly and accurately defined by Stern (1991) as "consecration through destruction" (see COMMENT F). This definition defies the usual understanding of *hērem* as a form of taboo, such as the alleged Mesopotamian equivalent *asakkam akālu* (most recently, Malul 1987b, modifying vol. 1.322). The *hērem* attested in the Bible is exercised by Israel against other nations as the result of either a vow (Num 21:2–3; implied in Josh 6:17) or God's command (Num 25:16–18; 31:1–12; Deut 7:2; 20:16–17; 1 Sam 15:3), or against its own rebels (Exod 22:19; Deut 13:13–19; Judg 20:48; 21:10–11). The antiquity of the word and the concept is confirmed by the ninth-century B.C.E. Mesha inscription:

> *w ʾhzh. w ʾhrs. kl[h]. šb ʿt. ʾlpn[.] g[b]m̂. w[gr]n/ wgbrt. w[gr]t. wrhmt/ ky. l ʿštr. kmš. hhrmth/*

> I seized it (Nebo) and I slew everybody in it—seven thousand m[e]n, b[oy]s, women, gi[rl]s and maidens—for to the warrior Kemosh I proscribed them. (ll. 16–17, following Stern 1991: 23–38, 55)

The antiquity of the concept, if not the term, is illustrated by an old Babylonian inscription, cited and discussed by Stern (1991: 39–40), in which *uqadissu*, augmented by *uḫalliqma*, is the Akkadian equivalent of Moabite / Hebrew *heḥĕrîm*:

awassu ᵈAdad ᵈIštar ù ᵈNisba išmûma ālam uḫalliqma ana ilī šunūti uqad-disu.

Adad, Ishtar and Nisba lent an ear to his word. He (Anzabazuna) destroyed the city and consecrated it to those Gods.

The biblical *ḥērem* manifests different degrees: (1) death of all persons and animals, and burning of all property on the site itself (Deut 13:16–17); (2) death of all persons and animals, and consecration of all precious metals to the sanctuary (Josh 6:16–19); (3) death of all persons, but animals and goods are kept as booty (Deut 2:34–35; 3:6–7; 20:16; Josh 8:2, 26–27; 10:28–39 [presumably, but proved by 11:14]; 1 Sam 15:9; see COMMENT F); (4) death of all persons, with the exception of virgins (Num 31:9–11, 17–18); and (5) death of all men and married women (Judg 21:11–12; Dillmann and Ryssel 1897).

Apparently, a curse pronounced against those who would settle a sacked enemy city takes effect because the city is declared *ḥērem*, consecrated to the deity. For example, the Hittite Anitta inscription reads: "I consigned it (the city) to the Weather-god of Heaven [ ] and to the Weather-god we [consigned it] once again" (Neu 1974: 13, l. 20; for other examples from the Anatolian and Greek spheres, see Gevirtz 1963: 53–59). Thus Joshua's *ḥērem* on Jericho implies that not only have its people and property been consigned to God, but also their very land—all are "most holy." Therefore, a curse against resettlement (Josh 6:26, fulfilled according to 1 Kgs 16:34) can be pronounced (D. Stewart).

Thus far, the war-*ḥērem*. What of the "peace-*ḥērem*" of Lev 27? Its only biblical example is the *ḥērem* imposed by Ezra on the property of those who deliberately would absent themselves from the national assembly (Ezra 10:8). Hoffmann (1953) contends that the imposition of the *ḥērem* on property but not the persons proves that the *ḥērem* (of Lev 27) on persons must be earlier. Supporting this view is that Ezra's banishment of persons (unattested elsewhere in Scripture) is proleptic of Rabbinic Hebrew *niddûy* (Dillmann and Ryssel 1897). Therefore, the *ḥērem* on persons must have been ameliorated by the time of Ezra; banishment replaced death and, hence, it must be, at least, older than the time of Ezra. Stern (1991: 125–35, 210), however, claims that the "peace-*ḥērem*" is postexilic—secondary to and later than the war-*ḥērem*. But he has to rationalize Ezra's expulsion of the miscreants rather than having them executed by speculating that "the Jewish authorities were not in a position to take lethal measures against a large group" (211). Also, he ignores the evidence of the Mesha inscription that *ḥērem* property was consecrated to the deity in earliest times:

w'qḥ. mšm. ʾ[t.k]ly. YHWH. w'sḥb.hm.lpny.kmš

I took from there t[he ves]sels of YHWH and I dragged them before Kemosh (ll. 17–18; cf. ANET 320)

One should also not forget that David consigned his precious metallic spoils to YHWH (2 Sam 8:10–11) and that Jericho's precious metals (in an otherwise total *ḥērem*) are consecrated by divine command to the sanctuary (Josh 6:19, 24). To be sure, these examples may ostensibly be dismissed because they reveal the practice of only the war-*ḥērem*, not that of the *ḥērem* of Lev 27. However, no one can doubt that the consecration of valuables was an important source of revenue for temples throughout the ancient Near East (e.g., as the result of a vow, see INTRODUCTION to vv. 3–7). It is, therefore, most plausible to infer that coevally with the war-*ḥērem*, there must have been a "peace-*ḥērem*," whereby a person's property could, voluntarily or forcibly, irredeemably be consecrated to the deity. I have no objection to the notion that the peace-*ḥērem* is a secondary development. I submit, however, that this development occurred early in the history of Israel's cult.

28. *However. 'ak.* This particle of exclusion clearly refers to the prior case of the impure firstling (v. 27): neither sale nor redemption is permitted with *ḥērem*.

anything a man proscribes to YHWH. kol-ḥērem 'ăšer yaḥărîm 'îš laYHWH. The nominal form of the root *ḥrm* connotes destruction (Ug.), possibly by fire (Akk., Eblaite), and a person who has become sacred or entitled to respect (Arab.); its verbal form means "destroy, extirpate" (eighth form of Arab. *ḥarama*) (Stern 1991: 5–17). Some scholars aver that this clause refers to someone sentenced to surrender part of his property as banned possessions (Noth 1977) or to someone who fails to uphold his oath *ḥārê 'ălay běḥērem* 'I owe (this) under the penalty of proscription' (rabbinic formula), resulting in the confiscation of his property by the Temple (Levine 1989). However, the active verb *heḥĕrîm* (*Hip'il*) with YHWH as the indirect object belies either claim. The subject is the person, not an outside institution or authority. It should be compared with *wěhaḥărmtî la-YHWH biṣ'ām* 'and I shall proscribe to YHWH their riches' (Mic 4:13a). Here, as the next clause "of what he owns" testifies, the subject *'îš* "man" proscribes his own property. Unfortunately, no actual case is recorded in Scripture.

of what he owns. "A principal purpose of [this clause of] v. 28 is to prevent the powerful landowner from devoting people other than those under his ownership, such as relatives or other freemen. In other words, his power to devote people was limited to [his non-Israelite] slaves" (Stern 1991: 132). Here Stern is in agreement with the rabbinic teaching that a person may proscribe his Canaanite slaves (*m. 'Arak.* 8:4), but "if a man proscribed his son or his daughter, his Hebrew bondman or bondwoman, or his bought field, they are not deemed proscribed, for a man may not proscribe what is not his" (*m. 'Arak.* 8:5). However, Stern's (1991: 135) contention that this clause was framed as a conscious imitation of *wěhaḥăramtem 'et-kol-'ăšer-lô* (1 Sam 15:3) in order to establish continuity with the war-*ḥērem* must be rejected. As he indicates, the purpose of this clause is to state unambiguously the limitation of the proscriber's powers.

quadrupeds. ûběhēmâ. According to Sperber (1966d), texts around the second century B.C.E. showed an attached *mib* prefix, in keeping with the two adjoining nouns (Pesh.; *m. 'Arak.* 8:4; *Sipra* Beḥuqotay 12:3).

or his tenured land. ûmiśśĕdēh 'ăhuzzātô. "A landowner, despairing of his prospects, might be moved to devote irrevocably his property—from his land to his slave—hoping for YHWH to respond favorably and restore him to prosperity" (Stern 1991: 192).

May he proscribe his movable property? In that case, he needs but consecrate (*hiqdîš*) it; redemption and jubilee do not apply to movables. Why, then, are houses (vv. 14–15) omitted as part of his validly proscribed property? Perhaps this is an indication that the consecration of houses (vv. 14–15) is not by the same hand and is a later gloss (Elliger 1966).

may not be sold. Even by the sanctuary.

totally consecrated to YHWH. qōdeš-qŏdāšîm hû' laYHWH, literally "it is most holy to YHWH." What happens to a proscribed field? "Sometimes selected conquered territory was emptied of all its inhabitants and consecrated to gods. It was, e.g., dedicated as pasture to the bulls drawing the Storm God's chariot" (Goetze 1963: 129), to which Stern (1991: 120) responds, "as devoted cities become grazing ground for the sacred bulls in early Hittite religion, so *mutatis mutandis* YHWH granted the priests the right to use the field of *ḥērem* of Lev 27:21 in Num 18:14."

Here Stern harmonizes Lev 27 and Num 18. He equates Num 18:9 and 14, declaring *ḥērem* as "most holy," a status that allows the priest, but not his family, to benefit while disregarding vv. 11 and 19, which conclusively place *ḥērem* property in the lesser holy category, from which the priest's family indeed may benefit. (True, Num 18:14 reads *lĕkā yihyeh* 'it is yours', [i.e., the priest's], ostensibly ruling out the priest's family. However, the same phrase is used for first-processed foods [v. 13] and firstling [v. 18], which indubitably may nourish the priest's family. Thus the identification of the *ḥērem*'s sacred category in Num 18:14 is determined by its context, which explicitly assigns all the priestly perquisites to the priest and his family [vv. 11–19]). Is there, then, a contradiction between Leviticus and Numbers? Not at all. Regarding food, *ḥērem* is of lesser sanctity and is eligible to be eaten by a priest's family (Num 18); regarding its irredeemability, it is most sacred (Lev 27), in contrast to an impure votive animal (vv. 11–13), a consecrated house or field (vv. 14–25), and an impure firstling (v. 27).

According to Stern (1991: 127), "The violation of *qōdeš haqqŏdāšîm* involves such an immediate infringement on YHWH's person, as it were, that God's immediate intervention was the consequence." So one gathers from 2 Sam 6:7–8 and, by implication, from Num 4:19 (Stern 1991: 127). But these verses deal with the Ark, which is super-holy in both popular and priestly Torah—it kills even by sight (1 Sam 6:19; see vol. 1.29 on Num 4:20; *Num. R.* 5:9). Moreover, in the priestly views, encroachment on sancta is punishable by death through human agency, namely, by the priestly and Levitic guardians of the sanctuary. Divine intervention takes place only when the clerical guards themselves are guilty of encroachment (Milgrom 1970: 16–36). In any event, the laws of sancta encroachment apply solely to most holy sancta, those confined to the sanctuary precincts. The use of the term "most holy" in regard to *ḥērem*, as mentioned above, thus has nothing to do with its innate state. As demonstrated above, *ḥērem* produce actually falls into the category of the lesser holy, eligible as food for the priest's family. Its claim to severity, as stated explicitly in this verse, rests in its unsalability and irredeemability.

The rabbis distinguish two recipients for sanctuary consecrations: the priests (*lakkōhen*) and the sanctuary (*laYHWH*). *Ḥērem* consecrations designate both these recipients (vv. 21b, 28b), thereby instigating a controversy among the rabbis: "R. Judah b. Bathyra says: What is proscribed without a condition goes for Temple maintenance, for it is written, 'every proscribed thing is totally consecrated to YHWH' (v. 27). But the sages say: What is proscribed without a condition goes to the priests, for it is written, 'a proscribed field: it belongs to the priest' (v. 28)" (*m. 'Arak.* 8:6; cf. *t. 'Arak.* 3:34). The discrepancy is chimerical: all proscriptions (and consecrations) fall to the sanctuary and benefit the priests (see NOTE on "it belongs to the priests," v. 21).

29. *has been proscribed. 'ăšer yoḥăram.* Drawing on the fact that the verb is passive (*Hop'al*), Hoffmann (1953, in the wake of *t. 'Arak.* 4:34; *Sipra* Beḥuqotay 12:7; Rashbam; Ramban; Wessely 1846) concludes that the death sentence is imposed by an authorized body after due process of law. This interpretation is bolstered by the absence of the object *laYHWH* 'to YHWH' (Shadal; Dillmann and Ryssel 1897; Heinisch 1935) and by the fact that this *Hop'al* is once again attested in *zōbēaḥ lā'ĕlōhîm yoḥŏrām* 'He who sacrifices to any god shall be proscribed' (Exod 22:19a; see also Deut 13:13–19), a law that again implies a judicial sentence (Ramban; Wessely 1846). S. Nikaido adds the argument that whereas *'îš* in v. 28 testifies that an individual is proscribing, the unstated subject in v. 29 indicates that the subject is no longer an individual, but a collective body.

What would motivate an authorized body to impose the extreme *ḥērem*, the death penalty, on a human being? R. Akiba (*Yalqut*, Judg 76) avers that the king or the Sanhedrin (i.e., the highest court) might impose the death penalty on Israel's enemies, citing the example of the oath taken by the Israelite tribes against the people of Jabesh Gilead (Judg 21:5; cf. Ramban; Wessely 1846; Dillmann and Ryssel 1897; Driver and White 1894–98). In other words, this law reflects the war-*ḥērem*—for example, Achan (Josh 7:25 [Bekhor Shor]), Arad (Num 21:2), Mesha—which would bespeak its antiquity.

Stern (1991: 134), however, would ameliorate the harshness of the penalty, claiming that "the priests (representing YHWH) had the right of refusal. . . . The priests had nothing to gain by approving human slaughter. . . . As Leviticus 22, a chapter which deals with the lower level of 'sacred donations' or *qōdeš*, illustrates, these donations were highly regulated to screen out the unacceptable." Elliger (1966), too, on the supposition that the text is postexilic, assumes that the death penalty is not literal, but is a vestige of an older law that became unenforceable. In addition, Stern (1991: 133) is surprised that Israel's priests did not act as their Babylonian counterparts, who employed their proscribed slaves on their temple estates (cf. Oelsner 1976). Interestingly, he was long before anticipated by Abravanel, who suggested that proscribed persons, whether by their owners (i.e., slaves) or by the court (i.e., miscreants), became sanctuary servants, "choppers of wood and drawers of water" (cf. Josh 9:27). Indeed, this Gibeonite precedent, suggested by Abravanel, may well indicate that Joshua, who could not destroy the wily Gibeonites because of his oath, nevertheless imposed on them a lesser, but acceptable, form of *ḥērem*.

However, one can seriously question whether the priests "had the right of refusal," the reference to Lev 22 notwithstanding. This chapter is hardly analogous: it refers to other conditions, the impure and the defective in the *qōdeš*, the less sacred category. The *ḥērem*, however, precisely because it is *qōdeš qŏdāšîm*, cannot be altered by the priests. Thus two alternatives remain:

1. Vv. 28–29 speak of two different fates that await a proscribed person: consigned as a slave to the sanctuary by his owner (v. 28), and sentenced to death by a judicial body (v. 29).
2. Only one fate awaits a proscribed person: whether proscribed by his owner (a slave, v. 28) or by a court (an enemy of the state, v. 29), he is put to death.

One consideration, I submit, decides the issue. If all proscribed persons were put to death, the term *mē'ādām* 'persons' would not appear in v. 28, since persons would not suffer the same fate as (impure) animals and tenured fields. Or, at least, v. 29 would have begun with the particle *'ak*, to indicate that the fate of persons mentioned in v. 28 is the death penalty specified in v. 29.

In sum, the *ḥērem* imposed voluntarily by the owner on his property, whether it is his slaves, animals, or tenured fields, transfers it to permanent sanctuary ownership where it may be neither sold nor redeemed because of its most sacred status. But persons who are declared *ḥērem* by some outside body (presumably, an authorized court) must be put to death.

he must be put to death. môt yûmāt. That this term denotes judicial execution (and not by divine agency), see Milgrom (1970: 5–8). The contrast between this law and Exod 22:19 (quoted above) adds further support to the conclusion. In Exodus, the death penalty is omitted because the consequence of the *ḥērem* sentence was self-understood. Here, however, since it was possible to consign proscribed persons as slaves to the sanctuary, the old death penalty must be specified.

Vv. 30–33. Tithes

Vv. 30–31. The Crop Tithe

This tithe is also discussed in detail in COMMENTS G–I.

30. *All tithes from the land. wĕkol-maʿăśar hāʾāreṣ.* The use of *'ereṣ* instead of *śādeh* (vv. 16–24) indicates that tithes are due from the entire land: not only from crops of cultivated fields, but also from wild crops such as fruits. This generalization is doubted by Wellhausen (1963: 157) and Eissfeldt (1917: 85–87), who claim that this verse refers to measurable agricultural goods—grain, must,

and (olive) oil—precisely as prescribed in Deut 14:23. The early rabbinic sources rule differently: "A general principle they (the rabbis) stated concerning the tithes: Anything that is food, cultivated, and which grows from the earth is subject to tithes" (*m. Ma'aś*. 1:1; cf. *Sipra* Beḥuqotay 12:9). Thus, paradoxically, both Wellhausen and the rabbis turn harmonistic, Wellhausen interpreting the tithe in Lev 27 to comport with Deut 14, and the rabbis employing the reverse strategy. They do not limit the tithe to the grain, must, and oil specified in Deut 14:23 (cf. Neh 10:38–40; 13:5, 12) but, most likely, consider these three crops, which constitute the main agricultural produce of the land, as a metonym for all cultivated, edible vegetation. In support of their contention, one need but turn to Mesopotamian sources that testify that tithes, royal and sacral alike, were taken from every possession (see COMMENT G) and to the earliest biblical sources: Jacob (Gen 28:22) and, presumably, Abraham (Gen 14:20). The rabbis further harmonize the two tithes not only in their composition but also in their disposal, claiming that both are second tithes, an addition to the Levite tithe of Num 18, which have to be consumed in Jerusalem (cf. *m. Ma'aś. Š*. 4:3). For recent harmonistic attempts and their failures, see COMMENTS I and G.

seed (from the ground). mizzera' (*hā'āreṣ*). This word, no differently from its occurrence in v. 16, means "seed," and not "produce" (see NOTE on v. 16).

fruit from the tree. mippĕrî hā'ēṣ. The Versions, Sam., and *Tg. Ps.-J.* read *ûmippĕrî* 'fruit from the tree'. The subdivision of vegetation, plants and fruit, in the creation story (Gen 1:11) is also followed here. Tob 1:7–8 and Josephus (*Ant*. 4.205, 240) declare fruit to be an additional (third) tithe.

are YHWH's. laYHWH hû'. Surely this clause is extraneous in view of the following one, "they are holy to YHWH," the normal expression for sanctuary dues (e.g., vv. 14, 21, 23, 28). Herein may lie a polemic against P (Num 18:21–24), which reflects a controversy within priestly circles concerning the recipients of the tithe. Lev 27 (H) does not deny that the Levites are *also* tithe recipients, but it explicitly prescribes that the tithe must be brought to the sanctuary—that is, into the authority of the priests. Num 18 (P), however, assumes that the tithe is given directly to the Levites; indeed, they may even seize it (*tiqḥû*, v. 26; cf. Milgrom 1970: 67, n. 246) from the landowner. Both positions are corroborated by textual evidence (see COMMENT G), but these two points of view are not in conflict. Judging from contemporary Mesopotamian practices, temple agents—in Israel's case, the Levites—would collect the tithes at their source and bring them to the temple storehouses under the supervision of the priests. P and H, however, differ on the recipients of the tithe: P (Num 18) claims that the Levites are the exclusive beneficiaries, while H (Lev 27) opts for the sanctuary (i.e., the priests) as the recipient, but is silent concerning its distribution. To be sure, food that is *qōdeš* is barred to a nonpriest (22:10–13). But it may plausibly be conjectured that just as the tithe exceptionally may revert to its owner, provided that it is redeemed (v. 31), and presumably be bought at its valuation price by any other layperson (see next NOTE), so it may be distributed gratis to the Levites, but at the discretion of the priests. This conclusion was correctly deduced by Rashi (on *b. Mak*. 23b) following the opinion of R. Eleazar b. Azariah (*b. Yeb*.

86b), that Ezra's innovation was not that the tithes should be brought to the Temple—a procedure that had long been practiced—but that they should be shared equally by priests and Levites. For details on the history of the tithe, see COMMENT G.

They are holy to YHWH. qōdeš laYHWH. Although Deuteronomy calls the tithe *qōdeš* 'holy' (Deut 26:13), it is eaten in Jerusalem by its owners (Deut 14:22–27), and every third and sixth year it is given to the local underprivileged (Deut 14:28–29). The probability, therefore, exists that the term *qōdeš* in Deut 26:13 is a terminological vestige of the original practice to bring the tithe to the sanctuary, before it was transferred by D to its owner.

31. *If a man wishes to redeem. wĕ'im-gā'ōl yig'al 'îš.* But what if someone besides the owner wishes to purchase the tithe, as might happen in the case of consecrated impure animals (v. 12), houses (v. 14), fields (v. 16), or impure firstlings (v. 27)? The absence of such a provision for the tithe leads Elliger (1966) to conclude that this verse is a gloss. Not at all. Purchases by valuation may be assumed, as is the free distribution of the tithe to the Levites, who, after all, need to be rewarded for collecting it (see previous NOTE).

The rabbis, who insist on harmonizing this text with Deuteronomy, claim that this redemption clause refers to the landowner who lives too far to haul his tithe to the Temple. He, therefore, may sell it, add one-fifth to the sale price, and then spend the entire amount in Jerusalem (Deut 14:24–26). The unsoundness of their interpretation is shown by its illogical demand that only those who live far away, and have to make a special effort to bring their tithes to the Temple, must pay a surtax. It also contradicts the basic purpose of redemption—to get back one's property, not its monetary value. Besides, Deuteronomy says nothing about a surtax.

Vv. 32–33. The Animal Tithe

This law is not in JE, P, or D—only here, in H. Its existence, however, cannot be doubted. Jacob's tithe (Gen 28:22) must have been of animals (Hoffmann 1953). And in earliest Israel, where herding played a dominant role, it would have been surprising if an animal would not have been required (Dillmann and Ryssel 1897). Certainly, the imposition of tithes in Babylonia on all goods, including cattle (see COMMENT G), would have provided a precedent. Equally, the coexistence of royal and sacral tithes in Babylonia indicates that Israel's royal tithe on livestock (cf. 1 Sam 8:15–17) would have been matched by a Temple tithe.

Furthermore, this law, as presently worded, can hardly be attributed to an interpolator (Elliger 1966): "An interpolator, it might be urged, would probably have asserted a fresh claim in a more emphatic and direct way" (Driver and White 1894–98; cf. Dillmann and Ryssel 1897). That the other law codes omit it, as does Nehemiah (cf. Neh 10:37–39; 12:44; 13:5, 12), only indicates that the animal tithe was a theoretical system, which may have been practiced *voluntarily* by well-to-do ranchers, but never became a universal and annual mandatory obligation followed by all of Israel (cf. Dillmann and Ryssel 1897). Perhaps these omissions, particularly in D and Nehemiah, more realistically also reflect the transformation from a pastoral to an agrarian economy. Herdsmen abounded during the time of Samuel and Saul, but by the eighth and seventh centuries, the pastoral life no longer existed anywhere near the main sanctuaries, but was relegated to the border regions: the Transjordan and the Judean wilderness (Num 32; Amos 7:14; 1 Chr 5:9). Certainly, with the centralization of all worship in the Jerusalem Temple, it is inconceivable that herdsmen from these border regions would drive their herd and flock tithes to the Temple. To be sure, animal sacrifices were brought to the Temple (or, more likely, purchased there) for the festivals. Jerusalem's pilgrim throngs could be described "like Jerusalem's sheep during its festivals" (Ezek 36:38), but these animals were probably votive offerings, firstlings and Paschal Offerings, not tithes. (The insertion of the firstling into the law of Deut 14:23 may be an interpolation [cf. 15:20], but at least it exemplifies D's attempt to make it practicable.)

The rabbis' description of the tithing procedure may reflect the actual practice at the end of Second Temple times: "How do we tithe the animals? We bring them to a shed and make for them a small opening so that two shall not go out at the same time, and we count [with the rod; see NOTE on "all that passes under the shepherd's staff," v. 32], one, two, three, four, five, six, seven, eight, nine, and he marks every tenth lamb that goes out with red chalk and says, 'this is (the tithe)' " (*m. Bek.* 9:7); "He also places their mothers outside (the shed) when the offspring are inside, so that (the mothers) low, and the offspring go out to meet the mothers" (*b. Bek.* 58b).

When were the tithe animals brought to the Temple? "There are three periods [lit. "threshing floors"] for the tithe of cattle (i.e., for those born between the periods), corresponding to the three periods when animals give birth so that animals are available to pilgrims for the three pilgrimage festivals" (*b. Bek.* 57b–58a), but R. Meir limits it to once yearly: Ellul (*m. Bek.* 9:5; cf. *m. Roš Haš.* 1:1). According to *Jub* 13:25–26; 32:15; Tob 1:6, and Qumran (*MMT* B 63–64; 11QT 60:3–4), the animal tithe was a priestly perquisite; that is, it was sacrificed in the manner of a well-being offering, but its meat belonged to the priests (see below). However, neither Josephus nor Philo includes it among the priestly prebends—an indication that the law was not observed.

2 Chr 31:5–6, which attributes the fulfillment of this law to pious Hezekiah, is problematic. Perhaps a realistic note is struck by the ascription of its practice to "the Israelites who dwelt in the cities of Judah" (v. 6), those who lived near the Temple (J. Thompson). But v. 6a is probably an interpolation:

1. *ûmaʿśar qŏdāšîm*, literally "and the tithe of sacred donations" is improbable since *qŏdāšîm* are not tithable; hence *ûmaʿśar* is a dittography (Benzinger 1899, cited by Eerdmans 1912).
2. *wîhûdâ* makes no sense; it, too, is a dittography.
3. *ʿărēmôt* 'heaps' fits agricultural produce, not animals.

Thus v. 6a, containing the animal tithe, looks like an interpolation to account for the law of Lev 27:32 (Eerdmans 1912), and this verse must be discounted as evidence for the practice of the animal tithe.

32. *the herd or flock. bāqār wāṣō'n.* The animal tithe is limited to sacrifice-able quadrupeds and, thus, is intended for the altar. Note that the royal tithe as described in 1 Sam 8:15–17 seems to conform to this limit, for whereas crops and flock animals are tithed (vv. 15, 17), donkeys are seized (*yiqqaḥ,* v. 16). If, however, *bahûrêkem* (v. 16), also the object of *yiqqaḥ* 'seize', is read *biqrêkem* 'your cattle' (LXX), then a distinction is made between the royal tithe, limited to flock animals, and the sacral tithe that falls on cattle (i.e., all sacrificeable quadrupeds).

all that passes under the shepherd's staff. kōl 'ăšer-ya'ăōr taḥat haššābeṭ. This procedure is verified in Jer 33:13 and metaphorized in Ezek 20:37a. That the shepherd leads with a staff, see Mic 7:14 and Ps 23:4.

holy to YHWH. qodeš la YHWH. The animal can either end up on the altar as a burnt offering (*Jub* 32:8), sacrificed as a well-being offering whereby the meat returns to the owner (according to the rabbis), or become one of the priestly prebends. That the latter option is the probable intent of this phrase, see the INTRODUCTION to vv. 32–33. It was certainly interpreted so by the sectaries of Qumran:

WM'ŚR HBQR WHṢWN LKWHNYM HW'

And the tithe of the herd and the flock should be given to the priests (4Q MMT B 63–64)

WKWL TNWPWTMH WKWL BKWRWT[Y]HMH HZKRYM WKWL [M']Ś[R] LBHMTMH WKWL QWDŠYHMH 'ŠR YQDYŠW LY 'M KWL QWD[Š] HLWLYHMH

And all their elevation offerings and all their firstborn males and all the [tith]e of their cattle and all their sacred gifts that they sanctify to me, with all their sacred (fruit offerings) of praise (11QT 60:2–4)

For the reconstruction of the latter text, see Milgrom (1980: 102–103, supported by Qimron 1983: 141). The rabbis, however, regarded this tithe to be equivalent to their second tithe, to be consumed by its owner at the Temple (*m. Zebaḥ.* 5:8; cf. Baumgarten 1985a).

33. *seek out. yĕbaqqēr.* This can also be rendered as "search out, examine" (Levine 1989; see NOTE on 13:36). This verb is applied metaphorically by Ezekiel: "I am going to take thought for my flock, and I will seek them out [*ûbiqqartîm*]. As a shepherd seeks out [*kĕbaqqārat*] his flock (when some of the animals have gotten separated), so will I seek out [*'ăbaqqēr*] my flock" (Ezek 34:11b–12; see NOTE on 19:20).

the healthy as against the emaciated. bên-tôb lāra'. Alternative translations are "between fine (good) and poor (bad)" (Speiser 1960: 40, n. 19) and "(distinguish) the more valuable from the less valuable" (Herman 1991: 53). However, on the basis of a Hittite analogy (see NOTE on v. 10), the concrete physical conditions of "healthy" and "emaciated" are preferred.

substitute. yāmîr. An animal of the same species (see NOTE on v. 10) is meant. The other means of deception *heḥĕlîp* 'exchange' (v. 10) is irrelevant in this context. An exchange of species, such as goat for sheep, is possible in the case of a vow to consecrate a sacrificeable animal, but a tithe replacement can come from only the same species.

they cannot be redeemed. lo' yiggā'ēl. This prohibition is missing in the pericope on vowed sacrificeable animals (vv. 9–10) not because redemption is possible, but, on the contrary, because the animal must end up on the altar and thus may not be legitimately desanctified. Why, then, is it mentioned here, considering that the animal tithe also devolves on sacrificeable animals? The answer simply is one of style and logic: in contrast to the previously mentioned crop tithe, which may be redeemed (v. 31), the animal tithe may not be redeemed. Similarly, just as the sale of the crop tithe by the sanctuary is assumed to be permitted, so the sale of the tithe animal by the sanctuary is assumed to be forbidden.

The postulate underlying all sacrificeable animals, whether vowed (vv. 9–10) or tithed (vv. 32–33), is that they must not be substituted, exchanged, sold, or redeemed, but must be offered on the altar (see COMMENT A).

V. 34. Summary

The fact that this subscript follows and resembles the one in Lev 26 renders the entire chapter as a glaring appendix. As noted by Levinson (1991: 150), "The very assertion of the authority of the text precludes credulity; the text, which doth protest too much, betrays its own textuality and compels its interpretation."

It is clear that this verse is a subscript, but of what: Lev 27, H, or the book of Leviticus? The answer hinges on a comparison with the previous subscript, 26:46 (similar words are in boldface):

> *'ēlleh haḥuqqîm wĕhammišpāṭîm wĕhattôrōt 'ăšer nātan* **YHWH** *bênô ûbên* **bĕnê yiśrā'ēl** *bĕhar sînay bĕyad-mōšeh*

> **These are** the laws, rules, and rituals **that YHWH** established between himself and **the Israelites on Mount Sinai** through **Moses.** (26:46)

> *'ēlleh hammiṣwôt 'ăšer siwwâ* **YHWH** *'et-mōšeh 'el-bĕnê yiśrā'ēl bĕhar sînay*

> **These are** the commandments **that YHWH** commanded **Moses** for the **Israelites on Mount Sinai.** (27:34)

Thus *hammiṣwot* 'commandments' replaces or supplements *haḥuqqîm wĕhamišpāṭîm wĕhattôrōt* 'the laws, rules, and rituals'; *siwwâ* 'commanded' replaces *nātan* 'established', creating a paronomasia with *hammiṣwôt* 'the commandments'; *'el* 'for' replaces *bênô ûbên* 'between'; and *'et* replaces *bĕyad* 'through', changing the relationship among God, Israel, and Moses. In 26:46, there is a direct relationship between God and Israel, with Moses as an intermediary, almost an afterthought; in 27:34, Moses' rule as the indispensable intermediary is stressed (D. Stewart).

This comparison shows that the author of 27:34 was keenly aware of 26:46. Perhaps he wrote *miṣwôt* 'commandments' precisely because it was not in 26:46, and hence he regarded both verses as a combined subscript to the book of Leviticus. He could not, however, have had in mind only the H source, chaps. 17–26, since *tôrōt* 'rituals', as pointed out in the NOTE on 26:46, clearly refers to the sacrifice and impurity laws of chaps. 1–16. Alternatively, one may argue that the fact that the writer of 27:34 does not repeal the categories of 26:46, but adds his own category *miṣwôt* 'commandments', indicates his intention to have this subscript apply solely to chap. 27.

In any event, the repetition of *běhar sînay* 'Mount Sinai' shows that the editor is deliberately completing 26:46. Thus the two interpretations may not differ at all, but complement each other. The purpose of the second subscript (27:34) is, indeed, to provide a separate ending for chap. 27. However, it also supplements and completes the previous subscript (26:46) so that both effect a proper closure for the entire book, the *tôrat kōhănîm* 'the priestly manual', in distinction to the laws (not the narrative) in the book of Numbers, which, in the main, could be called *tôrat halěwiyyîm* 'the levitic manual' (see Introduction I M).

commanded Moses for the Israelites. ṣiwwâ ʾet-mōšeh ʾel-běnê yiśrāʾēl. This expression uniquely differs from the customary *ṣiwwâ běyad-mōšeh ʾel-běnê yiśrāʾēl* 'commanded the Israelites through Moses' (e.g., 36:13, the closure to the book of Numbers) in order to emphasize the indispensability of Moses as the mediator between God and Israel.

COMMENTS

A. The Organizing Principle of Leviticus 27 and a Hittite Confirmation

Lev 27 discloses a consistent criterion for all consecrations: offerable animals must be consumed on the altar; all other sancta, being unofferable, are therefore redeemable.

The rabbis also agree that anything destined for the altar may never be released from it (*t. Tem.* 1) and that it is even forbidden to consecrate an offerable animal specifically for nonsacrificial use in the sanctuary (*Sipra* Emor 7; *b. Tem.* 7b [bar.]), though the consecration takes effect and cannot be revoked (*b. Tem.* 6a [bar.]). However, they differ as to whether offerable animals must be sacrificed if the use of the animal by the sanctuary is not specified in the consecration (*m. Šek.* 4:7). R. Joshua and R. Papyas hold that males must be sacrificed as burnt offerings, and females must be sold as offerings of well-being and their sale price used to purchase burnt offerings. R. Eliezer holds that males should be sold as burnt offerings and females as offerings of well-being and their sale price accrue to the Temple treasury (*m. Tem.* 7:2). However, there is no disagreement that the animals themselves, since they are offerable, must be sacrificed on the altar—in accord with the biblical postulate.

This criterion can now be demonstrated as the postulate underlying all the redemption rules of Lev 27:

1. The redemption of consecrated animals (vv. 9–13) is informed by this postulate: only impure (unofferable) animals may be redeemed, whereas offerable ones must be sacrificed on the altar.
2. Consecrated land may be redeemed (vv. 14–19, 22–25) because land is unofferable. Only *ḥērem* consecrations (man, animal, or land, vv. 20–21; 28–29) may not be redeemed. However, if one objects that *ḥērem*-land is a nonofferable category and should therefore be redeemable, let him note the explanatory clause: "all *ḥērem* may neither be sold nor redeemed *because it is totally consecrated to YHWH*" (v. 28). In other words *ḥērem*-land *is distinguished from all other consecrated land* in that it remains the permanent property of the sanctuary.
3. It clearly holds true for firstborn animals: they must be sacrificed on the altar unless they are unofferable (i.e., impure), in which case they are redeemed or sold (v. 27; cf. Num 18:17).
4. Finally, it is the shamir stone that cleaves the two tithe laws (vv. 30–33) into logically differentiated categories: the unofferable crop tithe is redeemable, but the animal tithe, being offerable, is therefore irredeemable.

The underlying postulate of Lev 27 is also its organizing principle. The laws of redemption in Lev 27 fit into a graded system that is simple, logical, and clear:

1. *ḥērem* is "most sacred" and irredeemable.
2. *Offerable animals*, be they firstborn, tithes, or consecrations are also irredeemable.
3. *Nonofferable* consecrations, such as impure animals, land, houses, and crops (except when they are *ḥērem*) are redeemable.

Only one postulate has been needed to explain the gradations: offerable animals are irredeemable because they must be sacrificed on the altar, and nonofferable animals and other consecrations are always redeemable unless they are *ḥērem*.

There are two glaring omissions in the sancta list of Lev 27:

1. The *firstfruits*. The problem, I believe, is clarified when it is recalled that the subject matter of Lev 27 is legitimate desanctification by redemption or purchase. Since firstfruits, in biblical times, were only a token gift (e.g., a sheaf of barley, Lev 23:10; two loaves, Lev 23:17; a basket of fruit, Deut 26:1–4), it is inconceivable that anyone would want to go through the bother of redeeming them.
2. *The tithe of impure animals*. The omission is also easily explained: impure animals were not subject to the tithe. Whereas the firstborn of all animals

(and Israelites) are *inherently* sacred, the tithe possesses an *acquired* sanctity. By definition it falls only on pure animals. Practice substantiates theory since the animal tithe recorded in Hezekiah's reign consisted of "the tithe of cattle and sheep" (2 Chr 31:6). Moreover, this distinction seems to have obtained in the royal tithe as well. Samuel warns that the king will tithe (*yʿśr*) the flock, and he will *seize* (*yqḥ*) the donkeys (1 Sam 8:16–17).

Further light on Lev 27 is cast by comparing it with Lev 5:14–26. First, both pericopes deal with the problem of desanctification: Lev 5:14–26 with illegal desanctification or desecration (*maʿal*), whereas Lev 27:9–25. allows for legal desanctification for sanctuary property outside its precincts and for sanctuary animals not permitted inside. Moreover, for either desanctification a fine of one-fifth is imposed. The importance of this similar fine cannot be overemphasized, for it appears only where desanctification has taken place and/or the telltale root *ʾšm* occurs (Lev 22:14–16; Lev 5:20–26; Num 5:6–8). This one-fifth fine is the common denominator in desanctification, and it points to the conclusion that just as in Lev 27 it is a *charge* imposed for the *right* to convert the sacred into the profane, in Lev 5 it is a *penalty* for the *crime* of doing the same. The *ʾāšām*, which accompanies the monetary fine in Lev 5:14–16, is therefore the sacrifice for desecration: it is a reparation (*ʾāšām*) owing to God for accidentally depriving him of his sancta; it expiates on behalf of the wrongdoer that he may be forgiven (vv. 16b, 18b, 26b).

A passage in the Hittite text "Instructions to Temple Officials" throws unexpected light on another section of Lev 27:

> 15. (iv) [Further: You who are the plowmen of the gods, . . .]. The young animals which you, the plowmen, are supposed to have ready, have them promptly ready at the correct time. (5) Before a man has eaten from them, carry them promptly to the presence of the gods; let the gods not wait for them. If you delay them, you commit a sin. They will consult the oracles about you, and just as the gods, my lords, direct, so they will do to you. (10) They will fine you an ox and ten sheep and will pacify the mind of the gods.
>
> 16. Further: If you plant grain, and if the priest does not send you a man to plant the seed, you shall manage by yourselves. Should you plant much, (15) but tell the priest (that) it (was) little, or should the gods' field be thriving, but the field of the plowmen be barren and you call the gods' field yours, but your field is that of the god, or should you when you store the grain declare one half, but conceal the other half (20) and should you proceed to divide it afterward among yourselves and should it(!) afterward become known — you may get away with appropriating it from a man, but you cannot appropriate it from a god —, you will commit a sin. They will take all the grain away from you and put it in the magazines of the gods.
>
> 17. (25) Further: You who hold the plow-oxen of [the gods], if you sell a plow-ox, or kill it and consume it, (if) you appropriate it for yourselves (while

it belongs) to the god (saying): "It died from emaciation, or it broke (its legs), or it ran away, or the bull gored it" (30) and consume it yourselves, and it afterwards becomes known, you will replace that ox. If however it does not become known, you will go before the god. If you are acquitted, (it is due to) your patron god; if you are convicted, it is considered a capital sin for you.

18. Further: You who are the gods' cowherds (and) the gods' shepherds, (35) if there is a rite for any god at the time of bearing young and you are supposed to have ready for him either a calf, a lamb, a kid or *choice animals*, do not delay them! Have them ready at the right time; do not let the gods wait for them. Before a man eats of the young animals, (40) bring it promptly to the gods. Or if there is a "festival of the cup" for any god, (even) while they repair the cup, do not allow it to lapse; celebrate it for him. If you do not bring the young animals promptly to the gods, but eat first of them yourselves (45) or send them to your superiors, but it afterward becomes known, it is considered a capital sin for you. If it does not become known—at whatever time you will bring them, you will bring them with these words: "If we have given this young animal to ourselves first, (50) or have given it to our superiors, or to our wives, our children or to anyone else, we have offended the gods' feelings." Then you will drink dry the rhyton of the god of life. If you are found innocent, (it is due to) your patron god; but if you are found guilty, you will perish together with (55) your wives (and) your children.

19. Further: If you ever make a selection (of animals) and drive them up to the gods, your lords, the cowherd and the shepherd shall go with that selection. In the same condition in which they are selected from the pen (and) the fold, (60) shall they bring them to the gods. On the road they must not exchange them. But if any cowherd or shepherd does wrong on the road, exchanges either a fattened ox or a fattened sheep, or makes a deal or kills it and (65) they eat it up, and put in its place an emaciated (animal), and it becomes known, it is considered a capital sin for them; they have taken the gods' *most valued possession*. But if it does not become known, whenever they arrive they shall take the rhyton of the god of life from the cult stand, (70) and while doing so they shall declare as follows: "If we have for ourselves withheld from the mouth of the gods their *most valued possession*, and have given it to ourselves, or (if) we have sold it for ourselves, or if we have exchanged it, made a deal (75) and substituted in its place an emaciated (animal), then do thou, O god, pursue us together with our wives (and) our children on account of thy *most valued possession*!" (ANET 210)

The list of trespasses by the outside staff of the temple—the farmers and the herdsmen—corresponds in many ways to a similar list in Lev 27:9–31 (table 8). The differences between the lists are vast. One has already been discussed: the "Instructions" speaks solely of trespass on sancta, whereas Lev 27 deals with legitimate desanctification. But the differences should not obscure the similarities. Both texts deal with (1) desanctification (2) of property outside the temple (3) that has been dedicated, but (4) in the case of animals has been trespassed upon by

TABLE 8

SUBJECT	LEV 27	HITTITE "INSTRUCTIONS"
Animals	vv. 9–13	IV, 56–77
Fields	vv. 16–25	IV, 12–24
Firstborn	vv. 26–27 (32–33)	IV, 34–55
Firstfruits/grain	vv. 30–31	IV, 3–10

the same technique—substitution. This last similarity carries an ancillary boon. It clarifies the anomaly that Lev 27 prescribes no penalties for substitution save the confiscation of the substitute (Lev 27:10, 33). This provision is also paralleled in the Hittite "Instructions": he who substitutes for the god's grain with his own ends up by losing both (IV, 12–24). Does the silence of the biblical text imply that deliberate trespass with a sacred animal otherwise goes unnoticed by heaven? How is this possible, since unintentional trespass, surely a lesser crime, is penalized by both sacrificial and monetary fines (Lev 5:14–16)? Furthermore, is it conceivable that one who redeems or substitutes for a sacred tithe animal (v. 33) or—what constitutes a greater sacrilege—redeems or sells ḥērem property (v. 28) will be absolved by the Deity? The answer lies in the purpose of the biblical legislator of Lev 27. He assumes, with all biblical law, that all sacrilege is punished by God. Therefore, his only concern is to set down what constitutes legal and illegal desanctification as enforceable in human courts. It must therefore be assumed that the codifier of Lev 27 takes for granted that deliberate trespass is punishable with death by God and unintentional trespass is expiable with an ʾāšām.

This conclusion would accord with the tannaitic premise that trespass begins from the time of dedication, for offerable and nonofferable animals alike (*m. Tem.* 1:1; *m. Meʿil.* 2:1–9; 3:6; 4:1). However, the rabbis differ regarding the penalties: for deliberate substitution, they prescribe flogging (*m. Tem.* 1:1), as with all cases of trespass, but they exempt inadvertent substitution from any penalty (*b. Tem.* 17a; with the exception of R. Hezekia, *m. Tem.* 2:3) as well as substitution with nonofferable animals (*Sipra* Beḥuqotay, 9:2; *m. Tem.* 1:6).

Is the redemption postulate of Lev 27 unique to Israel? The Hittite "Instructions," I submit, operates with a similar premise. True, there is no legitimate desanctification in this Hittite text. Nonetheless, a distinction exists between its offerable and nonofferable sancta that clearly resembles our biblical postulate. It will be noted that the penalties for sancta trespass are not the same for the herdsman and the farmer, even for the same offense. When the herdsman is apprehended expropriating sancta (outside the sanctuary), he is put to death (ll. 34–68), in contrast to the farmer, who suffers only the confiscation of his grain (ll. 12–24). The only postulate that best explains this distinction is that the animal is offerable (indeed, the shepherd is actually apprehended while bringing the animals to the gods [i.e., to the altar], ll. 56–57, 60). It is therefore of a higher sanctity than the grain. The case of the farmer's plow-ox provides further support. Its appropriation is subject to the least penalty of all: if the farmer is apprehended by man, he has but to replace the animal (with no fine, ll. 25–33); if by the gods (i.e., the ordeal), he faces death, not with his family, as would be expected as a result of conviction by ordeal (ll. 55–77), but alone (ll. 25–33). But the entire family of the herdsman is put to death if he is convicted by oracle (ll. 55–77). Again, there is but one answer for the leniency to the farmer: since his plow-ox is not eligible for the altar, its trespass is a lesser crime.

Thus the many contributions that the Hittite "Instructions" has made to the understanding of Lev 27 have been reciprocated, even if in a slight way. The biblical distinction between offerable and nonofferable sancta in regard to redemption may also operate in the Hittite cult in regard to penalties for trespass.

In sum, the Hittite "Instructions for Temple Officials" provides vivid glimpses into the economy and management of the temple and its holdings: offerable animals grazing on sanctuary lands until called for by the priests for sacrifice on the altar; nonofferable animals being put up for sale or working sanctuary fields, the fields being tilled for grain and grapes to provide the daily loaves and libations for the gods.

Lev 27 predicates that the Israelite sanctuary effected a similar economy. It provides rules for the purchase or redemption of sancta (legitimate desanctification) and therefore complements Lev 5:14–16, which deals with the desecration of sancta (illegitimate desanctification). The organizing principle of Lev 27 is that offerable consecrations may never be legitimately desanctified, but nonofferable consecrations (with the exception of *ḥērem*) may be desanctified by their sale or redemption. The distinction between offerable and nonofferable sancta may also have prevailed in the Hittite cult.

B. Leviticus 27: Its Function and Date

There is general agreement that the logical closure of H with the blessings and curses of chap. 26 mandates the conclusion that chap. 27 is an appendix. On the one hand, it cannot precede chap. 25, since it assumes the jubilee laws of that chapter (see NOTES on vv. 16–24). On the other hand, it complements the jubilee laws of chap. 25: whereas one chapter (25) deals with the effect of the jubilee on property whose usufruct was sold, the other (chap. 27) deals with the effect of the jubilee on property whose usufruct was consecrated to God (D. Stewart).

Chap. 27 is of priestly origin, as demonstrated by its vocabulary: *'ăḥuzza'* (vv. 16, 21, 22, 24, 28), *hiplî' neder* (v. 2), *'erkĕkā* (vv. 2–8, 12–13, 15–19, 23, 25, 27), *māk* (v. 8), *hiśśîgâ yādô* (v. 8), *biqqēr* (v. 33; for a complete list, see Dillmann and Ryssel 1894–98: 684–85). It probably stems from the school of H, as indicated by its style: its introduction follows H usage elsewhere (17:1–2; 18:1–2; 19:1–2; 22:17–18; 23:1–2, 9–10; 25:1–2; Elliger 1966), and its use of extraneous, ostensibly redundant, phrases (e.g., vv. 9b, 11a; see the NOTES) is typical of H's quest for structural symmetry.

What is its function or, to word the question differently, why was it placed here? Scanning the scholarly literature produces four answers:

1. Chap. 27 is connected with chap. 26 through an association of ideas. Blessings and curses (chap. 26) are, in a sense, vows taken by God, and they are followed by vows taken by persons (chap. 27). Also, since vows are taken during times of stress, it is only logical that they should follow curses (Wenham 1979a). The problem with this answer is the assumption that all of chap. 27 deals with vows, whereas, in fact, they are limited to vv. 1–13.

2. Chap. 27 provides for "the funding of the sanctuary, in particular, to procure silver, not the actual commodities that were consecrated or pledged" (Levine 1989; Porter 1976 [personal communications]). This answer also must be rejected. No sanctuary could subsist on the currency provided by this chapter. Votive pledges and consecrations are purely voluntary and, therefore, undependable to meet an annual budget. True, the impure firstlings (v. 27) and the crop tithe (vv. 30–31) are mandatory and must be transferred to the sanctuary. But their redemption is voluntary, and given the 20 percent penalty, probably rare—again, no sure basis for guaranteed income.

Moreover, monetary exchange is not the innovation of chap. 27. The provisions for the *'āšām* offering specify a monetary equivalent, indeed, prefer it (see NOTE on "as a reparation offering," v. 15). That this proviso was practiced in pre-exilic times is shown by 2 Kgs 12:17: *kesep 'āšām wĕkesep ḥaṭṭā'ôt lō' yûbā' bêt YHWH lakkōhănîm yihyû* 'Money brought as a reparation offering or as purification offerings was not deposited in the House of YHWH; it went to the priests'. This verse, in fact, points the development in the opposite direction: a monetary *ḥaṭṭā't* turning into an animal *ḥaṭṭā't* (vol. 1.287–88). Above all, the entire pericope of 2 Kgs 12, which in every respect appears authentic, speaks of silver donated to the sanctuary from a variety of sources:

kōl kesep haqqŏdāšîm 'ăšer yûbā' bêt-YHWH kesep 'ôbēr 'îš kesep napšôt 'erkô kol-kesep 'ăšer ya 'āleh 'al leb-'îš lĕhābî' bêt YHWH

All the money, current money, brought into the House of the Lord as sacred donations—any money a man may pay as the money equivalent of person, or any other money that a man may be minded to bring to the house of the Lord (2 Kgs 12:5 NJPS)

Thus, in addition to corroborating the vows of chap. 27 pledged on persons (vv. 2–8), this verse speaks of—indeed, emphasizes—monetary sacred donations. If chap. 27 were intent on enumerating the monetary income available to the sanctuary, why were the wide-ranging voluntary sacred donations omitted, which, in Joash's time, sufficed to guarantee the *bedeq habbayit* 'the repair of the house' (2 Kgs 12:7, 8 [twice], 9)?

3. The redactor did not want to end the book on the dour note of curses; indeed, a similar reason may account for the addition of Deut 30–34 to the curses of chaps. 28–29 (Hartley 1992). Supporting this answer is the Masoretic requirement that other biblical books ending on a negative note—Isaiah, Malachi, Lamentations, and Kohelet—must be supplemented by a contiguous, more pos-

itive verse (*Sop.* 14.2). This suggestion, admittedly, is attractive, but the support for it, the Masora, is late.

4. "The Book of Leviticus concludes, as it opened, with a chapter of Sanctuary regulations—voluntary contributions to the upkeep of the sanctuary" (Hertz 1941: 2.547). Chap. 27 is "the latch . . . (it) locks on to the beginning by speaking both of things consecrated and things belonging to YHWH" (Douglas 1993a: 10). This solution makes sense in view of the attempt by the redactor(s) of Leviticus to compose the diverse material of Leviticus into a cohesive and orderly structure (see Introduction I E, M). Douglas (forthcoming) further suggests that Lev 27, rather than Lev 26, is the natural close to the book by regarding chaps. 25–27 as a unit whose common theme is redemption. Chap. 25 "only tells the people of Israel to free their brothers from servitude and grant redemption for the land. . . . [Chap. 27] extends the liberation theme. . . . God also will allow persons, land and animals dedicated to his service to be redeemed." These chapters flank chap. 26 to project the importance of covenant (Douglas, forthcoming). I would carry her suggestion further: whereas Lev 25 and 27 speak of Israel's redemptive responsibility, Lev 26 focuses on YHWH's responsibility, by virtue of the covenant, to redeem Israel (vv. 39–45; echoed by Smith 1996: 29).

A final question concerns the possible date of this chapter and, hence, of the closure of the book of Leviticus. Unfortunately, this chapter, in my opinion, sheds little light. Its only innovation is its tithe laws: the crop tithe belongs to the sanctuary, as does the animal tithe. However, that this claim of the sanctuary is ancient can be demonstrated (see COMMENT G), and the absence of the animal tithe in the tithe laws of the other legal collections, including Nehemiah (postexilic!), is attributable to its impractical demands (see INTRODUCTION to vv. 32–33). There is, however, one datum in this chapter that possibly points to the period of its composition. The valuation price of 50 shekels for an adult male (v. 3) corresponds with Assyrian slave-market prices during the eighth and seventh centuries (Kitchen 1995: 52, citing Johns 1924: 3.542–46). It is thus possible that the tax imposed by King Pul of Assyria on Menahem, king of North Israel (eighth century), of 50 shekels per "every man of means" (2 Kgs 15:20) was also based on the going rate for slaves. There can be no doubt, however, that this figure hardly comports with that in the exilic and postexilic periods, when the price of slaves soared to twice that amount (Dandamaev 1984: 195–206). These facts undermine any attempt to attribute the composition of this chapter to a late H tradent. Thus reason no. 4, which can withstand criticism, looms more attractively (see Introduction I E, M). In sum, the most that can plausibly be conjectured is that since parts of H are demonstrably exilic (see NOTES on 23:2–4; 26:33b–35), this chapter, whose placement (but not its composition) is due to the redactor, was also put in its present place during the exile.

C. Oaths, Vows, and Consecrations

The common denominator of oaths, vows, and consecrations is that all are statements that invoke the name of God. Oaths are of two types: assertory and promissory. Assertory oaths are taken to clear oneself of a charge—for example, of misappropriating property (Exod 22:7; Lev 5:20–25). Promissory oaths, the more prevalent type, impose an obligation on the oath taker—for example, David's reputed oath that Solomon would reign after him (1 Kgs 1:13, 17, 30). A covenant, by definition, is a promissory oath (e.g., Gen 21:22–32; 31:44–53). The promissory oath (*šĕbûʿat ʾissār*) is restricted to an abstention and is exemplified in the case of a married woman who denies to herself (and probably to her husband) a pleasurable (or necessary) act (Num 30). Oaths are generally made in the name of the Deity: *nišbaʿ ba-YHWH* 'swear by YHWH'. But when the oath entails a promise to God (i.e., God is the recipient of the promissory oath), the term used is *nišbaʿ la-YHWH* 'swear to YHWH' (e.g., 2 Chr 15:14). In this case, the oath approximates the vow, which is also made "to YHWH" (e.g., Num 30:3). Thus it is possible for the Psalmist to say of David: "how he swore to YHWH [*nišbaʿ la-YHWH*], vowed [*nādar*] to the Mighty One of Jacob" (Ps 132:2).

Vows are promissory by definition, but they differ from promissory oaths in that they are conditional: they are to be fulfilled, for example, if Jacob returns home safely (Gen 28:20–21), if Israel is victorious over the Canaanites (Num 21:2), if Jephthah is granted victory over the Ammonites (Judg 11:30–31), if Hannah is granted a son (1 Sam 1:11), and if Absalom returns home safely (2 Sam 15:8). Moreover, all vows in the Bible are consecrations to the sanctuary. Thus, in the cases just cited, Jacob promises to build a sanctuary, Israel consecrates the Canaanite spoils as *ḥērem* (see COMMENT F), Jephthah sacrifices his daughter, Hannah dedicates her son to the sanctuary as a Nazirite, and Absalom offers sacrifices at the Hebron sanctuary. Ostensibly, the Nazirite vow resembles the negative promissory oath, since the Nazirite incurs a set of abstentions. However, it is the positive aspect of his status that is underscored in his vow. As one who is "consecrated to YHWH" (Num 6:5, 8), he belongs to God, as with any consecrations, for the duration of his vow. Moreover, the Nazirite has also vowed a minimum number of sacrifices if he completes his Nazirite period without mishap (Num 6:21). Therefore, the text is correct in viewing the Nazirite pledge as a vow and not as an oath. The context of Absalom's vow is also instructive: "Absalom said to the king, 'Let me go to Hebron and fulfill a vow I made to YHWH. For your servant made a vow when I lived in Geshur of Aram: If YHWH ever brings me back to Jerusalem I will worship YHWH [in Hebron'" (LXX)] (2 Sam 15:7–8). Thus the term "vow" not only automatically denotes a consecration to YHWH, but can be directed, as in Absalom's case, to a specific sanctuary. A singular example where the promissory oath and vow are fused is the case of King David, of whom the Psalmist says: "O Lord, remember in David's favor his extreme self-denial [*ʿunnôtô*], how he swore to YHWH [*nišbaʿ la-YHWH*], vowed [*nādar*] to the Mighty One of Jacob" (Ps 132:2). David denied himself rest (his oath) until he provided a resting place for the Ark (his vow).

Furthermore, the examples cited demonstrate that dedications stemming from a vow need not be animals, but can also be persons (Jephthah's daughter, Samuel) and even a sanctuary (for the Ark, Jacob's Bethel). To prevent the tragic case of Jephthah and to discourage the proliferation of Nazirites, priestly law provides that vows of persons (except as a Nazirite) must be redeemed by their fixed monetary worth, even allowing for a reduction of the evaluation in cases of indigence (Lev 27:1–8). That such vows were popular in early Israel is evidenced by King Jehoash's reference to monetary contributions to the Temple of Jerusalem that stem exclusively from "the money equivalent of persons" (2 Kgs 12:5). This kind of votive dedication also obtained elsewhere in the ancient Near East. A Ugaritic epic declares: "There [Ke]ret the Noble vo[ws]: As Asherah of Tyre exists, As Elath of Sidon. If Hurriya to my house I take, Bring the lass into my court, Her double I'll give in silver, And her treble in gold" (text cited in INTRODUCTION to vv. 3–7; see also RS 24.266. v. 99, in Margalit 1981: 78). Vowing the monetary equivalent of persons is attested at the end of the Second Temple period as well: "Once the mother of Yurmatia (or Domitia) said, 'I vow my daughter's weight,' and she went up to Jerusalem and weighed her and paid her weight in gold" (*m. 'Arak.* 5:1). That all vows, biblical and ancient Near Eastern alike, are conditional has been convincingly demonstrated by Cartledge (1992).

Consecrations, composing the third category, are like vows in that they are gifts to the sanctuary. However, they are neither future nor conditional but become effective the moment they are uttered. See, for example, the *ḥērem* consecration of Jericho (Josh 6:17–19) and the story of the consecrated silver (Judg 17:3). The following sacred gifts, according to the wording of the text, were consecrated before they were brought to the sanctuary: first-ripe and -processed fruits (Num 18:12–13), tithes (Lev 27:30–33), and most sacred offerings (Lev 6:18; 7:1–2). Thus the tannaitic dictum "oral dedication is equivalent to transfer [to the sanctuary]" (*m. Qidd.* 1:6; *t. Qidd.* 1:9) prevails in the Bible as well (see COMMENT D).

The regular occurrence of vows in the sacrificial laws indicates that a vow was usually fulfilled by a sacrifice (Lev 7:16; 22:18, 21, 23; 23:38; Num 15:3, 8; 29:39; Deut 12:6, 11, 17, 26). The prominent role of vows in the life of the individual is even better evinced by their frequent mention in Psalms (22:26; 50:14; 61:6; 65:2; 66:13; 116:14, 18). The popularity of vows is also attested by admonitions in law, wisdom teaching, and prophetic rebuke concerning their potential abuse. A harlot would invite a prospective client to the sacrificial feast that she had prepared in fulfillment of her vows (Prov 7:14), and Deuteronomy finds it necessary to warn that "you shall not bring the fee of a whore or the pay of a dog [i.e., a male prostitute] into the house of YHWH your God in fulfillment of any vow" (Deut 23:19). Vows were made to the Queen of Heaven (Jer 44:25) and, presumably, to other gods. The concern in the biblical literature, however, is that impulsive vows may go unfulfilled and thus arouse the divine wrath: "When you make a vow to God, do not delay to fulfill it. For He has no pleasure in fools; what you vow, fulfill. It is better not to vow at all than to vow and not fulfill. Don't let your mouth bring you into disfavor, and don't plead before the messenger [of God] that it was an error; else God may be angered by your talk and destroy your possessions" (Koh 5:3–5; see Deut 23:22–24; Prov 20:25).

The rabbis evolved an elaborate procedure for annulling vows: they looked for circumstances that would have discouraged the individual from making the vow if he or she had been aware of them at the time. Although they took for granted the right to annul vows (*m. Ned.* 2:1, 5, etc.), they readily admitted that "the procedure for annulling vows hovers in the air and has nothing to support it" (*m. Ḥag.* 1:8). They were well aware of the example of Jephthah (Judg 11:30–35) and of others (see Josh 9:19–20; Judg 21:7) whose vows and oaths, although made in error, could not be annulled. The absence of annulment in those cases, for which there were rabbinic grounds, is attributed to the ignorance of the vow maker. The rabbis set forth the grounds for the annulment of vows: "Four kinds of vows the sages have declared not to be binding: vows of incitement, vows of exaggeration, vows made in error, and vows of constraint" (*m. Ned.* 3:1). There is a basic distinction between the annulment of a woman's vows by her father or husband and the annulment of vows by the rabbis. In the former case, the vows are annulled henceforth; in the latter, the vows are retroactively uprooted so that the sage can say, "The vow or oath is nonexistent" (*y. Ned.* 10:8; *b. Ket.* 74b; *y. Ket.* 7:7). The Karaites also allow for the annulment of mistaken vows (Bashyazi 1966: chaps. 7, 16), but their biblical (and only) support (1 Sam 14:44–45; 25:22, 33) is untenable. Saul would have put Jonathan to death as a result of his oath (not a vow, 1 Sam 14:24) were he not prevented from doing so by his army. Similarly, Abigail's intervention prevented (rather, pursuaded) David from carrying out his oath (also not a vow, 1 Sam 25:22, 34).

D. Sanctifications

Sanctification means the transition from the realm of the profane to that of the holy. It is invariably expressed by the root *qdš* in all its conjugations. There is sanctification of time, space, persons, and objects.

1. Of Time

Certain time is inherently holy because it was sanctified by God—for example, the sabbath (Gen 2:3), the festivals (Lev 23:4–38; Neh 8:9–11), the jubilee (Lev 25:12). Israel is enjoined to sanctify these holy periods by adhering to the special rules that govern them.

2. Of Space

The land of Canaan is YHWH's land and therefore is holy (Exod 15:13; Isa 11:9). This is the premise of the Holiness Source, which states that offenses against God pollute the land (Lev 18:27–28), and hence all its inhabitants, including the resident alien, must observe God's prohibitions (Lev 17:8–12; 18:26; 20:2; 24:16). All other land is impure (Josh 22:19; Amos 7:17), except where a theophany has occurred (Exod 3:5; Josh 5:15).

The doctrine that Jerusalem is the holy city par excellence has its origins in First Isaiah, who proclaims Jerusalem as the divine residence (Isa 8:18; 18:7; 30:29). Its future inhabitants will *eo ipso* be sanctified (Isa 4:3). Jeremiah predicts that the future Jerusalem will extend beyond its former limits and will be "holy to YHWH," despite the inclusion of burial ground (31:38–40). Since recent excavations in the old Jewish quarter have unearthed a city wall dating to the time of Hezekiah or Manasseh, and excavations in the nearby Tyropoeon Valley have divulged empty tombs of approximately the same period, it seems safe to conclude that Jerusalem had expanded to three or four times its former size. It was by then conceived of as a holy city, for its dead were apparently disinterred and removed beyond its new walls (the kings excepted, Ezek 43:7b–9; cf. 'Abot R. Nat. B. 39). By the time of the Babylonian Exile, it had received the appellation "the holy city" (Isa 48:2; 52:1).

3. Of Persons

Certain persons become holy when they undergo consecration. Priests are holy, according to P, because they received the most-sacred oil of anointment (Exod 30:30–32; 40:13 ff.) in conjunction with a sacrificial service. The high priest Aaron's head is doused with the oil before the service, and his sons are sprinkled with the oil after the service (Exod 29:7, 21; Lev 8:12, 30; vol. 1.542–68).

In the person of the Nazirite, the layman attains quasi-priestly status, for he is "holy to YHWH" (Num 6:8; cf. Philo, *Laws* 1.249). Indeed, by his taboos, the Nazirite approximates the higher sanctity of the high priest, since he may not contaminate himself by contact with the dead, even of his immediate family (Num 6:7; cf. Lev 21:11), and, like the high priest, the head is the focus of his sanctity (Num 6:11b; cf. Exod 29:7). Since, however, the Nazirite period (in P) is for only a fixed term, the parallel to sanctified land (see below) is more instructive. Both terms are limited, the land reverting to its owner at the jubilee (Num 6:13; cf. Lev 27:21). Both periods can be terminated earlier, the Nazirite's by contamination (Num 6:9–12) and the land's by redemption (Lev 27:16–19). In such cases, a penalty is exacted: the Nazirite pays a reparation offering to the sanctuary (vol. 1.279–81), and the land owner pays a 20 percent surcharge to the sanctuary.

All pentateuchal sources agree that the people Israel is innately holy or is enjoined to holiness. In JE, all that is involved is refraining from eating flesh torn by a beast (Exod 22:30), whereas in P and H, Israel's sanctification can be achieved through a comprehensive behavior pattern that embraces fine points of ethics as well as ritual (e.g., Lev 19). D, however, mentions Israel's sanctification only in connection with ritual prohibitions (idolatry, Deut 7:5–6; certain mourning rites, 14:1–2; forbidden foods, 14:3–21). Jeremiah uses Israel's sanctity to weave a haggadic midrash to condemn its enemies (2:3), whereas Ezra fashions a halakhic midrash to condemn intermarriages (9:2). The term "consecrate" is also used of a prophet (Jer 1:5), but its use is metaphorical.

4. Of Objects

A. THE SANCTUARY. The Tabernacle, its sancta, and the priestly clothing are sanctified with the anointment oil (Exod 30:25–29; 40:9–11; Lev 8:10–12, 30). If the polluted altar has to be resanctified, the blood of the purification offering is sprinkled on it seven times (Lev 16:19). The Tabernacle sancta, being "most-sacred," sanctify other objects on contact (Exod 29:37; 30:29), but they are not contagious to person. This also holds true of the most-sacred offerings: the *minḥâ* and the *ḥaṭṭā't* (Lev 6:11, 20), and probably the *'āšām* and *'ōlâ*. Ezekiel, however, affirms that the sancta—including the priestly clothing—are contagious even to persons (44:19; 46:20). The Temple of Solomon was probably consecrated on its completion, though the verb *qdš* is used only in connection with the extension of the sanctity of the altar into the court in order to accommodate the overwhelming number of offerings (1 Kgs 8:64 [= 2 Chr 7:7]).

B. THE SACRED GIFTS. Three categories of objects become sanctuary property by virtue of sanctification: (1) objects whose sanctity is inherent, such as firstborn males of female animals and human beings (Exod 13:2, 12 ff.; Lev 27:26; see COMMENT F), first-ripe fruits (e.g., Neh 10:36) and first-processed fruits (Num 15:20; 18:12), and the fourth-year yield of fruit trees (Lev 19:24); (2) objects whose sanctification is required, such as tithes of crops and pure animals (Lev 27:30–33; Deut 26:13); and (3) objects whose sanctification is voluntary, partially listed in Lev 27, such as votive dedications of person (rather, their fixed value; vv. 1–8) and animals (vv. 9–13), consecrations of houses (vv. 14–15) and fields (vv. 16–25), and proscriptions of persons, animals, and property (vv. 28–29). The underlying postulate is that if the object is permissible as an offering on the altar, it is irredeemable; if it is not permissible, it is redeemable, except for *ḥērem* (something to be "utterly destroyed"), which may never be redeemed (see COMMENT F). The sanctifications recorded in Lev 27 are the result of individual initiative, but more likely the sanctuary received most of them as spoils of war (e.g., Num 31). Historical sources also attest that captured vessels were dedicated to the Temple (2 Sam 8:10–12; 1 Kgs 7:51; 15:15; 1 Chr 26:27–28), including precious weapons (2 Sam 8:7; 1 Kgs 14:26 ff.; 2 Kgs 11:10).

5. Inception

When did the sanctification of an object take effect? It took effect not when it was brought to the sanctuary, as might be expected, but when a declaration of dedication was made (contra Kugler 1997: 11). This is the only possible deduction from the consecration of Jericho (Josh 6:17–19) and the story of the consecrated silver (Judg 17:3). Also the wording of the following sacred gifts indicates that they were sanctified before they were brought to the sanctuary: firstripe and first-processed fruits (Num 18:12–13), tithes (Lev 27:30–33), and mostsacred offerings (Lev 6:18; 7:1 ff.). The tannaitic dictum "Oral dedication is equivalent to transfer" (*m. Qidd.* 1.6; *t. Qidd.* 1.9) prevails in the Bible as well. Within the sanctuary, sanctification could take place by means of the elevation offering (vol. 1.461–82).

6. Purification as Sanctification

The ablutions prescribed before a theophany effect sanctification (e.g., Exod 19:10, 14, 22; Num 11:18; Josh 3:5; 7:13; 1 Sam 16:5). In these cases, the ablutions take place the day before God appears, except for the theophany at Sinai, whose uniqueness requires two days of prior sanctification. The Priestly Code always enjoins severely contaminated persons to undergo ablutions the day before they appear in the sanctuary with their required offerings (the gonorrheic, Lev 15:13–14; the scale-diseased person, Lev 14:9 ff.; etc.). It is highly suggestive that "nonpriestly purification before a theophany, in which God appears in the presence of the people, is analogous to priestly purification before appearing before God" (B. S. Schwartz, personal communication). However, P never designates this process by the root *qdš*, which it reserves exclusively for the sanctification of objects and persons (see above). The historical and prophetic books attest that solemn gatherings and fasts are also designated by *qdš* (e.g., 2 Kgs 10:20; Joel 1:14; 2:15–17), as is the call to war (e.g., "prepare," Jer 6:4; Joel 4:9 [H]; "declare," Mic 3:5), originating in the sanctity of the war camp so that God would abide within (cf. Deut 23:11–15).

E. The Firstborn

The firstborn male of human beings and animals is usually called *běkôr*, less frequently *peṭer reḥem*, and, in the case of human beings, occasionally *rab* (Gen 25:23) and *rē'šît 'ônî* (Gen 49:3). The denominative *bikker* (*Pi'el*) is also found (Deut 21:16). The animal firstborn is always that of the mother. For human beings, *běkôr* can be either of the mother or of the father or even a metaphor (e.g., Exod 4:22); *peṭer reḥem* 'the first issue of the womb' refers exclusively to the firstborn of the mother; the remaining terms refer to only the firstborn of the father. In most instances, it is the firstborn of the father. The firstborn of the mother is mentioned for three limited purposes: (1) to stress the child's sanctity (e.g., Exod 34:19), (2) to emphasize that he is not his father's firstborn (e.g., 1 Chr 2:50), and (3) to underscore the mother's status at the time of his birth (Deut 25:6; cf. Jos. *Life* 76; Luke 2:7).

The genealogical lists point to the importance of the firstborn male. He is first in the list, even if the genealogical line is given for all the sons (e.g., 1 Chr 6:1–14). The family line is continued through the firstborn, even if other sons are named (1 Chr 7:1–4); at times, the firstborn is the only one named (Gen 11:12–13). Daughters, even the firstborn (*běkîrâ*), are listed at the end (1 Sam 14:49). More significantly, the status of the firstborn is indicated by the formula "father / mother / brother / sister of" (Gen 36:22), indicating that he is the point of reference for the rest of the family.

The hegemony of the firstborn is reflected in the early narratives (Gen 27:1–45; 37:22; cf. 29:32), as in other literature of the ancient Near East (e.g., *Širpu* 2.35, 89; 4:58; 8:59 [Reiner 1958]). More important, it is concretized in his rights of inheritance: in Israel, the law of Deut 21:15–17 ordains that the firstborn should receive double the portion allotted to each of his brothers (*pî šěnayim* means "two portions" of the estate), a division that also obtained in the ancient Near East (MAL B.1). But other systems are also attested—for example, one-tenth more, the entire inheritance, the same amount. D. N. Freedman (personal communication) opines that the oldest son gets a special portion (*rē'šît*) and then shares equally with the rest of the heirs in the remaining portion of the estate.

The polemical wording of Deut 21:15–17 indicates that in practice, fathers discriminated in favor of other sons. Indeed, the right of the father to transfer the birthright is evidenced among Israel's neighbors (for Mesopotamia [Nuzi], see Lacheman 1962; for Egypt, see Mattha 1958). According to Mendelsohn (1959), preferential status for the eldest son was practiced only in agricultural or semi-nomadic societies such as Nuzi, Middle Assyria, Syria, and Israel, whereas in economically well-developed civilizations of Lipit-Ishtar (Neo-Sumerian period) and Hammurabi (First Babylonian dynasty), the younger brothers were given equal status with the eldest. In Israel, however, though a younger brother might gain the birthright (běkôrâ), he never acquired the title běkôr (cf. rō'š 'chief', 1 Chr 26:10–11; nāgîd 'chief prince', 2 Chr 11:22). Thus the transfer of the birthright—even without the title—is generally recorded as taking place solely by the intervention of God and not by the whim of the father or intrigue of the brothers (e.g., Jacob, Gen 25:23; Ephraim, Gen 48:19; David, 1 Chr 28:4; Solomon, 1 Kgs 2:15). In the ancient Near East as well, Ashurbanipal, the youngest son, supports his right to the throne because of divine election (Parapola 1970: 1.letter 132).

The laws declaring the sanctity of the firstborn of the mother consist of a general statement (Exod 13:1–2; 13:12a; 34:19a; Num 18:15) and a threefold application: to pure animals, impure animals, and human beings (Exod 13:12b–13; 34:19b–20; Num 18:16–18; cf. Exod 22:28–29; Lev 27:26–27; Deut 15:19–23). In the case of the pure animals, the law codes differ: in JE (Exod 13:12–13; 22:28–29; 34:19), the firstborn is transferred (nātan, he'ĕbîr) to YHWH, sanctified either as an 'ōlâ or as the šĕlāmîm of the priest; P holds that it is the priest's (Num 18:17); and D maintains that it is the owner's (Deut 15:20). The law codes again differ in the case of the impure animal: JE requires that only the ass be ransomed, but P extends the ransom requirement to all impure animals, while D is silent. Here, however, the difference may reflect socioeconomic changes: in JE's time, the ass may have been the only domestically impure animal (cf. Ibn Ezra on Exod 13:13). The ransom also varies. In JE, it is a sheep. However, P's law of Lev 27:26–27 stipulates that it is ransomed (pādâ) by its worth as evaluated (bě-'erkěkā) by the priest, but if the owner redeems it (gā'al), he adds one-fifth to its value. Since the value of an ass is greater than that of a sheep, the change from JE to P favors the sanctuary.

The verbs used in the laws of the human firstborn, "nātan, qiddēš, he'ĕbîr to YHWH," as well as the use of pādâ 'ransom', clearly indicate that the firstborn male of the mother is the property of the Deity. This may be a literary reflex of an ancient rule whereby the firstborn was expected to care for the burial and worship of his deceased parents. Traces of ancestor worship are found in Mesopotamia: the firstborn inherits the family gods at Nuzi and the cultic objects at Nippur; the kudduru curses include lack of a son to pour a libation after death. Ancestor worship is also attested in Egypt, among pre-Islamic Arabs, and popularly in Israel (Isa 8:19; cf. Deut 26:14). Indeed, Samuel's dedication to the Shilo sanctuary by his mother, Hannah, may reflect an older tradition that the firstborn male was set apart for priestly service. Thus the Bible may be preserving the memory of the firstborn bearing a sacred status (Rashbam on Exod

13:2; see chap. 18, COMMENT B), and the replacement of the firstborn by the Levites (Num 3:11–13, 40–51; 8:14–18) may reflect the establishment of a professional priestly class (Milgrom 1990a: 17–18). The ransom of the firstborn is unspecified in JE, but P sets it at 5 shekels (Num 18:16; cf. Lev 27:6). There is no support for the theory that the firstborn was originally offered as a sacrifice. The biblical texts (e.g., Exod 13:2; 22:28b) may imply that *theoretically* the firstborn should be sacrificed, but YHWH rejects human sacrifice (Gen 22) and insists on the alternative of ransom. This conclusion can also be deduced from the etiology of the firstborn tradition that the firstborn of Israel would also have perished at the hands of "the Destroyer" had it not been for YHWH's intervention (Exod 12:23; cf. Schwartz 1987: 249–50, n. 36).

D. N. Freedman (personal communication) asks whether Ezek 20:25–26, stating that YHWH deliberately gave Israel bad laws in order to induce it to sacrifice the firstborn males, is not in itself testimony that many people were convinced that YHWH did desire, and on occasion even demand, human sacrifice. He is right, and I said as much in chap. 18, COMMENT B. I presented three explicit laws (Exod 13:2; 22:28–29; Num 18:15a) and an additional prophetic statement (Mic 6:7b) that ostensibly point to the same conclusion. Moreover, as noted by Greenberg (1983a: 36a), the polemic against child sacrifice *to YHWH* in Deut 12:29–31; Jer 7:31; 19:5; 32:35 (NOTE on "and thereby not desecrate the name of your God: I YHWH," 18:21) clearly indicates that at the end of the First Temple period it was widely practiced. This, indeed, is what Ezek 20:25–26 is saying. The people have *misinterpreted* God's laws, for child sacrifice is a practice "which I never commanded and never entered my mind" (Jer 32:35; see Jer 7:31, and NOTE on 18:21).

F. The Ḥērem

Stern's (1991) monograph on *ḥērem* is comprehensive, insightful, and, in its major thesis, convincing. He focuses on the mythopoetic background of the oldest form of the *ḥērem*, the war-*ḥērem*:

> "The struggle for land and the willingness to fight for it (and one's freedom) were taken up into the emotional and intellectual life of the people and transformed by myth into a chaos vs. order paradigm or set of paradigms. A great biblical result of such myth-forming process is Joshua 6, a cosmogonic myth in which order wins over chaos (the enemy forces) . . . the struggle for land was equally an effort to create "sacred space," a space consecrated by the presence of God" (Stern 1991: 226).

This thesis, in my opinion, effectively resolves the paradoxical antimony of destruction and consecration represented in the *ḥērem* by understanding it as a process of consecration through destruction. *Ḥērem* does not evoke a crusader or "holy war" mentality. *Ḥērem* involves acting as the Deity does: it is an act of creation, bringing order out of chaos.

The term *ḥērem* is generally rendered as "proscription or ban." It can be defined as "the status of that which is separated from common use or contact either because it is proscribed as an abomination to God or because it is consecrated to Him" (Greenberg 1971d). In effect, it is the ultimate in dedication. In the priestly view, *ḥērem* may never be redeemed: *ḥērem* land belongs permanently to the sanctuary; *ḥērem* animals, if pure, must be sacrificed on the altar and, if impure, become—like land—the permanent property of the sanctuary; and *ḥērem* persons (i.e., Canaanite slaves, prisoners of war) must be killed.

Although it is designated within the category of most-sacred offerings, *ḥērem* proves to be anomalous. It is called "most sacred" in Lev 27:28 only to indicate that the object cannot be redeemed. In other respects, however, it is certainly not "most sacred," for both the priests and their families are allowed to partake of this offering (cf. Num 18:11–19 with 18:9–10).

Ḥērem objects may apply not only to animals, but also to lands and human beings. Any animal, whether pure or impure, may become "devoted," in contrast to dedicated impure animals, which may be redeemed. Furthermore, *ḥērem* fields, as distinguished from all other dedicated lands, remain the permanent property of the sanctuary. (Note that despite their holy status, *ḥērem* lands may be farmed by the priests, and the produce may be used by them.) With respect to humans placed under the *ḥērem*, there is to be no redemption (Lev 27:29), which means that there is no alternative whatsoever to death. (For an excellent example of this practice, see 1 Sam 15:3, 33, noting the cultic implications of v. 33: "And Samuel cut Agag down before YHWH at Gilgal.")

The *ḥērem* is found in other narrative sections (Josh 7:1; 22:20; 1 Chr 2:7; 1 Kgs 20:42), and in addition to Lev 27:28 and Num 18:14, it is adduced in three other legal documents (Exod 22:19; Deut 7:25–26; Ezek 44:29).

Violation of the *ḥērem* is classified as *maʿal* (Josh 7:1; 22:20), a legal term denoting a sin against God. More specifically, *maʿal* means "trespassing upon the divine realm either by poaching on his sancta or breaking his covenant oath; it is a lethal sin which can destroy both the offender and his community" (Milgrom 1976a: 21). Although the *ḥērem* was also practiced at Mari, it differed in crucial ways from this case. In the Bible, the *ḥērem* belongs to God, not the king; the death penalty is unquestionably irrevocable; and *ḥērem* property may not be used by the laity or soldiers.

The *ḥērem* injunction of Deuteronomy (Deut 20:16–17) is unique in the pentateuchal sources. Exod 23:20–33 comes closest by demanding the total expulsion of the indigenous population. But expulsion is not extermination. True, *ḥērem* is enjoined once in the Covenant Code: "Whoever sacrifices to a god other than YHWH shall be proscribed" (Exod 22:19). However, as this injunction is addressed solely to the Israelites (as is the entire Covenant Code; cf. *běʿammĕkā*, Exod 22:27), it cannot refer to the residents of Canaan. Clearly, as Greenberg (1971) has pointed out, the hand of the Deuteronomist has been at work. He has taken both the expulsion law of Exod 23:20–33, directed against the inhabitants of Canaan, and the *ḥērem* law of Exod 22:19, directed against the individual Israelite, and fused them into a new law that applies *ḥērem* to all idolaters, Israelites (cf. Deut 13:13–19), and non-Israelites alike, as well as to their sancta (Deut 7:5, 25–26).

The Deuteronomist, however, does not claim that his law is innovative. To the contrary, he says, "as YHWH your God has commanded you" (Deut 20:17), implying that his *ḥērem* is based on an unambiguous and unimpeachable source (Milgrom 1976h: 6–9). This source is nowhere in Scripture. Nonetheless, there is evidence that at least once in Israel's history, the Deuteronomist's *ḥērem* against the Canaanites was actually invoked. Let us first bear in mind his definition of *ḥērem*: the population is destroyed as well as its cult objects, but its cities and property may be expropriated as spoils (Deut 2:35; 3:7). Now it is true that this is precisely the kind of *ḥērem* that Joshua frequently carried out in his conquests. It was imposed on Makkedah, Libnah, Lachish, Eglon, Debir, and other towns in both the south and the north (Josh 10:28–40; 11:10–20). However, the possibility must be reckoned with that the record of the conquest has been made to conform to the deuteronomic *ḥērem*, a possibility that is reinforced when we notice that the execution of *ḥērem* continues with the formula, "as YHWH commanded" (e.g., Josh 10:40; 11:12, 15, 20). Then, too, every example of *ḥērem* that stems from an indisputably non-deuteronomic source actually differs from the deuteronomic conception: Arad (Num 21:1–9) and Jericho (Josh 6:17–19) are subject to total *ḥērem*; Ai and Hazor are burned (Josh 8:2, 28; 11:11–13).

Does this mean, then, that the Deuteronomist's *ḥērem* is indeed a midrash, "a tendentious revision of history," and that his claim of "as YHWH your God commanded you" is a fiction (Greenberg 1971)?

I submit that there is one clear historical precedent for his *ḥērem*: Saul and the Gibeonites. Saul attempted to exterminate the Gibeonites (2 Sam 21:1). That some Gibeonites succeeded in escaping to Gath (2 Sam 4:3) underscores the fact that their only haven was outside Saul's jurisdiction, in non-Israelite territory. Saul confiscated their real property and divided it among his fellow Benjaminite officers (1 Sam 22:7). Thus Saul's campaign against the Gibeonites follows the precise rules of the deuteronomic *ḥērem*: the extermination and despoliation of the inhabitants of Canaan. It is clear, when we consider the total picture of Saul's personality and program, that his motives were primarily religious and not economic (although the force of the latter should not be discounted). He stamps out illegitimate divination (1 Sam 28:3, 9), purifies the cult (1 Sam 14:32–35), and resorts to prophetic ecstasy (1 Sam 10:10–12; 19:23–24). Indeed, the text itself labels his persecution of the Gibeonites by the root *qnʾ*, implying religious fanaticism. Thus it is hardly likely that a God-fearing king would have undertaken the genocide of the Gibeonites unless he felt compelled to do so by divine imperative.

True, Saul is twice portrayed as a rebel against YHWH (1 Sam 13:13; 15:9 ff.). But these texts stem from a Davidide (that is, anti-Saulide) author. The former text probably mirrors Samuel's attempt to contain Saul's desire to officiate at national sacrifices, a royal prerogative attested for later kings (e.g., 1 Kgs 8:63–64; 2 Kgs 16:15b), and the latter text may in fact be an example of Saul's obedience to God, not his rebelliousness. For it should be remembered that *ḥērem* animals fit for the altar need not be put to the sword, but may be sacrificed. Indeed, according to the priestly rules, they must be sacrificed (Lev 27:28; cf. Num 18:14; Ezek 44:29, which include nonsacrificial proscriptions). The fact that Samuel does not accuse Saul of sparing Agag and actually slaughters Agag as a sacrifice ("before YHWH," 1 Sam 15:33), also in keeping with the priestly ḥērem (Lev 27:29), is an indication that this is probably what Saul intended to carry out himself. Moreover, that Saul had the "cheap and worthless" animals destroyed on the spot (1 Sam 15:9) and retained only the best animals accords with the cultic requirement that sacrificial animals must be unblemished (Lev 22:19). There is, therefore, no reason to doubt Saul's statement that "the troops spared the choicest of the sheep and oxen for sacrificing to YHWH your God" (1 Sam 15:15). Further evidence that this verse harbors Saul's true intention is that he spared only "sheep and oxen," a fact confirmed by his antagonist Samuel (1 Sam 15:14): Saul took back with him *sacrificial* animals, but presumably destroyed animals ineligible for the altar, such as donkeys and camels (1 Sam 15:3). Thus Saul's assertion that "I have fulfilled YHWH's command" (1 Sam 15:13) can be fully justified, and it is only the anti-Saulide writer who misrepresents his valid execution of the ḥērem as an act of heresy.

Stern (1991), however, takes issue with my admittedly "unorthodox" interpretation (originally stated in 1990a: 430). His arguments will be answered point by point:

1. "The idea that Saul was afraid of the people (1 Sam 15:24) seems questionable in view of his previous dealings with them; cf. the episode of eating on the blood, in 1 Sam 14:31ff., where he upbraided the people with the cry, 'sinners!' " (Stern 1991: 173). Stern does not reckon with the possibility that, on the contrary, v. 24 betrays the author's pro-Davidic (anti-Saulide) bias.

2. So, too, Saul's *wayyaḥmōl* 'spared' (v. 9), which allegedly defied the divine injunction *wĕlô taḥmōl* 'you shall not spare' (v. 3), again reveals only the writer's intention, not Saul's.

3. "On capturing a king during the ḥērem, it was incumbent on Saul to kill him, i.e., by hanging, as Joshua did" (Stern 1991: 173, n. 30). Here, a correction is in order. Joshua hanged the five kings *after* he slew them (Josh 10:26); nothing is stated concerning the method of execution. The purpose of hanging was clearly that of deterrence (Deut 21:22–23). The execution, however, probably would have taken place at some improvised field altar so that the ḥērem would be enacted literally *lipnê YHWH* 'in the presence of YHWH'. Note that when the Gibeonites impale Saul's seven sons, it is "for YHWH," and it is enacted *lipnê YHWH* 'before YHWH' (2 Sam 21:6, 9), probably at an improvised altar. Stern (1991: 70–72) himself cites the case of the Sumerian Utuḥegal (ca. 2110 B.C.E.), who brings his conquered enemy king, the Gutian Tirigan, to the temple. Similarly, the Mesha inscription testifies: "I brought back from there the chief of the (clan of) Areli and I dragged him before Kemosh at Kerioth" (*ANET* 320, ll. 12–13). The strongest evidence for the writer's bias against Saul is his unwitting admission that Samuel does slay Agag the Amalekite king at Gilgal *lipnê YHWH* (v. 33; Gilgal indeed did possess a sanctuary, 1 Sam 13:8–12), thereby fulfilling Saul's openly stated intention (1 Sam 15:20–21).

4. Stern (1991: 175) claims that since only the worst of the inanimate (and animate–J.M.) booty was proscribed (1 Sam 15:9), Saul indeed must have flouted the requirements of the *ḥērem*. This verse actually may prove the opposite: Saul spared the best of the booty as sacrifices and consecrations to YHWH; the worst, being ineligible or unworthy of sacrifice or consecration, was proscribed.

5. Stern (1991: 176) recognizes correctly that "the text is far less slanted against Saul than it could easily have been." The reason, I submit, is clear: the facts, some of which vindicated Saul, were too well known and could not be entirely obliterated or altered.

6. Stern (1991: 173) seems puzzled "how lightly Saul and the people were treated. Compare what happened to Achan! The reason may be that the motive was not to steal from the *ḥērem*, but at least ostensibly to sacrifice the proscribed cattle to YHWH." Inadvertently, Stern has stumbled on my thesis, but did not follow through this insight to the obvious conclusion that Saul had intended to carry out a legitimate *ḥērem*.

Finally, I wish to restate my underlying reason for seeking a fresh reading of Saul's actions in 1 Sam 13, 15: in these two chapters, Saul is totally out of character. In chap. 13, the circumstances are transparent. The clash between Saul and Samuel is not ideological but personal: Saul had every right to officiate, especially in view of Samuel's tardiness, which endangered the welfare of his troops. In chap. 15, the tendentious nature of the composition is so blatant that Saul's claim that "he had fulfilled the word of YHWH" (v. 13b) must be upheld.

G. The Tithe: Its History

Although the rendering of tithes of property for sacral purposes was common all over the ancient Near East, well-documented, firsthand evidence concerning tithes comes mainly from Mesopotamia (*ešru/eširtû*). These documents date from the Neo-Babylonian period (sixth century B.C.E.), but there is no doubt that the institution as such is much older. In the Syro-Palestine area, the tithe (*maʿšārtu*; cf. Heb. *maʿăśēr*) is found in Ugarit in the fourteenth century B.C.E. (*PRU* 3.147, 9, 11).

The tithe was not assigned only to temples. As may be learned from 1 Sam 8:15, 17 and from Ugarit, it could also be a royal tax that the king might exact and give to his officials (Anderson 1987). This ambiguity of the tithe, as a royal due, on the one hand, and as a sacred donation, on the other, is to be explained by the fact that the temples to which the tithe was assigned were royal temples (see esp. Amos 7:13). As such, the property and treasures in them were at the king's disposal. This can best be exemplified by the two instances of tithe mentioned in older sources of the Pentateuch (JE). In Gen 14:20, Abraham gives a tithe (after his battle with the four kings of the north) to Melchizedek, the king-priest of Shalem (= Jerusalem; but see Vawter 1977: 199–200), and in Gen 28:22 (cf. Amos 4:4), Jacob vows to pay a tithe at Bethel, the "royal chapel" of the Northern Kingdom (Amos 7:13). The specific mention of these two "royal temples" in connection with the tithe is not a coincidence. It seems that these two traditions have an etiological slant. The institution of collecting tithes in the royal chapel at Bethel is linked to Jacob, the ancestor hero par excellence of the northern tribes, whereas the institution of the tithe in the royal sanctuary of Jerusalem is traced back to Abraham, whose traditions are mainly attached to the south. As is well known, the kings controlled the treasures of palace and Temple alike (1 Kgs 15:18; 2 Kgs 12:19; 18:15), which is understandable since they were responsible for the maintenance of the sanctuary and its service not less than for the service of the court (cf. Ezek 45:17). It stands to reason that the tithe, which originally was a religious tribute, came to be channeled to the court and was therefore supervised by royal authorities. This is actually attested in 2 Chr 31:4–21, where Hezekiah is said to organize the collection and the storage of the tribute, including the tithe. Although the description of the event comes from a late and tendentious source, its authenticity is supported by the fact that the Mesopotamian tithe, attested in earlier sources, was organized along similar lines (see also the organization in Neh 10:38; 12:44, 47; 13:5, 12). The annual tithe of the Carthaginians, which was sent to the Temple of Melqart in Tyre (Diodorus 20.14), is to be understood in a like manner. The Temple of Melqart was the state treasury of Tyre, and so the tribute paid by the Carthaginians had a political as well as a sacred aspect.

A further analogy between the sacred tithe and the royal tithe may be found in the priestly ordinance, according to which the tithes of grain and "flow from the vat" are allocated to the Levites in return for the services that they perform in the Tabernacle (Num 18:21, 27). A similar procedure is attested in Ugaritic grants whereby the king of Ugarit gives the tithe of a whole city to his official for his loyal service (*PRU* 16.153, 224), and, like the tithe given to the Levites, it consists of grain and beverage. The same phenomenon is encountered in 1 Sam 8:15, where the king is said to give to his servants the tithe (grain and wine) taken from the people.

The property that was subject to the tithe in Israel was grain, new wine, and new oil (Deut 14:23, etc.), as well as cattle and sheep (Lev 27:32). In a general context, however, the tithe appears to have embraced all kinds of property. Abraham gives Melchizedek one-tenth of everything, which seems to refer to the booty of the war, and Jacob vows that "of all that you give me, I will set aside a tithe for you" (Gen 28:22). In Mesopotamia, there is evidence of tithes from agricultural produce, cattle and sheep, slaves, donkeys, wool, cloth, wood, metal production, silver, gold, and so on. It seems, therefore, that the specification in the priestly and deuteronomic codes refers to only the most common objects of tithing in Israel.

Despite the view of most moderns, the tithe in Num 18 is not voluntary but mandatory, a conclusion supported by the following evidence:

1. The verb *tiqḥû* means "take by force," implying that the Levite is not dependent on the whims of the landowner (Milgrom 1970: 67, n. 246; Ben-Barak 1981).

2. It would be hard to conceive that the tithes, the only income assigned to the Levites, takes the form of charity—and this in compensation for the ongoing risks involved in laboring for the sanctuary. (The case of Deut 14:22–29, in which the tithe is indeed a charity, has a totally different sociological motivation: the Levites are unemployed priests and are literally the wards of society.)

3. Since the perquisites for the priestly family of Aaron from the annual produce of the land are mandatory (vv. 12–13), how could the Levitic perquisites from the land, which are supposed to feed a whole tribe (numbering 8580 males between the ages of thirty and fifty, according to Num 4:48), be purely voluntary?

4. The history of the Babylonian temple tithe demonstrates that no sooner was a centralized government established than it would have met the need of the sanctuary personnel for a fixed income by imposing an annual sacral tithe (see COMMENT H).

Underlying all the ancient Near Eastern sources dealing with the tithe is the notion of a tax that is indispensable for the maintenance of the temple and its personnel (except Deuteronomy, to be discussed below). As may be learned from the Mesopotamian documents, the tithe was stored in the temple treasuries, and some of the temple representatives were put in charge of these stores. The cattle were marked with the temple mark, and the tithe of grain and dates could be converted into money when desirable. The Babylonian documents also provide evidence on the question of how the tithe was spent by the temple. Most agricultural produce was destined for consumption by the temple personnel, but some was also applied to the maintenance of various enterprises and institutions attached to the temple. Cattle and sheep were used mainly for sacrificial purposes. The tithe was collected by representatives of the temple authorities, who were also responsible for transporting the products to the temple personnel; these collectors themselves were not exempted from the tithe.

A similar picture is obtained when the biblical sources dealing with the tithe are examined in conjunction with the nonbiblical sources. Admittedly, as will be shown, one has to take into account the fact that the various sources of the Pentateuch evince different attitudes to the tithe and that this institution underwent some development during the Second Temple period. However, in general, the nature of the tithe and the way of processing and spending it are quite similar in biblical and nonbiblical sources. That the tithe was kept in the storehouse of the Temple may be learned from Malachi (3:10), Nehemiah (10:38, 39; 12:44; 13:5, 12, 13), and 2 Chronicles (31:4–11). The same sources provide information about the custodians of these stores and about the way in which the tithe was distributed among the Temple personnel (e.g., Neh 13:13). Furthermore, the evidence in Neh 10:38 about Levites as tithe collectors in the provincial cities, which some have regarded as a gloss, is now corroborated by Mesopotamian data, according to which tithe collectors were recruited from the temple administration. Although the Mesopotamian data are from later sources, this does not mean that the whole procedure was a late invention, especially given that the same procedure is attested in outside sources. In fact, this is the only realistic way in which the tithe can be conceived. The conversion of tithes of the produce of the land into money, found in Mesopotamian sources, is also mentioned in Lev 27:31 and Deut 14:24–25 (but with the difference that in Deuteronomy, one is not bound to pay an additional one-fifth of the tithe for the redemption), and the information that the Mesopotamian tithe collectors themselves are bound to pay tithes helps clarify the biblical law that the Levites have to remove the tithes from their income (Num 18:25–32).

The law of Deuteronomy (14:22–27) prescribes the setting aside of a tithe of grain, wine, and oil every year and its consumption at the chosen place (i.e., the central sanctuary). The tithe may be converted into money to be spent on the festive meal in the chosen place. Every third year, however, the tithe has to be left in the local settlement, for the benefit of the Levite, who has no land of his own, the stranger, the fatherless, and the widow (Deut 14:28–29). After giving away the tithe to these *personae miserabiles*, the owner has to proclaim a confession in which he declares that he has given it to the indigent and not desecrated it by using it for impure purposes (Deut 26:13–15).

This novelty of eating the tithe instead of giving it away to the sanctuary and its ministrants (as was the case before) is to be explained against the background of the cultic reform that stands at the basis of the deuteronomic law code, especially Deut 12:19. After the abolition of the provincial sanctuaries and the provincial cultic officials, the Levites, there was no further need for the tithe, which had been destined for the maintenance of these institutions. The tithe was reduced primarily to a sacred gift. However, in order to preserve this ancient, sacred institution, the Israelite is commanded to observe the custom of setting aside a tithe from his yield and guarding its holiness by eating it only in the chosen place and by not letting it be defiled. The preservation of another feature of the tithe is also expressed in the allocation of the tithe to the Levite every third year. Called "the year of the tithe" (Deut 26:12), this year seems to preserve the old notion of the connection between the Levite and the tithe. It must, however, be admitted that the Levite appears here not as a sacred official—but as a destitute person—that is, on the same level as the stranger, orphan, and widow.

The various tithe laws are not in accord on the matter of either the composition of the tithe or the recipient of the tithe. According to Lev 27:30–33, the tithe falls due on all produce and pure animals. Deut 14:23 ignores the animal tithe and restricts the vegetable tithe to grain, new wine, and olive oil. Num 18:21–32 says nothing explicit about either tithe. But from the language of v. 29, it is certain that the animal tithe was ignored ("you shall set aside . . . from . . . its best portion, the part . . . to be consecrated"); and it is possible that the crop tithe of v. 30, like that of Deut 14:23, was restricted to grain, new wine, and oil ("as the yield of the threshing floor or vat"). In the two historical attestations of the tithe in biblical times, the one attributed to King Hezekiah falls due on livestock and "on everything" (2 Chr 31:5–6), in full agreement with

Lev 27; and the one attributed to Nehemiah falls due on "the tithes from our ground" (Neh 10:38), explained as "the contribution of grain, wine and oil" (v. 40), in keeping with Deut 14. Certainly by rabbinic times, there was no doubt that all vegetables were subject to the tithe (m. Ma'aś. 1:1).

On the matter of the tithe recipients, the discrepancies are indisputable. Leviticus assigns them to the sanctuary priests; Numbers, to the Levites; and Deuteronomy, to the Israelite owners. Yet these prescriptions, ostensibly so contradictory, may be related to one another. The produce tithe of Leviticus is redeemable by the owner and thus bears the same status as the tithe of Deuteronomy: every third year, it is turned over to the Levites and to other indigents; otherwise, it is eaten by its owner. Although Numbers assigns the tithe to the Levites, it admits that the tithe has been "set aside for YHWH," in conformance with Leviticus. Thus the change of beneficiary betrays a chronological relationship. Deuteronomy assigns the tithe to its owner, but implies that the Levite once had title to it, as ordained in Numbers. Numbers, in turn, acknowledges that the tithes originally belonged to YHWH (e.g., sanctuary, priests), a claim asserted only by Leviticus. Thus the pentateuchal codes affirm that the tithe beneficiary has undergone two changes: from the sanctuary to the Levite to the owner.

At the beginning of the Second Temple period, the tithe was considered to be indispensable for the maintenance of the sanctuary and its personnel. Thus Malachi (3:10) urges the people to bring "the full tithe into the storehouse" that there may be food in the house of God, apparently for the priests. Nehemiah stands on guard so that the people give their tithe to the Levites and do not neglect it (Neh 10:38; 12:44; 13:10, 13). As has already been indicated, the method of organizing the tithe in this period was not different from what is known about the organization of the tithe in Mesopotamia. Representatives of the Temple were in charge of collecting the tithes from the fields (Neh 10:38b), and the tithes were kept in the storehouses of the Temple (Mal 3:10; Neh 10:39–40; 12:44; 13:5, 12, 13; cf. 2 Chr 31:6–11) under the supervision of priestly officials, who were in charge of their proper distribution (cf. Neh 13:13). In contrast to the common view, there is no real contradiction between Neh 10:38, which speaks of "the Levites who collect the tithe in all our towns," and passages such as Mal 3:10 and Neh 12:44; 13:12, which speak of the people bringing tithes to the storehouses. The latter statements mean that the people made their contribution, not that the people brought the tithes with them in the literal sense of the word. According to the Mesopotamian practice, the temple authorities were responsible for the transportation of the tithe, and there is no reason to conclude that the same practice did not prevail in Judah, especially when this is explicitly stated in Neh 10:38. On the one hand, this view is supported by the rabbinic tradition, according to which the tithe was given to the Levites (or, rather, to the priests; see below) on the threshing floor (t. Pe'a 4:3, 6; b. Ket. 26a; y. Ket. 2:7; Jos. Ant. 20.181). Indeed, Josephus (Ant. 20.181, 206–7) relates that some high priests sent their men to the farmers' barns to take the tithe by force. On the other hand, it is possible that the petty farmers brought their tithes with them to Jerusalem. This was the ancient custom (Deut 14:22–25; Amos 4:4), a practice dutifully recorded (and fancifully interpreted) by Philo (*Laws* 1.132–50), though it was probably obsolete by his time.

Although the purpose of the tithe and its method of organization in the period under discussion seem quite clear, religious-halakhic factors complicated the issue. From Ezra's time, the entire body of pentateuchal literature was considered to be a unity (the Torah of Moses), and the people were expected to comply with the Torah as a whole. This required that the various attitudes toward the tithe, as reflected in the different sources (especially in the Priestly Code, on the one hand, and Deuteronomic Code, on the other), be combined in a way that reconciled contradictions. Thus, for instance, the two types of tithes prevalent at this period, "the first tithe" (*ma'ăśēr ri'šôn*) and the "second tithe" (*ma'ăśēr šēnî*), are the outcome of the contradiction between Num 18:21–24 and Deut 14:22–27. According to the Priestly Code, the tithe is to be given to the Levite, whereas according to the Deuteronomic Code, it is to be consumed by the owner at the central sanctuary. The rabbis, taking it for granted that both laws are of Mosaic origin and therefore equally binding, interpreted them as two different tributes: one to be given to the Levite, "the first tithe," and the other to be brought to Jerusalem and consumed there, "the second tithe." Theoretically, this was an excellent solution. However, from the practical point of view, the implementation of these laws was almost impossible. The excise of 20 percent of the yield was too high, and the destination of the tithe posed an even more serious problem.

There were very few Levites during the Second Temple period, compared with their number in the monarchical period, and so the tithe was automatically shifted to the priests. Because this allocation does not comply with the law, all kinds of explanations had to be provided in order to do away with the legal anomaly. A common explanation was that Ezra punished the Levites for not having gone up from Babylon to Jerusalem—he allocated the tithe to the priests (*b. Yeb.* 86b). Another source affirms that until John Hyrcanus's time, the Levites received one-third of the tithes (*y. Sot.* 9, 240a). The Mishna records that Hyrcanus abolished the tithe confession (Deut 26:13–15), possibly because he transferred all the tithes to the priests (Alon 1957: 1.83–92). The rabbis made unsuccessful efforts to restore the ancient custom (*y. Ma'aś. Š.* 5, 59b). But for obvious economic reasons, very few people observed the laws of tithe properly. Many priests and Levites were affluent landowners; thus tithing was pointless (Safrai 1976: 824). A conscientious observer of the law could not partake of his yield without first tithing it, and the common people were suspected of not putting aside the sacred portion. This situation caused a lot of problems whose legal aspects are dealt with extensively in a special tractate called Demai. (This COMMENT supplements Weinfeld 1971b.)

H. The Tithe: Mandatory or Voluntary?

Kaufmann (1937: 1.148–57; 1960: 190–91) holds that all tithes in P are votive and that Lev 27:30–31 contradicts Num 18:21–24 in assigning them to the priests and not to the Levites. Haran (1968), followed by Weinfeld (1971b), accepts Kaufmann's thesis, but he harmonizes the contradiction concerning their recipients by assuming that the crop tithe of Lev 27:30–31 belongs to the Levites, in accordance with Num 18:21–24, and that only the animal tithe, Lev 27:32–33, is given to the priests. As proof, he cites the difference in the law: only the crop tithe is redeemable. This, he claims, is explicable only by positing that the crop tithe is of lesser sanctity than the animal tithe and is given to the Levites (anticipated by *Seper Hamibḥar* and followed by Levine 1989).

There are many objections to the Kaufmann–Haran voluntary tithe thesis:

1. No verb is used on the order of *yaqrîb* or *yaqdîš* that might allow for a voluntary votive or dedicatory act. Indeed, the absence of a verb in v. 30 gives the crop tithe the same structure as the firstborn (vv. 26–27), which clearly is nondedicatory; contrast v. 9, where the clause *kol 'ăšer yittēn mimmennû laYHWH* is purposefully added to indicate that the dedication is voluntary. (True, a verb occurs with the animal tithe, *ya'ăbōr* [v. 32], but it is *Qal*, not *Hip'il*, as the dedicatory verbs *hiqdîš, hiqrîb, heḥĕrîm*. It is impersonal and passive in meaning, implying that the tithing is not a special act but takes place during the regular procedure for taking inventory; Jer 33:13; Ezek 20:37; cf. Milgrom 1970: 67, n. 246.)

2. The animal tithe appears only once again, in the Chronicler's account of Hezekiah's reform, together with the crop tithe (2 Chr 31:6), where they are termed *mĕnāt hakkōhănîm wĕhalĕwiyyim* 'the revenue of the priests and the Levites' (v. 4). If the Chronicler's account is correct, then it testifies to a fixed income for Levites as well as for priests, in the form of an annual tithe (see COMMENT G).

3. The very fact that the tithe in D is annual and compulsory (Deut 14:22–29) implies that it rests on an earlier tradition. If hitherto the tithe had been voluntary, why should D have enjoined that an animal tithe be brought to Jerusalem if it were to be eaten by the owner himself? Let him eat his tithe in the comfort of his home! Moreover, that the tithe for D is holy (26:13) indicates that it rests on earlier tradition (cf. Lev 27:31); hence, that it is compulsory and annual may also rest on earlier tradition. The elimination of the local sanctuaries meant that the tithe, heretofore the main source of their income, was henceforth superfluous, for the Jerusalem Temple could subsist on the voluntary offerings of the people (Deut 12:6, 11, 17–18, 26–27) and on the king's subsidies (1 Kgs 9:25; Ezek 45:17; 2 Chr 8:12–13; 31:3–11). Thus D ordained that the tithes should revert to their owners. But by insisting that the tithes be brought to Jerusalem, D endeavored to maintain their sacred character. They were to be eaten in a state of purity (Deut 26:13–14) and in the Temple environs (14:23).

4. Both Leviticus tithes are called "holy to YHWH," implying that they belong to the priests. Haran (1968) parries this argument by claiming that P reckons the Levites' tithes as sancta, citing Num 18:32, where the tithes are designated as "the Israelites' sancta." However, he overlooks the fact that the tithes are called sancta in this verse only to emphasize that they may not be eaten by the Levites until a tithe of the tithe is given to the priests (v. 26). It is this priestly

portion of the tithe that renders it sacred, as the text itself avers by calling it *miqdāšô* 'its sacred portion' (v. 29). Moreover, P consistently refrains from using *qdš* in regard to the Levites; this root is absent from even the Levites' ordination account, where the surrogate verb *ntn* is employed (Num 8:5–22; Milgrom 1970: 29, n. 103).

5. Kaufmann (1937) himself has ably shown that the royal tithe, an annual tax, was an ancient institution (1 Sam 8:15, 17; cf. *ma'šaru, mē'šertu*, RS) that the king could award to his officials. A case is even recorded where the king of Ugarit awarded the tithes of an entire city to a loyal official (see COMMENT G). In Israel, as elsewhere, the demarcation between the royal and the temple tithe is indistinct, since temples were ipso facto royal temples (Amos 7:13) and the kings controlled their treasuries (1 Kgs 15:18; 2 Kgs 12:19; 18:15) and were responsible for their maintenance (2 Kgs 12:7–17; 22:3–7; Ezek 45:17; 2 Chr 31:3–14; cf. Weinfeld 1973).

6. Israel's environment demonstrates the existence of not only a royal tithe, but also an annual temple tithe, especially in Babylonia. Because this point has not been widely recognized, a detailed exposition is indicated.

The antiquity of the royal tithe in Israel's environment is certain. But are there any written sources that attest to an annual temple tithe? From Babylonia, at least, the answer is unequivocally yes. Material on the Babylonian *ešrū* (pl. *ešrētu*) has been collected by the Russian Assyriologist Dandamaev (1965). His examination of more than 100 tithe documents of the Neo-Babylonian period leads him to the following conclusions:

1. In contrast to previously held views, the tithe in sixth-century Babylonia was paid to the temples, not to the royal treasury. Indeed, even kings and princes, not to speak of lesser officials, are recorded as paying annual tithes to temples.

2. The tithe was imposed on all goods: barley, dates, sesame, flax, oil, garlic, wool, clothes, cattle, sheep, birds, wood, and products of silver and gold. The tithe of Lev 27 (H) is imposed on all the produce of land and animals, but the tithes of Numbers (P) and Deuteronomy (D) are of narrower compass. However, the (allegedly voluntary) tithes could embrace all one's possessions, at least according to the early sources (Gen 28:22).

3. The tithe was imposed on the entire population. The persons appearing in the tithe documents include farmers, shepherds, gardeners, bakers, smiths, weavers, potters, and various administrative officials (e.g., generals, canal overseers, head accountants). Priests and other temple officials are not exempt from the tithe and, as mentioned, not even kings and princes. (Of course, they did not pay one-tenth of their income. According to Dandamaev [1965], only tenant farmers were compelled to pay the full tithe.) Even tenant farmers on temple lands were required to pay the tithe in addition to the annual rent to the temple.

4. Tithes fell due at the end of the year or when crops ripened. Extensions up to several years occasionally were granted to those who could not pay the tithe on time, interest being charged for each month's delay. If the extension was not granted, barley or dates were borrowed from banking institutions, homes

were rented or mortgaged, and slaves were sold. An instance is recorded that a defaulting tither was required to hand over his young son to the temple until the son's labors paid off the tithe obligation. This event may throw new light on the "ways of the king" (1 Sam 8:11–17), where the statement on the confiscation of property and the enslavement of the population twice follows the prescription of the tithe: "He will tithe your grain and your vintage to give to his eunuchs and lackeys; he will seize your slaves, both men and women; the best of your cattle [*bĕqarkem*, LXX] and your asses and put them to his own use. He will tithe your flocks and you yourselves will become his slaves" (vv. 15–17). The sequence may be causal: tithe default will lead to confiscation and enslavement by the Crown.

5. The tithes provided the temples with capital in excess of their other cultic revenues that enabled them to branch out into business enterprises. Temples would even function as banks, lending tithe produce to businessmen at profitable interest rates.

Annual temple tithes are attested in Greece, Egypt, Rome, and South Arabia (Dandamaev 1965: 15–16, n. 14). These sources are admittedly late. A similar demurrer should be voiced regarding the Babylonian tithe. Dandamaev's studies are limited to documents from mainly the sixth century B.C.E. and no earlier than the seventh, and caution should be exercised in drawing retroactive conclusions. However, it has also been demonstrated that a compulsory temple tithe was enforced during the reign of Ammiṣaduqa (1646–26 B.C.E.). The sacred object was "carried in procession from field to field in the countryside; at each stop the owner of the field would declare in its presence that so much barley was indeed the tenth of his harvest which was due the temple" (Harris 1965: 222). Indeed, it stands to reason that cultic procedures, conservative by nature, would not have been invented ad hoc by the Neo-Babylonian Empire. Similarly, that Israel's postexilic priests innovated the Temple tithe on the basis of a royal tithe must be abandoned (cf. Cazelles 1951).

The Babylonian temple tithe is of direct relevance to the biblical tithe, especially its formulation in Lev 27:30–33.

1. Corresponding to the redemption of the crop tithe in Lev 27:30–31, the Babylonian tithe of dates and barley (constituting more than half the tithe documents investigated by Dandamaev) was commutable into silver. Strikingly, the documents fail to record any commutation of the animal tithe. The likelihood of its being discovered in a new document is diminished by the fact that in Babylonia, the animal tithe was branded as permanent temple property. Bearing the indelible seal of the temple, the animal could hardly have been desanctified and allowed to reenter the profane realm. These considerations lead to the conclusion that in Babylonia, as in Israel, the animal tithe could not be redeemed (Lev 27:32–33).

2. That even temple officials in Babylonia were obligated to tithe recalls the tithe law imposed on the Levites (Num 18:25–32) and suggests that a similar requirement originally obtained in Israel as well and that even priests, regardless of whether they officiated at sacrifices, were subject to the law of tithe. If so,

then the exemption of Aaronid priests from the tithe would have to be attributed to a later stage or to a different school of thought.

3. The Babylonian tithe was not brought to the temples directly, but was collected from the people by temple officials especially assigned for this purpose, *amēlu ša (ina) muḫḫi ešrū (ešrē)*. Their counterpart in Israel is the Levites, for, according to Neh 10:38, *halĕwiyyim hamĕ'aśśĕrîm bĕkōl 'ārê 'ăbōdātēnû* 'it is the Levites who collect the tithes in all our farming villages' and, according to the Priestly Source, have the right to take them by force (Num 18:26–28; cf. Milgrom 1970: 67, n. 246).

4. In Babylonia, the tithe was payable to the local sanctuary. Thus there is no need to postulate that the annual tithe in Israel could have begun only after the deuteronomic centralization was put into effect. In keeping with the Babylonian example, Josiah's predecessors on the throne could have ordained that each local sanctuary have jurisdiction over the tithes in its district.

The question may justifiably be asked: Was there ever a voluntary tithe in Israel? If so, the codes do not recognize it. To the contrary, H, P, and D posit an annual, fixed tithe. The laws of JE, unfortunately, do not even mention the tithe. This omission has been taken by some commentators, as noted above, as an indication that the tithe, in JE's time, could not have been compulsory. However, it should be noted that JE's cultic provisions are contained mainly in two versions of an agricultural calendar (Exod 23:10–19; 34:18–26), which, aside from sabbath and sabbatical year provisions, focus primarily on the three pilgrimage festivals, which were the fixed occasions for worship at the sanctuary. There is the possibility that one verse in the Covenant Code does refer to a tithe: *mēlē'ātĕkā wĕdim'ăkā lō' tĕ'aḥēr* 'You shall not delay the first (processed) fruits of your vat and granary' (Exod 22:28a). If so, then it would clearly refer to a fixed tithe, since its delayed payment is forbidden. However, it is not yet known what the two technical terms *mēlē'â* and *dema'* mean, and until they are deciphered their evidence must be ruled out of court (cf. Milgrom 1976a: 61, n. 216).

Most of the other references to the Temple tithe are in postexilic sources, where it is clearly a fixed, annual institution (Mal 3:8, 10; Neh 10:38–39; 12:44; 13:5, 12; 2 Chr 31:5–6, 12). However, there are three occurrences in nonlegal sources that are clearly preexilic. One is in Amos (4:4), but its nature, unfortunately, is enigmatic. That the tithe is brought three days after voluntary offerings does not compel the deduction that the tithe is also voluntary. Later practice actually attests the contrary: the fixed tithe was brought to Jerusalem in conjunction with another cultic occasion (1 Sam 1:21; LXX [Jos *Ant.* 5.34b]; Tob 1:6–7; *m. Bek.* 9:5; *m. Ma'aś Š.* 5:6; see Safrai 1968: 125–30). The other two preexilic references are in the patriarchal narratives, and the tithes are indeed voluntary: Abraham at Salem (Gen 14:20) and Jacob at Bethel (Gen 28:22). However, it is no accident, as has been recognized, that Bethel and (Jeru)Salem are the sites of the main sanctuaries of the kingdoms of Israel and Judah, respectively. The purpose of these narratives may be etiological: to prove that the rights of these two sanctuaries are hallowed by tradition, traceable, in fact, to the patriarchs themselves. Thus rather than attesting to the early existence of a voluntary tithe, these etiological tales may testify to the reverse: the subsequent claim of these sanctuaries to receive a divinely sanctioned income through the annual tithe.

This is not to gainsay the possibility that at an early stage in Israel's history the tithes were purely voluntary. But on this matter all biblical sources are silent, and it can remain only a conjecture. Moreover, even if we assume that a voluntary tithe at one time existed, then, as the history of the Babylonian tithe demonstrates, no sooner was a centralized government established in the post-conquest period than it would have met the need of the sanctuaries for a fixed income by imposing an annual sacral tithe.

A by-product of our conclusion that the biblical codes know of only an annual fixed tithe is that D's cultic innovations are not radical, at least in regard to the tithe. Indeed, if D's prescription for an annual tithe is precisely what it inherited from its past (see COMMENT G), and the tithe originally was a sanctuary revenue, then perhaps other elements in its tithe law are likewise rooted in Israel's cultic traditions. The demonstration of this, however, is irrelevant to this volume.

To summarize: the entire kingdom of Babylonia was subject to an annual temple tithe during the sixth century B.C.E. It was incumbent on all subjects, including sovereigns and clerics; imposed on all goods, not just on produce of lands and herds; and collected by special officials in each temple district. Delinquents were forced to borrow on their property or to enslave members of their household. Alternatively, late payment might be allowed and interest charged. The Babylonian temple tithe was a mandatory institution and only after the sixth century did it lose this status.

Parallels with the Bible abound: tithes of produce, but not of animals, are commutable (Lev 27:31–32); temple officials are not exempt from the tithe (e.g., Levites, Num 18:25–32); and tithes are collected at the source, not brought to the sanctuary by the owner (Num 18:26a; Neh 10:38).

The parallels also lend themselves to a historical conclusion. In Babylonia, the trend is from a compulsory annual tithe to a voluntary one. Beginning with Nabonidus and continuing through the Achaemenids, the temple tithes are expropriated by the Crown and, after Alexander's conquest, cease to be compulsory. In view of this verifiable historical process, it is difficult to argue that in contemporary Israel the reverse took place—that an allegedly voluntary tithe became mandatory in Second Temple days, precisely at the time when the tithe lost its mandatory status in Babylonia. This argument gains force on the realization that all the pentateuchal codes predicate a fixed, annual sanctuary tithe and that, if the institution of a voluntary tithe did exist in early Israel—a possibility before the united kingdom—there is no evidence for it in the Bible.

I. Can the Tithe Laws Be Harmonized?

As has been shown (see COMMENT G), the three pentateuchal tithe laws conflict with one another regarding recipients—sanctuary, or priests (H), Levites (P), and laity (D)—and compass—all agricultural and pastoral products (H), agricultural products (P), and grain, must, and olive oil (D). The rabbis harmonize these laws by equating H and D, and by calling their tithes a second tithe. Thus the tithes of H and D become a supplement to those of P. This kind of harmonization is what we would expect. The rabbis are jurists, not exegetes. The Torah for them is not an antiquarian document calling for critical analysis, but a binding revelation demanding implementation of all its laws. Yet the rabbis, too, betray disagreement on one of the two major discrepancies in the tithe laws: their compass (see NOTE on v. 30). It is, therefore, all the more surprising to find that the two most recent scholarly treatments of the tithe laws are unabashedly harmonistic (McConville 1984: 68–87; Herman 1991). Are they successful?

The merit of McConville's book on the deuteronomic laws is that he raises serious questions about long-held axioms of deuteronomic research. He is anything but convincing, however, in his attempt to demonstrate that H, P, and D comprise a single tithe law.

McConville (1984: 70–71) cites Deut 10:9 as proof that D was aware of Num 18:20, which declares, using similar terms, that YHWH is Aaron's portion and inheritance. This correspondence, however, does not mean that ipso facto both priests and Levites are subject to the same tithe law. On the contrary, the more precise referent for Deut 10:9 is not Num 18:20, which addresses the priests, but Num 18:24, which refers to the Levites, as the following comparison will demonstrate:

> 'al-kēn lō'-hāyâ lēlēwî ḥēleq wĕnaḥălâ 'im-'eḥāyw YHWH hū' naḥălātô ka'ăšer dibbēr YHWH 'ĕlōhêkā lô

Therefore the Levites have received no hereditary portion along with their kinspeople. YHWH is their inheritance, as YHWH your God promised [lit. "said"] concerning them. (Deut 10:9)

To be sure, the phrase in Deuteronomy ka'ăšer dibbēr means "as promised" and specifically refers to a previous ordinance (cf. Milgrom 1976h). That ordinance, however, is not Num 18:20, but 18:24:

> kî 'et-ma'ăśar bĕnê-yiśrā'ēl 'ăšer yārîmû laYHWH tĕrûmâ nātattî lalewiyyim lĕnaḥălâ 'al-kēn 'āmartî lāhem bĕtôk bĕnê yiśrā'ēl lō' yinḥălû naḥălâ

for it is the tithes set aside by the Israelites as a gift to YHWH that I grant to the Levites as their **inheritance. Therefore I have said concerning them:** They shall not receive an **inheritance** among the Israelites.

The parallels (boldface) should be noted. Only this verse (and v. 21) states explicitly that the tithes are the Levites' inheritance. D, on the contrary, never links the two: the tithe of Deuteronomy is never termed their naḥălâ. To be sure, P also echoes the deuteronomic phrase YHWH hû' naḥălātô 'YHWH is their inheritance' (Deut 10:9; 18:2) in Num 18:20: 'ănî ḥelqĕkā wĕnaḥălātĕkā 'I am your hereditary portion'. But whereas Deuteronomy uses it in regard to the Levites, Numbers reserves its use exclusively for the priests.

Herein lies a polemic. D maintains that "the levitical priests, the whole tribe of Levi . . . shall live off the food offerings of YHWH as their inheritance" (Deut 18:1), and all Levites have the right to officiate in the central sanctuary (Deut 18:6). P, though, separates the Levites from the priests by an unbridgeable chasm: Levites may never officiate at the altar (cf. Num 18:3; Milgrom 1970: 16–18) or benefit from its sacrifices. Hence, P is intrinsically incapable of admitting to the notion that "YHWH is their (the Levites') inheritance" (for the polemic thrust of Deut 18:1, see Milgrom 1976h: 11–12).

McConville (1984: 73–74) further harmonizes D and P/H by arguing that the inclusion within D's tithe law (Deut 14:22–29) of "But do not neglect the Levite in your community, for he has no hereditary portion as you have" (Deut 14:27) proves that D mandates the distribution of the festal meal at the Temple to the Levites. Again, the invitation to the Levite to join the family meal bought in Jerusalem with the tithe money (see also Deut 12:11–12) only *suggests* that D is fully aware of the Levites' prior claim to the entire tithe, as prescribed by P. There is no indication, however, that the Levites' inclusion is even mandatory or any reason to believe that a Levite would join the family pilgrimage to Jerusalem just for the sake of a free meal. The very fact that the alien, orphan, and widow are also not invited (seeing that they, together with the Levite, are the recipients of the third-year tithe, Deut 14:28–29; 26:12) demonstrates conclusively that the Levites are invited to the meal not as a matter of Deuteronomy's well-attested charity, but as a consequence of Deuteronomy's guilt for having deprived the Levites of their prior rights to the tithe.

Herman (1991: 96–98) continues and expands McConville's harmonistic approach. Following McConville (1984: 83), he avers that H, P, and D impose the tithe on all agricultural products; that Deuteronomy's ostensible limitation of the tithe to grain, must, and olive oil is only a *pars pro toto* idiom for all crops; and that all three sources explicitly or tacitly agree that the tithe is also incumbent on all "pastoral yield." This is not so. First, in no manner can it be inferred from D that livestock is subject to the tithe. Similarly, neither can *kol-maʿăśar* in Num 18:21 (P) be interpreted as including livestock (Gray [1904: 233] is mistakenly adduced for support).

Herman also commits a number of exegetical errors. He presumes that every "tithe is subject to monetary conversion." This is nowhere stated in H and P and is, indeed, implicitly denied for H's animal tithe (v. 33). Furthermore, P's tithe payments are not (like H's) deposited at the sanctuary. The fact that the Levites may "take, seize" the tithe (Num 18:26) indicates that they may expropriate the tithe directly from the farmer's land (Milgrom 1970: 25, n. 246).

Finally, Herman's (1991: 130) main thesis that the tithe is an expression of Israel's covenant loyalty, which can be described as a presentation or gift-exchange system, is belied by P and missing in H. P's rationale for the tithe is crystal clear: it is the Levites' reward or wages for their life-threatening risks in protecting the sanctuary against encroachment and not, as Herman argues, that the

Levites protect the sanctuary as repayment for the tithes (Milgrom 1970: 22–23). The difference is critical: the Levites are receiving wages commensurate with their precarious service, not gifts for fulfilling covenantal obligations. The covenant idea is also missing in H's tithe law, which, to be sure, is followed by "These are the commandments that YHWH commanded Moses for the Israelites on Mount Sinai" (v. 34). However, this verse is not an integral part of the tithe law, but, as does the concluding verse of Leviticus, it emphasizes that all the commandments prescribed in the entire book (or, at least, in chap. 27; see NOTE on v. 34) stem from God and are part of the Sinaitic covenant. In no manner can the sacrificial or purity regulations in chaps. 1–16 or, for that matter, the laws of vows and dedications in chap. 27 be conceived as an aspect of prestation.

Thus there is no recourse but to confront the discrepancies and contradictions in the pentateuchal tithe laws head-on. To ignore them or smooth them over only blocks the disclosure of a vital chapter in the development of the religious history of ancient Israel.

J. Ancient Seed Mensuration and Leviticus 27:16 (Jean Sheldon)

The use of "seed" and the "homer of barleycorns" to determine the value ratio of inherited property dedicated to YHWH in Lev 27:16 seems difficult to modern Western thinking. The proposal could be made to understand the construction *zeraʿ ḥōmer* as referring to the area measurement of a piece of property, not the seed sown on that property (Powell 1992: 901).

From this text alone, it is not clear just what is meant or how the "measurement"—in terms of cost—is to be defined. The term "homer" must be compared with the ancient Near Eastern usage of this term. This COMMENT focuses on examples from Mesopotamian property contracts, where the "seed" mensuration of property is denoted, with an effort to understand the common basis lying behind Lev 27:16. Although not directly related to the passage, Powell's (1984) study of the measurement of land in Mesopotamia will be used to facilitate understanding of ancient Near Eastern mensuration.

According to Powell (1984: 34), ancient surface mensuration consisted of two methods: the "reed" and "seed" methods. "Reed" mensuration was used on surfaces equal to or smaller than a *sūtu* (1800 cubits). Areas over a *sūtu* were measured in seed. Thus seed measurements applied to large tracts of land, whereas reed measurements were used on houses or smaller plots of land (1984: 34–36).

In very early seed mensuration, the area of land appears to have been measured according to the quantity of seed sown, though this is a great simplification of the practice as it ultimately developed (Powell 1992: 901). In the Akkadian texts, the measurements given always correlate to exact lengths; the farmer used a line to measure a section in order to determine how much seed would be needed (1984: 37). Nevertheless, it is not clear which came first, line measurement or seeding the land (1984: 46–47). The "seed" was used anciently to express measure; thus its function was denotative rather than expressive of the sole means of mensuration (1984: 34–35).

Eventually, ancient Mesopotamian surface mensuration developed into a highly scientific system. The amount of seed needed to produce the highest yield per section of land was carefully, though not minutely, calculated, from the length and number of furrows (and their distance apart) to the finger-length distances between seeds sown. Cost accounting also came to be included (Powell 1984: 47–53).

Numerous texts illustrate Powell's insistence that "seed" (ANŠE) represents a term not unsimilar to "acre," thus denoting land area rather than means of measurement in terms of seed sown (see *CAD*'s renderings of *Nbn* 178:11, 18, 20 in 10:123; *JEN* 528:9 in 7:114; *TCL* 3:208 from the Sargonic period in 7:114). The same is true regarding the use of ANŠE (*imēru*), the Sumerian and Akkadian terms paralleling the Hebrew *ḥōmer*. In all three languages, ANŠE originally meant "a donkey," a meaning it never contained; it came to denote the load that an ass could carry (Scott 1951: 31). Thus it would naturally designate the dry-goods measurement used for large quantities of seed. In a number of texts from the seventh century or later, the phrase x ANŠE A.ŠÀ (*x imēr eqlim*) appears (e.g., *ADD* 58:5; 414:4; 419:5; 622:3; 385:4; 622:3; *TCL* 3:208; *VAS* 5 4:9; *Nbn* 178:20). If interpreting the *imēru* as denoting "hectare" (Kwasman and Parpola 1991:72), the rendering would be appropriate: "x hectares of land." Thus Powell (1984) generally restricts ŠE.NUMUN to a technical term for "land/area" that lost its original meaning once transferred to the complicated system of measurement; likewise Kwasman and Parpola (1991) render ANŠE as "hectare."

One wonders, though, if the underlying notion of seed was completely lost. In *VAS* (5 4:9–14) GUR ŠE.NUMUN *mi-šiḫ-ti kirî šumāti*, GUR would have to be rendered as technical term, along with ŠE.NUMUN and ANŠE. Presumably, then, all such words, when connected with land measurement, should be rendered as technical terms denoting a type of "area." Originally, however, it seems that ŠE.NUMUN did mean literally "seed"; ANŠE, literally "homer" (an assload); and *sūtu* was another dry-measure unit. Is it possible that, though the terms came to represent surface area, they still carried with them something of their original meaning and, perhaps, even a hint of the process of mensuration by the quantity of seed sown? It may be that Powell has this in mind, but the question might be raised regarding whether one could employ his system of definition so rigidly as to lose sight of this point.

This question is especially pertinent to Lev 27:16, the biblical passage under consideration. If one interprets the Hebrew text according to Powell's (1984) conclusions, an entirely new translation is merited. The clause of the law in question in Lev 27:16b reads *wĕhāyâ ʿerkĕkā lĕpî zarʿô zeraʿ ḥōmer śĕʿōrîm baḥămiššîm šeqel kāsep*. Rendered literally, it reads "And the evaluation shall be according to its sowing: a seed-homer of barley to 50 shekels of silver." Clearly, a ratio proportion underlies the text, not unsimilar to the 1:1 ratios preferred in ancient Near Eastern metrology. An attempt to render the clause after the manner of the more technical Akkadian texts would be: "The evaluation shall be according to its land area: land area of one hectare to 50 shekels of silver."

Although Powell (1992: 901) favors this rendering, several factors make it difficult. ŠE.NUMUN does not exactly correspond to *zera*ʿ. Powell correctly notes that ŠE.NUMUN represents the Akkadian *zēru*; however, ŠE.NUMUN literally (if taken separately) represents both *šeʾu* and *zēru*. Although both of these words are found in the Hebrew clause, they are not constructed together in order to make a single term, as is the case with their Akkadian counterpart.

Furthermore, the Akkadian construction is the reverse of the Hebrew construction in Lev 27:16, and the word order does not correspond exactly. It seems that the construction — *zera*ʿ *ḥōmer ṭěʿōrîm* (= ŠE.NUMUN ANŠE ŠE.MEŠ?) — contains syntactic problems that mitigate the possibility of a technical rendering corresponding to the actual length of surface measurements found possible in the Akkadian texts of the Neo-Babylonian period. It could be, though, that the syntactic difference represents not an actual difference in methodology of measurement, but in the way that methodology is expressed.

One remains hopeful that some internal system of terminology for surface mensuration (peculiar to the Israelite community) is meant by the terms used, though other biblical uses of the term do not prove helpful to understanding Lev 27:16. It may yet be found in extra-biblical sources; Powell (1992: 901) notes that the "seed" system did not originate in Mesopotamia, but is West Semitic in origin.

Perhaps a fairly close translation of the clause in Lev 27:16 is that of the *Tanakh* (*NJPS*): "Its assessment shall be in accordance with its seed requirement fifty shekels of silver to a *ḥōmer* of barley seed." While this rendering does not solve all the potential ramifications of the text, it implies both the use of ratio proportion and the sowing of seed in land measurements.

From the ample representation of seed mensuration demonstrated in the ancient Near Eastern property texts, it may be concluded that the estimated value of inherited property was originally determined by the amount of seed needed to sow it. Thus whether or not one renders Lev 27:16 using technical terms for land measurement, the background of measurement and evaluation of land by the amount of seed required for sowing is clearly indicated.

APPENDIXES

◆

A. RESPONSE TO HENRY SUN

In November 1992, the Society of Biblical Literature sponsored a symposium on *Leviticus 1–16*, to which it invited four specialists on Leviticus: Rolf Rendtorff, emeritus, University of Heidelberg; Baruch Levine, New York University; Henry Sun, Lexington Theological Seminary; and Israel Knohl, Hebrew University of Jerusalem. The first two have written or are writing comprehensive commentaries on Leviticus; the latter two have written seminal doctoral dissertations on Leviticus—in all a distinguished panel. Rendtorff's (1993) comments and my response (1993a) were published separately and need not be reprinted here. Knohl (1995: 225–30) published his comments in the English version of his thesis, and a gist of the comments made by the two other panelists is contained in my responses to them.

I am deeply grateful to all four colleagues for investing the time and energy to contribute, in each case, a challenging critique.

Henry Sun is right: we should not neglect the findings of the social sciences, especially the field of cultural anthropology. However, such comparative analysis inheres with fatal dangers. I shall take Eilberg-Schwartz's *Savage in Judaism* (1990) as a parade example (see APPENDIX F). His book is occasionally insightful, always stimulating, frequently speculative, and, just as frequently, wrong.

His basic approach is, indeed, that of cultural anthropology, as pioneered by Emile Durkheim, whose basic premise is that animal taxonomy reflects societal values. Contemporary biblicists are aware of the relevance of his work primarily through the writings of Mary Douglas, particularly her groundbreaking examination of Lev 11 (1966). Even if her own theory may be in need of correction (see vol. 1.719–21), its Durkheimian approach has opened the door to a more illuminating understanding of the animal listings and their structural arrangement in other parts of the Bible (for example, the relationship between 21:16–23 and 22:17–25).

In truth, this kind of interpretation of Lev 11 is not at all modern. It can be traced back to the Letter of Aristeas (ll. 145–58) and Philo (*Laws* 4.100–31). However, we do not regard these ancient precedents as cultural anthropology, but allegory: one is a scientific discipline; the other, a literary hermeneutic—a homiletical midrash, far removed from the plain meaning of the biblical text. Its inherent defect is its subjectivity: it can lead to any result the interpreter desires. In other words, it lacks controls. (For a critique of Eilberg-Schwartz [1990] from an anthropological perspective, see Gabril 1992.)

Another example of Eilberg-Schwartz's (1990: 129) use of allegory under the guise of cultural (more precisely, structural) anthropology is his claim that "the rule against boiling a kid-goat (in its mother's milk; see Exod 23:19; 34:26; Deut 14:21) parallels the prohibition against a male child having intercourse with his mother." That is to say, this alimentary rule is, in effect, an incest prohibition (Soler 1979; fully developed by Marlens 1977). This modern allegory, however, is as much suspect as its ancient predecessors, if nothing else, for its erroneous exegesis. As I pointed out (vol. 1.740), the term gĕdî 'kid' is generic for both male and female (hapacious gĕdiyyōtayik, though feminine in form, refers to both male and female kids). If the priestly text wished to specify the male, it would have written gĕdî zākār (as in śeh zākār, Exod 12:5) or zākār bāʿizzîm (as in zākār babbāqār, Lev 22:19). Moreover, as pointed out by Hurowitz (1994: 220), if Eilberg-Schwartz were right, it would be the only example of allegory in the laws of the Bible and the ancient Near East. For a more comprehensive critique of Eilberg-Schwartz's lack of grounding in ancient Near Eastern and biblical texts and disciplines, see Greenstein 1984b.

I do not wish to give the impression that everything Eilberg-Schwartz has written on ancient Israel's diet laws is faulty. Occasionally, a valid and valuable insight burgeons from his treatment. For example, the laws and structure of Lev 4 are based on Gen 1. This conclusion might have been anticipated, since both chapters were penned in the same priestly (P) school. (I have developed this point in vol. 1.656 and in further detail in 1992c.) Indeed, insights are not lacking in any of Eilberg-Schwartz's topics, some of which I have accepted and acknowledged. The (overwhelming) remainder, which I reject, I have found necessary to discuss because of its initial attractiveness, which can entrap the untrained reader.

In sum, cultural anthropology is here to stay; it is no longer an irrelevant diversion. It has proved its value again and again, and today it forms an indispensable tool for biblical research. But its indiscriminate use is fraught with perils. However, it is certain to provide even a modicum of success if its practitioner possesses a mastery of the biblical text and its ancient Near Eastern background.

B. RESPONSE TO BARUCH LEVINE

Both Baruch Levine and I share a premise: theology begins with philology. When Levine speaks, I listen; in philology he is nonpareil. We differ, however, on its use. For example, I no longer will accept the occurrence of Aramaisms as a (late) dating criterion.

First, we now possess Aramaic inscriptions from the Syro-Palestinian area, such as Bar Hadad, Hazael, and Zakkur, that stem from the ninth and eighth centuries B.C.E. — that is, a time preceding the composition of the priestly material in the Pentateuch.

Moreover, during this period trade and commerce between North Israel and Aramaic principalities flourished, characterized by the negotiation of reciprocal-trade agreements and the establishment of trading posts in both countries (1 Kgs 20:34; cf. Malamat 1973: 144; Bright 1981: 240–41). David and Solomon controlled Aramaic-speaking areas and established garrisons in them (2 Sam 8:6). After all, Hadadezer of Zobah and Rezin of Damascus, to mention two Aramaens with whom they had contact (2 Sam 8:3; 1 Kgs 11:23), assuredly did not communicate in Hebrew!

Thus the intrusion of an occasional Aramaic word into a biblical text is of no chronological significance. Only if a plethora of Aramaisms floods the text is it suspect of being a late composition and, even then, only if the Aramaisms are accompanied by characteristically late Biblical Hebrew words (details in Hurvitz 1968). I turn now to three other of Levine's points.

1. Two chapters deal with the priestly consecration: Exod 29 and Lev 8. Levine (1963) opts for the chronological priority of the latter. I cannot agree. First, the prescriptive text for Lev 8 is not all of Exod 29, but only its first five verses, which give instructions about the materials needed for the priestly consecration, on which Lev 8 is based. Moreover, the assembling of the *'ēdâ* and the consecration of the sanctuary (Lev 8:3–4, 10–11) are two items that are not mentioned in Exod 29. If Exod 29 were later, why was this salient information omitted?

Thus the conclusion is inescapable: Lev 8 is a revision of Exod 29. The consecration of the sanctuary (8:10–11) had to be added before the description of the sacrificial rites (8:12–30) because one cannot offer sacrifice in an unconsecrated sanctuary (for fifteen other stylistic and lexicographical differences and for the chronological priority of Exod 29, see vol. 1.545–49).

2. Levine questions my rendering of *welo'- yādā' wĕ'āšēm* 'without knowing it and he feels guilt' (5:17) by asking: "When the act was committed the person didn't realize he was doing something wrong. So how is it that he felt guilt?" (cf. also Levine 1989a). The answer, for me, is obvious. When a person is suffering because illness or misfortune has befallen him, he may not and probably does not know what sin of his was responsible. That is why all over the ancient Near East confessionals invariably include the phrase "the sin I know and the sin I do not know" (for examples, see vol. 1.361–63).

3. Finally, Levine gently upbraids me for not mentioning him concerning his gift theory of sacrifice. I admit my guilt. However, I devoted only three pages to the multifarious hypotheses on the origin of sacrifice (vol. 1. 440–43). Hence, I mentioned only one of Levine's forerunners, E. B. Tylor (mid-nineteenth century). Of the regnant theories, it is probably the best. However, it fails because it cannot explain the expiatory sacrifices; no one can possibly claim that the *ḥaṭṭāʾt*, the purification offering, is a gift. Indeed, even the *šĕlāmîm*, the gift offering par excellence, has an expiatory aspect: to ransom its offerer from the charge of murder because he killed the animal for the sake of eating it (see NOTE on 17:4; vol. 1.704–13; and chap. 17, COMMENT C), a rationale not unique to the priestly legists, but already adumbrated in Sumerian mythology (vol. 1.713; Hallo 1987). I continue to stand by my conclusion that "no single theory can encompass the sacrificial system of any society" (vol. 1.442).

C. REJOINDER TO ISRAEL KNOHL

As Israel Knohl (1995: 225–26) acknowledges, it was with exuberant delight that I greeted his announcement that he had drafted a thesis demonstrating that H is subsequent to and the redactor of P. For the previous decade, I had pondered this possibility, realizing in particular that indisputable H passages placed at critical interstices in the P document could only be the work of a redactor (vol. 1.13). I was thus happy to play the role of devil's advocate over the following four summers in Jerusalem. I was especially pleased to see that Knohl's source-critical skills were matched by a penetrating analysis of the text's underlying theology. Now that his dissertation has been published in a superb translation by Jackie Feldman and Peretz Rodman, it is happily available to the wider audience it richly deserves.

My disagreements with Knohl are noted throughout this Appendix and at length in the Introduction. It should not be forgotten, however, that in my opinion his major theses stand firm, except for the alleged influence of H over Hezekiah's reform (see Introduction II D, and chap. 17, COMMENT D) and his questionable assertions on P's theology (vol. 1.21–26; expanded in Introduction II D). Herein, I have reserved further remarks on P's ethical stance in view of Knohl's (1995: 225–30) appendix to his book.

Knohl's (1995: 175) major thesis concerning P is that it exhibits a "total disjunction of the cultic system, centered on the name of Yahweh, from the moral consciousness that regulates the social order." As for P's generalization that the *ḥaṭṭā't* sacrifice is brought for violation of *mikkōl miṣwōt YHWH 'ăšer lō' tē'āśênâ* (Lev 4:2), he remarks, "The comprehensive language of 'any of the Lord's commandments about things not to be done' refers only, I think, to the totality of cultic imperatives" (1995: 228). He lists them as follows: Exod 30:32, 37; Lev 7:15, 19; 11:4–5, 11–20; 12:4 (cf. 1995: 138, n. 55). In fact, his list should be even shorter. Lev 11 should be stricken from the list. Those who touch impure (*ṭāmē'*) foods only have to purify themselves (see NOTES on 11:24–40; Milgrom 1994a); but a *ḥaṭṭā't* is mandated if they neglect their purificatory rites (5:2–3, 5–13; cf. vol. 1.307–18). Thus the prohibitions requiring a *ḥaṭṭā't* for their involuntary violation are, in Knohl's view, making or using sacred anointment oil or incense offered on the incense altar (Exod 30:32, 37), not eating (or burning) the meat of the thanksgiving offering by morning (Lev 7:15), eating of a defiled well-being offering (Lev 7:19), and contact with the sanctuary or sancta by a parturient during the first seven (or fourteen) days following birth (Lev 12:4). Is it conceivable that these few cultic prohibitions constitute *kōl miṣwōt YHWH 'ăšer lō' tē'āśênâ* '*all* the Lord's prohibitive commandments'?

Moreover, Knohl (1995: 159, 226, 227) readily grants that P predicates (in Genesis) the existence of a universal, ethical imperative, which is the "first step in the development of the religious personality." Would not P also demand punishment for its infraction and expiation before God? For example, would P's theology allow a defrauder who voluntarily returned his stolen object *without* taking an imprecatory oath (cf. 5:20–26; Knohl 1995: 239–40) to be exempt (after paying his civil fine) from any responsibility to atone before God? If it were Abraham, would Israel's priests still say of him that he was "blameless" and "walked with God"? Indeed, as P's negative *ḥāmās* 'violence, lawlessness' (Gen 6:11–13; 49:5) and positive *tāmîm* 'blameless' (Gen 6:9; 17:1) and *ṣaddîq* (Gen 6:9; 18:23; 20:4) indicate the existence of a basic ethical code in its narrative, so P uses the expression *kōl miṣwōt YHWH 'ăšer lō' tē'āśênâ* 'all YHWH's commandments that may not be done' (Lev 4:2, 13, 22, 27; 5:17) for the violation *of its laws*. For example, as I have demonstrated (vol. 1.704–42), the fundamental ethical principle of the sanctity and inviolability of life lies behind the diet laws (chap. 11). Since the priests are commanded to teach these laws to Israel (11:1–2a), would they exclude their ethical import from their teaching?

Furthermore, the exhortation *wě'attâ 'im-šāmôa' tišmě'û běqōlî ûšěmartem 'et-běrîtî* 'Now then, if you will hearken to my voice and keep my covenant' (Exod 19:5a [JE]) is "not limited to the ritual-cultic sphere" (Knohl 1995: 181, n. 38). "Covenant" here refers to the Decalogue (Exod 20:1–17). To be sure, the entire pericope is nonpriestly, but P surely would not deny the Decalogue's imperatives. Nor would it defer the adjudication of all its ethical commands to the civil courts, since some of them (e.g., commandments 5 and 10, Exod 20:12, 17) are sins committed in private and would fall to the jurisdiction of the heavenly court, the exclusive curriculum of the priests. Moreover, wouldn't P, in keeping with its basic postulates, have barred such deliberate violators from the sanctuary and required some sacrificial expiation from inadvertent sinners?

Moreover, the word for moral perfection is *tāmîm*, —for example, H's Abraham (Gen 17:1) and D's idealized Israel (Deut 18:13). It is no coincidence that in D, the two passages that stress the unblemished requirement of sacrifices avoid *tāmîm* (Deut 15:21; 17:1; Paran 1983: 195). The reason is that D has preempted the term for moral perfection. The reverse holds true in the priestly legal literature, where *tāmîm* is consistently used for sacrificial animals (e.g., 1:3, 10; 4:3, 23; 22:19–25), but is absent in the physical requirements for priests (21:16–23; cf. the adjoining animal list, 22:19, 21). The reason can only be that H, just as P (Gen 6:9; 17:1), has reserved *tāmîm* for moral perfection. Why, then, is *tāmîm* absent in H's ethical imperatives (e.g., chap. 19)? The answer is that ethics are encapsulated in H's term *qādōš* (see chap. 19 the COMMENT) and in P's term *kol-hammiṣwōt* (above). Indeed, from an anthropological perspective, in a society such as Israel, basic ethics inhere in its structure: "the person in a closed and strongly positional society would know what is moral and what is immoral. Injunctions to be compassionate would not be necessary because kindness would be predicated in the rules of behavior as well as exemplified in the narratives" (Douglas forthcoming).

Finally, it can be demonstrated that P's ethics are not just implicit, but are visible in one instance in an unambiguous explicit statement, which Knohl surprisingly overlooks. He (1995: 140, n. 58) cites my conclusion on 5:20–26: "The understanding of Lev 5:20ff. is based on the realization that it concerns religious and not civil law . . . all that matters to the Priestly legislator is to enumerate those situations whereby the defrauding of man leads, by a false oath, to the 'defrauding' of God." True, the reason why this is religious law (*fas*) and not civil law (*jus*) is the false oath (*fas*) in every case. But P imposes a 20 percent fine for each case of fraud. Furthermore, the defrauder must pay the fine to his victim *before* he makes restitution to God (the *'āšām*) for the false oath (Milgrom 1976a: 110–11). Clearly, even if the cases were not compounded by a false oath, P would have maintained the 20 percent fine for the sin against man (*jus*)! Can there be any doubt that in P's system, though not expressed in P's cultic legislation, is hidden an entire regimen of ethics?

Knohl's claim concerning the lack of ethical interest or content in P appears even more extreme against the backdrop of the ancient Near East. In vol. 1.21–23, I quoted from Mesopotamian Šurpu and "Lipšur" Litanies to demonstrate that cultic and ethical violations are given equal space (shades of Lev 19!) in their enumeration of the sins that anger the gods. Here I wish to offer some additional evidence. Sumerian proverbs collected by Hallo (1985: 23–28), stemming from an even earlier period (the beginning of the second millennium), exhibit similar ethical sensitivity: "A judge who perverts justice . . . To seize someone with unauthorized force . . . Adding property to property . . . To reach for [i.e., to steal] alms . . . is an abomination of Ninurta / Utu" (for the problems in rendering the last evil, see Klein and Sefati 1988: 135, n. 15). One will recognize close biblical parallels in Exod 23:6–8; Lev 25:35–37; Isa 5:8, respectively (stealing from communal charity, however, is not found in Scripture). It can be argued that the texts I have cited thus far from Mesopotamia stem from either divinatory or wisdom literature and are irrelevant to the practices of the temple. This objection, however, collapses in view of the evidence culled from the sacral sphere. In the "Hymn to Enlil," according to its translator, S. N. Kramer (*ANET* 573–76), Enlil sets up his dwelling in the temple complex of Nippur (ll. 1–13) because the city is the exemplar of the loftiest moral and spiritual values (ll. 20–26; for slight variations in the rendering, see Klein and Sefati 1988: 139):

> Hypocrisy, distortion,
> Abuse, malice, unseemliness
> Insolence, enmity, oppression,
> Envy, (brute) force, libelous speech
> Arrogance, violation of agreement, breach of contract,
>   abuse of (a court) verdict
> (All these) evils the city does not tolerate

The city of Nippur is endowed with sanctity and deemed a worthy residence for the god Enlil because it eschews abuses of an exacting, refined moral standard. And if one further objects that this hymn is the exaggerated (probably propagandistic) boast of a temple poet, it nonetheless represents a vision of the ideal society in which ethical behavior rather than cultic practice is paramount. A similar standard is exemplified in Egypt by an inscription incised on the lintel of the southwest door of the Temple of Edfu (Weinfeld 1982a: 233–35):

he who initiates wrongfully
he who speaks falsehood in your house
he who knows (to discern) right from wrong
he who is pure
he who is upright and walks in righteousness . . .
he who loves your attendants exceedingly
he who receives bribes . . .
he who covets the property of your temple
he who is careful . . .
he who does not take rewards or the share of any man.
I (Seshat the mistress of writing) write down good for the doer of good in your (Horus's) city, I reject the character of the evildoer . . . (he who does righteousness) in your house (is) enduring forever, but the sinner perishes everlastingly.

Positive exhortations include purity, integrity, and respect for the god's servants. Negative ones include dealing wrongfully, speaking lies, accepting bribes and gifts, and coveting temple property (for the biblical analogies, Pss 15, 24; Isa 33:15–16; Weinfeld 1982a: 234, 245, n. 14). There can be no doubt that all those who enter the temple would see this inscription, and they would know that if they violate these instructions they are personae non grata in the temple. Would not, then, the Israelite worshiper know and would he not have heard from the priests that if he willfully violates "any of the Lord's prohibitive (ethical) commandments," he is not acceptable in his sanctuary?

The question, however, remains: If *kōl miṣwōt YHWH* 'all the Lord's commandments' (4:2) includes ethical prohibitions, why are they completely missing in P? Why, indeed, are only the few cultic prohibitions (cited above) specified? Knohl (1995: 145) himself, I submit, unwittingly provides the answer: "the laws of PT are not arranged in the form of a *sēper bĕrît*, a covenant book, nor do they terminate with a list of blessings and curses." Indeed, it should be kept in mind that H is not only a source, but a redaction. In its original form, P probably was of much larger scope, perhaps in the form of a covenant containing moral laws in addition to instructions for building the Tabernacle and inaugurating the cult. H, however, selected from P only that which interested it: P's sacrificial and purificatory procedures in Leviticus, the establishment of the cult and priesthood in Exodus (cf. Otto 1997: 50), the function of the Levites in the wilderness march (contra Knohl) and some of its events and laws in Numbers. It would have omitted P's ethical commandments because it replaced them with its own, in more nuanced and refined language (see below), and arranged its code in covenant form, beginning with laws concerning sacrifice (Lev 17) and terminating in blessings and curses (Lev 26).

Knohl (1995: 138, n. 55) denies the possibility that H eliminated P's moral commandments on the grounds that "moral-social laws such as the law of slavery, gifts to the poor and others, reappear in different formulations in the corpora of PT, HS and D in spite of some repetition." But this precisely is the point.

H and D have no outside redactor. P does. Thus the fact that there are no "so-cial-moral laws" in P indicates the likelihood that H omitted them in favor of its own. It should not be overlooked that, to all intents and purposes, H regards itself as the legitimate successor to P. Whereas H cites JE's social-moral laws and even polemicizes against them (e.g., the laws of slavery; see NOTES on 25:39–43, and Introduction I I), it feels fully justified in presenting, in place of P's social-moral laws, its own loftier version. Thus P might have contained ex-hortations to care for the poor, just as we find in the sabbatical laws of JE (Exod 23:11) and D (Deut 15:1–11). But H was not content to provide for the poor merely from meager pickings of the sabbatical aftergrowth. (In fact, it denied them to the poor; see NOTE on 25:6.) Hence it asserts the rights of the poor to the yearly harvest (19:9–10). Similarly, P might have had a general prohibition against taking interest, just as in JE (Exod 22:24) and D (Deut 23:20–21). But H insisted on defining interest more precisely, to include advance as well as ac-crued interest in relation to the substance of the principal (25:36–37).

Rather than hypothesizing P's purported ethical laws, let us see what H ac-tually does with the two ethical laws found in P. First, there is no need in H for a law against murder, because one is already present in P's Noahide covenant (Gen 9:5–6). But H certainly alludes to this law and refines it. It bans common slaughter to the Israelite as being equivalent to murder (17:3–4), and, if Num 35 stems from H (Knohl 1995: 99–100), it distinguishes between deliberate and involuntary homicide, providing asylums for those who committed the latter un-til a general amnesty is declared with the death of the high priest. It again al-ludes to the murder prohibition when it bans slander precisely because it may lead to murder (see NOTE on 19:16).

A second example is even more instructive. Because H cites P's entire sacri-ficial system, it also includes in its portfolio of P laws a series of ethical infrac-tions (fraud) requiring a reparation ('āšām) offering (5:20–26). H, therefore, has no need to repeat them. Instead, it supplements them (19:11–13). That is, it enumerates ethical wrongs missing in P's list, such as theft (gnb) and lies (šqr), so it can cover all kinds of deceitful acts that are not limited to P's category of misappropriated property (see NOTES on 19:11–13). Here, one is tempted to in-quire why H did not assume P's cases of fraud (5:20–26), as, according to my claim, it did with P's other ethics? The answer is that H needed to keep P where it was for its comprehensive portfolio on the 'āšām offering, as it does again in the case of the betrothed slave (19:20–22 [P]). H, therefore, did not have to list a charter of basic ethics. It may already have absorbed them from P. Instead, it carried them to rarified, sublime heights, such as condemning cursing the deaf and tripping the blind (19:14), rising before the elderly (19:32), cheating your fellow (in calculating a field's yield, 25:17), overworking your Israelite hireling / "slave" (25:43). These are all furtive crimes, matters of conscience, adjudica-ble not in the human court but in the court of God, as indicated by H's au-thoritative signature 'ănî YHWH or wĕyārē'tā mē'ĕlōhêka.

Now, let me turn to the example I cited in my earlier arguments (vol. 1.24–25) to bolster the case of an ethical P, but which Knohl (1995: 227–29) wishes to dispute, namely, the ʿăwōnōt confessed by the high priest on the head of the scapegoat (16:21). Knohl (1995: 229) denies that this term refers to moral transgressions: "The rectification of moral misconduct is effected by the return of stolen property to its owner, and not by the offering of a sacrifice or the sending out of a scapegoat." In other words, moral injustices fall in the realm of the civil juridical system, not of the priestly cult. First, his statement needs correction: the term ʿăwōnōt applies to only the scapegoat, not the sacrifice. The latter is characterized by ṭumʾōt (16:16), not by ʿăwōnōt· Both, however, are called pěšāʿîm 'transgressions' (i.e., deliberate sins), but the blood of the sacrifice (ḥaṭṭāʾt), not the scapegoat, purges the sanctuary of its accumulated impurities (ṭumʾōt). It may be conjectured, as can be deduced from other ancient Near Eastern elimination rites (vol. 1.1071–79), that originally the scapegoat did remove these impurities (see NOTE on "iniquities," 16:21). However, the fact that the term "impurities" (ṭumōʾt), used for the purgation of the sanctuary, is altered to "iniquities" (ʿăwōnōt) can only mean that the people of Israel is purified of its moral sins. If Israel's transgressions carried off by the scapegoat were the same cultic sort that polluted the sanctuary, the term ṭumʾōt would continue to be used. Indeed, whereas the sacrifice kipper 'purges' the sanctuary (found five times in the sacrificial rites of vv. 16–20), this term is conspicuously missing in the rite of the scapegoat (vv. 21–22; for the ostensible exception in v. 10, see its NOTE).

Finally, let us consider the case of P's Abram. He is commanded hithallēk lěpānay wehyēh tāmîm 'Walk in my ways, and be blameless' (Gen 17:1bβ). Here he is surely being urged to ethical, not cultic, perfection. As Israel's founding religious personality, he is the model for all his progeny; hence his ethical behavior is also incumbent on them (Gen 18:19). And if they have violated Abraham's ethical pattern, they must be purified before God, an action assumed annually by the high priest when he confesses Israel's ʿăwōnōt on the head of the scapegoat. Thus, according to P, it is insufficient to pay the penalties imposed by the civil court for crimes committed against one's fellow. God, too, demands expiation, which symbolically takes the form of sacrificial purgation for inadvertent violations (Lev 4:1–5:13) and fasting and abstinence from work (Num 29:7 [P]) for advertent violations as they are confessed on the scapegoat on the Day of Purgation (16:21). And what of Israel's furtive violations, whose number is legion, which will never be brought before a human court? These, too, must be what P surely encompasses in its term ʿawōnōt, which are also expiated in the scapegoat rite.

What is P's theology once it is stripped of its ethical substratum? Knohl (1995: 197) ascribes to it a metaphysical function: after Moses, it "is focused on the numinous essence (of God), essentially detached from morality or the principle of providence and recompense." God is impersonal, withdrawn, and feared: "Such an encounter [with God in the sanctuary] engenders feelings of guilt and the need for atonement. This guilt is not associated with any particular sins; rather it is a result of human awareness of insignificance and contamination in comparison with the sublimity of God's holiness" (1995: 151). As a footnote, Knohl cites Rudolf Otto's *Idea of the Holy* (1958), and Knohl's terminology clearly betrays Otto's influence. Otto would undoubtedly have distanced himself from Knohl's remarks. Knohl's notion of the numinous corresponds with only Otto's (1958: 75) "lower stage of numinous consciousness, viz. daemonic dread (which) has already been superseded by the time we reach the Prophets and Psalmists. . . . The venerable religion of Moses marks the beginning of a process which from that point onward proceeds with ever increasing momentum, by which the numinous is throughout rationalized and moralized, i.e., charged with ethical import, until it becomes the 'holy' in the fullest sense of the word." It is of no small moment that when Otto (1958: 72) wishes to cite an example of the "lower stage of numinous consciousness, viz. daemonic dread" in the Pentateuch, he resorts to Exod 4:24 (JE; cf. Exod 15:11b) but not to P's sanctuary and its cult (Lev 10:1–4 [P] and Num 4:15, 17–20 [possibly H! Knohl 1995: 85] are exceptions).

Moreover, Knohl's claim that "guilt is not associated with any particular sin" is a blatant distortion of P, which always attaches guilt (*'āšēm*) to specific sins (Lev 4–5). Indeed, in Lev 16 the one place in P where the sin is generalized, *'āšēm* is absent. And Knohl's notion that guilt is "a result of human awareness of insignificance and contamination" is nonexistent in P and is found only in Knohl's ill-founded extrapolations from Otto's concept of the numinous, which, ironically, is characteristic of Isa 6:5 — but not P.

In sum, P's *kōl miṣwōt YHWH* includes the moral behavior that it demands of Abraham and his progeny, who "will keep the way of the Lord by doing what is just and right" (Gen 18:19). If they violate these *miṣwōt* inadvertently, they are required to bring a purification offering to purge the sacrificial altar of its resultant pollution (Lev 4:23–35); if advertently, the high priest (but not the barred offenders) purges the entire sanctuary by confessing their *'ăwōnōt* on the dispatched scapegoat (Lev 16:21–22). All of P is a continuum. Its Genesis is assumed by its Leviticus. Israel's immoral behavior, as much as its cultic infractions, pollutes the sanctuary and, in aggregate, drives out YHWH's presence. Why doesn't P enumerate the moral obligations? Why doesn't it specify what it means by "what is just and right"? I think it did, but H replaced P's moral commands (and, in two cases, supplemented them) for a superior version of its own.

D. RESPONSE TO ADRIAN SCHENKER

Congratulations are in order to Adrian Schenker for his intensive study of ancient Israel's expiatory sacrifices and, particularly, for discerning that in the priestly texts they compose a coherent system. I heartily welcome the fruitful *Auseinandersetzung* that surely lies before us. We agree on major issues, but I differ with him on a number of his theses, which I find beset with logical difficulties and exegetical errors. My analysis is based on three seminal articles (Schenker 1990; 1992; 1994) and will focus, in the main, on his exegesis of the enigmatic, marginal cases of Lev 5:1–4 and 5:17–19. An annotated version was published in Milgrom (1996b), but a slightly expanded text appears here. In addition, I append a brief analysis of Schenker's (1998) most recent article on the stages of destitution and their alleviation through redemption and the jubilee.

Schenker (1994: 60–61) argues that the verb *'āšēm* always means "be liable, responsible" and the expression *wĕ'āšēm wĕnāśā' 'ăwōnô* (Lev 5:17) cannot be a tautology, as I claim, because a person must first be held liable (*wĕ'āšēm*) before he is sentenced (*wĕnāśā' 'ăwōnô*). But how can he be liable if neither he nor anyone else is aware of what he has done? The text states explicitly, not once but twice, *wĕ(hû')lō' yāda'* 'and (he) did not know' (Lev 5:17, 18). To be sure, Schenker (1990: 118) parries this objection by claiming "er wusste es nicht *sogleich*, sondern es wurde ihm *später bewusst*" [he did not know it immediately, but it was made known to him later]. However, that he subsequently becomes aware of his act is pure hypothesis; it is nowhere mentioned in the text. Indeed, if this were so, one would have expected the text to add *'ô hôda' 'ēlāyw ḥaṭṭā'tô* 'or (someone) informs him of his wrong' (as in Lev 4:23–28), namely, either he himself becomes aware of his act, or he is informed of it by someone else. If, however, he never comes to know what he has done, why must he bring a reparation offering? The answer, I aver, is that he *suspects* he has done wrong, and his troubled conscience, expressed by the verb *'āšēm·* is absolved by the *'āšām·* the reparation offering (see below). Thus there is no need, with Schenker (1990: 120), to speculate that the case of Lev 5:17–19 should require a *ḥaṭṭā't* 'a purification offering' rather than an *'āšām*, but the latter is prescribed because the sin was undisclosed for a purported long period. The *'āšām* expiates for sacrilege, not for prolonged, undisclosed sins (see below).

Schenker (1997: 697) defends his argument in response to this criticism (Milgrom 1996b: 511), claiming that liability comes with fear and guilt. Be that as it may, his rendering does not fit the text. In the *ḥaṭṭā't* pericope, the verb *wĕ'āšēm* is always followed by *ô' hôda' 'ēlāyw / wĕnôda' haḥaṭṭā't* 'if he is informed (of his wrongdoing) / when the wrongdoing becomes known' (4:14, 23, 28; cf. vol. 1). Two options are set forth: the wrongdoer realizes on his own, or he is informed. If *'āšēm* means "responsible, liable," why isn't it also found in the second option; that is, if he knows by himself, he is liable or if he is informed, *he is liable*. Alternatively, as I wrote (1996b: 512), *wĕ'āšēm* should come at the end of both options "only after he himself knows or someone else lets him know what he has done, *does he become liable*." I submit that my rendering eliminates Schenker's problem. The wrongdoer will seek expiation for his act only if he feels guilty, but if he is "caught" doing the wrong by someone else, conscience plays no part. He has no choice but to bring a *ḥaṭṭāt*.

In truth, Schenker and I differ by a semantic hair. By stating that liability comes with guilt, he admits that guilt must play a role. Note that in the case of 5:17–19, the sinner is explicitly unaware of his act (*wĕlō' yāda'*, v. 17). Why should he be liable unless he *first* felt guilt? If he had not been struck by guilt to begin with, then there is no liability because there is no motivation to seek expiation. Since he does not know, nor will he ever know, his wrongdoing, he only *suspects* he has done wrong. The essence of his guilt cannot be fact, but only *suspicion*. Rather than saying, with Schenker, that liability contains guilt, it would be more correct to turn the terms around: *guilt entails liability*. This is precisely the message of this pericope. And since the guilt is not based on fact, but only on suspicion, one can only conclude that the *'āšām* offering is brought for the *suspicion* that one may have committed *ma'al* 'sacrilege'.

Schenker (1990: 118) also asks why a suspected sin must be expiated by a more costly animal, a ram, than a known sin, which requires only a lamb or goat. As I have suggested (vol. 1.33), the person may have committed a *ma'al*, a sacrilege, the severest of sins, expiable only by a ram (Lev 5:15). Note as well that Lev 5:17–19 is inserted between two *ma'al* cases, vv. 14–16 and vv. 20–26, which supports my thesis that vv. 17–19 deal with a case of suspected *ma'al*. Incidentally, I also contend that *'āšām* is prescribed for a scale-diseased person (Lev 14:12, 24) because of suspected *ma'al*, a supposition supported by the *ma'al* of King Uzziah (2 Chr 26:16–19; cf. vol. 1.856–57).

Another difficulty in rendering *'āšēm* as "be liable" is the statement found in the *ḥaṭṭā't* pericope, mentioned above: *wĕ'āšēm 'ô hôda' 'ēlāyw ḥaṭṭā'tô* (Lev 4:23, 28). If *wĕ'āšēm* means "becomes liable" (Schenker 1990: 117), it should not begin but end these words; that is, only after he himself knows or someone else lets him know what he has done, does he become liable. Here again, I maintain (vol. 1.344–45), this statement makes sense only if it is rendered as "he feels guilt (as a result of knowing what he did) or he is informed by someone else."

In this regard, I believe that Schenker mistranslates *wĕhāyâ kî* (Lev 5:5) as "*Dann* [Then]." These words invariably begin a protasis, and must be rendered as "When." The following word, *ye'ĕšam*, according to Schenker (1992: 49), would not be translated "wird er schuldig sein" [he will become liable] but "Wenn er schuldig ist," [when he is liable] which is nonsense. Here, too, I claim (vol. 1.300–301, 342–45), the rendering should be "When he feels guilt."

Schenker (1992: 45, n. 2) claims that impurity and sin are sharply differentiated in all respects so that both cannot lead to the contamination of the sanctuary. However, this is precisely what is stated by the Yom Kippur rite of Lev 16:16: the high priest purges the sanctuary of the impurites caused by *all* of Israel's sins (vol. 1.1034). Moreover, Schenker's assertion that the purpose of Lev 16 is to expiate Israel's unconscious sins is refuted by this chapter's unique use of *peša* 'rebellious, presumptuous sins' for both Israel's unexpiated impurities (*ṭum'ōt*, v. 16) and moral misdemeanors (*'āwōnōt*, v. 21).

Turning now to Lev 5:1–4, Schenker (1992: 48, n. 7) sets forth the thesis that intentional and presumptuous sins make up two distinct categories and that only the latter are ineligible for sacrificial expiation (Num 15:30–31), whereas the former, if committed "in guter Absicht," [with good intention] are expiable by sacrifice. In my view, this distinction is nonexistent. The absence of the key term *šĕgāgâ* 'unintentionality' from all four cases of Lev 5:1–4 is a clear indication that they include the possibility of intentionally committed acts. Yet not a single case contains the qualification that the wrong was committed for an exonerable reason. For example, Schenker (1994: 66, 69) avers that the person who refuses to testify (v. 1) or fails to fulfill his oath (v. 4) does so legitimately. But this is stated nowhere in the text! Indeed, his claim that the oath (v. 4) was taken "in guter Absicht" (1992: 47) is refuted by the statement that all oaths are involved, even those *lĕhāra'* 'for evil purpose'!

Regarding Lev 5:2–3, Schenker once again introduces his unfounded distinction between presumptuous and intentional sins. Although he admits that intentionality is presupposed by the text, he claims that the offender's contact with impure carcasses or persons was committed with no *"verwerfliche* Absicht" [*blameable* intention] (1990: 120). Furthermore, according to Schenker (1990: 120), the sin consists of "Berührung von Heiligem mit Unreinen" [contact of the body with the impure]. Eisegesis thus occurs twice: presumptuous sins are excluded, and contact between impurity and holiness is presumed. But neither presumption nor holiness is stated or even intimated in the text.

That the contamination of the holy is not the subject of Lev 5:2–3 removes the ground from Schenker's claim that the four cases of Lev 5:1–4 actually require an *'āšām* offering, the sacrifice for desecration. To be sure, Schenker admits that the sacrifice actually offered is a *ḥaṭṭā't*, but he justifies the switch from a (purported) *'āšām* to a *ḥaṭṭāt* by assuming that "Zwei verschiedene *Opferarten* können unter bestimmten Bedingungen *derselben Zweck* erfüllen" [Two different kinds of sacrifices can, under certain conditions, fulfill the same good] (1990: 118). This assumption must be categorically denied, certainly in the case of the *ḥaṭṭā't* and *'āšām·* These two sacrifices should never be fused or confused. The *'āšām* expiates for desecration; the *ḥaṭṭā't·* for contamination. The reason that Lev 5:2–3 require a *ḥaṭṭā't* (v. 6) is that the prolonged defilement has contaminated the sanctuary (vol. 1.307–18). Similarly, cases 1 and 4, dealing with oaths, also involve the sanctuary's contamination (vol. 1.314). These oaths are not lying oaths, perjury, which can be expiated, under certain ameliorating circumstances (Lev 5:20–26), only by an *'āšām*. Rather, these sins involve an unfulfilled oath (v. 4) or an imposed but rejected oath (vol. 1.314–15), which calls for a *ḥaṭṭā't·* To be sure, Lev 5:1–4 are borderline cases, which explains why the *ḥaṭṭā't* is scaled according to the offender's financial status.

Schenker's (1990: 119) main evidence that Lev 5:1–4 prescribe an *'āšām* is the explicit statement *wĕhēbî' 'et-'ăšāmô* (v. 6), implying that an *'āšām* sacrifice is required. However, the word *'āšām*, in addition to its sacrificial designation, also denotes "penalty, reparation" (as in vv. 15, 25; cf. Lev 19:21; Num 5:7, 8; vol. 1.339–45).

Schenker (1997: 698–99) defends his position. Rather than repeating my argument as a counterargument, I would suggest to the reader to set our two positions side by side and reach his or her own conclusion.

To recapitulate, Schenker holds four untenable positions:

1. His distinction between intentional and presumptuous sins is nonexistent. All deliberate sins are regarded as presumptuous unless they are tempered by *subsequent* acts of repentance, such as voluntary confession and restitution specified by Lev 5:20–26; Num 5:5–8.
2. The *ḥaṭṭā't* and *'āšām* are discrete sacrifices that never can be substituted

one for the other. The *ḥaṭṭā't* expiates for the *contamination* of the sanctuary and its sancta by both severe impurities and moral transgressions. The *'āšām* expiates for the *desecration* of the sanctuary and its sancta (including God's personal sanctum—his name).

3. The text should not be subjected to eisegesis, such as reading excusable, intentional sins in Lev 5:1–4; direct contact with holiness in Lev 5:2–3; and eventual awareness of sin in Lev 5:17–19.

4. Rendering the verb *'āšēm* as "be liable" runs into the logical contradiction of Lev 5:17b and the logical difficulty of Lev 4:23, 28; 5:23. These texts, however (and all other usages of *'āšēm*), are resolved by rendering the verb as "feel guilt," which emphasizes the action of conscience in the expiation of sin. For further details, see Milgrom (1996b).

Schenker (1998) claims that Lev 25 supplements and completes the slave laws of Exod 21:1–7. In case of insoluble debt, the paterfamilias will sell his children (Exod 21:1–7); if he falls again into debt, he will sell part of his estate (Lev 25:25–28). If this is still not enough, he will sell all his land, and he and his family will become itinerants (*gērîm*); he will seek loans for food and some capital in return for his work (25:35–38), but in extremis he and his sons will have to be sold as slaves (25:39–43). H urges the Israelite creditor to take in the *gēr* and his family, to give him interest-free loans (vv. 36–37), to treat him not as a slave but as a hired laborer (v. 40), and not to work him harshly (v. 43). But if he is sold to an alien creditor, the latter may treat him as a slave (v. 47), and it is urgent to redeem him. All these stages are subject to the manumission laws of the jubilee, and sold land and sold (enslaved) Israelites are redeemable ahead of the jubilee year by the nearest kinsman (vv. 23–25, 28, 41, 48–49, 54).

Schenker's major thesis is that Lev 25 completes Exod 21. The fusion of these two laws implies that the paterfamilias will sell his sons and daughters as slaves before he sells any part of his land (Lev 25:25–28). I cannot imagine such an eventuality in biblical society, all the more so in H, which—alone of all the corpora—calls for the total abolition of Israelite slavery. After all, why would H legislate that if a son is indentured with his father he is not a slave (vv. 39–40), but if he is sold by himself, *without his parents to care for him* (Exod 21), he can be enslaved! Note as well that Lev 25 does not in fact complete Exod 21: there is no manumission law in either corpus for the wife of the paterfamilias (for my tentative solution, see NOTE on "he and his children," v. 41).

I also differ with Schenker on some of the basic terminology. This is particularly evident in v. 35. I render *'immak* 'under your authority' (of the creditor); *wĕheḥĕzaqtā bô gēr wĕtôšāb* 'and you (the creditor) would seize him (as) a resident alien'. Thus instead of Schenker's "then you shall relieve him: (as) a stranger and a sojourner, he will live with you," I have rendered "and you (would) hold him (as) a resident alien, let him subsist under your authority."

The upshot of this difference is that, according to my rendering, the Israelite is not reduced to a *gēr* status, living on the extraordinary goodwill (interest-free loans!) of the creditor, but, to the contrary, he is not to be treated as a *gēr*. He is working on his forfeited estate (not wandering throughout the land), probably as a tenant farmer, and paying off his debt from the usufruct. Indeed, where is there a creditor who would give a loan to a landless, kinless gēr, who cannot provide collateral? Schenker also faces the difficulty that in v. 35 the gēr is an Israelite, and the next time we confront the gēr (v. 47) he is a non-Israelite.

Schenker explains the absence of the principle of redemption in this case (vv. 35–38) because it applies to only sold land and persons. He is correct (see IN-TRODUCTION to vv. 39–43). But if in stage 2 (vv. 35–38) the debtor is reduced to the penury of a gēr, he is more than ever in need of redemption. The only reason that redemption is denied to him is that he is still working on his forfeited land and, with its usufruct, is paying off his interest-free loan (to buy seed and support his family) as well as his debt. Such a case is indeed envisaged in the final stage of destitution (vv. 39–43), when instead of being a slave his status is that of a hired laborer, and, as such, he is not eligible for redemption. I would also ask Schenker how he can regard the stage of a hired laborer (v. 40; stage 2) to be lower than that of a landless, kinless, itinerant gēr (stage 3).

Finally, Schenker (1998: 38) posits that alien creditors can reduce their insolvent Israelite debtors to slavery, resulting in "an asymmetry in the manumission laws between Israelite and foreign creditors residing in Israel, in favour of the latter, and in disfavour of the Israelite debt-slaves." Schenker (1998: 35, n. 28) reaches this conclusion by claiming that the śākîr 'hireling' clauses (vv. 50b, 53a) refer not to the debtor's status, as usually interpreted, but to the terms of redemption. This alleged superior status of the alien creditor leads Schenker (1988: 40, n. 32) to the politico-historical conclusion that "it seems difficult to date Lev 25:47–55 to a time where Israelites and Judeans were alone the masters of their state and society, that is, before the exile." Hence this pericope reflects "postexilic society in the land of Judah, dependent upon a foreign occupation which granted an autonomous social organization within certain limits, but imposed certain rights in favour of alien residents in the land of Israel" (1998: 40).

Initially I accepted Schenker's powerful arguments, and I was willing to assign 25:47–55 to the latest postexilic H tradent. Upon further reflection, however, I can see that Schenker's case does not hold up:

1. If Israel can enforce redemption and jubilee on the alien creditor, as if he were an Israelite creditor (v. 40), then Israel must be in full control of the land. Consider that the redeemer takes priority over the alien creditor at all times — hardly "a prerogative in favour of foreigners" (Schenker 1998: 40).

2. Schenker (1998: 35, n. 28) focuses on v. 53, but overlooks v. 50b: *kiymê śākîr yihyeh 'immô* 'as the term (or "days") of a hired laborer he shall be under the other's authority'. Schenker correctly emphasizes that this clause refers to the terms of redemption (vv. 50–53). But why should the redeemer be required to pay the creditor the higher rate of a hireling instead of the much lower rate of a slave? The only answer is that the alien has been paying a hireling's wages to his Israelite "slave" and, hence, the remaining years to the jubilee without his labor have to be figured on the same basis. In other words, the alien redemption terms of the Israelite imply his status even if he is in the hands of an alien.

3. How does the redeemer recover his "investment" in his indentured kinsman? Of certainty, until the jubilee he enjoys the usufruct of the debtor's land, which has been redeemed with him, while the redeemed debtor and his sons work on the land until the jubilee and receive the wages of a *śākîr* 'hireling' (v. 40). Thus the status of the Israelite debtor is the same under his kinsman as it was under the alien. To put it differently: the change for the redeemed Israelite debtor is that his working conditions are transferred from the alien creditor to the kinsman-redeemer without any monetary change.

4. The nexus between the Israelite and the alien creditor is broken in regard to the debtor's status. The principle that redemption applies to only sold property and persons still holds. But as long as an Israelite is sold to an alien, he must be redeemed regardless of his status in the alien's home. Although he receives the wages of a hireling, he is the *captive of an alien* and his redemption is required.

5. Schenker's postexilic dating is, in my opinion, flawed. As I have argued, it is precisely in the preexilic period that we find *gērîm* rising to high economic (and social) status, owning slaves and fields, whereas in postexilic times there is no attested group of aliens entrenched in the Persian province of Judea when the returnees from the Babylonian Exile occupy it (see NOTE on "has prospered," v. 47).

Again, I wish to express my gratitude to Adrian Schenker for his finely reasoned theses and for his trenchant critique of my views. I learn much from him. Above all, he always makes me rethink my own positions, and for that alone I am grateful. I hope that our fruitful *Auseinandersetzung* will continue for years to come.

E. RESPONSE TO VICTOR HUROWITZ

I can only wish that every author will be blessed with a reviewer like Victor Hurowitz. His fourteen-page essay-review (1994) reveals that he is in total command of the cultic material of the Bible and the ancient Near East and, thus, is fully equipped to evaluate critically every page of my commentary. Moreover, he has not only subjected each page to a close reading, but, as a friendly dybbuk, has penetrated through the text into my soul and extracted some of my unexpressed intentions. For example, consider his (1994: 221) remark:

> Milgrom *claims* that what is construed as new, revolutionary, and molded for and by Judaism's post-Temple existence was actually integral to the thought of the biblical Priestly and Holiness schools. . . . He *declares emphatically* that the worlds of biblical Israel and postbiblical Judaism are not to be torn asunder and analyzed as two distinct, unrelated, unlinked entities. Quite to the contrary, they are organically bound together and therefore may be mutually illuminating. (my emphasis)

The fact of the matter is that nowhere in my commentary did I make such a sweeping generalization. Yet clearly that was my intention. I preferred instead to state the evidence and hoped that perceptive readers, like Hurowitz, would draw (and accept) this conclusion. I intend now to contend with Hurowitz's quibbles, but in a significant number of cases, particularly due to his superior familiarity with Mesopotamian cultic texts, I gratefully acknowledge his corrections. My rejoinder follows his review's pagination:

(215) The "outline or synopsis of the book's overall thematic structure," omitted in vol. 3, was intentionally postponed to vols. 3A and 3B (see the complete translation in either volume).

(216) The three levels of P (surmised in vol. 1.63) have been reduced to two (for the elimination of P₃ in favor of H, see NOTE on "He shall not eat," 22:8). The source divisions are now graphically visible in the translation of the entire book.

(223–25) Would that VH's corrections of typographical errors and stylistic inelegancies were available for the second printing of vol. 1. They have been carefully (wishfully) noted for the third printing. However, "ovines" (see NOTE on "Aaron came forward to the altar," 9:8) should not be changed to "bovines."

(225 on p. 3) Perhaps Aaron's Judahite connection reflects an old tradition. The camps of Aaron and Judah were contiguous in the wilderness (Num 2:3; 3:38), and the Aaronides' permanent settlements were, according to the priestly tradition, mainly in Judah's territory (Josh 21:4, 13–16). However, that Num 34:19–29 "is to be related to the split in the kingdom" must be rejected. Benjamin was never wholly included in the kingdom of Judah, and as cogently argued by 'Or Haḥayyim (ca. 1742), the omission of the title *nĕśî'îm* for the tribal leaders of Judah, Benjamin, and Simeon is more likely due to the placement of these tribes at the head of the list, which is introduced by the injunction "And you shall take a chieftain [lit. "one *nāśî'*, one *nāśî'*"] from each tribe . . ." (Num 34:18). The twice-repeated *nāśî'* obviated the need for it in the following three verses.

(225–26 on p. 30) Possibly, the Arad adytum was separated from the rest of the sanctuary by a veil, no differently than the Tabernacle adytum. Architecturally, there is no good reason to lower the Temple's adytum by 10 cubits (from 30 to 20) unless it was made to conform with that of the Tabernacle.

(226 on p. 31) Following VH (1984), I now reject Friedman's (1980) theory that the Tabernacle was inserted into the Temple adytum.

(226–27 on p. 60) VH's (1995: 155–56) demonstration that the *mĕzammĕrôt* employed *inside* Solomon's Temple (1 Kgs 7:50) are musical instruments undermines Knohl's (1995) thesis that the Temple service was conducted in a "sanctuary of silence" (for other refutations, see Introduction II P).

(227 on p. 140) Haran agrees (1978: 265) that JE's Ark remained inside the camp. Accordingly, I have maintained that the Ark must have been housed to protect it from nature's inclemencies and human encroachment (vol. 1.141). I doubt that the purpose of Joshua's permanent station in JE's Tent of Meeting

(Exod 33:11) was to "wait for revelations." Moses would have been notified personally by God to enter the Tent, by means of the divine cloud at the Tent's entrance (Num 12:4–5). Therefore, it was more likely that Joshua had to guard the Ark. That this guarding function was indispensable, see the unequivocal statement of the text regarding the Ark in the house of Abinadab, "they consecrated his son Eleazar to guard [*lišmōr*] the Ark of the Lord" (1 Sam 7:1b).

(227 on p. 223) I accept VH's suggestion that *liškâ* is more likely related to Akkadian *ašlukkatu* / *ašrukkatu*.

(228 on p. 224) I doubt that Samuel's blessing over the sacrifice (1 Sam 9:13) was for the purpose of extispicy, for which there is no biblical evidence. Moreover, Akkadian *puḫāda karābum* (CAD 8.198) refers to an act of dedication, not extispicy.

(228 on p. 224) VH is probably correct in presuming the "cultic supremacy of the male" sacrifice. I have also suggested that the exclusive criterion of a male for the *ʿōlâ* was transferred to the public *ḥaṭṭāʾt* and to the high priest and *nāśîʾ* for their individual wrongs (vol. 1.176).

(228 on p. 272) I (1994a) have addressed the enigma of why the ashes of the red cow defile even before they are used.

(228–29 on p. 279) VH correctly applies my suggestion that the *ḥaṭṭāʾt* originally served an apotropaic function for the Nazirite (Num 6:14, 16).

(229 on p. 301) The expression *tēn tôdâ* (Josh 7:19), as VH suggests, is indeed another attestation of the root *ydh*, meaning "confess."

(229 on p. 311) I now agree. The detailed acknowledgment of guilt in the Sabean inscription constitutes confession.

(229 on p. 355) No, the *ʾāšām* sacrifice is inappropriate for both the Korah and the Nadab and Abihu incidents because their wrongdoing was deliberate, not inadvertent.

(229 on pp. 363–64) That scale disease is a "traditional malediction attributed to the moon god Sin, regardless of the violation," does not negate desecration as one of the (likely) violations.

(229–30 on p. 364) In regard to VH's assumption that encroachment on prophets (such as Moses and Elisha) constitutes *maʿal* because they are "sancta," there is no evidence whatsoever and must be rejected.

(230 on pp. 388–89) I deny that the altar fire was doused and relit every morning. The ritual prescriptions beginning with *zōʾt hattôrâ* (chaps. 6–7) refer to the permanent, stationary sanctuary in the promised land, with the exception of the *ʿōlâ*, which was continually offered in the wilderness (Num 28:6). Thus *lōʾ tikbeh* (6:6) is no hyperbole, and the wilderness journey (Num 4:14) is irrelevant.

(230 on p. 447) It is technically possible that P (and H) is polemicizing against Ezekiel. That possibility has been refuted in chap. 26, COMMENT D. More likely, the conservative tradition that P battles against is even older.

(230 on p. 449) When Ezekiel mentions the sanctity of the priestly garments (Ezek 44:19), he refers to those worn by the authorized priests of the preexilic Temple (not the exile), which were sanctified with the sacred anointment oil.

(230–31 on p. 509) VH's evidence from Starr (1990) for the Neo-Assyrian *Šamaš Anfrage* is a fruitful source for understanding the modus operandi of the Urim and Thummim.

(231 on p. 512) The same holds for the *ezib* clauses in the *Šamaš Anfrage* concerning flawed rituals.

(231–32 on pp. 566–69) Indeed, there is no humiliation rite for the high priest—by inference also for the ordinary priests (clearly stated in vol. 1:569)—indicating the limits of comparative anthropology.

(232 on p. 571) It is not clear whether the wilderness chronology, particularly Exod 19:1–2, should be attributed to P or H. In any event, the tradition of a second set of tablets (Exod 34) belongs to neither P nor H.

(232 on pp. 624–25) I agree. My reading of the broken texts (Knudson 1959) is only a possibility.

(232 on p. 629) I now concur with VH; Jer 41:5 does not speak of an independent incense offering.

(232 on pp. 628–33) I indeed mention a possible politico-historical basis for the Nadab and Abihu story (citing Gradwohl 1963–64), among others, and I conclude that "the hypotheses thus far proposed are unadulterated speculation and that the historical background remains a mystery" (vol. 1.628).

(233 on p. 631) P could not just have had only Nadab and Abihu (10:1–4) in mind. As an obvious a fortiori deduction, P's message was clear: if *'ēš zārâ* 'unauthorized coals' (not from the altar) invalidated incense offerings that otherwise were perfectly in order, all the more so all private offerings, which not only contained unauthorized coals, but violated other incense prohibitions (Exod 30:34–38).

(233 on p. 717) The *halakhic* reason for the restrictions on animal slaughter is the prevention of *ṭĕrēpâ*, but the *moral* reason is the prevention of excessive pain to the animal. The rabbis were aware of both (*b. Ḥul.* 7b; *b. Šab.* 128b; esp. Maimonides, *Guide*, 3.48).

(233 on p. 736 [not 737]) The greater frequency of meat on the table reflects both D's concession of profane slaughter and the concurrent urbanization and commercialization of Israel's economy.

(233 on pp. 739–40) VH's outright rejection of any allegorical explanation of biblical and ancient Near Eastern law is a further argument against Soler (1979), followed by Eilberg-Schwartz (1990), who allegorizes the prohibition against cooking a kid in its mother's milk (see APPENDIX A).

(234 on p. 747) VH does not follow my reasoning (where I concur with Friedman 1976): if in Mesopotamia, oaths were taken over the symbols of gods, in aniconic Israel, the circumcised penis—the divine covenant in the flesh—could have substituted as the symbol for the presence of the Deity. That oaths in Mesopotamia may also have been taken on the genital organs without any indication of a covenant ceremony (Malul 1987c) does not negate the possibility of precisely such an association in Israel.

(234 on p. 759) The presumption is that the priestly theology, including the contamination of the altar from afar, took root in the Shilo sanctuary, not at a local *bāmâ*, and subsequently was transferred to the Jerusalem Temple.

(234 on p. 765) The reaction of the human psyche to all bodily impurity is that it is unclean, dirty, Comfort's *Joy of Sex* notwithstanding. P carries this natural revulsion one step further: unclean is death-like.

(234 on p. 794) I have noted VH's correction that *ṣalmāt qaqqadim* refers to all humanity, including the Sumerians.

(234 on p. 814) VH cogently explains 13:55b as a horizontal dittograph from 13:42b that should be deleted.

(235 on pp. 823–24) David Wright's comment on the ubiquitous identification of *ṣāraʿat* with Hanson's disease is hardly irrelevant.

(235 on p. 833) I have anticipated VH concerning the reasons for the wild birds in the scale-disease ritual.

(235 on p. 855) I have cited a Ugaritic restoration and then dismissed it for heuristic reasons, as a glimpse into the scholarly enterprise.

(235 on p. 871) *miqtu* has been corrected to *samu* 'red'.

(235 on p. 941) I can now offer a better reason why a man having intercourse with a menstruant is defiled for seven days. Direct contact has been made with her genital life-blood, but contact with her body or objects (underneath her, 15:19–23), causes a one-day defilement. Analogously, a newborn boy, having emerged from his mother's blood, is also defiled for seven days (clearing my doubts expressed in vol. 1.746). The double impurity period for a newborn girl remains a mystery (vol. 1.750–51).

(235 on p. 951) I disagree: *musukkatu* and *ḥarištu* texts do deal with the menstruant (*CAD* 10.2.239; 5:105).

(235 on p. 962) I agree: Akkadian *mû* shall be deleted in favor of Sumerian A.

(235–36 on p. 1004) VH asks: "Were the rabbis of Yavneh sectarians in their treatment of biblical scrolls?" The answer is—yes, even more so. The sectarians (of Qumran) hold that blemishes defile. The rabbis declare that "all sacred scrolls defile the hands," on which I comment: "That something sacred can transmit impurity is unprecedented, illogical, and ostensibly inexplicable."

(236 on p. 1071) Another possible reason for the omission of the Yom Kippur observance in the dedicatory rites of Solomon's Temple is that it was still an emergency rite, before it became an annual event (given in an H appendix, 16:29–33).

F. ON *THE SAVAGE IN JUDAISM*

In his book, *The Savage in Judaism* (1990), Howard Eilberg-Schwartz frequently cites my published writings (prior to the appearance of *Leviticus 1–16*), often in disagreement. I would like to address his points, following his book's pagination:

(130–31) On Lev 11 and the prohibition against cooking a kid in its mother's milk, see vol. 1.740, my comments that follow, and my remarks on Henry Sun (APPENDIX A).

(135) On the fallacies inherent in the substitutionary theory of sacrifice, see the NOTE on "to ransom your life," 17:11, and vol. 1.441. Furthermore, the blood

daubed on people, priests, and scale-diseased persons does not come from the *ḥaṭṭā't*, the only sacrifice that purges the sanctuary. Exod 13:9 implies that the sacrifice of every firstling male animal is a reminder of the death of the Egyptian firstborn, not an everlasting substitution for the long-ago survival of Israel's firstborn in Egypt.

(183) The prohibition against sexual intercourse with a menstrual woman is not listed in chap. 15 because that chapter focuses on bodily symptoms of impurity (vol. 1. 986–1000) without prohibiting or penalizing them.

(186–87) All eight objections raised by Eilberg-Schwartz to my life–death rationale for the impurity rules of Lev 11–15 (vol. 1. 766–68, 1000–1004) are erroneous:

1. Nonseminal fluids do not pollute. The only exception is the saliva of a *zāb* (15:9), but not saliva per se.
2. Menstrual blood is more polluting than semen, though both represent the reproductive forces, for the obvious reason that menstruation can last up to a week, but the ejaculation of semen is instantaneous (see also below).
3. The loss of semen is a symbol of the death force, hence it continues to pollute during intercourse, even though it is a procreative act.
4. Yes, sexual relations are not prohibited during pregnancy, but neither is masturbation. These are one-day impurities (15:16–18), which are diagnostic, not judgmental, prescriptions (see NOTE on 18:22).
5. Although a bloody birth is a sign of "reproductive success," it renders the mother impure because it exudes from her body, the main criterion of the symbolic system (see no. 8).
6. Excrement does not contaminate (Ezek 4:12–15, however, shows other priestly views) because in P, an impurity source has to represent the loss of life, not the loss of waste.
7. Raw flesh (*ḥay*), though called "living" (13:10, 14), is impure on the body of a scale-diseased person because it is a sign that the disease has not healed. On the body of any other person, it is not impure.
8. The *ḥaṭṭā't* does not mark the "symbolic passing of a *person* from the death of impurity to life [my emphasis]." It removes the impurity of the sanctuary, not the person.

The bottom line is that the entire impurity system (Lev 11–15) is ritualistic symbolism for the opposition of life and death. It therefore focuses on the *visible* signs of the *appearance* of death, namely, the loss of reproductive fluid, the degenerative appearance of the scale-diseased person, and the corpse itself (vol. 1.766–68, 1000–1004). Paradoxically, Eilberg-Schwartz writes approvingly of the life–death principle in priestly circles (190–91), but does not apply it to the impurity rules.

Eilberg-Schwartz offers an alternative theory: controllability. Thus urine, the most controllable exudation, never pollutes; semen, usually controllable, pollutes for one day; "menstrual blood, non-menstrual blood, and nonseminal discharges are completely uncontrollable, and consequently make the body impure for seven days." In this statement lies the irreparable flaw in his theory. Nonmenstrual blood (e.g., from wounds) and nonseminal discharges (e.g., from sores) do not contaminate and, like menstrual blood, are completely uncontrollable.

(219, 255–56 nn. 8–10) Eilberg-Schwartz's five reasons demonstrating that Lev 11 reworks Deut 14 have been refuted in vol. 1. 698–704.

(227) Lev 11, no less than *m. Kel.* 17:14, reflects the distinctions between the days of creation by means of its distribution of the terms *šeqeṣ* and *ṭāmē'* (vol. 1.658–59; Milgrom 1992a). Eilberg-Schwartz does, however, offer a valuable insight into the structure of Lev 11: the land animals (11:24–28) were not placed more logically after v. 8, in keeping with the order of creation (Gen 1:20–25): fish (11:9–12), birds (11:13–23), and land animals (11:24–28).

(253–54, n. 12) Eilberg-Schwartz asks: "If the only issue is the purity of the Temple, why can't the priests simply sacrifice animals continually on the altar? It appears therefore that sacrifice is also part of the individual's purification process." Eilberg-Schwartz misses the point. The *ḥaṭṭāt* (not all sacrifices) must be brought by the person (and not by his/her proxy) who pollutes the sanctuary by his or her inadvertent moral or physical impurity (Lev 4, 12, 15). But the high priest acts on behalf of advertent wrongdoers on Yom Kippur (Lev 16) and on the festivals (Num 28–29; vol. 1.254–61).

G. RESPONSE TO HYAM MACCOBY

Hyam Maccoby sees the Bible through rabbinic eyes. Thus the rabbis' interpretation of P would correspond to its plain meaning. This tour de force is achieved by the principle of ellipsis. Whenever the text speaks of the pollution of the sanctuary, it takes for granted that the perpetrator entered it. The sanctuary is never polluted miasmatically, from afar.

Ellipsis, however, is a dangerous principle. It can prove anything. I am reminded of the quip: How can it be proved from the Torah that Jews must wear a skullcap (yarmulka)? It is written: "Jacob left Beer-sheba" (Gen. 28:10). Now would a pious Jew like Jacob go anywhere without a yarmulke?

Indeed, because the rabbis presume that pollution of the sanctuary occurs only by direct contact, does it necessarily follow that this is the plain meaning of the text? There is no evidence for the rabbis' assumption, not even the barest hint. References to the pollution of the sanctuary are spread throughout the priestly texts, and not once is there an allusion that it occurs by entry.

To be sure, ellipses can be found in P. Maccoby cites the case of Lev 5:4, which presumes that an oath (not a vow; for the difference, see Milgrom 1990a: 488–90) has broken due to temporary amnesia. This example, however, is not a bona fide ellipsis. Note that in the expression *wĕne'lam mimmennû wĕhû' yādā'* 'and though he has known (it; the fact) escapes him' the words *wĕhû' yādā'* 'though he has known (it)' are entirely superfluous. He surely was aware of the oath when he made it. However, the legist was bound by structural constraints. He wanted to retain the same wording as in the two previous cases (vv. 2–3).

But had he added that the vower forgot his oath, it would have overburdened the sentence and disturbed the style. Besides, it was self-evident. It was therefore eliminated.

Actually, Maccoby could have chosen more genuine P ellipses. The hand-leaning rite is omitted in the sacrificial regimen for the inauguration of the Tabernacle service (9:8, 17, 15, 18) and for the Day of Purgation (16:11, 15). Because the legist wished to focus on the altar rites, he omitted the preliminary rite of handleaning since it had previously been prescribed (chaps. 1–5) and implemented (chap. 8). A more striking example of ellipsis is the consistent omission of ablutions in the purification prescribed for contact with prohibited carcasses (11:27–28, 31, 32, 39, 40). Not a word alludes to ablutions. Note, however, that if the more serious requirement of laundering is mentioned, the more minor one of ablutions is surely implied. Moreover, the conjoining of ablutions and laundering is mentioned frequently enough (e.g., 15:5–11, 21–22, 27).

Maccoby (1999: 174) challenges that my concept of delay (vol. 1.307–19) also resorts to ellipsis. Note, however, that my assumption is deduced from the text itself. The basic question—overlooked by both Maccoby (1999: 189–91) and the rabbis—is why minor impurities (5:2–3) that as a rule require no sacrificial purification in fact do require it in 5:6–13. The answer, again, is provided by the seemingly superfluous words *wĕne'lam mimmennû*: the defiled person forgot that he had incurred impurity. In other words, something happened to the impurity between the time it occurred and the time it was remembered. My conclusion: the impurity was transformed from minor to major; it had grown. Initially, a simple same-day ablution would have eliminated it. Now, having waxed virulently, it polluted the sanctuary and, hence, requires the purifactory *ḥaṭṭā't*.

My conclusion is verified by other references to the incursion of minor impurity. For example, if a person eats from a carcass (17:16), "but does not launder (his clothes) and bathe his body he shall bear his punishment" (v. 16). There is a sense of urgency here. Delay is dangerous, indeed, fatal (see its NOTE). Why? Not because he might enter the sanctuary while impure. His very neglect to purify himself is sinful and punishable. The only possible reason, I submit, is that his minor impurity will become major and pollute the sanctuary.

My theory of delay fits hand and glove with my general theory of the *ḥaṭṭā't*. Wherever it is prescribed, pollution of the sanctuary has taken place. Moreover, it provides further evidence that in P impurity is virulent, dangerous to man and God alike. However, the threat to God is not from nonexistent demons, but from humans who willfully or inadvertently violate the divine commandments and ultimately drive YHWH out of the sanctuary.

In sum: all ellipses either are derivable from the text or are fleshed out elsewhere. Were there among the plethora of texts dealing with the pollution of the sanctuary or its sanctums even one that stated or even implied entrance into the sanctuary, I might have conceded to Maccoby. But there is neither a textual nor an ideological basis in any of them to justify the claim of ellipsis. Indeed, it turns out that Maccoby's ellipsis is nothing but the old argument from silence multiplied many times over. I am, therefore, forced to conclude that the pollution of the sanctuary and its sanctums results from impurity, not only by direct contact, but wherever it occurs. P represents a prerabbinic stage when the pollution of the sanctuary could take place miasmatically from afar.

My response to Maccoby's (1999) additional arguments follow his Book's pagination:

(169) Maccoby claims that according to my system everyone would be scared to death of becoming "ritually impure unawares" lest they pollute the sanctuary at a distance. Maccoby overlooks a basic requirement of the ḥaṭṭā't awareness. An individual has no responsibility for polluting the sanctuary unconsciously. Presumably, the accumulation of pollution generated unconsciously would be purged by the high priest at the annual Day of Purgation (note lĕkol-ḥaṭṭō'tām 'including all of their sins' (16:16–21).

Rejecting my claim (vol. 1.920) that P's purpose in allowing the zāb to remain at home provided that he washed his hands (Lev 15:11), Maccoby (1999: 56) asks: Why wasn't this concession also granted to the menstruant, parturient, and the zābâ herself? The last source can be dismissed out of hand. The pericope on the zābâ is abbreviated from that of the zāb in other respects as well (see NOTES on 15:25–27).

The absence of this "concession" from the menstruant and parturient is explicable on other grounds. Their discharge is natural; they are not ill, whereas the zāb has a chronic disease. The older (wilderness) tradition understandably banished him (Num 5:1–4), and the people continued to ostracize him even in postrabbinic times. Hence in a daring move, P allows the zāb to remain with his family and community if he washes his hands. The menstruant needs no concession. She may touch others *without washing* (vol. 1.936). The same holds for the parturient, whose initial (severe) impurity is that of the menstruant (12:2). Maccoby's theory that the zāb's concession is a vestige of an older tradition that P failed to excise has nothing on which to base itself. Besides, the older tradition (Num 5:1–4) prescribing banishment was more severe. Hence P's concession makes sense.

(169) Maccoby wonders about the continuous "existence of the dead rodents and even dead human beings." A basic postulate of the miasmatic theory has to be clarified. Corpses and carcasses do not contaminate the sanctuary from *afar.* The dead are dead. The corpse does exude impurity, but only within a confined space (ʾōhel 'tent', Num 19:14), and it does not threaten the sanctuary. Only live humans generate unbounded miasma. The miasma is created not through magic, but by disobedience. Either the person violates (even inadvertently) any of the divine commandments (mikkōl miṣwōt YHWH (4:2), or he refuses or neglects to undergo purification (e.g., 5:2–13; Num 19:13, 20). Only if he himself is the source of severe (ritual) impurity (e.g., bearing certain genital or skin diseases) do we find a residue of automatically generated miasma. Otherwise, it is only the product of the human will.

Maccoby (1999: 107–8) takes issue with my rendering of mê niddâ (Num 19:9; Zech 13:1) as "lustration." (vol. 1. 745). I write (one sentence earlier) that this term also bears "the meaning of expulsion: 'waters of expulsion [of impurity]' or simply 'water of lustration.' " I would have been more precise had I written that the fuller form of my suggested ellipsis was *mê* [*ḥaṭṭaʾt*] *niddâ*, literally "waters [of the elimination] of impurity." It would be grammatically equivalent to another priestly ellipsis *leḥem happānîm* 'Bread of Presence' (Exod 35:13), shortened from *leḥem šulḥan happānîm* 'the bread of the table of the Presence' (cf. Num 4:7). The term *niddâ* is used metaphorically in Ezek 7:19, 20; Zech 13:1; Lam 1:8, 17; Ezra 9:11; 2 Chr 9:5. But it also exists in a priestly text (Lev 20:21). Meyers and Meyers (1993: 364) find an elliptic *niddâ* in Zech 13:1.

(170) Maccoby contends that if "impurity acts at a distance, it is just as offensive to be outside the Temple as in it." Not true. Deliberate contact with the sacred while impure is subject to (delayed) *kārēt* (Lev 7:20, 21). But if it occurs inside the sanctuary, death is immediate by either God (Lev 10:1–3) or man (the sanctuary guards, Num 18:1–7; Milgrom 1990a: 341–43).

(170) Maccoby objects to my miasmatic theory because it implies that "God has been compelled to withdraw in the face of a non-moral power." As shown above, P's concept of impurity is a far cry from pagan (demonic) impurity, which indeed is "a non-moral evil power." Miasma is the product of human activity. Without the violation of YHWH's commandments, virulent impurity does not exist. Miasma is independently generated in three sources: the parturient, the *zābzābâ*, and the *měṣōrāʿ*. Their impurity is totally eliminated by the requisite purificatory rites. Thus P's impurity is not an evil power. For the rabbis (and Maccoby), however, P's revolutionary advance over its environment was not enough. Miasma still smacked of magic, and they excised it from the Torah.

(173) Maccoby claims that if the meaning of Lev 15:31 is conditional, "Milgrom's theoretical edifice collapses. This verse is saying that Israelites will die of their impurity *if* they enter and contaminate the Tabernacle." First, the "if" can stand without implying that the Tabernacle has been entered. Moreover, Maccoby's "if" is nonexistent. He achieves it by translating *běṭamměʾam* as "when (if) they contaminate." This word is preceded by the *beth* of means and it must be rendered "by their polluting" (not "through their impurity," which Maccoby attributes to me) or "by defiling" (*NJPS, NRSV, NAB, NJB*). Maccoby's "if" is what collapses.

(173) When confronted with the umambiguous statement of Num 19:13, 20 that a corpse-contaminated person (wherever he may be) *has contaminated the tabernacle/sanctuary* (*ṭimmēʾ*; note the perfect), Maccoby still resorts to his ellipsis, but with a new twist. The impure one may have unwittingly touched a priest, who then entered and contaminated the sanctuary. Why should the corpse-contaminated person have to purify himself? According to Maccoby, this should have been the responsibility of the one who entered the sanctuary—the priest!

(176) Maccoby contends that I offer "no evidence that sins such as theft . . . have any defiling effect on the sanctuary." Here he borders on Knohl's (1995) contention that in P moral sins do not generate impurity. My reply is given extensively in APPENDIX C and Introduction II H. Maccoby also avers that the *ḥaṭṭāʾt* purifies the person, not the sanctuary. Unfortunately, he overlooks philological evidence:

1. *ḥaṭṭā't* is a *Pi'ēl* construction from the verb *ḥiṭṭē'* meaning "decontaminate." It is not a sin offering, but a purification offering.
2. The *ḥaṭṭā't* blood, the purifying agent, is never smeared on the human being; therefore, it does not purify him.
3. The person is never the direct object of *kipper* 'purge, atone'. If the *ḥaṭṭā't* had purified him, we should expect the text to read *wĕkipper 'ōtô* (used only for objects; Lev 16:20; Ezek 43: 20, 26). But when the object is a person, the text invariable reads *wĕkipper 'ālāyw* 'on his behalf'.

(179) Maccoby contends that *mēḥaṭṭā'tô* (4:26) refers back to *nāsî yeḥĕṭā'* (v. 22) and, hence, it seems that "the offering atones for the sin not for the contaminating effect." Again, Maccoby fails to take into account that the latter is a *Qal*, whereas the former is a *Pi'ēl*. Thus the expression *wĕkipper ālāyw hakkōhen mēḥaṭṭā'to* (4:26) is precisely equivalent to *wĕkipper ālāyw hakkōhen miṭṭum'ātô* (14:19). Thus *mēḥaṭṭā'tô* refers to his impurity, not to his sin. His repentence (*wĕ'āšēm*) has wiped out his sin. What remains is its contaminating effect, necessitating a purification offering.

(198) Maccoby avers that "a system in which the altars are a particular focus of concentration . . . to a system (rabbinic) in which they are of no concern at all . . . seems a change that defies the tempo of religious evolution." More than 500 years had ensued between H's incorporation of P in the eighth century B.C.E. (P's composition was even earlier, see Introduction IL, IIR and vol. 1.29–35) and the dawning of the rabbinic age in the second century. In the interim, cataclysmic events had befallen Israel, beginning with the destruction and exile. This more than half millennium is, unfortunately, shrouded in darkness, but with the emergence of the rabbinic age the halakha of the Torah undergoes a transformation. See what the rabbis did with the insubordinate son (Deut 21:18–21). According to R. Jose the Galilean, such an incorrigible son is put to death—not for his demonstrable disobedience (an unjustifiable basis for a death penalty), but for his predictable [*sic*] life of criminality (*m. Sanh.* 8:5; *Sipre* Deut. 21:8). His immediate execution is necessary to obviate his potentially greater harm to society. Happily, no other tannaitic sage, to my knowledge, tries similarly to justify the death penalty. Instead they resort to circumscribing its implementation. For example, R. Judah deduces from the fact that the text twice places the mother on a par with the father (vv. 18–19) that for the court to hand down a death sentence, the mother must be of equal worth (*rĕ'ûyâ*) with the father (*m. Sanh.* 8:4; cf. Philo, *Laws* 2.232), namely, as the amoraic sages understand it, "equal in voice, looks, and height" (*b. Sanh.* 71a). The tannaites, furthermore, reduce the accused's age of culpability to a few months of his puberty (*m. Sanh.* 8:1); they set up evidentiary rules (for all capital crimes; see below) that make it virtually impossible to carry out the law (*m. Sanh.* 8:5); and they make the astonishing statement that "the case of the insubordinate son never occurred nor will ever occur. Why was this law written? To tell us 'expound and receive a reward' " (*t. Sanh.* 11:1). In the end, this law has been reduced to an academic exercise (for additional documentation and analysis, see Halbertal 1999:46–62).

The most radical change effected by the rabbis is their virtual abolition of the death penalty. This they accomplish by making it virtually impossible to carry it out. The two biblically required witnesses (Deut 17:6; 19:15) must testify not only that they saw the accused commit the crime, but that beforehand they warned him against committing the offense (*hatrā'â*) and that the accused had responded that he knew the law and was going to violate it (*t. Sanh.* 11:1–3; cf. *m. Sanh.* 5:1; 8:1, 4; 10:4; *Mak.* 1:8,9; *Sipre Zuṭ* on Num 35:12).

Finally, I shall also cite one example (out of many) of a revolutionary change in the sphere of the cult. In an act attributed by the rabbis to Ezra, they assert that Ezra transferred the Levitic tithe (Num 18:21–23) to the priests (*b. Yeb.* 86b; see also *b. Soṭ.* 47b–48a) without any support from a biblical law.

I have chosen these three examples because, in contrast to my miasmic theory of the *ḥaṭṭā't*, they do violence to the plain meaning of the text. Can there be any doubt that the incorrigible son was put to death, that the Torah's death sentence for capital crime was carried out, and that the tithe awarded to the Levites was "a law for all time throughout the ages" (Num 18:23)? In comparison with the magnitude of these changes, the rabbinic abolition of miasma fades into insignificance.

I cannot close this appendix without offering special thanks to Dr. Mark J. H. Fretz, Senior Editor of Religious Publishing at Doubleday, who graciously accepted it as well as other insertions while the manuscript was in his hands about to enter production.

Addendum. I am grateful to Maccoby (1999: 31) for pointing out the flaw in my claim that the effusion of blood symbolizes the loss of life and is therefore a source of impurity. I had paid no attention to the fact that blood oozing from a wound is not a source of impurity. I now realize that I must amend my theory: not all blood from living persons is an impurity source, only *reproductive blood*. Now my theory of life/holiness versus death/impurity (see chap. 19, COMMENT) is actually strengthened. The *zāb* and *zābâ* (blood) are functionally equal. Their issue produces life; their loss wastes life.

H. ADDENDA AND CORRIGENDA

The comments follow the pagination of vols. 1 and 1A.

(31) According to a more recent statement by Finkelstein (1986: 39–40), Shilo "became a central culture site serving the population of the surrounding area, especially in the first part of Late Bronze (LB I). . . . [R]egions with the greatest concentrations of earliest Israelite settlements are in the territories of Manasseh and Ephraim—in the north—from there the Israelite population spread southward to Benjamin and Judah. . . . Shilo preceded Bethel and Gilgal as cult centers serving the population of the hill country."

Thus archaeology provides solid evidence that Shilo was a regional sanctuary, probably the major one before Jerusalem, and it supports my contention that if P was created by and practiced in a sanctuary that preceded the Jerusalem Temple, it would have been the oldest and most prestigious sanctuary—Shilo.

Further supporting my supposition that the line of P's transmission was Shilo to Jerusalem is the evidence that the divine appellation *haṣṣĕbāʾôt* was originally a Shilonic tradition (1 Sam 4:4; 17:45), which was adopted in the Jerusalem Temple (Ps 24:10; cf. Kraus 1962: 213–14).

(161–62) For another demonstration that the term *ʾiššeh* is not related to *ʾēš* fire but to Ugaritic *iṯṯ* 'gift', see Greenfield (1993).

(205–6) I had asserted that suet (*ḥēleb*) was inedible and wondered why it was a divine portion. Mary Douglas has informed me that my premise is wrong: the English not only eat suet, but even favor it in their meat dishes. Nonetheless, as shown below (van Straten 1995: 126), in Greece the gods' portions were inedible. The question still remains why the Deity would choose it above all other portions. My surmise is that a major reason is that the entirety of suet goes up in smoke and leaves no traces (ashes). Moreover, its incineration is fragrant (*rēaḥ nīḥōaḥ*). Because it was the Deity's portion, it was considered the *best* of the sacrifice and led, in my view, to the secondary meaning of *ḥēleb* as "best."

(220–26) I have culled from van Straten (1995) many remarkable correspondences between Greek sacrifice and the *šĕlāmîm*, thus yielding further evidence that Greek and Semitic cultures were in many respects a single, organic continuum (cf. Brown 1969: 79, 80, 81, 83). I have noted the following:

104–5.   The blood is poured on all sides of the altar. This corresponds with *wĕzārĕqû ʾet-haddām ʿal-hammizbēaḥ sābîb* (Exod 29:16; Lev 1:5, 11; 3:2b, 8b, 13b; 7:2b; 9:18; all the blood sacrifices except the *ḥaṭṭāʾt*, which has its own ritual, Lev 4:6, 25, 30).

120.   The god's portion includes the curved end (*osphûs*) and the adjoining tail. The two compose the biblical *ʾalyâ* (Lev 3:9), also YHWH's portion.

123–24.   "The gods savoring the smell of the thigh bones burning in the fat" defines the *reaḥ nīḥōaḥ* (see above). Placing the god's portions wrapped in the suet on the altar (cf. Homer, *Odyssey* 14.427–29) may be the procedure implied in the sacrifices of the priestly consecration (Lev 8:25–27).

126.   "What the gods (received) are *mainly inedible parts*: thighbones wrapped in fat [more precisely the *omentum*, or suet]; the *osphûs* (also bone) and tail; and the gall bladder (also bare) and pieces of meat laid beside the bones [my emphasis]."

The differences should not be overlooked. The *splanchna* (heart, lungs, liver, spleen, kidneys) is not incinerated on the altar, but is burned on a spit and shared by persons and gods. It is placed "into the hands and onto the knees of a seated cult image" and ultimately eaten by the priest. In one respect, it resembles the *šĕlāmîn*, which is also shared among the offerer, god, and priest, but the portions are radically different (cf. Lev 1:8; 3:5).

(228–40, 339–45) In Gary Anderson's (1992: 875–82) excellent update on the priestly system of sacrifice, he points to two problems with my contention that the inadvertent violation of God's commandments demonstrates remorse as indicated by the term 'āšēm which I render "feel guilt." He asks: "If such an important atoning function is present in the act of feeling remose, why is this term absent in Num 15:22–31? Or why is it absent in the case of the priest (Lev 4:1–12)" (880)?

Num 15:22–31 (H) takes for granted its precedent Lev 4 (P). It therefore deletes many details of the sacrificial procedure. If it can omit the offender's indispensable hand leaning, why shouldn't it feel free to omit his remorse ('āšēm)? The reason for both (and other) omissions is transparent. Num 15:22–31 is the product of H, which regularly assumes P—except when it *differs*. The clearest example of H's policy with P is Lev 23 (see NOTE on "you shall offer a food gift to YHWH" 23:8).

The omission of 'āšēm in Lev 4:1–12 rests in the unique expression lĕ'ašmat hā'am '(the high priest) bringing guilt on the people' (v. 3 NRSV, REB; cf. NAB, NJB, NJPS). If the people feel guilt, all the more the one who misled them—their spiritual leader, the high priest!

(254–61) Confirmation of the ḥaṭṭā't theology. An OB incantation against the evil eye reads as follows:

> She passed by the door of the babies, and created rash among the babies
> She passed by the door of the women in childbed and strangled their babies
> She entered the storage room and broke the seal
> She dispersed the secluded fireplace and turned the locked house into ruins
> She destroyed the išertum, and the god of the house is gone.
> (Farber 1981: 61–63, cited in van der Toorn 1996b: 122)

In this incantation, the evil eye makes her first stop at the door of the babies and the door of the women in childbed, located at the outskirts of the house where they were isolated. The eye first brings rashes to the babies, causing them to cry; then strangles the babies; enters the storage room; disperses the fireplace (the family hearth = the altar?); and finally destroys the išertum (in the recesses of the house = the adytum?) and forces the god to depart.

One should keep in mind that every home was a miniature sanctuary. The family god's residence was located at the rear, and it was preceded by the room with the fireplace (where the family worshiped the god). The evil eye was not content with just killing the new offspring; her real objective was to drive the god out of his or her sanctuary.

The structure of the OB house is precisely the model for Israel's sanctuary: the rear room (adytum), where YHWH would reside on his throne / chariot, preceded by the shrine where he would be worshiped by the priest who officiated at the menorah, table of presence, and incense altar. The new mother and baby were isolated—since the mother (not the child) was cultically impure.

It is the procedure with the ḥaṭṭā't that exhibits the greatest parallels with this incantation. This sacrifice's use by the (high) priest on the courtyard altar, on the inner altar, and in the adytum (Lev 4, 16) shows precisely how impurity (human kind, not demonic) penetrates into the sanctuary and ultimately drives YHWH out.

It should be noted that the word *ṭāmē'* 'impure' is absent from Lev 4, which refers to *moral* impurity (v. 2). This is so because the wrongdoer contaminates the sanctuary *but not himself*. He remains in a ritually pure state. Therefore (contra Douglas 151 and many others) he is not contagious either to the sacred, to persons or to things. He undergoes no purification rites as do the *physically* impure (*ṭāmē*); cf. chaps. 11–15).

(339–45) Van der Toorn (1985: 92–93) disputes my rendering of *'āšēm* 'feel guilt', opting instead (with Knierim, *THAT* 1.251–57) to define it as denoting "legal liability and its consequences." For the first part of his definition, he cites Lev 5:2, rendering *wĕ'āšēm* 'he will be held responsible for his sin'. But what will van der Toorn do with the relative clause found just three verses later: *wĕhāyâ kî-ye'šam lĕ'aḥat mē'ēlleh*? It cannot be rendered as a main clause (a judicial sentence), but only as the conditional clause: "and it shall be if he feels guilt in any of these matters."

I agree wholeheartedly, however, with the second part of his definition: "its [the sin's] consequences." This corresponds with my claim that verbs of behavior connote their respective reward or punishment (Milgrom 1976a: 3–4); thus *'āšēm* 'incur liability' also refers to the "inner experience of liability," to feel guilt (Milgrom 1976a: 5–12).

Hendel (1995: 190, n. 20) disputes my contention (1983c: 119–21) that Jer 7:21–22 and Amos 5:22, 25 indict individual sacrifices, not the public cult, and therefore the prophets are not in opposition to the cult. He points out that the term *'ōlâ wāzebaḥ* is a synecdoche for all animal sacrifices, which would include the *ḥaṭṭā't* and *'āšām*. Even if so, this idiom would still apply to individual, private sacrifices, not public ones. Weiss (1995: 207, 13) argues that Amos (above) rejects the public cult. But the sacrifice called *šelem* (Amos 5:22) is not a public sacrifice, except in the unique case of the wheat festival (Lev 23:19), where the probability exists that originally (certainly so in Amos's days) it was an individual offering (see NOTE on 23:19).

(359–61) Japhet (1988: 112) claims that the source Ezra uses to declare intermarriage a sin is Lev 5:17–18. But the key terms defining the people's sin are *ma'al* 'sacrilege' and *qōdeš* 'sanctum' (Ezra 9:2), terms that are absent in Lev 5:17–18, but are present in vv. 15–16, where the desecrated sanctums are objects. However, the sin of intermarriage refers to persons, not objects. Ezra therefore creates an *halakhik midrash* specifying the desecrated sanctum as *zera' haqqōdeš* 'the holy seed', namely Israel (for details see Milgrom 1191: 345–55).

(397) Bar-On (1999:149, n. 21) notes these typos: Josh 3:6 should read Josh 3:16; 2 Kgs 23:23 should read 2 Kgs 23:33. But the correct verse for the typo 7:32 is not 7:17 but 7:36; see below. He also states categorically that my rendering for the *Beth* of *byom* as "from" (Lev 6:13) is "senseless." *Beth*, he claims, is partitive, never temporal. Unfortunately he overlooks the numerous places

where *byom* is temporal and must be rendered "from the day" or "when." I shall cite only one P text: the chieftains' gift in Num chap. 7. Verse 84 presents the total of all the chieftains' gifts for the altar over a period of twelve days. How then can *byom* mean "on the day"? Similarly, v. 10 states that the chieftains brought their offering to the altar *byom* it was annointed. This offering was brought throughout twelve days? Finally, only by rendering *byom* as "from the day" in v. 1 can a host of textual and chronological problems be resolved (see Milgrom 1990a: 53; 364, n. 1) where many other texts are cited.

On Bar-On's reading of Lev 6:13, the high priest's cereal offering was brought to the sanctuary only "on the day." But he had already brought one (Lev 9:4, 17)! In my reading the high priest brought this offering "from the day" of his consecration; it was his daily obligation—which not only makes exegetical sense, but also reflects the practice.

(656) The distinction between *šeqeṣ* and *ṭāmēʾ* (Milgrom 1992b) was also noted by Paran (1989: 345–48), but he did not distinguish between P and H, nor did he recognize the crucial element of P's *Weltanschauung*.

A further question: Why did H interject its differing and confusing notion of metaphoric impurity (*iṭimmēʾ*) three times into the land-swarmers pericope (vv. 43 [bis], 44)? The answer is that H was fully aware that P's distinction between *šeqeṣ* (nonedible but nondefiling) and *ṭāmēʾ* (nonedible and defiling) carcasses on the basis of water and land creatures, respectively, breaks down in the case of land swarmers: instead of falling into the *ṭāmēʾ* category, they are labeled *šeqeṣ* (vv. 41–42). Since their nondefiling (*šeqeṣ*) nature is fixed in P, H cannot alter the text, but covers the discrepancy by declaring that land swarmers are *ṭāmēʾ* only *metaphorically* (but not ritually, P's designation).

(671–72) Another reason for declaring the eight swarmers (11:29–30) as impure is that they are four-legged and contiguous with the pericope on impure quadrupeds (vv. 24–28), which by definition are also impure.

(715–16) D consistently uses the verb *zābaḥ* to denote sacrificial slaughter (Deut 15:21; 16:2, 4, 5, 6; 17:1; 27:7; 32:17; 33:19). The only ostensible exception is Deut 12:15, 21, when it clearly occurs in the context of common slaughter. However, as demonstrated in vol. 1.715–16, *zābaḥ* there also retains its original sacrificial meaning, implying that even though sacrificeable animals may henceforth be treated as game (cf. Lev 17:13–14), they must be slaughtered *as if* they were sacrifices, namely, by the approved sanctuary method of slaughter.

Levinson (1991: 199–200) has demurred on the grounds that when D indeed refers to sacrifices in the same chapter (Deut 12:27), it uses the verb *ʿāśâ* not *zābaḥ*, thereby indicating that in the verses under discussion (Deut 12:15, 21), *zābaḥ* exclusively denotes common slaughter. This alleged exception is chimerical. The relevant clause in Deut 12:27a reads *wěʿāśîtā ʿōlōtêkā habbāśār wěhaddām ʿal-mizbaḥ* YHWH *ʾělōhêkā* 'You shall offer your burnt offerings, both the flesh and the blood, on the altar of YHWH your God'. Since the object of the verb is explained as "the flesh and the blood," the use of *zābaḥ* 'slaughter' would be wholly inappropriate: one does not slaughter blood! Hence the verb *ʿāśâ* is used, referring to the performance of the entire sacrificial ritual.

(**1368, par. 3**) This deduction is implied by R. Ishmael "*Generalizations* (N.B.) were stated at Sinai, details were stated in the Tent of Meeting" (*b. Zebah.* 115b).

(**1378, par. 3**) The two positions, amximalist and minimalist, actually converge. Both claim that the words attributed to Moses are correct, not their ipsissima verba (the maximalist contention) but only their principles (the minimalist contention). The Torah shows evidence of historical development, a process of addition and redaction prior to reaching its final form, the MT.

(**1696 Sabbath and Sanctuary**) This verse is repeated verbatim in 26:2. The rabbis (*b. Yoma* 6a) teach that the Sabbath (Exod 31:12–17; 35:1–3) interrupts the pericopes on the building of the Sanctuary to prove that the Sabbath must not be violated even in the course of building the Sanctuary. Levenson (1984 292) further notes the same connection in Isa 56:4–7, namely, that the projected Temple will admit eunuchs and foreigners (contra Deut 23:2–4) on condition that they observe the Sabbath. The wider theological association was brought out by Weinfeld (1981); the completion of the Sanctuary (Exod 39–40 is described in the same way as the creation of the Sabbath (Gen 2:1–3). In contrast to the Mesopatamian Creation story (theomachy) where grateful gods build a temple to the creator and savior god Marduk, in the priestly narrative it is grateful Israel which builds a Temple to their creator and savior God.

(**1738**) In the Torah only three moral sins are named. They are so heinous they defile and bring disaster on the community. These moral sins are sexual violations (18:24–29; cf. Jer 3:1; Ezek 33:26), idolatry (20:1–5; cf. Jer 2:7; Ezek 36:18; Ps 106:36–39), and bloodshed (Num 35:33–34; cf. Ps 106:38–39).

According to the rabbis, "If a person is told 'transgress or you will be killed, then transgress and do not be killed, except' (for the three above-mentioned sins)" (*b. Sanh* 74a). Why should these threes sins be the only ones that can never be transgressed, even at the cost of one's life? It cannot be that these sins are from Sinai or that they are the most egregious. The reason lies deeper. It is because their impurity is virulent; polluting the Sanctuary and the land and leading to exile. In other words, these transgressions affect all of society whereas all the others only affect their transgessors. To save one's life (*pikkuah nepes*) one may sin, but not to the detriment of others.

BIBLIOGRAPHY

◆

SELECT COMMENTARIES:
A. MEDIEVAL AND PRE-CRITICAL

1. Saadiah (ben Joseph) Gaon
   1963   *The Commentaries of R. Saadiah Gaon on the Torah.* Excerpted and trans. J. Kapach. Jerusalem: Mosad Harav Kook. (Hebrew)
2. Ibn Janah, Jonah
   1964   *Seper Ha-Riqmah.* 2 vols. Ed. M. Wilensky. Jerusalem: Academy. (Hebrew)
   1968   *The Book of Roots.* Ed. A. Neubauer. Oxford: Clarendon Press. (Hebrew) [Originally published 1875]
3. Rashi (Solomon ben Isaac)
   1946   *Pentateuch with Rashi's Commentary.* 2 vols. Trans. and annotated A. H. Silbermann and M. Rosenbaum. London: Shapiro, Vallentine.
4. Rashbam (Samuel ben Meir)
   1969   *Commentary of the Rashbam on the Torah.* Ed. A. I. Bromberg. Jerusalem: Author. (Hebrew)
5. Ibn Ezra, Abraham
   1961   *Leviticus with Ibn Ezra's Commentary* Mehoqeqe Yehudah. Ed. J. L. Krinsky. Horeb: Bnai-Brak. (Hebrew)
6. Bekhor Shor (Joseph ben Isaac)
   1994   *The Commentaries of Joseph Bekhor Shor on the Torah.* Ed. Y. Nebo. Jerusalem: Mosad Harav Kook. (Hebrew)
7. Kimhi, David (Radak)
   1847   *The Book of Roots.* Ed. J. H. R. Bresenthal and F. Lebrecht. Berlin: Friedlander (Hebrew). [Reprint, Jerusalem: 1966–67]
   1970   *R. David Kimhi (Radak) on the Torah.* Ed. M. Kamleher. Jerusalem: Mosad Harav Kook. (Hebrew)
8. Ramban (Moses ben Nahman, also called Nahmanides)
   1960   *Comments of the Ramban on the Torah.* 2 vols. Ed. H. D. Chavel. Jerusalem: Mosad Harav Kook. (Hebrew)
9. Bahya, R.
   1967   *Comments of R. Bahya on the Torah.* 2 vols. Ed. H. D. Chavel. Jerusalem: Mosad Harav Kook. (Hebrew)
10. Hazzequni, H. (Hezekiah ben Manoah)
    1981   *The Torah Commentaries of R. Hizqiah b. Manoah.* Ed. H. D. Chavel. Jerusalem: Mosad Harav Kook. (Hebrew)

11. Aaron ben Joseph
    1935   *Seper Hamibḥar*. Eupatoria: Finkleman. (Karaite, Hebrew).
12. Aaron ben Elijah
    1866–67   *Keter Torah*. 5 vols. Ed. J. Saraskan. Eupatoria: Gozlow. (Karaite, Hebrew)
13. Abravanel (Isaac ben Jehuda)
    1964   *Commentary on the Torah*. 3 vols. Jerusalem: Bnai Arbel. (Hebrew)
14. Sforno (Obadiah ben Jacob)
    1980   *The Commentary of Sforno*. Ed. A. Darom and Z. Gottlieb. Jerusalem: Mosad Harav Kook. (Hebrew)
15. Wessely, Naphtali Herz
    1846   *Netivot Ha-shalom*. Vol. 3, *Leviticus*. Ed. M. Mendelssohn. Vienna: von Schmid and Busch.
16. Luzzatto, Samuel David (Shadal)
    1965   *Commentary to the Pentateuch and Hamishtadel*. Ed. P. Schlesinger. Tel Aviv: Dvir. (Hebrew)
17. Malbim
    1891   *The Torah and Commandment*. 2 vols. Vilna: Romm. (Hebrew)
18. Boleh, M.
    1991–92   *The Book of Leviticus*. Vols. I and II. Jerusalem: Mosad Harav Kook. (Hebrew)

SELECT COMMENTARIES:
B. CRITICAL

1. Kalisch, M. M.
   1867–72   *Leviticus*. 2 vols. London: Longmans.
2. Dillmann, A., and V. Ryssel
   1897   *Die Bucher Exodus und Leviticus*. 3rd ed. Leipzig: Hirzel. [Originally published 1880]
3. Driver, S. R., and M. A. White
   1894–98   *The Book of Leviticus in Hebrew*. Leipzig: Hinrichs.
4. Bertholet, A.
   1901   *Leviticus*. Tübingen: Mohr (P. Siebeck).
5. Baentsch, B.
   1903   *Exodus, Leviticus und Numeri*. Göttingen: Vandenhoeck & Ruprecht.
6. Hoffmann, D. Z.
   1953   *Leviticus*. 2 vols. Trans. Z. Har-Shafer and A. Lieberman. Jerusalem: Mosad Harav Kook. (Hebrew) [Trans. of *Das Buch Leviticus, I–II* (Berlin: Poppelauer, 1905–6)]
7. Eerdmans, B. D.
   1912   *Das Buch Leviticus*. Alttestamentliche Studien 4. Giessen: Töpelmann.

8. Heinisch, P.
   1935 *Das Buch Leviticus.* Bonn: Hanstein.
9. Keil, C. F., and F. Delitzsch
   1874 *Biblical Commentary on the Old Testament.* Vol. 2, *The Pentateuch.* Trans. J. Martin. Grand Rapids, Mich.: Eerdmans, 1956.
10. Noth, M.
    1977 *Leviticus: A Commentary.* Rev. ed. OTL. Philadelphia: Westminster Press. [Originally published 1965]
11. Elliger, K.
    1966 *Leviticus.* HAT 4. Tübingen: Mohr (P. Siebeck).
12. Snaith, N. H.
    1967 *Leviticus and Numbers.* London: Nelson. [Reprint, London: Oliphants, 1977]
13. Kornfeld, W.
    1972 *Das Buch Leviticus.* Düsseldorf: Patmos.
14. Porter, J. R.
    1976 *Leviticus.* CBC. Cambridge: Cambridge University Press.
15. Wenham, G. J.
    1979 *The Book of Leviticus.* Grand Rapids, Mich.: Eerdmans.
16. Harrison, R. K.
    1980 *Leviticus: An Introduction and Commentary.* Leicester: Inter-Varsity Press.
17. Levine, B. A.
    1989 *Leviticus.* Philadelphia: Jewish Publication Society.
18. Hartley, J. E.
    1992 *Leviticus.* Waco, Tex.: Word Books.
19. Gerstenberger, E. S.
    1996 *Leviticus.* Trans. D. W. Stott. Louisville, Ky.: Westminster–John Knox Press. [Trans. of *Das dritte Buch Mose: Leviticus* (Göttingen: Vandenhoeck & Ruprecht, 1993)]
20. Budd, P. J.
    1996 *Leviticus.* Grand Rapids, Mich.: Eerdmans.
21. Milgrom, J.
    1991 *Leviticus 1–16.* AB 3. New York: Doubleday.

SELECT BIBLIOGRAPHY

Aaron ben Elijah
   1866–67 *Keter Torah.* 5 vols. Ed. J. Saraskan. Eupatoria: Gozlow. (Karaite, Hebrew)
Aaron ben Joseph
   1935 *Seper Hamibḥar.* Eupatoria: Finkleman. (Karaite, Hebrew)
Abba, R.
   1962 Name. *IDB* 3:500–508.

Abramsky, S.
1968 *mattākôt. EM* 5:644–62.

Abravanel (Isaac ben Jehuda)
1964 *Commentary on the Torah.* 3 vols. Jerusalem: Bnai Arbel. (Hebrew)

Ackerman, S.
1992 *Under Every Green Tree.* Atlanta: Scholars Press.

Adler, E. J.
1989 The Background for the Metaphor of Covenant as Marriage in the Hebrew Bible. 2 vols. Ph.D. diss., University of California, Berkeley.

Aharoni, Y.
1968 Arad: Its Inscriptions and Temple. *BA* 31:2–32.
1974 The Horned Altar at Beer-sheba. *BA* 37:1–6.

Ahituv, Y.
1971b ṣō'n. *EM* 6:645–49.

Ahuvya, A.
1973 What Is *hônā'â? BM* 18:51–57. (Hebrew)

Albeck, Ch.
1930 Das Buch der Jubiläen und die Halakha. *Bericht der Hochschule für die Wissenschaft des Judentums in Berlin* 47:3–60.
1952 *Seder Moʻed.* Jerusalem: Bialik Institute. (Hebrew)
1953 *Seder Neziqin.* Jerusalem: Bialik Institute. (Hebrew)
1954 *Seder Nashim.* Jerusalem: Bialik Institute. (Hebrew)
1957 *Seder Zeraʻim.* Jerusalem: Bialik Institute. (Hebrew)

Albertz, R.
1976 *pl'. THAT* 2:413–20.
1978 Hintergrund und Bedeutung des Elterngebots im Decalog. *ZAW* 90:348–74.
1994 *The History of Israelite Religion in the Old Testament Period,* 2 vols. Trans. J. Bowden. Louisville, Ky.: Westminster–John Knox.

Albrektson, K.
1967 *History and the Gods.* Lund: Gleerup.

Albright, W. F.
1942 *From the Stone Age to Christianity.* Baltimore: Johns Hopkins Press.
1945 Review of *HUCA* 16–18. *JBL* 64:285–96.
1946 *Archaeology and the Religion of Israel.* Baltimore: Johns Hopkins University Press.
1949 *The Archaeology of Palestine.* Harmondsworth: Penguin.
1950a Review of *Ugaritic Grammar,* by C. H. Gordon. *JBL* 69:388–94.
1957 The High Place in Ancient Palestine. *SVT* 4:242–58.
1968 *Yahweh and the Gods of Canaan.* Garden City, N.Y.: Doubleday.

Almagro-Gorbea, M.
1980 Les Reliefs orientalisants de Pozo Moro. Pp. 123–36 in *Mythe et personification: Travaux et memoires. Actes du colloque du Grande Palais (Paris).* Paris: Société d'Edition "Les Belles Lettres."

Alon, G

1957 *Studies in the History of Israel During the Days of the Second Temple and the Period of the Mishna and Talmud.* 2 vols. Tel Aviv: Hakibbutz Hameuhad. (Hebrew). *Jews, Judaism, and the Classical World.* Trans. I. Abrahams. Jerusalem: Magnes, 1977.

1970 *Studies in Jewish History.* Vol 2. Tel Aviv: Hakibbutz Hameuchad. (Hebrew)

Aloni, J.

1984 The Place of Worship and the Place of Slaughter According to Leviticus 17:3–9. *Shnaton* 7–8:21–49. (Hebrew)

Alt, A.

1953 *Die Heimat des Deuteronomiums: Kleine Schriften.* Vol. 2. Munich: Beck.

1968 The Origins of Israelite Law. In *Essays in Old Testament History and Religion,* trans. R. A. Wilson, 101–71. Garden City, N.Y.: Doubleday. [Trans. of *Die Ursprünge des israelitischen Rechts* (Leipzig: Hirzel, 1934)]

1972 Zur Talionsformel. Pp. 407–11 in *Um das Prinzip der Vergeltung in Religion und Recht des Alten Testaments,* ed. K. Koch, 407–11. Darmstadt: Wissenschaftliche Buchgesellschaft.

Amir, Y.

1992 Measure for Measure in Talmudic Literature and in the Wisdom of Solomon. In *Justice and Righteousness* [Fest. B. Uffenheimer], ed. H. G. Reventhlow and Y. Hoffman, 29–46. Sheffield: JSOT Press.

Amit, Y.

1992 The Jubilee Law—An Attempt at Instituting Social Justice. Pp. 47–59 in *Justice and Righteousness* [Fest. B. Uffenheimer], ed. H. G. Reventhlow and Y. Hoffman. Sheffield: JSOT Press.

1997 Creation and the Calendar of Holiness. Pp. 13*–29* in *Tehillah Le-Moshe* [Fest. M. Greenberg], ed. M. Cogan et al. Winona Lake, Ind.: Eisenbrauns.

Andersen, F. I.

1974 *The Sentence in Biblical Hebrew.* The Hague: Mouton.

Anderson, F. I., and D. N. Freedman

1989 *Amos.* New York: Doubleday.

Anderson, B. W.

1993 The Biblical Circle of Homosexual Prohibition. *BR* 9:10, 52.

Anderson, G. A.

1987 *Sacrifices and Offerings in Ancient Israel: Studies in Their Social and Political Importance.* Atlanta: Scholars Press.

1991 *A Time to Mourn, a Time to Dance.* University Park: Pennsylvania State University Press.

1992 Sacrifice and Sacrificial Offerings. *ABD* 5:870–86.

Archi, A.

1973 Fêtes de printemps et d'automne et réintégration rituelle d'images de culte dans l'Anatolie Hittite. *UF* 5:7–27.

Ardzinba, V.
1982	On the Structure and the Functions of Hittite Festivals. Pp. 11–16 in *Gesellschaft und Kultur im alten Vorderasien*, ed. H. Klengel. Berlin: Akademie-Vorlag.

Arnold, W. R.
1917	*Ephod and Ark*. Cambridge, Mass.: Harvard University Press.

Ashbel, D.
1967	For Your Ancestors Dwell in Booths When They Left Egypt. *BM* 29:100–104. (Hebrew)

Auerbach, E.
1966	Das Zehngebot-allgemeines Gesetzes-form—in der Bibel. *VT* 16: 255–76.

Avigad, N.
1954	*Ancient Monuments in the Kidron Valley*. Jerusalem: Bialik Institute. (Hebrew)

Avishur, Y.
1979	The Ways of the Amorites. Pp. 17–47 in *Seper Meir Wallenstien*, ed. C. Rabin. Jerusalem: Kiryat Sefer. (Hebrew)
1981	The Ghost-Expelling Incantation from Ugarit. *UF* 13:13–25.
1987	Structure of Lev 18: 24–30. P. 128 in *Leviticus. World of the Bible*. Ramat-Gau: Revivim (Hebrew)

Baḥya, R.
1967	*Comments of R. Baḥya on the Torah*. Ed. H. D. Chavel. 2 vols. Jerusalem: Mosad Harav Kook. (Hebrew)

Baentsch, B.
1903	*Exodus, Leviticus un Numeri*. Göttingen: Vandenhoeck & Ruprecht.

Baersema, J. J.
1997	*Thora Nen Stoa Over Nens En Natur: Een Bijdraga Aen Het Milieu Debat Over Duurzaamheid En Kwalitit*. Nijkerk: Callenbach.

Baillet, M.
1982	*Qumran Grotte*, Cave 4. DJD 7. Oxford: Clarendon Press.

Baltzer, K.
1987	Liberation from Debt Slavery After the Exile in Second Isaiah and Nehemiah. Pp. 477–84 in *Ancient Israelite Religion*, ed. P. D. Miller, Jr. Philadelphia: Fortress Press.

Bar-Maoz, Y.
1980	The "Misharum" Reform of King Ammisaduqa. Pp. 40–74 in *Researches in Hebrew and Semitic Languages*. Tel Aviv: Bar-Ilan. (Hebrew)

Bar-On, S.
1995	Zur literarkritischen Analyse von Ex 12,21–27. *ZAW* 107:107–31.
1998	The Festival Calendars in Exod XIII 14–19 and XXXIV 18–26. *VT* 48:161–95
1999	The History of the Tamid Sacrifice and its Status in the Priestly Sacrificial Calendar. Pp. 143–53 in the *Proceedings of the Twelfth In-*

ternational World Congress, Section A, Jerusalem: World Union of Jewish Studies.

Barkay, G.
    1984   Excavations on the Hinnom Slope in Jerusalem. *Qadmoniot* 17:94–108. (Hebrew)
    1987   *Gerah* in *Leviticus*. Ed. B. A. Levine and M. Paran. Ramat-Gan: Revivim. (Hebrew)
    1991   "Your Poor Brother": A Note on an Inscribed Bowl from Beth Shemesh. *IEJ* 41:239–41.
    1992a The World's Oldest Poor Box. *BAR* 18:48–50.
    1992b The Priestly Benediction in Silver Plaques from Ketef Hinnom in Jerusalem. *Tel Aviv* 19:139–92. [Trans. from *Cathedra* 52 (1989) 37–76 (Hebrew)].

Baron, S.
    1952   *A Social and Religious History of the Jews*. Vol. 1. Philadelphia: Jewish Publication Society.

Barr, J.
    1963   Sacrifices and Offerings. In *Dictionary of the Bible*, ed. J. Hastings, 868–76. Rev. ed. F. C. Grant and H. H. Rowley. New York: Scribner.
    1986   *Migraš* in the Old Testament. *JSS* 29:15–31.

Barrick, W. B.
    1975   The Funerary Character of "High Places" in Ancient Palestine: A Reassessment. *VT* 25:565–94.
    1980   What Do We Really Know About "High Places"? *Svensk exegetisk årsbok* 45:50–57.
    1992   High Place. *ABD* 3:196–200.
    1996   On the Meaning of *bêt ha/bāmôt* and *bāttê-habbāmôt* and the Composition of the Kings History. *JBL* 115:621–42.

Barth, Ch.
    1975   *bōqer*. *TDOT* 2:219–28.

Bashyazi, E.
    1966   *Aderet Eliyahu*. (Hebrew) [Originally published 1530; reprint of 1870 edition]

Basset, F. W.
    1971   Noah's Nakedness and the Curse of Canaan: A Case of Incest? *VT* 21:232–37.

Batto, B.
    1987   The Covenant of Peace: A Neglected Ancient Near Eastern Motif. *CBQ* 49:187–211.
    forthcoming.   The Use of *mê niddâ* for General Purification.

Baumgarten, J. M.
    1966   The Counting of the Sabbath in Ancient Sources. *VT* 16:277–86.
    1982   Some Problems of the Jubilees Calendar in Current Research. *VT* 32:485–89.

1984   On the Non-Literal Use of *ma'aser/dekate*. *JBL* 103:245–51.

1985   Halakhic Polemics in New Fragments from Cave 4. In *Biblical Archaeology Today*, ed. J. Amitai, 390–99. Jerusalem: Israel Exploration Society.

1987a   The Sabbath Trumpets in 4Q493M'. *RevQ* 48:555–59.

1987b   The Laws of Orlah and First Fruits in Light of Jubilees, the Qumran Writings, and the Targum Ps.-Jonathan. *JJS* 38:195–202.

1992   The Disqualification of Priests in 4Q Fragments of the "Damascus Document," a Specimen of the Recovery of Pre-Rabbinic Halakha. In *The Madrid Qumran Congress*, ed. J. T. Barrera and L. V. Montaner, 2:503–14. Leiden: Brill.

1995   A Qumran Text with Agrarian Halakha. *JQR* 96:1–8.

Bayliss, M.
1973   The Cult of Dead Kin in Assyria and Babylonia. *Iraq* 35:115–25.

Beck, P.
1990   A Note on the "Schematic Statues" from the Stelae Temple at Hazor. *Tel Aviv* 17:91–95.

Beckman, G.
1982a   The Anatolian Myth of Illuyanka. *JNES* 14:11–25.

1982b   The Hittite Assembly. *JAOS* 102:435–42.

1983   *Hittite Birth Rituals*. Wiesbaden: Harrassowitz.

1996   Treaty Between Suppiluliuma I of Hatti and Huqqana of Hayasa. Pp. 22–30 in *Hittite Diplomatic Texts*, ed. and trans. G. M. Beckman. Atlanta: Scholars Press.

Beit-Arieh, I.
1996   Edomites Advance into Judah. *BAR* 22:28–36.

Bekhor Shor (Joseph ben Isaac)
1994   *The Commentaries of Joseph Bekhor Shor on the Torah*. Ed. Y. Nebo. Jerusalem: Mosad Harav Kook. (Hebrew)

Belkin, S.
1940   *Philo and the Oral Law*. Cambridge, Mass.: Harvard University Press.

Ben-Barak, Z.
1981   Meribaal and the System of Land Grants in Ancient Israel *Biblica* 62:73–91.

Ben-Hayyim
1936   "And She is a Slave Betrothed to Another Man, Leviticus 19:20" *Leshonenu* 7:362–66.

Ben Zvi, E.
1990   Who Wrote the Speech of Babshakeh and When? *JBL* 109:79–92.

1991a   *A Historical-Critical Study of the Book of Zephaniah*. Berlin: de Gruyter.

1991b   The Account of the Reign of Manasseh in II Reg 21,1–18 and the Redactional History of the Book of Kings. *ZAW* 103:355–74.

Ben-Shaḥar, Z.
1979   The Day After the Sabbath. *BM* 77: 225–26. (Hebrew)

Bendavid, A.
1972   *Parallels in the Bible.* Jerusalem: Carta.
Bendavid, S.
1986   *The Bet-Ab in Israel from the Settlement to the End of the Monarchy.* Oranim: Sifriyat Poalim. (Hebrew)
Benzinger, I.
1899   *Die Bücher der Könige.* Friedburg: J.C.B. Mohr.
Berger, P. L.
1967   *The Sacred Canopy: Elements of a Sociological Theory of Religion.*
Garden City, N.Y.: Doubleday.
Bergman, J.
1995   *kōhēn*, Egypt. *TDOT* 7:61–63.
Bergmann, J.
1980   *ḥālam, ḥălôm*, Egypt. *TDOT* 4:421–23.
Berlin, A.
1987   On the Interpretation of Psalm 133. Pp. 141–47 in *Directions in
Biblical Hebrew Poetry*, ed. E. R. Follis. Sheffield: Sheffield Acade-
mic Press.
1994   *Zephaniah.* AB 25A. New York: Doubleday.
Berlin, N. Z. Y.
1959   *Commentary on the Pentateuch Ha'ameq Davar.* Jerusalem: El
Hamekoroth. (Hebrew) [Reprint of 2nd ed., 1938]
Berlinerblau, J.
1996   *The Vow and the "Popular Religious Groups" of Ancient Israel.*
Sheffield: Sheffield Academic Press.
Berman, S.
1972   Law and Morality. *EJ* 10:1480–85.
Bertholet, A.
1901   *Leviticus.* Tübingen: Mohr (P. Siebeck).
Bess, S. H.
1963   Systems of Land Tenure in Ancient Israel. Ph.D. diss., University
of Michigan.
Beyse, K.-M.
1987   *'eṣem. ThWAT* 6:326–32.
Biale, D.
1992   *Eros and the Jews.* New York: Basic Books.
Bieger, G. and N. Lipschitz
1996–97   The Etrog—Was it "The Fruit of the *Hadar* Tree?" *BM*:28–33
(Hebrew)
Bigger, S. F.
1979   The Family Laws of Leviticus 18 in Their Setting. *JBL* 98:188–203.
Binger, T.
1997   *Asherah. Goddesses in Ugarit, Israel and the Old Testament.* JSOT
Suppl. 232. Sheffield: Sheffield Academic Press.
1981   To the God Who Is in Dan. Pp. 142–51 in *Temples and High Places*

        in Ancient Palestine, ed. A. Biran. Cincinnati: Hebrew Union Col-
        lege and Jewish Institute of Religion.

Biran, A.
    1992   Dan. *ABD* 2:12–17.
    1998   Sacred Spaces of Standing Stones, High Places and Cult Objects at
            Tel Dan. *BAR* 24:38–45, 70.

Blackman, A. M.
    1918–19   The Sequence of the Episodes in the Egyptian Daily Temple
            Liturgy. *Journal of the Manchester Egyptian and Oriental Society*:
            27–53.
    1951   Purification (Egypt). *ERE* 10:476–82.

Blenkinsopp, J.
    1966   Are There Traces of the Gibeonite Covenant in Deuteronomy?
            CBQ 28:207–19.
    1972   *Gibeon and Israel.* Cambridge: Cambridge University Press.
    1987   The Mission of Vdjahoresnet and Those of Ezra and Nehemiah.
            JBL 106:409–21.
    1995   Deuteronomy and the Politics of Post-Mortem Existence. *VT*
            45:1–16.
    1996   An Assessment of the Alleged Pre-Exilic Date of the Priestly Mate-
            rial in the Pentateuch. *ZAW* 108:495–518.

Block, D. J.
    1992   Beyond the Grave: Ezekiel's Vision of Death and Afterlife. *BBR*
            2:113–41.

Bloch-Smith, E.
    1991   Review of *Cults of the Dead in Ancient Israel and Ugarit,* by T. J.
            Lewis. *JBL* 110:327–30.
    1992a   *Judahite Burial Practices and Beliefs About the Dead.* Sheffield:
            JSOT Press.
    1992b   The Cult of the Dead in Judah: Interpreting the Material Remains.
            JBL 111:213–24.

Blome, F.
    1934   *Die Opfermaterie in Babylonian und Israel.* Rome: Biblical Institute
            Press.

Blosser, D.
    1981   The Sabbath Year Cycle in Josephus. *HUCA* 52:129–39.

Blum, E.
    1990   *Studien zur Komposition des Pentateuch.* Berlin: de Gruyter.

Boersma, J. J.
    1997   *Thora en Stoa over Mens en Natur.* Baarn: Callenbach.

Boleh, M.
    1991–92   *The Book of Leviticus.* Vols. I and II. Jerusalem: Mosad Harav
            Kook. (Hebrew)

Boling, R. G.
    1960   "Synonymous" Parallelism in the Psalms. *JSS* 5:221–55.

Bonnet, H.
   1952   Reinheit. *RLAR*:631–37.
Borger, R.
   1961   Zu don Asserhadon–Verträgen aus Nimrud. *ZA* 20: 191–92.
   1973   Die Weihe eines Enlil-Priesters. *BiOr* 30:163–76.
Borowski, O.
   1987   *Agriculture in Iron Age Israel: The Evidence from Archaeology and the Bible.* Winona Lake, Ind.: Eisenbrauns.
   1995   Hezekiah's Reforms and the Revolt Against Assyria. *BA* 58:148–55.
Boswell, J.
   1980   *Christianity, Social Tolerance, and Homosexuality.* Chicago: University of Chicago Press.
Bottéro, J.
   1995   *Textes culinaires mesopotamiens.* Winona Lake, Ind.: Eisenbrauns.
Bottéro, J., and H. Petschow
   1975   Homosexualität. *RLA* 4:459–68.
Botterweck, J. G.
   1980   *ḥālam, ḥălôm,* Mari. *TDOT* 4:425–26.
Branson, R. D., and G. J. Botterweck
   1990   *yāsar, mûsâr. TDOT* 6:127–34.
Braude, W. G., and I. J. Kapstein
   1975   *Pesikta de-Rab Kahana.* Philadelphia: Jewish Publication Society.
Braun, R.
   1986   *I Chronicles.* Waco, Tex.: Word Books.
Brauner, R. A.
   1974   Some Aspects of Offense and Penalty in the Bible and the Literature of the Ancient Near East. *Gratz College Annual* 3:9–18.
Breasted, J. H.
   1906   *Ancient Records of Egypt.* Vol. 4. Chicago: University of Chicago Press.
Brettler, M.
   1978–79   The Promise of the Land of Israel to the Patriarchs in the Pentateuch. *Shnaton* 5–6:vii–xxiv.
Brichto, H. C.
   1963   *The Problem of "Curse" in the Hebrew Bible.* Philadelphia: Society of Biblical Literature.
   1973   Kin, Cult, Land and Afterlife—A Biblical Complex. *HUCA* 44:1–54.
   1975   The Case of the Sota and a Reconsideration of Biblical Law. *HUCA* 46:55–70.
   1976   On Slaughter and Sacrifice, Blood and Atonement. *HUCA* 47:19–56.
Bright, J.
   1973   The Apodictic Prohibition: Some Observations. *JBL* 92:195–204.
   1980   *A History of Israel.* 3rd ed. London: SCM Press.

Brin, G.
    1971   The First-Born in Israel in the Biblical Period. Ph.D. diss., Univer-
            sity of Tel-Aviv. (Hebrew)
    1990   *Studies in the Biblical Exegesis of R. Joseph Qara.* Tel-Aviv: Tel-Aviv
            University Press. (Hebrew)
    1994   *Studies in Biblical Law.* Sheffield: JSOT Press.
Brown, J. P.
    1980   The Sacrificial Cult and Its Critique in Greek and Hebrew (II). *JSS*
            25:1–21.
    1983   Men of the Land and the God of Justice in Greece and Israel. *ZAW*
            95:376–402.
Brueggemann, W.
    1965   Amos IV 4–13 and Israel's Covenant Worship. *VT* 15:1–15.
Brunner, H.
    1978   The Teachings of Amenemope. Pp. 49–62 in *Near Eastern Reli-
            gious Texts Relating to the Old Testament,* ed. W. Beyerlin et al.
            Trans. J. Bowden. Philadelphia: Westminster Press.
Buber, M.
    1964   *The Way of the Bible.* Jerusalem: Mosad Bialik. (Hebrew) [Abridged
            as *On the Bible,* by N. M. Glatzer (New York: Schocken, 1982)]
Buck, R. J.
    1959   Communalism on the Lipari Islands. *Classical Philology* 54:35–39.
Budd, P. J.
    1996   *Leviticus.* Grand Rapids, Mich.: Eerdmans.
Buhl, F.
    1899   *Die socialen Verhältnisse der Israeliten.* Berlin: Reuther and
            Richard.
Buis, P.
    1974   Comment au septième siècle envisageait-on l'avenir de l'Alliance?
            Étude de Lv. 26, 3–45. In *Questions disputèes d'Ancient Testament:
            Méthode et Theologie,* ed. C. Brokelmans, 131–40. Louvain: Ducu-
            lot and Leuven University Press.
Buleh, M.
    1992   *Commentary on Leviticus.* Jerusalem: Mosad Bialik. (Hebrew)
Bultmann, C.
    1992   *Der Fremde im antiken Juda.* Göttingen: Vandenhoeck & Ruprecht.
Burrows, M.
    1925   *The Literary Relations of Ezekiel.* Philadelphia: Jewish Publication
            Society.
Businck, T.
    1970–80 *Der Tempel von Jerusalem. Von Salomo bis Herodes,* 2 vols.
            Leiden: Brill.
Caloz, M.
    1968   Exode XIII, 3–16 et son rapport au Deuteronome (Planches 1–11).
            RB 75:5–62.

Campbell, A.
1986   Of Prophets and Kings: A Ninth Century Document (1 Samuel 1–2 Kings 10). Grand Rapids, Mich.: Eerdmans.

Caplice, R.
1974   The Akkadian Namburb: Texts. In Sources for the Ancient Near East. Los Angeles: Undena.

Cardascia, G.
1980   Égalité et megalité des sexes en matière d'atteinte aux moeurs dans le Proche-Orient ancien. WO 11.

Cardellini, I.
1981   Die biblischen "Sklaven"—Gesetze im Lichte des keilschriftlichen Sklavenrechts. Bonn: Hanstein.

Carmichael, C. M.
1976   On Separating Life and Death: An Explanation of Some Biblical Laws. HTR 69:1–7.
1979   A Common Element in Five Supposedly Disparate Laws. VT 29:129–42.
1982   Forbidden Mixtures. VT 32:394–415.
1985a Biblical Laws of Talion. HAR 9:107–26.
1985b Law and Narrative in the Bible. Ithaca, N.Y.: Cornell University Press.
1994   Laws of Leviticus 19. HTR 87:433–48.
1995   Forbidden Mixtures in Deuteronomy XXII 9–11 and Leviticus XIX 19. VT 45:433–48.
1997   Law, Legend, and Incest in the Bible. Ithaca, N.Y.: Cornell University Press.

Carr, D. M.
1995   Reaching for Unity in Isaiah. JSOT 57:61–80.

Cartledge, W. W.
1992   Vows in the Hebrew Bible and the Ancient Near East. Sheffield: JSOT Press.

Cassuto, U.
1949   A Commentary on the Book of Genesis. Part 1, From Adam to Noah. Part 2, From Noah to Abraham. Jerusalem: Magnes. (Hebrew)
1951a A Commentary on the Book of Exodus. Jerusalem: Magnes. (Hebrew)
1951b The Goddess Anath. Jerusalem: Bialik Institute. (Hebrew)
1954a Leviticus. EM 2:878–87. (Hebrew)
1954b bĕṣiqlōn. EM 2:307–8. (Hebrew)
1961   From Adam to Noah. Trans. I. Abrahams. Jerusalem: Magnes. (Hebrew, 1944).
1964   From Noah to Abraham. Trans. I. Abrahams. Jerusalem: Magnes. (Hebrew, 1959)

Catron, J. E.
1995   Temple and bāmāh: Some Considerations. Pp. 150–65 in The Pitcher Is Broken [G. W. Ahlström Memorial], ed. S. W. Holloway and L. K. Handy. Sheffield: Sheffield Academic Press.

Cazelles, H.
    1946   *Études sur le code de l'alliance.* Paris: Letouzey et Ané.
    1951   La Dime. *VT* 1:131–34.
Černy, J.
    1954   Consanguineous Marriages in Pharaohnic Egypt. *Journal of Egypt-ian Archaeology* 40:23–29.
Chambon, A.
    1984   *Tell el-Far'ah I.* Paris: Éditions Recherche sur les Civilisations.
Charpin, D.
    1990   L'andurârum à Mari. *Mari* 6:253–70.
Chassinat, E.
    1928–34   *Le Temple d'Edfou.* 14 vols. Cairo: Institute Francais d'arche-ologie orientale du Caire.
Chavel, S.
    1998   Vocal Worship and the Role of the Blasphemy Pericope (Lev 24:10–23) in the Priestly Composition. Master's thesis, Hebrew Uni-versity. (Hebrew)
Childs, B. S.
    1974   *Exodus.* Philadelphia: Westminster Press.
    1986   *Old Testament Theology in a Canonical Context.* Philadelphia: Fortress Press.
Chinitz, J.
    1993   Altars and Tables. *CJ* 45:46–58.
Chirichigno, G. C.
    1987   The Narrative Structure of Exod 19–24. *Biblica* 68:457–79.
    1993   *Debt-Slavery in Israel and the Ancient Near East.* Sheffield: JSOT Press.
Cholewinski, A.
    1976   *Heiligkeitsgesetz und Deuteronomium: Eine vergleichende Studie.* AnBib 66. Rome: Pontifical Biblical Institute.
Clay, A. T.
    1912   *Babylonian Business Transactions of the First Millennium B.C.* 2 vols. New York.
Clements, R. E.
    1961–62   Temple and Land: A Significant Aspect of Israel's Worship. *Transactions of the Glasgow University Oriental Society* 19:16–28.
    1965   *God and Temple.* Oxford: Blackwell.
    1972   *Exodus.* Cambridge: Cambridge University Press.
    1982   The Unity of the Book of Isaiah. *Interpretation* 36:117–29.
    1985   Beyond Tradition-History: Deutero-Isaianic Development of First Isaiah's Themes. *JSOT* 31:95–113.
Clines, D. J. A.
    1974   The Evidence for an Autumnal New Year in Pre-Exilic Israel Re-considered. *JBL* 93:22–40. Reprinted in D. J. A. Clines *On the Way to the Postmanden: Old Testament Essays, 1967–1998,* vol. I, 371–94. Sheffield 1998.

Cogan, M.
  1974   *Imperialism and Religion*. Missoula, Mont.: Scholars Press.
Cogan, M., and H. Tadmor
  1988   *II Kings*. AB 11. New York: Doubleday.
Cohen, C.
  1969   Was the P Document Secret? *JNES* 1:39–44.
  1979   Neo-Assyrian Elements in the First Speech of the Biblical Rab-Šaqe. *Israel Oriental Studies* 9:32–47.
  1981–82   Studies in Extra-Biblical Hebrew Inscriptions I: The Semantic Range and Usage of the Terms *ʾāmâ* and *šipḥâ*. *Shnaton* 5–6:xxv–liii.
  1993   The Biblical Priestly Blessing (Num 6:24–26) in the Light of Akkadian Parallels. *TA* 20:228–38.
Cohen, H. H.
  1972   Divine Punishment. *EJ* 6:120–22.
Cohen, H. R.
  1978   *Biblical Hapax Legomena in the Light of Akkadian and Ugaritic*. Missoula, Mont.: Scholars Press.
Cohen, M.
  1990a   Le "Ger" biblique et son statut socio-religiux. *RHR* 207:131–58.
  1990b   A Diachronic and Synchronic Examination of the Concept "*gēr*" in the Bible. Pp. 11–18 in *Proceedings of the Tenth World Congress of Jewish Studies*, Division A. Jerusalem: World Union of Jewish Studies. (Hebrew)
  1993   The Terms Impurity and Purity in Biblical Hebrew and Their Relation to the Concept of Prohibition and Permission in Rabbinic Hebrew. *BM* 38:289–306.
Cohen, M. E.
  1993   *The Cultic Calendars of the Ancient Near East*. Bethesda, Md.: CDL Press.
Cohen, M. M.
  1971   Capital Punishment. *EJ* 5:142–45.
Cohen, M. S.
  1990   The Biblical Prohibition of Homosexual Intercourse. *Journal of Homosexuality* 19:3–20.
Cohen, R., and Y. Israel
  1995   *On the Road to Edom: Discoveries from ʿEn Ḥaṣeven*. Jerusalem: Israel Museum.
  1996   Smashing the Idols: Piecing Together an Edomite Shrine in Judah. *BAR* 22:40–51, 65.
  1970   *Peʾer Hador*. Vol. 3. Jerusalem: B'nai B'rak. (Hebrew)
Cohen, S. J. D.
  1983   From the Bible to the Talmud: The Prohibition of Intermarriage. *HAR* 7:23–40.
  1985   The Matrilineal Principle in Historical Perspective. *Judaism* 34:5–13.

Cohen, Y. A.
    1969   Ends and Means in Political Control: State Organization and the Punishment of Adultery, Incest, and the Violation of Celibacy. *American Anthropologist* 71:658–87.

Cohn, H. H.
    1976   *Jewish Law and Modern Israel*. New York: Ktav.

Collier, P.
    1983   Malfunctioning of African Rural Markets. *Oxford Bulletin of Economics and Statistics* 45:141–72.

Collins, O. E.
    1977   The Stem ZNH and Prostitution in the Hebrew Bible. Ph.D. diss., Brandeis University.

Colson, M.A.
    1968–71   *Philo*, 10 vols. Translation and Notes. Cambridge, Mass.: William Heineman.

Conrad, J.
    1980   *zāqēn*. TDOT 4:122–31.
    1987   *plʾ*. TWAT 6:570–83.

Cooley, R. E.
    1983   Gathered to His People: A Study of a Dothan Family Tomb. Pp. 47–58 in *The Living and Active Word of God* [Fest. S. J. Schultz], ed. M. Tuchand and R. Youngblood. Winona Lake, Ind.: Eisenbrauns.

Cooper, A., and B. R. Goldstein
    1992   Exodus and *Maṣṣot* in History and Tradition. *Maarav* 8:15–38.
    1993   The Cult of the Dead and the Theme of Entry into the Land. *BI* 1:285–30.

Cornelius, F.
    1970   Das Hethitische ANTAHŠUM (ŠAR) -Fest. In *Actes de la XVIIᵉ Rencontre assyriologique internationale*, 171–74. Hamsur-Heure: Comité belge de recherches en Mesopotamie.

Costecalde, C.-B.
    1985   Sacre. *DBSup* 10:1346–93.

Coulanges, F. de
    n.d.   *The Ancient City*. Garden City, N.Y.: Doubleday.

Countryman, L. W.
    1988   *Dirt, Greed, and Sex*. Philadelphia: Fortress Press.

Cover, R.
    1983   Nomos and Narrative. *Harvard Law Review* 97:4–68.

Cross, F. M.
    1973   *Canaanite Myth and Hebrew Epic*. Cambridge, Mass.: Harvard University Press.
    1998   *From Epic to Canon*. Baltimore: Johns Hopkins University Press.

Crüsemann, F.
    1996   *The Torah*. Minneapolis: Fortress Press. [Flawed trans. of *Die Tora*:

Theologie und Sozialgeschichte des altestamentlichen Gesetzes, by A. W. Mahnke. (Munich: Kaiser, 1992)]

Cryer, F. H.
1994 *Divination in Ancient Israel and its Near Eastern Environment.* Sheffield: Sheffield Academic Press.

Dahl, G., and A. Hjort
1976 *Having Herds: Pastoral Herd Growth and Household Economy.* Stockholm Studies in Social Anthropology 2. Stockholm: Department of Social Anthropology, University of Stockholm.

Dahood, M.
1970 *Psalms III.* AB 17a. Garden City, N.Y.: Doubleday.

Dalley, S.
1984 *Mari and Karana: Two Old Babylonian Cities.* New York: Longman.

Dalman, G.
1928–39 *Arbeit und Sitte in Palästina.* 6 vols. Gütersloh: Bertelsmann.

Dandamaev, M. A.
1984 *Slavery in Babylonia: From Nabopolassar to Alexander the Great (626–331 B.C.),* ed. M. A. Powell. Trans. V. A. Powell. Dekalb: Northern Illinois University Press.

Dandamaev, M. S.
1965 Charmowaja Desjatina w Pozdnej Babilonii. *Vestnik Drevney Istorii:* 29:14–34.

Daube, D.
1941 Codes and Codas in the Pentateuch. *Juridical Review* 53:242–61.
1947 *Studies in Biblical Law.* Cambridge: Cambridge University Press. [Reprint, New York: Ktav, 1969]
1956 *The New Testament and Rabbinic Judaism.* London: University of London Press.
1963 *The Exodus Pattern in the Bible.* Westport, Conn.: Greenwood Press.
1969 The Culture of Deuteronomy. *ORITA* 3:27–52.
1973 The Self-Understood in Legal History. *Juridical Review,* n.s., 18:126–34.

Davies, G. I.
1979 A Note on the Etymology of HIŠTAḤăWāH. *VT* 29:493–95.

Davies, P. R.
1983 Calendrical Change and Qumran Origins. *CBQ* 45:80–89.

Davies, W. D.
1976 *The Gospel and the Land.* Berkeley: University of California Press.

Day, J.
1989 *Molech: A God of Human Sacrifice in the OT.* Cambridge: Cambridge University Press.

Dearman, J. A.
1988 *Property Rights in the Eighth-Century Prophets.* Atlanta: Scholars Press.

Degen, R.
    1969   *Altaramäische Grammatik der Inschriften*. Wiesbaden: Kommission Verlag Franz Stimer.

Deller, K.
    1965   Review of *Les Sacrifices de l'Ancien Testament*, by R. de Vaux. *Or*, n.s., 34:182–86.

Derrett, S. D. M.
    1971   Love Thy Neighbor as a Man Like Thyself? *ET* 83:55–56.

Deshen, S.
    1977   Tunisian *Hilluloth* in *The Generation of Transition*. Ed. M. Shokeid and S. Deshen. Jerusalem: Bialik Institute. (Hebrew)

Detienne, M.
    1979   *Dionysos Slain*. Trans. M. Muellner and L. Muellner. Baltimore: John Hopkins University Press.

Diamond, A. S.
    1957   An Eye for an Eye. *Iraq* 15:151–55.
    1971   *Primitive Law, Past and Present*. London: Watts.

Dietrich, M., and O. Loretz
    1980   Die Bannung von Schlangengift. *UF* 12:153–70.

Dillard, R. B.
    1987   *2 Chronicles*. Waco, Tex.: Word Books.

Dillmann, A.
    1886   *Die Bücher Numeri, Deuteronomium und Josua*. 2nd ed. Leipzig: Hirzel.

Dillmann, A., and V. Ryssel
    1897   *Die Bucher Exodus und Leviticus*. 3rd ed. Leipzig: Hirzel. 1st ed. 1880

Dinçol, A. M., and M. Darga
    1969–70 Die Feste von Karahna. *Anatolica* 3:99–118.

Dohmen, C.
    1985   *nāsak*. *TWAT* 5:488–93.
    1989   *pesel*. *TWAT* 6:688–97.

Dommen, E. C.
    1972   Social Justice and Economic Development. *Rural Life* 17:13–20.

Dommershausen, W.
    1982   *kōhēn*. *TWAT* 4:62–79. [Reprinted in *TDOT* 7 (1995): 60–75]
    1984   *lāham, lehem*. *TWAT* 4:538–47.

Doron, P.
    1969   A New Look at an Old Lex. *JNES* 1:21–27.

Dossin, G.
    1938   Signaux lumineux au pays de Mari. *RA* 35:174–86.

Douglas, M.
    1966   *Purity and Danger*. London: Routledge & Kegan Paul.
    1972   Deciphering a Meal. *Daedalus* 101:61–81.
    1993a The Forbidden Animals in Leviticus. *JSOT* 59:3–23.

1993b *In the Wilderness: The Doctrine of Defilement in the Book of Numbers.* Sheffield: JSOT Press.

1994 The Stranger in the Bible. *Archives europeénnes de sociologie* 35: 283–98.

1995 Poetic Structure in Leviticus. Pp. 239–56 in *Pomegranates and Golden Bells* [Fest. J. Milgrom], ed. D. P. Wright et al. Winona Lake, Ind.: Eisenbrauns.

1996 Sacred Contagion. Pp. 86–106 in *Reading Leviticus,* ed. J. F. A. Sawyer. Sheffield: Sheffield Academic Press.

1999a *Leviticus as Literature.* Oxford: Oxford University Press.

1999b Impurity of Land Animals. Pp. 35–45 in *In Purity and Holiness,* eds. M. J. H. M. Poorthuis and J. Schwartz. Leiden: BriU.

Driver, G. R.

1931a Studies in the Vocabulary of the Old Testament II. *JTS* 32:250–57.

1931b Studies in the Vocabulary of the Old Testament III. *JTS* 32:361–65.

Driver, G. R., and J. C. Miles

1952 *The Babylonian Laws.* Vol. 1. Oxford: Clarendon Press.

Driver, S. R.

1881 *A Treatise on the Use of the Tenses in Hebrew.* Oxford: Clarendon Press.

1895 *Deuteronomy.* ICC. New York: Scribner.

1906 *The Book of Genesis.* 5th ed. WC. London: Methuen.

1913 *An Introduction to the Literature of the Old Testament.* New York: Scribner.

1929 *The Book of Exodus.* Cambridge: Cambridge University Press. [Originally published 1911]

Driver, S. R., and M. A. White

1894–98 *The Book of Leviticus in Hebrew.* Leipzig: Hinrichs.

Duhm, B.

1922 *Das Buch Jesaja.* 4th ed. Göttingen: Vandenhoeck & Ruprecht.

Dumbrell, W. J.

1984 *Covenant and Creation.* Exeter: Paternoster Press.

Dunash Ibn Labrat

1855 *Responsa.* Ed. Z. Filipowski.

Durham, J. J.

1987 *Exodus.* Waco, Tex.: Word Books.

Dybdahl, J. L.

1981 Israelite Village Land. Ph.D. diss., Fuller Seminary.

Ebach, J. H.

1971 *Pgr* = (Toten-) Opfer? *UF* 3:365–68.

Ebach, J., and U. Rutersworden

1977, 80 Unterweltsbeschwörung in Alton Testament: *UF* 9:58–70; 12: 205–20.

Edelman, D.
    1987   Biblical *Molek* Reassessed. *JAOS* 107:727–31.
Eden, A.
    1987   According to Its Seed. In *Leviticus*, ed. B. A. Levine and M. Paran, 217. Ramat-Gan: Revivim. (Hebrew)
Edzard, D. O.
    1965   *The Near East: The Early Civilizations*, ed. J. Bottéro et al., chaps. 2, 4, 5. Trans. R. F. Tannenbaum. London: Weidenfeld and Nicolson.
    1974   "Sociale Reformen" in Zweistrom land. *Acta Antiqua* 22:145–46.
Eerdmans, B. D.
    1912   *Das Buch Leviticus*. Alttestamentliche Studien 4. Giessen: Töpelmann.
Ehelolf, H.
    1916   *Ein Wortfolgeprinzip im Assyrisch-Babylonishen*. Marburg: Pries.
    1930   Zum hethitischen Lexicon. *Kleinasiatische Forschungen Weimar* 1:393–400.
Ehrlich, A.
    1899–1900   *Hamiqra kifshuto*. 3 vols. Berlin: Poppelauer. (Hebrew)
    1908–14   *Randglossen zur hebräischen Bibel*. 7 vols. Leipzig: Hinrichs.
Ehrlich, D.
    1987   *pissēaḥ*. P. 152 in *World of the Bible: Leviticus*, ed. B. A. Levine et al. Ramat-Gan: Revivim. (Hebrew)
Eichler, B. L.
    1973   *Indenture at Nuzi*. New Haven, Conn.: Yale University Press.
    1976   Bestiality. *IDBS*: 96–97.
    1985   Slavery. In *Harper's Bible Dictionary*, ed. P. J. Achtemeier, 959. San Francisco: Harper & Row.
Eilberg-Schwartz, H.
    1990   *The Savage in Judaism*. Bloomington: Indiana University Press.
Eisenman, R. H., and M. Wise
    1992   *The Dead Sea Scrolls Uncovered*. New York: Penguin.
Eissfeldt, O.
    1917   *Erstlinge und Zehnten im Alten Testament*. Leipzig: Hinrichs.
    1935   *Molk als Opferbegriff im Punischen und Hebräischen und das Ende das Gott Moloch*. Halle: Niemeyer.
Eitam, D., and H. Shomroni
    1987   Research of the Oil Industry During the Iron Age at Tel Miqne. Pp. 37–56 in *Olive Oil in Antiquity*, ed. M. Heltzer and D. Eitam. Haifa: University of Haifa.
Elgabish, D.
    1994   Sukkot—A Place Name or a Name for Temporary Structures? *BM* 39:367–76. (Hebrew)
Eliezer of Beaugency
    1909   *Kommentar zu Ezechiel*. Ed. S. A. Poznanski. Warsaw.

Elliger, K.
    1955   Das Gesetz Leviticus 18. ZAW 67:1–24.
    1966   *Leviticus.* HAT 4. Tübingen: Mohr (P. Siebeck).
Elliott-Binns, L. E.
    1955   Some Problems of the Holiness Code. ZAW 67:26–40.
Ellison, H. L.
    1973   The Hebrew Slave: A Study in Early Israelite Society. *EQ* 45:30–35.
Emerton, J. A.
    1977   The Etymology of *hištaḥawāh. OTS* 20:41–55.
    1997   The Biblical High Place in the Light of Recent Study. *PEQ* 129:116–32.
Engelhard, D. H.
    1970   *Hittite Magical Practices: An Analysis.* Dissertation, Brandeis University. Ann Arbor, Mich.: University Films.
Engelken, K.
    1990   *Frauen im Alten Israel.* Stuttgart: Kohlhammer.
Engnell, I.
    1969   A *Rigid Scrutiny,* ed. J.T. Willis. Nashville: University of Vanderbilt Press.
Enker, A.
    1991   *Lex Talionis:* The "Plain Meaning" of the Text. *S'vara* 2:52–55.
Eph ʿal, I.
    1996   *Siege and Its Ancient Near Eastern Manifestations.* Jerusalem: Magnes. (Hebrew)
Erman, A.
    1907   A *Handbook of Egyptian Religion.* Trans. A. S. Griffith. London: Constable.
Evans, G.
    1958   Ancient Mesopotamian Assemblies. *JAOS* 78:1–11, 114–15.
Eynikel, E.
    1996   *The Reform of King Josiah and the Composition of the Deuteronomic History.* Leiden: Brill.
Fabry, H.-J.
    1985   *nāḥāš. TWAT* 5:384–97.
Fager, J. A.
    1987   *Land Tenure and the Biblical Jubilee: A Moral World View.* Ann Arbor, Mich.: University Microfilms.
    1993   *Land Tenure and the Biblical Jubilee.* Sheffield: JSOT Press.
Falk, Z. W.
    1964   *Hebrew Law in Biblical Times.* Jerusalem: Wahrmann.
    1969   Hebrew Legal Terms: III. *JSS* 14:39–44.
    1980   Holiness (Leviticus 19): Ethics and Aesthetics. *BM* 34:138–43. (Hebrew)
    1990   Spirituality and Jewish Law. Pp. 127–39 in *Religion and Law.* Winona Lake, Ind.: Eisenbrauns.

Falkenstein, A., and W. von Soden
1953   *Sumerische und akkadische Hymnen und Gebeten.* Vol. 1. Zurich: Antemis.
Faust, A.
1996   Archaeological Findings for the *migrāšîm. BM* 42:20–27. (Hebrew)
Feldman, E.
1977   *Biblical and Post-Biblical Defilement and Mourning. Law as Theology.* New York: Ktav.
Feliks, Y.
1968   *Plant World of the Bible.* Tel-Aviv: Massada Press. (Hebrew)
1973   "Go Out and Sow in the Sabbatical Year Because of (the Roman) Taxes." *Sinai* 73:253–79. (Hebrew)
1985   On Neh 8:15. In *Ezra and Nehemiah: The World of the Bible,* ed. M. Heltzer and M. Kochman, 158. Jerusalem: Revivim. (Hebrew)
1986   The Four Species. In *Leviticus: The World of the Bible,* ed. B. A. Levine and M. Paran, 173–74. Jerusalem: Revivim. (Hebrew)
1990   *Agriculture in Eretz-Israel in the Period of the Bible and Talmud.* Jerusalem: Mass. (Hebrew)
1992   *Nature and Land in the Bible.* Jerusalem: Mass. (Hebrew)
1997   The Fruit of the Majestic Tree — The Citron. *BM* 42:288–92. (Hebrew)
Fensham, F. C.
1977   The Numeral Seventy in the Old Testament. *PEQ* 109:113–15.
Feucht, C.
1964   *Untersuchungen zum Heiligkeitsgesetz.* Berlin: Evangelische Verlagsanstalt.
Finesinger, S. B.
1931–32 The Shofar. *HUCA* 8:193–228.
Finkel, L. L.
1983–84 Necromancy in Ancient Mesopotamia. *AfO* 29–30:1–17.
Finkelstein, I.
1986   Shilo. *BAR* 12:22–41.
1988   *The Archaeology of the Israelite Settlement.* Jerusalem: Israel Exploration Society.
Finkelstein, J. J.
1961   Ammiṣaduqa's Edict and the Babylonian Law Codes. *JCS* 15:91–104.
1966   The Genealogy of the Hammurapi Dynasty. *JCS* 20:95–118.
1968   Some New *Misharum* and Its Implications. *Assyriological Studies* 16:233–46.
1981   *The Ox that Gored.* Philadelphia: American Philosophical Society.
Finley, M. I.
1968   The Alienability of Land in Ancient Greece: A Point of View. *Eirene* 7:25–32.

Firmage, E., Jr., and J. Milgrom
   1987   ʿārak. TWAT 6:380–84.
Fishbane, M.
   1985   Biblical Interpretation in Ancient Israel. Oxford: Clarendon Press.
Fisher, E. J.
   1982   Explorations and Responses: Lex Talionis in the Bible and Rabbinic Tradition. Journal of Ecumenical Studies 19:582–87.
Fisher, L. R.
   1970   A New Ritual Calendar from Ugarit. HTR 63:485–501.
   1975   Ras Shamra Parallels. Vol. 2. Rome: Pontifical Biblical Institute.
Fitzmeyer, J.
   1971   A Re-Study of an Elephantine Aramaic Marriage Contract (AP 15). Pp. 137–68 in Near Eastern Studies in Honor of W. F. Albright, ed. M. Goedicke. Baltimore: Johns Hopkins University Press.
Fleming, D. E.
   1990   The Installation of Baal's High Priestess at Emar: A Window on Ancient Syrian Religion. Ph.D. diss., Harvard University.
   1995   More Help from Syria: Introducing Emar to Biblical Study. FA 58:139–47.
Foley, W. A., and R. D. Van Valin, Jr.
   1984   Functional Syntax and Universal Grammar. Cambridge: Cambridge University Press.
Fox, E.
   1995   The Five Books of Moses. New York: Schocken Books.
Fox, M. V.
   1974   The Sign of the Covenant: Circumcision in the Light of the Priestly ʾôt Etiologies. RB 81:557–96.
Frankel, D.
   1994   The Stories of Murmuring in the Desert in the Priestly School. Ph.D. diss., Hebrew University. (Hebrew)
   1998   Two Priestly Conceptions of Guidance in the Wilderness. JSOT 81:31–37.
Freedman, D. N.
   1975   The Aaronic Benedictions. In No Famine in the Land, ed. J. W. Flanagan, 411–42. Missoula, Mont.: Scholars Press.
   1992   The Unity of the Hebrew Bible. Ann Arbor: University of Michigan Press.
Freedman, D. N., and K. A. Mathews
   1985   The Paleo-Hebrew Leviticus Scroll (11QPaleoLev). Winona Lake, Ind.: Eisenbrauns.
Freedman, D. N., and P. O'Connor
   1982   kěrûb. TWAT 4:322–34.
Freedy, K. S., and D. B. Redford
   1970   The Dates of Ezekiel in Relation to Biblical, Babylonian and Egyptian Sources. JAOS 90:462–85.

Freiberg, J.
1992 Numbers and Counting. *ABD* 4:1139–46.

Friedman, R. D.
1976 "Put Your Hand Under My Thigh"—The Patriarchal Oath. *BAR* 22:3–4, 22.

Friedman, R. E.
1981a From Egypt to Egypt: Dtr 1 and Dtr 2. In *Traditions in Transformation*, ed. B. Halpern and J. Levenson, 167–92. Winona Lake, Ind.: Eisenbrauns.
1981b Sacred History and Theology: The Redaction of the Torah. Pp. 25–34 in *The Creation of Sacred Literature*, ed. R. E. Friedman. Berkeley: University of California Press.
1988 *Who Wrote the Bible?* London: Cape.

Friedman, S.
1971 "The Law of Increasing Numbers" in Mishnaic Hebrew. *Leshonenu* 35:117–29, 192–206. (Hebrew)

Friedman, S. J.
1996 The Scholars' Dictionary of Tannaitic Hebrew, the Entry: *Biqqoret, Hefqer/Hevqer. Sidra* 12:113–27. (Hebrew) [English summary, VII–VIII]

Fritz, V.
1981 Die Bedeutung von *ḥammān* in Hebräischen und von *ḥmn'* in den palmyrischen Inschriften. *BN* 15:9–20.

Fröhlich, J.
1994 Themes, Structure, and Genre of Pesher Genesis. *JQR* 85: 83–90.

Fromm, E.
1955 *The Sane Society*. Greenwich, Conn.: Fawcett.

Frymer-Kensky, T.
1977 The Atrahasis Epic and Its Significance for Our Understanding of Genesis 1–9. *BA* 40:147–55.
1979 Israel and the Ancient Near East: New Perspectives on the Flood. *Proceedings of the Rabbinical Assembly* 41:213–25.
1980 Tit for Tat: The Principle of Equal Retribution in Near Eastern and Biblical Law. *BA* 43:230–34.

Füglister, N.
1977 Sühne durch Blut. Zur Bedeutung von Leviticus 17:11. Pp. 143–64 in *Studien zum Pentateuch* [Fest. W. Kornfeld], ed. G. Braulik. Salzburg: Herder.

Fuhs, H. F.
1978 *gāʾal. TDOT* 3:45–48.
1990 *yārēʾ. TDOT* 6:290–315.

Gabel, J. B., and C. B. Wheeler
1980 The Redactor's Hand in the Blasphemy Pericope of Leviticus XXIV. *VT* 30:227–29.

Gabril, A. H.
>   1992   Review of *The Savage in Judaism*, by H. Eilberg-Schwartz. *JAAR*
>   60:153–58.

Gadd, C. J.
>   1948   *Ideas of Divine Rule in the Ancient East*. Schweich Lectures 1945.
>   London: Oxford University Press.

Gaine, R. E.
>   1992   "Bread of Presence" and Creator-in-Residence. *VT* 42: 179–203.

Galatzer-Levy, R., and M. Gruber
>   1992   What an Affect Means: A Quasi-Experiment About Disgust. *Annual
>   of Psychoanalysis* 20:69–92.

Galil, G.
>   1987   The Literary Structure of 22:1–6 and 24:15–22. Pp. 154–55, 177 in
>   *Leviticus: The World of the Bible*, ed. B. A. Levine and M. Paran.
>   Jerusalem: Revivim. (Hebrew)

Galling, K.
>   1962   Incense Altar. *IDB* 2:699–700.
>   1973   Ba'al Ḥamman in Kition und die Ḥammanîm. Pp. 65–70 in *Wort
>   und Geschichte* [Fest. K. Elliger], ed. H. Gese and H. P. Rüger.
>   Neukirchen: Neukirchener Verlag.

Gammie, J. G.
>   1989   *Holiness in Israel*. Minneapolis: Fortress Press.

Gamoran, H.
>   1971   The Biblical Law Against Loans on Interest. *JNES* 38:11–22.

Gane, R. E.
>   1992a Ritual Dynamic Structure: Systems Theory and Ritual Syntax Ap-
>   plied to Selected Ancient Israelite, Babylonian and Hittite Festival
>   Days. Ph.D. diss., University of California, Berkeley.
>   1992b "Bread of Presence" and Creator-in-Residence. *VT* 42:179–203.
>   1998   *The Nanshe New Year and the Day of Atonement*. Berrien Springs,
>   Mich.: Andrews University Press.

Gane, R., and J. Milgrom
>   1990   *qārab*. *TWAT* 7:147–61.

Gardiner, F.
>   1881   The Relation of Ezekiel to the Levitical Law. *JBL* 1:173–205.

Gaster, T. H.
>   1952   *Festivals of the Jewish Year*. New York: Sloane.
>   1961   *Thespis: Ritual, Myth, and Drama in the Ancient Near East*. Rev.
>   ed. Garden City, N.Y.: Doubleday.
>   1962   Sacrifices. *IDB* 4:147–59.
>   1969   *Myth, Legend, and Custom in the Old Testament*. New York: Harper
>   & Row.

Geiger, A.
>   1857   *Urschrift und Uebersetzungen der Bibel*. Breslau: Hainauer.
>   1865   Neuere Mittheilungen über die Samaritaner IV. *ZDMG* 19:601–15.

Geller, M. J.
1990 Taboo in Mesopotamia. *JCS* 42:105–17.

Geller, P.
forthcoming *Recovering the Sanctity of the Galilee: The Veneration of Sawl Relics in Classical Kabbalah.*

Gennup, A.
1960 *The Rites of Passage.* Chicago: University of Chicago Press.

George, A. R.
1986 Sennacherib and the Tablet of Destinies. *Iraq* 48:133–45.

Gerlemann, G.
1977 Nutzrecht und Wohnrecht. Zur Bedeutung von *'ăhuzza* und *naḥălâ.* ZAW 89: 313–25.

Gerstenberger, E. S.
1996 *Leviticus.* Trans. D. W. Stott. Louisville, Ky.: Westminster-John Knox Press. [Trans. of *Das dritte Buch Mose: Leviticus* (Göttingen: Vandenhoeck & Ruprecht, 1993)]

Gevaryahu, H. M. Y.
1960 The Priestly Prebends in Egypt and Israel in *Sefer Tur-Sinai.* Jerusalem: Kirat Sefer. (Hebrew)

Gevirtz, S.
1963 Jericho and Shechem: A Religo-Literary Aspect of City Destruction. *VT* 13:52–62.

Gianto, A.
1987 Some Notes on the Mulk Inscription from Nebi Yunis (RES 367). *Biblica* 68:397–401.

Gibson, J. C. L.
1971 *Textbook of Syrian Semitic Inscriptions.* Vol. 1, *Hebrew and Moabite Inscriptions.* Oxford: Clarendon Press.
1978 *Canaanite Myths and Legends.* Edinburgh: Clark.
1985 *Textbook of Syrian Semitic Inscriptions.* Vol. 2, *Aramaic Inscriptions.* Oxford: Clarendon Press.

Gilat, Y. D.
1980 A Note on "The Acceptance of Sacrifices from Gentiles." *Tarbiz* 49:422–23. (Hebrew)
1995 Did the Jubilee Remit Debts? *Tarbiz* 64:229–36. (Hebrew)

Gilbert-Peretz, D.
1996 Ceramic Figures. In *Excavations at the City of David (1978–85).* *Qedem* 35: 29–41.

Ginsberg, H. L.
1945 Ugaritic Studies and the Bible. *BA* 8:41–58.
1963 Towards a Lexicon of the Biblical Language. Pp. 167–73 in *H. Yalon Jubilee Volume,* ed. S. Lieberman et al. Jerusalem: Kiryat Sefer. (Hebrew)
1967 Lexicographical Notes. *SVT* 16:71–82.
1971 Hosea. *EJ* 8:1010–24.

1979–80   The Grain Harvest Laws of Lev. 9–22 and Num. 28:26–31 . *PAAJR* 46–47:141–53.

1982   *The Israelian Heritage of Judaism.* New York: Jewish Theological Seminary.

Ginzberg, E.
1932   Studies in the Economics of the Bible. *JQR* 22:343–408.

Ginzburg, C. D.
1966   *Introduction to the Masoretic—Critical Edition of the Hebrew Bible.* New York: Ktav.

Gispen, W. H.
1961   De Gelofte. *Gereformeerd Theologisch Tijdschrift* 61:37–45.

Goetze, A.
1963   Warfare in Asia Minor. *Iraq* 25:124–30.

Goldberg, A.
1977   *Leviticus and Numbers.* Tel Aviv: Author. (Hebrew)

Goldstein, B. R., and A. Cooper
1990   The Festivals of Israel and Judah and the Literary History of the Pentateuch. *JAOS* 110:19–31.

Goldziher, I.
1889   *Muhammedanische Studien.* Vol. 1. Halle: Niemeyer.

1971   *Muslim Studies.* Chicago: Aldine.

Gonnet, H.
1982   La "Grande Fête d'Arinna." Pp. 43–71 in *Mémorial Atatürk: Études d'archéologie et de philologie anatoliennes.* Institut français d'études anatoliennes. Paris: Éditions Recherche sur les Civilisations.

1992   Hittite Religion. *ABD* 3:225–28.

Goodfriend, E. A.
1989   The Background for the Metaphor of Covenant as Marriage in the Hebrew Bible. Ph.D. diss., University of California, Berkeley.

1992   Cultic Prostitution. *ABD* 5:507–9.

Goodman, L. E.
1986   The Biblical Laws of Diet and Sex. In *Jewish Law Association Studies II,* ed. B. S. Jackson, 17–57. Atlanta: Scholars Press.

Goody, J.
1962   *Death, Property and the Ancestors.* London: Tavistock.

Gordis, R.
1945   On the Structure of Early Hebrew Poetry. Pp. 27, 144 ff. in *The Yearbook of American Jewry,* ed. M. Ribalow. New York: Histadruth Ivrith. (Hebrew)

Gordon, C. H.
1965   *Ugaritic Textbook.* Rome: Pontifical Biblical Institute.

Görg, M.
1980   Eine rätzelhafte Textilbezeichung im Alten Testament. *BN* 12:13–17.

Gorman, F. H.
1990   *The Ideology of Ritual.* Sheffield: JSOT Press.

Gottwald, N. K.

1979 *The Tribes of Yahweh: A Sociology of the Religion of Liberated Israel, 1350–1050* B.C.E. Maryknoll, N.Y.: Orbis.

forthcoming Is the Mediation of Israel Necessary for the Eschatological Conversion of the Nations? In *The U. Simon Fst.*

Gradwohl, R.

1963–64 Das "Fremde Fauer" von Nadab und Abihu ZAW 75–76: 288–95.

Graf, K. H.

1869 *Die sogenannte Grundschrift des Pentateuchs Archiv für wissenschaftliche Erforschung des Alten Testament, I.* Halle.

Gray, J. B.

1903 *Numbers* ICC. New York: Scribner.

Greenberg, M.

1957 The Hebrew Oath Particle *ḥay/ḥē*. *JBL* 76:34–39.

1959 The Biblical Concept of Asylum. *JBL* 78:125–32.

1960 Some Postulates of Biblical Criminal Law. Pp. 5–28 in *Yehezkel Kaufmann Jubilee Volume*, ed. M. Haran. Jerusalem: Magnes

1970 Prolegomenon. Pp. xi–xxxv in *Pseudo-Ezekiel and the Original Prophecy*, by C. C. Torrey and Critical Articles by S. Speigel. New York: Ktav.

1971a Sabbath. *EJ* 14:558–62.

1971b The Sabbath Pericope in Jeremiah. Pp. 27–37 in *Studies in the Book of Jeremiah*, vol. 2. Jerusalem: n.p. (Hebrew)

1971c Sabbatical Year and Jubilee. *EJ* 14:574–78.

1971d Ḥerem. *EJ* 8: 344–50.

1979 Religion: Stability and Ferment. Pp. 79–123, 296–302 in *The Age of the Monarchies: Culture and Society*, ed. A. Malamat. Jerusalem: Massada Press.

1983a *Ezekiel, 1–20*. AB 22. Garden City, N.Y.: Doubleday.

1983b *Biblical Prose Prayer*. Berkeley: University of California Press.

1985 *On the Bible and Judaism: A Collection of Writings*. Tel-Aviv: Am Oved. (Hebrew)

1990 Three Conceptions of Torah in Hebrew Scripture. Pp. 365– 78 in *Die hebräische Bibel und ihre zweifache nachgeschichte* [Fest. R. Rendtorff], ed. E. Blum et al. Neukirchen: Neukirchener Verlag.

1993 Notes on the Influences of Tradition on Ezekiel. *JNES* 22:29–37.

1995a The Etymology of *niddâ* "(Menstrual) Impurity." Pp. 69–77 in *Solving Riddles and Untying Knots* [Fest. J. C. Greenfield], ed. Z. Zevit et al. Winona Lake, Ind.: Eisenbrauns.

1995b Three Concepts of the Torah in Hebrew Scriptures. Pp. 11–24, in *Studies in the Biblical and Jewish Thought*, ed. M. Cogan, et al. Philadelphia: The Jewish Publication Society.

1996a A Problematic Heritage: The Attitude Toward the Gentile in the Jewish Tradition—an Israeli Perspective. *CJ* 48:23–35.

1996b The Value of Controversy. Pp. 4–9 in Judaism and Humanism, ed. N. Guber et al. Jerusalem. (Hebrew).

Greenfield, J. C.
1973   Un Rite religieux araméen et ses parallèles. *RB* 80:46–52.
1976   The Aramaic God Rammān/Rimmōn. *IEJ* 26:195–98.
1982   *Adi balṭu*—Care for the Elderly and Its Rewards. *AfO* 19: 309–15.
1993   Etymological Semantics. *ZAH* 6:33–34.
Greenfield, J. C., and A. Shaffer
1983   Notes on the Bilingual Inscription from Tell-Fekkerye. *Shnaton* 5: 119–29. (Hebrew)
1985   Notes on the Curse Formulae of the Tell Fekkerye Inscription. *RB* 92:47–59.
Greengus, S.
1969   The Old Babylonian Marriage Contracts. *JAOS* 8–9:505–32.
1975   Sisterhood Adoption at Nuzi and "Wife-Sister" in Genesis. *HUCA* 46:5–31.
1992   Law. *ABD* 4:242–52.
Greenspahn, F. E.
1984   *Hapax Legomena in Biblical Hebrew.* Chico, Calif.: Scholars Press.
Greenstein, E. L.
1984a Biblical Law. In *Back to the Sources*, ed. R. W. Holtz, 83–103. New York: Summit.
1984b Review-Essay of *The Savage in Judaism*, by H. Eilberg-Schwartz. *Judaism* 43:101–9.
1985   The Torah as She Is Read. *Response* 47:17–40.
1989   The Torah as She Is Read. In *Essays on Biblical Method and Translation*, 29–51. Atlanta: Scholars Press.
Greger, B.
1992   Beobachtungen zum Begriff *gēr*. *BN* 63:30–34.
Grintz, Y. M.
1966   Do Not Eat over the Blood. *Zion* 31:1–17. (Hebrew)
1970–71 Do Not Eat over the Blood. *ASTI* 8:78–105.
Gropp, D. M., and T. J. Lewis
1985   Notes on Some Problems in the Aramaic Text of the Hadd-Yitbʿi Bilingual. *BASOR* 259:45–62.
Grossfeld, B.
1988   *The Aramaic Bible.* Vol. 8. Wilmington, Del.: Glazier.
Gruber, M. I.
1983a The *qādēš* in the Book of Kings and in Other Sources. *Tarbiz* 52:167–76. (Hebrew)
1983b The Many Faces of Hebrew *nāśā' pānîm* 'Lift up the Face'. *ZAW* 95:252–60.
1986   Hebrew *qĕdēšâh* and Her Canaanite and Akkadian Cognates. *UF* 18:133–48.
1987a Hebrew *daʿbôn nepeš* 'Dryness of Throat': From Symptom to Literary Convention. *VT* 37:365–69.

1987b Women in the Cult According to the Priestly Code. Pp. 35–48 in
       Judaic Perspectives on Ancient Israel, ed. J. Neusner et al. Philadel-
       phia: Fortress Press.
1988   The *qĕdēšāh*: What Was Their Function? *Beer-Sheva* 3:45–52.
1990a Fear, Anxiety and Reverence in Akkadian, Biblical Hebrew and
       Other North-West Semitic Languages. *VT* 40:411–22.
1990b *ykḥ*. TDOT 6:64–71.

Gumpertz, Y. G.
1963   *wĕkol-ʿerkĕkā*. *Leshonenu* 27:44–48. (Hebrew)

Gurney, O. R.
1952   *The Hittites*. London: Penguin.

Güterbock, H. G.
1960   An Outline of the Hittite ANṬAHṢUM Festival. *JNES* 19:80–89.
1964   Religion und Kultus der Hethiter. Pp. 54–73 in *Neuere Hethiter-
       forschung*, ed. G. Walser. Historia Einzelschriften 7. Wiesbaden:
       Franz Steiner Verlag.
1970   Some Aspects of Hittite Festivals. Pp. 175–80 in *Actes de la XVIIᵉ
       Rencontre assyriologique internationale*. Hamsur-Heure: Comité
       belge de recherches en Mesopotamie.

Haas, V.
1970   *Der Kult von Nerik: Ein Beitrag zur hethitischen Religionsgeschichte*.
       Rome: Pontifical Biblical Institute.
1982   *Hethitische Berggotter und hurritische Steindämonen: Riten, Kulte
       und Mythen*. Kulturgeschichte der antiken Welt 10. Mainz: Verlag
       Philipp von Zabern.
1988   Betrachtungen zur Rekonstruction des hethithischen Frujahrfestes.
       Zeitschrift für Assyriologie und vorderasiastische Archäologie
       78:284–98.

Haas, V., and L. Jakob-Rost
1984   Das Festritual des Gottes Telipinu in Hanhana und in Kašha: Ein
       Beitrag zum hethitischen Festkalender. *AoF* 11:10–91.

Haberman, A. M.
1955–56 The Burial of Rachel and the Word *nepeš*. *Tarbiz* 25:363–68.
         (Hebrew)

Hachlili, R., and R. Merhav
1985   The Mennah in the First and Second Temple Times in the Light
       of the Sources and Archaeology *EI* 18 (Avigad Volume): 255–67.
       (Hebrew)

Hadasi, Y.
1836   *Eshkol Hakofer*. Koslow. (Hebrew)

Hadley, J. M.
1994   Yahweh and "His Ashera": Archaeological and Textual Evidence
       for the Cult of the Goddess. Pp. 235–68 in *Ein Gott Allein?* ed.
       W. Dietrich and M. A. Klopfenstein. Freiburg: Vandenhoeck &
       Ruprecht.

Halbe, J.
    1980   Die Reihe der Inzestverbote Lev 18:7–18. ZAW 92:60–88.
Halbertal, M.
    1999   *Interpretative Revolutions in the Making.* Jerusalem: Magnes. (Hebrew)
Halevi, B.
    1975   Additional Traces of Ancestral Worship. *BM* 64:101–17. (Hebrew)
Halivni, D. W.
    1989   On Man's Role in Revelation. Pp. 29–49 in *From Ancient Israel to Modern Judaism*, Vol. 2 [Fest. M. V. Fox], ed. J. Nausner et al. Atlanta: Scholars Press.
    1993   From Midrash to Mishnah: Theological Repercussions and Further Clarifications: "Chate'u Yisrael." Pp. 23–44 in *The Midrashic Imagination*, ed. M. Fishbane. Albany: State University of New York Press.
Halkin, A.
    1985   Letter to Yemen. Pp. 11–49 in *Crisis and Leadership*, ed. D. Hartman. Philadelphia: Jewish Publication Society.
Hallo, W. W.
    1983   Cult Statue and Divine Image: A Preliminary Study. Pp. 1–18 in *Scripture in Context*, Vol. 2, ed. W. W. Hallo et al. Winona Lake, Ind.: Eisenbrauns.
    1985   Biblical Abominations and Sumerian Taboos. *JQR* 86:21–40.
    1987   The Origins of the Sacrificial Cult: New Evidence from Mesopotamia and Israel. In *Ancient Israelite Religion*, ed. P. D. Miller et al., 3–13. Philadelphia: Fortress Press.
    1991   *The Book of the People.* Atlanta: Scholars Press.
    1992   Royal Ancestor Worship in the Biblical World. Pp. 381–401 in *Sha'arei Talmon*, ed. M. Fishbane and E. Tov. Winona Lake, Ind.: Eisenbrauns.
    1993   Disturbing the Dead. Pp. 183–92 in *Minḥah le-naḥum* [Fest. N. M. Sarna], ed. M. Brettler and M. Fishbane. JSOT Suppl. 154. Sheffield: Sheffield Academic Press.
    1995   Slave Release in the Biblical World in Light of a New Text. Pp. 79–83 in *Solving Riddles and Untying Knots* [Fest. J. C. Greenfield], ed. Z. Zevit et al. Winona Lake, Ind.: Eisenbrauns.
    1996   *Origins: The Ancient Near Eastern Background of Some Modern Origins Western Institutions.* Leiden: Brill.
Halpern, B.
    1981a The Uneasy Compromise: Israel Between League and Monarchy. Pp. 59–96 in *Traditions in Transformation*, ed. B. Halpern and J. D. Levenson. Winona Lake, Ind.: Eisenbrauns.
    1981b Sacred History and Ideology: Chronicles Thematic Structure— Indications of an Earlier Source. Pp. 35–54 in *The Creation of Sacred Literature*, ed. R. E. Friedman. Berkeley: University of California Press.

1987   "Brisker Pipes than Poetry": The Development of Israelite Monothe-
        ism. Pp. 77–116 in *Judaic Perspectives on Ancient Israel*, ed. J.
        Neusner et al. Philadelphia: Fortress Press.

1991   Jerusalem and the Lineages in the Seventh Century B.C.E.: Kinship
        and Rise of Individual Morality. Pp. 11–107 in *Law and Ideology in
        Monarchic Israel*, ed. B. Halpern and D. W. Hobson. Sheffield:
        JSOT Press.

Halpern, B., and D. Vanderhooft

1991   The Editions of Kings in the 7th–6th C. B.C.E. *HUCA* 62:179–244.

Hals, R. M.

1989   *Ezekiel*. Grand Rapids, Mich.: Eerdmans.

Hammershaimb, E.

1971   History and Cult in the Old Testament. Pp. 269–82 in *Near East-
        ern Studies in Honor of W. F. Albright*, ed. M. Goedicke. Baltimore:
        Johns Hopkins University Press.

Hamp, V.

1986   *ḥāṣēr*. *TDOT* 5:131–34.

Handy, L. K.

1988   Hezekiah's Unlikely Reform. *ZAW* 100:111–15.

Hannemann, G.

1975–76 On the Preposition *bet* in the Mishna and the Bible. *Leshonenu*
         40:33–53.

Haran, M.

1961   Studies in the Account of the Levitical Cities I: Preliminary Con-
        siderations. *JBL* 80:45–52.

1962a   Shilo and Jerusalem: The Origins of the Priestly Tradition in the
        Pentateuch. *JBL* 81:14–24.

1962b   *mĕlē'â*. *EM* 4:975. (Hebrew)

1963   *ma'ăkālîm ûmašqā'ôt*. *EM* 4:543–58.

1968a   *Ma'ăśēr*. *EM* 5:204–12. (Hebrew)

1968b   *miqdāš yĕḥezkēl*. *EM* 5:347–60.

1968c   *sēper haqqĕdûšâ* *EM* 5:1093–99.

1965   The Priestly Image of the Tabernacle. *HUCA* 36:191–226.

1970   The Religion of the Patriarchs: Beliefs and Practices. *WHJP* 2:219–
        45, 285–88.

1971   *'ărākîm*. *EM* 6:391–94.

1973   Studies in the Bible: The Idea of Centralization of the Cult in the
        Priestly Apprehension. *Beer-Sheva* 1:114–21. (Hebrew)

1978   *Temples and Temple Service in Ancient Israel*. Oxford: Clarendon
        Press

1979   The Law-Code of Ezekiel XL–XLVIII and its Relation to the Priestly
        School *HUCA* 50:45–71.

1981a   Temples and Cultic Open Areas as Reflected in the Bible. Pp. 31–37
        in *Temples and High Places in Biblical Times*, ed. A. Biran. Jerusalem:
        Hebrew Union College.

1981b Behind the Scenes of History: Determining the Date of the Priestly Source. *JBL* 100:321–33.

1992 Holiness Code. *EJ* 8:1820–25.

Hareuveni, N.

1980 *Nature in Our Biblical Heritage*. Givratayim: Japhet.

Harland, B. J.

1998 Vertical or Horizontal: The Sin of Babel. *VT* 48:515–33.

Harrington, D. J.

1993 2 Maccabees. Pp. 1691–1722 in *The HarperCollins Study Bible*. New York: HarperCollins.

Harris, R.

1955 The Archive of the Sin Temple in Khafajah (Tuṭub). *JCS* 9:31–38.

1965 The Journey of the Divine Weapon. *Assyriological Studies* 16: 217–24.

Harris, R. L.

1990 Leviticus. In *The Expositor's Bible Commentary*, 2:499–564. Grand Rapids, Mich.: Zondervan.

Harrison, J.

1922 *Prolegomena to the Study of Greek Religion*. 3rd ed. Cambridge: Cambridge University Press.

Harrison, R. K.

1980 *Leviticus: An Introduction and Commentary*. Leicester: Inter-Varsity Press.

Hartley, J. E.

1992 *Leviticus*. Waco, Tex.: Word Books.

Hartom, S., and S. E. Loewenstamm

1958 Day and Night. *EM* 3:600–603. (Hebrew)

Hasel, G. F.

1981 The Meaning of the Animal Rite in Genesis 15. *JSOT* 19:61–78.

Hayes, J. H.

1982 Restitution, Forgiveness, and Victim in Old Testament Law. *Trinity University Studies in Religion* 11:1–23.

Hazzequni, H. (Hezekiah ben Manoah)

1981 *The Torah Commentaries of R. Ḥizqiah b. Manoaḥ*. Ed. H. D. Chavel. Jerusalem: Mosad Harav Kook. (Hebrew)

Heawood, P. J.

1945–46 The Beginning of the Jewish Day. *JQR* 36:404–14.

Heider, G. C.

1985 *The Cult of Molek: A Reassessment*. Sheffield: JSOT Press.

1992 Molech. *ABD* 4:895–98.

1995 Molech. Pp. 1090–1097 in *Dictionary of Deities and Demons in the Bible*, ed. K. van der Toorn, B. Becking, W. van der Horst Leiden: Brill.

Heimpel, W.

1981 The Nanshe Hymn. *JCS* 33:65–139.

Heinemann, I.
    1932   *Philons griechische und jüdische Bildung.* Hildesheim: Olms.
Heinemann, J.
    1947   *prš. Leshonenu* 15:108–15. (Hebrew)
    1950   *The Ways of the Agadah.* Jerusalem: Magnes. (Hebrew)
Heinisch, P.
    1935   *Das Buch Leviticus.* Bonn: Hanstein.
Held, M.
    1957   Studies in Ugaritic Lexicography and Poetic Style. Ph.D. diss., Johns Hopkins University.
Helfmeyer, F. J.
    1978   *hālakh. TDOT* 3:388–403.
Heltzer, M.
    1976   *The Rural Community in Ancient Ugarit.* Wiesbaden: Reichert.
    1987   The Hunter in Biblical Times. Pp. 119–20 in *Leviticus: The World of the Bible,* ed. B. A. Levine and M. Paran. Jerusalem: Revivim. (Hebrew)
    1989   The Royal Economy of King David Compared with the Royal Economy of Ugarit. *EI* 20:175–80. (Hebrew)
Hempel, J.
    1915   Die israelitischen Anschauungen von Segen und Fluch im Lichte altorientalischen Parallen. *ZDMG,* n.s., 4:1520–110.
Hendel, R. S.
    1988   The Social Origin of the Aniconic Tradition in Early Israel. *CBQ* 50:365–82.
    1995   Prophets, Priests, and the Efficacy of Ritual. Pp. 185–96 in *Pomegranates and Golden Bells* [Fest. J. Milgrom], ed. D. P. Wright et al. Winona Lake, Ind.: Eisenbrauns.
Herman, M.
    1991   *Tithe as Gift.* San Francisco: Mellen Press.
Herr, M. D.
    1987   The Calendar. Pp. 834–64 in *The Jewish People in the First Century,* Vol. 2, ed. S. Safrai and M. Stern. Philadelphia: Fortress Press.
Hertz, J. H.
    1941   *The Pentateuch and Haftorahs.* 2 vols. New York: Metzudah.
Herzog, Z.
    1981   Israelite Sanctuaries at Arad and Beer-sheba. In *Temples and High Places in Biblical Times,* ed. A. Biran, 120–22. Jerusalem: Hebrew Union College.
    1987   Arad—An Ancient Israelite Fortress with a Temple to Yahweh. *BAR* 13:16–35.
    1992   Cities in the Levant. *ABD* 1:1032–43.
Herzog, Z., M. Aharoni, A. F. Rainey, and S. Moskovitz
    1984   The Israelite Fortress at Arad. *BASOR* 254:1–34.
Heschel, A. J.
    1951   *The Sabbath.* New York: Farrar, Straus, and Young.

Hillers, D. R.

1964 *Treaty-Curses and the Old Testament Prophets.* Rome: Pontifical Biblical Institute.

1984 *Covenant: The History of a Biblical Idea.* Baltimore: Johns Hopkins University Press.

Hoenig, S. B.

1969 Sabbatical Years and the Year of Jubilee. *JQR* 59:222–36.

Hoffmann, D. Z.

1928 Decisive Evidence Against Wellhausen. Jerusalem: Darom (Hebrew). Trans. by E. Barishansky from *Die wichtigsten Instanzen gegen die Graf-Wellhausenische Hypothese.*

1954 *Leviticus.* 2 vols. Trans. Z. Har-Shafer and A. Lieberman. Jerusalem: Mosad Harav Kook. (Hebrew) [Trans. of *Das Buch Leviticus, I–II.* (Berlin: Poppelauer, 1905–6)]

Hoffmann, H. D.

1980 *Reform und Reformen.* Zurich: Theologische Verlag.

Hoffner, H. A.

1973 Incest, Sodomy and Bestiality in the Ancient Near East. In *Orient and Occident* [Fest. C. H. Gordon], ed. H. Hoffner, 81–90. Kevelar: Butzon and Bercher.

1974 *Alimenta Hethaeorum: Food Production in Hittite Asia Minor.* New Haven, Conn.: American Oriental Society.

Hoftijzer, J., and B. Jongeling

1995 *Dictionary of Northwest Semitic Inscriptions.* Leiden: Brill.

Huffner, H. A.

1967 Second Millenium Antecedents to the Hebrew *ʾōb. JBL* 86: 385–401.

Holladay, J. S.

1987 Religion in Israel and Judah Under the Monarchy: An Explicitly Archaeological Approach. Pp. 249–99 in *Ancient Israelite Religion: Essays in Honor of Frank Moore Cross,* ed. P. D. Miller, Jr., P. D. Hanson, S. D. McBride. Philadelphia: Fortress Press.

Holland, T. A.

1977 A Study of Palestinian Iron Age Baked Figurines with Special Reference to Jerusalem: Cave I. *Levant* 9:121–55.

1995 A Study of Palestinian Iron Age Baked Clay Figurines with Special Reference to Jerusalem: Cave 1. Pp. 159–89 in *Excavations by K. M. Kenyon in Jerusalem, 1961–67,* Vol. 4, ed. I. Eshel and K. Prag. Oxford: Oxford University Press.

Honigwachs, Y.

1991 *The Unity of the Torah.* Jerusalem: Feldheim.

Hooks, S. M.

1985 Sacred Prostitution in the Bible and the Ancient Near East. Ph.D. diss., Hebrew Union College.

Hopkins, D. C.

1985 *The Highlands of Canaan.* Sheffield: JSOT Press.

Horst, F.
  1961   Das Eigentum nach dem Alten Testament. Pp. 203–21 in *Gottes Recht*, ed. H. W. Wolff. Munich: Kaiser Verlag.
Horton, F. L.
  1973   Form and Structure in Laws Relating to Women: Leviticus 18:6–18. In *SBLSP*, ed. G. MacRae, 1:20–33. Cambridge, Mass.: Society of Biblical Literature.
Houten, C. van
  1991   *The Alien in Israelite Law*. Sheffield: JSOT.
Houtman, C.
  1984   Another Look at Forbidden Mixtures. *VT* 34:226–28.
Houwink ten Cate, P. H. J.
  1966   Mursilis' Northwestern Campaigns—Additional Fragments of His Comprehensive Annals. *JNES* 25:162–91.
Hudson, M.
  1999   Proclaim Liberty Throughout the Land. *BR* 15:26–33, 44.
Huehnergard, J.
  1985   Biblical Notes on Some Akkadian Texts from Emar. *CBQ* 47:428–34.
Huffmon, H. B.
  1992   Lex Talionis. *ABD* 4:321–22.
Humbert, P.
  1960   Le Substantif *to'eba* et le verb *t'b* dans l'Ancien Testament. *ZAW* 72:217–37.
Hurowitz, V.
  1984   Review of *The Exile and the Biblical Narrative*, by R. E. Friedman. *IEJ*: 67–69.
  1992   "His Master Shall Pierce His Ear with an Awl" (Exodus 21.6)—Marking Slaves in the Bible in Light of Akkadian Sources. *PAAJR* 58: 47–77.
  1994   Ancient Israelite Cult in History, Tradition and Interpretation. *Association of Jewish Studies Review* 19:213–36.
  1995   Solomon's Golden Vessels (1 Kings 7:48–50) and the Cult of the First Temple. Pp. 151–64 in *Pomegranates and Golden Bells* [Fest. J. Milgrom], ed. D. P. Wright et al. Winona Lake, Ind.: Eisenbrauns.
  1997   Picturing Imageless Deities: Iconography in the Ancient Near East. *BR* 23: 46–51, 68–69.
  1999   *'eben maskît*: A New Interpretation. *JBL* 118:201–8.
Hurvitz, A.
  1968   The Chronological Significance of "Aramaisms" in Biblical Hebrew. *IEJ* 18:234–40.
  1972   *The Transition Period in Biblical Hebrew*. Jerusalem: Mosad Bialik. (Hebrew)
  1982   *A Linguistic Study of the Relationship Between the Priestly Source and the Book of Ezekiel*. Paris: Gabalda.
  1983   The Language of the Priestly Source and Its Historical Setting—

The Case for an Early Date. Pp. 83–94 in *Proceedings of the Eighth World Congress of Jewish Studies: Panel Sessions — Bible Studies and Hebrew Language*. Jerusalem: Hebrew University.

1988 Dating the Priestly Source in the Light of the Historical Study of Biblical Hebrew a Century After Wellhausen. ZAW 100 (Supplement):88–99.

1995 Terms and Epithets Relating to the Jerusalem Compound in the Book of Chronicles: The Linguistic Aspect. Pp. 165–83 in *Pomegranates and Golden Bells* [Fest. J. Milgrom], ed. D. P. Wright et al. Winona Lake, Ind.: Eisenbrauns.

Hyatt, J. P.
1955 Yaweh as "the God of My Father." VT 5:130–36.

Ibn Ezra, Abraham
1961 *Leviticus with Ibn Ezra's Commentary* Meḥoqeqe Yehudah. Ed. J. L. Krinsky. Horeb: Bnai-Brak. (Hebrew)

Ibn Janaḥ, Jonah
1964 *Seper Ha-Riqmah.* 2 vols. Ed. M. Wilensky. Jerusalem: Academy. (Hebrew)

1968 *The Book of Roots.* Ed. A. Neubauer. Oxford: Clarendon Press. (Hebrew) [Originally published 1875]

Irwin, B. P.
1995 Molek Imagery and the Slaughter of Gog in Ezekiel 38 and 39. *JSOT* 65:93–112.

Irwin, W. H.
1967 The Smooth Stones of the Wadi? Isaiah 57, 6. CBQ 29:31–40.

Israeli, Y.
1972a Second Temple, Mishna and Talmud Periods. Pp. 160–270 in *Inscriptions Reveal*. Jerusalem: Israel Museum. (Hebrew) [English trans., 1976]

1972b In *Inscriptions Reveal*, ed. Eitan. Jerusalem: Israel Museum.

Jackson, B. S.
1972 *Theft in Early Jewish Law.* Oxford: Clarendon Press.

1973 The Problem of Ex. 21:22–5 (Ius Talionis). VT 23:273–304.

1988 Biblical Laws of Slavery: A Comparative Approach. Pp. 86–101 in *Slavery and Other Forms of Unfree Labor*, ed. L. J. Archer. New York: Routledge.

1996 Talion and Purity: Some Glosses on Mary Douglas. Pp. 107–23 in *Reading Leviticus*, ed. J. F. A. Sawyer, 107–23. Sheffield: Sheffield Academic Press.

Jacob, B.
1934 *Das erste Buch der Torah: Genesis.* Berlin: Schoken

1974 *The First Book of the Bible: Genesis.* Trans. W. Jacob. Hoboken, N.J.: Ktav.

Jacobsen, Th.
1943 Primitive Democracy in Ancient Mesopotamia. *JNES* 2:159–72.

1957 Early Political Developments in Mesopotamia. ZA, n.s., 18:91–140.

1976 *The Treasures of Darkness: A History of Mesopotamian Religion.* New Haven, Conn.: Yale University Press.

1987 *The Harp that Once . . . : Sumerian Poetry in Translation.* New Haven, Conn.: Yale University Press.

Janowski, B.

1982 *Sühne als Heilsgeschehen.* Neukirchen: Neukirchener Verlag.

1995 Satyrs. Pp. 1381–84 in *Dictionary of Deities and Demons in the Bible,* ed. K. van der Toorn et al. Leiden: Brill.

Japhet, S.

1968 The Supposed Common Authorship of Chronicles and Ezra–Nehemiah Investigated Anew. *VT* 18:330–71.

1977 *The Ideology of the Book of Chronicles and its Place in Biblical Thought.* Jerusalem: Mosad Bialik. (Hebrew)

1986 The Relationship Between the Legal Corpora in the Pentateuch in Light of Manumission Laws. Pp. 63–89 in *Studies in the Bible,* ed. S. Japhet. Jerusalem: Magnes.

1998 Law and "The Law" in Ezra-Nehemiah. Pp. 96–115 in *Proceedings of the Ninth World Congress of Jewish Studies.* Jerusalem: Perry Foundation. (Hebrew)

1992 The Israelite Legal and Social Reality as Reflected in Chronicles: A Case Study. In *Shaʿarei Talmon,* ed. M. Fishbane and E. Tov, 79–91. Winona Lake, Ind.: Eisenbrauns.

1993 *I & II Chronicles.* OTL. Louisville, Ky.: Westminster Press.

1996 Ownership of Land and Inheritance of the Land. Pp. 36–50 in *Zion Shall Be Redeemed with Justice.* Jerusalem: Presidential Residence.

Jastrow, M.

1943 *A Dictionary of the Targum, The Talmud Babli and Yerushalmi and the Midrashic Literature.* New York: Title.

Jaubert, A.

1957 *La Date de la cène.* Paris: Gabalda.

Jensen, P. P.

1992 *Graded Holiness: A Key to the Priestly Conception of the World.* Sheffield: Sheffield Academic Press.

Jirku, A.

1929 Die israelitische Jobeljahr. Pp. 169–79 in *Reinhold-Seeberg-Festschrift,* Vol. 2, ed. W. Kaepp. Leipzig: Scholl.

Johns, C. H. W.

1898–1924 *Assyrian Deeds and Documents Recording the Transfer of Property Including the So-Called Private Contracts, Legal Decisions and Proclamations Preserved in the Kouyunjik.* 3 vols. Cambridge: Deighton Bell.

Johnson, A.

1947 Aspects of the Use of the Term *pānîm* in the Old Testament. In *Festschrift Otto Eissfeldt,* ed. J. Fück, 155–59. Halle in der Saale: Niemeyer.

Johnson, L. T.
1982　The Use of Leviticus 19 in the Letter of James. *JBL* 101:391–401.
Johnstone, W.
1969　Old Testament Technical Expressions in Property Holding Contributions from Ugarit. *Ugaritica* 6:313.
Jones, J. W.
1956　*The Law and Legal Theory of the Greeks.* Oxford: Clarendon Press.
Joosten, J.
1994　The People and Land in the Holiness Code. Ph.D. diss., Universitaire Protestantse Godgeleerdheid te Brussel.
1996　*The People and Land in the Holiness Code.* Leiden: Brill.
1998　Covenant Theology in the Holiness Code. *ZABR* 4:145–64.
Joosten, J.
1996　Moise a-t-il recèle le Code de Sainteté *BN* 84:75–86.
1998　Covenant Theology in the Holiness Code. *Zeitschrift fur altorientalische und biblische Rechtsgeschichte* 4:147–64.
2000　L'imbrication des codes législatifs dans le récit du pentatech; le cas du code de sainteté (Lévitique 17–26). Pp. 125–40 in La codification des lois dans l'antiquité. Ed. E. Levy. Strassbourg: De Boceard.
Joüon, P. P.
1923　*Grammaire de l'hébreu biblique.* Rome: Pontifical Biblical Institute.
1965　*Grammaire de l'hébreu biblique.* Corrected ed. Rome: Pontifical Biblical Institute.
Junker, H.
1959　Vorschriften für der Tempelkeult in Philä. *Analecta Biblica* 12:151–60.
Kalisch, M. M.
1858　*Genesis.* London: Longmans.
1867–72　*Leviticus.* 2 vols. London: Longmans.
Kampen, J.
1993　A Fresh Look at the Masculine Plural Suffix in CD iv 2. *REVQ* 61:91–98.
Kapach, J., ed.
1963　*Comments of R. Saadiah Gaon on the Torah.* Jerusalem: Mosad Harav Kook. (Hebrew)
Kaufman, S. A.
1979　The Structure of the Deuteronomic Law. *Maarav* 1:105–58.
1982　Reflections on the Assyrian–Aramaic Bilingual from Tell Fakhariyeh. *Maarav* 3:137–75.
1984　A Reconstruction of the Social Welfare Systems of Ancient Israel. In *In the Shelter of Elyon*, ed. W. B. Barrick and J. R. Spencer, 277–86. Sheffield: JSOT Press.
Kaufmann, Y.
1937–56　*The History of Israelite Religion.* 4 vols. Tel Aviv: Dvir (Hebrew).
1959　*The Book of Joshua.* Jerusalem: Kiryat Sefer. (Hebrew)

1960   *The Religion of Israel.* Trans. and abridged M. Greenberg. Chicago: University of Chicago Press.

1962   *The Book of Judges.* Jerusalem: Kiryat Sepher. (Hebrew)

1977   *History of the Religion of Israel.* Vol. 4. Trans. C. W. Efroymson. New York: Ktav.

Kedar-Kopfstein, B.

1980   *ḥag.* TDOT 4:201–13.

Keel, O.

1972   Erwägungen zum Sitz im Leben vormosäischen Pascha und zur Etymologie von *psḥ.* ZAW 84:414–34.

1978   *The Symbolism of the Biblical World.* New York: Seabury Press.

Keil, C. F., and F. Delitzsch

1874   *Biblical Commentary on the Old Testament.* Vol. 2, *The Pentateuch,* Trans. J. Martin. Grand Rapids, Mich.: Eerdmans, 1956.

Kellerman, G.

1981   Towards the Further Interpretation of the *Purulli*-Festival. *Slavica Hiersosolymitana* 5–6:35–46.

Kellermann, D.

1984   *maṣṣâ. TWAT* 4: 1074–81.

1990   *rēaʿ. TWAT* 7: 545–55.

Kennedy, C. A.

1981   The Mythological Reliefs at Pozo Moro, Spain. *SBLSP* 20:209–16.

1987   The Cult of the Dead in Corinth. Pp. 227–36 in *Love and Death in the Ancient Near East* [Fest. M. H. Pope], ed. J. H. Marks and R. M. Good. Guilford, Conn.: Four Quarters.

Kent, R. G.

1950   *Old Persian.* American Oriental Series 33. New Haven, Conn.: American Oriental Society.

Kenyon, K.

1967   *Jerusalem. Excavating 3000 Years of History.* London: Thames and Hudson.

1974   *Digging Up Jerusalem.* New York: Praeger.

Keter Torah   See Aaron ben Joseph.

Kikawada, I. M.

1974   The Shape of Genesis 11:1–9. Pp. 18–32 in *Rhetorical Critisism* (Fest. J. Muilenberg), ed. J. J. Jackson and M. Kessler. Pittsburg: Penn Pickwick.

Kilian, R.

1963   *Literarkritische und formgeschichtliche Untersuchung des Heiligkeitsgesetezes.* Bonn: Haustern.

1970   *R. David Kimḥi (Radak) on the Torah.* Ed. M. Kamleher. Jerusalem: Mosad Harav Kook. (Hebrew)

Kimḥi, David (Radak)

1847   *The Book of Roots.* Ed. H. R. Bresenthal and F. Lebrecht. Berlin: Friedlander (Hebrew). Reprinted Jerusalem, 1966–67

King, P. J.
    1988   The *Marzeaḥ* Amos Denounces—Using Archaeology to Interpret a Biblical Text. *BAR* 15:34–44.
King, T.
    1996   The Priestly Literature and Its Northern Component. Ph.D. diss., Graduate Theological Union, Berkeley.
Kirby, E. J. M.
    1984   Significant Stages of Ear Development in Winter Wheat. Pp. 7–24 in *Wheat Growth and Modelling*, ed. W. Day and R. K. Atkin. New York: Plenum.
Kirkbride, D.
    1969   Ancient Arabian Ancestor Idols. *Archaeology* 22:116–22, 188–95.
Kissane, E. J.
    1960   *The Book of Isaiah.* Dublin: Brown and Nolan.
Kister, M.
    1992   Some Aspects of Qumran Halakha. Pp. 571–89 in *The Madrid Qumran Congress*, Vol. 2, ed. J. T. Barrera and L. V. Montaner. Leiden: Brill.
Kitchen, K. A.
    1995   The Patriarchal Age: Myth or History? *BAR* 21:48–57, 88–95.
Kiuchi, N.
    1987   *The Purification Offering in the Priestly Literature.* Sheffield: JSOT Press.
Klawans, J.
    1995   Notions of Gentile Impurity in Ancient Judaism. *AJSR* 20:285–312.
Klein, J.
    1992   Akitu. *ABD* 1:138–39.
Klein, J., and Y. Sefati
    1988   The Concept of "Abomination" in Mesopotamian Literature and the Bible. *Beer-Sheva* 3:131–48. (Hebrew)
Klein, M. L.
    1986   *Genizah Manuscripts of Palestinian Targum to the Pentateuch.* 2 vols. Cincinnati: Hebrew Union College Press.
Klengel, H.
    1960   Zu den *šībutum* in altbabylonischer Zeit. *Or* 29:357–75.
    1965   Die Rolle der "Ältesten" (LÚ^MEŠ ŠU.GI) im Kleinasian der Hethiterzeit. *ZA*, n.s., 57:223–36.
Kletter, R.
    1990   *The Judean Pillar-Figurines and the Archaeology of Asherah.* Oxford: BAR International Series.
Klostermann, A.
    1893   *Der Pentateuch: Beitrage zu seinem Verstandis und seiner Entstehumgsgeschichte.* Leipzig: Bohme.
Knauf, E. A.
    1989–90   "You Shall Have No Other Gods": Eine notwendige notiz zu einer überflüssigen Diskussion. *DBAT* 26: 238–45.

Kniern, R.
1971 *ʾāšām* Schuldverpflichtung. *THAT* 1:251–57.
Knobel, A. W.
1857 *Die Bücher Exodus und Leviticus.* Leipzig: Hirzel.
Knobloch, F. W.
1992 Adoption. *ABD* 1:76–79.
Knohl, I.
1979 The Acceptance of Sacrifices from Gentiles. *Tarbiz* 48:341–47. (Hebrew)
1988 The Conception of God and Cult in the Priestly Torah and in the Holiness School. Ph.D. diss., Hebrew University. (Hebrew)
1991 Between Cult and Morality. *S'vara* 2:29–34.
1992 Post-Biblical Sectarianism and the Priestly Schools of the Pentateuch: The Issue of Popular Participation in the Temple Cult on Festivals. Pp. 601–10 in *The Madrid Qumran Congress,* Vol. 2, ed. J. T. Barrera and L. V. Montaner. Leiden: Brill.
1993 *Sanctuary of Silence.* Jerusalem: Magnes. (Hebrew) [Publication of diss.]
1995 *The Sanctuary of Silence: The Priestly Torah and the Holiness School.* Trans. E. Feldman and P. Rodman. Minneapolis: Fortress Press.
1996 Between Voice and Silence: The Relationship Between Prayer and the Temple Cult. *JBL* 115:17–30.
Knohl, I., and S. Naeh
1994 Studies in the Priestly Torah: Lev. 7:19–21, Pages 601–12 in *The Bible in the Light of Its Interpreters,* ed. S. Saphet. 601–12. Jerusalem: Magnes. (Hebrew)
Knoppers, G.
1993 *Two Nations Under God.* Vol. 1, *The Reign of Solomon Until the Reign of Jeroboam.* Atlanta: Scholars Press.
1996 Ancient Near Eastern Royal Grants and the Davidic Covenant: A Parallel? *JAOS* 116:670–97.
Knudsen, E. E.
1959 An Incantation Tablet from Nimrud. *Iraq* 21:54–61.
Koch, K.
1962 Der Spruch "Sein Blut bleibe auf seinim Haupt." *VT* 12:396–416.
1972 *Um das Prinzip der Vergeltung im Religion und Recht des Alten Testament.* Darmstadt: Wissenschaftliche Buchgesellschaft.
Kochman, M.
1985 Neh 8:15. In *Ezra and Nehemiah: The World of the Bible,* ed. M. Heltzer and M. Kochman, 157–59. Jerusalem: Revivim. (Hebrew)
1987 Lev 23:1–25. Pp. 157–67 in *Leviticus: The World of the Bible,* ed. B. A. Levine, et al. Ramat Gan: Revivim. (Hebrew)
Kogut, S.
1994 *Correlations Between Biblical Accentuation and Traditional Jewish Exegesis.* Jerusalem: Magnes. (Hebrew)
Kohler, I. V., and A. Ungnad
1913 *Assyrische Rechtsurkunden.* Leipzig: Pfeiffer.

Kohn, R. L.
　　1997　A New Heart and a New Soul: Ezekiel, the Exodus, and the Torah. Ph.D. diss., University of California, San Diego.
Kornfeld, W.
　　1952　*Studien zum Heiligkeitsgesetz.* Vienna: Herder.
　　1972　*Das Buch Leviticus.* Düsseldorf: Patmos.
Kornfeld, W., and H. Ringgren
　　1989　*qdš. TWAT* 6:1179–1204.
Kottackal, J.
　　1983　Jubilee in the Old Testament. *Bible Bashyam* 9:157–67.
Košak, S.
　　1976　The Hittite Nuntarrijashas-Festival (CTH 626). *Linguistica* [Ljubljana] 16:55–64.
Kraeling, E. G.
　　1953　*The Brooklyn Museum Aramaic Papyri.* New Haven, Conn.: Yale University Press.
Kraemer, D.
　　1996　*Reading the Rabbis: The Talmud as Literature.* Oxford: Oxford University Press.
Krahmalkov, C.
　　1996　Paper (untitled) presented at the annual meeting of the Society of Biblical Literature.
Kramer, S. N.
　　1963　*The Sumerians.* Chicago: University of Chicago Press.
Kraus, F.R.
　　1939　Die sumerische Entsprechung der Phrase ANA ITIŠU. Pp. 50–60 in *Symbolae L.L. Koschaker,* Vol. 11. Ed. J. Friedrich et al. Leiden: Brill.
Kraus, H.-J.
　　1966　*Worship in Israel.* Trans. G. Buswell. Richmond, Va.: John Knox Press.
Krašovec, J.
　　forthcoming　*The Antithesis Blessing/Curse and Renewal.*
Krebs, W.
　　1963　Zur kultischen Kohabitation mit Tieren im Alten Orient. *FF* 37:19–21.
Kreuzer, S.
　　1985　Zur Bedentung und Etymologie von *hištaḥăwāh/yšthwy. VT* 35:39–60.
Kselman, J. S.
　　1978　The Recovery of Poetic Fragments form the Pentateuchal Priestly Source. *JBL* 97:161–73.
Kuenen, A.
　　1886　*An Historico-Critical Inquiry into the Origin and Composition of the Hexateuch.* Trans. P. H. Wicksteed. London: Macmillan.
Kugel, J.
　　1987　On Hidden Hatred and Open Reproach: Early Exegesis of Leviticus 19:17. *HTR* 80:49–61.

1996   The Holiness of Israel and the Land in Second Temple Times. Pp.
        21–32 in *Texts, Temples and Traditions* [Fest. M. Haran], ed. M. V.
        Fox et al. Winona Lake, Ind.: Eisenbrauns.

Kugel, J. L.
1997   *The Bible as it Was.* Cambridge, Mass.: Harvard University Press.

Kugler, R. A.
1997   Holiness, Purity, the Body and Society: The Evidence for Theo-
        logical Conflict in Leviticus. *JSOT* 76:3–27.

Kutsch, E.
1953   *miqrā'.* ZAW 65:247–53.
1971   ". . . am Ende des Jahres": Zur Datierung des israelitischen Hebst-
        festes in Ex 23,16. ZAW 83:15–21.
1986   *ḥrp* TDOT 5:203–15.

Kutscher, Y.
1956–57 Regarding the Biblical Lexicon. *Leshonenu* 21:253–54. (Hebrew)

Kuwabara, T.
1983   The Netherworld in Sumero-Akkadian Literature. Ph.D. diss., Uni-
        versity of California, Berkeley.

Kwasman, T., and S. Parpola, eds.
1991   Legal Transactions of the Royal Court of Nineveh, Part I. In *State
        Archives of Assyria*, Vol. 6. Helsinki: Helsinki University Press.

Lacheman, E. C.
1962   *Family Law Documents.* Cambridge, Mass.: Harvard University
        Press.
1976   Tablets from Arraphe and Nuzi in the Iraq Museum. *Sumer*
        32:113–48.

Lack, R.
1962   Les Origines de Elyon, le Tres-Haut dans le tradition culturelle d'Is-
        rael. *CBQ* 24:44–64.
1973   *La Symbolique du livre d'Isaïe* Rome: Biblical Institute Press.

Lackenbacher, S.
1971   Note sur l'ardat-Lillî. *RA* 65:119–54.

Laessøe, J.
1955   *Studies on the Assyrian Ritual and Series bît rimki.* Copenhagen:
        Munksgaard.

Lambdin, T. O.
1953   Egyptian Loan Words in the Old Testament. *JAOS* 73:145–75.

Lambert, M.
1901   Notes et mélanges: De la consécration (Levitique, xxvii, 1–24). *Re-
        vue des études juives* 43:129–32.
1972   L'Expansion de Lagash au temps d'Entemena. *RSO* 47:1–22.

Lambert, W. G.
1960   *Babylonian Wisdom Literature.* Oxford: Clarendon Press.
1967   Enmeduranki and Related Matters. *JCS* 21:126–33.
1980   The Theology of Death. In *Death in Mesopotamia*, ed. B. Alster,
        53–68. Copenhagen: Akademisk.

Landsberger, B.
   1968   Jung fräulichkeit, ein Beitrag zum Thema "Beilager und Eheschlies-
          sung." Pp. 41–105 in Symbolae ivridicae et historicae Montino
          David dedicatae. Vol. 2, ed. J. A. Ankum et al. Leiden: Brill.
Lang, B.
   1982   *kippoer. TWAT* 4:303–18.
   1983   *Monotheism and the Prophetic Minority.* Sheffield: Almond Press.
Langdon, S. H.
   1912   *Die neubabylonischen Königsinschriften.* Leipzig: Hinrichs.
Langlamet, F.
   1969   Israel et "l'habitant du pays": Vocabulaire et formules d'Ex xxxiv,
          11–16. *RB* 76:321–50, 481–507.
Lans, B.
   1988   Life After Death in the Prophetic Promise. Pp. 144–56 in *Congress
          Volume, Jerusalem 1986*, ed. J. A. Emerton. VT Supp. 40. Leiden:
          Brill.
Lappé, F. M., and J. Collins
   1986   *World Hunger: Twelve Myths.* New York: Grove Press.
Leach, E.
   1976   *Culture and Communication,* Cambridge: Cambridge University
          Press.
Leemans, W. F.
   1991   Quelques considerations à propos d'une étude récente du doit du
          Proche-Orient ancien. *BiOr* 48:409–37.
Leggett, D. A.
   1974   *The Levirate and Goel Institutions in the Old Testament.* Cherry
          Hill, N.J.: Mack.
Leibowitz, J., and J. Licht
   1962   *mûm. EM* 4:724–28.
Leibowitz, N.
   1984   *New Studies in the Book of Leviticus.* Jerusalem: World Zionist Or-
          ganization. (Hebrew)
Lemche, N. P.
   1976   The Manumission of Slaves–the Fallow Year–the Sabbatical
          Year–the Yobel Year. *VT* 26:38–59.
Lesky, A.
   1966   Ein ritueller Scheinkampf bei den Hethitern. In *Gesammelte
          Schriften*: Herausgegeben von Walter Kraus, 310–17. Bern: Francke
          Verlag.
Leslau, W.
   1976   *Concise Amaharic Dictionary.* Wiesbaden: Harrassowitz.
Levenson, J. D.
   1984   The Temple and the World, *Journal of Religion* 64:275–98.
   1985   *Sinai and Zion.* Minneapolis: Winston.
   1986   The Jewish Temple in Devotional and Visionary Experience.
          Pp. 32–36 in *Jewish Spirituality*, ed. A. Green. New York: Crossroad.

1988   *Creation and the Persistence of Evil.* San Francisco: Harper & Row.
1993   *The Death and Resurrection of the Beloved Son.* New Haven, Conn.:
        Yale University Press.

Levi, A.
1981   Aspects of Bondage and Release in the Bible: Comparative Studies
        of Exodus 21:2–6, Leviticus 25:25–55, Deuteronomy 15:12–18.
        Ph.D. diss., Jewish Theological Seminary. (Hebrew)

Levi-Feldblum, A.
1986   The Prohibition of Interest in Relation to the Laws of Redemption
        and Jubilee—A Legal and Linguistic Interpretation (Leviticus
        25:35–38). Pp. 29–44 in *Studies in Bible and Exegesis*, Vol. 2 [Fest.
        Y. Elitzur], ed. U. Simon. Ramat-Gan: Bar-Ilan.

Levin, M. Z.
1984   Ḥallalah (Profane). *BM* 29:180–81. (Hebrew)

Levine, B. A.
1963   Ugaritic Descriptive Rituals. *JCS* 17:105–11.
1965   The Descriptive Tabernacle Texts of the Pentateuch. *JAOS*
        85:307–18.
1974   *In the Presence of the Lord.* Leiden: Brill.
1978   The Temple Scroll: Aspects of Its Historical Provenance and Liter-
        ary Character. *BASOR* 23:5–23.
1982   Research in the Priestly Source: The Linguistic Factor. *EI*
        16:127–29.
1983a   In Praise of the Israelite *Mišpāḥâ*: Legal Themes in Ruth. Pp.
        95–106 in *The Quest for the Kingdom of God* [Fest. G. E. Menden-
        hall], ed. H. B. Huffmon et al. Winona Lake, Ind.: Eisenbrauns.
1983b   Late Language in the Priestly Source. In *Proceedings of the Eighth
        World Congress of Jewish Studies*, 5: 69–82. Jerusalem: Hebrew Uni-
        versity.
1987   The Epilogue to the Holiness Code: A Priestly Statement on the
        Destiny of Israel. Pp. 9– 34 in *Judaic Perspectives on Ancient Israel*,
        ed. J. Neusner et al. Philadelphia: Fortress Press.
1989a   *Leviticus.* Philadelphia: Jewish Publication Society.
1989b   Capital Punishment. Pp. 11–32 in *What the Bible Really Says*, ed. M.
        Smith and R. J. Hoffmann. Buffalo, N.Y.: Prometheus Books.
1992   Leviticus, Book of. *ABD* 4:311–21.
1993   *Numbers 1–20.* AB 4A. New York: Doubleday.
1995   The Semantics of Loss: Two Exercises in Biblical Hebrew Lexi-
        cography. Pp. 137–58 in *Solving Riddles and Untying Knots* [Fest.
        J. C. Greenfield], ed. Z. Zevit et al. Winona Lake, Ind.: Eisenbrauns.
1997   The Next Phase in Jewish Religion: the Land of Israel as Sacred
        Space. Pp. 245–58 in *Tehillah le-Moshe* [Fest. M. Greenberg], ed.
        M. Cogan et al. Winona Lake, Ind.: Eisenbrauns.

Levine, B. A., and J.-M. de Tanagon
1984   Dead Kings and Rephaim: The Patrons of the Ugaritic Dynasty.
        JAOS 104:649–59.

Levine, L. D.
1985   Sennacherib's Southern Front. *JCS* 34:28–58.

Levinson, B. M.
1981   The Right Chorale: From the Poetics to the Hermeneutics of the Hebrew Bible. Pp. 129–47 in *"Not in Heaven": Coherence and Complexity*. Pp. 129–47 in *Biblical Narrative*, ed. J. P. Rosenblatt and J. T. Sitterson. Bloomington: Indiana University Press.
1990   Calum M. Carmichael's Approach to the Laws of Deuteronomy. *HTR* 83:227–57.
1991   The Hermeneutics of Innovation: The Impact of Centralization upon the Structure, Sequence, and Reformation of Legal Material in Deuteronomy. Ph.D. diss., Brandeis University.
1995   Thou Shall Surely Kill Him. In *Studien zum Deuteronomium*, ed. G. Braulik, 37–63. Freiburg: Herder.
1997   *Deuteronomy and the Hermeneutics of Legal Innovation*. Oxford: Oxford University Press.

Lewis, T. J.
1989   *Cults of the Dead in Ancient Israel and Ugarit*. Atlanta: Scholars Press.
1991   The Ancestral Estate (*naḥălat ʾĕlōhîm*) in 2 Samuel 14:16. *JBL* 110:597–612.
1998   Divine Images and Aniconism in Ancient Israel. *JAOS* 118:1–28.

Lewy, J.
1958   The Biblical Institution of *Dĕrôr* in the Light of Akkadian Documents. *EI* 5:21–31.

Lewy, J., and M. Lewy
1942–43   The Origin of the Week and the Oldest West Asiatic Calendar. *HUCA* 17:1–152c.

Licht, J.
1965   *The Rule Scroll*. Jerusalem: Bialik Institute. (Hebrew)
1968   *Sukkôt. EM* 6:1037–43 (Hebrew)
1976   *Šābûʿôt. EM* 7:482–94 (Hebrew)
1982   Some Considerations Concerning the Law of Restitution. *Teʿuda* 2:197–201. (Hebrew)
1985   *A Commentary on the Book of Numbers I–X*. Jerusalem: Magnes. (Hebrew)

Licht, J., and Y. Leibowitz
1962   *mûm. EM* 4:724–28. (Hebrew)

Lichtheim, M.
1973–80   *Ancient Egyptian Literature*. 3 vols. Berkeley: University of California Press.

Lieberman, S.
1951   Discipline in the So-Called Dead Sea Manual of Discipline. *JBL* 71:199–206.
1962   *Greek and Helenism in the Land of Israel*. Jerusalem: Bialik Institute. (Hebrew)

1965　Some Aspects of After Life in Early Rabbinic Literature. Pp. 495–532 in *Harry Austryn Wolfson Jubilee Volume*, ed. Leo W. Schwarz. New York: American Academy for Jewish Research.

1967　*Tosefta Ki-feshuṭah*. Vol. 5, *Seder Nashim*. New York: Jewish Theological Seminary.

Liebreich, L. J.

1955–56　The Composition of the Book of Isaiah. *JQR*, n.s., 46:259–77.

1956–57　The Composition of the Book of Isaiah. *JQR*, n.s., 46:114–38.

Lindenberger, J. M.

1991　How Much for a Hebrew Slave? The Meaning of *mišneh'* in Deuteronomy 15:18. *JBL* 110:479–82.

Lipinski, E.

1986　Syro-Palestinian Iconography of Woman and Goddess. *IEJ* 36, 1–2:87–96.

1988　Sacrifices d'enfants à Carthage et dans le monde sémitique oriental. Pp. 151–85 in *Studia Phoenicia VI Carthago*, ed. E. Lipinski. OLA 26. Leuvain: Peters.

1990　*rkl. TWAT* 7:522–23.

1992　*śākar. TWAT* 7:795–801.

Livingston, D. H.

1986　The Crime of Leviticus XXIV 11. *VT* 36:352–54.

Loewenstamm, S. E.

1956　Review of Cyrus H. Gordon, *Ugaritic Manual*, Rome 1955. *Ta* 25: 468–72. (Hebrew)

1958a　Jubilee. *EM* 3:578–82. (Hebrew)

1958b　*yôm hakkippûrîm. EM* 3:595–600. (Hebrew)

1962a　The Laws of the Adulterer and the Murderer in Biblical and Mesopotamian Jurisprudence. *BM* 13:55–56. (Hebrew)

1962b　Measure for Measure. *EM* 4:840–46. (Hebrew)

1963–64　*šě'ēr. Leshonenu* 27–28:295. (Hebrew)

1965　*The Tradition of the Exodus in Its Development*. Jerusalem: Magnes. (Hebrew)

1968　Law, Biblical. *EM* 5:614–37. (Hebrew)

1969　*nšk* and *m/trbyt. JBL* 88:78–80.

1971a　*'ārāyôt. EM* 6:388–90. (Hebrew)

1971b　*'ebed 'ibrî. EM* 6:13–14. (Hebrew)

1971c　Law, Biblical. In *WHJP*, ed. B. Mezar, 3:231–67. Tel Aviv: Massada Press.

1971d.　The Investiture of Levi. *EI* 10:169–72. (Hebrew)

1974　Did the Goddess Anath Wear a Beard and Side-Whiskers? *Israel Oriental Studies* 4:1–3.

1976a　Oath. *EM* 7: 479–94.

1976b　*rešep EM* 7:437–41.

1977　Exodus 21:22–25. *VT* 27: 352–60.

1980a　*biqqōret tihyeh. Shnaton* 4: 94–97 (Hebrew).

1980b Review of Cyrus H. Gordon, *Ugaritic Manual,* Rome 1955. In *Comparative Studies in Biblical and Ancient Oriental Literature,* 30–38. Neukirchen: Neukirchener Verlag.

1980c Did the Goddess Anath Wear a Beard and Side-Wiskers? Pp. 459–62 in *Comparative Studies in Biblical and Ancient Oriental Literature,* 459–62. Nuekirchen: Neukirchener Verlag.

1984   *naḥălat YHWH.* Pp. 155–92 in *Studies in the Bible,* ed. S. Japhet. Scripta Hierosolymitana 31. Jerusalem: Magnes.

1992   *The Evolution of the Exodus Tradition.* Trans. B. J. Schwartz. Jerusalem: Magnes. [Trans. of *The Tradition of the Exodus in Its Development* (Jerusalem: Magnes, 1968, 1987)]

Lohfink, N. F.

1973   Abänderung der Theologie des priesterlichen Geschictswerks im Segen des heilgkeitsgesetzes: Zu Lev. 26, 9.11–13. Pp. 129–36 in *Wort und Geschichte* [Fest. K. Elliger], ed. H. Gese and H. P. Rüger. Neukirchen: Neukirchener Verlag.

1986   *ḥopšî. TDOT* 5:114–18.

1992   Deuteronomy 6:24: *lĕhayyōtēnû* 'To Maintain Us'. Pp. 111–19 in *Shaʿarei Talmon,* ed. M. Fishbane and E. Tov. Winona Lake, Ind.: Eisenbrauns.

1993   *Option for the Poor.* Berkeley, Calif.: Bibal Press.

1994   *Theology of the Pentateuch.* Minneapolis: Fortress Press.

Loretz, O.

1962   Ugaritisches *ṣamātu* und hebräisches *ṣm(y)tt BZ* 6:269–79.

1989   Die babylonischen Gottesnamen Sukkot und Kajjamanu in Amos 5:26. *ZAW* 101:286–89.

1992   Die Teraphim als "Ahnen-Götter-Figur(in)en" im Liche der Texte aus Nuzi, Emar und Ugarit. *UF* 24:133–78.

Lucian

1976   *De Dea Syria.* Ed. H. W. Altridge and R. A. Oden. Missoula, Mont.: Scholars Press.

Luciani, D.

1992   "Soyez Saints, can je suit saint." Un commentar de Levitique 19. *Nouvelle revue théologique* 114:212–36.

1999   Le jubilé dans Levitique 25. *Revue Théologique de Louvain* 30:456–86.

Luckenbill, D. D.

1924   *The Annals of Sennacherib.* Chicago: University of Chicago Press.

Lund, N. W.

1942   *Chiasmus in the New Testament.* Chapel Hill: University of North Carolina Press.

Luria, S.

1965   Tochterschänderung in der Bibel. *ArOr* 33:207–8.

Lust, J.

1974   On Wizards and Prophets. Pp. 133–42 in *Studies in Prophecy.* VT Supp. 26. Leiden: Brill.

Lutzky, H. C.
1996 On "The Image of Jealousy" (Ezekiel VIII 3,5). *VT* 46:121–25.

Luzzatto, Samuel David (Shadal)
1965 *Commentary to the Pentateuch and Hamishtadel.* Ed. P. Schlesinger. Tel Aviv: Dvir. (Hebrew)

Macalister, R. A. S.
1912 *Excavation of Gezer.* 3 vols. London: Palestine Exploration Fund.

Maccoby, H.
1996 Holiness and Purity: The Holy People in Leviticus and Ezra–Nehemiah. In *Reading Leviticus,* ed. J. F. A. Sawyer, 153–70. Sheffield: Sheffield Academic Press.

1999 *Ritual and Morality.* Cambridge: Cambridge University Press.

MacRae, G. W.
1960 The Meaning and Evolution of the Feast of Tabernacles. *CBQ* 22:251–76.

Magonet, J.
1983 The Structure and Meaning of Leviticus 19. *HAR* 7:151–67.

1996 "But If It Is a Girl She Is Unclean for Twice Seven Days": The Riddle of Leviticus 12.5. Pp. 144–52 in *Reading Leviticus,* ed. J. F. A. Sawyer, 144–52. Sheffield: Sheffield Academic Press.

Maiberger, P.
1987 *pāgar, paegaer.* TWAT 6:508–14.

Maine, H. J. S.
1890 *Village Communities in the East and West.* London: Murray.

Malamat, A.
1956 "Prophecy in the Mari Documents." *EI* 4:74–94. (Hebrew)

1962 Mari and the Bible: Some Patterns of Tribal Organization and Institutions. *JAOS* 82:143–50.

1973 The Arameans. In *Peoples of Old Testament Times,* ed. D. J. Wiseman, 134–55. Oxford: Clarendon Press.

1988 Pre-Monarchical Social Institutions in Israel in the Light of Mari. *SVT* 40:165–76.

1989 *Mari and the Early Israelite Experience.* Schweich Lectures 1984. Oxford: Oxford University Press.

1990 "You Shall Love Your Neighbor as Yourself": A Case of Misinterpretation? Pp. 111–16 in *Die hebräische Bibel und ihre zweifache Nachgeschichte* [Fest. R. Rendtorff], ed. E. Blum et al. Neukirchen: Neukirchener Verlag.

Malbim
1891 *The Torah and Commandment.* 2 vols. Vilna: Romm. (Hebrew)

Maloney, R. P.
1974 Usury and Restrictions on Interest Taking in the Ancient Near East. *CBQ* 36:1–20.

Malul, M.
1987a *Bě'erkěkā.* In *Leviticus: The World of the Bible,* ed. B. Levine and M. Paran, 215. Ramat Gan: Revivim. (Hebrew)

1987b *Ḥerem.* In *Leviticus: The World of the Bible,* ed. B. A. Levine and M. Paran, 219–20. Ramat-Gan: Revivim. (Hebrew)

1987c Touching the Sexual Organs in an Oath Ceremony in an Akkadian Letter. *VT* 37:491–92.

Mansur, Y.

1959–60 *'Eben maśkit. Leshonenu* 24:181–82. (Hebrew)

Marco, A. di

1975 Der Chiasmus in der Bibel. *Lilnguistica Biblica* 36:21–97.

Marcus, J. M. and J. J. Francis

1975 Eds. *Masturbation: From Infancy to Senescence,* New York: International University Press.

Margaliot, E.

1951 The Laws Concerning Priests and Sacrifices in Ezekiel. *Ta* 22:21–27. (Hebrew)

Margalit, B.

1976 Studies in *KRT* and *Aqht,* Section II: The Ugaritic Analogue of the Biblical *'O(w)b* (CTA 16:I, II). *UF* 8:145–50.

1981 A Ugaritic Prayer for a City Under Siege. Pp. 63–83 in *Proceedings of the Seventh World Congress of Jewish Studies,* Vol. 1. Jerusalem: Perry Foundation. (Hebrew)

1990 The Meaning and Significance of Asherah. *VT* 40:264–97.

Margalit, S.

1993 *Maṣṣôt* of Egypt and Subsequent *maṣṣôt. BM* 38:328–31. (Hebrew)

Marlens, F.

1977 Diététhique on la cuisine de Dieu. *Communications* 26:16–45.

Marx, A.

1989 Sacrifice pour les péchés or rites du passage? Quelques réflexions sur la fonction de *ḥaNāʾt. RB* 96:27–48.

Mathys, H.-P.

1986 *Liebe deinen Nächsten wie dich selbst (Lev 19, 18).* Göttingen: Vandenhoeck & Ruprecht.

Mattha, G.

1958 Rights and Duties of the Eldest Son. *Bulletin of the Faculty of Arts, Cairo University* 12:113–18.

Matthiae, P.

1979 Princely Cemetery and Ancestor Cult at Ebla During Middle Bronze II: A Proposal of Interpretation. *UF* 11:563–69.

Mayer, G.

1989 *ʿāral. TWAT* 6:385–87.

Mazar, A.

1990 *Archaeology of the Land of the Bible.* Garden City, N.Y.: Doubleday.

Mazar, B.

1950 *'adrammelek. EM* 1:116–17. (Hebrew)

1954 Canaan on the Threshold of the Age of the Patriarchs. *EI* 3:18–32. (Hebrew)

1957 The Tobiads. *IEJ* 7:137–45, 229–38.

Mazar, B., et al.
1960   *Views of the Biblical World*. Vol. 3. Jerusalem: International.
McCarter, P. K.
1980   *I Samuel*. AB 8. New York: Doubleday.
McCarthy, D. J.
1969   The Symbolism of Blood and Sacrifice. *JBL* 88:166–76.
1973   Further Notes on the Symbolism of Blood and Sacrifice. *JBL* 92:205–10.
McClellan, T. L.
1987   Review of *Tell el-Far'ah* I, by A. Chambon. *BASOR* 267:84–86.
McConville, J. G.
1983   Priests and Levites in Ezekiel: A Crux in the Interpretation of Israel's History. *Tyndale Bulletin* 34:3–31.
1984   *Law and Theology in Deuteronomy*. Sheffield: JSOT.
McEvan, G. J. P.
1981   *Priest and Temple in Hellenistic Babylonia*. Wiesbaden: Franz Steiner Verlag.
1982   A Babylonian *Leitourgia?* WO 13:25–30.
McEvenue, S. E.
1971   *The Narrative Style of the Priestly Writer*. Rome: Biblical Institute.
McKane, W.
1961–62   Ruth and Boaz. *Transactions of the Glasgow University Oriental Society* 19:35.
1970   *Proverbs*. Philadelphia: Westminster Press.
1986   *Jeremiah*. Vol. 1. ICC. Edinburgh: Clark.
McKay, J. W.
1972   The Date of Passover and Its Significance. *ZAW* 84:435–47.
1973   *Religion in Judah Under the Assyrians*. Naperville, Ill.: Allenson.
McKeating, H.
1979   Sanctions Against Adultery in Ancient Israelite Society, with Some Reflections on Methodology in the Study of Old Testament Ethics. *JSOT* 11:57–72.
McKenzie, S. L.
1992   Deuteronomistic History. *ABD* 2:160–68.
McVey, K. E.
1989   *Ephrem the Syrian: Hymns*. 4 vols. New York: Paulist Press.
Meacham, T.
1997   The Missing Daughter: Leviticus 18 and 20. *ZAW* 109:254–59.
Mead, M.
1968   Incest. *IESS* 7:115–20.
Meeks, D.
1979   Pureté et purification en Égypte. *SDB* 9:430–52.
Melamed, E. Z.
1944–45   Hendiadys in the Bible. *Ta* 16:173–89, 242. (Hebrew)
1964   Linguistic Expressions that Were Split in Poetry. Pp. 188–219 in

Seper Segal, ed. J. Liver and Y. M. Grintz. Jerusalem: Kiryat Sefer. (Hebrew)

Melcher, S. J.
1996   The Holiness Code and Human Sexuality. In *Biblical Ethics and Homosexuality,* ed. R. L. Brawley, 87–102 . Louisville, Ky.: Westminster–John Knox Press.

Menahem ibn Saruq
1854   *Maḥberet.* Ed. Z. Filipowski. London: Hevrat Me'orere Yeshenim. (Hebrew)

Mendelsohn, I.
1949   *Slavery in the Ancient Near East.* New York: Oxford University Press.
1962   Slavery in the OT. *IDB* 4:383–91.

Mendelssohn, M., ed.
1846   *Netivot Ha-shalom.* Vol. 3. Vienna: von Schmid and Busch. (Hebrew)

Mendenhall, G.
1973   *The Tenth Generation.* Baltimore: Johns Hopkins University Press.
1983   Ancient Israel's Hyphenated History. Pp. 95–104 in *Palestine in Transition: The Emergence of Ancient Israel,* ed. D. N. Freedman and D. F. Graf. Sheffield: Almond Press.

Merras, M.
1995   *The Origins of the Celebration of the Christian Feast of Epiphany.* Joensuu, Finland: Joensuu University Press.

Meshel, Z.
1982   An Explanation of the Journey of the Israelites in the Wilderness. *BA* 45:18–20.

Mettinger, T. N. D.
1995   *No Graven Image? Israelite Aniconism in Its Ancient Near Eastern Context.* Stolkholm: Almqvist & Wiksell International.

Meuli, K.
1946   Griechische Opferbräuche. Pp. 185–288 in *Phyllobolia für Peter von der Mühll,* ed. O. Gigon et al. Basel: Schwabe.

Meyers, C.
1976   *The Tabernacle Menorah.* Missoula, Mont.: Scholars Press.
1983   Procreation, Production and Protection: Male–Female Balance in Early Israel. *JAAR* 51:569–93.
1988   *Discovering Eve.* Oxford: Oxford University Press.
1996   Realms of Sanctity: The Case of the "Misplaced" Incense Altar in the Tabernacle Texts of Exodus. Pp. 33–46 in *Texts, Temples and Traditions* [Fest. M. Haran], ed. M. V. Fox et al. Winona Lake, Ind.: Eisenbrauns.

Meyers, C. L., and E. M. Meyers
1993   *Zechariah 9–14.* AB 25C. New York: Doubleday.

Mikliszanski, J. K.
1947   The Law of Retaliation and the Pentateuch. *JBL* 66:295–304.

Milgrom, J.

1955 The Date of Jeremiah, Chapter 2. *JNES* 14:65–69.

1964 Did Isaiah Prophesy During the Reign of Uzziah? *VT* 14:164–82.

1970 *Studies in Levitical Terminology.* Berkeley: University of California Press.

1971 A Prolegomenon to Leviticus 17:11. *JBL* 90:149–56.

1972 'Eglah 'Aurfah. *EJ* 6:475–77.

1973 The *těnûpâ.* Pp. 38–55 in *Zer LiGevurot* [Fest. Z. Shazar], ed. B. Z. Luria. Jerusalem: Kiryat Sepher. (Hebrew)

1976a *Cult and Conscience: The Asham and Priestly Doctrine of Repentance.* Studies in Judaism in Late Antiquity 18. Leiden: Brill.

1976b Encroachment. *IDB* Supp.:264–65.

1976c First Born. *IDB* Supp.:337–38.

1976d Sanctification. *IDB* Supp.:782–84.

1976e First Fruits. *IDB* Supp.:336–37.

1976f The Legal Terms *šlm* and *br'šw* in the Bible. *JNES* 35:236–47.

1976g *qěṭōret. EM* 7:112–20. (Hebrew)

1976h Profane Slaughter and a Formulaic Key to the Composition of Deuteronomy. *HUCA* 47:1–17.

1977a The Betrothed Slave-girl. *ZAW* 86:43–50.

1977b Concerning Jeremiah's Repudiation of Sacrifice. *ZAW* 89:273–75.

1978a Studies in the Temple Scroll. *JBL* 97:501–23.

1978b "Sabbath" and "Temple City" in the Temple Scoll *BASOR* 232:25–27.

1978–79 Priestly Terminology and the Political and Social Structure of Pre-Monarchic Israel. *JQR* 69:65–81.

1979 The Offering of Incense in Second Temple Times. Pp. 330–34 in Ben-Zion *Seper Luria.* Jerusalem: Kiryat Sefer. (Hebrew)

1980 Further Studies in the Temple Scroll. *JQR* 81:1–17, 89–106.

1981a Vertical Retribution: Ruminations on Parashat Shelah. *CJ* 34:11–16.

1981b The Case of the Suspected Adulteress, Numbers 5:11–31: Redaction and Meaning. Pp. 69–75 in *The Creation of Sacred Literature,* ed. R. E. Friedman. Berkeley: University of California Press.

1981c *The Tassil and the Tallit.* The Fourth Annual Rabbi Louis Feinberg Lecture. Cincinnati: University of Cincinnati Press.

1982a The Levitic Town: An Exercise in Realistic Planning. *JJS* 33:185–88.

1982b Religious Conversion and the Revolt Model for the Formation of Israel. *JBL* 101:169–76.

1982c *tô'ēbâ. EM* 8:466–68. (Hebrew)

1983a Magic, Monotheism and the Sin of Moses. Pp. 251–66 in *The Quest for the Kingdom of God* [Fest. G. E. Mendenhall], ed. H. H. Huffmon et al. Winona Lake, Ind.: Eisenbrauns.

1983b Of Hems and Tassels. *BAR* 9:61–65.

1983c *Studies in Cultic Theology and Terminology.* Leiden: Brill.

1983d The Ideological and Historical Importance of the Office of Judge in Deuteronomy. Pp. 129–35 in *Isac Lev Seligmann Volume 2*, ed. A. Rofé and Y. Zakovitch. Jerusalem: Rubinstein.

1983e The Tassels Pericope, Num 15:37–41. *BM* 92:14–22. (Hebrew)

1985a *Numbers* [with contributors]. *The World of the Bible*. Ramat-Gan: Revivim. (Hebrew)

1985b You Shall Not Boil a Kid in Its Mother's Milk. *Bible Review* 1:48–55.

1985c The Ideological Importance of the Office of Judge in Deuteronomy. Pp. 129–39 in *I. L. Seligmann Volume II*, ed. A. Rofé and Y. Zakovitch. Jerusalem: Rubenstein.

1985d On the Suspected Adulteress. *VT* 35:368–69.

1989a The Qumran Cult: Its Exegetical Principles. In *Temple Scroll Studies*, ed. G. J. Brooke, 165–80. Sheffield: Sheffield Academic Press.

1989b "The Alien in Your Midst": Reflections on the Biblical *Ger*. Daniel E. Koshland Memorial Lecture. San Francisco: Congregation Emanu.

1990a *Numbers*. Philadelphia: Jewish Publication Society.

1990b The Scriptural Foundations and Deviations in the Laws of Purity of the Temple Scrolls. In *Archaeology and History in the Dead Sea Scrolls*, ed. L. H. Schiffman, 83–99. Sheffield: Sheffield Academic Press.

1990c The Hebrew Prophets on Eschatological Repentance. *Explorations* 4:2–3.

1991 *Leviticus 1–16*. AB 3. New York: Doubleday.

1992a Two Biblical Hebrew Terms: *šeqeṣ* and *ṭāmē'*. *Maarav* 8: 07–16.

1992b Two Biblical Priestly Terms: *šeqeṣ* and *ṭāmē'*. *Tarbiz* 60:423–28. (Hebrew)

1992c Priestly ("P") Source. *ABD* 5:454–61.

1993a Response to Rolf Rendtorff. *JSOT* 60:83–85.

1993b Leviticus: Introduction. Pp. 151–97 in *The HarperCollins Study Bible*. New York: HarperCollins.

1993c Does the Bible Prohibit Homosexuality? *BR* 9/6:11.

1994a Confusing the Sacred and Impure: A Rejoinder. *VT* 44:554–58.

1994b Sex and Wisdom: What the Garden of Eden Story Is Saying. *BR* 10:21.

1994c The Festival of Booths. Paper delivered at the University of Pennsylvania.

1994d How Not to Read the Bible *BR* 10/2:14.

1996a Law and Narrative and the Exegesis of Leviticus XIX. *VT* 46:544–48.

1996b Further on the Expiatory Sacrifices. *JBL* 115:511–14.

1996c The Changing Concept of Holiness. Pp. 65–75 in *Reading Leviticus*, ed. J. Sawyer. Sheffield: Sheffield University Press.

1999 The Antiquity of the Priestly Source: A Reply to Joseph Blenkinsopp. *ZAW* 111:10–22.

2000 Did H Advocate the Centralization of Worship? *JSOT* 88.

forthcoming The Nature and Extent of Idolatry in Eighth–Seventh Century Judah. *HVCA*.

Milgrom, J., and D. P. Wright
1984   mĕlāʾkâ. TWAT 4:905–11.

Milik, J. T.
1954   Un Contrat juif de l'an 134 après J.-C. RB 61:182–90.
1957a   Deux documents inedits du desert de juda. Biblica 38:245–68.
1957b   Le Travail d'édition des manuscrits du désert de juda. Pp. 17–26 in Volume du imagrès Strasbourg, 1956, ed. VT Supp. 4. Leiden: Brill.
1959   Ten Years of Discovery in the Wilderness of Judea. Trans. J. Strugnell. London: SCM Press.
1972   Milki-sedeq et milki-resa dans les écrits juifs et chrétiens (I). JJS 23:95–144.

Millar, J. E.
2000   Notes on Leviticus 18. ZAW.

Millard, A. R.
1995   Adrammelech, Anammelech. Pp. 17–29, 58–60 in Dictionary of Deities and Demons in the Bible, ed. K. van der Toorn et al. Leiden: Brill.

Millard, A. R., and P. Bordreuil
1982   A Statue from Syria with Assyrian and Aramaic Inscriptions. BA 45:135–42.

Miller, J. M., and J. H. Hayes
1986   A History of Ancient Israel and Judah. Philadelphia: Westminster Press.

Miller, P. D.
1980   El, the Creator of Earth. BASOR 239:43–46.

Möller, H.
1976   Lösungsvorschlag für eine Crux interpretum (Lev 25, 33). ZAW 90:411–12.

Moltmann, J.
1985   God in Creation. Trans. M. Kohl. San Francisco: Harper & Row.

Monkhouse, W.
1989   Consanguinous Marriage in the Ancient Near East (B.A. honors thesis).

Montgomery, J. A.
1908   The Holy City and Gehenna. JBL 27:24–47.

Moor, J. C. de
1972   New Year with Canaaʾnites and Israelites. Kampen: Kok.
1986   The Ancestral Cult in KTU 1.17:I.26–28. UF 17:407–9.

Moore, S. F., and B. G. Myerhoff
1977   Introduction: Secular Ritual: Forms and Meanings. Pp. 3–24 in Secular Ritual, ed. S. F. Moore and B. G. Myerhoff. Amsterdam: Van Gorcum.

Moran, W. L.
1959   The Scandal of the "Great Sin" at Ugarit. JNNES 18:280–81.
1962   The Ancient Near Eastern Background of the Love of God in Deuteronomy. CBQ 25:77–87.
1969   New Evidence from Mari on the History of Prophecy. Biblica 50:15–56.

Morgenstern, J.
  1935   The Calendars of Ancient Israel: The Moment of Beginning. *HUCA*
          10:15–28.
  1955   The Decalogue of the Holiness Code. *HUCA* 26:1–27.
  1958   The Message of Deutero-Isaiah in its Sequential Unfolding *HUCA*
          29:1–67.
  1962   The Book of the Covenant. *HUCA* 33:59–105.
  1966   *Rites of Birth, Marriage, Death and Kindred Occasions Among the
          Semites.* Cincinnati: Hebrew Union College Press.
Mosca, P. G.
  1975   Child Sacrifice in Canaanite and Israelite Religion: A Study in Mulk
          and Molech. Ph.D. diss., Harvard University.
Mowinckel, S.
  1937   Zur Geschichte der Decaloge. ZAW 55:218–35.
  1967   *The Psalms in Israel's Worship.* 2 vols. Trans. D. R. Ap-Thomas. Ox-
          ford: Blackwell.
Moyer, J. C.
  1969   The Concept of Ritual Purity Among the Hittites. Ph.D. diss., Bran-
          deis University.
  1983   Hittite and Israelite Cult Practices: A Selected Comparison. In *Scrip-
          ture in Context*, ed. W. W. Hallo et al., 2:19–38. Winona Lake, Ind.:
          Eisenbrauns.
Muffs, Y.
  1965a   Covenant Traditions in Deuteronomy. Pp. 1–9 in *Readings in the
          History of Biblical Thought*, Vol. 3. Lectures at the Jewish Theo-
          logical Seminary. New York: Jewish Theological Seminary.
  1965b   *Studies in Biblical Law II, IV.* Lectures at the Jewish Theological
          Seminary. New York: Jewish Theological Seminary.
  1969   *Studies in the Aramaic Legal Papyri from Elephantine.* Leiden: Brill.
Müller, H.-P.
  1984   *Moloek.* TWAT 4:957–67.
  1995   Malik. Pp. 1005–12 in *Dictionary of Deities and Demons in the
          Bible*, ed. K. van der Toorn et al. Leiden:Brill.
Müller, M.
  1971   Soziale und wirtschaftspolitische Rechtserlässe im Landa Arrapha.
          Pp. 53–60 in *Schriften zur Geschichte und Kultur des Alten Orients
          I: Beiträge zur sozialen Struktur des alten Vorderasian*, ed.
          H. Klengel. Berlin: Akademie-Verlag.
Muraoka, T.
  1978   A Syntactic Problem in Lev. XIX 18b. *JSS* 23:291–97.
  1985   *Emphatic Words and Structures in Biblical Hebrew.* Leiden: Brill.
Murray, M. A.
  1927   Notes on Some Genealogies of the Middle Kingdom. *Ancient Egypt*
          13:45–51.
Myers, J. M.
  1965   *Ezra and Nehemiah.* New York: Doubleday.

Na'aman, N.
1986 Habiru and Hebrews: The Transfer of a Social Term to the Literary Sphere. *JNES* 45:271–88.
1995 The Debated Historicity of Hezekiah's Reform in the Light of Historical and Archaeological Research. *ZAW* 107:179–95.

Nach, S.
1992 The Consonantal Biblical Text is NOT Authoritative. *Ta* 62: 401–48. (Hebrew)

Nakhai, B. A.
1994 What's a Bamah? How Sacred Space Functioned in Ancient Israel. *BAR* 20:18–29, 77–78.

Nasuti, H.
1986 Identity, Identification, and Imitation: The Narrative Hermeneutics of Biblical Law. *Journal of Law and Religion* 4:9–23.

Negev, A.
1971 The Necropolis of Mampis (Kurnub). *IEJ* 21:115–17.

Neiman, D.
1948 *PGR*: A Canaanite Cult-Object in the Old Testament. *JBL* 67:55–60.

Nelson, R. D.
1981 *The Double Redaction of the Deuteronomistic History*. Sheffield: JSOT Press.

Neu, E.
1974 *Der Anitta Text. StBoT* 18:1–15.

Neudecker, R.
1990 Lev 19, 18 in Jewish Interpretation. *Biblica* 73:515–17.

Neufeld, E.
1944 *Ancient Hebrew Marriage Laws*. London: Green.
1955 The Prohibitions Against Loans at Interest in Ancient Hebrew Laws. *HUCA* 26:355–412.
1958 Socio-economic Background of *Yōbēl* and *Šĕmiṭṭâ*. *RSO* 33:15–124.

Newman, L. E.
1983 *The Sanctity of the Seventh Year: A Study of Mishnah Tractate Shebiit*. Chico, Calif.: Scholars Press.

Newsom, C. A.
1985 *Songs of the Sabbath Sacrifice*. Atlanta: Scholars Press.

Nicholson, E. W.
1967 *Deuteronomy and Tradition*. Philadelphia: Fortress Press.
1982 The Covenant Ritual in Exodus XXIV 3–8. *VT* 32:74–86.

Niehr, H.
1996 The Rise of YHWH in Judahite and Israelite Religion. Pp. 45–74 in *The Triumph of Elohim*, ed. D. V. Dedelman. Grand Rapids, Mich.: Eerdmans.

Nielson, K.
1992 Incense. *ADB* 3:404–9.

Nikolsky, N. M.
1927 Pascha im Kulte des jerusalemischen Tempels. ZAW 55:171–90, 241–53.

Noordtzij, A.
1982 Leviticus. Trans. R. Togtman. Grand Rapids, Mich.: Zondervan. [Trans. of Het boek Levitikus (Kampen: Kok, 1955)]

North, R.
1950 Biblical Echoes in the Holy Year. American Ecclesiastical Review 123:416–36.

1951 The Biblical Jubilee and Social Reform. Scripture 4:323–35.

1954 Sociology of the Biblical Jubilee. Rome: Pontifical Biblical Institute.

1990 Yobel. TDOT 6:1–6.

Noth, M.
1962 Exodus. Trans. J. S. Bowden. Philadelphia: Westminster Press. [Trans. of Das zweite Buch Mose, Exodus (Gottingen: Vandenhoeck & Ruprecht, 1959)]

1966 Office and Vocation in the Old Testament. Pp. 229–49 in The Laws in the Pentateuch and Other Studies. Philadelphia: Fortress Press.

1977 Leviticus: A Commentary. Rev. ed. OTL. Philadelphia: Westminster. [Originally published 1965]

Novak, D.
1991 Lex Talionis: A Maimonidean Perspective on Scripture, Tradition, and Reason. S'vara 2:61–64.

Nussbaum, D.
1974 The Priestly Explanation of Exile and Its Bearing upon the Portrayal of the Canaanites in the Bible. Master's thesis, University of Pennsylvania.

Obermann, J.
1941 Votive Inscriptions from Ras Shamua. JAOS 61:31–45.

Oded, B.
1993 "I Will Grant Peace in the Land"—Assyrian Version: A Chapter in the Ideology of the Assyrian Kingdom. EI 24:148–57.

1996 Scriptural Issues in the Light of the Assyrian Inscriptions. BM 42:1–7. (Hebrew)

Oelsner, J.
1976 Erwägungen zum Gesellschaftsaufbau Babyloniens von der neubalaylonischen biz zur archamenidischen Zeit (7.–4Jh. v.u.Z.). AoF 4:131–49.

Oesterley, W. O. E., and T. H. Robinson
1930 The Hebrew Religion: Its Origin and Development. London: Society for Promoting Christian Knowledge.

Ohana, M.
1974 Prosélytisme et targum palistinien: Données nouvelles pour la datation de Neofiti I. Biblica 55:317–32.

Olivier, H.
1984 The Effectiveness of the Old Babylonian Mēšarum Decree. JNSL 12:107–13.

Olyan, S. M.
  1988   *Asherah and the Cult of Yahweh in Israel.* Atlanta: Scholars Press.
  1991   The Oaths of Amos 8.14. Pp. 121–49 in *Priesthood and Cult in Ancient Israel,* ed. G. A. Anderson and S. M. Olyan. Sheffield: JSOT Press.
  1994   "And with a Male You Shall Not Lie the Lying Down of a Woman": On the Meaning and Significance of Leviticus 18:22 and 20:13. *Journal of the History of Sexuality* 5:179–206.
  1996a   Honor, Shame, and Covenant Relations in Ancient Israel and Its Environment. *JBL* 115:201–18.
  1996b   Why an Altar of Unfinished Stones? Some Thoughts on Ex 20,25 and Dtn 27,5–6. ZAW 108:161–71.
  1997a   "And with a Male You Shall Not Lie the Lying Down of a Woman": On the Meaning and Significance of Leviticus 18:22 and 20:13. Pp. 398–414 in *Que(e)rying Religion,* ed. G. D. Comstock and S. E. Henking. New York: Continuum.
  1997b   Cult. In *Archaeology in the Near East,* ed. E. M. Meyers, 2:79–86. Oxford: Oxford University Press.
Oppenheim, A. L.
  1956   *The Interpretation of Dreams in the Ancient Near East, with a Translation of an Assyrian Dream-Book.* Transactions of the American Philosophical Society 46: 179–354. Philadelphia: American Philosophical Society.
  1967   *Letters from Mesopotamia.* Chicago: University of Chicago Press.
Orlinsky, H. M.
  1939   *Ḥāṣēr* in the OT. *JAOS* 59:22–37.
  1944   The Hebrew Root *škb. JBL* 63:37–39.
  1969   *Notes on the New Translation of the Torah.* Philadelphia: Jewish Publication Society.
Otten, H.
  1956   Ein Text zum Neujahrfest aus Bogazköy. *Orientalistiche Literaturzeitung* 51:102–5.
  1958   *Hethitische Totenrituale.* Berlin: Akadamie-Vorlag.
Otto, E.
  1988   Zur Semantik von hebr. *psḥ / pisseăḥ* und akk. *pessû(m) / pessātu(m).* BN 41:31–35.
  1994   *Theologische Ethik des Alten Testaments.* Stuttgart: Kohlhammer.
  1995a   Biblische Altersversorgung im altorientalischen Rechtsvergleich. ZABR 1:83–110.
  1995b   Gesetzesfortschreibung und Pentateuchredaktion. ZAW 107:373–92.
  1997   Forschungen zur Priesterschift. *ThR* 62:1–50.
Otto, R.
  1958   *The Idea of the Holy.* Trans. J. W. Harvey. Oxford: Oxford University Press.
Ottosson, M.
  1974   *ʾākhal. TDOT* 1:236–41.
  1975   *gebhûl. TDOT* 2:361–66.

1980 *ḥālam, ḥălôm*, Hittites, West Semites. *TDOT* 4:423–25, 426–27.

Paebel, A.
1932 *Das appositionell bestimmte Pronomen der 1 Pers. Sing. in den west-semitischen Inschriften und im A. T.* Assyriological Studies 3. Chicago: Oriental Institute.

Palmer, L. R.
1963 *The Interpretation of Mycenaean Greek Texts.* Oxford: Clarendon Press.

Pap, E.
1933 *Die israelitische neujahr fest* (Diss. Theo. Utrecht).

Paradise, J.
1987 Daughters as "Sons" at Nuzi. Pp. 203–13 in *Nuzi and the Hurrians*, ed. D. I. Owens and M. A. Morrison. Winona Lake, Ind.: Eisenbrauns.

Paran, M.
1983 Literary Features of the Priestly Code: Stylistic Patterns, Idioms and Structures. Ph.D. diss., Hebrew University. (Hebrew)
1989 *Forms of the Priestly Style in the Pentateuch.* Jerusalem: Magnes.

Parapola, S.
1970 *Letters from Assyrian Scholars to the Kings Esarhaddan and Assurbanipal.* Neukirchen: Kevelaer Butzon and Becker.

Parker, R.
1983 *Pollution and Purification in Early Greek Religion.* Oxford: Clarendon Press.

Parker, R. A.
1950 *Calendars of Ancient Egypt.* Chicago: University of Chicago Press.

Parker, R. A., and W. H. Dubberstein
1956 *Babylonian Chronology: 626 B.C.–75 A.D.* Providence, R.I.: Brown University Press.

Parker, S. B.
1991 The Hebrew Bible and Homosexuality. *QR* 11:4–19.

Paschen, W.
1970 *Rein und Unrein.* SANT 24. Munich: Kösel.

Patai, R.
1939 Control of Rain in Ancient Palestine. *HUCA* 14:251–86.
1959 *Sex and Family in the Bible and the Middle East.* Garden City, N.Y.: Doubleday.

Paton, L. B.
1894 The Relation of Lev. 20 to Lev. 17–19. *Hebraica* 10:111–21.
1896 The Holiness-Code and Ezekiel. *Presbyterian and Reformed Review* 7:98–115.
1897 The Original Form of Leviticus XVII–XIX. *JBL* 16:31–77.

Patrick, D.
1985 *Old Testament Law.* Atlanta: John Knox Press.

Paul, S. M.
1970a *Studies in the Book of the Covenant in the Light of Cuneiform and Biblical Law.* Leiden: Brill.

1970b Types of Formulation in Biblical and Mesopotamian Law. *Leshon-enu* 34:257–66. (Hebrew)

1990 Biblical Analogues to Middle Assyrian Law. Pp. 333–55 in *Religion and Law*, ed. E. B. Firmage et al. Winona Lake, Ind.: Eisenbrauns.

1991 *Amos*. Minneapolis: Fortress Press.

Pecham, B.

1993 *History and Prophecy*. New York: Doubleday.

Pedersen, J.

1926 *Israel: Its Life and Culture*. 2 vols. Copenhagen: Branner.

Peels, H. G. L.

1994 *The Vengeance of God: The Meaning of the Root NQM and the Function of the NQM-Texts in the Context of Divine Revelation in the Old Testament*. Leiden: Brill. [Trans. of *De wraak van God: De betekenis van de wortel NQM en de functe van de NQM-teksten in het kader van de oudtestamentiche godsopenbarung* (Zoetermeer: Boekencentrum, 1992)]

Pelletier, A.

1967 Une particularilé du rituel des "pains d'oblation" conserveé par la septante. *VT* 17:364–67.

Pemmath, D. N.

1988 Latifundialization and Isaiah 5.8–10. *JSOT* 40:49–60.

Peterson, R. F.

1965 *Wheat: Botany, Cultivation, and Utilization*. London: Hill Books.

Phillips, A. J.

1970 *Ancient Israel's Criminal Law: A New Approach to the Decalogue*. Oxford: Blackwell; New York: Schocken Books.

1973 Some Aspects of Family Law in Pre-exilic Israel. *VT* 23:349–61.

1980 Uncovering the Father's Skirt. *VT* 30:38–43.

1981 Another Look at Adultery. *JSOT* 20:3–25.

Picket, W.

1986 The Meaning and Function of T'B/TO'EBAH in the Hebrew Bible. Ph.D. diss., Hebrew Union College.

Pinsker, S.

1968 *Liqquṭe, Qadmoniyyot, Nispaḥim*. Jerusalem: Makor. [Reprint of Vi-enna, 1860]

Pitard, W. T.

1982 Amarna *ekēmu* and Hebrew *nāqam*. *Maarav* 3:5–25.

1994 The "Libation Installation" of the Tombs at Ugarit. *BA* 57:20–37.

Plataroti, D.

1978 Zum Gebrauch des Wortes *MLK* im Alten Testament. *VT* 28:286–300.

Ploeg, J. P. M. van der

1972 Slavery in the Old Testament. *SVT* 22:72–87.

Poebel, A.

1932 *Das appositionell bestimmte der l. pers. sing. in den westsemitischen In-schriften und im Alten Testament*. Chicago: Chicago University Press.

Polliack, M.
   1993–94   Alternate Renderings and Additions in Yeshu'ah ben Yehuda's
             Arabic Translation of the Pentateuch. *JQR* 84:209–25.
Pope, M. H.
   1976   Homosexuality. *IDB Sup*: 415–17.
   1977   *Song of Songs*. Garden City, N.Y.: Doubleday.
   1981   The Cult of the Dead at Ugarit. Pp. 159–79 in *Ugarit in Retrospect*,
          ed. G. D. Young. Winona Lake, Ind.: Eisenbrauns.
Popko, M., and P. Taracha
   1988   Der 28. und der 29. Tag des hethitischen ANṬAH.ŠUM-festes. *AoF*
          15:82–113.
Porten, B.
   1968   *Archives from Elephantine*. Berkeley: University of California Press.
Porter, J. R.
   1967   *The Extended Family in the Old Testament*. Occasional Papers in
          Social and Economic Administration 6. London: Edutext.
   1976   *Leviticus*. CBC. Cambridge: Cambridge University Press.
Portugali, J.
   1984   *'Arim, Bamot, Migrashim* and *Haṣerim* in the Spatial Organization
          of Eretz-Israel in the 12th–10th Centuries B.C.E. According to the
          Bible. *EI* 17:282–90. (Hebrew, with English abstract)
Postgate, J. N.
   1971   Land Tenure in the Middle-Assyrian Period. *Bulletin of the School
          of African and Oriental Studies* 34:496–520.
Powell, M. A.
   1984   Late Babylonian Surface Mensuration. *AfO* 31:32–66.
   1992   Weights and Measures. *ABD* 6:897–908.
Poznanski, S.
   1913   *Komnentar zu Ezechiel und den XII Propheten von Eliezer aus Beau-
          gancy*. Warsaw.
Preuss, H. D.
   1974   *'ĕlîl. TDOT* 1:285–87.
   1977   *'eth. TDOT* 1:449–63.
   1980   *ḥwh. TDOT* 4:248–56.
Propp, W. H. C.
   1996   The Priestly Source Recovered Intact? *VT* 46:458–78.
Qimron, E.
   1983   Notes on the Text of the Temple Scroll. *Tarbiz* 53:139–41.
   1987   Further New Readings in the Temple Scroll. *IEJ* 37:31–35.
   1989   Biblical Philology and the Dead Sea Scrolls. *Ta* 58: 297–316. (He-
          brew)
   1990   Times for Praising God: A Fragment of a Scroll from Qumran
          (4Q409). *JQR* 80:341–47.
Qimron, E., and J. Strugnell
   1994   *Qumran Cave 4.V: Miqṣat Ma'aśe Ha-Torah*. Discoveries in the Ju-
          daean Desert 10. Oxford: Clarendon Press.

Raban, N.
  1950   The Problem of Meat Consumption in the Creation Story. *Tarbiz*
         21: 25–29. (Hebrew)
  1951   In the Presence of the Lord. *Tarbiz* 23:1–8 (Hebrew)
  1956   The Law of the Bamot. Pp. 228–53 in *Seper Biram*, ed. H. Y. M.
         Gevaryahu et al. Jerusalem: Kiryat Sepher. (Hebrew)

Rabast, K.
  1948   *Das apodiktische Rechtum Deuteronomium und im Heiligkeitsgesetz.*
         Berlin: Heimatdienstverlag.

Rabin, C.
  1954   *The Zadokite Documents.* Oxford: Clarendon Press.

Rabinowitz, J. J.
  1957   A Clue to the Nabatean Contract from the Dead Sea Region.
         BASOR 139:14.
  1958   A Biblical Parallel to a Legal Formula from Ugarit. *VT* 8:95.
  1959   The "Great Sin" in Ancient Egyptian Marriage Contracts. *JNES*
         18:73.

Rad, G. von
  1962   *Old Testament Theology*, Vol. 1. Trans. D. M. G. Stalker. New York:
         Harper & Row.
  1966   Faith Reckoned as Righteousness. Pp. 125–30 in *The Problem of the
         Hexateuch*, trans. E. W. T. Dicken. New York: McGraw-Hill.

Radday, Y. T.
  1981   Chiasmus in Hebrew Biblical Narrative. Pp. 50–117 in *Chiasmus
         in Antiquity*, ed. J. W. Welch. Hildesheim: Gerstenberg Verlag.

Rahmani, L. Y.
  1981   Ancient Jerusalem's Funerary Customs and Tombs. *BA44*: 171–77,
         229–36.

Rainey, A.
  1967   *A Social Structure of Ugarit.* Jerusalem: Bialik Institute. (Hebrew)

Ralbag
  1992   *Comments on the Torah by Rabbi Levi ben Gershon* Jerusalem:
         Mosad Harav Kook. (Hebrew)

Ramban (Moses ben Naḥman, also called Naḥmanides)
  1960   *Comments of the Ramban on the Torah.* 2 vols. Ed. H. D. Chavel.
         Jerusalem: Mosad Harav Kook. (Hebrew)

Rashbam (Samuel ben Meir)
  1969   *Commentary of the Rashbam on the Torah.* Ed. A. I. Bromberg.
         Jerusalem: Author. (Hebrew)

Rashi (Solomon ben Isaac)
  1946   *Pentateuch with Rashi's Commentary.* 2 vols. Trans. and annotated A.
         H. Silbermann and M. Rosenbaum. London: Shapiro, Vallentine.

Rattray, S.
  1987   Marriage Rules, Kinship Terms and Family Structure in the Bible. In
         SBLSP, ed. K. Richards, 26:537–44. Atlanta: Scholars Press.

1992   The Tense-Mood-Aspect System of Biblical Hebrew, with Special Emphasis on 1 and 2 Samuel. Ph.D. diss., University of California, Berkeley.

Reichert, A.
1972   Der Jehowist und die sogenannten deuteronomistischen Erweiterungen im Buch Exodus. Ph.D. diss., University of Tübingen.

Reiner, E.
1958   *Šurpu*. *AfO* 11.

Rendsburg, G. A.
1993   The *Inclusio* in Leviticus XI. *VT* 43:418–21.

Rendtorff, R.
1967a   *Studien zur Geschichte des Opfers im Alten Israel.* WMANT 24. Neukirchen: Neukirchener Verlag.
1967b The Background of the Title *ʿelyôn* in Gen XIV. Pp. 367–70 in *Proceedings of the Fourth World Congress of Jewish Studies,* Vol. 1. Jerusalem: World Union of Jewish Studies.
1991   Der Text in seiner Endgestalt. Uberlegungen zu Exodus 19. Pp. 459–70 in *Ernten, was man sät* [Fest. K. Koch], ed. D. R. Daniels et al. Neukirchen: Neukirchener Verlag.
1992   *Leviticus,* III, 3. Biblischer Kommentar: Altes Testament. Neukirchen: Neukirchener Verlag.
1993   Two Kinds of P? Some Reflections on the Occasion of the Publishing of Jacob Milgrom's Commentary on Leviticus 1–16. *JSOT* 60:75–81.
1995   Another Prolegomenon to Leviticus 17:11. Pp. 23–28 in *Pomegranates and Golden Bells* (Fest. J. Milgrom), ed. D. P. Wright et al. Winona Lake, Ind.: Eisenbrauns.
1996   Is It Possible to Read Leviticus as a Separate Book? In *Reading Leviticus,* ed. J. F. A. Sawyer, 22–35. Sheffield: Sheffield Academic Press.

Renkema, J.
1995   Does the Hebrew *ytwm* Really Mean "Fatherless"? *VT* 45:119–21.

Reventlow, H. G.
1960   Sein Blut komme uber sein Haupt. *VT* 10:311–27.
1961   *Das Heiligkeitsgesetz formgeschichtlich untersucht.* WMANT 6. Neukirchen: Neukirchener Verlag.

Reviv, H.
1982   *śākîr. EM* 8:285–87. (Hebrew)

Richards, K. H.
1992   Blessing. *ABD* 1:753–55.

Riesenfeld, H.
1947   *Jésus transfiguré.* Lune: Ohlssons.

Rin, S.
1993   More on the Rephaim. *BM* 39:34–38. (Hebrew)

Ringe, S. H.
1985   *Jesus, Liberation, and the Biblical Jubilee: Images for Ethics and Christology.* Philadelphia: Fortress Press.

Ringgren, H.
    1966   *Israelite Religion.* Trans. D. E. Green. Philadelphia: Fortress Press.
    1990   *yānâ. TDOT* 6:104–6.
Robinson, G.
    1990   Das Jobel-Jahr: Die Losung einer sozial-ökonomischen Krise des Volkes Gottes. Pp. 471–94 in *Die hebräische Bibel und ihre zweifache Nachgeschichte* [Fest. R. Rendtorff], ed. E. Blum et al. Neukirchen: Neukirchener Verlag.
Rochbers-Halton, F.
    1992   Calendars, Ancient Near East. *ABD* 1:810–14.
Rodriguez, A. M.
    1979   *Substitution in the Hebrew Cultus.* Berrien Springs, Mich.: Andrews University Press.
Rofé, A.
    1985   The Covenant in the Land of Moab (Dt 28, 69–30, 20). Pp. 310–20 in *Das Deuteronomium,* ed. N. Lohfink. Louvain: Leuven University Press.
    1986   Methodological Aspects of the Study of Biblical Law. In *Jewish Law Association Studies,* ed. B. S. Jackson, 2:1–16. Atlanta: Scholars Press.
    1988   *Introduction to Deuteronomy, Part I.* Jerusalem: Akademon. (Hebrew)
Rogerson, J. W.
    1978   *Anthropology and the Old Testament.* Oxford: Blackwell.
Rooker, M. F.
    1990   *Biblical Hebrew in Transition: The Language of the Book of Ezekiel.* Sheffield: JSOT Press.
Rothenberg, B.
    1972   *Timna: Valley of the Biblical Copper Mines.* London: Thames and Hudson.
Rouillard, H., and J. Tropper
    1987   Vom kanaänaischen Ahnenkult zur Zauberi: Eine Auslegungsgeschichte zu den hebräischen Begriffen ʾwb und ydʿny. *UF* 19:235–54.
Rowley, H. H.
    1962   Hezekiah's Reform and Rebellion. *BJRL* 44:395–431.
Rubenstein, J. L.
    1994   The Symbolism of the *Sukkah. Judaism* 43:371–87.
Rubenstein, S. T.
    1959   *Annotations to Maimonides Book of Love.* Jerusalem: Mosad Harev Kook. (Hebrew)
Ruesche, F.
    1930   *Blut, Leben und Seele.* Paderborn: F. Schoningh.
Saadiah (ben Joseph) Gaon
    1963   *The Commentaries of R. Saadiah Gaon on the Torah.* Excerpted and trans. J. Kapach. Jerusalem: Mosad Harav Kook. (Hebrew)

Saalschütz, J. L.
1853   *Das mosaische Recht.* 2nd ed. Berlin: Heymann.
Sabourin, L.
1966   Nefesh, sang et expiation (Lv. 17.11–14). *Sciences ecclesiastiques* 18:25–45.
Safrai, S.
1968   *Pilgrimages at the Time of the Second Temple.* Tel Aviv: Am Hassefer.
1976   *The Jewish People in the First Century.* 2 vols. Philadelphia: Fortress Press.
Safren, J. D.
1999   Jubilee and the Day of Atonement. Pp. 107*–14* in *Proceedings of the Twelfth World Congress of Jewish Studies. Jerusalem: World Union of Jewish Studies.*
Saggs, H. W. F.
1984   *The Might that Was Assyria.* London: Sidgwick and Jackson.
San Nicolò, M.
1922   *Die Schlussklaaseln der altbabylonischen Kauf-und Tauschverträge.* Munich: Beck.
Šanda, A.
1911–12   *Die Bücher der Könige.* 2 vols. Münster: Aschendorffschen Verlag.
Sanmartin-Ascaso, J.
1978   *dôdh. TDOT* 3:143–56.
Sarna, N. M.
1959   The Interchange of the Prepositions *Beth* and *Mem* in Biblical Hebrew. *JBL* 78:310–16.
1973   Zedekiah's Emancipation of Slaves and the Sabbatical Year. *AOAT* 22:143–48.
1989   *Genesis.* Philadelphia: Jewish Publication Society.
1991   *Exodus.* Philadelphia: Jewish Publication Society.
1992   Legal Terminology in Psalm 3:8. Pp. 175–82 in "Sha'arei Talmon" (Fest. Talmon), ed. M. Fishbane and E. Tov. Winona Lake, Ind.: Eisenbrauns.
Sasson, V.
1985   The Aramaic Text of the Tell Fakhriyeh Assyrian–Aramaic Bilingual Inscription. *ZAW* 97:86–103.
Satlow, M. L.
1994   "Wasted Seed": The History of a Rabbinic Idea. *HUCA* 65:137–75.
Sauermann, O.
1952   *Untersuchungen zu der Wortgruppe nḥš.* Vienna: Mayer and Company.
Sauneron, S.
1960   *The Priests in Ancient Egypt.* New York: Grove Press.
1938   Les Fouilles de Ras Shamra-Ugarit, neuvième campagne (printemps 1937): Rapport sommaire. *Syria* 19:193–255, 313–27.

Schaeffer, C. F.-A.

1929–38 Les Fouilles de Minet-el-Beida et de Ras Shamra. *Syria* 10:28–303; 12:1–14; 13:1–27; 14:93–127; 15:105–31; 16:141–76; 17:105–48; 18:125–54; 19:193–255, 313–34.

1939 *The Cuneiform Texts of Ras Shamra-Ugarit.* Schweich Lectures 1936. Oxford: Oxford University Press.

Schaeffer, H.

1915 *The Social Legislation of the Primitive Semites.* New Haven, Conn.: Yale University Press; London: Oxford University Press.

1922 *Hebrew Tribal Economy and the Jubilee as Illustrated in Semitic and Indo-European Village Communities.* Leipzig: Hinrichs.

Schapiro, I.

1909 Leviticus XXVII im Lichte des Talmud. *Monatsschrift für Geschichte und Wissenschaft des Judentums* 53:269–85.

Scharbert, J.

1975 brk. *TDOT* 2:279–308.

1986 nāqab. *ThWAT* 5:589–91.

1990 qillēl. *ThWAT* 7:40–49.

Schechter, S.

1898 The Rabbinical Conception of Holiness. *JQR* 10:1–12.

Scheil, V.

1918 Quelques remèdes pour les yeux. *RA* 15:75–80.

Schenker, A.

1983 Das Zeichen des Blutes und die Gewissheit der Vergebung im Alten Testament: Die sünende Function des Blutes auf dem Altar nach Lev 17:10–12. *MTZ* 34:195–213.

1990 Der Unterschied zwischen Sündopfer *Chaṭṭat* und Schuldopfer *Ascham* im Licht von Lev 5:17–19 und 5:1–6. Pp. 115–23 in *Pentateuchal and Deuteronomic Studies,* ed. C. Brekelmans and J. Lust. Louvain: Leuven University Press.

1992 Die Anlässe zum Schuldopfer Ascham. In *Studien zu Opfer und Kult in Alten Testament,* ed. A. Schenker, 45–65. Tübingen: Mohr.

1994 Interprétations récentes et dimensions spécifiques du sacrifice ḥaṭṭāt. *Biblica* 75:59–70.

1997 Once Again, the Expiatory Sacrifices. *JBL* 116:697–99.

1998 The Biblical Legislation on the Release of Slaves: The Road from Exodus to Leviticus. *JSOT* 78:23–41.

Schiffman, L. H.

1975 *The Halakha at Qumran.* Leiden: Briss.

1983 *Sectarian Law in the Dead Sea Scrolls.* Chico, Calif.: Scholars Press.

1989a *Miqṣat Maʿseh Ha-Torah* and the Temple Scroll. *REVQ* 14:435–57.

1989b The Systems of Jewish Law. Pp. 239–59 in *Temple Scroll Studies,* ed. G. J. Brooke. Sheffield: JSOT Press.

1995 Sacral and Non-Sacral Slaughter According to the Temple Scroll.

Pp. 69–84 in *Time to Prepare the Way in the Wilderness*, ed. D. Dimant and L. H. Schiffman. Leiden: Brill.

Schmidt, B. B.

1996a *Israel's Beneficent Dead*. Winona Lake, Ind.: Eisenbrauns.

1996b The Aniconic Tradition. In *The Triumph of Elohim*, ed. D. V. Edelman, 75–106. Grand Rapids, Mich.: Eerdmans.

Schmidtke, F.

1967 Träume, Orakel und Totengeister als Künder der Zukunft in Israel und Babylonian *BZ* 11:420–46.

Schorr, M.

1971 *Urkunden des altbabylonischen Zivil- und Prozessrechts*. Hildesheim: Olms. (reprint of 1913)

Schottroff, W.

1966 *Gedenken im alten Orient und im Alten Testament*. Neukirchen: Neukirchener Verlag.

Schuler, E. von

1957 *Hethithische Dienstanweisungen II. Bēl madgalti. AfO* 10.

Schult, H. S.

1974 Lev 24:15b und 16a. *DBAT* 7:31–32.

Schulz, H.

1969 *Das Todesrecht im Alten Testament*. Berlin: Topelmann.

Schwartz, B. J.

1986 A Literary Study of the Slave-Girl Pericope—Leviticus 19:20–22. *Scripta* 31:341–55.

1987 Selected Chapters of the Holiness Code—A Literary Study of Leviticus 17–19. Ph.D. diss., Hebrew University. (Hebrew)

1991 The Prohibition Concerning the "Eating" of Blood in Leviticus 17. Pp. 34–66 in *Priesthood and Cult in Ancient Israel*, ed. G. A. Anderson and S. M. Olyan. Sheffield: Sheffield Academic Press.

1994 "Term" or Metaphor: Biblical *nāśā' 'āwōn/peša'/ḥēṭ'. Tarbiz* 63: 149–71. (Hebrew)

1995a The Bearing of Sin in the Priestly Literature. Pp. 3–21 in *Pomegranates and Golden Bells* [Fest. J. Milgrom], ed. D. P. Wright et al. Winona Lake, Ind.: Eisenbrauns.

1995b Week, Weeks, Seven Weeks. *Ta* 65:189–4. (Hebrew)

1996a The Priestly Account of the Theophany and Lawgiving at Sinai. Pp. 103–34 in *Texts, Temples and Traditions* [Fest. M. Haran], ed. M. V. Fox et al. Winona Lake, Ind.: Eisenbrauns.

1996b "Profane" Slaughter and the Integrity of the Priestly Code. *HUCA* 67:15–42.

1997 What Really Happened at Mount Sinai. *BR* 13:20–30, 46.

1999 *The Holiness Legislation*. Jerusalem: Magner (Hebrew)

Schwartz, D. R.

1992 Law and Truth: On Qumran—Sadducean and Rabbinic Views of Law. Pp. 229–40 in *The Dead Sea Scrolls: Forty Years of Research*, ed. D. Dimnat. Leiden: Brill.

Scolnic, B. E.
  1995   How to Read the Torah's Laws of Slavery. *CJ* 47:37–41.
Scott, R. B. Y.
  1960   Weights and Measures of the Bible. *BA* 22:22–40.
Scott, W. R.
  1993   The Booths of Ancient Israel's Autumn Festival. Ph.D. diss., Johns Hopkins University.
Seebass, M.
  1986   *nepeš*. *TDOT* 5:531–55.
Seeligmann, I. L.
  1954   *Gēr*. *EM* 2:546–50. (Hebrew)
  1978   Lending, Pledge and Interest in Biblical Law and Biblical Thought. Pp. 183–206, 209–10 in *Studies in Bible and the Ancient Near East* [Fest. S. E. Loewenstamm], ed. I. Avishur and J. Blau. Jerusalem: Rubinstein. (Hebrew)
Segal, P.
  1989   The "Divine Penalty" in the Harna Inscriptions and the Mishnah. *JJS* 40:46–52.
Seidel, M.
  1955–56   Parallels Between Isaiah and Psalms. *Sinai* 38:149–72, 229–40, 272–80, 333–55. (Hebrew)
  1978   Parallels Between Isaiah and Psalms. Pp. 1–97 in *Studies in Scripture*, M. Seidel. Jerusalem: Mosad Harav Kook. (Hebrew)
Seidler, M.
  1998   "It and Its Young" and the Problem of the Rationales for Commandments. *Weekly Page* 225:1–4. (Hebrew)
Sellin, E., and G. Foher
  1968   *Introduction to the Old Testament*. Trans. D. Green. Nashville, Tenn.: Abingdon Press.
Selms A. van
  1954   *Marriage and Family Life in Ugaritic Literature* London: Luzac.
Sen, A.
  1979   Starvation and Exchange Entitlement. *Cambridge Journal of Economics*, 33–59.
Seper Hamibḥar   See Aaron ben Joseph.
Sforno (Obadiah ben Jacob)
  1980   *The Commentary of Sforno*. Ed. A. Darom and Z. Gottlieb. Jerusalem: Mosad Harav Kook. (Hebrew)
Shadal (Luzzato, Samuel David)
  1965   *Commentary on the Pentateuch and Hamishtadel* Ed. P. Schlesinger Tel Aviv: Dvir. (Hebrew)
Shalit, A.
  1967   *Josephus' Antiquity of the Jews.* 2 vols. Jerusalem: Mosad Bialik. (Hebrew)
Sharon, I.
  1996   Appendix E: Analysis of Homogeneity for the Distribution of Figurines in Strata 13–10. Pp. 100–108 in *Excavations at the City of*

David (1978–1985): Final Report IV, ed. D. T. Ariel and A. de Groot. *Qedem* 35.

Sheffer, A.
1978 The Textiles in Z. Meshel *Kuntillet ʿAjrud: A Religious Centre from the Time of the Judean Monarchy on the Border of Sinai*. Jerusalem: Israel Museum.

Shilo, Y.
1979 Iron Age Sanctuaries and Cult Elements in Palestine. Pp. 147–57 in *ASOR Symposia*, ed. F. M. Cross.

Shutt, R. J. H., trans.
1985 The Letter of Aristeas. Pp. 7–34 in *The Old Testament Pseudepigrapha*, Vol. 2, ed. J. H. Charlesworth. New York: Doubleday.

Siebesma, P. A.
1991 *The Function of the* Niphʿal *in Biblical Hebrew in Relationship to Other Passive-Reflexive Verbal Stems and to the* Puʿal *and* Hophʿal *in Particular*. Assen: Van Gorcum.

Silberman, L. H.
1949 The Sefirah Season. *HUCA* 22:221–37.

Silver, A. H.
1964 The Lunar and Solar Calendars in Ancient Israel. Pp. 300–309 in *Essays in Honor of S. B. Freehof*, ed. W. Jacob and E. C. Schwartz. Pittsburgh: Rodef Shalom Congregation.

Simon, V.
1985 On the Exegetical Method of Ibn Ezra According to Three of his Interpretations on one Verse. *Bar Ilan* 3:92–138.

Singer, I.
1983 *The Hittite KI.LAM Festival*. Studien zu den Bogazkhoy-Texten 27–28. Wiesbaden: Harrassowitz.

Skinner, J.
1910 *Genesis*. ICC. New York: Scribner.

Smelik, K. A. D.
1995 Moloch, Molekh or Molk-Sacrifice. *SJOT* 9:133–41.

Smith, C. R.
1996 The Literary Structure of Leviticus. *JSOT* 70:17–32.

Smith, M.
1971 *Palestinian Purities and Politics that Shaped the Old Testament*. New York: Columbia University Press.
1975a A Note on Burning Babies. *JAOS* 95:477–79.
1975b The Veracity of Ezekiel, the Sins of Manasseh, and Jeremiah 44:18. *ZAW* 87:11–16.

Smith, M. S.
1984 The Magic of Kothar, the Ugaritic Craftsman God in KTU 1.6 VI 49–50. *RB* 91:377–80.
1990 *The Early History of God*. San Francisco: Harper & Row.
1993 The Invocation of Deceased Ancestors in Psalm 49:12c. *JBL* 112:105–7.

1996   *The Pilgrimage Pattern in Exodus.* Sheffield: Sheffield Academic Press.
1997   *The Pilgrimage Pattern in Exodus.* JSOT Supp. 239. Sheffield: Sheffield Academic Press.

Smith, M. S., and E. M. Bloch-Smith
1988   Death and Afterlife in Ugarit and Israel. Review of *Beatific Afterlife in Ancient Israel and the Ancient Near East,* by K. Spronk. *JAOS* 108:277–84.

Smith, W. R.
1907   *Kinship and Marriage in Early Arabia.* London: Black.
1927   *Lectures on the Religion of the Semites.* 3rd ed. Annotated S. A. Cook. New York: Macmillan.

Snaith, N. H.
1967   *Leviticus and Numbers.* London: Nelson. [Reprint, London: Oliphants, 1977]

Soden, W. von
1952   Zur Wiederherstellung der Geburtsomen—Seice *summa izbu.* ZA 50:182–93.

Soler, J.
1979   Sémiotique de la nourriture dans la Bible. *Annales* 28:943–55. [Trans. as The Dietary Prohibitions of the Hebrews, *New York Review,* 14 June 1979, 24]

Soltero, C.
1968   Nota Critica a Lev 18,30. *Biblica* 49:370–72.

Soss, N. M.
1973   Old Testament Law and Economic Society. *Journal of the History of Ideas* 34:323–44.

Speiser, E. A.
1932   New Kirkuk Documents Relating to Security Transactions. *JAOS* 52:350–67.
1933   New Kirkuk Documents Relating to Security Transactions. *JAOS* 53:22–46.
1964   *Genesis.* Garden City, N.Y.: Doubleday.
1960   Leviticus and the Critics. In *Yehezkel Kaufmann Jubilee Volume,* ed. M. Haran, 29–45. Jerusalem: Magnes.
1963   Unrecognized Dedication. *IEJ* 13:69–73.

Sperber, A.
1966   *A Historical Grammar of Biblical Hebrew.* Leiden: E. J. Brill.

Sperber, D.
1966   A Note on Leviticus XXVII 28. *VT* 16:515–18.

Sperling, A. I.
1957   *Seper Ṭa ʿame Ha-minhagim Umeqore ha-dinim.* Jerusalem: Eshcol Press.

Spieckermann, H.
1982   *Judah unter Assur in der Sargonidenzeit.* Göttingen: Vandenhoeck & Ruprecht.

Spiegelberg, W.
1914   *Die Sogenannte demotische Chronik des Pap. 215 der Bibliothèque*

Nationale zu Paris, nebst der auf der Ruckseite des Papyrus stehen-den Texten. Demotische Studien 17. Leipzig.

Spronk, K.
  1986   *Beatific Afterlife in Ancient Israel and in the Ancient Near East.* Kevalaer: Butzon and Bercker.

Stager, L. E.
  1980   The Rite of Child Sacrifice at Carthage. Pp. 1–12 in *New Light on Ancient Carthage,* ed. J. G. Pedley. Ann Arbor: University of Michigan Press.
  1985   The Archaeology of the Family in Ancient Israel. *BASOR* 260:1–35.

Stager, L. E., and S. R. Wolff
  1981   Production and Commerce in Temple Courtyards: An Olive Press in the Sacred Precinct at Tel Dan. *BASOR* 243:95–102.
  1984   Child Sacrifice at Carthage — Religious Rite or Population Control? *BAR* 10:30–51.

Starr, J.
  1990   Queries to the Sun God: Divination and Politics in Sargonid Assyria. In *State Archives of Assyria,* Vol. 4. Helsinki: Helsinki University Press.

Steele, F. R.
  1943   *Nuzi Real Estate Transactions.* New Haven, Conn.: American Oriental Society.

Steiner, M.
  1997   Two Popular Cult Sites of Ancient Palestine: Cave 1 in Jerusalem and E207 in Samaria. *SJOT* 11:16–28.

Stendebach, F. J.
  1973   Das Verbot des Knochenzerbrechuns bei den Semiten *Biblische Zeitschrift* 17:29–38.

Stern, E.
  1991   Phoenicians Sikils and Israelites in the Light of Recent Excavations. Pp. 85–94 in *Phoenicia and the Bible,* ed. E. Lipinski. Leuven: Peters.

Stern, E., and E. Gilboa
  1987   On Lev 26:26. P. 211 in *Leviticus: World of the Bible,* ed. B. A. Levine and M. Paran. Ramat Gan: Revivim. (Hebrew)

Stern, P. D.
  1992   The Origin and Significance of "the Land Flowing with Milk and Honey". *VT* 42:554–57.

Stewart, D. T.
  1992   Does Joshua 6:26 Reflect a Hittite Analogue? Term paper.
  1994   Disabilities in the Ancient Near East. Term paper.

Stohlman, S.
  1983   The Judean Exile after 701 B.C.E. Pp. 171–90 in *Scripture in Context,* ed. W. W. Hallo et al., Vol. 2. Winona Lake, Ind.: Eisenbrauns.

Stol, M.
  1995a   Kaiwan. In *Dictionary of Deities and Demons in the Bible,* ed. K. van der Toorn et al., 899–900. Leiden: Brill.

1995b Sakkuth. In *Dictionary of Deities and Demons in the Bible*, ed. K. van der Toorn et al., 1364–65. Leiden: Brill.

Strassmaier, J. N.
1889 *Inschriften von Nabonidus, König von Babylon von den Throntafeln des Britischen Museums*. Leipzig: Pfeiffer.

Stratem, F. T. von
1995 Hiera Kate: *Images of Animal Sacrifice in Archaic and Classical Greece*. Leiden: Brill.

Stroes, H. R.
1966 Does the Day Begin in the Evenings or Mornings? VT 16: 460–75.

Stulman, L.
1992 Sex and Familial Crimes in the D Code: A Witness to Mores in Transition. *JSOT* 53:47–64.

Sukenik, E. L.
1940 Arrangements for the Cult of the Dead in Ugarit and Samaria. Pp. 59–65 in *Mémorial Lagrange*. Paris: Gabalda.

Sun, H. T. C.
1990 An Investigation into the Compositional Integrity of the So-Called Holiness Code (Leviticus 17–26). Ph.D. diss., Claremont Graduate School.
1993 The Incest Laws of Leviticus 18 and 20. Paper presented at the annual meeting of the Society of Biblical Literature.

Sussmann, Y.
1990 The History of the Halakha and the Dead Sea Scrolls: Preliminary Observations on *Miqṣat Maʿase Ha-Torah* (4QMMT). *Tarbiz* 59:11–76. (Hebrew)

Swanson, D. D.
1995 *The Temple Scroll and the Bible*. Leiden: Brill.

Sweeny, M. A.
1983 Sefirah at Qumran: Aspects of the Counting Formulas for the First-Fruits Festivals in the Temple Scroll. *BASOR* 251:61–66.
1988 *Isaiah 1–4 and the Post-Exilic Understanding of the Isaianic Tradition.*

Szlechter, E.
1954 *Les Lois d'Esnunna*. Paris: Recueil Siriey.

Szubm, H. Z.
forthcoming A New Interpretation of Kraeling 2. *Israel Law Review* 29.
forthcoming The Matrimonial Status of the Reputed Spouse. Paper presented at the meeting of the International SBL, Louven, 1994.
forthcoming The "Beloved Son" in the Hebrew Bible and the "Beloved Disciple" in the New Testament in Light of Ancient Near Eastern Legal Texts.

Taber, C. R.
1976 Marriage, Sex, Sexual Behavior. *IDBSup*: 573–76, 817–20.

Tadmor, H.
    1962   Chronology. *EM* 4:245–310. (Hebrew)
    1968   The People and the Kingship in Ancient Israel: The Role of Political
            Institutions in the Biblical Period. *Journal of World History* 11:3–23.
Tal, A.
    1981   *The Samaritan Targum of the Pentateuch.* 2 vols. Tel-Aviv: Tel-Aviv
            University.
Talmon, S.
    1944   Whence the Day's Beginning in the Biblical Period and in the Be-
            ginning of the Second Temple Period? Pp. 109–29 in *The Bible as
            Reflected in Its Commentators* [S. Kamin Memorial], ed. S. Japhet.
            Jerusalem: Magnes. (Hebrew)
    1958   The Calendar Reckoning of the Sect from the Judean Desert. In
            Aspects of the Dead Sea Scrolls, 162–99. Scripta Herosolymitana 4.
            Jerusalem: Hebrew University.
    1967   The Judaean 'Am Ha'areṣ in Historical Perspective. Pp. 71–76 in
            Proceedings of the Fourth World Congress of Jewish Studies, Vol. 1.
            Jerusalem: World Union of Jewish Studies.
    1971   'am hā'ārez. *EM* 6:239–42.
Talmon, S. and I. Knohl
    1995   A Calendrical Scroll from a Qumran Cave: *Mišmarot* Bᵃ, 4Q 321.
            Pp. 267–302 in *Pomegranates and Golden Bells* [Fest. J. Milgrom],
            ed. D. P. Wright et al. Winona Lake, Ind.: Eisenbrauns.
Taracha, P.
    1986   Zum Festival des Gottes Telipinu in Hanhana und in Kasha. *AF*
            13:180–83.
Tatum, L.
    1991   King Manasseh and the Royal Fortress at Ḥorvat 'Usa. *BA* 54:136–
            45.
Tawil, H.
    1977   A Curse Concerning Crop-Consuming Insects in the Sefire Treaty
            and in Akkadian: A New Interpretation. *BASOR* 225:61.
Taylor, J. G.
    1994   *Yahweh and the Sun: Biblical and Archaeological Evidence for Sun
            Worship in Ancient Israel.* Sheffield: JSOT Press.
Telushkin, J.
    1997   *Biblical Literacy.* New York: William Monsow.
Thackeray, H. S. J.
    1986   *Josephus, Antiquities.* Vols. 1–4. Loeb Classics. Cambridge, Mass.:
            Harvard University Press.
Theophrastus
    1968   *Enquiry into Plants.* Vol. 1. Trans. W. Heineman. Cambridge,
            Mass.: Harvard University Press.
Thureau-Dangin, F.
    1921   *Rituals Accadiens.* Osnabrück: Zeller.

Thurston, T. M.
    1990   Leviticus 18:22 and the Prohibition of Homosexual Acts. Pp. 7–23 in *Homophobia and the Judaeo-Christian Traditions*, ed. M. L. Stemmeler and J. M. Clark. Dallas: Monument Press.

Tigay, J. H.
    1972   Adoption. *EJ* 2:298–301.
    1976   Sabbath. *EM* 7:504–17.
    1978a *Lifnê haššabbāt* and *'aḥar haššabbāt* = "on the day before the sabbath" and "on the day after the sabbath." *VT* 28:362–65.
    1978b Notes on the Development of the Jewish Week. *EJ* 14:111–121.
    1986   *You Shall Have No Other Gods*. Atlanta: Scholars Press.
    1996   *Deuteronomy*. Philadelphia: Jewish Publication Society.

Toeg, A.
    1977   *Law Giving at Sinai*. Jerusalem: Magnes. (Hebrew)

Tolkovsky, S.
    1966   *The Fruit of the Hadar Tree*. Jerusalem: Bialik Institute. (Hebrew)

Tomasino, A. J.
    1993   Isaiah 1:1–2:4 and 63–66 and the Composition of the Isaianic Corpus. *JSOT* 57:81–98.

Toorn, K. van der
    1985   *Sin and Sanction in Israel and Mesopotamia*. Assent: Van Gorcum.
    1988   Echoes of Judaean Necromancy in Isaiah 28:7–22. *ZAW* 100:199–218.
    1989a Female Prostitution in Payment of Vows in Ancient Israel. *JBL* 108:193–205.
    1989b The Babylonian New Year Festival: New Insights from the Cuneiform Texts. *SVT* 43:331–44.
    1990   The Nature of the Biblical Teraphim in the Light of Cuneiform Evidence. *CBQ* 52:203–22.
    1991   Funerary Rituals and Beatific Afterlife in Ugaritic Texts and in the Bible. *BO* 48:40–66.
    1992   Prostitution (Cultic). *ABD* 5:510–13.
    1995   The Domestic Cult at Emar. *JCS* 47:35–49.
    1996a Ancestors and Anthroponyms: Kinship Terms as Theophoric Elements in Hebrew Names. *ZAW* 108:1–11.
    1996b *Family Religion in Babylonia, Syria and Israel*. Leiden: Brill.
    1997   Worshipping Stones: On the Deification of Cult Symbols. *JNSL* 23:1–14.

Toorn, K. van der, and C. Houtman
    1994   David and the Ark. *JBL* 113:209–31.

Torat Ḥayyim
    1992   *The Book of Leviticus*. Ed. M. L. Katzenelbogen. Jerusalem: Mosad Harav Kook.

Tosato, A.
    1984   The Law of Leviticus 18:18: A Reexamination. *CBQ* 36:199–214.

Tov, E.
 1982 *TaNaK*: Greek Translations. *EM* 8: 774–803. (Hebrew)
 1995 4QLev^c,c,g (4Q25, 26a, 26b). In *Pomegranates and Golden Bells* [Fest. J. Milgrom], ed. D. P. Wright et al., 257–66. Winona Lake, Ind.: Eisenbrauns.

Tropper, J.
 1995 Spirits of the Dead. Pp. 1524–30 in *Dictionary of Deities and Demons in the Bible*, ed. K. van der Toorn et al. Leiden: Brill.

Tsevat, M.
 1958 Alalakhiana. *HUCA* 29:109–43.
 1970 The Connection of the Sabbatical to Mount Sinai. Pp. 282–88 in *Seper Showel Yeivin*, ed. Y. Aharoni et al. Jerusalem: Kiryat Sefer. (Hebrew)
 1972 The Basic Meaning of the Biblical Sabbath. *ZAW* 84:447–59.
 1975a Ishbosheth and Congeners: The Names and Their Study. *HUCA* 46:71–87.
 1975b *bĕtûlâ*. *TDOT* 3:340–43.
 1994 The Hebrew Slave According to Deuteronomy 15:12–18: His Lot and the Value of His Service with Special Attention to the Meaning of *mišneh*. *JBL* 113:587–95.

Tsukimoto, A.
 1985 *Untersuchungen zur Totenpflege (kispum) im alten Mesopotamien*. Neukirchen: Neukirchener Verlag.

Tucker, G.
 1993 The Sayings of the Wise Are Like Goads: An Appreciation of the Works of Robert Cover. *CJ* 45:17–39.
 1956 The Origin of the Sabbath. Pp. 205–28 in *Halashon Wehaseper*, Vol. 3. Jerusalem: Mosad Bialik Institute. (Hebrew)

Tuell, S. S.
 1992 *The Law of the Temple in Ezekiel 40–48*. Atlanta: Scholars Press.

Tur-Sinai, N. H. (Torczyner, H.), et al.
 1938 *Lachish I: The Lachish Letters*. Oxford: Oxford University Press.
 1945 '*lappetah ḥaṭṭā't rōbeṣ*' *Ta* 16:8–10 (Hebrew)
 1957 The *'etrôg*. In *The Book of Job*. Jerusalem: Kiryat Sepher. (Hebrew)
 1962 *The Plain Meaning of Scripture*, Vol. 1. Jerusalem: Kiryat Sepher. (Hebrew)

Turner, V.
 1979 The Anthropology of Performance. Pp. 60–93 in *Process, Performance, and Pilgrimage: A Study in Comparative Symbology*. New Delhi: Concept.

Ullendorf, E.
 1966 Thought Categories in the Hebrew Bible. Pp. 276–78 in *Studies in Rationalism, Judaism and Universalism in Memory of L. Roth*, ed. R. Lowe. New York: Humanities Press.

Urbach, E. E.
　　1959　The Rabbinical Laws of Idolatry in the Second and Third Centuries in the Light of Archaeological and Historical Facts. *IEJ* 9:149–65, 229–45.
　　1979　*The Sages.* Trans. I. Abrahams. Cambridge, Mass.: Harvard University Press.
　　1988　*The World of the Sages.* Jerusalem: Magnes. (Hebrew)
Urbrock, W. J.
　　1992　Blessings and Curses. *ABD* 1:755–61.
VanderKam, J. C.
　　1992　Calendars, Ancient Israelite and Early Jewish. *ABD* 1:814–20.
Vaughan, P. H.
　　1974　*The Meaning of Bāmâ in the Old Testament.* London: Cambridge University Press.
Vaux, R. de
　　1961　*Ancient Israel.* Trans. J. McHugh. New York: McGraw-Hill.
　　1964　*Studies in Old Testament Sacrifice.* Cardiff: University of Wales Press.
　　1968　Le Pays de Canaan. *JAOS* 88:23–29.
Vawter, B.
　　1977　*On Genesis.* Doubleday: New York.
Vermes, G.
　　1981　Leviticus 18:21 in Ancient Jewish Bible Exegesis. Pp. 108–24 in *Studies in Aggadah, Targum and Jewish Liturgy in Memory of Joseph Heinemann,* ed. J. J. Petuchowski and E. Fleischer. Jerusalem: Magnes.
　　1987　*The Dead Sea Scrolls.* 3rd ed. London: Penguin.
Vieyra, M.
　　1961　Les Noms du "mundus" un hittite et assyrien et la pythonisse d'Endor. *RHA* 19:47–55.
Vilnay, Z.
　　1951　*Holy Monuments in the Land of Israel.* 2 vols. Jerusalem: Mosad Harav Kook. (Hebrew)
　　1991　*Holy Monuments in the Land of Israel.* Rev ed. 2 vols. Jerusalem: Ahiavar. (Hebrew)
Vital, H.
　　1963　*Sha`ar Ha-Kawanot.* Jerusalem.
Volz, P.
　　1912　*Das neujahrfest yahwes.* Tübingen: Mohr.
Wacholder, B.-Z.
　　1975　Chronomessianism: The Timing of Messianic Movements and the Calendar of Sabbatical Cycles. *HUCA* 46:201–18.
　　1973　The Calendar of Sabbatical Cycles During the Second Temple and the Early Rabbinic Period. *HUCA* 44:153–96.
　　1983　*The Dawn of Qumran.* Cincinnati: Hebrew Union College Press.

Wacholder, B.-Z., and M. Abegg
1992   A *Preliminary Edition of the Unpublished Dead Sea Scrolls*. 2 vols. Washington, D.C.: Biblical Archaeology Society.

Wallace Budge, E. A., trans.
1960   *The Book of the Dead*. New York: University Press.

Waltke, B. K.
1988   The Phenomenon of Conditionality Within Unconditional Covenants. In *Israel's Apostasy and Restoration*, ed. A. Gileadi, 123–39. Grand Rapids, Mich.: Baker.

Wapnish, P., and B. Hesse
1991   Faunal Remains from Tel Dan: Perspectives on Animal Production at a Village, Urban and Ritual Center. *Archaeozoologica* 4:9–86.

Warmuth, G.
1978   *Hādār. TDOT* 3:335–41.

Warning, W.
1999   *Literary Artistry in Leviticus*. Leiden: Brill.

Watson, W. G. E.
1986   *Classical Hebrew Poetry: A Guide to Its Techniques*. Sheffield: JSOT Press.

Watts, J. D. W.
1985   *Isaiah 1–33*. Waco, Tex.: Word Books.

Watts, J. W.
1995a   The Rhetorical Strategy in the Composition of the Pentateuch. *JSOT* 68:3–22.
1995b   Public Readings and Pentateuchal Law. *VT* 45:540–57.

Weber, M.
1952   *Ancient Judaism*. Ed. H. H. Gerth and D. Martindale. Glencoe, Ill.: Free Press.

Wegner, J. R.
1992   Leviticus. Pp. 36–44 in *The Woman's Bible Commentary*, ed. C. A. Newsom and S. H. Ringe. Louisville, Ky.: Westminster Press.

Weidner, E.
1954–56 Hof- und Harems-Erlässe assyrichen Könige aus dem 2 Jahrtausend v. Chr. *AfO* 17:256–93.

Weinberg, J. P.
1992   *The Citizen-Temple Community*. Trans. D. L. Smith-Christopher. JSOT Suppl. 151. Sheffield: Sheffield Academic Press.

Weinfeld, M.
1964a   Cult Centralization in the Light of a Neo-Babylonian Analogy. *JNES* 23:202–12.
1964b   Towards an Understanding of the Law in Israel and Its Neighbors. *BM* 8:59–65. (Hebrew)
1968   Eve the Creator in Genesis 1 and in Second Isaiah. *Tarbiz* 37:105–32. (Hebrew)

1969   The Molech Cult in Israel and Its Background. Pp. 137–61, 182 in
        Proceedings of the Fifth World Congress of Jewish Studies, Vol. 1,
        ed. P. Peli. Jerusalem: World Union of Jewish Studies.

1970   The Covenant of Grant in the Old Testament and in the Ancient
        Near East. *JAOS* 90:184–203; 92: 468–69.

1971a   Molech, Cult of. *EJ* 12:230–32.

1971b   Tithe. *EJ* 15:1156–62.

1972a   The Worship of Molech and of the Queen of Heaven and Its Back-
        ground. *UF* 4:133–54.

1972b   Congregation. *EJ* 5:893–95.

1972c   *Hbrt whḥsd*—Their Development in Israel and the Ancient World.
        Leshonenu 36:85–105. (Hebrew)

1972d   *Deuteronomy and the Deuteronomic School.* Oxford: Clarendon
        Press.

1973   The Royal and Sacred Aspects of the Tithe in the Old Testament.
        Beer-Sheva 1:121–31. (Hebrew)

1975a   *Berith. TDOT* 2:253–79.

1975b   *Genesis.* Tel-Aviv: Gordon. (Hebrew)

1976   Curse. *EM* 7:185–92. (Hebrew)

1977   Notations on (Recent) Publications. *Shnaton* 2:249–58. (Hebrew)

1978   Burning Babies in Ancient Israel: A Rejoinder to Morton Smith's
        Article in *JAOS* 95 (1975), pp. 477–79. *UF* 10:411–13.

1980   Julius Wellhausen's Understanding of the Law of Ancient Israel and
        Its Fallacies. *Shnaton* 4:62–93. (Hebrew)

1981   Sabbath, Temple, and the Enthronement of the Lord. Pp. 501–12
        in *Mélanges bibliques et orientaux en l'honneur de M. Henri
        Cazelles,* ed. A. Caquot. AOAT 12.

1982a   Instructions for Temple Visitors in the Bible and in Ancient Egypt.
        Herosolymitana 28: 223–50.

1982b   "Justice and Righteousness" in Ancient Israel Against the Background
        of "Social Reforms" in the Ancient Near East. In *Mesopotamien und
        seine Nachbaren,* ed. H.-J. Nissen and J. Renger, 491–519. Berlin:
        Reimer Verlag.

1983a   Social and Cultic Institutions in the Priestly Source Against Their
        Ancient Near Eastern Background. Pp. 95–129 in *Proceedings of the
        Eighth World Congress of Jewish Studies,* Vol. 5. Jerusalem: World
        Union of Jewish Studies.

1983b   *Ḥillûl, kĕbîsâ ûmirmas regel* Pp. 195–200 in *Meḥqĕrê lāšôn* [Fest. Z.
        Ben-Hayyim], ed. M. Bar-Asher et al. Jerusalem: Magnes. (Hebrew)

1985a   *Justice and Righteousness in Israel and the Nations.* Jerusalem:
        Magnes. (Hebrew)

1985b   The Emergence of the Deuteronomic Movement: The Historical
        Antecedents. Pp. 76–98 in *Das Deuteronomium,* ed. N. Lohfink.
        Leuven: Leuven University Press.

1985c Freedom Proclamation in Egypt and in the Ancient Near East. Pp. 317–27 in *Pharaonic Egypt*, ed. S. Israelitz Groll. Jerusalem: Magnes.

1986 The Uniqueness of the Decalogue and Its Place in Jewish Tradition. Pp. 1–34 in *The Ten Commandments*, ed. B.-Z. Segal. Jerusalem: Magnes.

1988 The Pattern of Israelite Settlement in Canaan. SVT 40:270–83.

1990a Sabbatical Year and Jubilee in the Pentateuchal Laws and Their Ancient Near Eastern Background. Pp. 39–62 in *The Law in the Bible and in Its Environment*, ed. T. Veijola. Göttingen: Vandenhoeck & Ruprecht.

1990b Traces of the Hittite Cult in Shiloh and Jerusalem. *Shnaton* 10:107–14. (Hebrew)

1990c Traces of Hittite Cult in Shilo, Bethel and in Jerusalem. Pp. 455–72 in *Religionsgeschichtliche Beziehungen zwischen Kleinasien, Nordsyrian und dem Alten Testament*, ed. B. Janowski et al. Göttingen: Vandenhoeck & Ruprecht.

1991 *Deuteronomy 1–11*. AB 5. New York: Doubleday.

1992 *From Joshua to Josiah*. Jerusalem: Magnes. (Hebrew)

1993 *The Promise of the Land*. Berkeley: University of California Press.

1995 *Social Justice in Israel and in the Ancient Near East*. Jerusalem: Magnes; Minneapolis: Fortress Press. [Trans. of *Justice and Righteousness in Israel and the Nations* (Jerusalem: Magnes, 1985)]

Weingreen, J.
1972 The Case of the Blasphemer. *VT* 22:118–23.

Weingrod, A.
1990 *The Saint of Beersheba*. Albany: State University of New York Press.

Weippert, M.
1990 Synkretismus and Monotheismus. Pp. 143–79 in *Kultur und Konflikt*, ed. J. Assmann and D. Harth. Frankfurt: Suhrkamp.

Weismann, J.
1972 Talion und offentliche Strafe in mosaishen Rechte. Pp. 325–406 in *Um das Prinzip der Vergeltung in Religion und Recht des Alten Testamens*, ed. K. Koch. Darmstadt: Wissenschaftliche Buchgesellschaft.

Weiss, I. M.
1924 *Dor Dor weDorshaw*. 5 vols. Berlin: Platt and Minkus.

Weiss, M.
1978 The Differences Between the Present Days and the Days to Come According to Amos 9:13. *EI* 14:69–73. (Hebrew)

1984 *The Bible from Within—The Method of Total Interpretation*. Jerusalem: Magnes.

1995a Conceiving Amos' Repudiation of the Cult. Pp. 199–214 in *Pomegranates and Golden Bells* [Fest. J. Milgrom], ed. D. P. Wright et al. Winona Lake, Ind.: Eisenbrauns.

　　　　1995b　Concerning Amos' Redemption of the Cult. Pp. 199–214 in *Pome-granates and Golden Bells* (Fest. J. Milgrom}. Ed. D. P. Wright et al. Winona Lake, Ind.: Eisenbrauns.

Weiss, R.
　　　　1962　Concerning Chiasmus in Scripture. *BM* 13:46–51. (Hebrew)

Welch, A. C.
　　　　1924　*The Code of Deuteronomy.* London: Clark.
　　　　1925　Note on Lev 21:1–6. ZAW 43:135–37.

Welch, J. W.
　　　　1990　Chiasmus in Biblical Law; an Approach to the Structure of Legal Texts in the Hebrew Bible. *JLAS* 4:5–22.

Wellhausen, J.
　　　　1885　Prolegomena to the History of Israel. Edinburgh: A. C. Black. Reprinted New York, 1957.
　　　　1963　*Die Composition des Hexateuchs und die historischen Bücher des Alten Testaments.* 4th ed. Berlin: de Gruyter. [Originally published 1885]

Wenham, G. J.
　　　　1972　Betulah: "A Girl of Marraigeable Age." *VT* 22:326–48.
　　　　1978　Lev 27:2–8 and the Price of Slaves. ZAW 90:264–65.
　　　　1979a　*The Book of Leviticus.* Grand Rapids, Mich.: Eerdmans.
　　　　1979b　The Restoration of Marriage Reconsidered. *JJS* 30:36–40.
　　　　1983　Why Does Sexual Intercourse Defile (Lev. 15:18)? ZAW 95:432–34.
　　　　1987　*Genesis 1–15.* Waco, Tex.: Word Books.
　　　　1994　*Genesis 16–50.* Dallas, TX: Word.
　　　　1999　The Priority of P. *VT* 49:240–58.

Werman, C.
　　　　1994　Consumption of the Blood and Its Covering in the Priestly and Rabbinic Traditions. *Tarbiz* 63:173–84. (Hebrew)

Wessely, Naphtali Herz
　　　　1846　*Netivot Ha-shalom.* Vol. 3, *Leviticus.* Ed. M. Mendelssohn. Vienna: von Schmid and Busch.

West, M. L.
　　　　1972　IAMBI ET ELEGI GRAECI, Vol. 2. Oxford: Oxford University Press.

Westbrook, R.
　　　　1971a　Jubilee Laws. *Israel Law Review* 6:209–25.
　　　　1971b　Redemption of the Land. *Israel Law Review* 6:367–75.
　　　　1985　The Price Factor in the Redemption of Land. *RIDA* 32: 97–127.
　　　　1986　Lex Talionis and Ex 21:22–25. *RB* 93:52–69.
　　　　1988　*Studies in Biblical and Cuneiform Law.* Paris: Gabalda.
　　　　1990　Adultery in Ancient Near Eastern Law. *RB* 97:542–80.
　　　　1991a　The Price Factor in the Redemption of Land. Pp. 90–117 in *Property and the Family in Biblical Law.* Sheffield: Sheffield Academic Press.
　　　　1991b　Jubilee Laws. Pp. 36–57 in *Property and the Family in Biblical Law.* Sheffield: Academic Press.

1992   Punishments and Crimes. *ABD* 5:546–56.

1995   Social Justice in the Ancient Near East. Pp. 149–63 in *Social Justice in the Ancient World*, ed. K. D. Irani and M. Silver. Westport, Conn.: Greenwood Press.

Westbrook, R., and R. D. Woodard

1990   The Edict of Tudhaliya IV. *JAOS* 110:641–59.

Westendorf, W.

1972   Homosexualität. In *Lexikon der Ägyptologie*, Vol. 2, 1272–74, ed. H. W. Helck. Wiesbaden: Otto Harrassowitz.

Westenholz, J. G.

1989   Tamar, *qĕdēšâ, qadištu* and Sacred Prostitution in Mesopotamia. *HTR* 82:245–65.

Westermann, C.

1985   *Genesis 12–36*. Trans. J. S. Scullion. Minneapolis: Augsburg.

White, S. A.

1992   *4Q364 + 365:* A Preliminary Report. In *The Madrid Qumran Congress*, ed. J. T. Barrera and L. V. Montaner, 1:217–28. Leiden: Brill.

Whitelaw, T.

1894   Ezekiel and the Priests' Code. *Presbyterian and Reformed Review* 5:434–54.

Wiesenberg, E. J.

1986   Exogamy or Moloch Worship. Pp. 193–95 in *Jewish Law Association Studies*, ed. B. S. Jackson, Vol. 2. Atlanta: Scholars Press.

Wilcken, U., ed.

1963   *Grundzüge und Christomathie der Papyruskunde*. 2 vols. Hildesheim: Olds Verlag.

Williamson, H. G. M.

1985   *Ezra, Nehemiah*. Waco, Tex.: Word Books.

1988   History. Pp. 25–38 in *It Is Written: Scripture Citing Scripture* [Fest. B. Lindars], ed. D. A. Carson and H. G. M. Williamson. Cambridge: Cambridge University Press.

1994   *The Book Called Isaiah*. Oxford: Clarendon Press.

Willis, J. T.

1969   The Authenticity and Meaning of Micah 5,9–14. *ZAW* 81:353–68.

Wintermute, O. S.

1985   Jubilees. Pp. 35–142 in *The Old Testament Pseudepigrapha*, ed. J. H. Charlesworth, Vol. 2. Garden City, N.Y.: Doubleday.

Wirth, E.

1962   *Agrargeographie des Irak*. Hamburg: Instituts für Geographie und Wirtschaftgeographie der Universität Hamburg.

1971   *Syrien*. Darmstadt: Wissenschaftliche Buchges.

Wiseman, D. J.

1953   *The Alalakh Tablets*. London: British Institute of Archaeology at Ankara.

1958   The Vassal-Treaties of Esarhaddon. *Iraq* 20, Part I.

Witman, Z.
    1987   The Release and the Sanctuary. *Megadim* 3:9–20. (Hebrew)
Wold, D.
    1979   The KARETH Penalty in P: Rationale and Cases. *SBLSP* 1:1–45.
Wolff, H. W.
    1961   Das Kerygma des deuteronomistischen Geschichtswerk. *ZAW* 73:171–86.
    1974   *Anthropology of the Old Testament.* Philadelphia: Fortress Press.
    1977   *Joel and Amos.* Philadelphia: Fortress.
Wright, C. J. H.
    1984   What Happened Every Seven Years in Israel? Old Testament Sabbatical Institutions for Land, Debts, and Slaves. *EQ* 56:129–38, 193–201.
    1990   *God's People in God's Land.* Grand Rapids, Mich.: Eerdmans.
    1992   Jubilee, Year of. *ABD* 3:1025–30.
    forthcoming   Holiness, Sex, and Death in the Garden of Eden. *JSOT.*
Wright, D. P.
    1991   The Spectrum of Priestly Impurity. Pp. 150–82 in *Priesthood and Cult in Ancient Israel,* ed. G. A. Anderson and S. M. Olyan. Sheffield: Sheffield Academic Press.
    1992   Holiness. *ABD* 3:237–49.
Wright, D. P., and R. N. Jones
    1986   The Gesture of Hand Placement in the Hebrew Bible and in Hittite Literature *JAOS* 106:433–46.
    1992   Discharge. *ABD* 2.204–207.
Wright, G. E.
    1953   The Book of Deuteronomy. In *The Interpreter's Bible.* Vol. 2. New York: Abingdon Press.
Xella, P.
    1978   Un testi ugaritico recente (RS 24.266, verso, 9–19) e il "sacrificio dei prima nati" *RSO* 6:127–36.
    1979   KTU1.91 [RS 19.15] e i sacrifici del re-*UF* 11:833–38.
Yadin, Y.
    1965   *Masada, First Season of Excavations, 1963–64.* Jerusalem: Israel Exploration Society.
    1980   Is the Temple Scroll a Sectarian Document? Pp. 162–67 in *Humanizing America's Iconic Book,* ed. G. M. Tucker and D. A. Knight. Chico, Calif.: Scholars Press.
    1983   *The Temple Scroll.* 3 vols. and suppl. Jerusalem: Israel Exploration Society. [Hebrew, 1977]
Yalon, H.
    1971   *Pirqê lāšôn* Jerusalem.
Yardeni, A.
    1991   Remarks on the Priestly Blessing on Two Ancient Amulets from Jerusalem. *VT* 41:176–85.

Yaron, R.
  1959 Redemption of Persons in the Ancient Near East. *RIDA* 6:155–76.
  1961 *The Laws of the Aramaic Papyri*. Oxford: Clarendon Press.
  1963 Matrimonial Mishaps at Eshnunna. *JSS* 8:1–16.
  1969 *The Laws of Eshnunna*. Jerusalem: Magnes.
  1970 The Middle Assyrian Laws and the Bible. *Biblica* 51:549–57.
  1988 *The Laws of Eshnunna*. 2nd ed. Jerusalem: Magnes; Leiden: Brill.
  1995 Stylistic Conceits II. The Absolute Intuitive in Biblical Law. Pp. 449–60 in *Pomegranates and Golden Bells* (Fest. J. Milgrom). Winona Lake, Ind.: Eisenbrauns.

Yellin, D.
  1939 *Ketavim nivḥarim*, Vol. 2. Jerusalem: Kiryat Sepher.

Young, I.
  1992 The Style of the Gezer Calendar and Some "Archaic Biblical Hebrew" Passages. *VT* 42:362–75.

Zakovitch, Y.
  1977 The Pattern of the Numerical Sequence Three-Four in the Bible. Dissertation, Hebrew University. (Hebrew)
  1978 The Literary Paradigm 3–4 in Scripture, Hebrew University dissertation (Hebrew)
  1985 *Texts in the Land of Mirrors*. Kibbutz: Hakibbutz Hameuchad. (Hebrew)

Zatelli, I.
  1998 The Origin of the Biblical Scapegoat Ritual: The Evidence of Two Eblaite Texts. *VT* 48:254–63.

Zeitlin, S.
  1939–40 The Book of Jubilees: Its Character and Significance. *JQR* 30:1–31.
  1945–46 The Beginnings of the Jewish Day During the Second Commonwealth. *JQR* 36:403–14.
  1962 *The Rise and Fall of the Judean State*. Vol. 1. Philadelphia: Jewish Publication Society.

Zevit, Z.
  1996 The Earthen Altar Laws of Exodus 20:24–26 and Related Sacrificial Restrictions in Their Cultural Context. Pp. 53–62 in *Texts, Temples, and Traditions* [Fest. M. Haran], ed. M. V. Fox et al. Winona Lake, Ind.: Eisenbrauns.

Zias, J.
  1991 Death and Disease in Ancient Israel. *BA* 54:146–59.

Zimmerli, W.
  1953 Ich bin Yahweh. Pp. 179–209 in *Geschichtle und Altes Testament* [Fest. A. Alt]. Tübingen: Mohr.
  1954 Die Eigenart der prophetischen Rede des Ezechel. *ZAW* 66:1–26.
  1960 Sinaibund und Abrahambund *ThZ* 16:268–80.

1979, 83   *Ezekiel I*. Philadelphia: Fortress Press. 2 vols. Trans. R. Clements [Trans. of *Ezechiel I* (Neukirchen: Neukirchener Verlag, 1969)]

1980   "Heiligkeit" nach dem sogenannten Heiligkeitsgesetz. *VT* 80. 493–512.

1982   I Am Yahweh. In *I Am Yahweh*, trans. D. W. Stott, 1–28. Atlanta: John Knox Press.

Zimmern, H.

1901   *Beiträge zur Kenntnis der babylonischen Religion*. Leipzig: Hinrichs.

Zimmern, H., and H. Wincklen, eds.

1905   *Die Keilinschriften und das Alte Testament*. 3rd ed. Berlin: Reuther and Reichard.

Zipor, M.

1987a   Restrictions on Marriage for Priests (Lev 21, 7.13–14). *Bib* 68:259–67.

1987b   Clothing Made of Two Yarns, *ša'aṭnez*. *The World of the Bible*. Ed. B. A. Levine et al. Ramat Gan: Revivim. (Hebrew)

1991   A Note on Gen vi 13. *VT* 41:366–69.

Ziskind, J. R.

1988   Legal Rules on Incest in the Ancient Near East. *RIDA* 35:79–107.

1996   The Missing Daughter in Leviticus XVIII. *VT* 46:125–30.

Zobel, H. J.

1987   *'āmît*. *TWAT* 6:210–13.

1990   *rādâ*. *TWAT* 7:351–58.

Zohar, Z.

1991   Dialogue. *S'vara* 2:50–51.

Zohary, M. A.

1982   *Plants of the Bible*. Cambridge: Cambridge University Press.

Zorell, F.

1945   Zur Vokalisation des Wortes *'erkĕkā* in Lev 27 und Anderwärts. *Biblica* 26:112–14.

Zucker, M.

1959   *On R. Saadiah Gaon's Translation of the Torah*. New York: Feldheim. (Hebrew)

1984   *R. Saadiah Gaon on Genesis*. New York: Jewish Theological Seminary. (Hebrew)

Zwickel, W.

1994   *Der Tempel Kult in Kanaan und Israel*. Tübingen: Mohr.

INDEX OF SUBJECTS

◆

confession, 24–25, 301–3, 369–73, 374–75,
2330, 2332
 purification offerings, 1273
 and sacrifices, 293, 1042–43, 1901–2
congregation, 242–43
conscience, 369–73
 intentional wrongs, 25, 295, 1034, 1043–44
conscription age, 2373
consecration, 1941–43, 2365–67, 2368, 2375,
2376, 2380, 2381, 2411
 altars, 278–79, 523–24, 1039–40, 1294
 animals, 1941–42, 2365
 fields, see fields, consecration of
 firstlings, 1942, 2366
 houses, 1942, 2366, 2381, 2394, 2403
 jubilee system, 2380, 2381, 2385, 2386,
2394, 2407
 ordination offerings, 534–35
 persons, 1941–42, 2365
 of persons, 1941–42, 2365
 priestly assessment, 2381–82
 priests, 493–570, 519, 558–66, 1278–79,
1906–7
 proscriptions, 1942, 2366
 quadrupeds, 1941–43, 2365–67
 redemptions, 1941–43, 2365–67
 summary, 1943, 2367
 tithes, 1942–43, 2366–67
 valuations, 1941–43, 2365–67
 vows distinguished from, 2380, 2411
consequential offerings, 231–32, 295–96, 303,
339–42, 422–23, see also reparation
offerings
consumption, see eating
contamination, 270–78, 283–84, 564, 996,
1844, see also decontamination;
impurity
 from corpses, 46, 270–78, 283–84, 564, 996,
1844, 1924, 2461–62
counting, 1998–99, 2001–2
covenant, 9, 1307, 1941, 2277, 2288, 2302–3,
2333, 2343–46
 Abrahamic, 2297–98, 2302, 2305, 2334–35,
2340–41, 2345
 Covenant Code, 2106, 2342
 Davidic, 2341
 Hittite covenant, 2341
 with Isaac, 2334
 with Jacob, 2334
 Mosaic, 2302
 Noahide, 2344–45
 patriarchal, 1394–95, 2334–35, 2338–39,
2363
 Sinaitic, 1394–97, 2302, 2305, 2335,

2337–43, 2363
creation, 1967
crickets, 1283
crime and punishment, 1420–23, 1728–59,
1866
crissum, 169–71
crops, 2294–95
 failure of, 2191, 2193, 2204
 tithes, see tithes
cult, 482–485, 2279, 2288, 2289, 2315–29,
2333
cultural anthropology, 2437–38
curses, 1311–13, 1939–40, 2272–73, 2287–88,
2304–5, 2346–2347, 2350
 blasphemy, 1935–36, 2081, 2101–19,
2131–33, 2140–45
 cannibalism, 2288, 2290, 2315–16, 2351
 destruction of cult places, 2288, 2289,
2315–29
 draught and poor harvests, 2307–9
 exile, 2289, 2290
 illness and famine, 2288, 2289, 2293,
2305–7, 2313–15, 2351
 plague, 2288, 2289, 2312–13
 remorse and recall of the covenant, 2329–42
 reviling vs. cursing, 2109
 sword, 2288, 2289, 2296, 2311
 war, pestilence, and famine, 2310–15
 wild beasts, 2288, 2289, 2296, 2309–10,
2350, 2351

D, 8–13, 29, 54, 698–704, 741, 2132–33, 2161,
2172–74, 2186–87, 2207, 2222–23,
2230, 2245, 2252–57, 2280, 2328,
2364, 2377, 2388, 2398, 2413, 2416,
2427, 2428, 2430, 2431, 2432, 2433
 eighth day, 2032
 Festival of Booths, 2027
 Festival of Unleavened Bread, 1976, 1978,
1980, 1981
 Festival of Weeks, 1996, 2042
 first fruits, 1993
 grain offerings, 1996
 and P, 8–13, 29, 54, 698–704, 741
 paschal offerings, 2070–71, 2058
 pesah, 1970
 pilgrimages, 1975, 1996
 Sabbath weeks, 1998
 sacrifices, 2034
 sanctuaries, 1969, 1977
 terminology, 2039
 work prohibition, 1961
Dan, tribe of, 2110
dates, 2363–65

altar consecration, 278–79
ashes, 274–75
birds, 304–5
burnt, 239–40, 261–64, 407–8, 525, 580–81
cereal, 305–7
chieftain, 227, 1272, 1900
childbirth, 1284
commoner, 227–28, 1272–73, 1900–1901
community, 226–27, 1271–72, 1899–1900
confession, 1273
consumption, 261–64, 402, 622–27, 635–40
corpse contamination, 270–78, 283–84
date, 288–89
decontamination, 521–23
desanctification, 280
eaten, 261–64, 402
Ezekiel's, 281–84
Ezra's, 284–85
function, 254–58
genital discharges, 269–70
graduated, 292–93, 292–18, 1273–74, 1901–2
Hezekiah's, 285–87
high priest, 226, 1271, 1899
and impurity, 404–7
Joash's, 287–88
Levites', 278
name, 253–54
Nazirite's, 10, 179–81, 996
Num 15:22–26, 264–69
origin, 177
priestly, 996, 1271
public, 281
as rite of passage, 289–92, 889
as sacrifices, 1271–73, 1275–76, 1279–1280,
    1281, 1284, 1288–89, 1291–92, 1305
scale disease, 827–28, 1288–89, 1916–17
theology, 258–61
types, 261–64
purity, 1004–9, *see also* impurity
and land ownership, 2185

quadrupeds, 645, 667–71, 727–29, 1283–84,
    1313
camels, 648, 1282
consecration, 1941–43, 2365–67
dietary laws, 643, 1910
dogs, 650, 653
firstlings consecrated, 1942, 2366
flock animals, *see* flock animals
hares, 648–649, 1282
herd animals, *see* herd animals
hoofed, 646–48, 668–69, 723, 1282
impurity, 297–98, 425–26, 647–54, 681–82,
    1282, 1727

kids (goats), 10, 703–4, 732–42
pawed, 669
pigs, 649–53, 1282
rock badger, 648, 1282
ruminant, 647
testing, 727–28
quarantine
fungous houses, 871, 1290
scale disease, 779–80, 782, 795–96,
    1285–87
Qumran, 165, 194, 394, 405, 558–66, 620,
    789, 969–71, 1064, *see also* Index of
    Sources
Qumran calendar, 2060–61, 2063, 2071, 2072

rabbinic age
emergence of, 2463–64
talionic law and, 2136–40
rain, 1980, 2000, 2018, 2031, 2043–44, 2045,
    2055
sirocco, 1980, 1999–2000, 2031
rationales, 1371–75, 1456–63, 1472–79
ravens, 1283
raw flour cereal offerings, 177, 1897
reconciliation, 245, 1941, 2272–73
red, 272, 835
Red Cow, 270–78
redemption, 2234, 2411, 2414
consecrated items, 1941–43, 2365–67
definition of, 2189, 2262
irredeemable items, 2368, 2378, 2379, 2380,
    2384, 2385, 2402–3, 2403, 2406, 2407,
    2411, 2414, 2417–21
Israel's redemption, 2212
laws, 2368, 2379, 2380, 2394, 2403, 2407
property, 1309–11, 1937–38, 2146, 2183–91
redeemable items, 2368, 2378, 2379, 2380,
    2390, 2402–3, 2407
remorse, 245, 1941, 2272–73, 2326–27,
    2329–42
reparation offerings, 11, 50, 319–378, 408–10,
    466–84, 801, 850–51, 856–57, 861,
    1274, 1276, 1288–89, 1595, 1902, *see
    also* sacrifices
administrative order, 380, 1904
betrothed slave-woman, 1671–75
commutability, 326–28, 408–9
conscience, 342–45
Num 5:6–8, 368–79
origin, 177
psychology, 342–45
scale disease, 363–64
repentance, 5, 373–78, *see also* atonement
reproof, 1646–50

INDEX OF TERMS

◆

Akkadian
abālu, 2169
abātu, 2332
abu, 1768
abu bītim, 247
aḫāzu, 1750
akālu, 347, 1683
ākil dami, 708, 1470
ā-kil šīri, 709, 1470
akītu, 1078
alālu, 1682
amam našû, 1488
amīlū, 498
ana dāriātim, 614
ananiḫu, 738
ana ṣeri ašri elli šuṣima, 262, 387
andurāru, 2163, 2167, 2168, 2169, 2178, 2226, 2254, 2255
anzillu, 1621
apsû, 1079
apum, 1492
arnabu, 648
arnu, 339
arrat la napšuri maruštu, 820
arrat la pašāri, 820
ašāgu, 1078
asakka akālu, 1865
asakkam akālum, 1621
asakku, 322
āšipu, 294
āšipu/mašmaššu, 52
ašlukkatu, 2454
ašru, 403
ašrukkatu, 2454
ašru parsu, 1046
a-wi-lum me-iḫ-ri-šu, 2135
bi'āru, 774
balālu, 1828
ballukku, 1028
baluḫḫa, 1026
barûtu umallû qata'a, 539

batultu, 1799
bītāti, 1080
bît rimki, 968
dāgil iṣṣūrē, 52
dâku, 2119
daku/duaku, 1752
dallu, 860
daqqu, 1827
dawû, 745
dinanu, 1079
dišip suluppi, 189
dišpu, 1760
dullu, 7
dullulu, 860
egubbu, 1067
emēdu qātu, 153
ēmēšu, 188
emu, 1551
emūtu, 335, 1551
entu, 979
epattu/, epadu505
eperu, 775, 873
epēšu, 578
epqu, 799
epušuši, 2125
erbu/aribu, 665
erēbu, 809, 1683
ērīb bīti, 52
ergilu, 666
erretu lemuttu, 820
erretu maruštu, 820
erretu rabītu, 820
erretum/šertu rabitum/lemuttum, 364
erṣetu, 686
esettu, eṣemtu, eṣenṣēru, 213
eṭemmu, 1768
garābu, 1828
garakku, 201, 628
gubbuḫu, 800
ḫalāṣu, 872
ḫamātu, 671
ḫarištu, 746, 2456

ḫaruṗ, 1666
ḫarāpu, 1667
ḫarāṣu, 1877
ḫatanu, 747
ḫatnūtu, 747
ḫaṭṭi'u, 243
ḫaṭû, 230, 1084
ḫiāṭṭu, 1084
ḫīṭu, 339
ḫiṭam našû, 1488
ḫubbu, 1040
ḫubullu, 2209
ḫulmittu, 671
ḫupšu, 807
ḫurbātu, 1072
ḫīṭu, 230
idequ, 1067
ikkibu, 1570, 1621
ilānu, 1774
imeru 895, 901
imēru, 2383, 2435
ina, 397
ina durāri uṣû, 2197
iqbiu, 552
irâm, 475
irêm, 473
isinnu, 2076
išku, 1828
istu qaqqādisu adî šēpēšu, 785
kabru, 184
kaiītû, 207
kajamānu, 1383
kalû, 52
kamunu, 864, 870
kamānu/kamānātu, 201
kānu patīra, 628
kapāru, 1080
karmu, 1072
karṣî akālu, 1644
kaṣāru, 1982
katarru, 864, 870
kawu, 790
kīdi, 1072

2573

INDEX OF AUTHORS

◆

INDEX OF SOURCES

◆